PSYCHOLOGY

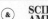

· A PARTNERSHIP BETWEEN ·

WORTH
PUBLISHERS & SCIENTIFIC
AMERICAN

PSYCHOLOGY

DEBORAH M. LICHT | MISTY G. HULL | COCO BALLANTYNE

Pikes Peak Community College,
Colorado

Pikes Peak Community College,
Colorado

Custom Edition for Washington State University

· A PARTNERSHIP BETWEEN ·

WORTH PUBLISHERS & SCIENTIFIC AMERICAN

macmillan learning
curriculum solutions

bedford/st.martin's ▪ hayden-mcneil ▪ w.h. freeman ▪ worth publishers

Senior Vice President, Editorial and Production: Catherine Woods

Publisher: Kevin Feyen

Acquisitions Editor: Rachel Losh

Marketing Manager: Lindsay Johnson

Associate Director of Market Development: Carlise Stembridge

Developmental Editors: Burrston House, Marna Miller

Executive Media Editor: Rachel Comerford

Director of Development, Print and Digital: Tracey Kuehn

Editorial Assistant: Katie Garrett

Photo Editor: Cecilia Varas

Photo Researcher: Jacqui Wong, Deborah Anderson

Art director, Cover Designer and Interior Designer: Barbara Reingold

Infographic Designer: DeMarinis Design LLC

Layout Designer and Infographic Illustrator: Clea Chmela

Chapter Opener Designer: Charles Yuen

Associate Managing Editor: Lisa Kinne

Project Editor: Robert Errera

Art Manager: Matthew McAdams

Illustrations: Todd Buck, Northeastern Graphic

Production Manager: Sarah Segal

Composition: Jouve

Printing and Binding: Mercury Print Production

Library of Congress Control Number: 2013957268

ISBN-13: 978-1-319-09741-7

ISBN-10: 1-319-09741-3

Worth Publishers
41 Madison Avenue
New York, NY 10010
www.worthpublishers.com

A Practical Guide to Study Skills

Amy Himsel
El Camino College

Learning How to Learn
Let Go of What You Think You Know
How Your Brain Really Works
Getting Things into Your Head: Brain-Change Fundamentals

Crafting Your Mental Workout Plan
Exercise Your Brain by Reading Before Class
Go to Class and Train with an Expert
Train Your Brain for Exams and Other Assessments

The Moment of Truth: Exam Day
The First Thing to Do Is to Manage Your Stress
Be Strategic in Completing the Exam

Actually Doing It
Developing Habits of Self-Regulation and Self-Control

If At First You Don't Succeed

Like most of you, I had never been taught the best way to study. I am writing this chapter because I want studying to be less confusing and frustrating for you than it was for me, and I want you to know about study techniques that are effective and efficient. So, if you are ready for a change in your study habits, prepare to open your mind to some of the surprising findings from the science of studying. They reveal successful study strategies that will help you improve specific class and overall school performance. You'll discover that the brain has an incredible capacity to change when given the proper exercise—an ability you can apply to any area of your life.

Learning How to Learn

How do we learn? It's a simple question, but the answer is more complicated than you might expect.

Let Go of What You Think You Know

My study plan as a college freshman was straightforward: to memorize as many words as possible from my textbooks and professors' lectures. I was pretty good at this, furiously taking notes in class or as I read the course materials. I spent countless hours repeating the information in an effort to make it sink into my brain, and I earned a reputation for being one of the most studious (okay, obsessive) students in my dorm. So why wasn't I, master memorizer with a will of steel, earning straight As? Like many students, my assumptions about studying were guided more by "common sense" than by scientific reality. Unfortunately, then as now, "common-sense" notions are frequently incorrect (Stanovich, 2010).

It's easy to get tricked into thinking rote methods work because they *feel* so effective in the moment. During my marathon sessions of rote learning, I certainly *felt* like I was doing the right thing. But the proof is in the pudding, and my grades that first year did not match my feeling of mastery. Has this ever happened to you? If so, you are not alone. We are poor judges of how well we have learned something, and we chronically underestimate how much we know about a topic we have studied. Furthermore, the less we know about a topic, the less we realize we *don't* really know it (Kruger & Dunning, 1999). In the quest to become a better and more efficient learner, you must let go of what you think you know about studying and follow methods backed by science.

No matter what your grades were in the past or what your current habits or attitudes are, you can change for the better. Please don't underestimate the brain's potential for change. It is constantly changing due to experience, and you are capable of creating new experiences while you study. As you'll find out, if you learn how the brain works and give it proper attention and exercise, it can change to your benefit.

How Your Brain Really Works

Studying is about making memories, but memories are not made in a straightforward manner. We do not "place" information in one spot—like placing an item on a closet shelf, returning later to pick it up, dust it off, and then use it to answer a question on a test. Instead, we make memories when our brain's networks of connections are activated in patterns. Basically, here's what science tells us: Mental exercise creates and strengthens networks of connections in your brain similar to the way lifting weights strengthens your muscles (Medina, 2008). The more you "work" the information (for example, by explaining a concept in your own words), the more neural connections are made or strengthened and the stronger your memory becomes. As a result, you remember more when it's time to take a test.

But here's a surprising fact: Memories—including those formed while you study—are deeply personal, customized to fit your brain and nobody else's in exactly the same way. Why? Because learning is not like painting on a blank canvas. Rather, you start with a backdrop of networks that represent your current knowledge, preferences, and habits.

Simply put, you are your connections. You make long-lasting memories by weaving the new information into your unique brain cell connections. No two people will do this in exactly the same way. Likewise, there is no magic formula for studying well. With this in mind, start experimenting with the techniques described in this chapter to find out what works best for your brain. But please don't worry: You don't have to become an expert in neuroscience to learn how best to exercise your brain cell networks. Take a look at Figure 1, and then stay with me to learn the basics of brain change and how to apply that information to your everyday life as a student.

(a)

(a) Tom Barrick, Chris Clark, SGHMS/Photo Researchers

(b) Image courtesy of Dr. Sebastian Seung: Neural "wiring" reconstructed from the retina V. Jain, J. Murray, S. Turaga, and S. Seung (MIT); K. Briggman, M. Helmstaedter, and W. Denk (MPG)

(b)

FIGURE 1 The Connectome These images are models created to represent the incredibly complex and unique networks of connections among brain cells. Nobody's connections are exactly the same as yours. Shown in (a) is a model of neuronal connections across different regions of the brain as a whole. The model in (b) shows a close-up of the complex connections that have formed between individual neurons.

Getting Things into Your Head: Brain-Change Fundamentals

When you study, you start by bringing new information into your brain, a process referred to as encoding. Basically, when you pay attention to information, you encode it. Reading, listening to lectures, taking notes, and reviewing notes are all forms of encoding. But not all forms of encoding are equally helpful. Common study strategies—like rereading the text or notes, or trying to memorize definitions word for word—are rote methods that involve shallow processing, which results in very limited brain change. This kind of encoding produces only the weakest of neural connections, without generating enough raw material from which to later construct an accurate memory.

To study better, move beyond shallow encoding to process information at a deeper level. For example, relate the new information you are trying to learn to something that is already familiar to you. Let's say you need to learn the definition of the term *homeostasis* ("the maintenance of a steady internal state in the body"). That may seem very abstract until you think about your actual experiences with homeostasis—say, a time when you have felt hot and sweaty. That's your body trying to cool itself off, and that's a homeostatic experience. Ever felt dehydrated? That's your body signaling that more liquid is needed. Thinking in this way, you will find that homeostasis now seems far more familiar because you've connected it to knowledge and experiences that are already represented in your networks of brain cells. Even the simple act of putting things into your own words triggers deeper processing because you are converting the material into words that are more familiar to you. (See more about this in Table 1.)

Quality studying also requires practice in getting the learned information out again, a process referred to as *retrieval*. As a student, when I tried to remember the exact words of a definition, I was practicing retrieval—but only in a very shallow form. It is much better exercise for the brain when studying involves deeper methods of retrieval, like restating definitions in your own words (without peeking at your notes first!) or trying to explain the material to someone else.

TABLE 1 Rote Method Makeover

Common rote strategy	New and improved strategy
Reading	• Previewing each section before you read, and writing questions • Using questions to think while you read, and to test yourself after reading
Copying definitions	• Writing definitions in your own words
Memorizing definitions	• Stating definitions in your own words, as though you were trying to explain the terms to someone else
Copying notes	• Elaborating on your notes • Noting connections between your notes and your past knowledge or experience • Making connections between terms and concepts within the material
Rereading the text or your notes	• Processing your notes or the text in different ways • Self-testing with questions you wrote or those provided in the text • Testing yourself to see if you can repeat in your own words the material you have just read
Taking notes focused on the professor's words	• Writing down not only what is on the slide, board, or outline, but also supplementing with your own words • Marking spots of confusion and asking the professor for clarification later
Comparing your notes with a classmate to make sure you "got everything down"	• Discussing your notes with a classmate; explaining to each other the material in your notes • Filling in any gaps with your own words

The mental exercise involved in studying takes time to sink in and stabilize into last-ing brain change. This is a process called *memory consolidation,* one that is similar to how your muscles need some rest after exercise in order to develop best. Memories settle into the fabric of the brain gradually, aided by time, sleep, and further mental ex-ercise. Imagine what happens when you spend several hours drilling with rote methods and skimping on sleep in an effort to cram it all in: You actually make the task of learn-ing harder on yourself by shortchanging your brain's memory consolidation process.

How do you apply these fundamentals to studying? What follows are some basic study tips to keep in mind.

Keep Things Challenging

Learning should not feel easy. To be more specific, creating strong, reliable memo-ries—memories that are still there for you on the day of the exam—should not feel easy. Sorry, but that is true. Ignoring this fact is like expecting to housetrain your new puppy on day one. It's funny how this same advice is completely non-contro-versial when it comes to physical exercise. Who expects to develop impressive biceps by doing curls with only 1-pound weights? Challenging study stimulates deeper brain change, resulting in stronger memories that are more easily retrieved on de-mand. Scientists call this a "desirable difficulty" because the more you struggle to learn now, the stronger your neural networks become—and the less likely you are to forget the information later (Bjork & Bjork, 2011).

It all makes sense when you spell it out, but it's fascinating how quickly we forget and get tricked by our feelings in the moment. I used to parrot back all kinds of infor-mation and definitions in the midst of my marathon rote-method study sessions. It didn't feel difficult, especially after three hours of memorizing. I felt like I was really learning something, which made it all the more disappointing when my test scores showed otherwise. Sound familiar? If so, it's time once again to let go of what you think you know. When studying feels easy in the moment, that's exactly when you should doubt your mastery the most. In contrast, when you feel frustrated and unsure while studying, smile and pat yourself on the back—you are engaging in a vigorous mental workout. Those difficulties are desirable and will pay off big time later.

Space Out Your Study Sessions

I used to study for long stretches of time for each class. I figured the longer I kept at it, the better I would learn the material. Wrong. Contrary to common sense, it's much better exercise for your brain if you space out your study sessions for each class. Consider a weight-lifting analogy: If you wanted to tone up, would you expect your muscles to respond better to one five-hour workout a week than to five one-hour sessions a week? Of course not. Similarly, the brain responds best to short, fo-cused study sessions spaced across several days.

Learning experts recommend you spend two to three hours studying for every hour spent at lectures. That's a lot of time, but it's much less overwhelming if you spread it out across several days. You'll see possible study schedules in the calendars in Figure 2.

Mix Things Up

Exercise your brain connections with some cross-training—that is, by varying the way you encode new information (see Figure 3 on page 6). Of course, it's a great idea to engage in traditional tasks like reading. But monitor your encoding: Are you just fo-cused on memorizing words? If so, you are focused only on *visual encoding.* At that level, processing is shallow. So take another step and encode the information further. For example, the definition of a term will be most memorable if you focus on the meaning *(semantic encoding),* which is aided by putting the definition into your own words. Perhaps also try relating what you read to a body movement or gesture (Cook,

Marisol

2011	Sunday, Jul 17	Monday, Jul 18	Tuesday Jul 19	Wednesday, Jul 20	Thursday Jul 21	Friday, Jul 22	Saturday, Jul 23
11 AM						11:00 AM Study Psychology	11:00 AM Study English
Noon						12:00 PM Study Biology	12:00 PM Study Biology
1 PM	1:00 PM Study Chemistry			1:00 PM Study English			1:00 PM Study Chemistry
2 PM					2:00 PM Study Biology		
3 PM			3:00 PM Study English		3:00 PM Study English		
4 PM			4:00 PM Study Psychology		4:00 PM Study Psychology	4:00 PM Study Psychology	
5 PM			5:00 PM Study Chemistry	5:00 PM Study Chemistry		5:00 PM Study English	
6 PM		6:00 PM Study Psychology		6:00 PM Study Psychology		6:00 PM Study Chemistry	
7 PM		7:00 PM Study Chemistry		7:00 PM Study Biology			
8 PM		8:00 PM Study Biology	8:00 PM Study Biology				
9 PM		9:00 PM Study English					
10 PM							

Noah

2011	Sunday, Jul 17	Monday, Jul 18	Tuesday Jul 19	Wednesday, Jul 20	Thursday, Jul 21	Friday, Jul 22	Saturday, Jul 23
11 AM						11:00 AM Study Psychology	11:00 AM Study English
Noon						12:00 PM Study Biology	12:00 PM Study Biology
1 PM	1:00 PM Study Chemistry					1:00 PM Study English	1:00 PM Study Chemistry
2 PM	2:00 PM Study Psychology					2:00 PM Study Chemistry	2:00 PM Study Psychology
3 PM	3:00 PM Study Biology						
4 PM	4:00 PM Study English						
5 PM							
6 PM							
7 PM		7:00 PM Study Chemistry	7:00 PM Study Chemistry	7:00 PM Study Chemistry	7:00 PM Study Biology		
8 PM	8:00 PM Study Biology	8:00 PM Study English	8:00 PM Study English	8:00 PM Study English			
9 PM		9:00 PM Study Psychology	9:00 PM Study Biology	9:00 PM Study Psychology	9:00 PM Study Psychology		
10 PM							

FIGURE 2 **Two Possible Study Calendars** With this customized plan, both Marisol and Noah spend 2 to 3 hours studying for each hour of lecture. They space their studying out across the week in 1-hour blocks per subject—this practice allows rest between subjects for the brain connections they have exercised.

FIGURE 3 Levels of Processing

Processing a word deeply—by its meaning (semantic encoding)—produces better recognition of it at a later time than does shallow processing by attending to its appearance or sound. (From Craik & Tulving, 1975.)

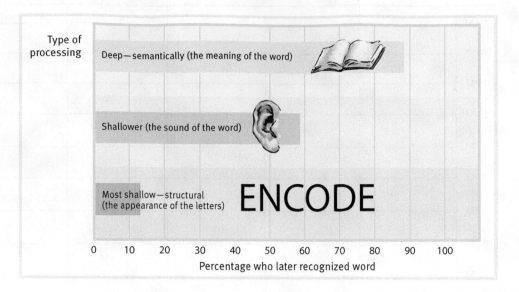

Type of processing

Deep—semantically (the meaning of the word)

Shallower (the sound of the word)

Most shallow—structural (the appearance of the letters)

ENCODE

0   10   20   30   40   50   60   70   80   90   100

Percentage who later recognized word

Mitchell, & Goldin-Meadow, 2008). For example, to remember that two variables move in opposite directions in a negative correlation, try moving your arms in different directions as you rehearse the material. You could also try linking the material with a catchy phrase or tune, anything to add an auditory component to the memory. Each encoding experience will present an opportunity to make connections; with more connections formed, more paths will lead to the memory. Remember to never turn down the opportunity to strengthen your memory with more connections!

Test Yourself, Early and Often

If just the mention of the word *test* increases your heart rate, then here's another opportunity to let go of what you think you know: Testing is your friend. Self-testing is one of the best ways to overcome the tendency to overestimate how much you know by providing a reality check of your actual knowledge (Rohrer & Pashler, 2010).

For everyone, self-testing not only reveals current competence but also provides another set of exercises to train the brain. Every time you test yourself, you engage the brain in an attempt to retrieve a memory. This act alone helps strengthen connections among your brain cells. Nevertheless, networks strengthened through study weaken over time. The fact that you once knew something provides no guarantee that you will know it when you are assessed. So test yourself repeatedly to ensure that those memories stay strong.

Combining self-testing with well-spaced study sessions is an even more useful strategy. Spread your self-testing out to create the best opportunity for a strenuous mental workout. When some time has elapsed, even just a day or two, some forgetting will inevitably occur. You would think that's bad, right? It's not. Experts are finding that forgetting helps us learn (Kornell, 2009). Basically, a little forgetting now provides you with a lot of desirable difficulties the next time you study the material. Think of it as one step backward that leads to two steps forward.

SECTION REVIEW

- Rote methods, like rereading the text or memorizing definitions, may *feel* like they work, but they are not very effective for long-term learning.
- The best way to study is to work the to-be-learned information into the unique set of connections that already exist among your brain cells.
- You exercise your brain (and learn best) when you keep study sessions challenging but brief, utilizing a variety of strategies and testing yourself often.

Test Yourself

Hint: Don't look back at the text until you have pulled out of your memory as much information as you can.

- What are rote methods, and why are they less effective than other study methods?
- Why is self-testing such a valuable study skill?

Try It

- Set a timer to go off at regular intervals (perhaps every 15 minutes) while you study. When the buzzer sounds, simply ask yourself: "Does this feel easy?" If so, evaluate your study methods and strive to create more desirable difficulties.
- Give yourself an exam reality check. After you take your next assessment in a class, predict the grade you earned and write it down in your notebook. When the assessment is returned, write your actual grade next to your prediction. Is there a discrepancy? If so, consider why.
- Create your own study calendar for the week ahead. Remember to allow 2 to 3 hours of study for each hour of lecture, and be sure to space out your study sessions for each class.

Crafting Your Mental Workout Plan

Let's get practical and discuss how to translate brain-change knowledge into your everyday life as a student before, during, and after classes.

Exercise Your Brain by Reading Before Class

Reading before class is one of the most overlooked ways to boost your learning in a college course. Think of how a warm-up prepares the body for a workout. Reading the material before class serves a similar function. If you first process this new information and get the neural networks primed, the result will be a much more productive time in class. Why? You will have an easier time figuring out which information is most important. What you hear in class will more easily connect with the networks in your brain because of the mental warm-up. So make the most of your reading by following these tips:

Invite Desirable Difficulties

Get a good workout while you read: If you feel your eyes skimming across the page, or if you reach the bottom and don't remember much (if anything) of what you just read, then you are barely processing the information at all. It happens to the best of us. The important thing is to catch yourself, shake the cobwebs out of your head, and start again with the goal of staying more engaged. Awareness is a step in the right direction. See Table 2 on the next page for specific tips on how to keep your brain active while reading.

Space It Out

If you have a 50-page chapter to read for Monday's class, break it down into smaller chunks (perhaps 15- to 20-page sections), and spread your reading out across a couple of days. Here's another reason to space things out: If you are zipping through a 50-page chapter in one sitting, I doubt that you are engaging desirable difficulties! Pace yourself. Course materials are often organized into sections with headers. Read one or two sections in one sitting, but no more than that. Remember, your brain needs breaks in order for memories to consolidate. Also, this will help you manage your attention better and help reading become more enjoyable.

TABLE 2 Desirable Difficulties While You Read

Here are two specific methods to trigger challenges that help you get the most out of your reading.

SQ3R: The Survey, Question, Read, Rehearse, and Review Strategy
One structured approach to reading for deep processing is SQ3R (Robinson, 1970). Here are the steps:

- Before you read, survey the section to get a general idea of what information you will encounter.
- Next, formulate a question to keep in mind as you read. Your text may already include learning objectives or preview questions that help with this step.
- Now you are ready to read, but you should read with your question in mind, actively considering what the answer might be. Take notes, putting things in your own words as much as you can.
- After you have finished reading a section, take time to rehearse: put the text material in your own words, then ask yourself the question again (but no peeking at the text or your notes until you have answered!).
- The last step is to review what you have learned, paying special attention to the notes in your own words.

3R: The Read-Recite-Review Strategy
The 3R approach (McDaniel, Howard, & Einstein, 2009) is another method to encourage deep processing while reading. You can use this technique repeatedly with your texts or your notes.

- Read a brief section or passage.
- Close your book or cover the text, then recite in your own words anything you can remember about what you have just read.
- Open the book and review the passage to check yourself.

Self-Test While You Read

As you read, think of questions you could ask yourself to test your learning. Write them down somewhere. When you reach the end of the section, use these questions as a self-test quiz. How much did you remember? Take note of the information that you left out, and go back to review that material.

Work the Information in Different Ways

First and foremost, make sure you are focused on the meaning of the words, not memorizing the author's words, which triggers only shallow encoding. How can you do this? Take notes while you read, but don't just copy from a book or screen. Instead, put things into your own words. Consider how this new information fits in with your uniquely wired brain. How does it link to your experiences? Does an image come to mind? If so, draw it. Does a silly thought occur to you? For example, I remember reading about the hippocampus, a brain structure involved with memory, and I immediately thought: "Hippos are similar to elephants, and elephants supposedly have good memories." It stuck. It worked for me, but it might not work for you. Remember, you are your connections, so make what you read stick in a way that makes sense to you!

Go to Class and Train with an Expert

Go to your classes—each and every one of them. These are golden opportunities your brain shouldn't miss. This is a chance to have a mental workout with an expert on the topic. At the very least, a missed class is a lost opportunity to find out what the professor thinks is most important (in other words, what material is most likely to appear on assessments).

Your professor will present the material in at least a slightly different way than it is presented in the readings, so that alone will provide some helpful cross-training to strengthen your neural networks. But it's ultimately up to you to make class worth your time. Just as simply moving your eyes across the page fails to result in much learning, sitting there and simply writing down whatever is on the board or slides only triggers the most shallow processing. So try the following procedures.

Create a Set of Complete and Personally Meaningful Notes

Notice that I said "create" instead of "take." This is an important distinction. When you "take" notes, you write down the exact words from the board or a slide, and that's it. Some students who are obsessive (as I was) attempt to write down as many words spoken by the professor as possible. In both cases, there is a misconception that the professor's words are magical: If you can just transfer them directly into your brain, you will be in good shape. It's simply not true. Research indicates that students who "create" comprehensive and elaborated notes tend to earn better grades (Peverly et al., 2007).

How do you do this? Of course you should write down the outline, terms, or key examples the professor has provided on the board or slides. And it's wise to jot down additional helpful details your professor may state, as long as you are not attempting to transcribe the words verbatim. What's most important is that you churn the information through your brain so it makes sense to you. You have to work with the information, and transform it in some way so it will become embedded within your neural networks. This strategy can range from simply putting things into your own words to jotting down a related example or a personal experience. It will build bridges that connect the professor's words with your brain.

Try some of these strategies to "create" your own notes:

- *Remind yourself to focus on the meaning, not just the words.* As much as possible, put things into your own words. Make your notes personally meaningful. If note taking seems quick and easy, view this as a warning sign. Keep desirable difficulties in mind.

- *Listen for organizational cues from your professor* (Kiewra, 2002). For example, a statement like "So we have just discussed X, and now I'd like to move to Y" is a clear signal that the lecture is shifting to a new topic. If the instructor tells you "There are four components of Z," use that as a signal to start a numbered list in your notes.

- *Develop a set of abbreviations and symbols.* Save time by abbreviating or using symbols whenever possible. Include those an individual professor uses and invent some of your own (see examples in Table 3). Just make sure the abbreviations and symbols help you make sense of the material.

- *Draw a representation of how concepts relate to each other.* Try venturing outside the standard outline structure. Consider using arrows, for example. Create drawings to represent the information.

- *Check yourself by noting spots where you got lost or confused.* I used to do this by writing a big question mark next to the spot where I got lost. After you mark the spot, shake out the mental cobwebs and then move on to keep up with the pace of the class. Stay after class to discuss the confusing part with the professor or a classmate. Do not wait.

- *As soon as possible after class, review your notes and jot down any additional information that comes to mind.* It's important to do this while the information is still fresh. Better yet, do this with a classmate. You may be able to fill in some blanks for each other. Kiewra (2002) calls this "the reconstruction strategy." But beware of shifting into rote mode! Don't just read and copy verbatim; actually discuss the notes, explain what they mean, and focus on which parts of the meaning either of you may have missed or misunderstood.

TABLE 3 Using Abbreviations in Your Notes

Allow your hands to keep up with the pace of class by using abbreviations in your notes. Here are just a few ideas to get you started, but the most important thing is to use symbols that make sense to your brain. What abbreviations could you add for some of the common words or phrases in your classes?

w/o	without
w/n	within
b/c	because
diffs	differences
beh	behavior
♂	male
♀	female
Ψ	psychology
?	ask professor
+	and
→	leads to, causes
≈	is similar to
≠	is not the same as

Train Your Brain for Exams and Other Assessments

Students often ask me how best to prepare for exams. It's a great question, but the problem is that most ask it less than a week before the exam. When should you start preparing for the exam? Today! But that doesn't mean you have to spend hours studying today. A little goes a long way, especially when you revisit the material several times a week. It's like going to the gym a few times a week instead of spending 10 hours there on Saturday to make up for a week of sloth. Here are some suggestions for how to proceed.

Process Your Notes Regularly

Research indicates that you will learn more from processing your notes than you learned while taking them (Kiewra, 2002; Knight & McKelvie, 1986). Rereading is not enough, and neither is copying notes verbatim. Oh, how I wish someone had told me this when I was a student! I wasted loads of time on this particular rote method. Of course, there is nothing wrong with rereading your notes the first time you revisit them. The problem is expecting that you will somehow be able to "write" the contents of your notes directly into your brain (Bjork & Bjork, 2011). This ignores the reality that each of us begins with a brain full of unique connections, where new information sticks best by being woven into the networks that already exist.

Use your notes as a springboard to organize and integrate the course material (see Figure 4). Consider how the different pieces of information connect to one another (*internal connections*), and then think about how the information relates to your prior knowledge and experiences (*external connections*) (Mayer, 1996). This is great exercise for the brain, helping to form and strengthen neural networks that can later consolidate into stronger memories.

- *Make internal links.* There are often numerous ways that the course material could be organized to show internal links, such as terms that can be grouped by some shared characteristic or terms that are notable for how they reveal opposite tendencies. Experiment with different ways to show internal links. You could construct a memory matrix, where you identify categories and appropriately place terms, concepts, or other information. Concept maps are another option; these are diagrams or figures you draw to show relationships among the various aspects of the material (see Figure 5).

- *Make external links.* You can relate the course material to information you currently know by forming mental representations. Depending on the way your mind works, this could come out in many different ways. The links could be visual. For example, I think of neural connections as colorful strands of yarn and of building strong memories as similar to knitting a blanket with that yarn. With further processing (strands/connections), the blanket (memory) becomes more and more resilient.

The links could also be verbal—for instance, analogies. Does a certain concept remind you of something else? If so, write in your notes: "It's like . . ." To understand how brain cells communicate, for example, you could note: "It's like a conversation." You could also imagine methods of linking the material to movements or sounds. Studies indicate that engaging the senses and motor skills when creating a memory yields additional cues that can help embed the new information more deeply into your brain (Glenberg, Brown, & Levin, 2007; Stevanoni & Salmon, 2005). The bottom line: You create stronger memories when you process the new information in a variety of ways.

FIGURE 4 Internal and External Links
While making notes, try to connect the new information with things you already know. This is one specific way to weave the material into your uniquely connected brain, as shown in blue. In addition, pay attention to the connections you see between the bits of new information you encounter, as shown in green. Both methods help you process the material deeply. (Illustration after Kiewra, 2002)

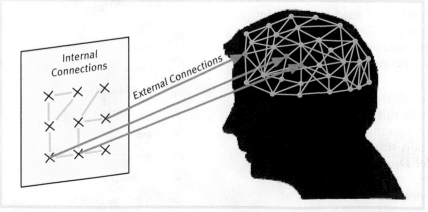

Internal Connections

External Connections

- *Simply ask "why"?* Doing so is a very effective and straightforward way to make external links. This method of triggering self-explanation has been shown to improve learning more than does simple summarizing or rereading of notes (Kiewra, 2002). Why does it work? It forces you to think about the meaning of the material instead of focusing on the memorization of words.

(a)

FIGURE 5 Memory Matrixes (a) and Concept Maps (b) (a) This memory matrix shows the distinctions a student made between two theories about learning. **(b)** This concept map shows how one student has organized her learning about energy and the natural laws governing it.

(b)

Check Your Learning Through Self-Testing—Repeatedly

How did you know that you could ride a bicycle? I remember the exhilarating feeling I had when the training wheels on my bike were removed and I rode down the driveway all on my own. It was scary at first, but eventually I brought the wobbles under control.

How do you know when you have really learned something? Most students rely on how familiar the material seems as they reread it or on how well they do on multiple-choice quizzes or test questions. Think about why that might be the case. Your notes, readings, and multiple-choice questions all contain the verbal equivalent of training wheels: words and organizational features that act as cues for your performance. The trouble is that, unlike training wheels on a bike, we don't realize how much our performance is assisted by these aids. The wheels come off for the exam—questions are in random order, unfamiliar wording is used, you're required to apply what you've learned—and suddenly your confidence is shaken. You feel wobbly. You discover that you really didn't know the material well.

Let's take the training wheels off for a moment, right now. Without looking back on the chapter, answer this question: How are memories formed in the brain?

Now look back to page 2 to check your answer. How much did you remember?

When you self-test like this, you get a more accurate view of how much you understand. This is especially true when you ask open-ended questions, like the one I used above—to answer, you are required to pull all of the information you can from the depths of your own brain. The real challenge is to put the course material away (for a few hours or a day) and then later see what you can still retrieve from the strands of information that were encoded. This strategy tests recall memory—a good countermeasure against that annoying human tendency to overestimate what you know.

There is another excellent reason to self-test: The act of trying to retrieve information helps us embed the information in the brain more deeply, which leads to stronger and more readily accessible memories. Remember, brain cell connections are strengthened by both encoding and retrieval. Making yourself come up with an answer (especially to an open-ended question) is one of the most effective exercises for your memory networks (Bjork & Bjork, 2011).

In short, self-testing is a great workout that will show you what you really do and don't know. Don't be surprised to find that there are some big gaps in your memory. Be happy you found them and can remedy the problem! Also, remember that if it's difficult while you're studying, it's more likely to be easier while you're being tested later. Self-testing creates desirable difficulties that strengthen your memories for long-term retention.

Here are some self-testing options you can try:

- *Use the tools the professor or text author gave you.* Many professors and texts provide lists of objectives, preview questions, or review questions. Just make sure to move beyond multiple-choice questions because, to begin with, they are easier. Focus on open-ended questions, like fill-in-the-blank or essay questions.

- *Make your own tests.* This is a lot easier than you might think. For example, go back to the questions you wrote in your notes while reading. Create flashcards and, on the back of each, write where in your notes the answer can be found. This will remind you not to try to rote-memorize "answers." You can also use the 3R method (look back at Table 2) as a simple and effective way to check your understanding while you study.

- *Mix up the order of questions.* This is a form of brain cross-training. If you always study everything in the same order, the order itself becomes a context cue that fools you into overestimating what you really know. Besides, many professors arrange their exam items in random order.

- *Try out a variety of study locations.* Even without our conscious awareness, cues from the places where we study help us form associations with the new material we are trying to learn (Smith, 2007; Smith & Vela, 2001). If we study in only one location, we create only one set of context cues to link to the material. Studying in many different locations gives you the chance to form multiple context cues. In other words, trying out different study locations can actually help you form more connections between brain cells relevant to the material. More connections equal stronger memories.

- *Sort items back into their categories.* Shuffle your flashcards and then sort them into piles by chapter or topic. Now you are forced to think about how the items are similar to or different from one another, which is excellent exercise for the mind. Even if this seems too hard, it can trigger deep learning because of the workout it gives your brain (Kornell, in press). Remember, difficulties help you learn!

- *Pretend it is your job to teach someone else this material, someone who really needs the information.* This makes you think about the meaning of the material instead of just focusing on the literal words. Actors often use this method (Noice & Noice, 2006). They are encouraged not to rote-memorize the script but to think of the motivations, goals, and reasons why the person would be saying these things. Even just talking to someone about the material—a classmate, friend, or family member—can serve as a self-test. The concepts that are hard for you to explain are those that need more attention.

- *It is never too early to self-test.* In fact, some research shows that it helps to start testing yourself even *before* you've read the text or attended a lecture on the topic, especially if you follow up by investigating the correct answer afterwards (Richland, Kornell, & Kao, 2009). Aren't you likely to answer incorrectly? Yes, but creating that initial challenge of retrieval for your brain cells prepares you for longer-term retention of the material over time. The answer is less important than the mental exercise the question triggers.

- *Self-test to keep memories strong.* Knowing something now doesn't mean you'll know it at test time. Why? Because your brain has undoubtedly changed, at least a little bit, since you first made that memory. Some students make the mistake of studying only the difficult material, assuming that they already know the easier material. But if brain cell pathways haven't been exercised, even if that material once felt "easy," you may fail to retrieve the information when it matters at a later date (like during an exam!). Remember, the brain responds like a muscle. Imagine that you have finally reached the point where your biceps are perfectly toned. Congratulations! But that doesn't mean you never have to work them again. The same is true of memory.

Remember: Self-test to study; test early and often. Don't wait until it's too late!

SECTION REVIEW

- Warm up your brain by taking a deep-processing approach to reading the assigned material before class.
- View each class as an opportunity to further exercise your brain. Create notes that go beyond the professor's words, and compare your notes with those of classmates afterwards.
- To find out what you have really learned, and to continue the workout of your brain cells, test yourself early and often.

Test Yourself
Hint: Don't look back at the text until you have pulled out of your memory as much information as you can.

- From the perspective of training your brain, what is the purpose of reading the assigned material before class?

- What is the difference between rereading your notes and processing your notes?
- How early and how often should you test yourself while studying?

Try It

- Flip back to a section of this chapter that you found challenging, and use the 3R method (look back at Table 2): Read the section, cover it, then recite anything at all that you remember from the passage. Be patient and give yourself enough time to truly drain the contents of your brain. Finally, uncover the section and review it to check your understanding. Remember, you can use this strategy anytime you read a text or process your notes.
- Ask another student to "reconstruct" lecture notes with you shortly after a class. Discuss the content of your notes to see if either of you missed any information. Resist the urge to simply copy missed information. Instead, explain the material to each other in your own words, focusing on the meaning.
- Examine a set of notes you have recently taken during class. "Re-create" these notes, putting the material in your own words and making internal or external linkages as much as possible. Then devise a plan for how to incorporate more note-creating techniques during the next class.
- Create a "cheat sheet" list of self-testing strategies to keep close at hand as a reminder while you study. During every session of studying on your calendar for the week ahead, strive to incorporate one or two of these strategies at regular intervals.

The Moment of Truth: Exam Day

I am a very anxious test-taker. I dealt with my anxiety by getting to class early on the day of a test and frantically scanning my notes to pack in as many last-minute bits of information as possible. I thought I was improving my chances of success. In reality, I was stressing myself out and making things worse. I was usually sleep-deprived as well, heaping another unnecessary burden on my maxed-out brain (see the feature Help Your Brain Help You: The Importance of Sleep).

The First Thing to Do Is to Manage Your Stress

Of course you are nervous: You feel motivated to do your best yet worried about the uncertainty inherent in testing. (What questions will be on the test? Will I know the answers?) The stress is even greater with past experiences of disappointment related to testing. Stress makes us feel threatened, and the body responds by increasing heart rate, generating sweat, and pumping stress hormones through the bloodstream. Unfortunately, those worries steal valuable brain energy and make it difficult for you to function at top capacity. Instead of worrying about your stress response, take action. Here are some ways to manage test-day stress:

Breathe Deeply to Reduce Your Stress Response

This advice is simple but absolutely true. You may not be able to prevent the stress reaction, but you can have an impact on how long it lasts and how intense it becomes. Your body is simply unable to sustain that intense fight-or-flight reaction forever. And you can hasten its decline by taking charge of the things you can control, like the rate of your breathing.

HELP YOUR BRAIN HELP YOU

The Importance of Sleep

Take care of yourself. This advice is obvious when it comes to physical health; for example, no runner in her right mind would suggest staying up all night before a marathon. Yet, like me, I bet many of you have treated your brain poorly in pursuit of better grades. Pressed for time, we assume we must skimp on sleep to learn the material. Let go of what you think you know, and let sleep improve your memory!

No, I'm not talking about sleeping with your book beneath your pillow. Getting a good night's sleep helps the brain form and keep memories. How? A well-rested brain is better at encoding (Walker, 2008). In other words, if you're chronically sleep deprived, your brain has a harder time processing new information. You make learning harder on yourself.

Sleep also helps us strengthen and maintain the networks of memories we have recently formed. While you sleep, the brain reactivates the memories you worked on during the day, a form of mental exercise that knits those memories more deeply into your network of connections (Rasch & Born, 2008). Even a short period of daytime sleep can trigger the consolidation process that helps stabilize new memories in the brain (Mednick, Cai, Kanady, & Drummond, 2008).

Why not just power through sleepiness with caffeine? That was my "solution." I thought that Diet Coke and coffee made up for the hours of sleep I regularly skipped. Nope. In fact, research suggests that a nap may benefit your brain more than a double-shot latte. One study found that a 60- to 90-minute nap boosted memory significantly more than a 200- to 300-mg dose of caffeine (Mednick et al., 2008). Sure, caffeine makes you feel more alert, but a nap actually helps you *strengthen* the memories you've studied so hard to create.

I'm sure it's obvious why all-nighters before an exam are an absolutely terrible idea: You harm your brain's natural ability to cement memories at the very time it's most critical that your brain be working at top capacity! But even skipping a couple of hours of sleep is enough to decrease your brain's potential. Of all the advice in this chapter, this is the piece I most desperately wish I had known back when I was in college. I could have studied less and slept more? That's right! And I probably would have earned the same, or even better, grades. It's too late for me, but not for you: Get plenty of sleep and help your brain help you learn!

Have a Stress-Reduction Plan for the Moments Before the Test Is Passed Out

Figure out what helps reduce your stress response, and take action. Are you a social person who relaxes by talking to others? If so, engage in conversation with another student. Or do you need to focus inward in order to calm yourself down? Does music help you relax? Recent research suggests that highly test-anxious students relax and perform better when they write out their test-related worries for 10 minutes before the exam (Ramirez & Beilock, 2011). Try some of these suggestions, and find out what works best for you.

Identify Factors That Influence Your Ability to Stay Focused During the Exam, and Ask About Possible Accommodations

For minor requests, ask your professor. For example, if you are easily distracted by noise, ask your professor if you can use earplugs (not earbuds) during the exam. If it is noisy in the hallway, ask if the professor could close the door. If you think you may have a disability that warrants more significant accommodations, make an appointment with the disabilities services department on campus well in advance of any exams. Typically, professors are unable to make significant accommodations without this kind of expertise involved.

Be Strategic in Completing the Exam

Try some of these tips to give your brain the best chance to perform.

Start by Skimming

Skim the exam from start to finish before starting to answer questions. Why? On a practical level, skimming lets you take stock of what is coming. It reminds you of how many items are on the exam. It allows you to check whether the exam is printed on both sides of the page, so you don't accidentally fail to answer any of the questions. But skimming is also an overlooked strategy for warming up your brain. As you quickly read each question, you are exposing yourself to a treasure-trove of cues that will spark activation of your neural networks. This may not happen immediately, and you may not be fully aware of it happening. But, when it helps, you will be happy you gave it a chance!

Write on the Exam (if permitted)

Your brain is very busy while you are taking an exam, so anything you can do to ease the cognitive strain can make a big difference. Circle important words (e.g., *not*, *all*, *except for*). Cross out answers you know are incorrect. Jot down notes, charts, figures—anything that comes to mind that could help you answer the question.

If You Are Uncertain, Mark the Question, Move On, and Return to It Later

As you work on other questions, the cues you encounter may begin to jostle connections and activate a pathway to the answer. When I was taking the statistics portion of my comprehensive exams in graduate school, I kept going back to the same question again and again. I just didn't know the answer. But eventually, after working on other parts of the test, the answer just popped into my head like a gift from the universe. I can't tell you how it happened, but obviously my work on the test shook up my neural networks and spread the activation to enough spots that allowed me to construct the memory. Sometimes you have to give your brain time to activate the proper networks. Remember, each memory may consist of thousands of connections, and any of these could serve as a lifeline to the information you need.

A Special Tip for Multiple-Choice Questions: Cover the Answer Choices, and Read Only the Stem of the Question First

Basically, treat a multiple-choice question like an open-ended question first, and try to recall the answer. Think of it as a strategy to warm up the relevant neural networks. Next, uncover the answer choices and make a decision. Why do this? Sometimes it's easy to overanalyze the answer choices, which can lead to confusion. Answer choices often contain a variety of cues that can lead you down the wrong neural pathways. Focus on the stem first, trigger those associations, and then consider the answer choices.

Don't Assume Your First Hunch Is Always Correct

Many of us have received the well-intentioned but misguided advice to trust our instincts and not change our initial answers. Let go of what you think you know! To the contrary, research indicates that students more often change from an incorrect to a correct answer than vice versa (Lilienfeld, Lynn, Ruscio, & Beyerstein, 2010). If you really don't know the answer, randomly making changes is not going to help improve your score. But if you are struck by compelling reasons that suggest your initial answer is incorrect, trust your reasoning.

A Special Tip for Essay Questions: Brainstorm and Outline First

You probably get more nervous about essay questions than multiple-choice ones, but don't let this fear freeze your brain. In the margins or on the back (if writing on the exam is permissible), sketch out any ideas that come to mind in response to the essay question. Try to organize these thoughts into some structure. This helps activate the relevant brain cell networks, basically warming up the brain. If the answer isn't coming to you, move on to other questions and come back to it later. Sometimes the act of answering other questions will remind you of other bits of relevant information. As that happens, write those ideas alongside the others. When you are ready to answer the essay question, make sure you provide the information that is requested. For example, compare/contrast questions require you not only to define concepts but also to show how they are similar to and different from one another. Application questions require that you not only provide definitions but also show how terms or concepts relate to a given example.

Don't Rush Through the Exam Just to "Get It Over With"

We all look forward to unpleasant experiences coming to an end. My dentist is a terrific person, but dental work is unpleasant, and I want appointments to be over as quickly as possible. It's only natural that you would feel the same way about exams. However, unlike being at the dentist, you decide how quickly to work on a test; within the overall testing-time framework, you decide when the ordeal is over. The anticipation is enticing: You look forward to the feeling of relief.

In my class, I often hear audible sighs as students walk out the door after taking a test. This desire for relief can lead you to work faster than you should, increasing your odds of misreading questions or making other careless mistakes. So take all the time you are given to show all of what you know on an exam.

SECTION REVIEW

- Manage your pre-exam stress so you can devote more of your brain's resources to demonstrating your mastery.
- Be strategic in completing the exam: Skim to get an overview, make notes to aid your memory, and allow the experience of taking the exam to activate the connections you made while studying.
- Do not rush. Take the time you are given to show what you really know!

Test Yourself

Hint: Don't look back at the text until you have pulled out of your memory as much information as you can.

- What impact does stress have on your brain?
- How can skimming the exam influence your memory?
- What should you do if you are having second thoughts about an answer you chose?

Try It

- Reflect on your typical pre-exam experience. What changes could you make to improve your brain's ability to do its best for you? Identify at least one strategy you could incorporate when you take your next exam.
- Evaluate the strategies you typically follow while taking exams, and plan out the changes you could make to improve your performance on the next one.
- The next time you take an exam, introduce a "mindful moment" whenever you feel overwhelmed. Try the S.T.O.P. method (Stahl & Goldstein, 2010): *Stop* (simply take a brief moment to pause). *Take* a deep breath. Without passing judgment, *Observe* what's going on in your mind and body (Is your heart rate elevated? Are anxious thoughts interfering with your reasoning?). Finally, *Proceed* (check the time, note how many more items you have to complete, and decide which test-taking strategies to use next). Remind yourself of this strategy by writing "STOP" at the top of your exam.

Actually Doing It

Consider this question: What are the observable behaviors that successful students engage in consistently? At this point, you should have all kinds of answers. That's the easy part. But consider a trickier question: Once successful, how do you prevent yourself from slipping back into old, ineffective patterns of study behavior, like cramming, depriving yourself of sleep, and rote memorizing? Unfortunately, "saying" is much easier than "doing." But take heart: Any pattern of behavior or thinking you engage in that is detrimental to your learning is still just a habit. Habits reflect well-worn pathways in the neural networks of the brain, like a map of our current default settings. Habits are not eliminated overnight, but they can be changed through awareness, persistence, and motivation (see the feature Help Your Brain Help You: The Trouble with Multitasking to learn about a common habit that makes learning more difficult).

Developing Habits of Self-Regulation and Self-Control

Changing habits requires plenty of self-regulation, something that is challenging for most of us. If you've ever known what you needed to do but had trouble actually doing it, you know what this is like. We need to exercise self-control, putting off something very interesting right now in order to do something else that is less interesting but will pay off big time later. Luckily, we can build self-control over time; it's another mental muscle that responds to training (Muraven, 2010). The benefits extend well beyond studying, too; our strengthened self-control helps us modify any habit or learn any new skill—from quitting smoking to learning a new job.

HELP YOUR BRAIN HELP YOU

The Trouble with Multitasking

Are you easily bored? I am. I get bored while I'm cleaning or doing laundry, so I often listen to a podcast or audiobook. It makes the time pass more quickly. As long as one of the tasks is virtually mindless (like folding laundry), multitasking can work just fine. But when you try to do two cognitively complex tasks at once—like studying while texting or IMing—the brain protests. Why? The brain cannot simultaneously engage in two tasks requiring complex cognition. Instead, it shifts back and forth between tasks. When you study, you exercise one set of networks in the brain. When you read and answer a text message, you switch to a completely different network. All of this switching puts a lot of stress on your brain. It's like requiring one conductor to switch back and forth between two different orchestras performing different pieces. Your brain is designed to do its best work when focused on one task (Rubenstein, Myer, & Evans, 2001). When you try to multitask while studying, you activate a less flexible and more basic area of the brain capable of only the most shallow processing (Foerde, Knowlton, & Poldrack, 2006).

You may feel like multitasking is necessary in order to keep you from feeling so bored. Maybe it seems like you're able to study longer while watching TV, using Facebook, or talking to friends. If this is the case, I need you to let go of what you think you know. Yes, time may seem to pass more quickly, but you are making things much harder on your brain by providing it with a very weak form of exercise. By eliminating distractions, you make your studying more efficient and effective. In short, multitasking wastes time; performing one task at a time saves time.

What if you are a chronic multitasker? Can you train your brain to switch between tasks without any declines in brain performance? The scientific evidence suggests the answer is no: Practice does not make perfect. In fact, those who multitask most often tend to show the steepest declines in their cognitive performance while multitasking (Ophir, Nass, & Wagner, 2009)!

If you are easily bored while studying, evaluate your study habits. Spending several hours memorizing definitions or rereading notes? That's boring. Instead of pulling out your cell phone or turning on the TV, use the strategies discussed in this chapter. Remember, studying that feels challenging now pays off the most later, and it also happens to be much less boring than memorizing flashcards. So try something different. Spend shorter periods of time on each subject, and alternate between subjects. Make a concept map. Create some open-ended questions and test yourself. Pretend you are teaching the material to someone else. Focus on having a high-quality mental workout, and your urge to multitask won't be so strong.

Procrastination is one of the biggest self-control challenges we face. It feels good in the moment because we have avoided an aversive task. In regard to studying, students procrastinate for many reasons. Some are afraid of failure, and some believe they do their best work under the pressure of the last minute. Whatever the reason, procrastination gives us an escape from an unpleasant feeling. But it always catches up with us in the end. One study found that students who procrastinated reported more health problems near the end of the term, perhaps because of the stress of all of that cramming. On top of that, their grades suffered as well (Tice & Baumeister, 1997). Here are some strategies you can use to strengthen your self-control.

Start with a Short Burst

If you are having trouble getting started with a task, make it very easy at first. Work on the dreaded task for only 10 minutes, and then take a 2-minute break to do something more interesting. Go back for another 10-minute work session, and then take another 2-minute break. Repeat as necessary! I do this to kick-start my grading, which at first leaves me feeling overwhelmed. But when I think about only spending 10 minutes on grading, it's no longer a big deal. What usually happens next is that the simple act of getting started breaks the spell of procrastination. I find that after a few 10-minute bursts, I can work longer.

Make Sure You Are Spacing Out Your Studying

Remember, it's better for your brain if your study sessions are short and frequent. This helps with procrastination as well, because a 1-hour study session seems far less dreadful than a 5-hour marathon.

Capitalize on Your Strengths and Interests

Fuse something that provides immediate rewards with something that advances you toward your long-term goal (Steel, 2007). For example, if you are a very social person who loves meeting new people, form a study group early in the semester and start meeting regularly. If you love nature, incorporate a short session of reading into your next hike. In other words, find ways to link studying with some of the things you love.

Make Small Changes in Your Environment to Stay Focused on Your Goals

People striving to meet health-related goals do this by eliminating unhealthy foods from their pantry at home. You can do something similar to advance your academic goals. Reduce distractions by turning off any indicators of new texts or e-mails. Better yet, put your cell phone in a different room. Is the Internet a constant temptation? Temporarily disable your online access. Do you have trouble staying focused in class? Sit where you are not able to see the clock, or put your watch or cell phone away so you can't see the time. Why? The more we check the time, the more slowly time seems to pass (Sackett, Meyvis, Nelson, Converse, & Sackett, 2010). Try sitting in the front row, where the professor is more likely to notice your behavior. That way, you're less likely to feel tempted to give into your urge to text, sleep, or daydream.

Act "As If"

Have you ever felt your attitude needed an adjustment? Try changing your behavior first. Do you think this is the most boring class in the world? Act "as if" you are interested: Get to class early, sit near the front, listen intently with an expression of interest, and create great notes. Quite literally, play the role of "interested student." Do this to boost your studying outside class (if necessary) as well. Obviously, this will feel very strange at first, but research indicates that our attitudes often shift to line up with our behaviors (Festinger, 1957). This may not become your favorite class, but acting "as if" is likely to help improve your attitude and motivation. As a result, you have more energy to apply effective study strategies!

SECTION REVIEW

- Habits are behaviors learned over time. As such, habits can be unlearned through persistence and patience.
- Self-control and self-regulation habits are central to long-term, effective studying.
- You should focus on making small changes first.

Test Yourself

Hint: Don't look back at the text until you have pulled out of your memory as much information as you can.

- How is practicing self-control like engaging a muscle?
- Why can it be beneficial to your studying to act "as if" you are more interested and motivated than you sometimes really feel?

Try It

- Think back to a time when you successfully changed a habit. How did you do it? Adapt elements of that experience to change your least effective study habits.
- If you tend to put things off, choose one procrastination-reduction method to apply in the week ahead.
- Identify the biggest distractions you face while studying, and make changes to your environment to minimize these distractions the next time you study.

If At First You Don't Succeed . . .

Effective habits for studying and self-regulation come from the same place: the well-trained brain. Imagine your brain cells lifting weights, getting stronger and building more connections every day. It will take time to figure out which strategies work best for you, so be prepared to experiment. Remember, your brain is wired uniquely; the strategies that work best for you may be different from those that work best for others. You may also find that different classes require different strategies, so prepare to modify your approach accordingly.

Allow yourself to be human. You will probably lapse back into ineffective strategies or habits occasionally. What matters most is what you do next. Take a lesson from a recent study on procrastination (Wohl, Pychyl, & Bennet, 2010). Students who forgave themselves for procrastinating before Exam 1 were much less likely to procrastinate before Exam 2. Self-forgiveness prevented them from spiraling into apathy, like a dieter who slips up with one cookie and decides he might as well eat the whole box. The self-forgivers acknowledged their slip-up and took the next opportunity to get back on track again. So with these findings in mind, keep persisting!

Whether your future plans include academics or not, I hope the practical advice offered in this chapter will help you make long-lasting changes in the way you approach any type of learning experience.

References

Bjork, E., & Bjork, R. (2011). Making things hard on yourself, but in a good way: Creating desirable difficulties to enhance learning. In M. A. Gernsbacher, R. W. Pew, L. W. Hough, & J. R. Pomerantz (Eds.), *Psychology and the real world: Essays illustrating fundamental contributions to society* (pp. 56–64). New York: Worth Publishers.

Cook, S. W., Mitchell, Z., & Goldin-Meadow, S. (2008). Gesturing makes learning last. *Cognition, 106* (2), 1047–1058. doi:10.1016/j.cognition.2007.04.010

Craik, F.I.M., & Tulving, E. (1975). Depth of processing and the retention of words in episodic memory. *Journal of Experimental Psychology: General, 104,* 268-294.

Festinger, L. (1957). *A theory of cognitive dissonance.* Evanston, IL: Row, Peterson.

Foerde, K., Knowlton, B. J., & Poldrack, R. A. (2006). Modulation of competing memory systems by distraction. *Proceedings of the National Academy of Sciences, 103*(31), 11778–11783. doi:10.1073/pnas.0602659103

Glenberg, A., Brown, M., & Levin, J. (2007). Enhancing comprehension in small reading groups using a manipulation strategy. *Contemporary Educational Psychology, 32*(3), 389–399. doi:10.1016/j.cedpsych.2006.03.001

Karpicke, J. D., & Blunt, J. R. (2011). Retrieval practice produces more learning than elaborative studying with concept mapping. *Science, 331*(6018), 772–775. doi:10.1126/science.1199327

Kiewra, K. A. (2002). How classroom teachers can help students learn and teach them how to learn. *Theory into Practice, 41*(2), 71–80.

Knight, L. J., & McKelvie, S. J. (1986). Effects of attendance, note-taking, and review on memory for a lecture: Encoding vs. external storage functions of notes. *Canadian Journal of Behavioural Science/Revue canadienne des sciences du comportement, 18*(1), 52–61. doi:10.1037/h0079957

Kornell, N. (in press). Discrimination learning: Training methods. In H. Pashler (Ed.), *Encyclopedia of the mind.* Thousand Oaks: Sage Reference.

Kornell, N. (2009). Optimising learning using flashcards: Spacing is more effective than cramming. *Applied Cognitive Psychology, 23*(9), 1297–1317. doi:10.1002/acp.1537

Kruger, J., & Dunning, D. (1999). Unskilled and unaware of it: How difficulties in recognizing one's own incompetence lead to inflated self-assessments. *Journal of Personality and Social Psychology, 77*(6), 1121–1134. doi:10.1037/0022-3514.77.6.1121

Lilienfeld, S. O., Lynn, S. J., Ruscio, J., & Beyerstein, B. L. (2010). *50 great myths of popular psychology: Shattering widespread misconceptions about human behavior.* Malden, MA: Wiley-Blackwell.

Mayer, R. E. (1996). Learning strategies for making sense out of expository text: The SOI model for guiding three cognitive processes in knowledge construction. *Educational Psychology Review, 8*(4), 357–371. doi:10.1007/BF01463939

McDaniel, M. A., Howard, D. C., & Einstein, G. O. (2009). The Read-Recite-Review study strategy: Effective and portable. *Psychological Science, 20*(4), 516–522. doi:10.1111/j.1467-9280.2009.02325.x

Medina, J. (2008). *Brain rules: 12 principles for surviving and thriving at work, home, and school.* Seattle, WA: Pear Press.

Mednick, S., Cai, D., Kanady, J., & Drummond, S. (2008). Comparing the benefits of caffeine, naps and placebo on verbal, motor and perceptual memory. *Behavioural Brain Research, 193*(1), 79–86. doi:10.1016/j.bbr.2008.04.028

Muraven, M. (2010). Practicing self-control lowers the risk of smoking lapse. *Psychology of Addictive Behaviors, 24*(3), 446–452. doi:10.1037/a0018545

Noice, H., & Noice, T. (2006). What studies of actors and acting can tell us about memory and cognitive functioning. *Current Directions in Psychological Science, 15*(1), 14–18.

Ophir, E., Nass, C., & Wagner, A. D. (2009). From the cover: Cognitive control in media multitaskers. *Proceedings of the National Academy of Sciences, 106*(37), 15583–15587. doi:10.1073/pnas.0903620106

Peverly, S. T., Ramaswamy, V., Brown, C., Sumowski, J., Alidoost, M., & Garner, J. (2007). What predicts skill in lecture note taking? *Journal of Educational Psychology, 99*(1), 167–180. doi:10.1037/0022-0663.99.1.167

Ramirez, G., & Beilock, S. L. (2011). Writing about testing worries boosts exam performance in the classroom. *Science, 331*(6014), 211–213. doi:10.1126/science.1199427

Rasch, B., & Born, J. (2008). Reactivation and consolidation of memory during sleep. *Current Directions in Psychological Science, 17*(3), 188–192.

Richland, L. E., Kornell, N., & Kao, L. S. (2009). The pretesting effect: Do unsuccessful retrieval attempts enhance learning? *Journal of Experimental Psychology: Applied, 15*(3), 243–257. doi:10.1037/a0016496

Robinson, F. P. (1970). *Effective study*. New York: HarperCollins.

Rohrer, D., & Pashler, H. (2010). Recent research on human learning challenges conventional instructional strategies. *Educational Researcher, 39*(5), 406–412. doi:10.3102/0013189X10374770

Rubinstein, J. S., Meyer, D. E., & Evans, J. E. (2001). Executive control of cognitive processes in task switching. *Journal of Experimental Psychology: Human Perception and Performance, 27*(4), 763–797. doi:10.1037//0096-1523.27.4.763

Sackett, A. M., Meyvis, T., Nelson, L. D., Converse, B. A., & Sackett, A. L. (2010). You're having fun when time flies: The hedonic consequences of subjective time progression. *Psychological Science, 21*(1), 111–117. doi:10.1177/0956797609354832

Smith, S. M. (2007). Context and human memory. In H. L. Roediger, Y. Dudai, & S. M. Fitzpatrick (Eds.), *Science of memory: Concepts* (pp. 111–114). Oxford: Oxford University Press.

Smith, S. M., & Vela, E. (2001). Environmental context dependent memory: A review and meta analysis. *Psychonomic Bulletin and Review, 8*, 203–220.

Stahl, B., & Goldstein, E. (2010). *A mindfulness-based stress reduction workbook*. Oakland, CA: New Harbinger Publications.

Stanovich, K. (2010). *How to think straight about psychology* (9th ed.). Boston: Allyn & Bacon.

Stanovich, K. E. (2010). *Rationality and the reflective mind*. New York: Oxford University Press.

Steel, P. (2007). The nature of procrastination: A meta-analytic and theoretical review of quintessential self-regulatory failure. *Psychological Bulletin, 133*(1), 65–94. doi:10.1037/0033-2909.133.1.65

Stevanoni, E., & Salmon, K. (2005). Giving memory a hand: Instructing children to gesture enhances their event recall. *Journal of Nonverbal Behavior, 29*(4), 217–233. doi:10.1007/s10919-005-7721-y

Tice, D. M., & Baumeister, R. F. (1997). Longitudinal study of procrastination, performance, stress, and health: The costs and benefits of dawdling. *Psychological Science, 8*(6), 454–458. doi:10.1111/j.1467-9280.1997.tb00460.x

Walker, M. P. (2008). Sleep-dependent memory processing. *Harvard Review of Psychiatry, 16*(5), 287–298. doi:10.1080/10673220802432517

Wohl, M. J., Pychyl, T. A., & Bennett, S. H. (2010). I forgive myself, now I can study: How self-forgiveness for procrastinating can reduce future procrastination. *Personality and Individual Differences, 48*(7), 803–808. doi:10.1016/j.paid.2010.01.029

The Basics of Scientific Writing in APA Style

Pam Marek
Kennesaw State University

This chapter was prepared with the expert assistance of Terrence D. Jorgensen, M.S., Applied Statistics, Kennesaw State University (Ph.D, Quantitative Psychology, University of Kansas, expected 2016)

Common Genres of APA-Style Articles

Step 1: Planning—Locating, Reading, and Taking Notes on Source Material
 Locating Appropriate Source Material
 Reading Source Material
 Constructing an Outline and Taking Notes

Step 2: Writing a First Draft
 General Information About APA-Style Formatting
 Title Page
 The Abstract
 The Introduction
 Citations in Scientific Writing
 Method Section of an Empirical Report
 Results Section of an Empirical Report
 Discussion Section of an Empirical Report
 References

Step 3: Editing and Proofreading
 Grammar and Punctuation Rules for All Writing
 Rules Pertaining Specifically to APA Style
 Things to Avoid in APA-Style Writing

Appendix A: Sample Annotated Manuscript

Appendix B: Constructing Grammatical Sentences

For quite some time, the three Rs—Reading, 'Riting, and 'Rithmetic—have been the cornerstone of education. When it comes to "'Riting," scientists use specific scientific writing styles to communicate their findings in a way that generalizes across many disciplines. By utilizing these styles, they effectively organize their material; communicate with clarity, precision, and logic; and cite source materials to avoid plagiarism (inappropriate use of someone else's ideas or expressions). Familiarity with the elements of scientific writing in the field of psychology—specifically, APA (American Psychological Association) style—will enhance successful report writing and assignment preparation in psychology courses. An understanding of scientific writing style also provides a tool that sharpens critical thinking about ideas and evaluation of conclusions.

Scientific writing, like all formal writing, requires a firm foundation in English sentence construction, usage, and punctuation. The abbreviated communication used in instant messages or tweets among friends—such as "RUOK with this?"—would likely cause confusion and, possibly, consternation from those who read scientific writing. When studying this chapter, consider its contents a challenge to learning how to organize ideas about science and to expressing science-related thoughts with clear but formal language. Use the chapter as a reference to guide formal scientific writing and APA style, specifically.

Writing for any discipline involves a cycle (or multiple cycles) that includes (1) planning, which encompasses locating and reading source materials; (2) writing a rough draft; and (3) editing and proofreading. Writers aim for continuity and a logical flow of ideas. In scientific writing, all ideas must be supported by evidence, with appropriate citations of the source of the evidence. Of course, different instructors have different requirements for writing assignments. Thus, it is important for you to be thoroughly familiar with the criteria for specific assignments and to assume responsibility for clarifying the answers to questions that arise.

In psychology courses, the "ultimate source" for appropriate writing style is the *Publication Manual of the American Psychological Association*, 6th edition.* The guidelines for APA style include instructions for formatting, organization, content, citations, lan-

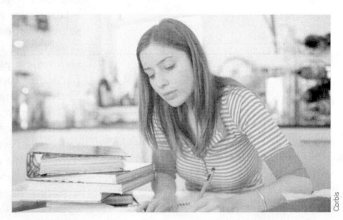

* This content is adapted from Publication Manual of the American Psychological Association (6th ed.). Washington, DC, US: American Psychological Association (2010). Copyright (c) 2010 by the American Psychological Association. Adapted with permission.

This content is not a substitute for the *Publication Manual of the American Psychological Association,* 6th edition (2010), which contains broad and comprehensive guidance on all aspects of scientific writing.

APA has a number of resources to help individuals learn APA style, including free tutorials, FAQs, and an APA Style blog. Visit http://www.apastyle.org for more information, and join APA Style on Facebook http://www.facebook.com/APAStyle and Twitter http://twitter.com/#!/APA_Style.

guage, and sentence construction. Unless your instructor says otherwise, use formal language when writing APA-style papers because the typical audience includes researchers and academics. Precise and clear writing is crucial, with adjectives or adverbs used only to advance accurate and objective description. For instance, a scientific writer might describe participants in an experiment as "preschool children"; in this case, the adjective "preschool" helps to clarify the age and experience of the subjects. If this writer had written "cute little children," the word "cute" would express only the writer's opinion, and the word "little" would be a less precise description of the participants' age or experience.

When learning about the elements of APA style, students are sometimes surprised to find that many psychology textbooks do not use it. For example, to engage a student such as yourself, many textbooks (and this very chapter!) frequently use a more conversational tone, addressing the reader as "you." As you will notice in the "Things to Avoid in APA Style" section of this chapter, when writing in APA style, writers avoid the word "you." Instead, rather than addressing the reader directly, they use terms such as "people" or "individuals." To help you make these kinds of distinctions, this chapter outlines several "dos and don'ts" for writing in APA style (see Table 6, page 20).

Further, to illustrate APA style items, Appendix A (pages 1–16) presents an annotated manuscript for an article published in the *Psi Chi Journal of Undergraduate Research* (http://www.psichi.org/pubs/journal/). The annotated comments point out ways in which science writing may or may not meet APA criteria and emphasizes correct APA style. Appendix B (pages B-1–B-2) summarizes and illustrates important rules for proper sentence construction. All examples are drawn from students' final reports of an experimental psychology class project that focused on ageism in the workplace. Armed with this information, you will be prepared to complete written assignments effectively in a variety of psychology courses.

COMMON GENRES OF APA-STYLE ARTICLES

The types of written assignments that instructors may ask you to complete will vary across courses. In an introductory psychology class, for example, your instructor may require an article summary, a book review, or a brief paper on a specific topic. In research methods, experimental psychology, and laboratory courses (e.g., some cognitive psychology or learning and behavior courses), your instructor may require a laboratory report, an empirical report on a project you have completed, or a research proposal. In senior-level courses, instructors may also require an empirical report on an individual project, or they may require that you prepare a comprehensive review paper to compare and contrast different theoretical perspectives on a particular topic. Thus, during the course of your academic career, you will most likely be using APA style to prepare a variety of different types of reports.

To prepare for most of the assignments described above, you will be reading articles from professional journals. Typically, these articles will be classified as empirical reports or review articles. An **empirical report** describes original research that the authors have conducted, typically with human participants or animals. In these reports, authors provide a structured framework for their new research by topically integrating relevant findings of existing studies in a literature review, presenting their hypotheses, describing their methodology and results, and then concluding with a discussion to position the new research in the context of existing knowledge. A **review article** integrates, summarizes, and provides suggestions for extending prior research on a particular topic. Rather than initiating a new investigation with individual participants, authors of review articles study the existing literature on a topic. The information contained in a review article is an expansion of the information contained in the literature review portion of the introduction to an empirical report.

APA style specifies guidelines for the order of report sections. Table 1 lists these sections sequentially. To guide both your reading and writing, it also includes a brief

TABLE 1 **Organization of Empirical Reports and Review Articles**

Section	Information in Section	Page (typed manuscript)
Title page	Identifies topic/variables studied and provides authorship information	1
Abstract	Provides very brief summary of information from major sections of report	2
Introduction (or Body of empirical report)	Indicates purpose and importance of research and reviews prior research literature and theory • In an empirical report, the introduction typically concludes with specific hypotheses that follow from information in the literature review • In a review article, the literature review and theoretical information are more extensive than in an empirical report and constitute the body (main part) of the report	Start on p. 3
Method	In an empirical report, provides sufficient information about participants, design, materials, and procedures so that interested readers might replicate (repeat) the research	No new page
Results	In an empirical report, provides detailed information about the findings and includes results of statistical analysis for quantitative research	No new page
Discussion (or Conclusion)	Offers interpretation of results, their theoretical implications, limitations of the research, potential applications of the findings, and ideas for further research • In an empirical report, the discussion typically includes a focus on whether results supported specific hypotheses presented in the introduction and an explanation of why hypotheses were (or were not) supported	No new page
References	Lists authorship and source information for all items cited in report or article to enable readers to locate original sources	Start on new page

statement of the information contained in each section. Finally, it indicates which sections should start on a new page in a manuscript.

Supplementary information (e.g., Appendix, tables) follows the References section, and page numbers continue from the end of the References section. In a typed manuscript, you would present supplementary information in the following order, with each section starting on a new page: tables, figures, and then appendices. In a published article, these sections are integrated within the text rather than appearing in a separate section.

STEP 1: PLANNING—LOCATING, READING, AND TAKING NOTES ON SOURCE MATERIAL

Scientific papers are not written in a vacuum; rather, they build on and extend prior research. Thus, becoming familiar with existing scientific literature on the topic of interest is a crucial first step in planning a paper. Planning a scientific writing assignment involves locating appropriate source articles, reading the articles, and taking notes in a manner that will ultimately facilitate preparation of a first draft that includes accurate citations.

Locating Appropriate Source Material

When locating appropriate source material, it is important to distinguish between scientific material and articles targeted at the general public that may or may not be firmly based on scientific research. Multiple sources are available on the internet, in books, in newspapers, and in trade publications that may be tempting to use. However, unlike articles in professional, peer-reviewed literature, these sources often do not contain citations to support their claims, may be based on anecdotal evidence such as personal experience, or may include conclusions that are not justified by the data presented. In other words, there may be no "check" on the accuracy of the facts or logic of the arguments.

The peer review process is a safeguard against these weaknesses. If an article is peer reviewed, it means that professionals who are experts in a particular field have carefully evaluated the article on dimensions such as inclusion and citation of relevant background material, methodology, analysis, and interpretation of results. Thus, before you begin a writing project, you will often need to search the professional, peer-reviewed literature on your topic. Computerized databases typically allow users to limit their searches to peer-reviewed sources. PsycINFO is a comprehensive database for psychology-related sources. After entering search terms, you will be able to retrieve a listing of published articles, books, and book chapters. In this database, as in many others, searches can be restricted to terms found in specific fields (e.g., author, title, abstract, source) of database records. As shown below, a search for the term "writing" in the title and "assessment" in the abstract yielded 541 results.

These results suggest that your initial topic may be too broad to cover in a single paper. Generally, a literature review is more effective if writers probe deeply into a more limited topic rather than skim over a wide range of material. A more limited topic allows you to compare and contrast different approaches or theories rather than simply describing them. Careful selection of articles will make it easier to write a cohesive literature review. Reading the abstract will indicate how closely an article relates to your specific topic of interest. Often, you may decide to restrict your search to specific subtopics or populations. For example, narrowing the results above by adding the term "college students" in the "subjects" field led to a list of 31 potential items.

After locating appropriate sources, the next step is to obtain the full text of the material. In some instances, full text articles are available for downloading directly from the database. When given the choice between .html and .pdf, the .pdf version is preferable because it integrates tables and figures in the text for ease of reference. Although some students are tempted to limit their sources to those that are available for immediate download, yielding to such temptation often leads to the omission of highly relevant information from the literature review. To avoid this potential problem, attempt to locate the material by checking the catalogue at your school's library. If the library does not have the material, check with a librarian (or on the library web page) to determine the procedures for ordering material via interlibrary loan. Typically, school libraries share materials with each other; thus, if the material is not available at your school, your library may be able to borrow it from another school for your use. The time needed to obtain materials from other libraries varies across institutions and by the type of resource requested.

Prior to searching for sources or after reading just a few that have been collected, it is helpful to develop a topical outline for the literature review. This outline can guide the search process, and you can refine it as the search progresses. Then, when reading and taking notes about theories, findings, and relevant terms in the source articles, you can position the notes in the appropriate section of the outline.

Reading Source Material

It takes considerable time to select and collect sources and to extract the appropriate material from each source. Professional articles are not necessarily easy to read and "digest." Reading the abstract first will give you an idea of what to expect. However, if you just read the abstract, you definitely will not have a sufficient depth of understanding (or content) to integrate information into a literature review.

Before reading an article thoroughly, familiarize yourself with the article's structure (the information contained in each section). Table 1 on page 3 indicates what to expect in each section. Then, as you read the article more carefully, direct your attention to issues such as the research purpose and importance, how it relates to prior research on the topic, the hypotheses, general methodology, major findings, and interpretation of the findings. As you read, consider how the material relates to what you plan to write.

As you confront potentially unfamiliar terminology and theories, your first experience reading articles from the professional literature is apt to be quite challenging. If you plan to include information from a source in your written report, be sure that you take the time to understand it. Otherwise, you will not be able to express the ideas correctly in your own words or to integrate them with related material in your report. Early in your academic career, the material in the Results section, which often includes multiple statistical tests, is particularly daunting. To gain a better understanding of the results, read the verbal information that indicates, for example, whether one group performed better than another did or whether one variable predicted another variable. In addition, in the Discussion section, authors often reiterate key results in a straightforward verbal form when they examine support for a hypothesis or explain the findings.

Constructing an Outline and Taking Notes

It is important to develop a topical outline. Do this as early as possible in the literature review process. A topical outline helps overcome the tendency to summarize one article after another. Organizing information by topic encourages you to compare and contrast the findings from one study with those of other studies on the same topic in a single paragraph (integrating information from multiple sources). Your topical outline serves as a framework for presentation of past research and provides an underlying structure for writing.

> *Note:* For a review article, you may opt to use your outline to develop headings for subsections. The outline for a review article encompasses the entire article, leading to the conclusions. For an empirical study, the items in an outline will guide the flow of information relevant to explaining the particular research question, illuminating prior research related to the variables being investigated, and providing a rationale for the research hypothesis.

Good note taking during a literature review typically leads to a higher quality paper. Because a source article may address one or more topics, it is helpful to categorize notes topically and to include identifying information from source articles for citation purposes. To avoid plagiarism in the writing stage, do not copy phrases directly from articles and do not simply change one or two words in a sentence when you add the information to your notes. Instead, describe the ideas and findings in your own words. *Be sure that your notes include all the information you need for citations* that are required for each factual item that is not very common knowledge. If in doubt, cite! Although using quotations in psychological writing is discouraged, if it seems absolutely necessary to use a brief quote (and assignment criteria permit doing so), remember to include quotation marks (and a page number) as well as a citation! Highlighting the sections of source articles from which you draw information will assist subsequent self-checks for signs of plagiarism, which encompass both missing or incorrect citations and use of similar words or expressions. (See Table 5 on page 10 for more details about these topics.)

STEP 2: WRITING A FIRST DRAFT

This section focuses on the types of information that you need to organize and include in each section of a research report. It begins with general guidelines for formatting and provides additional information about formatting for each individual part of the paper. To emphasize the importance of citations in APA-style writing, it includes a special section about citations and their formatting both in the text of the report and in the References section.

General Information About APA-Style Formatting

APA-style formatting includes rules for margins, line spacing, alignment, and font as outlined in the table below. Using the options provided by word processing software, select the appropriate formatting choices before starting your first draft. When preparing the paper, adjust the formatting options for the Abstract and References as noted in Table 2.

There are also APA-style formatting rules for the headings and subheadings, which do not include what APA-style considers section labels (e.g., "Abstract," the title, and "References"). On her APA-style blog, Chelsea Lee includes a table that concisely summarizes these rules at http://blog.apastyle.org/apastyle/2009/07/five-essential-tips-for-apa-style-headings.html or http://tinyurl.com/ykqzm6s. For their respective sections, the words Method, Results, and Discussion are typed using Level 1 bold-faced headings. However, the first section of an APA-style report (the Introduction) begins with the title of the paper (not the word "Introduction"). Although it is centered, the title is not shown in boldface font. "Abstract" and "References" titles are also centered, but not boldfaced.

TABLE 2 How to Format APA-Style Manuscripts

Line spacing	• Double-spaced throughout • No extra spaces between paragraphs
Spacing after punctuation	• Use two spaces after punctuation at the end of a sentence; otherwise, use one space after punctuation
Alignment	• Left for all paragraphs and most headings, but Level 1 headings (for major sections, see illustration) are centered
Margins	• All (top, bottom, left, right) set at 1" for the body of the manuscript, with header ½" from top
Typeface	• 12-point font, Times New Roman

First line of paragraph	• Set indent at .5" paragraph
	• Exceptions:
	  ▪ The abstract is a single block paragraph (without .5" indent for the first line)
	  ▪ Reference items are formatted using a "hanging" indent (with the first line of each citation beginning at the margin and subsequent lines using a .5" ["hanging"] indent)

Page number & running head	• On the first line of the header in a Word document, the running head appears at top left of all pages, and the page number appears at top right on the same line • Explained in Title Page section

There are five levels of headings in APA style. An example illustrating the use of the first three levels from an empirical paper is shown at right. Level 1, used for the main section heading (Method), is centered and in boldface font. If there were multiple words in the Level 1 heading, all words with four letters or more would begin with a capital letter. Level 2, used for the Participants and Materials subsections in the example, is also in boldface font, but it is positioned flush with the left margin. Capitalization rules are the same as those for Level 1 headings. Level 3, used for Scenarios and related questions in the example, is positioned .5" from the left margin (as is the indent for the first line of a new paragraph), is in boldface font, and is followed by a period (with text beginning thereafter). Only the first word of Level 3 headings is capitalized unless the heading includes proper nouns, which would also be capitalized.

Level 4 and Level 5 headings, if needed, would also be positioned .5" from the left margin and would be followed by a period. Level 4 and Level 5 headings are italicized and follow the same capitalization rules used for Level 3 headings. However, the font style used for Level 4 and Level 5 headings differs: boldface for Level 4 and regular for Level 5.

Method

Participants

Participants included 301 individuals from a community sample (180 women and 115 men, $M_{age} = 38.64$, $SD_{age} = 14.15$.

Participants had a variety of ethnic backgrounds, (text continues)

Materials

Scenarios and related questions. Participants read a brief scenario about a mother (Maggie) who was offered the measles, mumps, and rubella (MMR) vaccine for (text continues)

Title Page

The title should clearly and concisely (maximum 12 words) indicate the topic of the manuscript. For an empirical report, it should include the primary variables that you are studying. For a review article, it should contain the major issue that you are investigating. Use Table 3 as a guide for the Title Page.

TABLE 3 What to Include on a Title Page

Title	• Centered horizontally on upper half of page • Capitalize first letters of important words and all words of four of more letters
Author's name and	• Centered, on a line double-spaced below title, including first name, middle initial, last name • If there are two authors from the same institution, both names are typed on the same line with "and" between them
Institutional affiliation	• Centered • On a line double-spaced below author's name
Running head (appears at top of page in published articles)	• In header area (use header feature in word processing programs) • Type the words "Running head:" left-justified • After the words Running head: (on the same line in the header area) type an abbreviated title *in all capital letters* (maximum 50 characters including spaces and punctuation)
IMPORTANT NOTE	• The actual running head appears on all pages, but the words "Running head:" appear on the title page only. For instructions on creating a unique header for the first page, see http://www.apastyle.org/learn/faqs/running-head.aspx
Page number	• In header on every page, on same line as running head, on right • Title page is page 1 • Do not use dashes or the word "page," just the number • Use automatic page numbering feature in word-processing programs

In manuscripts submitted for publication, title pages also contain an Author's Note. Guidelines specify that an Author's Note should include departmental affiliation, acknowledgments, and contact information for the author. However, your instructor may not require an Author's Note on student papers.

The Abstract

An abstract summarizes a report in 120 to 250 words with maximum length requirements varying across journals (and instructors). When you search databases, the abstract is the only section of a manuscript shown in the database record. By reading the abstract, you typically learn whether a source is directly relevant to your paper.

When you actually write a report, you prepare the Abstract last because it summarizes the entire paper (see Table 4). The Abstract should not contain any information that is not included in the actual paper. Moreover, information in the Abstract should be consistent with information that is included in the body of the report. Abstracts are concise, specific, and self-explanatory.

TABLE 4 **What to Include in an Abstract**

Empirical Reports	Review Articles
Purpose/problem investigated	Topic/purpose or thesis
Number, type, age, sex (or species) of participants	Types of sources used
Method (materials used, basic procedures)	
Major findings	Major findings
Conclusions and implications	Conclusions and implications

In manuscripts submitted for publication, authors itemize keywords used for database searches. To do so, double-space after the last line of the abstract, indent .5", and type *Keywords* (italicized and followed by a colon). Then, add a few words that indicate key topics of your manuscript. For example, keywords for the manuscript in Appendix A (see pages 1–16) might include "communication" and "self-disclosure." Your instructor may not require keywords on student papers.

The Introduction

The Introduction of an empirical report or the body of a review article begins on page 3 (after the Title Page and Abstract) with the title of the paper. The opening paragraphs highlight general information about the issue under investigation and prepare readers for the detailed literature review that follows. For example, in the opening paragraphs of their Introduction in the sample manuscript, Bruss and Hill (2010) incorporated key facts about communication and self-disclosure that indicated why the issue is important. The paragraphs included specific statements, supported by citations, rather than broad generalities without citations. Typically, the opening paragraphs also include a statement of the goal or purpose of the research. However, in the sample manuscript, the explicit statement of purpose was positioned as a lead-in to the hypothesis at the end of the introduction.

The Thesis Statement

When you write a review article (or an analytical, explanatory, or argumentative paper), you typically begin with a thesis statement, a short, precise statement that indicates what issue you are analyzing, what you are explaining to readers, or what argument you are making. The thesis statement presents the main idea of your paper. If you have prepared an outline, check to be sure it includes information relevant to your thesis statement. You may need to add topics (perhaps searching for additional sources), or you may need to eliminate topics that are only peripherally related to your thesis. An outline that conforms to your thesis will serve as an effective framework for your paper, guiding your subsequent writing.

The Literature Review

As described at http://www.writing.utoronto.ca/advice/specific-types-of-writing/literature-review or http://tinyurl.com/mt22ly, the purpose of a literature review is "... to convey to your reader what knowledge and ideas have been established on a topic, and what their strengths and weaknesses are" (para. 1). In a literature review, do not simply summarize a series of articles sequentially. Rather, integrate material from multiple articles into paragraphs focused on specific subtopics linked to the purpose of your research. In the sample manuscript, Bruss and Hill (2010) integrated information about self-disclosure, online communication, and face-to-face communication in their literature review. For articles published in professional, peer-reviewed journals, literature reviews are quite comprehensive. However, instructors' expectations for literature reviews typically reflect the extent of your experience with reading professional literature and preparing scientific reports. Regardless of requirements for length or a minimum number of sources, typical expectations include thorough reading of source articles, precise and accurate reporting, appropriate organization, proper citations, and use of formal grammar and sentence construction.

An outline helps you integrate the information from multiple articles into a series of paragraphs about a specific topic rather than summarizing one article after another. If coverage of a particular topic area seems weak, the weakness should be a cue that you need to search for additional articles on the topic. If you do not understand something that seems important when you read it, make sure to clarify the meaning before using the information in a written assignment. Avoid simply trying to reorganize the original author's words without understanding them! Such "reorganization without understanding" tends to result in plagiarism. If there are conflicting findings or opinions on a topic, compare and contrast them in the same paragraph, perhaps commenting on the possible reason (e.g., different methodologies) for the conflict. You seldom need to report detailed information about the number of participants or methodology in a literature review unless the methodology relates to a point about a particular finding. Instead, emphasize the research findings and their theoretical underpinnings. In an empirical report, the literature review provides information needed to justify the hypotheses. In a review article, the literature review provides evidence to support the conclusion.

Concluding the Introduction of an Empirical Report

The final paragraphs of the Introduction of an empirical report typically lead in to the Method section. To do so, they provide a brief description of the research design, a rationale for the hypotheses, and specific hypotheses. A rationale is a statement that indicates the reasoning that underlies a hypothesis based on prior findings or theories introduced in the literature review. In the sample manuscript, Bruss and Hill (2010) clearly stated their rationale for each of two hypotheses based on prior findings about online anonymity and on the concept of reciprocity. Their actual hypotheses identified specific variables and indicated how they expected these variables to relate to or influence each other.

Citations in Scientific Writing

Scientific writing relies heavily on providing evidence from existing research and theoretical perspectives. One of the most important requirements for scientific writing is the obligation to cite the original source of ideas or findings (see Table 5). Not only is such citation an indication of academic "etiquette," but the lack of citation of ideas is considered *plagiarism*. Principle 8.11, Plagiarism, of the Ethical Principles of Psychologists and Code of Conduct, states, "Psychologists do not present substantial portions or elements of another's work or data as their own, even if the other work or data source is cited occasionally" (see http://www.apa.org/ethics/code/index.aspx?item=40 or http://tinyurl.com/749vrw6). The phrase "elements of another's work" refers to even single sentences!! Moreover, although it may be tempting to adapt someone else's sentence from a source article by changing a few words, such minor changes are NOT permissible, *even if you cite the source article*. Rather, in addition to citing sources, use paraphrasing (expressing ideas using your own words and sentence structure).

TABLE 5 **Focus on Citations and Plagiarism**

Paraphrases

Paraphrasing involves reading something that someone else has written (the original source); "digesting," synthesizing, and otherwise integrating the material with other topically relevant information; and showing accurate understanding of the material by presenting it in your own words. Rather than attempting to paraphrase a single sentence, carefully read an entire paragraph. Then, present the gist of the paragraph in your own words. Below you will find an original source and examples indicating inappropriate paraphrasing (plagiarism) and acceptable paraphrasing.

- **Original source** (Fallahi, Wood, Austad, & Fallahi, 2006): "In conclusion, we recommend that instructors of undergraduate psychology courses incorporate a student-friendly didactic model into their course curricula. Our findings demonstrate that the instructors' time and effort is well spent because it improved students' basic writing skills. Writing proficiency is an essential element of effective communication for future psychology clinicians or academicians that requires ongoing training and feedback, and students are unlikely to master it in a single college-level English course."
- **Plagiarized version #1** (missing quotation marks and ellipsis dots [three dots with spaces between them] to indicate omitted material): Writing proficiency is an essential element of effective communication that requires ongoing training and feedback (Fallahi, Wood, Austad, & Fallahi, 2006).
- **Plagiarized version #2** (a few words changed, sentence structure not changed): Writing well is a key component of meaningful communication that entails continuous training and feedback (Fallahi, Wood, Austad, & Fallahi, 2006).
- **Acceptable paraphrase:** Because writing is an important communication skill, instructors should incorporate writing assignments and provide feedback in multiple courses (Fallahi, Wood, Austad, & Fallahi, 2006).

Quotations

A quotation is an exact copy of the language from a source. If you do use a quote, be sure to include quotation marks, cite the source, and include a page number.

Quotations are very rare in scientific writing. Overuse of quotations may detract from a paper in both style and content. On occasion, instructors may perceive that use of quotations reflects a lack of effort or understanding. Thus, it is extremely important that you thoroughly understand the material that you incorporate into your manuscripts; otherwise, it will be extremely difficult to accurately paraphrase and integrate the material into a written report without using quotes. If your instructor permits you to use quotes, remember the quotation marks, citation, and page number! If you do not include quotation marks, the material may be considered plagiarized even if the source is cited! Below is the correct format for quotations, based on the Fallahi et al. (2006) example:

- **Correct quotation** (Illustrates use of ellipsis dots for omitted material): "Writing proficiency is an essential element of effective communication . . . that requires ongoing training and feedback" (Fallahi, Wood, Austad, & Fallahi, 2006, p. 174).

Citation Format

APA style incorporates author–date referencing for all citations in all sections of any report. The application of this author–date referencing varies slightly (e.g., in the use of "and" versus "&") for citations that are included in the body of a narrative (see Example 1) or in parentheses (see Example 2). The first time a source is cited, if the source includes fewer than six authors, an APA-style citation includes the surnames of all authors, followed by the year of publication.

- Example 1 (in body of narrative): Marek, Griggs, and Christopher (1999) noted that students prefer pedagogical aids that relate directly to test content.

- Example 2 (parenthetical): Students prefer pedagogical aids that most directly assist in preparing for tests (Marek, Griggs, & Christopher, 1999).

If there are more than two authors, all subsequent citations include the name of the first author followed by et al. (and others). There is no period after "et," but there is a period after "al" (an abbreviation for alia).

- Within body of narrative: Marek et al. (1999) indicated that introductory psychology textbooks differed in the number and type of pedagogical aids used.

- Parenthetical: Introductory psychology textbooks differed in the number and type of pedagogical aids used (Marek et al., 1999).

If a source contains six or more authors, only the surname of the first author followed by et al. appears both in the first and subsequent citations. For example, Lynn Fuchs collaborated with five other authors on an article about assessment of learning. Even the first time this source is cited, the citation would read either Fuchs et al. (2011) or (Fuchs et al., 2011), depending on its positioning in the body of narrative or in parenthesis.

If an article has a single author, the author's name is included in all citations. If an article has two authors, both authors' names are always included in all citations. For citations in the body of the narrative, include the year the first time the article is cited in each paragraph but omit the year for subsequent citations to the same article in the *same* paragraph. For parenthetical citations, the year is included in *all* citations. If you include more than one citation in the same parenthesis, put the citations in alphabetical order (by last name of first author) and separated by semicolons. Do not change the order of authors for any citation!

Instructors may require that you obtain copies of all sources cited in your writing. However, in some instances, instructors will permit you to cite a source mentioned in your textbook (or in another published work) when you are unable to obtain the source itself. In such instances, you must distinguish what you actually read from the item cited (the original source of the information). For example, suppose you were reporting information from a textbook by Richard Griggs that included coverage of an article by Schwartz (1999). Although textbooks are seldom cited in formal APA writing, suppose your instructor permits you to do so without obtaining the primary source article. In that case, the citation would read as follows:

> When constructing a survey, researchers should remember that question wording may influence participants' answers (Schwartz, 1999, as cited in Griggs, 2012).

The unread, original source is *not* included in the Reference list. Remember, before citing a source that you did not personally read, *check the criteria for your assignment!* Remember that such citations, whether they are from a textbook, another article, an edited book, or a book chapter, are extremely rare in published manuscripts.

Method Section of an Empirical Report

The Method section provides enough information for readers to replicate the research and to determine if findings are valid and reliable. This section is typically divided into three subsections: Participants, Materials (or Apparatus), and Design and Procedures. Although content of specific subsections may vary somewhat, the paragraphs below highlight typical content, as does the sample manuscript in Appendix A (see pages 1–16).

Participants

This subsection includes information about the number of participants, the overall "group" to which they belong (e.g., college students, workers at Company ABC, children from a specific day care center), and basic demographic characteristics (e.g., age, gender, ethnicity). In addition, this section often includes information about recruiting participants (e.g., random sample from Registrar's list, convenience sample of adults, sign-up sheet posted in a particular area) and incentive offered (entered in drawing for prize, small amount of money or credit, no incentive). In some manuscripts, information about recruiting and incentive is included in a Design and Procedures subsection instead of in the Participants subsection.

Materials (or Apparatus)

The description of materials provides sufficient detail for readers to replicate the research. For an experiment, the Materials section includes a description of the stimuli, and explicitly identifies differences in materials used for different groups. For a survey, the Materials section includes a description of the overall questionnaire (number of questions asked, type of answer options), and identifies key topics covered. For each existing scale (a series of items measuring the same construct) included in a questionnaire, descriptions often encompass the following information: what it measures, original source/citation, number of items, type of answer options, anchor points and descriptions, sample item, and reliability and validity data.

Design and Procedures

This subsection describes how the investigation was conducted. For an experiment, it indicates whether the design was between subjects (each participant was in only one condition) or within subjects (each participant was in all conditions). For a between-subjects design, it clarifies how you assigned participants to conditions. For a within-subjects design, it clarifies how you counterbalanced the order of conditions (systematically changed the order for different participants). It includes information about participants' tasks, the order in which tasks were completed, instructions, and time limits if applicable. For a survey, this section includes information about how questionnaires were distributed and collected, instructions given to participants, and the approximate time it took participants to complete the questionnaire.

Results Section of an Empirical Report

This section contains verbal and statistical information describing the findings. Section organization varies according to the types of analyses involved and the research hypotheses. An opening paragraph often includes information about the type of analyses used and clarification of variables analyzed. Next, following specific rules for formatting of statistics, it presents the results that relate to the hypotheses. For example, in the sample manuscript, Bruss and Hill (2010) reported results for an independent-samples *t* test, an analysis designed to compare ratings or scores for two unrelated groups of participants. If assignment criteria indicate that you should provide tables or figures to clarify complex arrays of data, refer to and comment on the highlights of each table or figure in the text of the Results section even though the actual tables and figures appear at the end of the report.

Discussion Section of Empirical Report

This section serves as an arena for interpretation of the results. It often begins with an explicit statement or statements regarding whether results supported the hypotheses. Subsequent discussion positions the results in the context of theoretical perspectives and explains similarities to and differences from prior research on the topic. The Discussion section also contains information about the limitations of the study (e.g., the generalizability of findings). It includes coverage of the implications of the findings and potential applications of the results. The section often concludes by indicating how the research extends the existing literature and by offering suggestions for future investigations that emanate from questions raised by the results of the current study. In Appendix A, annotations identify the elements of a discussion section.

References

This section contains a listing in a standardized format (with "hanging indent") of all sources that you have read and cited in your paper. Unlike a bibliography, the References section does *not* include any material that you read but do not cite in the manuscript. Each item in the References contains detailed information that enables readers to obtain the source material. Alphabetize reference entries by the surname (last name) of the first author. Do not change the order of authors for any source!

Individual Reference Entries

Authors' names appear in the same order as they appear on the original source, because the ordering of names typically reflects the extent to which authors contributed to the article or book. The components of each reference entry typically include the authors' names, year of publication, title, and publisher-related information. Authors' names include both surnames and initials. For the most common types of references used in scientific writing, the year is shown within parentheses and then followed by a period. References without a doi (digital object identifier) end with a period. The *doi* (digital object identifier) is a recently added reference component designed to facilitate location of items on the internet (http://www.doi.org/). It is most often applicable to articles in professional journals rather than other types of sources. The order of reference components varies somewhat. Instructions for and examples of reference entries to three common sources (journal article, book, and chapter in edited book) and to an online resource follow. Additional examples of references to journal articles, books, and an online newsletter are included in the sample manuscript in Appendix A (see pages 1–16).

A Citation to a Journal

Include the following components in the following order: author(s) name(s), year, article title, journal name, volume number, page numbers, and doi (digital object identifier). As illustrated, when there are multiple authors, an ampersand (&) is used before the name of the last author. The date and title are also followed by a period. In the title, only proper nouns, the first word, and the first word after a colon (if applicable) are capitalized. The journal name, followed by a comma and a volume number (also followed by a comma) are both italicized, but the page numbers are not. Here is an example of a reference to a journal article.

Luttrell, V. R., Bufkin, J. L., Eastman, V. J., & Miller, R. (2010). Teaching scientific writing: Measuring student learning in an intensive APA skills course. *Teaching of Psychology, 37,* 193–195. doi:10.1080/00986283.2010.488531

If a doi is not available, include the words "Retrieved from" followed by the URL (web site address) of the journal's publisher. In the References of the sample manuscript, the citation for Chiou (2006) illustrates use of a journal URL when a doi has not been assigned.

A Citation to a Book

Include the following components in the following order: author(s) name(s), year, book title, publisher's location, and publisher's name. Information about the publisher is found in database records and on one of the first pages in a book. The title of the book is italicized and follows the same capitalization rules used for article titles. Regarding publisher location, standard (postal code) abbreviations are used for states (e.g., GA for Georgia). If the publisher is an association or a press, as in the example below, the publisher's name should be complete; however, if the publisher's name ends with Publishers, Company, or Incorporated, these words are not included in the citation.

Graham, S., MacArthur, C. A., & Fitzgerald, J. (2007). *Best practices in writing instruction: Solving problems in the teaching of literacy.* New York, NY: Guilford Press.

A Citation to a Chapter in an Edited Book

Include the following components in the following order: author(s) name(s), year, chapter title, editors' names, book title, pages for chapter, publisher's location, and publisher's name. For editors' names, initials precede surnames. The editors' names are followed by the abbreviation "Eds." within parentheses and then followed by a comma. The title of the book is italicized and follows the same capitalization rules used for article titles. Unlike a reference to an article, the abbreviation "pp." precedes the chapter page numbers that are in parentheses. Here is an example of a reference for a chapter in an edited book.

Schmidt, M. E., & Dunn, D. S. (2007). Teaching writing in statistics and research methods: Addressing objectives, intensive issues, and style. In D. S. Dunn, R. A. Smith, & B. Beins (Eds.), *Best practices for teaching statistics and research methods in the behavioral sciences* (pp. 257–273). Mahwah, NJ: Erlbaum.

If there are eight or more authors for a chapter (or for a journal article or book), APA style follows a somewhat unusual guideline for the citation in the References section. The citation should include the surnames and initials for the first six authors, followed by an ellipsis (three periods with a space between them . . .) and the surname and initials of the last author. An example for a chapter with eight authors in an edited book follows.

Rijlaarsdam, G., Van den Bergh, H., Couzijn, M., Janssen, T., Braaksma, M., Tillema, M., . . . Raedts, M. (2012). Writing. In K. R. Harris, S. Graham, T. Urdan, A. G. Bus, S. Major, & H. Swanson (Eds.), *APA educational psychology handbook, Vol 3: Application to teaching and learning* (pp. 189–227). Washington, DC: American Psychological Association. doi:10.1037/13275-009

A Citation to an Online Resource

To cite a web page or nonperiodical web document, include the following components in the following order: author(s) name(s), year, title of resource, and URL (website address).

> Seas, K., & Brizee, A. (2010). *APA style workshop*. Retrieved from http://owl.english.purdue.edu/owl/resource/664/01/

STEP 3: EDITING AND PROOFREADING

After the first draft is written, the next step is the initial proofreading, a task that encompasses grammar, sentence construction, punctuation, spelling, and use of APA style, as well as a review of the content. The following sections illuminate rules that are specific to APA-style writing and general rules that apply to all formal writing. These general rules are available in most grammar books. The Purdue Online Writing Lab (OWL, http://owl.english.purdue.edu/) is an excellent source of information for both grammar and APA-style guidelines.

Other online educational sites also offer a variety of exercises for practicing grammar and the mechanics of writing. For clarification and additional practice, you are encouraged to consult any (or all) of the following sites:

> Butte College
> http://www.butte.edu/departments/cas/tipsheets/grammar/parts_of_speech.html
> or http://tinyurl.com/6vvclno

> Indiana State University
> http://libguides.indstate.edu/content.php?pid=18359&search_terms=
> writing+center

> University of North Carolina at Chapel Hill
> http://www.unc.edu/depts/wcweb/handouts/index.html or
> http://tinyurl.com/72ykcmk

> Diana Hacker's *A Writer's Reference* http://bcs.bedfordstmartins.com/
> writersref7e or http://tinyurl.com/6mnqmop

Grammar and Punctuation Rules for All Writing

The principles outlined below (and summarized in Appendix B, pages B-1–B-2) are applicable to scientific writing across disciplines. The principles include fundamental rules of formal English grammar and punctuation. Some of the topics covered include construction of complete sentences, subject-verb agreement, noun-pronoun agreement, parallel construction, and punctuation. *When editing your manuscript, it is particularly important to leave sufficient time to check these items and to correct any errors.*

Construct Complete Sentences and Avoid Sentence Fragments.

A sentence must contain an independent clause (a clause containing a subject and a verb that expresses a complete thought). In contrast, a group of words (including a subject and a verb) that does not express a complete thought is called a dependent (or subordinate) clause. An independent clause can stand alone as a sentence, but a dependent clause is not a sentence; if you use a dependent clause alone, you have created a sentence fragment (e.g., "Because consumers perceive that generic brands are not as healthy as name brands"). To help you identify dependent clauses that cannot stand alone, remember that they often begin with words such as "although," "because," "if," or "when."

Use Parallel Construction.

Parallel construction applies to using the same grammatical form to express a series of elements in the same sentence. Using parallel construction tends to improve the clarity of a sentence. For example, the sentence "People at the sporting event were either cheering, talking, or had a program to look at" does not use parallel construction. The words "had a program to look at" involve a different grammatical form than do "cheering" and "talking." An improved version of the sentence would read as follows: "People at the sporting event were cheering, talking, or looking at a program."

Make Sure the Subject "Agrees With" the Verb.

The subject of a clause is who or what the clause is about, and the verb describes the action or state of being. If the subject is plural, then the verb must be in the plural form as well. For example, it is *incorrect* to say, "One reason for smoking habits are that young adults may tend to conform." The subject "reason" is singular; thus, the verb should be "is." The correct sentence would read, "One reason for smoking habits is that young adults may tend to conform."

Make Sure a Pronoun "Agrees With" the Noun to Which It Refers.

A pronoun is a word that takes the place of a noun (a name of a person, place, or thing). A pronoun must "agree in number" with the noun that it replaces. If a noun is singular (e.g., participant), then the pronoun must also be singular (e.g., he or she). If a noun is plural (e.g., participants), then the pronoun must also be plural (e.g., they). For example, it is *incorrect* to say, "Each participant was assigned to a group based on a number they had chosen." The subject "participant" is singular; thus, the pronoun should be "he or she." Because the use of "he or she" (to avoid gender bias) may seem somewhat awkward, most sources suggest that you change the sentence so that the subject is plural (e.g., Participants were assigned to a group based on a number they had chosen).

Make Sure a Pronoun Clearly Refers to a Specific Noun or Noun Phrase.

Although the referents for words such as "this," "that," or "it" may be clear to you as a writer, the referents may be unclear to readers. For example, the referent for the word "this" in the second sentence that follows is ambiguous. "To identify each participant, I will assign a number to each individual who submits an informed consent form. This will serve as identification for later analysis." The word "this" could refer to the informed consent form or to the number (the intended meaning). To correct the ambiguity, you may simply add the word "number" after "this."

Use Similar Words Appropriately.

Words such as "then" and "than" are sometimes confused. "Then" typically refers to a point in time (e.g., "Then, we ended the session with a debriefing."), whereas "than" is used in comparisons (e.g., "Women responded more quickly than did men."). Other word sets or pairs that tend to be confused include "there," "their," and "they're"; "to," "too," and "two'; "affect" and "effect"; "who's" and "whose"; "accept" and "except"; "adolescents" and "adolescence"; and "compliment" and "complement." If you have any doubt about which word is appropriate in a particular context, checking a dictionary should resolve the uncertainty.

Use Apostrophes Appropriately.

Apostrophes indicate possession (e.g., the participant's scores). When a sentence involves a plural noun (e.g., participants), the apostrophe is placed after the "s" (e.g., the participants' scores). *One particularly confusing situation involves the use of "its," a* possessive form that does *not* require an apostrophe (e.g., "The committee was doing its work."). There is no such word as "its'." In forms of writing other than APA style, "it's" is used as a contraction for "it is." However, in APA style, you should avoid using contractions.

Punctuation

It is sometimes difficult to notice errors in punctuation if you are not actively looking for them. With this in mind, prior to editing, you might develop a list of the types of errors you are personally most apt to make. You can then use this list to systematically check for and correct these types of errors.

- *Use a comma before a coordinating conjunction that connects two independent clauses.* Seven coordinating conjunctions are available for connecting two independent clauses in the same sentence. To help remember these connecting words, you may use the acronym FANBOYS, which represents For, And, Nor, But, Or, Yet, and So. When you use one of these words as a coordinating conjunction, you should use a comma before the word (e.g., "The independent variable will be the condition, and the dependent variable will be attitudes toward the anti-smoking policy."). In contrast, the following sentence is incorrect because it lacks a comma before the coordinating conjunction: "Some parents claimed that health care professionals provided vaccination-related information that was too general and other parents noted that information about side effects was vague or lacking (Austvoll-Dahlgren & Helseth, 2010)." Please remember that the rule about using a comma before FANBOYS applies *specifically* to the use of these words to connect two independent clauses. Do *not* place a comma before every "and" in your manuscript (see section about avoiding unnecessary commas)!

- *Use a comma after introductory phrases, clauses, or words* before *the main independent clause but not if the dependent clause* follows *the main clause.* In the sentence "Because people are distracted, they may not notice changes in their environment," the dependent clause precedes the main clause; therefore, it is correct to use a comma between the two. The sentence "People may not notice changes in their environment because they are distracted" is also correct. In this second example, the dependent clause follows the main clause; therefore, there is no comma separating the two.

- *Use a comma after each item in a series of three or more items.* The following sentence illustrates correct use of commas in a series because it includes a comma after both "eggs" and "bacon": "Ten patrons ordered a combination of eggs, bacon, and waffles." The next sentence is *incorrect* because it is missing a comma after "equity theory": "Theories of work motivation emphasizing the cognitive effects of information include expectancy theory, equity theory and goal-setting theory."

- *Avoid comma splices.* A comma splice occurs when you use only a comma to separate two sentences (independent clauses)—for instance, "Many public emergency rooms are understaffed, some may attract homeless people who are seeking shelter." There are two equally acceptable ways of creating a correct compound sentence. One way is to add a conjunction such as "and" after the comma (e.g., "Many public emergency rooms are understaffed, and some may attract homeless people who are seeking shelter."). A second way is to change the comma to a semicolon (e.g., "Many public emergency rooms are understaffed; some may attract homeless people who are seeking shelter."). You may also solve the problem by creating two simple sentences.

- *Avoid using commas when they are not necessary.* There are three relatively common types of "comma abuse." First, commas are not used between a subject and a predicate. The subject indicates who or what the sentence is about. The predicate includes a verb or verbs that tell something about the subject. The sentence "One important attribute of learning, involves elaboration of material" is *incorrect* because it has an unnecessary comma between "learning" and "involves." Second, commas are not used between two parts of a compound subject (a subject with more than one noun). The sentence "Magazines, and televisions often portray models who are very slim." is *incorrect* because it includes a comma between "magazines" and "and." Third, commas are not used between two parts of a compound predicate. The sentence "Fifteen women talked on their cell phones, and crossed the street." is *incorrect* because it includes an unnecessary comma between "phones" and "and."

- *Use semicolons correctly.* The most common use of a semicolon is to separate two closely related sentences (independent clauses) that are not connected with a conjunction (e.g., "and"). The following example illustrates the correct use of a semicolon: "People show remorse in different ways; some cry, and others are apologetic." A semicolon should *not* be used to separate an independent from a dependent clause. The following example illustrates an *incorrect* use of a semicolon: "Students in a cooperative learning environment typically enjoy it; particularly when a single grade is given for a group assignment." To correct this sentence, remove the semicolon and replace it with a comma.

- *Use colons correctly.* The most common use of a colon is to separate a grammatically complete (independent) clause from a final phrase that extends it. The following example illustrates the correct use of a colon: "The routine included three types of exercises: knee bends, sit ups, and running in place." A colon should *not* be used after a clause that is not an independent clause. The following example illustrates an *incorrect* use of a colon: "According to Freud, the mind is made up of: the ego, the id, and the superego." To correct this sentence, remove the colon.

Rules Pertaining Specifically to APA Style

In addition to rules about grammar and mechanics that apply to formal writing in general, APA style also includes specific guidelines that relate to unnecessary words, use of numerals, use of abbreviations, use of active voice, and distinctions between words such as "while" and "since." These guidelines are summarized in this section.

Economy of Expression

Avoid redundancy by using as few words as possible to express your ideas. For example, the phrase "due to the fact that" can be consolidated to a single word, "because." Another way to reduce redundancy is to consider the precise meaning of words. For example, because "unanimous" means endorsed by everyone, it is redundant to use the phrase "completely unanimous."

Use of Numerals Versus Numbers Expressed as Words

When referring to numbers 10 and above, use numerals except when the number begins a sentence (in which case use words to express the number). To express numbers less than 10, APA style requires that you use words rather than numerals most of the time. For example, the description of a sample of students might read, "The sample included 14 first-year students, nine sophomores, 10 juniors, and five seniors." The most common exceptions to the rule about using words to express numbers less than 10 include using numerals in the Abstract and in tables; for values that precede a unit of measurement (e.g. 9 cm) including time (e.g., 5 min); and for values designating age, scores, points on a scale, or placement in a sequence (e.g., Test 3). Numbers that begin a sentence are always expressed in words (e.g., "Thirty-five participants did not complete the survey.").

Use of Abbreviations

The examples for numerals illustrate two of the more common abbreviations in APA style: "cm" for centimeters and "min" for minutes. Other common abbreviations include "hr" for hour, "s" for second, "m" for meter, and "v" for volt. However, APA guidelines state that you should not abbreviate the words "day," "week," "month," and "year." Before using other abbreviations (e.g., "CG" for control group), consider whether the abbreviation is helpful or potentially confusing. With a few exceptions for words familiar to psychologists (e.g., IQ), abbreviations are explained when initially used. You might say, for example, that participants in the control group (CG) did not listen to any type of music. After an abbreviation is introduced, use it consistently throughout the paper.

Use of Active Voice

In general, APA-style guidelines suggest that you use active voice whenever possible. In sentences that use active voice, the subject of the sentence performs an action. For example, the sentence "men completed the task in small groups" is in active voice. In contrast, the sentence "the task was performed by the men" is in passive voice.

Use "While" and "Since" to Refer Only to Time.

To be precise, APA guidelines suggest that you should use the word "while" only when referring to events that occur simultaneously. For example, it is correct to say, "While participants were learning the words, they heard either music or static." It is incorrect to say, "While many reasons parents offered for not vaccinating their children related to potential side effects, others emphasized emotional factors rather than risks (Wroe, Turner, & Salkovskis, 2004)." In this latter instance, you should substitute "although" or "whereas" for "while." Similarly, you should use the word "since" only to indicate that an event occurred after another event. For example, it is correct to say, "Since the time when the data were initially published, there have been divergent interpretations of the findings." It is incorrect to say, "Since studies (e.g., Hedge, 2000) indicate that people spend a majority of the time indoors, it is important to investigate the effect of different types of artificial lighting on performance." In this latter instance, you should substitute "because" for "since."

Things to Avoid in APA-Style Writing

Although the APA guidelines explicitly mention only some of the items in Table 6 (on the next page), the listing encompasses widespread conventions for scientific writing in psychology. Reviewing your writing to adhere to these suggestions will improve the quality of your manuscript!

CONCLUDING THOUGHTS

Manuscript editing and revision completes your first writing cycle. Ideally, if you have time, put the manuscript away for a few days. After some time has elapsed, read it again. Some sources even suggest that you take the time to read your work aloud in order to locate possible discontinuities or awkward phrases. Prior to submitting your written assignment, it is particularly important to check that you have cited all sources accurately and that all articles cited in the body of the report are included in the manuscript. Overall, although you may find these guidelines cumbersome at first, continued practice with formal, scientific APA-style writing, complemented by instructors' feedback and the material included in this chapter, should enable you to develop and enhance your scientific writing skills. In turn, you may approach your written assignments with greater confidence and with heightened potential for academic success.

TABLE 6 Clarification of and Commentary on Items to Avoid

Items to avoid	Clarification	Comment
Using sexist language	Do not use "he" to refer to a person in general.	Unless you are specifically referring to a man or woman, it is often easier to work with plurals (with the nouns "participants" or "people") and the gender-neutral pronoun "they."
Using informal language and colloquial expressions	Phrases such as "kind of," "sort of," "lots of," "pretty much," and "write up," although used in conversation, are not appropriate in formal writing.	Be as precise as possible. Find data that allow you to specify numbers or percentages if possible, or use words such as "many" or "few."
Using the word "prove"	Seek alternatives such as "support the hypothesis" or "gathered evidence for."	In psychology, conclusions are generally probabilistic, not certain, which is why we avoid the use of "prove."
Using the word "you" to refer to the reader	Rather than stating "it is important for you to exercise regularly," report "it is important for people to exercise regularly."	
Using the words "we," "us," or "our" to refer to people in general	Seek alternatives such as "individuals," "students," "respondents," or "people."	"We" or "our" is appropriate only to refer to the opinions or behaviors of the authors if there is more than one author (e.g., "We recruited a convenience sample.").
Using phrases such as "The first article indicated," "The next article demonstrated."	Use citations such as "Myers (2008) reported" or "_____ and _____ indicated."	In a literature review, integrate material topically, using meaningful transitions such as "Similarly," "In contrast," or "Moreover."
Using titles of articles (except in References) or authors' first names.	Use citations as illustrated above.	
Using males and females as nouns	Use "men" and "women" as nouns (e.g., 30 men and 30 women).	Use "male" and "female" as adjectives (e.g., Male participants read a scenario.)
Using contractions	Write "have not" rather than "haven't."	

References

Austvoll-Dahlgren, A., & Helseth, S. (2010). What informs parents' decision-making about childhood vaccinations? *Journal of Advanced Nursing, 66,* 2421–2430. doi:10.1111/j.1365-2648.2010.05403.x

Bruss, O. E., & Hill, J. M. (2010) Tell me more: Online versus face-to-face communication and self-disclosure. *Psi Chi Journal of Undergraduate Research, 15,* 3–7. Retrieved from http://www.psichi.org/pubs/journal/

Chiou, W. (2006). Adolescents' sexual self-disclosure on the Internet: Deindividuation and impression management. *Adolescence, 41,* 547–561. Retrieved from http://www.vjf.cnrs.fr/clt/php/va/Page_revue.php?ValCodeRev=ADO

Fallahi, C. R., Wood, R. M., Austad, C., & Fallahi, H. (2006). A program for improving undergraduate psychology students' basic writing skills. *Teaching of Psychology, 33,* 171–175. doi:10.1207/s15328023top3303_3

Fuchs, L. S., Compton, D. L., Fuchs, D., Hollenbeck, K. N., Hamlett, C. L., & Seethaler, P. M. (2011). Two-stage screening for math problem-solving difficulty using dynamic assessment of algebraic learning. *Journal of Learning Disabilities, 44,* 372–380. doi:10.1177/0022219411407867

Griggs, R. A. (2012). *Psychology: A concise introduction* (3rd ed.). New York, NY: Worth.

Hedge, A. (2000). Where are we in understanding the effects of where we are?. *Ergonomics, 43,* 1019–1029. doi:10.1080/001401300409198

Marek, P., Griggs, R. A., & Christopher, A. N. (1999). Pedagogical aids in textbooks: Do college students' perceptions justify their prevalence?. *Teaching of Psychology, 26*(1), 11–19. doi:10.1207/s15328023top2601_2

Schwarz, N. (1999). Self-reports: How the questions shape the answers. *American Psychologist, 54,* 93–105. doi:10.1037/0003-066X.54.2.93

Wroe, A. L., Turner, N., & Salkovskis, P. M. (2004). Understanding and predicting parental decisions about early childhood immunizations. *Health Psychology, 23,* 33–41. doi:1037/0278-6133.23.1.33

Appendix A

Sample Annotated Manuscript

Note: The copy above the line below constitutes the name of this section. The material below this line and in the running head above is part of the sample copy itself.

Tell Me More: Online Versus Face-to-Face Communication and

Self-Disclosure

Olivia E. Bruss and Jennifer M. Hill

Wisconsin Lutheran College

> Page numbering starts on the title page, right-justified in the header area.

> Running head—The running head is left-justified. The words "Running head" (followed by a colon, with only the R capitalized) appear in the header area for the title page only. The actual running head that appears on all pages is typed in all capital letters

> Key words (and all words with four or more letters) in the title begin with capital letters. The title, authors' names, and byline (affiliation) are all centered.

> Authors' names are on a line double-spaced below the title and affiliation is on the next double-spaced line.

The abstract is a single block paragraph. Length limits vary for different journals.

Information from Introduction (purpose).

Information from Method (participants and design).

Citations in the Abstract do not "count" as the first citation within the text of the manuscript.

Information from Results that includes specific measure used.

Information about Discussion.

Abstract

The purpose of this study was to examine the effect of type of communication (online or face-to- face) on self-disclosure. A group of 58 college students engaged in a conversation either face-to-face or using an instant-messaging system. Those who conversed online reported a significantly higher amount of personal and perceived partner self-disclosure as measured by an adapted version of the Revised Self-Disclosure Scale (Wheeless, 1978) than those who conversed face-to-face. Implications regarding online communication and its impact on counseling, educational, and personal relationships are discussed.

In the Abstract, *all* numbers are expressed as numerals. Do not begin a sentence with a number in the Abstract. Elsewhere in the manuscript, any number greater than or equal to 10 is also expressed as a numeral (unless it begins a sentence). However, numbers less than 10, with some exceptions, are expressed in words.

Tell Me More: Online Versus Face-to-Face Communication and Self-Disclosure

In today's technology-centered world, people are no longer required to communicate and form relationships in face-to-face situations alone. In fact, the use of electronic forms of communication, such as text-messaging or online interaction, is rapidly becoming a primary tool for many people to form and maintain many of their relationships. For instance, a recent online survey of 439 college students showed that nearly 20% of college students spent over 20 hr per week online (Burst Media, 2007). This shift in communication impacts several different categories of relationships people have: familial relationships, friendships, romantic relationships, professional relationships, and educational relationships. Consequently, the impact of online communication on building and maintaining relationships is important to understand.

Self-disclosure has been viewed as a key component in developing close relationships (Altman & Taylor, 1973). Jourard and Lasakow (1958, p. 91) defined self-disclosure as "the process of making the self known to other persons." According to this perspective, self-disclosure builds trust which leads to closer relationships. When one individual takes a risk by disclosing to another individual, the receiver feels as though he or she is trusted. In return, the receiver is more likely to disclose information as well. Trust and security are developed when two people respond to one another positively over repeated interactions, which continually strengthen the relationship. A key element of the relationship is that the individuals involved must perceive that their disclosures are being accepted. Therefore, the process is mutually reinforcing (Bennis, Schien, Berlew, & Steele, 1964).

With the rapid growth of technology, people can now self-disclose

---

The introduction begins with the title, not the word Introduction.

There are two spaces between sentences.

Note the comma after the introductory phrase.

Abbreviate units of time.

Note the use of a colon after an independent clause that is extended with additional information.

Initial paragraph emphasizes the relevance of the topic.

Example of parenthetical citation with use of an ampersand (&).

Example of citation in narrative with use of "and." Because this citation involves a quote, it also includes a page number.

If a citation contains three to five authors, all are included in the first citation in the text, with a comma between them and between the last author and the year.

Note the use of a comma before the coordinating conjunction that separates two independent clauses.

If multiple citations are included in the same parentheses, the citations are listed in alphabetical order by the name of the first author.

Note the appropriate use of a semicolon between two closely related independent clauses.

The year is always included in parenthetical citations.

Notice the logical organization of information in this paragraph about disparate results. The systematic use of the terms first, second, and third provide a structure to the coverage.

If a citation includes more than two authors, only the first author's name (followed by et al.) is used after the initial citation. Et al. means "and others." There is a period after "al" (because it is an abbreviation for alia) but not after "et" (because it is an unabbreviated word).

using more indirect means like the Internet, and several recent studies have begun to more closely examine self-disclosure during online communication (Chiou, 2006; Punyanunt-Carter, 2006; Valkenburg & Peter, 2007). One of the most common explanations proposed for people's tendency to self-disclose online is the fact that online communication increases anonymity. This anonymity can then produce a state of deindividuation in which others are not seen as individuals; consequently, people lose their inner restraints (Chiou, 2006). In other words, people may feel more comfortable with self-disclosure online because others do not necessarily know who they are as individuals and their disclosures online are less likely to produce immediate social repercussions.

Online Versus Face-to-Face Communication and Self-Disclosure

Although numerous researchers have compared the self-disclosure of participants in online situations versus those in face-to-face situations, results have been mixed. Tidwell and Walther (2002) found that participants in online situations demonstrated higher self-disclosure than those in face-to-face situations. Conversely, others found that participants in a face-to-face situation reported greater self-disclosure than those interacting online (Mallen, Day, & Green, 2003; Skinner & Latchford, 2006).

Factors that may have contributed to the different results should be noted. First, researchers have studied the relationship between type of communication and self-disclosure in different ways. Some have assigned participants to one of two communication conditions (online versus face-to-face) and looked for differences in self-disclosure (Mallen et al., 2003; Tidwell & Walther, 2002). Others examined differences in perceived self-disclosure between those who self-reported using online communication regularly, compared to those who said they used it less frequently (Cho, 2007; Skinner & Latchford, 2006). Second, different forms of computer-mediated communication (CMC) were used in these studies, including synchronous (instant messaging) and asynchronous (e-mail and support group webpage) methods. Third, these studies differed in their measurements of self-disclosure as well; some employed self-reports and some used judges to rate the degree and quality of self-disclosure, often by rules of linguistics.

An abbreviation is initially introduced by putting it in parentheses after the term to which it refers. In subsequent mentions of the concept, only the abbreviation is used. Although APA guidelines suggest that it is preferable not to introduce an abbreviation for a term that is subsequently used less than three times, this manuscript does not follow that guideline.

Another facet of self-disclosure is the phenomenon of reciprocity. This states that if people perceive that their discussion partners are self-disclosing to them, they will in-turn self-disclose more to their partners (Barak & Gluck-Ofri, 2007). The extant literature indicates that reciprocity does occur online (Barak & Gluck-Ofri, 2007) and describes the factors that impact reciprocity online (Rollman, Krug, & Parente, 2000; Rollman & Parente, 2001). However, to our knowledge, no studies exist that have investigated whether people perceive their partners as self-disclosing more in an online situation or a face-to-face situation. This would be necessary to determine if reciprocity occurs to a greater degree online than face-to-face.

In this paragraph, after introducing the topic of reciprocity, the authors discuss a gap in the literature that provides justification for their own study.

Purpose and Hypotheses

The goal of the present research is to gain more clarity regarding the relationship between type of communication and self-disclosure. Specifically, the current study extends previous research in the area by (a) employing an experimental rather than retrospective design and (b) comparing whether the perception of partner self-disclosure is greater online or face-to-face situation. First, we hypothesized that because online communication increases anonymity (Chiou, 2006), participants in the online group will report higher levels of personal self-disclosure than those in the face-to-face group. Second, based on the concept of reci-

The authors state explicitly the goal of their research.

Within this sentence, notice how the authors identify elements in a series by lowercase letters in parentheses.

In the hypotheses, the authors identify specify variables and how they expect them to influence each other.

procity (Barak & Gluck-Ofri, 2007), we hypothesized that those participating in online discussions would perceive that their conversation partners disclose more to them than those participating in face-to-face discussions.

Method

Participants

Participants were recruited through an undergraduate psychology department-sponsored research activity. Initially, 60 participants completed the study, but two participants were not included in the final analyses due to incomplete data. The remaining participants included 58 (25 men, 33 women) undergraduate students attending a small liberal arts college in the Midwest, and the majority of the sample was Caucasian (97%). The participants' ages ranged from 18 to 28 ($M = 20.10$, $SD = 1.78$). Two conditions existed: the online communication group and the face-to-face communication group. The participants in the online group consisted of 14 men and 15 women, whose ages ranged from 18 to 28 ($M = 20.38$, $SD = 2.19$). The participants in the face-to-face group consisted of 11 men and 18 women, and their ages ranged from 18 to 22 ($M = 19.83$, $SD = 1.23$).

Instruments and Apparatus

The researchers employed an adapted version of the Revised Self-Disclosure Scale (RSDS; Wheeless, 1978) to determine participants' level of self-disclosure. Nineteen items from the original scale were reworded to be more applicable to the interaction in this particular experiment. Nine items were used to measure the amount and quality of each participant's disclosure in this situation (personal self-disclosure). Sample items include "In this experience, I often disclosed intimate personal things about myself without hesitation" and "In this experience, I did not often talk about myself."

The heading of the Method is centered and is in boldface type.

This Level 2 heading is flush left and boldface.

Numbers less than ten are typically expressed using words (with some exceptions). More common exceptions include consistent use of numbers for time, age, scores, points on a scale, and for numbers that indicate a position in a series (such as Table 2).

Note the appropriate placement of an apostrophe to indicate plural possessive.

Abbreviations for statistics (mean and standard deviation) are italicized.

This Participants section contains basic, required demographic information about number of participants, age, gender, and ethnicity.

This Level 2 heading is flush left and boldface with capital letters at the beginning of key words.

Always use words to express a number that begins a sentence.

In this and the following paragraph, notice the detailed information provided about the scale (source, number of items that measured each construct, sample items, the type of answer options, and the numerical and verbal anchors for the answer options).

The remaining 10 items measured the amount and quality of disclosure from the partner in this situation (perceived partner self-disclosure). Sample items included "In this experience, my partner talked about his/herself for fairly long periods at a time" and "In this experience, my partner did not seem honest in his/her self-disclosures." Participants were asked to indicate their agreement with the items on a 7-point Likert scale ranging from 1 (*strongly disagree*) to 7 (*strongly agree*).

The participants used five of Aron, Melinat, Aron, Vallone, and Bator's (1997) Closeness-Generating Questions, which were designed to encourage self-disclosure. One example question is, "If you have to move from where you consider home, where would you go, and what would you miss the most about home?". Lastly, participants responded to an eight-question demographic survey on which they reported their age, gender, year in school, and the extent to which they felt they knew their partner before this experiment.

In addition, the participants in the online condition used computers in the following manner. The researchers placed 15 laptops in two rooms (A and B) on two different floors. Each computer had a number 1 through 15. Each computer also had a mock instant messaging (IM) account already on the screen. The individual IM accounts on each screen allowed the participant to communicate with only one other account, which was already up on the screen of the corresponding computer in another room on a different floor. Therefore, participants communicated online with the person in the other room sitting at the computer with the same number. For instance, the participant seated at Computer 1 in Room A communicated online only with the person seated at Computer 1 in Room B. Each participant was assigned a gender-neutral pseudonym that appeared at the top of each IM account (e.g.,

Numbers representing points on a scale are expressed in numerals, an exception to the rule about using words to express numbers less than 10.

Verbal anchor points for a scale are italicized.

Typically the period goes inside the quotation marks when the material occurs at the end of a sentence, but in this case the material is a question, even though the sentence itself is not.

This is example of the use of a numeral to express a number less than 10 that designates a place in a series.

Capitalize words that indicate placement within a series.

Sam024689753, Taylor035798642, and Jess035798642). In addition, all participants were asked not to reveal their real names to their partners.

Procedure

In this opening paragraph of the Procedure, the authors describe the experimental design and identify the independent and dependent variables.

The independent variable was type of communication (online versus face-to-face) and participants were assigned to one of these two conditions as they arrived at the study. We randomly assigned partners only in the face-to-face condition. The dependent measures were personal self-disclosure and perceived partner self-disclosure.

Online condition. Participants entered the room and picked a computer by seating themselves. Consequently, pairs were created through convenience sampling. Each pair then was given five questions to discuss, and each topic was designed to encourage self-disclosure (Aron et al., 1997). The researchers asked participants not to reveal their names to each other and to stop the conversation and notify the researchers if they suspected that they knew their partner. This, however, did not occur. The researchers then informed the participants to keep conversing until instructed to do otherwise. After 15 min, the researchers stopped the conversations and the participants filled out the survey packet, which included an adapted version of the RSDS (Wheeless, 1978) and a demographic survey. Participants took approximately 3 min to complete these surveys.

Min is the standard APA style abbreviation for minutes. The abbreviation is not followed by a period.

Numbers referring to time are also always expressed in numerals, another exception to the less than 10 rule.

This description of the face-to-face condition includes information about informed consent and debriefing.

Face-to-face condition. All participants entered the same room and received an informed consent. The researchers randomly assigned pairs by having participants pick numbers out of a container and pair up with the person with the same number. Participants were asked if they knew their partners (more than just in passing) before this interaction, and if they did, they would have been reassigned. However, this did not happen. Pairs then were given the same choices of topics as the online condition and the same time limit. After 15 min, the researchers stopped the conversations and handed out the survey packets, which contained all the same instruments as the packets for the online group. The participants in both the online and face-to-face groups were given debriefing statements after they handed in their survey packets.

Results

For the entire sample, mean response scores for personal self-disclosure on the adapted version of the RSDS (Wheeless, 1978) ranged from 3.56 to 6.56 ($M = 5.09$, $SD = 0.68$) on a scale from 1 to 7. The Cronbach's αα for the personal self-disclosure items was .64. An independent t test was conducted to explore the impact of communication group (online or face-to-face) on levels of personal self-disclosure. Mean personal self-disclosure responses for the online group ($M = 5.30$, $SD = 0.66$) were significantly higher than the face-to-face group ($M = 4.88$, $SD = 0.65$), $t(56) = 2.45$, $p = .02$. The partial eta squared statistic was .10, indicating a large effect.

For perceived partner self-disclosure, entire sample mean response scores on a scale from 1 to 7 ranged from 1.90 to 6.10 ($M = 4.80$, $SD = 0.69$). The Cronbach's αα for perceived partner self-disclosure items was .71. An independent t test was conducted to explore the impact of communication group (online or face-to-face) on levels of perceived partner self-disclosure. Mean perceived partner self-disclosure responses for the online group ($M = 5.02$, $SD = 0.57$) were significantly higher than the face-to-face group ($M = 4.58$, $SD = 0.74$), $t(56) = 2.49$, $p = .02$. The partial eta squared statistic was .10, indicating a large effect.

The opening paragraph is the analysis of the first dependent variable. Cronbach's alpha is a measure of internal consistency, which means that it measures how closely all the items on a scale relate to each other.

This sentence describes the results of one type of inferential statistical test, a t test. This type of t test is used to determine whether the difference between two sample groups is likely to occur in the population or whether the difference is attributable to random fluctuation (chance). The authors state that the difference was significant, meaning that the difference is likely to be attributable to the independent variable (communication group) rather than to chance.

Discussion

Type of Communication and Self-Disclosure

The purpose of the study is restated.

The authors explicitly state whether the hypothesis about the predicted results was supported.

Current findings are placed in the context of existing literature.

This research study sought to examine the relationship between online or face-to-face communication and self-disclosure. As predicted, the participants in the online communication group reported higher levels of personal self-disclosure and perceived partner self-disclosure than those in the face-to-face group. These results are in line with Tidwell and Walther's (2002) findings, but contradict Mallen et al.'s (2003) results, which indicated that those in face-to-face pairs self-disclosed more than those in online pairs. These differences may reflect measurement issues.

A possible explanation is offered for why results differ from those of a prior investigation.

Mallen et al. (2003) measured self-disclosure with one item that focused on the amount of self-disclosure. Specifically, they asked participants to rate their own self-disclosure from 1 (*no self-disclosure*) to 6 (*extreme self-disclosure*), whereas the present study's measure contained nine items that were also meant to assess one's perception of both the quality and amount of self-disclosure.

Information in this paragraph expands on possible reasons for personal self-disclosure results in the present research.

Results from the current study suggest that online communication may increase people's personal self-disclosure in general, helping them along in the early stages of relationship building. Several previous researchers have provided possible explanations for the present results. A common explanation is the anonymity that an online environment provides, which allows people to feel safer self-disclosing (Chiou, 2006). Tidwell and Walther (2002) proposed another explanation for greater disclosure in an online setting. They noted that many of the ways people get to know others (e.g., reading and interpreting nonverbal cues) are not possible in online communication. Therefore, people communicating online may actually be limited to using self-disclosure as a means to get to know one another. Because this form of communication is fairly commonplace in present times, people may now expect self-disclosure by themselves and others in online communication because no other means of getting to know each other is possible. If this norm of self-disclosure does in fact exist online, it may explain why the online group in this study reported higher personal self-disclosure.

Finally, results indicated that people perceive their communication partners as disclosing more in an online situation than in a face-to-face situation. This suggests that the phenomenon of reciprocity may occur to a greater degree online than face-to-face. Therefore, these findings may serve as another explanation of why people disclose more online in general. The online participants may have felt that their partners were self-disclosing more than the face-to-face participants felt their partners were self-disclosing. In turn, this may have then influenced the online group to self-disclose more to their partners than the face-to-face group felt necessary to disclose to theirs.

This paragraph focuses on participants' perceptions of their partners' disclosure. Again, potential explanations are offered, expanding readers' understanding of the results rather than just iterating the findings.

Practical Applications and Future Directions

Due to the prevalence of online communication in the world today, the results of this study can be applied to practical situations. This study can contribute to the debate concerning the effectiveness of online counseling (Mallen & Vogel, 2005; Murphy & Mitchell, 1998; Rochlen, Zack, & Speyer, 2004; Young, 2005). Because online communication elicited more self-disclosure, online communication may be an effective venue for forming therapeutic relationships. Online therapy may appeal to and benefit clients for several other reasons, which are discussed extensively in other research articles; therefore, we provide only a brief overview of the benefits here. The anonymity of online communication may make clients feel more open when disclosing to counselors (Chiou, 2006). Furthermore, because the Internet can hide the client's and thera-

In this section, the authors highlight the importance of their study by indicating how results can be applied. In the first paragraph, the authors discuss clinical applications; in the second paragraph, they discuss academic applications. Such organization enhances readers' understanding.

pist's age, race, other physical features, and clothing style or quality, the harmful assumptions and judgments about others that people often make in person will not exist. This may allow for less biased communication from the client and genuine therapeutic guidance (Rochlen et al., 2004). Despite the possible benefits of online therapy, research on its effectiveness is still needed. Therefore, counselors should practice online counseling cautiously by taking extra ethical precautions, such as ensuring confidentiality, formulating an emergency protocol, and obtaining informed consent for treatment (Casper, 2004).

Furthermore, the present results may also be useful in academic settings. Because online communication elicited more self-disclosure, teachers may consider using it to form closer relationships with their students so they can better meet their students' needs. Using online communication may make students feel more comfortable asking teachers or other students' questions because of the anonymity it can provide. Similarly, online communication may be used in this way for students to assist each other with academic assignments. Naturally, the present study's results suggest that future research examine whether online communication may be used to increase disclosure and strengthen new business relationships between colleagues as well as personal relationships (familial, romantic, and platonic).

This paragraph addresses limitations of the present research and possible ways to overcome them in future investigations.

Given that online communication will likely continue to grow rapidly, research about the impact of online communication on self-disclosure and relationships is necessary. Due to the small and racially homogenous sample size, future studies should employ a larger and more ethnically diverse sample. Because this study took place on a small campus of less than 1000 students, the anonymity of online communication may have played a role in producing more self-disclosure in the online group. This may have occurred because participants in the face-to-face group may have guarded their disclosures more than those in the online group if they thought they were likely to see their partners on campus later. This phenomenon may not occur in a larger sample from a bigger university or from a noncollege sample.

Additionally, future researchers should consider other important moderating variables to better understand the relationship between type of communication (online versus face-to-face) and self-disclosure. In particular, it would be helpful to consider the impact of certain personal characteristics, such as age, personality, race, culture, socioeconomic status, intelligence, and writing ability. Furthermore, the present study did not consider the effects of large amounts of self-disclosure on relationships; for example, future studies could examine how and in which situations excessive self-disclosure can harm a relationship. Finally, it would be beneficial to examine how online versus face-to-face communication impacts self-disclosure for particular types of relationships, such as student–teacher, client–therapist, romantic, and familial.

The concluding paragraph also addresses future research, highlighting specific variables that researchers may investigate.

- Every reference included in the article is listed in the References section.
- References are listed in alphabetical order by the last name of the first author.
- Citations use a "hanging" indentation.
- There is only a single space after the period that follows each reference element (e.g., year, title,).
- If there is more than one author, an ampersand (preceded by a comma) is used before the last author's surname.

For books and book chapters, include city and state (or city and country, if not in the United States).

This citation is an example of a reference to an entire book. For a book, the title is italicized.
- If an author's middle initial is provided in the article, the middle initial is included in the citation (with a space after the period between initials).

This citation is an example of a reference to a journal article, the most common type of source in a typical article.
- Note the order of reference elements, the use of capitalization in the article compared to the journal title, and the use of italics for the journal name and volume number (but not for the article title or page numbers).
- There is a period after the page numbers, but not after the doi (digital object identifier).

This citation is for an online newsletter. As is the case for a doi, make sure not to put a period after a URL because it could be confused as part of the URL rather than as punctuation.

If a journal article does not have an assigned doi, provide the URL of the journal's home page.

References

Altman, I., & Taylor, D. (1973). *Social penetration: The development of interpersonal relationships*. New York, NY: Holt, Rinehart, & Winston.

Aron, A., Melinat, E., Aron, E. N., Vallone, R. D., & Bator, R. J. (1997). The experimental generation of interpersonal closeness: A procedure and some preliminary findings. *Personality and Social Psychology Bulletin, 23,* 363–377. doi:10.1177/0146167297234003

Barak, A., & Gluck-Ofri, O. (2007). Degree and reciprocity of self-disclosure in online forums. *CyberPsychology & Behavior, 10*, 407–417. doi:10.1089/cpb.2006.9938

Bennis, W. G., Schien, E. H., Berlew, D. E., & Steele, F. I. (1964). *Interpersonal dynamics*. Homewood, IL: Dorsey Press.

Burst Media (2007). *Online insights*. Retrieved from http://www.burst-media.com/assets/newsletter/items/2007_07_01.pdf

Casper, F. (2004). Technological developments and applications in clinical psychology and psychotherapy: Introduction. *Journal of Clinical Psychology, 60,* 221–230. doi:10.1002/jclp.10260

Chiou, W. (2006). Adolescents' sexual self-disclosure on the Internet: Deindividuation and impression management. *Adolescence, 41,* 547–561. Retrieved from http://www.vjf.cnrs.fr/clt/php/va/Page_revue.php?ValCodeRev=ADO

Cho, S. H. (2007). Effects of motivations and gender on adolescents' self-disclosure in online chatting. *CyberPsychology & Behavior, 10,* 339–345. doi:10.1089/cpb.2006.9946

Jourard, S. M., & Lasakow, P. (1958). Some factors in self-disclosure. *Journal of Abnormal and Social Psychology, 56,* 91–98. doi:10.1037/h0043357

Mallen, M. J., Day, S. X., & Green, M. A. (2003). Online versus face-to-face conversations: An examination of relational and disclosure variables. *Psychotherapy: Theory, Research, Practice, Training, 40,* 155–163. doi:10.1037/0033-3204.40.1-2.155

Mallen, M. J., & Vogel, D. L. (2005). Introduction to the major contribution: Counseling psychology and online counseling. *The Counseling Psychologist, 33,* 761–776. doi:10.1177/0011000005278623

Murphy, L., & Mitchell, D. (1998). When writing helps to heal: E-mail as therapy. *British Journal of Guidance & Counseling, 26,* 21–32. doi:10.1080/03069889800760031

Punyanunt-Carter, N. M. (2006). An analysis of college students' self-disclosure behaviors on the Internet. *College Student Journal, 40,* 329–331. Retrieved from http://www.projectinnovation.biz/csj_2006.html

Rochlen, A. B., Zack, J. S., & Speyer, C. (2004). Online therapy: Review of relevant definitions, debates, and current empirical support. *Journal of Clinical Psychology, 60,* 269–283. doi:10.1002/jclp.10263

Rollman, J. B., Krug, K., & Parente, F. (2000). The chat room phenomenon: Reciprocal communication in cyberspace. *CyberPsychology & Behavior, 3,* 161–166. doi:10.1089/109493100316003

Rollman, J. B., & Parente, F. (2001). Relation of statement length and type and type of chat room to reciprocal communication on the Internet. *CyberPsychology & Behavior, 5,* 617–622. doi:10.1089/109493101753235214

Skinner, A. E. G., & Latchford, G. (2006). Attitudes to counseling via the Internet: A comparison between in-person counseling clients and Internet support group users. *Counseling and Psychotherapy Research, 6,* 158–163. doi:10.1080/14733140600853641

This citation illustrates the correct use of capitalization after a colon.

Alphabetize entries with the same first author according to the first difference between the two citations (ignoring "&"), not necessarily by the year of publication.

This article title illustrates correct use of a hyphen; all "self" compounds should be hyphenated.

Tidwell, L. C., & Walther, J. B. (2002). Computer-mediated communication effects on disclosure, impressions, and interpersonal evaluations: Getting to know one another a bit at a time. *Human Communication Research, 28,* 317–348. doi:10.1111/j.1468-2958.2002.tb00811.x

Valkenburg, P. M., & Peter, J. (2007). Preadolescents' and adolescents' online communication and their closeness to friends. *Developmental Psychology, 43,* 267–277. doi:10.1037/0012-1649.43.2.267

Wheeless, L. R. (1978). A follow-up study of the relationships among trust, disclosure, and interpersonal solidarity. *Human Communication Research, 4,* 143–157. doi:10.1111/j.1468-2958.1978.tb00604.x

Young, K. S. (2005). An empirical examination of client attitudes towards online counseling. *CyberPsychology & Behavior, 8,* 172–177. doi:10.1089/cpb.2005.8.172

This article title illustrates correct usage of apostrophes for plural possessives.

Appendix B

Constructing Grammatical Sentences

Proper sentence structure	Explanation	Correct example	Incorrect usage (see bolding)
Construct complete sentences and avoid sentence fragments.	A sentence expresses a complete thought and typically contains a subject and a verb. A fragment does not express a complete thought.	Because employers may consider being young as a plus (Finkelstein & Burke, 1998), older applicants may have difficulty obtaining an interview.	**Because employers may consider being young as a plus (Finkelstein & Burke, 1998).**
Use parallel construction.	Use a similar grammatical form to express each item in a series.	Limitations of this online research included convenience sampling, potential for socially desirable responding, and lack of control over the experimental environment.	Limitations of this online research included convenience sampling, **participants who may have responded in a socially desirable manner,** and the fact that the researcher did not control the experimental environment.
Make sure the subject agrees with the verb. (Remember, the word "data" is pural.)	The verb should be consistent with the subject in number (singular or plural) and person (1st, 2nd, or 3rd).	High scores on the ageism scale indicate more negative attitudes about older individuals.	High **scores** on the ageism scale **indicates** more negative attitudes about older individuals.
Make sure a pronoun agrees with the noun to which it refers.	A pronoun should be consistent in number (singular or plural) and person (1st, 2nd, or 3rd) with the noun that it replaces.	When individuals feel stereotyped, they may fall victim to self-fulfilling prophecies (Hilton & Von Hippel, 1996).	When **an individual** feels stereotyped, **they** may fall victim to self-fulfilling prophecies (Hilton & Von Hippel, 1996).
Make sure pronouns have a clear referent.	There should be no doubt about the noun to which a pronoun refers.	If older job applicants are viewed as resistant to change, employers may be less likely to hire them particularly when the pool of job applicants is large. This stereotyping of older applicants could lead to problems of discrimination.	If older job applicants are viewed as resistant to change, employers may be less likely to hire them particularly when the pool of job applicants is large. **This** could lead to problems of discrimination.
Use similar words appropriately.	Correctly distinguish between words that sound or look alike (e.g., "then" and "than, " "their" and "there").	Participants perceived that younger workers performed more efficiently than did older workers (Finkelstein & Burke, 1998).	Participants perceived that younger workers performed more efficiently **then** did older workers (Finkelstein & Burke, 1998).
Use apostrophes appropriately.	Apostrophes indicate possession or contraction, never whether a word is plural, and their placement differs for singular and plural nouns.	Kwong See and Heller (2004) explained how shifting standards for what is good across age groups may affect participants' responses.	Kwong See and Heller (2004) explained how shifting standards for what is good across age groups may affect participant**'s** responses.
Use a comma before a conjunction that separates two independent clauses.	Use a comma before a "coordinating conjunction" when the conjunction is used to connect two independent clauses. Coordinating conjunctions include For, And, Nor, But, Or, Yet, and So (FANBOYS).	Martens et al. (2004) reported that people do not want to be reminded of their own mortality, and older adults only serve as a reminder of the reality of aging and dying.	Martens et al. (2004) reported that people do not want to be reminded of their own **mortality and** older adults only serve as a reminder of the reality of aging and dying.

Proper sentence structure	Explanation	Correct example	Incorrect usage
Use a comma after introductory phrases, clauses, or words before the main independent clause.	If a sentence begins with a phrase or clause that does not express a complete thought, put a comma at the end of that phrase or clause.	Because of the increasing number of older workers, ageism in employment has become a topical issue (William & Nussbaum, 2001).	Because of the increasing number of older workers ageism in employment has become a topical issue (William & Nussbaum, 2001).
Do not use a comma between clauses when the dependent clause follows the main clause.	If a sentence includes an independent clause followed by a dependent clause, do not put a comma between the two clauses.	Ageism in employment has become a topical issue because of the increasing number of older workers (William & Nussbaum, 2001).	Ageism in employment has become a topical **issue, because** of the increasing number of older workers (William & Nussbaum, 2001).
Use a comma after each item in a series of three or more items.	If a sentence includes a series of items, put a comma between them.	Laczko and Philipson (1991) found that older workers exhibited high energy, flexibility, and a willingness to learn.	Laczko and Philipson (1991) found that older workers exhibited high energy, **flexibility and** a willingness to learn.
Avoid comma splices.	When only a comma connects two independent clauses, it is called a comma splice. Avoid this error by using a semicolon or a period.	We hypothesized that participants would perceive older workers as more resistant to change than younger workers. We derived this hypothesis from Reio and Sanders-Reio's (1999) findings that older adults were set in their ways.	We hypothesized that participants would perceive older workers as more resistant to change than younger **workers, we** derived this hypothesis from Reio and Sanders-Reio's (1999) findings that older adults were set in their ways.
Do not use a comma between a subject and a predicate (the part of a sentence including the verb).	There is no comma used between these two primary sentence components.	Another factor that may influence the reporting of discrimination is the accountability of employees.	Another factor that may influence the reporting of **discrimination, is** the accountability of employees.
Do not use a comma between two parts of a compound subject.	A subject may include more than one noun. If it does, do not put a comma between them.	Media and advertisements may reinforce ageist attitudes.	**Media, and** advertisements may reinforce ageist attitudes.
Do not use a comma between two parts of a compound predicate.	A predicate may contain more than one verb or verb phrase. If it does, do not put a comma between them.	Older employees can contribute considerably to a company and should be valued for their achievements.	Older employees can contribute considerably to a **company, and** should be valued for their achievements.
Use semicolons correctly.	The most common use of a semicolon is to separate two independent clauses not connected with a conjunction.	Lawmakers enacted the Age Discrimination Act to protect older workers from discrimination; legislators designed the Act to provide guidance to employers.	Lawmakers enacted the Age Discrimination Act to protect older workers from discrimination; **providing** guidance to employers.
Use colons correctly.	The most common use of a colon is to separate a grammatically complete (independent) clause from a final phrase that extends it.	Fraboni, Saltstone, and Hughes (1990) indicated that their ageism scale included three primary factors: antilocution, avoidance, and discrimination.	The three primary factors of the ageism scale **were:** antilocution, avoidance, and discrimination (Fraboni, Saltstone, & Hughes, 1990).

References

Finkelstein, L. M., & Burke, M. J. (1998). Age stereotyping at work: The role of rater and contextual factors on evaluations of job applicants. *Journal of General Psychology, 125,* 317–345. doi:10.1080/00221309809595341

Fraboni, M., Saltstone, R., & Hughes, S. (1990). The Fraboni Scale of Ageism (FSA): An attempt at a more precise measure of ageism. *Canadian Journal on Aging, 9,* 56–66. doi:10.1017/S0714980800016093

Hilton, J. L., & von Hippel, W. (1996). Stereotypes. *Annual Review of Psychology, 47,* 237–271. doi:10.1146/annurev.psych.47.1.237

Kwong See, S. T., & Heller, R. B. (2004). Judging older targets' discourse: How do age stereotypes influence evaluations?. *Experimental Aging Research, 30,* 63–73. doi:10.1080/03610730490251487

Laczko, F., & Philipson, C. (1991). *Changing work and retirement.* Buckingham: Open University Press.

Martens, A., Greenberg, J., Schimel, J., & Landau, M. J. (2004). Ageism and death: Effects of mortality salience and perceived similarity to elders on reactions to elderly people. *Personality and Social Psychology Bulletin, 30,* 1524–1536. doi:10.1177/0146167204271185

Reio Jr., T. G., & Sanders-Reio, J. (1999). Combating workplace ageism. *Adult Learning, 11*(1), 10–13. Retrieved from http://www.aaace.org

Williams, A., & Nussbaum, J. F. (2001). *Intergenerational communication across the life span.* Mahwah, NJ: Lawrence Erlbaum Associates.

To our husbands, and most precious children: You are everything to us. Thank you for the endless support throughout this journey.

about the authors

Courtesy Deborah Licht

Becky Kyle, www.good-photo.org

Courtesy Coco Ballantyne

Deborah Licht is a professor of psychology and co-chair of the Department of Psychology at Pikes Peak Community College in Colorado Springs, Colorado. She has over two decades of teaching and research experience in a variety of settings, ranging from a small private university in the midwest to a large public university in Copenhagen, Denmark. She has taught introductory psychology, psychology of the workplace, abnormal psychology, the history of psychology, child development, and elementary statistics. She has experience in traditional, online, and hybrid courses, and is particularly inspired by first-generation college students who turn to community colleges to pursue their education. She received a BS in psychology from Wright State University, Dayton, Ohio; an MS in clinical psychology from the University of Dayton; and a PhD in psychology (experimental psychopathology) from Harvard University. She continues to be interested in research on causal beliefs and their influence on behavior, particularly in relation to how college students think about their successes and failures as they pursue their degrees.

Misty Hull is a professor of psychology and co-chair of the Department of Psychology at Pikes Peak Community College in Colorado Springs, Colorado. She has taught a range of psychology courses at Pikes Peak Community College, including introductory psychology, human sexuality, and social psychology in a variety of delivery formats (traditional, online, and hybrid). Her love of teaching comes through in her dedication to mentoring new and part-time faculty in the teaching of psychology. She received her BS in human development and family studies from Texas Tech University in Lubbock, Texas, and an MA in professional counseling at Colorado Christian University in Lakewood, Colorado. She has served in a variety of administrative roles at Pikes Peak Community College, including interim associate dean, and coordinator of the Student Crisis Counseling Office. In addition, she has helped to facilitate the state system's approach to teaching psychology, as the state psychology discipline chair of the Colorado Community College System from 2002 to 2010. One of her many professional interests is research on the impact of student persistence in higher education.

Coco Ballantyne is a New York–based journalist and science writer with a special interest in psychology. Before joining forces with Misty Hull and Deborah Licht to write *Scientific American: Psychology*, Coco worked as a reporter for *Scientific American* online, covering the health, medicine, and neuroscience beats. She has also written for *Discover* magazine and *Nature Medicine*. Coco earned an MS from Columbia University School of Journalism, where she received a Horgan Prize for Excellence in Critical Science Writing. Prior to her journalistic career, Coco worked as a teacher and tutor, helping high school and college students prepare for standardized tests such as the SAT, GRE, and MCAT. She also worked as a physics and math teacher at Eastside College Preparatory School in East Palo Alto, California, and as a Human Biology course associate at Stanford University, where she earned a BA in human biology.

brief contents

A Practical Guide to Study Skills   v
Amy Himsel, El Camino College

The Basics of Scientific Writing in APA Style   xxvii
Pam Marek, Kennesaw State University

Preface   lxxvii

CHAPTER **1** introduction to the science of psychology   1

CHAPTER **2** biology and behavior   49

CHAPTER **3** sensation and perception   93

CHAPTER **4** consciousness   139

CHAPTER **5** learning   185

CHAPTER **6** memory   231

CHAPTER **7** cognition, language, and intelligence   281

CHAPTER **8** human development   331

CHAPTER **9** motivation and emotion   383

CHAPTER **10** sexuality and gender   425

CHAPTER **11** personality   465

CHAPTER **12** stress and health   505

CHAPTER **13** psychological disorders   541

CHAPTER **14** treatment of psychological disorders   583

CHAPTER **15** social psychology   623

APPENDIX **A** introduction to statistics   A-1

APPENDIX **B** careers in psychology   B-1

APPENDIX **C** check your answers   C-1

Glossary   G-1

References   R-1

Name Index   N-1

Subject Index   S-1

contents

A PRACTICAL GUIDE TO STUDY SKILLS   v
Amy Himsel, El Camino College

THE BASICS OF SCIENTIFIC WRITING IN APA STYLE   xxvii
Pam Marek, Kennesaw State University

PREFACE   lxxvii

CHAPTER 1 introduction to the science of psychology 1

Presenting Psychology 1
AND IT ALL CAME FALLING DOWN 1
What Is Psychology? 4
The Goals of Psychology 7
Roots, Schools, and Perspectives of Psychology 8
Philosophy and Physiology 8
Psychology Is Born 9
Psychology's Perspectives 11
THE FIRST 17 DAYS 15
Science and Psychology 16
FRUSTRATED MINERS 16
THINK again What's in a Number? 17
Critical Thinking 18
from the pages of SCIENTIFIC AMERICAN Murder,
    She Wrote 19
The Scientific Method 19
Steps of the Scientific Method 20
Research Designs 24
THE BIG WAIT 24
Research Basics 26
THE MINERS GET THEIR WAY 27
Descriptive Research 28
Naturalistic Observation 28
Case Study 29
Survey Method 30

Correlational Method 31
across the WORLD The Many Faces of Facebook 32
Experimental Research 34
Experimental Method 35
didn't SEE that coming Sponge Bob on the Brain 40
Important Issues in Psychology 41
Research Ethics 41
THINK again Psychology in the Media 42
THE RESCUE 43
Positive Psychology 44

CHAPTER 2 biology and behavior 49

An Introduction to the Brain 49
IN THE LINE OF FIRE 49
Biology and Behavior: Studying the Last Frontier 50
THE AWAKENING 52
Neurons and Neural Communication 52
Just the Basics 53
Communication Within and Between 54
Major League Players: Neurotransmitters 58
The Supporting Systems 61
The Spinal Cord and Simple Reflexes 61
What Lies Beyond: The Peripheral Nervous
    System 63
THINK again Male Brain, Female Brain 65
The Endocrine System and Its Slowpoke
    Messengers 66
The Hemispheres 68
THE GIRL WITH HALF A BRAIN 68
Right Brain, Left Brain: The Two Hemispheres 68
CHRISTINA MAKES THE DECISION 69
Split Brain 69
Language and the Left 71
The Role of the Right 72
The Amazing Brain 73
Neuroplasticity 73
across the WORLD The Plastic Brains of
    Our Children 74

From Bumps to Brain Scans: We've Come a
Long Way. 75

SOCIAL MEDIA and psychology Facebook in
the Brain 76

from the pages of *SCIENTIFIC AMERICAN* Electric
Surprise. 77

The Cortex: A Peek Beneath the Skull 79
The Lobes: Up Close and Personal 80

Digging Below the Cortex 84
Drama Central: The Limbic System. 84
Deeper Yet: The Brainstem and Cerebellum 85
Wrapping It Up 86
WHERE ARE THEY NOW? 87

CHAPTER 3 sensation and perception 93

An Introduction to Sensation
and Perception 93
GOOD MORNING TRIPLETS 93
Sensation and Perception 101 94
Studying Sensation. 96

Vision. 100
THE EYES OF THE TRIPLETS. 100
Light Is Sight 101
The Colors We See 102
You Won't Believe Your Eyes. 103
The Retina 104
In Living Color. 107
across the WORLD Colors and Culture 109

Hearing 110
THE EARS OF THE TRIPLETS. 110
Listen, Hear 110
from the pages of *SCIENTIFIC AMERICAN* Physically
Out of Tune. 112
All Ears. 112
CONTROVERSIES Conflicted Feelings About
Cochlear Implants 115
Pitch and the Cochlea. 115
I Can't Hear You 116

Smell, Taste, Touch: The Chemical and
Skin Senses 117
Smell: Nosing Around. 117
didn't SEE that coming The Scent of Money 119
Taste: Just Eat It 119
Touch: Feel the Magic 121
Oh, the Pain 122
from the pages of *SCIENTIFIC AMERICAN* Brain
Freeze Explained 122
Kinesthesia. 126

Perception 127
The Mind's Imperfect Eye. 127
Perceptual Organization. .128
Depth Perception 130
Perceptual Constancy 132
Extrasensory Perception: Where's the Evidence? 133
THINK again Extrasensory Perception. 133
MOVING FORWARD 134

CHAPTER 4 consciousness 139

An Introduction to Consciousness 139
MIND-ALTERING MEDICINE .139
Studying Consciousness. .143
Wrap Your Mind Around This. 143

Sleep 147
ASLEEP AT THE WHEEL 147
An Introduction to Sleep .147
The Stages of Sleep 151
nature AND nurture What Kind of Sleeper Are You?. . .154
PROBLEM IDENTIFIED 155
Sleep Disturbances. 156
from the pages of *SCIENTIFIC AMERICAN* More
Than Just a Bad Dream. 159
Who Needs Sleep? 159
THINK again 7 Sleep Myths. 162

Dreams 163
SLEEP, SLEEP, GO AWAY. 163

In Your Dreams 164
Dream a Little Dream 165

Altered States of Consciousness 166
DRUGS, DRUGS, EVERYWHERE 166
Depressants 167
Alcohol 170
Stimulants and Hallucinogens 171
Overuse and Addiction 176
SOCIAL MEDIA and psychology Can't Get Enough 176
Hypnosis 178
CONTROVERSIES False Claims About Hypnosis 179
Fade to Black? 180

CHAPTER 5 learning 185

An Introduction to Learning 185
ATHLETES IN THE MAKING 185

What Is Learning? 187
AN OMINOUS SMELL 188

Classical Conditioning 189
What Salivating Dogs Can Teach Us 189
Time for Some Terms 190
Nuts and Bolts of Classical Conditioning 192
From Dogs to People: Extending Pavlov's
Understanding 194
Yuck: Conditioned Taste Aversion 195
didn't SEE that coming Rescuing Animals with
    Classical Conditioning 196
from the pages of *SCIENTIFIC AMERICAN* The Taste
    of Immune Suppression 197
Little Albert and Conditioned Emotional Response . .197
Real-Life Examples of Classical Conditioning 198

Operant Conditioning 200
THE JEREMY LIN SHOW 200
Operant Conditioning and the Law of Effect 201
Behaviorism and the Shaping of Behavior 203
THINK again Chickens Can't Play Baseball 205
Acquisition to Extinction, and Everything in
Between 205

SOCIAL MEDIA and psychology Contagious
    Behaviors 209
The Power of Partial Reinforcement 209
Timing Is Everything: Reinforcement Schedules 211
The Trouble with Punishment 213
CONTROVERSIES Spotlight on Spanking 215
THINK again Think Positive Reinforcement 217
Classical and Operant Conditioning: What's the
Difference? 218

Observational Learning and Cognition 219
BASKETBALL IQ 219
The Power of Observational Learning 219
didn't SEE that coming Monkey See, Monkey Do:
    Can Apes Learn by Observation, Too? 222
Learning and Cognition: A Map That Cannot Be
Seen 223
IT KEEPS GETTING BETTER 225

CHAPTER 6 memory 231

An Introduction to Memory 231
MEMORY BREAKDOWN: THE CASE OF CLIVE WEARING 231
An Overview of Memory 234
Memory: Encoding, Storage, and Retrieval 234
MEET THE MEMORY ATHLETES 235
The Information-Processing Model of Memory 236
Levels of Processing 237
from the pages of *SCIENTIFIC AMERICAN* Why
    Testing Boosts Learning 238

Flow With It: The Stages of Memory 240
Sensory Memory: The Here and Now 240
Short-Term Memory 243
THINK again Multitasking and Memory 243
Working Memory: Where the Action Is 244
Long-Term Memory: Save It for Later 246
Memory Aids: Put Your Memory to the Test 248
Processing, Effort, and Improving Long-Term
Memory 249
across the WORLD Memory and Culture 252

Retrieval and Forgetting. 254

What Can You Retrieve?. 255

How Easily We Remember: Memory Savings. 258

How Easily We Forget: Memory Slips Explained 259

didn't SEE that coming Google Brain 262

The Reliability of Memory 263

Misinformation. 263

False Memories 264

CONTROVERSIES The Debate over Repressed
Childhood Memories 265

The Biology of Memory 267

Amnesia. 267

Where Memories Live in the Brain—A Macro
Perspective 269

from the pages of SCIENTIFIC AMERICAN What
Marijuana Reveals About Memory 272

Where Memories Live in the Brain—A Micro
Perspective 273

FINAL THOUGHTS. 276

CHAPTER **7** cognition, language,
and intelligence 281

**An Introduction to Cognition and
Thinking** 281

BLEEDING BRAIN. 281

Cognition and Thinking 284

HOSPITAL HUBBUB. 284

Concepts 285

Mental Imagery 287

Biology of Cognition. 290

Problem Solving 292

THE BIG DILEMMA 292

What's the Problem? 292

Approaches to Problem Solving 293

from the pages of SCIENTIFIC AMERICAN Laughter
Leads to Insight 295

Barriers to Problem Solving 297

across the WORLD Problem Solving in Different
Cultures 297

Decision Making 299

UNDER THE KNIFE 299

Decisions, Decisions 299

Decisions, Heuristics, and the Confirmation Bias . . . 300

THINK again Fearing the Friendly Skies. 301

You've Been Framed! 302

THINK again Let Them Eat Cake 303

Language. 304

ELVES, PIRATES, AND READING TROUBLES 304

Language, Amazing Language 305

The Basic Elements of Language 305

didn't SEE that coming The Perks of Being
Bilingual 306

THINK again Language Without Sound. 309

Thinking What We Say or Saying What
We Think? 310

CONTROVERSIES Do Animals Use Language Too? . . . 311

Intelligence 312

What Is Intelligence?. 312

Theories of Intelligence .313

Measuring Brainpower 315

Let's Test the Intelligence Tests. 316

But Are They Fair? 318

The Diversity of Human Intelligence 320

Life Smarts. 321

DR. JILL'S NEWFOUND INTELLIGENCE. 322

nature AND nurture Why Dyslexia?. 322

Origins of Intelligence. 323

Creativity 324

didn't SEE that coming Inside the Brain
of a Rapper. 325

Closing Thoughts 325

CHAPTER **8** human development 331

The Study of Human Development 331

A DAY IN THE LIFE 331

Three Debates. 334
Three Methods 336

Genetics, Conception, and Prenatal Development. 338
16 AND PREGNANT. 338
Chromosomes and Genes 339
From Zygote to Embryo to Fetus 341

Infancy and Child Development. 344
26 AND PREGNANT. 344
Newborn Growth and Development. 344
The Language Explosion 348
THINK again Genie the "Feral Child" 350
Piaget and Cognitive Development: Blossoming of a Young Mind 351
Vgotsky and Cognitive Development 355
SOME THINGS NEVER CHANGE 355
Temperment and Attachment 356
nature AND nurture Destiny of the Difficult Baby 357
Erikson's Psychosocial Stages. 359

Adolescence. 361
THE WALKING, TALKING HORMONE 361
Physical and Cognitive Development in Adolescence. .361
Socioemotional Development in Adolescence 363
SOCIAL MEDIA and psychology The Social Networking Teen Machine. 365
Kohlberg's Stages of Moral Development 365
Emerging Adulthood 367

Adulthood 369
A WORK IN PROGRESS. 369
Physical Development 370
Cognitive Development 371
Socioemotional Development: Early, Middle, and Late Adulthood 373
from the pages of SCIENTIFIC AMERICAN Changing Social Roles Can Reverse Aging. 375
Death and Dying. 376
across the WORLD Death in Different Cultures 377
LATEST DEVELOPMENTS. 377

CHAPTER 9 motivation and emotion 383

Introduction to Motivation. 383
THE FIRST DAY OF SCHOOL 383
What Is Motivation? 385

Theories of Motivation. 388
GOODBYE, SOMALIA 388
Instinct Theory 388
FOUR YEARS IN KENYA 389
Drive-Reduction Theory. 389
Arousal Theory 390
Needs and More Needs: Maslow's Hierarchy 390
SOCIAL MEDIA and psychology Network Needs. 394

Back to Basics: Hunger. 395
STARVING IN SOMALIA 395
Hungry Brain, Hungry Body. 395
Let's Have a Meal: Cultural and Social Context 396
from the pages of SCIENTIFIC AMERICAN Lunchtime Leniency 398
Obesity. 399
Eating Disorders 400
across the WORLD A Cross-Cultural Look at Eating Disorders. 402

Introduction to Emotion 403
SHARK ATTACK 403
What Is Emotion? 403

Theories of Emotion 405
FIGHT BACK 405
Emotion and Physiology. 405
Cognition and Emotion 407
CONTROVERSIES Problems with Polygraphs 410
FACE VALUE 411
across the WORLD Can You Feel the Culture?. 412

Types of Emotion .414
Fascinating Fear 414
The Biology of Fear .414
Happiness 417

from the pages of *SCIENTIFIC AMERICAN* Happy in
    the Morning 418
Gender and Emotions. 418
Closing Thoughts 419

"Normal" Is Relative 456
CONTROVERSIES Are You My Natural Selection?. . . . 459
BACK TO THE FUTURE 460

CHAPTER 10 sexuality and gender   425

Sex and Sexuality 425
GUESS THE PROFESSION. 425
Let's Talk About Sex 426
Sex: It's in Your Biology 426
The Biology of Sexual Determination 428
Vive la Différence 429
Differences of Sexual Development 431

Gender 434
A MASCULINE TOUCH. 434
Gender: Beyond Biology 434
nature AND nurture The Case of Bruce Reimer 437

The Birds and the Bees 439
THE MAKING OF A SEXPERT. 439
Everything You Always Wanted to Know
About Sex 440
from the pages of *SCIENTIFIC AMERICAN* Crying
    Women Turn Men Off 441
Sexual Orientation 442
How Sexual Orientation Develops. 443
across the WORLD Homosexuality and Culture 445
didn't SEE that coming Great Ape Sex 446
The Sex We Have 446
across the WORLD What They Are Doing in Bed . . .
    or Elsewhere. 449
Contemporary Trends in Sexual Behavior 450
THINK again Sext You Later 450

The Trouble with Sex: Sexual
Dysfunctions. 452
NOT TONIGHT, BABE 452
Sexual Difficulties 452

Sex, Its Consequences, and Culture 454
Sexually Transmitted Infections. 454

CHAPTER 11 personality   465

An Introduction to Personality. 465
MEET TANK 465
What Is Personality? 467
nature AND nurture The Funny Thing About
    Personality 469

Psychoanalytic Theories 470
NEVER GOOD ENOUGH FOR DAD 470
Freud and the Mind. 470
Id, Ego, and Superego: The Structural Model of
the Mind 471
Defense Mechanisms 473
Freud's Stages of Development 475
Taking Stock: An Appraisal of Psychoanalytic
Theory 478
TANK'S ONGOING TROUBLES 478
The Neo-Freudians 479
CONTROVERSIES How Birth Order May—or May
    Not—Affect Your Personality 480
Questioning Freud 481

Humanistic Theories. 482
The Brighter Side: Maslow and Rogers. 482
Taking Stock: An Appraisal of the Humanistic
Theories 484

Learning and Social-Cognitive Theories . . . 484
ROBOTS CAN LEARN, TOO 484
The Role of Learning, Thought, and
Environment 485
Taking Stock: An Appraisal of Learning and
Social-Cognitive Theories 488

Trait Theories and Their Biological Basis . . 489
A FEW WORDS ABOUT TANK 489
Who's Who in Trait Theories 489
across the WORLD Culture of Personality 492

Taking Stock: An Appraisal of the Trait Theories. . . . 492

from the pages of *SCIENTIFIC AMERICAN* Open Mind,
Longer Life 493

Personality Assessment 494

A LIFETIME OF MISHAPS. 494

Is It Legit? Reliability and Validity 494

What Brings You Here Today?. 495

What Do *You* See? Projective Personality Tests . . . 495

Taking Stock: An Appraisal of Projective
Personality Tests. 497

SOCIAL MEDIA and psychology It's Written All Over
Your Facebook. 498

Objective Personality Tests 498

Taking Stock: An Appraisal of Objective
Personality Tests. 499

Technology and Personality Assessment. 500

FINAL THOUGHTS 500

CHAPTER **12** stress and health 505

An Introduction to Stress 505

DRIVE. 505

Stress and Stressors 506

EVERYTHING HAPPENS FOR A REASON 508

Major Life Events. 509

Posttraumatic Stress Disorder. 510

It's Nonstop: Chronic Stressors 511

across the WORLD The Stress of Starting Anew 512

THE PARAMEDIC'S ROLLERCOASTER. 513

What a Hassle, What a Joy 513

Stress and Your Body 515

TROUBLE UNDERCOVER 515

Fight or Flight 515

Stress and Your Health 518

Is Stress Making You Sick?. 518

Stress, Insidious Stress 520

ADRENALINE JUNKIES 521

Too Much Cortisol 522

Factors Related to Stress 524

Conflicts. 524

AMBULANCE BURNOUT 525

I Can Deal: Coping with Stress. 525

IT'S A PERSONAL THING. 526

I Am in Control 529

FROM AMBULANCE TO FIREHOUSE 530

Tools for Healthy Living 530

CONTROVERSIES Meditate on This 531

from the pages of *SCIENTIFIC AMERICAN* Meditate
That Cold Away 532

THINK again Think Positive. 535

TO PROTECT, SERVE, AND NOT GET TOO STRESSED 535

CHAPTER **13** psychological disorders 541

**Psychological Disorders and Abnormal
Behavior** 541

WINTER NIGHT 541

What's Normal, What's Not 542

THINK again The Insanity Plea 545

DISPELLING STIGMA: ROSS FINDS HIS VOICE 545

**Classifying and Explaining Psychological
Disorders** 547

The *Diagnostic and Statistical Manual of Mental
Disorders (DSM–5)* 547

didn't SEE that coming "On Being Sane in Insane
Places" 549

"Abnormal," But Not Uncommon 550

What Causes Psychological Disorders? 550

UNWELCOME THOUGHTS: MELISSA'S STORY 552

Anxiety Disorders 553

Extreme Anxiety 553

Panic Disorder. 553

Specific Phobias and Agoraphobia. 555

Social Anxiety Disorder 556

across the WORLD The Many Faces of Social
Anxiety 556

Generalized Anxiety Disorder 557

Obsessive-Compulsive Disorder 558

DSM–5 and Obsessive-Compulsive Disorder 558

Depressive Disorders 560
MELISSA'S SECOND DIAGNOSIS 560
DSM–5 and Major Depressive Disorder 560
The Biology of Depression 563
from the pages of *SCIENTIFIC AMERICAN*
   Inflammation Brings on the Blues 564
Psychological Roots of Depression 564

Bipolar Disorders 566
HIGHEST HIGHS, LOWEST LOWS 566
DSM–5 and Bipolar Disorders 566

Schizophrenia 568
Degrees of Psychopathology 568
Schizophrenia, Take 5 568
Untangling the Roots of Schizophrenia 569
nature AND nurture Four Sisters 570

Personality Disorders 573
Antisocial Personality Disorder 574
Borderline Personality Disorder 574

Dissociative Disorders 575
Dissociative Amnesia 575
Dissociative Identity Disorder 576
What Causes Dissociative Disorders? 576

Postscript: Where Are They Now? 577
DEFYING STIGMA: ROSS LEARNS TO THRIVE 577
OUTSMARTING OCD: MELISSA FINDS A THERAPY THAT WORKS 578

CHAPTER **14** treatment of psychological
   disorders 583

An Introduction to Treatment 583
VOICES 583
Who Gets Treatment? 585
A Primitive Past: The History of Treatment 586
Treatment Today: An Overview of Major
Approaches 588
from the pages of *SCIENTIFIC AMERICAN* A Brighter
   Tune 590

Insight Therapies 591
AWARENESS EQUALS POWER 591
Taking It to the Couch, Freudian Style:
Psychoanalysis 591
Goodbye, Couch; Hello, Chairs: Psychodynamic
Therapy 593
You Can Do It! Humanistic Therapy 593
THE CLIENT KNOWS 593

Behavior Therapies 596
Get to Work! Behavior Therapy 596
didn't SEE that coming Virtual Reality Exposure
   Therapy 597

Cognitive Therapies 601
FOLLOW-UP 601
You Are What You Think: Cognitive Therapy 601

Group Therapies 604
Let's Get Through This Together:
Group Therapy 604
We Are Family: Family Therapy 605

Biomedical Therapies 607
Medicines That Help: Psychopharmacology 607
When Drugs Aren't Enough: The Other
Biomedical Therapies 612

Psychotherapy Today 614
WHEN TO LISTEN, WHEN TO TALK 614
across the WORLD Know Thy Client 614
Does Psychotherapy Work? 615
I Think I Need Help. What Should I Do? 616
Nonstandard Treatment: Self-Help and
e-Therapy 616
SOCIAL MEDIA and psychology Therapist
   or Friend? 617
PASSIONATE PROVIDERS 618

CHAPTER 15 social psychology   623

An Introduction to Social Psychology 623
LOVE STORY 623
What Is Social Psychology? 624

Social Cognition 627
THE DATING GAME 627
Attributions 627
Attitudes 630
nature AND nurture Why the Attitude? 632
didn't SEE that coming Something Doesn't
    Feel Right 633

Social Influence 635
11 ORPHANS 635
Power of Others 636
Persuasion and Compliance 637
Conformity 640
BOY SOLDIERS 643
Obedience 643

Groups and Relationships 647
LET'S DO THIS TOGETHER 647
When Two Heads Are *Not* Better Than One 647
across the WORLD Slackers of the West 648
THE BYSTANDER WHO REFUSED TO STAND BY 650

Aggression 652
THE ULTIMATE INSULT 652
Stereotypes and Discrimination 652
from the pages of *SCIENTIFIC AMERICAN* Following
    the Crowd 653
CONTROVERSIES The Stanford "Prison" 656
from the pages of *SCIENTIFIC AMERICAN* Rudeness
    on the Internet 657
Prosocial Behavior 658
On the Up Side 659

Attraction and Love 660
Interpersonal Attraction 660
SOCIAL MEDIA and psychology Relationships
    Online 660
What Is Love? 663
Making This Chapter Work for You 664

APPENDIX A introduction to statistics   A-1

APPENDIX B careers in psychology   B-1

APPENDIX C check your answers   C-1

Glossary   G-1
References   R-1
Name Index   NI-1
Subject Index   SI-1

preface

In this new work, we have combined our efforts with Scientific American to produce an innovative textbook designed to engage and motivate introductory psychology students as they explore and learn the fundamental concepts of psychology. In planning and writing this book, we benefited significantly from extensive needs-based research conducted by Worth Publishers. This research focused on identifying the most common challenges facing instructors teaching the introductory course, both in traditional classrooms and online.

Written in a stimulating, journalistic style and featuring distinct pedagogical and content characteristics, this text is meant to be a student-friendly introduction to psychology that readily applies compelling scientific information to everyday life. Many years of teaching introductory psychology have taught us the value and necessity of helping students connect with the material. They want to learn about concepts and issues that are practical and relevant to their lives. The research conducted by Worth Publishers clearly and consistently reinforced the importance of achieving a higher degree of student engagement. Thus, we set out to write a text with stimulating content that would offer students a model for thinking critically about a complex world filled with behaving, emoting, and thinking humans.

We also recognize that a student's learning experience does not end with the printed text. Accordingly, we have created a text that marries the printed page with the online space, and uses multimedia to seamlessly reinforce concepts. The online experience of this text—and the digital authorship of its components—are not an afterthought. We have worked equally hard in curating the online lessons that accompany the book in LaunchPad and in composing the questions in LearningCurve, its online adaptive quizzing system.

What's Different and Why
An emphasis on engagement and comprehension

The combination of our teaching experience, our partnership with Scientific American, and the knowledge we have gleaned from needs-based research has led to the creation of an innovative text with several distinctive characteristics. These characteristics, which combine to enhance student engagement and comprehension, are described here:

1. Stories of real people, which provide a relevant and meaningful context for the psychological concepts presented, are seamlessly integrated throughout each chapter. These stories also provide real-world examples of strength and resilience.

Infancy and Child Development

26 AND PREGNANT The circumstances surrounding the birth mine's second child were strikingly different from those of her first Eddie came into the world, Jasmine was a married, working woma 10 more years of life experience; and a decade can make a world o ence in development. As Jasmine can testify, "The mental capacity different between a 16- and a 26-year-old." By this time in life, Jasmine h become much more aware of how her decisions impacted others, especially her children.

2. There are free, easy-to-access *Online Video Profiles* of people featured in the chapters. These "In Their Own Words" and "You Asked, They Answered" segments engage students on a personal level. Assessable versions of the Online Video Profiles also exist in LaunchPad and incorporate thoughtful questions that tighten the link between the video and the chapter content, creating a more relevant and memorable learning experience.

Christina, in Her Own Words:

http://qrs.ly/uy3jpbp

You Asked, Christina Answers

http://qrs.ly/5a3jpcq

Which medical professional had the biggest impact on your recovery?

3. Our authorship extends beyond the printed book and into the digital space. As instructors with experience teaching traditional, online, and hybrid courses, we have curated LaunchPad, the online course space, ourselves—ensuring that the online experience complements the printed text and supports assessment in accordance with learning outcomes.

4. The unique partnership with Scientific American has infused a journalistic style throughout the text, particularly through the involvement of co-author Coco Ballantyne, a science writer who came to the project directly from *Scientific American*. In addition, enrichment material from the magazine is provided in a feature titled From the Pages of *Scientific American*—one or more of which appear in each chapter.

from the pages of SCIENTIFIC AMERICAN

Meditate That Cold Away

Practicing meditation or exercising might make you sick less often

To blunt your next cold, try meditating or exercising now. A new study from the University of Wisconsin–Madison found that adults who practiced mindful meditation or moderately intense exercise for 8 weeks suffered less from seasonal ailments during the following winter than those who did not exercise or meditate.

The study appeared in the July issue of *Annals of Family Medicine*. Researchers recruited about 150 participants, 80

group did neither. The researchers then monitored the respiratory health of the volunteers with biweekly telephone calls and laboratory visits from September through May—but they did not attempt to find out whether the subjects continued meditating or exercising after the initial eight-week training period.

Participants who had meditated missed 76 percent fewer days of work from September through May than did the control subjects. Those who had exercised missed 48 percent fewer days during this period. The severity of the colds also differed between the two groups. Those who had exercised or meditated suffered for an average of five days; colds of participants in the control group lasted eight. Lab tests confirmed that the self-reported length of colds correlated with the level of antibodies in the body, which is a biomarker for the presence of a virus.

"I think the big news is that mindfulness meditation training appears to have worked" in preventing or reducing the length of

5. *Infographics*, 50+ full-page visual presentations are integrated throughout the text, combining concepts and/or data into a single, storyboard format (patterned after those featured in *Scientific American*). The majority illuminate concepts identified through research as the most challenging for instructors to teach and students to master. Examples include communication within neurons, and positive and negative reinforcement and punishment.

6. *Integrated thematic features* emphasizing conceptual relationships and everyday relevance are woven throughout the text. There are seven feature themes representing different topics in contemporary psychology. For each chapter, we have chosen only those themes that logically and directly reinforce content. They are seamlessly integrated into the narrative, never relegated to a "box" or an aside.

7. *Connections* appear liberally throughout, beginning in Chapter 2. These annotated cross-references to material covered in previous chapters explain the relationships between topics, helping students understand the "big picture" issues in psychology.

8. All substantive content, including the stories and thematic features, flows within the narrative in an uninterrupted fashion. This absence of boxes places all coverage on an equal footing and allows examples to occur precisely where they are needed to illuminate and reinforce concepts.

CONNECTIONS

Compelling Life Stories Woven Through Each Chapter

Stories stimulate interest and help students connect concepts with real life.

Stories are often the key to how we organize information and apprehend meaning in the world around us. Most textbook authors understand this, and many texts contain opening vignettes to introduce each chapter. Similarly, their pages are peppered with examples to help students apply and grasp material along the way.

This text is different. It integrates the compelling stories of real people with essential psychological content throughout the chapter. Students encounter both famous figures, such as NBA star Jeremy Lin (Chapter 5), and everyday people who find themselves in extraordinary circumstances, like Liz Allen, the mother of deaf-blind triplets (Chapter 3). The stories of these people are tightly interwoven into the body of the chapter, helping students comprehend and recall critical material. Students do not have to guess how psychology relates to everyday life because our stories dovetail the content with the application. In other words, we return to the same human stories throughout the chapter, linking psychology content to the lives of real people.

We have intentionally chosen people from all walks of life, providing a diverse spread of gender, culture, race, age, nationality, and occupation. (See **TABLES P.1** and **P.2** on pages xx–xxi for a full list of gender and cultural coverage throughout the book.) Your students will read about an Iraq War veteran, an immigrant from Somalia, a neuroanatomist, and a community college student balancing work, school, and parenting. Our goal is for every student to see aspects of him- or herself in the stories presented in this book. We also aim to convey a strong sense of optimism. Our stories typically feature ordinary people who encounter difficult circumstances but persevere and grow nevertheless.

When we say this book has a journalistic element, we really mean it. Most of the chapter stories are based on direct interviews with subjects—not simply background information gathered from secondary sources. Interview questions have been content driven, or designed to gather information that reinforces chapter concepts.

Table P.1 CULTURE AND MULTICULTURAL COVERAGE

Culture and multicultural topics are covered on the following pages:

Aggression, pp. 28, 431

Alcohol, p. 170

Attractiveness, pp. 460, 662

Body ideal, p. 402

Classical music and cognitive benefits, pp. 75–76

Colors, meaning of, p. 109

Conformity, p. 640

Cultural norms, pp. 161, 460

Daily hassles, p. 514

Deaf culture, p. 115

Death, p. 377

Depression, pp. 512–513; 561

Development
adolescence, protracted, pp. 367–368
attachment, pp. 358–359
child rearing, p. 355
cognitive development, p. 355
moral development, pp. 365–367

Dreams, meaning of, p. 481

Eating disorders, pp. 400–402

Facebook and other social media, pp. 32, 34, 617

Facial expression
display rules, pp. 412–413
universality, pp. 411–412

Family therapy, p. 651

Fasting and hierarchy of needs, p. 393

Homosexuality
genes, p. 443
views on, pp. 445–446

Hunger, p. 393

Hypnosis, pp. 178–179

Intelligence, p. 312
cultural aspects, p. 312
culture-fair intelligence tests, pp. 318, 320
problem solving, pp. 297–298
socioeconomic factors and, p. 318
testing bias, pp. 318, 320

Intrinsic motivation, pp. 386–387

Language
bilingualism, p. 306
and environment, p. 349
and personality, p. 491
syntax, p. 307
and thought, p. 310

Learning outcomes, in children, p. 355

Marriage, p. 368

Mate preferences, pp. 459–460, 662

Memory, pp. 252–253

Media violence, pp. 221–222

Minorities in psychology, pp. 10–11

Motivation, learning a new culture, pp. 383–385

Obesity, p. 399

Observational learning, pp. 188, 219, 222

Perceptual illusions, pp. 127–128

Personal control, p. 529

Prejudice and stereotyping, p. 654

Problem solving, pp. 296–297

Psychological disorders
antisocial personality disorder, p. 574
dissociative identity disorder, p. 576
eating disorders, pp. 400–402
schizophrenia, pp. 583–585
social anxiety, pp. 556–557

Psychotherapy, pp. 585–586

Racism
stress, pp. 512–513

Reasoning, pp. 297–298

Safety needs, p. 392

Sex, pp. 449–450, 459, 460

Sexually transmitted infections around the world, pp. 456, 457

Sleep, p. 160

Smoking, pp. 173–174

Social loafing, pp. 647–648

Social anxiety disorder, pp. 556–557

Social support, p. 533

Stereotype threat, p. 654

Stereotyping, pp. 492, 652–653

Stress
adjusting to a new culture, pp. 512–513
poverty and inequality, pp. 317, 511–512

Suicide, pp. 561–562

Therapy, pp. 614–615

Table P.2 GENDER COVERAGE

Topics relating to gender are covered on the following pages:

Aggression and biology, pp. 430–431

Alcohol

    binge drinking, p. 170

    pregnancy, p. 171

Attraction, pp. 104, 441

Beauty, standards of, pp. 653, 662

Biological sex/gender, pp. 428–431

Body image, pp. 401, 662

Cancer and stressors, p. 519

Cognition, pp. 430, 436

Couples therapy, p. 605

Dating, pp. 623–625

Development, motor skills, pp. 355–356

Dieting, p. 529

Early maturation, p. 362

Eating disorders, pp. 398, 400–402

Emotions, pp. 418–419

Freud's views, pp. 470–478, 481

Gender roles, pp. 434–435

Hardiness, pp. 528–529

Hormones, p. 563

Jealousy, p. 605

Life expectancy, p. 376

Marriage, pp. 368, 447

Mate preferences

    biological, pp. 459–460

    cultural, p. 460

MDMA, p. 175

Menarche, pp. 361–362

Moral development, p. 367

Personal control, p. 529

Personality, pp. 491–492

Physical development, pp. 361–362

Pregnancy

    teen, pp. 338–339

Psychological disorders

    anxiety, p. 553

    bipolar disorder, p. 567

    depression, pp. 561, 565

    dissociative identity disorder, p. 576

    panic disorder, pp. 553–554

    schizophrenia, pp. 568–569

Psychodynamic therapy, p. 593

REM sleep behavior disorder, pp. 157–158

Sensory, branding, p. 119

Sex

    gender differences, pp. 448–449

    motivation for, pp. 440–442, 459–460

    and relationships, pp. 447–448

Sexual activity, pp. 448–449

Sexual orientation, pp. 442–443

Sexually transmitted infections, p. 362

Smoking, pp. 520–521

Stereotyping, pp. 65, 309, 418–419

Stress, coping, pp. 529–530

Suicide, pp. 561–562

Tend and befriend, p. 65

Women and work, pp. 65, 439

Women in psychology, pp. 10–11

Online Video Profiles of Featured Stories

Videos allow students to know the people we have featured in a more personal way.

Videos of people featured in the book accompany most chapters and are strategically placed to complement written content. All videos are free and easily accessed via students' mobile devices (by scanning the QR code in the text) and computers (by using the URL that appears under the QR code).

The first video, "In Their Own Words," introduces the person and important themes of his or her story, answers questions, and provides thought-provoking, and often poignant, commentary. The shorter "You Asked, They Answered" clips are interspersed elsewhere in the chapter, showing the same individuals answering questions posed by students who reviewed the manuscript. These student-generated questions are associated with chapter concepts and provide perspective as to how the reader perceives the person being interviewed. Within LaunchPad, our curated online course space, students find the Online Video Profiles again, only this time as assessable capstone activities for each chapter. Instructors can assign the Online Video Profiles within LaunchPad and require students to answer questions linking the video to important chapter content. Students will never wonder how these stories relate to the course material: The quizzes highlight the connection and reinforce key concepts.

Digital Authorship That Extends Beyond the Book
The online course space complements the printed text.

As professors who have taught traditional, online, and hybrid courses, we understand the importance of digital materials. Many texts divorce their media content from the written content, so that the online experience seems bolted onto the text. Our book is integrated with digital materials in LaunchPad, Worth's online course space. There, you'll find online materials that truly echo the features of the book—and use online tools to enhance them. Examples are the assessable versions of the Online Video Profiles and infographics. We've composed the LearningCurve adaptive quizzes in LaunchPad ourselves, to ensure that they match the text seamlessly. And we've curated the LaunchPad units so that they reflect the online lessons we use in our own classes. We truly believe that it is not enough for writing and multimedia simply to exist side by side. For instructors to teach effectively, they must be in conversation with each other. Our goal has been to create a text and online system that is in tune with the way contemporary students experience the text and multimedia together.

Engaging Visual Program with Unique Infographics
Our visuals help students understand processes and combine related concepts.

Students are bombarded with different forms of visual media, and they have come to expect visual representations of concepts. Textbooks have responded to this development with flashy magazine-style images and engaging photos. Again, based on extensive research with instructors and students, including those in our own classes, our text seeks to find a desirable middle ground between the visual clutter of contemporary texts and the traditional, less stimulating pages of those from the past. Ours is one in which visuals are consciously used to augment and reinforce students' understanding of critical and more challenging concepts.

Working closely with experienced science illustrators, we have developed infographics with introductory psychology students in mind. Our visuals are attractive and modern, but they have been conceived and developed for their pedagogical value, not their flash. Many of these infographics were inspired by the whiteboard illustrations we create to elucidate concepts in our own classes. Others have been suggested by our thoughtful and creative manuscript reviewers.

Clear and easy to navigate, these full-page infographics combine stimulating images with straightforward explanations in a format that is accessible to the novice psychology student. All chapters include at least two infographics, and many contain three or more. These learning tools are designed to accomplish one or more of the following:

- Describe a step-by-step process or tell a sequential story.
- Compare two concepts that are distinct but well suited to being presented together in a fresh context. For example, we've included four theories of emotion in one infographic to show how each explains the sequence of events leading to an emotion.
- Provide visual representations of data so students who are new to statistics can easily grasp complex analyses.

There is another reason our infographics differ from those found in other texts: They can stand alone. By reviewing and studying an infographic, students can examine concepts without necessarily referring to the main text, making them a great study

INFOGRAPHIC 12.2

The Process of Coping

Coping refers to the cognitive, emotional, and behavioral methods we employ to manage stressful events. But we don't always rely on the same strategies to manage stressors in our lives. Coping is an individual *process* through which we appraise a stressor to determine how it will affect us and how we can respond.

INFOGRAPHIC 2.1

Communication Within Neurons

Neural communication involves different processes *within* and *between* neurons. In this infographic, we follow the electrical action that conveys messages *within* the neuron, from one end to the other.

2. THE ACTION POTENTIAL
This graph shows the characteristic electrical trace of the action potential. When the neuron is stimulated, positive ions enter the cell, making the axon less negative (A). When the charge reaches threshold (–55 mV), an action potential is triggered. Positive ions flood the cell, quickly reversing the charge from negative to positive (B). Afterward, the cell is restored to resting potential (C).

3. ACTION POTENTIAL TRAVELS LENGTH OF AXON
The action potential occurring in one axon segment causes a voltage change in the next, initiating an entirely new action potential there. This sequential action travels along the axon like a wave, carrying the message from axon hillock to terminal buds.

and review tool. That being said, our infographics also provide an excellent way to reinforce material in the narrative. Finally, use of the infographics is not limited to the printed page. Online in LaunchPad, we've made assessable versions of the infographics, which quiz students on their content and encourage them to make connections with everyday life.

Integrated Thematic Features

Our thematic features seamlessly enhance understanding of core material.

Most introductory textbooks contain a standard or uniform set of boxes that provide enrichment content. Unfortunately, many students see the outline of the box and skip right over it because they believe it lacks importance or is "unnecessary" content they will not need to master for tests. Instructors may not even assign these boxes if they seem superfluous—not only to their students, but also to them.

We strongly believe enrichment features should deepen and build on students' understanding of chapter concepts. This perspective, fully reinforced by the publisher's research, led us to eliminate boxes and embed this content within the narrative. Our thematic examples and applications always occur precisely where they provide maximal reinforcement of concepts, and seamlessly flow within the chapter narrative. The intent of this approach is to have students continue reading, that is, not stop because they see a box with information (sometimes set off to the side, at other times marginalized by a surrounding border). In other words, we have taken this important content out of the box. We use small labels to identify the features so that they are recognized, but not set apart.

The seven themes for the integrated features are described below. We chose these features because they are both *relevant* and *practical* in their content and placement. We've created them with the knowledge that the more students are able see how psychology is relevant to their lives, the easier it will be for them to learn and retain the information. In utilizing these thematic features, we follow one simple guideline: Features (typically, four or five per chapter) are *only* included in a chapter where there is a *clear and meaningful relationship* to the main discussion. In other texts, a fixed set of topics is selected for presentation in boxes and statically appear in each chapter, regardless of fit. Our thematic topics vary: Sometimes they are applications of a concept introduced in the chapter; other times they can be used to launch lectures or classroom discussion. As a result, these features are unlikely to be skipped. They offer high-interest content you and your students can use in and out of the classroom—not to mention information you can include on exams. Each theme is briefly described on page xxvi. (For a full list of thematic pieces, see **TABLE P.3.**)

SOCIAL MEDIA and psychology

The Social Networking Teen Machine

Around 95% of U.S. teens use the Internet, and 80% of them have established identities on social media sites, primarily Facebook. Twitter is less popular, but still used by a substantial 16% (Lenhart et al., 2011). Most teenagers now have cell phones, which means they can engage in digital communication virtually 24 hours a day (Lenhart, 2012).

How does all this social media activity affect young people? Networking sites are places where friendships are created and cultivated, but some experts worry that teens place excessive importance on the number of online interactions they have, rather than the depth of those interactions (*How many Twitter followers do you have?*) (FoxNews.com, 2013, March 20). Others are concerned that overreliance on digital communication is making teenagers less attuned to facial expressions and social cues normally conveyed in real-life interactions (Stout, 2010, April 30). Social media sites can also serve as staging grounds for negative behaviors like bullying. Just take a look at some data from a survey of several hundred Internet-using teenagers (Lenhart et al., 2011): Approximately 8% say they have been bullied online in the past year; 88% have observed others being "mean or cruel" on a social media

NETWORK BULLIES AND

Table P.3 INTEGRATED THEMATIC FEATURES

Topics grouped under this book's themes can be found on the listed pages:

SA......from the pages of *SCIENTIFIC AMERICAN*

Murder, She Wrote, p. 19
Electric Surprise, p. 77
Physically Out of Tune, p. 112
Brain Freeze Explained, p. 122
More Than Just a Bad Dream, p. 159
The Taste of Immune Suppression, p. 197
Why Testing Boosts Learning, p. 238
What Marijuana Reveals About Memory, p. 272
Laughter Leads to Insight, p. 295
Changing Social Roles Can Reverse Aging, p. 375
Lunchtime Leniency, p. 398
Happy in the Morning, p. 418
Crying Women Turn Men Off, p. 441
Open Mind, Longer Life, p. 493
Meditate that Cold Away, p. 532
Inflammation Brings on the Blues, p. 564
A Brighter Tune, p. 589
Following the Crowd, p. 653
Rudeness on the Internet, p. 657

......SOCIAL MEDIA and psychology

Facebook in the Brain, p. 76
Can't Get Enough, p. 176
Contagious Behaviors, p. 209
The Social Networking Teen Machine, p. 365
Network Needs, p. 394
It's Written All Over Your Facebook, p. 498
Therapist or Friend?, p. 617
Relationships Online, p. 660

!......didn't SEE that coming

Sponge Bob on the Brain, p. 40
The Scent of Money, p. 119
Rescuing Animals with Classical Conditioning, p. 196
Monkey See, Monkey Do: Can Apes Learn by Observation, Too?, p. 222
Google Brain, p. 262
The Perks of Being Bilingual, p. 306
Inside the Brain of a Rapper, p. 325
Great Ape Sex, p. 446
"On Being Sane in Insane Places," p. 549
Virtual Reality Exposure Therapy, p. 597
Something Doesn't Feel Right, p. 633

......nature AND nurture:

Why Dyslexia?, p. 322
Destiny of the Difficult Baby, p. 357
The Case of Bruce Reimer, p. 437
The Funny Thing About Personality, p. 469
Four Sisters, p. 570
Why The Attitude?, p. 632

......across the WORLD

The Many Faces of Facebook, p. 32
The Plastic Brains of Our Children, p. 74
Colors and Culture, p. 109
Memory and Culture, p. 254
Problem Solving in Different Cultures, p. 297
Death in Different Cultures, p. 377
A Cross-Cultural Look at Eating Disorders, p. 402
Can You Feel the Culture?, p. 412
Homosexuality and Culture, p. 445
What They Are Doing in Bed . . . or Elsewhere, p. 449
Culture of Personality, p. 492
The Stress of Starting Anew, p. 512
The Many Faces of Social Anxiety, p. 556
Know Thy Client, p. 614
Slackers of the West, p. 648

......CONTROVERSIES

Conflicted Feelings About Cochlear Implants, p. 115
False Claims About Hypnosis, p. 179
Spotlight on Spanking, p. 215
The Debate over Repressed Childhood Memories, p. 265
Do Animals Use Language, Too?, p. 311
Problems with Polygraphs, p. 410
Are You My Natural Selection?, p. 459
How Birth Order May—or May Not—Affect Your Personality, p. 480
Meditate on This, p. 531
The Stanford "Prison," p. 656

......THINK again

What's in a Number?, p. 17
Psychology in the Media, p. 42
Male Brain, Female Brain, p. 65
Extrasensory Perception, p. 133
7 Sleep Myths, p. 162
Chickens Can't Play Baseball, p. 205
Think Positive Reinforcement, p. 217
Multitasking and Memory, p. 243
Fearing the Friendly Skies, p. 301
Let Them Eat Cake, p. 303
Language Without Sound, p. 309
Genie the "Feral Child," p. 350
Sext You Later, p. 450
Think Positive, p. 535
The Insanity Plea, p. 545

1. **from the pages of SCIENTIFIC AMERICAN** Offers thought-provoking articles from *Scientific American,* a publication with a long history and reputation for providing accessibly written reports on cutting-edge scientific findings. We have chosen brief articles that focus on some of the most fascinating aspects of behavior and mental processes, which logically fit within the content of the chapter. *Example:* "Rudeness on the Internet" (Chapter 15).

2. **SOCIAL MEDIA and psychology** Highlights contemporary research exploring how social media applications, such as Facebook and Twitter, impact behavior. *Example:* "Facebook in the Brain" (Chapter 2).

3. **didn't SEE that coming** Raises student interest by detailing an unexpected, high-interest, and newsworthy development related to the chapter's focus. *Example:* "Monkey See, Monkey Do: Can Apes Learn by Observation, Too?" (Chapter 5).

4. **nature AND nurture** Presents important findings related to twin studies, genetic research, and heritability studies. Students will get a sense of how difficult it is to gauge the relative degrees to which nature and nurture shape human behavior. *Example:* "The Case of Bruce Reimer" (Chapter 10).

5. **across the WORLD** Focuses on cross-cultural studies, highlighting salient findings on behavior variation across cultures. *Example:* "Death in Different Cultures" (Chapter 8).

6. **CONTROVERSIES** Examines debates over contemporary research and provocative issues in the psychological community. *Example:* "Conflicted Feelings About Cochlear Implants" (Chapter 3).

7. **THINK again** Helps students zero in on key concepts or deconstruct popular psychological myths, providing a fun and interesting way to hone their critical thinking skills. *Example:* "Fearing the Friendly Skies" (Chapter 7).

Connections: Emphasizing the "Big Picture"

Frequently occurring short asides point out conceptual links across chapters.

As instructors, we have spent years consistently pointing out important conceptual relationships among psychology topics and subdisciplines. Research by Worth Publishers confirms that the vast majority of instructors (over 90%) believe it is important for students to grasp the "big picture" issues of psychology. Yet most texts fall short in this respect. Many present psychology's subdisciplines as "silos" or independent areas of study and then, in an attempt to counter this limitation, include brief cross-references (frequently limited to a page number), or boxed inserts that are nicely annotated, but used too infrequently.

With considerable help from our reviewers, we believe we've overcome this long-standing problem. Beyond the introductory chapter, students will encounter numerous **Connections,** clearly annotated to establish the most important conceptual relationships across chapters. In Chapter 6 on memory, for example, we connect our discussion of attention to the topic of consciousness (Chapter 4), pointing out that we can only attend to, and thus remember, a certain amount of information at any given time. In Chapter 8 on human development, we link our discussion of language development to the principles of learning (Chapter 5), noting that operant conditioning and observational learning play a role in language acquisition. For those instructors who wish to test on these connections, related questions are provided and earmarked within our Test Bank.

CONNECTIONS

In **Chapter 1** we presented the four major goals of psychology: describe, explain, predict, and control behavior. These four goals guide psychologists' investigation of how biology influences behavior. As you read through this chapter, try to keep these goals in mind.

From Administrator to Adjunct: Assessment That Helps

Our assessment components encourage students to become more proactive about learning.

In the interest of more student engagement, psychology instructors continue to request that authors provide more applications and exercises. We have noted that the use of these "learning by doing" tools has become increasingly popular and very effective in our own classrooms. Accordingly, our chapters contain Try This exercises that ask students to apply key concepts by performing simple activities. These exercises are typically fast and easy-to-do, and reinforce chapter content. For example, in Chapter 7 on cognition, we provide students with a list of six words and ask them to create as many sentences as possible. The point of this activity is to show that language is a creative medium. In Chapter 9 on motivation and emotion, we ask students to hold a pen in their mouth in two different ways and then reflect on how they feel. The results of this mini-experiment demonstrate the facial feedback hypothesis.

try this

Take 15 seconds and try to memorize these seven words in the order they appear.

puppy stop sing sadness soccer kick panic

Now close your eyes, and see how many you recall. How did you do?

Another key pedagogical tool is the Show What You Know at the end of each major section. Our questions are carefully tied to the chapter's learning objectives, and rather than limit their assessment purpose to recall and recognition, each set includes one or more questions that require application and conceptual synthesis. In turn, these questions serve to continuously remind students of the importance of achieving a deeper understanding of key principles. A typical example of such a question comes from Chapter 2 on biology and behavior: "When confronted with a potentially threatening situation, the sympathetic nervous system sometimes prepares for 'fight or flight' and/or 'tend and befriend.' How would you explain these two very different responses using the evolutionary perspective?"

 show what you know

As instructors, we understand the value of both formative and summative assessment. We've read the research and we have seen it play out in the classroom: Students learn better when they are tested on the material. But testing needn't be restricted to high-stakes exams and stressful pop quizzes. We can build assessment into the learning process using end-of-section and end-of-chapter questions that reward students for reading carefully and encourage them to think critically. This is the purpose of our Show What You Know and *Test Prep* features. We can also incorporate fun explorative activities where appropriate (the Try This feature), and give students the opportunity to challenge themselves further with online assessment. Worth's research-driven LearningCurve adaptive quizzing system (available via LaunchPad) provides

try this

show what you know

TEST PREP are you ready?

*LEARNING*Curve

franckreporter/Getty Images

students with formative assessment and immediate and personalized feedback. We, the authors, have written the entire bank of quiz questions for LearningCurve, so instructors and students can be confident that the online formative assessment is seamlessly aligned with the text.

Alignment with the American Psychological Association and Disciplines Beyond Psychology

APA Learning Guidelines 2.0

We aim to prepare students for successful careers in psychology and other fields. For this reason, we have aligned our content with the newly revised goals of psychology's principal professional organization, the American Psychological Association (APA). Even more granular alignment can be found in our Test Bank, which allows instructors to sort questions by APA learning goal.

ALIGNMENT WITH APA LEARNING GUIDELINES 2.0

GOAL 1: KNOWLEDGE BASE IN PSYCHOLOGY

APA LEARNING OBJECTIVES:

1.1 Describe key concepts, principles, and overarching themes in psychology

1.2 Develop a working knowledge of psychology's content domains

1.3 Describe applications of psychology

APA Learning Goal 1 aligns with the following *Scientific American: Psychology* content and *Scientific American: Psychology* objectives (numbered by chapter).

CHAPTER 1: 1.1—1.11

CHAPTER 2: 2.1—2.16

CHAPTER 3: 3.1—3.15

CHAPTER 4: 4.1—4.12

CHAPTER 5: 5.1—5.15

CHAPTER 6: 6.1—6.15

CHAPTER 7: 7.1—7.12

CHAPTER 8: 8.1—8.21

CHAPTER 9: 9.1—9.15

CHAPTER 10: 10.1—10.11

CHAPTER 11: 11.1—11.15

CHAPTER 12: 12.1—12.12

CHAPTER 13: 13.1—13.11

CHAPTER 14: 14.1—14.12

CHAPTER 15: 15.1—15.12

APPENDIX A: Introduction to Statistics

APPENDIX B: Careers in Psychology

INTEGRATED THEMATIC features in each chapter

ALL CONNECTIONS in Chapters 2-15 and Appendix A

INFOGRAPHICS in each chapter

TRY THIS application activities in Chapters 1—9, 12, 14, 15, and Appendix A: Introduction to Statistics

LAUNCHPAD RESOURCES

LEARNINGCURVE

INSTRUCTOR'S RESOURCE MANUAL

GOAL 2: SCIENTIFIC INQUIRY AND CRITICAL THINKING

APA LEARNING OBJECTIVES:

2.1 Use scientific reasoning to interpret psychological phenomena

2.2 Demonstrate psychology information literacy

2.3 Engage in innovative and integrative thinking and problem solving

2.4 Interpret, design, and conduct basic psychological research

2.5 Incorporate sociocultural factors in scientific inquiry

APA Learning Goal 2 aligns with the following *Scientific American: Psychology* content and *Scientific American: Psychology* objectives (numbered by chapter).

CHAPTER 1: 1.7—1.11; Think Again: What's in a Number?; Think Again: Psychology in the Media; and Didn't See That Coming: Sponge Bob on the Brain; From the Pages of *Scientific American:* Murder She Wrote; Infographic 1.2: How to Read a Scientific Article; Infographic 1.3: The Scientific Method; Infographic 1.4: The Correlation Coefficient: What's in a Number?; Infographic 1.5: The Experimental Method: Are You in Control?

CHAPTER 2: 2.12; Think Again: Male Brain, Female Brain; Social Media and Psychology: Facebook in the Brain; Infographic 2.3: Ways to Study the Living Brain

CHAPTER 3: 3.11, 3.15; Controversies: Conflicted Feelings About Cochlear Implants; Didn't See That Coming: The Scent of Money; Think Again: Extrasensory Perception; From the Pages of *Scientific American:* Physically Out of Tune; From the Pages of Scientific American: Brain Freeze Explained; Infographic 3.4: Gestalt Organizational Principles: The Whole is Greater

CHAPTER 4: Nature and Nurture: What King of Sleeper Are You?; Think Again: 7 Sleep Myths; Controversies: False Claims About Hypnosis; From the Pages of *Scientific American:* More than Just a Bad Dream; Social Media and Psychology: Can't Get Enough

CHAPTER 5: Didn't See That Coming: Rescuing Animals with Classical Conditioning; Think Again: Chickens Can't Play Baseball; Controversies: Spotlight on Spanking; Think Again: Think Positive Reinforcement; Didn't See That Coming: Monkey See, Monkey Do: Can Apes Learn by Observation, Too?;

ALIGNMENT WITH APA LEARNING GUIDELINES 2.0 (CONTINUED)

From the Pages of *Scientific American:* The Taste of Immune Suppression; Infographic 5.1: Learning Through Classical Conditioning; Infographic 5.2: Learning Through Operant Conditioning; Infographic 5.3: Learning: Punishment and Reinforcement

CHAPTER 6: Think Again: Multitasking and Memory; Didn't See That Coming: Google Brain; Controversies: The Debate Over Repressed Childhood Memories; From the Pages of *Scientific American:* Why Testing Boosts Learning; From the Pages of *Scientific American:* What Marijuana Reveals About Memory; Infographic 6.1: Sensory Memory; Infographic 6.2: Study Smarter: Methods of Improving Your Memory

CHAPTER 7: Think Again: Fearing the Friendly Skies; Think Again: Let Them Eat Cake; Didn't See That Coming: The Perks of Being Bilingual; Think Again: Language Without Sound; Controversies: Do Animals Use Language Too?; Nature and Nurture: Why Dyslexia?; Didn't See That Coming: Inside the Brain of a Rapper; From the Pages of *Scientific American:* Laughter Leads to Insight; Infographic 7.1: Concepts and Prototypes; Infographic 7.2: Problem Solving; Infographic 7.4: How Smart Are Intelligence Tests?

CHAPTER 8: 8.19; Think Again: Genie the "Feral Child"; Nature and Nurture: Destiny of the Difficult Baby; From the Pages of *Scientific American:* Changing Social Roles Can Reverse Aging; Infographic 8.1: Research Methods in Developmental Psychology; Infographic 8.3: Piaget's Theory of Cognitive Development

CHAPTER 9: Controversies: Problems with Polygraphs; From the Pages of *Scientific American:* Lunchtime Leniency; From the Pages of *Scientific American:* Happy in the Morning; Infographic 9.2: Mechanisms in Hunger Regulation; Infographic 9.4: The Anatomy of Fear

CHAPTER 10: 10.11; Nature and Nurture: The Case of Bruce Reimer; Didn't See That Coming: Great Ape Sex; Think Again: Sext You Later; Controversies: Are you My Natural Selection; From the Pages of *Scientific American:* Crying Women Turn Men Off

CHAPTER 11: Nature and Nurture: The Funny Thing About Personality; Controversies: How Birth Order May—or May Not—Affect Your Personality; From the Pages of *Scientific American:* Open Mind, Longer Life; Infographic 11.1: Ego Defense Mechanisms; Infographic 11.2: The Social-Cognitive Perspective on Personality; Infographic 11.3: Examining the Unconscious: Projective Personality Tests

CHAPTER 12: 12.2—12.3; Controversies: Meditate on This; Think Again: Think Positive; From the Pages of *Scientific American:* Meditate that Cold Away; Infographic 12.1: Physiological Responses to Stress; Infographic 12.2: The Process of Coping; Infographic 12.3: Stressed Out

CHAPTER 13: 13.9; Think Again: The Insanity Plea; Didn't See That Coming: "On Being Sane in Insane Places"; Nature and Nurture: Four Sisters; From the Pages of *Scientific American:* Inflammation Brings on the Blues

CHAPTER 14: 14.10; Didn't See That Coming: Virtual Reality Exposure Therapy; From the Pages of *Scientific American:* A Brighter Tune

CHAPTER 15: 15.10; Nature and Nurture: Why the Attitude?; Didn't See That Coming: Something Doesn't Feel Right; Controversies: The Stanford "Prison"; From the Pages of *Scientific American:* Following the Crowd; From the Pages of *Scientific American:* Rudeness on the Internet

APPENDIX A: Introduction to Statistics

DIVERSE CHARACTER profiles integrated throughout each chapter

INTEGRATIVE CONNECTIONS found in Chapters 2-15 and Appendix A

LAUNCHPAD

LEARNINGCURVE

INSTRUCTOR'S RESOURCE MANUAL

GOAL 3: ETHICAL AND SOCIAL RESPONSIBILITY IN A DIVERSE WORLD

APA LEARNING OBJECTIVES:

3.1 Apply ethical standards to evaluate psychological science and practice

3.2 Build and enhance interpersonal relationships

3.3 Adopt values that build community at local, national, and global levels

APA Learning Goal 3 aligns with the following *Scientific American: Psychology* content and *Scientific American: Psychology* objectives (numbered by chapter).

CHAPTER 1: 1.11; Across the World: The Many Faces of Facebook

CHAPTER 2: Across the World: The Plastic Brains of Our Children

CHAPTER 3: Across the World: Colors and Culture

CHAPTER 5: Social Media and Psychology: Contagious Behaviors

CHAPTER 6: Across the World: Memory and Culture

CHAPTER 7: Across the World: Problem Solving in Different Cultures

CHAPTER 8: Across the World: Death in Different Cultures; Social Media and Psychology: The Social Networking Teen Machine

CHAPTER 9: Across the World: A Cross-Cultural Look at Eating Disorders; Across the World: Can You Feel the Culture?; Social Media and Psychology: Network Needs

CHAPTER 10: Across the World: Homosexuality and Culture; Across the World: What They Are Doing in Bed...or Elsewhere

CHAPTER 11: Across the World: Culture of Personality; Social Media and Psychology: It's Written All Over Your Facebook

CHAPTER 12: Across the World: The Stress of Starting Anew

CHAPTER 13: Across the World: The Many Faces of Social Anxiety

CHAPTER 14: 14.10; Across the Word: Know Thy Client; Social Media and Psychology: Therapist or Friend?

CHAPTER 15: 15.5—15.8, 15.11—15.12; Across the World: Slackers of the West; From the Pages of *Scientific American:* Rudeness on the Internet; Social Media and Psychology: Relationships Online; Infographic 15.3: Discrimination, Stereotype, and Prejudice

DIVERSE CHARACTER profiles integrated throughout each chapter.

CORRELATION WITH APA LEARNING GUIDELINES 2.0 (CONTINUED)

GOAL 4: COMMUNICATION

APA LEARNING OBJECTIVES:

4.1 Demonstrate effective writing for different purposes

4.2 Exhibit effective presentation skills for different purposes

4.3 Interact effectively with others

APA Learning Goal 4 aligns with the following *Scientific American: Psychology* content and *Scientific American: Psychology* objectives (numbered by chapter).

CHAPTER 1: Infographic 1.2: How to Read a Scientific Article

CHAPTER 7: 7.8—7.9; Infographic 7.3: The Building Blocks of Language

CHAPTER 8: 8.8—8.9; Social Media and Psychology: The Social Networking Teen Machine

CHAPTER 9: 9.13; Social Media and Psychology: Network Needs; Across the World: Can You Feel the Culture?

CHAPTER 10: From the Pages of *Scientific American:* Crying Women Turn Men Off; Think Again: Sext You Later

CHAPTER 11: Nature and Nurture: The Funny Thing About Personality; Social Media and Psychology: It's Written All Over Your Facebook

CHAPTER 14: Across the World: Know Thy Client; Social Media and Psychology: Therapist or Friend?

CHAPTER 15: 15.3—15.6, 15.12; From the Pages of *Scientific American:* Rudeness on the Internet; Social Media and Psychology: Relationships Online

SHOW WHAT YOU KNOW AND TEST PREP: *Are you ready?* assessment questions in each chapter; "You Asked, They Answered" Online Video Profile questions

TEST BANK essay questions

LAUNCHPAD

LEARNINGCURVE

INSTRUCTOR'S RESOURCE MANUAL

GOAL 5: PROFESSIONAL DEVELOPMENT

APA LEARNING OBJECTIVES:

5.1 Apply psychological content and skills to career goals

5.2 Exhibit self-efficacy and self-regulation

5.3 Refine project-management skills

5.4 Enhance teamwork capacity

5.5 Develop meaningful professional direction for life after graduation

APA Learning Goal 5 aligns with the following *Scientific American: Psychology* content and *Scientific American: Psychology* objectives (numbered by chapter).

CHAPTER 1: 1.1

CHAPTER 2: Across the World: The Plastic Brains of Our Children

CHAPTER 3: From the Pages of *Scientific American:* Physically Out of Tune; Didn't See that Coming: The Scent of Money

CHAPTER 4: Nature and Nurture: What Kind of Sleeper Are You?; From the Pages of *Scientific American:* More Than Just a Bad Dream; Think Again: 7 Sleep Myths

CHAPTER 5: Social Media and Psychology: Contagious Behaviors; Think Again: Think Positive

CHAPTER 6: 6.6; From the Pages of *Scientific American:* Psychology: Why Testing Boosts Learning; Think Again: Multitasking and Memory; Didn't See That Coming: Google Brain; Infographic 6.2: Study Smarter: Methods of Improving Your Memory

CHAPTER 7: 7.5—7.7; From the Pages of *Scientific American:* Laughter Leads to Insight; Think Again: Let Them Eat Cake; Didn't See That Coming: The Perks of Being Bilingual; Didn't See That Coming: Inside the Brain of a Rapper; Infographic 7.2: Problem Solving; Infographic 7.3: The Building Blocks of Language

CHAPTER 8: Nature and Nurture: Destiny of the Difficult Baby; Social Media and Psychology: The Social Networking Teen Machine; From the Pages of *Scientific American:* Changing Social Roles Can Reverse Aging

CHAPTER 9: 9.1—9.7, 9.9; Social Media and Psychology: Network Needs

CHAPTER 11: 11.6—11.7; Across the World: Culture of Personality; From the Pages of *Scientific American:* Open Mind, Longer Life; Social Media and Psychology: It's Written All Over Your Facebook; Infographic 11.1: Ego Defense Mechanisms

CHAPTER 12: 12.7, 12.10, 12.12; Across the World: The Stress of Starting Anew; Controversies: Meditate on This; From the Pages of *Scientific American:* Meditate That Cold Away; Think Again: Think Positive; Infographic 12.2: The Process of Coping; Infographic 12.3: Stressed Out

CHAPTER 13: Infographic 13.2: Suicide in the United States

CHAPTER 14: 14.11—14.12; From the Pages of *Scientific American:* A Brighter Tune; Didn't See That Coming: Virtual Reality Exposure Therapy; Across the World: Know Thy Client; Social Media and Psychology: Therapist or Friend?

CHAPTER 15: 15.2—15.6, 15.8, 15.10—15.12; Across the World: Slackers of the West; From the Pages of *Scientific American:* Following the Crowd

APPENDIX B: Careers in Psychology

LAUNCHPAD

LEARNINGCURVE

INSTRUCTOR'S RESOURCE MANUAL

Psychology Content on the MCAT—Starting in 2015

The Medical College Admission Test (MCAT) will begin including psychology on its exam in 2015. This new requirement stipulates that 25% of the test will include questions pertaining to the "Psychological, Social, and Biological Foundations of Behavior." Many of these topics are covered during the introductory psychology course, so we've made a useful chart that aligns the psychology topics to be covered on the MCAT with the location of that material in the book. A sample version appears below, and the entire chart is available for download from the *Scientific American: Psychology* page at worthpublishers.com.

PSYCHOLOGY CONTENT ON THE MCAT

MCAT 2015: Categories in Sensation and Perception

Content Category 6e: Sensing the environment	Scientific American: Psychology Section Topic	Page Number(s)	Content Category 6e: Sensing the environment	Scientific American: Psychology Section Topic	Page Number(s)
Sensation	Sensation and Perception (Ch 3)	92–137	The cerebral cortex controls voluntary movement and cognitive functions.	The Cortex: A Peek Beneath the Skull	79–83
	Studying Sensation	96–126			
Thresholds	Absolute Threshold	96–97	*Information processing in the cerebral cortex*	The Cortex: A Peek Beneath the Skull	79–83
	Difference Threshold	97–100			
	Infographic 3.1: Studying Sensation	98	*Lateralization of cortical functions*	Lateralization	71
Signal Detection Theory	Signal Detection Theory	99–100		Split Brain	69
Sensory Adaptation	Sensory Adaption	97		Language and the Left	71–72
Sensory receptors transduce stimulus energy and transmit signals to the central nervous system.	Transduction	95		The Role of the Right	72
			Vision	Vision	100–109
			Structure and Function of the Eye	You won't believe your eyes	103–107
Sensory pathways	Light Is Sight	101	Visual Processing	Feature Detectors	107
	All Ears	112–113	*Visual pathways in the brain*	Infographic 3.2: Seeing	105
	Smell: Nosing Around	117–119	*Parallel processing*		
	Taste: Just Eat It	119–121	*Feature detection*	Feature Detectors	107
	Touch: Feel the Magic	121–123	Hearing	Hearing	110–116
Types of sensory receptors	The Retina	104–107	Auditory processing	All Ears	112–113
	All Ears	112–113	*Auditory pathways in the brain*	From Sound Wave to Bone Movement	112–113
	Smell: Nosing Around	117–119	*Perceiving loudness and pitch*	Listen, Hear	110–112
	Taste: Just Eat It	119–121	*Locating sounds*		
	Touch: Feel the Magic	121–122			

PSYCHOLOGY CONTENT ON THE MCAT (CONTINUED)

Content Category 6e: Sensing the environment	*Scientific American: Psychology* Section Topic	Page Number(s)
Sensory reception by hair cells	From Bone Movement to Moving Fluid	113
Other senses	Extrasensory Perception	133
Somatosensation		
Sensory systems in the skin	Oh, the Pain	122–125
	The Reflex Arc	62–63
Tactile pathways in the brain	Figure 3.6: Fast and Slow Pain Pathways	123
Types of pain	Oh, the Pain	122–125
Factors that influence pain	Gate Control	124–125
	Psychology of Pain	125
Taste	Taste: Just Eat it	119–121
Taste buds/ chemoreceptors that detect specific chemicals in the environment	Taste: Just Eat it	119–121
Gustatory pathways in the brain	Gustation	120
	Figure 3.4: Tasting	120

Content Category 6e: Sensing the environment	*Scientific American: Psychology* Section Topic	Page Number(s)
Smell	Smell: Nosing Around	117–119
Olfactory cells/ chemoreceptors that detect specific chemicals in the environment	Olfaction	117
Pheromones		
Olfactory pathways in the brain	Olfaction and the Brain	118
Role of smell in perception of taste	Chemical Sense	117
Perception	Perception	127–133
Bottom-up/Top-down processing	Data-based and Knowledge-based Processing	96
Perceptual organization (i.e., depth, form, motion, constancy)	Perceptual organization	128–130
	Depth Perception	130–131
	Perceptual Constancy	132–133
	Extrasensory Perception	133
Gestalt principles	Infographic 3.4: Gestalt Organizing Principles: The Whole is Greater	129

15 Chapters, 27 Ordinary People, 27 Extraordinary Stories

The scope and sequence of our text are consistent with the typical 15 chapters covered in most introductory psychology books. We've also included two appendices. The first provides coverage of statistical concepts, allowing instructors to choose how deeply they want to explore statistics and experimental design. The second addresses careers in psychology. Both appendices supplement the related material in Chapter 1.

We have described the innovations that set this book apart, but how do they all connect? If we could identify the two unifying themes of this textbook, they would be the following: thinking critically and thinking positively. Our experiences in academia and journalism have taught us to question what we see on television, encounter on the Internet, read in newspapers, and hear in conversation. Being a scientist means being a critical thinker, and we have made a conscious effort to impart a healthy dose of skepticism in our readers: highlighting areas where research is preliminary or inconclusive, where correlation does not imply causation, and where human bias may color research findings.

Being skeptical does not mean being negative, however. We believe that human beings are intrinsically good: capable of learning, evolving, and contributing to society in positive ways. The people described in this book display the extraordinary sensibility and strength that all of us possess at some deep level. Their stories, and the chapters and content they illustrate, can be taught in any order. However, we do recommend that students start with Chapter 1, which lays the groundwork for all the other chapters. Here is a brief overview of what lies ahead:

CHAPTER 1 introduction to the science of psychology demonstrates how psychology was intensely relevant to the 33 Chilean miners who spent over 2 months trapped underground. One of the key pedagogical tools in this chapter is an elegant infographic showing students how to read a research article.

CHAPTER 2 biology and behavior interweaves psychology concepts with the story of Iraq War veteran Brandon Burns, who experienced a miraculous recovery from a brain injury, and Christina Santhouse, a young woman who has thrived in school, work, and life in general—after having an operation to remove nearly half her brain. One of the highlights in this chapter is a Social Media and Psychology feature revealing a relationship between the number of Facebook friends and structural features of the brain.

CHAPTER 3 sensation and perception tells the story of Liz Allen, a mother raising deaf and blind triplets. This chapter is rich with colorful and engaging perceptual illusions.

CHAPTER 4 consciousness offers a peek into the life of anesthesiologist Dr. Robert Julien, and explores the experiences of Matt Utesch, a young man with narcolepsy. Here, we feature a detailed infographic illustrating how different drugs combine to amplify or dampen neural activity.

CHAPTER 5 learning illustrates the principles of classical conditioning, operant conditioning, and observational learning using the examples of basketball pro Jeremy Lin and blind marathon runner/triathlete Ivonne Mosquera-Schmidt. Demonstrating the application aspect of psychological research, a Didn't See That Coming feature explores how conservationists are using conditioned taste aversion to protect endangered species.

CHAPTER 6 memory tells the poignant tale of the amnesiac Clive Wearing and follows Dorothea Seitz, a memory expert, to the World Memory Championships. A Think Again feature gets students to think critically about multitasking while doing schoolwork.

CHAPTER 7 cognition, language, and intelligence explores the cognitive breakdown of stroke survivor Dr. Jill Bolte Taylor and the reading difficulties of actor Orlando Bloom, who has dyslexia. A From the Pages of *Scientific American* feature reveals that a good laugh can set the stage for a flash of insight.

CHAPTER 8 human development details the lives of two community college students—Jasmine Mitchell, a single mother juggling education and career responsibilities with child rearing, and Chloe Ojeah, a young woman who cares for her aging grandparents between classes and homework. A useful infographic compares cross-sectional, longitudinal, and cross-sequential research designs.

CHAPTER 9 motivation and emotion relates the life experiences of Mohamed Dirie, a young man who immigrated to the United States from Somalia, and Lucy Mangum, a child who survived a shark attack. A Social Media and Psychology feature explores how people use Facebook to satisfy psychological needs (or not).

CHAPTER 10 sexuality and gender presents insights on gender and sex from the perspectives of Stephen Patten, a male nurse, and Dr. Stephanie Buehler, a female sex therapist. A Think Again feature examines the risks and benefits of "sexting," or sending sexually explicit text messages.

CHAPTER 11 personality introduces the digital personality of Tank, a robot receptionist at Carnegie Mellon University. A From the Pages of *Scientific American* feature unveils the relationship between longevity and the personality trait of openness.

CHAPTER 12 stress and health examines stress from the perspectives of Eric Flansburg, a police officer, and Kehlen Kirby, an emergency medical services (EMS) provider. An Across the World feature looks at the stressors associated with immigration.

7 8 9 10 11 12 13 14 15

CHAPTER 13 psychological disorders tells the story of Ross Szabo, a young man with bipolar disorder, and Melissa Hopely, a young woman with obsessive-compulsive disorder. Here, we have carefully aligned chapter content with the changes outlined in the *DSM–5*.

CHAPTER 14 treatment of psychological disorders focuses on Dr. Dan Foster, a psychologist working on an Indian reservation, and Laura Lichti, a therapist just beginning her career. An Across the World feature explores some of the cultural issues therapists should consider when serving a diverse client population.

CHAPTER 15 social psychology explores the life of Olympic runner Julius Achon, who adopted 11 orphans from his homeland of Uganda. In fact, his story is so inspirational that we chose to have him adorn our cover. This chapter also includes the story of Joe and Susanne Maggio, a married couple whose union was made possible by the Internet, and a From the Pages of *Scientific American* feature that helps explain why people can be so cruel on the Internet.

Multimedia to Support Teaching and Learning

☐ LaunchPad for *Scientific American: Psychology*

LaunchPad offers Worth's acclaimed online content curated by the authors themselves and organized for easy assignability. LaunchPad includes a full e-Book, LearningCurve quizzing, student self-assessment, simulations, videos, instructor resources, and an easy-to-use gradebook. It also includes Video Profile Assessments—versions of the text's Online Video Profiles that contain questions to help students connect the book's stories to core content. Infographic Assessments within the e-Book turn the printed infographics into mini-quizzes.

LearningCurve quizzing combines adaptive question selection, personalized study plans, and state-of-the-art question analysis reports. Written by Deborah Licht and Misty Hull, LearningCurve provides a unique learning experience—a gamelike feel that keeps students engaged in the material while helping them learn the concepts.

LaunchPad is a breakthrough user interface distinguished by its powerful simplicity. Learn more and request access at worthpublishers.com/launchpad.

Broca's area

Wernicke's area

☐ e-Book for *Scientific American: Psychology*

With LaunchPad, the *Scientific American: Psychology* e-Book integrates the text with an assortment of media-powered learning tools, and a variety of customization options for both students and instructors. Worth's acclaimed *e-Book* platform was developed by a cognitive psychologist (PhD, Yale University) who taught undergraduate psychology at the University of Massachusetts. *Scientific American: Psychology* is also available as an online or downloadable e-Book at CourseSmart (www.coursesmart.com).

☐ Presentation and Video Resources

Worth Video Anthology for Introductory Psychology

Instead of having to search through all of Worth's vast video collection, users can now access a "best of" collection that showcases 250 videos from:

- Video Tool Kit for Introductory Psychology (including 30 new videos co-produced by Nature and Scientific American)
- Digital Media Archives, Volumes 1 and 2
- *Scientific American Frontiers Teaching Modules,* Third Edition

Interactive Presentation Slides for Introductory Psychology

This series of "next generation" PowerPoint® lectures gives instructors a dynamic, yet easy-to-use way to engage students during classroom presentations. Each lecture provides opportunities for discussion and interaction, and includes a wide array of embedded video clips and animations (including activities from Worth's ActivePsych).

ActivePsych: Classroom Activities, Projects, and Video Teaching Modules

ActivePsych is a series of interactive activities and video clips that will captivate your classroom and inspire student participation, with minimal instructor preparation necessary. ActivePsych includes more than 30 interactive activities, PowerPoint®-based demonstrations, 22 new short video clips, plus the new *Scientific American Frontiers Teaching Modules,* Third Edition.

Presentation Slides

- Illustration Slides feature all of the text art and illustrations (including infographics, tables, charts, and graphs) in PowerPoint® format.
- Lecture Slides focus on key concepts and themes from the text, and feature tables, graphs, and figures from both the text and selected videos from the Worth Anthology.
- Chapter Photos, Figures, and Tables give you access to all of the photographs from *Scientific American: Psychology,* organized by chapter.

Assessment Tools

Diploma Computerized Test Bank (Windows 6.71 and Macintosh 6.71 on one CD-ROM)

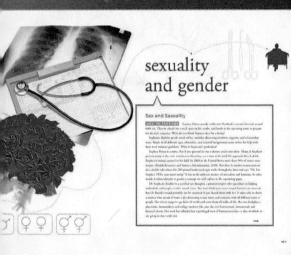

This comprehensive Test Bank includes approximately 4,000 multiple-choice, true/false, and essay questions. Each question is keyed to a learning objective, page and section reference, and APA goal. Questions are also rated for level of difficulty and identified as either factual/definitional or conceptual/application. The CD-ROM allows you to add an unlimited number of questions, edit questions, format a test, scramble questions, and incorporate pictures, equations, or multimedia links. The computerized Test Bank also allows you to export into a variety of formats compatible with many Internet-based testing products.

iClicker Radio Frequency Classroom Response System

Offered by Worth Publishers, in partnership with iClicker.

Instructor's Resources

Instructor's Resource Manual

Written and compiled by experienced instructors of introductory psychology, the *Instructor's Resource Manual* is the perfect tool for busy instructors who want to make the introductory psychology course more engaging for their students. This manual includes chapter objectives; chapter summaries; lecture, discussion, and classroom activity suggestions organized by section; multimedia suggestions from Worth's rich video and student media offerings; plus tips for embracing new classroom technologies and teaching online.

Faculty Lounge

Free to psychology instructors, Worth's Faculty Lounge is the place to find and share teaching ideas and materials that work best in the classroom. In no time, you'll be browsing through a wealth of publisher- and peer-provided resources—or uploading your own. All resources in the Lounge are faculty-reviewed for accuracy and quality, which means you can feel calm, cool, and collected in front of your class at a moment's notice!

- Videos, animations, and images
- News articles
- Lecture ideas and classroom activities
- Useful Web sites and images
  Explore at http://psych.facultylounge.worthpublishers.com.

TLC (Teaching, Learning, Community)

A breakthrough teaching service supervised by a team of faculty experts, Worth's TLC allows you to:

- Consult with leading psychology educators
- Participate in online symposia and events that may qualify for continuing education credit
- Share teaching tips and challenges
- Connect with your colleagues
  Explore at http://worthpublishers.com/tlc.

☐ Student Study and Research Tools

Psychology and the Real World, FABBS Foundation

This reader provides a collection of brief, personal, original essays, ranging in length from 2,500 to 3,500 words, in which leading academic psychologists describe what their area of research has contributed to society. Free when packaged.

Pursuing Human Strengths: A Positive Psychology Guide, Martin Bolt, Calvin College

This workbook provides an overview of nine positive personality traits, such as hope, self-respect, and joy. It also offers self-assessment tools to help students gauge how much of the trait they have developed, and how they might work toward fostering these traits. Free when packaged.

☐ Enhanced Course Management Solutions and Single Sign-On

Blackboard, Angel, Desire2Learn, Moodle, Sakai, and more

Course packs offer a completely integrated solution that you can easily customize and adapt to meet your teaching goals and objectives. Examples of instructor content now included in our enhanced solutions are the complete Test Bank, the complete Instructor's Resources, a variety of PowerPoint® slides, and much more. Course packs are available at www.bfwpub.com/lms. For information about arranging single sign-on/grade-sync between your department's course management system and LaunchPad, inquire with your local sales representative.

Acknowledgments

Four years ago, we met in Manhattan to discuss the possibility of creating a bold new psychology textbook. Sipping coffee and watching taxis zoom past the window, we discussed our burgeoning partnership with Worth Publishers, and our excitement about creating an introductory text that would bring relevance and student engagement to a whole new level. We believe that dream has finally materialized, but it would not have been possible without the hard work and talent of reviewers, focus group attendees, students, interview subjects, contributors, and editors.

We are forever grateful to publisher Kevin Feyen and acquisitions editor Erik Gilg for having the vision to go forward with this project, and believing in our ability to execute it. Thank you for bringing the three authors together and for your continued friendships. President Liz Widdicombe and Senior Vice President Catherine Woods, what an honor it has been to work with your exceptional team. Sales representative Matt Ours, we joke with you about "getting us into this mess!" but it turns out we really do love this mess. Thank you for planting the seed for our involvement at Worth.

Early manuscript developer Jim "period-end-of-sentence" Strandberg, you guided us through the early drafts, supplying the right balance of honest feedback and kind encouragement. Your steady stream of insight and humor kept us afloat while we navigated the unknown waters of textbook publishing. Acquisitions editor Rachel Losh, you picked up this project and ran with it in all the right directions. It's hard to imagine a more enterprising and market-savvy leader to see this project through. Thank you for listening and responding to our concerns, trusting our judgment about critical issues, and throwing your heart and soul into this book. Editorial assistant Katie Garrett, you juggled a variety of essential editing and production responsibilities. Thank you for your hard work. Manuscript consultant Moira Lerner, your guidance was essential during the development process. Thank you for your painstaking chapter reviews and sound advice.

Working by our side from development through production was developmental editor Marna Miller, whose brilliant ideas for infographics now appear as full-page spreads in every chapter of this book. Marna, you have repeatedly blown us away with your creative spins on concept presentation. Your figures and photos are original and thought provoking; students will be drawn in by their relevance and interest, just as we have been. Anne DeMarinis, Dawn Albertson, Emily Stark, and Leah Georges, thank you for making the infographics come to life so elegantly. Photo editor Cecilia Varas and photo researchers Jacqui Wong and Deborah Anderson, your patience and persistence have paid off; thank you for working so hard to secure use of the desired photographs; we know it was challenging.

Brad Rivenburgh, Glenn and Meg Turner of Burrston House, you came to this project just when we were in great need of your extensive publishing experience and vast fund of research knowledge. You knew what the market demanded, and you provided explicit directions for supplying it. Thank you for selecting an exceptional panel of reviewers, and distilling their feedback into practical suggestions for us to consider. The focus groups you organized have been an invaluable tool for fine-tuning our efforts.

Producing a high-quality college textbook is a formidable task, but no one is better qualified for this mission than project editor Robert Errera. Thank you, Rob, for maintaining such high standards and personally seeing to it that our requests were fulfilled. Director of Development Tracey Kuehn, you made the transition from development to production smooth and manageable—and perhaps more importantly, you kept us sane during production. We knew your heart was really in it when you spent part of your honeymoon with us! Copy editor Patti Brecht, we are grateful to you for going the extra mile to ensure consistency of content and copy. Art director Babs Reingold, what can we say? You are a design genius! Flipping through the pages of this textbook, we are dazzled by its uncomplicated beauty.

To all the managers, designers, illustrators, editors, and other team members with whom we did not have direct contact, please know that we are thoroughly impressed with your work; we feel lucky to have had you on our team. A huge thanks to production manager Sarah Segal, associate managing editor Lisa Kinne, layout designer Clea Chmela, chapter opener designer Charles Yuen, illustration coordinator Matthew McAdams, illustrator Todd Buck, designer Lyndall Culbertson, supplements production manager Stacey Alexander, and market development assistant Stephanie Ellis.

Peter Levin, John Philp, and Barbara Parks of Splash Studios, your videos give us goose bumps, and some of them move us to tears. Thank you for conveying the chapter stories in a way that was real, yet respectful to the interview subjects. No one could have done it better. Jessica Bayne, your guidance on this project has been invaluable.

Rachel Comerford and Gayle Yamazaki, you have provided essential support to us in our development of online learning activities. Thanks to your expertise, our readers can take full advantage of Worth's online learning space, LaunchPad.

Marketing gurus Carlise Stembridge and Lindsay Johnson, thank you for helping us bond with the sales team and ensuring that real college students read this book! Without you, our work would be pointless. We also acknowledge the excellent work of Andrea Musick Page, who has developed the supplements, and Debra Hollister, who assissted with Appendix C—in addition to many other contributions.

We have benefited in countless ways from an exceptional group of academic reviewers. Some have been our greatest champions, and others our sharpest critics. We needed both. We are grateful for the hundreds of hours you spent examining this text, writing thoughtful critiques, and offering bright ideas— many of which we have incorporated into our text. This is your book, too.

Mary Beth Ahlum, *Nebraska Wesleyan University*

Winifred Armstead-Hannah, *City College of Chicago, Richard R. Daley College*

Sandra Arntz, *Carroll University*

Shaki Asgari, *Iona College*

Sherry Ash, *San Jacinto College Community College*

Diane Ashe, *Valencia College, West*

Nani Azman, *University of Hawaii, Maui College*

Rosenna Bakari, *Des Moines Area Community College*

Michael E. Barber, *Sante Fe College*

Nazira Barry, *Miami Dade College, Wolfson*

Holly Beard, *Midlands Technical College*

Patrick Bennett, *Indiana State University*

Garrett L. Berman, *Roger Williams University*

Leslie Berntsen, *University of Southern California*

John Bickford, *University of Massachusetts, Amherst*

David Biek, *Middle Georgia State College*

Andrew Blair, *Palm Beach State College*

Marilyn Bonem, *Eastern Michigan University*

Leanne Boucher, *Nova Southeastern University*

Saundra Boyd, *Houston Community College*

Amy A. Bradshaw, *Embry-Riddle Aeronautical University*

Karen Brakke, *Spelman College*

Lauren Brown, *Mott Community College*

Amy Buckingham, *Red Rocks Community College*

Michelle A. Butler, *U.S. Air Force Academy*

Judith Caprio, *Rhode Island College*

Jessica Carpenter, *Elgin Community College*

Gabriela Carrasco, *University of North Alabama*

Sharon Chacon, *Northeast Wisconsin Technical College*

Daniel Chadborn, *Southeastern Louisiana University*

Gabriela Chavira, *California State University–Northridge*

Regina Chopp, *University of Southern California*

Diana Ciesko, *Valencia College–East*

Shirley Clay, *Northeast Texas Community College*

Deborah Conway, *Community College of Allegheny County, South Campus*

Kristie Coredell-McNulty, *Angelo State University*

Cheryl Cotten, *Wor-Wic Community College*

Baine B. Craft, *Seattle Pacific University*

Margaret Davidson, *Rockwall– Heath High School*

Amber DeBono, *Winston- Salem State University*

David Devonis, *Graceland University*

Rebekah Phillips DeZalia, *Coastal Carolina Community College*

Amanda di Bartolomeo, *University of California, Los Angeles*

Matthew D. Diggs, *Collin College*

Evelyn Doody, *College of Southern Nevada*

Karen Trotty Douglas, *Alamo Colleges, San Antonio College*

Kimberly Duff, *Cerritos College*

Jeanne Edman, *Consumnes River College*

Mitchell Estaphan, *Bristol Community College*

Roel Evangelista, *Community College of Baltimore–Essex*

Frank Eyetsemitan, *Roger Williams University*

Kelvin Faison, *Pasco Hernando Community College*

Robert Fauber, *Temple University*

Dan Fawaz, *Georgia Perimeter College–Clarkston*

Christopher Ferguson, *Stetson University*

Frank M. Ferraro III, *Nebraska Wesleyan University*

Stephen Fox, *University of Hawaii–Maui College*

Lisa Fozio-Thielk, *Waubonsee Community College*

Susan Frantz, *Highline Community College*

Jeanette Gassaway, *Ohio University–Chillicothe*

Rachel Gentry, *Ball State University*

Sherry Ginn, *Rowan–Cabarrus Community College*

Gladys Green, *State College of Florida*

Jerry Green, *Tarrant County College, Northwest*

Donnell Griffin, *Davidson County Community College*

Bettye P. Griffin, *West Hills Community College District*

Lynn Haller, *Morehead State University*

Julie Hanauer, *Suffolk County Community College*

Keith Happaney, *Lehman College*

Christine Harrington, *Middlesex County College*

Carol Kozak Hawk, *Austin Community College*

Cathy Hawkins, *North Hennepin Community College*

Rickye Heffner, *University of Toledo*

Byron Heidenreich, *Illinois State University*

Bryan Hendricks, *University of Wisconsin, Madison*

Jennifer Higa-King, *Honolulu Community College*

Mia Holland, *Bridgewater State University*

Debra Hollister, *Valencia College–Lake Nona*

Amy Holmes, *Davidson County Community College*

Karen Y. Holmes, *Norfolk State University*

Nancy Honeycutt, *Alamance Community College*

Mary Susan Horton, *Mesa Community College*

Vivian Hsu, *Rutgers University*

Christopher Hubbell, *Rensselaer Polytechnic Institute*

Ken Hudson, *Florida Community College*

Mayte Insua-Auais, *Miami Dade College–North*

Judy Jankowski, *Grand Rapids Community College*

Joan Jensen, *Central Piedmont Community College*

Barry Johnson, *Davidson County Community College*

Jessica Jolly, *Gloucester County College*

Judith Josephs, *Salem State University*

Diana Joy, *Community College of Denver*

Nora Kametani, *Nunez Community College*

Carolyn Kaufman, *Columbus State Community College*

Zelida Keo-Trang, *Saddleback College*

Lynnel Kiely, *City Colleges of Chicago, Harold Washington College*

Yuthika Kim, *Oklahoma City Community College*

Cheri Kittrell, *State College of Florida*

Nicole Korzetz, *Lee College*

Michelle LaBrie, *College of the Canyons*

Cindy Lahar, *York County Community College*

Jennifer Lee, *Cabrillo College*

Juliet Lee, *Cape Fear Community College*

Kris Leppien-Christensen, *Saddleback College*

Christine Lofgren, *University of California–Irvine*

Pamela Joan Marek, *Kennesaw State University*

Alexander Marvin, *Seminole State College of Florida*

Kirsten Matthews, *Harper College*

Brent Mattingly, *Ashland University*

Cindy Matyi, *Ohio University, Chillicothe Campus*

Ashley Maynard, *University of Hawaii*

Dan McConnell, *University of Central Florida*

Cheryl McGill, *Florence-Darlington Technical College*

Lisa Moeller, *Devry University*

Thurla Moore, *Tallahassee Community College*

Kristie Morris, *SUNY Rockland Community College*

Julie Morrison, *Glendale Community College*

Paige Muellerleile, *Marshall University*

Robin Musselman, *Lehigh Carbon Community College*

Margaret Nauta, *Illinois State University*

Roderick Neal, *Patrick Henry Community College*

Ronn Newby, *Des Moines Area Community College*

John L. Oliver, *Florida Community College*

Jennifer Ounjian, *Contra Costa College*

Joanna Palmer, *Baker College of Flint*

Carol Pandey, *Los Angeles Pierce College*

Jan Pascal, *Johnson County Community College*

Linda Perrotti, *University of Texas at Arlington*

Kristin Price, *Owens Community College*

Judy Quon, *California State University–Long Beach*

Marianna Rader, *Rockingham Community College*

Barbara Radigan, *Community College of Allegheny County*

Elena Reigadas, *Los Angeles Harbor College*

Tanya Renner, *Kapiʻolani Community College*

Nan Rice, *Springfield Tech Community College*

Vicki Ritts, *St. Louis Community College, Meramec*

Michelle Robinson, *Saddleback College*

Fredric E. Rose, *Palomar College*

Karen Saenz, *Houston Community College*

Ronald Arthur Salazar, *San Juan College*

Carol Schachat, *Orange Coast College*

Rebecca E. Shepherd, *College of the Canyons*

Melinda Shoemaker, *Broward College–North*

Maria Shpurik, *Florida International University*

Joan Siebert, *Community College of Allegheny County*

Debra Silverman, *Keiser University*

Theresa Simantirakis, *Wright College*

Valerie A. Simon, *Wayne State University*

Karyn Skaar, *Northeast Texas Community College*

Don Smith, *Everett Community College*

Jerry Snead, *Coastal Carolina Community College*

Jonathan Sparks, *Vance-Granville Community College*

Jason Spiegelman, *Community College of Baltimore County–Catonsville*

Susan Nash Spooner, *McLennan Community College*

Chris Stanley, *Winston-Salem State University*

Betsy Stern, *Milwaukee Area Technical College*

Lara Tedrow, *Tidewater Cimmunity College*

Jennifer Thompson-Watson, *City Colleges of Chicago, Kennedy–King College*

Carole Toney, *Polk State College*

Elizabeth Tuckwiller, *George Washington University*

Mary Ann Valentino, *Fresno City College*

Jennifer M. Verive, *Western Nevada College*

Jeff Wachsmuth, *Napa Valley College*

Linda Walsh, *University of Northern Iowa*

Martha Weaver, *Eastfield College*

Melissa B. Weston, *El Centro College*

Tanya Whipple, *Missouri State University*

Ric Wynn, *County College of Morris*

Clare Zaborowshi, *San Jacinto College Community College*

Valerie Zurawski, *St. John's University*

Thank you to the following student reviewers who provided valuable feedback and contributed questions for our video interviews:

Nicole Adamcyzk, *Suffolk County Community College*

Hilary Allen, *Waubonsee Community College*

Wes Armstrong, *Georgia Perimeter College*

Michael Baker, *Suffolk County Community College*

Michael Blackburn, *Valencia College*

Rebecca Blackburn, *Valencia College*

Zandi Bosua, *Suffolk County Community College*

Michael Burt, *Valencia College*

Joseph Calabrese, *Waubonsee Community College*

Paul Calzada, *College of Southern Nevada*

Tracy Cleary, *Valencia College*

James Ferguson, *Suffolk County Community College*

Amanda Flood, *Suffolk County Community College*

Marie Forestal, *Valencia College*

Casey Frisque, *Northeast Wisconsin Technical College*

Jordana Gaines, *Suffolk County Community College*

Chris Henderson, *Georgia Perimeter College*

Daisy Hidalgo, *Valencia College*

Matthew Hirschland, *Georgia Perimeter College*

Eric Hollenback, *Waubonsee Community College*

Michael Hollenback, *Waubonsee Community College*

Meridith Hollister, *Valencia College*

Zane Howard, *Georgia Perimeter College*

Caitlyn Ingram, *Suffolk County Community College*

Carole Keef, *Valencia College*

Zoe Kiefer, *Waubonsee Community College*

Donya Kobari, *Georgia Perimeter College*

Emily Kolk, *Suffolk County Community College*

Deanna Krane, *Suffolk County Community College*

Kayla Krasnee, *Suffolk County Community College*

Amanda Landolt, *Northeast Wisconsin Technical College*

Joline Ledbetter, *College of Southern Nevada*

Adam R. Leicht, *Georgia Perimeter College*

Amanda Meyer, *Waubonsee Community College*

Justin Oge, *Tarrant County College–Northwest*

Melissa Ortiz, *Suffolk County Community College*

Kimberly Peterson, *Suffolk County Community College*

Jacob Rodgers, *Tarrant County College–Northwest*

Jared Rodgers, *Tarrant County College–Northwest*

Chloe Rodriguez, *Tarrant County College–Northwest*

Sarah Rogers, *Suffolk County Community College*

Carolina Rosales, *Waubonsee Community College*

Amber Roth, *Georgia Perimeter College*

Danika Sanders, *College of Southern Nevada*

Olivia Schlabra, *Georgia Perimeter College*

Whitney Schmidt, *Tarrant County College–Northwest*

Cheyenne Sharpe, *Tarrant County College–Northwest*

Monica Sheehan, *Tarrant County College–Northwest*

Lydia Simone, *College of Southern Nevada*

Analiese Smith, *Tarrant County College–Northwest*

Victoria Vallance, *Suffolk County Community College*

Katherine Weinmann, *Tarrant County College–Northwest*

Stephanie Willes, *College of Southern Nevada*

Courtney Williams, *Tarrant County College–Northwest*

Owen Wood, *Tarrant County College–Northwest*

Sarah Woolf, *Tarrant County College–Northwest*

The following instructors graciously attended our focus groups. Their feedback both informed and influenced many key aspects of the text, as well as the resources that accompany it.

Anora Ackerson, *Kalamazoo Valley Community College*

Winifred Armstead-Hannah, *City Colleges of Chicago, Richard R. Daley College*

Marina Baratian, *Brevard Community College*

Nazira Barry, *Miami College, Dade, Wolfson*

Sonia Bell, *Prince George's Community College*

Christopher Beverly, *St. Johns River State College*

Andrew Blair, *Palm Beach State College*

Marilyn Bonem, *Eastern Michigan University*

Leanne Boucher, *Nova Southeastern University*

Winfield Brown, *Florence-Darlington Technical College*

Alison Buchanan, *Henry Ford Community College*

Jessica Cail, *Pepperdine University*

Christie Cathey, *Missouri State University*

Shakiera Causey, *Guilford Technical Community College*

Ruby Christian-Brougham, *Los Angeles Valley College*

Julia Cohen, *Los Angeles Pierce College*

Bonnie Dennis, *Virginia Western Community College*

Dianne DeSousa, *Prairie State Community College*

Peggy Dombrowski, *Harrisburg Area Community College*

Susan Edwards, *Mott Community College*

Urminda Firlan, *Kalamazoo Valley Community College*

Amanda Frei, *University of Phoenix*

Sherry Ginn, *Rowan–Cabarrus Community College*

Marlene Groomes, *Miami Dade–Homestead*

Julie Hernandez, *Rock Valley College*

Sallie Herrin, *Rowan–Cabarrus Community College*

Debra Hollister, *Valencia College–Lake Nona*

Nancy Honeycutt, *Alamance Community College*

Kathleen Hughes-DeSousa, *Pasco Hernando Community College*

Susan Johnson, *Cypress College*

Paul Johnson, *Oakton Community College*

Lynda Karlis, *Macomb Community College–Center Campus*

Ken Kikuchi, *College of Lake County*

Andrew Kim, *Citrus College*

Cherl Kittrell, *State College of Florida*

Rachel Laimon, *Mott Community College*

Samuel Lamb, *Tidewater Community College, Virginia Beach*

Deborah Maher, *Orange Coast College*

Jeni Maijala, *University of Phoenix*

Richard Manley, *Antelope Valley College*

Randy Martinez, *Cypress College*

Myssie Mathis, *Cape Fear Community College*

Dan McConnell, *University of Central Florida*

Cheryl McGill, *Florence–Darlington Technical College*

David McGrevy, *Palomar Community College*

Russ McGuff, *Tallahassee Community College*

William Mellan, *Hillsborough Community College–Plant City*

Charles Miron, *Community College of Baltimore County–Catonsville*

Paulina Multhaupt, *Macomb Community College–Center Campus*

Sonia Nieves, *Broward Community College–South Campus*

James O'Brien, *Tidewater Community College, Virginia Beach*

Marco O'Brien, *Milwaukee Area Technical College*

Denise Orme, *Golden West College*

Jennifer Pemberton, *Community College of Baltimore County–Catonsville*

Kathleen Peters, *Brevard Community College*

Debbie Podwika, *Kankakee Community College*

James Previte, *Antelope Valley College*

Christopher Raye, *Santa Fe College*

Alan Richey, *Wilkes Community College*

Debra Rowe, *Oakland Community College-Royal Oak*

Carlos Sandoval, *Cypress College*

Spring Schaefer, *Delta College*

Alex Schwartz, *Santa Monica College*

Maria Shpurik, *Florida International University*

Morgan Slusher, *Community College of Baltimore County–Essex*

Steven Smith, *California State University, Fullerton*

Jason Spiegelman, *Community College of Baltimore County–Catonsville*

Eli Stav, *Broward Community College–North Campus*

Betsy Stern, *Milwaukee Area Technical College*

Cari Stevenson, *Kankakee Community College*

Krishna Stilianos, *Oakland Community College–Highland Lakes*

Shawn Talbot, *Kellogg Community College*

Anne Taylor-Spitzer, *Antelope Valley College*

Khia Thomas, *Broward Community College–North Campus*

Chris Thomas, *Florence–Darlington Technical College*

Jennifer Thompson-Watson, *City Colleges of Chicago, Kennedy–King College*

Lora Vasiliauskas, *Virginia Western Community College*

Rebekah Wanic, *Grossmont College*

Linda Weldon, *Community College of Baltimore County–Essex*

Rhonda Whitten, *Tri-County Technical College*

Steve Withrow, *Guilford Technical Community College*

Dreama Witt, *Guilford Technical Community College*

Brandy Young, *Cypress College*

There is one "unofficial" reviewer whose contributions cannot be quantified. Working behind the scenes from start to finish, reading every line of this text alongside us was Dr. Eve Van Rennes. Dr. Van Rennes, thank you for your intelligent critiques and unwavering support.

It goes without saying that this project would not have been the same without the hard work and dedication of our author team. Every sentence in this textbook has been a group effort: We have written and reviewed everything together. Our minds work differently and we have distinct skill sets, but we recognize and appreciate those in each other. Writing this book has been an arduous task (who knew three women could live on just a few hours of sleep every night?), but we have encouraged and supported each other along the way. We are more than a work team—we are lifelong friends. We should acknowledge that none of us would have written these words if it hadn't been for our parents and grandparents, who made our education their top priority.

Last, but certainly not least, we would like to thank the extraordinary people whose life stories are woven throughout these chapters. We selected you because your stories touched and inspired us. Learning about your lives has helped us become more thoughtful and compassionate people. We believe you will have the same effect on college students across the country.

A special thanks to Julius Achon and the late James Fee, who made it possible for us to use the beautiful photo gracing the cover of this text. We hope the inclusion of Julius's story raises awareness about the challenges facing people in Northern Uganda, and about the efforts of the Achon Uganda Children's Fund.

Deborah M. Licht
Misty G. Hull
Coco Ballantyne

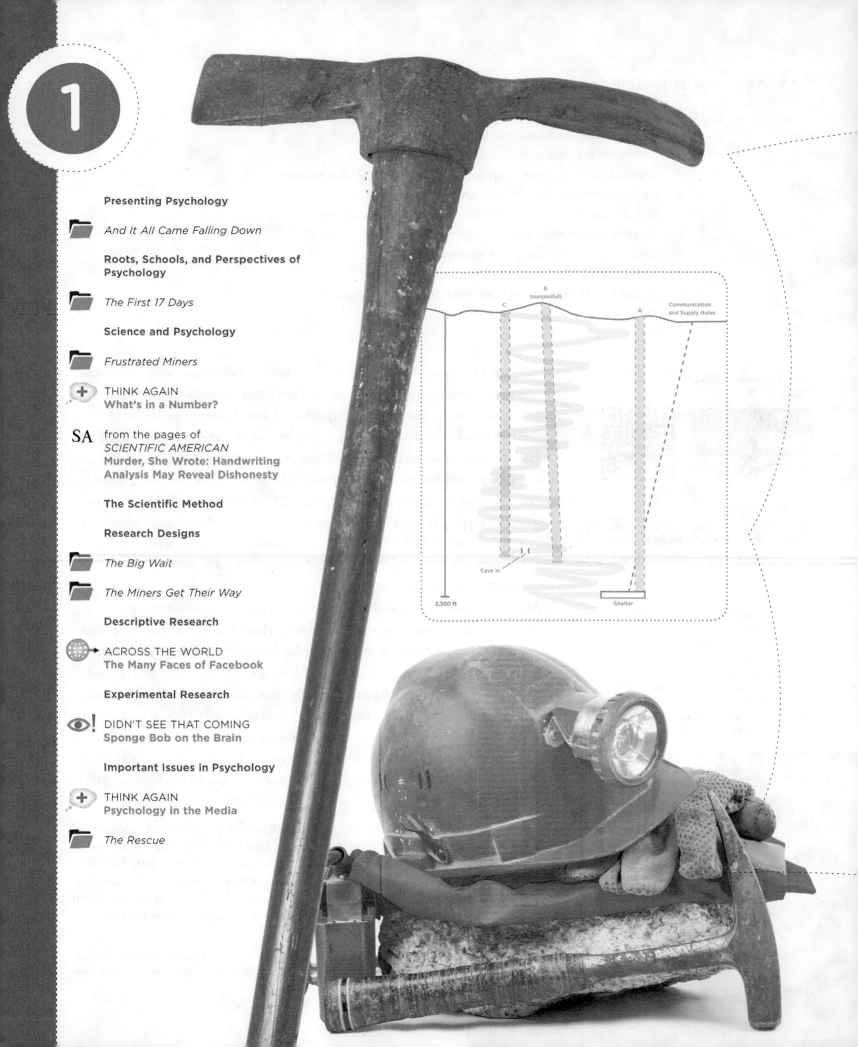

1

Presenting Psychology

📁 *And It All Came Falling Down*

Roots, Schools, and Perspectives of Psychology

📁 *The First 17 Days*

Science and Psychology

📁 *Frustrated Miners*

➕ THINK AGAIN
What's in a Number?

SA from the pages of
SCIENTIFIC AMERICAN
Murder, She Wrote: Handwriting Analysis May Reveal Dishonesty

The Scientific Method

Research Designs

📁 *The Big Wait*

📁 *The Miners Get Their Way*

Descriptive Research

🌐➔ ACROSS THE WORLD
The Many Faces of Facebook

Experimental Research

👁! DIDN'T SEE THAT COMING
Sponge Bob on the Brain

Important Issues in Psychology

➕ THINK AGAIN
Psychology in the Media

📁 *The Rescue*

B
(successful)

C

A

Communication
and Supply Holes

Cave in

2,300 ft

Shelter

1

LEARNING OBJECTIVES
after reading and studying this chapter, you should be able to:

LO 1 Define psychology.

LO 2 Describe the scope of psychology and its subfields.

LO 3 Summarize the goals of the discipline of psychology.

LO 4 Identify influential people in the formation of psychology as a discipline.

LO 5 List and summarize the major perspectives in psychology.

LO 6 Evaluate pseudopsychology and its relationship to critical thinking.

LO 7 Describe how psychologists use the scientific method.

LO 8 Summarize the importance of a random sample.

LO 9 Recognize the forms of descriptive research.

LO 10 Explain how the experimental method relates to cause and effect.

LO 11 Demonstrate an understanding of research ethics.

Beyond the Book: Watch the Video

http://qrs.ly/kc3jiz1

SCIENTIFIC AMERICAN PSYCHOLOGY

► Hello from Below

A government video shows a handful of the trapped miners standing in *el refugio,* a safety shelter half a mile beneath the earth's surface. At the time this footage was captured, the men had been trapped for 23 days. They appear worn and weary, but if you look closely, you might notice a glimmer of hope in their eyes, for they know that rescue teams are working 24-7 to bring them home. AP Photo/Chile's Government Video

At about 11:30 A.M., the mountain issued its warning call. A loud splintering sound reverberated through the mine's dim caverns. Then about 2 hours later, the mountain hit its breaking point. A section of tunnel collapsed some 1,300 feet underground (a depth of four football fields), sending a thick whoosh of stones and dirt howling through the shaft (Associated Press, 2010, August 25; Franklin, 2011). The blast of air was so strong it knocked loose Victor Zamora's false teeth. "It was like getting boxed in the ears," Segovia remembers (Franklin, 2011, p. 21). As miners scrambled up the dark passageways slipping on loose rocks and gravel, the mountain shook again, delivering a fresh downpour of debris. The final rumble ended with an enormous thunk—the sound of a massive boulder plugging their only viable escape. The estimated weight of the rock: 700,000 tons (Franklin, 2011).

Meanwhile above ground, workers stood by as a plume of dust collected at the entrance. They knew something was terribly wrong. Those thunderous noises from inside the mountain did not sound like routine dynamite detonations. Below the cave-in site, 33 men began making their way to "el refugio," a safety shelter half a mile underground at the base of the mine. About the size of a studio apartment, the shelter contained two oxygen tanks, a few medical supplies, and enough food to sustain 10 miners for 2 days. Once all the men arrived, they closed the doors, turned off their lamps to save energy, and began to ponder what had just occurred. As journalists throughout the world would soon report, they had been buried alive (Franklin, 2011).

Take a minute and put yourself in the place of the Chilean miners. Squeezed into a small, dark hole half a mile beneath the earth's surface, a place where it's approximately 90°F with 90% humidity (Cohen, 2011), you are crowded among 32 other sweaty men. The main supply of drinking water is tainted with oil and dirt, and your daily food ration amounts to one spoonful of canned tuna fish and

The story of the Chilean miners is largely based on Jonathan Franklin's 33 Men: *Inside the Miraculous Survival and Dramatic Rescue of the Chilean Miners.* Publisher: G.P. Putnam's Sons.

a few sips of milk (Franklin, 2011). Sleep is dangerous because you never know when a slab of rock might break off the ceiling and crush you. Besides, there is no dry spot to lie on; water trickles through every vein and crevice of this miserable dungeon. Crouched on the wet rock floor, you wonder what your family is doing. Have they heard about the accident? Surely, they will worry when you don't show up for dinner tonight. Maybe a rescue team is on its way. Maybe there is no rescue team.

In this type of situation, our first concern tends to be physical safety. The average healthy adult can only survive about 3 to 5 weeks without food (Lieberson, 2004); the humid, filthy mine shaft is an ideal breeding ground for dangerous skin infections; and the dust and noxious air particles are a perfect recipe for lung disease (Associated Press, 2010, September 7; Franklin, 2011). Clearly, the miners were in grave physical danger. But is that the only type of danger they faced? Think about what might happen to a man's mind when he is crowded into a sweltering rock pit for a prolonged period. How might it affect his thoughts and emotions? How might it affect his behavior? We could rewrite the miners' story and point out where their story intersects with our knowledge of human behaviors, thoughts, emotions, and a variety of other topics to be covered in this textbook. For example, you can read about sleep–wake cycles (Chapter 4), stress and health (Chapter 12), and how we perceive our environments (Chapter 3). As you progress through the chapters of this book, keep in mind that you are reading the stories of real people who feel and react (with one notable exception in Chapter 11). We can better understand these individuals through the field of psychology.

Table 1.1   MENTAL HEALTH PROFESSIONALS

Degree	Occupation	Training	Focus	Prescribes Medications
Medical Doctor, MD	Psychiatrist	Medical school and residency training in psychiatry	Treatment of psychological disorders; may include research focus	Yes
Doctor of Philosophy, PhD	Clinical or Counseling Psychologist	Graduate school; includes dissertation and internship	Research-oriented and clinical practice	Varies by state
Doctor of Psychology, PsyD	Clinical or Counseling Psychologist	Graduate school; includes internship; may include dissertation	Focus on professional practice	Varies by state
Master's Degree, MA or MS	Mental Health Counselor	Graduate school; includes internship	Focus on professional practice	No

Mental health professionals come from a variety of backgrounds. Here, we present a handful of these, including general information on training, focus, and whether the training includes licensing to prescribe medication for psychological disorders.

What Is Psychology?

···▶ **LO 1**   Define psychology.

Psychology is the scientific study of behavior and mental processes. Running, praying, and gasping were observable activities of the miners when the mountain collapsed above them, all potentially a focus of study in psychology. And although their thoughts and emotions were not observable, they are valid topics of study in psychology as well.

Psychologists are scientists who work in a variety of fields, all of which include the study of behavior and underlying mental processes. People often associate psychology with therapy, and many psychologists do provide therapy. These *counseling psychologists* and *clinical psychologists* might also conduct research on the causes and treatments of psychological disorders (**TABLE 1.1**; Chapters 13 and 14). Clinical practice is just one slice of the gigantic psychology pie. There are psychologists who spend their days observing rats in laboratories or assessing the capabilities of children in schools. Psychologists may also be found poring over brain scans in major medical centers, spying on monkeys in the Brazilian rainforest, and meeting with corporate executives in skyscrapers (**FIGURE 1.1**; see Appendix B for more on careers in psychology).

FIGURE 1.1

Fields of Psychology

The pie charts on the right show the primary place of work for full-time doctorate-level psychologists working in 2009 and their areas of specialty. As you can see, psychologists work in diverse contexts and specialize in many subfields. The young clinical psychologist pictured above is counseling one of the survivors of China's Great Sichuan earthquake, a 7.9 trembler that killed 70,000 people in 2008 (*The New York Times*, 2009, May 6). Adapted from: Michalski et al. (2011); Photo: AP Photo/Greg Baker

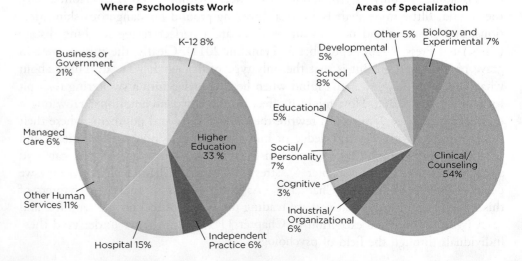

Where Psychologists Work

- K–12 8%
- Business or Government 21%
- Managed Care 6%
- Other Human Services 11%
- Hospital 15%
- Higher Education 33%
- Independent Practice 6%

Areas of Specialization

- Other 5%
- Biology and Experimental 7%
- Developmental 5%
- School 8%
- Educational 5%
- Social/Personality 7%
- Cognitive 3%
- Industrial/Organizational 6%
- Clinical/Counseling 54%

⇢ LO 2   Describe the scope of psychology and its subfields.

SUBFIELDS OF PSYCHOLOGY   Psychology is a broad field that includes many perspectives and subfields. The American Psychological Association (APA), one of the major professional organizations in the field, has over 50 divisions representing various subdisciplines and areas of interest (APA, 2012a). The Association for Psychological Science (APS), another major professional organization in the field, offers a list on its Web site of over 100 different societies, organizations, and agencies that are considered to have some affiliation with the field of psychology (APS, 2012). In fact, each of the chapters in this textbook covers a broad subtopic that represents a subfield of psychology.

BASIC AND APPLIED RESEARCH   Psychologists conduct two major types of research. Basic research, which often occurs in university laboratories, focuses on collecting data to support (or refute) theories. The goal of basic research is not to find solutions to specific problems, but rather to gather knowledge for the sake of knowledge. Explorations of human sensory abilities, trauma, and memory are examples of basic research. Applied research, on the other hand, focuses on changing behaviors and outcomes, and often leads to real-world applications. This type of research has helped generate behavioral interventions for children with sensory issues and autism, natural disaster response planning, as well as keyboard layout and improved typing performance. Applied research may use findings from basic research for ideas and inspiration, but it is often conducted in natural settings outside the laboratory and its goals are more pragmatic or practical.

MISCONCEPTIONS ABOUT PSYCHOLOGY   Looking at Figure 1.1, you may have been surprised to learn about the variety of subjects that psychologists study. If so, you are not alone. Researchers report that students often have misconceptions about the field of psychology and psychological concepts (Landau & Bavaria, 2003). Truth be told, we can't blame students. Most of what the average person knows about psychology comes from the popular media, which fails to present an accurate portrayal of the field, its practitioners, and its findings. Frequently, guests who are introduced as "psychologists" or "therapists" by television talk show hosts really aren't psychologists as defined by the leading psychological organizations (Stanovich, 2010).

One common misconception is that psychology is simply common sense, meaning it is just a collection of knowledge that any reasonably smart person can pick up through everyday experiences. This sense of the obviousness of psychological findings might be related to the *hindsight bias*, or the feeling that "I knew it all along." When a student learns of a finding from psychology, she may believe she knew it all along because the finding seems obvious to her in retrospect, even though she wouldn't necessarily have predicted the outcome beforehand. We fall prey to the hindsight bias in part because we are constantly seeking to explain events; we come up with plausible explanations after we learn of a finding from psychological research (Lilienfeld, 2012).

Or sometimes, students insist they know all there is to know about child development, for example, because they are parents. Just because a young man has experience as a father does not necessarily mean he can observe his family like a scientist. As you learn more about the human mind and how it works, you will start to see that it is quite fallible and prone to errors (Chapter 6), which calls into question the accuracy of our observations and common sense. The problem is that common sense and "popular wisdom" are not always correct (Lilienfeld, 2012). Common sense is an important ability that helps us survive and adapt, but it should not take the place of scientific findings. **TABLE 1.2** identifies some commonsense myths that have been dispelled through research.

▲ **FIGURE 1.2**
What Is This?
Throughout this book, you'll find parenthetical notes like this one for the research published by Stanovich in 2010. This citation tells you the source of research being discussed. If you want to know more about a topic, you can look up the source and read the original article. Information provided in this brief citation allows you to locate the full reference in the alphabetized reference list at the back of the book (page R-1). There are many systems for citing sources, but this textbook uses the format established by one of psychology's main professional organizations, the American Psychological Association (APA).

psychology The scientific study of behavior and mental processes.
psychologists Scientists who study behavior and mental processes.

Table 1.2   DISPELLED: SEVEN "COMMONSENSE" MYTHS

Myth	Reality
"Blowing off steam" or expressing anger is good for you.	Unleashing anger actually may make you more aggressive (Lilienfeld, Lynn, Ruscio, & Beyerstein, 2010).
Most older people live sad and solitary lives.	People actually become happier with age (Lilienfeld et al., 2010).
Once you're married and have kids, your sex life goes down the tubes.	According to the Global Sex Survey (2005), people ages 35–44 are having more sex than any other age group.
Once you are born, your brain no longer generates new neurons.	Neurons in certain areas of the brain are replenished during adulthood (Eriksson et al., 1998).
Listening to Mozart and other classical music will make an infant smarter.	There is no solid evidence that infants who listen to Mozart are smarter than those who do not (Hirsh-Pasek, Golinkoff, & Eyer, 2003).
When people reach 40 years of age, they are bound to have a "midlife crisis."	Evidence suggests that only a quarter of middle-aged people hit a breaking point and suffer from such a crisis (Almeida, 2009).
People with schizophrenia and other mental disorders are dangerous.	Only 3–5% of violent crimes are committed by people with serious mental disorders (Arkowitz & Lilienfeld, 2011).

Psychological research has debunked many pieces of commonsense wisdom, including the notion that "opposites attract." Similarity turns out to a better predictor of romantic attraction, with studies suggesting that people are more drawn to those with cultural backgrounds, values, and interests resembling their own (Lott & Lott, 1965).

Photo: Jessie Cowan/Getty Images

PSYCHOLOGY IS A SCIENCE   Unlike common sense, which is based on casual observations, psychology is a rigorous science based on meticulous and methodical observation, as well as data analysis. You may be surprised to learn that psychology is a *science,* in the same sense that chemistry and biology are sciences. And although people often feel as if they can explain others' behaviors, we probably would all agree that we are bewildered by some of the things people do. In some of these types of situations, the methods used by psychologists can help explain what prompts behaviors.

You don't have to pour chemicals into test tubes or crunch numbers on a computer to be considered a scientist. Science is not defined by the subject studied or the equipment used. It is a systematic approach to gathering knowledge through careful observation and experimentation. It requires sharing results and doing so in a manner that permits others to duplicate and therefore verify work. Using this scientific approach, psychologists have determined that many popular commonsense beliefs, such as *people only use 10% of their brains,* are not true. It appears there is a great deal of "psychomythology," which is "the collective body of misinformation about human nature" (Lilienfeld et al., 2010, p. 43). Reading this textbook, you might discover that some of your most cherished nuggets of commonsense wisdom do not stand up to scientific scrutiny. (Did you recognize any of them among the myths listed in Table 1.2?)

The Goals of Psychology

⋯➤ **LO 3**   Summarize the goals of the discipline of psychology.

Now that we've defined psychology, it's time to explore the goals of this discipline. What exactly does psychology aim to accomplish? The answer to this question varies according to subfield, but there are four main goals: to describe, explain, predict, and control behavior. These goals lay the foundation for the scientific approach used in psychology and the experiments designed to carry out research. Let's take a closer look at each goal.

DESCRIBE   Goal 1 is simply to describe or report what is observed. We also can use findings from observations to help plan future research. Imagine a psychologist who wants to *describe* the aftereffects of being trapped in a mine for a prolonged period. What kind of study would she conduct? To begin with, she would need access to a group of people who have survived this type of ordeal, such as the 33 Chilean miners. Following the men's rescue, she might request permission to perform some assessments to evaluate their moods, social adjustment, and physical health. She might even monitor the miners over time, conducting more assessments at a later date. Eventually, she would *describe* her observations in a scientific article published in a respected journal.

EXPLAIN   Goal 2 is to organize and understand observations of behaviors. Researchers gathering data must try to make sense of what they have observed. If the psychologist noticed an interesting pattern in her assessments of the miners, she might develop an explanation for this finding. Let's say the miners' health after confinement seemed to be poor compared to their prior status; then the psychologist might look for factors that could influence immunological health. Searching the scientific literature for clues, she might come across studies of people with experiences in similar situations, for example, sailors living and working for long periods in submarines. If she determined that health-related changes were associated with the confinement experienced in a submarine, this could help *explain* the changes in the miners' medical status, although she still would have to conduct a controlled experiment to identify a causal relationship between confinement in a mine and health-related issues.

PREDICT   Goal 3 is to predict behaviors or outcomes. When we observe behavior patterns, we can make predictions about what will happen in the future. If the researcher determined that the miners' reduced immunological status resulted from sleep deprivation caused by confinement, then she could predict that prolonged confinement in another setting (such as a submarine) might lead to the same outcome: sleep deprivation, and therefore decreased immunity.

CONTROL   Goal 4 is to use research findings to shape, modify, and control behavior. When we say "control behavior," your mind might conjure up the image of an evil inventor who takes control of someone's mind and makes him carry out a malicious plot. This is *not* the kind of control we are talking about. Instead, we are referring to how we can *apply* the findings of psychological research to shape and change behaviors in a beneficial way. Perhaps the researcher could use her findings to help a mining company hire workers who might be better suited to the confining characteristics of mining. Working in small spaces like mines and submarines is not for everyone.

Down We Go
The cramped environment of a submarine provides an ideal setting for studying the psychological effects of confinement. Naval officers, like those working on the USS *Annapolis* (SSN 760) pictured here, may spend weeks at a time crowded into cramped quarters—a living arrangement that can affect mood, memory, and disease immunity (Thomas et al., 2003). © Gary Coronado/The Palm Beach Post/ZUMAPRESS.com

You have now learned the definition, scope, and goals of psychology. You will soon explore the ins and outs of psychological research: how psychologists use a scientific approach, the many types of studies they conduct, and the ethical standards or guidelines for acceptable conduct that guide them through the process. But we will start with some history, meeting the people whose philosophies, insights, and research findings molded psychology into the vibrant science it is today.

✓ show what you know

1. Psychology is the scientific study of _____ and _____.

2. A researcher is asked to devise a plan to help improve behavior in the confined space of subway trains. Based on his research findings, he creates some placards that he believes will modify the behavior of subway riders. This attempt to change behaviors falls under which of the main goals of psychology?
   a. describe
   b. explain
   c. predict
   d. control

3. How is common sense different from the findings of psychology? If one of your friends says, "I could have told you that!" when you describe the findings of various studies on confinement, how would you respond?

✓ CHECK YOUR ANSWERS IN APPENDIX C.

Roots, Schools, and Perspectives of Psychology

The field of psychology is a little over 130 years old, very young compared to other scientific disciplines, but its core questions are as old as humanity itself. Look at the works of the ancient Greeks, and you will see that they asked some of the same questions as modern psychologists—questions such as, *What is the connection between the body and mind? How do we obtain knowledge? Where does knowledge reside?* Making your way through this book, you will see answers to these questions take many forms.

Philosophy and Physiology

> **LO 4** Identify influential people in the formation of psychology as a discipline.

The roots of psychology lie in disciplines as diverse as philosophy and physiology. In ancient Greece, the great philosopher Plato (427–347 BCE) believed that truth and knowledge exist in the soul before birth, that is, humans are born with some degree of innate knowledge. Plato raised an important issue psychologists still contemplate: the contribution of *nature* in the human capacity for cognition.

One of Plato's most renowned students, Aristotle (384–322 BCE), eventually went on to challenge his mentor's basic teachings. Aristotle believed that we know

Nature or Nurture
Would you believe that these trees belong to the same species? Both are Jeffrey pines (*Pinus jeffreyi*), but they have been exposed to dramatically different environmental pressures. Jeffrey pines typically reach 80 to 130 feet. The tree on the left appears to be growing in fertile soil in a thriving forest, whereas the one on the right has virtually sprung from a slab of rock on an 8,122-foot peak in Yosemite National Park (St. John, 2003, August 19). A testament to the power of nurture. left: Kent and Donna Dannen/Science Source; right: Bob Gibbons/Science Source

reality through our perceptions, and we learn through our sensory experiences, an approach now commonly referred to as *empiricism*. Aristotle has been credited with laying the foundation for a scientific approach to answering questions, including those pertaining to psychological concepts such as emotion, sensation, and perception (Slife, 1990; Thorne & Henley, 2005). Ultimately, because he believed knowledge is the result of our experiences, Aristotle paved the way for scientists to study the world through their observations.

This notion that experience (or *nurture*) plays an all-important role in how we acquire knowledge contradicts Plato's belief that it is inborn (the result of *nature*). Aristotle thus provided the opposing position in the discussion of the relative contributions of *nature and nurture,* a central theme in the field of psychology. Today, psychologists agree that nature and nurture both play important roles, and current research explores the contribution of each through studies of heredity and environmental factors.

If Aristotle placed great confidence in human perception, French philosopher René Descartes (dā-'kärt; 1596–1650) practically discounted it. Famous for saying, "I think, therefore, I am," Descartes believed that most everything else was uncertain, including what he saw with his own eyes. He proposed that the body is like a tangible machine, and the mind has no physical substance. The body and mind interact as two separate entities, a view known as *dualism,* and Descartes (and many others) wondered how they were connected. Descartes' work allowed for a more scientific approach to examining thoughts, emotions, and other topics previously believed to be beyond the scope of study.

About 200 years later, another scientist experienced a "flash of insight" about the mind–body connection. It was October 22, 1850, when German physicist Gustav Theodor Fechner (1801–1887) suddenly realized that he could "solve" the mind–body conundrum, that is, figure out how they connect. Fechner reasoned that by studying the physical ability to sense stimuli, we are simultaneously conducting experiments on the mind. In other words, we can understand how the mind and body work together by studying sensation. Fechner is considered one of the founders of physiological psychology, and his efforts laid the groundwork for research on sensation and perception (Benjamin, 2007; Robinson, 2010).

Psychology Is Born

Thus far, the only people in our presentation of the history of psychology have been philosophers and a physicist. You might ask where all the psychologists were during the time of Descartes and Fechner. The answer is simple: There were no psychologists until 1879. That was the year Wilhelm Wundt (1832–1920) founded the first psychology laboratory, at the University of Leipzig in Germany, and for this he generally is considered the "father of psychology." Equipped with its own laboratory and research team, psychology finally became a discipline in its own right. Wundt also created and edited the first psychological journal and published numerous books, including meticulous accounts of his psychological experiments and methods, which provided details of the scientific nature of this new area of study.

The overall aim of Wundt's early experiments was to measure psychological processes through **introspection,** a method used to examine one's own conscious activities. For Wundt, introspection involved effortful reflection on the sensations, feelings, and images experienced in response to a stimulus, followed by reports that were *objective,* meaning free of opinions, beliefs, expectations, and values. In order to ensure

Descartes and Dualism
French philosopher René Descartes proposed that the eye and other body parts worked like machines. The mind, he suggested, was separate and intangible. But as you will discover in this textbook, many activities of the mind have already been traced back to physical interactions among nerve cells. National Library of Medicine.

Wundt Measures the Mind
In 1861 Wilhelm Wundt conducted an experiment on reaction time, which was a turning point in the field of psychology. Using a pendulum that hit a bell upon reaching its outer limits, Wundt demonstrated a 10th of a second delay between hearing the bell and noting the position of the pendulum (and vice versa), and it was during that very brief period that a mental process occurred. Finally, activities of the mind could be measured (Thorne & Henley, 2005). Archives of the History of American Psychology, The Center for the History of Psychology, The University of Akron.

introspection The examination of one's own conscious activities.

reliable data, Wundt required all his participants to complete 10,000 "introspective observations" prior to starting data collection. His participants were asked to make quantitative judgments about physical stimuli—how strong they were, how long they lasted, and so on (Boring, 1953; Schultz & Schultz, 2012). The following Try This should give you a better sense of Wundt's method of introspection.

try this

The next time your cell phone vibrates or rings, take the opportunity to engage in some introspection. Grab the cell phone and hold it in your hands (try to resist answering the call). Pay attention to what you experience as you wait for the vibrations to stop. Then put down the phone and consider your experience. Report on your sensations (the color, the shape, the texture, and so on) and feelings (anxiety, excitement, frustration), but make your observations *objective*.

STRUCTURALISM   A student of Wundt's, Edward Titchener (1867–1927) developed the school of psychology known as **structuralism.** In 1893 Titchener set up a laboratory at Cornell University (in Ithaca, New York) where he conducted introspection experiments aimed at determining the structure and "atoms" (or most basic elements) of the mind. Titchener's participants, also extremely well trained, were asked to describe the elements of their current consciousness. In contrast to Wundt's focus on objective, quantitative reports of conscious experiences, Titchener's participants provided detailed reports of their subjective (unique or personal) experiences (Hothersall, 2004). The school of structuralism did not last past Titchener's lifetime, and even most of his contemporaries regarded structuralism as outdated. Nevertheless, Titchener demonstrated that psychological studies could be conducted through observation and measurement.

FUNCTIONALISM   In the late 1870s, William James (1842–1910) offered the first psychology classes in the United States, at Harvard University, where he was granted $300 for laboratory and classroom demonstration equipment (Croce, 2010). James had little interest in pursuing the experimental psychology practiced by Wundt and other Europeans; instead, he was inspired by the work of Charles Darwin (1809–1882). Studying the elements of introspection was not a worthwhile endeavor, James believed, because consciousness is an ever-changing "stream" of thoughts. Consciousness cannot be studied by looking for fixed or static elements, because they don't exist, or so he reasoned. But James believed consciousness does serve a function, and it is important to study the purpose of thought processes, feelings, and behaviors, and how they help us adapt to the environment. This focus on purpose and adaptation in psychological research is the overarching theme of the school of **functionalism.** Although it didn't endure as a separate field of psychology, functionalism has continued to influence the practice of psychology, as evidenced by educational psychology, studies of emotion, and comparative studies of animal behavior (Benjamin, 2007).

HERE COME THE WOMEN   Like most sciences, psychology began as a "boys' club," with men earning the degrees, teaching the classes, and running the labs. There were, however, a few women, as competent and inquiring as their male counterparts, who beat down the club doors long before women were formally invited. One of William James's students, Mary Whiton Calkins (1863–1930), completed all the requirements for a PhD at Harvard, but was not allowed to graduate from the then all-male college because she was a woman. Nonetheless, she persevered with her work and established her own laboratory at Wellesley College, eventually becoming the first female president of the American Psychological Association (APA). If you are wondering, the first woman to actually earn a PhD in psychology was Margaret Floy Washburn (1871–1939), a

Breaking Ground ◄
Margaret Floy Washburn is perhaps most famous for becoming the first woman psychologist to earn a PhD, but her scholarly contributions cannot be underestimated. Her book *The Animal Mind: A Textbook of Comparative Psychology* (1908), which drew on her extensive research with animals, had an enduring impact on the field (American Psychological Association, 2013b; Washburn, 2010).

structuralism An early school of psychology that used introspection to determine the structure and most basic elements of the mind.

functionalism An early school of psychology that focused on the function of thought processes, feelings, and behaviors and how they help us adapt to the environment.

behaviorism The scientific study of observable behavior.

student of Titchener's. Her degree, which was granted in 1894, came from Cornell, which—unlike Harvard—allowed women to earn doctorates at the time.

Mamie Phipps Clark (1917–1983) was the first Black woman to be awarded a PhD in psychology from Columbia University. Her work, which she conducted with her husband Kenneth Bancroft Clark, examined the impact of prejudice and discrimination on child development. In particular, she explored how race recognition impacts a child's self-esteem (Lal, 2002). Her husband held a faculty position at City University of New York, but she was never allowed to teach there. Instead, she found a job analyzing research data and eventually became executive director of the Northside Center for Child Development in upper Manhattan (Benjamin, 2007).

Thanks to trailblazers such as Calkins, Washburn, and Clark, the field of psychology is no longer dominated by men. In fact, about three quarters of students earning master's degrees and PhDs in psychology are women, a statistic that now has some experts worrying about the need for more men in various subfields of psychology (Cynkar, 2007).

For the Children
The work of Mamie Phipps Clark raised awareness about the unique psychological issues affecting African American and other minority children. She and her husband founded Harlem's Northside Center for Child Development, an organization that continues to provide psychological and educational support to children in the community.

Psychology's Perspectives

> **LO 5** List and summarize the major perspectives in psychology.

Some of the early schools of psychology had a lasting impact and others seemed to fade. Nevertheless, they all contributed to the growth of the young science. To appreciate the vast field of psychology, it is useful to examine the influences of the early schools, and how some developed into perspectives. Each perspective described below provides a unique vantage point for explaining the complex nature of human behavior. **INFOGRAPHIC 1.1** shows how the early roots of psychology and the perspectives fused and flow together (see p. 13).

PSYCHOANALYTIC Toward the end of the 19th century, while many early psychologists were busy investigating the "normal" functioning of the mind (in experimental psychology), Sigmund Freud (1856–1939) focused much of his attention on the "abnormal" aspects. Freud believed that behavior and personality are influenced by the conflict between one's inner desires (such as sexual and aggressive impulses) and the expectations of society—a clash that occurs for the most part unconsciously or outside of awareness (Gay, 1988; Chapter 11). The *psychoanalytic* perspective is used as an explanatory tool in many of psychology's subfields.

BEHAVIORAL As Freud worked on his new theories of the unconscious mind, Ivan Pavlov (1849–1936), a Russian scientist, was busy studying canine digestion. A physiologist by training, Pavlov got sidetracked by an intriguing phenomenon. The dogs in his study had learned to salivate in response to stimuli or events in the environment, a type of learning that eventually became known as *classical conditioning* (Chapter 5). Building on Pavlov's conditioning experiments, American psychologist John B. Watson (1878–1958) established **behaviorism,** which viewed psychology as the scientific study of behaviors that could be seen and/or measured. Consciousness, sensations, feelings, and the unconscious were not suitable topics of study, according to Watson.

Carrying on the behaviorist approach to psychology, B. F. Skinner (1904–1990) studied the relationship between behaviors and their consequences. Skinner's research focused on *operant conditioning,* a type of learning that occurs when behaviors are rewarded or punished (Chapter 5). Skinner acknowledged that mental processes such as memory and emotion might exist, but they are not topics to be studied in psychology.

Freud Takes Off
Psychology's most famous icon boards his first airplane in 1928, years after psychoanalysis had gotten off the ground in Europe and America. Freudian ideas are still alive and well, though people often overestimate their importance in psychology. About 90% of American Psychological Association members do not practice psychoanalysis, and most science-minded psychologists have distanced themselves from Freudian notions because they are not supported by solid experimental data (Stanovich, 2010; Hobson, 2006). AP Photo

To ensure that psychology was a science, he insisted on studying behaviors that could be observed and documented.

HUMANISTIC   Psychologists such as Carl Rogers (1902–1987) and Abraham Maslow (1908–1970) took psychology in yet another direction. The founders of **humanistic psychology** were critical of the deterministic tilt of psychoanalysis and behaviorism, and the presumed lack of control people have over their lives. The humanistic perspective suggests that human nature is essentially positive, and that people are naturally inclined to grow and change for the better (Chapter 11) (Maslow, 1943; Rogers, 1961). Humanism challenged the thinking and practice of researchers and clinicians who had been "raised" on Watson and Skinner. Reflecting on the history of psychology, we cannot help but notice that new developments are often reactions to what came before. The rise of the humanistic perspective was, in some ways, a rebellion against the rigidity of psychoanalysis and behaviorism.

COGNITIVE   During the two-decade prime of *behaviorism* (1930–1950), many psychologists only studied observable behavior. Yet prior to behaviorism, psychologists had emphasized the study of thoughts and emotions. The situation eventually came full-circle in the 1950s, when a new force in psychology brought these unobservable elements back into focus. This renewed interest in the study of mental processes falls under the field of *cognitive psychology* (Wertheimer, 2012). And George Miller's (1920–2012) research on memory is considered an important catalyst for this cognitive revolution (Chapter 6). The cognitive perspective examines mental processes that direct behavior, focusing on concepts such as thinking, memory, and language. The *cognitive neuroscience* perspective, in particular, explores physiological explanations for mental processes, searching for connections between behavior and the human nervous system, especially the brain. With the development of brain-scanning technologies, cognitive neuroscience has flourished, interfacing with fields such as medicine, computer science, and psychology.

May the Biggest Beak Win
In a population of finches, some have little beaks that can only crack open small, soft seeds; others have big beaks that can open big seeds; and still others fall somewhere in between. During times of food scarcity (such as a drought), the big-beaked birds are more likely to survive and reproduce because they have a greater variety of seeds to choose from. Looking at the finch population during this period, you will see more birds being born with bigger beaks. It's natural selection right before your eyes (Grant, 1991).
© A. & J. Binns/ VIREO

EVOLUTIONARY   According to the evolutionary perspective, behaviors and mental processes are shaped by the forces of evolution This perspective is based on Charles Darwin's theory of evolution and the principles of **natural selection.** As Darwin saw it, great variability exists in the characteristics that humans and other organisms exhibit. Natural selection is the process through which inherited traits in a given population either increase in frequency because they are adaptive or decrease in frequency because they are maladaptive. Humans have many adaptive traits and behaviors that appear to have evolved through natural selection.

BIOLOGICAL   The biological perspective uses knowledge about underlying physiology to explain behavior and mental processes. Psychologists who take this approach explore how biological factors, such as hormones, genes, and the brain, are involved in behavior and cognition. Chapter 2 provides a foundation for understanding this perspective.

humanistic psychology An approach suggesting that human nature is by and large positive, and the human direction is toward growth.

natural selection The process through which inherited traits in a given population either increase in frequency because they are adaptive or decrease in frequency because they are maladaptive.

SOCIOCULTURAL   The sociocultural perspective suggests that we must examine the influences of social interactions and culture, including the roles we play. Lev Vygotsky (1896–1934) proposed that we must examine how social and cultural features in children's lives influence their cognitive development (Chapter 8). Researchers such as Mamie Phipps Clark study the impact of prejudice, segregation, and discrimination, with the realization that we must consider the importance of sociocultural factors as they relate to the development of the self (Lal, 2002).

Psychology's Roots

The first laboratory dedicated to the new science of psychology was founded by Wilhelm Wundt at the University of Leipzig in Germany in 1879. But psychology's roots go back further than that. Philosophers and scientists have long been interested in understanding how the mind works. Early schools of thought like Structuralism and Functionalism developed into contemporary perspectives, each defined by different sets of interests, prompting different kinds of questions.

BIOPSYCHOSOCIAL PERSPECTIVE
Examine the biological, psychological, and sociocultural factors influencing behavior.

HUMANISTIC PERSPECTIVE
Maintain an optimistic focus on human behavior; believe that each person is a master of his own fate.

Carl Rogers 1902–1987
Abraham Maslow 1908–1970

Will tending to and nurturing this tree help me reach my fullest potential?

SOCIOCULTURAL PERSPECTIVE

Mamie Phipps Clark 1917–1983
Lev Vygotsky 1896–1934

Understand behavior by examining influences of other people and the larger culture.

What biological, psychological, and social factors influence the way I manage my allergy to tree pollen?

PSYCHOANALYTIC PERSPECTIVE
Sigmund Freud 1856–1939
Interested in abnormal functioning and unconscious thought; personality is shaped by unconscious conflict.

How do cultures differ in their attitudes toward nature?

Charles Darwin 1809–1882

EVOLUTIONARY PERSPECTIVE
Use knowledge about evolutionary forces to understand behavior.

How do your feelings about the size of this tree relate to your unconscious aggression toward your father?

BEHAVIORAL PERSPECTIVE

B. F. Skinner 1904–1990
Ivan Pavlov 1849–1936
John Watson 1878–1958

Interested in studying only behavior that can be observed and measured.

COGNITIVE PERSPECTIVE
George Miller 1920–2012
Renewed focus on mental processes, including physiological explanations.

How am I able to remember where this tree is in the forest?

Is my fear of heights inherited? Could it have contributed to my survival?

Is spending time relaxing under this tree reinforced? If yes, I will come back again.

STRUCTURALISM
Edward Titchener 1867–1927
Margaret Floy Washburn 1871–1939
Wilhelm Wundt 1832–1920

Used reports of subjective experience (introspection) to describe the structure of the mind.

BIOLOGICAL PERSPECTIVE
Use knowledge about underlying physiology to explain behavior and mental processes.

How do my eyes and brain work together to sense and perceive this tree?

FUNCTIONALISM
Mary Whiton Calkins 1863–1930
William James 1842–1910

Interested in how the mind functions to help us adapt and survive.

How does resting under this tree promote my long-term survival?

Describe in detail each element of this tree, including color, shape, size, etc.

Wilhelm Wundt, "Father of Psychology," founded the first laboratory dedicated to psychology.

PHILOSOPHICAL AND SCIENTIFIC ROOTS

Plato 427–347 BCE
Aristotle 384–322 BCE
Descartes 1596–1650
Gustav Fechner 1801–1887

Ancient and modern philosophers and scientists explored the connection between mind and body.

Does this tree exist in the physical world or only in my mind?

Credits: Aristotle, The National Library of Medicine; Descartes, The National Library of Medicine; Edward Titchener, The National Library of Medicine; Wilhelm Wundt with his colleagues (Friedrich Sander), Wilhelm Wundt with his colleagues (Friedrich Sander; Otto Klemm; Ottmar Dittrich; Wilhelm Wirth; and Hartmann), circa 1910, © INTERFOTO/Alamy; INTERFOTO/Alamy; Sigmund Freud, Pictorial Press Ltd/Alamy; William James, Time Life Pictures/Mansell/Time Life Pictures/Getty Images; John Watson, © Underwood & Underwood/Corbis; Carl Rogers, Courtesy Everett Collection; Gustav Fechner, Science Source/Photo Researchers, Inc.; George A. Miller, Princeton University, Office of Communications; John I. Miller; Charles Darwin, The National Library of Medicine; Lev Vygotsky, Lev Vygotsky, RIA Novosti/Alamy; Plato, © Vladimir Korostyshevskiy/Dreamstime.com

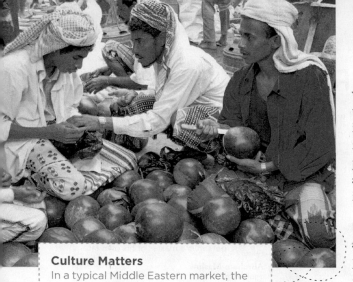

Culture Matters
In a typical Middle Eastern market, the customer is expected to bargain with the seller. How does this compare to shopping in the U.S., where prices are pre-established? When it comes to studying human thoughts and behavior, understanding cultural context is key.
Craig Pershouse /Getty Images.

In the past, researchers often assumed that the findings of their studies were applicable to people of all ethnic and cultural backgrounds. Then in the 1980s, cross-cultural research began to uncover differences that called into question the presumed universal nature of these findings. New studies revealed that Western research participants are not always representative of people from other cultures. We also must remain aware that groups within a culture can influence behavior and mental processes; thus, we need to take into account these various settings and subcultures.

BIOPSYCHOSOCIAL   Many psychologists use the **biopsychosocial perspective** to explain behavior; in other words, they examine the biological, psychological, and sociocultural factors influencing behavior (Beauchamp & Anderson, 2010). The biopsychosocial perspective suggests that these factors are highly interactive: It's not just the convergence of factors that matters, but the way they interact.

SUMMARY OF PERSPECTIVES   You can see that the field of psychology abounds with diversity. With so many perspectives (**TABLE 1.3**), how do we know which one is the most accurate and effective in achieving psychology's goals? Human behavior is complex and requires an integrated approach to explain its origins. Sometimes it is also necessary to create a *model* to help clarify a complex set of observations, as a model frequently allows us to picture in our minds what we seek to understand. Many psychologists pick and choose among theories and models, as needed, to explain and understand behavior. Remember this integrated approach as you learn more about the miners. What biological, psychological, social, and cultural factors were involved in their survival? How did these factors combine to form their overall experience?

Table 1.3 CURRENT PERSPECTIVES IN PSYCHOLOGY

Perspective	Main Idea	Questions Psychologists Ask
Psychoanalytic	Illustrates the underlying conflicts that influence behavior.	How do our unconscious conflicts affect our decisions and behavior?
Behavioral	Explores human behavior as learned primarily through associations, reinforcers, and observation.	How does learning shape our behavior?
Humanistic	Focuses on the positive and growth aspects of human nature.	How do choice and self-determination influence behavior?
Cognitive	Examines the mental processes that direct behavior.	How do thinking, memory, and language direct behavior?
Evolutionary	Examines characteristics in terms of how they influence adaptation to the environment and survival.	How does natural selection advance our behavioral predispositions?
Biological	Uses knowledge about underlying physiology to explore and explain behavior and mental processes.	How do biological factors, such as hormones, genes, anatomy, and brain structures, influence behavior and mental processes?
Sociocultural	Examines the influences of other people as well as the larger culture to help explain behavior and mental processes.	How do culture and environment shape our attitudes?
Biopsychosocial	Investigates the biological, psychological, and sociocultural factors that influence behavior.	How do the interactions of biology, psychology, and culture influence behavior and mental processes?

Psychologists draw on a variety of theories in their research and practice. Listed above are the dominant theoretical perspectives, all of which reappear many times in this textbook. Human behaviors are often best understood when viewed through more than one theoretical lens.

THE FIRST 17 DAYS What took place inside the mine during the first 17 days after the cave-in is not totally clear. The men made a "pact of silence," promising each other they would never disclose the unpleasant details of that dark period—unless they did so as a group (Gardner & Wade, 2010, October 18). According to miner Juan Illanes, "The first 17 days were a nightmare" (translated from Agence France Presse, 2010, October 15).

Immediately following the mine collapse, the men switched to survival mode. When faced with a life-or-death situation, the brain responds by unloading stress hormones. This stress response, which we will discuss in more detail in Chapter 12, leads to a boost of physical energy, alertness, and an overwhelming sense of urgency to deal with a threat. The miners found it difficult to stay calm and think rationally. Some lost their tempers and started to shout. They argued about what to do next: Should they stay in the safety shelter awaiting a rescue team or search the mine for exit routes? The shift foreman Luis Urzúa attempted to take command, but some of the miners refused to recognize his authority. That first night underground, all bets were off. There was no plan, no cooperation. It was every man for himself (Franklin, 2011).

After a sleepless night on the wet floor, the men arose in darkness (morning, noon, and midnight all look the same when you're half a mile beneath the earth's surface). But the day started off on a bright note when one of the older miners, José Henríquez, led the group in a prayer. With restored optimism, one group of men began to search the mine's winding tunnels for escape passages. Another team tried to alert rescue workers by blasting through rock with dynamite sticks, banging the roof with heavy machinery, and beeping the horns of trucks that had been sealed underground with them. Both missions failed, and the miners spent yet another night splayed on jagged slabs of rock (Franklin, 2011).

Several days passed without a sign from the world above, and the miners grew weak and weary. To stretch their food supply over several days, they had been forced to limit their intake to one spoonful of tuna fish, half a glass of milk, and one cracker every 24 hours—about 100 calories per day. Their only source of hydration was oil-tainted water so foul-tasting that one man opted to try his own urine as an alternative. For a toilet, they used an old oil drum, the smell of which was almost unbearable (Franklin, 2011).

At the 2-week mark, the food supply had been reduced to two cans of tuna fish (Franklin, 2011). "Our bodies were eating away at themselves," miner Richard Villarroel told journalists (translated from *El Mercurio*, 2010, October 15). Although they heard drills humming for several days, a sure sign that a recovery effort was under way, no rescue team had actually reached the part of the mine where they were trapped. Time was not on their side (Franklin, 2011).

By Day 16, each of the miners had lost what appeared to be about 20 pounds (Healy, 2010, August 23). Some had written goodbye letters to their wives and children. "Take care and protect your mother, your sister, you are now the man of the house," Mario Sepúlveda wrote his teenage son (Franklin, 2011, p. 111). Then at 5:50 A.M. the next morning, a miracle came crashing through the roof of their dank dungeon: the tip of a drill bit. The rescue team had finally found them (Franklin, 2011).

Above ground, rescuers waited anxiously as the drill slowly emerged from underground. The tip of the bit emerged with orange paint on the bottom and bags of letters—sure signs that at least one man had survived. But the real celebrations began with the discovery of a note scrawled in red marker: "Estamos bien en el refugio los 33" or "We are okay in the shelter, the 33 of us." It was a miracle: All 33 men were alive (Franklin, 2011, p. 124).

Are You There? What do you see in the eyes of miner Florencio Ávalos? The image was captured on August 23, 2010, after the miners had endured over 2 weeks of starvation and isolation. © Ho New/Reuters

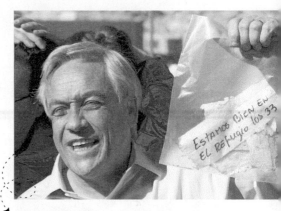

Estamos Bien After 2 weeks of drilling the earth in search of the miners, rescuers finally pierced into a cavern located almost half a mile underground. When the drill bit resurfaced, it carried a bag full of notes, one of which read, "Estamos bien en el refugio los 33" or "We are okay in the shelter, the 33 of us." The rescuers—and eventually people all around the world—went wild in celebration. Now the challenge was drilling a hole wide enough to hoist the men to safety. © DPA/ZUMApress.com

biopsychosocial perspective Explains behavior through the interaction of biological, psychological, and social factors.

Now that the miners had a lifeline, a tiny borehole through which food, medicine, and other essentials could be delivered, attention in the media began to shift to their psychological status. Drilling a rescue tunnel wide enough to hoist them out of the mine could take up to 4 months: Were the miners emotionally prepared to wait that long?

✓ show what you know

1. Wilhelm Wundt's research efforts all involved _____, which is the examination of one's own conscious activities.
   a. functionalism
   b. structuralism
   c. reaction time
   d. introspection

2. Your psychology instructor is adamant that psychologists should only study observable behaviors. She acknowledges consciousness exists, for example, but insists it cannot be observed or documented, so should not be a topic for psychological research. Which of the following perspectives is she using?
   a. psychoanalytic
   b. behavioral
   c. humanistic
   d. cognitive

3. The process through which inherited traits in a given population either increase in frequency because they are adaptive or decrease in frequency because they are maladaptive is called:
   a. natural selection.
   b. functionalism.
   c. structuralism.
   d. psychology.

4. We have presented eight perspectives in this section. Describe how two of them are similar to each other. Pick two other perspectives and explain how they differ.

✓ CHECK YOUR ANSWERS IN APPENDIX C.

Science and Psychology

FRUSTRATED MINERS Extreme circumstances tend to awaken the darker elements of human nature, and the Chilean mining ordeal was no exception. During those first 17 days underground, the men split into three factions, each with its own designated leader and sleeping territory. They squabbled over pieces of cardboard that they used as mattresses, and a few arguments reportedly escalated into fistfights (CBS News/Associated Press, 2010, October 16; Franklin, 2011). But the same life-or-death situations that elicit what is most ugly about humankind can also summon what is most beautiful—our ability to feel compassion, to comfort and support one another, and to sacrifice personal needs for the benefit of the group. In the case of Los 33, the beautiful triumphed over the ugly.

The men were able to move beyond their personal disputes and see the big picture. They realized that banding together was the only sensible way to endure. Like players on a team, they began to assume special roles and responsibilities. The "pastor" José Henríquez led the group in regular prayers; the "electrician" Edison Peña cobbled together a bootleg lighting system; and the "doctor" Yonny Barrios drew from the knowledge of medicine he learned while caring for his sick mother. The miners selected two very different yet complementary leaders: the foreman Luis Urzúa and a second unofficial leader named Mario Sepúlveda. Formerly known as "El Loco" or the "Crazy One," Sepúlveda once pole-danced on the bus the miners daily rode, sending them into fits of laughter. Now they looked to him for strength and inspiration (Franklin, 2011).

To break the monotony of their subterranean existence, the miners coordinated their daily activities, starting their morning with a prayer, holding a midday "town-hall" meeting where they voted democratically on all major decisions, and praying again in the afternoon. When it was time for their daily meal, they gathered like a family, politely waiting to eat until all 33 members had been served (Franklin, 2011).

The men experienced their share of psychological meltdowns during those first 17 days, but they found comfort in the bonds of brotherhood. "We were like a family," said Samuel Ávalos. "When someone falls, you pick them up" (Franklin,

2011 p. 103). And like very close family members, they could almost feel each other's pain. "I was more worried about my companions," said Ávalos, referring to the younger men who had just started to raise families. "They had little babies, pregnant wives. That broke me. . . . To see my compañeros cry and cry" (p. 109).

The roles these men assumed, the ways in which they cooperated, and the emotional support they offered to each other are just the types of social dynamics that social scientists would be interested in studying (Chapter 15). Equally interesting from the standpoint of social psychology was the manner in which people throughout the world responded when they learned that rescuers had made contact with the miners.

THINK again

What's in a Number?

When news broke that Los 33 were alive and well, Chile erupted in celebration (Reuters, 2010, August 22). News of the trapped miners was headlined, broadcast, and tweeted across the globe. It was difficult to believe that all 33 men had survived the rockfall and endured 17 days in a sweltering hole with no food or clean water—and done so with honor and dignity. Some said it was testament to the goodness of the human spirit. Others called it a miracle of God. Still others pointed to the mystical nature of numerology, which attempts to provide explanations for a variety of events and observations. The number 33, which numerologists consider a "master healer" (Culbertson, 2009, October 15), was thought to play an important role in the rescue of the Chilean miners. Here is some of the "evidence" presented to support this claim (AFP, 2010, October 13; freedomflores, 2010, October 18; The Vigilant Citizen, 2010, October 14):

- There were **33** miners.
- They sent up a note saying, "Estamos bien en el refugio los **33**." This statement contains **33** characters and spaces.
- The eventual rescue date was 10/13/10; the sum of these digits equals **33**.
- Drilling the rescue tunnel took **33** days, and the width of the rescue tunnel was said to be 66 centimeters, which is **33** times two.

Are you detecting a pattern? Anyone can draw a connection or find a pattern if they try hard enough, and these patterns do not necessarily represent a unifying theory or provide a scientific explanation. They are just coincidences.

NUMEROLOGY TO THE RESCUE?

While the beliefs surrounding numerology may have provided a meaningful way for some people to interpret the miners' experiences, such beliefs have no scientific validity. In the following section, we'll examine "pseudosciences" like numerology and explain how we use *critical thinking* to evaluate them in comparison to scientific research and thought.

LO 6   Evaluate pseudopsychology and its relationship to critical thinking.

As intriguing as this apparent 33 theme may be, it has no scientific meaning. Numerology is a prime example of **pseudopsychology,** an approach to explaining and predicting behavior and events that appears to be psychology but is not supported by empirical, objective evidence. Another familiar pseudopsychology is *astrology,* which uses a chart of the heavens called a *horoscope* to predict everything from the weather to romantic relationships. Surprisingly, many people have difficulty

pseudopsychology An approach to explaining and predicting behavior and events that appears to be psychology, but has no empirical or objective evidence to support it.

"What's nice about working in this place is we don't have to finish any of our experiments."

distinguishing between pseudosciences, like astrology, and true sciences. One study found that nearly half of college science majors could not tell the difference between astrology, the pseudoscience, and astronomy, the actual scientific study of stars and other celestial bodies (De Robertis & Delaney, 1993).

Why do horoscopes often seem to be accurate in their descriptions and predictions? Consider this excerpt from a monthly Cancer horoscope: "Life at home or time spent dealing with your family will require more patience and cooperation than usual. Others might need advice or help and you may have to make yourself available" (Horoscope. com, 2012). When you think about it, this statement could apply to just about any human being on the planet. Doesn't dealing with family inevitably require extra "patience and cooperation"? And isn't it true that family and friends often ask for help and advice? How could you possibly prove such a statement wrong? You couldn't. That's why astrology is not science. A telltale feature of a pseudopsychology, like any pseudoscience, is its tendency to make assertions so broad and vague that they cannot be refuted (Stanovich, 2010).

Critical Thinking

Why can't we use pseudopsychology to help predict and explain behaviors? Because there is no solid evidence for its effectiveness, no scientific support for its findings. *Critical thinking* is absent from the "pseudotheories" used to explain the pseudopsychologies (Rasmussen, 2007). What is critical thinking and when should we use it? **Critical thinking** is the process of weighing various pieces of evidence, synthesizing them (putting them together), and determining how each contributes to the bigger picture. Critical thinking requires one to consider the source of information and the quality of evidence before making a decision on the validity of material. The process involves thinking beyond definitions, focusing on underlying concepts and applications, and being open-minded and skeptical at the same time. Psychology is driven by *critical thinking;* pseudopsychology is not (Rasmussen, 2007).

Let's put our critical thinking skills to work by examining the numerological "evidence" pertaining to Los 33. First, can we trust the data? One source suggests the rescue hole was 66 centimeters, but another says it was 68 centimeters. Some miners were rescued on 10/13/10, but others emerged on 10/14/10 (the rescue took place over the course of 2 days). Hmm, some of the 33s appear to be fading into thin air. Lesson learned: We should use critical thinking to evaluate the evidence for a claim.

But critical thinking goes far beyond verifying the facts (Yanchar, Slife, & Warne, 2008). Even if every piece of numerological evidence was spot-on, you would still have to weigh the relative importance of each piece of information and combine them all in a logical way: What do all these 33s mean, and can your conclusion predict what happens next? Here, we run into trouble again. Numerology and other pseudosciences cannot effectively predict future events.

Critical thinking is an invaluable skill, whether you are a trapped miner struggling to survive, a psychologist planning an experiment, or a student trying to earn a good grade in psychology class. For example, has anyone ever told you that choosing "C" on a multiple-choice question is your best bet when you don't know the answer? There is little research showing this is the best strategy (Skinner, 2009). Next time you're offered a tempting niblet of folk wisdom, think before you bite: What kind of evidence exists to support this claim? Can it be used to predict future events?

Using the principles of critical thinking, see what you can gather from the findings related to handwriting analysis and dishonesty presented in From the Pages of *Scientific American*.

S.Harris/Cartoonstock.

from the pages of **SCIENTIFIC AMERICAN**

Murder, She Wrote

Handwriting Analysis May Reveal Dishonesty

A new study adds "writing with large strokes and applying high pressure on paper" to the list of telltale signs that someone might be lying. Researchers at Haifa University in Israel could tell whether or not students were writing the truth by analyzing these physical properties of their handwriting.

Lying requires more cognitive resources than being truthful, says lead author Gil Luria. "You need to invent a story, make sure not to contradict yourself, etcetera." Any task done simultaneously, therefore, becomes less automatic. Tabletop pressure sensors showed this effect in the students' handwriting, which became more belabored when they fibbed.

Handwriting analysis could eventually complement other lie detection methods and would add a new dimension because, unlike almost all other techniques, it doesn't rely on verbal communication, Luria says.

 show what you know

1. An instructor in the psychology department assigns a project requiring students to read several journal articles on a controversial topic. They are then required to weigh various pieces of evidence from the articles, synthesize the information, and determine how the various findings contribute to understanding the topic. This process is known as:

   a. pseudotheory.

   b. critical thinking.

   c. hindsight bias.

   d. applied research.

2. _____ is an approach to explaining and predicting events that appears to be psychology but is not supported by empirical, objective evidence.

3. How would you explain to someone that astrology is a pseudopsychology?

✓ CHECK YOUR ANSWERS IN APPENDIX C.

The Scientific Method

--→ **LO 7**   Describe how psychologists use the scientific method.

Critical thinking is an important component of the **scientific method,** the process scientists use to conduct research. The goal of the scientific method is to provide *empirical evidence,* or data from systematic observations or experiments. An **experiment** is a controlled procedure involving scientific observations and/or manipulations by the researcher to influence participants' thinking, emotions, or behaviors. In the scientific method, an observation must be objective, or outside the influence of personal opinion and preconceived notions. Humans are prone to biases (Chapter 7), but the scientific method helps to minimize their effects.

Suppose a researcher had tried to determine whether any of the Chilean miners was running a fever. He might have asked the crew's "doctor," Yonny Barrios, to place his hand on each man's forehead, but Barrios' measurement of "fever" could have been different from the researcher's. A more objective approach would have been to send down a thermometer to the mine. Observations that are truly objective do not differ from one person to the next based on beliefs or opinions. A thermometer will read the same whether it's being used by Yonny Barrios or a new mom.

critical thinking The process of weighing various pieces of evidence, synthesizing them, and evaluating and determining the contributions of each.

scientific method The process scientists use to conduct research, which includes a continuing cycle of exploration, critical thinking, and systematic observation.

experiment A controlled procedure that involves careful examination through the use of scientific observation and/or manipulation of variables (measurable characteristic).

It's in the Data
Sian Beilock, a psychologist from the University of Chicago, examines an fMRI scan. Using brain imaging and other types of objective data such as behavioral observations and cortisol levels in the saliva, Dr. Beilock studies the psychological mechanisms that underlie "choking under pressure," or faltering under stress (University of Chicago, 2013). AP Photo/M. Spencer Green

Steps of the Scientific Method

STEP 1: DEVELOP A QUESTION   The scientific method typically begins when a researcher observes something interesting in the environment and comes up with a research question. A great way to start this process is to read books and articles written by scientists. (See **INFOGRAPHIC 1.2** to get a sense of how best to find and read an article.) Imagine that a psychologist has decided to study the psychological health of the trapped miners. While reviewing the literature on this topic, he comes across several studies suggesting that disaster survivors face an elevated risk for depression (Bonanno, Brewin, Kaniasty, & La Greca, 2010). This makes the psychologist wonder: Will Los 33 experience rates of depression similar to those of other disaster victims, or do their unique circumstances place them in a category all their own?

STEP 2: DEVELOP A HYPOTHESIS   Once a research question has been developed, the next step in the scientific method is to formulate a **hypothesis** (hī-'pä-thə-səs), a statement that can be used to test a prediction. The psychologist might come up with a hypothesis that reads something like this: "If we treat half of the survivors from the San José mining disaster with therapy and put the other half on a waiting list for therapy, those on the waiting list will be more likely to receive a diagnosis of depression within 5 years of rescue." The data collected by the experimenter will either support or refute the hypothesis. Hypotheses are difficult to generate for studies on new and unexplored topics; in this situation, a general prediction may take the place of a formal hypothesis.

While developing research questions and hypotheses, researchers should always be on the lookout for information that could offer explanations for the phenomenon they are studying. For a study on depression, this might entail reviewing theories about the causes of depression. **Theories** synthesize observations in order to explain phenomena, and they can be used to make predictions that can then be tested through research. Many people believe scientific theories are nothing more than unverified guesses or hunches, but they are mistaken (Stanovich, 2010). A theory is a well-established body of principles that often rests on a sturdy foundation of scientific evidence. Evolution is a prime example of a theory that has been mistaken for an ongoing scientific controversy. Thanks to inaccurate portrayals in the media and elsewhere, many people have come to believe that evolution is an active area of "debate" among scientists when, in reality, it is a theory embraced by the overwhelming majority of scientists, including most psychologists. We all have opinions about various issues and events in our environments, but how are these opinions different from theories? Please use what you have just learned about critical thinking to answer this question.

STEP 3: DESIGN STUDY AND COLLECT DATA   Once a hypothesis has been developed, the researcher designs a procedure to test it. **Operational definitions** specify the precise manner in which the characteristics of interest are defined and measured. For example, the psychologist might have used a depression scale to measure the mood of the miners, and then defined depression based on a cutoff point (anyone with a score greater than 40, for example). According to the scientific method, a good operational definition helps others understand how to perform an observation or take a measurement.

The researcher then collects the data to test the hypothesis. Gathering data must be done in a very controlled fashion to ensure there are no errors, which could arise from recording problems, or biases from different environmental factors. We will address the basics of data collection later in the chapter.

STEP 4: ANALYZE THE DATA   The researcher now has data that need to be analyzed, or organized in a meaningful way. As you can see from **FIGURE 1.3**, rows and columns of numbers are just that, numbers. In order to make sense of the "raw"

hypothesis (hī-'pä-thə-səs) A statement that can be used to test a prediction.

theory Synthesizes observations in order to explain phenomena and guide predictions to be tested through research.

operational definition The precise manner in which a variable of interest is defined and measured.

How to Read a Scientific Article

Psychologists publish their research findings in peer-reviewed, scientific journals. Scientific journal articles are different from news articles or blog posts that you might find through a typical Internet search. When you read news articles or blog posts about a research study, you can't assume these sources accurately interpret the study's findings or appropriately emphasize what the study's original authors think is important. For a full description of the background, methodology, results, and the application of a research study's findings, you must read a scientific article.

How Do I Find a Scientific Article?

You can find scientific journal articles through online journal databases such as PsycINFO, available through your school library, or Google Scholar, a search engine accessible on any computer. Search results can provide **references** that follow a standard format, like this:

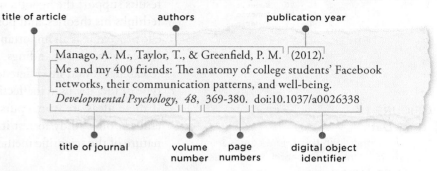

title of article — authors — publication year

Manago, A. M., Taylor, T., & Greenfield, P. M. (2012). Me and my 400 friends: The anatomy of college students' Facebook networks, their communication patterns, and well-being. *Developmental Psychology, 48,* 369-380. doi:10.1037/a0026338

title of journal — volume number — page numbers — digital object identifier

What's In a Scientific Article?

At first glance, scientific articles can seem overwhelming. It helps to know what you will find in a typical article. Scientific articles follow a specific organizational style and include the following elements:

Developmental Psychology
2012, Vol. 48, No. 2, 369–380

© 2012 American Psychological Association
0012-1649/12/$12.00 DOI: 10.1037/a0026338

TITLE

Me and My 400 Friends: The Anatomy of College Students' Facebook Networks, Their Communication Patterns, and Well-Being

AUTHORS

Adriana M. Manago, Tamara Taylor, and Patricia M. Greenfield
University of California, Los Angeles

ABSTRACT
- ✔ Brief description of entire article.
- ✔ Helps you quickly decide if the article describes research you are interested in.

Is there a trade-off between having large networks of social connections on social networking sites such as Facebook and the development of intimacy and social support among today's generation of emerging adults? To understand the socialization context of Facebook during the transition to adulthood, an online survey was distributed to college students at a large urban university; participants answered questions about their relationships by systematically sampling their Facebook contacts while viewing their Facebook profiles online. Results confirmed that Facebook facilitates expansive social networks that grow disproportionately through distant kinds of relationship (acquaintances and activity connections), while also expanding the number of close relationships and stranger relationships, albeit at slower rates. Those with larger networks estimated that larger numbers of contacts in their networks were observing their status updates, a form of public communication to one's entire contact list. The major function of status updates was emotional disclosure, the key feature of intimacy. This finding indicates the transformation of the nature of intimacy in the environment of a social network site. In addition, larger networks and larger estimated audiences predicted higher levels of life satisfaction and perceived social support on Facebook. These findings emphasize the psychological importance of audience in the Facebook environment. Findings also suggest that social networking sites help youth to satisfy enduring human psychosocial needs for permanent relations in a geographically mobile world—college students with higher proportions of maintained contacts from the past (primarily high school friends) perceived Facebook as a more useful tool for procuring social support.

KEYWORDS
- ✔ Identify themes or topics of article.
- ✔ Can be used to search for similar articles.

Keywords: social network site, peer relationships, emerging adulthood, intimacy development, wellbeing

INTRODUCTION

Explains topic of study, relevant previous research, and specific goals and hypotheses.

Psychological development during the transition from childhood to adulthood happens within the context of an expanding network of social relations, the details of which depend on cultural and historical context, socialization environments, and material affordances (Schlegel & Barry, 1991). One of the most striking aspects of the socialization environment in Western cultures in the early part of the 21st century is that adolescents and emerging adults have a variety of communication technologies at their disposal to manage quickly and efficiently very large webs of social connections. Nowhere is this expanse of social connections more clearly articulated than on social networking sites such as Facebook, the most popular social network in the United States and the fourth most visited website on the Internet (Comscore, 2010). From a sociocultural and historical perspective on human development (Co'te & Levine, 2002), it is not hard to imagine that the prominence of Facebook as a cultural phenomenon in the lives of college students in the United States would frame and shape developmental issues salient to them. Certainly, the current generation of college students has experienced an adolescence permeated by online peer interactions

This article was published Online First January 30,

Other elements not shown here:

METHOD
- ✔ Describes how study was conducted.
- ✔ Provides details about participants, materials and procedures, allowing the study to be replicated.

RESULTS
- ✔ Describes data collected and outcome of study.
- ✔ Often includes tables, graphs or figures.

DISCUSSION
- ✔ Interprets results to determine support or lack of support for the research hypotheses.
- ✔ Often reports study's limitations, contributions, and implications for future research.

REFERENCES
- ✔ Listing of all articles cited.
- ✔ A *great* place to look for additional research articles!

Variable	Record Number	Columns	Format
FAMILYID	1	3 - 7	Numeric
FROMWHO	1	9 - 12	Numeric
WHICHATT	1	14 - 17	Numeric
INT_T_	1	19 - 24	Numeric
INT_S_	1	26 - 31	Numeric
CON_T_	1	33 - 38	Numeric
CON_S_	1	40 - 46	Numeric
PERS	1	48 - 52	Numeric
GLOB	1	54 - 58	Numeric
STA_C_	1	60 - 64	Numeric
STA_O_	1	66 - 70	Numeric
BARR	1	72 - 76	Numeric
BREW	2	1 - 5	Numeric

165	1	1	0	1	0	0	1
165	1	2	1	0	1	0	0
165	1	3	1	0	9	0	0
165	1	4	1	0	0	0	

▲ **FIGURE 1.3**
Raw Data
The information in this figure comes from a data file. Until the researcher analyzes the data, these numbers will have little meaning.

Misguided Marchers?
Actors Jenny McCarthy and Jim Carrey lead a rally calling for changes in childhood vaccines. Studies suggest that routine vaccinations are safe, but some parents believe they trigger autism, a misconception stemming from a widely publicized but problematic study published in a peer-reviewed journal.
REUTERS/Yuri Gripas (UNITED STATES)

data, one must use statistical methods. There are two basic types of statistical analyses. Descriptive statistics are used to organize and present data, often through tables, graphs, and charts. Inferential statistics go beyond simply describing the data set. Using this type of statistical analysis, it is possible to make inferences and determine the probability of events occurring in the future (for a more in-depth look at statistics, see Appendix A).

Once the data have been analyzed, the researcher must ask several questions: Did the results support the hypothesis? Were the predictions met? He evaluates his hypothesis, rethinks his theories, and possibly designs a new study based on the analyses. This cyclic procedure is an important part of the scientific method because it allows us to think critically about our findings. In the hypothetical depression study of Los 33, what if the researcher found no differences between the therapy and nontherapy groups? Was the type of therapy used ineffective? Were the tools for measuring depression problematic? If these ideas are worth pursuing, the researcher could develop a new hypothesis and embark on a study to test it. Look at **INFOGRAPHIC 1.3** to get a sense of the cyclical nature of the scientific method.

STEP 5: PUBLISH THE FINDINGS   Once the data have been analyzed and the hypothesis tested, it's time to share findings with other researchers who might be able to build on the work. What is the point of doing research if no one ever reads about it or has access to the findings? This typically means writing a scientific article and trying to get it published in a scholarly, peer-reviewed journal. Journal editors send a submitted manuscript to subject-matter experts, or peer reviewers, who review it and make recommendations for publishing, revising, or rejecting the article altogether.

The peer-review process is notoriously meticulous, and it helps provide us with more certainty that findings from research can be trusted. This approach is not foolproof, of course. There have been cases of fabricated data slipping past the scrutiny of peer reviewers. In some cases, these oversights have serious consequences for the general public. Case in point: the widespread confusion over the safety of routine childhood vaccines.

In the late 1990s, researchers published a study suggesting that vaccination against infectious diseases caused autism (Wakefield et al., 1998). The findings sparked panic among parents, including the actress Jenny McCarthy, who led a march in Washington, D.C., calling for changes in vaccination policies. Concerned that their children would develop autism, many parents shunned the shots, putting their children at risk for life-threatening infections such as the measles. The study turned out to be fraudulent and the reported findings were deceptive, but it took 12 years for journal editors to retract the article (Editors of *The Lancet*, 2010). Why did the retraction take so long? One reason is that it took years for researchers to investigate all the accusations of wrongdoing and data fabrication (Godlee, Smith, & Marcovitch, 2011). The investigation included interviews with the parents of the children discussed in the study, which ultimately led to the finding that the information in the published account was inaccurate (Deer, 2011).

Since the publication of that flawed study, several high-quality investigations have found no solid support for the autism-vaccine hypothesis (Honda, Shimizu, & Rutter, 2005; Madsen et al., 2002; Taylor et al., 2002). Still, the publicity given to the original article continues to cast a shadow: Approximately 18% of Americans believe that vaccines cause autism and 30% are "not sure" (Harris Interactive/HealthDay poll, 2011). Ultimately, even though the peer-review process is a safeguard against fraud and inaccuracies, sometimes the process is not successful, and problematic findings make their way into peer-reviewed journals.

The Scientific Method

Psychologists use the scientific method to conduct research. The scientific method allows researchers to collect empirical (objective) evidence by following a sequence of carefully executed steps. In this infographic, you can trace the steps taken in an actual research project performed by two psychologists who were interested in the effect of "counting your blessings" (Emmons & McCullough, 2003). Notice that the process is cyclical in nature. Answering one research question often leads researchers to develop additional questions, and the process begins again.

The researchers see an article suggesting happiness is related to greater overall health. The researchers think about their own study and wonder:

ASK NEW QUESTIONS

Does counting your blessings also lead to better overall health?

To develop a question, a researcher will:
• observe the world around him;
• identify a personally interesting topic;
• review scientific literature on this topic.

To develop a hypothesis (a testable prediction), a researcher will:
• look for existing theories about the topic;
• establish operational definitions to specify variables being studied.

STEP 1: DEVELOP A QUESTION

Grandma always says, "Count your blessings." Why? What is the impact of a grateful outlook?

STEP 2: DEVELOP A HYPOTHESIS

HYPOTHESIS:
People who think about positive events in their lives will report greater psychological well-being than people who think about negative events.

STEP 5: PUBLISH THE FINDINGS

A researcher writes a description of the study and submits it to an academic journal, where it will be peer-reviewed and if approved, published for other researchers to read and use in their own research.

The researchers write an article titled, "Counting blessings versus burdens: An experimental investigation of gratitude and subjective well-being in daily life." It is published in the *Journal of Personality and Social Psychology*.

STEP 4: ANALYZE THE DATA

Group 1 participants reported significantly greater well-being than other groups. Researchers conclude that people who count their blessings feel better about their lives as a whole.

1 2 3 Researchers randomly assign participants to three groups. Every week, Group 1 participants list five things they are grateful for; Group 2 participants list five things that bother them; and Group 3 participants list any five things that happened. All three groups are surveyed weekly to determine their psychological well-being.

STEP 3: DESIGN STUDY & COLLECT DATA

A researcher organizes and analyzes the data and determines whether the hypothesis is supported.

A researcher plans a well-controlled study. Data are collected when the study is performed.
• A study can be experimental or descriptive.
• Data are collected using controlled measurement techniques.

Publishing an article is a crucial step in the scientific process because it allows other researchers to **replicate** the experiment, which might mean repeating it with other participants or altering some of the procedures. This repetition is necessary to ensure that the initial findings were not just a fluke or the result of a bias in one particular experiment.

In the case of Wakefield's fraudulent autism study, other researchers tried to replicate the study for over 10 years, but could never establish a relationship between autism and vaccines (Godlee et al., 2011). This fact alone made the Wakefield findings suspect. The more a study is replicated and produces similar findings, the more confidence we can have in those findings.

ASK NEW QUESTIONS   Most studies generate more questions than they answer, and here lies the beauty of the scientific process. The results of one scientific study raise a host of new questions, and those questions lead to new hypotheses, new studies, and yet another collection of questions. This continuing cycle of exploration uses critical thinking at every step in the process.

  show what you know

1. We all hold opinions about various issues and events in our environments, but how are those opinions different from theories?

2. A researcher identifies affection between partners by counting the number of times they gaze into each other's eyes while in the laboratory waiting room. The cutoff for those who would be considered very affectionate partners is gazing more than 10 times in 1 hour. The researcher has created a(n) _____ of affection.

    a. theory   **c.** replication
    b. hypothesis   **d.** operational definition

3. A _____ synthesizes observations to try to explain phenomena, and we can use it to help make predictions.

    a. theory
    b. hypothesis
    c. descriptive statistic
    d. peer-reviewed journal

    ✓ CHECK YOUR ANSWERS IN APPENDIX C.

Research Designs

► Note from Above
The wife of trapped miner Mario Gomez writes him a letter. © Ronald Patrick/Action Press/ZUMApress.com

THE BIG WAIT   The miners' first 17 days underground were intense and grueling, but now they faced the ultimate test of psychological endurance: waiting up to 4 months for rescuers to bore an escape tunnel. Could they go the distance? The circumstances of their cave-home were not exactly conducive to mental stability: no personal space, zero privacy, stifling heat, nauseating odors, minimal contact with family and friends, and loads of time to kill.

Recognizing the extraordinary psychological battle the miners faced, a team of psychologists was assembled to oversee their mental health (Franklin, 2011). Physicians and the lead psychologist Alberto Iturra began holding daily conference calls using a makeshift telephone line running through one of the boreholes. [A total of three narrow bore holes were drilled in order to facilitate communication and the delivery of food, medicine, and other necessities (Associated Press, 2010, August 30).] The therapist–patient relationship was congenial at first, but those feelings soon turned sour when Iturra began to meddle with the miners' communications. He recommended, for example, that the men be allotted only

1 minute for their first conversation with family members. According to one miner, Iturra actually got on the line and said "cut" when a miner's time was up. The psychologists also began to read personal letters sent from the miners to their families, and vice versa, censoring every piece of mail flowing in and out of the mine. Apparently, they were concerned that certain types of news (such as problems in the family or financial troubles) might be too much for the already stressed miners to bear. But this censorship incited something of a rebellion among the group (Franklin, 2011).

When the miners started to skip their conference calls, the psychologists punished them by taking away their few pleasures. "OK, you don't want to speak with psychologists? Perfect. That day you get no TV, there is no music—because we administer these things," lead physician Dr. Jorge Diaz admitted to reporters (Franklin, 2010, September 18). The rewards and punishments did not go over so well. "These government psychologists . . . they are treating these strong men like children," one of the miner's partners told journalists. "They are humiliating them. They are punishing them, like in a reality show. If they are bad, they don't get treats or special food. If they rebel, they are chastised. You cannot treat grown men, tough miners, like this" (McDougall & Allen-Mills, 2010, October 18).

Mental health experts across the globe weighed in on the matter. Psychiatrist Nick Kanas of the University of California deemed it unwise to censor communications between the miners and the outside world. "I would not screen anything. . . . Otherwise you are setting up a basis for mistrust," Kanas told journalist Jonathan Franklin (Franklin, 2011, p. 152). "Any attempt to be not entirely forthcoming [by rescuers] could be seen as a lack of trust," said psychologist Lawrence Palinkas of the University of Southern California in an interview with *Discovery News* (O'Hanlon, 2010, August 31).

The situation, in terms of the number of victims trapped, their distance underground, and the length of time they were buried, was entirely unprecedented (Spotts, 2010, September 7). No psychologist had ever studied human beings in a scenario quite like this. There were no "lessons learned" from past experience, no guidelines to follow, and certainly no research on the subject. The best Iturra and his colleagues could do was draw on studies of people in similar situations—such as miners who had been trapped for shorter periods of time, sailors confined in submarines, and astronauts on long-term space missions (Franklin, 2011).

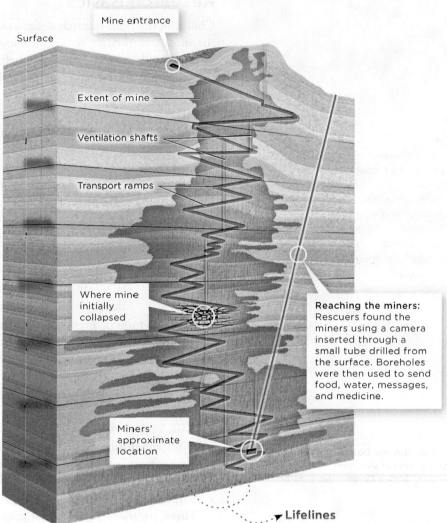

Mine entrance

Surface

Extent of mine

Ventilation shafts

Transport ramps

Where mine initially collapsed

Reaching the miners: Rescuers found the miners using a camera inserted through a small tube drilled from the surface. Boreholes were then used to send food, water, messages, and medicine.

Miners' approximate location

Lifelines
The miners communicated with the outside world through six-inch wide boreholes running from inside the mine to the ground above. Using one of these passageways, rescuers sent the men small containers known as *palomas,* or "doves," containing letters from family members (BBC News, 2010, October 14; Quilodran, 2010, August 24). Staff/MCT/Newsroom

replicate To repeat an experiment, generally with a new sample and/or other changes to the procedures, the goal of which is to provide further support for the findings of the first study.

Research Basics

Choosing the right research design, or type of scientific study, is crucial for collecting the most useful data. We will discuss two major categories of research design—descriptive and experimental—but before we do so, let's take a look at some of the concepts relevant to nearly all types of scientific research.

VARIABLES   Virtually every psychology study includes **variables,** or measurable characteristics that vary, or change, over time or across people. In chemistry, a variable might be temperature, mass, or volume. In psychological experiments, researchers study a variety of characteristics pertaining to humans and other organisms. Examples of variables include personality characteristics (shyness or friendliness), cognitive characteristics (memory), number of siblings in a family, gender, socioeconomic status, and so forth. A psychologist studying the miners might be interested in variables related to mood, leadership qualities, competitiveness, or educational background. In many experiments, the goal is to see how changing one variable affects another. In the Chilean miner example, you might be interested in knowing how the delivery of empanadas, a delicious stuffed pastry, affected the miners' moods. Once the variables for a study are chosen, researchers must create operational definitions that offer their precise descriptions and manners of measurement.

Yum ◄
On Chile's Independence Day, the miners received a special delivery from on high: *empanadas,* or delicious pastries filled with meat, olives, raisins, and egg (Penhaul, 2010, September 18). How might such comfort food have affected the men's moods? Juanmonino/iStockphoto

····► **LO 8   Summarize the importance of a random sample.**

POPULATION AND SAMPLE   How do researchers decide who should participate in their studies? It depends on the **population,** or overall group, the researcher wants to examine. If the population is large (all college students in the United States, for example), then the researcher selects a subset of that population called a **sample.**

There are many methods for choosing a sample. One way is to pick a **random sample,** that is, theoretically any member of the population has an equally likely chance of being selected to participate in the study. Think about the problems that may occur if the sample is not random. Suppose a researcher is trying to assess attitudes about banning supersized sugary sodas in the United States, but the only place she recruits participants is New York City, where there is a ban on supersized sugary sodas. How might this bias her findings? New York City residents do not constitute a **representative sample,** whose members' characteristics closely reflect those of the population of interest.

It is important for the researcher to make sure she chooses a representative sample, because this allows her to generalize the findings, meaning to apply the information from the sample to the population at large. Let's say that 44% of the respondents in her study believe supersized sugary sodas should be banned. If her sample were representative, then she may be able to infer that this finding from the sample is representative of the entire population: "Approximately 44% of people in the United States believe that supersized sugary sodas should be banned."

INFORMED CONSENT   The researcher has chosen the population of interest, and she has identified her sample, but she needs to make certain that these people are comfortable participating in her research. Before she can begin to collect data, she must obtain **informed consent,** or acknowledgment from the participants that they understand what their participation will entail, including any possible harm that could result. Informed consent is the participant's way of saying, "I understand my

Synonyms

Institutional Review Board (IRB) reviewing committee, Animal Welfare Committee, Independent Ethics Committee, Ethical Review Board

variables Measurable characteristics that can vary over time or across people.

population All members of an identified group about which a researcher is interested.

sample A subset of a population chosen for inclusion in an experiment.

random sample A subset of the population chosen through a procedure that ensures all members of the population have an equally likely chance of being selected to participate in the study.

representative sample A subgroup of a population selected so that its members have characteristics that closely reflect those of the population of interest.

informed consent Acknowledgment of study participants that they understand what their participation will entail.

debriefing Sharing information with participants after their involvement in a study has ended, including the purpose of the study and deception used in it.

Institutional Review Board (IRB) A committee that reviews research proposals to protect the rights and welfare of all participants.

role in this study, and I am okay with it," and it's the researcher's way of ensuring that participants know what they are getting into.

DEBRIEFING   Following the study, there is another step of disclosure known as **debriefing.** In a debriefing session, researchers provide participants with useful information related to the study. In some cases, participants are informed of the deception or manipulation they were exposed to in the study, information that couldn't be shared with them beforehand. You will soon learn why a small dose of duplicity sometimes comes in handy for scientific research. And rest assured, all experiments on humans and animals must be approved by an *Institutional Review Board (IRB)* to ensure the highest degree of ethical standards.

The topics we have touched on thus far—variables, operational definitions, samples, informed consent, and debriefing—apply to psychology research in general. You will see how these concepts are relevant to studies when we explore descriptive and experimental research, in the upcoming sections.

Super Sample

If a researcher aims to understand American attitudes about supersize soda bans, she would be foolish to limit her study to residents of New York City. Michael Bloomberg, the mayor of the Big Apple, called for a ban on the sale of supersized sugary drinks in 2012. The controversial law probably affected attitudes about the issue, even though the law was subsequently struck down by a judge. Thus, the people of New York City do not constitute a representative sample. AP Photo/ Kathy Willens

THE MINERS GET THEIR WAY   After nearly a month of working with lead psychologist Alberto Iturra, the miners demanded that he be dismissed. They were tired of the psychologists reading and editing their letters, searching care packages, and punishing them for refusing to go along with Iturra's agenda. The miners issued an ultimatum: Either Iturra goes, or we stop eating. Their strategy worked, at least temporarily; Iturra agreed to take a 1-week break, while another psychologist, Claudio Ibañez, took charge (Franklin, 2011).

Ibañez was much more relaxed in his approach. He put an end to the letter-editing and package-tampering and, in doing so, he placed more faith in the miners' ability to cope with whatever news might arrive from the world above. Ibañez was trained in *positive psychology* (Franklin, 2011), a relatively new approach to psychology that focuses on the positive aspects of human nature (a topic we will return to at the end of the chapter).

Ibañez's more laid-back style was a welcome relief to some of the miners, but soon it became clear that his method had its drawbacks as well. With much of the censorship stopped, families reportedly began to sneak forbidden items like marijuana, amphetamines, and chocolate into their care packages. Yes, chocolate. Sweets were a "no-no" because they could aggravate the miners' fragile dental health. Try living with an untreated toothache for days, weeks, or months. The arrival of prohibited items soon sparked envy and resentment among some of the men, disrupting the delicate social structure within the mine (Franklin, 2011).

show what you know

1. Psychology studies focus on _____, which are characteristics that vary or change over time or across people.

2. A researcher is interested in studying college students' attitudes about banning supersize sodas. She randomly selects a sample of students from across the nation, trying to pick a _____ that will closely reflect the characteristics of college students in the United States.
   a. variable
   b. debriefing
   c. representative sample
   d. representative population

3. Why do researchers need to ensure that they collect data from a representative sample?

✓ CHECK YOUR ANSWERS IN APPENDIX C.

Descriptive Research

▶ **LO 9**   **Recognize the forms of descriptive research.**

Suppose a researcher is interested in studying how the sudden arrival of drugs, sweets, and other prohibited goods affected the miners' social interactions. This is a great topic for **descriptive research,** the type of investigation psychologists conduct when they need to describe and explore a phenomenon or topic. Descriptive research is primarily concerned with describing, and is useful for studying new or unexplored topics when researchers might not have specific expectations about outcomes. But there are some things descriptive research cannot achieve. This method provides us with clues to the causes of behaviors, but it *cannot* unearth cause-and-effect relationships, a point that we will return to later in the chapter. But first, we will explore four types of descriptive research methods.

Naturalistic Observation

One form of descriptive research is **naturalistic observation,** which involves studying participants in their natural environments using systematic observation. And when we say "natural environments," we don't necessarily mean the "wild." It could be an office, a home, or even a preschool. In one naturalistic study of families with young children, researchers explored the interactions that occurred when parents dropped off their children at preschool. One variable of interest was the length of time it took parents to leave the children once they arrived at school. The researchers found that the longer parents or caregivers took to leave, the less time the children played with their peers and the more likely they were to stand by and watch other kids playing. The researchers also noted that women were somewhat more likely than men to hold the children and physically pick them up during drop-off. These drop-off interactions seemed to get in the way of children "settling into" the classroom (Grady, Ale, & Morris, 2012).

The most important feature of naturalistic observation is that researchers do not disturb the participants or their environment. Why? Imagine you were a participant in the naturalistic observation of families dropping off preschoolers. Researchers have been deployed throughout your child's preschool, and every time you walk through the doors, you feel as if you're under surveillance. Parking your car, you spot a researcher peeping at you from behind a tree; at the front office, you catch another one videotaping you. It would be extremely difficult for most people to behave naturally under these circumstances. It is important for researchers to be unobtrusive so participants don't change their normal behaviors.

As with any type of research, naturalistic observation centers around variables, and those variables must be pinned down with operational definitions. Let's say a researcher is interested in studying aggressiveness in enclosed spaces and decides to examine aggression among Los 33: an intriguing topic given that research has linked stress and hot temperatures to more aggressive behaviors (Anderson, 2001; Bushman, Wang, & Anderson, 2005; Kruk, Halász, Meelis, & Haller, 2004). At the beginning of the study, the researcher would need to operationally define aggression, including detailed descriptions of specific behaviors that illustrate it. Then she might create a checklist of aggressive behaviors like shouting and pushing, and a coding system to help keep track of them.

AVOIDING THE PITFALLS   Naturalistic observation allows psychologists to observe participants going about their business in their normal environments, without the disruptions of artificial laboratory settings. Some problems arise with this arrangement, however. Natural environments are cluttered with a variety of unwanted variables, and

Please Wash Your Hands
According to one naturalistic study, male college students are less conscientious about hand-washing in the restroom than female college students. Even after a reminder was placed in the restroom, only 35% of men washed their hands, compared to 97% of women (Johnson et al., 2003). Researchers in this study took great care to look as though they were regular people who just happened to be using the restroom themselves. Do you think more men would have washed their hands if they knew they were being observed? Jutta Klee/Getty Images

descriptive research Research methods that describe and explore behaviors, although the findings cannot definitively state cause-and-effect relationships.

naturalistic observation A type of descriptive research that studies participants in their natural environment through systematic observation.

observer bias Errors introduced into the recording of observations due to the researcher's value system, expectations, or attitudes.

case study A type of descriptive research that closely examines one individual or small group.

removing them alters the natural state of affairs you are striving to maintain. These environments are also very hard to control, making replication of the research more difficult. Suppose you opted to study the behavior of Los 33 during their heated dominoes matches. In this natural setting, you could not control who played and when; whoever showed up at the dominoes table became a participant in your study. You simply had to record the behaviors of your participants—whomever they ended up being.

OBSERVER BIAS   How can we be sure observers will do a good job recording behaviors? For example, a researcher who detests dominoes might be less inclined to pay attention to different aspects of domino-related behaviors than a researcher who relishes the game. One way to ensure that these types of issues do not intrude on a study is to include multiple observers and then determine how similarly they record the behaviors. If the observers don't all rate in the same way, this suggests the presence of **observer bias,** which refers to errors introduced into the recording of observations due to a researcher's value system, expectations, attitudes, and so forth.

Case Study

Another type of descriptive research method is the **case study,** a detailed examination of an individual or small group. Case studies typically involve collecting a vast amount of data on one particular person or group, often using multiple avenues to gather information. The process might include in-depth interviews with the person being studied and her friends, family, and co-workers, and questionnaires about medical history, career, and mental health. The goal of a case study is to provide a wealth of information from a variety of resources. Case studies are invaluable for studying rare events, like 33 Chilean miners cooped up in a subterranean hole, offering a window into this unusual experience. Unlike naturalistic observation, where the researcher assumes the role of detached spectator, the case study may require complete immersion in the participant's environment. How do you think this might impact the researcher's observations and the conclusions of the study? See **TABLE 1.4** for some examples of classic case studies, many of which we will examine in later chapters to help us answer this question.

Rain Man
The subject of one of the most famous case studies in the history of psychology, Kim Peek was able to simultaneously read two pages of a book—one with each eye—and memorize nearly all the information it contained. Like the movie character he inspired ("Raymond Babbitt" in the movie *Rain Man),* Peek had extraordinary intellectual abilities but a low IQ (Brogaard & Marlow, 2012, December 11). Case studies are often used to study rare psychological conditions relating to cognition, personality, and behavior. Barton Glasser/Deseret News

Table 1.4	CLASSIC CASE STUDIES IN PSYCHOLOGY	
Case Study	**Description**	**Outcome**
Phineas Gage	A railroad worker who survived after an iron rod blasted through his skull	Suggested the role that frontal lobes play in personality
H. M.	A man who suffered from profound memory loss following brain surgery	Showed how brain damage can be linked to memory loss
Little Albert	An 11-month-old who was conditioned to fear rats	Revealed the ability to classically condition fear in humans
The Genain Quadruplets	Identical quadruplet sisters who all developed schizophrenia	Demonstrated a genetic factor is involved in schizophrenia
"Rat Man"	A man with obsessive thoughts, including a punishment involving rats	Exemplified a case study on which Sigmund Freud based his theories
Lorenz's Geese	Goslings that became attached to Konrad Lorenz	Documented the imprinting phenomenon

Summarized here are some of the most colorful case studies in the history of psychology. These classic studies have provided psychologists with valuable insights into human behaviors, and you will read about many of them in the chapters to come.

PROVIDING CLUES No matter how colorful or thought-provoking a case study may be, it cannot be used to support or refute a hypothesis (Stanovich, 2010). Like direct observation, the case study method can help to further develop theories, but it can't provide answers to what is causing behaviors. This descriptive method can offer guidance for designing new studies on topics that may be relatively underexplored (Stanovich, 2010). But as knowledge advances and researchers are more concerned with testing hypotheses, the case study becomes increasingly irrelevant. Hypothesis testing involves drawing comparisons between different conditions (Stanovich, 2010). Case studies do not allow us to compare conditions to determine if there are other explanations for behaviors.

Suppose you are trying to examine how parent–child interactions at home might relate to preschoolers' transitions during morning drop-off. What would happen if you limit your research to a case study of a family with two working parents and 10 children? The dynamics of this family may not be representative of those in other families. We must always be vigilant against drawing conclusions from a single person or group; the chosen case may be unique, thus making generalizations inaccurate.

Survey Method

One of the fastest ways to collect descriptive data is the **survey method,** which relies on questionnaires or interviews. A survey is basically a series of questions that can be administered on paper, in face-to-face interviews, via telephone, or through a few mouse clicks. Your college might send out surveys to gauge student attitudes about new online classes and e-books (How often do you encounter technical difficulties with your online courses? How would you rate your overall satisfaction with an assigned e-book?). The benefit of the survey method is that one can gather data from numerous people in a short period of time. Surveys can be used in conjunction with other research methods, but sometimes researchers use only surveys to gather their data. Survey findings often complement demographic data, psychological assessments, and other types of information.

WORDING AND HONESTY Like any research design, the survey method has its limitations. The wording of surveys can lead to biases in responses. A question with a positive or negative spin may sway a participant's response one way or the other: Do you prefer a half-full glass of soda or a half-empty glass of soda? Take a look at **FIGURE 1.4** for an example of how the wording of a survey can influence participant responses.

More importantly, participants in studies using the survey method are not always forthright in their responses, particularly when they have to admit to things they are uncomfortable discussing face-to-face. In short, people lie. In one study, psychologists asked thousands of American women if they had ever cheated on their husbands. When a researcher questioned them in person, 1% of the wives admitted cheating; but when asked through a computer-based questionnaire, 6% confessed their infidelity (Whisman & Snyder, 2007). People often exhibit a desire not to reveal attitudes or behaviors that are embarrassing or deal with sensitive topics (Tourangeau & Yan, 2007). This may lead to an inaccurate representation of the attitudes and beliefs of participants.

SKIMMING THE SURFACE Another disadvantage of the survey method is that it tends to skim the surface of people's beliefs or attitudes, failing to tap into the complex issues underlying responses. Ask 1,000 people if they *intend* to exercise regularly, and you might get more than a few affirmative responses. But *yes* might mean something quite different from one person to the next ("Yes it crosses my

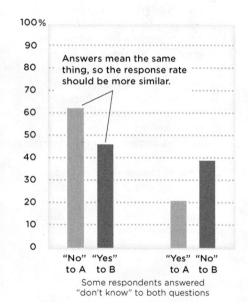

▲ **FIGURE 1.4**

It Depends How You Ask

In a classic study, researchers asked two versions of the same question:

(A) Do you think the United States should allow public speeches against democracy?

(B) Do you think the United States should forbid public speeches against democracy?

Answering "no" to Question A ("not allow speeches") *should* be the same as answering "yes" to Question B ("forbid speeches"). However, far more respondents answered "no" to Question A than answered "yes" to Question B. According to the researchers, "the 'forbid' phrasing makes the implied threat to civil liberties more apparent" than the "not allow" phrasing does (Rugg, 1941). And that's something fewer people were willing to support.

mind, but I can never go through with it" versus "Yes, I have a specific plan, and I have been able to follow through"). A simple yes/no question cannot distinguish between these vastly different answers, so the types of possible responses the survey includes (for example, yes/no, scale of 1 to 4) will certainly direct participants' answers. To obtain more precise responses, researchers often ask people to respond to statements using a scale that indicates the degree to which they agree or disagree (for example, a 5-point scale ranging from *strongly agree* to *strongly disagree*), or the degree to which they have had an experience (for example, a 5-point scale ranging from *never* to *almost always*).

REPRESENTATIVE SAMPLES AND SURVEYS The representativeness of survey samples can also be called into question. Some surveys fail to achieve representative samples because their *response rates* fall short of ideal. If a researcher sends out 100 surveys to potential participants and only 20 people return them, how can we be sure that the answers of those 20 responders reflect those of the entire group? Without a representative sample, we cannot generalize the survey findings.

"87% of the 56% who completed more than 23% of the survey thought it was a waste of time."

Correlational Method

The final form of descriptive research we will cover is the **correlational method,** which examines relationships among variables and assists researchers in making predictions. When researchers collect data on many variables, it can be useful to determine if these variables are related to each other in some way. A **correlation** represents a relationship or link between variables (**INFOGRAPHIC 1.4**, p. 33). For example, there is probably a correlation between the years of working in a mine and yearly salary. The more time a miner has put in, the more cash he takes home. This is an example of a positive correlation. As one variable increases, so does the other. A negative correlation, on the other hand, means as one variable goes up the other goes down (an inverse relationship). A good example would be the number of days trapped in the mine and body weight (at least before rescuers started delivering food). As the number of days increased, the miners' weight decreased. You have probably noticed correlations between variables in your own life. Increase the hours you devote to studying, and you will likely see your grades go up (a positive correlation). The more you hold a baby, the less she cries (a negative correlation).

CORRELATION COEFFICIENT Some variables are not related to each other whereas others have a link between them. Correlations indicate this type of information by representing the strength of a relationship between variables. Some relationships are strong and clear. Others are weak and barely noticeable. Lucky for researchers, there is one number that tells us how strong a relationship is and whether a relationship is positive or negative. Both of these characteristics of the relationship are portrayed by a **correlation coefficient** (symbolized as r), which is a statistical measure that indicates the strength and the direction of the relationship. Correlation coefficients range from $+1.00$ to -1.00, with positive numbers indicating a positive relationship between variables and negative numbers indicating an inverse relationship between variables. The closer r is to $+1.00$ or to -1.00, the stronger the relationship is. The closer r is to .00, the weaker the relationship is. When the correlation coefficient is very close to zero, there may be no relationship at all between the variables. An example of a nonexistent correlation might be shoe size and intelligence. Are people with bigger (or smaller) feet more intelligent? Probably not; there would be no link between the two variables, so the correlation coefficient between

survey method A type of descriptive research that uses questionnaires or interviews to gather data.

correlational method A type of descriptive research examining the relationships among variables.

correlation An association or relationship between two (or more) variables.

correlation coefficient The statistical measure (symbolized as r) that indicates the strength and direction of the relationship between two variables.

Eking Out an Existence
Darío Segovia began to work at the San José mine just three months before its collapse, so he would have been at the low end of the pay scale. But working at the notoriously risky mine paid well compared to other mining gigs. Laboring in dangerous conditions is a "third variable" that could influence the positive relationship between years worked in the mine and salary (Webber, 2010, October 11). DPA/ZUMApress.com

these variables (the *r* value) is around zero. Take a look at Infographic 1.4 to see how correlation coefficients are portrayed on graphs called *scatterplots*.

THIRD VARIABLE   Even if there is a very strong correlation between two variables, this does not indicate that a causal link exists between them; no matter how high the *r* value is or how logical the relationship seems, it does not prove a cause-and-effect link. If you discover a positive relationship between the years worked in the mine and salary, it's easy to jump to the conclusion that experience causes higher salary. However, it is possible that although they appear to be directly linked, there may be some other variable or characteristic influencing both of them. What additional variables might "cause" increased salary? One possibility is productivity, which could increase with the number of years on the job; more productive workers are rewarded with higher salaries. Another possibility is attendance: Seasoned workers may tend to miss fewer workdays as a result of on-the-job injuries; maybe they earn more money simply because they are able to clock more hours. In each case, we have a **third variable,** some unaccounted for characteristic of the participants or their environment that explains the changes in the two other variables. When you observe strong links between variables, consider other factors that could be related to both.

Now let's consider the direction of the relationship between variables. With a positive correlation between years of mining experience and salary, you might have assumed that experience leads to increased salary. The longer you are at a job, the more raises you get. But maybe well-paid employees are more likely to retain their jobs than their lower-earning coworkers, and the salary level leads them to stay on the job. For most people, a large paycheck is a compelling reason to hold onto a job. If this is the case, then salary level leads to the number of years on the job, not the other way around; the direction of the relationship matters.

Remember this type of method can't provide answers to what is causing behaviors or what the effects of behaviors are. It provides clues (description) to what underlies behaviors, but not definitive answers. Yet, correlational research is used when other types of experiments are unethical or impossible to do. If we wanted to determine the causal relationship between salary and years at work, we would not ethically be able to manipulate either variable. We couldn't ask the mining company to fire people, keep people on, or change salaries just so we can determine what is really happening between these two variables. Sometimes descriptive research is our best choice, as you will see in the following example.

across the WORLD

The Many Faces of Facebook

You probably know that Facebook is the most widely used social networking site in the world, far more popular than Twitter, LinkedIn, and MySpace (EBizMBA.com, 2012). But you may be surprised to learn that 81% of Facebook's one billion users reside outside of North America (Facebook, 2012). Why do people in different parts of the world use this American invention? Do they use Facebook to rekindle an old friendship, create a new alliance, or spy on an ex?

WHAT'S THE NUMBER ONE REASON PEOPLE USE FACEBOOK?

Curious about patterns of Facebook use across time and culture, a team of European researchers set out to gather data from users in different countries (Vasalou, Joinson, & Courvoisier, 2010). With the help of Facebook walls and networks, they recruited 423 Facebook users from the United States, the United Kingdom, Italy, Greece, and France. Then they asked the participants to complete an online questionnaire and conducted a statistical analysis of the responses. Their findings were intriguing.

Synonym
third variable third factor

third variable An unaccounted for characteristic of participants or environment that explains changes in the variables of interest.

The Correlation Coefficient: What's in a Number?

A correlation indicates a relationship between two variables, such as the amount of time you spend studying and the grade you get on a test. This relationship is often indicated using a correlation coefficient, symbolized as *r*. To interpret the relationship using a correlation coefficient *(r)*, ask yourself two questions:

(1) What is the *direction* of the relationship?

(2) What is the *strength* of the relationship?

A *scatterplot* helps us see what the correlation looks like.

And remember, a correlation between two variables does not necessarily mean that one variable caused the change in the other variable.

$$r = +.73$$

↕ What Is the **Direction** of the Correlation?

- *positive (+) correlation*
  as one variable increases, the other also increases

- *negative (−) correlation*
  as one variable increases, the other decreases (an inverse relationship)

Example: +.73 is a positive number, showing a **positive correlation**. As hours spent studying increase, test grades also increase.

▬ What Is the **Strength** of the Correlation?

strength ranges from +1.00 to −1.00

- a value close to +1.00 or −1.00 is a **strong** correlation
- a value close to 0.00 is a **weak** correlation

Example: +.73 is close to 1.00. This shows a **strong correlation** between hours spent studying and test grades.

⚠ BEWARE of the potential Third Variable

Correlation does not indicate that one variable *causes* a change in the other. A **third variable** may have influenced the results.

Example: Although time spent studying and exam grades are strongly and positively correlated, attendance is another variable. Students who attend classes regularly tend to spend more hours studying. Likewise, students who attend classes regularly know what to expect on the test and are therefore likely to get better grades.

👁 What does the Correlation **look** like?

Using a scatterplot, we can express the relationship between two variables. One variable is labeled on the horizontal axis, and the second variable is labeled on the vertical axis. Each dot represents one participant's scores on the two variables. Notice how the shape of the graph changes depending on the direction and strength of the relationship between the variables.

example:
+.73 (strong positive correlation)

perfect positive correlation (+1.00)

no relationship (.00)

perfect negative correlation (−1.00)

Credits: Push Pin Note, PicFive/Veer; Push Pin note paper, PicFive/Veer; Blank yellow sticky note, iStockphoto/Thinkstock

▲ FIGURE 1.5
Friend Finder
Social searching, or connecting with people one already knows, is a leading reason for using Facebook across countries (Vasalou et al., 2010).

Across cultures, the primary motivation for using Facebook was "social searching," or connecting with people already known outside of Facebook (friends, family, colleagues, and so on). In second place was "social browsing," or looking for new acquaintances, which was particularly popular among French and Italian users. When it came to total time investment in Facebook, the British led the pack, averaging between 2 and 5 hours per week (compared to 2 hours or less for those in other countries). The British and the Italians invested a significant amount of time in groups, and the Italians showed a strong interest in games and applications. French and Greek users were not particularly interested in status updates, and the French did not place a high value on photographs (Vasalou et al., 2010). Take a look at **FIGURE 1.5** for more information.

What do all these findings mean? Surely, there is a reason that French and Italian users are more inclined than their American counterparts to shop around for new contacts, and an explanation must exist for the French indifference toward photos. Finding answers to these phenomena was outside the scope of the study by Vasalou and colleagues. Surveys and other forms of descriptive research are information-gathering tools that illuminate behavioral tendencies, but they cannot explain the causes of those behaviors, which is the goal of experimental research, the focus of our next section. 🌐➡

Before moving on, let's hammer home a few points about descriptive research, which is particularly useful when it comes to relatively unexplored topics. Data gleaned from descriptive research often steer the course for future studies and help psychologists develop hypotheses and fine-tune their theories. But for testing hypotheses and uncovering cause-and-effect relationships, descriptive research cannot provide us with definitive answers, only hints.

✓○○○ show what you know

1. _____ is primarily useful for studying new or unexplored topics.
   a. An operational definition
   b. Observer bias
   c. Descriptive research
   d. A correlation

2. A researcher was interested in studying the behaviors of parents dropping off children at preschool. He trained several teachers to use a checklist and a stopwatch to record how long it took a caregiver to enter and leave the classroom, as well as the subsequent behaviors of the children. This approach to collecting data is referred to as:
   a. naturalistic observation.
   b. representative sampling.
   c. informed consent.
   d. applied research.

3. The longer a miner has worked for a mining company, the more money he makes. This is an example of a _____.

4. Describe the strengths and weaknesses of descriptive research.

✓ CHECK YOUR ANSWERS IN APPENDIX C.

Experimental Research

The nation of Chile went to heroic lengths to ensure that Los 33 made it out of the mountain alive. Most search-and-rescue missions are run by mine owners, but this was an extraordinary situation that demanded extraordinary measures. Lucky for the miners, Chilean President Sebastián Piñera decided that the government would lead the operation (Weiner, 2011, January 1). Engineers from the Chilean navy built the rescue capsule that ultimately lifted all 33 men back into the light of day, and the Health Ministry created a plan to care for the miners, which included voluntary psychological counseling for at least 6 months after the rescue (Kofman & Hopper, 2010, October 13; Kraul, 2010, October 11).

But the Chilean government was not in it alone. Governments, businesses, and individuals from all over the world flooded the Atacama Desert offering whatever help they could. Twenty privately run mining outfits deployed their employees and state-of-the-art drilling technology to help bore the escape tunnel; volunteers took charge of making over 500 daily meals for the miners' family members (*Los Angeles Times*,

2010, October 12); and the Red Cross provided round-the-clock first aid and psychological support to the miners' families (American Red Cross, 2010, October 13). Even a group from the National Aeronautics and Space Administration (NASA) showed up to lend a hand: two doctors, one engineer, and a psychologist named Albert Holland who had trained astronauts to cope with the stressful living conditions of outer space. The NASA crew was impressed with the efforts of the Chileans, but they also offered a few bits of advice, including a recommendation to increase the men's daily intake of vitamin D (Prengaman, 2010, September 3; Spotts, 2010, September 7).

You may wonder what's so special about vitamin D. The average person gets a substantial amount of vitamin D from the sun and, as you may recall, the miners were half a mile underground—where the sun doesn't shine. When the sun's UV rays strike the skin, its cells begin synthesizing vitamin D. (You also can obtain small amounts of this nutrient from a few foods, but not enough—unless your diet includes cod liver oil and lots of fatty fish.) Deprived of sunlight for weeks on end, the miners were at risk of becoming vitamin D deficient. Not a trivial matter, as this "sunshine vitamin" is essential for maintaining healthy bones, a strong immune system, and normal cellular activity. If you don't get enough of it, you may be at risk for a variety of ailments, including osteomalacia (softening of the bones) and heart disease (Lee, O'Keefe, Bell, Hensrud, & Holick, 2008; Medline Plus, 2010). Preliminary studies even suggest that a lack of vitamin D may be linked to cognitive functioning and perhaps certain problems with cognitive performance (Przybelski & Binkley, 2007; Wilkins, Sheline, Roe, Birge, & Morris, 2006).

Imagine you are a psychologist who has been following the Chilean miner saga. You've read the news reports about NASA recommending more vitamin D, which makes you wonder if giving vitamin D supplements will, in fact, improve the men's cognitive abilities. Here's the hypothesis you come up with: If one group of miners is given vitamin D supplements and the other group of miners a sugar pill, those receiving the vitamin D supplement will show improvements in cognitive functioning.

Eager to begin your study, you ask the Chilean government for permission to study the cognitive effects of vitamin D supplementation on Los 33. Sadly, your request is promptly denied. Not to worry. You have another option that may be even better: taking your study to a laboratory setting. Performing research in a controlled laboratory setting has huge benefits. You have greater control over who participates in your study, freedom to control the variables you desire, and the ability to draw comparisons between groups that differ only with respect to your target variables. In other words, you have the opportunity to use the *experimental method*.

Experimental Method

LO 10 Explain how the experimental method relates to cause and effect.

At last, we arrive at the type of research design we have been alluding to all along, a design that reveals cause and effect. Unlike the descriptive studies discussed earlier, the **experimental method** can tell us about cause and effect, because it aims to ensure that every variable except those being manipulated by the researcher is held constant, or controlled (**INFOGRAPHIC 1.5** on p. 39). To identify a particular cause of an outcome, we assign research participants to two or more groups, and with the exception of some sort of manipulation or treatment done by the experimenter, these groups are equivalent. If following the manipulation or treatment the groups differ on a measure of interest, we can say with confidence that the experimental manipulation caused that change. This allows researchers to observe the variable of interest without interference from other variables.

If you are having trouble understanding what it means to control variables, consider this analogy: You are outside a football stadium, desperately trying to follow

To the Rescue
A photo taken on October 7, 2010, shows two of the three drills used to bore rescue shafts for the miners. The rescue of Los 33 was truly an international collaboration, as workers and equipment from countries all over the world were deployed to the Atacama Desert. AP Photo/ Roberto Candia, POOL

experimental method A type of research that manipulates a variable of interest (independent variable) to uncover cause-and-effect relationships.

a friend lost in a swarm of people. Everyone is moving in different directions, making it exceedingly difficult to pinpoint your friend's location and direction of movement. But what if everyone in the crowd except your friend froze for a moment in time? Would it be easier to observe him now that he is the only one moving? This is similar to what researchers try to do with variables—hold everything steady except the variables they are examining.

Returning to the sun-deprived miners, let's examine how you might design a simple research study using the experimental method to investigate the cognitive effects of a vitamin D boost. Your hypothesis is that participants housed in a laboratory setting without natural light who are given vitamin D supplements will perform better on a cognitive task than participants in the same laboratory setting who receive a sugar pill. Although we cannot study Los 33 per se, it's possible for us to put together a group of men who are very similar to the miners in age, educational background, physical health, and other variables that might affect their cognitive performance, and then subject them to a prolonged period of sun deprivation. Next you would divide the men into two groups—one receives vitamin D supplements and the other gets a sugar pill—and compare their performance on various mental tasks after a designated amount of time has passed. If the group receiving the vitamin D performs better than the other group, then you can attribute the difference to vitamin D. Although this may sound fairly straightforward, there are still a few more things you need to know.

RANDOM ASSIGNMENT   Assigning participants to groups is a crucial step of the experimental process. Fail to assign participants in the correct way and your whole study is compromised. For this reason, researchers use **random assignment** to ensure that the likelihood of placement in a given group is identical for every participant. Randomly choosing which treatment the participants receive reduces the possibility of some participant characteristics influencing the findings. You may have noticed some similarities between random assignment and the "random sample" introduced earlier in the chapter. But here's the difference: Random sampling is used at the onset of a study to gather participants from a larger population. Random assignment comes into play later, when you are assigning participants to different groups. You can flip a coin, roll dice, or use a computer to generate numbers, but the goal of random assignment is always the same: to ensure that the groups are roughly equal on all characteristics. If the groups are lopsided with respect to some variable, the results may be affected. Getting back to your study on vitamin D and cognition, imagine that you assigned all the highly educated participants to one group and less educated participants to the other. Might educational experience influence the results of a cognitive test? Perhaps. Random assignment helps reduce some of the interference resulting from these types of characteristics.

EXPERIMENTAL AND CONTROL GROUPS   Let's assume you did use random assignment to divvy your participants into two groups. One will receive the treatment (a daily dose of vitamin D), and the other will receive no treatment at all (they will, however, be handed a sugar pill that looks identical to the vitamin D supplement). Those members of the group who get the treatment (the real vitamin D supplements) comprise the **experimental group,** and those participants who get the sugar pill are members of the **control group** (the group that does not receive the treatment). You may be wondering why the sugar pill is even necessary. We call this fake or "pretend" treatment a **placebo** (plə-ˈsē-ˌbō), and it is a key element of the experimental method. Our goal is to hide from participants whether they are receiving the treatment (in this case, the vitamin D). This is because human beings frequently feel better simply as a result of believing they are being treated. More on the peculiar *placebo effect* in a moment.

random assignment The process of appointing participants in a research study to the experimental or control groups, ensuring that every person has an equal chance of being assigned to either.

experimental group The members of an experiment who are exposed to the treatment variable or manipulation by the researcher; represents the treatment group.

control group The participants in an experiment who are not exposed to the treatment variable; this is the comparison group.

placebo (plə-ˈsē-ˌbō) An inert substance given to members of the control group; the fake treatment that has no benefit, but is administered as if it does.

independent variable (IV) In an experimental design, the variable manipulated by the researcher to determine its effect on the dependent variable.

dependent variable (DV) In an experimental design, the characteristic or response that is measured to determine the effect of the researcher's manipulation.

extraneous variable A variable in the environment or of the participants that could unintentionally influence the outcome of the study.

confounding variable A type of extraneous variable that changes in sync with the independent variable, making it difficult to discern which one is causing changes in the dependent variable.

INDEPENDENT AND DEPENDENT VARIABLES   Let's restate a point we already made earlier in the section, this time using our new vocabulary terms: The only difference between the experimental and control groups should be the variable the researchers are manipulating—in this case, vitamin D intake. The different treatments the two groups receive is called the **independent variable (IV),** because it is the one variable the researchers are deliberately changing (in this case, some participants get vitamin D, the others a placebo). In the experimental method, an independent variable is that which the researcher is manipulating, and due to the complex nature of human behavior, often more than one independent variable may be used. The **dependent variable (DV)** is the characteristic or response the researchers are trying to observe or measure. In the hypothetical study, the dependent variable is the participants' performance on cognitive tests. Just remember, the independent variable is what is manipulated and the dependent variable is what is being measured as a result of that manipulation. Stated slightly differently: The dependent variable, in this case, performance on the cognitive tests, "depends" on or is caused by the treatment (either vitamin D or the placebo).

"*Well, I guess we're the control group.*"

EXTRANEOUS VARIABLES   Another issue that must be considered by researchers as they plan their experiment is making sure that **extraneous variables** are not allowed to interfere with their measures. Extraneous variables are characteristics of the environment or participants that potentially interfere with the outcome of the research. While conducting your study of vitamin D supplements, you discover that three of the participants are reacting to the artificial light in the lab, making it very difficult for them to sleep. And this sleeplessness can definitely influence performance on cognitive tasks. Unfortunately, you failed to consider this very important variable in your research design, making it an extraneous variable. Researchers have to carefully contemplate the different kinds of variables that might unintentionally influence the dependent variable.

There is a specific type of extraneous variable that can *confound* the results of an experiment. **Confounding variables** are a type of extraneous variables that change in sync with the independent variable, making it very difficult to discern which one is causing changes in the dependent variable. Imagine you house the participants in your study in a very nice lab setting, but because the lab can only hold half the participants at a time, you decide to wait and collect data from the control group later in the year. At that point, your lab assistant has gone on maternity leave, so you need to hire a new lab assistant, a young man who will administer the placebos to the control group. When the data are collected on cognitive performance, you can't be sure whether differences between groups on test scores result from the vitamin D pills, or some variables related to the gender of the lab assistants or even the time of year that the data were collected. These other variables could be confounding variables.

The good news is that there are numerous ways of eliminating the influence of an extraneous variable. This is called *controlling* a variable. As we mentioned earlier, random assignment to the treatment and control groups can help to lessen the impact of such types of variables. In this example, that means ensuring both groups have approximately the same number of participants who are having trouble sleeping in the lab. Or, if you wanted to control how sleep impacts the outcome of your study, you could just remove the poor sleepers from your sample and not include their information in your statistical analyses.

If you succeed in holding all variables constant except the independent variable, then you can make a statement about cause and effect. Let's say your study does uncover cognitive differences between the experimental and control groups. It is relatively

Synonyms

experimental group treatment group
independent variable explanatory variable
dependent variable response variable

Looks Real ◄┄┄┄
One of these pills contains an active ingredient; the other is a placebo. In placebo-controlled drug trials, researchers give some participants drugs and others placebos. People taking the placebos often experience effects that are similar to those reported by the participants taking the actual drug.
Cordelia Molloy/Science Source

"Good Morning, Here's your placebo— I mean medicine... well, I'm fired."

Cartoonstock

Synonyms

experimenter bias experimenter effect, researcher expectancy effect

double-blind study Type of study in which neither the researchers who are administering the independent variable nor the participants know what type of treatment is being given.

experimenter bias Researchers' expectations that influence the outcome of a study.

safe to attribute that disparity to the independent variable. In other words, you can presume that the vitamin D caused the superior performance of the experimental group.

DOUBLE-BLIND STUDY   Earlier in the chapter, we mentioned that deception can sometimes be useful in scientific research. You are about to learn why. One way researchers use deception is by conducting a *single-blind study* in which participants do not know what treatment they are receiving. An even stronger experimental design is a **double-blind study,** an experiment in which neither the participants nor the researchers working directly with those participants know who is getting the treatment and who is getting the placebo. In our example, neither the person administering the pills nor the participants would know who was receiving the vitamin D supplement and who was receiving the placebo. Keeping participants in the dark is relatively easy; just make sure the treatment and placebo look the same from the outside (here, the vitamin D and sugar pill look identical). Blinding the researchers is a little trickier but can be accomplished with the help of clever assistants who make it appear that all participants are getting the same treatment.

THINKING IS BELIEVING   There are some very compelling reasons for making a study double-blind. Prior research tells us that the expectations of the participants can influence the results. If someone hands you a sugar pill but tells you it is real medicine, you might end up feeling better simply because this is what you expect. Apparently, thinking is believing. When people ingest a placebo pill, they often get better even though the contents of the pill were inert. The *placebo effect* works through individual expectations for getting better, suggesting that the strength of our beliefs can change our behavior and physical outcome. The placebo effect has been shown to ease pain, anxiety, depression, and the symptoms of Parkinson's disease. There are even some reports that, on occasion, the use of placebos has been linked to a reduction in the size of tumors (Niemi, 2009). Researchers believe that the placebo effect arises through both conscious expectations and unconscious associations between treatment cues and healing. One's expectation of the effect of the placebo influences the actual effect.

EXPERIMENTER BIAS   We've discussed the rationale for keeping participants in the dark, but why is it necessary to keep the researchers clueless as well? A great deal of evidence suggests that researchers' expectations can influence the outcome of a study, a phenomenon known as **experimenter bias.** A researcher may unwittingly color a study's outcome through subtle, verbal, and/or non-verbal communication with the participants, perhaps suggesting to them what the researcher hopes or believes may happen as a result of the experiment. Saying something like "I really have high hopes for this treatment we are giving you" might influence how the participant reacts to the treatment or describes its effect. The researcher's value system may also impact the results in barely noticeable but very important ways. How the researcher frames questions, decides to test hypotheses, or interprets findings can be influenced by her particular beliefs and attitudes (Rosenthal, 2002b).

Congratulations! You have now learned the nuts and bolts of experimental research, one of psychology's greatest myth-debunking, knowledge-gathering tools. This method gives us more control over variables than any other type of study we have discussed; it also stands out in its ability to establish cause and effect. However, like any scientific approach, the experimental method is not without its flaws. Laboratory settings are inherently unnatural and therefore cannot always paint an accurate picture of behaviors that would occur in a natural setting. Remember, when people know they are being observed, their behavior changes. Other weaknesses of the experimental method include cost (it's expensive to maintain a laboratory) and time (collecting data in a laboratory setting can be much slower than, say, sending

The Experimental Method: Are You in Control?

The experimental method is the type of research that can tell us about causes and effects. It is different from descriptive studies in that key aspects of an experiment—participants, variables, and study implementation—are tightly controlled. An experiment typically includes at least two groups—an experimental group and a control group. This allows the researcher to isolate the effects of manipulating a single variable, called the independent variable.

When is it important to use the experimental method? Imagine you want to know if laws that ban texting while driving are worthwhile. Does texting really *cause* more accidents? Perhaps texting is merely correlated with higher accident rates in certain populations, such as college students, because college students are both more likely to text and more likely to have accidents. In order to find out, you have to perform an experiment.

VARIABLES

INDEPENDENT VARIABLE

The variable that researchers deliberately manipulate.

Example: The independent variable is texting while driving.

- **Experimental group** drives through obstacle course while texting
- **Control group** drives through obstacle course without texting

DEPENDENT VARIABLE

The variable measured as an outcome of manipulation of the independent variable

Example: The dependent variable is the number of accidents (objects hit in obstacle course).

EXTRANEOUS VARIABLE

An unforeseen factor of the participants that could unintentionally interfere with the outcome.

Example: Some participants have more driving experience than others. Without controlling the amount of driving experience, we can't be certain the independent variable caused more accidents.

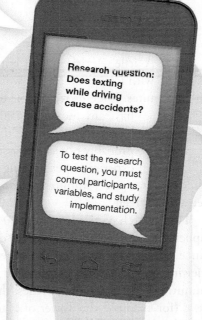

Research question: Does texting while driving cause accidents?

To test the research question, you must control participants, variables, and study implementation.

STUDY IMPLEMENTATION

PARTICIPANTS

REPRESENTATIVE SAMPLE

Subset of the population chosen to reflect population of interest.

Example: Participants must be college students. Other groups might be affected differently by the independent variable.

RANDOM SAMPLE

Method used to ensure participants do not introduce unexpected bias.

Example: Researchers recruit participants by randomly selecting students from the college directory.

RANDOM ASSIGNMENT

Process by which researcher randomly assigns participants to experimental or control group.

Example: Experimenter flips coin to determine participant's group.

EXPERIMENTER BIAS

Researchers' expectations and unintentional behaviors can unwittingly change the outcome of a study.

Example: Without thinking, researcher says "good luck" to one group. This might unintentionally cause them to try harder.

Researchers control for these effects by using a **double-blind study** in which neither researcher nor participant knows what group participants are assigned to.

FIGURE 1.6
Research Methods
How does a researcher choose which method to use? It depends on the research question. Each research method has advantages and disadvantages

ADVANTAGES		DISADVANTAGES
Good for new research questions; can study phenomena in their naturally occurring environment.	Descriptive	Very little control; increased experimenter/participant bias; cannot determine cause and effect.
Shows whether two phenomena are related; useful when an experiment is not possible.	Correlational	Directionality and third-variable problem; cannot determine cause and effect.
Can determine cause and effect; increased levels of control over variables.	Experimental	Results may not generalize beyond lab setting; potential for extraneous variables.

out a survey study). **FIGURE 1.6** gives an overview of some of the advantages and disadvantages of the research methods we have described.

Now it's time to test our understanding of the experimental method with the help of a sprightly yellow square named Sponge Bob.

didn't SEE that coming

Sponge Bob on the Brain

👁️❗ A little television won't hurt a child, will it? Kids' programs are interspersed with lessons on colors, words, and numbers, and only run for periods of 20 to 30 minutes. It seems reasonable to assume that little snippets of TV can't possibly have any measurable effect.

TURNING YOUNG BRAINS TO "SPONGE"?

When it comes to the rapidly developing juvenile brain, however, it's probably not safe to assume anything. Consider the following controlled experiment examining the cognitive changes observed in preschool children after just 9 minutes of exposure to a talking yellow sponge zipping across a television screen.

The research participants were 60 four-year-olds, most of whom came from White, upper-middle-class households. Researchers randomly assigned the children to one of three conditions: watching the extremely fast-paced cartoon *SpongeBob SquarePants,* viewing an educational program, or drawing with crayons and markers. Following 9 minutes of the assigned activities, the children took a series of four commonly used tests (for example, the Tower of Hanoi task) to assess their executive function—the collection of brain processes involved in self-control, decision making, problem solving, and other higher-level functions. The results were shocking: Children in the Sponge Bob group performed considerably worse than those in the other groups (Lillard & Peterson, 2011). Just 9 minutes of Sponge Bob produced a temporary lapse in cognitive function.

How do we know that this was not the result of a different variable, such as some children's preexisting attentional issues or television-watching habits at home? Those factors were accounted for in the study. In an experimental design, researchers hold nearly all variables constant except the one they want to manipulate—the 9-minute activity, in this case. This is the independent variable (IV). That way, the researchers can be somewhat confident that changes in

Sponge Brain
No one expects cartoons to make kids smarter, but can they hurt them? One study suggests that preschool children watching just 9 minutes of the high-energy, ultra-stimulating kids' show *SpongeBob SquarePants* experience a temporary dip in cognitive function.
PRNewsFoto/Nickelodeon

the IV are driving changes in the dependent variable (DV)—performance on the cognitive tests.

What aspect of the cartoon caused these effects is not yet known, but the researchers suspect that it has something to do with the show's "fantastical events and fast pacing" (Lillard & Peterson, 2011, p. 648). Further studies are in the works, so stay tuned. ⊙!

◯✓◯◯ show what you know

1. The experimental method can provide findings on the _____ of variables.
   a. experimenter bias
   b. confounding
   c. random assignment
   d. cause-and-effect relationship

2. A researcher studying the impact of vitamin D on cognitive functioning gave supplements to the experimental group and a placebo to the control group. After 2 months, she tested the participants' cognitive functioning, which is a measure of the _____ variable.
   a. dependent
   b. independent
   c. extraneous
   d. confounding

3. A study of preschool children looked at the impact of watching fast-paced cartoons on executive functioning. Half of the children were assigned to watch *SpongeBob SquarePants* in a room alone. The other half were assigned to draw for the same amount of time while sitting at a table with other children. The researcher mistakenly introduced a confounding variable, which in this case was:
   a. whether the child watched the cartoon or not.
   b. whether the child was alone or with others.
   c. whether the child was drawing or not.
   d. that both groups spent the same amount of time in their activity.

4. Describe what a double-blind study is and explain why deception is necessary in this case.

✓ CHECK YOUR ANSWERS IN APPENDIX C.

Important Issues in Psychology

Throughout this chapter, we have used the Chilean mining disaster as a subject for many hypothetical research endeavors, including studies on depression, aggression, and cognition. What we haven't yet addressed is the enormous ethical responsibility psychologists take on when they decide to conduct these types of studies. Psychologists do not study dinosaur fossils or atomic particles. They study humans and other living creatures who experience pain, fear, and other complex feelings, and it is their professional duty to treat them with dignity and respect.

Research Ethics

LO 11 Demonstrate an understanding of research ethics.

Like most other professionals, psychologists have agreed that it is important to follow specific guidelines to help ensure ethical behavior in the field. Professional organizations such as the American Psychological Association (APA), the Association for Psychological Science (APS), and the British Psychological Society (BPS) provide written guidelines their members agree to abide by. These guidelines ensure the ethical treatment of research participants (human and animal). They encourage psychologists to do no harm; safeguard the welfare of humans and animals in their research; know their responsibilities to society and community; maintain accuracy in research, teaching, and practice; and respect human dignity, to name a few (APA, 2010a).

CONFIDENTIALITY Confidentiality is a primary issue in psychology. Researchers must take steps to safeguard research data from misuse or theft. Psychologists who offer therapy services are obligated to keep client and therapy session information confidential; in fact, they are required to keep this information safeguarded in their offices. Confidentiality enables clients to speak freely about deeply personal issues. Furthermore, it also ensures that participants will feel confident when they share sensitive information

A Lofty Responsibility
Researchers study a newborn baby responding to smells such as curry and garlic. Certain flavors are familiar to babies because they were exposed to them in utero (through their mothers' diets). Conducting research on infants and other minors involves additional ethical considerations, and informed consent must be obtained from parents or legal guardians. Thierry Berrod, Mona Lisa Production/Science Source Model Released

obtained by researchers (such as information on sexuality or controversial issues), because they may rest assured it will be maintained securely.

DECEPTION   Other important ethical topics are informed consent and debriefing, both of which we discussed earlier. Informed consent is the process by which research participants acknowledge their understanding of their role in the study and sign off on it. Debriefing refers to the process in which researchers disclose important information to their participants after wrapping up a study. This would include informing participants about any deception. Remember that researchers sometimes use deception in order to uncover characteristics of human behavior. Throughout this textbook, you will read about experiments in which the participants did not know ahead of time what was being studied. In addition, they were often purposely lied to as a part of the manipulation, or to conceal what was being studied until the debriefing phase. It is important to note that no one is ever forced to become a participant in a research study. Participation in research is completely voluntary, and participants can drop out of studies at any time.

THINK again

Psychology in the Media

As you venture deeper into the study of psychology, you may find yourself becoming increasingly skeptical of media reports on psychological research. We encourage a healthy dose of skepticism. Although many news stories on scientific findings are accurate and balanced, others are flawed and overhyped. Look at these headlines about a 2012 study on the psychological impact of pacifier, or "Binkie," use:

SCIENCE, SPIN OR SOUND BITES?

"Pacifier use can lead to emotional problems in boys, study finds" (Fox News, 2012, September 19).

"UW study says boys' pacifier use limits social development" (Seely, 2012, September 19).

It sounds as if pacifiers are *causing* emotional problems in males. We must have a cause-and-effect relationship, right? Wrong. The following is a rough description of the research, which is actually a combination of three studies described in one article. In a study of elementary school children, researchers found that boys (but not girls) who had used pacifiers during infancy were more likely to have trouble mimicking the facial expressions of others. (Mirroring facial expressions is believed to promote *empathy*, or the ability to put oneself in someone else's shoes, and pacifiers could potentially interrupt the development of this skill by blocking muscles around the mouth.) Additional studies of college students linked pacifier use during infancy to lower levels of empathy and emotional intelligence, but only in males (Niedenthal et al., 2012).

Provocative as these findings may be, they do not allow us to conclude that pacifiers cause emotional impairments. Isn't it possible that the reverse is true? Infants with emotional problems are more likely to be given pacifiers (thus the emotional problems are leading to the pacifier use)? The authors explicitly highlight this problem: "The studies do not allow us to draw causal conclusions, as the children were not randomly assigned to pacifier use" (Niedenthal et al., 2012, p. 392). And while the researchers did control for some variables such as the mother's education and the child's anxiety level, it is impossible to control for every third variable that might influence emotional health. Can you think of any other factors that could impact the results?

The take-home message: If a news report claims that *X causes Y*, don't automatically assume that the media has it right. The only way to really understand the results and limitations of a psychological study is to read it for yourself.

Binkie Brouhaha
In 2012 researchers published a study showing a correlation between pacifier use in boys and lower levels of emotional intelligence later in life. The findings of this study could easily be interpreted as "pacifier use stunts emotional development," but this is a reckless conclusion. Think of all the other variables that might affect emotional development: parenting style, exposure to television, nutrition, interactions with siblings. Need we go on? © Jochen Tack/ imagebrok

THE RESCUE   Tuesday, October 12, 2010: The miners had been dreaming of this day for the last 10 weeks. Rescuers had finally blasted an escape tunnel down to the workshop area, a small cavern located above the safety shelter (Franklin, 2011). They would soon be lowering an elevator-like contraption known as the "Phoenix" down the tunnel to retrieve the miners. One by one, each man would travel back to the surface of the earth and into the arms of his family and friends. There would be a few onlookers, including President Piñera, a thousand journalists, and one billion people watching the rescue live on television (Craze & Crooks, 2010, October 13).

The first to ascend would be those believed to be most mentally stable. If something went wrong during the initial ascent, the rescuers wanted someone who could keep his cool onboard (Kraul, 2010, October 11). Florencio Ávalos, the soft-spoken 31-year-old father of two young boys, would go first, followed by the charismatic Mario Sepúlveda, 39; Juan Illanes, 51; and a 23-year-old Bolivian named Carlos Mamani. Next to go would be the men with medical problems, followed by those in good physical shape. The very last man to surface would be the determined and devoted leader, 54-year-old Luis Urzúa (CBS/AP, 2010, October 12; Craze & Crooks, 2010, October 13; Kraul, 2010, October 11).

The image of the first miner, Florencio Ávalos, emerging from the Phoenix capsule, greeting the president, and reuniting with his family is beyond description. Even the most stoic among us were moved by the image of his 9-year-old son weeping and trembling.

When Sepúlveda, otherwise known as "Super Mario," emerged, the mood was also dramatic, but in a different way. "Hey old woman!" Sepúlveda said to his wife through the metal mesh of the rescue capsule (Franklin, 2011, p. 253). Leaping from the capsule, he fell to his knees and began to unload a bag of rocks—souvenirs from his 10-week entombment. Then he threw his arms around President Piñera three times in a row, ran around giving high fives and hugs to rescuers, and led the crowd in a "Viva Chile!" chant.

The rescue effort spanned 2 days. When all was said and done, all 33 men had been brought to safety. Now everyone wondered how the miners would cope with their new celebrity status. These 33 men had gone from being ordinary working people to the most sought after interview subjects in the world. Reporters, publishing companies, and Hollywood all wanted a piece of Los 33. The group met with movie stars, attended galas, and led parades through Disneyland. One of the miners, Edison Peña, ran the New York City Marathon just weeks after emerging from the mine (Pearson & Siemaszko, 2010, November 6). He also appeared on *The Late Show with David Letterman* doing an Elvis impression (Pearson & Siemaszko, 2010, November 6).

But the same Peña who was seen gyrating on the *The Late Show* was later hospitalized for depression and anxiety. Other miners have also suffered from psychological troubles, including nightmares, sleep disturbances, and difficulty readjusting to family life. Some are taking medications, and nearly a third have suffered from *posttraumatic stress disorder* (Chapter 12) (Barrionuevo, 2011, October 12; CBS News, 2011, February 11). Despite these stark aftereffects, the rescue of these 33 men gives us many reasons to be hopeful.

13 Down, 20 to Go ▼
Carlos Barrios emerges from the Phoenix rescue capsule. He was the 13th miner to be hoisted to safety. AP Photo/Jorge Saenz

Positive Psychology

Let's end this chapter on a "positive" note, a positive psychology note. As mentioned earlier, **positive psychology** is a relatively new approach to psychology that focuses on the positive aspects of human nature, and is one of the many recurring themes presented throughout this text (**TABLE 1.5** on p. 44). It refers to the study of human

positive psychology An approach that focuses on the positive aspects of human beings, seeking to understand their strengths and uncover the roots of happiness, creativity, humor, and so on.

At Last
Dario Segovia's family members erupted in celebration as they witnessed him emerge from the mine on October 13, 2010. They had waited 10 weeks for him to come home. AP Photo/Natacha Pisarenko, File

strengths and virtues—happiness, creativity, love, and all that is positive (Seligman & Csikszentmihalyi, 2000). Historically, psychologists have tended to focus on the abnormal and maladaptive patterns of human behavior. Positive psychology does not deny the existence of these darker elements; it just directs the spotlight elsewhere, illuminating what is best about human nature. This has much in common with the humanistic perspective you learned about earlier. In fact, positive psychologists often refer to the early work of the humanists as setting the stage for the current field of positive psychology, including the topics they now study (Robbins, 2008).

There is a lot to be said for this approach to psychology and to life in general. Evidence suggests that people who have a positive outlook tend to flourish and have better mental health than their less optimistic peers (Catalino & Fredrickson, 2011).

As you reflect on the Chilean miner story, contemplate the positive aspects of the people involved—the teamwork, selflessness, and love the miners showed for each other; the rescue workers who worked around the clock to save the men from their underground nightmare; the wives, mothers, fathers, siblings, cousins, and friends who dropped everything and moved to the Atacama Desert to await the return of their loved ones; and the strangers all over the world who sat crying as Florencio Ávalos became the first man to emerge from the darkness. It is tragic that many of the miners now face a new set of psychological challenges, but as you will learn in this book, humans have an amazing way of overcoming adversity. Do not underestimate the positive potential of humanity.

Table 1.5	**RECURRING THEMES**	
Theme	**Definition**	**What to look for**
Nature and Nurture	The relative weight of heredity and environment in relation to behaviors, personality characteristics, etc.	Adaptation, heredity, environment, genes, instincts, reflexes, upbringing, peers, parents
Culture	The relative importance of cultural influences on behaviors, personality characteristics, and so on	Diversity, ethnicity, ethnic groups, cultural context, cross-cultural factors, ethnocentrism
Gender	The relative importance of one's gender as it relates to behaviors, personality characteristics, and so on	Gender bias, gender differences, social roles, masculinity, femininity, gender roles
Positive Psychology	The focus on positive aspects of human beings, as opposed to the more traditional focus on abnormality and maladaptive behavior	Strengths, optimal behavior, happiness, well-being, achievement, self-confidence, human potential

Throughout this textbook, you will come across four important themes: nature and nurture, culture, gender, and positive psychology.

show what you know

1. _____ is the process through which research participants acknowledge their understanding of their role in a study.
   a. Informed consent
   b. Research ethics
   c. Debriefing
   d. Positive psychology

2. Following a study involving a double-blind procedure with a treatment and a placebo, a researcher met with each participant individually to discuss important information about the study. This is known as:
   a. informed consent.
   b. debriefing.
   c. deception.
   d. naturalistic observation.

3. In the study about pacifier use, newspapers and websites ran headlines that were somewhat misleading with regard to the findings. How would you write a headline for an article on the findings of this study so that it draws readers in but still represents the findings fairly?

✓ CHECK YOUR ANSWERS IN APPENDIX C.

1 summary of concepts

LO 1 Define psychology. (p. 4)

Psychology is the scientific study of behavior and mental processes. Psychologists are scientists who work in a variety of fields, studying behavior and mental processes.

LO 2 Describe the scope of psychology and its subfields. (p. 5)

Psychology is a broad field that includes many perspectives and subfields. Psychologists conduct two major types of research: basic research and applied research. Basic research focuses on collecting data to support or refute theories, gathering knowledge for the sake of knowledge. Applied research focuses on changing behaviors and outcomes, often leading to real-world applications.

LO 3 Summarize the goals of the discipline of psychology. (p. 7)

The goals of psychology are to describe, predict, explain, and control behavior. These goals lay the foundation for the scientific approach and the experimental designs used to carry out research.

LO 4 Identify influential people in the formation of psychology as a discipline. (p. 8)

The roots of psychology lie in disciplines such as philosophy and physiology. The early philosophers established the foundation for some of the long-standing issues in psychology (nature and nurture). In 1879 psychology was officially founded when Wilhelm Wundt created the first psychology laboratory, located in Leipzig, Germany. Edward Titchener established structuralism to study the elements of the mind. In the late 1870s, William James offered the first psychology class in the United States, at Harvard, and developed the early school of psychology known as functionalism.

LO 5 List and summarize the major perspectives in psychology. (p. 11)

Psychologists use different perspectives to understand and study issues and topics in the field. Each perspective provides a different vantage point for uncovering the complex nature of human behavior. The psychoanalytic perspective looks at the unconscious conflicts at the root of personality development. The behavioral perspective examines human behavior as learned primarily through associations, reinforcers, and observation. The humanistic perspective focuses on the positive and growth aspects of human nature. The cognitive perspective considers the mental processes that direct behavior. The evolutionary perspective examines the aspects of human behavior that are genetically passed across generations. The biological perspective identifies the physiological and neurological basis of behavior. The sociocultural perspective looks at the social and cultural influences that impact behavior. The biopsychosocial perspective explains human behavior in terms of biological, psychological, and sociocultural interactions.

LO 6 Evaluate pseudopsychology and its relationship to critical thinking. (p. 17)

Pseudopsychology is an approach to explaining and predicting behavior and events that appears to be psychology, but is not supported by empirical, objective evidence. Critical thinking, on the other hand, is the process of weighing various pieces of evidence, synthesizing them, and determining how each contributes to the bigger picture. Critical thinking is absent from the "pseudotheories" used to explain the pseudopsychologies.

LO 7 Describe how psychologists use the scientific method. (p. 19)

Psychologists use the scientific method to provide empirical evidence based on systematic observation or experiments. The scientific method includes five basic steps: develop a question, develop a hypothesis, collect data, analyze the data, and publish the findings. The scientific method is a continuing cycle of exploration, which uses critical thinking as it looks at each and every step in the process, and asks new questions along the way.

LO 8 Summarize the importance of a random sample. (p. 26)

A population includes all members of an identified group a researcher is interested in exploring. If it is a large population, then the researcher will select a subset, called a sample. A random sample ensures that all members of a population have an equally likely chance of being selected to participate in a study, thus increasing the likelihood of a representative sample being used.

LO 9 Recognize the forms of descriptive research. (p. 28)

Descriptive research is a type of investigation psychologists conduct when researchers need to describe and explore a phenomenon or topic. It is especially useful for studying new or unexplored topics, when researchers might not have specific expectations about outcomes. Descriptive research

methods include naturalistic observation, case studies, the survey method, and the correlational method.

LO 10 Explain how the experimental method relates to cause and effect. (p. 35)

The experimental method is a type of research that incorporates independent and dependent variables to uncover cause-and-effect relationships. A well-designed experiment holds everything constant, except for the variables being manipulated by the researcher. If following the manipulation the groups of participants differ on the measure of interest, we can say with confidence that the experimental manipulation caused that change. This allows researchers to observe the variable of interest without interference from other variables.

LO 11 Demonstrate an understanding of research ethics. (p. 41)

Researchers must abide by guidelines to ensure the ethical treatment of research participants. These guidelines encourage psychologists to do no harm; safeguard the welfare of humans and animals in their research; know their responsibilities to society and community; maintain accuracy in research, teaching, and practice; and respect human dignity.

key terms

behaviorism, p. 11
biopsychosocial perspective, p. 14
case study, p. 29
confounding variable, p. 37
control group, p. 36
correlation, p. 31
correlation coefficient, p. 31
correlational method, p. 31
critical thinking, p. 18
debriefing, p. 27
dependent variable (DV), p. 37

descriptive research, p. 28
double-blind study, p. 38
experiment, p. 19
experimental group, p. 36
experimental method, p. 35
experimenter bias, p. 38
extraneous variable, p. 37
functionalism, p. 10
humanistic psychology, p. 12
hypothesis, p. 20
independent variable (IV), p. 37
informed consent, p. 26

Institutional Review Board (IRB), p. 27
introspection, p. 8
natural selection, p. 12
naturalistic observation, p. 28
observer bias, p. 29
operational definition, p. 20
placebo, p. 36
population, p. 26
positive psychology, p. 43
pseudopsychology, p. 17
psychologists, p. 4

psychology, p. 4
random assignment, p. 36
random sample, p. 26
replicate, p. 24
representative sample, p. 26
sample, p. 26
scientific method, p. 19
structuralism, p. 10
survey method, p. 30
theory, p. 20
third variable, p. 32
variables, p. 26

TEST PREP　are you ready?

1. Researchers at a large university were asked to devise a stop-smoking campaign. They created a program based on findings from research on learning to help students, faculty, and staff quit smoking. This is an example of:
   a. basic research.
   c. naturalistic observation.
   b. applied research.
   d. case studies.

2. _____ is a collection of knowledge that any reasonably smart person can pick up through casual observations of everyday experiences.
   a. Common sense
   c. Psychology
   b. Hindsight bias
   d. Psychomythology

3. The Greek philosopher Plato believed that truth and knowledge exist in the soul before birth and that humans have innate knowledge. This positions supports:

   a. empiricism.
   b. the nurture side of the nature–nurture issue.
   c. the nature side of the nature–nurture issue.
   d. dualism.

4. Inspired by the work of Charles Darwin, William James proposed that the purpose of thought processes, feelings, and behaviors is to adapt to the environment, which is an important concept of:

   a. introspection.
   b. behaviorism.
   c. structuralism.
   d. functionalism.

5. _____ suggests that human nature is by and large positive.

   a. Natural selection
   b. Psychoanalysis
   c. Structuralism
   d. Humanistic psychology

6. Psychology is driven by _____, but pseudopsychology is not.

   a. unverified guesses
   b. critical thinking
   c. lessons learned
   d. folk wisdom

7. The goal of _____ is to provide empirical evidence or data based on systematic observation or experimentation.

   a. operational definitions
   b. critical thinking
   c. the scientific method
   d. a hypothesis

8. _____ allow us to make inferences and determine the probability of certain events occurring.

   a. Inferential statistics
   b. Descriptive statistics
   c. Operational definitions
   d. Theories

9. A psychologist studying the Chilean miners was interested in their leadership qualities and educational backgrounds. These characteristics are generally referred to as:

   a. operational definitions.
   b. hypotheses.
   c. variables.
   d. empiricism.

10. One way to pick a random sample is to make sure every member of the population has:

    a. no extraneous variables.
    b. no confounding variables.
    c. an equally likely chance of having a characteristic in common.
    d. an equally likely chance of being picked to participate.

11. Descriptive research is invaluable to psychologists at the beginning stages of a study. Some forms of descriptive research can provide information on:

    a. cause-and-effect relationships.
    b. random assignment.
    c. relationships among variables.
    d. experimenter bias.

12. A researcher interested in learning more about the effect of isolation might choose the Chilean miners as a(n) _____, which is a type of descriptive research invaluable for studying rare events.

    a. experiment
    b. case study
    c. naturalistic observation
    d. correlational study

13. The _____ variable is what the researcher manipulates, and the _____ variable is the response the researcher measures.

    a. confounding; extraneous
    b. extraneous; confounding
    c. dependent; independent
    d. independent; dependent

14. With a _____ study, neither the researchers nor the participants know who is getting the treatment or who is getting the placebo.

    a. double-blind
    b. experimental
    c. correlational
    d. blind

15. The members of the _____ include those participants who receive the real treatment as opposed to a placebo.

    a. control group
    b. experimental group
    c. population
    d. sample

16. Explain how a thorough review of the literature plays a part in the scientific method.

17. A researcher has suggested that handwriting analysis may reveal dishonesty through stroke size and pressure used. If you were to use an experimental design to further study this topic, what would your treatment and control groups be?

18. Which survey is potentially more accurate: a face-to-face interview or written questions to be answered in private? Explain your answer.

19. Find an article in the popular media that presents variables as providing cause-and-effect relationships, but that is really a correlational study.

20. Reread the feature on the Sponge Bob study. If you were to replicate the study, what would you do to change or improve it?

✓ CHECK YOUR ANSWERS IN APPENDIX C.

Get personalized practice by logging into LaunchPad at **http://www.worthpublishers.com/launchpad/Licht** to take the LearningCurve adaptive quizzes for Chapter 1.

2

An Introduction to the Brain

📁 *In the Line of Fire*

📁 *The Awakening*

Neurons and Neural Communication

The Supporting Systems

💭➕ THINK AGAIN
Male Brain, Female Brain

The Hemispheres

📁 *The Girl with Half a Brain*

📁 *Christina Makes the Decision*

The Amazing Brain

🌐➡ ACROSS THE WORLD
The Plastic Brains of Our Children

💬 SOCIAL MEDIA AND PSYCHOLOGY
Facebook in the Brain

SA from the pages of
SCIENTIFIC AMERICAN
Electric Surprise

The Cortex: A Peek Beneath the Skull

Digging Below the Cortex

📁 *Where Are They Now?*

biology and behavior

An Introduction to the Brain

IN THE LINE OF FIRE   It was November 9th, 2004, and U.S. Marine Brandon Burns was surrounded on all sides by gunfire. The enemy was everywhere, in the buildings, streets, and alleyways of Fallujah. "I was in the deepest part of the city [and] there was chaos," remembers Brandon. At age 19, Brandon was on the front lines in the Iraq War, fighting in the battle of Fallujah.

"I was on top of the Humvee automatic grenade launcher shooting round after round," Brandon remembers. Suddenly, there was darkness. A bullet from an enemy sniper impaled Brandon's helmet, pierced his skull, and ricocheted through the back left side of his brain. Bleeding and unconscious, Brandon was rushed from Fallujah to Baghdad. Medics had to resuscitate him on five separate occasions during that ambulance ride. Brandon explains, "Five times I died."

After arriving in Baghdad, Brandon was transferred to a hospital in Germany. Doctors concluded that some parts of his brain were no longer viable. "They removed part of my skull and dug out the injured part of my brain," and now, Brandon says, "one third of my brain is gone."

2

LEARNING OBJECTIVES

after reading and studying this chapter, you should be able to:

LO 1 Define neuroscience and explain its contributions to our understanding of behavior.

LO 2 Label the parts of a neuron and describe an action potential.

LO 3 Illustrate how neurons communicate with each other.

LO 4 Summarize various neurotransmitters and the roles they play in human behavior.

LO 5 Recognize the connections between the central and peripheral nervous systems.

LO 6 Describe the organization and function of the peripheral nervous system.

LO 7 Evaluate the role of the endocrine system and how it influences behavior.

LO 8 Describe the functions of the two brain hemispheres and how they communicate.

LO 9 Explain lateralization and how split-brain operations affect it.

LO 10 Identify areas in the brain responsible for language production and comprehension.

LO 11 Define neuroplasticity and recognize when it is evident in brains.

LO 12 Compare and contrast tools scientists use to study the brain.

LO 13 Identify the lobes of the cortex and explain their functions.

LO 14 Recognize the association areas and identify their functions.

LO 15 Distinguish the structures and functions of the limbic system.

LO 16 Distinguish the structures and functions of the brainstem and cerebellum.

Ready for Duty
Brandon Burns poses for a photo at the Marine Corps Recruit Depot in Parris Island, South Carolina in the fall of 2003. The following year, he was shot by an enemy sniper in the Battle of Fallujah. Laura Burns

neuroscience The study of the brain and nervous system.

biological psychology The branch of psychology that focuses on how the brain and other biological systems influence human behavior.

Biology and Behavior: Studying the Last Frontier

Imagine that you lost a sizable chunk of your brain. How would it impact your life? Would you be the same person as before? Your brain houses your thoughts, emotions, and personality, and orchestrates your behavior. It files away all your memories and dark secrets, and is involved in your every move, from the beat of your heart to the blink of your eye.

However, the human brain is only one part of the most complex living entity known. The human *nervous system* is a communication network that conveys messages throughout your body, using electrical and chemical processes. The nervous system contains the brain, spinal cord, and other nerves and fibers, and includes some 100 billion (10^{11}) nerve cells. For a sense of what that number represents, consider that, in 2013, the population of the United States was approximately 314 million people; the number of nerve cells is approximately 333 times the number of people living in the United States. These cells are interlinked through some quadrillion (10^{15}) connections (Tang, Nyengaard, De Groot, & Gundersen, 2001). This intricate, ever-adapting web of connections gives us the power to think and feel in ways that are different from—and vastly more complex than—the thinking and feeling capacities of other organisms.

LO 1 Define neuroscience and explain its contributions to our understanding of behavior.

Consider the many tasks your brain is juggling at this very moment. As you scan the words on this page, your brain helps control the tiny muscles moving your eyes back and forth as well as the larger muscles in your neck and torso that keep you sitting upright. Light-sensitive cells in the back of your eyes relay signals, using electricity and chemicals, to various brain regions that transform the black marks on

Note: Quotations attributed to Brandon Burns and Christina Santhouse are personal communications.

this page into words, sentences, and ideas for you to remember. And all the while, your brain is processing nonvisual sensory input such as sounds and smells, working with other nerve cells in your body to make sure your heart keeps pumping, your lungs keep breathing, and your glands and organs keep releasing hormones properly.

NEUROSCIENCE Brandon's injury resulted in a significant loss of his brain tissue. Remarkably, not only did he survive, but he can still talk about what occurred, think about the events, and feel emotions regarding what happened to him. How exactly does his brain orchestrate all these complex functions, especially after severe trauma? And how does a noninjured brain carry out these complicated processes? Scientists have developed a decent understanding of how individual brain cells communicate with each other, but they have yet to provide definitive answers to "big questions" involving the brain and other parts of the nervous system such as: How do we think? What is consciousness? Why must we sleep? This is why the brain may be regarded as the last frontier of medicine. **Neuroscience,** the study of the brain and nervous system, actually extends far beyond the borders of medicine and into disciplines as diverse as engineering, computer science, and our personal favorite—psychology. The subfield of psychology concerned with understanding how the brain and other biological systems influence human behavior is called **biological psychology,** which brings us to the **goal of this chapter:** to examine how biology influences our behavior.

► CONNECTIONS

In **Chapter 1,** we presented the four major goals of psychology, which are to describe, explain, predict, and control behavior. These four goals guide psychologists' investigations of how biology influences behavior. As you read through this chapter, try to keep these goals in mind.

Synonyms

biological psychology biopsychology, psychobiology, neuropsychology, physiological psychology, behavioral neuroscience

In the pages to come, we will discuss some exciting new research findings and technologies used in neuroscience, but first we must get down to the basics: an examination of the nervous system, and how its various components work together to create sensations, movement, thoughts, and emotions. Our chapter-long "learning tour" of the nervous system will begin in the microscopic world of nerve cells, or **neurons.** Neurons are specialized cells that communicate with each other through both electrical and chemical signals. They are the building blocks of the brain, spinal cord, and nerves.

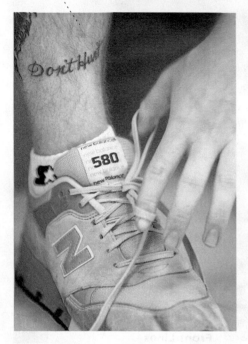

▲ One-Handed
Brandon ties his shoelaces with his left hand. His traumatic brain injury occurred on the left side of his brain, causing paralysis and loss of sensation on the right side of his body.
A.J. Wolfe/The Commercial Appeal

THE AWAKENING   Two weeks after the shooting, Brandon finally awoke from his coma. He could not move or feel the right side of his body, and he had lost the ability to use language. There were so many things he wanted to say to his family, but when he opened his mouth, the only sound that came out was "ugh." Weeks went by before Brandon uttered his first word: "no." That was all he could say for months, even when he was dying to say "yes." During Brandon's recovery, for example, his parents asked if he wanted some pizza, but all he could spit out was the word "no" (while nodding his head "yes"), even though he craved a hot, dripping slice like never before.

Apart from the paralysis to his right side and his difficulty with language, Brandon's other abilities seemed fine. He could remember people, places, and objects, and he reported no trouble hearing, smelling, or tasting (The pizza tasted so good when he finally got it!). Although Brandon was not as outgoing and self-assured as before, he hadn't changed much overall.

Why did the trauma to Brandon's brain cause deficits in language, but not memory? Why was the right side of his body paralyzed, while the left side worked fine? Our discussion of the brain's organization later in this chapter will clear up these mysteries for you. But first, let's find out how neurons communicate.

◉✓◯◯◯   show what you know

1. Comprised of the brain, spinal cord, and other nerves, _____ is a communication network that conveys messages throughout the body, using electrical and chemical processes.
   a. consciousness
   b. the human nervous system
   c. a neuron
   d. the skull

2. A researcher studying the impact of Brandon's brain injury might work in the field of _____, which includes the study of the brain and nervous system.

3. In the next section, you will learn much more about neurons, which are often referred to as the "building blocks" of the nervous system. What building blocks are you familiar with in other fields of study?

✓ CHECK YOUR ANSWERS IN APPENDIX C.

Neurons and Neural Communication

In the next few pages, you will be introduced to some fairly tough biology concepts. Stay focused, do not give up, and reread the section as necessary. Communication among the cells in your nervous system underlies every behavior and mental process. In order to fully understand psychology, you need to understand the biology of the nervous system. So prepare to learn about something truly electrifying: the human neuron.

Cell body

Dendrites: receive messages

Axon: sends messages from cell body to terminal buds

Nodes of Ranvier

Myelin sheath: speeds communication

Terminal buds: transmit messages to other neurons

▲ FIGURE 2.1
The Neuron
The neuron, the basic building block of the nervous system, has three main components: (1) the *cell body,* which contains vital cellular structures; (2) bushy *dendrites* that receive messages from neighboring neurons; and (3) a long, thin *axon* that sends messages to other neurons through its branchlike *terminal buds.* above: James Cavallini/Photo Researchers, Inc.

Just the Basics

········> **LO 2** Label the parts of a neuron and describe an action potential.

THE STRUCTURE OF A TYPICAL NEURON   A typical neuron has three basic parts: a cell body, dendrites, and an axon (**FIGURE 2.1**). The **cell body** of a neuron contains the standard components found in most human cells: a nucleus containing DNA, protein-producing mechanisms, and other structures that nourish the cell. Extending from the cell body are many **dendrites** (den-drīts), which are tiny, branchlike fibers. Generally projecting in the opposite direction from the dendrites is a single **axon,** which is a long, skinny, tubelike extension of the cell body, with branches ending in *terminal buds.* Many axons are surrounded by a **myelin sheath** (mī-ə-lən shēth), a fatty substance that provides insulation. The axon is not entirely enclosed, but rather, covered in segments of myelin. The gaps between segments of the myelin are called *nodes of Ranvier.* The **synapse** (si-naps) is the tiny gap between a terminal bud of one axon and a neighboring dendrite of the next neuron (see photo on page 57). Just for perspective, the synaptic gap is only about 0.000127 millimeters (1.27 $\times$ 10^{-4}) wide, whereas a single sheet of printer paper is 0.1 millimeters thick.

HOLDING IT TOGETHER: GLIAL CELLS   The function of neurons is to transmit information up and down the body all day and night, and neurons need a little support and nurturing to get this tough job done. This is where the **glial cells** (glē-əl) come into play. In the human brain, glial cells outnumber neurons by approximately 50 to 1 (Yuhas & Jabr, 2012). They hold neurons together (*glia* means "glue" in Greek) and maintain the structure of the nervous system. For many years, scientists believed that glial cells simply kept things together, but we now know they do much more (Ndubaku & de Bellard, 2008).

Glial cells come to the rescue if the brain is injured. When Brandon was shot in the head, glial cells called *microglia* began multiplying and secreting substances to defend his brain from infection and inflammation (d'Avila et al., 2012; Streit, 2000).

Synonyms

cell body soma

terminal buds axon buds, synaptic knobs, terminal buttons

synapse synaptic cleft, synaptic gap

neurons The building blocks of the nervous system that transmit electrical and chemical signals in the body.

cell body The region of the neuron that includes a nucleus containing DNA, protein-producing mechanisms, and other structures that nourish the cell.

dendrites (den-drīts) Tiny, branchlike fibers extending from the cell body that receive messages from other neurons and send information in the direction of the cell body.

axon Skinny tubelike structure of a neuron that extends from the cell body, and which sends messages to other neurons.

myelin sheath (mī-ə-lən, shēth) Fatty substance that insulates the axon and speeds the transmission of neural messages.

synapse (si-naps) The tiny gap between a terminal bud of one axon and a neighboring dendrite of the next neuron; junction between neurons where communication occurs.

glial cells (glē-əl) Cells that support, nourish, and protect neurons; produce myelin that covers axons.

Glia to the Rescue ▼

A scanning electron micrograph shows neurons (green) and glia (orange). Glial cells serve as the "glue" of the nervous system, providing cohesion and support for the neurons. Thomas Deerinck, NCMIR

Another class of glial cells called *astrocytes* began restoring the barrier between his brain and blood (Gruber, 2009). Astrocytes have been found to support communication between neurons as well (Araque & Navarrete, 2010). Another type of glial cells, *Schwann cells,* make the myelin that envelops axons.

Communication Within and Between

Neurons have properties that allow them to communicate with other cells. But what information do they convey? In essence, the message is simple: "I have been activated." Neurons are activated in response to sensations, thoughts, and other neurons, and this forms the basis for all that we think, feel, and do.

PROCESSES INSIDE THE NEURON A neuron is surrounded by and contains electrically charged solutions (**INFOGRAPHIC 2.1**). If the total charge in each of these solutions is different, a voltage will be generated between the outside and the inside of the cell. This voltage is determined by the electrical characteristics of particles called *ions.* (Some ions are negatively charged; others are positively charged.) The difference in the charges inside and outside of the neuron determines its *polarity,* the degree to which it is positive or negative overall. Two processes direct the flow of positive and negative ions into or out of the cell. *Diffusion* is the natural tendency of the ions to spread out or disperse, and *electrostatic pressure* causes similarly charged ions to spread apart and oppositely charged ions to move toward each other (like the behavior of magnets). The concentrations, inside and outside of the cell, of positively charged ions (sodium and potassium) and negatively charged ions (protein molecules) determine the activity in most neurons. A neuron is encased in a membrane that is selectively permeable, allowing only some of the ions to pass in and out of its channels. The membrane is impermeable to positive sodium ions and negative protein ions (it does not allow these ions to enter or exit). Positive sodium ions move toward the membrane from the outside, and negative protein ions move toward the membrane from the inside; each moves closer to its side of the membrane wall (because the opposite charges are attracted to each other).

Inside the neuron, the concentration of potassium ions is greater than that outside the membrane. Also inside the cell are negatively charged protein ions, which do not exist outside the cell. These protein ions are attracted to the excess positive charge outside and move toward the membrane, but they are too big to go through. Because the protein ions can't get out, the inside of the neuron is negatively charged when the neuron is not active. The concentration of sodium ions inside the cell is much less than its concentration on the outside of the cell. As a result, the sodium ions on the outside are attracted to the cell wall. This is due not only to the force of diffusion, but also to the force of attraction that occurs between oppositely charged ions. An electrical potential is created by the differences in charge between the outside and the inside of the neuron, which is its *resting potential.*

RESTING POTENTIAL The **resting potential** represents the electrical potential of a cell "at rest," the condition of a cell when it is not activated. The solutions on either side of the membrane wall come into equilibrium with a slightly more negative charge inside. In the resting state, the voltage inside the cell is about -70 millivolts (mV) compared to the voltage on the outside. (Think of a resting neuron like a battery, which holds a charge. For comparison, one double A battery has a 1,500 mV charge.) This resting potential is only one part of the story. Let's look at what happens when a neuron stops "resting" and goes into "action."

ACTION POTENTIAL Although the positive sodium ions are being pulled toward the inside of the cell, they cannot move into the cell until the neuron is stimulated by neighboring cells. When this happens, a signal instructs the channels

resting potential The electrical potential of a cell "at rest"; the state of a cell when it is not activated.

Communication Within Neurons

Neural communication involves different processes *within* and *between* neurons. In this infographic, we follow the electrical action that conveys messages *within* the neuron, from one end to the other.

Dendrites

Neuron cell body

Axon hillock

Axon

Myelin sheath

Node of Ranvier

Terminal buds

1. THE NEURON AT REST

Before communication begins, the neuron is "at rest." Closed channels in the cell membrane prevent some positive ions from entering the cell, and the inside of the cell is slightly more negative than the charge outside. At –70 mV, the cell is at its resting potential.

2. THE ACTION POTENTIAL

This graph shows the characteristic electrical trace of the action potential. When the neuron is stimulated, positive ions enter the cell, making the axon less negative (A). When the charge reaches threshold (–55 mV), an action potential is triggered. Positive ions flood the cell, quickly reversing the charge from negative to positive (B). Afterward, the cell is restored to resting potential (C).

Axon

Node of Ranvier

Myelin

3. ACTION POTENTIAL TRAVELS LENGTH OF AXON

The action potential occurring in one axon segment causes a voltage change in the next, initiating an entirely new action potential there. This sequential action travels along the axon like a wave, carrying the message from axon hillock to terminal buds.

in the cell membrane to open up. The channels, or gates, open, freeing the positive sodium ions to move into the cell, through the dendrites, to the cell body, and to finally reach the beginning of the axon, known as the *axon hillock*. The positive sodium ions cannot leave the cell, because the channels in the dendrites closed immediately after they entered.

The influx of the positive sodium ions at the axon hillock raises the internal cell voltage of the first segment of the axon from the resting voltage of -70 mV to the **threshold potential** of -55 mV relative to the outside. This change in voltage causes the sodium gates to open, and the positive sodium ions flood into the cell. The voltage inside that section of the axon rises rapidly, increasing from -55 mV to $+30$ mV, after which the sodium gates immediately close. This produces a spike in the value of the voltage within the cell, as the charge inside the cell becomes more positive than that outside of the cell. This is the **action potential**, or the spike in electrical energy that passes through the axon of a neuron.

The potassium gates open, and the positive potassium ions, now repelled by the much more positively charged cell interior, flow out of the cell as the similarly charged ions repel each other. This segment of the neuron returns to the resting potential. However, because the proportion of sodium and potassium ions inside and outside the cell is not the same as before (the ions are no longer at equilibrium), a sodium/potassium pump within the cell membrane brings them back to their original values by pumping the excess positive sodium ions back outside the cell and the positive potassium ions back in. In this way, the solutions inside and outside this segment of the axon return to equilibrium.

MOVING DOWN THE AXON   The firing of the first segment of the axon produces excess positive sodium ions on the inside of the cell, and these positive sodium ions diffuse to the next segment within the axon. This causes the voltage of the second segment of the axon to reach the threshold potential (-55 mV), opening its sodium gates and causing a spike of voltage there ($+30$ mV). Meanwhile, the first segment of the axon returns to its resting potential so that the electrical spike cannot go in that direction. This process repeats through each segment of the axon, like a row of dominos tumbling down. Every time a segment of the axon fires, the positive sodium ions flood in from the outside of the cell, while the prior segment returns to its resting potential, all along the length of the axon to its end. Each action potential takes about 1 millisecond to complete, and a typical neuron can fire several hundred times per second.

EXCITATORY AND INHIBITORY SIGNALS   How do neighboring cells initially signal for the channels to open up to let the positive sodium ions move into the dendrites of a neuron? The message to fire begins at the dendrites. Chemical messages from surrounding neurons are sent to the cell body. If enough sending neurons signal the receiving neuron to pass along the message, their combined signal becomes *excitatory* and the neuron will fire. However, not all neighboring neurons send an excitatory signal. Some will send an *inhibitory* signal, instructing the neuron not to fire. For an excitatory signal to occur, there have to be more excitatory than inhibitory signals, and the difference between the two has to meet the threshold potential of -55 mV. If "enough" positively charged ions enter the cell, the potential of the neuron increases and reaches the threshold, or trigger point, and the cell "fires."

ALL-OR-NONE   Action potentials are **all-or-none:** They either happen or they don't. Their strength remains the same no matter what occurs. A neuron conveys the strength of a stimulus by firing more often and delivering its message to more

Synonyms

threshold potential stimulus threshold

action potential spike potential

action potential The spike in electrical energy that passes through the axon of a neuron, the purpose of which is to convey information.

all-or-none A neuron either fires or does not fire; action potentials are always the same strength.

neurotransmitters Chemical messengers that neurons use to communicate at the synapse.

receptor sites The location where neurotransmitters attach on the receiving side of the synaptic gap.

reuptake Process by which neurotransmitters are reabsorbed by the sending terminal bud.

neurons. This is how we sense the difference between a quiet sound and a loud bang, for example. When we hear a loud bang: (1) The number of sensory neurons being fired is greater than the number that would have been fired for a quiet sound, and (2) each individual neuron fires more often than it would for a quiet sound. Thus, there is no such thing as a partial action potential, or a strong or weak action potential.

MYELIN SHEATH The firing of a neuron is facilitated by the myelin sheath, which insulates and protects the tiny spikes in electricity happening inside the axon. Because myelin is such a good insulator, it does not allow the exchange of ion fluid between the inside and the outside of the cell membrane. However, the axon is not covered with myelin at the nodes of Ranvier (you can see this in the photograph to the right). The exchange of ion fluid can only happen at the nodes of Ranvier, where there is no myelin. The action potential thus appears to "jump" from node to node, as opposed to traversing the entire axon in one continuous movement, speeding the transmission of the signal. The speed of the action potential in an unmyelinated axon is approximately 1.1 to 4.5 miles per hour (mph), and a myelinated axon has transmission speeds of approximately 157 to 268 mph (Susuki, 2010). Unmyelinated axons, or those damaged from multiple sclerosis or other diseases, have slower transmission speeds, because the signal must make its way down the entire length of the axon. The damaged myelination caused by multiple sclerosis can lead to many symptoms, including fatigue, trouble with vision, and cognitive disabilities (Su, Banker, Bourdette, & Forte, 2009).

LO 3   Illustrate how neurons communicate with each other.

COMMUNICATION BETWEEN   Neurons communicate with each other via chemicals called **neurotransmitters.** (Infographic 2.2 on page 59 demonstrates communication of neurotransmitters in detail.) An action potential moves down the axon, eventually reaching the branches of the terminal buds. The signal to release neurotransmitters is the voltage change from the action potential, which results in *vesicles* (small fluid-filled sacs) that contain neurotransmitters attaching to the membrane on the terminal bud. This allows the neurotransmitter to be released into the synaptic gap. The majority of these neurotransmitters drift across the synaptic gap and come into contact with **receptor sites** of the receiving neuron's dendrites. Because there are a variety of neurotransmitters, a variety of receptor sites also exist. Just as it takes the right key to unlock a door, it is necessary for the right neurotransmitter to fit a corresponding receptor site to convey the message.

When the neurotransmitters latch onto the receptors of the dendrites of the receiving neuron, tiny gates in the receiving cell's membrane fly open, ushering positively charged particles into the cell and thus restarting the cycle of the action potential (if the threshold is met). Keep in mind that the firing of one neuron contributes to the potential for neighboring neurons to fire as a result of its chemical message.

REUPTAKE   When neurotransmitters are released into the synapse, many of them bind to receptors. Neurotransmitters can be reabsorbed by the sending terminal bud in a process known as **reuptake.** Those that are not reabsorbed drift out of the synaptic gap, through diffusion. This is how the synaptic gap is cleared of neurotransmitters, in preparation for the next release of a new batch of chemical messengers.

So Fast
Action potentials may travel as fast as 268 miles per hour through a myelinated axon (Susuki, 2010). Myelin is a protein that envelops and insulates the axon, facilitating faster transmission of the impulse. The action potential "skips" over the segments of myelin, hopping from one node of Ranvier to the next (see small space in the center), instead of traversing the entire length of the axon. Jean-Claude Revy, ISM/Phototake

The Synapse
The axon terminal of a sending neuron interacts with the dendrites of a receiving neuron by releasing chemical messengers (neurotransmitters) into the synapse. Once the neurotransmitters migrate across the gap and latch onto the dendrite's receptor sites, the message has been conveyed. Carol and Mike Werner/ Science Source

Major League Players: Neurotransmitters

···► **LO 4**   Summarize various neurotransmitters and the roles they play in human behavior.

As we have already mentioned, there are different types of neurotransmitters. Researchers have identified approximately 100 of them, with many more yet to be discovered. We already know that neurotransmitters secreted by one neuron under certain conditions can cause neighboring neurons to fire. Now let's turn to how different neurotransmitters influence us in a variety of ways. The secretion of neurotransmitters can lead to a neuron firing, which can effect the regulation of mood, appetite, muscles, organs, arousal, and a variety of other outcomes. By examining what happens when neurotransmitters are not at their ideal levels, we can understand their effect at normal levels. We will describe only a handful of neurotransmitters, starting with the first neurotransmitter discovered, *acetylcholine.*

ACETYLCHOLINE   Acetylcholine is a neurotransmitter that relays messages from motor neurons (see page 62) to muscles, enabling movement. Any time you move some part of your body, whether dancing your fingers across a keypad or bouncing your head to one of your favorite songs, you have, in part, acetylcholine to thank for this. Too much acetylcholine leads to muscle spasms; too little causes paralysis. Acetylcholine is also known to be involved in memory. In particular, low levels of acetylcholine in the brain have been linked to Alzheimer's disease (Kihara & Shimohama, 2004), which can lead to problems with memory, language, and thinking.

GLUTAMATE AND GABA   Much of the transmission of information involves two neurotransmitters: *glutamate* and *GABA* (short for gamma-aminobutyric acid). Glutamate is an excitatory neurotransmitter, so its main job is to kick neurons into action (make them fire), whereas GABA is inhibitory (it puts the brakes on firing). Glutamate plays a central role in learning and memory (Riedel, Platt, & Micheau, 2003); its overactivity may be associated with strokes (Castellanos et al., 2008); and its underactivity is theorized to be involved in some of the symptoms of schizophrenia (Gordon, 2010).

NOREPINEPHRINE   *Norepinephrine* has a variety of effects in the nervous system, but one of its most important functions is to help prepare the body for stressful situations. Think about how Brandon was surrounded by gunfire on every side while serving in Fallujah. Norepinephrine was working to enable Brandon's nervous system to initiate action. In the brain, norepinephrine is involved in regulating arousal and sleep (Jones, 2003).

SEROTONIN   Serotonin is a neurotransmitter that plays a key role in controlling appetite, aggression, and mood, and also regulates sleep and breathing. Abnormally low serotonin activity is thought to drive depression. Many of the popular antidepressants called serotonin reuptake inhibitors (SSRIs), including Prozac and Zoloft, work to boost the effects of this "feel good" neurotransmitter (Chapter 14). Normally, neurotransmitters that do not connect with receptor sites can be reabsorbed by the sending terminal bud in the reuptake process. SSRIs work to prevent the reabsorption of serotonin back into the sending neuron. The longer the neurotransmitters (in this case, serotonin) are available in the gap, the more time they have to attach to a receptor.

DOPAMINE   The neurotransmitter *dopamine* is known to play a role in problems with drug use. Repeated use of drugs overstimulates and damages the functioning of the neurons in the brain's reward circuit, theoretically making it more difficult to enjoy non-drug-related activities that would otherwise be rewarding. Dopamine also plays a key role in learning through reinforcement, attention, and regulating body movements. Deterioration of neurons that produce dopamine is linked to Parkinson's

Synonyms
norepinephrine noradrenaline

Communication Between Neurons

Messages travel within a neuron using electrical currents. But communication *between* neurons depends on the movement of chemicals—neurotransmitters. Though they all work in the same way, there are many different types of neurotransmitters, each linked to unique effects on behavior. However, drugs and other substances, known as *agonists* and *antagonists,* can alter this process of communication between neurons by boosting or blocking normal neurotransmitter activity.

NORMAL NEUROTRANSMISSION

1 Action potential reaches terminal buds.

2 Action potential triggers vesicles to release neurotransmitters into synaptic gap.

Sending neuron

Neurotransmitters

Synaptic gap

Receptor sites

Receiving neuron

Excess neurotransmitter being reabsorbed by the sending neuron

3 Neurotransmitters bind to their matching receptor sites on receiving neuron's dendrite, causing positively charged particles to enter cell. Action potential is created.

4 After binding, neurotransmitters are reabsorbed or diffuse out of synaptic gap.

BOOST

BLOCK

Drugs and other substances can alter normal neurotransmission.

AGONIST

Agonists boost normal neurotransmitter activity. Nicotine mimics acetylcholine and causes this same activation. More receptors are activated, and more messages are sent.

Agonists

ANTAGONIST

Antagonists block normal neurotransmitter activity. Curare, the paralyzing poison used on blowgun darts, acts as an acetylcholine antagonist. It blocks acetylcholine receptors, preventing the neurotransmitter from activating them, so fewer messages are sent.

Antagonists

disease, an incurable disorder that causes trembling of the hands, arms, legs, and face, and difficulty with movement, coordination, and balance.

ENDORPHINS   *Endorphins* are a group of naturally produced opioids (Chapter 4) that regulate the secretion of other neurotransmitters. The term endorphin is derived from the words "endogenous," meaning it is created within, and "morphine." With brisk exercise the production of endorphins is increased. This reduces the experience of pain and elevates mood. Endorphins are released in response to pain, thereby blocking pain receptor sites to prevent the pain message from being sent.

AGONISTS AND ANTAGONISTS   Drugs and other substances influence behavior by interfering at the level of the synapse (Chapters 4 and 14). Certain substances can be used to act like neurotransmitters and others can be used to block normal neurotransmitter activity. *Agonists* are substances that increase the normal activity of the neurotransmitter (whether it normally sends an excitatory or inhibitory signal) and *antagonists* reduce the activity or block the release of the neurotransmitter (**INFOGRAPHIC 2.2**). For example, some substances, such as nicotine and muscarine (found in poisonous mushrooms), increase the secretion of acetylcholine, causing sweating, pupil constriction, nausea, and respiratory distress. These substances increase the normal activity of acetylcholine; thus, they are agonists. On the other hand, the popular anti-wrinkle treatment Botox is an antagonist because it blocks acetylcholine release, paralyzing the facial muscles so they can no longer wrinkle the overlying skin (Kim, Oh, & Paik, 2006).

istockphoto/Thinkstock

CAFFEINE AND NEUROTRANSMITTERS   Did you jump-start your day with coffee? Or perhaps you sipped a caffe latte, tea, or soda this morning? Caffeine works its magic, perking you up at the crack of dawn or jolting you from that mid-afternoon daze by manipulating the nervous system. One way caffeine works is by blocking the receptors for a neurotransmitter called *adenosine*. (Thus, caffeine's primary role is as an antagonist.) When adenosine latches onto receptors, it slows down their activity (making them less likely to fire), and this tends to make you feel drowsy. Caffeine resembles adenosine enough that it can dock onto the same receptors ("posing" as adenosine), which makes fewer receptors available for adenosine. With caffeine occupying its receptors, adenosine can no longer exert its calming effect on the brain (Julien, Advokat, & Comaty, 2011). The result: More neurons fire and you feel full of energy. But note that continued use of caffeine can lead to anxiety, restlessness, and headaches if you reduce your consumption (Ozsunger, Brenner, & El-Sohemy, 2009; Chapter 4).

The effects of caffeine do not stop at the brain. As anyone who has enjoyed a double latte can testify, caffeine kicks the body into high gear by increasing activity in the branch of the nervous system serving the body (Corti et al., 2002). In the next section, we will examine the nervous system running through your arms, legs, fingers, toes—and everywhere else.

◉✓◯◯   **show what you know**

1. Many axons are surrounded by a _____, which is a fatty substance that insulates the axon.

2. When Brandon was injured, _____ played an important role in his recovery by defending against infection and inflammation of the brain, as well as holding neurons together and maintaining the structure of the nervous system.
   a. glial cells
   b. dendrites
   c. action potentials
   d. sodium ions

3. _____ are released into the _____ when an action potential reaches the branches of the terminal buds.
   a. Sodium ions; synaptic gap
   b. Neurotransmitters; synaptic gap
   c. Potassium ions; cell membrane
   d. Neurotransmitters; sodium gates

4. Neural communication is very complicated. Draw a diagram depicting the process of neural communication, then explain it to yourself while looking at what you have drawn.

✓ CHECK YOUR ANSWERS IN APPENDIX C.

The Supporting Systems

Like any complex system, the brain needs a supporting infrastructure to carry out its directives and relay essential information from the outside world. Running up and down your spine and branching throughout your body are neurons that provide the connections between brain and body. The **central nervous system (CNS)** is made up of the brain and spinal cord. The **peripheral nervous system (PNS)** includes all the neurons that are not in the central nervous system and is divided into two branches: the *somatic nervous system* and the *autonomic nervous system*. The peripheral nervous system provides the communication pathway between the central nervous system and the rest of the body. Thanks to your *spinal cord* and peripheral nervous system, you can flex your facial muscles into a smirk, feel a soft breeze, and flip through the pages of this book. **FIGURE 2.2** provides an overview of the entire nervous system.

The Spinal Cord and Simple Reflexes

Brandon suffered a devastating brain injury that temporarily immobilized half of his body. The paralysis would have affected his entire body if the bullet had pierced his **spinal cord,** the bundle of neurons that allows communication between the brain and the peripheral nervous system, connecting with the body's muscles, glands, and

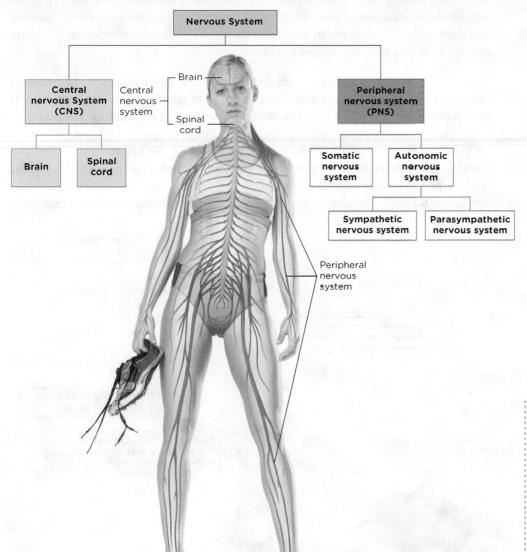

FIGURE 2.2
Overview of the Nervous System
The nervous system is made up of the central nervous system, which includes the brain and spinal cord, and the peripheral nervous system.
moodboard/Alamy

central nervous system (CNS) A major component of the human nervous system that includes the brain and spinal cord.

peripheral nervous system (PNS) The part of the nervous system that connects the central nervous system to the rest of the body.

spinal cord The bundle of neurons that allows communication between the brain and the peripheral nervous system, connecting with the body's muscles, glands, and organs.

organs. The spinal cord has two major responsibilities: (1) receiving information from the body and sending it to the brain; and (2) taking information from the brain and sending it throughout the body. If this pathway is blocked, commands from the brain cannot reach the muscles responsible for making you walk, dance, and wash dishes, and sensory information from the skin and elsewhere has no way of communicating crucial information to the brain, like "Ooh, that burner is hot," or "Oh, this massage feels good."

LO 5   Recognize the connections between the central
and peripheral nervous systems.

How do the brain and spinal cord, which make up the *central nervous system,* communicate with the rest of the body through the *peripheral nervous system*? In essence, there are three types of neurons participating in this back-and-forth communication. **Sensory neurons** receive information about the environment from the sensory systems and convey this information to the brain for processing. **Motor neurons** carry information from the central nervous system to produce movement in various parts of the body, such as muscles and glands. Motor neurons provide a mechanism for performing activities determined or commanded by the spinal cord and brain. **Interneurons,** which reside exclusively in the brain and spinal cord, act as bridges connecting sensory and motor neurons. By assembling and processing sensory input from multiple neurons, interneurons facilitate the nervous system's most complex operations, from solving tough problems to forming life-long memories. They are also involved in a relatively simple operation, the reflex.

THE REFLEX ARC   Some activities don't involve the interneurons in the brain (at least at the start). Consider the withdrawal reaction to painful stimuli (**FIGURE 2.3**). If you accidentally touch a hot pan, you activate a pathway of communication that goes from your sensory neurons through interneurons in your spinal cord and right back out through motor neurons, without initially involving the brain. In the following example, you can see how the pain reflex includes a number of steps: (1) Your hand touches the hot pan, activating sensory receptors, which cause the sensory neurons to carry a signal from your hand to the spinal cord. (2) In the spinal cord, the signal from

FIGURE 2.3

The Spinal Cord and Reflex Arc
Without any input from the brain, the spinal cord neurons are capable of creating some simple reflexive behavior. While the spinal reflex occurs, sensory neurons also send messages to the brain, letting it know what has happened.

(5) Brain receives message.

Spinal cord (section)   to brain

(2) Sensory neurons carry information from environment to interneuron in spinal cord.

(3) Interneuron in spinal cord activates motor neuron.

(4) Motor neuron exits spinal cord and excites muscle, initiating motion that pulls hand away.

(1) Heat activates sensory neurons.

the sensory neurons is received by interneurons. (3) The interneurons quickly activate motor neurons and instruct them to respond. (4) The motor neurons then instruct your muscles to contract, causing your hand to withdraw quickly. A sensory neuron has a rendezvous with an interneuron, which then commands a motor neuron in the spinal cord to react—no brain required. We refer to this process, in which a stimulus causes an involuntary response, as a **reflex arc.**

Eventually, your brain does process the event; otherwise, you would have no clue it ever happened. However, you become consciously aware of your reaction *after* it has occurred (*my hand just pulled back; that pan was hot!*). Although many sensory and motor neurons are involved in this reaction, it happens very quickly, hopefully in time to reduce damage or injury in cases when the reflex arc involves pain. Think about touching a flame or something sharp. You want to be able to respond, without waiting for information to get to the brain or for the brain to send a message to the motor neurons instructing the muscles to react.

Test your knowledge of the reflex arc using Brandon as an example. As you recall, Brandon's brain injury led to paralysis on the right side of his body. What do you think would happen if a doctor tapped on his right knee—would he experience a reflex?

try this

Check your answers in Appendix C.

What Lies Beyond: The Peripheral Nervous System

It is now time to look more specifically at how the peripheral nervous system is organized and how it allows for communication between the central nervous system and the rest of the body.

LO 6   Describe the organization and function of the peripheral nervous system.

The peripheral nervous system includes all the neurons that are not in the central nervous system. These neurons are bundled together and act like electrical cables carrying signals from place to place. The collections of neurons are called **nerves.** Nerves are the primary mechanism for communication of information by the peripheral nervous system, supplying the central nervous system with information about the body's environment—both the exterior (for example, sights, sounds, and tastes) and the interior (for example, heart rate, blood pressure, and temperature). The central nervous system, in turn, makes sense of all this information and then responds by dispatching orders to the muscles, glands, and other tissues through the nerves of the peripheral nervous system. Information flows from the peripheral nervous system (via sensory nerves) into the central nervous system, and then new information is sent back out through the peripheral nervous system (via motor nerves). The PNS has two functional branches: the *somatic nervous system* and the *autonomic nervous system.*

THE SOMATIC NERVOUS SYSTEM   The **somatic nervous system** includes sensory nerves and motor nerves. (*Somatic* means "related to the body.") The sensory nerves gather information from sensory receptors, sending it to the central nervous system. The motor nerves receive information from the central nervous system and send this information to the muscles, instructing them to initiate *voluntary* muscle activity (which results in movement). The somatic nervous system controls the skeletal muscles that give rise to voluntary movements, like using your arms and legs. It also receives sensory information from the skin and other tissues, providing the brain with constant feedback about temperature, pressure, pain, and other stimuli.

Synonyms

sensory neurons afferent neurons

motor neurons efferent neurons

interneurons association neurons, relay neurons

sensory neurons Neurons specialized for receiving information about the environment from the sensory systems and transmitting this information to the brain for further processing.

motor neurons Neurons specialized for transmitting information from the central nervous system to other parts of the body, such as muscles and glands.

interneurons A type of neuron that resides exclusively in the brain and spinal cord; acts as a bridge connecting sensory and motor neurons.

reflex arc An automatic response to a sensory stimulus, such as the "knee jerk" reaction; a simple pathway of communication from sensory neurons through interneurons in the spinal cord back out through motor neurons.

nerves Bundles of neurons that carry information to and from the central nervous system; provide communication between the central nervous system and the muscles, glands, and sensory receptors.

somatic nervous system The branch of the peripheral nervous system that includes sensory nerves and motor nerves; gathers information from sensory receptors and controls the skeletal muscles responsible for voluntary movement.

FIGURE 2.4 ▶
The Sympathetic and Parasympathetic Nervous Systems
The autonomic nervous system has two divisions, the sympathetic and parasympathetic nervous systems. In a stressful situation, the sympathetic nervous system initiates the "fight-or-flight" response. The parasympathetic nervous system calms the body when the stressful situation has passed.
PhotoObjects.net/Thinkstock

Sympathetic

Dilates pupils (improves vision)

Increases respiration

Increases heart rate

Slows digestion (energy diverted to muscles)

Increases blood flow to muscles

Parasympathetic

Constricts pupils

Decreases respiration

Lowers heart rate

Activates digestive processes

autonomic nervous system
(ȯ-tə-ˈnä-mik) The branch of the peripheral nervous system that controls involuntary processes within the body, such as contractions in the digestive tract, and activity of glands.

sympathetic nervous system
The division of the autonomic nervous system that mobilizes the "fight-or-flight" response to stressful or crisis situations.

parasympathetic nervous system
The division of the autonomic nervous system that orchestrates the "rest-and-digest" response to bring the body back to a noncrisis mode.

THE AUTONOMIC NERVOUS SYSTEM   Meanwhile, the **autonomic nervous system** (ȯ-tə-ˈnä-mik) is working behind the scenes, regulating *involuntary* activity, such as the pumping of the heart, the expansion and contraction of blood vessels, and digestion. Most of the activities supervised by the somatic nervous system are voluntary (within your conscious control and awareness), whereas processes under the control of the autonomic nervous system tend to be involuntary (automatic) and outside of your awareness. Just remember: Autonomic controls the automatic. But this is not a hard-and-fast rule. The knee-jerk reflex, for instance, is managed by the somatic, or "voluntary," system even though it is an involuntary response.

The autonomic nervous system has two divisions involved in our physiological responses to stressful or crisis situations (**FIGURE 2.4**). The **sympathetic nervous system** initiates what is often referred to as the "fight-or-flight" response, which is how the body prepares to deal with a crisis. When faced with a stressful situation, the sympathetic nervous system prepares the body for action, by increasing heart rate and respiration, slowing digestion and other bodily functions. Earlier, we mentioned that caffeine makes you feel physically energized. This is because it activates the fight-or-flight system (Corti et al., 2002).

The **parasympathetic nervous system,** on the other hand, oversees the "rest-and-digest" process, which basically works to bring the body back to a noncrisis mode. The parasympathetic nervous system takes over when the crisis has ended by reversing the activity of these processes (for example, lowering heart rate and respiration, increasing digestion and other maintenance activities). The two systems work together, balancing the activities of these primarily involuntary processes. Sometimes they even work toward a common goal. For example, parasympathetic stimulation increases blood flow to the penis to create an erection, but it is the sympathetic system that causes ejaculation (Goldstein, 2000). Working together, these two systems allow us to fight if we need to, flee when necessary, and calm down when danger has passed.

The fight-or-flight response would certainly come in handy if fleeing predators was part of your day-to-day life (as it may have been for our primitive ancestors), but you probably are not chased by wild animals very often. You may, however, notice your heart racing and your breathing rate increase during other types of anxiety-producing situations—going on a first date, taking a test, or speaking in front of an audience. You have your sympathetic nervous system to thank for these effects (Chapter 12).

TEND AND BEFRIEND   Fighting and running like mad are not the only ways we respond to stress. Many women have an inclination to "tend and befriend" in response to a threat, or direct energy toward nurturing offspring and forging social bonds (Taylor et al., 2000). The tend-and-befriend response is also evident in men, especially in high-pressure situations. In one small study, men placed in a stressful situation were more likely to show increased trust of others; those others, in turn, were more likely to feel that these men were trustworthy. The trusting men were also more willing to share resources than were those who were not subjected to stress (von Dawans, Fischbacher, Kirschbaum, Fehr, & Heinrichs, 2012). Brandon likely experienced this increase of trust while serving in Iraq with his fellow soldiers.

Women are generally more likely to "tend and befriend," but are there other gender disparities related to the nervous system? Many of us believe males and females are "hardwired" differently or socially conditioned to develop certain tendencies. Let's take a look at some of the evidence.

THINK again

Male Brain, Female Brain

It is a well-known fact that the numbers of women employed in certain fields, such as science, math, engineering, and technology, continue to be low (Blickenstaff, 2005; FIGURE 2.5 on page 66). Does society encourage boys to pursue science and technology interests while pushing girls into the social sciences and humanities? There is no denying that social and cultural factors influence female achievement in math and science. Studies suggest, for example, that gender stereotypes, which are commonly held beliefs about the nature of men and women, can influence performance in math and science. When exposed to statements such as "women possess poor math ability" just before taking a test, some women will actually perform at a lower level (Josephs, Newman, Brown, & Beer, 2003; Chapter 15).

SCIENCE AND THE SEXES

But there might also be something biological at play. Research shows that male and female brains are far more alike than they are different, but some intriguing differences exist, both in terms of anatomy and function. An fMRI study by Goldstein and colleagues (2001) found that certain regions of the limbic cortex and the frontal lobes were larger in women, while areas of the parietal cortex, the amygdala, and hypothalamus were larger in men. How these differences translate into behavior is not totally clear, but we know, for example, these regions are involved in spatial reasoning, memory, and emotion (Cahill, 2012). It appears that both **nature and nurture** are responsible for the gender imbalance in math and the sciences. While women are statistically underrepresented in math and science, their presence in these fields has grown dramatically over the past 50 years, a clear sign of positive change. For more on gender differences, see Chapter 10.

CONNECTIONS

In **Chapter 1,** we presented the nature–nurture issue and its importance in the field of psychology. Here, we can see this issue in relation to the gender imbalance in math and science. Researchers continue to evaluate the relative influence of nature and nurture in the development of academic and career goals.

All Fields

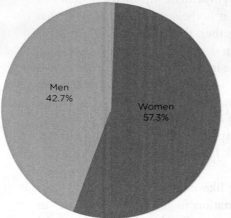

Men
42.7%

Women
57.3%

STEM Fields

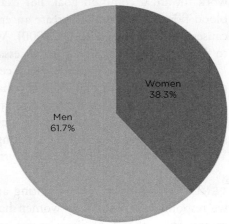

Women
38.3%

Men
61.7%

······· ➤

FIGURE 2.5

Bachelor's Degrees Awarded in the United States

Women earn the majority (57.3%) of all bachelor's degrees awarded in the United States. But when it comes to degrees awarded in science, math, and engineering (STEM), the numbers look very different (National Science Foundation, 2011). Why do so many fewer women receive degrees in STEM fields?

The Endocrine System and Its Slowpoke Messengers

Imagine that you are 19-year-old Brandon Burns fighting in the battle of Fallujah. How would it feel to be immersed in one of the bloodiest battles of the Iraq War? The sound of gunfire rings through the air. Bullets zip past your helmet. People are dying around you. Your life could end at any moment. Unless you have been in a similar situation, it would be difficult to fathom how it feels. But one thing seems certain: You would feel extremely stressed.

When faced with imminent danger, the sympathetic nervous system responds almost instantaneously. Activity in the brain triggers the release of neurotransmitters that cause increases in heart rate, breathing rate, and metabolism—changes that will come in handy if you need to defend yourself or flee the situation. But the nervous system does not act alone. The endocrine system is also hard at work, releasing stress hormones, such as cortisol, which prompt similar physiological changes.

···➤ **LO 7**   Evaluate the role of the endocrine system and how it influences behavior.

The **endocrine system** (en-də-krən) is a communication system that uses glands, rather than neurons, to convey messages (**FIGURE 2.6**). These messages are delivered by **hormones,** chemicals released into the bloodstream that can cause aggression and mood swings, as well as influence growth, alertness, cognition, and appetite. Like neurotransmitters, hormones are chemical messengers that can influence many processes and behaviors. In fact, some chemicals, such as norepinephrine, can act as both neurotransmitters and hormones depending on where they are released. Neurotransmitters are unloaded into the synapse, whereas hormones are secreted into the bloodstream by glands stationed around the body. These glands collectively belong to the endocrine system.

Following an action potential, neurotransmitters are released into the synaptic gap and their effects can be almost instant. Hormones usually make long voyages to faraway targets by way of the bloodstream, creating a relatively delayed but usually longer-lasting impact. A neural impulse can travel over 250 mph, which means signals arrive at their destinations within fractions of a second, much faster than messages sent via hormones, which take minutes (if not longer) to arrive where they are going. Although not as fast as neurotransmitters, the messages sent via hormones are more widely spread because they are disseminated through the bloodstream.

If the endocrine system had a chief executive officer, it would be the **pituitary gland,** a gland about the size of a pencil eraser located in the center of the brain, just

endocrine system (en-də-krən) The communication system that uses glands to convey messages by releasing hormones into the bloodstream.

hormones Chemical messengers released into the bloodstream that influence mood, cognition, appetite, and many other processes and behaviors.

pituitary gland The pea-sized gland located in the center of the brain just under the hypothalamus; secretes hormones that dictate the release of hormones by other glands; known as the master gland.

thyroid gland Gland of the endocrine system that regulates the rate of metabolism by secreting thyroxin.

adrenal glands (ə-drē-nəl) Part of the endocrine system involved in responses to stress as well as the regulation of salt balance.

FIGURE 2.6
The Endocrine System
This system of glands communicates
within the body by secreting hormones
directly into the bloodstream. left: (face)
Hemera/Thinkstock, (body) Yuri Arcurs; right:
Asiaselects/Getty Images

Labels on figure: Pineal gland, Hypothalamus, Pituitary gland, Thyroid gland, Adrenal gland, Pancreas, Ovaries, Testes

under the *hypothalamus* (a structure of the brain we will return to later). Controlled by the hypothalamus, the pituitary gland influences all the other glands, as well as promoting growth through the secretion of hormones. The **thyroid gland** regulates the rate of metabolism by secreting *thyroxin,* and the **adrenal glands** (ə-drē-nəl) are involved in responses to stress as well as the regulation of salt balance.

Other endocrine glands and organs directed by the pituitary include the pineal gland, which secretes melatonin (controls sleep–wake cycles); the pancreas, which secretes insulin (regulates blood sugar); and the ovaries and testes, whose secretion of sex hormones is one reason that men and women are different. Together, these glands and organs influence a variety of processes and behaviors: (1) growth and sex characteristics, (2) regulation of some of the basic body processes, and (3) responses to emergencies. Just as our behaviors are influenced by neurotransmitters we can't see and action potentials we can't feel, the hormones secreted by the endocrine system are also hard at work behind the scenes.

Now that we have discovered how information moves through the body via electrical and chemical signals, let's turn our attention toward the part of the nervous system that integrates this activity, creating a unified and meaningful experience. Let's explore the brain.

✓○○○   show what you know

1. _____ carry information from the central nervous system to activate various parts of the body, such as muscles and glands.
   a. Interneurons
   b. Dendrites
   c. Sensory neurons
   d. Motor neurons

2. When a stimulus causes an involuntary response, we refer to it as a reflex arc; the simple communication pathway goes from a sensory neuron through interneurons in the _____ and back out through motor neurons.
   a. brain
   b. spinal cord
   c. axon hillock
   d. nodes of Ranvier

3. The _____ gland, located in the center of the brain, just under the hypothalamus, is in charge of the endocrine system.

4. When confronted with a potentially threatening situation, the sympathetic nervous system sometimes prepares for "fight or flight" and/or "tend and befriend." How would you explain these two very different responses using the evolutionary perspective?

✓ CHECK YOUR ANSWERS IN APPENDIX C.

The Hemispheres

THE GIRL WITH HALF A BRAIN   As Brandon Burns began his long journey to recovery, a 17-year-old girl in Bristol, Pennsylvania, was enjoying a particularly successful senior year of high school. Christina Santhouse was an honor roll student for the fourth year in a row, and she had been named captain of the varsity bowling team. But these accomplishments did not come so easily. It took Christina twice as much time as classmates to do homework assignments and projects because her brain needed extra time to process information. She had to invent a new bowling technique to use in games because the left side of her body was partially paralyzed, and she was constantly aware of being "different" from the other kids at school. Christina wasn't simply *different* from her classmates, however. She was *extraordinary* because she managed to do everything her classmates did (and more) with nearly half of her brain missing.

Christina's remarkable story began when she was 7 years old. She was a vibrant, healthy child who loved soccer and playing outside with her friends. Barring an occasional ear infection, she basically never got sick—that is, until the day she suffered her first seizure. It was the summer of 1995 and Christina's family was vacationing on the Jersey Shore. While playing in a swimming pool with her cousins, Christina hopped onto the deck to chase a ball. At that moment, she noticed that something wasn't quite right. She looked down and saw her left ankle twitching uncontrollably. Her life was about to change dramatically.

Christina continued to experience tremors in her ankle. As the days and weeks wore on, those tremors moved up her left side and eventually spread throughout her body. In time, she was having seizures every 3 to 5 minutes. Christina was evaluated by various doctors, who suspected she had Rasmussen's encephalitis, a rare disease that causes severe swelling in one side of the brain, impairing movement and thinking and causing seizures that come as often as every few minutes (National Institute of Neurological Disorders and Stroke, 2011b). As one doctor put it, "The disease eats away at your brain like a Pac-Man."

Christina and her mother decided to seek treatment at The Johns Hopkins Hospital in Baltimore, the premiere center for children with seizure disorders. They met with Dr. John Freeman, a pediatric neurologist and an expert in *hemispherectomy*, a surgery to remove nearly half of the brain. A rare and last-resort operation, the hemispherectomy is only performed on patients suffering from severe seizures that can't be controlled in other ways. After examining Christina, Dr. Freeman made the same diagnosis of her condition—Rasmussen's encephalitis—and indicated that the seizures would get worse, and they would get worse fast. He recommended a hemispherectomy and told Christina (and her mother) to let him know when she had reached her limit with the seizures. Then they would go ahead with the operation.

Why did Dr. Freeman recommend this drastic surgery to remove nearly half of Christina's brain? And what side of the brain did he suggest removing? Before addressing these important questions, we need to develop a general sense of the brain's geography.

► Staying Strong
Christina Santhouse relaxes with her mother at Johns Hopkins, where she had a dramatic brain surgery known as a hemispherectomy. Prior to the operation, Christina experienced over 100 seizures a day. William Johnson

Christina, in Her Own Words:
http://qrs.ly/uy3jpbp

cerebrum The largest part of the brain, includes virtually all parts of the brain except primitive brain structures; has two distinct hemispheres.

split-brain operation A rare procedure used to disconnect the right and left hemispheres by cutting the corpus callosum.

corpus callosum (kȯr-pəs ka-lō-səm) The thick band of nerve fibers connecting the right and left cerebral hemispheres; principal structure for information shared between the two hemispheres.

Right Brain, Left Brain: The Two Hemispheres

► LO 8   Describe the functions of the two brain hemispheres and how they communicate.

If you look at a photo or an illustration of the brain, you will see a walnut-shaped wrinkled structure—this is the **cerebrum** (Latin for "brain"), the largest and most conspicuous part of the brain. The cerebrum includes virtually all parts of the brain except the brainstem structures, which you will learn about later. Like a pecan or walnut, the cerebrum has two distinct halves, or *hemispheres*. Looking at the brain from above, you can see a deep groove running from the front of the head to the back, dividing it into the right cerebral hemisphere and the left cerebral hemisphere. Although the hemispheres look like mirror images of one another, with similar structures on the left and right, they do not have identical jobs nor are they perfectly symmetrical. Generally speaking, the right hemisphere controls the left side of the body, and the left hemisphere controls the right. This explains why Brandon, who was shot on the left side of his head, suffered paralysis and loss of sensation on the *right* half of his body. Christina's situation is roughly the opposite. Rasmussen's encephalitis struck the *right* side of her brain, which explains why her *left* ankle started twitching at the pool and why all of her subsequent seizures affected the left side of her body. Thus, it might come as no surprise that Dr. Freeman recommended the removal of the right hemisphere of her brain.

Two Hemispheres
The cerebrum looks like a walnut with its two wrinkled halves. Regions of the left and right hemispheres specialize in different activities, but the two sides of the brain are constantly communicating and collaborating. Science Source/Photo Researchers, Inc. Colorization by: Eric Cohen

CHRISTINA MAKES THE DECISION Within 2 months, Christina's seizures were occurring every 3 minutes, hundreds of times a day. She was unable to play soccer or go outside during school recess, and she sat on a beanbag chair in class so she wouldn't hurt herself when overcome with a seizure. "I couldn't do anything anymore," Christina says. "I wasn't enjoying my life." In February 1996 the doctors at Johns Hopkins removed the right hemisphere of Christina's brain. The operation lasted some 14 hours.

When Christina emerged from the marathon surgery, her head was pounding with pain. "I remember screaming and asking for medicine," she recalls. The migraines persisted for months but eventually tapered off, and ultimately the surgery served its purpose: Christina no longer experienced debilitating seizures.

Pre-Op
Christina is wheeled into the operating room for her 14-hour hemispherectomy. She had a seizure in the elevator on the way to the surgery. William Johnson

Split Brain

LO 9 Explain lateralization and how split-brain operations affect it.

Removing nearly half of a brain may sound barbaric, but hemispherectomies have proven to be effective for eliminating and reducing seizures. In a study of the 111 children who had hemispherectomies at Johns Hopkins between 1975 and 2001, 65% no longer suffered seizures at all, and 21% experienced infrequent, "nonhandicapping" seizures. The remaining 14% still had seizures described as "troublesome" (Kossoff et al., 2003).

Hemispherectomies are exceptionally rare, used only when seizures occur many times a day, cannot be tempered with drugs, and stem from problems in one hemisphere (Choi, 2007, May 24). A less extreme, last-resort surgery for drug-resistant seizures is the **split-brain operation,** which essentially disconnects the right and left hemispheres. Normally, the two hemispheres are linked by a bundle of nerve fibers known as the **corpus callosum** (kȯr-pəs ka-lō-səm). Through the corpus callosum, the left and right sides of the brain communicate and work together to process information. But this same band of nerve fibers can also serve as a passageway for the electrical storms responsible for seizures. With the split-brain operation, the corpus callosum is severed so that these storms can no longer pass freely between the hemispheres (Wolman, 2012, March 15).

SPECIALIZATION AND THE SPLIT-BRAIN OPERATION In addition to helping many patients with severe, drug-resistant epilepsy (Abou-Khalil, 2010), the consequences of split-brain operations have provided researchers with an excellent opportunity to explore the *specialization* of the hemispheres. Before we start to look at

Synonyms
split-brain operation callosotomy

Hemispherectomy
On the left is an MRI scan of a brain with both hemispheres intact. The scan on the right shows the brain of a person who has undergone a hemispherectomy. The green area, once occupied by the removed hemisphere, is now filled with cerebrospinal fluid.
left: Medical Body Scans/Science Source.
Colorization by Matthew Bologna; right: Medical Body Scans/Science Source

this research, you need to understand how visual information is processed. Each eye receives visual sensations, but that information is sent to the opposite hemisphere, and shared between the hemispheres via the corpus callosum (Chapter 3). Specifically, information presented in the right visual field is processed in the left hemisphere, and information presented in the left visual field is processed in the right hemisphere.

Equipped with this knowledge, American neuropsychologist Roger Sperry (1913–1994) and his student Michael Gazzaniga (1939–) conducted groundbreaking research on epilepsy patients who had undergone split-brain operations to alleviate their seizures. (This research ultimately led to Sperry's 1981 Nobel Prize in Physiology or Medicine.) Not only did Sperry and Gazzaniga's "split-brain" participants experience fewer seizures, they had surprisingly normal cognitive abilities and showed no obvious changes in "temperament, personality, or general intelligence" as a result of their surgeries (Gazzaniga, 1967, p. 24). But under certain circumstances, the researchers observed, they behaved as though they had two separate brains (Gazzaniga, 1967, 1998; **FIGURE 2.7**). Because the hemispheres were disconnected, the researchers could study each hemisphere separately to explore its own unique capabilities (or "specializations").

FIGURE 2.7
The Split-Brain Experiment
The image to the right shows a top view of the corpus callosum, the bundle of neurons linking the right and left hemispheres. When the corpus callosum is severed, we can easily see functional differences between the two sides of the brain. Studies of people who have undergone this procedure are known as "split-brain" experiments. An example of this type of experiment is shown here. Terence H. Williams, Nedzad Gluhbegovic/Wolters Kluwer

Touch the object matching the image on the screen.

I see an apple.

I don't see anything.

Information presented to right visual field is processed in left hemisphere where language processing occurs. Subject can speak the answer.

Information presented to left visual field is processed in right hemisphere. Subject can't use language to say what he was shown.

The subject can touch the correct object even if he can't say what has been projected in his left visual field. The subject uses his left hand, which is controlled by the right hemisphere, where the visual information has been processed.

Imagine that the researchers flashed an image (let's say an apple) on the right side of a screen, ensuring that it would be processed by the brain's left hemisphere. The split-brain participant could articulate what she had seen (*I saw an apple*). If, however, the apple appeared on the left side of the screen (processed by the *right* hemisphere), she would claim she saw nothing. But when asked to identify the image in a nonverbal way (pointing or touching with her left hand), she could do this without a problem (Gazzaniga, 1967, 1998). These findings are extremely useful in understanding the capabilities of the left and right hemispheres.

LATERALIZATION   The split-brain experiments offered an elegant demonstration of **lateralization,** the tendency for the left and right hemispheres to excel in certain activities. When images are flashed in the right visual field, the information is sent to the left side of the brain, which excels in language processing. This explains why the split-brain participants were able to articulate the image they had seen on the right side of the screen. Images appearing in the left visual field are sent to the right side of the brain, which is generally not responsible for processing language but instead excels at visual spatial tasks. This is why the participants were tongue tied when asked to report what they had seen on the left side of the screen. They could, however, reach out and point to it. What hand do you think they used? The image was flashed in the left visual field and the sensory information was sent to the right hemisphere, which is unable to put into words what was seen. The left hand, which is controlled by the right hemisphere, pointed to the object (Gazzaniga, 1998; Gazzaniga, Bogen, & Sperry, 1965). The bottom line: The left hemisphere plays a crucial role in language processing and the right hemisphere plays a crucial role in managing visual spatial tasks.

This is only a generalization, however. While there are clear differences in the way the hemispheres process information (and the speed at which they do it), they can also process the same types of information. In a split-brain patient, communication between the hemispheres is limited. This is *not* the case for someone with an intact corpus callosum. Regardless of the type of information coming in or being processed, our hemispheres are constantly integrating and sharing information (Lilienfeld, Lynn, Ruscio, & Beyerstein, 2011). Next time you hear someone claim that some people are more "left-brained" or "right-brained," ask him to identify the research that backs up such a claim. Similarly, beware of catchy sales pitches for products designed to increase your "logical and analytical" left-brain thinking or to help you tap into the "creative" side of your right brain. This way of thinking is oversimplified.

Keep this in mind while reading the upcoming sections on specialization in the left and right sides of the brain. The two hemispheres may each have certain areas of expertise, but they work as a team to create your experience of the world.

Language and the Left

Armed with this new knowledge of the split-brain experiments, let's return our focus to Brandon. Brandon's injury occurred on the left side of his brain, devastating his ability to use language. Before the battle of Fallujah, he had breezed through western novels at breakneck speeds. After his injury, even the simplest sentence baffled him. Words on a page looked like nothing more than black lines and curls. Brandon remembers, "It was like a puzzle that I couldn't figure out."

HANDEDNESS AND LANGUAGE DOMINANCE   Brandon's difficulties with language are fairly typical for someone with a brain injury to the left hemisphere, because regions on the left side of the brain tend to predominate in language. This is not true for everyone, however. In a study examining handedness and language

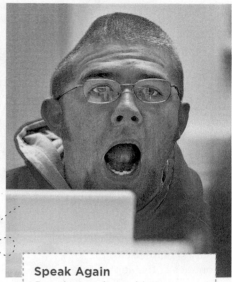

Speak Again
Brandon works on his pronunciation in front of a mirror during a speech therapy session at the Memphis VA hospital. You can see the extent of his injury on the left side of his head. Upon awaking from his coma, Brandon could not articulate a single word. Today, he can hold his own in complex conversations. A.J. Wolfe/The Commercial Appeal

lateralization The idea that each cerebral hemisphere processes certain types of information and excels in certain activities.

dominance, researchers administered a test to participants to determine degree of handedness (righty or lefty) and used brain scan technology to determine their predominant side for language processing. They found that around 27% of strongly left-handed participants and 4% of strongly right-handed participants had language dominance in the *right* hemisphere (Knecht et al., 2000). What does this mean? The left hemisphere controls language in most but not all people, and it doesn't necessarily correspond to right- or left-handedness.

> **LO 10** Identify areas in the brain responsible for language production and comprehension.

BROCA'S AREA Evidence for the "language on the left" trend appeared as early as 1861, when a French surgeon by the name of Pierre Paul Broca (1824–1880) encountered two patients who had, for all practical purposes, lost the ability to talk. One of the patients could only say the word "tan," and the other had an oral vocabulary of only five words. When Broca later performed autopsies on the men, he found that both had sustained damage to the same area on the side of the left frontal lobe (right around the temple; **FIGURE 2.8**). Over the years, Broca identified several other speech-impaired patients with damage to the same area, a region now called **Broca's area** (brō-kəz) (Greenblatt, Dagi, & Epstein, 1997), which is involved in speech production.

WERNICKE'S AREA Around the same time Broca was doing his research, a German doctor named Karl Wernicke (1848–1905) pinpointed a different place in the left hemisphere that seemed to control speech comprehension. Wernicke noticed that patients suffering damage to a small tract of tissue in the left temporal lobe, now called **Wernicke's area** (ver-nə-kəz), struggled to make sense of what others were saying. Wernicke's area is the brain's headquarters for language comprehension. Broca's and Wernicke's work, along with other early findings, highlighted the left hemisphere's critical role in language. Scientists initially suspected that Broca's area was responsible for speech creation and Wernicke's area for comprehension, but it is now clear the use of language is far more complicated. These areas may perform additional functions, such as processing music and interpreting hand gestures (Koelsch et al., 2002; Xu, Gannon, Emmorey, Smith, & Braun, 2009), and they cooperate with multiple brain regions to allow us to produce and understand language. Furthermore, some speech processing appears to occur in the right hemisphere.

Broca's area

Wernicke's area

▲ **FIGURE 2.8**
Language Areas of the Brain
For most people, the left hemisphere controls language. Broca's area plays a critical role in language production, and Wernicke's area language comprehension.

Broca's area (brō-kəz) An area of the cortex that is critical for speech production.

Wernicke's area (ver-nə-kəz) A region of the cortex that plays a pivotal role in language comprehension.

neuroplasticity The brain's ability to heal, grow new connections, and reorganize in order to adapt to the environment.

The Role of the Right

Research involving two split-brain patients suggests the right hemisphere is more proficient than the left in some visual tasks (Corballis, 2003), such as determining whether two objects are identical as opposed to mirror images of one another (Funnell, Corballis, & Gazzaniga, 1999), or judging if lines are oriented in the same direction (Corballis, Funnell, & Gazzaniga, 2002). Other findings suggest the right hemisphere is crucial for understanding abstract and humorous use of language (Coulson & Van Petten, 2007); somewhat better than the left for following conversations that change topic (Dapretto, Lee, & Caplan, 2005); and important for our ability to recognize faces (Kanwisher, McDermott, & Chun, 1997).

show what you know

1. The left hemisphere excels in language and the right hemisphere excels in visual spatial tasks. This specialization of the two hemispheres is known as:
   a. split-brain.
   b. callosotomy.
   c. hemispherectomy.
   d. lateralization.

2. A man involved in a car accident suffered severe brain trauma. As he recovered, it became clear he was having difficulty producing speech, even though he could understand what people were saying to him. It is very likely he had suffered damage to the left frontal lobe in a part of the brain referred to as:
   a. Wernicke's area.
   b. Broca's area.
   c. the visual field.
   d. the corpus callosum.

3. On rare occasions, medication does not work for people with severe seizures. In those cases, doctors might suggest a procedure known as a _____, which essentially disconnects the right and left hemispheres.

4. The corpus callosum enables information sharing between the two hemispheres. In some cases, surgeons sever the corpus callosum to prevent seizures from spreading between the two hemispheres. How would you explain to a middle school student why this surgical procedure is used and how it is helpful?

✓ CHECK YOUR ANSWERS IN APPENDIX C.

The Amazing Brain

When Christina was wheeled out of surgery, her mother approached, grabbed hold of her right hand, and asked her to squeeze. Christina squeezed, demonstrating that she could understand and respond to language. Remember, she still had her left hemisphere.

Christina may not have lost her language abilities, but losing the right hemisphere did come at a cost. We know that Christina suffers partial paralysis on the left side of her body; this makes sense, because the right hemisphere controls movement and sensation on the left. We also know that it took Christina extra time to do her schoolwork. But if you ask Christina whether she has significant difficulty with any of the "right-brain" tasks described earlier, her answer will be no.

Christina's recovery has been nothing short of astonishing. After the surgery, she went back to school and outperformed many of her classmates. In addition to making the honor roll and leading the bowling team, she managed to get her driver's license (even though some of her doctors said she never would), graduate from high school, and go to college. These accomplishments are the result of Christina's steadfast determination, but also a testament to the brain's amazing ability to heal and regenerate.

Neuroplasticity

--▶ **LO 11** Define neuroplasticity and recognize when it is evident in brains.

The brain undergoes constant alteration in response to experiences and is capable of some degree of physical adaptation and repair. Its ability to heal, grow new connections, and make do with what is available is a characteristic we refer to as **neuroplasticity.** New connections are constantly forming between neurons, and unused ones are fading away. Vast networks of neurons have the ability to reorganize in order to adapt to the environment and an organism's ever-changing needs, a quality particularly evident in the young. After brain injuries, younger children have better outcomes than do adults; their brains show more plasticity (Johnston, 2009).

In one study, researchers **removed the eyes** of newborn opossums and found that brain tissues normally destined to become visual processing centers took a

Brain Games
Christina's dramatic recovery was facilitated by physical, occupational, vision, and speech therapy. "The more therapy," says Christina, "the better chance of recovery." William Johnson

You Asked, Christina Answers
http://qrs.ly/jo3jpcn
What kind of therapy did you have and for how long?

CONNECTIONS

In **Chapter 1,** we described the guidelines psychologists use to ensure the ethical treatment of humans and animals in their studies. In the study described here, the researchers were required to get approval from an ethics board to conduct their study. The board determined the proposed research required the surgery on the baby opossums and that they would be treated humanely.

Cure All?
Because stem cells can differentiate into any type of cell in the body, they have great therapeutic potential. The cells pictured here are derived from a human embryo, but stem cells also reside in various adult tissues such as the brain and bone marrow. Professor Miodrag Stojkovic/Science Source

Baby Beethoven
For millions of Chinese children, learning to play an instrument like the violin or piano begins early. Children with musical training outperform their untrained peers on tests of IQ and language skills. Is this because music lessons make children smarter, or because smart children are more likely to take them? Researchers are still trying to get to the bottom of this conundrum. Lou Linwei/Sinopix

neurogenesis The generation of new neurons in the brain.

stem cells Cells responsible for producing new neurons.

phrenology An early approach to explaining the functions of the brain by trying to link the physical structure of the skull with a variety of characteristics.

developmental turn. Instead, they became areas that specialize in processing other types of sensory stimuli, such as sounds and touch (Karlen, Kahn, & Krubitzer, 2006). The same appears to happen in humans. Brain scans reveal that when visually impaired individuals learn to read Braille early in life, a region of the brain that normally specializes in handling visual information becomes activated, suggesting it is used instead for processing touch sensations (Burton, 2003; Liu et al., 2007).

Remarkably, this plasticity is evident even with the loss of an entire hemisphere. Researchers report that the younger the patient is when she has a hemispherectomy, the better her chances are for recovery. In fact, even with the loss of an entire left hemisphere (the primary location for language processing), speech is less severely impacted (though some impact is inevitable) in young patients. The younger the person undergoing the procedure, the less disability is evident in speech (Choi, 2008).

STEM CELLS Scientists once thought that people were born with all the neurons they would ever have. Brain cells might die, but no new ones would crop up to replace them. Thanks to research beginning in the 1990s, that dismal notion has been turned on its head. In the last few decades, studies with animals and humans have shown that some areas of the brain are constantly generating new neurons, a process known as **neurogenesis,** which might be tied to learning and creating new memories (Eriksson et al., 1998; Gould, Beylin, Tanapat, Reeves, & Shors, 1999; Reynolds & Weiss, 1992).

The cells responsible for churning out these new neurons are known as **stem cells,** and they are quite a hot topic in biomedical research. Scientists hope to harness these little cell factories to repair tissue that has been damaged or destroyed. Imagine that you could use stem cells to bring back all the neurons that Brandon lost from his injury or replace those that Christina lost to surgery. Cultivating new brain tissue is just one potential application of stem cell science. These cellular cure-alls might also be used to alleviate the symptoms of Parkinson's disease, or replenish neurons of the spine, enabling people with spinal cord injuries to regain movement. Both have already been accomplished in mice (Keirstead et al., 2005; Wernig et al., 2008). Although embryonic stem cells can be used for such purposes, some stem cells can be found in tissues of the adult body, such as the brain and bone marrow.

Earlier we explained how neuroplasticity is more evident in young people. So what can we do to promote positive brain changes in our children? Some people think that early exposure to music is a critical factor, but is there evidence to support this belief?

across the WORLD

The Plastic Brains of Our Children

Some 40 million children in China are learning to play the piano. Special piano kindergartens have sprung up across that country, their 4- and 5-year-old pupils studying scales and chords on top of traditional subjects. After school, these children may devote another 2 to 3 hours to piano practice (Lebrecht, 2010, February 1; Trelawny, 2008, June 5). The reason many Chinese parents push the piano so hard? Learning an instrument, they believe, will help their children thrive in school and life (Trelawny, 2008, June 5).

Meanwhile on the other side of the Pacific, American parents are playing classical music to their unborn fetuses and showing "Baby Mozart" DVDs to their babies and toddlers. Many of these moms and dads have been led to believe that early exposure to classical music promotes brain development, and they will do whatever it takes to give their kids a leg up on their peers (Hirsh-Pasek, Golinkoff, & Eyer, 2003).

Some evidence suggests that learning an instrument may indeed have cognitive benefits. Studies show that people with musical training generally score higher on language, auditory, and overall IQ tests than those without such training (Schellenberg, 2011; Schellenberg & Winner, 2011). But such research is correlational; **the link between the variables is not necessarily causal.** Even with a strong correlation or link between playing a musical instrument and increased cognitive abilities, we cannot be sure that one of these variables *causes* changes in the other. The only way to determine a cause-and-effect link is to conduct a study using the experimental method. As for playing Mozart to babies, there is no solid data demonstrating that merely listening to music enhances intelligence (Hirsh-Pasek et al., 2003). Enjoying the dynamic melodies of Mozart stimulates the brain and may improve mood, which can provide temporary cognitive benefits, but the same could be said for a host of other activities (Schellenberg, 2011). 🌐➔

DOES MUSICAL TRAINING MAKE YOU SMARTER?

From Bumps to Brain Scans: We've Come a Long Way

Both Brandon and Christina underwent many brain scans before and after their surgeries, which allowed doctors to get a detailed look inside their heads without lifting a scalpel. But had Brandon and Christina lived in a different era, brain scans would not have been an option.

Before there were technologies to study the brain, people could only speculate about what was going on beneath the skull of a living person. One theory was that bumps on a person's skull could reveal characteristics about him. Judging the topography of a person's head was a core part of **phrenology,** the now discredited brain "science" that achieved enormous popularity at the beginning of the 19th century through its founder Franz Joseph Gall (1757–1828). But **flaws in the theory** behind phrenology were recognized early on. Another early (but more scientific) way of studying the brain was through *ablation*, a technique used by physiologist Pierre Flourens (1794–1867) to determine the functions of different brain regions

CONNECTIONS

In **Chapter 1,** we discussed the problems with assuming a correlation between two variables can demonstrate a causal relationship. In this example, we cannot assume that music playing causes increased cognitive abilities. The direction may be the opposite (increased cognitive abilities leads to more interest in playing music) or some third variable may be involved (higher socioeconomic status linked to both music and better scores on tests).

CONNECTIONS

If phrenology were practiced today, we would consider it a *pseudoscience,* or an activity that resembles science but rests upon false assumptions and is unsubstantiated (see **Chapter 1** to read more on pseudoscience).

All in Your Head
Are you a secretive person? How high is your self-esteem? The answers to these questions lie on the surface of the skull, or so claimed 19th-century phrenologists, such as the one depicted in this 1886 illustration (left). The phrenological map (right) shows the locations of brain "organs" thought to be responsible for various psychological traits. left: ©North Wind Picture Archives/The Image Works; right: Image Asset Management Ltd./SuperStock

(Pearce, 2009). This technique involved destroying parts of the brain of living animals and then determining whether some functioning was lost following this surgery.

These days, scientists no longer try to interpret what's going on inside living brains by running fingers over people's heads. There are now technologies that allow us to sift through the brain's constant buzz of activity, behold its three-dimensional structure, and identify interesting hot spots (**TABLE 2.1**). Nevertheless, one of Gall and Flourens' major contributions was the idea that there might be areas of the brain that have particular functions. In other words, there are locations in the brain that are responsible for specific brain activities: there is a *localization* of function.

Table 2.1 TOOLS FOR STUDYING THE BRAIN

	Function	Use	Limitations
Electroencephalogram (EEG)	Detects electrical energy in the brain and displays information that can be interpreted.	Monitors and studies brain processes, diagnoses brain conditions, and sheds light on the way substances affect brain function.	Records activity happening on the surface of the brain.
Computerized Axial Tomography (CAT scan or CT scan)	X-rays create many cross-sectional images of the brain (or body); similar to bread slices, you can examine the pieces individually.	Spots tumors and brain damage and presents the brain's structural features.	Exposes people to radiation, potentially increasing cancer risk (National Cancer Institute, 2010).
Positron Emission Tomography (PET)	Uses radioactive glucose; scanner sensitive to radioactivity, detects active areas of the brain, which have absorbed the most sugar.	Captures the brain in a variety of activities (e.g., dreaming, hallucinating, or appreciating the scent of a rose).	From injection to scan, PET scans are time-consuming. This procedure can be expensive, and it exposes people to radiation.
Magnetic Resonance Imaging (MRI)	Using radio frequency waves, the MRI produces cross-sectional images (slices) of the brain; detects tumors, bleeding, infections, and the size and shape of various brain structures.	Provides information on the anatomy of the brain.	MRIs produce more detailed images than CTs, but are more time-consuming and expensive.
Functional Magnetic Resonance Imaging (fMRI)	Captures changes in brain activity.	Reveals patterns of blood flow in a particular area of the brain, providing a good indicator of how much oxygen is being used as a result of activity.	Indirectly measures neural activity via blood flow, not necessarily identifying the precise location of cognitive processes.

Technologies to study the brain are continuing to evolve. Summarized here are the most commonly used technologies.

SOURCE: YASMIN ET AL., 2012.

SOCIAL MEDIA and psychology

Facebook in the Brain

One of the main themes of this chapter is specialization, the idea that certain areas of the brain tend to become active during certain tasks. When we say "tasks," we mean just about any activity you can imagine, from riding a bicycle to managing friend networks on Facebook.

The average number of Facebook "friends" is 245, but the friend tally varies significantly from one person to the next, ranging from zero to 5,000, the maximum allowed by Facebook (Ball, 2010, May 28; Tsukayama, 2012, February 3). What does a Facebook friend number reveal about a person—job networking skills, offline popularity, time wasted at work? According to one preliminary study, friend volume may reflect something about the brain of the user.

Using MRI technology, researchers studied the brain structures of a sample of Facebook users. What they discovered was a correlation between the number of Facebook friends and the density of gray matter (the primary tissue of the cerebral cortex) in areas of the brain important for social interaction. One of those regions, the *superior temporal sulcus*, is thought to be important for detecting socially meaningful movements such as hand gestures and eye shifts. Another, known as the *entorhinal cortex,* appears to play a key role in matching faces to names, a critical skill for Facebookers (Kanai, Bahrami, Roylance, & Rees, 2012). As anyone with a few hundred friends can testify, keeping track of all those names and faces can be challenging.

FACEBOOK FRIENDS: A GRAY MATTER.

We should point out that this study is merely correlational. It does not reveal whether the number of friends causes changes in brain structure, or whether the characteristics of brain structures determine the number of friends. Perhaps some other variable is responsible for both. This single study needs replication, but it has generated intriguing questions for researchers to tackle in the future.

LO 12 Compare and contrast tools scientists use to study the brain.

In the past, most of what scientists learned about the brain came from probing the skulls of cadavers and observing the behavior of people suffering from brain damage. But the last century, and particularly the last few decades, has witnessed an explosion of brain research technologies. Such technological advances have made it possible to observe the brain as it makes decisions, sleeps, and even tells lies (Dang-Vu et al., 2008; Hampton & O'Doherty, 2007; Kozel et al., 2009). See Table 2.1 for information on the different types of technologies, their function, uses, and limitations (also see **INFOGRAPHIC 2.3** on the next page). With the technology available today, we can even track the activities of strings of neurons.

from the pages of **SCIENTIFIC AMERICAN**

Electric Surprise

Stimulating brain cells may be trickier than we thought

Scientists and doctors have long used electricity to both study and treat the brain. But a report in the August 27, 2009, issue of *Neuron* indicates that the brain's response to electricity is exceptionally complex. Using a new type of optical imaging, Harvard Medical School researchers observed neurons as they were stimulated by an electrode. Instead of activating a small sphere of surrounding neurons as expected, the electrodes caused sparse strings of neurons to fire across the brain. The finding suggests that brain surgeons and the designers of neural prosthetics have a much smaller margin of error than previously thought—shifting an electrode even slightly could activate an entirely different set of neurons. **Melinda Wenner. Reproduced with permission. Copyright © 2010 Scientific American, a division of Nature America, Inc. All rights reserved.**

Ways to Study the Living Brain

For hundreds of years, scientists interested in the brain were limited to surgical techniques, often on cadavers. Imaging and recording technologies now allow us to investigate the living brain by assessing structure, function, or both. CAT and MRI techniques provide static pictures of brain structures, while functional imaging and recording techniques allow us to see the relationship between brain activity and specific mental functions. Functional techniques can also be used to diagnose injuries and diseases earlier than techniques that look at structure.

New technologies are continually being developed, allowing us to study the brain in ways we couldn't imagine just a few years ago.

Looking at Brain STRUCTURE

COMPUTERIZED AXIAL TOMOGRAPHY — CAT

Using X-rays, a scanner creates multiple cross-sectional images of the brain. Here, we see the brain from the top at the level of the ventricles, which form the butterfly-shaped dark spaces in the center.

MAGNETIC RESONANCE IMAGING — MRI

An MRI machine's powerful magnets create a magnetic field that passes through the brain. A computer analyzes the electromagnetic response, creating cross-sectional images similar to those produced by CAT, but with superior detail.

What's Next?
Making Connections

The intricate pathways of myelinated axons in the brain can't be seen in the imaging techniques above. But new technologies like diffusion spectrum imaging (DSI), which tracks the diffusion of water molecules through brain tissue, are being used to map neural connections. The resulting images show a complex information superhighway, with different colors indicating directions of travel.

Watching Brain FUNCTION

EEG — ELECTROENCEPHALOGRAM

Electrodes placed on the scalp record electrical activity from the cortical area directly below. When the recorded traces are lined up, as in the computer readout seen here, we can see the scope of functional responses across the lobes.

PET — POSITRON EMISSION TOMOGRAPHY

A radioactively labeled substance called a tracer is injected into the bloodstream and tracked while the subject performs a task. A computer then creates 3-D images showing degrees of brain activity. Areas with the most activity appear in red.

fMRI — FUNCTIONAL MAGNETIC RESONANCE IMAGING

The flow of oxygen-rich blood increases to areas of the brain that are active during a task. fMRI uses powerful magnets to track changes in blood-oxygen levels. Like PET, this produces measurements of activity throughout the brain.

Credits: Cat Scan, Southern Illinois University/Science Source; EEG, Science Source; MRI, Living Art Enterprises, LLC/Science Source; Person in MRI, Science Source; PET Scan, National Institute on Aging/Science Source; Syringe, Thinkstock; Horizontal cross-section of brain, Laboratory of Neuro Imaging at UCLA and Martinos Center for Biomedical Imaging at MGH, Consortium of the Human Connectome Project

show what you know

1. Scientists hope that in the future they will be able to discover how we can use stem cells to help people like Brandon and Christina. The goal would be for doctors to induce the process of _____ to restore the lost brain tissue.
   a. ablation
   b. agonists
   c. neurogenesis
   d. lateralization

2. You have been asked to set up an experiment to determine if playing classical music to infants leads to improved cognitive abilities. What would your independent and dependent variables be? How would your experimental and control groups be treated differently?

3. _____ are responsible for creating new neurons.

4. The brain is constantly undergoing alterations in response to experiences and is capable of a certain degree of physical adaptation and repair. This ability is known as:
   a. neuroplasticity
   b. phrenology
   c. ablation
   d. lateralization

✓ CHECK YOUR ANSWERS IN APPENDIX C.

The Cortex: A Peek Beneath the Skull

Imagine you were one of the surgeons performing Christina's hemispherectomy. What exactly would you see when you peeled away the scalp and cut an opening into the skull? Before seeing the brain, you would come upon a layer of three thin membranes, the *meninges,* which envelop and protect the brain and spinal cord. Perhaps you have heard of meningitis, a potentially life-threatening condition in which the meninges become inflamed as a result of an infection. The meninges are bathed in a clear watery substance called cerebrospinal fluid, which offers additional cushioning and helps in the transport of nutrients and waste in and out of the brain and the spinal cord. Once you peeled back the meninges, you would behold the pink cerebrum.

CEREBRAL CORTEX   As Christina's surgeon, your main task would be to remove part of the cerebrum's outermost layer, the **cerebral cortex** (sə-rē-brəl). The cerebral cortex processes information and is the layer of cells surrounding nearly all the brain's structures. You'll remember from our earlier presentation that the cerebrum looks like a wrinkled walnut. This is because the cortex is scrunched up and folded onto itself to fit inside a small space (the skull).

> **LO 13**   Identify the lobes of the cortex and explain their functions.

THE LOBES OF THE BRAIN   The cortex overlaying each hemisphere is separated into different sections, or lobes (**INFOGRAPHIC 2.4** on p. 81). The major function of the **frontal lobes** is to organize information among the other lobes of the brain. The frontal lobes are also responsible for higher-level cognitive functions, such as thinking, perception, and impulse control. The **parietal lobes** (pə-rī-ə-təl) receive and process sensory information such as touch, pressure, temperature, and spatial orientation. Visual information goes to the **occipital lobes** (äk-si-pə-təl) for processing, and hearing and language comprehension are largely handled by the **temporal lobes.** We'll have more to say about the lobes shortly.

> **LO 14**   Recognize the association areas and identify their functions.

THE ASSOCIATION AREAS   In addition to these broad functions of the brain lobes, there are specific functions associated with particular areas of the lobes. Some areas in the lobes are home to networks of neurons that specialize in certain activities. The *motor areas* direct movement, the *sensory areas* receive and analyze sensory stimuli, and the **association areas** integrate information from all over the brain. The association areas are located in all four lobes of the brain; however, they are much harder to pinpoint than are the motor and sensory areas. The association areas allow us to learn (just as you're doing now), have abstract thoughts (for example, 2 + 2 = 4), and carry out complex behaviors like texting and tweeting. The language-processing hubs we learned about earlier, *Broca's area* and *Wernicke's area*, are association areas

Synonyms

association areas intrinsic processing areas

cerebral cortex (sə-rē-brəl) The wrinkled outermost layer of the cerebrum, responsible for higher mental functions, such as decision making, planning, and processing visual information.

frontal lobes The area of the cortex that organizes information among the other lobes of the brain and is responsible for higher-level cognitive functions and behavior.

parietal lobes (pə-rī-ə-təl) The area of the cortex that receives and processes sensory information such as touch, pressure, temperature, and spatial orientation.

occipital lobes (äk-si-pə-təl) The area of the cortex in the back of the head that processes visual information.

temporal lobes The area of the cortex that processes auditory stimuli and language.

association areas Regions of the cortex that integrate information from all over the brain, allowing us to learn, think in abstract terms, and carry out other intellectual tasks.

that play a role in the production and comprehension of speech. In humans, the vast majority of the cortical surface is dedicated to the association areas.

The Lobes: Up Close and Personal

Prior to her hemispherectomy, Christina was extroverted, easygoing, and full of energy. "I had absolutely no worries," she says, recalling her pre-Rasmussen's days. After her operation, Christina became more introverted and passive. She felt more emotionally unsettled. "You go into surgery one person," she says, "and you come out another."

The transformation of Christina's personality may be a result of many factors, including the stress of dealing with a serious disease, undergoing a major surgery, and readjusting to life with disabilities. But it could also have something to do with the fact that she lost a considerable amount of brain tissue, including her right frontal lobe. Networks of neurons in the frontal lobes are involved in processing emotions, making plans, controlling impulses, and carrying out a vast array of mental tasks that each person does in a unique way (Williams, Suchy, & Kraybill, 2010). The frontal lobes play a key role in the development of personality (Stuss & Alexander, 2000). A striking illustration of this phenomenon involves an unlucky railroad foreman, Phineas Gage.

PHINEAS GAGE AND THE FRONTAL LOBES   The year was 1848, and Phineas Gage was working on the railroad. An accidental explosion sent a 3-foot iron tamping rod clear through his frontal lobes (Infographic 2.4). The rod, about as thick as a broom handle, drove straight into Gage's left cheek, through his brain, and out the top of his skull (Macmillan, 2000). What's peculiar about Gage's mishap (besides the fact that he was walking and talking just hours later) is the extreme transformation it caused. Before the accident, Gage was a well-balanced, diligent worker whom his supervisors referred to as their "most efficient and capable foreman" (Harlow, 1848, as cited in Neylan, 1999, p. 280). After the accident, he was unreliable, unpleasant, and downright vulgar. His character was so altered that people acquainted with him before and after the accident claimed he was "no longer Gage" (Harlow, 1848, as cited in Neylan, 1999, p. 280). As he could not continue working as a foreman, Gage eventually began to travel to the larger towns of New England, "exhibiting himself and the tamping iron" (Macmillan, 2000, p. 55).

Modern scientists have revisited Gage's case, using measurements from his fractured skull and brain imaging data to estimate exactly where the damage occurred. Their studies suggest that the metal rod caused destruction in both the left and right frontal lobes (Damasio, Grabowski, Frank, Galaburda, & Damasio, 1994). The only good thing about Gage's horrible accident, it seems, is that it illuminated the importance of the frontal lobes in defining personality characteristics.

CANINES AND THE MOTOR CORTEX   Toward the rear of the frontal lobes is a strip of the brain known as the **motor cortex,** which works with other areas to plan and execute voluntary movements (Infographic 2.4). Persuasive evidence pointing to this region's involvement in muscle movement came initially from a study of dogs by Gustav Fritsch (1838–1927) and Edvard Hitzig (1838–1907). Working from a makeshift lab, the two doctors discovered they could make the animals move by electrically stimulating their brains (Gross, 2007). A mild shock to the right side of the cortex might cause a twitch in the left forepaw or the left side of the face, whereas stimulating the left would spur movement on the right (Finger, 2001).

ALBERT EINSTEIN AND THE PARIETAL LOBES   Directly behind the frontal lobes on the crown of your head are the parietal lobes (Infographic 2.4). The parietal lobes help orient the body in space, are involved in tactile processing (for example, interpreting sensations related to touch, such as pain and pressure), and may play

motor cortex A band of tissue toward the rear of the frontal lobes that works with other brain regions to plan and execute voluntary movements.

Getting Into the Brain

Finding Personality in the Brain

In 1848 an accidental blast drove a 3-foot iron bar through the head of railroad worker Phineas Gage. He survived, but his personality was disastrously affected. Previously reliable and agreeable, post-injury Gage was prone to angry outbursts and became unable to hold down a job.

Phineas Gage holding the iron bar that injured him.

Using measurements from his fractured skull, modern scientists have been able to connect Gage's personality changes to frontal lobe damage. Cases like this have helped psychologists understand the role of different structures in the brain.

Getting TO the Brain

Scalp

Meninges

Cortex

Skull

In order to study the brain, we must get to it first. Peel away the scalp and cut away the bony skull, and you will find still more layers of protection. Three thin membranes—the meninges—provide a barrier to both physical injury and infection. Bypass them, and the outermost layer of the brain, the cortex, is revealed.

Frontal lobe
higher-level cognitive functions like thinking, planning, and personality characteristics

Parietal lobe
integration of sensory information like touch and temperature

Occipital lobe
processing of visual formation

Temporal lobe
hearing and language comprehension

Lobes of the Brain

This drawing shows the left hemisphere of the brain. Each hemisphere is divided into lobes, which are known for the major functions found there.

Primary motor cortex
commands the body's movements

Somatosensory cortex
receives sensory information from the body

Wernicke's area
language comprehension

Broca's area
language production

Specialized Areas of the Brain

Unlike the lobes, which are associated with many functions, some areas of the brain have one specialized function.

CONNECTIONS

This research study compared one man's brain to a control group of 35 men. In **Chapter 1,** we discussed the importance of having a large enough sample size to give us reliable findings, which might be a consideration here. Also, we discussed the potential problems with using case studies for making generalizations to the population, and in the current study, the use of Einstein as a single participant to compare to the control group could be considered a type of case study.

Superbrain

A recently rediscovered photo of Einstein's brain shows what researchers have referred to as his "extraordinary pre-frontal cortex" (Falk, Lepore, & Noe, 2012, p. 1). The irregularities in Einstein's parietal lobes may explain some of his spectacular mathematical and visuospatial abilities (Witelson et al., 1999; Falk et al., 2012). Could it be that Einstein's mathematical activities caused changes to his parietal lobes? Harvey Collection. Otis Historical Archives, National Museum of Health and Medicine

FIGURE 2.9
The Motor and Somatosensory Cortex

This drawing shows how the motor and somatosensory cortex correspond to the various regions of the body. Parts of the body that are shown larger, such as the face and hands, indicate areas of greater motor control or sensitivity. The size of each body part reflects the amount of cortex allocated to it.

a role in mathematical reasoning associated with spatial cognition (Grabner et al., 2007; Wolpert, Goodbody, & Husain, 1998). Let's take a closer look at one study **comparing the brain of Albert Einstein** to a control group of 35 brain specimens from men who had donated their bodies for use in research. Prior to their deaths, these men had normal cognitive functioning, average intelligence, and no mental health issues. The researchers reported that Einstein's brain did not weigh more than the average brain of the control group, but a region of his parietal lobe believed to be important for visual–spatial processing was 15% larger than those of the control group. They proposed that the differences in that specific region of the parietal lobe in Einstein's brain may be linked to his "exceptional intellect" in areas of visuospatial cognition and mathematical thinking (Witelson, Kigar, & Harvey, 1999). But again, the link between the size of the parietal region and "exceptional intellect" is correlational in nature, so we should be cautious in our interpretations.

PENFIELD, THE HOMUNCULUS, AND THE SOMATOSENSORY CORTEX North American neurosurgeon Wilder Penfield (1891–1976) used a method similar to Fritsch and Hitzig with humans to create a map showing which points along the motor cortex corresponded to the various parts of the body (Penfield & Boldrey, 1937). Penfield's map is often represented by the oversimplified "homunculus" (hō-ˈmäŋ-kyə-ləs; Latin for "little man") cartoon, a distorted image of a human body with huge lips and hands and a tiny torso (**FIGURE 2.9**). The size of each body part roughly reflects the amount of cortex devoted to it, which explains why parts requiring extremely fine-tuned motor control (the lips and hands) are gigantic in comparison to the other body parts in the figure.

Primary Motor Cortex

Somatosensory Cortex

somatosensory cortex A band of tissue running parallel to the motor cortex that receives and integrates sensory information from all over the body.

The parietal lobes are home to the **somatosensory cortex**, a strip of the brain running parallel to the motor cortex that receives and integrates sensory information from all over the body, for example, pain and temperature. Penfield, the neurosurgeon who created the homunculus for the primary motor cortex, mapped the somatosensory cortex in the same way (Penfield & Boldrey, 1937; Figure 2.9). As you might expect, the most sensitive areas of the body like the face and tongue are oversized on the homunculus, whereas areas less sensitive to stimulation, such as the forearm and the calf, are smaller.

THE TEMPORAL LOBES AND THE AUDITORY CORTEX Behind the parietal lobes, on the sides of your head, are the temporal lobes, which process auditory stimuli, recognize visual objects, especially faces, and play a key role in language comprehension and memory (Hickok & Poeppel, 2000; Infographic 2.4 on page 81). The temporal lobes are home to the *auditory cortex,* which receives information from the ears and allows us to "hear" sounds. In particular, researchers have supported the notion, based on studies of primate vocalizations, that the ability to recognize language has evolved over time and is processed within the temporal lobes (Scott, Blank, Rosen, & Wise, 2000; Squire, Stark, & Clark, 2004).

THE OCCIPITAL LOBES AND THE PRIMARY VISUAL CORTEX Visual information is initially processed in the occipital lobes, in the lower back of the head (Infographic 2.4). If you have ever suffered a severe blow to the rear of your head, you may remember "seeing stars," probably because activity in the occipital lobes was disrupted (hopefully only for a few seconds). It is here, where the optic nerve connects to the *primary visual cortex,* that our visual information is received and interpreted, and where we process information (for example, about color, shape, and motion). (See Chapter 3 on sensation and perception for a full discussion.) Even for a person with healthy eyes, if this area were damaged, severe visual impairment could occur. At the same time, the individual would still be able to "see" vivid *mental* images (Bridge, Harrold, Holmes, Stokes, & Kennard, 2012).

The cortex is the outermost section of the brain. It is also the part that is "newest," or most recently evolved compared to the "older" structures closer to the core. We know this because researchers have compared the brains of humans with other primates. Those structures we share with our primate relatives are considered more primitive, or less evolved.

Now that we have surveyed the brain's outer terrain, identifying some of the hotspots for language and other higher cognitive functions, let's dig deeper and examine some of its older structures.

Seeing Stars
If you have ever been struck or fallen on the back of the head, you may recall perceiving bright blobs or dots floating by. The occipital lobes at the rear of the brain are home to the visual processing centers. Anthony J. Causi/Icon SMI 942/Anthony J. Causi/Icon SMI/Newscom

---

✓ **show what you know**

1. The major function of the _____ is to organize information among the other lobes of the brain.
   a. parietal lobes
   b. frontal lobes
   c. corpus callosum
   d. temporal lobes

2. The _____ integrate information from all over the brain, allowing us to learn, have abstract thoughts, and carry out complex behaviors.

3. This section introduces the lobes of the cortex and their associated functions. Create a way to remember the lobes and their specific functions using a rhyme or another memorization technique you know.

4. Phineas Gage suffered a horrific accident in the mid-1800s, when an explosion sent a metal rod through his brain and out the top of his skull. Which of the following caused the sudden change in his personality following the accident?
   a. damage to his occipital lobes
   b. damage to his temporal lobes
   c. damage to his frontal lobes
   d. damage to his somatosensory cortex

✓ CHECK YOUR ANSWERS IN APPENDIX C.

Digging Below the Cortex
Drama Central: The Limbic System

> **LO 15** Distinguish the structures and functions of the limbic system.

Buried beneath the cortex is the **limbic system,** a group of interconnected structures that play an important role in our experiences of emotion, motivation, and memory. It also fuels our most basic drives, such as hunger, sex, and aggression. The limbic system includes the *hippocampus, amygdala, thalamus,* and *hypothalamus* (**FIGURE 2.10**).

FIGURE 2.10
The Limbic System
The limbic system fuels basic drives and processes emotions and memories. Stockbyte/Getty Images

HIPPOCAMPUS   The largest structure in the limbic system is the hippocampus, a pair of seahorse-shaped structures. The **hippocampus** is primarily responsible for processing and forming new memories from experiences, but is not where memories are permanently stored (Eichenbaum, 2004). Given its key role in memory, it may come as no surprise that the hippocampus is one of the brain areas affected by Alzheimer's disease (Henneman et al., 2009; Wang et al., 2003). On the brighter side of things, the hippocampus is also one of the few places in the brain known to give birth to new neurons throughout life (Eriksson et al., 1998).

AMYGDALA   Another structure of the limbic system is the **amygdala** (ə-mig-də-lə), which processes basic emotions like fear and aggression and the memories associated with them (Kalin, Shelton, & Davidson, 2004; Kluver & Bucy, 1939; LeDoux, 2000). Having spent many months in a war zone, Brandon encountered more than his fair share of fear-provoking near-death experiences. On one occasion, he was riding at nearly 60 mph in a Humvee that spun out of control and almost flipped over. "My heart was beating faster than ever before," Brandon recalls. In dangerous situations like this, activity in the nervous system increases drastically, including in the amygdala, triggering an emotional reaction (for example, terror) and orchestrating a whole-body response to the threat (racing heart, sweaty palms, and the like).

THALAMUS   Seated at the center of the limbic system is the **thalamus** (tha-lə-məs), whose job is to process and relay sensory information to the appropriate parts of the cortex (visual information to the visual cortex, and so on). The great majority of the data picked up by all the sensory systems, except olfaction (sense of smell), pass through the thalamus before moving on to the cortex for processing (Kay & Sherman, 2007). You might think of the thalamus as an air traffic control tower guiding incoming aircraft; when pilots communicate with the tower, the controllers direct the route to take or the runway to use.

HYPOTHALAMUS   Just below the thalamus is the **hypothalamus** (hī-pō-tha-lə-məs; *hypo* means "under" in Greek), which keeps the body's systems in a steady state, making sure functions like blood pressure, body temperature, and fluid/electrolyte balance remain within a healthy range. The hypothalamus is also involved in regulating sleep–wake cycles (Saper, Scammell, & Lu, 2005), sexual arousal (Laan & Janssen, 2007), and appetite (Ahima & Antwi, 2008). For example, neurons from the digestive system send signals to the hypothalamus (such as "stomach is empty"), which then sends signals to higher regions of the brain (such as "it's time to eat"). But deciding what and when to eat does not always come down to being hungry or full. Other brain areas are involved in eating decisions and can override the hypothalamus, driving you to polish off the French fries or scarf down that chocolate bar even when you are not that hungry.

Deeper Yet: The Brainstem and Cerebellum

The brain is made up of structures responsible for processes as complex as being able to rebuild a car's engine to selecting the right classes for a degree program. Yet delving deeper in the brain, we find structures that control more primitive functions.

> **LO 16** Distinguish the structures and functions of the brainstem and cerebellum.

The brain's ancient core consists of a stalklike trio of structures called the *brainstem* (**FIGURE 2.11** on page 86). The brainstem extends from the spinal cord to the **forebrain,** which is the largest part of the brain and includes the cerebral cortex and the limbic system. Located at the top of the brainstem is the **midbrain,** and although there is some disagreement about which brain structures belong to the midbrain, most agree it plays a role in levels of arousal. The midbrain is also home to neurons that help generate movement patterns in response to sensory input (Stein, Stanford, & Rowland, 2009). An example would be flinching when someone shouts, "Look out!"

RETICULAR FORMATION   Part of the **reticular formation** is located in the midbrain. The reticular formation is an intricate web of neurons that is responsible for levels of arousal—whether you are awake, dozing off, or somewhere in between. It is also involved in your ability to attend selectively to important incoming information by sifting through sensory data on its way to the cortex, picking out what's relevant and ignoring the rest. Imagine how overwhelmed you would feel by all the sights, sounds, tastes, smells, and physical sensations in your environment if you didn't have a reticular formation to help you discriminate between the important (the sound of a honking car horn) and trivial (the sound of a dog barking in the distance) information.

The **hindbrain** includes areas of the brain responsible for fundamental life-sustaining processes. The **pons,** which helps regulate sleep–wake cycles and coordinates movement between the right and left sides of the body, is an important structure of the hindbrain. The pons sits atop the **medulla** (mə-ˈdŭl-ə), a structure that oversees some

Synonyms
reticular formation reticular activating system

limbic system A horseshoe-shaped collection of structures that regulates emotions and basic drives like hunger, and aids in the creation of memories.

hippocampus A pair of seahorse-shaped structures located in the limbic system; primarily responsible for creating new memories.

amygdala (ə-mig-də-lə) A pair of almond-shaped structures in the limbic system that processes basic emotions, such as fear and aggression, as well as associated memories.

thalamus (tha-lə-məs) A structure in the limbic system that processes and relays sensory information to the appropriate areas of the cortex.

hypothalamus (hī-pō-tha-lə-məs) A small structure located below the thalamus that maintains a constant internal environment within a healthy range; helps regulate sleep-wake cycles, sexual behavior, and appetite.

forebrain Largest part of the brain; includes the cerebral cortex and the limbic system.

midbrain The part of the brainstem involved in levels of arousal; responsible for generating movement patterns in response to sensory input.

reticular formation A network of neurons running through the midbrain that controls levels of arousal and quickly analyzes sensory information on its way to the cortex.

hindbrain Includes areas of the brain responsible for fundamental life-sustaining processes.

pons A hindbrain structure that helps regulate sleep-wake cycles and coordinate movement between the right and left sides of the body.

medulla (mə-ˈdŭl-ə) A structure that oversees vital functions, including breathing, digestion, and heart rate.

Midbrain
Reticular formation
Pons
Hindbrain
Cerebellum
Medulla

of the body's most vital functions, including breathing and heart rate maintenance (Broadbelt, Paterson, Rivera, Trachtenberg, & Kinney, 2010).

CEREBELLUM Behind the brainstem, just above the nape of the neck, sits the orange-sized **cerebellum** (ser-ə-be-ləm). (Latin for "little brain," the cerebellum looks like a mini-version of the whole brain.) Centuries ago, scientists found that removing parts of the cerebellum from animals caused them to stagger, fall, and act clumsy. Although the cerebellum is best known for its importance in muscle coordination and balance, scientists are beginning to understand just how much this "little brain" influences higher cognitive processes in the "big brain," such as abstract reasoning and language production (Fine, Ionita, & Lohr, 2002). People with damaged cerebellums struggle with certain fine distinctions, such as telling the difference between words that sound somewhat alike (for example, "pause" versus "paws") or for producing emotional reactions that are appropriate to a given situation (Bower & Parsons, 2003).

▲ **FIGURE 2.11**
The Brainstem and Cerebellum
Located beneath the structures of the limbic system, the brainstem includes the midbrain, pons and medulla. These structures are involved in arousal, movement, and life-sustaining processes. The cerebellum is important for muscle coordination and balance and, when paired with the pons and medulla, makes up the hindbrain. © Fabrice Lerouge/Onoky/Corbis

Wrapping It Up

We've come a long way in our journey. Let's step back and review some of the key points we have learned. The body has two main systems of communication: the fast-acting nervous system and the slower endocrine system. Commanding and coordinating the activity of the nervous system is the brain, whose various regions excel in performing certain tasks. While it may be tempting to view the brain as a collection of parts doing various jobs independent of each other, the reality is that most everything the brain does is the result of many components working in sync. Violins alone won't make a symphony; you need the flutes, trumpets, and all the instruments in the orchestra to create a unified sound. If one violin in the orchestra breaks, there are other violinists to play the same part, compensating for the loss. Likewise, the brain houses many networks of neurons that have the ability to carry out the same job. When one stops working, another can take over (Doidge, 2007).

This allows us to dispel an urban myth: we do use more than 10% of our brains! In fact, people use 100% of their brains, but they don't always use them effectively, efficiently, or wisely. Brandon Burns and Christina Santhouse have made the most of their brains, and they are living rich and meaningful lives because of it.

✔○○○ show what you know

1. The _____ represents a group of interconnected structures that process emotions, memories, and basic drives.
   a. left hemisphere
   b. limbic system
   c. corpus callosum
   d. superior temporal sulcus

2. The specific part of the brain that processes basic emotions, such as fear and aggression and the memories associated with them, is the _____.

3. How might the specific structures of the limbic system, the brainstem, and the cerebellum come into play if you were out on a first date?

4. The primary role of the thalamus is to:
   a. relay sensory information.
   b. keep the body's systems in a steady state.
   c. generate movement patterns in response to sensory input.
   d. regulate sleep–wake cycles.

✔ CHECK YOUR ANSWERS IN APPENDIX C.

WHERE ARE THEY NOW? You may be wondering what became of Brandon Burns and Christina Santhouse. Three years after returning from Iraq, Brandon married a young woman named Laura who has witnessed the dramatic unfolding of his recovery. When Laura first met Brandon, he had a lot of trouble communicating his thoughts. His sentences were choppy; he often omitted words and spoke in a flat and emotionless tone. "His speech was very delayed, very slow," Laura recalls. Over the years, however, Brandon's vocabulary has expanded considerably, and he can now express himself with greater feeling and fluidity. "He is able to use more humor and emotion when he's speaking," Laura says. This young veteran, who was once unable to talk, read, or write, can now articulate his thoughts in lengthy, complex sentences; read a book; and write for his Web site.

These days, Brandon is quite a busy fellow. Much of his time is spent at home in Bartlett, Tennessee, caring for his sons, 4-year-old Porter and 2-year-old Morgan, and his newborn daughter MacCrea Iona. He also works in a church ministry providing much-needed help to people in the inner city of Memphis, and he has traveled to numerous countries, including Haiti, Kenya, and Honduras, to assist pastors in developing new strategies for reaching out to their communities.

As for Christina, she continues to reach for the stars—and grab them. After studying speech–language pathology at Misericordia University in Dallas, Pennsylvania for 5 years (and making the dean's list nearly every semester), Christina graduated with both a bachelor's and master's degree. Those years in academia were not smooth sailing. When Christina first embarked upon her major, she remembers the department chairman telling her that she wouldn't be able handle the rigors of the program. According to Christina, on graduation day, that same chairman presented her with the department's Outstanding Achievement Award. "This is the man who said I would never be able to make it, that I should try a new major," Christina says. "People often don't expect too much from people with disabilities."

Today, Christina works as a full-time speech–language pathologist in Pennsylvania's public school system. She spends her days helping elementary schoolchildren overcome their difficulties with stuttering, articulation, and other speech problems. She is also a member of the local school district's Brain STEPS team, which supports students who are transitioning back into school following brain injuries. "Hopefully, I have opened some doors for other people with disabilities," Christina offers. "There were never doors open for me; I've had to bang them down."

Brandon and Christina provide breathtaking illustrations of neuroplasticity—the brain's ability to heal, grow new connections, and make do with what is available. And although neuroplasticity played a role in these two people's recoveries, we would be remiss not to recognize the vast number of medical professionals, such as neuropsychologists, physical therapists, occupational therapists, speech pathologists, nurses, and doctors, who assisted them in their rehabilitation. The recoveries of Brandon and Christina bear testimony to the awesome tenacity of the human spirit.

You Asked, Christina Answers
http://qrs.ly/5a3jpcq
Which medical professional had the biggest impact on your recovery?

Life Is Good◄
Three years after his traumatic brain injury, Brandon celebrated his marriage to Laura. The couple recently had their third child, a daughter named MacCrea Iona. Laura Burns

Hard at Work▼
With her master's degree in speech–language pathology, Christina now works full time in Pennsylvania's public school system. Courtesy, Bucks County Courier Times

cerebellum (ser-ə-be-ləm) Structure located behind the brainstem that is responsible for muscle coordination and balance; Latin for "little brain."

2 summary of concepts

LO 1 Define neuroscience and explain its contributions to our understanding of behavior. (p. 50)

Neuroscience is the study of the nervous system and the brain, extending into a variety of disciplines and research areas. Our understanding of behavior is further explored in biological psychology, a subfield of psychology focusing on how the brain and other biological systems influence behavior. Neuroscience helps us explore physiological explanations for mental processes, searching for connections between behavior and the human nervous system, particularly the brain.

LO 2 Label the parts of a neuron and describe an action potential. (p. 53)

A typical neuron has three basic parts: a cell body, dendrites, and an axon. The dendrites receive messages from other neurons, and the branches at the end of the axon send messages to neighboring neurons. The messages are in the form of electrical and chemical activity. When a neuron fires, the action potential moves down the axon. Action potentials are all-or-none, meaning they either fire or do not fire.

LO 3 Illustrate how neurons communicate with each other. (p. 57)

Neurons communicate with each other via chemicals called neurotransmitters. An action potential moves down the axon and reaches the branches of the terminal buds, where the command to release neurotransmitters is conveyed. The neurotransmitters are released into the synapse. Most of these neurotransmitters drift across the gap and come into contact with receptor sites of the receiving neuron's dendrites.

LO 4 Summarize various neurotransmitters and the roles they play in human behavior. (p. 58)

Neurotransmitters are chemical messengers that neurons use to communicate. There are many types of neurotransmitters, each with its own type of receptor site, including: acetylcholine, glutamate, GABA, norepinephrine, serotonin, dopamine, and endorphins. Neurotransmitters can influence mood, cognition, and many other processes and behaviors.

LO 5 Recognize the connections between the central and peripheral nervous systems. (p. 62)

The brain and spinal cord make up the central nervous system (CNS), which communicates with the rest of the body through the peripheral nervous system (PNS). There are three types of neurons participating in this back-and-forth communication: Motor neurons carry information from the CNS to various parts of the body such as muscles and glands; sensory neurons relay data from the sensory systems (for example, eyes and ears) to the CNS for processing; and interneurons, which reside exclusively in the CNS and act as bridges connecting sensory and motor neurons. Interneurons mediate the nervous system's most complex operations. They assemble and process sensory input from multiple neurons and, in addition, connect what is happening now to our memory of experiences in the past. They also give rise to our thoughts and feelings, and direct our behaviors.

LO 6 Describe the organization and function of the peripheral nervous system. (p. 63)

The peripheral nervous system is divided into two branches: the somatic nervous system and the autonomic nervous system. The somatic nervous system controls the skeletal muscles, and the autonomic nervous system regulates involuntary processes within the body. The autonomic nervous system is made up of the sympathetic nervous system and the parasympathetic nervous system. The sympathetic nervous system initiates the fight-or-flight response. The parasympathetic nervous system is responsible for the rest-and-digest process.

LO 7 Evaluate the role of the endocrine system and how it influences behavior. (p. 66)

The endocrine system is a communication system that uses glands to convey messages and is closely connected with the nervous system. Its messages are conveyed by hormones, chemicals released into the bloodstream that can cause aggression and mood swings, as well as influence growth and alertness.

LO 8 Describe the functions of the two brain hemispheres and how they communicate. (p. 68)

The cerebrum includes virtually all parts of the brain except for the primitive brainstem structures. It is divided into two hemispheres: the right cerebral hemisphere and the left cerebral hemisphere. The left hemisphere controls most of the movement and sensation on the right side of the body. The right hemisphere controls most of the movement and sensation on the left side of the body. Language is processed primarily in the left hemisphere. Running between the two hemispheres is the corpus callosum, a band of fibers that connects the activities of the two hemispheres, allowing for communication between them.

LO 9 Explain lateralization and how split-brain operations affect it. (p. 69)

Each hemisphere excels in certain activities, which is known as lateralization. The left hemisphere excels in language and the right hemisphere excels in visual spatial tasks. Under certain experimental conditions, split-brain operation participants act as if they have two separate brains, each hemisphere exhibiting its own specialization.

LO 10 Identify areas in the brain responsible for language production and comprehension. (p. 72)

There are several areas in the brain that together are responsible for speech. Broca's area is primarily responsible for speech production, and Wernicke's area is primarily responsible for language comprehension.

LO 11 Define neuroplasticity and recognize when it is evident in brains. (p. 73)

Neuroplasticity refers to the ability of the brain to form new connections between neurons and adapt to changing circumstances, including structural changes in the brain. Vast networks of neurons have the ability to reorganize in order to adapt to the environment and an organism's ever-changing needs—a quality that is particularly evident in the young.

LO 12 Compare and contrast tools scientists use to study the brain. (p. 77)

There are a variety of technologies used to study the brain. The EEG detects electrical impulses in the brain. The CT uses X-rays to create many cross-sectional images of the brain. The MRI uses pulses of radio frequency waves to produce more detailed cross-sectional images than does a CT scan; however, both study the structure of the brain. The PET uses radioactivity to track glucose consumption to construct a map of the brain. The fMRI also captures changes in activity in the brain. However, instead of tracking glucose consumption, it reveals patterns of blood flow in a particular area of the brain, which

is a good indicator of how much oxygen is being used as a result of activity in that particular area.

LO 13 Identify the lobes of the cortex and explain their functions. (p. 79)

The outermost layer of the cerebrum is the cerebral cortex. The cortex is separated into different sections called lobes. The major function of the frontal lobes is to organize information among the other lobes of the brain. The frontal lobes are also responsible for higher-level cognitive functions, such as thinking and personality characteristics. The parietal lobes receive and process sensory information such as touch, pressure, temperature, and spatial orientation. Visual information goes to the occipital lobes, where it is processed. The temporal lobes are primarily responsible for hearing and language comprehension.

LO 14 Recognize the association areas and identify their functions. (p. 79)

The lobes include networks of neurons that specialize in certain activities: motor areas, sensory areas, and association areas. The motor areas direct movement, the sensory areas receive and analyze sensory stimuli, and the association areas integrate information from all over the brain, allowing us to learn, have abstract thoughts, and carry out complex behaviors.

LO 15 Distinguish the structures and functions of the limbic system. (p. 84)

The limbic system is a group of interconnected structures that play an important role in our experiences of emotion and our memories. The limbic system includes the hippocampus, amygdala, thalamus, and hypothalamus. In addition to processing emotions and memories, the limbic system fuels the most basic drives, such as hunger, sex, and aggression.

LO 16 Distinguish the structures and functions of the brainstem and cerebellum. (p. 85)

The brain's ancient core consists of a stalklike trio of structures called the brainstem, extending from the spinal cord to the forebrain, which is the largest part of the brain and includes the cerebral cortex and the limbic system. Located at the top of the brainstem is the midbrain, and although there is some disagreement about which brain structures belong to the midbrain, most agree it plays a role in levels of arousal. The hindbrain includes areas of the brain responsible for fundamental life-sustaining processes.

key terms

action potential, p. 56
adrenal glands, p. 67
all-or-none, p. 56
amygdala, p. 84
association areas, p. 79
autonomic nervous system, p. 64
axon, p. 53
biological psychology, p. 51
Broca's area, p. 72
cell body, p. 53
central nervous system (CNS), p. 61
cerebellum, p. 86
cerebral cortex, p. 79
cerebrum, p. 68
corpus callosum, p. 69

dendrites, p. 53
endocrine system, p. 66
forebrain, p. 85
frontal lobes, p. 79
glial cells, p. 53
hindbrain, p. 85
hippocampus, p. 84
hormones, p. 66
hypothalamus, p. 85
interneurons, p. 62
lateralization, p. 71
limbic system, p. 84
medulla, p. 85
midbrain, p. 85
motor cortex, p. 80
motor neurons, p. 62
myelin sheath, p. 53

nerves, p. 63
neurogenesis, p. 74
neurons, p. 52
neuroplasticity, p. 73
neuroscience, p. 51
neurotransmitters, p. 57
occipital lobes, p. 79
parasympathetic nervous system, p. 64
parietal lobes, p. 79
peripheral nervous system (PNS), p. 61
phrenology, p. 75
pituitary gland, p. 66
pons, p. 85
receptor sites, p. 57
reflex arc, p. 63

resting potential, p. 54
reticular formation, p. 85
reuptake, p. 57
sensory neurons, p. 62
somatic nervous system, p. 63
somatosensory cortex, p. 83
spinal cord, p. 61
split-brain operation, p. 69
stem cells, p. 74
sympathetic nervous system, p. 64
synapse, p. 53
temporal lobes, p. 79
thalamus, p. 85
thyroid gland, p. 67
Wernicke's area, p. 72

TEST PREP are you ready?

1. _____ are the specialized cells found in the nervous system that are the building blocks of the central nervous system and the peripheral nervous system.
   a. Neurotransmitters
   b. The hemispheres
   c. Neurons
   d. Hormones

2. When positive ions at the axon hillock raise the internal cell voltage of the first segment of the axon from its resting voltage to its threshold potential, the neuron becomes activated. This spike in electrical energy causes _____ to occur.
   a. an action potential
   b. reuptake
   c. a reflex arc
   d. lateralization

3. A colleague of yours tells you that she has been diagnosed with multiple sclerosis. Luckily, the disease was diagnosed early and she is getting state-of-the-art treatment. So far, it does not appear that she has experienced problems with the _____ covering the axons in her nervous system.
   a. myelin sheath
   b. reticular formation
   c. glutamate
   d. neurotransmitters

4. Match the neurotransmitter with its primary role(s).
   ____ 1. acetylcholine
   ____ 2. glutamate
   ____ 3. endorphins
   ____ 4. serotonin
   a. reduces experience of pain
   b. learning, memory
   c. enables movement
   d. mood, aggression, appetite

5. A neuroscientist studying the brain and the spinal cord would describe her general area of interest as the:
   a. central nervous system.
   b. peripheral nervous system.
   c. autonomic nervous system.
   d. neurons.

6. A serious diving accident can result in damage to the _____, which is responsible for receiving information from the body and sending it to the brain, and for sending information from the brain throughout the body.
   a. corpus callosum
   b. spinal cord
   c. reflex arc
   d. somatic nervous system

7. While sitting at your desk, you hear the tone signaling an incoming e-mail. That sound is received by your auditory system and information is sent via sensory neurons to your brain. Here, we can see how the _____ provides a communication link between the central nervous system and the rest of the body.
   a. endocrine system
   b. cerebrum
   c. corpus callosum
   d. peripheral nervous system

8. After facing a frightening situation in a war zone, Brandon's parasympathetic nervous system is in charge of the:
   a. "fight-and-rest" response.
   b. "fight-or-flight" response.
   c. "tend-and-befriend" process.
   d. "rest-and-digest" process.

9. Lately, your friend has been prone to mood swings and aggressive behavior. The doctor has pinpointed a problem in his _____, which is a communication system that uses _____ to convey messages via hormones.
   a. endocrine system; action potentials
   b. endocrine system; glands
   c. central nervous system; glands
   d. central nervous system; peripheral nervous system

10. Which of the following statements is correct regarding the function of the right hemisphere in comparison to the left hemisphere?
    a. The right hemisphere is less competent handling visual tasks.
    b. The right hemisphere is more competent handling visual tasks.
    c. The left hemisphere is more competent judging if lines are oriented similarly.
    d. The right hemisphere is more competent with speech production.

11. Although Gall's phrenology has been discredited as a true brain "science," Gall's major contribution to the field of psychology is the idea that:
    a. locations in the brain are responsible for certain activities.
    b. the left hemisphere is responsible for activity on the right side of the body.
    c. the left hemisphere is responsible for language production.
    d. stem cells can be used to repair tissue that has been damaged.

12. Broca's area is involved in speech production, and _____ is critical for language comprehension.
    a. the corpus callosum   c. the parietal lobe
    b. the right hemisphere   d. Wernicke's area

13. Match the structures with their principle functions:
    ____ 1. association area
    ____ 2. temporal lobes
    ____ 3. meninges
    ____ 4. occipital lobes
    ____ 5. parietal lobes

    a. three thin membranes protect brain
    b. integrates information from all over brain
    c. hearing and language comprehension
    d. receives sensory information, such as touch
    e. processes visual information

14. The limbic system is a group of interconnected structures in the brain. Match the structures below with their principle functions:
    ____ 1. amygdala
    ____ 2. hippocampus
    ____ 3. hypothalamus
    ____ 4. thalamus

    a. responsible for making new memories
    b. processes basic emotions
    c. relays sensory information
    d. keeps body systems in steady state

15. The _____ is located in the midbrain and is responsible for levels of arousal and your ability to selectively attend to important stimuli.
    a. cerebellum   c. hippocampus
    b. thalamus   d. reticular formation

16. Describe the differences between the agonists and antagonists and develop an analogy to help you remember these differences.

17. The "knee-jerk" reaction that occurs when a doctor taps your knee with a rubber hammer provides a good example of a reflex arc. Describe this involuntary reaction and then draw your own diagram to show the reflex arc associated with it.

18. Describe two major differences between neurotransmitters and hormones and how they influence behavior.

19. The research conducted by Sperry and Gazzaniga examined the effects of surgeries that severed the corpus callosum. Describe what these split-brain experiments tell us about the lateralization of the hemispheres of the brain and how they communicate.

20. We described a handful of tools scientists use to study the brain. Compare their functions and weaknesses.

✓ CHECK YOUR ANSWERS IN APPENDIX C.

Get personalized practice by logging into LaunchPad at **http://www.worthpublishers.com/launchpad/Licht** to take the LearningCurve adaptive quizzes for Chapter 2.

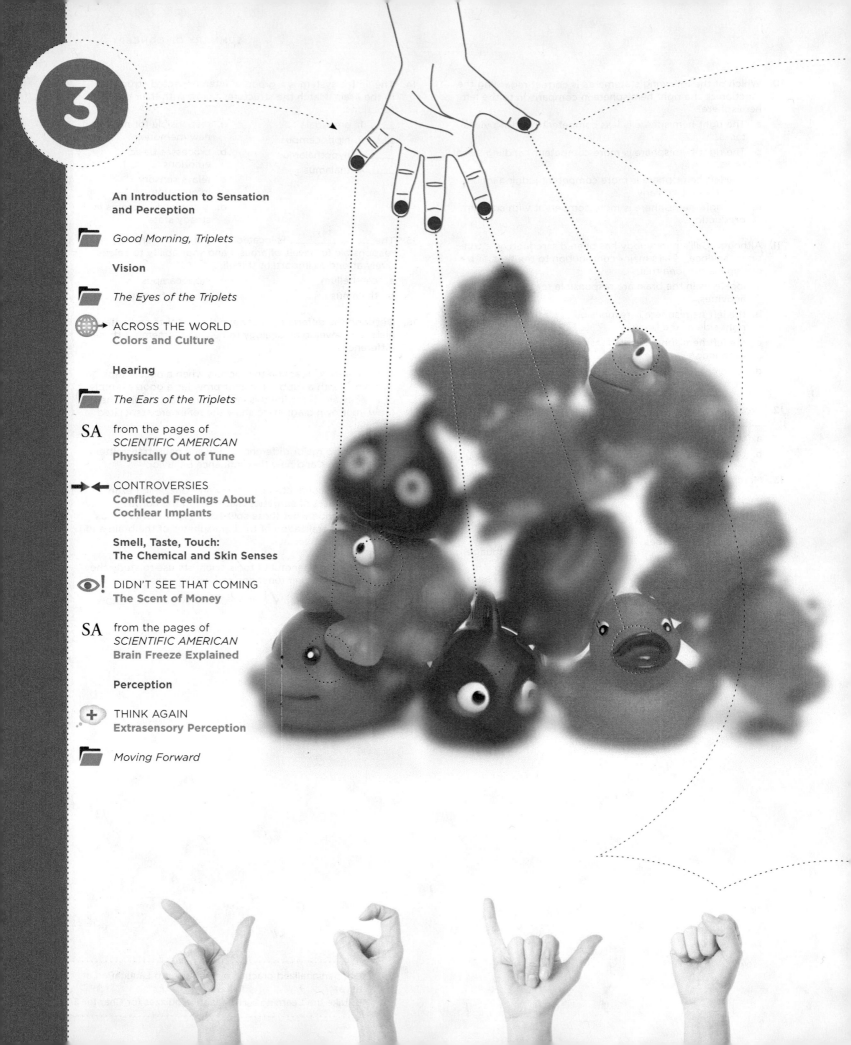

3

An Introduction to Sensation and Perception

📁 *Good Morning, Triplets*

Vision

📁 *The Eyes of the Triplets*

🌐➤ ACROSS THE WORLD
Colors and Culture

Hearing

📁 *The Ears of the Triplets*

SA from the pages of
SCIENTIFIC AMERICAN
Physically Out of Tune

➡◀ CONTROVERSIES
Conflicted Feelings About Cochlear Implants

Smell, Taste, Touch: The Chemical and Skin Senses

👁! DIDN'T SEE THAT COMING
The Scent of Money

SA from the pages of
SCIENTIFIC AMERICAN
Brain Freeze Explained

Perception

➕ THINK AGAIN
Extrasensory Perception

📁 *Moving Forward*

sensation and perception

An Introduction to Sensation and Perception

GOOD MORNING, TRIPLETS Long before the sun rises, Liz Allen is awake, making sure that her 13-year-old triplets Emma, Zoe, and Sophie make it to school on time. First she walks into the bedroom of Emma and Zoe.

The floor may be sprinkled with toys if Emma has been awake in the night. She likes to climb inside her toy box and toss out everything. Zoe is a better sleeper, but she too might be up for several hours at a time. "They're pretty active at night," explains Liz, who occasionally finds the girls wearing bathing suits in the morning. "They both love swimming." Whatever they may be wearing, Emma and Zoe are almost certain to be sleeping in the same position: cuddled lengthwise, feet-to-head.

Gently shaking the girls, Liz says, "Wake up. Let's get ready," but she needn't utter a word. She "speaks" to Emma and Zoe by moving her hands, and they "listen" by feeling her fingers dance through the motions of sign language. Emma and Zoe are completely blind and deaf. During the day, the triplets use *cochlear implants,* electronic devices that provide them with some degree of hearing. But these implants only provide a hearinglike experience; they do not "fix" deafness (UCSF Medical Center, 2012). (More about these "bionic ears" later.) The third triplet Sophie is easier to rouse. Though she is deaf and legally blind, Sophie does have limited vision. Flipping the light switch is enough to get her started on her morning routine.

Welcome to the world of Zoe, Sophie, and Emma. They are, as far as we know, the world's only deaf and blind triplets.

3

LEARNING OBJECTIVES

after reading and studying this chapter, you should be able to:

LO 1   Define sensation and perception and explain how they are different.

LO 2   Define transduction and explain how it relates to sensation.

LO 3   Describe and differentiate between absolute thresholds and difference thresholds.

LO 4   Explain how electromagnetic energy is transduced into a sensation of vision.

LO 5   Describe the function of rods and cones.

LO 6   Compare and contrast the theories of color vision.

LO 7   Summarize how sound waves are transduced into the sensation of hearing.

LO 8   Illustrate how we sense different pitches of sound.

LO 9   Describe the process of olfaction.

LO 10   Discuss the structures involved in taste and describe how they work.

LO 11   Describe how the biopsychosocial perspective is used to understand pain.

LO 12   Illustrate how we sense the position and movement of our bodies.

LO 13   Identify the principles of perceptual organization.

LO 14   Identify concepts involved in depth perception.

LO 15   Define extrasensory perception and explain why psychologists dismiss its legitimacy.

Liz, in Her Own Words:

http://qrs.ly/zr3le9e

The Triplets
The Dunn sisters, Sophie (left), Zoe, and Emma (front), are the world's only deaf and blind triplets. Emma and Zoe can see nothing, while Sophie has very limited vision even when wearing corrective lenses. All three girls wear devices known as cochlear implants, which simulate the sensation of hearing.
Worldwide Features/Barcroft Media/Landov

Sensation and Perception 101

LO 1   Define sensation and perception and explain how they are different.

Have you ever wondered what it may feel like to be blind and deaf? Most people are dependent on sights and sounds to accomplish virtually every daily activity, from buttering toast to answering a ringing phone. Thanks to eyes and ears, we can tell the difference between 12:00 noon and 12:00 midnight, soft jazz and a screaming ambulance, and a bottle of shampoo and a bottle of ketchup. Sights and sounds are a source for our thoughts and memories. When we think about people, we "see" their faces and "hear" their voices in our minds.

How does a deaf-blind person function in the world? We humans are adaptive creatures; when faced with a disability, we make the best of what we have. Emma, Zoe, and Sophie have come to rely on their other senses—touch, smell, and taste—to compensate for what they cannot see or hear. Instead of rising to an alarm clock or the sunlight streaming through their window, Emma and Zoe feel their mother nudging their arms and signing "Wake up" and "Let's get ready" into their hands. They recognize Mom by touch and smell, and they find their way around new places by running their fingers along the edges and contours of objects and walls. "You would think . . . that they are missing out on a lot," Liz says, "but they don't miss much."

SENSATION AND PERCEPTION The subject of this chapter is sensation and perception, the absorbing and deciphering of information from the environment. **Sensation** is the process by which receptors in our sensory organs (such as in the eyes, ears, nose, mouth, skin and other tissues) and the nervous system receive and detect stimuli. **Perception** is the process through which information about these stimuli is organized, interpreted, and transformed into something meaningful. Sensation and perception work closely together to provide you with the experience of the world around you and inside you. The connection between sensation and perception allows you to experience the surrounding world as coherent and meaningful. But how does this happen without your effort

Note: Quotations attributed to Liz Allen are personal communications.

Sensory Blending
Painter David Hockney stands before his massive *Bigger Trees Near Warter* at an exhibition in London. Hockney reportedly has synesthesia, a rare condition whereby a person experiences a combination of perceptions in response to a "single sensory modality" (Rich & Mattingley, 2002). A synesthete may, for instance, describe the color green as having a scent, or the word "Tuesday" as being maroon with black stripes. Hockney created the stage sets for various operas by painting what he saw in the music (Ward, 2006, June 10). AP Photo/Sang Tan

or knowledge? How does the vast amount of stimuli outside and inside of your body get transformed into experiences that seem so personal—how do beams of light get turned into an image of a beautifully colored sunrise, and chemical sensations converted into your experience of a sweet strawberry? Let's find out.

LO 2 Define transduction and explain how it relates to sensation.

TRANSDUCTION   Sensation begins when your sensory systems receive input from the environment. Each of your sensory systems is designed to respond to stimuli of a certain kind. Light waves and sound waves accost your eyes and ears, heat waves bathe your skin, molecules of different chemical compositions float into your nostrils and descend upon your taste buds, and physical objects push against you (for example, the chair pushing against your back and the clothing gently pressing against your skin). But none of these stimuli can have an impact on your brain unless they are translated into a language it understands: **electrical and chemical signals.** This is the job of the specialized sensory cells located in the back of your eyes, the caverns of your ears and nose, the spongy surface of your tongue and within your skin, muscle, and other tissues. The process of transforming stimuli into the electrical and chemical signals of neurons is called **transduction,** and it is the first step of sensation. The neural signals are then processed by the **central nervous system,** resulting in what we consciously experience as *sensations* (*seeing* a person's face or *smelling* smoke).

In order for sensations to be useful, we must assign meaning to them (*that face belongs to my girlfriend* or *the scent of smoke signals fire*). This process of organizing and understanding incoming information is *perception*. Sensation is seeing a red burner on the stove; perception is thinking *hot*. Sensation is hearing a loud, shrill tone; perception is recognizing it as the warning sound of a fire alarm. In this chapter, we describe and explain sensation and perception as two distinct events, but there is no physical boundary in the brain marking the end of sensation and the beginning of perception. The processing of stimuli into sensations and perceptions happens quickly and effortlessly.

CONNECTIONS

In **Chapter 2,** we described how neurons work together to shape our experiences. The electrical signals are active within the axon, and the chemical signals are at work in the synapse.

CONNECTIONS

As discussed in **Chapter 2,** the brain and the spinal cord make up the central nervous system. The peripheral nervous system includes the somatic and autonomic branches of the nervous system.

sensation The process by which sensory organs in the eyes, ears, nose, mouth, skin, and other tissues receive and detect stimuli.

perception The organization and interpretation of sensory stimuli by the brain.

transduction The process of transforming stimuli into neural signals.

DATA-BASED AND KNOWLEDGE-BASED PROCESSING   Psychologists often distinguish between two ways that we process sensory and perceptual information. **Data-based processing** describes how the brain takes basic sensory information and processes the incoming stimuli. **Knowledge-based processing** generally involves the next step, utilizing our past experiences and knowledge to understand sensory information. Data-based processing is the equivalent to what cameras and video recorders do best—collect data without any preconceived notions or expectations. Knowledge-based processing is the arena where humans excel. Our brain constructs a representation of the world based on what we have learned and experienced in the past.

How do these concepts figure into *psychology,* the scientific study of behavior and mental processes? Sensation and perception are the starting points for every psychological process you can imagine, from problem-solving to building relationships. Psychologists continue to discover the many ways that sensation and perception affect such processes. How do they do it? Through careful and systematic observation of behavior.

Studying Sensation

Liz began to suspect that her triplets had vision and hearing impairments when she noticed irregularities in their behavior. When Zoe lost her hearing, for example, she became frustrated with one of her favorite toys—a cube that made music when she pushed its buttons. Liz's careful observation of her daughter's behaviors prompted her to consult a specialist. Eventually, it became clear that there was a problem with the *sensory* receptors in Zoe's ears, but Liz initially noticed a *behavioral* change.

HUMAN SENSATION   Studying sensation means studying human beings, and humans are complex and variable. Not everyone is born with the same collection of stimulus-detecting equipment. Some people have eyes that see 20/20; others have been wearing glasses since they were toddlers. There is even variation within a given individual. The ability to detect faint stimuli, for instance, depends on your state of mind and body (such as how preoccupied or bored you happen to be, how stressed you feel, or whether you've had your morning cup of coffee).

This variability in our ability to sense can have profound consequences. If you get in the car immediately following a heated argument with your spouse, you may be less likely to notice (that is, sense) the bicyclist in your rearview mirror—who on any other day would catch your eye. Research has found that, although approximately 2% of people might be able to multitask flawlessly, the great majority of us are limited in our ability to attend to our environments, especially when we are focusing on more than one task that demands our attention (Watson & Strayer, 2010). In particular, and perhaps of interest to you, researchers have demonstrated that activities used for social purposes, such as Facebook and text messaging, are linked with poorer grades in college students (Junco & Cotten, 2012). Unfortunately, human beings do not have sensory organs that are equivalent to light meters, sound meters, motion detectors, and thermometers. Our sensory systems are prone to interferences from outside and within, which challenge psychologists as they search for ways to accurately measure sensory abilities.

- -
LO 3   Describe and differentiate between absolute thresholds and difference thresholds.
- -

ABSOLUTE THRESHOLDS   Researchers can determine various types of sensory *thresholds,* which are the smallest levels of stimulation people can detect. One particular interest of psychologists is to determine **absolute thresholds,** defined as the weakest

Synonyms

data-based processing bottom-up processing

knowledge-based processing top-down processing

difference thresholds just noticeable differences

data-based processing Taking basic sensory information about incoming stimuli and processing it for further interpretation.

knowledge-based processing Drawing on past experiences and knowledge to understand and interpret sensory information.

absolute threshold The weakest stimuli that can be detected 50% of the time.

sensory adaptation Sensory receptors tend to become less sensitive to constant stimuli.

difference threshold The minimum difference between two stimuli that can be noticed 50% of the time.

stimuli that can be detected 50% of the time. The absolute threshold commonly cited for vision, for instance, is described as the equivalent of being able to see the flame of one candle 30 miles away 50% of the time (Galanter, 1962). But, remember, the state of a person's body and mind can influence his ability to sense a faint stimulus. **INFOGRAPHIC 3.1** on page 98 lists absolute thresholds for the population (Galanter, 1962), but consider these with the warning that absolute thresholds are not necessarily *absolute* for a particular person over time. Absolute thresholds are important, but there is more to sensation than noting the presence of a stimulus. Many everyday sensory experiences involve detecting *changes* in environmental stimuli.

SENSORY ADAPTATION   Have you ever put on cologne or perfume and wondered if it was too strong, but within a matter of minutes you don't even notice it? Or, have you ever jumped into an ice-cold swimming pool and not noticed the frigid temperature 30 minutes later? Our sensory receptors become less sensitive to constant stimuli through a process called **sensory adaptation,** a natural lessening of awareness of unchanging conditions. This allows us to focus instead on changes in our environment—a skill that has proven invaluable for **survival.**

DIFFERENCE THRESHOLDS   Intrigued by this keen sensitivity to change, early psychologists decided to figure out *how different* two stimuli needed to be in order for someone to notice. Through careful experimentation, they established various **difference thresholds,** or the minimum differences between two stimuli noticed 50% of the time.

Let's say you are blindfolded, holding a 100-gram stick of butter, and somebody places a thinly sliced pat of butter weighing only 0.5 grams on top of the stick (adding 0.5% of the weight of the stick of butter). Do you think you'd notice the added weight of the pat of butter? Probably not. But if someone added a much larger pat of butter on top, say, a pat weighing 5 grams (5% of the weight of the stick of butter), then you would almost definitely notice the change, right? Somewhere in between that tiny pat and the larger pat of butter is the difference threshold. In fact, the *just noticeable difference* for weight is 2%, which is the amount of added weight needed for you to feel the difference 50% of the time. Getting back to our stick of butter (which is getting a little soft now), we only need to add a slice of butter weighing 2 grams (2% of the weight of the stick) for you to notice someone has added to your burden. What if you were holding 500 grams (or 5 sticks) of butter? How much would need to be added for you to detect the difference in weight*?

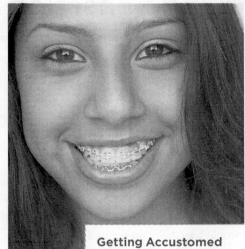

Getting Accustomed
Most people are painfully aware of their new braces, but after a while they begin to notice them less. If a stimulus is ongoing and steady, we tend to become less aware of it. This process of *sensory adaptation* helps keep us on alert for changes in the environment.
© Caroline Schiff/Blend Images/Corbis

CONNECTIONS

In **Chapter 1,** we presented the evolutionary perspective. Here, it is used to explain how sensory adaptation has evolved and contributed to the safety of humans. By ignoring unchanging stimuli, we are better prepared to detect changes in the environment. For our ancestors, picking up new information often meant the difference between life and death.

Ever So Subtle
Participants from China and the Netherlands were asked to choose the less colorful image. Can you tell there's a difference in brightness? The *difference threshold,* or just noticeable difference, is the minimum difference between two stimuli noticed 50% of the time. Qin, S., Ge, S., Yin, H., Xia, J., & Heynderickx, I. Displays, 31, 25-34 (2010)

---

*Answer: 2% of 500 grams is 10 grams.

Studying Sensation

An airplane manufacturer designs a control panel covered with dials and lights. In addition to checking the panel in a factory setting, the manufacturer must also be sure the panel works for the people who will be using it. For example, will pilots notice when a warning light is on?

Human factors engineers study how sensation and perception interact with machines and equipment. A pilot might be tested to see how dim a light she can detect 50% of the time (absolute threshold). A pilot might also be tested to determine how different the intensity of two lights would have to be for her to detect a change 50% of the time (difference threshold). Using information gathered by a human factors engineer, the manufacturer could accurately set the brightness of lights on the panel.

Absolute thresholds

are the weakest stimuli that can be detected 50% of the time. Absolute thresholds for each of the five senses (GALANTER, 1962):

Touch
a bee's wing falling on your cheek

Hearing
the tick of a clock at 20 feet

Smell
one drop of perfume throughout a six-room apartment

Vision
candle flame seen from 30 miles away on a clear dark night

Taste
1 teaspoon of sugar in 2 gallons of water

In order to be detected, a light must be bright enough to be seen. Lights weaker than the absolute threshold would be considered subliminal stimuli—stimuli so weak you don't sense them consciously and reliably.

percent of times you can see the light

absolute threshold

50%

subliminal stimuli

100 · 75 · 50 · 25

0 miles   15   30   45   60
distance from light

Signal detection theory

Our ability to detect a stimulus depends on sensory factors (such as the intensity of the stimulus or the presence of interfering stimuli) and our psychological state (such as how alert we are). After determining minimum brightness for airplane control panel lights, a human factors engineer would also use signal detection theory to assess real-life situations. Lights that are noticeable in a controlled, test situation might not be detected when other stimuli interfere.

During a real flight, natural light might be coming in through the cockpit windows.

The pilot might be busy communicating with air traffic control.

Credits: Airplane cockpit sunset, © Nikolai Sorokin – Fotolia.com; Airplane cockpit blue sky, © Nikolai Sorokin – Fotolia.com; Aircraft instruments (set #1), istockphoto.com

✳ How much more intense does a stimulus need to be for it to be detected in real-life situations?

Difference thresholds vary slightly from person to person because each of us has a unique sensory toolkit. But is there variation across people from **different cultures**? In a recent study, researchers compared participants' ability to detect changes to pictures (for example, their brightness and color) of flowers, balloons, rabbits, and other objects (see photo on page 97). The just noticeable difference was the same for the Chinese and Dutch participants "for most images" (Qin, Ge, Yin, Xia, & Heynderickx, 2010, p. 25). The implication is that this aspect of sensation and perception might not be influenced by cultural factors.

WEBER'S LAW   According to Ernst Heinrich Weber (1795–1878), thresholds are determined by ratios, not absolute numbers. Let's go back to our butter example. When we started with 100 grams of butter, we needed to add 2 grams to detect a difference— a ratio of 2/100 (that is, a 2% difference between 100 and 102 grams). If we started with 200 grams and added just 2 grams, we would not feel the difference; instead, we would need to add 4 grams to feel the difference (4/200 is equivalent to 2/100 or 2%). **Weber's law** states that the *ratios,* not the raw number values, determine these difference thresholds. The five senses each have their own constant Weber ratios.

SUBLIMINAL INFLUENCES   The absolute thresholds and difference thresholds discussed above pertain to stimuli that we can detect 50% of the time. What about stimuli below these thresholds? Do *subliminal* stimuli, which are well below our absolute thresholds (such as light that is too dim to see and sounds that are too faint to hear), have an impact on us? Perhaps you have heard of "subliminal advertising," or stealthy attempts by marketers to woo you into buying their products without you even being aware. Here's an example: You're watching a movie and suddenly the words "Buy Popcorn!" flash across the screen, but only for a few milliseconds. Your sensory receptors may detect this fleeting stimulus, but so briefly that it never penetrates your awareness; that is, you don't even notice it. To what degree, if at all, does this stimulus register on a "subconscious" level? **According to urban myth,** subliminal marketing can make you run out and buy popcorn, soft drinks, or whatever products happen to be advertised. But these messages cannot affect behavior in this way. They cannot manipulate you to purchase something you had not planned on purchasing, or to quit smoking, for example (Karremans, Stroebe, & Claus, 2006).

Findings from neuroimaging studies have shown that neural activity is evident with the "subliminal presentation" of stimuli (Kouider & Dehaene, 2007). The brain does respond to information presented at an unconscious or nonconscious level. What subliminal messages may be able to do is influence fleeting moods through *priming* (stimulating memories beneath awareness through previous exposure; Chapter 6). One study found that if you expose people to ugly scenes (for example, pictures of dead bodies or buckets of snakes) for several milliseconds (thus "priming" them) and then ask them to look at a neutral picture of a woman's face, people rate her as more unlikable than if they had been exposed to feel-good subliminal images (such as pictures of kittens and bridal couples) (Krosnick, Betz, Jussim, & Lynn, 1992).

Thus far, we have focused on the stimulus itself. But what about other environmental factors, such as background stimuli competing for the observer's attention, or internal factors like the observer's state of mind—do these variables enter the equation as well?

SIGNAL DETECTION THEORY   Our ability to detect weak stimuli in the environment is based on many factors, and the theory that draws them all together is called **signal detection theory** (Infographic 3.1). Factors such as the internal and external "noise" in our environment can interfere with our ability to detect weak

---

CONNECTIONS

In **Chapter 1,** we presented the sociocultural perspective, which helps us to understand how some behaviors differ across cultures, and how others are universal. Here, the sociocultural perspective is used to explain how difference thresholds are the same across cultures.

CONNECTIONS

In **Chapter 1,** we discussed critical thinking and psychomythology. The claim that subliminal advertising can make us buy things we don't want is an example of this type of "misinformation" about human behavior. An important component of critical thinking is determining if there is scientific evidence to support or refute claims conveyed in urban myths.

Weber's law The law stating that each of the five senses has its own constant ratio determining difference thresholds.

signal detection theory A theory explaining how various factors influence our ability to detect weak signals in the environment signals. Imagine you are participating in an experiment studying the detection of weak stimuli, and the researcher tells you to push a button when you see a light flash. The strength of the light will range from some flashes you will clearly notice to others you might not even detect. There will probably be some false alarms: "I *think* I saw the light," you press the button, and it turns out no light flash occurred. There will also be some "hits": "I *know* I saw a light that time," so you press the button, and you are correct. How many hits and false alarms you have depends on many internal factors, including how tired you are, if you have eaten, your expectations about the importance of success, your motivation, and so on. It also depends on external variables, such as the light level in the room and the dust in the air.

Signal detection theory is useful in a variety of real-world situations. In one study, researchers applied the theory to explain how nurses respond and make decisions about patient safety—how background noises influence their ability to hear patient alarm monitors, for example. One of the specific issues raised by these researchers was the impact of "missed signals," that is, medical errors resulting from interference with the nurses' ability to detect and interpret patient signs and symptoms (Despins, Scott-Cawiezell, & Rouder, 2010). In situations like these, the ability to sense and perceive may have life or death implications.

Sensation and perception make it possible for us to know the surrounding world. We rely on sensation, transduction, and perception to translate stimuli into electrical and chemical activity in the nervous system. Amazingly, this activity becomes our sensory experiences: an image of a billowy white cloud, the sound of a bird singing, the tickle of a breeze over the skin, and the smell and taste of sweet lemonade. But how exactly does the process work for each of the five senses? Let's start by exploring the sense that is generally considered most dominant: vision.

✓○○○ show what you know

1. _____ makes the information received by the sensory receptors more meaningful by drawing from experience to organize and interpret sensory data.
   a. Perception
   b. Transduction
   c. Sensation
   d. Signal detection

2. Imagine you have been asked to watch a neighbor's property while she is away. According to signal detection theory, what factors may influence your ability to detect an intruder's flashlight in the middle of the night?

3. At the supermarket, a woman next to you in line has some very strong-smelling cheese in her basket. You notice the odor immediately, but within a matter of minutes you can barely detect it. This reduced sensitivity to a constant smell results from the process of:
   a. sensation.
   b. transduction.
   c. perception.
   d. sensory adaptation.

✓ CHECK YOUR ANSWERS IN APPENDIX C.

Vision

 THE EYES OF THE TRIPLETS When Liz became pregnant back in 1999, she was busy caring for her firstborn child, 3-year-old Sarah. Her marriage wasn't working. In fact, she and her husband had already begun to contemplate divorce. It could not have been a worse time for Liz to discover she was going to have not one, not two, but three babies.

Many triplets are fraternal, meaning they come from three distinct egg–sperm combinations, each with its own genetic makeup. Liz was pregnant with *identical* triplets, which results when one fertilized egg splits three ways. The babies were born more than 3 months early by emergency cesarean delivery due to grave concerns about Zoe's fetal heartbeat. Each of the three babies entered the world weighing less than 2 pounds.

Liz remembers feeling shocked and "scared to death" as she lay on the operating table watching her newborns wheeling by in incubators. She was well aware of the health dangers associated with prematurity (breathing problems, brain bleeds, visual impairment, and so on). All Liz could do was hope for the best.

After spending their first months of life in the hospital, hooked to feeding tubes, breathing tubes, and IVs, the triplets finally came home—Sophie first, Emma second, and finally Zoe. But 2 days after Emma arrived home, Liz realized that something was wrong. Emma's eyes weren't "tracking," or following moving objects. Liz took Emma to a specialist, who said she was blind. Soon it became clear that Zoe and Sophie also had vision problems.

What happened to the triplets' eyes? To understand how the girls lost their vision, we must first learn how the eye turns light into electrical and chemical impulses for the brain to interpret.

Extreme Preemies
Emma, Zoe, and Sophie were born over 3 months early, long before fetal development had run its course. Infants born before 32 weeks of gestation are at risk for serious complications, including respiratory distress, heart irregularities, and vision problems (March of Dimes, 2012). Worldwide Features/Barcroft Media/Landov

Light Is Sight

> **LO 4** Explain how electromagnetic energy is transduced into a sensation of vision.

When you look at a stop sign, would you believe you are sensing light waves bouncing off the stop sign and into your eyes? The eyes do not sense faces, objects, or scenery. They detect light. Remember, if you don't have light, you don't have sight. But what exactly *is* light? Light is an electromagnetic energy wave, composed of fluctuating electric and magnetic fields zooming from place to place at a very fast rate. And when we say "fast," we mean from Atlanta to Los Angeles in a tenth of a second. Electromagnetic energy waves are everywhere all the time, zipping past your head, and bouncing off your nose. As you can see in **FIGURE 3.1** on page 102, light that is visible to humans falls along a spectrum or range of electromagnetic energy. **TABLE 3.1** summarizes this range.

Table 3.1 **ELECTROMAGNETIC (EM) WAVES IN EVERYDAY LIFE**	
EM Frequency	**Real-World Examples**
Gamma waves	Emitted by radioactive substances, such as the glucose tracers used in PET imaging
X-rays	X-ray machines (CT scanners included) used to generate pictures of the inside of the body
Ultraviolet	Sun rays that tan your skin (and can give you cancer)
Visible	What you see
Infrared	Heat emitted from human bodies
Microwaves	Microwave ovens, cell phones
Radio waves	AM and FM radios, televisions, wireless Internet

We use electromagnetic energy for a variety of purposes, from warming our dinners to carrying on digital conversations. Visible light is the only part of the spectrum detectable by human eyes.

SOURCE: ADAPTED FROM BERKELEY LAB (N.D.).

Light Visible to Humans

400   500   600   700
wavelength (in nanometers)

WAVELENGTH   The various types of electromagnetic energy can be distinguished by their **wavelengths,** which is the distance from one wave hump to the next (like the distance between the crests of waves rolling in the ocean; Figure 3.1). Gamma waves have short wavelengths and are located on the far left of the spectrum. At the opposite extreme (far right of the spectrum) are the long radio waves. The light humans can see falls in the middle of the spectrum, measuring between 400 to 700 nanometers (nm) or billionths of a meter (Brown & Wald, 1964). Wavelength also plays an important role in determining the colors humans and animals can detect.

The Colors We See

Although dogs can only see the world in blues, yellows, and grays (Coren, 2008, October 20), primates, including humans, can detect a wider spectrum of colors, including reds and oranges. This ability to see reds and oranges may be an adaptation to spot ripe fruits against the green backdrop of tree leaves (Rowe, 2002). Other creatures can see "colors" that we can't. Snakes can detect infrared waves radiating off the bodies of their prey, and birds size up potential mates using the ultraviolet waves reflected by feathers (Bennett, Cuthill, Partridge, & Maier, 1996; Gracheva et al., 2010).

I "See" You
This is what you might perceive if you were a snake searching for dinner in the dark. The western diamondback rattlesnake has facial sensors that detect infrared radiation from warm-blooded prey. Scientists have yet to determine exactly how the heat waves are transduced into neural signals, but the process depends on specialized channels in nerve fibers of the face (Gracheva et al., 2010). Julius Lab at UCSF

FEATURES OF LIGHT   The colors you see result from light reflecting off of objects and reaching your eyes. Every color can be described according to three factors: hue, brightness, and saturation. The first factor, **hue**, is what we commonly refer to as "color" (blue jeans have a blue hue). Hue is determined by the wavelength reflecting off of an object: Violet has the shortest wavelength in the visible spectrum (400 nm), and red has the longest (700 nm). The *brightness* of a color represents a continuum from bright to dim in terms of the intensity of the color. Brightness depends on wave height, or **amplitude,** the distance from midpoint to peak (or from midpoint to trough; Figure 3.1). Just remember, the taller the height, the brighter the light. **Saturation,** or color purity, is determined by uniformity of wavelength. Saturated colors are made up of same-size wavelengths. Objects we see as pure violet, for instance, are reflecting only 400-nm light waves. We can "pollute" the violet light by mixing it with other wavelengths and the result will be a less saturated, pale lavender. Most colors in the environment are not pure. The red pigments in Angelina Jolie's red lipstick probably reflect a mixture of waves in the 600–700 nm range, rather than pure 700-nm red. Combinations of these three basic features—hue, brightness, and saturation—can produce an infinite number of colors; our eyes are just not sensitive enough to tell them all apart. Amazingly, though, the average person sees some 2.3 million colors (Linhares, Pinto, & Nascimento, 2008).

THE PERCEPTION OF COLORS   And now, the 2.3 million-dollar question: Most of us agree that stop signs are red and taxicabs are yellow, but can we be sure that one person's *perception* of color is identical to another's? Is it possible that your "red" may be someone else's "yellow"? The colors we perceive do not actually exist in the world around us; they are the product of what is in our environment, including properties of the object and the wavelength of the light it reflects, and the brain's interpretation of that light. Without getting inside the mind of another person and perceiving the world as he does, this question is very difficult to answer. When these factors change, so, too, do the colors we see.

Really Red
Angelina Jolie sported intensely red lipstick at the 2012 Academy Awards. Her lipstick may appear to be a pure red, but the color is most likely a blend of various red wavelengths. Most colors we encounter in the real world are a mix of different wavelengths. AP Photo/Matt Sayles

Go find the brightest, most saturated object you possess that has a yellow hue, and grab a strong flashlight while you are at it. Wait until it is dark outside. Now put the object on a table right in front of you and look at it with a dim light shining overhead. Next, shine the flashlight directly onto the yellow object and notice how your perception of the color changes. Finally, turn off all the lights in the room and notice again how your perception of the color changes.

try this

Your three perceptions of this same yellow object will be very different—not because the object itself has changed, but rather because the light shining upon it (and thus, the light it reflects) has changed.

Color perception results from the interaction between light and brain activity. The eyes take light energy and transform it into neural code for the brain to interpret. The exquisite specificity of this code allows us to distinguish between electric blue and cobalt, lime green, and chartreuse. All this is made possible by the eye's remarkable biology.

You Won't Believe Your Eyes

The human eye is nothing short of an engineering marvel (**INFOGRAPHIC 3.2** on page 105). When you look in the mirror, you see only a fraction of each ping-pong-sized eyeball; the rest is hidden inside your head. Let's explore this biological wonder, starting from the outside and working our way toward the brain.

THE CORNEA   The surface of the eye looks wet and glassy. This clear outer layer over the colored portion of the eye is called the **cornea,** and it has two important jobs:

wavelength The distance between wave peaks (or troughs)

hue The color of an object, determined by the wavelength of light it reflects.

amplitude The height of a wave; the distance from midpoint to peak, or from midpoint to the trough of a wave.

saturation Color purity.

cornea The clear, outer layer of the eye that shields it from damage and focuses incoming light waves.

(1) shielding the eye from damage by dust, bacteria, or even a poke in the eye, and (2) focusing incoming light waves. About 65–75% of the focusing ability of the eye comes from the cornea, which is why imperfections in its shape can lead to blurred vision (National Eye Institute, 2012). Corneal flaws are primarily to blame for so many people (about a third of the American population) needing glasses or contact lenses. LASIK eye surgery, a popular alternative to corrective lenses, uses a laser to reshape the cornea so that it can focus light properly.

THE IRIS AND THE PUPIL   Directly behind the cornea is the donut-shaped **iris.** When you say someone has velvety brown eyes, you are really talking about the color of her irises. The black hole in the center of the iris is called the pupil. In dim lighting, the muscles of the iris relax, widening the pupil to allow more light inside the eye. In bright sunlight, the iris muscles squeeze, constricting the pupil to limit the amount of light. At first glance, the pupils may seem empty and boring. But pupils are actually quite sexy. Studies show, for example, that men are more enticed by women with enlarged pupils (Hess, 1975; Tombs & Silverman, 2004). When looking at someone she finds attractive, a woman's pupils dilate—and this response is magnified during the most fertile time of her monthly cycle (Laeng & Falkenberg, 2007).

THE LENS AND ACCOMMODATION   Behind the pupil is the lens, a tough, transparent structure that is similar in size and shape to an "M&M's candy" (Mayo Clinic, 2011). Like the cornea, the lens specializes in focusing incoming light, but it can also change shape in order to adjust to images near and far, a process called **accommodation.** If you take your eyes off this page and look across the room, faraway objects immediately come into focus because your lens changes shape. As we age, the lens begins to stiffen, impairing our ability to focus on up-close images like the letters on a computer screen. You can tell if a person has this condition, called presbyopia, when she strains to read a book or restaurant menu at arm's length. Most people develop some degree of presbyopia between 40 to 65 years old (Mayo Clinic, 2011).

The Retina

After passing through the cornea, pupil, and lens, light waves travel through the eyeball's jellylike filling and land on the **retina,** a carpet of neurons covering the back wall of the eye. This area of the eye was the source of the triplets' visual impairments. Emma, Zoe, and Sophie all suffered from retinopathy of prematurity (ROP), a condition in which blood vessels in the retina grow incorrectly. The last 3 months of pregnancy are critical for fetal eye development, when webs of blood vessels rapidly branch from the center of the retina outward, delivering crucial oxygen and nutrients to the developing tissue. The triplets were born over 3 months early, long before the blood vessel development was complete. The vessels began to branch abnormally, eventually pulling the retina from the back of the eye (Chawla et al., 2012).

The retina is responsible for the *transduction* of light energy into neural activity; that is, sensing light and relaying a message to the brain. Without the retina, vision is impossible.

LO 5   Describe the function of rods and cones.

PHOTORECEPTORS AND OTHER NEURONS   The retina is home to millions of specialized neurons called **photoreceptors,** which absorb light energy and turn it into chemical and electrical signals for the **brain to process.** Two types of photoreceptors are located along the back of the retina, *rods* and *cones,* which get their names from

CONNECTIONS

In **Chapter 2,** we noted that neurons are activated in response to sensations. In the case of vision, the sensation is light and the neurons being stimulated start with the photoreceptors in the retina. When a photoreceptor fires, its message is sent on its way to the brain.

iris The muscle responsible for changing the size of the pupil.
accommodation The process by which the lens changes shape in order to focus on images near and far.
retina The layer of the eye that contains photoreceptor cells and the location for the transduction of light energy into neural activity.
photoreceptors Cells that absorb light energy and turn it into chemical and electrical signals for the brain to process.

Seeing

"Seeing" involves more than simply looking at an object. Vision is a complex process in which light waves entering the eye are directed toward the retina where they are transduced into messages the brain can understand. The triplets all experienced vision loss from retinopathy of prematurity (ROP), a condition in which blood vessels in the retina grow incorrectly. Damage to this crucial structure has a severe impact on vision.

2 Iris dilates and contracts pupil to control amount of light entering eye.

3 Cornea and lens focus light waves toward the retina, bending the light and projecting an inverted image.

1 Light waves bouncing off an object enter your eye through the cornea, pupil, and lens.

4 Light strikes the retina, exciting photoreceptors.

5 Rods and cones fire, activating bipolar cells found in retina. This excites ganglion cells, which form the optic nerve carrying messages to the brain.

Ganglion cells

Bipolar cells

Photoreceptors

Rods

Cones

Light

Lens

Iris

Cornea

Pupil

Light waves

Retina

Blind spot

Optic disc

Fovea

Optic nerve

RETINOPATHY OF PREMATURITY (ROP)

is a condition characterized by irregular blood vessel growth in the eye. If a baby is born too early (before 31 weeks), blood vessels serving the retina may fail to develop properly, leaving part of the retina without blood vessels. Scar tissue may also pull the retina away from its normal position in the back of the eye (National Eye Institute, 2009). Even when light waves are received by the eye, vision is impossible without a healthy retina to transduce light into messages the brain can understand.

Detached retina

Abnormal blood vessel growth

Here we see the incomplete blood vessel growth characteristic of ROP. The vessels, shown here in yellow, stop before they reach the front of the eye.

Credits: Cute puppy, Thinkstock; Retinopathy in premature infant (retinal fluorescein angiogram showing hypoxia of the retinal periphery), BSIP/UIG Via Getty Images their characteristic shapes. **Rods** are extremely sensitive, firing in response to even a single *photon,* the smallest possible packet of light (Rieke & Baylor, 1998). If rods were all we had, the world would look something like an old black-and-white movie. **Cones** enable us to enjoy a visual experience more akin to HDTV (except for those of us with *color deficiencies,* which we will discuss later). In addition to providing color vision, cones allow us to see fine details, such as the small print on the back of a shampoo bottle.

The rods and cones are just the first step in a complex signaling cascade involving many neurons, which ultimately leads to a visual experience in the brain. The rods and cones are in close proximity to *bipolar cells,* which are also a specialized type of neuron located approximately in the middle of the retina. When a rod or cone is stimulated by light energy, it conveys its signal to nearby bipolar cells. These bipolar cells in turn convey their signal to *ganglion cells.* The ganglion cells, which comprise another type of neuron, are located toward the front of the retina. Axons of the ganglion cells bundle together in the **optic nerve,** which is like an electrical cable hooking the retina to the brain. The axons of the ganglion cells form one bundle for each eye in the *optic nerves,* which exit the retina at the *optic disc,* causing a **blind spot,** since it lacks rods or cones. You can find your blind spot by following the instructions in the Try This.

try this

Holding your book at arm's length, close your right eye and stare at the orange with your left eye. Slowly bring the book closer to your face. The apple on the left will disappear when light from that picture falls on your blind spot.

THE FOVEA The retina in each eye is home to some 120 million rods and 6 million cones (Amesbury & Schallhorn, 2003). Rods are found everywhere in the retina except for a tiny central spot called the *fovea.* Although cones are packed most densely in the fovea, they can also be found sprinkled throughout the rest of the retina. When you need to study something in great detail (like the tiny serial number on the back of a computer), hold it under a bright light and stare at it straight-on. The cones in the fovea excel at sensing detail and operate best in ample light. If, however, you want to get a look at something in the dim light, focus your gaze slightly to its side, stimulating the super-light-sensitive rods outside the fovea.

IS THAT OPRAH WINFREY OVER THERE? Let's stop for a moment and examine how information flows through the visual pathway (Infographic 3.2 on page 105). Suppose you are looking at Oprah Winfrey's face. Remember, you're actually seeing the light that her face reflects. Normally, light rays bouncing off Oprah would continue moving along a straight-line path, but they encounter the bulging curvature of the cornea covering your pupil, which bends them. (The light is later bent by the lens, but to a lesser extent.) The cornea redirects light rays on their way to the retina. Rays entering the top bend downward and those striking the base bend upward. The result is an inverted, or flip-flopped, projection on your retina. It's like your eye is a movie theater, the retina is its screen, and the feature film being played is "Your World, Turned Upside Down" (Kornheiser, 1976; Stratton, 1896). The neurons in the retina respond to the stimulus, sending signals from the photoreceptor cells to the bipolar cells, and then on to the ganglion cells, which bundle into the optic nerves.

FEATURE DETECTORS The optic nerves (one from each eye) intersect at a place in the brain called the *optic chiasm*. From there, information coming from each eye gets split, with about half traveling to the same-side thalamus and half going to the opposite-side thalamus. **Interneurons** then shuttle the data to the *visual cortex*, located in the occipital lobes in the back of your head. Neurons in the visual cortex called **feature detectors** specialize in detecting specific features of your visual experience, such as angles, lines, and movements. How these features are pieced together into a unified visual experience (*I see Oprah!*) is complex. Hubel and Wiesel (1979) proposed that visual processing begins in the visual cortex, where teams of cells respond to specifically oriented lines (as opposed to just pixel-like spots of light), and then continues in other parts of the cortex, where information from both eyes is integrated. Scientists have now identified at least 30 different areas in the brains of humans and other primates that play a role in visual processing (Ramachandran & Rogers-Ramachandran, 2009).

Now that we have outlined the general flow of information from eyes to brain, let's learn how the visual system adapts to the ever-changing environment.

DARK AND LIGHT ADAPTATION The eye has an amazing ability to adjust to drastic fluctuations in light levels. This process starts with the pupil, which rapidly shrinks and expands in response to light changes, and then continues with the rods and cones, which need more time to adjust to changes in lighting. When you walk into a dark movie theater after being outside in the bright sun, you can barely see an inch in front of your face. After a few minutes, your eyes start to adjust to the dark in a process called **dark adaptation,** which takes about 8 minutes for cones and 30 minutes for rods (Hecht & Mandelbaum, 1938; Klaver, Wolfs, Vingerling, Hoffman, & de Jong, 1998). Cones respond more quickly, so they are more useful in the first few minutes of dark adaptation. Then the rods kick into action, allowing you to make out silhouettes of objects and people. Why are these photoreceptors so sluggish in their responses to darkness? To restore their sensitivity to light, rods and cones must undergo a chemical change associated with protein molecules, and this takes time (Caruso, 2007, August 13; Ludel, 1978). Also keep in mind that, for most of human evolution, dark adaptation meant adjusting to the gradual setting of the sun (Caruso, 2007, August 13).

What happens when you *leave* the dark theater and return to the blinding light of day—do the eyes also adjust then? The answer is yes. With **light adaptation,** the pupil constricts to reduce the amount of light flooding the retina, and the rods and cones become less sensitive to light. Light adaptation occurs relatively quickly, lasting at most 10 minutes (Ludel, 1978). Dark and light adaptation demonstrate the eye's ability to accommodate to changes in brightness—an amazing feat. But the eye is capable of much more; remember, it can discern among millions of colors.

In Living Color

Although we have discussed the various features of color, we have not yet explained *how* waves of electromagnetic energy result in our perception of colors. How does the brain know red from maroon, green from turquoise, grey from charcoal? Two main theories explain human color vision—the *trichromatic theory* and the *opponent-process theory*—and you need to understand both because they address different aspects of the phenomenon.

▶ **LO 6** Compare and contrast the theories of color vision.

THE TRICHROMATIC THEORY Proposed in the 1800s by an English physician-scientist, Thomas Young (1773–1829), and then expanded upon several decades later by Hermann von Helmholtz (1821–1894), a Prussian physicist, the

CONNECTIONS

Interneurons are found in the central nervous system (the brain and the spinal cord). As described in **Chapter 2,** the interneurons receive and help process signals from sensory neurons.

rods Specialized light receptors in the retina that are responsible for sight when the light level is low; not sensitive to color, but useful for night vision.

cones Specialized light receptors responsible for our sensation of color and our ability to sense details.

optic nerve The bundle of axons from ganglion cells leading to the visual cortex.

blind spot The location where the optic nerve exits the retina.

feature detectors Neurons in the visual cortex specialized in detecting specific features of the visual experience, such as angles, lines, and movements.

dark adaptation Ability of the eyes to adjust to dark after exposure to brightness.

light adaptation Ability of the eyes to adjust to light after being in the dark.

trichromatic theory (trī-krō-'ma-tik) suggests that we have three types of cones. Red cones are excited by electromagnetic energy with wavelengths in the red range (about 620–700 nm); green cones fire in response to electromagnetic energy with wavelengths in the green realm (500–575 nm); and blue cones are activated by electromagnetic energy with wavelengths corresponding to blues (about 450–490 nm; Mollon, 1982).

So how is it that we can detect millions of colors when our cones are only sensitive to red, green, and blue? The primary colors of light are also red, green, and blue, and when mixed together in equal proportions, they appear as white light (see the photograph to the left). According to the trichromatic theory, the brain identifies a precise hue by calculating patterns of excitement among the three cone populations. When you look at a yellow banana, for example, both the red and green cones fire, but not the blue ones. The brain interprets this pattern of red and green activation as "yellow." And because white light is actually a mixture of all the wavelengths in the visible spectrum, it excites all three cone types, creating a sensation of "white" in the mind's eye. Thus, it is the relative activity of the three types of cones that the brain uses to make its color calculations.

COLOR DEFICIENCY AND COLOR BLINDNESS   Loss or damage to one or more of the cone types leads to *color deficiency,* more commonly known as "color blindness." These terms are often used interchangeably, but true color blindness is extremely rare. Sometimes color blindness is accompanied by extreme sensitivity to light and poor vision for detail, both resulting from deficient or missing cones (Tränkner et al., 2004). The condition associated with red–green color defects occurs in about 8% of men and less than 1% of women with European ancestors (Deeb, 2005). Color deficiencies may stem from problems with the cones. Most people with color deficiencies have trouble distinguishing between red and green because they are missing or deficient in the red or green receptors, but can see other colors very well. You can get an indication of red–green deficiency by looking at the Ishihara color plate to the left. If you can't see the number shown, then you may have a red–green deficiency (Wong, 2011).

Ample research backs up the trichromatic theory, but there are some color-related phenomena it cannot explain. A prime example is the *afterimage effect.* An **afterimage** is an *image* that appears to linger in your visual field *after* its stimulus, or source, is gone.

OPPONENT-PROCESS THEORY   German physiologist Ewald Hering (1834–1918) realized that the trichromatic theory could not explain the visual phenomenon of the afterimage effect and thus developed the **opponent-process theory** of color vision. Hering proposed that in addition to the color-sensitive cones, a special group of neurons responds to opponent colors—pairs of colors such as red–green and blue–yellow that cannot be perceived simultaneously (there is no such thing as reddish-green or bluish-yellow light). One neuron in an opponent pair fires when you look at red, but is inactive when you see green. The other neuron gets excited by green but turned off by red. If you spend enough time staring at the red and blue picture in the Try This on page 108, the neurons excited by these colors become exhausted and stop responding. When you shift your gaze to the white surface, the opponent neurons fire in response to the green and yellow wavelengths. Meanwhile, the red and blue neurons are too fatigued to rally (when not fatigued, they would normally respond). You end up seeing an afterimage of the box and a plus sign in green and yellow. Research has provided strong support for the opponent-process theory, identifying particular types of neurons located in a region of the thalamus (DeValois & DeValois, 1975; Jameson & Hurvich, 1989).

As it turns out, we need both the trichromatic and opponent-process theories to clarify different aspects of color vision. Color perception occurs in the light-sensing cones in the retina and in the opponent cells serving the brain. The ability to perceive color is not based on processing at a single point along the visual pathway, or even one area of the brain (Gegenfurtner, 2003; Solomon & Lennie, 2007).

Ultimately, these color perceptions lead to cognitive and emotional responses. You may believe blue is a sad color, and yellow is warm and comforting. What you think and feel about a particular color depends on many factors, including your culture.

across the WORLD

Colors and Culture

Red is a lucky color in China but a sign of bad fortune in Nigeria. People in the United States see white as a symbol of virginity and cleanliness; those in East Asia associate it with dying and bereavement (Sable & Akcay, 2010). Black is considered upscale and influential across cultures (Madden, Hewett, & Roth, 2000). And blue, the most popular "favorite color" in the world, carries different meanings for various groups: sanctity in the Jewish religion, warmth for the Dutch, and the color of the god Krishna for Hindus (Akcay, Dalgin, & Bhatnagar, 2011; Sable & Akcay, 2011).

How do you explain the similarities and differences in these responses to color? Like many questions in psychology, we can use the **biopsychosocial perspective** to explore this. Seeing certain colors can elicit measurable biological responses. In one study, for example, people exposed to blue light—but not red light—experienced significant drops in blood pressure and breathing rate (Visweswaraiah & Telles, 2006). In addition, some scholars suggest that learning is a key factor shaping the cultural meanings of color (Sable & Akcay, 2011). If a color is repeatedly presented in a certain context (black clothes at a funeral, pink clothes on a girl baby), mental associations begin to take hold (black is for grieving; pink is for girls). It appears our perception of color is the result of a complex mixture of biological, psychological, and sociocultural factors.

Perception of color may vary significantly across cultures, and even between individuals, but the early stages of sensation are virtually the same for everyone with normal vision. The fact that the complex visual system works so well for so many people is really quite amazing. Equally intricate is the auditory system. Next we'll discover how hearing works—and how easily it can be dismantled—using the triplets as our example.

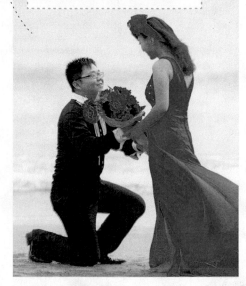

Wed in Red
A couple in China poses for a wedding photo. The bridal gown and roses are red, a color that connotes luck in Chinese culture. Many brides also wear red in India, where this color is associated with purity (Akcay, Dalgin, & Bhatnagar, 2011). © Hou Jiansen/Xinhua/ZUMAPRESS.com

SEEING RED IN CHINA

CONNECTIONS

In **Chapter 1,** we mentioned that psychologists use the biopsychosocial perspective to understand behavior. Here, we look at how biology, learning, and culture influence differences in color perception.

trichromatic theory (trī-krō-ˡma-tik) The perception of color is the result of three types of cones, each sensitive to particular wavelengths in the red, green, and blue spectrums.

afterimage An image that appears to linger in the visual field after its stimulus, or source, is removed.

opponent-process theory Perception of color derives from a special group of neurons that respond to opponent colors (red–green, blue–yellow).

✓◯◯◯   show what you know

1. The hue of a color is determined by the _____ of the light reflecting off an object.

2. Cells contained in the retina that absorb light energy and turn it into chemical and electrical signals are called _____.
   a. opponent-processing
   c. fovea
   b. photoreceptors
   d. feature detectors

3. Explain the two theories of color vision presented in the chapter and how they differ.

4. It's dark in your house, and you are struggling to see what time it is without turning on the light. You notice that if you turn your gaze slightly to the side of your watch, you can make out the large numbers. The ability to see these large details in the dark is due to your:
   a. presbyopia.
   c. cones.
   b. optic disc.
   d. rods.

✓ CHECK YOUR ANSWERS IN APPENDIX C.

Hearing

THE EARS OF THE TRIPLETS Taking care of three blind infants and a preschooler was no easy task, but Liz was strong, stubborn, and determined to see her girls thrive. And the triplets did thrive. By 20 months, they were beginning to reach the major developmental milestones of babyhood: walking and talking. But just as they were beginning to take their first steps and say their first words, "cup" and "Mama," everything fell apart.

It started with Zoe, who out of the blue stopped playing with her favorite toy, a cube that made different sounds when she pushed on its sides. Zoe would push the buttons over and over, then burst into tears. Eventually, Zoe and her sisters stopped responding to Liz's voice. Hearing had been the main portal connecting the triplets to the outside world. It allowed them to communicate their needs to Liz, babble among themselves, and take pleasure in music. But now that door had closed, too.

It was also during this period that the triplets began to act as if they had some kind of stomach illness—refusing to eat, vomiting during car rides, curling up in the fetal position, and banging their heads against the floor. These were not the symptoms of a tummy ache, but something much more troubling: vertigo, a dizzying sensation of spinning or whirling.

Both conditions—the deafness and the vertigo—arose from deterioration of the inner ear, home to the delicate structures responsible for hearing and balance. The damage dated back to the triplets' first few months in the hospital when doctors had given them antibiotics. The drugs may have saved the girls' lives, but they had a devastating side effect: ototoxicity, or "ear poisoning."

▶ **Toddling Triplets**
Liz sits with her firstborn Sarah (left back), and the triplets (left to right) Sophie, Emma, and Zoe. The triplets were about 12 months when this photo was taken.
Worldwide Features/Barcroft Media/Landov

Listen, Hear

▶ **LO 7**   Summarize how sound waves are transduced into the sensation of hearing.

The wind howling. A baby crying. Raindrops pelting the roof of the car. These sounds are perceived so differently, yet they all begin with the same type of stimulus: a sound wave moving through the environment. When we use our sense of hearing, or **audition,** we are detecting sound waves that enter our ears. Sound waves are the rhythmic vibrations of molecules traveling through a variety of forms of matter, such as air. Sound waves can also travel through materials like water, metal, and wood, which is why we can hear muffled sounds through the walls in an apartment or when swimming. Where do these sound waves originate?

SOUND WAVES Every sound wave begins with a vibration. That could mean a pulsating loud speaker, a quivering guitar string, or vocal chords fluttering in your throat. When an object vibrates, it sends a pressure disturbance of molecules moving through the air. Imagine a very quiet environment, such as late at night in a parked car; the molecules in the air in the car for the most part are evenly distributed. If you were to turn on the radio with its amplified speakers, the speaker's membrane would immediately bulge outward, pushing air particles out of its way. This creates a zone where the particles are tightly packed and the pressure is high; the particles directly in front of the speaker will hit the particles right in front of them, and so on throughout the interior of your car. As the speaker retracts, or pulls back, it gives the air particles ample room to move, creating a zone where particles are spread out and pressure is low. As the speaker rhythmically pushes back and forth, it sends *cycles* of waves of high pressure (with particles "bunched up") and low pressure (with particles "spread out") rippling through the air (Ludel, 1978). It's important to note that molecules are not being transmitted when you speak to a friend across the room; air particles from your mouth do not travel to his ears, only the sound wave does.

Now that we have established what sound waves are—alternating zones of high and low pressure moving through the environment—let's address the immense variation in sound quality. Why are some noises loud and others soft, some shrill like a siren and others deep like a bullfrog? Sounds can be differentiated by three main qualities: *loudness, pitch,* and *timbre.*

LOUDNESS   Let's begin by exploring loudness. We sense the loudness of a sound based on the amplitude, or height, of the wave it generates. A kitten purring generates low-amplitude sound waves; a NASCAR engine generates high-amplitude sound waves. Just remember: The taller the mound, the louder the sound. Loudness is measured in decibels (dB), with 0 dB being the absolute threshold for human hearing; normal conversation is around 60 dB. Noises at 140 dB can be instantly detrimental to hearing (Yost, 2007). But you needn't stand next to a 140-dB jet engine to sustain hearing loss. Prolonged exposure to moderately loud sounds such as traffic and loud music can also cause damage. Think twice the next time you crank up the volume on your iPod. **FIGURE 3.2** illustrates sound levels, some of which are capable of causing auditory damage.

PITCH   The **pitch** of a sound describes how high or low it is. An example of a high-pitched sound is a flute at its highest notes; a low-pitched sound is a tuba at its lowest notes. The pitch of a sound is based on the **frequency** of its waves. We measure frequency with a unit called the *Hertz* (Hz), which indicates the number of wave peaks passing a given point in 1 second. A higher-pitched sound, like the high note of a flute, will have a higher frequency of waves; the time between the "bunched up" particles and the "spread out" particles will be less than that for the lower-pitched sound of a tuba. If you are hearing a 200-Hz sound wave, then theoretically 200 waves enter your ear per second. Humans can detect frequencies ranging from about 20 Hz to 20,000 Hz, but we tend to lose the higher frequencies as we get older. **TABLE 3.2** on page 112 shows the range of frequencies that can be detected by humans and other species. And just remember, the faster the peaks, the higher the squeaks, and if waves are slow, the pitch is low.

When Emma, Zoe, and Sophie began to go deaf, they lost their ability to hear high frequencies first, which means they stopped hearing high-pitched sounds, like female voices, before they lost the ability to detect deeper sounds. It pains Liz to reminisce about this period because she wonders how her babies felt when it seemed like their Mom had stopped talking to them.

▲ **FIGURE 3.2**
Decibels and Damage
Loudness is measured in decibels (dB). The absolute threshold for human hearing—the softest sound a human can hear—is described as 0 dB. Loud noises, such as the 140 dB produced by a jet engine, cause immediate nerve damage leading to hearing loss. Chronic exposure to moderately loud noise, such as traffic or an MP3 player near maximum volume, can also cause damage (Keith, Michaud, & Chiu, 2008).
Airplane, istockphoto/Thinkstock; Motorcycle: Vasiliy Vishnevskiy/Alamy; Whispering women, Photosindia/ Getty Images

Synonyms

loudness volume

audition The sense of hearing.

pitch The degree to which a sound is high or low determined by the frequency of its sound wave.

frequency The number of sound waves passing a given point per second; higher frequency is perceived as higher pitch, and lower frequency is perceived as lower pitch.

People with normal hearing can generally tell the difference between high and low pitches, but singing notes on key is quite a different story. If you've ever been to a karaoke club, you know that plenty of people cannot carry a tune to save their lives. Why is this so?

from the pages of **SCIENTIFIC AMERICAN**

Physically Out of Tune

Poor muscle control, not aural perception, underlies most cases of bad singing

A cringe-worthy chorus of "Happy Birthday" is usually all it takes to earn the label of "tone-deaf." Yet fewer than 1 percent of the population is truly amusical, that is, lacking the ability to distinguish different pitches. Many more of us simply can't carry a tune. A study published online in the *Journal of Experimental Psychology: General* reinforces scientists' growing belief that the culprit is not the ear but the throat. In a series of pitch-matching experiments, nonmusicians were pretty good at adjusting an instrument to match a specific note, suggesting that they could hear it just fine. They had much more trouble, however, imitating the same note with their own voice. The authors suspect that poor motor control of vocal muscles is partly to blame—findings that reinforce the idea that almost anyone can learn to sing. **Lena Groeger. Reproduced with permission. Copyright © 2012 Scientific American, a division of Nature America, Inc. All rights reserved.**

Table 3.2 RANGE OF FREQUENCIES THAT CAN BE DETECTED BY SPECIES	
Species	**Approximate Frequency Range (Hz)**
Elephant	16–12,000
Human	64–23,000
Rabbit	360–42,000
Dog	67–45,000
Cat	45–64,000
Mouse	1,000–91,000
Bat	2,000–110,000
Beluga whale	100–123,000

Bats cannot see very well, but they have an exquisite sense of hearing. Like many animal species, bats can detect sound frequencies well beyond the range of human hearing.

SOURCE: ADAPTED FROM STRAIN (2003).

TIMBRE We know that sounds can have different levels of loudness and pitch, but how is it possible that two sounds with identical loudness and pitch (Beyonce and Shakira belting the same note at the same volume) can sound so different? The answer to this question lies in the timbre. The texture of a sound, or *timbre,* describes its unique combination of frequencies. Most of the "racket" you hear on a regular basis—people's voices, traffic noises, humming air conditioners—is made up of many frequencies. Timbre is the reason we can tell the difference between two sounds with exactly the same pitch and loudness.

All Ears

We have outlined the basic properties of sound. Now let's learn how the ears transform sound waves into the language of the brain. As you will see, your ears are extraordinarily efficient at what they do—transducing the physical motion of sound waves into the electrical and chemical signals of the nervous system (**INFOGRAPHIC 3.3** on page 114).

FROM SOUND WAVE TO BONE MOVEMENTS What exactly happens when a sound wave reaches your ear? First it is ushered inside by the ear's funnel-like structure. Then it sweeps down the auditory canal, a tunnel leading to a delicate membrane called the eardrum, which separates the outer ear from the middle ear. The impact of the sound wave bouncing against the eardrum sets off a chain reaction through the three tiny bones in the middle ear: the hammer, anvil, and stirrup. The chain reaction of the tiny bones moving each other amplifies the sound wave, turning it into a physical motion that has great strength. The hammer pushes the anvil; the anvil moves the stirrup; and the stirrup presses on a drumlike membrane called the *oval window* leading to the ear's deepest cavern, the inner ear. It is in this cavern that the amazing transduction occurs, eventually registering in the brain as sound.

FROM BONE MOVEMENT TO MOVING FLUID   The oval window marks the boundary to the inner ear. The **cochlea** (kō-klē-ə), a snail-shaped structure filled with liquid, is the primary component of the inner ear. It is also the place where the auditory receptors are. These cells take the information conveyed by the sound and transform it into neural messages: (1) The sound waves hit the eardrum, (2) which starts the vibrations of the tiny bones, (3) causing fluid in the cochlea to vibrate as well. Let's take a closer look at what is occurring inside the cochlea.

The entire length of the cochlea is lined with the *basilar membrane,* which contains about 16,000 hair cells. These hair cells are the receptor cells for the sound waves, which have been transformed into liquid waves. When the fluid in the cochlea moves, the hair cells bend in response to this motion. Below the base of the hair cells are dendrites of neurons whose axons form the *auditory nerve* (Ludel, 1978). If a vibration is strong enough in the cochlear fluid, the bending of the hair cells causes the nearby nerve cells to fire. Signals from the auditory nerve pass through various processing hubs in the brain, including the thalamus, and eventually wind up in the auditory cortex, where sounds are given meaning.

COCHLEAR IMPLANTS   The cochlea is an extremely delicate structure. If the hair cells are damaged or destroyed, they will not regrow like blades of grass (at least in humans and other mammals). So when Emma, Zoe, and Sophie lost their hearing around age 2, there was no magical drug or surgical procedure that could restore their hearing. Hope arrived about a year later, when the triplets were outfitted with cochlear implants, electronic devices that help those who are deaf or hard-of-hearing. These "bionic ears," as they are sometimes called, pick up sound waves from the environment with a microphone and turn them into electrical impulses that stimulate the auditory nerve, much as the cochlea would do were it functioning properly. From there, the auditory nerve transmits electrical signals to the brain, where they are "heard," or interpreted as human voices, hip-hop beats, and dog barks.

Cochlear implants have enabled many people to understand language and appreciate music, but "hearing" with a cochlear implant is not exactly the same as hearing with two ears. Voices may sound computerized or Mickey Mouse-like (Mayo Clinic, 2012, May 11). Liz had no idea how the girls would respond to their first experience hearing with the implants. They reacted the same way they do to most everything in life—each in her own way. Zoe broke into a huge grin; Emma sat still, just listening; and Sophie started crying (Hudson & Paul, 2007).

You might be wondering why the triplets were provided with cochlear implants, not *hearing aids.* Hearing aids work by increasing the amplitude of incoming sound waves (making them louder) so the hair cells in the inner ear can better detect them. If hair cells are damaged beyond repair, as was the case for Emma, Zoe, and Sophie,

cochlea (kō-klē-ə) Fluid-filled, snail-shaped organ of the inner ear lined with the basilar membrane.

Can You Hear Me Now?

Side effects of lifesaving drugs given to the triplets as newborns eventually led to deterioration of the inner ear, home of the delicate structures where vibrations are converted to electrical and chemical signals that the brain understands as sound. Without this conversion, sound waves may enter the ear, but we do not "hear." Hearing is a process in which stimuli (sound waves) are mechanically converted to vibrations that are transduced to neural messages. If one part of this complicated system is compromised, hearing loss results. In the triplets' case, cochlear implants provide a sense of sound.

1 The pinna funnels sound waves into the auditory canal, focusing them toward the eardrum.

2 Vibrations in the eardrum cause hammer to push anvil, which moves stirrup, which presses on oval window, amplifying waves.

3 Pressure on oval window causes fluid in cochlea to vibrate.

4 Vibrating fluid in cochlea bends hair cells on basilar membrane, triggering action potentials in the auditory nerve.

5 Auditory nerve carries signals to auditory cortex in brain, where sounds are given meaning.

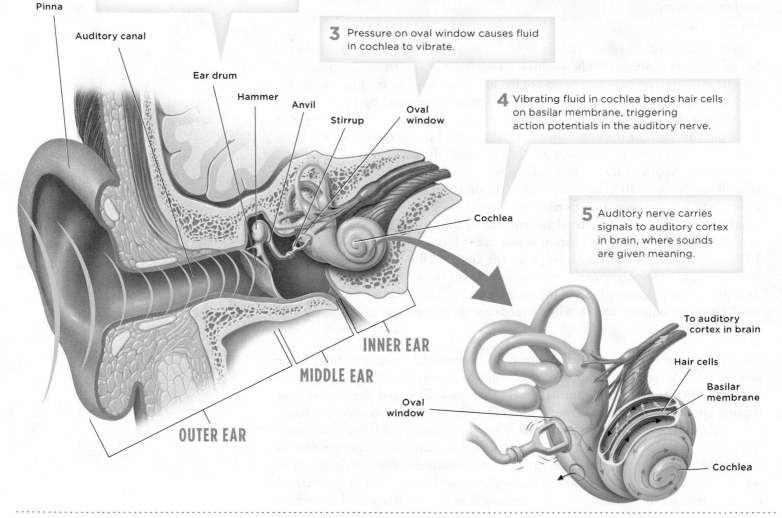

Pinna
Auditory canal
Ear drum
Hammer
Anvil
Stirrup
Oval window
Cochlea

OUTER EAR
MIDDLE EAR
INNER EAR

To auditory cortex in brain
Hair cells
Basilar membrane
Cochlea
Oval window

COCHLEAR IMPLANTS enable hearing by circumventing damaged parts of the inner ear. An external microphone gathers sound, which is organized by a speech processor. Internally, an implanted receiver converts this signal into electrical impulses that directly stimulate the auditory nerve.

This x-ray shows the cochlear implant's electrode array coiling into the cochlea, directly reaching nerve fibers leading to the auditory nerve.

Transmitter
Receiver/stimulator
Speech processor
Microphone
Auditory nerve
Cochlea
Electrode array

then the inner ear cannot pass along messages to the brain. There will be no sensation of hearing, no matter how much you turn up the volume.

CONTROVERSIES

Conflicted Feelings About Cochlear Implants

➡️⬅️ Cochlear implants are a marvel of modern technology. To take a brain full of silence and fill it with sound—now, that is an accomplishment worth celebrating, right? Not everyone in the deaf community thinks so. Cochlear implants may sound like a "miracle cure" for people with hearing difficulties, but they are not without controversy (Papsin & Gordon, 2007). The deaf community is divided on the issue, with many saying that deafness is not a medical problem that needs to be fixed, but instead is a culture with its own language, literature, art, and educational system (Swanson, 1997). Some individuals view their deafness as a gift and would choose to remain deaf even if given the opportunity to acquire normal hearing (Sparrow, 2005). Sign language bonds the deaf community, and cochlear implants threaten to weaken that bond by assimilating deaf people into the hearing world. The issue becomes particularly prominent in cases involving young children, whose parents are making decisions for them. When it comes to cochlear implants, there is no right or wrong—only choices appropriate for the unique circumstances facing each individual. ➡️⬅️

> SOME DEAF INDIVIDUALS VIEW THEIR DEAFNESS AS A GIFT....

Pitch and the Cochlea

We know how sound waves are transformed into auditory sensations, but there are many types of sounds. How does the brain know the difference between the yap of a Chihuahua and the deep bark of a Rottweiler, or the sweet song of a flute and the bellow of a tuba? In other words, how do we distinguish between sound waves of high and low frequencies? There are two complementary theories that explain how the brain processes pitch.

LO 8 Illustrate how we sense different pitches of sound.

PLACE THEORY According to **place theory,** the location of neural activity along the cochlea allows us to sense the different pitches of high-frequency sounds. Hair cells toward the end of the basilar membrane near the oval window vibrate more to higher-frequency sounds. Hair cells toward the opposite end of the basilar membrane vibrate more in response to lower-frequency sounds. The brain determines the pitch of high-frequency sounds by judging where along the basilar membrane neural signals originate.

But, place theory is better at explaining higher-pitch than lower-pitch sounds. Lower-frequency sounds result in vibrations that are more dispersed along the basilar membrane, with a less precise location of movement than higher-pitch sounds. This makes it difficult for the brain to determine the entire range of pitches in this manner.

FREQUENCY THEORY To understand how humans perceive lower pitches, we can use the **frequency theory,** which suggests it is not where along the cochlea hair cells are vibrating, but how frequently they are firing (the number of neural impulses per second). The entire basilar membrane vibrates at the same frequency as a sound wave, causing the hair cells to be activated at that frequency, too, leading to associated neural activity. The neurons fire at the same rate as the vibrations, sending signals through the auditory nerve at this rate. If the sound wave has a frequency of 200 Hz,

place theory States that pitch corresponds to the location of the vibrating hair cells along the cochlea.

frequency theory States that pitch is determined by the vibrating frequency of the sound wave, basilar membrane, and associated neural impulses.

then the basilar membrane vibrates at 200 Hz, and the neurons in the auditory nerve fire at this rate as well.

VOLLEY PRINCIPLE   Neurons, however, can only fire so fast, the maximum rate being about 1,000 times per second. How does the frequency theory explain how we hear sounds higher than 1,000 Hz? According to the **volley principle,** neurons can "work" together so that their combined firing can exceed 1,000 times per second. Imagine a hockey team practicing for a tournament. The coach asks the players if they can fire shots on goal at a faster rate than one individual. The team members get together and decide to work in small groups and alternate shots on the goal. The first group skates and shoots, and as they are skating away from the goal to return to the back of the line, the next group takes their shots. Each time a group is finished shooting, the next group is ready to shoot. Neurons grouped together in the same way will fire in *volleys;* as one group of neurons finishes firing and is "**recovering,**" the next group will fire. The sum of all the groups firing, one after another, allows for the frequency of their firing to result in our perception of the pitch of the sound.

FROM 20 TO 20,000   Let's draw this all together. Human beings can hear sounds ranging in frequency from 20 to 20,000 Hz. The frequency theory explains how we perceive sounds from 20 to 400 Hz; the volley principle covers the 400 to 4,000 Hz range; and the place theory accounts for frequencies between 4,000 to 20,000 Hz. And at times, both place theory and the volley principle can be used to explain perceptions of sounds between 1,000 and 4,000 Hz.

We have now examined what occurs in a hearing system working at an optimal level. But many of us have auditory functioning that is far from perfect.

I Can't Hear You

Hearing loss is extremely common, affecting 16% of American adults under 70 (Agrawal, Platz, & Niparko, 2008). At least one third of people over age 65 and half of those over 80 have difficulty hearing (Desai, Pratt, Lentzner, & Robinson, 2001; Gordon-Salant & Callahan, 2009). Initially, high frequencies become hard to hear, making it difficult to understand certain consonant sounds such as the "th" in thumb (American Speech-Language Hearing Association, 2012). Everyone experiences some degree of hearing loss as they age, primarily resulting from normal wear and tear of the delicate hair cells. Damage to the hair cells or the auditory nerve leads to sensorineural deafness. Conduction hearing impairment results from damage to the eardrum or the middle-ear bones that transmit sound waves to the cochlea.

But it's not just adults and older people who ought to be concerned. One large study found that about 20%, or 1 in 5, of American teenagers suffer from some degree of hearing loss, and the problem appears to be on the rise (Shargorodsky, Curhan, Curhan, & Eavey, 2010). Exposure to loud sounds, such as listening to music on MP3 players at high volume through earbuds, may play a role. A study of Australian children determined that using personal stereo devices increased the risk of hearing loss by 70% (Cone, Wake, Tobin, Poulakis, & Rickards, 2010).

As you know from the triplets' story, certain medications can also harm the fragile structures of the ear, as can ear infections, tumors, and trauma. Some babies (between 1 and 6 of every 1,000) are born with severe to profound hearing loss (Cunningham & Cox, 2003). How do you think those babies adjust to their hearing deficit? How does anyone with a sensory weakness cope? They find ways to compensate, and often that means fine-tuning other sensory systems. Case in point: Zoe and her exquisite sense of smell.

CONNECTIONS

In **Chapter 2,** we described how neurons must recover after they fire, so that each neuron can return to its resting potential. It is during this period that they cannot fire, that is, they are "recovering."

Not Too Loud
Next time you use your earbuds, remember that long-term exposure to loud music can cause hearing damage. A sound needn't be earsplitting to harm your delicate auditory system. Granger Wootz/Blend Images

volley principle States that the perception of pitches between 400 and 4,000 Hz is made possible by neurons working together to fire in volleys.

olfaction (ōl-ˈfak-shən) The sense of smell.

show what you know

1. The pitch of a sound is based on the _____ of its waves.
   a. frequency   c. amplitude
   b. timbre   d. purity

2. When a sound wave hits the eardrum, it causes vibrations in the bones of the middle ear, making the fluid in the cochlea vibrate. Hair cells on the basilar membrane bend in response to the motion, causing nerve cells to fire. This process is known as:
   a. the volley principle.   c. the frequency theory.
   b. transduction.   d. audition.

3. A researcher studying the location of neural activity in the cochlea finds that hair cells nearest the oval window vibrate more to high-frequency sounds. This supports the _____ theory of pitch perception.

4. The mechanisms underlying how we sense the pitch of a sound are complicated. We have included two theories and one principle to explain pitch sensation. Try to solidify your understanding of how we hear pitch by creating a sketch of the process.

✓ CHECK YOUR ANSWERS IN APPENDIX C.

Smell, Taste, Touch: The Chemical and Skin Senses
Smell: Nosing Around

One day when Zoe was walking in the park with a friend, Liz decided to pay her an unexpected visit. As soon as her mom came within 15 feet, Zoe turned off the trail and made a beeline toward her with outstretched arms. She knew her mother had arrived because she could smell her, and she could do it while strolling through the breezy outdoors and eating a potent-smelling orange. Zoe was so confident in her sense of smell, explains Liz, "[that] she was willing to walk off the path into the grass to unknown territory, positive that's where I was." Either Zoe's sense of smell is **extraordinarily** sharp, or she has learned to use it more effectively than the average person. Do you think your nose could accomplish the same?

At Play
Zoe rocks on a spring rider at the playground. The triplets spend much of their time outdoors—at the playground, the park, and the swimming pool. Worldwide Features/ Barcroft Media/Landov

▶ **LO 9**   Describe the process of olfaction.

OLFACTION   Many people take **olfaction** (ōl-ˈfak-shən)—the sense of smell—for granted. But such individuals might think twice if they actually understood how losing olfaction would affect their lives. People with the rare condition of *anosmia* are unable to perceive odors. They cannot smell smoke in a burning building or a gas leak from a stove. They cannot tell whether the fish they are about to eat is spoiled. Nor can they savor the complex palates of pesto, curry, chocolate, coffee, or prime rib. Because, without smell, food doesn't taste as good.

CHEMICAL SENSE   Olfaction and taste are called chemical senses, because they involve sensing chemicals in the environment. For olfaction, those chemicals are odor molecules riding currents of air. For taste, they are flavor molecules surfing on waves of saliva. Odor molecules, which are emitted by a variety of sources (for example, spices, fruits, flowers, bacteria, and skin), make their way into the nose by hitchhiking on currents of air flowing into the nostrils or through the mouth. About 3 inches into the nostrils is a patch of tissue called the *olfactory epithelium.* Around the size of a typical postage stamp, the olfactory epithelium is home to millions of olfactory receptor neurons that provide tiny docking sites, or receptors, for odor molecules (much as a lock acts as a docking site for a key; FIGURE 3.3 on page 118). When enough odor molecules attach to an olfactory receptor neuron, it fires, causing an **action potential,** illustrating how *transduction* occurs in the chemical sense of olfaction.

CONNECTIONS

In **Chapter 2,** we introduced the concept of *neuroplasticity,* which refers to the ability of the brain to heal, grow, and make do with what's available. Here, we suggest that Zoe's heavy reliance on other senses is made possible by the plasticity of her nervous system.

CONNECTIONS

In **Chapter 2** we discussed the properties that allow neurons to communicate with other cells. When sending neurons signal a receiving neuron to pass along its message, their combined signal becomes *excitatory* and the neuron will fire. Here we are discussing olfactory receptor neurons stimulated by odor molecules. If enough odor molecules are present, an *action potential* occurs, causing a spike in electrical energy to pass through the axon.

Olfactory nerve

Olfactory bulb

Odor molecules

Olfactory bulb

Glomerulus
(glomeruli communicate
information from olfactory
neurons to higher brain centers)

Olfactory receptor neurons

Olfactory epithelium

Odor molecules bind
to receptor sites

▲ **FIGURE 3.3**
Olfaction
When enough odor molecules attach to an olfactory receptor neuron, it fires, sending a message to the olfactory bulb in the brain. Glomeruli then communicate the signal to the higher brain centers.

OLFACTION AND THE BRAIN   Olfactory receptor neurons stimulate a part of the brain called the *olfactory bulb,* with similar neurons converging in clusters called *glomeruli* (Figure 3.3). Then the signal is passed along to higher brain centers, including the hippocampus, amygdala, and olfactory cortex (Firestein, 2001). The other sensory systems relay data through the thalamus before going to higher brain centers. But the wiring of the olfactory system is unique; olfaction is on a fast track to the limbic system, where emotions like fear and anger are processed.

OLFACTORY RECEPTORS   There is another reason smell is special. Olfactory receptor neurons are one of the few types of neurons that regenerate. Once an olfactory receptor neuron is born, it does its job for a minimum of 30 days, then dies and is replaced (Schiffman, 1997). This process slows with age, impairing odor sensitivity (Larsson, Finkel, & Pedersen, 2000). If it weren't for this continual replenishment of olfactory neurons, we wouldn't smell much of anything. Olfactory neurons are in direct contact with the environment, so they are constantly under assault by bacteria, dirt, and noxious chemicals. Some toxins—like the fumes and dust at New York City's World Trade Center site after the terrorist attacks in 2001—can even cause long-term damage to the olfactory system. Many workers involved in the clean-up effort following 9/11 may be permanently impaired in their ability to smell (Dalton et al., 2010).

Humans have about 350 different *types* of odor receptors, yet we can distinguish over 10,000 different odors (Buck, 2004). Each receptor type recognizes several odors, and each odor activates several receptors; a given scent creates a telltale pattern of electrical activity that the brain recognizes as lemon, garlic, or smelly feet. The types of receptors and the degree to which they are activated identify the odor (Firestein, 2001). Our sense of smell may be keen, but it pales in comparison to that of some dogs, who can detect millions of odors. Humans can discriminate thousands of different odors, yet we may have trouble naming them (Schmidt & Cain, 2010).

Scents have a powerful influence on human behavior and thought. Within minutes after birth, babies use the scent of their mother's breast to guide them toward the nipple, and they quickly learn to discriminate Mom's milk from someone else's (Makin & Porter, 1989; Porter & Winberg, 1999). Research also suggests that odor-induced memories are not necessarily more accurate than those evoked by touching, hearing, or seeing something (Herz, 1998), but they are more emotional and "associated with stronger feelings of being brought back in time" (Larsson & Willander, 2009, p. 318). Why are memories triggered by smell so drenched in emotion? Remember that olfactory information is communicated directly to the limbic system. Evidence suggests that smells activate this emotion-processing hub more than other sensations. Brain imaging research indicates smelling a perfume remembered from one's past activates the amygdala more than looking at its bottle (Herz, 2007; Herz, Eliassen, Beland, & Souza, 2004).

Given the power of scent, it is no surprise people become attached to certain perfumes and scented body products. But would you believe smells are capable of cultivating more positive reactions to entire stores and other commercial entities? This is what scent marketers are hoping.

didn't SEE that coming

The Scent of Money

👁❗ Next time you pass by an upscale hotel, walk into the lobby and perk up your nose. You may catch wind of lavender, white tea, or citrus. Hotel chains are among the many commercial establishments now using "scent marketing" to allure customers. Sony Style uses hints of orange, vanilla, and cedar; and Las Vegas casinos such as the Mirage have been piping odors through their gambling halls since the 1990s, apparently in an attempt to drive up customer satisfaction and boost revenues (Rosenblum, 2010; Vlahos, 2007, September 9). But what does the science say?

Some research suggests that ambient odors can sway customer perceptions of stores and products. In one study, clothing store shoppers were more satisfied with their experience and spent more money when ambient scents were "gender congruent." Men reacted more positively when the store smelled "masculine" (like rose maroc) as opposed to "feminine" (vanilla), and women reacted more positively when the store smelled feminine (Spangenberg, Sprott, Grohmann, & Tracy, 2006). Another study found that diffusing an orange essence through the waiting room of a dental office reduced patients' anxiety and lightened their moods (Lehrner, Eckersberger, Walla, Pötsch, & Deecke, 2000).

Liudmila Sundikova/ALAMY

DOES THIS MARKETING STRATEGY SMELL?

Researchers are still trying to determine the extent to which aromas and other sensory stimuli affect the numbers, but it's probably safe to say that no aroma, no matter how luscious and enticing, will force you to squander your hard-earned cash. 👁❗

Taste: Just Eat It

Your sense of smell may not affect your shopping habits, but it definitely impacts your culinary preferences. Eating is as much an olfactory experience as it is a taste experience. Just think back to the last time your nose was clogged from a really bad cold. How did your meals taste? When you chew, odors from the food float up into your nose, creating a flavor that you perceive as "taste," when it's actually smell. If this mouth–nose connection is blocked, there is no difference between apples and onions, Sprite and Coke, or wine and cooled coffee (Herz, 2007). Don't believe us? Then do the Try This experiment on page 120.

try this

Tie on a blindfold, squeeze your nostrils, and ask a friend to hand you a wedge of apple and a wedge of onion, both on toothpicks so that you can't feel their texture. Now bite into both. Without your nose, you probably can't tell the difference (Rosenblum, 2010).

LO 10 Discuss the structures involved in taste and describe how they work.

GUSTATION   If the nose is so crucial for flavor appreciation, then what role does the mouth play? Receptors in the mouth are sensitive to five basic but very important tastes: sweet, salty, sour, bitter, and umami. You are likely familiar with all these tastes, except perhaps umami, which is a savory taste found in seaweed, aged cheeses, protein-rich foods, mushrooms, and monosodium glutamate (MSG; Chandrashekar, Hoon, Ryba, & Zuker, 2006). We call the ability to detect these stimuli our sense of taste, or **gustation** (gəs-'tā-shən; **FIGURE 3.4**).

CHEMICAL SENSE   Receptor cells for taste are found in the taste buds on the tongue, the roof of the mouth, and lining the cheeks. Somewhere between 5,000 to 10,000 taste buds are embedded in the *papillae,* those bumps you can see on a person's tongue (Society for Neuroscience, 2012). Jutting from each of these buds are 50 to 100 taste receptor cells, and it is onto these cells that taste molecules bind (similar to the lock-and-key mechanism of an odor molecule binding to a receptor in the nose).

As you bite into a juicy orange and begin to chew, chemicals from the orange (sour acid and sweet sugar) are released into your saliva, where they dissolve and bathe the taste buds throughout your mouth. The chemicals find their way to matching receptors and latch on, sparking action potentials in **sensory neurons,** another example of *transduction.* Signals are then sent through sensory neurons to the thalamus, and then on to higher brain centers for processing.

Receptors for taste are constantly being replenished; but their life span is only about 10 days (Schiffman, 1997). If they didn't regenerate, you would be in trouble

CONNECTIONS

In **Chapter 2,** we learned that sensory neurons receive information from the sensory system and send it to the brain for processing. With gustation, the sensory neurons are sending information about taste. Once processed in the brain, information can be sent back through motor neurons signaling you to take another bite!

FIGURE 3.4
Tasting
Taste buds located in the papillae are made up of receptor cells that communicate signals to the brain when stimulated by chemicals from food and other substances. Omikron/ Science Source

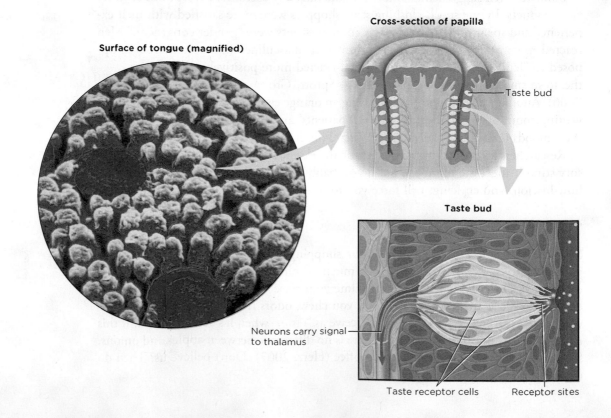

Surface of tongue (magnified)

Cross-section of papilla

Taste bud

Taste bud

Neurons carry signal to thalamus

Taste receptor cells   Receptor sites

every time you burned your tongue sipping hot coffee or eating hot soup. By age 20, you have already lost half of the taste receptors you had at birth. And as the years go by, their turnover rate gets slower and slower, making it harder to appreciate the basic taste sensations (Kaneda et al., 2000). Drinking alcohol and smoking worsen the problem by impairing the ability of receptors to receive taste molecules. Losing taste is unfortunate, and it may take away from life's simple pleasures, but it's probably not going to kill you—at least not if you are a modern human. But we can't be so sure about our primitive ancestors.

EVOLUTION AND TASTE   Taste has been essential to the survival of our species. Tastes push us toward foods we need and away from those that could harm us. We gravitate toward sweet, calorie-rich foods for their life-sustaining energy—an adaptive trait if you are a primitive human foraging in trees and bushes, not so adaptive if you are a modern human looking for something to eat at the food court in your local shopping mall. We are also drawn to salty foods, which tend to contain valuable minerals, and umami, which signals the presence of proteins essential for cellular health and growth. Bitter and sour tastes we tend to avoid, on the other hand. This also gives us an evolutionary edge because poisonous plants or rancid foods are often bitter and sour. And it is interesting to note that our *absolute threshold* for bitter is lower than the threshold for sweet. Can you see how this is advantageous to us?

In addition to evolutionary advantages, there are individual preferences. You like cilantro; your friend thinks it tastes like bath soap. Taste preferences may begin developing before birth, as flavors consumed by a pregnant woman pass into amniotic fluid and are swallowed by the fetus. Research suggests this early exposure shapes taste preferences later in life. For example, infants who were exposed in utero to the flavor of carrots (through their mothers' consumption of carrot juice in the last trimester) showed fewer disapproving facial expressions when fed carrot-flavored cereal compared to plain cereal. This suggests exposure to the carrot flavor before birth led to greater enjoyment of this taste compared to that of plain cereal. This taste preference was not evident in infants who had not been exposed to the flavor of carrots in utero (Mennella, Coren, Jagnow, & Beauchamp, 2001).

We have made some major headway in this chapter, examining four of the major sensory systems: vision, hearing, smell, and taste. Now it is time to get a feel for a fifth sense. Are you ready for tingling, tickling, and titillating touch?

Touch: Feel the Magic

If you were introduced to Zoe, she would probably explore your face for about 20 seconds, and then return to what she was doing. Emma would likely spend more time getting to know you. She might give you a hug, put her cheek against yours, and carefully explore your head with her fingers. Emma pores over things, paying close attention to detail. Zoe moves fast and focuses on the goal.

At the dinner table, Emma is neat and tidy, and does not like to get food on her hands and face. Zoe loves to dig in and make a mess. These two girls, who are genetically identical, experience the world of touch in dramatically different ways. But both rely on touch receptors that dwell within the body's main touch organ—the skin.

YOUR EPIDERMIS IS SHOWING   Take a moment to appreciate your vast *epidermis,* the outer layer of your skin. Weighing around 6 pounds on the average adult, the skin is the body's biggest organ and the barrier that protects our insides from cruel elements of the environment (bacteria, viruses, and physical objects) and distinguishes us from others (fingerprints, birth marks). It also shields us from the cold, sweats to cool us down, and makes vitamin D (Bikle, 2004). And perhaps most importantly, skin is a data collector. Every moment of the day, receptors in our skin gather

Supertaster
A graduate student performs a taste test at Rutgers University's Sensory Evaluation Laboratory. Researchers have found that some people are more sensitive than others to bitter-tasting foods. These "supertasters" tend to eat fewer vegetables because of their texture and slightly bitter taste (Marris, 2006). AP Photo/Brian Branch-Price

Feeling Around
Zoe approaches eating in a very tactile way, digging in and feeling the food on her skin. While Zoe cannot see or hear, her senses of smell, taste, and touch are extremely fine-tuned. Worldwide Features/Barcroft Media/Landov

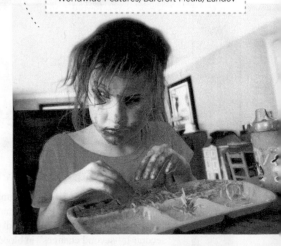

gustation (gəs-ˈtā-shən) The sensation of taste.

FIGURE 3.5
Touch
The sensation of touch begins with our skin, which houses a variety of receptors including those shown here.

Thermoreceptors (senses hot or cold)

Meissner's corpuscles (senses touch)

Hair follicle receptors (flutter and pressure)

Pacinian corpuscles (detect vibrations)

information about the environment. Among them are *thermoreceptors* that sense hot or cold, *Pacinian corpuscles* that detect vibrations, and *Meissner's corpuscles* sensitive to the slightest touch, like a snowflake landing on your nose (Bandell, Macpherson, & Patapoutian, 2007; **FIGURE 3.5**).

Oh, the Pain

Not all touch sensations are as pleasant as the tickle of a snowflake. Touch receptors can also communicate signals that are interpreted as pain. *Nociceptive pain* is caused by heat, cold, chemicals, and pressure. *Nociceptors* that respond to these stimuli are primarily housed in the skin, but they also are found in muscles and internal organs.

Speaking of temperature, have you ever experienced a brief, piercing headache immediately after gulping down ice cream? What is this *brain freeze,* and why does it happen?

from the pages of **SCIENTIFIC AMERICAN**

Brain Freeze Explained

Cold drinks cause a major artery in the skull to dilate.

Ice cream headache is a familiar summertime sensation, but the pain's source has been mysterious until now. A team led by Jorge Serrador of Harvard Medical School produced brain scans of "second-by-second changes" in blood flow while subjects sipped iced water through a straw pressed against the roof of the mouth,

which caused the brain's major artery to widen. "Blood flow changes actually preceded the pain" that subjects reported, Serrador says. As the vessel narrowed again, the discomfort ebbed. He suspects that the influx of blood is meant to protect the brain from extreme cold and that increased pressure inside the skull could cause the pain. Serrador presented the results at Experimental Biology 2012 in April in San Diego. **Stephani Sutherland. Reproduced with permission.**

CAN'T FEEL PAIN   In very rare cases, some children are born without the ability to feel pain. Children with this type of genetic disorder are potentially at greater risk of serious injury (Romero, Simón, Garcia-Recuero, & Romance, 2008). Not knowing they have been hurt, some scrapes and cuts might go unnoticed and untreated. Pain protects us from minor bangs and bruises as well as serious bodily harm. The "ouch" that results from the stub of a toe or the prick of a needle tells us to stop what we are doing and tend to our wounds. Let's find out how this protective mechanism works.

TWO PATHWAYS FOR PAIN   Thanks to the elaborate system of nerves running up and down our bodies, we are able to experience unpleasant, yet very necessary, sensations of pain. *Fast nerve fibers,* made up of large, myelinated neurons, are responsible for conveying information about pain occurring in the skin and muscles, generally experienced as a stinging feeling in a specific location. If you stub your toe, your first perception is a painful sting where the impact occurred. *Slow nerve fibers,* made up of smaller, unmyelinated neurons, are responsible for conveying information about pain throughout the body. Pain conveyed by the slow nerve fibers is more like a dull ache, not necessarily located in a specific region. After the immediate sting of stubbing your toe, you might feel a more diffuse aching in that area, due to slow nerve fibers. As the names of these **fibers** suggest, fast nerve fibers convey information quickly (at a speed of 30–110 meters/sec) and slow nerve fibers convey information more slowly (8–40 meters/sec; Somatosensory Function, 2004). But where are they sending this information?

The axons of these fast and slow sensory nerve fibers band together as nerves on their way to the spinal cord and up to the brain (**FIGURE 3.6**). The bundled fast nerve

CONNECTIONS

In **Chapter 2,** we explained how a myelin sheath insulates the axon and speeds up the conduction of electrical impulses. The myelin covering the fast nerve fibers allows them to convey their information about pain more quickly than the slow nerve fibers that are unmyelinated.

Thalamus

Somatosensory cortex

Limbic system

Hypothalamus

Amygdala

Reticular formation

Slow nerve fibers
(convey information to the hypothalamus, thalamus, and amygdala [emotion])

Fast nerve fibers
(convey information to the reticular formation [arousal], thalamus, and somatosensory cortex)

Spinal cord (section)

FIGURE 3.6
Fast and Slow Pain Pathways
When you stub your toe, two kinds of pain messages can be communicated to your brain. Your first perception of pain may be a sharp, clear feeling where the impact occurred. The message quickly travels through your spinal cord to your brain, signaling arousal and alerting you to react. Slow nerve fibers also travel through your spinal cord to carry messages about the pain that lingers after the initial injury, often generating an emotional response.

fibers make their way to the reticular formation of the brain, alerting it that something important has happened. The information then goes to the thalamus and on to the somatosensory cortex, where sensory information from the skin is processed further (for example, indicating where it hurts most). The bundled slow nerve fibers start out in the same direction toward the brain, with processing occurring in the brainstem, the hypothalamus, thalamus, and limbic system. In the midbrain and amygdala, for example, emotional reactions to the pain are processed (Gatchel, Peng, Peters, Fuchs, & Turk, 2007). As with other neurons, the transmission of information about pain occurs through electrical and chemical activities. *Substance P* and glutamate are two important neurotransmitters that work together to increase the firing of the pain fibers at the injury location.

Just knowing the mechanisms at the neural level does not explain how we perceive pain and why our experiences of pain are so varied. A bump on the head that causes one person to shriek in agony may not faze someone else. No two people experience pain exactly the same way.

···▶ **LO 11**   Describe how the biopsychosocial perspective is used to understand pain.

As with most complex topics in psychology, we need to explore the phenomenon of pain using a multilevel method, such as the biopsychosocial perspective. Chronic pain can be explained by biological factors (the neurological pathways involved), psychological factors (distress, cognition), and social factors (immediate environment, relationships; Gatchel et al., 2007). Prior experiences, environmental factors, and cultural expectations influence how the pain is processed (Gatchell & Maddrey, 2004).

Researchers studying pain initially tried to find a direct path from pain receptors to specific locations in the brain, but this simple relationship does not exist (Melzack, 2008). Instead, there is a complex interaction between neurological pathways and psychological and social factors, and a *gate* involved in the shuttling of information back and forth between the brain and the rest of the body.

GATE CONTROL   The most influential theory of pain perception is the **gate-control theory.** Melzack and Wall (1965) proposed that a person's perception of pain is either increased or decreased by how the brain interprets pain through an interaction of biopsychosocial factors. Once pain messages are received in the brain (through the mechanisms outlined above), the brain interprets the incoming information, and then sends signals back down through the spinal cord to either open or close the "gates" that control the neurological pathways for pain. Depending on the situation, psychological factors, and social influences, the gates will open, to increase the experience of pain, or close, to decrease the experience of pain. The gates might be instructed to close in situations when it's important to keep going in spite of an injury (athletes in competitions, soldiers in danger). This "close the gate" message can happen with distractions, which interfere with the ability to attend to pain, causing the pain to be perceived as less intense. Or the gates might be instructed to remain open, for example, when it is important for pain to be felt intensely (when you are ill, and your body needs to rest).

Signals to shut the gate do not always come from the brain (Melzack, 1993, 2008). Information sent from the pain receptors in the body can also open and close the neurological gates from the bottom-up, depending on which type of fiber is active. If the small unmyelinated fibers are active, the gates are more likely to open, sending the pain message up the spinal cord to the brain. If the large myelinated fibers are active, the gates are more likely to close, inhibiting pain messages from being sent on. Suppose you stub your toe. One way to ease the pain is by rubbing the injured area, stimulating the pressure receptors of the large fibers. This activity closes the gates, interfering with the pain message that would have been sent to the brain.

gate-control theory Suggests that the perception of pain will either increase or decrease through the interaction of biopsychosocial factors; signals are sent to open or close "gates" that control the neurological pathways for pain.

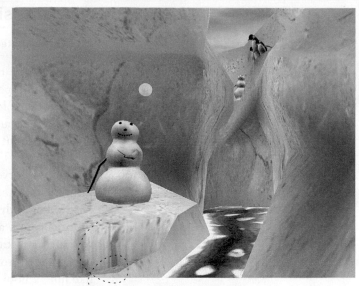

It is clear that everyone experiences pain in a unique way. But are there factors that predispose a person to be more or less sensitive to pain?

THE PSYCHOLOGY OF PAIN Pain sensitivity can ebb and flow for an individual, with psychological factors exerting a powerful effect (Gatchel et al., 2007; Raichle, Hanley, Jensen, & Cardenas, 2007). Negative feelings such as fear and anxiety can amplify pain, whereas laughter and distraction can soften it. Certain types of stress (for example, running in a marathon, giving birth) trigger the release of **endorphins.** Endorphins reduce pain by blocking the transmission of pain signals to the brain and spinal cord, possibly through the inhibition of substance P, a neurotransmitter in the spinal cord and brain (Rosenkranz, 2007).

As you can see, pain is a complex psychological phenomenon, dependent on many factors beyond the initial stimulus—so complex that a stimulus may not even be necessary. Can you imagine feeling a piercing burn or a stabbing cramp in a leg that you don't even have?

PHANTOM LIMB PAIN Sometimes people who have had an arm or leg amputated experience intense pain in their missing limb. Phantom limb pain occurs in 50–80% of people who have lost a limb through amputation, with reports of burning, tingling, cramping, and sharp feelings in the missing appendage (Ramachandran & Brang, 2009; Ramachandran & Hauser, 2010). One phantom limb sufferer reported feeling a burning itch in the place where his big toe used to be; to relieve the itch, he would scratch the air there (Rosenblum, 2010). Why amputees are haunted by their lost limbs is not entirely clear, and there are a variety of suggested mechanisms underlying this type of pain, ranging from changes in the structure of neurons to reorganization of the brain in relation to sensations felt in different locations in the body (Flor, Nikolajsen, & Jensen, 2006). When the brain doesn't receive normal signals from the limb, conflicting messages are sent to the brain from nerve cells and seem to be interpreted as pain.

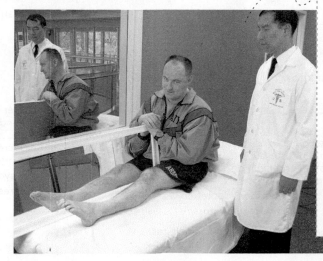

Escape the Pain

The last thing you want to look at while undergoing an unpleasant or painful medical procedure are the ceiling tiles in your hospital room. Being immersed in a virtual winter scene, complete with snowmen and penguins, can help take one's mind off the pain (Li, Montaño, Chen, & Gold, 2011). Army Sergeant Oscar Liberato (left) gets lost in the virtual reality video game SnowWorld (right) as he undergoes a painful procedure. left: Steve Elliot, U.S. Army Photo; right: Image by Ari Hollander and Howard Rose, Seattle, copyright Hunter Hoffman, UW, www.vrpain.com

CONNECTIONS

In **Chapter 2,** we reported that endorphins are naturally produced opioids that regulate the secretion of other neurotransmitters.

Mirror Therapy

Neurologist Jack Tsao uses mirror therapy to help Army Sergeant Nicholas Paupore at the Walter Reed Army Medical Center. The reflection of a leg in the mirror seems to take on the identity of the one that is missing, which may help the patient resolve his phantom limb pain. Mirror therapy is a promising development, but further studies are needed to evaluate its efficacy (Moseley, Gallace, & Spence, 2008). Donna Miles/American Forces Press Service

Kinesthesia

LO 12 Illustrate how we sense the position and movement of our bodies.

You may have thought "touch" was the fifth and final sense, but there is more to sensation and perception than the traditional five categories. Closely related to touch is the sense of **kinesthesia** (ki-nəs-ʹthē-zhē-ə), which provides feedback to us about body position and movement. Kinesthesia endows us with the coordination we need to walk without stumbling, dance the salsa, and put on our clothes without looking in the mirror. This knowledge of body location and orientation is made possible by specialized nerve endings called **proprioceptors** (proh-pree-uh-sep-tərs), which are primarily located in the muscles and joints. Proprioceptors monitor changes in the position of body parts and the tension in muscles. So as you are trying to dance, your proprioceptors are gathering information about where your right foot is in relation to your right knee, where your left arm is in relation to your head, allowing you to dance like a professional. When proprioception is impaired, the ability to do things like hold a book, walk without falling over, or drive is impacted.

VESTIBULAR SENSE You may recall from earlier in the chapter that Emma, Zoe, and Sophie began to curl up in the fetal position and vomit while riding in the car during the same period that they lost their hearing. This was because they were losing their **vestibular sense** (ve-ʹsti-byə-lər), which helps the body deal with the effects of gravity, movement, and position and which gives us the information we need to feel balanced and to be balanced. Astronauts often become nauseated during their first days in space because their vestibular systems are confused. The vestibular system comprises fluid-filled organs located in the inner ear: the *semicircular canals* and the nearby *vestibular sacs*. When the head tilts, fluid moves the hairlike receptors in these structures, causing neurons to fire, sending messages to the cerebellum (transduction once again). Motion sickness, which many people experience on boats and roller coasters, is caused by conflicting information we receive from our eyes and from our vestibular systems. This is known as *sensory conflict theory* (Johnson, 2005).

We have made it through a long and challenging lesson on sensation. The senses we have explored enable us to see the intricate details of a painted masterpiece, hear cries of sorrow and joy, and feel the warm sand as we walk along the beach smelling the salty water. But how do simple sensations turn into perceptions that have meaning?

Walk the Wire
Without his sense of kinesthesia, stuntman Nik Wallenda never would have crossed the Niagara Falls on an 1,800-foot tightrope. Kinesthesia enables us to know our body position and movement. AP Photo/The Canadian Press, Frank Gunn

---

⦿⦿✓⦿⦿   **show what you know**

1. The chemical sense called _____ provides the sensation of smell.

2. Chemicals from food that is being eaten are released in saliva, where they dissolve and bathe the taste buds in your mouth. The chemicals find matching receptors and latch on, sparking action potentials. This is an example of:
   a. olfaction.
   b. transduction.
   c. sensory adaptation.
   d. thermoreceptors.

3. Describe the common features and characteristics of smell, taste, and touch.

4. Maya consulted her physician about severe back pain. In order to help her understand pain perception, her doctor recommended she consider _____, which suggests that the interpretation of pain can either increase or decrease the perception of pain through an interaction of biopsychosocial factors.
   a. the theory of evolution
   b. an absolute threshold
   c. the gate-control theory
   d. gustation

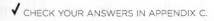 CHECK YOUR ANSWERS IN APPENDIX C.

Perception

After reading the first sections of this chapter, you can see that sensation is not a purely physiological process. *Perception,* which draws from experience to organize and interpret sensory data, makes the information from our sensory receptors more meaningful. Although Emma, Zoe, and Sophie receive less sensory input than many people, they are clearly able to perceive their worlds as meaningful and organized. The principles we discuss in the following apply to all of us, including the triplets.

The Mind's Imperfect Eye

What you see is not always what you get. Consider this experiment: Researchers asked a group of undergraduates studying *oenology* (the study of wine) to sample two wines. One was a white wine, and the other was the exact same white wine—colored red with flavorless dye. When it came time to evaluate the aromas, the students used the standard white-wine adjectives (for example, honey and apple) to describe the white wine, and this came as no surprise. When asked to describe the "red wine," which was really the same white wine, the tasters used the standard red-wine adjectives (for example, raspberry and peppery; Morrot, Brochet, & Dubourdieu, 2001). It appeared they were tricked by their eyes! What they *saw* was red wine, so what they *perceived* were red wine aromas, even though they were not actually smelling red wine aromas.

Perception is essential to our functioning, but as the wine-tasting example illustrates, it is far from foolproof. We don't see, hear, smell, taste, or feel the world exactly as it is, but as our brains judge it to be. At the start of the chapter, we introduced *data-based processing* (sensation), which refers to how we process basic sensory information (like pattern recognition), and *knowledge-based processing* (perception), which draws on past experiences and knowledge to understand sensory information. Let's take a basic example. Looking at :-) in an e-mail or text message, data-based processing allows us to recognize the hyphen, the dots, and a parenthesis, but knowledge-based processing enables us to recognize it as a smiley face. In this section, we are primarily concerned with knowledge-based processing.

ILLUSIONS   Do we all perceive the world in the same way? Many of us certainly seem to get *tricked* in the same way (we will talk more about exceptions to this a little later). A case in point is an **illusion,** which is a perception incongruent with real sensory data. Studying illusions is useful for detecting distortions in our perceptual processes. Looking at perception when it is working "incorrectly" allows us to examine knowledge-based processing. If a clock stops ticking, you can open it up to see what's wrong, to better understand how it works. Illusions serve a similar purpose. Let's examine one.

Look at the Müller-Lyer Illusion on page 128 (**FIGURE 3.7**). It appears lines (b) and (d) are longer, but in fact all 4 lines (a–d) are equal in length. Why does this illusion happen? Our experience with buildings tells us that the corner presented in line (c) is nearer because it is jutting toward us. The corner presented in line (d) seems to be farther away because it is jutting away from us. Two objects that are the same size will project different images on the retina if one is farther away; the farther object will project a smaller image on the retina. People living in "carpentered

LOL :-)
When your friend texts you a smiley face, your brain sees two dots, a hyphen, and a parenthesis. But how does it know what these symbols mean collectively? Through knowledge-based processing, you draw on past experience to make sense of the new information you encounter. Mathias Wilson/Getty Images

kinesthesia (ki-nəs-ˈthē-zhē-ə) Sensory system that conveys information about body position and movement.

proprioceptors (proh-pree-uh-sep-tərs) Specialized nerve endings primarily located in the muscles and joints that provide information about body location and orientation.

vestibular sense (ve-ˈsti-byə-lər) The sense of balance and equilibrium.

illusion A perception incongruent with sensory data.

FIGURE 3.7
The Müller-Lyer Illusion
Which line looks longer? They are actually the same length. Visual depth cues cause you to perceive that (b) and (d) are longer because it appears farther away

(a)   (b)   (c)   (d)

▶ **Stroboscopic**
The golf club and golf ball seem to be moving because their images appear in rapid succession. Stroboscopic motion is an example of a visual illusion. Vandystadt/ Michael Hans/Science Source

gestalt (gə-ˈstält) The natural tendency for the brain to organize stimuli into a whole, rather than perceiving the parts and pieces.

figure–ground A central principle of Gestalt psychology, involving the shifting of focus; as attention is focused on one object, all other features drop or recede into the background.

worlds" (that is, surrounded by structures constructed with corners, angles, and straight lines, as opposed to living in more "traditional" settings) are more likely to be tricked by this illusion because of their experiences with manufactured structures. People in more traditional settings, without all the hard edges and straight lines, are less likely to fall prey to such an illusion (Segall, Campbell, & Herskovits, 1968). We have expectations about these types of corners because of our experiences with them, and this influences our perceptions.

Another visual illusion is evident with *stroboscopic motion,* which occurs when a set of still images appears to be moving when shown in rapid progression. (Think of drawing stick figures on the edges of the pages of your book and then flipping the pages to see your figure "move.") The brain interprets this as movement. Even infants evidently are able to perceive this kind of motion (Valenza, Leo, Gava, & Simion, 2006). Although illusions can provide us with some clues to how perception works, they cannot explain it in its entirety. Let's take a look at principles of perceptual organization, which provide universal guidelines on how we perceive.

Perceptual Organization

▶ **LO 13** Identify the principles of perceptual organization.

The majority of psychologists first turn to the **Gestalt** (gə-ˈstält) psychologists to explain how perception works. Gestalt psychologists, who were active in Germany in the late 1800s and early 1900s, were initially interested in perception as a result of noticing illusions of motion. They wondered how something that is stationary could be perceived by the human brain as moving and thus attempted to explain how the human mind organizes stimuli in the environment. Noting the tendency for perception to be organized and complete, they realized that the whole is greater than the sum of its parts; the brain naturally organizes stimuli in their entirety rather than perceiving the parts and pieces. Gestalt means "whole" or "form" in German. The Gestalt psychologists, and others who followed, studied the rules, or principles, that explain how the brain perceives objects in the environment as wholes or groups (**INFOGRAPHIC 3.4**).

FIGURE–GROUND   One central principle illuminated by the Gestalt psychologists is **figure–ground** (Fowlkes, Martin, & Malik, 2007). As you focus your attention on a figure (for example, the vase in Infographic 3.4), all other features drop into the background. If, however, you direct your gaze onto the faces, the vase falls into the

Gestalt Organizing Principles: The Whole is Greater

The Gestalt psychologists identified principles that explain how the brain naturally organizes sensory information into meaningful wholes rather than distinct parts and pieces. These principles help you navigate the world by allowing you to see, for example, that the path you are walking on continues on the other side of an intersection. Gestalt principles also help you make sense of the information presented in your textbooks. Let's look at how this works.

figure-ground

We tend to perceive visual stimuli as figures existing on a background. On this map, one area becomes the focus, while the rest functions as background context.

Some stimuli, such as this classic figure ground vase, are *reversible figures*. You see something different depending on whether you focus on the yellow or the black portion.

LAW OF
proximity

We tend to perceive objects that are near each other as a unit. This set of dots is perceived as three groups rather than six separate columns or 36 individual dots.

men
women

Proximity helps us read graphs like this one. We understand that bars close together should be compared.

LAW OF
similarity

We see objects as a group if they share features such as color or shape. In this example, we perceive eight vertical columns rather than four rows of alternating squares and dots.

Canada
U.S.
Mexico

0   5   10   15   20   25

Similarity helps us read color-coded charts and graphs. We understand the graph above as having horizontal bars because we naturally group the similarly colored icons.

LAW OF
connectedness

We tend to see objects as a group if there is something that connects them. In this group of dots, the ones enclosed in or connected by lines appear related even though all dots are the same.

Scalp
Meninges
Skull

In a textbook figure, connectedness helps us understand what is being labeled.

LAW OF
closure

We tend to fill in incomplete parts of a line or figure. In this example, we perceive a circle even when the line is broken.

Closure allows us to read letters and images that are interrupted. We can read this letter even though it is made up of unconnected lines.

LAW OF
continuity

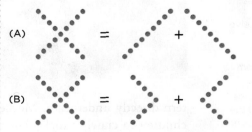

(A)

(B)

We perceive groups where objects appear to be going in the same direction. In this example, we perceive the figure as made up of two continuous lines that intersect (A) rather than two angles that are brought together (B).

Continuity helps us read graphs like this scatterplot, where we perceive the overall pattern.

background with everything else. The figure and ground continually change as you shift your focus. Other gestalt organizational principles include the following:

- **Proximity**—Objects close to each other are perceived as a group.
- **Similarity**—Objects similar in shape or color are perceived as a group.
- **Connectedness**—Objects that are connected are seen as a group.
- **Closure**—Gaps tend to be filled in if something isn't complete.
- **Continuity**—Parts tend to be perceived as members of a group if they head in the same direction.

Although these organizational principles have been demonstrated for vision, it is important to note they apply to the other senses as well. Take the mother who can distinguish her child's voice at the busy playground: Her child's voice is the figure and the other noises are the ground.

Depth Perception

> **LO 14** Identify concepts involved in depth perception.

That same mother can tell that the slide extends from the front of the jungle gym, thanks to her brain's ability to pick up on cues about depth. How is it that two-dimensional images projected on retinas are perceived in three dimensions? There appear to be inborn abilities and learned cues for perceiving depth and distance. Let's start by examining an inborn capability to recognize depth and its potential for danger. Watch out, baby.

VISUAL CLIFF In order to determine whether **depth perception** is innate or learned, Gibson and Walk (1960) studied the behavior of babies approaching a "visual cliff," a glass device that gives the illusion of a drop-off. They placed infants ages 6 to 14 months at the edge of the glass with a checkered tablecloth-like pat-

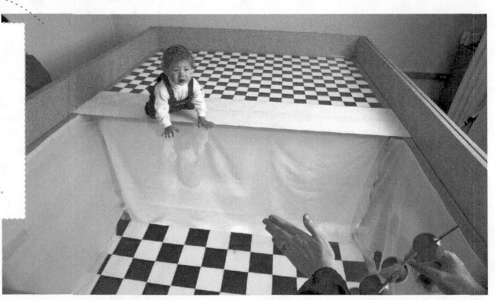

Visual Cliff
A baby appears distressed when he encounters the visual cliff, a supportive glass surface positioned over a drop-off, or "cliff." Most babies will not proceed, even when coaxed by a trusted caregiver. This finding suggests that depth perception is already in place by the time a child is crawling (Gibson & Walk, 1960). Mark Richards/Photo Edit

depth perception The ability to perceive three-dimensional objects and judge distances.

binocular cues Information gathered from both eyes to help judge depth and distance.

convergence A binocular cue used to judge distance and depth based on the tension of the muscles that direct where the eyes are focusing.

retinal disparity A binocular cue that uses the difference between the images the two eyes see to determine the distance of objects.

monocular cues Depth and distance cues that require the use of only one eye.

tern directly underneath. Mothers were at the other end of the glass, coaxing their children to crawl to them. For the most part, the children refused to move toward what they perceived to be a drop-off, suggesting that the perception of depth was innate. These infants had never been in a situation where someone tried to get them to go toward the edge of an abyss, but they seemed to instinctively know better than to go near the edge.

BINOCULAR CUES   Some cues for perceiving depth are the result of information gathered by both eyes. **Binocular cues** provide information from the right and left eyes to help judge depth and distance. For example, **convergence** is the brain's interpretation of the tension (or lack thereof) in the muscles of the eyes that direct where both eyes focus. If the object is close, there is more muscular tension (the muscles used to turn our eyes inward toward our nose), and the object is perceived as near. This perception of distance is based on experiences with objects; throughout life, we have learned that the more muscular tension, the closer the object is. Let's take a moment and feel that tension.

> Point your finger up to the ceiling at arm's length with both eyes open. Now slowly bring your finger close to your nose. Can you feel the tension and strain in the muscles of your eyes? Your brain uses this type of convergence cue to determine distance.

try this

Another binocular cue is **retinal disparity,** which is the difference between the two images the eyes see. The greater the difference in these two images, the closer the object. The more similar the two images, the farther the object is. With experience, our brains begin to interpret these differing image sizes to help us judge distance. The following Try This provides an example of retinal disparity.

> Hold your index finger about 4 inches in front of your face pointing up to the ceiling. Quickly open your right eye as you are closing your left eye, alternating this activity for a few seconds; it should appear as if your finger is jumping back and forth. Now do the same thing, with your finger out at arm's length. The image does not seem to be jumping as much as it did when your finger was closer to your face.

try this

MONOCULAR CUES   We can also use **monocular cues** to make judgments about depth and distance, but these do not necessitate the use of both eyes. Imagine how an artist uses paint to transform a white canvas into a three-dimensional perceptual experience. How can a two-dimensional object be perceived as having depth? This is accomplished by using techniques that take advantage of monocular cues. The monocular cues include (but are not limited to):

- **Relative Size**—If two objects are similar in actual size, but one is farther away, it appears to be smaller. We interpret the larger object as being closer.

- **Linear Perspective**—When two lines start off parallel, then come together, where they converge appears farther away than where they are parallel.

- **Interposition**—When one object is in front of another, it partially blocks the view of the other object, and the object that is partially blocked appears more distant.

- **Texture Gradient**—When objects are closer, it is easier to see their texture. As they get farther away, the texture becomes less distinct or less clear.

Monocular Cues
You can gauge the distance and depth in this photo with at least four types of monocular cues: (1) People that are farther away look smaller (relative size). (2) The two sides of the street start out parallel but converge as distance increases (linear perspective) (3) The trees in the front block those that are behind (interposition). (4) Textures are more apparent for closer objects (texture gradient). Yoan Valat/epa/Corbis

Once a Rectangle, Always a Rectangle
How do you know that all these doors are the same size and shape? The images projected onto your retina suggest that the closing doors are narrower, nonrectangular shapes. Your brain, however, knows from experience that all the doors are identical rectangles. This phenomenon is known as shape constancy.
Getty Images/Image Source

Letters or Numbers? ◄
Look in the green square. What do you see? That depends on whether you viewed the symbol as belonging to a row of letters (A B C) or a column of numbers (12 13 14). Perceptions are shaped by the context in which a stimulus occurs, and our expectations about that stimulus.

Perceptual Constancy

All these perceptual skills are great—if you are standing still—but the world around us is constantly moving. How do our perceptual systems adapt to changes? We possess the ability to perceive the objects in our world as having constant properties, although our environments are constantly changing. **Perceptual constancy** means that even when angle, lighting, and distance change, we know through experience that the objects themselves do not change in shape, size, or color although the sensory data might tell us otherwise. A door is shaped like a rectangle, but when it opens, the image on our retina is not a rectangle. Yet, we still perceive the door as having a rectangular shape. This is called **shape constancy.**

As you gaze on cars and trucks from the window of an airplane, they may look like bugs scurrying around, but you know some are as big as elephants because your perceptual toolkit includes **size constancy.** Through experience, we get to know the size of everyday objects and perceive them accordingly, regardless of whether they are far or near.

Similarly, **color constancy** allows us to see the world in stable colors, even when the sensory data arriving at our photoreceptors change. A bright red backpack appears bright red outside in the sunshine or inside a house. The color of the backpack does not change just because it is no longer in the bright light from the sun. The light waves bouncing off of the backpack have changed, but your understanding of the color of your backpack has not altered.

Although we can describe these organizational abilities with robust regularity, some of these perceptual skills are not necessarily universal, as the Müller-Lyer illusion demonstrates. Some studies suggest that children *learn* to perceive size constancy (Granrud, 2009), and this skill may not develop properly when children are deprived of certain types of stimuli.

PERCEPTUAL SET **Perceptual set** is the tendency to perceive stimuli in a specific manner based on past experiences and expectations. If someone handed you a picture of two women and said, "This is a mother and daughter," you would be more likely to rate them as looking alike than if you had been given the exact same picture and told, "These women are unrelated." Indeed, research shows that people who believe they are looking at parent–child pairs are more likely to rate the pair as similar than those participants who believe the pair are not related (with both groups looking at the same pairs of adults–children; Oda, Matsumoto-Oda, & Kurashima, 2005). In short, we tend to see what we are looking for.

Perceptual sets are also molded by the context of the moment. If you hear the word "sects" in a TV news report about feuding religious groups, you are unlikely to think the reporter is saying "sex" even though "sects" and "sex" sound the same. Similarly, if you see a baby swaddled in a blue blanket, you are probably more likely to assume it's a boy than a girl. Studies show that expectancies about male or female infants influence viewers' perceptions of gender (Stern & Karraker, 1989).

Simply labeling infants as *premature* or *full-term* will shape people's attitudes about them (Porter, Stern, & Zak-Place, 2009).

Although our perceptual sets may not always lead us to the right conclusions, they do help us organize the vast amount of information flooding our senses. But can perception exist in the absence of sensation? In other words, is it possible to perceive something without seeing, hearing, smelling, tasting, or feeling it?

Extrasensory Perception: Where's the Evidence?

LO 15 Define extrasensory perception and explain why psychologists dismiss its legitimacy.

Have you ever had a dream and the next day the event of that dream came to pass? Perhaps you have heard of psychics who claim they can read people's "auras" and decipher their thoughts. **Extrasensory perception (ESP)** is this purported ability to obtain information about the world without any sensory stimuli. And when we say "no sensory input," we are not referring to sights, sounds, smells, tastes, and feelings occurring subliminally, or below absolute thresholds. We mean absolutely no measurable sensory data. The study of these kinds of phenomena is called **parapsychology**.

THINK again

Extrasensory Perception

ESP, psychic powers, the sixth sense—call it what you will, there is no scientific evidence to support its existence (Farha, 2007; Wiseman & Watt, 2006). Nevertheless, a handful of respected researchers have published research suggesting it is valid. In 2011, Cornell University's Daryl Bem set off a firestorm of controversy with a journal article offering evidence for ESP. The article, which reported nine experiments involving some 1,000 participants, suggested that human beings have the ability to predict the future (Bem, 2011). Other psychologists pointed out flaws in Bem's statistical analysis (Wagenmakers, Wetzels, Borsboom, & van der Maas, 2011), which Bem then defended (Bem, Utts, & Johnson, 2011). The research was further called into question in 2012, when a team of scientists tried to **replicate** Bem's results using his same methodology and failed (Ritchie, Wiseman, & French, 2012).

Despite ESP's lack of scientific credibility, many people remain firm believers. Most often, their "evidence" comes in the form of personal anecdotes. Aunt Tilly predicted she was going to win the lottery based on a dream she had one night, and when she did win, it was "proof" of her ESP abilities. This is an example of what psychologists might call *illusory correlation,* or an apparent link between variables that are not closely related at all. Aunt Tilly dreamed she won the lottery, but so did 1,000 other people around the country, and they didn't win—what about that evidence? Although some may find the idea of ESP compelling, you should be *very* skeptical about its existence because there is no scientific evidence to support it (Farha, 2007; Wiseman & Watt, 2006).

. . .THERE IS NO SCIENTIFIC EVIDENCE TO SUPPORT ITS EXISTENCE.

CONNECTIONS

The importance of replicating experiments was discussed in **Chapter 1.** The more a study is replicated and produces similar findings, the more confident we can be in them; replication is a key step in the scientific method. If similar results cannot be reproduced using the same methods, then the original findings may have resulted from chance or experimenter bias.

perceptual constancy The tendency to perceive objects in our environment as stable in terms of shape, size, and color, regardless of changes in the sensory data received.

shape constancy An object is perceived as maintaining its shape, regardless of the image projected on the retina.

size constancy An object is perceived as maintaining its size, regardless of the image projected on the retina.

color constancy Objects are perceived as maintaining their color, even with changing sensory data.

perceptual set The tendency to perceive stimuli in a specific manner based on past experiences and expectations.

extrasensory perception (ESP) The purported ability to obtain information about the world without any sensory stimuli.

parapsychology The study of extrasensory perception.

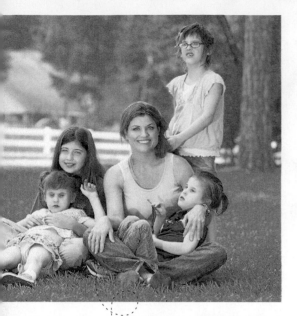

▶ Mother and Daughters
Liz and her eldest daughter Sarah (back left) relax with the triplets: Zoe (front left), Emma (front right), and Sophie (back right). Zoe and Emma currently attend the Texas School for the Blind and Visually Impaired, while Sophie goes to middle school in the local district. Worldwide Features/Barcroft Media/Landov

MOVING FORWARD When the triplets were about 5 years old, Liz and her husband got a divorce, and Liz faced the daunting task of caring for four young children. Today, Sarah is a high school student, Emma and Zoe are students at the prestigious Texas School for the Blind and Visually Impaired, and Sophie is holding her own in the public school system. Liz operates her own business and recently wed her true love from two decades past.

Although Emma, Zoe, and Sophie do not have personal tutors working 24-7, they have something more important—the absolute love and support of family. Emma and Zoe have made significant strides in their social and linguistic skills. Both can communicate with about 50 signs, but they understand many more and are building their vocabulary all the time. As for Sophie, having limited vision has enabled her to take classes in the local middle school.

Sensation and perception, distinct yet seamless processes, enable us to know our surroundings. We rely on sights, sounds, smells, tastes, and touch to interact with the surrounding world. If one or more of those senses fails, we fall back on the others to guide us. Every moment, we are flooded with sensory input that would be meaningless if our brains lacked systematic ways of interpreting and organizing it. With organizational principles of perception, perceptual sets, and contextual information, we experience our environments in a remarkably smooth manner.

✓ show what you know

1. _____ occur when perceptions are incongruent with real sensory data.

2. One binocular cue called _____ is based on the brain's interpretation of the tension in muscles of the eyes.
   a. convergence
   c. interposition
   b. retinal disparity
   d. relative size

3. Using what you have learned so far in the textbook, how would you try to convince a friend that extrasensory perception does not exist?

4. Have you ever noticed how the shape of a door seems to change as it opens and closes, yet you know its shape remains the same? This _____ refers to the fact that even though stimuli may change, we know that objects do not change in shape, size, or color.
   a. perceptual set
   c. convergence
   b. perceptual constancy
   d. texture-gradient

✓ CHECK YOUR ANSWERS IN APPENDIX C.

---

③ summary of concepts

LO 1 Define sensation and perception and explain how they are different. (p. 94)

Sensation is the manner in which physical stimuli are received and detected. Perception gives meaning to the information the sensory receptors receive. Data-based processing describes how the brain takes basic sensory information and processes the incoming stimuli. Knowledge-based processing utilizes our past experiences and knowledge in order to understand sensory information.

LO 2 Define transduction and explain how it relates to sensation. (p. 95)

Sensory organs receive stimuli from the environment (for example, sound waves, light energy) and these stimuli are transformed into neural signals in a process known as transduction. The neural signals are then processed by the central nervous system, resulting in what we consciously experience as sensations.

LO 3 Describe and differentiate between absolute thresholds and difference thresholds. (p. 96)

One of the important goals of studying sensation and perception is to determine absolute thresholds, the weakest stimuli that can be detected 50% of the time. Difference thresholds indicate the minimum difference between two stimuli noticed 50% of the time. Weber's law states the ratios that determine these difference thresholds. The ability to detect weak signals in the environment is based on many factors. *Signal detection theory* takes into consideration the factors interfering with our ability to detect weak signals; the "noise" in our environment can be internal and external.

LO 4 Explain how electromagnetic energy is transduced into a sensation of vision. (p. 101)

For vision, light is transduced into neural activity. The neural signals are processed by the central nervous system, resulting in visual experiences. The wavelength of the light shining on objects and reflecting back at our eyes determines the color. Our experience or perception of color results from the interaction between the light in our environment and the activities in our brains.

LO 5 Describe the function of rods and cones. (p. 104)

Rods are photoreceptors in the *retina* that are extremely sensitive to light. Rods do not provide the sensation of color. Cones, also in the retina, are responsible for our sensation of color and our ability to see the details of objects. Cones are not used when ambient light is low. Cones are concentrated in the fovea.

LO 6 Compare and contrast the theories of color vision. (p. 107)

The trichromatic theory of color vision suggests there are three types of cones, each sensitive to particular wavelengths in the red, green, and blue spectrums. The three types of cones fire in response to different electromagnetic wavelengths. The opponent-process theory of color vision suggests that in addition to the color-sensitive cones, we also have neurons that respond differently to opponent colors (for example, red–green, blue–yellow).

LO 7 Summarize how sound waves are transduced into the sensation of hearing. (p. 110)

Audition is the term used for the sense of hearing. When we hear, we are sensing sound waves, which are rhythmic vibrations of molecules traveling through a variety of forms of matter (including air). The cochlea is a fluid-filled, snail-shaped organ of the inner ear. When the oval window vibrates, it causes the fluid in the cochlea to move. The cochlea is lined with the basilar membrane, which contains hair cells. When the fluid moves, the hairs lining the basilar membrane bend in response. The hair cells cause the nerve cells nearby to fire, sending neural messages through the auditory nerve to the auditory cortex via the thalamus.

LO 8 Illustrate how we sense different pitches of sound. (p. 115)

Place theory suggests that the location of neural activity along the cochlea allows us to sense different pitches of high-frequency sounds. With a high-frequency sound, vibrations occur closer to the end of the basilar membrane near the oval window. Frequency theory suggests that the frequency of the neural impulses firing per second determines the experience of pitch. The entire basilar membrane vibrates at the same rate as the sound wave; the neural impulses occur at this same rate. The frequency theory explains how we perceive the pitch of sounds from 20 to 400 Hz. The volley principle explains our perception of the different pitches between 400 and 4,000 Hz. And, the place theory explains our perception of pitches from 4,000 to 20,000 Hz.

LO 9 Describe the process of olfaction. (p. 117)

The chemical sense referred to as olfaction provides the sensation of smell. Molecules from odor-emitting objects in our environments make their way into our nostrils up through the nose or mouth. The olfactory epithelium is home to millions of olfactory receptor neurons, which provide receptors for odor molecules.

LO 10 Discuss the structures involved in taste and describe how they work. (p. 120)

Gustation is the sense of taste. The receptor cells for taste are located in the taste buds, which are located on the tongue, the roof of the mouth, and inside the mouth on the cheeks. Taste buds are embedded in the papillae on the tongue. Jutting from each of these buds are 50 to 100 taste receptor cells. Taste is essential to the survival of species. Tastes push organisms toward needed foods and away from harmful ones.

LO 11 Describe how the biopsychosocial perspective is used to understand pain. (p. 124)

The biopsychosocial perspective explains the perception of pain by exploring biological, psychological, and social factors. This multilevel method examines how these factors play a role in the experience of pain. According to the *gate-control theory*, how the brain interprets pain will either increase or decrease the perception of pain. Neural activity makes its way to the brain where it is processed, and part of this processing includes prior experiences, environmental factors, or cultural expectations. Pain signals are sent through nerves to the brain, where they are processed. The brain is capable of blocking pain by sending a message through the interneurons to "close the gate" so the pain won't be felt.

LO 12 Illustrate how we sense the position and movement of our bodies. (p. 126)

Kinesthesia is the sense of position and movement of the body, including body parts. We are aware of where the parts of our bodies are in space because of specialized nerve endings called proprioceptors, which are primarily located in the muscles and joints. Our proprioceptors monitor changes in the position of body parts and the tension in our muscles. The vestibular sense helps us deal with the effects of gravity, movement, and body position to keep us balanced.

LO 13 Identify the principles of perceptual organization. (p. 128)

Gestalt psychologists sought to explain how the human mind organizes stimuli from the environment. They realized the whole is greater than the sum of its parts, meaning the brain naturally organizes stimuli as a whole rather than parts and pieces. Gestalt indicates a tendency for human perception to be organized and complete. The organizational principles include: proximity, similarity, connectedness, closure, and continuity.

LO 14 Identify concepts involved in depth perception. (p. 130)

Depth perception appears partially to be an innate ability. Children in the visual cliff experiment, for example, refuse to move toward what they perceived to be a drop-off. Binocular cues use information gathered from both eyes to help judge depth and distance. Monocular cues can be used by either eye alone and also help judge depth and distance.

LO 15 Define extrasensory perception and explain why psychologists dismiss its legitimacy. (p. 133)

Extrasensory perception (ESP) is the purported ability to obtain information about the world without any sensory stimuli. The study of these kinds of phenomena is called parapsychology. There is no scientific evidence to back up claims of ESP and other parapsychology phenomena.

key terms

absolute threshold, p. 96
accommodation, p. 104
afterimage, p. 108
amplitude, p. 102
audition, p. 110
binocular cues, p. 131
blind spot, p. 106
cochlea, p. 113
color constancy, p. 132
cones, p. 106
convergence, p. 131
cornea, p. 103
dark adaptation, p. 107
data-based processing, p. 96
depth perception, p. 130

difference threshold, p. 97
extrasensory perception (ESP), p. 133
feature detectors, p. 107
figure–ground, p. 128
frequency, p. 111
frequency theory, p. 115
gate-control theory, p. 124
gestalt, p. 128
gustation, p. 121
hue, p. 102
illusions, p. 127
iris, p. 104
kinesthesia, p. 126

knowledge-based processing, p. 96
light adaptation, p. 107
monocular cues, p. 131
olfaction, p. 117
opponent-process theory, p. 108
optic nerve, p. 106
parapsychology, p. 133
perception, p. 94
perceptual constancy, p. 133
perceptual set, p. 133
photoreceptors, p. 104
pitch, p. 111
place theory, p. 115

proprioceptors, p. 126
retina, p. 104
retinal disparity, p. 131
rods, p. 106
saturation, p. 103
sensation, p. 94
sensory adaptation, p. 96
shape constancy, p. 133
signal detection theory, p. 99
size constancy, p. 133
transduction, p. 95
trichromatic theory, p. 108
vestibular sense, p. 126
volley principle, p. 116
wavelength, p. 102
Weber's law, p. 99

TEST PREP are you ready?

1. Stimuli are detected through the process called:
   a. perception.
   b. data-based processing.
   c. sensation.
   d. knowledge-based processing.

2. You're listening to music on your iPod. The sound waves transmitted through the earbuds lead to vibrations in the fluid in your cochlea. This activity causes the hair cells to bend, which causes nearby nerve cells to fire. This process of transforming stimuli into electrical and chemical signals of neurons is:
   a. transduction.
   b. perception.
   c. knowledge-based processing.
   d. convergence.

3. According to signal detection theory, our ability to detect weak stimuli in the environment is based on many factors, including which of the following?
   a. characteristics of the experimenter
   b. fatigue and motivation
   c. false alarms
   d. hits

4. While rollerblading outside, you get something in your eye. As the day goes on, your eye still feels irritated. It is possible you've scratched your _____, which is the transparent outer layer, the function of which is to protect the eye and bend light to help focus light waves.
   a. lens
   b. retina
   c. iris
   d. cornea

5. The blind spot of the retina lacks _____ because it is the location where the optic nerve exits the retina.
   a. binocular cues
   b. rods and cones
   c. interposition
   d. feature detectors

6. In color vision, the opponent-process theory was developed to explain the _____, which could not be explained by the _____ theory.
   a. afterimage effect; trichromatic
   b. blind spot; place
   c. feature detectors; trichromatic
   d. color deficiencies; frequency

7. A developmental psychologist is interested in studying children's _____, which is the term we use for the sense of hearing.
   a. wavelength
   b. amplitude
   c. pitch
   d. audition

8. Frequency theory of pitch perception suggests it is the frequency of _____ that allows us to perceive differences in pitch.
   a. sound waves greater than 1,000 Hz
   b. the timbre
   c. neural impulses firing
   d. the amplitude

9. One large study conducted in the United States by Shargorodsky and colleagues (2012) found hearing loss in what percentage of teenagers?
   a. 5%
   b. 20%
   c. 50%
   d. 65%

10. The wiring of the olfactory system is unique, because other sensory systems relay data through the _____ before information is passed along to higher brain centers, but this is not the case for olfactory information.
    a. thalamus
    b. corpus callosum
    c. reticular formation
    d. basilar membrane

11. _____ specialize in recognizing specific characteristics of your visual experience, such as angles, lines, and movements.
    a. Feature detectors
    b. Rods
    c. Cones
    d. Photoreceptors

12. We are aware of where the parts of our bodies are in space because of specialized nerve endings called _____, which are primarily located in the joints and muscles.
    a. proprioceptors
    b. Meissner's corpuscles
    c. Pacinian corpuscles
    d. nociceptors

13. Hector is staring at the small print on the back of a credit card. Which of the following would be a binocular cue to indicate how close the credit card is to his face?
    a. tension of the muscles focusing the eyes
    b. relative size of two similar objects
    c. two lines initially some distance apart coming together
    d. interposition

14. One of the Gestalt organizational principles suggests that objects close to each other are perceived as a group. This is known as:
    a. continuity.
    b. closure.
    c. similarity.
    d. proximity.

15. When two objects are similar in actual size and one of these objects is farther away than the other, the object at a distance appears to be smaller than the closer object. This is a monocular cue called:
    a. linear perspective.
    b. interposition.
    c. relative size.
    d. texture gradient.

16. List and explain two different connections between vision and evolutionary psychology.

17. Why do you have a hard time seeing when you first walk into a dark room? Why then does your sight improve after approximately 8 minutes?

18. A sound wave transformed into the experience of something heard follows a complicated path. To better understand the process, draw a diagram starting with a sound in the environment and ending with a sound heard by an individual.

19. Why does placing ice on a sore shoulder stop the pain?

20. We described sensory adaptation as it relates to jumping into cold water. In the next 3 minutes, list as many examples as you can of your experiences with sensory adaptation.

✓ CHECK YOUR ANSWERS IN APPENDIX C.

Get personalized practice by logging into LaunchPad at **http://www.worthpublishers.com/launchpad/Licht** to take the LearningCurve adaptive quizzes for Chapter 3.

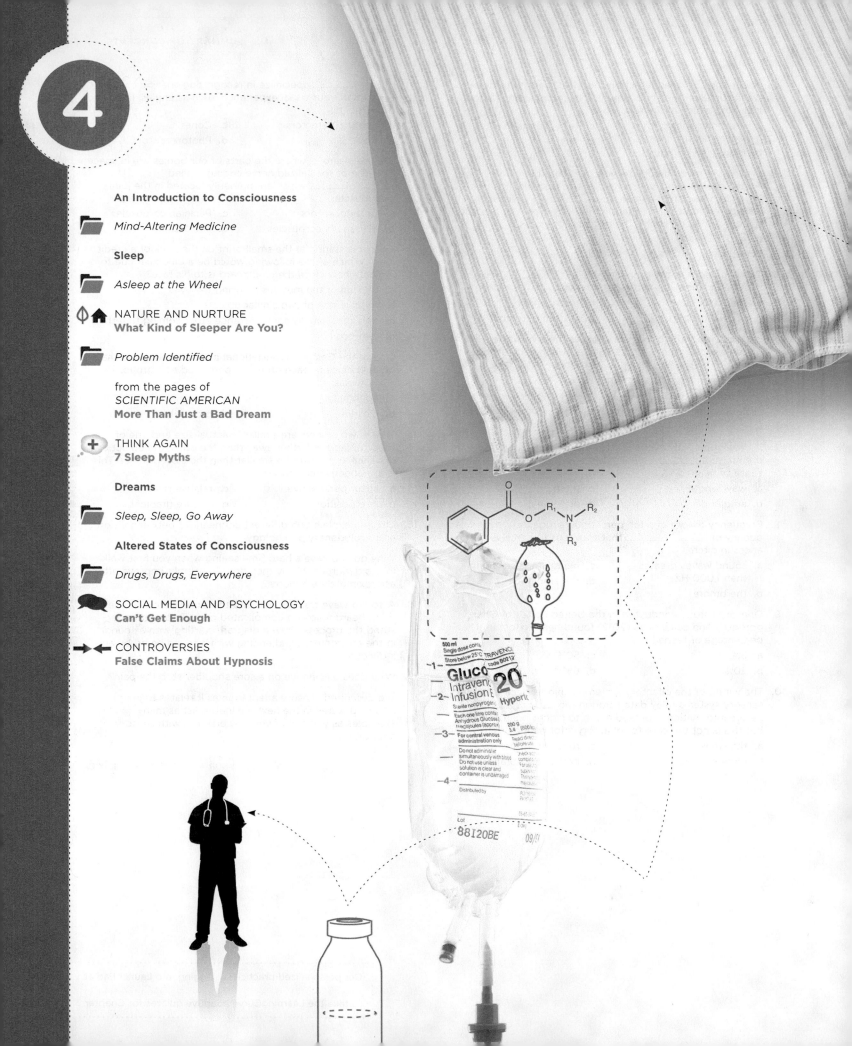

4

An Introduction to Consciousness

📁 *Mind-Altering Medicine*

Sleep

📁 *Asleep at the Wheel*

🌱🏠 NATURE AND NURTURE
What Kind of Sleeper Are You?

📁 *Problem Identified*

from the pages of
SCIENTIFIC AMERICAN
More Than Just a Bad Dream

➕ THINK AGAIN
7 Sleep Myths

Dreams

📁 *Sleep, Sleep, Go Away*

Altered States of Consciousness

📁 *Drugs, Drugs, Everywhere*

💬 SOCIAL MEDIA AND PSYCHOLOGY
Can't Get Enough

➡️◀ CONTROVERSIES
False Claims About Hypnosis

consciousness

An Introduction to Consciousness

MIND-ALTERING MEDICINE Robert Julien, M.D., did not choose a typical 9-to-5 job. His profession involves paralyzing people, interfering with their memory formation, and numbing their senses—but only temporarily. Dr. Julien is an *anesthesiologist,* a medical doctor whose primary responsibility is to monitor a patient's vital functions (for example, respiration and pulse) and manage pain before, during, and after surgery. With the help of powerful drugs that manipulate the nervous system, Dr. Julien has eased the pain and anxiety of over 30,000 patients undergoing procedures that otherwise would likely have been very unpleasant.

In ancient times, people may have sought pain relief by dipping their wounds in cold rivers and streams. They concocted mixtures of crushed roots, barks, herbs, fruits, and flowers to ease pain and induce sleep in surgical patients (Keys, 1945). Many of the plant chemicals discovered by these early peoples are still given to patients today, although in slightly different forms. Opium was used by the ancient Egyptians (El Ansary, Steigerwald, & Esser, 2003), and its chemical relatives are used by modern-day physicians and hospitals all over the world (for example, *morphine* for pain relief and *codeine* for cough suppression).

→

4

LEARNING OBJECTIVES

after reading and studying this chapter, you should be able to:

LO 1 Define consciousness.

LO 2 Explain how automatic processing relates to consciousness.

LO 3 Describe how we narrow our focus on specific stimuli to attend to them.

LO 4 Identify how circadian rhythm relates to sleep.

LO 5 Summarize the stages of sleep.

LO 6 Recognize various sleep disorders and their symptoms.

LO 7 Summarize the theories of why we dream.

LO 8 Define psychoactive drugs.

LO 9 Identify several depressants and stimulants and know their effects.

LO 10 Discuss some of the hallucinogens.

LO 11 Explain how physiological and psychological dependence differ.

LO 12 Describe hypnosis and explain how it works.

Seasoned Anesthesiologist

Dr. Robert Julien is an anesthesiologist, a physician who keeps patients comfortable and monitors their vital signs during surgery. Anesthesiologists administer drugs that interfere with pain, paralyze the muscles, and induce a sleeplike state. How these substances alter consciousness is still somewhat mysterious (Geddes, 2011, November 29). Judith Julien

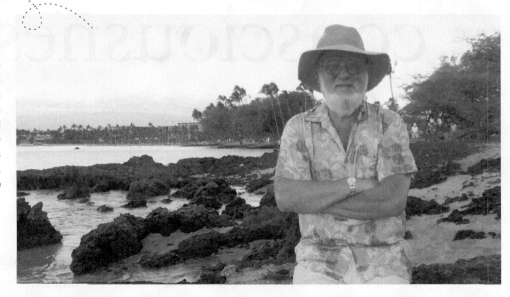

consciousness The state of being aware of oneself, one's thoughts, and/or the environment; includes various levels of conscious awareness.

Nevertheless, anesthesia's routine use during surgery did not occur for centuries. Before the mid-1800s, surgery was so painful, patients writhed and screamed on operating tables, sometimes held down by four or five people (Bynum, 2007). During the Mexican-American War, a band would play when Mexican soldiers had their limbs amputated so the men's cries would not be heard by others (Aldrete, Marron, & Wright, 1984). The only anesthetic available may have been whiskey, wine, or a firm blow to the head, that is, patients were literally knocked out. Fortunately, the science of anesthesia has come a long way. It is now possible to have a tooth extracted or a mole removed without a twinge of discomfort. A patient undergoing open heart surgery can lie peacefully as surgeons pry open his chest and poke around with their instruments, then leave the hospital with no memory of the actual surgery. But anesthesia is a curious thing. Drugs used to ease pain and anxiety also influence sensations, perceptions, and one's awareness of self and the environment: They can dramatically alter "conscious" experiences.

Note: Unless otherwise specified, quotations attributed to Dr. Robert Julien and Matt Utesch are personal communications.

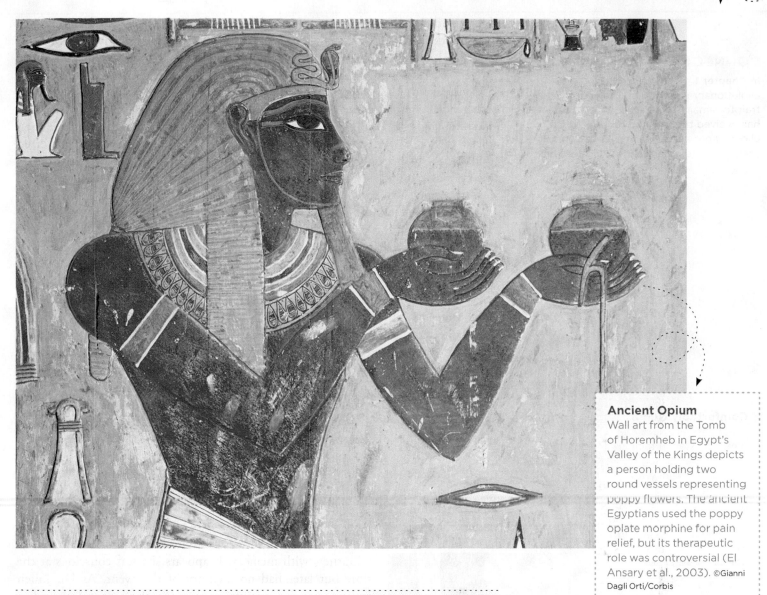

LO 1   Define consciousness.

WHAT IS CONSCIOUSNESS?   People usually think of *consciousness* as the state of being awake and *unconsciousness* as what happens when you are asleep, but as you will learn in this chapter, consciousness is a concept that can be difficult to pinpoint. Although some psychologists disagree about its precise definition, G. William Farthing offers a good starting point: **Consciousness** is "the subjective state of being currently aware of something either within oneself or outside of oneself" (1992, p. 6). Consciousness is best defined as the state of being aware of oneself, one's thoughts, and/or the environment. According to this definition of subjective awareness, one can be asleep and still be aware (Farthing, 1992). Consider this example: You are dreaming about a siren blaring and you wake up to discover it is your alarm clock; you were clearly asleep but aware at the same time, as the sound registered within your brain. This ability to register a sound while asleep is very important in the production of not only alarm clocks but also smoke detectors and fire alarms. **Human factors** researchers have conducted numerous studies to determine the types of sounds most likely to arouse a sleeping person, as well as individual differences (for example, age, gender, sleep deprivation, hearing

CONNECTIONS

In **Chapter 3**, we considered the subfield of human factors engineering. Just as we can study sensation and perception as they relate to machines and equipment, human factors engineers must be aware of issues related to consciousness and the design of machines.

ability, and sleep stage) that affect whether a person will register and/or wake up to a sound (Bruck & Ball, 2007). This ability to remain aware of our environment even while sleeping has served us well, allowing our **ancestors** to be vigilant about dangers day and night.

Consider this story: Several years ago, Dr. Julien had a patient who didn't want to have general anesthesia during her hysterectomy, an operation to remove the uterus. Anesthesiologists typically put patients "to sleep" for hysterectomies, but Dr. Julien agreed to honor the patient's unusual request. He gave her a drug called Versed (midazolam) to help her relax, but not enough to knock her out. (Versed belongs to a class of calming drugs called *depressants*, which you will learn about later.) The woman seemed to be wide awake throughout the two-and-a-half hour procedure, chatting with doctors and nurses and even requesting that certain music be played in the operating room (much to the dismay of the surgical team).

At 11:00 P.M. that night, Dr. Julien received a phone call from a nurse indicating that the patient was furious because he had used general anesthesia during the operation. Apparently, she could not remember any of the experience. The drug Dr. Julien had used to help the patient relax can also cause memory loss for events experienced while under its influence. Unable to remember the surgery, the patient logically assumed she had been given general anesthesia. "I went to the hospital at midnight to explain to the patient that I had honored her request and that she had been wide awake during the procedure but was unable to form memory proteins because the Versed had blocked their formation," Dr. Julien explained. In other words, the Versed had interfered with the production of a protein needed for memory creation. "To this day, I'm not sure she ever accepted my explanation or forgave me for taking away any memory of the procedure" (Julien & DiCecco, 2010, p. 11).

CONSCIOUSNESS AND MEMORY   Would you say Dr. Julien's patient was conscious during the operation? If consciousness is a "subjective state of being currently aware" (Farthing, 1992, p. 6), then it would appear she was conscious during the surgery. She was alert and talking, yet her awareness of the event vanished within hours, so was she conscious after all? Let's not confuse consciousness with memory. It appears she was conscious at the time but later had no memory of the event. As Dr. Julien explained to her, a failure occurred in the process involved in memory formation, for example, in the *encoding* or *storage* of the event (Chapter 6).

Millions of Americans suffer from memory problems similar to that experienced by Dr. Julien's patient. They are aware, alert, and able to have meaningful conversations, yet they cannot form new memories (they may suffer from Alzheimer's or another form of dementia; Chapter 6). Then there are those who cannot form memories because they are taking consciousness-altering drugs. In very rare cases, people taking certain types of prescription sleeping pills have been known to "sleep-drive" or get behind the wheel in a trance-like state (Dolder & Nelson, 2008; Southworth, Kortepeter, & Hughes, 2008; Zammit, 2009). If such a person causes a fatal accident while in this sort of state, is she to blame? Keep this question in mind as we delve the depths of consciousness in the pages to come.

CONNECTIONS

In **Chapter 1**, we introduced the evolutionary perspective. The adaptive trait to remain aware even while asleep has evolved through natural selection, allowing our ancestors to defend against predators and other dangerous situations.

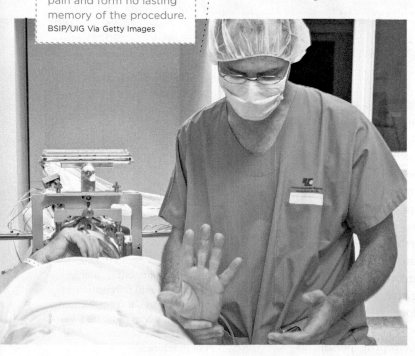

Comfortably Numb
A patient lies awake on the operating table as a neurophysiologist probes his brain. With the right combination of anesthetics, a patient can be wide awake yet feel no pain and form no lasting memory of the procedure.
BSIP/UIG Via Getty Images

Studying Consciousness

The field of psychology began with the study of consciousness. **Wilhelm Wundt and his disciple Edward Titchener** founded psychology as a science based on research that examined consciousness and its contents. Another early psychologist, William James, was also interested in studying consciousness. According to James, consciousness can be thought of as a "stream" that provides a sense of day-to-day continuity (James, 1890/1983). Think about how this "river" of thoughts is constantly rushing through your head. An e-mail from an old friend appears in your inbox, jogging your memory of the birthday party she threw last month, and that reminds you that tomorrow is your *mother*'s birthday (better not forget that one), and you need to swing by the mall after class to pick up a gift for her. You notice your shoe is untied. You think about dinner last night, school starting tomorrow, your utility bill sitting on the counter; all of these thoughts might cross your mind within a matter of seconds. Thoughts interweave and overtake each other like currents of flowing water; sometimes they are connected by topic, emotion, events, but other times they seem to not be connected by anything other than your stream of consciousness.

Although psychology started with the very introspective study of consciousness, American psychologists John Watson, B. F. Skinner, and other behaviorists insisted that psychology as a science should only study observable behavior. This attitude persisted until the 1950s and 1960s, when psychology underwent a revolution of sorts. Researchers began to direct their focus back on the unseen mechanisms of the mind. *Cognitive psychology,* the scientific study of conscious experiences such as thinking, problem solv ing, and language, emerged as a major subfield. Today, understanding consciousness is an important goal of psychology, and many believe science can be used to further investigate its mysteries.

Although advanced technology for studying brain processes and functions has added to our growing knowledge, there are several barriers to studying consciousness. One is that consciousness is *subjective,* pertaining only to the individual who experiences it. Because of this, it is impossible to *objectively* study another's conscious experience (Blackmore, 2005; Farthing, 1992). To make matters more complicated, consciousness is constantly changing; there is great variety in the conscious experiences within a person from moment-to-moment. Right now you are concentrating on these words, but in a few seconds you might be thinking of something else or slip into light sleep. In spite of these challenges, researchers around the world are inching closer to understanding consciousness by studying it from many perspectives.

Wrap Your Mind Around This

How exactly do psychologists understand this concept we call "consciousness"? We must first agree on what topics are relevant to the study of consciousness. There are many elements of conscious experience, including desire, thought, language,

CONNECTIONS

In **Chapter 1**, we discussed the contributions of these early psychologists. Wundt founded the first psychology laboratory, edited the first psychological journal, and used experimentation to measure psychological processes. Titchener was particularly interested in examining consciousness and the "atoms" of the mind.

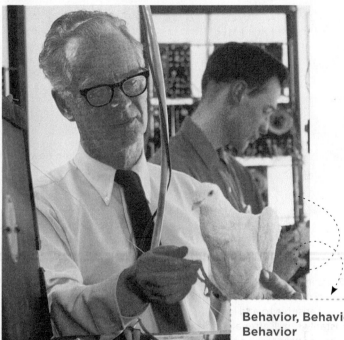

Behavior, Behavior, Behavior
B. F. Skinner works with a pigeon in the laboratory. A die-hard behaviorist, Skinner believed that psychology should restrict itself to the study of observable behaviors. Consciousness and other unseen mental activities were beyond the realm of psychological research. Sam Falk/Science Source

CONNECTIONS

In **Chapter 1**, we presented the concept of objective reports, which are free of opinions, beliefs, expectations, and values. Here, we note that descriptions of consciousness are more subjective in nature, and do not lend themselves to objective reporting.

sensation, perception, and knowledge of self—simply stated, any cognitive process is potentially a part of your conscious experience. Memory is definitely a key player, as conscious experiences usually involve the retrieval of memories. Let's look at what this means, for example, when you go shopping on the Internet. Your ability to navigate from page to page hinges on your ability to recognize visual images (*Is that the PayPal home page or my e-mail log-in?*), language aptitude (for reading), and motor skills (for typing and clicking). As you scroll through a page, or click on a hyperlink, your mind might wander from what you are looking at onscreen to a variety of memories (such as which link you just clicked, the shoes you saw last week while shopping, and the homework you were supposed to be doing)—all of this is part of your consciousness, your stream of thought.

try this

Stop reading and listen. Do you hear background sounds you didn't notice before—a soft breeze rustling through the curtains or a car passing by? *You* may not have picked up on these sounds, but your brain was keeping tabs. You are constantly monitoring all this activity whether you are aware of it or not.

- - - ▶ **LO 2**   Explain how automatic processing relates to consciousness.

AUTOMATIC PROCESSING   One of the important distinctions often made regarding consciousness is between cognitive activity that happens *automatically* (without effort, control, or awareness on our part) and cognitive processes that require us to focus our attention on sensory input (with effort, we choose what to attend to and we are aware of this focus). **Our sensory systems** absorb an enormous amount of information, and one of the major functions of the brain is to sift through that information, determining what is important and needs immediate attention, what can be ignored, and what can be processed and stored for later use if necessary. This **automatic processing** allows information to be collected and saved (at least temporarily) with little or no conscious effort (McCarthy & Skowronski, 2011; Schmidt-Daffy, 2011). If it weren't for automatic processing, we would be overwhelmed with data. Just imagine assuming some of your brain's behind-the-scenes responsibilities (for example, keeping track of your heart rate or filtering unimportant noises) while taking a psychology midterm exam.

Automatic processing can also refer to the involuntary cognitive activity guiding some of our behaviors. We are seemingly able to behave and act without focusing our attention. Behaviors seem to occur without intentional awareness, and without getting in the way of our other activities (Hassin, Bargh, & Zimerman, 2009). A few examples are in order here. Do you remember the last time you drove a car on a familiar route, daydreaming the entire time? Somehow you arrived at your destination without noticing much about your driving, the traffic, and so forth. Or have you ever found yourself listening to music while cleaning the kitchen, and then realizing you are almost finished cleaning up without once being aware that you had scrubbed the countertop or mopped the floor? You managed to be conscious enough to complete complex tasks, but not conscious enough to truly realize that you were doing so.

Although unconscious processes guide a great number of our behaviors, we are also able to focus our attention, making conscious decisions about what to attend to.

CONNECTIONS

In **Chapter 3**, we introduced the concept of *sensory adaptation,* which is the tendency to become less sensitive to and less aware of constant stimuli after a period of time. This better prepares us to detect changes in the environment, which can signal important activities that require our attention. Here, we see how this can occur through automatic processing.

automatic processing Refers to the processing of information with little or no conscious effort: detection, encoding, and sometimes storage of information without awareness.

selective attention The ability to focus awareness on a small segment of information that is available through our sensory systems.

When driving, you might focus intently on a conversation you just had with your friend or an exam you will take in an hour. With this type of conscious activity, we deliberately channel or direct our attention.

LO 3 Describe how we narrow our focus on specific stimuli to attend to them.

SELECTIVE ATTENTION   This brings us to an important concept in understanding consciousness; although we have access to a great deal of information in our internal and external environments, we can only focus our attention on a small portion of that information at one time. This narrow focus on specific stimuli is known as **selective attention.** Researchers have found selective attention can be influenced by emotions. Anger, for example, increases our ability to selectively attend to something or someone (Finucane, 2011). So too does repeated exposure to stimuli (Brascamp, Blake, & Kristjánsson, 2011). We also get better at ignoring distractions as we age (Couperus, 2011).

This doesn't mean other information isn't being processed. We generally adapt to continuous input, ignoring the millions of unimportant sensory stimuli constantly bombarding us. Yet, we are designed to pay attention to abrupt, unexpected changes in the environment, and to stimuli that are unfamiliar or especially strong (Bahrick & Newell, 2008; Daffner et al., 2007; Parmentier & Andrés, 2010). Think about how you approach reading this chapter, for example. Your sensory systems are hard at work, but your focus remains on your reading.

Imagine you are studying in a busy courtyard. You are aware the environment is bustling with activity, but you fail to pay attention to every person. If something changes, though, your attention might be directed to that novelty. The same thing occurs when you are in a crowded room talking to someone. You are able to pay attention to your conversation despite all the noise from the many other conversations. This is known as the *cocktail-party effect*; you can block out the chatter and noise of the party and get lost in a deep conversation, a very efficient use of selective attention (Koch, Lawo, Fels, & Vorländer, 2011).

INATTENTIONAL BLINDNESS   Selective attention is great if you need to study for a psychology test while others are watching TV, but it can also be dangerous. Suppose a friend sends you a hilarious text message while you are walking into a busy intersection. Thinking about the text can momentarily steal your attention away from signs of danger, like a car turning right on red without stopping. While distracted by the text message, it is completely possible you step into the intersection—without seeing the car turning in your path. This "looking without seeing" is referred to as inattentional blindness, and it can have serious consequences (Mack, 2003).

Ulric Neisser was the first to illustrate just how blind we can be to objects directly in our line of vision (see page 146). In one of his studies, participants were instructed to watch a video of men passing a basketball from one person to another (Neisser, 1979; Neisser & Becklen, 1975). As they diligently followed the basketball with their eyes, counting each pass, a partially transparent woman holding an umbrella was superimposed walking across the basketball court. Only 21% of the participants even noticed the woman (Most et al., 2001; Simons, 2010); the others had been too fixated on the basketball to see her (Mack, 2003).

Automatic Processing
Do you recall dropping your keys in your bag this morning? Many routine activities, such as putting away keys and locking the car, occur without our awareness. We might not remember these events because we never gave them our attention in the first place.
Garo/Phanie/SuperStock

What Umbrella?
In an elegant demonstration of *inattentional blindness*, researchers asked a group of participants to watch a video of men passing around a basketball. As the participants kept careful tabs on the players' passes, a semi-transparent image of a woman with an umbrella appeared among them. Only 21% of the participants (1 out of 5) even noticed; the others had been focusing their attention elsewhere (Most et al., 2001).

LEVELS OF CONSCIOUSNESS People often equate consciousness with being awake and alert, and unconsciousness as being passed out or comatose. But the distinction is not so clear, because there are different *levels of conscious awareness* including wakefulness, sleepiness, drug induced states, dreaming, hypnotic states, and meditative states, to name but a few. One way to define these levels of consciousness is to determine how much control you have over your awareness at the time. A high level of awareness might occur when focusing a lot of attention on a task (using a sharp knife); a lower level might occur when daydreaming, although you are able to snap out of it as needed. Sometimes we can identify an agent that causes a change in the level or state of consciousness. Psychologists typically delineate between *waking consciousness* and *altered states of consciousness* that may result from drugs, alcohol, or hypnosis—all topics covered later in the chapter.

Consciousness is like a swirling plume of smoke, always changing, seemingly impossible to grasp. But wherever your attention is focused at this moment, that is your conscious experience. There are times when attention essentially shuts down, however. What's going on when we lie in bed motionless, lost in a peaceful slumber? Sleep, fascinating sleep, is the subject of our next section. Welcome to the world of consciousness and its many shades of gray.

 show what you know

1. When researchers try to study participants' conscious experiences, one barrier they face is that consciousness is _____, pertaining only to the individual who experiences it.

2. While studying for an exam, your sensory systems absorb an inordinate amount of information from your surroundings, most of which you are not aware of. Because of _____, generally you do not get overwhelmed with incoming sensory data.

   a. consciousness   c. depressants
   b. automatic processing   d. encoding

3. Inattentional blindness is the tendency to "look without seeing." Researchers have determined that most people do not notice a variety of events. Given what you know about selective attention, what advice would you give someone about defending against "looking without seeing"?

✓ CHECK YOUR ANSWERS IN APPENDIX C.

Sleep

ASLEEP AT THE WHEEL When Matt Utesch reminisces about childhood, he remembers having a lot of energy. "I was the kid that would wake up at 6:00 A.M. and watch cartoons," Matt recalls. As a teenager, Matt channeled his energy through sports—playing basketball, running cross-country, and competing in one of the nation's top-ranking private soccer leagues. But everything changed during Matt's sophomore year of high school. That was the year the sleepiness hit.

At first it seemed like nothing serious. Matt just dozed off in class from time to time. But his mini-naps gradually became more frequent. Eventually, the sleepiness would take hold of him in every class except physical education. "Matt, you just fell asleep," his friends would say. "No I didn't," he would shoot back, unaware he had been sleeping. Most of Matt's teachers assumed he was just another teenager exhausted from late-night partying. Some even slammed their hands on his desk to rouse him. Nobody, not even Matt's doctor, suspected he had a serious medical condition—until the accident happened.

It was the summer before junior year, and Matt was driving his truck home from work at his father's appliance repair shop. One moment he was rolling along the street at a safe distance from other cars, and the next he was ramming into a brown Saturn that had slowed to make a left turn. What had transpired in the interim? Matt had fallen asleep. He slammed on the brake pedal, but it was too late; the two vehicles collided. Unharmed, Matt leaped out of his truck and ran to check on the other driver—a woman who, as he remembers, "was totally out of it." Her backrest had broken, and her back had nearly broken along with it. This woman already had a serious back problem, and a fresh injury was the last thing she needed. Matt was dismayed. A few weeks after the accident, he went to the woman's home to bring her flowers. She invited him inside, and they sat down and began to chat. Then, right in the midst of their conversation, Matt fell asleep. More on Matt's story in a bit.

Sleep Troubles
Matt Utesch was active and full of energy as a child, but come sophomore year in high school, he periodically fell asleep throughout the day. Matt was beginning to experience the symptoms of a serious sleep disorder.
Courtesy Matthew Utesch

Matt, In His Own Words
http://qrs.ly/oj3le7e

An Introduction to Sleep

All animals sleep or engage in some rest activity that resembles sleep (Horne, 2006). Dolphins snooze while swimming, keeping one eye cracked open at all times; horses usually sleep standing up; and some birds appear to doze mid-flight (U.S. Fish & Wildlife Service, 2006). There are animals that require loads of sleep—bats and opossums sleep 18 to 20 hours a day—and those that need barely any—elephants and giraffes get by on 3 or 4 hours (Siegel, 2005). Sleep needs vary greatly among people, ranging from as little as 4 hours a night to as long as 11 or more (Horne, 2006). But most of us require between 7 and 8 hours to stay mentally and physically healthy (Banks & Dinges, 2007). Do the math and that translates to more or less a third of the day. And that translates to a third of your *life*. Clearly, sleep must serve some important function, but what is it? And how does it relate to consciousness? How can sleep go so wrong, as happened for Matt? We will address these questions and many more in the pages to come, but first let's cover the basics.

Animal Sleep
Two mustang fillies sleep while standing. Horses are not the only animals that snooze in seemingly awkward positions. The bottlenose dolphin dozes while swimming, one brain hemisphere awake and the other asleep (McCormick, 2007; Siegel, 2005). J. L. Klein & M. L. Hubert/Science Source

---

LO 4 Identify how circadian rhythm relates to sleep.

CIRCADIAN RHYTHM Have you ever noticed that you often get sleepy in the middle of the afternoon? Even if you had a good sleep the night before, an afternoon daze invariably sets in at 2:00 or 3:00 P.M.; it's like clockwork. That's because it is clockwork. Many things your body does, including sleep, are regulated by a biological clock. Body temperature rises during the day, reaching its maximum in the early evening. Hormones are secreted in a cyclical fashion. Growth hormone is released at night, and levels of the stress hormone cortisol soar in the morning, reaching levels 10 to 20 times higher than at night (Wright, 2002). These are just a few of the body functions that follow predictable daily patterns affecting our behaviors, alertness, and activity levels. Such patterns in our physiological functioning roughly follow the 24-hour cycle of daylight and darkness, driven by our **circadian rhythm** (sər-ˈkā-dē-ən).

In the circadian rhythm for sleep and wakefulness, there are two times when the desire for sleep hits hardest. The first is between 2:00 and 6:00 A.M., the same window of time when most car accidents caused by sleepiness occur (Horne, 2006). The second, less intense desire for sleep strikes mid-afternoon, around 2:30 P.M., when many college students have trouble keeping their eyes open in class (Mitler & Miller, 1996).

Not all biological rhythms are circadian. Some occur over longer time intervals (monthly menstruation), and others cycle much faster (the 90-minute sleep cycles, to be discussed shortly). Many animals migrate or hibernate during certain seasons and mate according to a yearly pattern. Even when deprived of cues like changing levels of sunlight, some animals continue to follow these cycles. Birds caged indoors, for example, exhibit mood and behavioral changes at the times of year when they would normally be migrating (Wright, 2002). Biological clocks are everywhere in nature, acting as day planners for organisms as basic as bacteria and slime mold.

SUPRACHIASMATIC NUCLEUS   Where in the body do these inner clocks and calendars dwell? Miniclocks are found in cells all over your body, but a master clock is nestled deep within the **hypothalamus**, a brain structure whose activities revolve around maintaining homeostasis, or balance, in the body's systems. This king of clocks, known as the *suprachiasmatic nucleus* (*SCN*), actually consists of two clusters, each no bigger than an ant, totaling around 20,000 neurons (Forger & Peskin, 2003; Wright, 2002). The SCN plays a role in our circadian rhythm by communicating with other areas of the hypothalamus, which regulates daily patterns of hunger and temperature, and the reticular formation, which regulates alertness and sleepiness (**INFOGRAPHIC 4.1**).

Although tucked away in the recesses of the brain, the SCN knows the difference between day and night. That's because it receives signals from a special type of **light-sensing cells** in the eye, called *retinal ganglion cells*. With the help of these informants, the clock resets to the light and dark cycling of the planet. When light beams upon the earth, your clock tells you to rise and shine, and when darkness hits, it urges you to bed. One way the SCN keeps you on schedule is by indirectly communicating with the pineal gland, a part of the endocrine system, to regulate the release of *melatonin*, a hormone that promotes sleep. In dark conditions, the clock commands the pineal gland to produce melatonin, making it easier to sleep. When light hits the eye, melatonin secretion slows down. So if you want to sleep, turn down the lights, and let your brain turn up the melatonin.

What would happen if you lived in a dark cave with no watches or computers to help you keep track of time? Would your body stay on a 24-hour cycle or get confused? Studies of people living in conditions with no indication of the time of day show that the internal clock continues to hum along at a slightly slower pace, eventually settling on a cycle that runs a little over 24 hours (Carskadon, Labayak, Acebo, & Seifer, 1999; Czeisler et al., 1999). But depriving the clock of its external light cues is generally not a good idea. Sleep–wake cycles can be disrupted, leading to exhaustion, irritability, impairment of memory, and other **negative outcomes.**

CONNECTIONS

In **Chapter 2**, we explained the functions of the hypothalamus. For example, it maintains blood pressure, temperature, and electrolyte balance. It also is involved in regulating sleep–wake cycles, sexual arousal, and appetite.

In **Chapter 3**, we described how light enters the eye and is directed to the retina. The rods and cones in the retina are photoreceptors, which absorb light energy and turn it into electrical and chemical signals. Here, we see how light-sensing cells relay information to the SCN.

In **Chapter 1**, we presented the experiences of the 33 Chilean miners who spent 2 months trapped in the dark caverns of a collapsed mine. When they were rescued, actions were taken to protect their eyes because they had not been exposed to natural light for more than 2 months.

circadian rhythm (sər-ˈkā-dē-ən) The daily patterns roughly following the 24-hour cycle of daylight and darkness; 24-hour cycle of physiological and behavioral functioning.

The Suprachiasmatic Nucleus

The suprachiasmatic nucleus (SCN) of the hypothalamus is the body's internal master clock, playing a role in regulating our circadian rhythms. These rhythms roughly follow the 24-hour cycle of daylight and darkness. But one doesn't have to consciously perceive light for the SCN to function properly; there is a dedicated, *nonvisual* pathway that carries light information from the eyes to the SCN.

Pineal gland
produces melatonin

Hypothalamus
regulates patterns of hunger and temperature

Reticular formation
regulates alertness and sleepiness

The SCN is located deep in the brain, far away from visual processing areas. So how does it get information about light? Our eyes contain a separate nonvisual pathway made of retinal ganglion cells. This pathway goes directly to the SCN.

SCN

Suprachiasmatic nucleus (SCN)

The SCN is actually two tiny bundles of neurons within the hypothalamus. The SCN sends messages about light to the rest of the hypothalamus and the reticular formation, and regulates the pineal gland's production of melatonin, a sleep-inducing hormone.

Pathway for visual information

Visual processing area

Supra is Latin for "above."
Suprachiasmatic means "above the chiasm."
The SCN's long name helps you find it in the brain!

Optic chiasm

Nonvisual pathway for signals about light

For the 20% of the U.S. workforce doing shift work, normal sleep schedules are disrupted. This leads to health problems and increased accidents (Harrington, 2001). Using what we know about how the SCN works, researchers are helping industries ease these effects. Bright lights, such as those installed in this power station control room, contain a high proportion of the blue light found in morning sun, fooling the SCN into thinking it is daytime. That makes it easier for workers to synchronize sleep patterns with work activities.

Credits: Head, ©Alamy; Control room, ©Hank Morgan/Science Source

Jet Lag
Rapidly traveling through time zones puts a strain on the body and brain. It takes time for us to adjust to a new time zone—typically 1 or 2 hours per day (Cunha & Stöppler, 2011). ©Beard & Howell/Getty Images

LARKS AND OWLS   Everyone has his own unique clock, which helps explain why some of us are "morning people" or so-called larks, and others are "night owls." If you are a lark, likely you roll out of bed feeling energized and alert, get more accomplished early in the day, yet grow weary as the day drags on. One study characterized larks as preferring to go to bed before 11:00 P.M. and rising before 8:00 A.M. (Gale & Martyn, 1998). Owls, on the other hand, get up late and hit the sack late. If you slam the "snooze" button on your alarm clock five times every morning, shower with your eyes closed, and act like a grouch at breakfast, you're probably an owl. But being an owl often means your energy level builds throughout the day, making it easy to stay up late watching movies or reading your textbook. About 20% of us are true owls, 20% are genuine larks, and the rest fall somewhere in between (Horne, 2006).

try this

Check your answers in Appendix C.

College students tend to be portrayed as owls, but is this just a stereotype? Does something in the college environment influence sleep–wake cycles, or is there a biological reason some people keep late nights? If you were to explore this question, what kind of experiment would you design? What would your independent and dependent variables be?

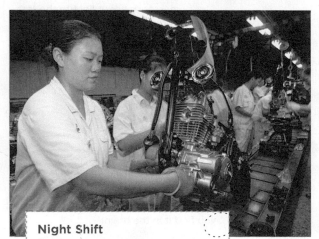

Night Shift
Factory workers are among the many professionals who clock in and out at all hours of the day. Working alternating or night shifts can disrupt circadian rhythms, leading to fatigue, irritability, and diminished mental sharpness. Physical activity and good sleep habits will help counteract the negative effects (Costa, 2003). Michael Reynolds/EPA/Newscom

JET LAG AND SHIFT WORK   Whether you are a lark or an owl, your clock is likely to become confused when you travel between time zones. If you take an airplane halfway around the globe, your biological clock does not automatically reset to match the new time. The physical and mental consequences of this delayed adjustment are known as "jet lag," and it is not an ideal way to start a business trip or honeymoon, as typical symptoms include difficulty concentrating, headaches, and gastrointestinal distress. Fortunately, the biological clock can readjust by about 1 or 2 hours each day, eventually falling into step with the new environmental schedule (Cunha & Stöppler, 2011). Jet lag is frustrating, but at least it's only temporary.

Now imagine plodding through life with a case of jet lag you just can't shake. This is the tough reality for some of the world's shift workers—firefighters, nurses, miners, power plant operators, and other professionals who work while the rest of the world is snuggled under the covers. Shift workers represent about 20% of the workforce in the United States and other developed countries, or 1 in 5 people who are employed (Di Lorenzo et al., 2003). Some work rotating shifts, which means they are constantly going to bed and waking up at different times; others consistently work the overnight shift, so their sleep–wake cycles are permanently out-of-step with the light and dark cycles of the earth. Constantly fighting the clock takes a heavy toll on the mind and body. An irregular sleep schedule may lead to symptoms of *insomnia*, or difficulty falling asleep and sleeping soundly. It's not hard to imagine why. Picture yourself coming off the nightshift and arriving home at 7:00 A.M.: The sun is shining brightly, the birds are chirping, and the rest of the family is chatting over their cornflakes. This is not an ideal environment for sleep. Insomnia resulting from shift work can lead to decreased job productivity, depression, anxiety, diabetes, and other chronic diseases (Morin et al., 2006; Vgontzas et al., 2009). Studies also show that shift workers face an elevated risk of becoming overweight, and developing stomach ulcers and heart disease (Di Lorenzo et al., 2003; Knutsson, 2003). In addition, an estimated 5% to 10% of shift workers have been diagnosed with *circadian rhythm sleep–wake disorders*, which are characterized by excessive sleepiness at work and insomnia at home (American Psychiatric Association [APA], 2013).

However, in our world of 24-hour pharmacies and round-the-clock customer service, shift work is a necessary evil. Dr. Lawrence J. Epstein, the director of the Sleep HealthCenters associated with Harvard, suggests ways in which night workers can minimize circadian disturbances and increase their productivity. Remember that light is the master clock's most important external cue. Dr. Epstein suggests maximizing light exposure during work time and steering clear of it close to bedtime. Some night shifters don sunglasses on their way home, to block the morning sun, and head straight to bed in a quiet, dark room (Epstein & Mardon, 2007). Taking 20- to 30-minute power naps in the middle of a night shift can also help shift workers stay awake and alert (Harvard Medical School, 2007).

Sleep Waves
A young man snoozes in a sleep laboratory. The electrodes attached to his head pick up electrical activity from his brain, which is transformed into a series of spikes on a computer screen. Through careful study of these brain waves, researchers have come to understand the various stages of sleep. Hank Morgan/Science Source

The Stages of Sleep

LO 5   Summarize the stages of sleep.

Have you ever watched someone sleeping? The person looks blissfully tranquil: body still, face relaxed, chest rising and falling like a lazy ocean wave. Don't be fooled. Underneath the body's quiet front is a very active brain, as determined by an electroencephalogram (EEG), a device that picks up electrical signals from the brain and displays this information on a screen. If you could look at an EEG trace of your brain right this moment, you would probably see a series of tiny, short spikes in rapid-fire succession. These high-frequency brainwaves are called **beta waves,** and they appear when you are solving a math problem, reading a book, or whenever you are alert. Now let's say you climb into bed, close your eyes, and relax. As you become more and more drowsy, the electrical activity measured by an EEG would likely begin showing **alpha waves,** which are lower in frequency than beta waves (Cantero, Atienza, Salas, & Gomez, 1999). At some point, you drift into a different level of consciousness known as sleep.

NON-REM SLEEP   A normal sleeper begins the night in **non-rapid eye movement (non-REM),** or nondreaming, sleep, which has four stages (INFOGRAPHIC 4.2 on p. 153). The first and lightest is Stage 1 sleep, also known as "light sleep." During Stage 1, muscles go limp and body temperature starts to fall. The eyeballs may move gently beneath the lids. If you looked at an EEG of a person in Stage 1, you would likely see **theta waves,** which are lower in frequency than both alpha and beta waves. This is the type of sleep many people deny having. Example: Your friend begins to snore while watching TV, so you poke her in the ribs and say, "Wake up!" but she swears she wasn't asleep. It is also during this initial phase of sleep that *hallucinations,* or imaginary sensations, can occur. Do you ever see blotches of color or bizarre

beta waves Brain waves that indicate an alert, awake state.

alpha waves Brain waves that indicate a relaxed, drowsy state.

non-rapid eye movement (non-REM) The nondreaming sleep that occurs during sleep Stages 1 to 4.

theta waves Brain waves that indicate the early stage of sleep.

Kitty Dreams
This cat may be dreaming of chasing mice and birds, but its body is essentially paralyzed during REM sleep. Disable the neurons responsible for this paralysis and you will see some very interesting behavior—the cat will act out its dream.
Thinkstock

delta waves Brain waves that indicate a deep sleep.

rapid eye movement (REM) The stage of sleep associated with dreaming; sleep characterized by bursts of eye movements, with brain activity similar to that of a waking state, but with a lack of muscle tone.

images floating past while you drift off to sleep? Or perhaps you have felt a sensation of falling or swinging and then jerked your arms or legs in response? False perceptions that occur during the limbo between wakefulness and sleep are called *hypnagogic hallucinations*, and they are no cause for concern, in most cases. More on this when we return to Matt's story.

After a few minutes in Stage 1, you move on to the next phase of non-REM sleep, called Stage 2 sleep, which is slightly deeper than Stage 1, so it is harder to awaken the sleeper. Theta waves continue showing up on the EEG, along with little bursts of electrical activity called *sleep spindles* and large waves called *K-complexes* appearing every 2 minutes or so. Researchers suspect sleep spindles are associated with memory consolidation and intelligence (Fogel & Smith, 2011). The exact function of K-complexes is up for debate: Some suggest they are the brain's way of being ready to awaken when the need arises, others believe they are the mechanism for remaining asleep in spite of disturbing stimuli (Colrain, 2005).

After passing through Stages 1 and 2, the sleeper descends into Stage 3, and then into an even deeper Stage 4, when it is most difficult to awaken. Both Stages 3 and 4 are known as slow-wave sleep, because they are characterized by tall, low-frequency **delta waves.** Stages 3 and 4 are really very similar, but Stage 4 contains a higher proportion of delta waves (delta waves are evident more than 50% of the time). Waking a person from slow-wave sleep is not easy, and if you succeed, be prepared. Most of us will feel groggy, disoriented, and downright irritated when jarred from a slow-wave slumber. This is also the time of greatest secretion of growth hormone, which helps children to grow taller and stronger, and to build tissue (Awikunprasert & Sittiprapaporn, 2012).

REM SLEEP   You will only remain in Stage 4 for around 40 minutes. You don't stay in deep sleep for the remainder of the night; your sleep becomes less deep as you work your way from Stage 4 back to Stage 1. And instead of waking up, you enter the fifth stage, known as **rapid eye movement (REM)** sleep, so called because during this stage, a person's eyes often dart around, even though they are closed. How else can you tell someone is in REM sleep? Brain activity changes from those slower brain waves to faster and shorter brain waves; an EEG recording of someone in REM sleep shows brain activity similar to that of a person who is wide awake. Meanwhile, the eyes make quick, sharp movements beneath the eyelids, pulse and breathing rate fluctuate, and blood flow to the genitals increases, which explains why people frequently wake up in a state of sexual arousal. Another name for REM sleep is *paradoxical sleep*, because the sleeper appears to be quiet and resting, but the brain is full of electrical activity. People roused from REM sleep often report having vivid, illogical dreams. Thankfully, the brain has a way of preventing us from acting out our dreams. During REM sleep, certain neurons in the brainstem control the voluntary muscles, keeping most of the body still.

What would happen if the neurons responsible for disabling the muscles during REM sleep were destroyed or damaged? Researchers led by Michel Jouvet in France and Adrian Morrison in the United States found the answer to that question in the 1960s and 1970s. Both teams showed that severing these neurons in the brains of cats caused them to act out their kitty dreams. Not only did the sleeping felines stand up; they arched their backs in fury, groomed and licked themselves, and hunted imaginary mice (Jouvet, 1979; Sastre & Jouvet, 1979).

Sleep

Looking in on a sleep study, you'll see that the brain is actually very active during sleep, cycling through non-REM (NREM) stages and ending in REM sleep approximately five times during the night. Transitions between stages are clearly visible as shifts in EEG patterns.

Graphs illustrating the human sleep cycle typically present an 8-hour time span, as shown here. But this doesn't tell the whole story of sleep. The amount of time spent sleeping and the content of our sleep changes across the life span. And while a *normal* night's sleep lasts approximately 7 hours for a healthy young adult, 30% of working adults get 6 hours or fewer of sleep per night (Centers for Disease Control and Prevention, 2012f).

This sleep study participant wears electrodes that will measure her brain waves and body movements during sleep.

Sleep

Looking at brain waves allows us to trace a person's stage of sleep. Here we can see a clear shift from waking to sleeping patterns.
(FROM DEMENT & VAUGHAN, 1999.)

A typical night's sleep has 4 or 5 multistage sleep cycles, each lasting approximately 90 minutes. Each cycle includes at least 1 NREM and 1 REM stage. Pattern and duration of stages differ over the course of the night.

Human Sleep Stages

REM duration increases.

Stages 3 and 4 vanish.

Awake
REM sleep
Stage 1 NREM
Stage 2 NREM
Stage 3 NREM
Stage 4 NREM

Hours of sleep

Alpha and Beta waves
Eye movement phase
Theta waves
Sleep spindle   K-complex
Delta waves (characterize slow wave sleep)

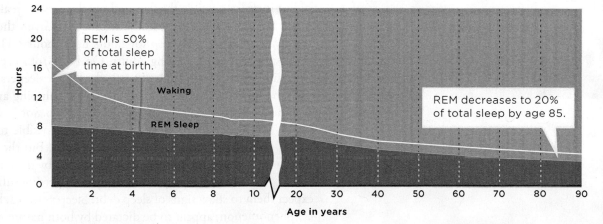

As we age, we need fewer hours of sleep, and the proportion of time spent in REM diminishes.

REM is 50% of total sleep time at birth.

REM decreases to 20% of total sleep by age 85.

Waking

REM Sleep

Hours

Age in years

SLEEP ARCHITECTURE Congratulations. You have just completed one sleep cycle, working your way up and down Stages 1, 2, 3, and 4 of non-REM sleep and ending with a dream-packed episode of REM. Each of these cycles lasts about 90 minutes, and the average adult sleeper loops through five of them per night. These cycles are not identical because they change in composition throughout the night. During the first two cycles, a considerable amount of time is devoted to the deep Stages 3 and 4. Halfway through the night, however, Stages 3 and 4 vanish. Meanwhile, the REM periods become progressively longer, and an adult will average approximately four to five REM cycles. The first REM episode may last a mere 5 to 10 minutes, whereas the final one may drag on for nearly a half-hour (Siegel, 2005). When all is said and done, the sleep stage where we spend the most time—nearly half the night—is Stage 2 (Epstein & Mardon, 2007). Therefore, we pack in most of our restorative sleep early in the night and most dreaming toward the end.

As we age, the makeup of our sleep cycles, or *sleep architecture*, changes. Older people spend less time in REM sleep and the deeply refreshing stages of non-REM sleep (3 and 4). Instead, their periods of light sleep (Stages 1 and 2, which can be interrupted easily by noises and movements) are longer (Ohayon, Carskadon, Guilleminault, & Vitiello, 2004). This may be why many older people complain of sleeping poorly, waking up often, and feeling drowsy during the day. Not all elderly people have trouble sleeping, of course. Like most everything in life, sleep patterns vary considerably from one individual to the next.

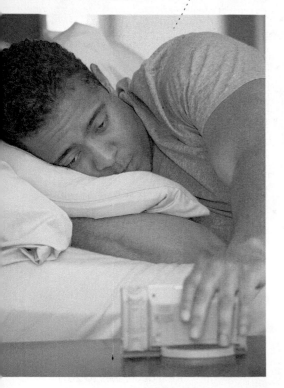

Wake Up! Some of us feel refreshed after sleeping 6 or 7 hours. Others can barely grasp a glass of orange juice without a solid 8. Sleep habits appear to be a blend of biological and environmental forces—both nature and nurture. ©Ariel Skelley/Blend Images/Corbis

nature AND nurture

What Kind of Sleeper Are You?

On a typical weeknight, the average American sleeps 6 hours and 40 minutes, but there is significant deviation from this "average." A large number of people—about 20% of the population—get fewer than 6 hours, and another 28% snooze longer than 8 hours (National Sleep Foundation, 2009). How do you account for so much variation in the duration of sleep?

When it comes to understanding sleep patterns, we cannot ignore what is in our *nature*, or biology. Some studies suggest sleep needs are inherited from parents, and there are probably many genes involved (He et al., 2009; Hor & Tafti, 2009). Evidence also suggests that "short sleepers" (people who average fewer than 6 hours per night) and "long sleepers" (those who sleep more than 9 hours) are running on different circadian rhythms. Nighttime increases in the "sleep hormone" melatonin, for example, tend to be reduced for those who get fewer zzz's (Aeschbach et al., 2003; Rivkees, 2003).

But it is also possible that some short sleepers are really just average sleepers getting by on less than an optimal amount of sleep. Given the opportunity to catch up for a few days, would they sleep for hours upon hours? This is just what happened in a small study of healthy young adults. On Day 1 of sleep catch-up, all the participants slept more than usual. But by Day 3, the longer sleepers were engaged in less catch-up than the shorter sleepers, who seemed to be chipping away at a "sleep debt" they had accumulated (Klerman & Dijk, 2004). We do not have access to the genetic codes of these participants, so it is impossible to know what heritable factors might have influenced the results. But the findings do suggest sleep patterns are, to some degree, shaped by the circumstances of our lives. If the short sleepers in the study were getting sufficient sleep, then we wouldn't expect them to show signs of sleep debt. Sleep patterns, like virtually every psychological phenomenon, appear to be dictated by both nature and nurture. ◊🏠

ARE "SHORT SLEEPERS" ALWAYS IN SLEEP DEBT?

PROBLEM IDENTIFIED Shortly after the car accident, Matt was diagnosed with **narcolepsy,** a neurological disorder characterized by excessive daytime sleepiness and other sleep-related disturbances. The most striking symptoms of narcolepsy include the "irrepressible need to sleep, lapsing into sleep, or napping occurring within the same day" (American Psychological Association, 2013a, p. 372). Sleepiness can strike anytime, anywhere—during a job interview, while riding a bicycle, or in the midst of a passionate kiss. One time Matt fell asleep while making a sandwich. When he woke up, he was still holding a slice of meat in his hand. Some people with narcolepsy report a waking alert level and then falling asleep, while others report an overwhelming feeling of sleepiness all the time. "Sleep attacks" can occur several times a day. Most are measured in seconds or minutes, but episodes of an hour or longer have been reported (National Institute of Neurological Disorders and Stroke, 2011a). By the time Matt was a junior in high school, his uncontrollable naps were striking upward of 20 to 30 times a day.

Tired Teen ◄
Matt's battle with narcolepsy climaxed during his junior year of high school. In addition to falling asleep 20 to 30 times a day, he was experiencing frequent bouts of cataplexy, or sudden episodes of muscle paralysis. Cataplexy struck Matt anytime, anywhere—up to 100 times a day. Courtesy Matthew Utesch

CATAPLEXY And that wasn't all. Matt developed another debilitating symptom of narcolepsy: *cataplexy,* or sudden episodes of total loss of muscle tone or strength that occur when a person is awake. During a severe cataplectic attack, some muscles go limp, and the body may collapse slowly to the floor like a rag doll. One moment Matt would be standing in the hallway laughing with friends; the next he was splayed on the floor unable to move a muscle. "It was like a tree being cut down [and] tipping over," he recalls. Usually, cataplexy wears off after several seconds, but severe attacks can render a person immobilized for minutes at a time.

Cataplexy may completely disable the body, but it produces no loss in consciousness. Even during the worst attack, Matt remained completely aware of himself and his surroundings. He could hear people talking about him; sometimes they snickered in amusement. "Kids can be cruel," Matt says. Cataplexy attacks come on suddenly, usually during periods of emotional excitement (APA, 2013). By junior year, Matt's cataplexy had spun out of control. He was having 60 to 100 attacks a day.

Sleep Attack
Eight-year-old Lucas Carlton of Liverpool, England, suffers from narcolepsy, a neurological disorder characterized by frequent bouts of uncontrollable sleepiness and other symptoms. Lucas sleeps as many as 20 hours per day. Mercury Press/ZUMAPRESS.com

SLEEP PARALYSIS AND HYPNAGOGIC HALLUCINATIONS Matt also developed two other common narcolepsy symptoms: sleep paralysis and hypnagogic hallucinations. *Sleep paralysis* is a temporary paralysis that strikes just before falling asleep or upon waking up (APA, 2013). Recall that the body becomes paralyzed during REM sleep, but sometimes this paralysis sets in prematurely or fails to turn off on time. Picture yourself lying in bed, awake and fully aware yet unable to roll over, climb out of bed, or even wiggle a toe. You want to scream for help, but your lips won't budge. Sleep paralysis is a common symptom of narcolepsy, but it can also strike ordinary sleepers. One study found that nearly a third of college students had experienced sleep paralysis at least once in their lives (Cheyne, Newby-Clark, & Rueffer, 1999). Episodes usually last a few seconds, but some go on for several minutes—a terrifying experience for most people.

Sleep paralysis may seem scary, but now imagine seeing bloodthirsty vampires standing at the foot of your bed just as you are about to fall asleep. Earlier we discussed the *hypnagogic hallucinations* people can experience during Stage 1 sleep (seeing strange images, for example). But not all hypnagogic hallucinations involve harmless blobs. They can also be realistic visions of axe murderers or space aliens trying to abduct you (McNally & Clancy, 2005). Matt had a recurring hallucination of a man with a butcher knife racing through his doorway, jumping onto his bed, and

narcolepsy A neurological disorder characterized by excessive daytime sleepiness, which includes lapses into sleep and napping.

stabbing him in the chest. Upon awakening, he would often quiz his mother with questions like, "When is my birthday?" or "What is your license plate number?" He wanted to verify she was real, not just another character in his dream. Like sleep paralysis, vivid hypnagogic hallucinations can occur in people without narcolepsy, too. Shift work, insomnia, and sleeping face-up are all factors that appear to heighten one's risk (Cheyne, 2002; McNally & Clancy, 2005).

Throughout junior year, Matt took various medications to control his narcolepsy, but his symptoms persisted. Narcolepsy was beginning to interfere with virtually every aspect of his life. At the beginning of high school, Matt had a 4.0 grade point average; now he was working twice as hard and earning lower grades. Playing sports had become a major health hazard because his cataplexy struck wherever and whenever, without notice. If he collapsed while sprinting down the soccer field or diving for a basketball, he might twist an ankle, break an arm, or worse. Narcolepsy also began to undermine Matt's social life. Some of his classmates viewed him as a source of entertainment. "Hey, you're like that guy out of *Rat Race* or *Deuce Bigalow*," they would say, drawing on Hollywood's inaccurate stereotypes. It was during those years that Matt realized who his true friends were. "The people that stuck with me [then] are still my close friends now," he says. Matt's loyal buddies learned to read the warning signs of cataplexy (for example, when he suddenly stands still and closes his eyes) and did everything possible to keep him safe, grabbing hold of his body and slowly lowering him to the ground. His buddies had his back—literally.

Sleep Disturbances

> **LO 6**   Recognize various sleep disorders and their symptoms.

Approximately 1 in 2,500 people suffer from narcolepsy (Ohayon, 2011). It is believed to result from a failure of the brain to properly regulate sleep patterns. Normally, the boundaries separating sleep and wakefulness are relatively clear—you are awake, in REM sleep, or in non-REM sleep. With narcolepsy, the lines separating these different realms of consciousness fade, allowing sleep to spill into periods of wakefulness. The loss of muscle tone during cataplexy, sleep paralysis, and dreamlike hypnagogic hallucinations experienced while falling asleep may be explained by occurrences of REM sleep in the midst of wakefulness (Attarian, Schenck, & Mahowald, 2000). In other words, REM sleep occurs in the wrong place, at the wrong time (see a summary of this and other sleep disturbances in **TABLE 4.1**).

REM SLEEP BEHAVIOR DISORDER   Problems with REM regulation can also lead to other sleep disturbances, including **REM sleep behavior disorder.** The defining characteristics of this disorder include "repeated episodes of arousal often associated with vocalizations and/or complex motor behaviors arising from REM sleep" (APA, 2013, p. 408). People with REM sleep behavior disorder are much like the cats in Morrison's and Jouvet's experiments; something has gone awry with the brainstem mechanism responsible for paralyzing their bodies during REM sleep, so they are able to move around and act out their dreams (Schenck & Mahowald, 2002). This is not a good thing, since the dreams of REM sleep behavior disorder sufferers tend to be unusually violent and action-packed, involving fights with wild animals and other attackers (Fantini, Corona, Clerici, & Ferini-Strambi, 2005). The sleeping partners of individuals with REM sleep behavior disorder often get kicked, punched, and screamed at. According to some research, up to 65% of REM sleep behavior disorder sufferers have injured either themselves or their bedmates at one point or another. Scrapes, cuts, and bruises are common, and traumatic brain injuries have also been

REM sleep behavior disorder A sleep disturbance in which the mechanism responsible for paralyzing the body during REM sleep is not functioning, resulting in the acting out of dreams.

obstructive sleep apnea hypopnea (hī-pop-ᴵnē-ə) A serious disturbance of non-REM sleep characterized by complete absence of air flow (apnea) or reduced air flow (hypopnea).

reported (APA, 2013; Aurora et al., 2010). REM sleep behavior disorder primarily affects older men (age 50 and up) and frequently foreshadows the development of serious neurodegenerative disorders— conditions such as Parkinson's disease and dementia that are associated with the gradual decline and death of neurons (Boeve et al., 2007; Fantini et al., 2005; Schenck & Mahowald, 2002). More recently, women and younger people are being diagnosed with this disorder as well (APA, 2013). Sadly, many people struggling with REM sleep behavior disorder (about half, according to some estimates) develop a neurodegenerative disease within a decade of being diagnosed (Postuma et al., 2009).

BREATHING-RELATED SLEEP DISORDERS There are several breathing related sleep disorders, but the most common is **obstructive sleep apnea hypopnea** (hī-'pop-nē-ə). This is a serious disturbance characterized by a complete absence of air flow (apnea) or reduced air flow (hypopnea). During normal sleep, the airway remains open, allowing air to flow in and out of the lungs. With obstructive sleep apnea hypopnea, the upper throat muscles go limp, allowing the upper airway to close shut (APA, 2013). Breathing stops for 10 seconds or more, causing blood oxygen levels to drop (Chung & Elsaid, 2009). Sensing an emergency, the brain responds by commanding the body to *wake up and breathe!* The sleeper awakes and gasps for air, sometimes with a noisy nasal sound, and then drifts back to sleep. This process can repeat itself several hundred times per night, preventing a person from experiencing the deep stages of sleep so crucial for feeling rested and refreshed in the morning. Most people have no memory of the repeated awakenings and wonder why they feel so exhausted during the day, with absolutely no idea they suffer from a serious sleep

Does Shaq Snore?
Basketball icon Shaquille O'Neal suffers from a breathing-related sleep disorder. At the request of Harvard researchers who studied his sleep behaviors, Shaq began wearing a special mask to keep his airway open at night. He now reports sleeping better and feeling more energized during the day (American Academy of Sleep Medicine, 2011; National Heart, Lung, and Blood Institute, 2011).
Robyn Beck/AFP/Getty Images

Table 4.1 SLEEP DISTURBANCES

Sleep Disturbance	Definition	Defining Characteristics
Narcolepsy	Neurological disorder characterized by excessive daytime sleepiness, which includes lapses into sleep and napping	Irrepressible need to sleep; daytime napping; cataplexy; sleep paralysis; hypnagogic hallucinations.
REM Sleep Behavior Disorder	The mechanism responsible for paralysis during REM not functioning, resulting in the acting out of dreams.	Dreamers vocalize and act out dreams; violent and active dreams are common; upon awakening the dream is remembered; risk of injury to self and sleeping partners.
Obstructive Sleep Apnea Hypopnea	Serious disturbance characterized by a complete absence of air flow (apnea) or reduced air flow (hypopnea).	Upper throat muscles go limp; airway closes; breathing stops for 10 seconds or longer; sleeper awakens, gasping for air.
Insomnia	Inability to fall asleep or stay asleep.	Poor sleep quantity or quality; tendency to wake up too early; can't fall back asleep; not feeling refreshed after a night's sleep
Sleepwalking	Disturbance of non-REM sleep characterized by complex motor behavior during sleep.	Expressionless face; open eyes; may sit up in bed, walk around, or speak gibberish; upon awakening has limited recall
Sleep Terrors	Disturbance of non-REM sleep generally occurring in children.	Screaming, inconsolable child; usually no memory of the episode the next day.

Problems can arise during both REM and non-REM sleep. This table outlines some of the most common sleep disturbances and their defining characteristics.

disturbance. Obstructive sleep apnea hypopnea is more common among men than women and is linked to increased risk of death in the elderly, increased traffic accidents, and reduced quality of life. This disorder is also associated with a rise in blood pressure, increasing the risk of cardiovascular disease. Research indicates that obstructive sleep apnea hypopnea is more prevalent in the obese, and in women after menopause (APA, 2013).

Restless Clooney
George Clooney glows as he accepts the Best Actor award at the 2012 Golden Globes. You would never guess that he struggles with two of the symptoms of insomnia: difficulty falling asleep and remaining asleep (Roth, 2007). Clooney says he needs to keep the television on to fall asleep and wakes up five times a night (*The Hollywood Reporter,* 2012, February 15). ©Paul Drinkwater/NBC/ NBCU Photo Bank via Getty Images

INSOMNIA   The most prevalent sleep disorder is **insomnia,** which is characterized by an inability to fall asleep or stay asleep; often people with insomnia will report that the quantity or quality of their sleep is not good. Some may complain they wake up too early and can't fall back to sleep, or they don't feel refreshed after a night's sleep. Sleepiness during the day and difficulties with cognitive tasks and processes are also reported (APA, 2013). About a third of adults experience some symptoms of insomnia, and 6% to 10% suffer from insomnia disorder (APA, 2013; Mai & Buysse, 2008; Roth, 2007). Insomnia symptoms can be related to factors such as the stress of a new job, college studies, depression, anxiety, jet lag, aging, and drug use.

OTHER SLEEP DISTURBANCES   A common sleep disturbance that can occur during non-REM (typically, Stages 3 and 4) is sleepwalking. A quarter of all children will experience at least one sleepwalking incident, and it seems to run in families (Licis, Desruisseau, Yamada, Duntley, & Gurnett, 2011). Here are some ways to spot a sleepwalker: Her face is expressionless; her eyes are open; and she may sit up in bed, walk around in confusion, or speak gibberish. (The garbled speech of sleepwalking is different from sleep *talking,* which can occur in either REM or non-REM sleep, but is not considered a sleep disturbance.) Sleepwalkers may have "limited recall" of the event upon awakening (APA, 2013). They are capable of accomplishing a variety of tasks such as opening doors, going to the bathroom, and getting dressed, all of which they are likely to forget by morning. Most sleepwalking episodes are not related to dreaming, and contrary to urban myth, awakening a sleepwalker will not cause sudden death or injury. What's dangerous is leaving the front door unlocked and the car keys in the ignition, as sleepwalkers have been known to wander into the streets and even attempt driving (APA, 2013).

Sleep terrors are a non-REM sleep disturbance primarily affecting children. Here's how a sleep terror typically presents itself: A child sits bolt upright in bed, staring fearfully at nothing, and utters a blood-curdling scream. Parents rush into the room to find the child crying hysterically, hyperventilating, and perhaps struggling frantically. No matter what the parents say or do, the child remains inconsolable. Fortunately, sleep terrors only last a few minutes, and most children outgrow them. Sleep terrors are often worse for parents, who are awakened by a screaming child, than they are for the child, who generally won't remember the episode the next day (APA, 2013).

"Wake up, Tom. You're having the American dream again."

Peter Steiner/The New Yorker Collection/ www.cartoonbank.com

Synonyms
sleep terrors night terrors
sleepwalking somnambulism
(säm-ˡnam-byə-ˌli-zəm)

Nightmares are frightening dreams that occur in REM sleep. They affect people of all ages. And unlike night terrors, nightmares can often be recalled in vivid detail. Because nightmares usually occur during REM sleep, they are generally not acted out (APA, 2013). But can nightmares cause any type of emotional harm?

from the pages of **SCIENTIFIC AMERICAN**

More Than Just a Bad Dream

Nightmares may fuel anxiety rather than serving as an emotional release

You awake with a pounding heart and clammy hands. Relax, you think to yourself—it was just a bad dream. But are nightmares truly benign? Psychologists aren't so sure. Although some continue to believe nightmares reduce psychological tensions by letting the brain act out its fears, recent research suggests that nocturnal torments are more likely to increase anxiety in waking life.

In one study Australian researchers asked 624 high school students about their lives and nightmares during the past year and assessed their stress levels. It is well known that stressful experiences cause nightmares, but if nightmares serve to diffuse that tension, troubled sleepers should have an easier time coping with emotional ordeals. The study, published in the journal *Dreaming,* did not bear out that hypothesis: not only did nightmares not stave off anxiety, but people who reported being distressed about their dreams were even more likely to suffer from general anxiety than those who experienced an upsetting event such as the divorce of their parents.

It is possible, however, that something is going wrong in the brains of individuals who experience a lot of anxiety, so that normal emotional processing during dreaming fails, says Tore Nielsen, director of the Dream and Nightmare Laboratory at Sacred Heart Hospital in Montreal. But Nielsen's most recent results, published in the *Journal of Sleep Research* last June, actually bolster the Australian findings. To tease out how REM sleep—during which most dreaming takes place—affects our emotions, the Canadian researchers showed disturbing images (such as gory scenes or a woman being forced into a van at knifepoint) to a group of healthy volunteers just before they went to bed. When the subjects viewed the same pictures in the morning, those who had been deprived of dream-filled REM sleep were less emotionally affected than those deprived of other sleep phases. The same was true for those who experienced fewer negative emotions in their dreams. In other words, having nightmares did not make dreamers more resilient in waking life—just the opposite.

What is not clear from these studies is whether nightmares play a causal role in anxiety or are merely an expression of an underlying problem. Most researchers agree that having an occasional nightmare is normal and not problematic. But if the dreams give rise to persistent anxiety and concern, something more serious could be going on—and it may be a good idea to talk to a mental health professional about it. **Frederik Joelving.**

Who Needs Sleep?

Matt's worst struggle with narcolepsy stretched through the last two years of high school. During this time, he was averaging 20 to 30 naps a day. You might think that someone who falls asleep so often would at least benefit from feeling well-rested while awake. This was not the case. Matt had trouble sleeping at night, and it was taking a heavy toll on his ability to think clearly. He remembers nodding off at the wheel a few times but continuing to drive, reassuring himself that everything was fine. (Such a decision was a poor one given that his narcolepsy had already caused at least one serious accident.) He forgot about homework assignments and simple things people told him. Matt was experiencing two of the most common symptoms of sleep deprivation: impaired judgment and lapses in memory (Goel, Rao, Durmer, & Dinges, 2009).

Let's face it. No one can function optimally without a good night's sleep. But the expression "good night's sleep" means something quite different from one person to

insomnia Sleep disorder characterized by an inability to fall asleep or stay asleep, impacting both the quality and the quantity of sleep.

sleep terrors A disturbance of non-REM sleep, generally occurring in children; characterized by screaming, staring fearfully, and usually no memory of the episode the following morning.

nightmares Frightening dreams that occur during REM sleep.

the next. Newborns sleep anywhere from 10.5 to 18 hours per day, toddlers 12 to 14 hours, school-aged children 10 to 11 hours, and teens about 9 hours (National Sleep Foundation, 2012a, 2012b). The average adult needs between 7 and 8 hours to feel restored, though others (including Madonna and Jay Leno) claim they get by on just 4 (Breus, 2009, May 6). People who average less than 4 or more than 11 hours, otherwise known as "extreme sleepers," are very rare (Horne, 2006).

SLEEP DEPRIVATION What happens to animals when they don't sleep at all? Laboratory studies show that sleep deprivation kills rats faster than starvation (Rechtschaffen & Bergmann, 1995; Siegel, 2005). Curtailing sleep in humans leads to rapid deterioration of mental and physical well-being. Stay up all night for 48 hours and you can expect your memory, attention, reaction time, and decision making to suffer noticeably (Goel et al., 2009; Lim & Dinges, 2010). Sleepy people find it especially challenging to accomplish tasks that are monotonous and boring; sleep deprivation impairs the ability to focus attention on a single activity, such as keeping your eyes on the road while driving (Lim & Dinges, 2010). Using driving simulators and tests to measure alertness, hand–eye coordination, and other factors, researchers report that getting behind the wheel while sleepy is similar to driving drunk. Staying awake for just 17 to 19 consecutive hours (which many of us with demanding jobs, children, and social lives do regularly) produces the same effect as having a blood alcohol content (BAC) of 0.05%, the legal limit in many countries. Stay up a few hours beyond that, and your driving will begin to look like that of a person whose BAC is 0.10%—enough to get you arrested in the United States (Williamson & Feyer, 2000). Sleep loss also makes you more prone to *microsleeps*, or uncontrollable mini-naps lasting several seconds—enough time to miss a traffic light turning red. When you take sleep deprivation to the extreme, staying awake for several days at a time (11 days is the current world record, based on experimental data; Gillin, 2002, March 25), a host of disabling effects may result, including fragmented speech, cognitive deficits, mood swings, and hallucinations (Gulevich, Dement, & Johnson, 1966).

Just because you don't pull all-nighters does not mean you are immune to problems of sleep deprivation. A large proportion of people suffer from a more chronic form of sleep loss, resulting from insufficient sleep night-upon-night for weeks, months, or years. These people are less likely than their well-rested peers to exercise, eat healthy foods, have sex, and attend family events (National Sleep Foundation, 2009), and they face a greater risk for heart disease, diabetes, and weight gain (Sigurdson & Ayas, 2007). People who do not get enough sleep have decreased immune system responses and slower reaction times (Besedovsky, Lange, & Born, 2012; Orzeł-Gryglewska, 2010). Many researchers suspect the obesity epidemic currently plaguing Western countries is linked to chronic sleep deprivation. Skimping on sleep appears to disrupt appetite-regulating hormones, which may lead to excessive hunger and overeating (Willyard, 2008).

REM DEPRIVATION So far we have only covered sleep loss in general, but remember there are two types of sleep: REM and non-REM. What happens if only one of these is compromised? Studies show that depriving people of Stages 3 and 4 sleep leads to increased physical symptoms such as fatigue and more overall pain (Roehrs, Hyde, Blaisdell, Greenwald, & Roth, 2006). Preliminary research suggests depriving people of REM sleep in particular can cause emotional overreactions to threatening situations (Rosales-Lagarde et al., 2012). One other important thing to note is that following REM deprivation, people experience **REM rebound,** an increased amount of time spent in REM sleep when they finally have an opportunity to sleep in peace.

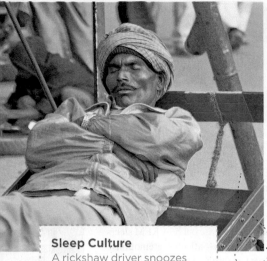

Sleep Culture
A rickshaw driver snoozes in the bright sun. Afternoon siestas are common in countries such as India and Spain, but atypical in the United States (Randall, 2012, September 22). Cultural norms regarding sleep vary significantly around the world. ©Christine Welman/Alamy

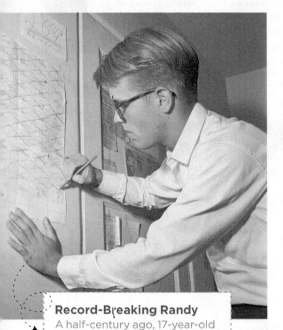

Record-Breaking Randy
A half-century ago, 17-year-old Randy Gardner set the record for the longest documented period of self-imposed sleep deprivation. With the help and encouragement of two friends, and no caffeine or stimulants of any sort, the young man went 11 consecutive days without snoozing (Gulevich et al., 1966). ©San Diego History Center

WHY DO WE SLEEP? Although we spend one third of our lives sleeping and we know what goes on while we are asleep, there is disagreement on the function of sleep. Drawing from sleep deprivation studies and other types of experiments, researchers have constructed various theories to explain *why* we spend so much time sleeping (**TABLE 4.2**). Here are three of the major ones:

- The restorative theory of sleep suggests we sleep because it allows for growth and repair of the body and brain. This makes sense, given that growth hormone is secreted during non-REM sleep and protein production ramps up in the brain during REM. Some have suggested that sleep is a time for rest and replenishment of neurotransmitters, especially those important for attention and memory (Hobson, 1989).

- An evolutionary theory of sleep suggests that sleep serves an adaptive function; it evolved because it helped us survive. For much of human history, before people became accustomed to illuminating their homes, nighttime was very dark—and very unsafe—for humans, who have poor night vision compared to animals hunting for prey. Given that our predators were more threatening in the dark, it was adaptive for us to stay out of environments where we couldn't see. The development of our circadian rhythms driving us to sleep thus served an important evolutionary purpose.

- Another compelling theory suggests that sleep helps with the consolidation of memories and learning. Researchers disagree which stage of sleep might facilitate such a process, but one thing seems clear: Without sleep, our ability to lay down complex memories, and thus learn difficult concepts, is hampered (Farthing, 1992). How do we know this? Studies show that areas of the brain excited during learning tasks are reawakened during non-REM sleep. When researchers monitored the neuronal activity of rats exploring a new environment, they noticed certain neurons firing. These same neurons became active again when the rats fell into non-REM sleep, suggesting that the neurons were involved in remembering the experience (Diekelmann & Born, 2010). Maquet (2000) found evidence of a similar phenomenon in humans. Using PET scans, he observed common patterns of brain activity when the participants were awake and learning and later while asleep.

Table 4.2	THEORIES OF SLEEP	
Theory	**Description**	**Reflection**
Restorative	Sleep allows for growth and repair of the body and brain.	Growth hormone secreted during non-REM sleep; protein production increases during REM; replenishment of neurotransmitters.
Evolutionary	Sleep serves adaptive function; evolved as it helped survival.	Dark environments were unsafe; humans have poor night vision compared to animals hunting at night.
Consolidation	Sleep aids in the consolidation of memories and learning.	Assists in creation of memories, learning difficult concepts; similar patterns of brain activity when learning and sleeping afterwards.

We spend approximately a third of our lives sleeping, yet the precise purpose of sleep is still to be established. Above are three of the dominant theories.

REM rebound An increased amount of sleep in the REM stage with the first sleep session following sleep deprivation.

The exact purpose of sleep has yet to be identified, but there is no denying its importance. After a couple of sleepless nights, we are grumpy, clumsy, and not able to think straight. Research has confirmed what we all know intuitively: Without good sleep, we don't feel like ourselves.

THINK again

7 Sleep Myths

 Everyone seems to have their own bits of "expert knowledge" about sleep. Read on to learn about claims (in **bold**) that are false.

- **Drinking alcohol before bed helps you sleep better:** Alcohol helps you fall asleep, but too much interferes with slow-wave sleep and may cause you to wake up during the night (Ballantyne, 2009). So, too, can one or two cups of coffee. Although moderate caffeine consumption heightens alertness (Epstein & Mardon, 2007), be careful not to drink too much or too close to bedtime; either action may lead to further sleep disruption (Landolt, Dijk, Gaus, & Borbély, 1995).

- **Exercising right before bed sets you up for a good night's sleep:** Generally speaking, exercise promotes slow-wave sleep, the type that makes you feel bright-eyed and bushy-tailed in the morning (Driver & Taylor, 2000; Youngstedt & Kline, 2006). However, working out too close to bedtime (2 to 3 hours beforehand) may prevent good sleep (National Institutes of Health [NIH], 2012).

- **Everyone needs 8 hours of sleep each night:** Most people require between 7 and 8 hours (Banks & Dinges, 2007), but sleep needs can range greatly from person to person. Some people do fine with 6; others genuinely need 9 or 10 hours.

- **Watching TV or tooling around on your computer just before bed will help get you into the sleep zone:** Screen time is not advised as a transition to sleep time. The stimulation of TV and computers can interfere with your slumber, and the ability to fall and remain asleep (National Sleep Foundation, 2012c).

- **You can catch up on accumulated sleep loss with one night of "super-sleep":** Settling any sleep debt is not easy. You may feel refreshed upon waking from 10 hours of "recovery" sleep, but the effects of sleep debt will likely creep up later on (Cohen et al., 2010).

- **Insomnia is no big deal. Everyone has trouble sleeping from time to time:** Insomnia is a mentally and physically debilitating condition that can result in mood changes, memory problems, difficulty with concentration and coordination, and other life-altering impairments (Pavlovich-Danis & Patterson, 2006).

NO iPADS ALLOWED IN THE BED!

- **Sleep aids are totally safe:** When taken according to prescription, sleep aids are relatively safe and effective, although they do not guarantee a normal night of sleep. That being said, research has linked some of these medications to an increased risk of death (Kripke, Langer, & Kline, 2012), as well as an increased risk of sleepwalking, sleep eating, and sleep driving. ●+

Before moving on to the next section, look at **TABLE 4.3** for some ideas on how to get better sleep.

Table 4.3 HOW TO GET A GOOD NIGHT'S SLEEP

To Get Good Sleep	Reasoning
Get on a schedule.	The body operates according to daily cycles, or circadian rhythms. Putting your body and brain on a regular schedule—going to bed and waking up at roughly the same time every day—is critical.
Set the stage for sleep.	Turn down the lights, turn off your phone, and slip into soft pajamas. Do everything possible to create a quiet, dark, and comfortable sleeping environment.
Watch eating, drinking, and smoking.	Beware of foods that create heartburn, and avoid excessive use of alcohol, caffeine, and nicotine (known enemies of sleep) especially late in the day.
Move it or lose it.	Exercise is associated with better sleep, but not right before bed. Exercise 2 to 3 hours before bed can actually prevent good sleep.

If you frequently wake up feeling groggy and unrestored, above are several simple measures you can take to improve the quality of your sleep.

SOURCE: NIH, 2012.

 show what you know

1. The suprachiasmatic nucleus obtains its information about day and night from:
   a. circadian rhythm.
   b. beta waves.
   c. K complexes.
   d. retinal ganglion cells.

2. In which of the following stages of sleep do we spend the most time at night?
   a. Stage 1
   b. Stage 2
   c. Stage 3
   d. Stage 4

3. Narcolepsy is a neurological disorder characterized by excessive daytime sleepiness and other sleep-related disturbances such as _____, which refers to the sudden loss of muscle tone that can occur when a person is awake.

4. Make a drawing of the 90-minute sleep cycle. Label each stage with the appropriate brain wave experienced.

✓ CHECK YOUR ANSWERS IN APPENDIX C.

Dreams

Sleep is an exciting time for the brain. As we lie in the darkness, eyes closed and bodies limp, our neurons keep firing. REM is a particularly active sleep stage, when the brain waves are fast and irregular. During REM, anything is possible. We can soar through the clouds, kiss superheroes, and ride roller coasters with frogs. Time to explore the weird world of dreaming.

SLEEP, SLEEP, GO AWAY Just 2 months before graduating from high school, Matt began taking a new medication that vastly improved the quality of his nighttime sleep. Taking this drug at set intervals was a key element in the dramatic improvement he experienced over the next few years. He also began strategic power napping, setting aside time in his schedule to go somewhere peaceful and fall asleep for 15 to 30 minutes. "Power naps are probably the greatest thing a person with narcolepsy can do," Matt insists. The naps helped eliminate the daytime sleepiness, effectively preempting all those unplanned naps that had fragmented his days. Matt also worked diligently to create structure in his life, setting a predictable rhythm of going to bed, taking medication, going to bed again, waking up in the morning, attending class, taking a nap, and so on.

You Asked, Matt Answers
http://qrs.ly/kl3le8d
What sorts of medications help to control narcolepsy?

Now a college graduate and working professional, Matt manages his narcolepsy quite successfully. All of his major symptoms—the spontaneous naps, cataplexy, sleep paralysis, and hypnagogic hallucinations—have faded. "Now if I fall asleep, it's because I choose to," Matt says. "Most people don't even know I have narcolepsy."

Not everyone with narcolepsy is so fortunate. The disorder is often mistaken for another ailment, such as depression or insomnia. Most people with narcolepsy don't even know they have it, and by the time an expert offers them a diagnosis (sometimes years after the symptoms began), they have already suffered major social and professional consequences (Stanford Center for Narcolepsy, 2012). While several medications are available to help control symptoms, there is no known cure for narcolepsy. Scheduling "therapeutic naps," avoiding monotonous activities, and controlling emotional highs are all behavioral treatments for narcolepsy.

Now when Matt goes to sleep at night, he no longer imagines people coming to murder him. And instead of having nightmares, he dreams about soaring through the skies like Superman. Sometimes he cruises at the altitude of an airplane; other times he penetrates the earth's outer atmosphere and barrels into outer space to visit the planets. "All my dreams are now pleasant," says Matt, "[and] it's a lot nicer being able to fly than being stabbed by a butcher knife." And if you wonder what Matt is doing these days, he works at a credit union (he was just promoted) and is very busy remodeling his new home. Onward and upward, like Superman.

▶ **Under Control**
After a few very challenging years, Matt developed effective strategies for managing his narcolepsy. In addition to using a medication that helps him sleep more soundly at night, Matt takes strategic power naps and sticks to a regular bedtime and wake-up schedule. Courtesy Matthew Utesch

In Your Dreams

LO 7   Summarize the theories of why we dream.

What are dreams, and why do we have them? Dreams have been interpreted as messages from God, revelations of the future, and communication from spirits. People have contemplated the significance of dreams for millennia, resulting in many theories to explain why we dream.

PSYCHOANALYSIS AND DREAMS   The first comprehensive theory of dreaming was developed by the father of psychoanalysis, Sigmund Freud (Chapters 11 and 14). In 1900 Freud laid out his theory in the now-classic *The Interpretation of Dreams*, proposing that dreams were a form of "wish fulfillment," or a playing out of unconscious desires. As Freud saw it, many of the desires expressed in dreams are forbidden ones that would produce great anxiety in a dreamer if she were aware of them. In dreams, these desires are disguised so they can be experienced without danger of discovery. Freud believed dreams have two levels of content: *manifest* and *latent*. **Manifest content,** the apparent meaning of the dream, is the actual story line of the dream itself—what you remember when you wake up. **Latent content** contains the hidden meaning of the dream, which represents unconscious conflicts and desires. During therapy sessions, psychoanalysts use the latent content of dreams to uncover the unconscious, by looking deeper than the actual story line of the dream. Freud would ask patients to recount the manifest content and then look for symbols and other clues that might expose what is otherwise hidden because of its threatening nature; that is, the latent content.

Here's an example: A painter arrives at Freud's office and recounts a dream in which his wife destroys the canvas he has been working on for weeks. Freud might suggest the brush used by the painter's wife is a symbol of the painter's fear of his mother controlling his sexual activity. But critics of Freud's approach to dream analysis would note there are an infinite number of ways to interpret any dream (all impossible to prove wrong). For example, maybe the underlying conflict in the painter is the lack of control he feels about his own work. Either interpretation could be correct, or perhaps his disturbing dream was simply the result of indigestion.

manifest content The apparent meaning of a dream; the remembered story line of a dream.

latent content The hidden meaning of a dream, often concealed by the manifest content of the dream.

activation–synthesis model This theory proposes that humans respond to random neural activity while in REM sleep as if it has meaning.

ACTIVATION–SYNTHESIS MODEL   In contrast to Freud's theory, the **activation–synthesis model** suggests that dreams have no meaning whatsoever (Hobson & McCarley, 1977). During REM sleep, the motor areas of the brain are inhibited (remember, the body is paralyzed), but sensory areas of the brain hum with the excitement of a great deal of neural activity. According to the activation–synthesis model, we respond to the random neural activity as if it has meaning. The brain tries to interpret this sensory excitement, which really is nothing more than neural chatter. This model suggests that our creative minds make up stories to match the neural activity. The brain is also trying to make sense of activity in the **vestibular system**, which is active during REM sleep. If the vestibular system is active while we are lying still, then the brain can interpret this as floating or flying—both common experiences reported by dreamers.

NEUROCOGNITIVE THEORY OF DREAMS   The neurocognitive theory of dreams proposes that a network of neurons exists in the brain, including some areas in the limbic system and the forebrain, that is necessary for dreaming to occur (Domhoff, 2001). People with damage to these areas of the brain either do not have dreams, or their dreams are not normal in some way. Another indication of the underlying neurocognitive nature of dreams is that children seem to develop the ability to dream, as their dreams are not like those of adults. For example, until children are around 13 to 15 years old, their reported dreams are less vivid and seem to have less of a story line. The underlying neural network must develop or mature before a child can dream like an adult. And as noted earlier, memory consolidation seems to be facilitated by sleep, with some theorists emphasizing the important role REM sleep plays in this process. The neurocognitive theory of dreams does not suggest, however, that dreams serve a purpose. Instead, they seem to be the result of how sleep and consciousness have evolved in humans (Domhoff, 2001).

Dream a Little Dream

Most dreams feature ordinary, everyday scenarios like driving or sitting in class. The content of dreams is repetitive and in line with what we think about when we are awake, and includes similar ideas about relationships, bad luck, people, and negative feelings. In fact, even over long periods of time and across cultures, the content of dreams is relatively consistent. Unfortunately, dreams are more likely to include sad events than happy ones. Despite popular assumptions, less than 12% of dream time is devoted to sexual activity (Yu & Fu, 2011). If you're one of those people who believe they don't dream, you are probably wrong. Most individuals who insist they don't dream simply fail to remember their dreams. If you're still skeptical, ask a bedmate to wake you next time it looks like you are in REM sleep (typical signs include eyes flitting side to side beneath the eyelids, and fingers and toes twitching). If awakened during a dream, you are more likely to be able to recall it at that moment than if asked to remember it at lunchtime. The ability to remember dreams is dependent on the length of time since the dream.

Most dreaming takes place during REM sleep and is jam-packed with rich sensory details and narrative. Dreams also occur during non-REM sleep, but they lack the vivid imagery and storylike quality of REM dreams. The average person starts dreaming about 90 minutes into sleep, then goes on to have about four to six dreams during the night. Add up the time and you get a total of about 1 to 2

CONNECTIONS

In **Chapter 3** we noted that the vestibular system is responsible for our balance. Accordingly, if its associated area in the nervous system is active while we are asleep, the sensations normally associated with this system when we are awake will be interpreted in a congruent manner.

Dreaming Brain
PET scans reveal the high levels of brain activity during REM sleep (left) and wakefulness (right). During REM, the brain is abuzz with excitement. (This is especially true of the sensory areas.) According to the activation–synthesis model, dreams may result when the brain tries to make sense of all this neural activity.
Hank Morgan/Science Source

"Uh-oh. I think I'm having one of those dreams again."

Jack Ziegler/The New Yorker Collection/www.cartoonbank.com

hours of dreaming per night. Dreams happen in real time. In one early study investigating this phenomenon, researchers roused sleepers after they had been in a 5-minute REM cycle and again after a 15-minute REM cycle, asking them how long they had been dreaming (5 or 15 minutes). The majority of the participants—four out of five—gave the right answer (Dement & Kleitman, 1957).

Have you ever experienced the realization that you are in the middle of a dream? A *lucid dream* is a dream in which you are aware you are dreaming, and research suggests that about half of us have had one (Gackenbach & LaBerge, 1988). There are two parts to a lucid dream: the dream itself and the awareness that you are dreaming. Some suggest lucid dreaming is actually a way to direct the content of dreams (Gavie & Revonsuo, 2010), but this is a controversial claim because there is no way to confirm people's subjective reports; dreams cannot be experienced by an outsider.

Fantastical, funny, frightening dreams can take many forms. Freud suggested that dreams unlock the mysteries of the unconscious mind. Contemporary scholars suspect that dreams are the result of neurocognitive activity. Others posit that dreams mean nothing and are merely the product of the brain's efforts to make sense of the electrical traffic from sensory networks. What do dreams mean, and why do they happen? These are two of the great puzzles facing today's psychologists. We know dreams represent a distinct state of consciousness, and consciousness is a fluid, ever-changing entity. But now it's time to explore how consciousness transforms when chemicals are introduced into our bodies.

✓✓✓ show what you know

1. Freud believed dreams have two levels. The _____ refers to the apparent meaning of the dream, whereas the _____ refers to its hidden meaning.

2. According to the _____, dreams have no meaning whatsoever. Instead, the brain is responding to random neural activity as if it has meaning.
   a. psychoanalytic perspective
   b. neurocognitive theory
   c. activation–synthesis model
   d. evolutionary perspective

3. What occurs in the brain when you dream?

4. Your 6-year-old cousin does not have dreams with a true story line; her dreams seem to be fleeting images. This supports the neurocognitive theory of dreams, as does the fact that:
   a. until children are around 13 to 15 years old, their reported dreams are less vivid.
   b. dream content is not the same across cultures.
   c. children younger than 13 can report very complicated story lines from their dreams.
   d. dream content is the same for people, regardless of age.

✓ CHECK YOUR ANSWERS IN APPENDIX C.

▶ Altered States of Consciousness

We have so far explored a range of levels of consciousness, from wide-awake to sound asleep. But we have not addressed states of consciousness that result from the influence of agents such as drugs and alcohol, or hypnosis. Let's take a look now at these altered states.

psychoactive drugs Substances that can cause changes in psychological activities such as sensation, perception, attention, judgment, memory, self-control, emotion, thinking, and behavior; substances that cause changes in conscious experiences.

depressants A class of psychoactive drugs that *depress* or slow down activity in the central nervous system.

DRUGS, DRUGS, EVERYWHERE   You awake in the middle of the night with a dull pain around your belly button. By morning, the pain is sharp and stabbing and has migrated to your lower right abdomen, so you head to the local emergency room where doctors diagnose you with appendicitis, an inflammation of the appendix often caused by infection. You need an emergency operation to remove your appendix, and a strong anesthetic is in order: a combination of drugs to paralyze the abdominal muscles, dull the pain, and wipe out your memory of the procedure. Dr. Julien, introduced at the start of the chapter, is your anesthesiologist.

For paralysis, Dr. Julien would probably give you a drug similar to *curare,* an arrowhead poison used by South American natives. Curare works by blocking the activity of the neurotransmitter called **acetylcholine**, which stimulates muscle contractions in the body. But curare does not cross into the brain, and therefore it does not have the power to transport you to another level of consciousness (Czarnowski, Bailey, & Bal, 2007). If curare were the only drug Dr. Julien administered, you would be lying on the operating table paralyzed yet completely awake and aware of your pain—not a pleasant scenario.

CONNECTIONS

In **Chapter 2**, we described neurotransmitters and the role they play in the nervous system. Acetylcholine is a neurotransmitter that relays messages from motor neurons to muscles, which enables movement. Too little acetylcholine causes paralysis. Here, we see how drugs can block the normal activity of acetylcholine, causing the paralysis useful during surgery.

LO 8   Define psychoactive drugs.

PSYCHOACTIVE DRUGS   To dull the perception of pain, Dr. Julien might administer Fentanyl, which belongs to a class of drugs called opioids that we will soon discuss. And to stamp out your memory of the surgery, he would lull you into a sleep-like stupor with a drug such as Propofol and then maintain that state of sleep with other drugs. One moment you are awake, sensing, perceiving, thinking, and talking. The next moment you see nothing, hear nothing, feel nothing. It's like you are gone. Fentanyl and Propofol are considered **psychoactive drugs** because the chemicals in these drugs can cause changes in psychological activities such as sensation, perception, attention, judgment, memory, self-control, emotion, thinking, and behavior—all of which may be associated with our conscious experiences.

You don't need to visit the hospital to have a psychoactive drug experience. Mind-altering drugs are everywhere—in the coffee shop around the corner, at the liquor store down the street, and probably in your own kitchen. About 90% of people in the United States regularly use *caffeine,* a psychoactive drug found in coffee, soda, tea, and medicines (Alpert, 2012; Gurpegui, Aguilar, Martínez-Ortega, Diaz, & de Leon, 2004). Trailing close behind caffeine are *alcohol* (found in beer, wine, and liquor) and *nicotine* (in cigarettes and other tobacco products), two substances that present serious health risks. Another huge category of psychoactive drugs is prescription medications—drugs for pain relief, depression, insomnia, and just about any ailment you can imagine. Don't forget the illicit, or illegal, drugs like LSD and Ecstasy. About a third of Americans aged 12 and older have tried an illicit drug at least once in their lifetime, and some 11% have used drugs in the past year, according to reported estimates (Substance Abuse and Mental Health Services Administration [SAMHSA], 2008).

Psychoactive drugs alter consciousness in an untold number of ways. They can rev you up, slow you down, let down your inhibitions, and convince you that the universe is on the verge of collapse. We will discuss the three major categories of psychoactive drugs—stimulants, depressants, and hallucinogens—but keep in mind that some drugs fall into more than one group.

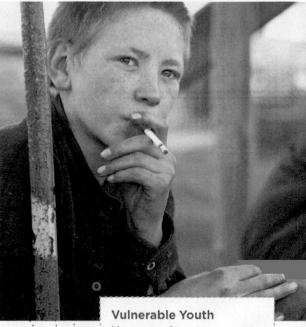

Vulnerable Youth
Young smokers are more inclined than their non-smoking peers to use illegal drugs, display aggression, and develop mental health problems. They also have a harder time quitting than those who start smoking in adulthood (American Cancer Society, 2012). Aaron Huey/ National Geographic/Getty Images

Depressants

LO 9   Identify several depressants and stimulants and know their effects.

In his 25 years as an anesthesiologist, Dr. Julien has primarily relied on a group of psychoactive drugs that *depress* activity in the central nervous system, or slow things down. For this reason, we call them **depressants.** Dr. Julien sometimes *premedicates* patients, administering drugs to calm them while they wait to be wheeled into the operating room. For this purpose, he might use a benzodiazepine, which would act as a *tranquilizer*—a type of depressant that has a calming, sleep-inducing effect. Other

Synonyms
depressants downers

Shooting Up
Heroin is one of the most pleasure-inducing—and dangerous—drugs in the world. About 23% of heroin users get hooked, and the consequences of chronic use are serious: boils on the skin, HIV and hepatitis (from contaminated needles), liver disease, spontaneous abortion, and many others (National Institute on Drug Abuse, 2013). ©PhotoAlto/Alamy

Opium Poppy
Naturally occurring opioids, or *opiates*, are found in the opium poppy, the same plant that produces those little black seeds on your breakfast bagel. Doctors have been using the poppy opiate *morphine* to alleviate pain since the early 1800s (Julien et al., 2011). Getty Images/Vetta

Synonyms
barbiturate yellow jackets, pink ladies, goof balls, reds, rainbows

barbiturate (bär-ˈbi-chə-rət) Depressant drug that decreases neural activity and reduces anxiety; a type of sedative.

opioids A class of psychoactive drugs that minimizes perceptions of pain.

opiates A class of psychoactive drugs that cause a sense of euphoria; a drug that imitates the endorphins naturally produced in the brain.

examples of tranquilizers are Valium (diazepam) and Xanax (alprazolam), which are used to treat anxiety disorders. A more recent addition to the tranquilizer family is Rohypnol (flunitrazepam), also known as the "date rape drug" or "roofies," which is legally manufactured and approved as a treatment for insomnia in other countries, but banned in the United States (Drug Enforcement Administration [DEA], 2012). Sex predators have been known to slip roofies into their victims' drinks, especially darker-colored cocktails where the blue pills dissolve unseen. Rohypnol can cause confusion, amnesia, lowered inhibitions, and sometimes loss of consciousness, preventing victims from defending themselves or remembering the details of a sexual assault.

BARBITURATES   Once a patient is in the operating room and ready for surgery, Dr. Julien puts him to sleep. This process is called "induction," and it is sometimes accomplished using another type of depressant termed a **barbiturate** (bär-ˈbi-chə-rət), which is a sedative drug that decreases neural activity. In low doses, barbiturates cause many of the same effects as alcohol—relaxation, lowering of spirits, or alternatively, aggression (Julien et al., 2011)—which may explain why they have become so popular among recreational users. But these substances are addictive and extremely dangerous when taken in excess or mixed with other drugs. If barbiturates are taken alongside alcohol, for example, the muscles of the diaphragm may relax to the point of suffocation (**INFOGRAPHIC 4.3**).

OPIOIDS   Recall from the beginning of the chapter that the brain continues receiving pain impulses even when a patient is out cold on the operating table. Without proper painkilling drugs, these signals can give rise to what Dr. Julien calls "autonomic instability," a disruption of heart rate, blood pressure, and other activities regulated by the autonomic nervous system. One way to maintain autonomic stability is to give the patient an **opioid,** a drug that minimizes the brain's perception of pain. "Opioid" is an umbrella term for a large group of similarly acting drugs, some found in nature and others concocted in laboratories (synthesized replacements such as methadone). Opioids block pain, induce drowsiness and euphoria, and slow down breathing (Julien et al., 2011). There are two types of naturally occurring opioids: the endorphins produced by your body, and the **opiates** found in the opium poppy. The poppy-derived opioid morphine alleviates patients' pain. Morphine is also the raw material used in making the street drug heroin, which enters the brain more quickly and has 3 times the strength (Julien et al., 2011).

PRESCRIPTION DRUG ABUSE   Few people in the United States actually use heroin (less than 1%), and some studies suggest that number is decreasing. But another class of opioids appears to be taking its place—synthetic painkillers such as Vicodin (hydrocodone) and OxyContin (oxycodone; Fischer & Rehm, 2007; SAMHSA, 2010). Unlike heroin, these medications are legally manufactured by drug companies and legitimately prescribed by physicians. Intentionally using a medication without a doctor's approval can lead to *prescription drug abuse,* and this behavior is shockingly common among teenagers, who are more vulnerable to becoming hooked or addicted (Zhang et al., 2009). Prescription drug abuse can also occur when a medication is used in a way that is not prescribed by a doctor (for example, taking too much of a medication). Nearly 1 in 10 high school seniors in the United States has abused Vicodin, and 1 in 20 has abused OxyContin. Over half report getting such prescription meds from friends and relatives (National Institute on Drug Abuse, 2011). Opioid abuse is an epidemic among high school students, and many don't understand how easy it is to become hooked on these drugs. Sadly, drug overdose deaths recently surpassed the number of deaths resulting from car accidents in the United States (Moisse, 2011, September 20).

The Dangers of Drugs in Combination

Taking multiple drugs simultaneously can lead to unintended and potentially fatal consequences because of how they work in the brain. Drugs can modify neurotransmission by increasing or decreasing the chemical activity. When two drugs work on the same system, their effects can be additive, greatly increasing the risk of overdose. For example, alcohol and barbiturates both bind to GABA receptors. GABA's inhibitory action has a sedating effect, which is a good thing when you need to relax. But too much GABA will relax physiological processes to the point where unconscious, life-sustaining activities shut down, causing you to stop breathing and die.

Hundreds of deaths are caused annually in the U.S. when drugs like alcohol and barbiturates are taken in combination (Kochanek et al., 2012). In 2009 alone, 519,650 emergency room visits were attributed to use of alcohol in combination with other drugs (SAMHSA, 2010).

NORMAL GABA ACTIVITY

- GABA
- Alcohol
- Barbiturate

Action potential

Sending neuron

GABA receptor

Receiving neuron

GABA message communicated

GABA activation, which calms nervous system activity, is essential for proper functioning of the central nervous system. Without GABA, nerve cells fire too frequently.

ALCOHOL

Alcohol activates the same receptors, increasing GABA's activity.

ALCOHOL + BARBITURATE

Barbiturates bind to and activate GABA receptors too, creating even more GABA-related inhibition.

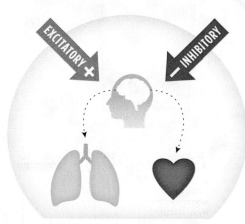

EXCITATORY +

INHIBITORY −

When systems are functioning normally, GABA's inhibitory signals perfectly balance excitatory signals in the central nervous system (CNS). This results in regular breathing and heart rate.

EXCITATORY +

INHIBITORY −

When alcohol increases GABA's inhibitory signals, excitatory and inhibitory signals in the CNS are out of balance. Along with increased relaxation, heart and breathing rates decrease. Increasing levels of alcohol could eventually lead to stupor and coma.

EXCITATORY +

INHIBITORY −

Together, alcohol and barbiturates further unbalance excitatory and inhibitory signals, suppressing heart rate and the impulse to breathe.

Alcohol

We end our coverage of depressants with alcohol, which, like other drugs in its class, has played a central role in the history of anesthesia. The ancient Greek doctor Dioscorides gave his surgical patients a special concoction of wine and mandrake plant (Keys, 1945), and 19th-century Europeans used an alcohol-opium mixture called *laudanum* for anesthetic purposes (Barash, Cullen, Stoelting, & Cahalan, 2009). These days, you won't find anesthesiologists knocking out patients with alcohol, but you will encounter plenty of people intoxicating themselves.

BINGE DRINKING   Alcohol is the most commonly used depressant in the United States. Around 15% of adults and 25% of teenagers report that they *binge drink* (consuming four or more drinks for women and five or more for men, on one occasion or within a short time span) at least once a month (Naimi et al., 2003; Wen et al., 2012). Many people think binge drinking is fun, but they might change their minds if they read the research. Studies have linked binge drinking to poor grades, aggressive behavior, sexual promiscuity, and accidental death. In 2005 almost 2,000 college students in the United States died in alcohol-related accidents (Hingson, Zha, & Weitzman, 2009). Think getting wasted is sexy? Consider this: Alcohol impairs sexual performance, particularly for men, who may have trouble obtaining and sustaining an erection.

You don't have to binge drink in order to have an alcohol problem (**FIGURE 4.1**). Some people cannot get through the day without a midday drink; others need alcohol to unwind or fall asleep. The point is there are many forms of alcohol misuse. About 8.5% of the adult population in the United States (nearly 1 in 10 people) struggles with alcohol dependence or some other type of drinking problem (Grant et al., 2004). Drinking can destroy families, careers, and human life.

FIGURE 4.1
Blood Alcohol Concentration (BAC) and Effects on Behavior
The effects of one drink—a 12-oz bottle of beer, 4-oz glass of wine, or 1-oz shot of hard liquor—vary depending on weight, ethnicity, gender, and other factors. Across most of the United States, a BAC of .08 is the legal limit for driving. But even at lower levels, our coordination and focus may be impaired. *Source:* Centers for Disease Control and Prevention, 2011, February 11; (Photos: left & center) Danny Smythe/Shutterstock; (right) Thinkstock

| BAC % | .02 | .05 | .08 | .10 | .15 | .30 | .40 | .50 |

Effects

Relaxation. Some loss of judgment.

Slurred speech. Clear deterioration of reaction time and control.

Loss of consciousness may occur.

Incapable of voluntary action.

Reduced coordination. Impaired judgment. Release of inhibition.

Major loss of balance. Vomiting may occur.

Poor muscle coordination. Impaired reasoning and memory. Drunk driving limit.

Comatose. Death may occur.

stimulants A class of drugs that increase neural activity in the central nervous system.

ALCOHOL AND THE BODY Let's stop for a minute and examine how alcohol influences consciousness (Figure 4.1). People sometimes say they feel "high" when they drink. How can such a statement be true when alcohol is a *depressant*, a drug that slows down activity in the central nervous system? Alcohol boosts the activity of GABA, a neurotransmitter that dampens activity in certain neural networks, including those that regulate social inhibition—a type of self-restraint that keeps you from doing things you will regret the next morning. It is this release of social inhibition that can lead to feelings of euphoria. Drinking affects other conscious processes, such as reaction time, balance, attention span, memory, speech, and involuntary life-sustaining activities like breathing (Howland et al., 2010; McKinney & Coyle, 2006). Drink enough, and these vital functions will shut down entirely, leading to coma and even death.

The female body is less efficient at breaking down (metabolizing) alcohol. Even when we control for body size and the muscle-to-fat ratio, we see that women achieve higher blood alcohol levels (and thus a significantly stronger "buzz") than men who have consumed equal amounts. Why? Because men have more of an alcohol-metabolizing enzyme in their stomachs, which means they start to break down alcohol almost immediately after ingestion. In a woman, most of the alcohol clears the stomach and enters the bloodstream and brain before the liver finally breaks it down (Toufexis, 2001).

- Having your friends or relatives express concern.
- Becoming annoyed when people criticize your drinking behavior.
- Feeling guilty about your drinking behavior.
- Thinking you should drink less but being unable to do so.

- Needing a morning drink as an "eye-opener" or to relieve a hangover.
- Not fulfilling responsibilities at work, home, or school because of your drinking.
- Engaging in dangerous behavior (like driving under the influence).
- Having legal or social problems due to your drinking.

THE CONSEQUENCES OF DRINKING Light alcohol consumption by adults—one to two drinks of wine, beer, or liquor a day—may have some cardiovascular and cognitive benefits (Cervilla, Prince, Joels, Lovestone, & Mann, 2000; Mukamal, Maclure, Muller, Sherwood, & Mittleman, 2001). Excessive drinking, on the other hand, is associated with a host of health problems. Overuse of alcohol can lead to malnourishment, cirrhosis of the liver, and *Wernicke–Korsakoff Syndrome,* which can include symptoms such as confusion and memory problems. It has also been linked to heart disease, various types of cancer, tens of thousands of traffic deaths every year, and fetal-alcohol syndrome in children with mothers who drank during pregnancy. Deaths due to overuse of alcohol, numbering about 75,000 annually, are the third most common type of preventable death in the United States (Centers for Disease Control and Prevention [CDC], 2004; Mokdad, Marks, Stroup, & Gerberding, 2004). Read through **FIGURE 4.2** for some warning signs of problematic drinking.

Stimulants and Hallucinogens

Not all drugs used in anesthesia are depressants. Did you know that some doctors use cocaine as a local anesthetic for nose and throat surgeries (Simmer, 2012)? Cocaine is a **stimulant**—a drug that increases neural activity in the central nervous system, producing effects such as heightened alertness, energy, and an elevated mood (Julien et al., 2011). When applied topically, cocaine blocks sensation in the peripheral nerves and thereby numbs the area.

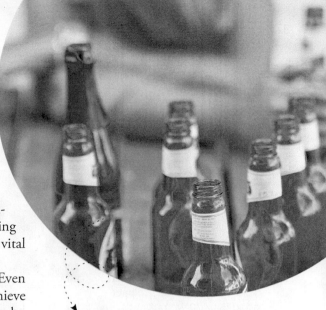

Binge Drinking
Binge drinking has been associated with reduced mental and physical health. This effect appears to intensify with increasing levels of alcohol ingestion (Wen et al., 2012). ©Pascal Deloche/GODONG/Godong/Corbis

FIGURE 4.2
Warning Signs of Problematic Drinking
The presence of one or more of these warning signs could indicate a developing problem with alcohol. *Sources:* American Psychological Association, 2012d; NIH, National Institute on Alcohol Abuse and Alcoholism, 2013.

Cocaine in Cola
The original recipe for Coca Cola included cocaine, but the company removed the drug from its cola in 1900, one year before the city of Atlanta banned its nonprescription use (Musto, 1991). ©Bettmann/CORBIS

This Is Your Face on Meth
This woman appears to have aged 15 or 20 years, but the time elapsed between these two photos is just 2 1/2 years. Methamphetamine ravages the body, the brain, and one's overall appearance. Some meth users have lingering symptoms: Imagine experiencing horrific tactile hallucinations that cause you to believe bugs have invaded your skin and are crawling underneath it, and that in response you tear your skin to the bone in order to kill them. Newscom

COCAINE The first to tap into cocaine's pain-zapping potential were the ancient Peruvians, who chewed the leaves of the coca plant (which contain about 1% cocaine) and then applied their saliva to surgical incisions. The coca plant, they believed, was a divine gift; chewing the leaves quenched their hunger, lifted their sadness, and restored their energy. Thousands of years later, in 1860, a German chemist named Albert Niemann extracted the active ingredient in the coca leaf and dubbed it "cocaine" (Julien et al., 2011; Keys, 1945). Within a few decades doctors were using cocaine for anesthesia, Sigmund Freud was giving it to patients (and himself), and Coca-Cola was putting it in soda (Keys, 1945; Musto, 1991).

While cocaine is illegal in the United States and most other countries, it is among the most widely used illicit drugs. Depending on the form in which it is prepared (powder, rocks, and so on), it can be snorted, injected, or smoked. The sense of energy, euphoria, and other alterations of consciousness that cocaine induces after entering the bloodstream and infiltrating the brain last anywhere from 5 to 30 minutes (National Institute on Drug Abuse, 2010a). Cocaine produces a rush of pleasure and excitement by amplifying the effects of dopamine and norepinephrine. But the coke high comes at a steep price. Any time you take cocaine, you put yourself at risk for suffering a stroke or heart attack, even if you are young and healthy. Cocaine is implicated in more emergency room visits than any other illegal drug (Drug Abuse Warning Network, 2009). It is also extremely addictive. Many users find they can never quite duplicate the high they experienced the first time, so they take increasingly higher doses, developing a physical need for the drug, increasing their risk of effects such as anxiety, insomnia, and schizophrenia-like psychosis when they stop using it (Julien et al., 2011).

Cocaine use grew rampant in the 1980s. That was the decade *crack*—an ultra-potent (and ultra-cheap) crystalline form of cocaine—began poisoning America's inner cities. Although cocaine is still a major problem, another stimulant has come to rival it in popularity—one that is ridiculously cheap, easy to make, and capable of producing a 24-hour high or euphoric rush—methamphetamine.

AMPHETAMINES Methamphetamine belongs to a family of stimulants called the **amphetamines** (am-ˈfe-tə-ˌmēnz). Doctors used amphetamines to treat medical conditions as diverse as head injury and excessive hiccups in the 1930s and 1940s (Julien et al., 2011). Methamphetamine was once used by soldiers and factory workers during World War II for energy and to enhance performance (Lineberry & Bostwick, 2006). Nonprescription use of methamphetamine is illegal, but people have learned how to brew it in their own laboratories, using ingredients from ordinary household products such as over-the-counter cough medicines, drain cleaner, and battery acid. "Cooking meth" is a dangerous enterprise. The flammable ingredients, combined with the reckless mentality of "tweaking" cookers, make for toxic fumes and thousands of accidental explosions every year (Lineberry & Bostwick, 2006). Despite the enormous risk, many people continue to cook meth at home, endangering and sometimes killing their own children.

Methamphetamine stimulates the release of the brain's pleasure-producing neurotransmitter dopamine, causing a surge in energy and alertness similar to a cocaine high. It also tends to increase one's sex drive and suppress appetite. But unlike cocaine, which the body eliminates quickly, meth lingers in the body (National Institute on Drug Abuse, 2006). Brain imaging studies show that chronic meth use causes serious brain damage in the frontal lobes and other areas, still visible even among those who have been clean for 11 months. This may explain why so many meth users suffer from lasting memory and movement problems (Krasnova & Cadet, 2009; Volkow et al., 2001). Other severe consequences of meth use include extreme weight loss; tooth decay

Synonyms

methamphetamine meth, crystal meth, crank

amphetamines (am-ˈfe-tə-ˌmēnz) speed, uppers, bennies

amphetamines Stimulant drugs; methamphetamine falls in this class of drugs.

("meth mouth"); psychosis with hallucinations that can come and go for months, if not years, after quitting; and sudden death (National Institute on Drug Abuse, 2006).

CAFFEINE   Most people have not experimented with illegal stimulants like cocaine and meth, but many have used caffeine. We usually associate caffeine with beverages like coffee, but this pick-me-up drug also lurks in places you wouldn't expect, such as in over-the-counter cough medicines, chocolate, and face creams. Caffeine works by blocking the action of adenosine, a neurotransmitter that normally muffles the activity of excitatory neurons in the brain (Julien et al., 2011). By interfering with adenosine's calming effect, caffeine makes you feel physically and mentally wired. A cup of coffee might help you stay up later, exercise longer and harder, and get through more pages in your textbooks. Moderate caffeine use (up to four cups of coffee per day) has been associated with increased alertness, enhanced recall ability, elevated mood, and greater endurance during physical exercise (Ruxton, 2008). Some studies have also linked moderate long-term consumption with lower rates of depression and suicide, and even reduced cognitive decline with aging (Lara, 2010; Rosso, Mossey & Lippa, 2008).

With all these promising data about caffeine, you may feel like running to your local coffee shop to order a triple-shot latte. But just because researchers find a link, for example, between caffeine and positive health outcomes, we should not necessarily conclude that caffeine is responsible for it. Maybe people who have a low risk for depression and dementia also enjoy drinking coffee. Or perhaps coffee drinkers are more likely to engage in regular exercise, an activity linked to improved mood and cognition. Remember, correlation does not prove causation. What's more, too much caffeine can make your heart race, your hands tremble, and your mood turn sour and irritable. It takes several hours for your body to metabolize caffeine, so a late afternoon mocha latte may still be present in your system as you lie in bed at midnight counting sheep—with no luck.

CONNECTIONS

In **Chapter 1**, we discussed the problem with possible third factors and correlations. Here, we need to be cautious about making too strong a statement about coffee causing positive health outcomes, because third factors could be involved in increased caffeine consumption and better health.

TOBACCO   What do you think is the number one cause of premature death worldwide—AIDS, illegal drugs, road accidents, murder, suicide? None of the above (**FIGURE 4.3**). Tobacco causes more deaths than any of these other factors combined (BBC News, 2010; World Health Organization [WHO], 2008b). The use of cigarettes and

FIGURE 4.3

Leading Causes of Death in the United States The leading killers in this country—heart disease, cancer, and chronic lower respiratory diseases—are largely driven by smoking. Tobacco exposure is behind nearly half a million deaths every year. *Source:* Kochanek et al., 2012; photo: ©David J. Green—Lifestyle/Alamy other tobacco products claims 5 million lives every year, and half a million in the United States alone (Kasisomayajula et al., 2010). Smoking can lead to lung cancer, emphysema, heart disease, and stroke (CDC, 2008b). The average smoker loses approximately 10 to 15 years of her life.

Despite these harrowing statistics, about 1 in 5 adults in the United States continues to light up (CDC, 2010). They say it makes them feel relaxed yet more alert, less hungry, and more tolerant of pain. And those who try to kick the habit find it exceedingly difficult to do so. Cigarettes and other tobacco products contain a highly addictive stimulant called *nicotine,* which sparks the release of epinephrine and norepinephrine. Nicotine use appears to be associated with activity in the same brain area that is activated with cocaine, another drug that is also extremely difficult to give up (Pich et al., 1997; Zhang, Dong, Doyon, & Dani, 2012). The few who do succeed face a steep uphill battle. Around 90% of quitters relapse within 6 months (Nonnemaker et al., 2011), suggesting that relapse is a normal experience when quitting, not a sign of failure.

Smoking is not just a problem for the smoker. It is a problem for spouses, children, friends, and anyone who is exposed to the *secondhand smoke.* Secondhand smoke is particularly dangerous for children, whose developing tissues are especially vulnerable (Chapter 8). By smoking, parents increase their children's risk for sudden infant death syndrome (SIDS), respiratory infections, asthma, and lung cancer (CDC, 2012e). Secondhand smoke contributes to 21,400 lung cancer deaths and 379,000 heart disease deaths worldwide (Öberg, Jaakkola, Woodward, Peruga, & Prüss-Ustün, 2011), and according to the Centers for Disease Control and Prevention (2012e), "There is no risk-free level of exposure" (p. 1). In recent years, researchers have also become concerned about the health implications of thirdhand smoke, the combination of cigarette toxins (including lead, which is a known neurotoxin) that linger in rooms, elevators, and other small spaces long after a smoker has left the scene. Thirdhand smoke is what you smell when you walk into a hotel room and think, *Hmm, someone's been smoking in here* (Winickoff et al., 2009).

···▶ **LO 10** Discuss some of the hallucinogens.

We have learned how various depressants and stimulants are used in anesthesia. Believe it or not, there is also a place for **hallucinogens** (hə-ˈlü-sə-nə-jənz)—drugs that produce hallucinations (sights, sounds, odors, or other sensations of things that aren't actually present), altered moods, and distorted perception and thought. Phencyclidine (PCP or *angel dust*) and ketamine (*Special K*) are sometimes referred to as *psychedelic anesthetics* because they were developed to block pain and memory in surgical patients during the 1950s and 1960s (Julien et al., 2011). PCP is highly addictive and extremely dangerous. Because users cannot feel normal pain signals, they run the risk of unintentionally harming or killing themselves. Long-term use can lead to depression and memory impairment. The milder of the two, ketamine, continues to be used in hospitals, but PCP was abandoned long ago. Its effect was just too erratic.

LSD The most well-known hallucinogen is probably **lysergic acid diethylamide (LSD;** lə-ˈsər-jik; dī-ˌe-thə-ˈla-ˌmīd)—the odorless, tasteless, and colorless substance that produces extreme changes in sensation and perception. People using LSD may report seeing "far out" colors and visions of spirals and other geometric forms. Some people experience a crossover of sensations, "tasting sound" or "hearing colors." Emotions run wild and bleed into one another; the person "tripping" can quickly flip between depression and joy, excitement and terror (Julien et al., 2011). Trapped on this sensory and emotional roller coaster, some people panic and injure themselves. Others believe that LSD opens their minds, offers new insights, and expands their consciousness. The outcome of a "trip" depends a great deal on the environment and people who are there.

Synonyms

secondhand smoke passive smoke

hallucinogens psychedelic drugs

---

hallucinogens (hə-ˈlü-sə-nə-jənz) A group of psychoactive drugs that can produce hallucinations (auditory, visual, or kinesthetic), distorted sensory experiences, alterations of mood, and distorted thinking.

lysergic acid diethylamide (LSD) (lə-ˈsər-jik; dī-ˌe-thə-ˌla-ˌmīd) A synthetically produced, odorless, tasteless, and colorless hallucinogen that is very potent; produces extreme changes in sensations and perceptions.

methylenedioxymethamphetamine (MDMA) (methˈlī-lēn-dī-okˈsē-methˈam-fetˈă-mēn) A synthetic drug chemically similar to the stimulant methamphetamine and the hallucinogen mescaline; produces a combination of stimulant and hallucinogenic effects.

LSD is not often overused, and its reported use has remained at an all-time low (Johnston, O'Malley, Bachman, & Schulenberg, 2012). Long-term use may be associated with depression and other psychological problems, including flashbacks that can occur weeks, months, or years after taking the drug. Fatigue, stress, and illness may trigger flashbacks (Thurlow & Girvin, 1971).

MDMA   In addition to the traditional hallucinogens, there are quite a few "club drugs," or synthetic "designer drugs," used at parties, raves, and dance venues. The most popular among them is **methylenedioxymethamphetamine (MDMA;** meth'ĭ-lēn-dī-ok'sē-meth'am-fet'ă-mēn**),** commonly known as *Ecstasy*. Ecstasy is chemically similar to the stimulant methamphetamine and the hallucinogen mescaline, and thus produces a combination of stimulant and hallucinogenic effects (Barnes et al., 2009; National Institute on Drug Abuse, 2010b).

An Ecstasy trip might bring on feelings of euphoria, love, openness, heightened energy, and floating sensations, as well as intense anxiety and depersonalization, with the user feeling like a detached spectator, watching himself from the outside without having any control. Ecstasy can also cause a host of changes to the body, including decreased appetite, lockjaw, blurred vision, dizziness, rapid heart rate, and dehydration (Gordon, 2001, July 5; Noller, 2009). Dancing in hot, crowded conditions while on Ecstasy can lead to severe heat stroke, seizures, even cardiac arrest and death (Parrott, 2004). Every year, thousands of Ecstasy users leave raves and all-night parties in ambulances. Between 2004 and 2009, the number of emergency room visits associated with the drug climbed by 123% (Drug Abuse Warning Network, 2009). Despite its dangers, Ecstasy is still a popular illicit drug (SAMHSA, 2012).

Ecstasy triggers a sudden general unloading of serotonin in the brain, after which serotonin activity is depleted until the **neurotransmitters'** levels are restored (Klugman & Gruzelier, 2003). Studies of animals have shown that even short-term exposure to MDMA can cause long-term, perhaps even permanent, damage to the brain's serotonin pathways, and there is mounting evidence that a similar type of damage in reuptake from the synapse and storage of serotonin occurs in humans as well (Campbell & Rosner, 2008; Reneman et al., 2001; Ricaurte & McCann, 2001). One study found evidence that women's brains are more susceptible to Ecstasy damage than men's, but larger studies are needed to confirm this finding (Reneman et al., 2001). The growing consensus is that even light-to-moderate Ecstasy use can handicap the brain's memory system, and heavy use may impair higher-level cortical functions, such as planning for the future and shifting attention (Klugman & Gruzelier, 2003). Studies also suggest that Ecstasy users are more likely to experience symptoms of depression (Guillot, 2007).

MARIJUANA   We end our discussion with the most widely used illegal (in most states) drug, and one of the most popular in all the Western world: marijuana (Compton, Grant, Colliver, Glantz, & Stinson, 2004; SAMHSA, 2008). Forty-two percent of American teenagers have already tried marijuana by the time they graduate from high school (National Institute on Drug Abuse, 2010c). Attitudes tend to be more casual about marijuana than other illegal drugs. "It's no big deal," a user might say, "you can't get addicted." But these kinds of assumptions are misleading. Recent studies suggest that marijuana use can lead to dependence, memory impairment, and deficits in attention and learning (Harvey, Sellman, Porter, & Frampton, 2007; Kleber & DuPont, 2012). Others identify it as a cause of some chronic psychological disorders (Reece, 2009). The long-term use of marijuana has also been associated with reduced motivation (Reece 2009), and linked to respiratory problems, impaired lung functioning, and suppression of the immune system (Iversen, 2003; Pletcher et al., 2012). In addition, the smoke from marijuana contains 50 to 70% more cancer-causing hydrocarbons than tobacco (Kothadia et al., 2012). Smoking marijuana also causes a temporary dip in sperm production and a greater proportion of abnormal sperm (Brown & Dobs, 2002).

LSD Sheets
Lysergic acid diethylamide, or LSD, is usually taken by mouth, administered through candy, sugar cubes, or blotter sheets like the one pictured here. A popular drug during the "hippie" era of the 1960s and 1970s, LSD has now fallen out of favor.
Science Source

CONNECTIONS

In **Chapter 2**, we reported that serotonin is critical for the regulation of mood, appetite, aggression, and automatic behaviors like sleep. Here, we see how the use of Ecstasy can alter levels of this neurotransmitter.

Synonyms

methylenedioxymethamphetamine E, X
marijuana Mary Jane, M.J., grass, reefer, weed, pot, ganja, hemp

Cannabis ◄┄┄┄┄
Marijuana is the most commonly used illicit drug in the world, consumed by 2.6 to 5% of the adult population. It is also the primary reason people seek drug treatment in many regions of the world, including North America (United Nations, 2012). Thinkstock

Marijuana comes from the hemp plant *Cannabis sativa*, which has long been used as—surprise—an anesthetic. The 3rd-century Chinese physician Hua T'o reportedly used hemp to put his patients to sleep before performing surgery (Keys, 1945). These days, doctors prescribe marijuana to stimulate patients' appetites and suppress nausea, but its medicinal use is not without debate. Studies suggest that marijuana does effectively reduce the nausea and vomiting linked to chemotherapy (Grotenhermen & Müller-Vahl, 2012; Iversen, 2003), but there is conflicting evidence about its long-term effects on the brain (Schreiner & Dunn, 2012).

Marijuana's active ingredient is **tetrahydrocannabinol (THC;** te-trə-hī-drə-kə-ˈna-bə-ˌnȯl**)**, which toys with consciousness in a variety of ways, making it hard to classify the drug into a single category (for example, stimulant, depressant, or hallucinogen). In addition to altering pain perception, THC can induce mild euphoria, and create intense sensory experiences and distortions of time. At higher doses, THC may cause hallucinations and delusions (Murray, Morrison, Henquet, & Di Forti, 2007).

Some of marijuana's effects linger long after the initial high is over. Impairments in learning and memory may persist for days in adults (weeks for adolescents), and long-term use may lead to *addiction* (National Institute on Drug Abuse, 2010c; Schweinsburg, Brown, & Tapert, 2008).

Overuse and Addiction

We often joke about being "addicted" to our coffee or soda, but do we understand what this really means? Historically, the term *addiction* has been used (both by laypeople and professionals) to refer to the urges people experience for using a drug or engaging in an activity to such an extent that it interferes with their functioning or may even be dangerous (see **FIGURE 4.4** on drug dependence in the United States). This could mean a gambling habit that depletes your bank account, a sexual appetite that destroys your marriage, or perhaps even a social media fixation that prevents you from holding down a job. It is important to note the term addiction has been omitted from the American Psychiatric Association's diagnostic manual due to its "uncertain definition and potentially negative connotation" (APA, 2013, p. 485).

SOCIAL MEDIA and psychology

Can't Get Enough

Is it difficult for you to sit through a movie without checking your Twitter "Mentions"? Are you constantly looking at your Facebook News feed in between work e-mails? Do you sleep with your iPhone? If you answered "yes" to any of the above, you are not alone. People around the world, from Indonesia to the United Kingdom, are getting hooked on social media—so hooked in some cases that they are receiving treatment for social media *addiction* (Maulia, 2013, February 15; NBC Universal, 2013, February 12).

Facebook and Twitter may be habit forming, but you would think these sites would be easier to resist than, say, coffee or cigarettes. Such is not the case, according to one recent study. With the help of smartphones, researchers kept tabs on the daily desires of 205 young adults and found the urge to use media was harder to resist than sex, spending money, alcohol, coffee, or cigarettes (Hofmann, Vohs, & Baumeister, 2012). These findings are thought provoking, and this line of research is one to follow, but don't allow one study to minimize the serious and long-standing issue of drug addiction. The American Psychiatric Association (2013) does not consider *behavioral* addictions to be mental disorders. Further, the National Institute on Drug Abuse (2009) defines addiction to drugs, in particular, as "a chronic, relapsing disease characterized by compulsive drug seeking and abuse and by long-lasting neurochemical and molecular changes in the brain" (p. 1). You read it right: Substance use changes your brain. ●

". . .THE URGE TO USE MEDIA WAS HARDER TO RESIST THAN SEX, SPENDING MONEY, ALCOHOL. . . ."

FIGURE 4.4
Rates of Drug Dependence in the United States
This graph depicts the rates of drug dependence/abuse in the United States. As you can see, alcohol tops the list, followed by marijuana, and then pain relievers such as Vicodin and OxyContin. The sedatives category includes barbiturates, which are powerful nervous system depressants.
Source: National Institute on Drug Abuse, 2012; (photo) ©Alec Macdonald / Alamy

> **LO 11** Explain how physiological and psychological dependence differ.

PHYSIOLOGICAL AND PSYCHOLOGICAL DEPENDENCE Substance use can be fueled by both *physiological* and *psychological* dependence. **Physiological dependence** means the body no longer functions normally without the drug. Want to know if you are physiologically dependent on your morning cup of Joe? Try removing it from your routine for a few days and see if you get a headache or feel fatigued. If your answers are yes and yes, odds are that you have experienced *withdrawal,* a sign of physiological dependence. **Withdrawal** is the constellation of symptoms that surface when a drug is removed or withheld from the body, and it's not always as mild as a headache and fatigue. An alcoholic who suddenly stops drinking (or significantly cuts down) may suffer from **delirium tremens (DTs),** withdrawal symptoms that include sweating, restlessness, hallucinations, severe tremors, and seizures. Withdrawal symptoms disappear when you take the drug again, and because the symptoms do go away, you are more likely to continue using the drug. The removal of the unpleasant symptoms acts as negative reinforcement for taking the drug (Chapter 5). In this way, withdrawal powers the addiction cycle.

Another sign of physiological dependence is **tolerance.** Persistent drug and alcohol use alters the chemistry of the brain and body. Over time, your system adapts to the drug and therefore needs more and more of the substance to re-create the original effect. If it once took you two beers to unwind, but now takes four, then tolerance has probably set in. Tolerance increases the risk for accidental overdose, because more drug is needed to obtain the desired effect.

Psychological dependence occurs without the evidence of tolerance or withdrawal symptoms, but is indicated by many other problematic symptoms. Individuals with psychological dependence believe, for example, they need the drug because it will increase their emotional or mental well-being. The "pleasant" effects of a drug can act as positive reinforcement for taking the drug (Chapter 5). Let's say a smoker has a cigarette, fulfilling her physical need for nicotine. If the phone rings, she might answer it and light up a cigarette, because she has become accustomed to smoking and talking on the phone at the same time. It is an urge or craving, not a physical need. The cues associated with using the telephone facilitated the smoker's urge to light up (Bold, Yoon, Chapman, & McCarthy, 2013).

Psychologists and psychiatrists have developed specific criteria for drawing the line between use and overuse. Overuse is maladaptive and causes significant impairment

tetrahydrocannabinol (THC) (te-trə-hī-drə-kə-ˈna-bə-ˌnȯl) The active ingredient of marijuana.

physiological dependence With constant use of some psychoactive drugs, the body no longer functions normally without the drug.

withdrawal With constant use of some psychoactive drugs, a condition in which the body becomes dependent and then reacts when the drug is withheld.

delirium tremens (DTs) Withdrawal symptoms that can occur when a heavy drinker suddenly stops or significantly cuts down alcohol consumption; can include sweating, restlessness, hallucinations, severe tremors, and seizures.

tolerance With constant use of some psychoactive drugs, a condition in which the body requires more and more of the drug to create the original effect; a sign of physiological dependence.

psychological dependence With constant use of some psychoactive drugs, a strong desire or need to continue using the substance occurs without the evidence of tolerance or withdrawal symptoms.

Table 4.4 PSYCHOACTIVE DRUGS

Drug	Classification	Effects	Potential Harm
Alcohol	Depressant	disinhibition, feeling "high"	coma, death
Barbiturates	Depressant	decreased neural activity, relaxation, possible aggression	loss of consciousness, coma, death
Caffeine	Stimulant	alertness, enhanced recall, elevated mood, endurance	heart races, trembling, insomnia
Cocaine	Stimulant	energy, euphoria, rush of pleasure	heart attack, stroke, anxiety, psychosis
Heroin	Depressant	pleasure-inducing, reduces pain, rush of euphoria and relaxation	boils on the skin, hepatitis, liver disease, spontaneous abortion
LSD	Hallucinogen	extreme changes in sensation and perception, emotional rollercoaster	depression, long-term flashbacks, other psychological problems
Marijuana	Hallucinogen	stimulates appetite, suppresses nausea, relaxation, mild euphoria, distortion of time, intense sensory experience	respiratory problems, immune system suppression, cancer, memory impairment, deficits in attention and learning
MDMA	Stimulant; hallucinogen	euphoria, heightened energy, anxiety, and depersonalization	blurred vision, dizziness, rapid heart rate, dehydration, heat stroke, seizures, cardiac arrest, and death
Methamphetamine	Stimulant	energy, alertness, increases sex drive, suppresses appetite	lasting memory and movement problems, severe weight loss, tooth decay, psychosis, sudden death
Opioids	Depressant	blocks pain, induces drowsiness, euphoria, slows down breathing	respiratory problems during sleep, falls, constipation, sexual problems, overdose
Tobacco	Stimulant	relaxed, alert, more tolerant of pain	cancer, emphysema, heart disease, stroke, reduction in life span

Most drugs can be classified under one of the major categories listed above, but there are substances, such as MDMA, that fall into more than one class. Psychoactive drugs carry serious risks.

or distress to the user and/or his family: problems at work or school, neglect of children or household duties, physically dangerous behaviors, and so forth. In addition, the behavior has to be sustained for a certain period of time (that is, over a 12-month period). The American Psychiatric Association (2013) has established these criteria to help professionals distinguish between drug use and substance use disorder.

Depressants, stimulants, hallucinogens, marijuana—every drug we have discussed, and every drug imaginable—must gain entrance to the body in order to access the brain. Some are inhaled, others snorted or injected directly into the veins, all altering the state of consciousness of the user (TABLE 4.4). But is it possible to enter an altered state of consciousness without using a substance? It is time to explore hypnosis.

Hypnosis

> **LO 12** Describe hypnosis and explain how it works.

Ask a random group of mothers to report their most physically painful experience, and we suspect most will say "childbirth." Some women welcome the pain of labor, viewing it as a rite of passage into motherhood. Others opt for some form of pain management, often taking drugs. Some choose meditation, a form of relaxation that has been associated with a reduction in "negative" emotions (Chapter 12). Many women choose deep-breathing. Some even call upon the use of *hypnosis*.

There is research suggesting that hypnosis does ease the pain associated with childbirth and surgery, reducing the need for painkillers (Cyna, McAuliffe, & Andrew, 2004;

hypnosis An altered state of consciousness allowing for changes in perceptions and behaviors, which result from suggestions made by a hypnotist.

Wobst, 2007). With the help of PET scans, some researchers have found evidence that hypnosis induces changes in the brain that might explain this diminished pain perception (Faymonville et al., 2000; Rainville, Duncan, Price, Carrier, & Bushnell, 1997). Dr. Julien agrees that hypnosis, meditation, and other relaxation techniques may indeed reduce anxiety and pain, but only to a certain extent. So if you plan to go under the knife with hypnosis as your sole form of pain management, don't be surprised if you feel the piercing sensation of the scalpel.

The term *hypnosis* was taken from the Greek root word for "sleep," but it is by no means the equivalent of sleep. Most would agree **hypnosis** is an altered state of consciousness that allows for changes in perceptions and behaviors, which result from suggestions made by the hypnotist. "Changes in perceptions and behaviors" can mean a lot of things, of course, and there is some debate about what hypnosis is. Before going any further, let's be clear about what hypnosis *isn't*.

CONTROVERSIES

False Claims About Hypnosis

➡️◀️ Popular conceptions of hypnosis often clash with scientists' understanding of the phenomenon. Let's take a look at some examples:

- **People can be hypnotized without consent:** You cannot force someone to be hypnotized; they must be willing.
- **Hypnotized people will act against their own will:** Stage hypnotists seem to make people walk like chickens or miscount their fingers, but these are things they would likely be willing to do when not hypnotized.
- **Hypnotized people can exhibit "superhuman" strength:** Hypnotized or not, people have the same capabilities (Druckman & Bjork, 1994). Stage hypnotists often choose feats that their hypnotized performers could achieve under normal circumstances.
- **Hypnosis helps people retrieve lost memories:** Studies find that hypnosis may actually promote the formation of false memories and one's confidence in those memories (Kihlstrom, 1985).
- **Hypnotized people experience age regression. In other words, they act childlike:** Hypnotized people may indeed act immaturely, but the underlying cognitive activity is that of an adult (Nash, 2001).
- **Hypnosis induces long-term amnesia:** Hypnosis cannot make you forget your first day of kindergarten or your wedding. Short-term amnesia is possible if the hypnotist specifically suggests that something will be forgotten after the hypnosis wears off. ➡️◀️

Mesmerizing ◀
A 19th-century doctor attempts to heal a patient using the hypnotic techniques created by Franz Mesmer in the 1770s. Mesmer believed that every person was surrounded by a magnetic field, or "animal magnetism," that could be summoned for therapeutic purposes (Wobst, 2007). The word "mesmerize" derives from Mesmer's name. Jean-Loup Charmet/ Science Source

NO ONE CAN FORCE YOU TO BECOME HYPNOTIZED

Now that some misconceptions about hypnosis have been cleared up, let's focus on what we know. Researchers propose the following characteristics are evident in a hypnotized person: (1) ability to focus intently, ignoring all extraneous stimuli; (2) heightened imagination; (3) an unresisting and receptive attitude; (4) decreased pain awareness; (5) high responsivity to suggestions (Kosslyn, Thompson, Costantini-Ferrando, Alpert, & Spiegel, 2000; Silva & Kirsch, 1992).

Does this process have any application to real life? With some limited success, hypnosis has been used therapeutically to treat phobias and commercially to help people change lifestyle habits (Green, 1999; Kraft, 2012). Hypnosis can also be used to reduce headaches and other pains associated with stress (Patterson & Jensen, 2003). Athletes use self-hypnosis to improve performance.

Imagine you are using hypnosis for one of these purposes, headaches, for example. How would a session with a hypnotist proceed? Probably something like this: The hypnotist talks to you in a calm, quiet voice, running through a list of suggestions on how to relax. She might suggest that you sit back in your chair and choose a place to

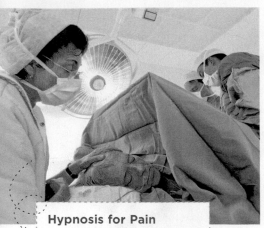

Hypnosis for Pain
A doctor in Belgium performs hypnosis on a patient undergoing a painful procedure. For those who are susceptible to hypnosis, this approach may diminish the need for anesthesia.
BSIP/UIG Via Getty Images

focus your eyes. Then she quietly suggests that your eyelids are starting to droop, and you feel like you need to yawn. You grow tired and more relaxed. Your breathing slows. Your arms feel so heavy that you can barely lift them off the chair. Or the hypnotist might suggest that you are going down steps, and ask you to focus attention on her voice. Hypnotists who are very good at this procedure can do an induction in less than a minute, especially if they know the individual being hypnotized.

Once you are in this altered state of consciousness, you may be open to suggestion. If, say, the hypnotist suggested you could not lift your feet off the ground, then you might actually feel this way. Or if she suggested that you will not remember your own middle name after coming out of hypnosis, this *posthypnotic suggestion* may very well play out.

People in hypnotic states sometimes report having sensory experiences that deviate from reality; they may, for example, see or hear things that are not there. In a classic experiment, participants were hypnotized to believe they wouldn't experience pain when asked to place one hand in a container filled with ice-cold water. With their other hand, they were asked to press a button if they experienced pain. Amazingly, the participants *reported* feeling no pain. However, they actually did press the button indicating pain during their hypnotic session (Hilgard, Morgan, & Macdonald, 1975). This suggests a "divided consciousness," that is, part of our consciousness is always aware, even when hypnotized and instructed to feel no pain. People under hypnotic states can also experience temporary blindness and deafness.

THEORIES OF HYPNOSIS   There are many theories to explain hypnosis. According to Hilgard (1977, 1994), hypnotized people experience a "split" in awareness, or consciousness. There is an ever-present hidden observer that oversees the events of our daily lives. You are listening to a boring lecture, picking up a little content here and there, but also thinking about that juicy gossip you heard before class. Your mind is working on different levels, and the hidden observer is keeping track of everything. In a hypnotic state, the hidden observer is still aware of what is transpiring in the environment, while another stream of mental activity focuses on the hypnotic suggestions.

Others have suggested that hypnosis is not a distinct state of consciousness, but more of a role-playing exercise. Have you ever watched a little boy pretend he was a firefighter? He becomes so enthralled in his play that he really believes he is a firefighter. His tricycle is now his fire engine; his baseball cap his firefighter's hat. He *is* the firefighter. Something similar happens when we are hypnotized. We have an expectation of how a hypnotized person should act or behave; therefore, our hypnotized response is nothing more than the role we think we should take on. And this is particularly true when good rapport exists between the hypnotist and the person being hypnotized.

Fade to Black?

It is time to conclude our discussion of consciousness, but first let's run through some of the big picture concepts you should take away from this chapter. Consciousness refers to a state of awareness—awareness of self and things outside of self—that has many gradations and dimensions. During sleep, awareness decreases, but it does not fade entirely (remember that alarm clock that becomes part of your dream about a wailing siren). Sleep has many stages, but the two main forms are non-REM and REM. Dreams may serve a purpose, but they may also be nothing more than your brain's interpretation of neurons signaling in the night. You learned from Dr. Julien that anesthetic drugs can profoundly alter consciousness. The same is true of recreational drugs, the use of which can lead to dependence, health problems, and death. Although somewhat controversial and misunderstood, hypnosis appears to induce an altered state of consciousness and may have useful therapeutic applications.

show what you know

1. Match the agent in the left column with the most appropriate outcome in the right column:

   _____ 1. depressant   a. blocks pain
   _____ 2. opioid   b. slows down activity in the CNS
   _____ 3. alcohol   c. increases neural activity in the CNS
   _____ 4. cocaine   d. cirrhosis of the liver

2. An acquaintance described an odorless, tasteless, and colorless substance he took many years ago. He discussed a variety of changes to his sensations and perceptions, including seeing colors and spirals. It is likely he had taken which of the following hallucinogens:

   a. alcohol   b. nicotine   c. LSD   d. cocaine

3. Dr. Julien uses a variety of _____ to dull the perception of pain, to inhibit memories of surgery, and to change a variety of psychological activities.

4. People often describe behaviors as being addictive. You might hear a character in a movie say that he is addicted to driving fast, for example. These descriptions often refer to dangerous or risky behaviors. Given what you have learned about physiological and psychological dependence, how would you determine if these behaviors should be considered problematic?

✓ CHECK YOUR ANSWERS IN APPENDIX C.

 # summary of concepts

LO 1 Define consciousness. (p. 141)

Consciousness is the state of being aware of oneself, one's thoughts, and/or the environment. There are various levels of conscious awareness, including wakefulness, sleepiness, drug-induced states, dreaming, hypnotic states, and meditative states, to name a few.

LO 2 Explain how automatic processing relates to consciousness. (p. 144)

Because our sensory systems absorb large amounts of information, being consciously aware of all of it is not possible. Without our awareness, the brain determines what is important, what requires immediate attention, and what can be processed and stored for later use if necessary. This automatic processing happens involuntarily, with little or no conscious effort.

LO 3 Describe how we narrow our focus on specific stimuli to attend to them. (p. 145)

We have access to a great deal of information in our internal and external environments, but we can only focus our attention on a small portion of that information. This narrow focus on specific stimuli is referred to as selective attention. We are designed to pay attention to changes in environmental stimuli, to unfamiliar stimuli, and to especially strong stimuli.

LO 4 Identify how circadian rhythm relates to sleep. (p. 147)

Predictable daily patterns influence our behaviors, alertness, and activity levels in a cyclical fashion. These daily patterns in our physiological functioning roughly follow the 24-hour cycle of daylight and darkness, driven by our circadian rhythm. In the circadian rhythm for sleep and wakefulness,

there are two times when the desire for sleep hits hardest. The first occurs in the early hours of the morning, between about 2:00 to 6:00 A.M., and the second, less intense desire for sleep strikes mid-afternoon, around 2:00 or 3:00 P.M.

LO 5 Summarize the stages of sleep. (p. 151)

Sleep begins in non-rapid eye movement (non-REM), or nondreaming sleep, which has four stages. The lightest stage of sleep is Stage 1; it is the time during which hallucinations, or imaginary sensations, can occur. This stage lasts only a few minutes before Stage 2 sleep begins. At this point, it is a little more difficult to rouse the sleeper before she drifts even further into Stage 3 sleep and then Stage 4 sleep, slow-wave sleep. Stage 4 is the deepest sleep. As the night progresses, the sleeper goes back to Stage 1 from Stage 4. And instead of waking up, the sleeper enters a 5th stage of sleep known as rapid eye movement (REM) sleep. During this stage, closed eyes dart around, and brain activity changes. People awakened from REM sleep often report having vivid dreams. Each cycle, from Stage 1 to REM, lasts about 90 minutes, and the average adult loops through five complete cycles per night. These cycles change in composition throughout the night.

LO 6 Recognize various sleep disorders and their symptoms. (p. 156)

Narcolepsy is a neurological disorder characterized by excessive daytime sleepiness and other sleep-related disturbances. REM sleep behavior disorder is a disorder of sleep in which the mechanism responsible for paralyzing the body during REM sleep does not function properly. The individual is able to move around and act out dreams. Obstructive sleep apnea hypopnea is a serious disturbance of non-REM sleep characterized by the periodic blockage of breathing. It results in the upper throat muscles going limp, allowing the airway to close. The sleeper awakens and gasps for air, then drifts back to sleep. Insomnia is the inability to fall asleep or stay asleep. People with insomnia report on the poor quantity or quality of their sleep, and some may complain about waking up too early and being unable to fall back to sleep.

LO 7 Summarize the theories of why we dream. (p. 164)

Freud believed dreams have two levels of content. Manifest content, the apparent meaning of the dream, is the actual story line of the dream itself—what you remember when you wake up. Latent content contains the hidden meaning of the dream, which represents the unconscious conflicts and desires. The activation–synthesis model suggests that dreams have no meaning whatsoever: we respond to random neural activity of the brain during sleep as if it has meaning. Neurocognitive theory suggests there is a network of neurons in the brain necessary for dreaming to occur. According to this theory, dreams are the result of how sleep and consciousness have evolved in humans.

LO 8 Define psychoactive drugs. (p. 167)

Psychoactive drugs can cause changes in psychological activities such as sensation, perception, attention, judgment, memory, self-control, emotion, thinking, and behavior. These drugs alter consciousness in an untold number of ways. They can depress activity in the central nervous system, produce hallucinations, and cause a sense of euphoria.

LO 9 Identify several depressants and stimulants and know their effects. (p. 167)

Depressants decrease the activities in the central nervous system. These include barbiturates, opioids, and alcohol. Stimulants are drugs that increase neural activity in the central nervous system, producing effects such as heightened alertness and energy and an elevated mood. These include cocaine, amphetamines, methamphetamine, caffeine, and nicotine.

LO 10 Discuss some of the hallucinogens. (p. 174)

Hallucinogens are drugs that produce hallucinations, altered moods, and distorted perception and thought. The most well-known hallucinogen is lysergic acid diethylamide (LSD). This odorless, tasteless, and colorless substance often produces extreme changes in sensation and perception. In addition to the traditional hallucinogens, a number of "club drugs," or synthetic "designer drugs," are commonly used at parties, raves, and dance venues. The most popular is methylenedioxymethamphetamine (MDMA), which is chemically similar to the stimulant methamphetamine, producing a combination of stimulant and hallucinogen effects. The most widely used illegal (in most states) drug is marijuana, and at high doses, tetrahydracannabinol (THC) can induce mild euphoria and create intense sensory experiences.

LO 11 Explain how physiological and psychological dependence differ. (p. 177)

With constant use of some psychoactive drugs, a condition can develop in which the body becomes dependent on the drug. Signs of this physiological dependence include tolerance and withdrawal. Psychological dependence occurs without the evidence of tolerance or withdrawal symptoms, but is indicated by many other problematic symptoms. People with psychological dependence believe they need the drug because it increases their emotional or mental well-being. Physiological dependence is physical and has serious physical consequences. Psychological dependence is associated with beliefs and emotions.

LO 12 Describe hypnosis and explain how it works. (p. 178)

Hypnosis is an altered state of consciousness that can create changes in perceptions and behaviors, usually resulting from suggestions made by a hypnotist. Hypnosis is known to ease pain associated with childbirth and surgery, and can reduce the need for painkillers. One theory suggests that hypnotized people experience a "split" in awareness or consciousness. Others suggest hypnosis is a role-playing exercise.

key terms

activation–synthesis model, p. 165
alpha waves, p. 151
amphetamines, p. 172
automatic processing, p. 144
barbiturate, p. 168
beta waves, p. 151
circadian rhythm, p. 148
consciousness, p. 141

delirium tremens (DTs), p. 177
delta waves, p. 152
depressants, p. 167
hallucinogens, p. 174
hypnosis, p. 179
insomnia, p. 158
latent content, p. 164
lysergic acid diethylamide (LSD), p. 174

manifest content, p. 164
methylenedioxymeth-amphetamine (MDMA), p. 175
narcolepsy, p. 155
nightmares, p. 158
non-rapid eye movement (non-REM), p. 151

obstructive sleep apnea hypopnea, p. 157
opiates, p. 168
opioid, p. 168
physiological dependence, p. 177
psychoactive drugs, p. 167
psychological dependence, p. 177

rapid eye movement (REM), p. 152
REM rebound, p. 160

REM sleep behavior disorder, p. 156
selective attention, p. 145

sleep terrors, p. 158
stimulant, p. 171
tetrahydrocannabinol (THC), p. 176

theta waves, p. 151
tolerance, p. 177
withdrawal, p. 177

TEST PREP are you ready?

1. William James was interested in studying _____, which he described as a "stream" that provides day-to-day continuity.
   a. dreams
   b. automatic processing
   c. selective attention
   d. consciousness

2. A great deal of information is available in our internal and external environments, but we can only focus on a small portion of it. This narrow focus on specific stimuli is known as:
   a. stream of consciousness.
   b. selective attention.
   c. waking consciousness.
   d. encoding of memories.

3. _____ refers to the ability to block out the chatter and noise in a busy environment so that you can pay attention to your ongoing conversation with someone.
   a. The cocktail-party effect
   b. Inattentional blindness
   c. Automatic processing
   d. The circadian rhythm

4. The daily patterns of our physiological functioning, such as our temperature, roughly follow the 24-hour cycle of daylight and darkness. This pattern is driven by our:
   a. blood pressure.
   b. need for sleep.
   c. levels of consciousness.
   d. circadian rhythm.

5. The suprachiasmatic nucleus (SCN) can be thought of as a master clock for our daily rhythm. The SCN sends messages to the _____, which regulates patterns of hunger and temperature, and the _____, which regulates alertness and sleepiness.
   a. reticular formation; retinal ganglion cells
   b. retinal ganglion cells; hypothalamus
   c. hypothalamus; reticular formation
   d. thalamus; hypothalamus

6. Shift workers can have problems with their sleep–wake cycles, sometimes resulting in _____, which refers to difficulty falling asleep and sleeping soundly.
   a. insomnia
   b. cataplexy
   c. narcolepsy
   d. hypnagogic hallucinations

7. If we hook you up to an electroencephalogram (EEG) as you become drowsy, the EEG would begin to show _____ waves.
   a. fast
   b. alpha
   c. beta
   d. theta

8. The fifth stage of sleep is known as _____, when brain activity looks similar to that of someone who is wide awake.
   a. sleep paralysis
   b. cataplexy
   c. non-REM sleep
   d. REM sleep

9. If you deprive people of REM sleep, this can result in:
   a. REM rebound.
   b. insomnia.
   c. more beta waves while they sleep.
   d. increased energy levels.

10. According to Sigmund Freud's theory, dreams are a form of:
    a. REM rebound.
    b. wish fulfillment.
    c. microsleep.
    d. sleep terror.

11. People with damage to specific areas of the limbic system and forebrain do not have dreams or experience abnormal dreams. Which of the following explains this finding?
    a. the theory of evolution
    b. the activation–synthesis model
    c. the psychoanalytic theory
    d. the neurocognitive theory

12. _____ such as caffeine, alcohol, and hallucinogens can cause changes in psychological activities, for example, sensation, perception, attention, and judgment.
    a. Tranquilizers
    b. Depressants
    c. Psychoactive drugs
    d. Stimulants

13. Methamphetamine stimulates the release of the brain's pleasure-producing neurotransmitter _____, causing a surge in energy and alertness.
    a. dopamine
    b. serotonin
    c. acetylcholine
    d. adenosine

14. Which is the number one cause of premature death worldwide?
    a. AIDS
    b. tobacco
    c. road accidents
    d. illegal drugs

15. Drug use can be fueled by dependence. _____ dependence means the body no longer functions normally without the drug, and one sign of this type of dependence is _____, as indicated by the symptoms that occur when the drug is withheld.
    a. Psychological; tolerance
    b. Physiological; substance abuse
    c. Physiological; withdrawal
    d. Psychological; withdrawal

16. Give an example showing that you are still conscious when asleep.

17. Describe automatic processing, and give two reasons why it is important.

18. Interns and residents in hospitals sometimes work 48-hour shifts. Why would you not want a doctor keeping such a schedule to care for you at the end of her shift?

19. Name and describe four different sleep disturbances. Differentiate them by describing their characteristics.

20. Give four examples of drugs that people use legally on a daily basis.

✓ CHECK YOUR ANSWERS IN APPENDIX C.

Get personalized practice by logging into LaunchPad at **http://www.worthpublishers.com/launchpad/Licht** to take the LearningCurve adaptive quizzes for Chapter 4.

5

An Introduction to Learning

📁 *Athletes in the Making*

📁 *An Ominous Smell*

Classical Conditioning

👁! DIDN'T SEE THAT COMING
Rescuing Animals with Classical Conditioning

SA from the pages of
SCIENTIFIC AMERICAN
The Taste of Immune Suppression

Operant Conditioning

📁 *The Jeremy Lin Show*

➕ THINK AGAIN
Chickens Can't Play Baseball

💬 SOCIAL MEDIA AND PSYCHOLOGY
Contagious Behaviors

➤◄ CONTROVERSIES
Spotlight on Spanking

➕ THINK AGAIN
Think Positive Reinforcement

Observational Learning and Cognition

📁 *Basketball IQ*

👁! DIDN'T SEE THAT COMING
Monkey See, Monkey Do: Can Apes Learn by Observation, Too?

📁 *It Keeps Getting Better*

learning

An Introduction to Learning

ATHLETES IN THE MAKING   Palo Alto, California: It was the spring of 1999, and Ivonne Mosquera was about to graduate from Stanford University with a bachelor's degree in mathematics. Math majors typically spend a lot of time manipulating numbers on paper, graphing functions, and trying to understand spatial relationships—all activities that draw on their sense of vision. But Ivonne had no memory of seeing an equation, a number, or even a piece of paper. She had been blind since the age of 2, when doctors removed both of her eyes to arrest the spread of an aggressive cancer.

Blindness never stopped Ivonne from doing much of anything. Growing up in New York City, she used to ride her bicycle across the George Washington Bridge as her father ran alongside. She went to school with sighted kids, climbed trees in the park, and studied ballet, tap, and jazz dance (Boccella, 2012, May 6; iminmotion.net, 2012). She tried downhill skiing, hiking, and rock climbing. Now Ivonne was graduating from college with a degree in one of the most rigorous academic disciplines, a great accomplishment indeed. Yet there were bigger things to come for Ivonne. In the next decade, she would become a world-class runner and triathlete.

That same year Ivonne graduated from college, just a few miles from the Stanford campus, a 10-year-old boy named Jeremy Lin was finishing fifth grade and working on his basketball game. In the evenings, Jeremy and his brothers would go with their father to the nearby YMCA, where they ran drills and shot hoops late into the night (Dalrymple, 2012). It was during this period that Jeremy's future high school coach, Peter Diepenbrock, first caught a glimpse of the scrappy young player. "He was very small," Coach Diepenbrock recalls, "but [had] just an incredible, incredible amount of confidence." There was a certain presence about Jeremy, the coach explains (P. Diepenbrock, personal communication, May 21, 2012). He knew exactly how to play and was determined to do so, regardless of his size.

As impressive as the young player's skills and spunk may have been, Coach Diepenbrock did not foresee the basketball heights Jeremy would eventually reach and the impact he would have on the global community. No one could have predicted the "Linsanity" he was capable of inspiring.

At first glance, Ivonne Mosquera (now Ivonne Mosquera-Schmidt) and Jeremy Lin don't seem to have much in common. But as you read their stories, you will see how their relentless determination, work ethic, and optimism led to their athletic achievements—Ivonne as a runner and triathlete and Jeremy as a basketball player. Were they destined to become star athletes, regardless of events in their lives? Perhaps they were not. As you read through this chapter, you will see how *learning* changed their lives and paved the way for their success.

5

LEARNING OBJECTIVES

after reading and studying this chapter, you should be able to:

LO 1 Define learning.

LO 2 Explain what Pavlov's studies teach us about classical conditioning.

LO 3 Evaluate the differences between the US, UR, CS, and CR.

LO 4 Recognize and give examples of stimulus discrimination and stimulus generalization.

LO 5 Summarize how classical conditioning is dependent on the biology of the organism.

LO 6 Evaluate the Little Albert study and explain how fear can be learned.

LO 7 Describe Thorndike's law of effect.

LO 8 Explain shaping and the method of successive approximations.

LO 9 Identify the differences between positive and negative reinforcement.

LO 10 Distinguish between primary and secondary reinforcers.

LO 11 Describe continuous reinforcement and partial reinforcement.

LO 12 Name the schedules of reinforcement and give examples of each.

LO 13 Explain how punishment differs from negative reinforcement.

LO 14 Summarize what Bandura's classic Bobo doll study teaches us about learning.

LO 15 Describe latent learning and explain how cognition is involved in learning.

World Champion
(left) Ivonne Mosquera-Schmidt runs in the Capital of Texas Triathlon on May 28, 2012. Blind since the age of 2, Ivonne has always been extremely active. She has danced across the stage of New York City's Lincoln Center, climbed Tanzania's Mount Kilimanjaro, and competed in over 20 triathlons. Brightroom.com

Swoosh
(right) Jeremy Lin of the Houston Rockets leaps for the basket in a game against the Boston Celtics on January 11, 2013. This young man's basketball accomplishments are the result of talent, motivation, and extensive *learning.* CJ GUNTHER/EPA/Newscom

Jeremy, in Coach Diepenbrock's Words
http://qrs.ly/373m610

Note: Quotations attributed to Ivonne Mosquera-Schmidt and Peter Diepenbrock are personal communications.

What Is Learning?

LO 1 Define learning.

When does learning begin? Studies suggest that learning can begin before we are even born—prior to birth, a baby has already begun to single out the sound of his mother's voice (Kisilevsky et al., 2008). And learning may continue until our dying day. But what exactly is learning? Psychologists define **learning** as a relatively enduring change in behavior or thinking that results from our experiences. Although learning leads to changes in the brain, including alterations to individual **neurons** as well as their networks, modifications of behavior and thinking are not always permanent (a fact that will be discussed later in the chapter).

The ability to learn is not unique to humans. Trout can learn to press a pendulum to get food (Yue, Duncan, & Moccia, 2008); orangutans can pick up whistling (Wich et al., 2009); and, research suggests, even honeybees can be trained to differentiate among photos of human faces (Dyer, Neumeyer, & Chittka, 2005). One of the most basic forms of learning occurs during the process of **habituation** (hah-bi-chü-ā-shən), which is evident when an organism does not respond as strongly or as often to an event or occurrence **following multiple exposures** to that event. This type of learning is apparent in a wide range of living beings, from humans to sea slugs (Chapter 6). Although an organism might initially *respond* to a **stimulus,** which is an event that generally leads to a response or reaction, with repeated exposures, the stimulus is increasingly ignored and habituation occurs. Essentially, an organism *learns* about a *stimulus* but begins to ignore it as it is repeated.

CONNECTIONS

In **Chapter 2,** we described circumstances in which learning influences the brain and how the brain influences learning. For example, dopamine plays an important role in learning through reinforcement, attention, and regulating body movements. *Neurogenesis* (the generation of new neurons) is also thought to be associated with learning.

In **Chapter 3,** we discussed *sensory adaptation,* which is the tendency to become less aware of constant stimuli. Becoming habituated to sensory input keeps us alert to changes in the environment.

learning A relatively enduring change in behavior or thinking that results from experiences.

habituation (hah-bi-chü-ā-shən) A basic form of learning evident when an organism does not respond as strongly or as often to an event following multiple exposures to it.

stimulus An event or occurrence that generally leads to a response.

CONNECTIONS

In **Chapter 1,** we described the theme of nature and nurture, which examines the relative weight of biology and environment. Some scientists who initially studied the biological and innate aspects (nature) of animals shifted their focus and began to study how experiences and learning (nurture) influenced these animals.

In **Chapter 1,** we discussed Institutional Review Boards, which must approve all research with human participants *and* animal subjects to ensure safe and humane procedures.

Synonym
observational learning social learning

▶ Suited Up to Swim
Ivonne and her guide prepare for the 2012 Paratriathlon World Championships in Auckland, New Zealand. Ivonne is about to begin the swim portion of the triathlon, which takes place in the frigid ocean waters along Queens Wharf. She wears a wetsuit to keep her warm. The red string just below her knee is the tether that keeps her connected to the guide.
G. John Schmidt/Courtesy Ivonne Mosquera-Schmidt

A great deal of research on learning has been conducted using a wide range of animals. The history of psychology is full of stories about **scientists** who began studying animal *biology* but then switched their focus to the study of animal *behavior* as unexpected events unfolded in the laboratory. These scientists were often excited to find the connections between biology and experience that became evident as they explored the principles of learning.

Animals are often excellent models for studying and understanding human behavior. Conducting research with them sidesteps many of the ethical dilemmas that arise with human research. It's generally considered okay to keep rats, cats, and birds in cages (as long as they are otherwise treated **humanely**) to ensure control over experimental variables, but locking up people in laboratories would obviously be unacceptable.

This chapter focuses on three major types of learning: *classical conditioning, operant conditioning,* and *observational learning.* As you make your way through these pages, you will begin to realize that learning is very much about creating associations. Through *classical conditioning,* we associate two different stimuli: for example, the sound of a bell and food. In *operant conditioning,* we make connections between our behaviors and their consequences: for example, through rewards and punishments. With ***observational learning,*** we learn by watching and imitating other people, establishing a closer link between our behavior and the behavior of others.

Learning can occur in predictable or unexpected ways. It allows us to grow and change, and it is a key to achieving goals. Now let's see how learning has shaped the lives of Ivonne Mosquera-Schmidt and Jeremy Lin. We begin in the most unexpected place: the locker room of a swimming pool.

AN OMINOUS SMELL   Ivonne is on her way to swim practice. As she walks through the locker room and approaches the entrance to the pool, she catches a whiff of chlorine. Immediately, her shoulders tense and her heart rate jumps. The smell of chlorine gives Ivonne the jitters, not because there is something inherent about the chemical that causes a physical reaction, but because it is associated with something she dreads: swimming.

"I've never been a strong swimmer," Ivonne says. "I just survive in water." Submerging her ears in water, which is necessary when she swims the freestyle stroke in triathlons, makes Ivonne feel disoriented. "I can't hear what's around me," she explains. "There aren't sounds or echoes for me to follow."

Feeling awkward in the water wouldn't be much of an issue were Ivonne just a recreational swimmer, taking occasional dips at the beach or in the pool. But swimming in triathlons is a serious and potentially dangerous proposition. Imagine navigating a mile in the frigid ocean bordering Canada in the Vancouver Triathlon, or plowing through choppy waves (not to mention dodging pieces of trash) in the Hudson River in New York City's Triathlon. Now imagine doing all of that swimming in the darkness. It's no surprise that Ivonne feels a little apprehensive about being in the water.

To understand why the smell of chlorine seems to evoke such a strong physiological response for Ivonne, we need to travel back in time to the lab of a young ▼ Russian scientist: Ivan Pavlov.

 show what you know

1. Learning is a relatively enduring change in _____ that results from our _____.

2. Learning can often be described as the creation of _____, for example, between two stimuli or between a behavior and its consequences.
   a. habituation
   b. ethical dilemmas
   c. associations
   d. unexpected events

✓ CHECK YOUR ANSWERS IN APPENDIX C.

Classical Conditioning

The son of a village priest, Ivan Pavlov (1849–1936) had planned to devote his life to the church. He changed his mind at a young age, however, when he discovered his love for science. His primary interest was physiology, a branch of biology that investigates the physical and chemical mechanisms underlying life's processes. Although he won a Nobel Prize in 1904 for his research on the physiology of digestion, Pavlov's most enduring legacy was his trailblazing research on learning (Fancher & Rutherford, 2012).

What Salivating Dogs Can Teach Us

LO 2 Explain what Pavlov's studies teach us about classical conditioning.

Pavlov spent the 1890s studying the digestive system of dogs at Russia's Institute of Experimental Medicine (Watson, 1968). One of his early experiments involved measuring how much dogs salivate in response to food. Initially, the dogs salivated as expected, but as the experiment progressed, they began salivating to other stimuli as well. After repeated trials with an assistant giving a dog its food and then measuring the dog's saliva output, Pavlov noticed that instead of **salivating** the moment it received food, the dog began to salivate at the mere sight or sound of the lab assistant arriving to feed it. The assistant's footsteps seemed to act like a trigger (the *stimulus*) for the dog to start salivating (the *response*). The dog was associating the sound of footsteps with the arrival of food; it had been *conditioned* to associate the sights and sounds with eating. The dog had learned to salivate when exposed to these stimuli, much like you might respond when seeing a sign for a favorite restaurant or a dessert you love.

Pavlov had discovered how associations develop through the process of learning, which he referred to as *conditioning*. He was so intrigued by his discovery that he decided to shift the focus of his research to investigate the dogs' salivation (which he termed "psychic secretions") in these types of scenarios (Fancher & Rutherford, 2012, p. 248; Watson, 1968).

PAVLOV'S BASIC RESEARCH PLAN Pavlov followed up on his initial observations with numerous studies in the early 1900s, examining the link between stimulus (for example, the sound of human footsteps) and response (the dog's salivation). The type of *behavior* Pavlov was studying (salivating) was not voluntary; it was involuntary or reflexive (Pavlov, 1906). The connection between food and salivating is innate or universal, whereas the link between the sound of footsteps and salivating is learned. Learning has occurred whenever a new, nonuniversal link between stimulus (footsteps) and response (salivation) is established.

Many of Pavlov's studies had the same basic format (**INFOGRAPHIC 5.1** on page 191). Prior to the experiment, the dog had a tube surgically inserted into its cheek to allow for the precise collection of its saliva. When the dog salivated, instead of the secretions being swallowed, they were emptied from that tube into a measuring device so Pavlov could figure out exactly how much the dog was producing.

CONNECTIONS

The dog naturally begins to salivate when exposed to the smell of food, even before tasting it. This is an involuntary response of the autonomic nervous system, which we explored in **Chapter 2**. Dogs do not innately salivate at the sound of footsteps. Here, we see this response is a *learned* behavior, as the dog salivates without tasting or smelling food.

Tick Tock
Pavlov conditioned his dogs to salivate in response to auditory stimuli, such as bells, tones, and ticking metronomes. A metronome is a device that musicians often use to maintain tempo. This "old-fashioned" metronome has a wind-up knob and a pendulum that ticks at various speed settings. Modern metronomes are digital and often come with additional features such as adjustable volume. Galina Ermolaeva/Dreamstime.com

CONNECTIONS

In **Chapter 1,** we discussed the importance of control in the *experimental method*. In this case, if the sound of footsteps was the stimulus, then Pavlov would need to *control* the number of steps taken, the type of shoes worn, the size of the approaching person, and so on, to ensure the stimulus was identical for each trial. Otherwise, it would be difficult to determine what exactly was causing the dog to salivate.

CONNECTIONS

In **Chapter 1,** we discussed operational definitions, which are the precise way in which characteristics of interest are defined and measured. Although in the preceding paragraphs we described the research in everyday language, here we provide operational definitions for the procedures of the study.

Synonym

classical conditioning Pavlovian conditioning

neutral stimulus A stimulus that does not cause a relevant automatic or reflexive response.

classical conditioning Learning process in which two stimuli become associated with each other; when an originally neutral stimulus is conditioned to elicit an involuntary response.

unconditioned stimulus (US) A stimulus that automatically triggers an involuntary response without any learning needed.

unconditioned response (UR) A reflexive, involuntary response to an unconditioned stimulus.

conditioned stimulus (CS) A previously neutral stimulus that an organism learns to associate with an unconditioned stimulus.

conditioned response (CR) A learned response to a conditioned stimulus.

acquisition The initial learning phase in both classical and operant conditioning.

Because Pavlov was interested in exploring the link between a stimulus and the dog's response, he had to pick a stimulus that was **more controlled** than the sound of someone walking into a room. Pavlov used a variety of stimuli, such as sounds from a metronome, a buzzer, and the tone of a bell, which under normal circumstances have nothing to do with food. In other words, they are *neutral* stimuli in relation to food and responses to food.

A typical Pavlovian experiment using the tone of a bell and meat powder went something like this: A dog was placed alone in a soundproof room and outfitted with equipment designed to keep it from moving around. On numerous occasions during an experimental trial, Pavlov and his assistants presented the dog with the sound of the tone, and then moments later gave the dog some meat powder. Each time the tone was sounded, the assistant would wait a couple of seconds and then offer the dog the meat powder. All the while, its saliva was being measured. As predicted, the dog learned to pair the sound of the tone with the meat powder. We know the procedure resulted in learning because after repeating the tone–food pairing several times, when only the sound of the tone was played, with no meat powder nearby, the dog salivated anyway. The dog had been conditioned to associate the sound of the tone with food.

Time for Some Terms

LO 3   Evaluate the differences between the US, UR, CS, and CR.

Now that you know Pavlov's basic research procedure, it is important to learn the **specific terminology** psychologists use to describe what is happening (Infographic 5.1). Before the experiment began, the sound of the tone was a **neutral stimulus**—something in the environment that *does not* normally cause a relevant *automatic* or reflexive response. In the current example, salivation is the relevant automatic response associated with food; dogs do not normally respond to the sound of a tone by salivating. But through experience, the dogs learned to link this neutral stimulus (the tone) with another stimulus (food) that prompts an automatic, unlearned response (salivation). This type of learning is **classical conditioning,** which occurs when an originally neutral stimulus is conditioned to *elicit* or induce an involuntary response, such as salivation, eye blinks, and other types of *reflex* reactions.

US, UR, CS, AND CR   At the start of Pavlov's experiment, before the dogs were conditioned or had learned anything about the neutral stimulus, they salivated when they smelled or were given food. The food is called an **unconditioned stimulus (US)** because it automatically triggers a response without any learning needed. Salivation by the dogs when exposed to food is an **unconditioned response (UR)** because it doesn't require any conditioning (learning); the dog just does it automatically. The salivation (the UR) is an automatic response elicited by the smell or taste of food (the US). After conditioning has occurred, the dog responds to the sound of the tone almost as if it were food. The tone, previously a *neutral stimulus,* has now become a **conditioned stimulus (CS)** because it triggers the dog's salivation. When the salivation occurs in response to the sound of the tone, it is called a **conditioned response (CR);** the salivation is a learned response.

THE ACQUISITION PHASE   The pairings of the neutral stimulus (the tone) with the US (the meat powder) occur during the **acquisition** or initial learning phase. Some points to remember:

Learning Through Classical Conditioning

During his experiments with dogs, **Ivan Pavlov** noticed them salivating before food was even presented. Somehow the dogs had learned to associate the lab assistant's approaching footsteps with eating. This observation led to Pavlov's discovery of the process of classical conditioning, in which we learn to associate a neutral stimulus with an unconditioned stimulus that produces an automatic, natural response. The crucial stage of this process involves repeated pairings of the two stimuli.

PAVLOV'S EXPERIMENT

Before conditioning

Dog salivates automatically when food is presented.

Unconditioned stimulus → Unconditioned response (salivates)

Bell means nothing to dog, so there is no response.

Neutral stimulus (ringing bell)   No response

During conditioning

In the process of conditioning, bell is repeatedly played right before dog receives food. Over time, dog learns that bell signals arrival of food.

Neutral stimulus (ringing bell) + Unconditioned stimulus = Unconditioned response (salivates)

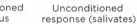

repeated over time

After conditioning

Dog has now learned to associate bell with food and will begin salivating when bell rings.

Conditioned stimulus (ringing bell)   Conditioned response (salivates)

HAVE YOU BEEN CONDITIONED?

Before conditioning

Neutral stimulus   No response

Unconditioned stimulus   Unconditioned response (stomach growls)

During conditioning

Neutral stimulus + Unconditioned stimulus

repeated over time

Unconditioned response (stomach growls)

After conditioning

Conditioned stimulus   Conditioned response (stomach growls)

Classical conditioning prompts learning that occurs naturally, without studying or other voluntary effort. And it happens every day. Do you feel hungry when you see a pizza box or McDonald's "golden arches"? Just like Pavlov's dogs, we learn through repeated pairings to associate these neutral stimuli with food, and the sight of a cardboard box or a yellow "M" can be enough to get our stomachs rumbling.

CONNECTIONS

In **Chapter 1,** we discussed *extraneous variables,* which are characteristics of the environment or participants that interfere with the outcome of research. Pavlov had to consider the sight and smell of meat powder as potential extraneous variables that could affect the conditioning procedure. He went to great lengths to control these variables so they did not interfere with measurements of the dependent variables.

CONNECTIONS

In **Chapter 1,** we described the scientific method and how it depends on *objective* observations. An objective approach requires scientists to make their observations without the influence of personal opinion and preconceived notions. Although we are prone to personal biases, the scientific method helps minimize their effects. Pavlov was among the first to insist that behavior must be studied objectively.

- The meat powder is always a US (the dog never has to learn how to respond to it).

- The dog's salivating is initially a UR to the meat powder, but eventually becomes a CR as it occurs in response to the sound of the tone (without the **sight or smell** of meat powder).

- The US is always different from the CS; the US automatically triggers the response, but with the CS, the response has been *learned* by the organism.

In order to determine the proper label of a response, you must know what caused that response. Knowing what elicited the response will help determine whether it is conditioned or unconditioned.

Pavlov's work paved the way for a new generation of psychologists who considered behavior to be a topic of **objective,** scientific study. His disdain for psychology and its early methods of introspection made him reluctant to pursue the surprising observation he made in the laboratory. Pavlov held firm to his belief that scientists should focus only on observable behaviors; his work transformed our understanding of learning and our approach to psychological research.

Nuts and Bolts of Classical Conditioning

LO 4   Recognize and give examples of stimulus discrimination and stimulus generalization.

We have learned about Pavlov's dogs and their demonstration of classical conditioning. We have described the process by which classical conditioning occurs and the terminology associated with that process. Now it's time to take our learning to the next level and examine some of the principles that guide the process.

Layland Masuda/
Shutterstock

STIMULUS GENERALIZATION   What would happen if a dog in one of Pavlov's experiments heard a slightly higher-frequency tone? Would the dog still salivate? Pavlov (1927/1960) asked this same question and found that a stimulus similar to the CS caused the dogs to salivate as well. This is an example of **stimulus generalization.** Once an association is forged between a CS and a CR, the learner often responds to similar stimuli as if they are the original CS. Here's an example: When Pavlov's dogs learned to salivate in response to a metronome ticking at 90 beats per minute, they also salivated when the metronome ticked a little more quickly (100 beats per minute) or slowly (80 beats per minute; Hothersall, 2004). Their response was *generalized* to metronome speeds ranging from 80 to 100 beats per minute. Many of you may have been classically conditioned to salivate at the sight of a tall glass of lemonade. Stimulus generalization predicts you would salivate when seeing a shorter glass of lemonade, or even a mug, if you knew it contained your favorite lemonade. Someone who has been bitten by a small dog may subsequently react with fear to all dogs, big and small. This would suggest she has generalized her fear, responding in this way to dogs of all sizes, even though the original CS was a small dog.

STIMULUS DISCRIMINATION   Next let's examine what happens when Pavlov's dogs are presented with two stimuli that differ significantly. You may be surprised to learn that the dogs can tell them apart. If you present the meat powder with a high-pitched sound, the dogs will associate that pitch with the meat powder. They will then only salivate in response to that pitch, but not to low-pitched sounds.

The dogs in the experiment are displaying **stimulus discrimination,** the ability to differentiate between a particular CS and other stimuli sufficiently different from it. Pavlov's dogs exhibited stimulus discrimination; with enough training, they could differentiate among various pitches, or high and low tones (Watson, 1968). Someone who's been stung by a bee might only become afraid at the sight of bees (and not flies, for example) because he has learned to discriminate among the stimuli represented by the wide variety of flying insects. He has only been conditioned to experience fear in response to bees.

EXTINCTION   Once the dogs associate the sound of the tone with meat powder, can they ever listen to its sound without salivating? The answer is yes—if they are repeatedly exposed to the sound of the tone *without* the meat powder. If the CS is presented time and again without being accompanied by the US, the association may fade. The CR decreases and eventually disappears in a process called **extinction.** In general, if dogs are repeatedly exposed to a CS (for example, a metronome or ringing bell) without any tasty treats to follow, they produce progressively less saliva in response to the stimulus and, eventually, none at all (Watson, 1968).

SPONTANEOUS RECOVERY   Take note: Even with extinction, the connection is not necessarily gone forever. We've already observed how Pavlov (1927/1960) used classical conditioning with a dog to form an association between a bell ringing and meat powder. Once the sound of the bell was associated with the salivation, he stopped presenting the meat powder, and the association was extinguished (the dog didn't salivate in response to the sound of the bell). Two hours following this extinction, Pavlov presented the tone again and the dog salivated because of a process called **spontaneous recovery.** With the presentation of a CS after a period of rest, the CR reappears. The link between the sound of the bell and the food was simmering beneath the surface. The dog had not "forgotten" the association when the pairing was extinguished. Rather, the CR was "suppressed" during the extinction, when the dog was not being exposed to the US. The association was not completely lost, as evidenced by its return 2 hours later when the bell (the CS) sounded in the absence of food (the US). Let's return to that refreshing glass of lemonade—perhaps a summer drink you do not get to enjoy for 9 months out of the year. It is possible that your CR (salivating) will be suppressed through the process of extinction (from September to the end of May), but when June rolls around, spontaneous recovery may find you once again salivating at the sight of that tangy sweet drink.

HIGHER ORDER CONDITIONING   After acquisition has occurred, is it possible to add another layer to the conditioning process? Suppose the sound of the tone has become a CS for the dog, such that every time the tone sounds, the dog has learned to salivate. Once this conditioning is established, the researcher can add a new neutral stimulus, such as a light flashing, every time the dog hears the sound of the tone. After pairing the sound and the light together (without the meat powder anywhere in sight or smell), the light will become associated with the sound and the dog will begin to salivate in response to seeing the light alone. This is called **higher order conditioning** (FIGURE 5.1). With repeated pairings of the CS (the tone) and a new neutral stimulus (the light), the second neutral stimulus becomes a CS as well. When all is said and done, both stimuli (the sound and the light) have gone from being neutral stimuli to conditioned stimuli, and either of them can elicit the CR (salivation). But in higher order conditioning, the second neutral stimulus is paired with a CS instead of being paired with the original US (Pavlov, 1927). In our example, the light is associated with the sound, not with the food directly.

CONNECTIONS

In **Chapter 3,** we introduced the concept of a *difference threshold,* which is the minimum difference between two stimuli that is noticed 50% of the time. Here, we see that difference thresholds can play a role in stimulus discrimination tasks. The conditioned stimulus and the comparison stimuli must be sufficiently different to be distinguished; that is, their difference is greater than the difference threshold.

stimulus generalization The tendency for stimuli similar to the conditioned stimulus to elicit the conditioned response.

stimulus discrimination The ability to differentiate between a conditioned stimulus and other stimuli sufficiently different from it.

extinction In classical conditioning, the process by which the CR decreases after repeated exposure to the CS in the absence of the US; in operant conditioning, the disappearance of a learned behavior through the removal of its reinforcer.

spontaneous recovery In classical conditioning, the reappearance of the conditioned response following its extinction; occurs in response to the conditioned stimulus after a period of rest.

higher order conditioning With repeated pairings of a conditioned stimulus and a neutral stimulus, the second neutral stimulus becomes a conditioned stimulus as well.

FIGURE 5.1
Higher Order Conditioning
Once a learned association has been made through classical conditioning, the new conditioned stimulus can be used to acquire new learned associations.

Here, when a conditioned stimulus (such as a bell that now triggers salivation) is repeatedly paired with a neutral stimulus (NS) such as a flashing light, the dog will learn to salivate in response to the light—without food ever being present! These multiple layers of learning help us understand how humans learn associations between many different stimuli. Jack Russell terrier: Thinkstock; Bell: Thinkstock; Dog bowl: Thinkstock

Humans also learn to salivate when presented with stimuli that signal the delivery of food. Next time you are really hungry and begin to open the wrapper of your favorite granola bar or energy snack, notice what's going on inside your mouth. You have come to associate the wrapper (CS) with the food (US), leading you to salivate (CR) at the unwrapping of the bar. Or perhaps your mouth begins to water when you prepare food, or when you are exposed to stimuli associated with making food. Let's say your nightly routine includes making dinner during television commercial breaks. Initially, the commercials are neutral stimuli, but you may have gotten into the habit of preparing food only during those breaks. Making your food (CS) causes you to salivate (CR), and because dinner preparation always happens during commercials, those commercials will eventually have the power to make you salivate (CR) as well, even in the absence of food. Here we have an example of higher order conditioning, wherein additional stimuli elicit the CR.

Classical conditioning is not limited to examples of salivation. It affects you in ways you may not even realize. Think of what happens to your heart rate, for example, when you walk into a room where you have had a bad experience. See Table 5.1 on page 199 for some additional real-life applications of classical conditioning. Now let's observe how classical conditioning might apply to Ivonne's experiences.

From Dogs to People: Extending Pavlov's Understanding

Getting in the water has always made Ivonne uneasy, making her muscles tighten and her heart pump faster. She experiences this physiological fear response (the UR) because she feels disoriented when her ears, which she uses for navigation, are submerged. This disorientation would be considered the *unconditioned stimulus* (US). During a period of acquisition, Ivonne begins to associate the smell of chlorine (a neutral stimulus) with the disorientation she feels (US) while swimming. Every time she goes to the pool, the odor of chlorine is in the air. With repeated pairings of the chlorine smell and the disorientation she feels when swimming, the neutral stimulus becomes linked with the US. Now, simply catching wind of chlorine evokes the same physiological response as the disorientation she feels when in the water. The chlorine odor goes from being a *neutral stimulus* to a *conditioned stimulus* that elicits the now *conditioned response* of her fear reaction.

Now let's explore a more hypothetical situation. If Ivonne were to smell dishes rinsed in a bleach solution or chlorine-smelling household cleaners, she might have a *CR*, suggesting *stimulus generalization* has occurred. This explains how we can react in

conditioned taste aversion A form of classical conditioning that occurs when an organism learns to associate the taste of a particular food or drink with illness.

adaptive value The degree to which a trait or behavior helps an organism survive.

ways that make no sense whatsoever to us; Ivonne may wonder to herself why she is reacting so strongly to those dishes.

Stimulus discrimination also applies to Ivonne's example. A gym locker room is filled with all sorts of odors: hair spray, shampoo, and sweaty socks, just to mention a few. Of all the scents in the locker room, chlorine is the only one that gets her heart racing. The fact that Ivonne can single out this one odor even when bombarded with multiple other smells and sounds demonstrates her ability to differentiate the CS from other extraneous stimuli.

It would be nice for Ivonne if the smell of chlorine no longer made her heart race. There are two ways that she could get rid of this classically conditioned response. First, she could stop swimming for a very long time, and the association might just fade away through *extinction.* But quite often avoidance does not extinguish a classically conditioned response, as the possibility of spontaneous recovery always exists. (Recovery in this sense means recovering the conditioned response of fear, not the more familiar sense of "getting better.") And clearly, this approach is not practical for Ivonne.

The second option is to pair a new response with the US or the CS. For example, Ivonne could practice relaxation skills and positive race visualization that includes a successful completion of the swim, until swimming itself no longer triggers the anxiety. With this accomplished, the chlorine would cease to stir up anxiety as well. Alternatively, Ivonne could work on her response to chlorine by gradually exposing herself to the smell while staying in a state of relaxation, thus preventing the learned anxiety and fear response. In Chapter 14, we will see how these techniques are actually used in therapy to help individuals struggling with anxiety and fear.

Yuck: Conditioned Taste Aversion

> **LO 5** Summarize how classical conditioning is dependent on the biology of the organism.

Have you ever experienced food poisoning? After falling ill from something you ate, whether it was sushi, uncooked chicken, or tainted peanut butter, you probably steered clear of that particular food for a while. This is an example of **conditioned taste aversion,** a *powerful* form of classical conditioning that occurs when an organism learns to associate the taste of a particular food or drink with illness. A grizzly bear avoids poisonous berries after vomiting all day from eating them. Often it only takes a single pairing between a food and a bad feeling—that is, one-trial learning—for an organism to learn its lesson. In the case of the bear, the US is the poison in the berries; the UR is the vomiting. After acquisition, the CS would be the sight of the berries, and the CR would be a nauseous feeling, as well as avoiding the berries in the future.

Avoiding foods that induce sickness has **adaptive value,** meaning it helps organisms survive, upping the odds they will reproduce and pass their genes along to the next generation. According to the evolutionary perspective, humans and other animals have a powerful drive to ensure that they and their offspring reach reproductive age, so it's critical to steer clear of tastes that have been associated with illness.

RATS WITH BELLYACHES American psychologist John Garcia and his colleagues provided a demonstration of taste aversion in their well-known studies with laboratory rats (Garcia, Ervin, & Koelling, 1966). Garcia and the other researchers designed a series of experiments to explore how rats respond to eating and drinking foods associated with sickness. In one study, the researchers provided the animals with flavored water followed by injections of a drug that upset their stomachs. The animals rejected the flavored drink thereafter.

Smells Like Chlorine
Although Ivonne has now completed over 20 triathlons, she is not particularly comfortable with the swimming portion of the event. Just smelling chlorinated pool water makes her heart beat faster and her muscles tense—physiological responses resulting from classical conditioning. How might this reaction be eliminated? If Ivonne were to stay away from the pool for some period of time, the association between the chlorine smell and the disorientation she feels in the water may fade in a process called extinction. Michael S. Wirtz, Used with permission of *Philadelphia Inquirer.* Copyright © 2013. All rights reserved.

CONNECTIONS

In **Chapter 1,** we introduced the *evolutionary perspective,* which suggests that adaptive behaviors and traits are shaped by *natural selection.* Here, the evolutionary perspective helps clarify why some types of learning are so powerful. In the case of conditioned taste aversion, species gain an evolutionary advantage through quick and efficient learning about poisonous foods.

Here's an example with humans: Imagine that you eat a foot-long hot dog a few hours before coming down with a stomach virus that's coincidentally spreading throughout your school. The hot dog wasn't the culprit—and you might even be aware of this—but the thought of eating another one would probably still make you feel sick. Physical experiences like this can sometimes be so strong that they override our knowledge of the facts.

The rats in Garcia's studies seemed naturally inclined to link their "internal malaise" (sick feeling) to tastes and smells and less likely to associate the nausea to other types of stimuli related to their hearing or vision, such as noises or things they saw (Garcia et al., 1966). This is clearly an adaptive trait, because nausea typically results from ingesting food that is poisonous or spoiled. In order to survive, an animal must be able to recognize and shun the tastes of dangerous substances. Garcia's research highlights the importance of **biological preparedness,** the predisposition or inclination of animals (including people) to form associations through classical conditioning. Now, let's examine how conditioned taste aversion can be used to save endangered species.

didn't SEE that coming

Rescuing Animals with Classical Conditioning

Using your newfound knowledge of conditioned taste aversion, imagine how you might solve the following problem: An animal is in trouble in Australia. The northern quoll, a meat-eating marsupial that might be described as a cute version of an opossum, is critically endangered because a nonnative "cane toad" is invading its territory. Cane toads may look delicious (at least to the quolls, who eat them right up), but they pack a lethal dose of poison—often enough to kill a quoll in just one eating. Wherever the toads have settled, quoll populations have diminished or disappeared (O'Donnell, Webb, & Shine, 2010). The quolls are now in danger of becoming extinct. How would you save them, using your knowledge of conditioned taste aversion?

EATING A POISONOUS TOAD CAN TAKE A QUOLL!

Remember that conditioned taste aversion occurs when an organism rejects a food or drink after consuming it and becoming very sick. To condition the quolls to stop eating the toxic toads, you must teach them to associate the little amphibians with a tummyache. You could do this by feeding them toads with the poisonous parts removed, but laced with a nausea-causing drug. A group of researchers from the University of Sydney recently used this approach with the quolls, and the strategy turned out to be quite successful. Quolls that were submitted to conditioned taste aversion were less likely than their unconditioned comrades to eat the poisonous toads and die (O'Donnell et al., 2010).

Similar approaches are being tried across the world. In Africa, researchers have found that conditioned taste aversion makes lions avoid beef. Dining on cattle is a

Learning to the Rescue Australia's northern quoll (left) is threatened by the introduction of an invasive species known as the cane toad (right). The quolls eat the toads, which carry a lethal dose of poison, but they can learn to avoid this toxic prey through conditioned taste aversion (O'Donnell et al., 2010). left: Eric and David Hosking/CORBIS; right: Chris Mattison/FLPA/ Science Source risky business for African lions, which often get killed by farmers trying to protect their livelihood (Platt, 2011, December 27). Faced with a similar problem, the U.S. Fish and Wildlife Service is using taste aversion to discourage endangered Mexican wolves from feasting on livestock in New Mexico and Arizona (Bryan, 2012, January 28). ☉!

As you see, **lessons** learned by psychologists working in a lab can have far-reaching consequences. The principles of psychology may even be used to manipulate the immune system.

from the pages of SCIENTIFIC AMERICAN

The Taste of Immune Suppression

An unusual flavor trains the brain to dampen the immune system

More than 100 years ago Ivan Pavlov famously observed that a dog salivated not only when fed but also on hearing a stimulus it associated with food. Since then, scientists have discovered many other seemingly autonomous processes that can be trained with sensory stimuli—including, most recently, our immune system.

Researchers have long been able to train an animal's immune system to respond to a nonpathogen stimulus. Pavlov's students even did so in the early 20th century, but the famous dogs overshadowed their work. Then, in the 1970s, researchers trained rats and mice to associate a taste, such as sugar water, with an immunosuppressive drug. They found that after repeated conditioning, ingesting the sugar water alone could tamp down the animals' immune response.

In 2002 a small study showed that the effect could be replicated in humans—at least on a onetime basis. By then, this training had already been used to prolong the survival of rats with heart transplants and slow the progression of lupus, arthritis and other autoimmune disorders in lab animals. But could human immune systems be trained to mimic a drug again and again?

"If it can be done only once, that's a very nice phenomenon for understanding the relation between the brain and the immune system," says Manfred Schedlowski, a medical psychologist at the University of Duisberg-Essen in Germany and a co-author of the 2002 paper. "But that's clinically useless." Last year Schedlowski published a study in the journal *Brain, Behavior, and Immunity* that aimed to find out whether the trained immunosuppressive response in humans could be sustained.

Thirty-two subjects were fed a green-colored, lavender-scented strawberry milk—an odd concoction designed to taste unique. For three days in a row, about half the subjects took an immunosuppressive drug along with the drink, whereas the other half took a placebo pill. After five days and then again another 11 days later, all the participants received a placebo pill along with the strawberry milk. Both times the immune systems of the experimental group were significantly inhibited after drinking the milk—as shown by levels of immunoresponsive molecules in their blood—whereas the control group was practically unchanged.

The study showed for the first time that learned immunosuppression can be recalled more than once in human subjects—encouraging news for patients on immunosuppressive regimens who must deal with the dangerous long-term side effects, such as high blood pressure and kidney failure. Although the researchers still need to figure out how to strengthen the conditioned effect and determine how long it will last, they hope one day to significantly reduce dosages of these drugs—and supplant them with harmless green milk and placebos.   Lauren F. Friedman. Reproduced with permission.

Little Albert and Conditioned Emotional Response

▶ **LO 6**   Evaluate the Little Albert study and explain how fear can be learned.

So far, we have focused on the classical conditioning of physical responses—salivation, nausea, and increased heart rate. We have also described some of the emotional reactions classical conditioning can produce, through the pairing of a stimulus with an emotional response. We call this a **conditioned emotional response:** an emotional reaction acquired via classical conditioning.

biological preparedness The tendency for animals to be predisposed or inclined to form associations.

conditioned emotional response An emotional reaction acquired through classical conditioning; process by which an emotional reaction becomes associated with a previously neutral stimulus.

Poor Albert

"Little Albert" was an 11-month-old baby who developed a fear of rats through his participation in an ethically questionable experiment by John B. Watson and Rosalie Rayner (Watson & Rayner, 1920). Watson and Rayner repeatedly showed the child a rat while terrifying him with a loud banging sound. Albert quickly learned to associate the sight of the rat with the scary noise, and his resulting fear of rats is known as a conditioned emotional response.
Archives of the History of American Psychology, The Center for the History of Psychology, The University of Akron

One famous illustration of conditioned emotional response is the classic "Little Albert" study by John B. Watson and Rosalie Rayner (Watson & Rayner, 1920). Little Albert was an 11-month-old baby who initially had no fear of rats. When he saw the white rats scurrying about Watson and Rayner's lab, he didn't seem the least bit scared. In fact, he was rather intrigued and sometimes would reach out to touch them. But all this changed when the researchers began making a loud sound (a US for a fear response in younger children) every time he reached for the rat by banging a hammer against a steel bar (Harris, 1979). (This type of study would be considered unethical by today's standards and would consequently not be allowed at research institutions.) After seven pairings of the loud noise and the appearance of the rat, Little Albert began to fear rats and generalized this fear to other furry objects, including a sealskin coat and a rabbit (Harris, 1979).

Let's use the Little Albert example to review the terminology of classical conditioning. When Little Albert heard the loud bang, it was an unconditioned stimulus (US) that elicited fear, the unconditioned response (UR). Through conditioning, the sight of the rat became paired with the loud noise, and thus the rat went from being a *neutral stimulus* to a conditioned stimulus (CS). Little Albert's fear of the rat became a conditioned response (CR).

Nobody really knows much about what happened to Little Albert after he spent time as Watson and Rayner's research subject. Some psychologists believe Little Albert's true identity is still unknown (Powell, 2010; Reese, 2010). More recent evidence suggests his real identity was Douglas Merritte, who at age 6 died of hydrocephalus (Harris, 2011), leaving us uncertain about the long-term effects of his exposure to this type of unethical conditioning.

Real-Life Examples of Classical Conditioning

The Little Albert study would never happen today; at least, we hope it wouldn't. Today's psychologists conduct research according to stringent ethical guidelines, and instilling terror in an innocent baby would not be considered acceptable. However, it is not too far out to imagine a similar scenario playing out in real life. Imagine a toddler who is about to reach for a rat on the kitchen floor. The parent sees this happening and shouts "NO!" It would not take many pairings of the toddler reaching for the rat and the parent shouting for the child to develop a fear of the rat. In this real-world scenario, you would be hard-pressed to find someone who would say the parent's behavior was unethical.

How does classical conditioning affect your own life? Perhaps you know a dog or cat that starts to salivate every time you turn on an electric can opener. It doesn't matter if you are opening a can of tuna fish, black beans, or coffee; the pet starts salivating (the CR) in anticipation of eating. The sound of the can opener is a neutral stimulus to begin with, but becomes a conditioned stimulus (CS) through repeated pairings with food (the US). Here's another example: Have you ever been taking a shower when someone flushes a toilet in a nearby bathroom? Depending on the plumbing in a building, flushing can divert cold water away from the shower, making the stream blistering hot for a few seconds. The first time you hear the toilet flush (neutral stimulus) and the water temperature rises (US), you might not make a connection. But after getting burned a few times and jerking away from the stream of water (UR), you begin to associate the sound of the toilet flushing (CS) with the unpleasant heat. Now, whenever you're in the shower and hear the toilet flush, you flinch in anticipation (CR).

CLASSICAL CONDITIONING: DO YOU BUY IT?

Classical conditioning may also have applications in marketing and sales (**TABLE 5.1**). Some research suggests that advertisements might instill emotions and attitudes toward product brands through classical conditioning, and that these responses can linger as long as 3 weeks (Grossman & Till, 1998). In one study, participants were shown pictures of pleasant scenes, such as tropical scenery, a snow-covered mountain, and a panda in a natural setting, paired with a fictitious mouthwash brand. Participants who were exposed to pairings of the fictitious brand of mouthwash (originally a neutral stimulus) and the favorable pictures (the US) were more likely to retain a positive enduring attitude (now the CR) toward the mouthwash (which became a CS) than participants who were exposed to the same pictures in random order. In other words, the researchers were able to create "favorable attitudes" toward the fictitious brand of mouthwash by pairing pictures of the mouthwash with scenery that induced positive emotions. The study did not address whether this favorable attitude leads to a purchase, however.

Do you think you are susceptible to this kind of conditioning? We would venture to say that we all are. Complete the following Try This to see if we are correct.

Does Sexy Sell?
Reality TV icon Kim Kardashian performs in a salad commercial for Carl's Jr. Restaurant. Research suggests that advertisements may instill attitudes toward brands through classical conditioning (Grossman & Till, 1998), but how do these attitudes affect sales? Now that is a question worth researching. Doria Anselmo/Carls Jr/Splash/Newscom

Classical conditioning is used in marketing to instill positive emotions and attitudes toward product brands. List examples of recent advertisements you have seen on television or the Internet that use this approach to get people to buy products. Which of your recent purchases were influenced by this type of ad?

try this

Table 5.1   REAL-LIFE EXAMPLES OF CLASSICAL CONDITIONING

Type	Pairing of Neutral and US	Expected Response
Advertising	Repeated pairing of products such as automobiles (neutral stimulus) with celebrities (US)	Automatic response to celebrity (UR), such as sexual response, heart racing, desire; pairing leads to similar response, such as sexual response, heart racing, desire (CR) to the product (CS).
Fears	Pairing of a dog lunging (US) at you on the street (neutral stimulus) where you take your morning run	Automatic response to the dog lunging at you is fear or startle (UR); pairing leads to similar response of fear (CR) to the street (CS) where the dog lives.
	One pairing of seeing a car in the rear-view mirror (neutral stimulus) and being rear-ended by that car (US)	Automatic response to the impact of the collision leads to a fear response (UR); with one pairing, the sight of a car approaching in the rearview mirror (CS) elicits a fearful reaction (CR).
Fetishes	Repeated pairings of originally nonsexual objects like shoes (neutral stimuli) and sexual activity (US)	Automatic response to sexual activity (UR) is sexual arousal, leading to an association of sexual pleasure (CR) with objects such as shoes or undergarments (CS).
Romance	Repeated pairings of a cologne (neutral stimulus) with your romantic partner (US)	Automatic response to your feelings for your partner is sexual arousal (UR); paired with the cologne (CS), leads to sexual arousal (CR).

The implications of classical conditioning extend far beyond salivating dogs. These are just a few examples of how this form of learning impacts human life.

Remember that classical conditioning is a type of learning associated with automatic (or involuntary) behaviors. You don't "learn" to go out and buy a particular brand of mouthwash through classical conditioning. Classical conditioning can influence our attitudes toward products, but it can't teach us voluntary behaviors. Well then, how do we learn these deliberate behaviors? Read on.

✓○○○ show what you know

1. A mother takes her 2-year-old son to the doctor for immunizations. The child sees a nurse approaching with a stethoscope around her neck. She gives him a shot and he automatically starts crying. After that, every time the boy sees anyone wearing a stethoscope, he starts to cry. Which of the following is the conditioned stimulus?

   a. the shot
   b. crying
   c. the stethoscope
   d. the mother

2. Because of _____, animals and people are predisposed or inclined to form associations that increase their chances of survival.

3. Hot dogs were once your favorite food, but ever since you ate a foot-long hot dog tainted with salmonella (which causes food poisoning), you cannot smell or taste one without feeling nauseous. Which of the following is the unconditioned stimulus?

   a. salmonella
   b. nausea
   c. hotdogs
   d. the hotdog stand

4. Watson and Rayner used classical conditioning to instill fear in Little Albert. Create a diagram of the neutral stimulus, US, UR, CS, and CR used in their experiment with Little Albert.

✓ CHECK YOUR ANSWERS IN APPENDIX C.

Operant Conditioning

▶**Rising Star**
Jeremy Lin appears on a 2012 cover of *Sports Illustrated*. This rookie player amazed the world on February 4 of that same year when he came off the bench and led the New York Knicks to victory against the New Jersey Nets. It was the beginning of a Lin-led winning streak—the beginning of "Linsanity."
Sports Illustrated/Getty Images

THE JEREMY LIN SHOW Madison Square Garden, February 4, 2012: The New York Knicks are playing their third game in three nights, hoping to end a losing streak. But they are already trailing far behind the New Jersey Nets in the first quarter. That's when Jeremy Lin, a third-string point guard who is dangerously close to being cut from his third NBA team, bounds off the bench and leads the Knicks to a stunning victory. By the end of the game, the crowd is going crazy, the Knicks players are laughing like giddy schoolboys, and the Pearl Jam song "Jeremy" reverberates through the stadium (Beck, 2012, February 4; Dalrymple, 2012). One commentator perfectly sums up the state of affairs: "It's the Jeremy Lin Show here at Madison Square Garden" (Dalrymple, 2012, p. 24).

Jeremy Lin was an overnight sensation. People around the world were fascinated by him for many reasons. He was the fourth Asian American player in NBA history; he was the first Harvard graduate to play in the league since the 1950s; and he had previously been a benchwarmer, who was not even drafted out of college (Beck, 2011, December 28). Everyone was asking the same question: Would Jeremy be a one-game wonder or something bigger?

Jeremy ended up leading the Knicks through a seven-game victory spree, the highlights of which included scoring 38 points against the Los Angeles Lakers—he scored more points in that game than the Lakers' mighty Kobe Bryant (ESPN.com, 2012, February 10). Suddenly, Jeremy's face was everywhere—on the covers of *TIME Magazine* and *Sports Illustrated* (twice) and all over the Internet. More people were typing "Jeremy Lin" into Google than "Tiger Woods" or "David Beckham" (Dalrymple, 2012, p. xv; Google, 2012, February 15).

Where did this guy come from? Like any of us, Jeremy is a unique blend of nature and nurture. He was blessed with a hearty helping of physical capabilities (nature), such as speed, agility, and coordination. But he was also shaped by the circumstances of his life (nurture). This second category is where learning comes in. ▼ Let's find out how.

Operant Conditioning and the Law of Effect

When Jeremy started Palo Alto High School, he was about 5′3″ and 125 pounds—not exactly NBA material. During his sophomore year, he learned to dunk, and by senior year, he was over 6 feet tall and leading his team to victory in the Division II state championship (Dalrymple, 2012; Tennis, 2012, February 19). Jeremy was a big fish in a small pond—so big that he didn't need to work very hard to maintain his level of success. However, college recruiters did not observe anything exceptional in his strength or overall athleticism (Viera, 2012, February 12). This may be the reason Jeremy did not receive any athletic scholarship offers from Division 1 colleges, despite his hoops prowess and 4.2 grade point average (McGregor, 2012, February 15; Spears, 2012, February 18).

Things changed when Jeremy found himself in a bigger pond, playing basketball at Harvard University. That's when Coach Diepenbrock says the young player began working harder on aspects of practice he didn't particularly enjoy, such as weight lifting, ball handling, and conditioning. After being picked up by the NBA, Jeremy's diligence soared to a new level. While playing with the Golden State Warriors, he would eat breakfast at the team's training facility by 8:30 A.M., three and a half hours before practice. "Then, all of sudden, you'd hear a ball bouncing on the floor," Keith Smart, a former coach told *The New York Times* (Beck, 2012, February 24). Between NBA seasons, Jeremy returned to his alma mater Palo Alto High School to run track workouts with Diepenbrock. He also trained with a shooting coach and spent "an inordinate amount of time" honing his shot (P. Diepenbrock, personal communication, May 21, 2012).

Jeremy's persistence paid off. The once-scrawny scrapper, now 6′3″ and 200 pounds (ESPN.com, 2013), is exploding with power and agility. According to Diepenbrock, "He has gotten to the point where now, as far as the strength and the athleticism, he is on par—or good enough—with veteran NBA athletes" (personal communication, May 21, 2012).

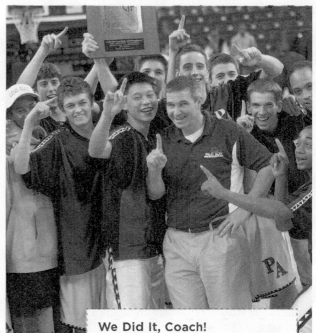

We Did It, Coach!
Jeremy and his teammates from Palo Alto High School celebrate a victory that led them to the 2006 state finals. Pictured in the center is Coach Peter Diepenbrock, who has maintained a friendship with Jeremy since he graduated. Prior to Jeremy's sensational season with the Knicks, Diepenbrock helped him with his track workouts. Keith Peters/Palo Alto Weekly

OPERANT CONDITIONING   What has kept Jeremy working so hard all these years? Psychologists might attribute Jeremy's ongoing efforts to **operant conditioning,** a type of learning in which people or animals come to associate their voluntary actions with their consequences. Whether pleasant or unpleasant, the effects of a behavior influence future actions. Think about some of the consequences of Jeremy's training—short-term results like seeing his free throw shot improve, and long-term rewards like victory, fame, and fortune. How do you think these outcomes might have shaped (and continue to shape) Jeremy's behavior? Before addressing this question, we need to take a closer look at operant conditioning.

LO 7   Describe Thorndike's law of effect.

THORNDIKE AND HIS CATS   One of the first scientists to objectively study the effect of consequences on behavior was American psychologist Edward Thorndike (1874–1949). Thorndike's early research focused on chicks and other animals, many of which he kept in his apartment. But after an incubator almost caught fire, his landlady insisted he get rid of the chicks (Hothersall, 2004). It was in the lab that Thorndike conducted his research on cats. His most famous experimental setup involved putting a cat in a latched cage called a "puzzle box" and planting enticing pieces of fish outside the door. When first placed in the box, the cat would

You Asked, Coach Diepenbrock Answers

http://qrs.ly/o83m611

What is your favorite memory of Jeremy?

operant conditioning Learning that occurs when voluntary actions become associated with their consequences.

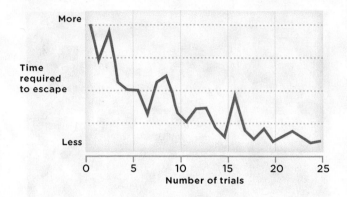

More

Time
required
to escape

Less

0   5   10   15   20   25

Number of trials

▲ **FIGURE 5.2**
Puzzle Box
Early psychologist Edward Thorndike
conducted his well-known cat experiments
using "puzzle boxes" like the one shown
here. At the start of the experiment,
Thorndike's cats pawed around haphazardly
until they managed to unlatch the cage and
then eat the fish treats outside the door. As
the trials wore on, the felines learned to free
themselves more and more quickly. After
several trials, the amount of time needed to
escape the box dropped significantly (see
graph above). Thorndike attributed this
phenomenon to the law of effect, which
states that behaviors are more likely to
reoccur if they are followed by pleasurable
outcomes. *Source:* Adapted from Thorndike, 1898.

law of effect Thorndike's principle
stating that behaviors are more likely to
be repeated when followed by pleasurable
outcomes, and those followed by something
unpleasant are less likely to be repeated.

reinforcers Consequences, such as events
or objects, that increase the likelihood of a
behavior reoccurring.

reinforcement Process by which an
organism learns to associate a voluntary
behavior with its consequences.

behaviorism The scientific study of
observable behavior.

shaping The use of reinforcers to guide
behavior to the acquisition of a desired,
complex behavior.

successive approximations A method
of shaping that uses reinforcers to condition
a series of small steps that gradually
approach the target behavior.

scratch and paw around randomly, but after a while, just by chance, it would pop
the latch, causing the door to release. The cat would then escape the cage to devour
the fish (**FIGURE 5.2**). The next time the cat was put in the box, it would repeat this
random activity, scratching and pawing with no particular direction. And again,
just by chance, the cat would pop the latch that released the door and freed it to
eat the fish. Each time the cat was returned to the box, the number of random
activities decreased until eventually it was able to break free almost immediately
(Thorndike, 1898).

We should highlight a few important issues relating to this early research. First,
these cats discovered the solution to the puzzle box accidentally, while exhibiting their
naturally occurring behaviors (scratching and exploring). So, they initially obtained
the fish treat by accident. The other important point to note is that the measure of
learning was not an exam or basketball shoot-off; instead, the amount of time it took
the cats to break free was the measure of learning.

The cats' behavior, Thorndike reasoned, could be explained by the **law of effect,**
which says that a behavior (opening the latch) is more likely to happen again when
followed by a pleasurable outcome (delicious fish). Behaviors that lead to pleasurable
outcomes will be repeated, while behaviors that don't lead to pleasurable outcomes
(or are followed by something unpleasant) will not be repeated. The law of effect is
not limited to cats, however. When was the last time your behavior changed because
of a pleasurable outcome that followed?

Most contemporary psychologists would call the fish in Thorndike's experiments
reinforcers, because the fish increased the likelihood that the preceding behavior
(escaping the cage) would occur again. Reinforcers are consequences that follow
behaviors, and they are a key component of operant conditioning. Our daily lives
abound with examples of reinforcers. Praise, hugs, good grades, enjoyable food, and
attention are all reinforcers that increase the probability the behaviors they follow will
be repeated. Through the process of **reinforcement,** an organism's behaviors become
more frequent. A child praised for sharing a toy is more likely to share in the future.
A student who studies hard to earn an A on an exam is more likely to prepare well
for upcoming exams.

Behaviorism and the Shaping of Behavior

Some of the earliest and most influential research on operant conditioning came out of the lab of B. F. Skinner (1904–1990), an American psychologist. Like Pavlov, Skinner had not planned to study learning. Upon graduating from college, Skinner decided to become a writer and a poet, but after a year of trying his hand at writing, he decided he "had nothing to say" (Skinner, 1976). Around this time, he began to read the work of Watson and Pavlov, which inspired him to pursue a graduate degree in psychology. He enrolled at Harvard, took some psychology classes that he found "dull," and eventually joined a lab in the Department of Biology, where he could study the subject he found most intriguing: animal behavior.

Skinner was devoted to **behaviorism,** which is the scientific study of observable behavior. Behaviorists believed that psychology could only be considered a "true science" if it was based on the study of behaviors that could be seen and documented. In relation to learning, Skinner and other behaviorists proposed that *all* of an organism's behaviors—all acts, thoughts, and feelings—are shaped by factors in the external environment.

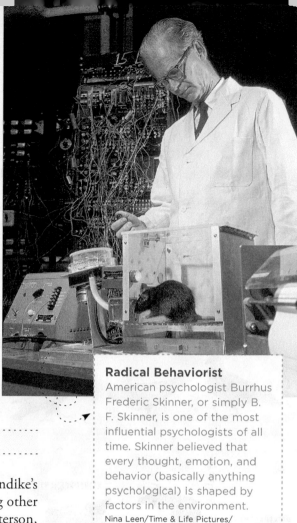

Radical Behaviorist
American psychologist Burrhus Frederic Skinner, or simply B. F. Skinner, is one of the most influential psychologists of all time. Skinner believed that every thought, emotion, and behavior (basically anything psychological) is shaped by factors in the environment.
Nina Leen/Time & Life Pictures/Getty Images

···▶ **LO 8**   Explain shaping and the method of successive approximations.

SHAPING AND SUCCESSIVE APPROXIMATIONS   Building on Thorndike's law of effect and Watson's approach to research, Skinner demonstrated, among other things, that rats can learn to push levers and pigeons can learn to bowl (Peterson, 2004). Since animals can't be expected to immediately perform such complex behaviors, Skinner employed **shaping,** the use of reinforcers to change behaviors through small steps toward a desired behavior (see **INFOGRAPHIC 5.2** on page 204). Skinner used shaping to teach a rat to "play basketball" (by dropping a marble through a hole) and pigeons how to "bowl" (by nudging the ball). As you can see in the photo on this page, Skinner placed the animals in chambers, or "*Skinner boxes,*" which were outfitted with food dispensers the animals could activate (by pecking a target or pushing on a lever, for instance) and recording equipment to monitor these behaviors. These boxes allowed Skinner to conduct carefully controlled experiments, measuring behaviors precisely and advancing the scientific and systematic study of behavior.

You may be wondering how Skinner was able to teach pigeons to bowl. The first task was to break the bowling lessons into small steps that pigeons could accomplish. Next, he introduced reinforcers as consequences for behaviors that came closer and closer to achieving the desired goal—bowling a strike! Choosing the right increments for the behaviors was crucial for the success of his experiment. If his expectations started too high, the pigeons would never be given any reinforcers. If his expectations were too low, the pigeons would get reinforcers for everything they did—and again would be unable to make the critical connection between desired behavior and reward. So Skinner devised a plan such that every time the animals did something that brought them a step closer to completing the desired behavior, they would get a reinforcer (usually food). The first reward might be given for simply looking at the ball; the second might be given for bending down and touching it; and the third, for nudging the ball with their beaks. Since each incremental change in behavior brings the birds closer to accomplishing the larger goal of bowling, this method is called shaping by **successive approximations.** By the end of the experiment, the pigeons were repeatedly driving balls down miniature alleys, knocking down pins with a swipe of the beak (Peterson, 2004).

Synonym
Skinner boxes operant chambers

Learning Through Operant Conditioning

Operant conditioning is a type of learning in which we associate our voluntary actions with the consequences of those actions. For example, a pigeon naturally pecks things. But if every time the pigeon pecks a ball, he is given a *reinforcer,* the pigeon will soon learn to peck the ball more frequently.

B. F. Skinner showed that operant conditioning could do more than elicit simple, isolated actions. Through the process of *shaping,* in which reinforcers are used to change behaviors toward a more complex behavior, Skinner taught his pigeons to perform behaviors involving a series of actions, like bowling and tennis. Today, shaping is used routinely by parents, teachers, coaches, and employers to train all kinds of complex behaviors.

SKINNER'S EXPERIMENT: TRAIN A PIGEON TO PLAY TENNIS

Pigeon is rewarded with seeds for pecking the ball.

peck **REINFORCEMENT**

reinforcement with seeds

Ball-pecking behavior increases.

peck **REINFORCEMENT** peck peck **REINFORCEMENT**

REINFORCEMENT

Now only the next step toward "tennis" is rewarded.

peck peck pushing the ball **REINFORCEMENT**

reinforcement with seeds

Ball-pushing behavior increases.

pushing the ball pushing the ball pushing the ball

REINFORCEMENT **REINFORCEMENT** **REINFORCEMENT**

After behavior has been shaped through reinforcement, the pigeon has learned to play tennis.

HAVE YOU BEEN TRAINED?

Not every child is born loving the healthy foods his parent offers. But shaping can help a child learn to eat his vegetables. Over a period of time, reinforcement is given for behaviors that are closer and closer to this goal. Can you think of anything that would be a reward for eating vegetables? Praise or the excitement of a contest may work in this way.

1 Child refuses to eat vegetables.

2 YES! Reinforced for touching fork

3 GOOD JOB! Now, reinforced for touching vegetables

4 After behavior has been shaped through reinforcement, the child has learned to eat his vegetables.

Successive approximations can also be used with humans, who are sometimes unwilling or unable to change problematic behaviors overnight. For example, psychologists have used successive approximation to change truancy behavior in adolescents (Enea & Dafinoiu, 2009). The truant teens were provided reinforcers for consistent attendance, but with small steps requiring increasingly more days in school.

It is amazing that the principles used for training animals can also be harnessed to keep teenagers in school. Is there anything operant conditioning *can't* accomplish?

THINK again

Chickens Can't Play Baseball

Rats can be conditioned to press levers; pigeons can be trained to bowl; and—believe it or not—chickens can learn to dance and play the piano (Breland & Breland, 1951). Keller and Marian Breland, a pair of Skinner's students, managed to train 6,000 animals not only to boogie but also to vacuum, dine at a table, and play sports and musical instruments (Breland & Breland, 1961). But as hard as they tried, the Brelands could not coax a chicken to play baseball.

Here's a rundown of what happened: The Brelands placed a chicken in a cage adjacent to a scaled down "baseball field," where it had access to a loop attached to a baseball bat. If the chicken managed to swing the bat hard enough to send the ball into the outfield, a food reward was delivered at the other end of the cage. Off the bird would go, running toward its meal dispenser like a baseball player sprinting to first base—or so the routine was supposed to go. But as soon as the Brelands took away the cage, the chicken behaved nothing like a baseball player; instead, it madly chased and pecked at the ball (Breland & Breland, 1961).

How did the Brelands explain the chickens' behavior? They believed that the birds were demonstrating **instinctive drift**, the tendency for instinct to undermine conditioned behaviors. A chicken's pecking, for example, is an instinctive food-getting behavior. Pecking is useful for opening seeds or killing insects (Breland & Breland, 1961), but it won't help the bird get to first base. Animal behavior can be conditioned, but instinct can interfere with the process. 💬+

BASEBALL? NO. PIANO? YES.

Musical Bunny
Keller and Marian Breland observe one of their animal performers at the IQ Zoo in Hot Springs, Arkansas, circa 1960. Using the operant conditioning concepts they learned from B. F. Skinner, the Brelands trained ducks to play guitars, raccoons to shoot basketballs, and chickens to tell fortunes. But their animal "students" did not always cooperate; sometimes their instincts interfered with the conditioning process (Bihm, Gillaspy, Lammers, & Huffman, 2010). The Central Arkansas Library System/Courtesy of Bob Bailey

The examples above involve researchers deliberately shaping behaviors with reinforcers in a laboratory setting. Skinner and others believe behaviors are being shaped all of the time, whether in a laboratory or not. Think of all the factors in the environment that might be involved in shaping your behavior.

Acquisition to Extinction, and Everything in Between

Both operant and classical conditioning are forms of learning, and they share many common principles (**TABLE 5.2** on the next page). As with classical conditioning, behaviors learned through operant conditioning go through an *acquisition* phase. When Jeremy Lin was a sophomore in high school, he learned how to dunk a basketball. Similarly, the cats in Thorndike's puzzle boxes learned the skills they needed to break free. In both cases, the acquisition stage occurred through the gradual process of shaping. Using successive approximations, the learner acquires the new behavior over time.

Behaviors learned through operant conditioning are also subject to *extinction*—that is, they may fade in the absence of reinforcers. A rat in a Skinner box eventually gives

instinctive drift The tendency for animals to revert to instinctual behaviors after a behavior pattern has been learned.

Table 5.2   CONDITIONING BASICS

Term	Classical Conditioning	Operant Conditioning
The Link	Links different stimuli, often through repeated pairings.	Links behavior to its consequence, often through repeated pairings.
Response	Involuntary behavior.	Voluntary behavior.
Acquisition	The initial learning phase.	The initial learning phase.
Extinction	The process by which the conditioned response decreases after repeated exposure to the conditioned stimulus in the absence of the unconditioned stimulus.	The disappearance of a learned behavior through the removal of its reinforcer.
Spontaneous Recovery	Following extinction, with the presentation of the conditioned stimulus after a rest period, the conditioned response reappears.	Following extinction due to the absence of reinforcers, the behavior reemerges in a similar setting.

These fundamental learning concepts apply to both classical and operant conditioning.

up pushing on a lever if there is no longer a tasty reinforcer awaiting. But that same lever-pushing behavior can make a sudden comeback through *spontaneous recovery*. After a rest period, the rat returns to his box and reverts to his old lever-pushing ways.

Do you think the cats in Thorndike's experiments would stop trying to escape from the puzzle box if they stopped getting fish? Perhaps they would not, because escaping the confines of the box might be a reinforcer for them. We will return to the issue of what makes something a reinforcer a little later in this section.

STIMULUS GENERALIZATION AND DISCRIMINATION   With operant conditioning, stimulus generalization occurs when a previously learned response to one stimulus occurs in the presence of a similar stimulus. A rat is conditioned to push a particular type of lever, but it may push a variety of other lever types similar in shape, size, and/or color. Horses also show stimulus generalization. With successive approximations using a tasty oat-molasses grain reinforcer, a small sample of horses learned to push on a "rat lever" with their lips in response to the appearance of a solid black circle with a 2.5-inch diameter. After conditioning, the horses were presented with a variety of black circles of different diameters, and indeed stimulus generalization was evident; they pressed the lever most often when shown circles closer in size to the original (Dougherty & Lewis, 1991).

Stimulus discrimination is also at work in operant conditioning, as organisms can learn to discriminate between behaviors that do and do not result in reinforcement. With the use of reinforcers, turtles can learn to discriminate among black, white, and gray wooden paddles. A turtle was rewarded with morsels of meat for choosing the black paddle as opposed to the white, for example, and then subsequently chose the black paddle over other colored paddles (Leighty et al., 2013).

Stimulus discrimination even applies to basketball players. Jeremy Lin certainly has learned to discriminate between teammates and opponents. It's not likely that he would get reinforcement from the crowd if he mistook an opponent for a teammate and passed the ball to the other team. Making a perfect pass to a teammate,

You Asked, Coach Diepenbrock Answers

http://qrs.ly/6i3m619

What was Jeremy's biggest strength and weakness?

positive reinforcement The process by which pleasant reinforcers are added or presented following the targeted behavior, increasing the likelihood of it occurring again.

on the other hand, would likely earn approval. This brings us to the next topic, *positive reinforcement,* where we start to see how classical and operant conditioning differ.

LO 9   Identify the differences between positive and negative reinforcement.

POSITIVE REINFORCEMENT   We have already defined reinforcement as a process through which an organism learns to associate voluntary behaviors with their consequences. *Any* stimulus that increases a behavior is a reinforcer. What we haven't addressed yet is that reinforcers can be added or taken away. In the process of **positive reinforcement,** reinforcers are added or presented following the targeted behavior, and reinforcers in this case are generally pleasant (see Infographic 5.3 on p. 214). By presenting positive reinforcers following the target behavior, we are increasing the chances that the target behavior will occur again in the future. If the behavior doesn't increase after the stimulus is presented, that particular stimulus should not be considered a reinforcer. The fish treats that Thorndike's cats received immediately after escaping the puzzle box and the morsels of bird feed that Skinner's pigeons got for bowling are examples of positive reinforcement. In both cases, the reinforcers were *added* following the desired behavior and were pleasurable to the cats and pigeons.

There were also many potential positive reinforcers driving Jeremy Lin. The praise that his coaches gave him following his passing a ball to a teammate would be considered an example of positive reinforcement. Back in high school, Coach Diepenbrock rewarded players with stickers to provide feedback on their performance ("kind of middle schoolish," he admits, but effective nonetheless). Each game statistic was assigned a value (for example, +2 points for making an assist, −2 for missing a shot, and so on); the sum of the positive and negative numbers gave players a numerical rating of their performance (*Today I had a +5 game*). "[If] all your stats added up—the minuses and the pluses—and you ended up with a +20 or above, then you did very well," explains the coach, noting that Jeremy averaged the highest of any player ever (P. Diepenbrock, personal communication, May 21, 2012). Did the sticker system have an effect on Jeremy? Coach Diepenbrock cannot be certain, but if it did, seeing his sticker-filled poster every day would have served as a positive reinforcer for him to practice.

You may be wondering if this approach could be used in a college classroom setting. The answer would inevitably depend on the people involved. What is a positive reinforcer to one person might not act that way for another. Remember, the definition of a positive reinforcer depends on the organism's response to its presence (Skinner, 1953). You may love getting stickers, but your classmate may be offended by them. Thus, stickers could be a positive reinforcer for you, but not for your classmate. Keep in mind, not all positive reinforcers are positive in the sense that we think of them as pleasant; when we refer to *positive* reinforcement, we mean that something has been *added.* For example, if a child is starved for attention, any kind of attention (including a reprimand) would be experienced as a positive reinforcer; the attention is added. Every time the child misbehaves, she gets reprimanded, and reprimanding is a form of attention, which the child craves. The scolding just reinforces the misbehavior.

Good Work
Georgia preschool teacher Inyite (Shell) Adle-Ikor with a bouquet of roses. She is the recipient of the Early Childhood Educator Award and a $10,000 check from the international education organization Knowledge Universe. Awards and money often reinforce the behaviors they reward, but every individual responds differently to reinforcement. Craig Bromley/Getty Images for Knowledge Universe

NEGATIVE REINFORCEMENT We have established that behaviors can be increased or strengthened by the addition of a stimulus. But it is also possible to increase a behavior by taking something away. Behaviors can increase in response to **negative reinforcement,** through the process of *taking away* (or subtracting) something unpleasant. Skinner used negative reinforcement to shape the behavior of his rats. The rats were placed in Skinner boxes with floors that delivered a continuous mild electric shock—except when the animals pushed on a lever. The animals would begin the experiment scampering around the floors to escape the electric current, but every once in a while they would accidentally hit the lever and turn off the current. Eventually, they learned to associate pushing the lever with the removal of the unpleasant stimulus (the mild electric shock). After several trials, the rats would push the lever immediately, reducing the amount of time being shocked.

Remember that either category of reinforcement—positive or negative—has the effect of increasing a desired behavior. Think about some examples of negative reinforcement in your own life. If you try to drive your car without your seat belt, does your car make an annoying beeping sound? If so, the automakers have found a way to use negative reinforcement to *increase* your use of seat belts. The beeping provides an annoyance (an unpleasant stimulus) that will influence most people to quickly put on their seat belts (the desired behavior increases) to make the beeping stop, and thus remove the unpleasant stimulus. The next time you get in the car, you will put on your seat belt more quickly, having learned that the annoying sound goes away immediately after you do so. Another example is putting the lid on a garbage can to cover its awful smell. Here, the desired behavior is to put the lid on the can, and the unpleasant stimulus that goes away is the bad smell. Finally, think about a dog that constantly begs for treats. The begging (the annoying stimulus) stops the moment the dog is given a treat, a pattern that increases *your* treat-giving behavior. The problem is that the dog's begging behavior is being strengthened through positive reinforcement; the dog has learned that the more it begs, the more treats it receives.

Notice that with negative reinforcement, the target behaviors increase in order to remove an unwanted condition. Returning to our example of Jeremy Lin, how might a basketball coach use negative reinforcement to increase a behavior? Of course, the coach can't build an electric grid in the flooring (as Skinner did with his rats) to get his players moving faster. He might, however, start each practice session by whining and complaining (a very annoying stimulus) about how slow the players are. But as soon as their level of activity increases, he stops his annoying behavior. The players then learn to avoid the coach's whining and complaining simply by running faster and working harder at every practice. Thus, the removal of the annoying stimulus (whining and complaining) increases the desired behavior (running faster). Keep in mind that the goal of negative reinforcement is to *increase* a desired behavior. Try to remember this when you read the section on punishment.

LO 10 Distinguish between primary and secondary reinforcers.

PRIMARY AND SECONDARY REINFORCERS There are two major categories of reinforcers: primary and secondary. The food with which Skinner rewarded his pigeons and rats is considered a **primary reinforcer** (innate reinforcer), because it satisfies a biological need. Food, water, and physical contact are considered primary reinforcers (for both animals and people) because they meet essential requirements. Many of the reinforcers shaping human behavior are **secondary reinforcers,** which

negative reinforcement The removal of an unpleasant stimulus following a target behavior, which increases the likelihood of it occurring again.

primary reinforcer A reinforcer that satisfies a biological need, such as food, water, physical contact; innate reinforcer.

secondary reinforcer Reinforcers that do not satisfy biological needs but often gain their power through their association with primary reinforcers.

means they do not satisfy biological needs but often derive their power from their connection with primary reinforcers. Although money is not a primary reinforcer, we know from experience that it gives us access to primary reinforcers, such as food, a safe place to live, and perhaps even the ability to attract desirable mates. Thus, money is a secondary reinforcer. The list of secondary reinforcers is long and varied, because different people find different things and activities to be reinforcing. Listening to music, washing dishes, taking a ride in your car—these would all be considered secondary reinforcers for people who enjoy doing them. Ready for a tongue twister? A reinforcer is only a reinforcer if the person receiving it finds it reinforcing. In other words, the existence of a reinforcer depends on its ability to increase a target behavior.

Secondary reinforcers are also evident in social interactions. Think about how your behaviors might change in response to praise from a boss, a pat on the back from a co-worker, or even a nod of approval from a friend on Facebook or Twitter.

SOCIAL MEDIA and psychology

Contagious Behaviors

In some respects, the behavioral effects of social media are obvious. Why do you keep glancing at your Facebook ticker, and what compels you to check your phone 10 times an hour? All those little tweets and updates you receive are reinforcing. It feels good to be re-tweeted, and it's nice to see people "like" your wall posts and photo albums.

With its never-ending supply of mini-rewards, social media often sucks away time that would otherwise be devoted to offline relationships and work—a clear drawback. But the reinforcing power of social media can also be harnessed to promote positive behaviors. A study by MIT researcher Damon Centola found that people are more likely to explore healthy behaviors when alerted that people in their social media networks are doing the same. This is especially true for those in "clustered" networks, where people share many of the same contacts. As Centola observed: "People usually require contact with multiple sources of 'infection' before being convinced to adopt a behavior" (Centola, 2010, p. 1194). Each of these sources of infection, it seems, provides social reinforcement for the positive behavior. Thus, if you want to develop a more healthy lifestyle, it can't hurt to surround yourself with online friends who exercise, eat well, and don't smoke.

WHY DO YOU CHECK YOUR PHONE 10 TIMES AN HOUR?

Now that we have a basic understanding of operant conditioning, let's take things to the next level and examine its guiding principles. Many of the principles of classical conditioning (acquisition, stimulus generalization, extinction, etc.) also apply to operant conditioning. Let's find out how.

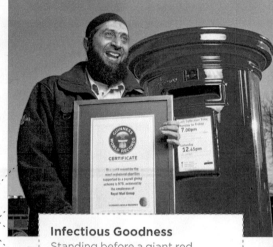

Infectious Goodness
Standing before a giant red mailbox, London postal worker Imtiyaz Chawan holds the Guinness World Records certificate. The Royal Mail Group's Payroll Giving Scheme incorporated a record-breaking 975 registered charities and causes (Guinness Book of World Records News, 2012, February 6). Charitable giving is the type of positive behavior that can spread through social networks. Many charities are now using social media for fundraising purposes. David Parry/PA Wire

The Power of Partial Reinforcement

LO 11 Describe continuous reinforcement and partial reinforcement.

A year after graduating from Stanford, Ivonne moved back to New York City and began looking for a new activity to get her outside and moving. She found the New York Road Runners Club, which connected her with an organization that supports and trains runners with all types of disabilities, including paraplegia, amputation,

For the Love of Running ◄----
Ivonne runs tethered to her husband, G. John Schmidt. She sets the pace, while he warns her of any changes in terrain, elevation, and direction. When Ivonne started running in 2001, her friends reinforced her with hot chocolate. These days, she doesn't need sweet treats to keep her coming back. The pleasure she derives from running is reinforcement enough. MICHAEL S. WIRTZ/The Inquirer/Daily News/Philly.com

Synonym

partial reinforcement intermittent reinforcement

continuous reinforcement A schedule of reinforcement in which every target behavior is reinforced.

partial reinforcement A schedule of reinforcement in which target behaviors are reinforced intermittently, not continuously.

partial reinforcement effect The tendency for behaviors acquired through intermittent reinforcement to be more resistant to extinction than those acquired through continuous reinforcement.

and cerebral palsy. Having no running experience (apart from jogging on a treadmill), Ivonne showed up at a practice one Saturday morning in Central Park and ran 2 miles with one of the running club's guides. The next week she came back for more, and then the next, and the next.

CONTINUOUS REINFORCEMENT When Ivonne first started attending practices, her teammates promised to buy her hot chocolate whenever she increased her distance. "Every time they would try to get me to run further, they'd say, 'We'll have hot chocolate afterwards!'" Ivonne remembers. "They actually would follow through with their promise too!" The hot chocolate was given in a schedule of **continuous reinforcement,** because the reinforcer was presented *every* time Ivonne ran a little farther. Continuous reinforcement can be used in a variety of settings: a child getting a sticker *every* time she practices the piano; a spouse getting praise *every* time she does the dishes; a dog getting a treat *every* time it comes when called. You get the commonality: reinforcement *every* time the behavior is produced.

PARTIAL REINFORCEMENT Continuous reinforcement comes in handy for a variety of purposes and is ideal for establishing new behaviors during the acquisition phase. But delivering reinforcers intermittently, or every once in a while, works better for maintaining behaviors. We call this approach **partial reinforcement.** Returning to the examples listed for continuous reinforcement, we can also imagine partial reinforcement being used in each instance: A child gets a sticker every other time she practices; a spouse gets praise almost all of the time she does the dishes; a dog gets a treat every third time it comes when called. The reinforcer is not given every time the behavior is observed, but only some of the time.

How might partial reinforcement have played a role in Ivonne's athletic development? It was 2002 when Ivonne became passionate about running marathons. She and her friends went to cheer on some disabled athletes competing in the New York City Marathon. As she stood on the sidelines listening to the runners whoosh by and the crowds whoop and scream, she knew she wanted a piece of the energy. Determined to run a marathon, Ivonne extended and intensified her workouts. Soon she began to focus her training on achieving faster and faster "splits"—the times taken to run certain distances. "You get a feeling of fulfillment when you meet your splits, and when you meet your splits that means your training has paid off," she says. "It makes you want to keep trying to improve."

How was Ivonne reinforced for hard training? As noted, early on, she received a reinforcer from her training buddies for *every* workout she increased her mileage. But how might partial reinforcement be used to help someone increase mileage? Perhaps instead of hot chocolate on every occasion, the treat could come after every other successful run. Or, a coach might praise the runner's hard work only some of the time. The amazing thing about partial reinforcement is that it happens to all of us, in an infinite number of settings, and we might never know how many times we have been partially reinforced for any particular behavior. Common to all of these partial reinforcement situations is that the target behavior is exhibited or a goal has been met (for example, running longer and faster), but the reinforcer is *not* supplied each time this occurs.

The hard work and reinforcement paid off for Ivonne. In 2003 she ran her first marathon—New York City—and has since competed in more than a dozen others.

PARTIAL REINFORCEMENT EFFECT   Partial reinforcement is more effective than continuous reinforcement when it comes to maintaining behaviors. When Skinner put the pigeons in his experiments on partial reinforcement schedules, they would peck at a target up to 10,000 times without getting food before giving up (Skinner, 1953). According to Skinner, "Nothing of this sort is ever obtained after continuous reinforcement" (p. 99). And the same seems to be true with humans. In one study from the mid-1950s, researchers observed college students playing slot machines. Some of the slot machines provided continuous reinforcement, delivering pretend coins every time students pulled their levers. Others followed partial reinforcement schedules, dispensing coins only some of the time. After the students played eight rounds, all of the machines stopped giving coins. Without any coins to reinforce them, the students stopped pulling the levers—but not at the same time. Those who had received coins with every lever pull gave up more quickly than did those rewarded intermittently. In other words, their lever-pulling behavior was less likely to be extinguished when established through partial reinforcement (Lewis & Duncan, 1956). Psychologists call this phenomenon the **partial reinforcement effect:** Behaviors take longer to disappear (through the process of *extinction*) when they have been acquired or maintained through partial or intermittent, rather than continuous, reinforcement.

Imagine how long it would take Skinner's pigeons to learn the first step in the shaping process (looking at the ball) if they were rewarded for doing so only 1 in 5 times. The birds learn fastest when reinforced every time, but their behavior will persist longer if they are given partial reinforcement thereafter. Here's another example: Suppose you would like to house train your puppy. The best plan is to start the training process with continuous reinforcement (praise the dog every time it goes outside), but then shift to partial reinforcement once the desired behavior is established.

But there are exceptions to every rule. Not all people respond well to partial reinforcement. Some research suggests that children with attention-deficit/hyperactivity disorder (ADHD) tend to become more frustrated than their non-ADHD peers when placed under partial reinforcement schedules. For these children, continuous reinforcement may be more effective (Aase & Sagvolden, 2006; Douglas & Parry, 1983).

Hope Springs Eternal
Why are slot machines so enticing? The fact that they deliver rewards occasionally and unpredictably makes them irresistible to many gamblers. Slot machines take advantage of the partial reinforcement effect, which states that behaviors are more persistent when reinforced intermittently, rather than continuously. David Sacks/Getty Images

Timing Is Everything: Reinforcement Schedules

LO 12   Name the schedules of reinforcement and give examples of each.

Skinner identified various ways to administer partial reinforcement, called *partial reinforcement schedules* (**FIGURE 5.3** on page 212). As often occurs in scientific research, he stumbled on the idea by chance. Late one Friday afternoon, Skinner realized he was running low on the food pellets he used as reinforcers for his laboratory animals. If he continued rewarding the animals on a continuous basis, the pellets would run out before the end of the weekend. With this in mind, he decided only to reinforce some of the desired behaviors (Skinner, 1956, 1976). The new strategy worked like a charm. The animals kept performing the desired

FIGURE 5.3 ▸

Schedules of Reinforcement
Continuous reinforcement is ideal for establishing new behaviors. But once learned, a behavior is best maintained with only *partial* reinforcement. Partial reinforcement can be delivered according to four different schedules of reinforcement, as shown here. Starbursts indicate that reinforcement has been given. Notice that fixed-interval and fixed-ratio graphs demonstrate a characteristic dip in the reinforced behavior after each reinforcement, as the learner seems to anticipate that reinforcement won't follow immediately.

FIXED-RATIO

Cumulative responses

Time

VARIABLE-RATIO

Cumulative responses

Time

FIXED-INTERVAL

Cumulative responses

Time

VARIABLE-INTERVAL

Cumulative responses

Time

✦ Reinforcer

behaviors, even though they weren't given reinforcers every time. But how often should research subjects be given reinforcers for the target behavior? Four different reinforcement schedules can be used: fixed-ratio, variable-ratio, fixed-interval, and variable-interval (**FIGURE 5.3**).

FIXED-RATIO SCHEDULE   In some situations, the best approach to reinforcement is a **fixed-ratio schedule.** With this arrangement, the subject must exhibit a predetermined number of desired responses or behaviors before a reinforcer is given. A pigeon in a Skinner box may have to peck a spot five times in order to score a delicious pellet (5:1). A third-grade teacher might give students prizes when they pass three multiplication tests (3:1). The students quickly learn this predictable pattern. Generally, the fixed-ratio schedule produces a high response rate, but with a characteristic dip immediately following the reinforcement. Pigeons peck away at the target with only a brief rest and students study for multiplication tests following the same pattern.

VARIABLE-RATIO SCHEDULE   Other times, it is best to use reinforcement that is unpredictable. In a **variable-ratio schedule,** the number of desired responses or behaviors that must occur before a reinforcer is given changes across trials and is based on an average number of responses to be reinforced. If the goal is to train a pigeon to peck a spot on a target, a variable-ratio schedule can be used: Trial 1, the pigeon gets a pellet after pecking the spot twice; Trial 2, the pigeon gets a pellet after pecking the spot once; Trial 3, the pigeon gets a pellet after pecking the spot three times; and so on. In the classroom, the teacher might not tell the students in advance how many tests they will need to pass to get a prize. She may give a prize after two tests, then the next time after seven tests. This variable-ratio schedule tends to produce a high response rate (pecking and studying in our examples) and behaviors that are difficult to extinguish because of the unpredictability of the reinforcement schedule.

FIXED-INTERVAL SCHEDULE   In some cases, researchers may determine that it is important to focus on the interval of time between reinforcers, as opposed to the number of desired responses. In a **fixed-interval schedule,** the reinforcer comes after a preestablished interval of time; the target behavior is only reinforced after the given time period is over. A reinforcer is given for the first target behavior that occurs *after* the time interval has ended. If a pigeon is on a fixed-interval schedule of 30 seconds, it can peck at the target as often as possible once the interval starts, but it will only get a reinforcer following its first response after the 30 seconds has ended. With a 1-week interval, the teacher gives prizes only on Fridays for children who do well on their math quiz that day, regardless of how they performed during the week on other math quizzes. With this schedule, the target behavior tends to increase as each time interval comes to an end. The pigeon pecks the spot more often when the time nears 30 seconds, and the students study harder as Friday approaches.

VARIABLE-INTERVAL SCHEDULE   In a **variable-interval schedule,** the length of time between reinforcements is unpredictable. In this schedule, the reinforcer comes after an interval of time goes by, but the length of the interval changes from trial to trial (within a predetermined range based on an average interval length). As with the fixed-interval schedule, reinforcement follows the first target behavior that occurs after the time interval has elapsed. Training a pigeon to peck a spot on a target using a variable-interval schedule might include: Trial 1, the pigeon gets a pellet after 41 seconds; Trial 2, the pigeon gets a pellet after 43 seconds; Trial 3, the pigeon gets a pellet after 40 seconds; and so on. In each trial, the pigeon must respond after the interval of time has passed (which varies from trial to trial). The third-grade teacher might think that an average of 4 days should go by between quizzes. So, instead of giving reinforcers every 7 days (that is, always on Friday), she gives quizzes separated by a variable interval. The first quiz might be after a 2-day interval, the next after a 3-day interval, and the students do not know when to expect them. The variable-interval schedule tends to encourage steady patterns of behavior. The pigeon tries its luck pecking a target once every 30 seconds or so, and the students come to school prepared to take a quiz every day (their amount of study holding steady).

So far, we have learned about *increasing* desired behaviors through reinforcement, but not all behaviors are desirable. Let's turn our attention to techniques used to suppress undesirable behaviors.

The Trouble with Punishment

In contrast to reinforcement, which makes a behavior more likely to recur, the goal of **punishment** is to *decrease* or stop a behavior (**INFOGRAPHIC 5.3** on the next page). Punishment is used to reduce unwanted behaviors by instilling an association between a behavior and some unwanted consequence (for example, between stealing and going to jail, or between misbehaving and a spanking). Punishment isn't always effective, however; people are often willing to accept unpleasant consequences to get something they really want.

fixed-ratio schedule A schedule in which the subject must exhibit a predetermined number of desired behaviors before a reinforcer is given.

variable-ratio schedule A schedule in which the number of desired responses or behaviors that must occur before a reinforcer is given changes across trials and is based on an average number of responses to be reinforced.

fixed-interval schedule A schedule in which the reinforcer comes after a preestablished interval of time goes by; the response or behavior is only reinforced after the given interval is over.

variable-interval schedule A schedule in which the reinforcer comes after an interval of time goes by, but the length of the interval changes from trial to trial.

punishment The application of a consequence that decreases the likelihood of a behavior recurring.

Learning: Punishment and Reinforcement

Behavior: *Driving Fast*

Do you want to increase this behavior?

YES!
It's Nascar! You have to drive faster than anyone else to win.
We will apply a reinforcer to **increase** the behavior.

NO!
We're not at the racetrack! Speeding is dangerous and against the law.
We will apply a punishment to **decrease** the behavior.

REINFORCEMENT

PUNISHMENT

Negative Reinforcement

You don't like working in the family auto-body shop. Your family says you can work fewer hours if you win the next race. **Taking away** unwanted work increases the speeding behavior.

Positive Reinforcement

You win a trophy and a cash prize for going fast at the race. **Adding** desirable rewards increases your speeding behavior.

Negative Punishment

The police officer confiscates your license. **Taking away** something desirable decreases your speeding behavior.

Positive Punishment

The police officer gives you a citation. **Adding** something undesirable decreases your speeding behavior.

---

test yourself

Which process matches each of the following examples?
Choose from **positive reinforcement**, **negative reinforcement**, **positive punishment**, and **negative punishment**.

1. Carlos' parents grounded him the last time he stayed out past his curfew, so tonight he came home right on time.

2. Jinhee spent an entire week helping an elderly neighbor clean out her basement after a flood. The local newspaper caught wind of the story and ran it as an inspiring front-page headline. Jinhee enjoyed the attention and decided to organize a neighborhood work group.

3. The trash stinks, so Sheri takes it out.

4. Gabriel's assistant had a bad habit of showing up late for work, so Gabriel docked his pay.

5. During food drives, the basketball team offers to wash your car for free if you donate six items or more to the local homeless shelter.

6. Claire received a stern lecture for texting in class. She doesn't want to hear that again, so now she turns off her phone when she enters the classroom.

Answers 1. negative punishment, 2. positive reinforcement, 3. negative reinforcement, 4. negative punishment, 5. positive reinforcement, 6. positive punishment

POSITIVE AND NEGATIVE PUNISHMENT　There are two major categories of punishment: *positive* and *negative.* With **positive punishment,** something aversive or disagreeable is applied following an unwanted behavior. For example, getting a ticket for speeding is a positive punishment, the aim of which is to decrease driving over the speed limit. Paying a late fine for overdue library books is a positive punishment, the goal of which is to decrease returning library books past their due date. In basketball, a personal foul (for example, inappropriate physical contact, like shoving) might result in positive punishment, such as a free throw for the opposing team. Here, the *addition* of something aversive (the other team getting a wide open shot) is used with the intention of decreasing a behavior (pushing, shoving, and the like).

The goal of **negative punishment** is also to reduce an unwanted behavior, but in this case, it is done by *taking away* something desirable. A person who drives while inebriated runs the risk of negative punishment, as his driver's license may be taken away. This loss of driving privileges is a punishment designed to *reduce* drunken driving. If you never return your library books, you might suffer the negative punishment of losing your borrowing privileges. The goal is to *decrease* the number of lost or stolen library books. What kind of negative punishment might be used to rein in illegal conduct in basketball? Just ask one of Jeremy Lin's former teammates, superstar Carmelo Anthony, one of many players suspended for participating in a 2006 brawl between the Knicks and the Denver Nuggets. Anthony, a Nuggets player at the time (how ironic that he was later traded to the Knicks), was dealt a 15-game suspension (and no salary for those games not played) for slugging a Knicks player in the face (Lee, 2006, December 19). Anthony's suspension is an example of negative punishment, because it involves subtracting something desirable (the privilege to compete and his salary for those games) to decrease a behavior (throwing punches on the court).

Punishment may be useful for the purposes of basketball, but how does it figure into everyday life? Think about the last time you tried using punishment to reduce unwanted behavior. Perhaps you scolded your puppy for having an accident, or snapped at your housemate for leaving dirty dishes in the sink. If you are a parent or caregiver of a young child, you may try to reign in misbehavior with various types of punishment, such as spanking.

CONTROVERSIES

Spotlight on Spanking

➡️⬅️　Were you spanked as a child? Would you or do you spank your own children? Statistically speaking, there is a good chance your answer will be *yes* to both questions. Studies suggest that about two thirds of American parents use corporal (or physical) punishment to discipline their young children (Gershoff, 2008; Regalado, Sareen, Inkelas, Wissow, & Halfon, 2004; Socolar, Savage, & Evans, 2007). But is spanking an effective and acceptable means of discipline?

TO SPANK OR NOT TO SPANK. . .

There is little doubt that spanking can provide a fast-acting fix: If a child is beating up his brother, a swift slap on his bottom will probably make him stop pronto. But think about the larger lesson the boy learns in the process. His parents are trying to teach him not to be aggressive toward his brother, but in doing so, they demonstrate an aggressive behavior (hitting). Children are experts at mimicking adults' behaviors (see the next section on observational learning), and several studies suggest that spanking is associated with future aggression and other antisocial behaviors (Gershoff, 2002; Taylor, Manganello, Lee, & Rice, 2010).

positive punishment The addition of something unpleasant following an unwanted behavior, with the intention of decreasing that behavior.

negative punishment The removal of something desirable following an unwanted behavior, with the intention of decreasing that behavior.

CONNECTIONS

In **Chapter 2,** we noted the primary roles of the *frontal lobes:* to organize information processed in other areas of the brain, orchestrate higher-level cognitive functions, and direct behaviors associated with personality. Here, we note that harsh physical punishment interferes with normal development of the frontal lobes—a good example of the ongoing interaction between nature (physical development of the brain) and nurture (physical punishment).

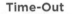

Time-Out

Sending a child to a corner for a "time-out" is an example of negative punishment because it involves removing something (the privilege to play) in order to decrease an unwanted behavior. Spanking is a positive punishment because it involves the addition of something (a slap on the bottom) to discourage an undesirable behavior. Design Pics/Ron Nickel/Getty Images

Apart from sending children the message that aggression is okay, corporal punishment may promote serious long-term mental health problems. Harsh physical punishment, which includes spanking, grabbing, and pushing, has been linked to an elevated risk for developing mood, anxiety, and personality disorders, as well as problems with drugs and alcohol. It may also interfere with cognitive development, retarding growth in various parts of the **frontal lobes** (Tomoda et al., 2009), a region of the brain that processes complex thoughts. One study even found that spanked children score lower on intelligence tests than their nonspanked peers (Straus & Paschall, 2009).

Critics argue that studies casting a negative light on spanking are primarily *correlational,* meaning they show only a link—not a cause-and-effect relationship—between physical punishment and negative outcomes (Larzelere & Baumrind, 2010). They point to other factors that might explain some of the problems spanked children seem to develop. Perhaps these children are aggressive and antisocial to begin with (that would explain why they were spanked in the first place), or maybe their parents are more likely to be abusive, and the abuse (not the spanking) is to blame (Baumrind, Larzelere, & Cowan, 2002). Spanking, which means striking the extremities or the bottom with an open hand without causing injury, may be an effective way to modify young children's behavior, according to some experts (Baumrind, Larzelere, & Cowan, 2002; Larzelere & Baumrind, 2010). But it must be delivered by a parent whose approach is "warm, responsive, rational, and temperate" (Baumrind, 1996, p. 857).

Scholars on both sides make valid points, but the debate is somewhat lopsided, as an increasing number of studies suggest that spanking is ineffective and emotionally damaging (Gershoff & Bitensky, 2008; Smith, 2012; Straus, 2005).

LO 13 Explain how punishment differs from negative reinforcement.

PUNISHMENT VERSUS NEGATIVE REINFORCEMENT   Punishment and negative reinforcement are two concepts that students often find difficult to distinguish (**TABLE 5.3**; also see Infographic 5.3 on p. 214). Remember that punishment (positive or negative) is designed to *decrease* the behavior that it follows, whereas reinforcement (positive or negative) aims to *increase* the behavior. Operant conditioning uses reinforcers (both positive and negative) to *increase* target behaviors, and punishment applies aversive stimuli to *decrease* unwanted behaviors.

If all the positives and negatives are confusing you, just think in terms of math: Positive always means adding something, and negative means taking it away. Punishment can be *positive,* which means the addition of something viewed as unpleasant ("Because you made a mess of your room, you have to wash all the dishes!"), or *negative,* which involves the removal of something viewed as pleasant or valuable ("Because you made a mess of your room, no ice cream for you!"). For basketball players, a positive punishment might be *adding* more wind sprints to *decrease* errors on the free throw line. An example of negative punishment might be benching the players for brawling on the court; *taking away* the players' court time *decreases* their fighting behavior.

Table 5.3 REINFORCEMENT VERSUS PUNISHMENT

Term	Defined	Goal	Example
Positive Reinforcement	Addition of a pleasant stimulus following a target behavior	Increase desired behavior	Students who complete an online course 15 days before the end of semester receive 10 points of extra credit.
Negative Reinforcement	Removal of an unpleasant stimulus following a target behavior	Increase desired behavior	Students who have perfect attendance for the semester do not have to take the final exam.
Positive Punishment	Addition of something unpleasant following an unwanted behavior	Decrease undesired behavior	Students who are late to class more than two times have to write an extra paper.
Negative Punishment	Removal of something pleasant following an unwanted behavior	Decrease undesired behavior	Students late to class on exam day are not allowed to use their notes when taking the exam.

The positive and negative forms of reinforcement and punishment are easy to confuse. Above are some concrete definitions, goals, and examples to help you sort them out.

THINK again

Think Positive Reinforcement

With all this talk of chickens, basketball players, and triathletes, you may be wondering how operant conditioning applies to *you*. Just think about the last time you earned a good grade on a test after studying really hard. How did this grade affect your preparation for the next test? If it made you study more, then it served as a positive reinforcer. A little dose of a positive reinforcer goes a long way when it comes to increasing productivity. Let's examine three everyday dilemmas and brainstorm ways we could use positive reinforcers to achieve better outcomes.

Problem 1: Your housemate frequently goes to sleep without washing his dinner dishes. Almost every morning, you walk into the kitchen and find a tower of dirty pans and plates sitting in the sink. No matter how much you nag and complain, he simply will not change his ways. *Solution:* Nagging and complaining are not getting you anywhere. Try positive reinforcers instead. Wait until a day your housemate takes care of his dishes and then pour on the praise. You might be pleasantly surprised the next morning.

Problem 2: Your child is driving you crazy with her incessant whining. She whines for milk, so you give it to her. She whines for someone to play with, so you play with her. Why does your child continue to whine although you are responding to all her needs? *Solution:* Here, we have a case in which positive reinforcers are driving the problem. When you react to your child's gripes and moans, you are reinforcing them. Turn off your ears to the whining. You might even want to say something like, "I can't hear you when you're whining. If you ask me in a normal voice, I'll be more than happy to help." Then reinforce her more mature behavior by responding attentively.

Problem 3: You just trained your puppy to sit. She was cooperating wonderfully until about a week after you stopped rewarding her with dog biscuits. You want her to sit on command, but you can't keep doling out doggie treats forever. *Solution:* Once the dog has adopted the desired behavior, begin reinforcing unpredictably. Remember, continuous reinforcement is most effective for establishing behaviors, but a variable schedule (that is, giving treats intermittently) is a good bet if you want to make the behavior stick (Pryor, 2002).

REINFORCEMENT STRATEGIES YOU CAN PUT TO GOOD USE

Classical and Operant Conditioning: What's the Difference?

Students sometimes have trouble differentiating classical and operant conditioning (**FIGURE 5.4**). After all, both forms of conditioning—classical and operant—involve forming associations. In classical conditioning, the learner links different *stimuli;* in operant conditioning, the learner connects her behavior to its *consequences* (reinforcement and punishment). Another key similarity is that the principles of acquisition, stimulus discrimination, stimulus generalization, extinction, and spontaneous recovery apply to both types of conditioning.

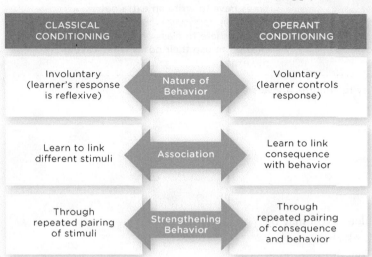

▲ FIGURE 5.4
Differences Between Classical and Operant Conditioning

But there are also key differences between classical and operant conditioning. In classical conditioning, the learned behaviors are involuntary, or reflexive. Ivonne cannot control her heart rate any more than Pavlov's dogs can decide when to salivate. Operant conditioning, on the other hand, concerns voluntary behavior. Jeremy Lin had power over his decision to practice his shot, just as Skinner's pigeons had control over swatting bowling balls with their beaks. In short, classical conditioning is an involuntary form of learning, whereas operant conditioning requires active effort.

Another important distinction is the way in which behaviors are strengthened. In classical conditioning, behaviors become more frequent with repeated pairings of stimuli. The more often Ivonne smells chlorine before swim practice, the tighter the association she makes between chlorine and swimming. Operant conditioning is also strengthened by repeated pairings, but in this case, the connection is between a behavior and its consequences. Reinforcers strengthen the behavior; punishment weakens it. The more benefits (reinforcers) Jeremy gains from succeeding in basketball, the more likely he will keep practicing.

Often classical conditioning and operant conditioning occur simultaneously. A baby learns that he gets fed when he cries; getting milk reinforces the crying behavior (operant conditioning). At the same time, the baby learns to associate milk with the appearance of the bottle. As soon as he sees his mom or dad take the bottle out of the refrigerator, he begins salivating in anticipation of gulping it down (classical conditioning).

Classical and operant conditioning are not the only ways we learn. We have one major category of learning yet to cover. Try to guess what it might be using these hints. How did you learn to tie your shoes, dance, rake leaves, and kick a soccer ball? Somebody must have shown you.

show what you know

1. According to Thorndike and the _____, if a behavior is followed by a pleasurable outcome, the likelihood that the behavior will happen again increases.

2. A third-grade teacher gives her students prizes for passing math tests. Not only do the students improve their math scores; they also begin to study more to improve their spelling scores as a result of this reinforcement schedule. Their increased studying of spelling is a good example of:
   a. classical conditioning.
   b. an unconditioned response.
   c. an unconditioned stimulus.
   d. stimulus generalization.

3. A child disrupts class and the teacher writes her name on the board. For the rest of the week, the child does not act up. The teacher used _____ to decrease the child's disruptive behaviors.
   a. positive punishment
   b. negative punishment
   c. positive reinforcement
   d. negative reinforcement

4. Think about a behavior you would like to change (either yours or someone else's). Devise a strategy using positive and negative reinforcement to change that behavior. Also contemplate how you might use successive approximations. What reinforcers would you use?

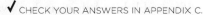 CHECK YOUR ANSWERS IN APPENDIX C.

Observational Learning and Cognition

BASKETBALL IQ Jeremy Lin is not the fastest runner or highest jumper on the planet, and he is certainly not the biggest guy in professional hoops. In the world of the NBA, where a player's average height is about 6′7″ and average weight is 220 pounds, Jeremy is actually somewhat small (NBA.com, 2007, November 20; NBA.com, 2007, November 27). So what is it about this benchwarmer-turned-big-shot that makes him so special? Jeremy's success, we suspect, is largely a result of qualities that are extremely hard to measure, like unstoppable confidence, dogged determination, and a penetrating *basketball IQ,* or mental mastery of the sport.

"He has a very natural understanding of the game, an ability to see the game and anticipate the game," Coach Diepenbrock explains. "There are very few people that have the same basketball IQ," he notes. "That's what separates him from other players" (P. Diepenbrock, personal communication, May 21, 2012).

The roots of Jeremy's hoops smarts reach back to his father's native country. Growing up in Taiwan, Gie-Ming Lin didn't have much exposure to basketball, but he was fascinated by what he saw of the sport. According to ESPN, "He dreamed of coming to the United States for two reasons: to complete his PhD and 'to watch the NBA'" (O'Neil, 2009, December 10). When Gie-Ming finally arrived in America, he fell head over heels in love with basketball, taping NBA games and watching them any chance he got. This 5′6″ engineering student had never picked up a basketball, but he managed to learn the techniques of the game by closely watching the moves of NBA legends like Kareem Abdul-Jabbar, Larry Bird, and Magic Johnson (O'Neil, 2009, December 10). Eventually, he tried those moves on the court, and passed them along to Jeremy and his other two sons.

Gie-Ming learned by observing and imitating NBA greats. These players served as **models** by demonstrating behaviors (for example, Kareem's hook shot; O'Neil, 2009, December 10). We call this process **observational learning,** as it results from watching the behavior of others. According to Bandura (1986), this type of learning is more likely to occur when the learner: (1) is *paying attention* to the model; (2) *remembers* what she observed (Bahrick, Gogate, & Ruiz, 2002); (3) is *capable of performing* the behavior she has observed; and (4) is *motivated* to demonstrate the behavior.

Lincredible
Playing for the Houston Rockets, Jeremy works the offense against the Brooklyn Nets. He may not be the tallest player in the NBA, but he more than makes up for that in confidence and game smarts. Song Qiong Xinhua News Agency/Newscom

Basketball Family
Baby Jeremy poses with his father Gie-Ming, a basketball aficionado who learned the game by studying NBA greats like Kareem Abdul-Jabbar and Larry Bird (O'Neil, 2009, December 10). HANDOUT/Reuters/Landov

The Power of Observational Learning

LO 14 Summarize what Bandura's classic Bobo doll study teaches us about learning.

Think about how observational learning impacts your own life. Speaking English, eating with utensils, and driving a car are all skills you probably picked up in part by watching and mimicking others. Do you ever use slang? Phrases like "gnarley" (cool) from the 1980s, "Wassup" (What is going on?) from the 1990s, and "peeps" (my

model The individual or character whose behavior is being imitated.

observational learning Learning that occurs as a result of watching the behavior of others.

Tandem Triathletes
Ivonne (rear) and her guide, Marit Ogin, ride together in the Nickel City Buffalo Triathlon. The guide is responsible for steering, breaking, and communicating to Ivonne when it is time to shift gears or adjust body position for a turn. G. John Schmidt/Courtesy Ivonne Mosquera-Schmidt

people, or friends) from the 2000s caught on because people copy what they observe others saying and writing. Consider some of the phrases trending today that 20 years from now people won't recognize.

But take note: Observational learning doesn't necessarily require sight. Let's return to Ivonne, who competes in triathlons, consisting of 1 mile of swimming, 25 miles of biking, and 6 miles of running. Ivonne performs the swimming and running sections of the triathlon attached to a guide with a tether, and the bike section on a tandem bike with the guide. To fine-tune her swimming technique, she *feels* her swim coach demonstrate the freestyle stroke. Standing in the water behind him, Ivonne places one hand on his back and the other on his arm while he goes through the motions of a stroke. She feels the angle of his arms as they break the water's surface, the distance between his fingers as he plows through the water, and the position of his wrist throughout the motion. Then she imitates the movement she *observed* through her sense of touch.

PLEASE PLAY NICELY WITH YOUR DOLL Just as observational learning can lead to positive outcomes like sharper basketball and swimming skills, it can also breed undesirable behaviors. The classic Bobo doll experiment conducted by psychologist Albert Bandura and his colleagues revealed just how fast children can adopt aggressive ways they see modeled by adults, as well as exhibit their own novel aggressive responses (Bandura, Ross, & Ross, 1961). In one of Bandura's studies, 76 preschool children were placed in a room alone with an adult and allowed to play with stickers and prints for making pictures. During their playtime, some of the children were paired with adults who acted aggressively toward a 5-foot-tall inflatable Bobo doll—punching it in the nose, hitting its head with a mallet, kicking it around the room, and yelling phrases such as, "Sock him in the nose," "Hit him down," and "Pow!" The other children in the study were paired with adults who played with toys peacefully (Bandura et al., 1961).

Bobo Doll
Preschool children in Albert Bandura's famous Bobo doll experiment performed shocking displays of aggression after seeing violent behaviors modeled by adults. Bandura's experiment highlights the impact of observational learning.
Courtesy Dr. Albert Bandura

At the end of the experiment, all the children were allowed to play with a Bobo doll themselves. Those who had observed adults attacking and shouting were much more likely to do the same. Boys were more likely than girls to mimic physical aggression, especially if they had observed it modeled by men. Boys and girls were about equally likely to imitate verbal aggression (Bandura et al., 1961).

Identify the independent variable and dependent variable in the experiment carried out by Bandura and colleagues. What might you change if you were to replicate or duplicate this experiment?

try this

Check your answers in Appendix C.

Bandura and his colleagues also looked at how children were influenced by observing the consequences of the adults' behaviors. Children were more likely to copy models who were rewarded for their aggressive behavior and less likely to mimic those who were punished (Bandura, 1986).

VIOLENCE IN THE MEDIA Psychologists have followed up Bandura's research with studies investigating how children are influenced by violence they see on television, movies and video games, and on the Internet. The American Academy of Pediatrics sums it up nicely: "Extensive research evidence indicates that media violence can contribute to aggressive behavior, desensitization to violence, nightmares, and fear of being harmed" (American Academy of Pediatrics, 2009, p. 1495). One large study found that children who watched TV programs with violent role models, such as *Starsky and Hutch* (a detective series from the 1970s that included violence and suspense), were at increased risk when they became adults of physically abusing their spouses and getting into trouble with the law (Huesmann, Moise-Titus, Podolski, & Eron, 2003). A more recent study conducted in New Zealand followed over 1,000 children from as early as birth until they were around 26 years old. The researchers found that the more television the children watched, the more likely they were to show antisocial behaviors as young adults. Interestingly, this association was between antisocial behaviors and excessive television viewing, regardless of the content (Robertson, McAnally, & Hancox, 2013).

Critics caution, however, that an *association* between media portrayals and violent behaviors doesn't mean there is a cause-and-effect relationship (establishing an association is not the same as pinning down a cause). As Huesmann and colleagues (2003) pointed out, there are other factors related to parenting that could influence *both* television viewing and aggression. If a parent is emotionally neglectful and places a child in front of the television all day, the child may eventually imitate some of the aggression she sees on TV. At the same time, the child may resent the parent for ignoring her, and this resentment could lead to aggression. But how do you know which of these factors—television exposure or parenting approach—is more important in the development of aggressive tendencies? This is an active area of psychological research, but experts agree that television and other forms of media may influence aggressive tendencies in children (Clemente, Espinosa, & Vidal, 2008; Office of the Surgeon General et al., 2001). The American Academy of Pediatrics has recommended that children should be limited to less than 1–2 hours of total screen time per day (American Academy of Pediatrics, 2001). Unfortunately, children and their parents have not responded to this recommendation. In fact, the

Sunny Days
The prosocial behaviors demonstrated by Big Bird and *Sesame Street* friends appear to have a meaningful impact on child viewers. Children have a knack for imitating positive behaviors such as sharing and caring (Cole et al., 2008). AP Photo/Mark Lennihan

average screen time has increased, with preschool-age children in the United States reported to have an average of 4.4 hours of daily screen time (Tandon, Zhou, Lozano, & Christakis, 2011). Instead of focusing on the number of hours children watch television, some have suggested that we should focus on program content, encouraging families and caregivers to reduce exposure to programs that contain violence and aggression, and to increase the amount of content with prosocial behavior (Christakis et al., 2013; McCarthy, 2013).

PROSOCIAL BEHAVIOR AND OBSERVATIONAL LEARNING Here's the flip side to this issue: Children also have a gift for mimicking positive behaviors. When children watch shows similar to *Sesame Street,* they receive messages that encourage **prosocial behaviors,** meaning they foster kindness, generosity, and forms of behavior that benefit others.

Let's look more closely at research designed to determine the impact of prosocial models. Using scales to measure children's stereotypes and cultural knowledge before and after they watch TV shows, a group of researchers found evidence that shows like *Sesame Street* can have a positive influence (Cole, Labin, & del Rocio Galarza, 2008). Based on their review of multiple studies, these researchers made recommendations to increase prosocial behaviors. Children's shows should have: intended messages; include prosocial information about people of other cultures and religions; be relevant to children in terms of culture and environment; and be age-appropriate and contain intentional and direct (unhidden) messages aimed at educating children about people from different backgrounds.

Adults can also pick up prosocial messages from media. In a multipart study, researchers exposed adults to prosocial song lyrics (as opposed to neutral lyrics). The first experiment found that listening to prosocial lyrics increased the frequency of prosocial thoughts. Findings from the second experiment indicated that listening to a song with prosocial lyrics increased empathy, or the ability to understand what another person is going through. The third experiment found that listening to a song with prosocial lyrics increased helping behavior. These researchers only looked at the short-term effects, but exposing people continuously to prosocial lyrics may also have a lasting impact (Greitemeyer, 2009).

You know from reading earlier sections that humans are not the only ones who can learn. Dogs, rats, pigeons, and all types of creatures can learn through classical and operant conditioning. As you might expect, our furry and feathered friends can also learn through observation.

didn't SEE that coming

Monkey See, Monkey Do: Can Apes Learn by Observation, Too?

👁! Bonnie the orangutan, a 142-pound ape living at the Smithsonian National Zoological Park in Washington, D.C., has always been fascinated by people. When crowds come to the zoo and gawk at the orangutans swinging through trees and chewing on branches, Bonnie returns their stares with equal

prosocial behaviors Actions that are kind, generous, and benefit others.
cognitive map The mental image of the layout of a physical space.

intensity. Years of people-watching have made this adult ape an expert in the art of "monkey see, monkey do." Bonnie particularly enjoys imitating the zookeepers; she can often be seen picking up handfuls of hay and using them to sweep floors, or scrubbing windows with fabric from her bedding (E. Stromberg, personal communication, June 21, 2010). But of all Bonnie's humanlike abilities, whistling is the one that has captured the most scientific interest.

No one deliberately taught Bonnie to whistle. It's not even clear when and how she picked up the talent. One day back in the 1980s, a zookeeper just happened to notice Bonnie alone in her cage, whistling to herself. Researchers think she probably acquired the skill through observational learning, perhaps by hearing and copying one of her caretakers (Stone, 2009; Wich et al., 2009). Previously, scientists had shown that orangutans and chimpanzees could learn to copy human vocalizations, but only with plenty of training (Furness, 1916; Hayes, 1951, cited in Wich et al., 2009). Until Bonnie came along, there were no documented cases of apes doing it on their own, without help or reinforcement (Wich et al., 2009).

"I get asked quite often if Bonnie's ability to teach herself to whistle surprises me," says Erin Stromberg, one of the zookeepers. "But working with these incredibly intelligent apes every day, I've stopped being surprised at their abilities, and simply am just amazed and impressed by them daily" (E. Stromberg, personal communication, June 21, 2010).

Bonnie's case not only illustrates the power of observational learning, it also suggests that primates might be capable of creating completely new sounds, possibly shedding light on how language evolved in one of the orangutan's not-so-distant relatives: human beings (Wich et al., 2009). 👁!

BUT CAN SHE CARRY A TUNE?

Whistling Ape
Bonnie the orangutan seems to have learned whistling by copying workers at the Smithsonian National Zoological Park in Washington, D.C. Her musical skill is the result of observational learning. Courtesy of Smithsonian National Zoological Park

Thus far we have focused on types of learning that are visible or observable in some way. You can actually observe the process leading up to the dog salivating, the rat pushing the lever, the child smacking the Bobo doll. But learning can also occur in ways that are much more internal and not so easily observed. Learning can be cognitive in nature.

Learning and Cognition: A Map That Cannot Be Seen

> **LO 15** Describe latent learning and explain how cognition is involved in learning.

Ivonne's feet pound the streets of Boston. She is among some 20,000 of the world's finest runners competing in its oldest annual 26.2-mile running race, the Boston Marathon. (Ivonne has nabbed first place in the Women's Visually Impaired division three times.) She runs with teammates who make sure the path is clear, allowing her to focus on her performance instead of becoming preoccupied with bumping into obstacles.

Before the race, Ivonne checks online to see if there is a description of the course or studies a map with her husband or a friend in order to learn the location of important landmarks such as hills, major turns, bridges, railroad tracks, and so on. "Doing this helps me feel that I have an idea of what to expect, and when to expect it," Ivonne says. The mental layout she creates is called a **cognitive map,** and it continues to come together when she's running the race. In fact, we all create

Feel the Map
Ivonne's husband guides her hand over the map of a race course. She is beginning to form a cognitive map of the route, one that will continue to crystallize as she races. While running, Ivonne's ears collect clues about the relative positions of objects and the direction of motion—information that goes into creating a cognitive map. MICHAEL S. WIRTZ/The Inquirer/Daily News/Philly.com

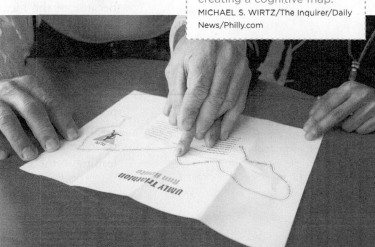

these cognitive maps, which provide a spatial representation to help us navigate our environment. As Ivonne runs, she hears sounds from all directions—the breathing of other runners, their feet hitting the ground, chatter from the sidelines—and uses these auditory cues to produce a mental map of her surroundings. These maps are created through **latent learning,** a type of learning that occurs without awareness and regardless of reinforcement, and that remains hidden until there is a need to use it.

FIGURE 5.5
Latent Learning
In a classic experiment, groups of rats learned how to navigate a maze at remarkably different rates. Rats in a group receiving reinforcement from Day 1 (the green line on the graph) initially had the lowest rate of error and were able to work their way through the maze more quickly than the other groups. But when a group began to receive reinforcement for the first time on Day 11, their error rate dropped immediately. This shows that the rats were learning the basic structure of the maze even when they weren't being reinforced. *Source:* Adapted from Tolman, 1948

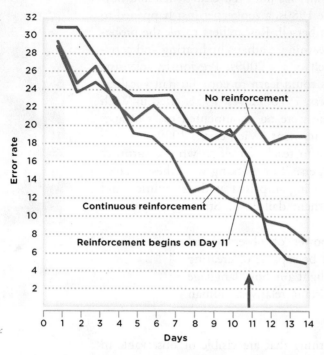

LATENT LEARNING: RATS THAT KNOW WHERE TO GO Edward Tolman and his colleague C. H. Honzik demonstrated latent learning in rats in their classic 1930 maze experiment (**FIGURE 5.5**). The researchers took three groups of rats and let them run free in mazes for several days. One group received food for reaching the goal boxes in their mazes; a second group received no reinforcement; and a third received nothing until the 11th day of the experiment, when they, too, received food for finding the goal box. As you might expect, rats getting the treats from the onset solved the mazes more and more quickly as the days wore on. Meanwhile, their unrewarded compatriots wandered through the twists and turns, showing only minor improvements from one day to the next. But on Day 11 when the researchers started to give treats to the third group, the behavior of the rats changed. After just one round of treats, the rats were scurrying through the mazes and scooping up the food as if they had been rewarded throughout the experiment (Tolman & Honzik, 1930). They had apparently been learning, even when there was no reinforcement for doing so—or in simpler terms, learning just for the sake of learning.

We all do this as we acquire cognitive maps of our environments. Without realizing it, we remember locations, objects, and details of our surroundings, and all of this information is brought together in a mental layout (Lynch, 2002). Research suggests that visually impaired people forge cognitive maps without the use of visual information. Instead, they use "compensatory sensorial channels" (hearing and sense of touch, for example) as they gather information about their environments (Lahav & Mioduser, 2008).

This line of research highlights the importance of cognitive processes underlying behavior and suggests that learning can occur in the absence of reinforcement. Because of the focus on cognition, this research approach conflicts with the views of Skinner and some other 20th-century psychologists who adhered to a strict form of behaviorism.

Many other studies have challenged Skinner's views. Wolfgang Köhler's (1925) research on chimpanzees suggests that animals are capable of thinking through a problem before taking action. He designed an experiment in which chimps were presented with out-of-reach bananas, and showed that the animals were able to plan a variety of banana-fetching strategies, including stacking crates to climb on. Here, the chimps displayed insight, a sudden coming together of awareness of a situation, leading to the solution of a problem (Chapter 7).

latent learning Learning that occurs without awareness and regardless of reinforcement, and is not evident until needed.

Today, most psychologists agree that both measurable behaviors and cognitive processes such as insight are necessary and complementary elements of learning. Environmental factors have a powerful influence on behavior, as Pavlov, Skinner and others discovered, but every behavior can be traced back to activity in the brain. Understanding how cognitive processes translate to behaviors remains one of the great challenges facing psychologists.

You Asked, Coach Diepenbrock Answers

http://qrs.ly/nm3m61e

How did it feel to watch Jeremy's dream run with the Knicks?

IT KEEPS GETTING BETTER   Wondering what became of Jeremy Lin following "Linsanity"? After suffering a knee injury in the spring of 2012, Jeremy was out of commission for the remainder of the season with the Knicks. He eventually signed a deal with the Houston Rockets, where he was still playing at the time of this printing. He has proven he can hold his own as a starting point guard in the NBA, and we suspect he will continue stirring up "Linsanity" in the future (Ogden, 2013, February 27).

Ivonne Mosquera-Schmidt isn't doing so badly herself. Running at the Paralympics National Trials in 2012, she set the U.S. record for the 1,500-meter event for totally blind women. Then in 2013, she won the gold medal at the Paratriathlon World Championships. Now she is beginning to prepare for the 2016 Paralympics, which are scheduled to be held in Rio de Janeiro, Brazil. In between all the training and racing, Ivonne works full time as a project manager at the Dow Chemical Company. What keeps her going? Apart from the obvious reinforcers, such as love of sport, Ivonne derives great satisfaction from bridging the gap between the able-bodied and disabled communities. Blind and sighted athletes have a common appreciation for exercise, and training and racing unite them in a very human way. "We can have the same dreams, the same goals, the same ambitions," Ivonne says, "and [exercise] gets us working together."

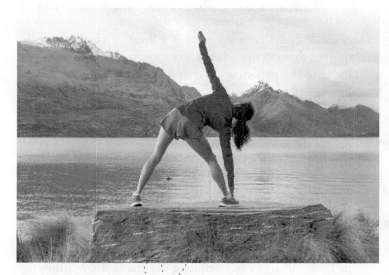

Peace of Mind ◄------
Ivonne does the triangle pose during a visit to Queenstown, New Zealand. Yoga helps develop the strength and flexibility she needs for racing, and keeps her grounded.
G. John Schmidt/Courtesy Ivonne Mosquera-Schmidt

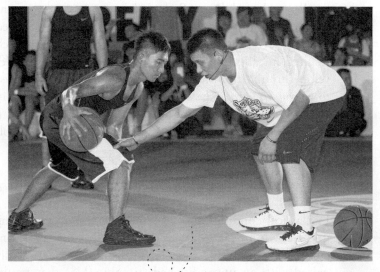

Shoot for the Stars ◄------
Jeremy works with an aspiring basketball player in Taipei, Taiwan, in 2012. His work with children continues through the Jeremy Lin Foundation, a nonprofit organization devoted to serving young people and their communities. AP Photo/Chiang Ying-ying

1. You want to learn how to play basketball, so you watch videos of Jeremy Lin executing plays. If your game improves as a result, this would be considered an example of:
   a. observational learning.
   b. association.
   c. prosocial behavior.
   d. your cognitive map.

2. Observational learning results in a wide variety of learned behaviors. Describe several types of behaviors you have learned through observation of a model.

3. Although Skinner was a strong advocate for the theory that reinforcement is the cause of learning, there is robust evidence that reinforcement is not always necessary. This comes from experiments studying:
   a. positive reinforcement.
   b. negative reinforcement.
   c. latent learning.
   d. stimulus generalization.

✓ CHECK YOUR ANSWERS IN APPENDIX C.

⑤ summary of concepts

LO 1 Define learning. (p. 187)

Learning is a relatively enduring change in behavior or thinking that results from experiences. Organisms as simple as fish and as complex as humans have the ability to learn. Learning is about creating associations. Sometimes we associate two different stimuli (*classical conditioning*). At other times we make connections between our behaviors and their consequences (*operant conditioning*), and we can also learn by watching and imitating others (*observational learning*), creating a link between our behavior and the behavior of others.

LO 2 Explain what Pavlov's studies teach us about classical conditioning. (p. 189)

Studies such as those on Pavlov's dogs teach us how organisms learn to respond. In Pavlov's work, the dogs associated a variety of stimuli with the anticipation of food, which resulted in salivating. He discovered how associations develop through the process of learning, which he referred to as *conditioning*. Classical conditioning is the process in which two stimuli become associated with each other; an originally neutral stimulus is conditioned to elicit an involuntary response.

LO 3 Evaluate the differences between the US, UR, CS, and CR. (p. 190)

In classical conditioning, a neutral stimulus is something in the environment that does not normally cause a relevant automatic or reflexive response. This stimulus is repeatedly paired with an unconditioned stimulus (US) that results in an unconditioned response (UR). The neutral stimulus thus becomes a conditioned stimulus (CS) that the organism learns to associate with the US. The CS elicits a conditioned response (CR), which is the learned response an organism has to the CS. The initial pairing of a neutral stimulus with a US is called acquisition.

LO 4 Recognize and give examples of stimulus discrimination and stimulus generalization. (p. 192)

Once the association is forged between a CS and a CR, the learner often responds to similar stimuli as if they are the CS. This is called stimulus generalization. For example, someone who has been bitten by a small dog and reacts with fear to all dogs, big and small, demonstrates stimulus generalization. Stimulus discrimination is the ability to differentiate between the CS and other stimuli sufficiently different from it. Someone who was bitten by a small dog may only be afraid of small dogs, but not large dogs, thus demonstrating stimulus discrimination.

LO 5 Summarize how classical conditioning is dependent on the biology of the organism. (p. 195)

A conditioned taste aversion is a form of classical conditioning that occurs when an organism learns to associate the taste of a particular food or drink with illness. Avoiding foods that induce sickness has adaptive value, increasing the odds the organism will survive and reproduce, passing its genes along to the next generation. Animals and people show biological preparedness, or are predisposed or inclined to learn such associations.

LO 6 Evaluate the Little Albert study and explain how fear can be learned. (p. 197)

The classic Little Albert experiment illustrated the conditioned emotional response, an emotional reaction (fear in Little Albert's case) acquired via classical conditioning. When Little Albert heard a loud bang, this was a US that elicited fear (the UR). Through conditioning, the sight of a rat became paired with the loud noise and went from being a *neutral stimulus* to a CS. Little Albert's fear became a CR.

LO 7 Describe Thorndike's law of effect. (p. 201)

Thorndike's law of effect was foundational in our understanding of operant conditioning, a type of learning in which people or animals come to associate their voluntary actions with the consequences of those actions. The law of effect states that if a behavior is followed by a pleasurable outcome, this increases the likelihood the behavior will occur again. Building on Thorndike's law of effect and Watson's behaviorism, Skinner used reinforcers to change behaviors through small steps toward a desired behavior.

LO 8 Explain shaping and the method of successive approximations. (p. 203)

Shaping allows us to reinforce each incremental change in behavior to accomplish a larger goal. When trying to shape animals' behavior through these successive approximations, we may run into trouble with instinctive drift. Animal behavior can be shaped using successive approximations, but instinct can interfere with parts of the process.

LO 9 Identify the differences between positive and negative reinforcement (p. 207).

Positive reinforcement refers to the process of applying reinforcers that increase future occurrences of a targeted behavior. The fish treats that Thorndike gave his cats are examples of positive reinforcers (strengthening the likelihood of the cats opening the latch). Behaviors can also increase in response to negative reinforcement through the process of taking away (or subtracting) something unpleasant. Putting on a seat belt in a car to stop an annoying beep is an example of negative reinforcement (strengthening the likelihood of wearing a seat belt). Both positive and negative reinforcement increase desired behaviors.

LO 10 Distinguish between primary and secondary reinforcers. (p. 208)

There are two major categories of reinforcers. Primary reinforcers satisfy biological needs. Food, water, and physical contact are considered primary reinforcers. Secondary reinforcers do not satisfy biological needs, but often derive their power from their connection with primary reinforcers. Money is an example of a secondary reinforcer; we know from experience that it gives us access to primary reinforcers, such as food, a safe place to live, and perhaps even the ability to attract desirable mates.

LO 11 Describe continuous reinforcement and partial reinforcement. (p. 209)

Reinforcers can be delivered on a constant basis (continuous reinforcement) or intermittently (partial reinforcement).

Continuous reinforcement is generally more effective for establishing a behavior, whereas partial reinforcement is more resistant to extinction (the partial reinforcement effect) and useful for maintaining behavior.

LO 12 Name the schedules of reinforcement and give examples of each. (p. 211)

B. F. Skinner, a leading behaviorist whose research with "Skinner boxes" illuminated the principles of operant conditioning, described several types of partial reinforcement schedules. In a fixed-ratio schedule, the participant must exhibit a predetermined number of desired responses or behaviors before a reinforcer is given. In a variable-ratio schedule, the number of desired responses or behaviors that must occur before a reinforcer is given changes across trials and is based on an average number of responses to be reinforced. In a fixed-interval schedule, the reinforcer comes after a preestablished interval of time goes by; the response or behavior is only reinforced after the given interval is over. In a variable-interval schedule, the reinforcement comes after an interval of time goes by, but the length of the interval changes from trial to trial. The lengths of these intervals are within a predetermined range based on a desired average interval length.

LO 13 Explain how punishment differs from negative reinforcement. (p. 216)

In contrast to reinforcement, which makes a behavior more likely to recur, the goal of punishment is to *decrease* a behavior. Negative reinforcement differs from punishment because it strengthens a behavior that it follows by removing something aversive or disagreeable. Punishment decreases a behavior by instilling an association between a behavior and some unwanted consequence (for example, between stealing and going to jail, or between misbehaving and a spanking).

LO 14 Summarize what Bandura's classic Bobo doll study teaches us about learning. (p. 219)

Watching a model demonstrate a behavior, observational learning can occur. Albert Bandura's classic Bobo doll experiment showed that children readily imitate aggression when they see it modeled by adults. Studies suggest that children and adults may be inclined to mimic aggressive behaviors seen in TV shows, movies, video games, and on the Internet. Prosocial behaviors, on the other hand, can encourage kindness, generosity, and forms of behavior that benefit others.

LO 15 Describe latent learning and explain how cognition is involved in learning. (p. 223)

Learning can occur without reinforcement. Edward Tolman showed that rats could learn to navigate mazes even when given no rewards. The animals developed cognitive maps, or mental images of the mazes, yet their learning only became apparent when it was needed (latent learning). The rats were learning without reinforcement, just for the sake of learning. This cognitive approach to learning reminds us that measurable behaviors and cognitive processes are necessary and complementary elements in the study of learning.

key terms

acquisition, p. 190
adaptive value, p. 195
behaviorism, p. 203
biological preparedness, p. 196
classical conditioning, p. 190
cognitive map, p. 223
conditioned emotional response, p. 197
conditioned response (CR), p. 190
conditioned stimulus (CS), p. 190
conditioned taste aversion, p. 195

continuous reinforcement, p. 210
extinction, p. 193
fixed-interval schedule, p. 213
fixed-ratio schedule, p. 212
habituation, p. 187
higher order conditioning, p. 193
instinctive drift, p. 205
latent learning, p. 224
law of effect, p. 202
learning, p. 187
model, p. 219
negative punishment, p. 215
negative reinforcement, p. 208

neutral stimulus, p. 190
observational learning, p. 219
operant conditioning, p. 201
partial reinforcement, p. 210
partial reinforcement effect, p. 211
positive punishment, p. 215
positive reinforcement, p. 207
primary reinforcer, p. 208
prosocial behaviors, p. 222
punishment, p. 213
reinforcement, p. 202
reinforcers, p. 202
secondary reinforcer, p. 208

shaping, p. 203
spontaneous recovery, p. 193
stimulus, p. 187
stimulus discrimination, p. 193
stimulus generalization, p. 192
successive approximations, p. 203
unconditioned response (UR), p. 190
unconditioned stimulus (US), p. 190
variable-interval schedule, p. 213
variable-ratio schedule, p. 212

TEST PREP are you ready?

1. One basic form of learning occurs during the process of _____, which is evident when an organism does not respond as strongly or as often to an event following multiple exposures to it.
   a. insight
   b. habituation
   c. classical conditioning
   d. operant conditioning

2. Even trout can learn through operant conditioning, as evidenced by their
   a. innate urge to get food.
   b. reaction to an unconditioned stimulus.
   c. ability to press a pendulum to get food.
   d. reactions to predators.

3. The behaviors learned with classical conditioning are _____, whereas those learned with operant conditioning are _____.
   a. involuntary; voluntary
   b. voluntary; involuntary
   c. voluntary; innate
   d. involuntary; innate

4. Every time you open the pantry where dog food is stored, your dog starts to salivate. His reaction to your opening the pantry door is a(n)
   a. unconditioned response.
   b. conditioned response.
   c. stimulus discrimination.
   d. reaction based on observational learning.

5. Your first love wore a musky-scented perfume, making your heart race every time he or she appeared. Even now when you smell that scent, your heart speeds up, suggesting the scent is a(n)
   a. unconditioned stimulus.
   b. conditioned stimulus.
   c. conditioned response.
   d. unconditioned response.

6. Avoiding foods that induce sickness have _____. This taste aversion helps organisms survive.
   a. adaptive value
   b. stimulus generalization
   c. stimulus discrimination
   d. higher order conditioning

7. Little Albert was an 11-month-old baby who originally had no fear of rats. In an experiment conducted by Watson and Rayner, he was classically conditioned to fear white rats through the pairing of a loud noise with exposure to a rat. His resulting fear is an example of
   a. unconditioned stimulus.
   b. operant conditioning.
   c. conditioned emotional response.
   d. biological preparedness.

8. _____ indicates that if a behavior is followed by a pleasurable outcome, it likely will be repeated.
   a. The primary principle of classical conditioning
   b. Classical conditioning
   c. Biological preparedness
   d. The law of effect

9. Which of the following is an example of negative reinforcement?
   a. working hard to get an A on a paper
   b. a child getting more computer time when he finishes his homework
   c. a dog whining in the morning, leading an owner to wake up and take it outside
   d. getting a speeding ticket and then not exceeding the speed limit afterward

10. All your friends tell you that you look fabulous in your new jeans, so you start wearing them all the time. This is an example of
    a. positive reinforcement.
    c. positive punishment.
    b. negative reinforcement.
    d. negative punishment.

11. A child is reprimanded for misbehaving. Following this, the child seems to misbehave even more! This indicates that reprimanding the child was
    a. negative punishment.
    b. positive reinforcement.
    c. positive punishment.
    d. unconditioned response.

12. In Bandura's Bobo doll study, children who saw an adult attacking and shouting at the doll:
    a. were more likely to imitate the adult's aggressive behavior.
    b. were less likely to imitate the adult's aggressive behavior.
    c. did not play with the Bobo doll at all.
    d. began to cry when they saw the adult acting aggressively.

13. Children who watch TV programs with violent role models are:
    a. more likely to have parents with legal troubles.
    b. less likely to get in trouble with the law as adults.
    c. at decreased risk of abusing their spouses when they become adults.
    d. at increased risk of abusing their spouses when they become adults.

14. Rats allowed to explore a maze, without getting reinforcers until the 11th day of the experiment, subsequently behaved in the maze as if they had been given reinforcers throughout the entire experiment. Their behavior is evidence of
    a. latent learning.
    c. classical conditioning.
    b. observational learning.
    d. operant conditioning.

15. Wolfgang Köhler's research on chimpanzees suggests that animals are capable of thinking through a problem before taking action, and having a sudden coming together of awareness of a situation, leading to the solution of a problem. This is called:
    a. observational learning.
    b. insight.
    c. modeling.
    d. higher order conditioning.

16. How are classical conditioning and operant conditioning different from each other? What characteristics do they share?

17. Why is biological preparedness important in the life of animals?

18. What is the difference between primary reinforcers and secondary reinforcers? Give an example of each and how they might be used to change a behavior.

19. How are punishment and negative reinforcement different? Give examples of negative reinforcement, positive punishment, and negative punishment and the goal of each for changing behavior.

20. Some studies show that watching violent films is associated with violent behaviors. Why are such studies unable to show a cause-and-effect relationship between a film's content and viewers' behavior?

✓ CHECK YOUR ANSWERS IN APPENDIX C.

Get personalized practice by logging into LaunchPad at **http://www.worthpublishers.com/launchpad/Licht** to take the LearningCurve adaptive quizzes for Chapter 5.

6

An Introduction to Memory

📁 *Memory Breakdown: The Case of Clive Wearing*

📁 *Meet the Memory Athletes*

SA from the pages of
SCIENTIFIC AMERICAN
Why Testing Boosts Learning

Flow With It: The Stages of Memory

➕ THINK AGAIN
Multitasking and Memory

🌐➤ ACROSS THE WORLD
Memory and Culture

Retrieval and Forgetting

👁! DIDN'T SEE THAT COMING
Google Brain

The Reliability of Memory

➡◀ CONTROVERSIES
**The Debate over Repressed
Childhood Memories**

The Biology of Memory

SA from the pages of
SCIENTIFIC AMERICAN
What Marijuana Reveals About Memory

📁 *Final Thoughts*

153   209   17

189   192

memory

An Introduction to Memory

MEMORY BREAKDOWN: THE CASE OF CLIVE WEARING Monday, March 25, 1985: Deborah Wearing awoke in a sweat-soaked bed. Her husband Clive had been up all night sweating, vomiting, and with a high fever. He said that he had a "constant, terrible" headache, like a "band" of pain tightening around his head (Wearing, 2005, p. 27). The symptoms worsened over the next few days, but the two doctors caring for Clive reassured Deborah that it was just a bad case of the flu. By Wednesday, Clive had spent three nights awake with the pain. Confused and disoriented, he turned to Deborah and said, "Er, er, darling. . . . I can't . . . think of your name" (Wearing, 2005, p. 31).

The doctor arrived a couple of hours later, reassured Deborah that her husband's confusion was merely the result of sleep deprivation, and prescribed sleeping pills. Deborah came home later that day, expecting to find her husband in bed. But no Clive. She shouted out his name. No answer, just a heap of pajamas. After the police had conducted an extensive search, Clive was found when a taxi driver dropped him off at a local police station; he had gotten into the cab and couldn't remember his address (Wearing, 2005). Clive returned to his flat (which he did not recognize as home), rested, and took in fluids. His fever dropped, and it appeared that he was improving. But when he awoke Friday morning, his confusion was so severe he could not identify the toilet among the various pieces of furniture in his bathroom. As Deborah placed urgent calls to the doctor, Clive began to drift away. He lost consciousness and was rushed to the hospital in an ambulance (Wearing, 2005; Wilson & Wearing, 1995).

Prior to this illness, Clive Wearing had enjoyed a fabulous career in music. As the Director of the London Lassus Ensemble, he spent his days leading singers and instrumentalists through the emotionally complex music of his favorite composer, Orlande de Lassus. A renowned expert on Renaissance music, Clive produced music for the prestigious British Broadcasting Corporation (BBC), including that which aired on the wedding day of Prince Charles and Lady Diana Spencer (Sacks, 2007; Wilson, Baddeley, & Kapur, 1995; Wilson, Kopelman, & Kapur, 2008). But Clive's work—and his whole life— tumbled into chaos when a virus that normally causes blisters on the mouth invaded his brain.

→

6

LEARNING OBJECTIVES

after reading and studying this chapter, you should be able to:

LO 1   Define memory.

LO 2   Identify the processes of encoding, storage, and retrieval in memory.

LO 3   Explain the stages of memory described by the information-processing model.

LO 4   Describe sensory memory.

LO 5   Summarize short-term memory.

LO 6   Give examples of how we can use chunking to improve our memory span.

LO 7   Explain working memory and how it compares with short-term memory.

LO 8   Define long-term memory.

LO 9   Illustrate how encoding specificity relates to retrieval cues.

LO 10   Identify some of the reasons why we forget.

LO 11   Explain how the malleability of memory influences the recall of events.

LO 12   Define rich false memory.

LO 13   Compare and contrast anterograde and retrograde amnesia.

LO 14   Identify the brain structures involved in memory.

LO 15   Describe long-term potentiation.

The Conductor
In 1985 conductor Clive Wearing (pictured here with his wife Deborah) developed a brain infection—viral encephalitis—that nearly took his life. Clive recovered physically, but his memory was never the same. © Ros Drinkwater/Alamy

Clive and Deborah, In Their Own Words
http://qrs.ly/fb3m62a

Millions of people carry herpes simplex virus type 1 (HSV-1). Usually, it causes unsightly cold sores on the mouth and face. (There is also HSV-2, more commonly associated with genital herpes.) But for a small minority of the adult population—as few as 1 in 500,000 annually—the virus invades the central nervous system and causes a life-threatening infection called *encephalitis*. Left untreated, herpes encephalitis causes death in over 70% of its victims. Most who survive have lasting neurological deficits (Sabah, Mulcahy, & Zeman, 2012; Whitley & Gnann, 2002).

Although Deborah saw to it that Clive received early medical attention, having two doctors visit the house day and night for nearly a week, these physicians mistook his condition for the flu with meningitis-like symptoms (Wilson & Wearing, 1995). Misdiagnosis is common with herpes encephalitis (even to this day), as its symptoms resemble those of other conditions, including the flu, meningitis, a stroke, and epilepsy (Sabah et al., 2012). When Clive and Deborah arrived at the hospital on the 6th day of his illness, they waited another 11 hours just to get a proper diagnosis (Wearing, 2005; Wilson & Wearing, 1995).

Clive survived, but the damage to his brain was extensive and profound; the virus had destroyed a substantial amount of neural tissue. And though Clive could still sing and play the keyboard (and spent much of the day doing so), he was unable to continue working as a conductor and music producer (D. Wearing, personal communication,

Note: Quotations attributed to Dorothea Seitz are personal communications.

June 18, 2013; Wilson & Wearing, 1995). In fact, he could barely get through day-to-day life. In the early stages of recovery, simple activities like eating baffled him. He ate the menu and attempted to spread cottage cheese on his bread, apparently mistaking it for butter. He confused basic concepts such as "scarf" and "umbrella," and shaved his eyebrows and nose (Wearing, 2005; Wilson et al., 1995).

In the months following his illness, Clive was overcome with the feeling of just awakening. His senses were functioning properly, but every sight, sound, odor, taste, and feeling registered for just a moment, and then vanished. As Deborah described it, Clive saw the world anew with every blink of his eye (Wearing, 2005). The world must have seemed like a whirlwind of sensations, always changing, never stable. Desperate to make sense of everything, Clive would pose the same questions time and again: "How long have I been ill?" he would ask Deborah and the hospital staff members looking after him. "How long's it been?" (Wearing, 2005, p. 181). For much of the first decade following his illness, Clive repeated the same few phrases almost continuously in his conversations with people. "I haven't heard anything, seen anything, touched anything, smelled anything," he would say. "It's just like being dead" (Wearing, 2005, p. 160).

The depth of Clive's impairment is revealed in his diary, where he wrote essentially the same entries all day long. On August 25, 1985, he wrote, "I woke at 8:50 A.M. and baught [sic] a copy of *The Observer*," which is then crossed out and followed by "I woke at 9:00 A.M. I had already bought a copy of *The Observer*." The next line reads, "This (officially) confirms that I awoke at 9:05 A.M. this morning" (Wearing, 2005, p. 182). Having forgotten all previous entries, Clive reported throughout the day that he had just become conscious. His recollection of writing in his journal—along with every experience in his life—came and went in a flash. The herpes virus had ravaged his memory system.

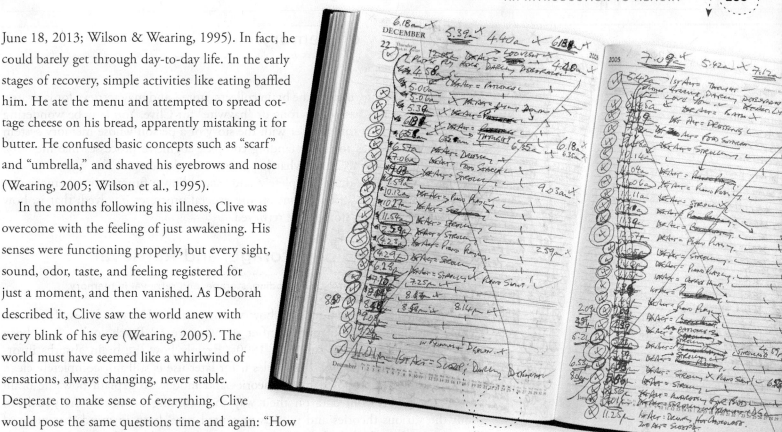

► **The Diary**
Looking at a page from Clive's diary, you can see the fragmented nature of his thought process. He writes an entry, forgets it within seconds, and then returns to the page to start over, often writing the same thing. Encephalitis destroyed areas of Clive's brain that are crucial for learning and memory, so he can no longer recall what is happening from moment to moment. Jiri Rezac/Polaris/Newscom

The story of Clive Wearing launches our journey through *memory*. This chapter will take us to the opposite ends of a continuum: from memory loss to exceptional memory. We will travel to the World Memory Championships, an annual competition where memory competitors from around the globe gather to see how many numbers, words, and images they can squeeze into their brains in 3 days. You will learn some of their tricks, which might help you remember material for exams and everyday life: terms, concepts, passwords, pin numbers, people's names, and where you left your keys. You, too, can develop superior memorization skills; you just have to practice using memory aids. But beware: No matter how well you exercise your memory "muscle," it does not always perform perfectly. Like anything human, memory is imperfect.

An Overview of Memory

> **LO 1**   Define memory.

Memory refers to information the brain collects, stores, and may retrieve for later use. Much of this process has gone wrong or "haywire" for Clive. You may be wondering why we chose to start this chapter with the story of a person whose memory system failed. When it comes to understanding complex cognitive processes like memory, sometimes it helps to examine what happens when elements of the system are not working. Although we don't completely understand how a functioning memory system works, there is basic agreement on the general processes involved; that is, how memories are encoded, stored, and retrieved.

Memory: Encoding, Storage, and Retrieval

> **LO 2**   Identify the processes of encoding, storage, and retrieval in memory.

What is your earliest memory and how was it created? Do you know if it is accurate? And how can you recall it after so many years? Psychologists have been asking questions like these since the 1800s. Exactly how the brain absorbs information from the outside world and files it for later use is still not completely clear, but scientists have proposed many theories and models to explain how the brain processes, or works on, data on their way to becoming memories. As you learn about the various theories and models presented here, keep in mind that none of them are perfect. Rather than labeling one as *right* and another as *wrong*, most psychologists embrace a combination of approaches, taking into consideration their various strengths and weaknesses.

One often used model likens the brain's memory system to a computer. Think about how a computer operates: It receives data from external sources, like your fingers typing on the keyboard, and that data must be converted into a code the computer can manipulate. Once this is accomplished, the information can be saved on the hard drive so you can open up the documents, mp3s, and other data files you need. The brain's memory system accomplishes similar tasks, but as you will learn in this chapter, it is very different from a computer. **Communication among neurons** in the brain is more complicated than signals running between electrical components in a circuit. And unlike a computer, which maintains your files exactly how you last saved them, memories are subject to modifications over time, and this means they may be somewhat different each time you access them. Finally, the brain has seemingly unlimited storage capabilities, and the ability to process many types of information simultaneously, both consciously and unconsciously. Despite these differences, the computer serves as a useful metaphor to explain memory processes, including the *encoding, storage,* and *retrieval* of information.

ENCODING   During the course of a day, we are bombarded with external information coming from all of our senses and internal data from thoughts and emotions. Some of this information we will remember, but the majority of it will not be retained for very long. What is the difference between what is kept and what is not? Most psychologists agree that it all starts with **encoding,** the process through which information enters our memory system. Think about what happens when you pay attention to an event unfolding before you; stimuli associated with that event (sights, sounds, smells) are taken in by your senses and then **converted to neural activity** that travels to the brain. Once in the brain, the neural activity continues, at which point the information takes one of two paths: Either it enters our memory system (it is encoded to be stored for a longer period of time) or it slips away. For Clive Wearing, much of this information slips away.

CONNECTIONS ◂

In **Chapter 2,** we described the electrical and chemical processes involved in the communication between neurons. We also reported that the human nervous system, which includes the brain, contains 100 billion cells interlinked by about 100 quadrillion (10^{15}) connections.

CONNECTIONS ◂

In **Chapters 2 and 3,** we described how sensory information is taken in by sensory receptors and transduced; that is, transformed into neural activity. Here, we will explore what happens after *transduction,* when information is processed in the memory system.

memory Information collected and stored in the brain that is generally retrievable for later use.

encoding The process through which information enters our memory system.

storage The process of preserving information for possible recollection in the future.

retrieval The process of accessing information encoded and stored in memory.

STORAGE The next step for information that is successfully encoded is **storage.** Storage is exactly what it sounds like: preserving information for possible recollection in the future. Before Clive Wearing fell ill, his memory was excellent. His brain was able to encode and store a variety of events and learned abilities. Following his bout with encephalitis, however, his ability for long-term storage of new memories was destroyed—he could no longer retain new information for more than seconds at a time.

RETRIEVAL After information is stored, how do we access it? Perhaps you still have a memory of your first-grade teacher's face, but can you remember his/her name? This process of coming up with the name is called **retrieval.** Sometimes information is encoded and stored in memory, but it cannot be accessed, or retrieved. Have you ever felt that a person's name or a certain vocabulary word was just sitting "on the tip of your tongue"? Chances are you were struggling from a retrieval failure, which we will discuss later in this chapter.

Before taking a closer look at the three processes of memory—encoding, storage, and retrieval—let's see what the memory system can do when it's functioning at an optimal level. Welcome to the world of memory sport.

Encephalitis ◄
The red area in this computerized axial tomography (CAT or CT) scan reveals inflammation in the temporal lobe. The cause of this swelling is herpes simplex virus, the same virus responsible for Clive's illness. Many people carry this virus (it causes cold sores), but herpes encephalitis is extremely rare, affecting as few as 1 in 500,000 people annually (Sabah et al., 2012). Even with early treatment, this brain infection frequently leaves its victims with cognitive damage (Kennedy & Chaudhuri, 2002). Airelle-Joubert/Science Source

MEET THE MEMORY ATHLETES The 18th Annual World Memory Championships had officially kicked off. Dorothea Seitz felt her heart pound as she flipped over her memorization sheet. The page was filled with row upon row of black-and-gray "abstract images" that any ordinary person would see as meaningless blobs, distinguishable only by subtle differences in shape, shade, and texture. But to Dorothea, these blobs were rabbits leaping off the page, fish splashing in water, or bizarre human faces—anything her mind could conjure up. Because one of the keys to memorization, most any memory champion will tell you, is a lively imagination. She had 15 minutes to memorize as many images as possible, a maximum of 330, in the order given.

Dorothea was the reigning junior champion, and she had come to defend her title. Sitting in that same London conference room with her were 73 other contestants from all over the world, including most of the hotshots in memory sport.

Silence saturated the room as contestants studied their memorization sheets. Many of them wore large ear plugs or earmuffs to cancel out any noises that might derail their train of thought—a sneeze, a pen hitting the floor, even the sound of someone breathing. Others wore dark glasses with tiny holes cut out of their centers, or side blinders like the kind racehorses wear—anything to keep their eyes from wandering from the task at hand.

Memory Jocks ◄
Germany's child memory champion Katharina Bunk studies a memorization sheet at a competition in Bad Wörishofen, Germany. In this "Names and Faces" event, the goal is to memorize as many name–face combinations as possible during the allotted time. Many competitors wear earmuffs and other devices to block out background noises that might interfere with their concentration. Karl-Josef Hildenbrand/picturealliance/dpa/AP Images

When the 15 minutes was up, contest supervisors circulated the room collecting memorization sheets and distributing "recall sheets"—pieces of paper with the same images arranged in a different order. The contestants had only 30 minutes to unscramble them. Speeding through the recall phase of the event, Dorothea managed to remember 214 images. That put her in fourth place overall—not bad for a 17-year-old high school student competing against adults.

Dorothea had started the competition strong, but there were still nine events to go. The competitors would spend the next 3 days memorizing meaningless strings of numbers, random lists of words, imaginary historic dates, and other pieces of contrived "information."

2,808 Cards
Memory master Dominic O'Brien took 54 decks of playing cards and memorized their correct order after flipping through them just once. By practicing memory techniques, Dominic went from being a person with an average memory to an eight-time World Memory Champion. musk/Alamy

MEMORY COMPETITORS AND THE REST OF US   The brains of memory champions are not wired in a special way; these are regular people who have trained themselves to excel in memory. Just ask eight-time World Memory Champion Dominic O'Brien if he thinks anyone can acquire an exceptional memory, and he will tell you there's no doubt about it. When O'Brien first began to train his memory at age 30, he could remember no more than 6 or 7 playing cards in a row. Eventually, he was able to memorize 2,808 cards (54 decks) after looking at each card only once. "I transformed my memory power very quickly as a result of applying simple techniques and practicing regularly," Dominic says. "If I can become a memory champion then anybody can" (D. O'Brien, personal communication, January 10, 2010). Just like a gymnast or a wrestler, a memory athlete prepares, trains, and practices. A powerful memory takes work!

One small study actually compared memory competitors to "normal" people and found nothing extraordinary about their intelligence or brain structure. What they did find was heightened activity in specific brain areas (particularly in regions used for spatial memory). This activity seemed to be associated with the use of a method for remembering items by associating them with an imagined "journey" (Maguire, Valentine, Wilding, & Kapur, 2003). As it turns out, memory champions like Dorothea and Dominic rely heavily on this type of imagined journey, which is rich with visual images. We will learn about this memory aid later in the chapter when we discuss memory improvement, but first we must get a grasp of how the entire system works. What exactly happens to data flowing into the memory system?

The Information-Processing Model of Memory

> **LO 3**   Explain the stages of memory described by the information-processing model.

CONNECTIONS

In **Chapter 1,** we described the importance of using theories and models to organize and conceptualize observations. In this chapter, we present several of these to explain the human memory system.

Psychologists employ **several models** that offer plausible explanations for how the memory system is organized. Among the most influential is the *information-processing model,* which suggests that memory operates in a series of stages (**FIGURE 6.1**). This model, first developed by Atkinson and Shiffrin, suggests that these stages represent a *flow of information* (Anderson, 1971; Atkinson & Shiffrin, 1968; Wood & Pennington, 1973).

FIGURE 6.1
The Information-Processing Model of Memory

According to the information-processing model, the brain has three types of memory storage, each associated with a stage of memory: **Sensory memory** can hold vast amounts of sensory stimuli for a sliver of time, **short-term memory** can temporarily maintain and process limited information for a longer stretch, and **long-term memory** has essentially unlimited capacity and stores enduring information about facts and experiences. In the upcoming pages, you will read much more about these stages of memory and how they relate to Clive Wearing, whose short- and long-term memory are severely impaired.

The information-processing model is a valuable tool for learning about and researching memory, but like any scientific model, it has flaws. Some critics contend

Synonym

sensory memory sensory register

sensory memory A stage of memory that captures near-exact copies of vast amounts of sensory stimuli for a very brief period of time.

short-term memory A stage of memory that temporarily maintains and processes a limited amount of information.

long-term memory A stage of memory with essentially unlimited capacity that stores enduring information about facts and experiences.

that *sensory memory* is really a primary component of **perception.** Others doubt that a clear boundary exists between *short-term* and *long-term memories* (Baddeley, 1995). And still others argue that this "pipeline" model is a simplistic representation because information does not necessarily flow through the memory system in a straight-line path (Cowan, 1988). Despite its weaknesses, the information-processing model remains an essential tool for explaining how memory works.

Levels of Processing

Another way to conceptualize memory is from a processing standpoint. To what degree does information entering the memory system get worked on? According to the *levels of processing* framework, there is a "hierarchy of processing stages" that corresponds to different depths of information processing (Craik & Lockhart, 1972). Thus, processing can occur along a continuum from shallow to deep (**FIGURE 6.2**). Shallow-level processing is primarily concerned with physical features—characteristics like the brightness or shape of an object, for instance. Deeper-level processing relies on characteristics related to patterns and meaning, and generally results in longer-lasting and easier to retrieve memories. So when you pay only a little attention to data entering your sensory system, shallow processing occurs, resulting in more transient memories. If you really contemplate incoming information and relate it to memories you already have, deeper processing occurs, and the new memories are more likely to persist (Craik & Tulving, 1975; Francis & Gutiérrez, 2012; Newell & Andrews, 2004).

Suppose you are trying to learn and remember the names of the three processes involved in memory: *encoding, storage,* and *retrieval.* You could try to memorize the words based on a shallow characteristic (storage has 7 letters, encoding has 8 letters, and retrieval has 9 letters), or you could think about the words on a deeper level, connecting them to concepts already stored in your memory system. Memory champion Dominic O'Brien came up with this one: *Encoding* makes him think of codes and secret agents, so he imagines a James Bond character going into a huge warehouse (*storage* facility) and seeing a golden retriever (*retrieval*) run out the door (D. O'Brien, personal communication, December 7, 2009). The more deeply you think about incoming information, considering its meaning or personal relevance, the greater success you will have learning and remembering it.

Shallow: notice some physical features

Intermediate: notice patterns and a little more detail

Deep: think about meaning

SHALLOW, INTERMEDIATE, AND DEEP Fergus Craik and Endel Tulving explored levels of processing in their 1975 classic study. After presenting college students with various words, the researchers asked them yes or no questions, prompting them to think about and encode the words at three different levels: shallow, intermediate, and deep. The shallow questions required the students to study the appearance of the word: "Is the word in capital letters?" The intermediate-level questions related to the sound of the word: "Does the word rhyme with 'weight'?" And finally, the deep questions challenged the students to consider the word's meaning: "Is the word a type of fish?" When the researchers surprised the students with a test to see which words they remembered best, without any cues or clues, the students were best able to remember those words whose meaning they had thought about (Craik & Tulving, 1975). The take-home message: Deep thinking leads to firm memories (Foos & Goolkasian, 2008), particularly if you are trying to remember information with no cues for retrieval. Ask several people

CONNECTIONS

In **Chapter 3,** we defined *sensation* as the process by which receptors receive and detect stimuli. *Perception* is the process by which sensory data are organized to provide meaningful information. Some critics of the information-processing model suggest that sensory memory is an important component of perception, not a stage of memory.

PROCESSING

FISH *fish* fish

fish/dish

▲ **FIGURE 6.2**
The Levels of Processing Framework of Memory
Information can be processed along a continuum from shallow to deep, affecting the probability of recall. Shallow processing, in which only certain details like the physical appearance of a word might be noticed, results in brief memories that may not be recalled later. We are better able to recall information we process at a deep level, thinking about meaning and tying it to memories we already have. Gunnar Pippel/Shutterstock

to do the following Try This and see if a *deeper* level of processing leads to better encoding and stronger memories, depending on which one of the three instructions you give them.

Try to remember the name "Clive Wearing" by (1) picturing it written out in uppercase letters (CLIVE WEARING), (2) imagining what it sounds like (*Clive Wearing rhymes with dive daring*), and (3) contemplating its underlying significance (*Clive Wearing is the musician who suffers from an extreme case of memory loss*).

Most people have the greatest success with (3), but the impact of depth of processing depends somewhat on how you are prompted to retrieve information. For example, if someone asks you to remember any words that rhyme with "dive daring," the name "Clive Wearing" will probably pop into your head regardless of whether you used deep processing.

Can you guess how deep thinking might help you succeed in school? Let's find out how testing, which often requires you to connect new and old information, can improve your memory.

from the pages of **SCIENTIFIC AMERICAN**

Why Testing Boosts Learning

Getting quizzed strengthens memory-jogging keyword clues

For more than a century scientists have known that individuals who are tested on material are more likely to remember it than those who simply study. But questions remain about why that is the case. Kent State University psychology researcher Katherine Rawson argues that part of the explanation is that testing gets people to come up with better keyword clues, which bridge the gap between familiar and new information— and it strengthens ties between these keywords and the newly learned information.

Rawson and former graduate student Mary Pyc asked 118 college students to learn four dozen Swahili words by matching them with their English counterparts, such as *wingu,* which means "cloud." After an initial study period, half were given practice tests before studying the words a second time, and half restudied the words without taking a practice test.

As expected, students in the practice test group were better at remembering the word pairs during a final exam a week later. But Rawson and Pyc also asked students to tell them their keywords— for instance, "bird" might serve as a bridge between *wingu* and cloud—and they revealed that the people in the practice test group not only remembered more of their keywords, but they were more likely to have changed their keyword before restudying the word pairs than those who had not been tested. As the researchers reported in *Science* last October, these results suggest that testing improves memory by strengthening keyword associations and weeding out clues that do not work. Andrea Anderson. Reproduced with permission. Copyright © 2010 Scientific American, a division of Nature America, Inc. All rights reserved.

Who knew that testing actually could improve memory? Will this change your approach to studying for exams? A recent review strongly supports the finding that "testing improves learning," as long as the stakes are low (Dunlosky, Rawson, Marsh, Nathan, & Willingham, 2013). The Show What You Know and Test Prep resources in this textbook are designed for just this purpose. Repeated testing, or the *testing effect,* results in a variety of benefits: better information retention; identification of areas needing more study; and increased self-motivated studying (Roediger, Putnam, & Smith, 2011; TABLE 6.1).

Table 6.1 STUDY TIPS	
Technique	**What to Do**
Survey	Skim the contents to determine what may be useful to you: review questions, learning objectives, chapter summaries. Identify main ideas and concepts.
Question	Note any questions that arise after your survey. Create an outline to help organize your study based on the questions you generate.
Read	Read through your chapter and take notes on the content.
Recall	Go over the material you have read in your mind. Identify key points and crucial processes. Discuss how other material supports the key points and processes.
Review	Reread the material, and include additional material to enhance your notes. "Teach" the material to someone else.
Individualize the process	Break down the reading into small sections you can read, recall, and review effectively.
Space your study	Build in breaks and spread the study sessions over time.
Minimize distractions	Focus on the task at hand; multitasking while studying diverts attention, resulting in more time spent learning the material.
Test frequently	Test yourself frequently. Low-stakes feedback provides an opportunity to learn the material and retain it longer.
Sleep	Get enough rest. Good sleep helps us learn new material and retain it.

Included in this table are tips for improving your memory and long-term retention of new information. These ideas can be applied not only in your psychology class, but also to other courses and life situations.

SOURCES: AL FIRDAUS (2012); ROEDIGER, PUTNAM, & SMITH (2011); ROHRER & TAYLOR (2006).

We have now introduced the information-processing model, which suggests that data travel through various memory stages: sensory, short-term, and long-term. We have also addressed the way in which levels of processing (shallow, intermediate, and deep) can influence our ability to retrieve information. In the next section, we will flesh out the concepts of sensory, short-term, and long-term memory, which are incorporated in most memory models. We will also examine a model that offers a more dynamic alternative to short-term memory.

show what you know

1. _____ refers to the information that your brain collects, stores, and may use at a later time.

2. _____ is the process whereby information enters our memory system.
   a. Retrieval
   b. Encoding
   c. Communication
   d. Spatial memory

3. After suffering from a devastating illness, Clive Wearing essentially lost the ability to use which of the following stages of the information-processing model?
   a. long-term memory
   b. sensory memory
   c. memory for keywords
   d. sensory register

4. How might you illustrate shallow processing versus deep processing as it relates to studying?

✓ CHECK YOUR ANSWERS IN APPENDIX C.

Flow With It: The Stages of Memory

Think of all the information streaming through your sensory channels at this very moment. Your eyes may be focused on this sentence, but you are also collecting data through your peripheral vision. You may be hearing noises (the hum of a fan), smelling odors (dinner cooking in the kitchen), tasting foods (if you are snacking), and even feeling things (your back pressed against a chair). Many of these sensory stimuli never catch your attention, but some are being registered in your *sensory memory*, the first stage of the information-processing model (INFOGRAPHIC 6.1).

Sensory Memory: The Here and Now

LO 4   Describe sensory memory.

The bulk of information entering sensory memory comes and goes like the images on a movie screen. A few things catch your attention—the beautiful eyes of Mila Kunis, the sound of her voice, and perhaps the color of her shirt—but not much more before the frame switches and you're looking at another image. Information floods our sensory memory through multiple channels—what we see enters through one channel, what we taste through another, and so on.

"MORE IS SEEN THAN CAN BE REMEMBERED"   Interested in how the brain processes data entering the visual channel, Harvard graduate student George Sperling (1960) designed an experiment to determine how much information can be detected in a brief exposure to visual stimuli. Sperling set up a screen that flashed multiple rows of letters for one-twentieth of a second, and then asked participants to report what they saw. His first goal was to determine how many letters the participants could remember when an *array* of letters (for example, three rows of 4 letters) was flashed briefly; he found that, on average, the participants only reported 4 letters. But Sperling wasn't sure if this meant they were only able to store one row at a time in their memory, or if they stored all the rows at once, but just not long enough to recite them before they were forgotten.

Sperling was convinced that "more is seen than can be remembered" (1960, p. 1), so he devised a clever method called *partial report* to provide evidence. As with the original experiment, he briefly flashed an array of letters (for example, three rows of 4 letters), with all rows visible. But instead of having the participants report what they remembered from all the rows, he asked them to report what they remembered from just one row at a time. Here's how the study went: The array of letters was flashed, and once it disappeared, a tone was sounded. When participants heard a high-pitched tone, they were to report the letters in the top row; with a medium-pitched tone, the letters in the middle row; and with a low-pitched tone, the letters in the bottom row. The participants were only asked to give a partial report, that is, to report on just one of the rows, but they did not know which row ahead of time. In this version of the study, the participants performed very well, recalling approximately 76% of the letters. They doubled their performance with the partial report method, suggesting that more *can* be seen than is remembered—even though these memories last less than 1 second (Sperling, 1960). Sperling's research suggests that the *visual impressions* in our sensory memory, also known as **iconic memory,** are photograph-like in their accuracy but dissolve in less than a second. Given the short duration of iconic memory, can you predict what would happen to the participants' performance if there were a delay before they reported what they saw?

iconic memory Visual impressions that are photograph-like in their accuracy but dissolve in less than a second; a form of sensory memory.

Sensory Memory

On your way to class, you notice a dog barking at a passing car. You see the car, smell its exhaust, hear the dog. All this information coming through your sensory systems registers in your *sensory memory*, the first in a series of stages in the information-processing model of memory.

But what happens to information once it enters your sensory memory? Sensory memory is difficult to study. Research such as George Sperling's classic experiment involving iconic memory helps us understand how sensory memories are registered and processed.

Sensory information is constantly taken in, creating different types of sensory memory.

woof!

Most information registers in sensory memory.

Echoic Memory

"*I hear the dog barking.*"
- auditory impressions/ sounds
- duration 1–10 seconds
- very accurate

Iconic Memory

"*I see the dog.*"
- visual impressions/ images
- duration less than 1 second
- very accurate

SENSORY MEMORY

woof!

→ **SHORT-TERM MEMORY*** → **LONG-TERM MEMORY**

*Not all information processed in sensory memory ends up in short-term memory.

"*I smell the car's exhaust.*"
- smell, pain, touch, taste, etc.
- duration and accuracy vary

How do we know how long iconic memory lasts?

George Sperling (1960) developed a creative way to measure how quickly iconic memories fade from awareness. Participants were shown an array of letters and were asked to recall one row. Participants performed well when recalling that one row, but couldn't recall other letters: Their sensory memory for them had faded. This technique is still used today to study fleeting sensory memories.

K Z R A
Q B T P
S G N Y

Letters flash on screen, then disappear.

High Tone
MediumTone
Low Tone

A tone sounds. Participants report only the row associated with that tone.

Q B T P

Participants can report row associated with tone, but no other row. All letters initially registered in their sensory memory, but the iconic memory dissolves before more letters can be reported.

EIDETIC IMAGERY   Perhaps you have heard friends talk about someone who claims to have a "photographic memory" that can record and store images with the accuracy of a camera: "My cousin can look at a textbook page, remember exactly what it says in a few seconds, and then recall the information days later, seeing the pages exactly as they were." That may be what your cousin claims, but is there scientific evidence to back up such an assertion? We doubt it.

According to some reports, though, researchers have documented a phenomenon that comes fairly close to photographic memory. It's called *eidetic imagery* (ī-'de-tik), and those who have this ability can "see" an image or object for as long as several minutes after it has been removed from sight, describing its parts with amazing specificity. However, the details they "see" are not always accurate, and thus their memories are not quite "photographic." Eidetic imagery is rare and usually only occurs in young children (Searleman, 2007).

ECHOIC MEMORY   Exact copies of the sounds we hear linger longer than visual impressions; **echoic memory** (ə-kō-ik) can last from about 1 to 10 seconds (Lu, Williamson, & Kaufman, 1992; Peterson, Meagher, & Ellsbury, 1970), and it can capture very subtle changes in sound. Research has shown that the introduction of a **single tone** played for 300 milliseconds initiates changes in cortical activity (Inui et al., 2010). Even if you are not aware of it, your auditory system is picking up slight changes in stimuli and storing them in echoic memory for a brief moment, so you don't have to pay attention to every incoming bit of auditory information. Perhaps you have had the following experience: During class, your instructor notices a classmate daydreaming and tries to bring him back to reality: "Eddy, could you please restate the question for us?" His mind was indeed wandering, but amazingly he could recall your instructor's last sentence, responding, "You asked us if brain scans should be allowed as evidence in courtrooms." For this, he can thank his echoic memory.

Although brief, sensory memory is critical to the creation of memories. Without it, how would information enter the memory system in the first place? We have discussed iconic and echoic memory, which register sights and sounds, but memories can also be rich in smells, tastes, and touch. Remember, data received from all the senses are held momentarily in sensory memory. And although the bulk of research has focused on iconic and echoic memories, psychologists propose that we also have similar sensory stores for the other senses.

Now that we have examined the initial sensory and perceptual experiences captured in sensory memory, let's move to the next stage of the information-processing model: short-term memory.

Short-Term Memory

> **LO 5**   Summarize short-term memory.

When information enters your sensory memory, it does not linger. So where does it go next? If not lost in the overwhelming array of sensory stimuli, the data proceed to *short-term memory,* the second stage in the information-processing model proposed by Atkinson and Shiffrin (1968). The amount of time information is maintained and processed in short-term memory depends on whether you are distracted by other cognitive activities, but the duration can be about 30 seconds (Atkinson & Shiffrin, 1968).

In a classic study examining the duration of short-term memory, an experimenter recited a three-letter combination, followed by a number. Participants were then asked to begin counting backward by 3 from the number given (if the experimenter said, "CHG 300," then participants would respond, "300, 297, 294. . .") until they saw a red light flash, which signaled them to repeat the three-letter combination. After 3 seconds of counting backward, participants could only recall the correct letter combinations approximately 50% of the time (**FIGURE 6.3**). Most of the participants were unable to recall the letter combination beyond 18 seconds (Peterson & Peterson, 1959). Why do you think it was so hard for them to remember? Think about what you normally do if you're trying to remember something; you probably say it over and over in your head (*CHG, CHG, CHG. . .*). But the participants were not able to do this because they had to count backward by 3s, which interfered with their natural inclination to mentally repeat the letter combinations.

What this experiment reveals is that short-term memory has a limited capacity. At any given moment, you can only concentrate on a tiny percentage of the data flooding your sensory memory. Items that capture your **attention** can move into your short-term memory, but most everything else disappears faster than you can say the word "memory." Please remember this when you are texting during class or watching TV while studying; if your goal is to remember what you *should be* concentrating on, you need to give it your full attention.

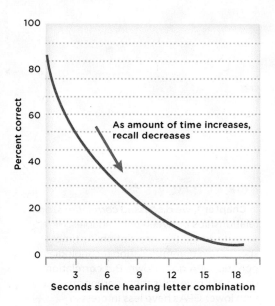

▲ **FIGURE 6.3**
Duration of Short-Term Memory
Distraction can reduce the amount of time information remains in short-term memory. When performing a distracting cognitive task, most people were unable to recall a letter combination beyond 18 seconds. *Source: From Peterson and Peterson (1959), Figure 3, p. 195.*

CONNECTIONS

Here, we see how memory is related to attention. In **Chapter 4,** we talked about the limited capacity of human attention. At any given point in time, there are only so many items you can attend to and thus move into your memory system.

THINK again

Multitasking and Memory

It's Sunday evening, and you need to catch up on the reading for your psychology class. You sit down in a quiet place and open your textbook. But just as you are getting into the psychology groove, a little "bloop bloop" jolts you out of the mental flow. A text bubble appears in the corner of the screen: OMG . . . blah blah blah . . . LOL! You begin an instant messaging (IM) conversation that continues on-and-off throughout your study session, periodically taking away your attention from psychology. By the evening's end, you do manage to finish a chapter, but how do you think your digital chitchat affected your memory of its material?

Psychologists from Central Connecticut State University wondered the same thing, so they did what any good researchers would do: They designed an experiment to find answers. The participants in their study were people very much like you—college students ranging from ages 17 to 46 who had enrolled in a general psychology course. All 89 students were asked to read a passage from a psychology textbook; some were allowed to read undisturbed, while others had to carry on IM conversations at the same time. Once the students had completed the assignment, the researchers quizzed them on their knowledge of the material (Bowman, Levine, Waite, & Gendron, 2010).

Here's what they found: The students who IMed during the reading task performed at roughly the same level as their non-IMing peers, but they needed much more time to

---

echoic memory (ə-ˈkō-ik) Exact copies of the sounds we hear; a form of sensory memory.

read the passage: about 22–59% longer, and that's not including the time they spent reading and writing instant messages (Bowman et al., 2010). Thus, in order to achieve the same level of understanding, the IMers had to spend a lot more time making their way through the text. What does this mean for you? IMing might be seriously slowing the rate at which you learn. Spend enough time bouncing text bubbles back-and-forth, and you might even see your grades head south; there is some evidence that college students who spend a lot of time IMing may have lower grade point averages than those who do not (Fox, Rosen, & Crawford, 2009). And it's not just IMing. Another large study found that students who frequently text and use Facebook while studying have lower GPAs than those who do not (Junco & Cotten, 2012). ●+

HOW TO LOWER YOUR GPA USING FACEBOOK

CONNECTIONS

In **Chapter 1,** we discussed *correlations,* or relationships between two variables. Here, we note a negative correlation: As time spent using communication technologies goes up, GPA goes down. But correlation does not prove causation; perhaps people with lower GPAs have less interest in studying, and thus more time to socialize. Or, maybe there is a *third factor,* such as the ability to manage time effectively, influencing both variables.

2390
45791
340982
0128957
93781256
501298347

▲ FIGURE 6.4
Digit Span Test
The Digit Span test is a simple way to assess memory. Participants are asked to listen to a string of numbers and then repeat them. The string of numbers grows longer as the test progresses. Ask a friend to give you this test and see how many numbers you can remember. For a real challenge, you can even try to recite the list backward!

chunking Grouping numbers, letters, or other items into meaningful subsets as a strategy for increasing the quantity of information that can be maintained in short-term memory.

working memory The active processing of information in short-term memory; the maintenance and manipulation of information in the memory system.

Multitasking, whether texting, using Facebook, or IMing, inevitably involves a shift in attention, and this is hard work for the brain, which has to engage and disengage different networks (Clapp, Rubens, Sabharwal, & Gazzaley, 2011). Keep this in mind the next time you consider texting while driving. Texting at the wheel increases the likelihood of crashing or coming close to crashing by 23 times (Olson, Hanowski, Hickman, & Bocanegra, 2009), and studies show that using a cell phone impairs driving to the same degree as drunkenness (Strayer & Watson, 2012).

Now that we have established how important attention is for your success and safety, let's return to the memory stage to which it is so intimately tied: short-term memory. We mentioned that people frequently try to remember numbers and letters by repeating them over and over in their minds. Mental rehearsal is useful, but how many digits can we realistically hold in our short-term memory at one time? Using a task called the Digit Span test (**FIGURE 6.4**), cognitive psychologist George Miller (1956) determined that most people can retain only five to nine digits: He called this the "magical number seven, plus or minus two."

LO 6   Give examples of how we can use chunking to improve our memory span.

Indeed, most people can only attend to about five to nine items at one time (Cowan, Chen, & Rouder, 2004; Cowan, Nugent, & Elliott, 2000; Miller, 1956), but what if those "items" are not numbers made up of single digits? Is it possible to expand short-term memory by packing more information into the items we need to remember?

Consider this example: Your friend has just gotten a new phone number, and she tells it to you as the elevator is closing between you. How are you going to remember her number long enough to create a new entry in your cell phone's address book? You could try memorizing all 10 digits in a row (8935550172), but a better strategy is to break the number into more manageable pieces (893-555-0172). Here, we have an example of **chunking,** Miller's name for grouping numbers, letters, or other items into meaningful subsets, or "chunks." Can you think of situations in which you might chunk information to help you remember it more easily?

Short-term memory can only hold so much, but we can increase its storage potential by chunking. The fact that short-term memory is actively processing information and is flexible in this regard suggests that it may be more than just a stage in which information is briefly stored. Indeed, many psychologists believe that short-term memory is more than an inactive storage facility.

Working Memory: Where the Action Is

LO 7   Explain working memory and how it compares with short-term memory.

More recent conceptualizations of the information-processing model include a concept known as **working memory** (Baddeley & Hitch, 1974), which refers to what is *going on* in short-term memory. Working memory is the active processing through which we maintain and manipulate information in the memory system. Let's use an analogy of a "bakery" and what goes on inside it. Think of short-term memory as the bakery, that is, the place that hosts your current thoughts and whatever your brain is working on at this very moment. According to this conceptualization, working memory is analogous to the making of bread inside the bakery.

But not everyone agrees on the distinctions between short-term and working memory (Cowan, 2008; Rose, Myerson, Roediger, & Hale, 2010). Some psychologists do not differentiate between short-term and working memory, and use the terms interchangeably. For our purposes, we will identify "short-term memory" as a stage in the original information-processing model as well as the "location" where information is temporarily held, and "working memory" as the activities and processing occurring within. So, let's take a closer look at the model of working memory originally proposed by psychologists Alan Baddeley and Graham Hitch (1974), which has been updated and revised throughout the years (Baddeley, 2002).

According to this model, the purpose of working memory is to actively maintain information, aiding the mind that is busily performing complex cognitive tasks. To accomplish this, working memory has four components with specific functions: the phonological loop, the visuospatial sketchpad, the central executive, and the episodic buffer (Baddeley, 2002; FIGURE 6.5).

PHONOLOGICAL LOOP   The *phonological loop* is responsible for working with verbal information for brief periods of time; when exposed to verbal stimuli, we "hear" an immediate corollary in our mind. This component of working memory is what we use, for example, when we are reading, trying to solve problems, or learning new vocabulary. Most of us can only manipulate about 2 seconds' worth of verbal material in this loop without actively trying to repeat it (Baddeley, 2000; Baddeley & Hitch, 1994).

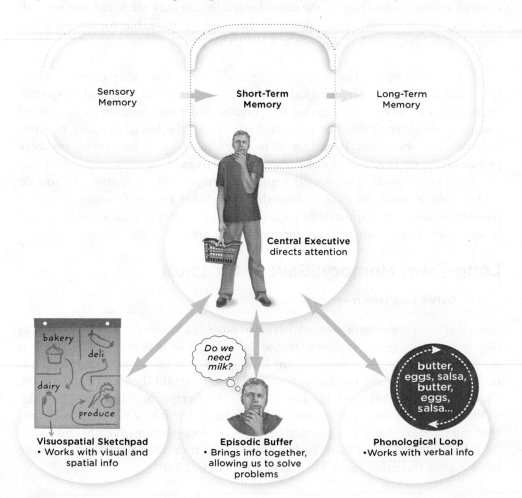

FIGURE 6.5
Model of Working Memory
Working memory represents the active processing occurring in short-term memory. Overseeing the big picture is the central executive, which directs attention and integrates processing among three subsystems: the phonological loop, the visuospatial sketchpad, and the episodic buffer. To see how this model works, imagine you have stopped by the supermarket to pick up groceries. You rehearse the shopping list with your phonological loop, produce a mental layout of the store with your visuospatial sketchpad, and use the episodic buffer to access long-term memories and determine whether you need any additional items. Tying together all these activities is the central executive. *Source:* Baddeley (2002).

Imagine you are trying to remember the passcode for your debit card. You know it is somehow related to your first zip code, so you retrieve your zip code from long-term memory. You then "hear" the five numbers played in your phonological loop as you desperately try to remember your passcode (*I remember it was 02138*). Once you figure out your passcode, the numbers of your zip code are no longer needed, and they slip quietly back into your long-term memory.

VISUOSPATIAL SKETCHPAD   The *visuospatial sketchpad* is where visual and spatial data are briefly stored and manipulated, including information about your surroundings, where things are in relation to each other and you. This working memory component allows you to close your eyes and reach for the coffee mug you just set down. We can also use information from long-term memory in our visuospatial sketchpad. Imagine you are standing at the entrance to the mall, determined to make your shopping excursion short and sweet. Thinking back to the last time you were there, you bring forth a mental image of how the stores are laid out. Excellent! You now have a map of the mall in your visuospatial sketchpad, which allows you to make more strategic decisions (*Victoria's Secret? No, JCPenney is closer*). But as you start considering the items you need to buy, the memory of the mall layout begins to slide back into your long-term memory. Studies by Baddeley and colleagues show that we have difficulty trying to perform just two visuospatial tasks at the same time (Baddeley, 1999, 2006).

CENTRAL EXECUTIVE   The *central executive* has responsibilities similar to those of the chief executive in any organization—it directs attention, makes plans, and coordinates activities (Baddeley, 2002). Part of its role is determining what information to attend to and what to ignore, helping with the juggling, organizing, focusing, and manipulating of consciousness. Why is it that we cannot actually text, eat, and safely drive all at once? Like a juggler, the central executive can only catch and toss one ball at a time. We may think we are doing all three tasks at once, but we are really just swapping the alternatives in and out at a fast pace.

EPISODIC BUFFER   The *episodic buffer* is the part of working memory where information from the phonological loop, visuospatial sketchpad, and long-term memory can all be brought together temporarily, under the direction of the central executive (Baddeley, 2000). The episodic buffer forms the bridge between memory and conscious awareness. It enables us to assign meaning to past events, to solve problems that we face, and to make plans for the future.

As you know, working memory is limited in its capacity and duration. So how do we maintain so much information over the years? What aspect of memory makes it possible to memorize thousands of vocabulary words, scores of names and facts, and lyrics to your favorite songs? Enter long-term memory.

Long-Term Memory: Save It for Later

LO 8   Define long-term memory.

Items that enter short-term memory have two possible fates: Either they fade away or they move into *long-term memory* (**FIGURE 6.6**). Think of how much information is stored in your long-term memory: funny jokes, passwords, images of faces, multiplication tables, and so many vocabulary words—between 30,000 (Lessmoellmann, 2006, October 4) and 60,000 words (Pinker, 1994) for the average English speaker. Could it be that long-term memory has an endless holding capacity? It may be impossible to answer this question, but for all practical purposes our long-term memory has no limits. And the memories stored there, such as street names from your childhood, may even last a lifetime (Schmidt, Peeck, Paas, & van Breukelen, 2000).

Synonym
explicit memory declarative memory

explicit memory A type of memory you are aware of having and can consciously express in words or declare, including memories of facts and experiences.

semantic memory The memory of information theoretically available to anyone, which pertains to general facts about the world; a type of explicit memory.

episodic memory (e-pə-sä-dik) The record of memorable experiences or "episodes" including when and where an experience occurred; a type of explicit memory.

flashbulb memory A detailed account of circumstances surrounding an emotionally significant or shocking, sometimes historic, event.

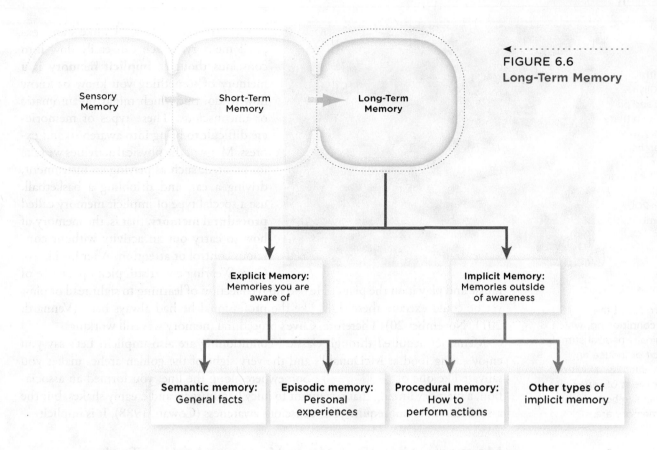

FIGURE 6.6
Long-Term Memory

EXPLICIT MEMORY   Long-term memory can be described in a variety of ways, but psychologists often distinguish between two categories: explicit and implicit. **Explicit memory** is the type of memory you are aware of having and can consciously express in words or declare: *Roses are red, guacamole is made with avocados; I wore blue jeans yesterday.* Tulving (1972) proposes two forms of explicit memory: semantic and episodic. **Semantic memory** pertains to general facts about the world (*the sky is blue; the United States holds presidential elections every four years*; Tulving, 1985). But there is also a type of memory you can call your own. This personal form is called **episodic memory** (e-pə-sä-dik). It is the record of the memorable experiences, or "episodes," you have had, including when and where they occurred (Tulving, 1985).

FLASHBULB MEMORIES   Often our most vivid episodic memories are associated with intense emotion. Think about an emotionally charged experience from your past: receiving news that a loved one has died, getting engaged, or being the victim of an assault. If recollecting these events feels like watching a 4-D movie, you might be experiencing what psychologists call a **flashbulb memory,** a detailed account of circumstances surrounding an emotionally significant or shocking, sometimes historic, event (Brown & Kulik, 1977). Some people remember what they were doing when they heard about the terrorist attacks of September 11, 2001, or the horrific events that unfolded at Sandy Hook Elementary School in Newtown, Connecticut, on December 14, 2012. They recall where they were, who or what source relayed the news, how it made them feel, what they did next, and other random details about their experience (Brown & Kulik, 1977).

Because flashbulb memories seem so strong, vivid, and rich in detail, we often place great confidence in them, but research suggests that we should be cautious about doing this. Sometimes these flashbulb memories may include inaccuracies or lack some specific details (Neisser, 1991; Talarico & Rubin, 2003).

Effortless
Following his bout with encephalitis in 1985, Clive could still read music and play the piano, demonstrating that his procedural memory was not destroyed. Researchers documented a similar phenomenon in a professional cello player who battled herpes encephalitis in 2005 (Vennard, 2011, November 20). Jiri Rezac/Polaris/Newscom

CONNECTIONS

In **Chapter 5,** we introduced the concept of classical conditioning, which occurs when an originally neutral stimulus is conditioned to *elicit* or induce an involuntary response, such as salivation, eye blinks, and other types of *reflex* reactions. Here we can see how closely linked learning and memory are.

IMPLICIT MEMORY Unlike an explicit memory, which can easily flow into conscious thought, **implicit memory** is a memory of something you know or know how to do, but which might be automatic or unconscious. These types of memories are difficult to bring into awareness and express. Many of the physical activities we take for granted, such as playing an instrument, driving a car, and dribbling a basketball, use a special type of implicit memory called **procedural memory,** that is, the memory of how to carry out an activity without conscious control or attention. After his illness, Clive Wearing could still pick up a piece of music and play it on the piano. He had no recollection of learning to sight read or play, yet he could execute these skills like the professional he had always been (Vennard, 2011, November 20). Therefore, Clive's procedural memory was still working.

Memories acquired through classical conditioning are also implicit. Let's say you enjoy eating food at McDonald's and the very sight of the golden arches makes you salivate like one of **Pavlov's dogs.** Somewhere along the line, you formed an association, a memory linking that restaurant to juicy hamburgers and creamy shakes, but the association does not require your conscious awareness (Cowan, 1988). It is implicit.

Memory Aids: Put Your Memory to the Test

try this

Take 15 seconds and try to memorize these seven words in the order they appear.

puppy stop sing sadness soccer kick panic

Now close your eyes, and see how many you recall. How did you do?

You just completed a mini-version of "Random Words," Dorothea's favorite event in the World Memory Championships. Dorothea won a gold medal in this category, committing 244 words to memory in 15 minutes. What's her secret? Dorothea uses **mnemonic** (nih-ˈmän-ik) devices—techniques for improving memory. You have probably used several mnemonic techniques yourself, perhaps not even realizing a discussion of them belongs in an introductory psychology textbook. For example, have you ever used the *first-letter technique,* such as *Every Good Boy Deserves Fudge,* to learn the line notes of the treble clef scale? Or perhaps you have used an *acronym,* such as ROY G BIV, to remember the colors of the rainbow? (See **FIGURE 6.7.**) Chunking, which we discussed earlier, is also a mnemonic technique. As you'll see in **INFOGRAPHIC 6.2** on page 251, mnemonic devices and other strategies can be used to improve retention when studying.

METHOD OF LOCI One of the mnemonics Dorothea relies on most is the *method of loci* (lō-ˌsī, meaning "places"). Here's how it works: When presented with a series of words to remember, Dorothea takes them on a mental journey through the place she knows best: her bedroom and bathroom. Walking through her room, she places the items to be remembered at predetermined spots along the way. Let's say she is trying to remember the seven words from the beginning of this section. Dorothea visualizes herself entering her bedroom. The first thing she comes upon is the bed, so she might imagine a cute *puppy* playing with the pillow. Then she encounters a bedside table, which suddenly is a bus *stop* with a bus parked in front. She walks over to the sofa,

Synonym

implicit memory
nondeclarative memory

implicit memory A memory of something you know or know how to do, but that might be automatic or unconscious; this type of memory is often difficult to brin to awareness and express.

procedural memory The unconscious memory of how to carry out a variety of skills and activities; a type of implicit memory.

mnemonic (nih-ˌmän-ik) Technique to improve memory.

climbs onto it, and begins to *sing*. The next object on her path is a box, but not an ordinary box, because it's weeping tears of *sadness*. Next in her path is a mirror that she shatters to pieces with a *soccer* ball. When she gets to the sink, she *kicks* it with her foot. Finally, she imagines aliens climbing out of the toilet, causing her to *panic*. If she needs to remember the items, she retraces the journey, stopping at each point to observe the image she left there.

You can make use of the method of loci, too. Just pick a familiar route—through your favorite restaurant, the college campus, even your own body—and mentally place things you need to remember at points along the way. For remembering short lists, memory champion Dominic O'Brien suggests tagging items to preestablished points along the body (O'Brien, 2005). Suppose you need to pick up five items at the grocery: *milk, eggs, olive oil, bananas,* and *cherries*. Choose some body parts and then visually connect them to the items you need. For example, your hair is slicked back in *olive oil;* your nose is a big long *banana;* you can't see because someone threw *eggs* in your eyes; *cherries* dangle from your ears like earrings; and you have a *milk* mustache.

HIERARCHICAL STRUCTURES   Another way to boost your memory is to arrange the material you are trying to memorize into a hierarchy, or a system of meaningful classes and subclasses. In a classic study, researchers found that if participants were given a list of words that followed a hierarchical structure, they were better able to recall the words than participants who were learning the same words not organized in any meaningful way. In fact, the participants who had learned the words using the hierarchy were able to recall 3 times as many words as the other group (Bower, Clark, Lesgold, & Winzenz, 1969).

► FIGURE 6.7

Mnemonics

Mnemonics help us translate information into a form that is easier to remember. For example, the common acronym ROY G BIV helps us remember the exact order of the seven colors in the rainbow. And when music students have trouble remembering the notes on the lines of the treble clef (EGBDF), they often rely on the first-letter technique, creating a sentence out of words beginning with these letters: *Every Good Boy Deserves Fudge.*

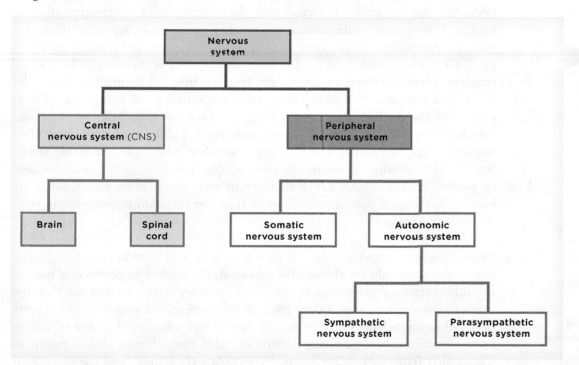

try this

Suppose you are trying to remember the various divisions of the nervous system. Sketch a diagram like the one here (this is from Figure 2.2 from Chapter 2) showing the relationships among the concepts, starting with the most general and ending with the most specific.

Processing, Effort, and Improving Long-Term Memory

While we're on the topic of memory improvement, how does *encoding,* that is, the process of moving data into the memory system, play a role in information going from short-term memory to long-term memory? Let's look at some of the different ways this can occur.

CONNECTIONS ◄┄┄┄┄

In **Chapter 4** we described *automatic processing,* the collection and retention (sometimes temporary) of information with little or no conscious effort. Automatic processing can also refer to the automatic cognitive activity that guides some behaviors, enabling us to act without focusing attention on what we are doing. Without our awareness, the brain determines what needs attention and what can be processed for later use.

Synonym

maintenance rehearsal rote rehearsal

effortful processing The encoding and storage of information with conscious effort, or awareness.

maintenance rehearsal Technique of repeating information to be remembered, increasing the length of time it can be held in short-term memory.

elaborative rehearsal The method of connecting incoming information to knowledge in long-term memory; a deep level of encoding.

AUTOMATIC AND EFFORTFUL PROCESSING As you may recall from earlier in the chapter, the *levels of processing* framework suggests that stronger memories result when you think about information on a deep level. But some encoding of information occurs through **automatic processing**—that is, with little or no conscious effort, or awareness (Hartlage, Alloy, Vázquez, & Dykman, 1993; Hasher & Zacks, 1979). For example, when Dorothea walked into the conference room at the World Memory Championships, she processed all sorts of information without even trying—like the fact that most of the people milling around the room were men, and that the team from China was wearing matching orange-and-white tracksuits. She did not make an effort to pick up on these details, but she remembers them nevertheless. Her memory system absorbed the data automatically; hence, we call it automatic processing. But this is not the type of encoding Dorothea and her rivals came to the championships to do; they came expecting to use **effortful processing.** As the name implies, effortful processing is not only intentional but also requires work (Hartlage et al., 1993; Hasher & Zacks, 1979). Linking hundreds of elaborate images (like a puppy playing on a pillow, or aliens rising out of a toilet) on a mental journey is no easy task, especially when you only have 15 minutes to complete it. This effortful processing, using patterns and meaning to encode information, occurs at a deeper level, and as the levels of processing framework suggests, it results in more successful learning and retention of information.

MAINTENANCE REHEARSAL There are different forms of effortful processing, some useful for extending the amount of time you can hold onto information in short-term memory, others for implanting information firmly into long-term storage. Short-term memory normally lasts between 20 and 30 seconds, but you can stretch it further and, theoretically, hold information there as long as desired using **maintenance rehearsal,** a technique of repeating what you want to remember over and over in your mind. Maintenance rehearsal comes in particularly handy when you need to remember a series of numbers or letters (for example, phone numbers or zip codes). Imagine this: While strolling down the street, you witness a hit-and-run accident; a truck runs a red light, smashes into a car, and then pulls away without the driver even stopping to assess the damage. As the truck races away, you manage to catch a glimpse of the license plate number, "PRZ-7659," but how will you remember it long enough before reaching the 911 operator? If you're like most people, you will say the plate number to yourself over and over, either aloud or in your mind, using maintenance rehearsal. But what if you want to do more than just maintain information in your short-term memory?

ELABORATIVE REHEARSAL If your goal is to hold onto information for the long term, you might try **elaborative rehearsal,** the method of connecting incoming information to knowledge in long-term memory. Here, we can see that the *level of processing* occurs at a deep level, which suggests the encoding of information will be more successful. Dorothea's mental walks involve this type of deeper processing (elaborative rehearsal) because she takes new information and puts it in the familiar framework of her home. By picturing the journey and the objects-to-be-remembered in her mind's eye, she is taking advantage of *visualization,* another effective encoding strategy. People tend to remember verbal information better when it's accompanied by vivid imagery. Some research suggests, for example, that children recall news stories better when they see them presented on television, as opposed to reading about them in a printed article (Walma van der Molen & van der Voort, 2000).

Study Smarter: Methods of Improving Your Memory

You may never need to memorize the order of 2,808 playing cards as memory champion Dominic O'Brien did. But you do need to be able to understand and recall hundreds of details when your teacher hands you an exam. Luckily, research shows that certain strategies and memory techniques will help you retain information when you study.

start studying

Recall details

Mnemonics translate information into a more easily remembered form.

Acronyms and first-letter technique
It's easier to remember a short phrase than a string of information.

ROYGBIV

Chunking
It's easier to remember a few chunks than a long string.

8935550172
893-555-0172

Method of loci
It's easier to remember information when you deliberately link it to locations along a familiar route.

Organize information

Hierarchical structures organize information into a meaningful system. The process of organizing aids encoding and, once encoded, the information is easier to recall.

furniture   fruit   flowers

Make connections

Elaborative rehearsal is deep processing that boosts transfer to long-term memory by connecting new information to older memories.

Give yourself time

Distributed practice creates better memory than study crammed into a single session.

NOVEMBER **13**   NOVEMBER **15**
NOVEMBER **18**   NOVEMBER **21**
↑ *study* ↗
NOVEMBER **23**   ↖ *test*

Get some rest

Sleep, or even wakeful resting after study, allows newly learned material to be encoded better.

ZZZ

A test

DISTRIBUTED PRACTICE   What other strategies, besides elaborative rehearsal and visualization, might improve encoding and help you move information into long-term memory? You've probably heard this before, but it couldn't be truer: Avoid cramming for long periods of time without breaks (also referred to as **massed practice**). Research dating back to the 1800s shows that **distributed practice**—spreading out study sessions, with breaks in between—is much more effective than packing information into your brain all at once (Ebbinghaus, 1885/1913; Rohrer & Taylor, 2006). Separating study sessions is also an important factor, with breaks facilitating better retention. When researchers asked students to learn a new mathematical skill, they found that the participants who practiced the new skill in two sessions (separated by a week) did better on a practice test (4 weeks later) than those who spent the same amount of time practicing in one session (Pashler, Rohrer, Cepeda, & Carpenter, 2007).

Surprisingly, how students apply distributed practice to studying may be associated with their culture and beliefs. In one intriguing study, researchers uncovered significant differences between European American students and Asian American students in their beliefs about studying and learning. Compared to the Asian Americans, the European Americans were more likely to think that learning takes more time and that knowledge is more complex. Students who believed that learning could happen quickly were more likely to choose strategies such as speeding through homework and tests—approaches that might make identifying the main points more difficult (Schommer-Aikins & Easter, 2008).

We should point out that this study merely found evidence of cultural trends. When it comes to studying the psychology of groups, there are no hard-and-fast rules that apply to every member. Each individual should be viewed as such—as an individual. Keep this in mind as you read on.

CONNECTIONS

In **Chapter 1,** we presented the sociocultural perspective of psychology, which suggests that we should examine the influences of social interactions and culture to understand behavior. Here, we see how culture can influence decisions about the way to study.

across the WORLD

Memory and Culture

Ask a person from the United States and a person from China to recount some life memories, and you may detect some interesting cultural themes in their reports. Research suggests that Chinese people are more likely than Americans to remember social and historical occurrences and focus their memories on other people. Americans, on the other hand, tend to recall events as they relate to their individual actions and emotions (Wang & Conway, 2004). Why is this so?

It may have something to do with the fact that China—like many countries in East Asia, Africa, and Latin America—has a collectivist culture, whereas the United States is more *individualistic.* People in *collectivist* societies tend to prioritize the needs of family and community over those of the individual. Individualistic cultures are more "me" oriented, or focused on autonomy and independence. Thus, it would make sense that participants from China, a collectivist culture, would have more community-oriented memories than their American counterparts.

MEMORIES OF WE, OR MEMORIES OF ME?   Think about how culture might shape your own childhood memories. Family members help you create memories of your past by telling you stories of events you may not be able to recall on your own (or that never even happened, a topic we will discuss later). Depending on your cultural background, those memories may have a collectivist or individualistic slant. Whichever way they lean, they are uniquely yours.

The memories you carry serve as reminders of your cultural and family identity. Who would you be without them? Put yourself in the shoes of Clive Wearing.

Memories East and West
A group of Chinese boys enjoy each other's company. China has a community-oriented, or collectivist, culture, which is reflected in the memories of its people. Compared to their U.S. counterparts, the Chinese are more inclined to recollect events in the context of society and history, emphasizing the roles played by other people (Wang & Conway, 2004).
Xinhua/ZUMApress/Newscom

Although Clive retained a strong sense of "self" (personal identity), his illness stamped out decades of episodic memories (D. Wearing, personal communication, June 10, 2013). This loss and the evident distress had a profound impact on him. For 6½ years following his illness, Clive lived on a psychiatric ward, often under the influence of potent prescription tranquilizers. He was not suffering from a mental disorder—if he had, you might expect the drugs to have been effective, but they were not. No, Clive was reacting to his condition in a very human way. As Deborah put it, "His behavioural problems were a rational response to his terrifying amnesia" (D. Wearing, personal communication, June 25, 2013).

SLEEP AND MEMORY   We have touched on many strategies for boosting memory, from chunking to visualization to distributed practice. If we could leave you with one final piece of advice, it would be the following: SLEEP. Exactly how **sleep** promotes memory is still not completely understood, but there is no question that good sleep makes for better processing of memories (Born, Rasch, & Gais, 2006; Diekelmann & Born, 2010; Marshall & Born, 2007). Even periods of "wakeful resting" following the learning of new material can increase the retention of that information. Participants who experienced a 15-minute period of wakeful resting (that is, they sat in a darkened quiet room) displayed better retention of newly learned material than did participants who played a game for 15 minutes. Wakeful resting seems to allow newly learned material to be encoded better, and thus retained in memory longer (Dewar, Alber, Butler, Cowan, & Della Sala, 2012). What might this mean for you? Make sure you allow yourself some quiet time following the learning of new material. Don't end your study sessions with an activity that might interfere with your encoding of the information. Of course, it takes more than good sleep to succeed in college; you need to be able to analyze, apply, and synthesize material, not just remember it (Table 6.1 on page 239).

▶CONNECTIONS

In **Chapter 4,** we discussed how sleep and dreams relate to memory. For example, researchers suspect that *sleep spindles* are associated with memory consolidation, and some theorists emphasize the importance of *REM* sleep in this process.

Synonym
distributed practice spacing effect

massed practice Studying for long periods of time without breaks.
distributed practice Spreading out study sessions over time with breaks in between.

"Wow, that's a lot to remember," you may be saying. Hopefully, you can retain it with the help of some of the mnemonic devices we have presented thus far. You might also take a wakeful resting break in preparation for the next section, which focuses on the topic of memory retrieval.

show what you know

1. Your best friend tells you to close your eyes because she has a present for you. Just after you close your eyes, you momentarily "see" an image of her face. This is an example of:
   a. echoic memory.
   b. iconic memory.
   c. spatial memory.
   d. semantic memory.

2. According to the information-processing model, our short-term memory can hold onto information for up to about _____ if we are not distracted by something else.
   a. 10 seconds
   b. 30 seconds
   c. 45 seconds
   d. 60 seconds

3. As you enter the airport, you try to remember the location of the baggage claim area. You remember the last time you picked up your friend at this airport, and using your visuospatial sketchpad, realize the area is to your left. This ability demonstrates the use of your:
   a. sensory memory.
   b. working memory.
   c. phonological loop.
   d. flashbulb memory.

4. _____ memory is the type of memory you are aware of having and can consciously declare, whereas _____ memory is a memory of something you know how to do, but which might be automatic or unconscious.

5. On 9/11 Tanya was watching television when a news bulletin announced the terrorist attacks. She has vivid memories of that moment, including what she was doing, the friends she was with, and many details of her surroundings. This type of memory is known as a(n):
   a. phonological loop.
   b. sensory memory.
   c. implicit memory.
   d. flashbulb memory.

6. Develop a mnemonic device to help you memorize the following terms from this section: explicit memory, semantic memory, episodic memory, flashbulb memory, implicit memory, and procedural memory.

✓ CHECK YOUR ANSWERS IN APPENDIX C.

Retrieval and Forgetting

Have you ever heard the saying "an elephant never forgets"? Granted, this might be somewhat of an overstatement, but as far as animals go, elephants do have fairly remarkable memories. Consider the story of two elephants who briefly worked together in the circus and then were separated for 23 years. When they reencountered one another at an elephant sanctuary in Tennessee, the two animals started to inspect each other's trunk scars and "bellowed" in excitement: The long-lost friends had recognized one other (Ritchie, 2009, January 12)! An elephant's memory—and yours, too—is only as good as its ability to retrieve stored memories. Let's return to the World Memory Championships and examine the critical process of retrieval.

Friends Forever
Elephants Jenny and Shirley remembered one another after being separated for 23 years. Reunited at the Elephant Sanctuary in Hohenwald, Tennessee, they examined one another's trunks and hollered with joy (Ritchie, 2009, January 12). Courtesy of Carolyn Buckley, www.carolbuckley.com

What Can You Retrieve?

LO 9 Illustrate how encoding specificity relates to retrieval cues.

Every event in the World Memory Championships begins with *encoding* data into the memory system and *storing* that information for later use. Contestants are presented with information—numbers, words, historic dates, and the like—and provided a certain amount of time to file it away in long-term memory. But no matter how much information they absorb, the contestants' efforts are meaningless if they can't *retrieve* it in the recall phase of the event.

RETRIEVAL CUES AND PRIMING One of the most grueling events in the World Memory Championships is "One Hour Numbers," a race to see who can memorize the greatest number of random digits in an hour. Contestants are given four sheets of paper, each containing 1,000 random digits, and 1 hour to cram as many as possible into their long-term memories. During the recall phase that follows, they get 2 hours to scrawl the correctly ordered numbers on blank sheets of paper. This is a backbreaker because there are no reminders, or *retrieval cues,* to help contestants locate the information in their long-term memory. **Retrieval cues** are stimuli that help you retrieve stored information that is difficult to access (Tulving & Osler, 1968). For example, let's say you were trying to remember the name of the researcher who created the working memory model introduced earlier in the chapter. If we gave you the first letter of his last name, *B,* would that help you retrieve the information? If your mind jumped to "Baddeley" (the correct answer), then *B* served as your retrieval cue.

Even Clive Wearing, who could not remember what was happening from one moment to the next, showed evidence of using retrieval cues. For instance, Clive spent 7 years of his life at St. Mary's Hospital in Paddington, England, yet had no conscious memory of living there. And, according to his wife Deborah, Clive was "completely devoid" of knowledge of his own location; the hospital name was not at all connected with his sense of location (D. Wearing, personal communication, June 25, 2013). But if Deborah prompted him with the words "St. Mary's," he would chime back, "Paddington," oblivious to its connection (Wearing, 2005, p. 188). In this instance, the *retrieval cue* in Clive's environment (the sound of the word "St. Mary's") was **priming** his memory of the hospital name. Priming is the process of awakening memories with the help of retrieval cues.

At this point, you may be wondering how priming can occur in a person with severe amnesia. Clive's conscious, *explicit* memory is diminished, but his unconscious, *implicit* memory still functions. Just because he could not articulate, or "declare," the name of the hospital does not mean that the previously known word combination had entirely vanished from his memory system.

RECALL AND RECOGNITION Now let's return to the "One Hour Numbers" event of the World Memory Championships. This type of challenge relies on pure **recall,** the process of retrieving information held in long-term memory without the help of explicit retrieval cues. Recall is what you depend on when you answer fill-in-the-blank or short-answer essay questions on exams. Say you are given the following prompt: "Using a computer metaphor, what are the three processes involved in memory?" In this situation, you must come up with the answer from scratch: "The three processes are *encoding, storage,* and *retrieval.*"

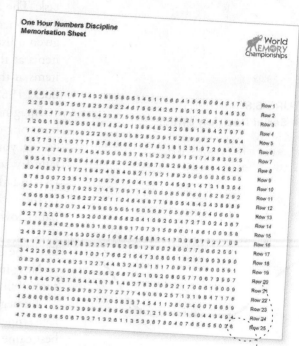

The Ultimate Test
"One Hour Numbers" is one of the most demanding events in the World Memory Championships. Contestants are given 1 hour to memorize as many numbers as possible, and then 2 hours to write them in order on paper. The world record, currently held by Wang Feng of China, is 2,660 digits (World Memory Statistics, 2013).
World Memory Championships

retrieval cues Stimuli that help in the retrieval of stored information that is difficult to access.

priming The stimulation of memories as a result of retrieval cues in the environment.

recall The process of retrieving information held in long-term memory without the help of explicit retrieval cues.

Now let's say you are faced with a multiple-choice question: "One proven way of retaining information is: (a) distributed practice, (b) massed practice, or (c) eidetic imagery." Answering this question relies on **recognition,** the process of matching incoming data to information stored in long-term memory. Recognition is generally a lot easier than recall because the information is right before your eyes; you just have to identify it (*Hey, I've seen that before*). Recall, on the other hand, requires you to come up with information on your own. Most of us find it easier to *recognize* the correct answer from a list of possible answers in a multiple-choice question than to *recall* the same correct answer for a fill-in-the-blank question.

SERIAL POSITION EFFECT   Recall and recognition come into play outside of school as well. Just think about the last time someone asked you to pick up a list of items at the store. In order to find the requested items, you had to recognize them (*There's the ketchup*), but even before that you had to recall them—a much harder task. The ability to recall items appearing in a list depends on where they fall in the list, a phenomenon psychologists call the **serial position effect** (FIGURE 6.8). When given a list of words to memorize, research participants are better able to remember items at the beginning of the list, which is known as the **primacy effect,** as well as items at the end, which is called the **recency effect** (Deese & Kaufman, 1957; Murdock, 1962).

Imagine you are on your way to the store to buy supplies for a dinner party, but your cell phone battery is about to die. Your phone rings; it's your housemate asking you to buy the following items: napkins, paper towels, dish soap, butter, laundry soap, paper plates, sparkling water, ice cream, plastic spoons, bread, pickles, and flowers. Without any way to write down this list, you are at the mercy of the serial position effect. In all likelihood, you will return home with napkins, paper towels, and a bottle of dish soap (due to the primacy effect), as well as bread, pickles, and flowers (due to the recency effect); the items in the middle will more likely be forgotten.

Now imagine you are a top executive at a television network, and one of your responsibilities is to decide which time slots advertisers should pay the most for—those at the beginning, middle, or end of a commercial break. One study looking at college students' viewings of TV commercials found that the brand names they *recalled* best came from ads appearing at the beginning and end of breaks (Terry, 2005). The first ads were etched most deeply in students' long-term memories because they had the most time to think about them (the primacy effect). The final ads, on the other hand, were easily recalled because they still lingered in short-term memory (the recency effect).

What do you think happened when the researchers allowed more time to pass, questioning students at the end of the program rather than immediately following commercial breaks? Memories of the first ads held strong (probably because they had been encoded in long-term memory), whereas those of the later ads faded (presumably because they had dropped out of short-term memory, never even transitioning to long-term storage). The solution to your dilemma is to charge big bucks for the first ads, because they will stick longest in the minds of viewers.

CONTEXT IS EVERYTHING   When it comes to retrieving memories, context matters. Where were you when you encoded the information, and what was occurring around you? Researchers have found that environmental factors play a key role in determining how easily memories are retrieved.

In a classic study conducted by Godden and Baddeley (1975), participants learned lists of words under two conditions: while underwater (using scuba gear) and on dry land. They were then tested for recall in both conditions: If they learned

---

FIGURE 6.8
The Serial Position Effect
Items at the beginning and the end of a list are more likely to be recalled.

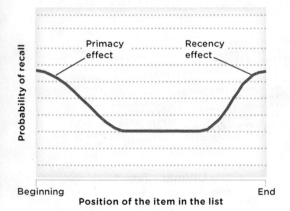

Primacy effect

Recency effect

Probability of recall

Beginning

End

Position of the item in the list

---

recognition The process of matching incoming data to information stored in long-term memory.

serial position effect The ability to recall items in a list depends on where they are in the series.

primacy effect The tendency to remember items at the beginning of a list.

recency effect The tendency to remember items at the end of a list.

encoding specificity principle Memories are more easily recalled when the context and cues at the time of encoding are similar to those at the time of retrieval.

the list underwater, they were tested underwater and on dry ground; if they learned the list on dry ground, they were tested on dry ground and underwater. The participants were better able to retrieve words when the learning and recall occurred in the same location (**FIGURE 6.9**). If they learned the words underwater, they had an easier time retrieving them underwater. The same was true for words learned on land. Here we have an example of *context-dependent memory;* memories are easier to access when the encoding and retrieval occur in similar contexts.

FIGURE 6.9

Does Context Influence Memory Retrieval?

Researchers asked participants to learn a list of words in two contexts: underwater and on dry land. The participants had an easier time recalling words when learning and recall happened in the same setting (learning underwater and recalling underwater or learning on dry land and recalling on dry land). *Source:* Godden and Baddeley, 1975

Context-dependent memory is part of a broader phenomenon conveyed by the **encoding specificity principle,** which states that memories are more easily recalled when the context and cues at the time of encoding are similar to those at the time of retrieval (Smith, Glenberg, & Bjork, 1978; Tulving & Thompson, 1973). There is even evidence that summoning a memory for an event reactivates the same brain areas that became excited during the event itself (Danker & Anderson, 2010).

This suggests that the activity in your brain at the time of encoding is similar to that at retrieval. In one study examining how odors and memories are linked, participants were asked to smell an odor (positive, negative, and neutral) at the same time they were presented with an image (animals, tools, vehicles). They were also asked to think of a link between the two that would help them remember the smell and the image. For example, one participant who smelled the odor of a rose while looking at an image of a duck came up with a story about being in a park feeding ducks with her grandmother. The researchers used fMRIs to examine the participants' brain activity while viewing images they had seen earlier, as well as new images. The findings indicated that areas of the brain associated with smell were more active when participants viewed (and presumably remembered) earlier-seen images that originally had been paired with an odor (Gottfried, Smith, Rugg, & Dolan, 2004).

CONNECTIONS

In **Chapter 2,** we presented a variety of technologies used to explore the brain. fMRI captures changes in brain activity by revealing patterns of blood flow in a particular area. This is a good indicator of how much oxygen is being used as a result of activity there. Here, researchers use fMRI scans to examine processes in the brain associated with the detection of odors.

IT ALL COMES FLOODING BACK   In your own life, you may have noticed that old memories tend to emerge from the woodwork when you return to the places where they were created. Dining at a restaurant you once frequented with an ex-boyfriend or girlfriend probably sparks memories of romantic moments (or perhaps a bitter argument) you had there. Going to a high school reunion might bring back memories of football games, dances, and classrooms not recalled in years.

How does returning to the birthplace of a memory help bring it to mind? The levels of processing framework would suggest that the deeper the processing, the greater the likelihood of retrieval (Andre & Sola, 1976; Baddeley, 1982). So if you once spent a lot of time reflecting on junior prom, chances are the memory will be rich in detail when it comes rushing back. But more important, perhaps, is that a memory's place of origin is rich in retrieval cues—sights, sounds, tastes, smells, and feelings present at the time of encoding.

Suppose you go to a friend's house to watch the James Bond movie *Skyfall.* While encoding a memory of the movie, you are exposed to all sorts of stimuli in the environment, such as the hum of an air conditioner, the taste of the chips and salsa you are munching on, the tabby cat purring next to you on the sofa. All these feelings have nothing to do with *Skyfall,* but they are strongly linked to your experience of watching the film. So the next time you are at your friend's house and you see that tabby cat purring on a sofa, thoughts of 007 might come back to you.

Context Matters

Using fMRI scans, researchers observed the brain activity of people trying to remember images they had first viewed in the presence of a specific scent (Gottfried et al., 2004). When recalling images they had linked to smells, odor-processing areas of the brain became noticeably excited, even in the absence of any odors. The scan shows the activity in the brain (see yellow on scan) of a person recalling an odor-linked image. Gottfried, J. A., Smith, A. P. R., Rugg, M. D., & Dolan, R. J. (2004). Remembrance of odors past: Human olfactory cortex in cross-modal recognition memory. *Neuron, 42,* 687–895.

Cues . . . Retrieval Cues
While watching your favorite James Bond movie, you pick up on all sorts of background stimuli from the environment. These sights, sounds, smells, tastes, and feelings have become entwined with your memory of the movie, so they can serve as retrieval cues for scenes in the film. Next time you smell buttery popcorn, don't be surprised if the ice blue eyes of Daniel Craig pop into your head.
Apc/ZUMAPRESS/Newscom

CONNECTIONS
As we noted in **Chapter 1,** case studies generally have only one participant. Here we see that Ebbinghaus, the researcher, was the sole participant. It is important to consider this when interpreting the findings, especially as we try to generalize to the population.

relearning Material learned previously is acquired more quickly in subsequent exposures.

MOODS AND MEMORY   The encoding specificity principle does not merely apply to the context of the surroundings. Remembering things is also easier when physiological and psychological conditions, including moods and emotions, are similar at the time of encoding and retrieval. Sometimes memories can be best retrieved under such circumstances; we call this *state-dependent memory*. One morning while arising from bed, you spot a red cardinal on your window ledge. You forget about the cardinal for the rest of the day—even when you pass the very same window. But come tomorrow morning when you are once again half-awake and groggy, memories of the red bird return. Here, your ability to recall the cardinal is dependent on your internal state being the same as it was at the time of encoding.

Retrieval is also easier when the content of a memory corresponds to our present emotional state. This phenomenon is known as mood congruence (Bower, Gilligan, & Menteiro, 1981; Drace, Ric, & Desrichard, 2010). If you are in a happy mood, you are more likely to recollect a happy-go-lucky character from a book, but if you are in a sour mood, you are more inclined to learn about and remember the character whose bad mood matches yours.

How Easily We Remember: Memory Savings

Retrieval is clearly at work in recall and recognition, the two processes we compared above. But there is another, less obvious form of retrieval that occurs in the process of **relearning.** Perhaps you've noticed that you learn material much more quickly a second time around. Math equations, vocabulary, and grammar rules seem to make more sense when you've seen them before. Some information seems to stick better when we learn it twice (Storm, Bjork, & Bjork, 2008).

HERMANN EBBINGHAUS   The first person to quantify the effect of relearning was Hermann Ebbinghaus (1850–1909), a German psychologist and pioneering researcher of human memory. Ebbinghaus was the **sole participant** in his experiments, so his research actually shed light on *his* memory, although the trends he uncovered in himself seem to apply to human memory in general.

The thorough scientist he was, Ebbinghaus spent hour upon hour, day after day memorizing lists of "nonsense syllables"—meaningless combinations of vowels and consonants such as DAZ and MIB. Once Ebbinghaus had successfully remembered a list, meaning he could recite it smoothly and confidently, he would put it aside. Later, he would memorize it all over again and calculate how much time he had saved in Round 2, a measure called the "savings score" (Ebbinghaus, 1885/1913). A study by Marmurek and Grant (1990) supports Ebbinghaus's theory of savings in relearning. Participants who were asked to memorize number–word pairs (for example, 17-snake, 23-crown) showed significant savings in the amount of time needed to relearn the number–word pairs 6 weeks later.

Since no one spends all day memorizing nonsense syllables, you may wonder how Ebbinghaus's research and the "savings score" apply to real life. At some point in school, you probably had to memorize a famous speech like Dr. Martin Luther King's "I Have a Dream." Let's say it took you 100 practice sessions to recite the speech flawlessly. Then a month later, you tried memorizing it again and it only took 50 attempts. Because you cut your learning time in half (from 100 practice sessions to 50), your savings score would be 50%.

A FOREIGN LANGUAGE?   Learning is a lot like blazing a trail through freshly fallen snow. Your first attempt plowing through the powder is hard work and slow going, but the second time (relearning) is easier and faster because the snow is packed and the tracks have been laid down for you. This also seems to be true for relearning a forgotten childhood language. One small study focused on native English speakers who as children had been exposed to either Hindi or Zulu to varying degrees. Although none of the adults in the study had any *explicit* memories of those languages, those who were under 40 were still able to distinguish sounds from their childhood languages better than members of a control group with no exposure to these languages (Bowers, Mattys, & Gage, 2009). The implication is that people who have some knowledge of a language (even if they don't realize it) benefit from this memory, by showing a "memory savings" if they try to learn the language again. They are a step ahead of other adults learning that language for the first time.

How Easily We Forget: Memory Slips Explained

········► **LO 10** Identify some of the reasons why we forget.

Once Dorothea has memorized numbers, images, and other bits of information for the World Memory Championships, how long do they stick in her mind—an hour, a day, a week? Dorothea reports that images and words can last for several days, but meaningless strings of numbers, like the hundreds of digits memorized for the "One Hour Numbers" event, tend to fade within a day.

This would probably come as no surprise to Hermann Ebbinghaus, who, in addition to demonstrating the effects of relearning, was the first to demonstrate just how rapidly memories vanish. Through his experiments with nonsense syllables, Ebbinghaus (1885/1913) found that the bulk of forgetting occurs immediately after learning. If you look at his *curve of forgetting* (**FIGURE 6.10**), you will see his memory of word lists plunging downward the hour following learning, then leveling off thereafter. Think about how the curve of forgetting applies to you. Some of what you hear in a psychology lecture will disappear from memory as soon as you walk out the door, but what you remember a week later will probably not differ much from what you recall in a month.

ENCODING FAILURE   What exactly causes us to forget? That may depend on the stage of memory processing—encoding, storage, or retrieval—at which a given instance of memory failure occurs. Sometimes details and events we think we have forgotten were actually never encoded in the first place. Take this example: After a long and stressful day, you stop at the supermarket to pick up a frozen dinner. While fumbling through your bag in search of your wallet, you take out your gloves and place them on the cashier's counter, but because your attention is focused on finding your wallet, you don't even notice where you've placed the gloves. Then you pay and

FIGURE 6.10
Ebbinghaus's Curve of Forgetting
Ebbinghaus discovered that most forgetting occurs within 1 hour of learning and then levels off.

walk out the door, only to wake up the next morning wondering where you left your gloves! This is an example of *encoding failure* because the data never entered your memory system. Because you never registered putting your gloves on the counter in the first place, how can you expect to remember where you left them? For a classic demonstration of encoding failure, take a look at the 10 pennies appearing in the Try This feature. You've looked at a penny hundreds of times in your life, so identifying the real penny should be no problem, right?

try this

Look at the 10 pennies to the right. Which one is correct?

If you're like most people, chances are you picked the wrong coin because you have never taken the time to study a penny and *encode* its visual details (Nickerson & Adams, 1979).

STORAGE FAILURE AND MEMORY DECAY   Memory lapses can also result from *storage* failure. Take a moment and try to remember your middle school or high school locker combination. The digits may have slipped your mind, but at one point in your life you knew them by heart. The number is inaccessible because you no longer use it; the memory may have decayed over time. However, there is plenty of evidence to suggest that we are capable of storing a vast fund of information, sometimes for a very long time. Such memories might include the name of the street you grew up on (Schmidt et al., 2000), grades in college (Bahrick, Hall, & Da Costa, 2008), and factual knowledge from college courses (Conway, Cohen, & Stanhope, 1991). However, these types of memories are subject to a variety of inaccuracies and distortions, and tapping into them is not always easy.

TIP-OF-THE-TONGUE PHENOMENON   Sometimes we know that we have knowledge of something but just can't pull it out of storage. The name of that college classmate or that new blockbuster movie, it's just sitting on the tip of your tongue but it won't slide off! This simple *retrieval* failure is called the *tip-of-the-tongue phenomenon*. Most of us have this feeling about once a week, but luckily we are able to retrieve the elusive phrase approximately 50% of the time (James & Burke, 2000; Schwartz, 2012). Often we can correctly guess the first letter of the word or how many syllables it has (Hanley & Chapman, 2008). Studies suggest this tip-of-the-tongue phenomenon becomes more common with age (Brown & Nix, 1996).

HYPERTHYMESTIC SYNDROME   What would happen if you had the opposite problem—that is, instead of forgetting all the time, you remembered everything? Imagine how overwhelming it would be to remember all the experiences you have

proactive interference The tendency for information learned in the past to interfere with the retrieval of new material.

retroactive interference The tendency for recently learned information to interfere with the retrieval of things learned in the past.

had, all the people you have met, the meals that you have eaten over the years, and so on. How would that impact your ability to calculate your grocery bill, remember where you parked your car, and carry out a myriad of other mental tasks required for survival in modern society? Great adaptive value seems to be associated with being able to forget, because it allows you to attend to what's going on in the here and now. Some people, however, cannot forget. This type of memory ability is known as *hyperthymestic syndrome* (Parker, Cahill, & McGaugh, 2006). The irony is that having this type of "super" memory has drawbacks, including problems with abstract thinking and the ability to make generalizations, although it doesn't necessarily impair day-to-day functioning.

PROACTIVE INTERFERENCE   You now know that forgetting can stem from problems in encoding and storage. And the tip-of-the-tongue phenomenon tells us that it can also result from glitches in *retrieval.* Let's take a closer look at some other retrieval problems. Studies show that retrieval is influenced, or in some cases blocked, by information we learn before and after a memory was made, which we refer to as *interference* (Waugh & Norman, 1965). If you have studied more than one foreign language, you have probably experienced interference. Suppose you take Spanish in middle school, and then begin studying Italian in college. As you try to learn Italian, you may find Spanish words creeping into your mind and confusing you; this is an example of **proactive interference,** the tendency for information learned in the past to interfere with the retrieval of new material. People who learn to play a second musical instrument experience the same problem; the fingering of the old instrument interferes with the retrieval of new fingering.

RETROACTIVE INTERFERENCE   Now let's say you are going on a trip to Mexico and need to use the Spanish you learned back in middle school. As you approach a vendor in an outdoor market in Costa Maya, you may become frustrated when the only words that come to mind are *ciao bello* and *buongiorno* (Italian for "hello handsome" and "good day"), when you really are searching for phrases with the same meaning in Español. Here, recently learned information interferes with the retrieval of things learned in the past. We call this **retroactive interference.** This type of interference can also impact the musician; when she switches back to her original instrument, the fingering techniques she uses to play the new instrument interfere with her old techniques. Thus, proactive interference results from knowledge acquired in the past and retroactive interference is caused by information learned recently (**FIGURE 6.11** on p. 262).

Although our memories fail us all the time, we manage to get by with a little help from our friends, who remind us to set our alarm clocks, study for tests, and say "happy birthday" to so and so. We have cell phones to store phone numbers and e-mail accounts to maintain addresses. Newspapers and television remind us what day it is. And then of course, there is Google.

FIGURE 6.11
Proactive and Retroactive Interference

Proactive Interference: Old information interferes with newly learned information

SPANISH → ITALIAN →

Italian Test (F)

Time

Retroactive Interference: New information interferes with information learned in the past

SPANISH → ITALIAN →

Spanish Test (F)

didn't SEE that coming

Google Brain

Google. What would life be like without it? Every day, we use Google to find the answers to questions we are too embarrassed to state out loud. It helps us stay abreast of the latest news, provides us with immediate access to the voices and faces of friends, and helps us schedule our lives. Google is, without doubt, one of the modern brain's greatest helpers. But here's the question: Is all of Google's hard work making us lazy?

Maybe "resourceful" is a better word. A study by Sparrow, Liu, and Wegner (2011) found that people essentially use computers as storage places for information they would otherwise have to remember. In one experiment, the researchers asked participants to read and type 40 statements referring to trivia-like information (for example, "An ostrich's eye is bigger than its brain"). Those who were told they would need the information later *and* that it would be available on the computer were less likely to try memorizing it than those denied computer access. Participants who were *not* asked to remember the information also showed better recall for the trivia if they had no expectations of later searching for it on the computer. And so it seems, we as a culture have adapted to being constantly "plugged in" and having information at our fingertips.

IS GOOGLE MAKING US LAZY?

In the past, people simply memorized new phone numbers or jotted them down in an address book. Now we rely on a few keystrokes and the click of a mouse. Imagine life without our digital sidekicks like Google, Yahoo, and Bing. Remember the last time you lost Internet service? "The experience of losing our Internet connection becomes more and more like losing a friend" (Sparrow et al., 2011, p. 4).

show what you know

1. _____ suggests that retrieving memories is easier in the context in which they were made.
   a. The encoding specificity principle
   b. Retroactive interference
   c. Proactive interference
   d. The curve of forgetting

2. Your friend remarks that her scores are better when she studies and takes her quiz in Starbucks than if she studies in Starbucks but takes the quiz at home. She is exhibiting:
   a. context-dependent memory.
   b. proactive interference.
   c. retroactive interference.
   d. mood-congruency of memory.

3. Ebbinghaus reported that his memory of word lists plunged the first hour after he learned them; he displayed this in his:
   a. encoding specificity principle.
   b. curve of forgetting.
   c. recency effect.
   d. serial position effect.

4. Imagine a friend is almost finished with her application for a job she really wants. Create two arguments for when she should submit her application using what you know about the serial position effect (applications are being accepted for a seven day period): one based on the primacy effect the other on the recency effect.

✓ CHECK YOUR ANSWERS IN APPENDIX C.

The Reliability of Memory

Why do we need computers to help us keep track of the loads of information flooding our brains throughout the day? The answer is simple. We can't remember everything. We forget, and we forget often. Sometimes it's obvious an error has occurred (*I can't remember where I left my cell phone*), but other times it's less apparent. Have you noticed that when you recall a shared event, your version is not always consistent with those of other people? As you will soon discover, memories are not **reliable records** of reality. They are malleable (that is, capable of being changed or reshaped by various influences) and constantly updated and revised, like a wiki. Let's see how this occurs.

Misinformation

···▶ **LO 11** Explain how the malleability of memory influences the recall of events.

Elizabeth Loftus, a renowned psychologist and law professor, has been studying memory and its reliability for the last 40 or more years. During the course of her career, she has been an expert witness in over 200 trials. The main focus of her work is the very problem we just touched upon: If two people have different memories of an event, whom do we believe? Loftus suggests that we should not expect our accounts of the past to be identical to those of other people or even of our own previous renditions of events. According to Loftus, episodic memories are not exact duplicates of past events (recent or distant). Instead, she and others propose a *reconstructionist* model of memory "in which memories are understood as creative blendings of fact and fiction" (Loftus & Ketcham, 1994, p. 5). Over the course of time, memories can fade, and because they are permeable, they become more vulnerable to the invasion of new information. In other words, your memory of some event might include revisions to what really happened, based on knowledge, opinions, and information you have acquired since the event occurred.

Suppose you watch a debate between two presidential candidates on live television. A few days later, you see that same debate parodied on *Saturday Night Live*. Then a few weeks later, you try to remember the details of the actual debate—the topics discussed, the phrases used by the candidates, the clothes they wore. In your effort to recall the real event, you may very well incorporate some elements of the *Saturday Night Live* skit (for example, words or expressions used by the candidates). Pulling information out of storage is not like pressing "play" on a digital recorder. The memories we make are not precise depictions of reality, but representations of the world as we perceive it. With the passage of time, we lose bits and pieces of a memory, and unknowingly we replace them with new information.

THE MISINFORMATION EFFECT If you witnessed a car accident, how good do you think your memory of it would be? Elizabeth Loftus and John Palmer (1974) tested the reliability of people's memories for such an event in a classic experiment. After showing participants a short film clip of a multiple-car accident, Loftus and Palmer quizzed them about what they had seen. They asked some participants, "About how fast were the cars going when they smashed into each other?" Replacing the word "smashed" with "hit," they asked others, "About how fast were the cars going when they hit each other?" Can you guess which version resulted in the highest estimates of speed? If you guessed "smashed," you are correct.

CONNECTIONS

In **Chapter 1,** we introduced the concepts of expectations and bias, noting that these can produce inaccuracies in thinking and research. Here, we will describe the ways in which our memories can fail. As accurate as our thoughts and memories may seem, we must be aware that they are vulnerable to error.

Comedy or Reality

Did former vice presidential candidate Sarah Palin (right) really say, "I can see Russia from my house!" during a one-on-one interview, or was that just Tina Fey (left) doing a Palin impersonation on *Saturday Night Live*? Sometimes, we unknowingly edit our memories, incorporating bits and pieces of information learned after the fact. left: Photo by Dana Edelson/NBC/NBCU Photo Bank Getty Images; right: WHITNEY CURTIS/EPA/Newscom

One week later, the researchers asked the participants to recall the details of the accident, including whether they had seen any broken glass in the film. Although no broken glass appears in the film, the researchers nevertheless predicted there would be some "yes" answers from participants who had initially been asked about the speed of the cars that "smashed" into each other, as opposed to those who had heard the cars "hit" each other. And their predictions were correct. Participants who had heard the word "smashed" apparently incorporated a faster speed in their memories, and were more likely to report having seen broken glass. Participants who had not heard the word "smashed" seemed to have a more accurate memory of the filmed car collision. The researchers concluded that memories can be changed in response to new information. In this case, the participants' recollections of the car accident were altered by the wording of a questionnaire (Loftus & Palmer, 1974). This research suggests that eyewitness accounts of accidents, crimes, and other important events might be altered by a variety of factors that come into play *after* the event occurs. Since memories are malleable, one must be careful when questioning people about the past, whether it's in a therapist's office, a police station, or at home talking with friends. The wording of questions can change the way events are recalled.

Researchers were fascinated with the findings from this initial study involving the car accident and have since conducted numerous studies on the **misinformation effect,** or the tendency for new and misleading information to distort one's memory of an incident. Studies with a variety of participants have resulted in their "remembering" a stop sign that was really a yield sign, a screwdriver that was really a hammer, and a barn that did not actually exist (Loftus, 2005).

Prosecutors often tell people who have witnessed crimes not to speak to each other, and with good reason. Suppose two people witnessed an elderly woman being robbed. One eyewitness remembers seeing a bearded man wearing a blue hoodie swiping the woman's purse. The other noticed the blue hoodie but *not* the beard. If, however, the two eyewitnesses exchange stories of what they saw, the second eyewitness may unknowingly incorporate the beard into his "memory." Information learned after the event (that is, the "fact" that the thief had a beard) can unknowingly get mixed in with memories of that event (Loftus, 2005; Loftus, Miller, & Burns, 1978). If we can instill this type of "false" information into a "true" memory, do you suppose it is possible to give people memories for events that never happened? Indeed, it is.

Memory Sketches
Comparing the two police sketches (left) and the more accurate drawing by sketch artist Jeanne Boylan (right), you see how renderings of the same individual can be dramatically different, even though all three were based on eyewitness information. Police sketches are based on the memories of eyewitnesses, each of whom has a unique—and potentially erroneous—memory of the suspect. Composite by Nate Caplin KRT/Newscom

False Memories

> **LO 12** Define rich false memory.

Elizabeth Loftus knows firsthand what it is like to have a memory implanted. Tragically, her mother drowned when she was 14 years old. For 30 years, she believed that someone else had found her mother's body in a swimming pool. But then her uncle, in the middle of his 90th birthday party, told her that she, Elizabeth, had found her mother's body. Loftus initially denied any memory of this horrifying experience, but as the days passed, she began to "recall" the event, including images of the pool, her mother's body, and numerous police cars arriving at the scene. These images continued to build for several days, until she received a phone call from her brother informing her that her uncle had been wrong, and that all her other relatives agreed Elizabeth was not the one who found her mother. According to Loftus, "All it took was a suggestion, casually planted" (Loftus & Ketcham, 1994, p. 40), and she was

misinformation effect The tendency for new and misleading information obtained after an incident to distort one's memory of it.

rich false memories Recollections of an event that never occurred, which are expressed with emotions and confidence and include details.

able to create a memory of an event she never witnessed. Following this experience, Loftus began to study **rich false memories,** that is, "wholly false memories" characterized by "the subjective feeling that one is experiencing a genuine recollection, replete with sensory details, and even expressed with confidence and emotion, even though the event never happened" (Loftus & Bernstein, 2005, p. 101).

Would you believe that about 25% of participants in rich false memory studies are able to "remember" an event that never happened? Using the "lost in the mall" technique, Loftus and Pickrell (1995) showed just how these imaginary memories take form. The researchers recruited a pair of family members (for example, parent–child or sibling–sibling) and then told them they would be participating in a study on memory. With the help of one of the members of the pair (the "relative"), the researchers recorded three true events from the pair's shared past and created a plausible story of a trip to a shopping mall that never happened. Then they asked the true "participant" to recall as many details as possible about each of the four events (remember, only three of the events were real), which were presented in a book provided by the researchers. If the participant could not remember any details from an event, he was instructed to write, "I do not remember this." In the "lost in the mall" story, the participant was told that he had been separated from the family in a shopping mall around the age of 5. According to the story, the participant began to cry, but was eventually helped by an elderly woman and was reunited with his family. Mind you, the "lost in the mall" episode was pure fiction, but it was made to seem real through the help of the participant's relative (who was working with the researchers). Following a series of interviews, the researchers concluded that 29% of the participants were able to recall either part or all of the fabricated "lost in the mall" experience (Loftus & Pickrell, 1995). These findings may seem shocking (they certainly caused a great uproar in the field), but keep in mind that the great majority of the participants did not "remember" the fabricated event (Hyman, Husband, & Billings, 1995; Loftus & Pickrell, 1995).

False Memories
Would you believe that looking at photoshopped pictures can lead to the creation of false memories? In one study, researchers discovered that participants could "remember" hot air balloon rides they never took after looking at doctored photos of themselves as children on balloon rides. The researchers speculate that a photo "helps subjects to imagine details about the event that they later confuse with reality" (Garry & Gerrie, 2005, p. 321). Mike Sonnenberg/ E+/Getty Images

CONTROVERSIES

The Debate over Repressed Childhood Memories

►◄ Given what you learned from the "lost in the mall" study, do you think it's possible that false memories can be planted in psychotherapy? Imagine a clinical psychologist or psychiatrist who firmly believes that her client was sexually abused as a child. The client has no memory of abuse, but the therapist is convinced that the abuse occurred and that the traumatic memory for it has been *repressed,* or unconsciously pushed below the threshold of awareness. Using methods such as **hypnosis** and dream analysis, the therapist helps the client resurrect a "memory" of the abuse (that presumably never occurred). Angry and hurt, the client then confronts the "abuser," who happens to be a close relative, and forever damages the relationship. Believe it or not, this scenario is very realistic. Consider these true stories picked from a long list:

- With the help of a psychiatrist, Nadean Cool came to believe that she was a victim of sexual abuse, a former member of a satanic cult, and a baby killer. She later claimed these to be false memories brought about in therapy (Loftus, 1997).

- Under the influence of prescription drugs and persuasive therapists, Lynn Price Gondolf became convinced that her parents molested her during childhood. Three years after accusing her parents of such abuse, she concluded the accusation was a mistake (Loftus & Ketcham, 1994).

- Laura Pasley "walked into her Texas therapist's office with one problem, bulimia, and walked out with another, incest" (Loftus, 1994, p. 44).

CONNECTIONS

In **Chapter 4,** we described *hypnosis* as an altered state of consciousness that allows for changes in perceptions and behavior that result from suggestions made by the hypnotist. Here, we discuss the use of hypnosis in a therapeutic setting, in which the hypnotist is a therapist trying to help a client "remember" an abuse that the therapist believes has been repressed.

In the history of psychology, few topics have stirred up as much controversy as repressed memories. Some psychologists believe that painful memories can indeed be repressed and recovered years or decades later (Knapp & VandeCreek, 2000). The majority, however, would agree that the studies supporting the existence of repressed memories have many shortcomings (Piper, Lillevik, & Kritzer, 2008). Although childhood sexual abuse is shockingly common, affecting some 30–40% of girls (about 1 in 3) and 13% of boys (about 1 in 8) in the United States (Bolen & Scannapieco, 1999), there is *not* good evidence that these traumas are repressed. Even if they were, retrieved memories of them would likely be inaccurate (Roediger & Bergman, 1998). Many trauma survivors face quite a different challenge—letting go of painful memories that continue to haunt them. (See the discussion of posttraumatic stress disorder in Chapter 12.)

REAL OR IMAGINED?

The American Psychological Association (APA) and other authoritative mental health organizations have investigated the repressed memory issue at length. In 1998 the APA issued a statement offering its main conclusions, summarized below:

- Sexual abuse of children is very common and often unrecognized, and the repressed memory debate should not detract attention from this important issue.
- Most victims of sexual abuse have at least some memory of the abuse.
- Memories of past abuses can be forgotten and remembered at a later time.
- People sometimes do create false memories of experiences they never had.
- We still do not completely understand how accurate and flawed memories of childhood abuse are formed (APA, 1998a). ➤◄

The main message of this section is that memory is malleable, or changeable. What are the implications for eyewitness accounts, especially those provided by children? If we are aware of how questions are structured and understand rewards and punishments from the perspective of a child, then the interview will produce fewer inaccuracies (Sparling, Wilder, Kondash, Boyle, & Compton, 2011). Researchers have found that having children close their eyes increases the accuracy of the testimony (Vredeveldt, Baddeley, & Hitch, 2013), but relying solely on their accounts has contributed to many cases of mistaken identity. In addition, the presence of someone in a uniform appears to put added pressure on child eyewitnesses, resulting in more guessing and inaccurate recall (Lowenstein, Blank, & Sauer, 2010).

Before you read on, take a minute and allow the words of Elizabeth Loftus to sink in: "Think of your mind as a bowl filled with clear water. Now imagine each memory as a teaspoon of milk stirred into the water. Every adult mind holds thousands of these murky memories. . . . Who among us would dare to disentangle the water from the milk?" (Loftus & Ketcham, 1994, pp. 3–4). What is the basis for all this murkiness? Time to explore the biological roots of memory.

✓○○○   show what you know

1. The _____ refers to the tendency for new and misleading information to distort memories.

2. Your uncle claims he attended a school play in which you played the "Cowardly Lion." He has described the costume you wore, the lines you mixed up, and even the flowers he gave you. At first you can't remember the play, but eventually you seem to. Your mother insists you were never in that school play, and your uncle wasn't in the country that year, so he couldn't have attended the performance at all. Instead, you have experienced a:

   a. curve of forgetting.
   b. state-dependent memory.
   c. savings score.
   d. rich false memory.

3. Loftus and Palmer (1974) conducted an experiment in which the wording of a question (using "smash" versus "hit") significantly influenced participants' recall of the event. What does this suggest about the malleability, or changeability, of memory?

✓ CHECK YOUR ANSWERS IN APPENDIX C.

The Biology of Memory

What did you do today? Did you have breakfast, brush your teeth, put your clothes on, drive your car, read an assignment, text a friend? Whatever you did, we are sure of one thing: It required a whole lot of memory. Every task described here, and probably every task you completed today, draws on a vast fund of memories residing in your brain. You could not send a text message without knowing how to spell, read, and use a cell phone—all things you had to learn and remember. Likewise, you could not drive without remembering how to unlock your car, start the engine, use the pedals. Memory is involved in virtually everything you do.

If memory is behind all your daily activities, important processes must be occurring in the brain to make this happen: both on the macro (large) and micro (small) scale. But as we learned from Clive's experiences, the process is fragile and can be profoundly disrupted. Exploring the causes of memory failure in cases of amnesia can help us understand the biological basis of memory.

Amnesia

LO 13 Compare and contrast anterograde and retrograde amnesia.

In the months and years following Clive's illness, researchers administered many tests to assess his cognitive functioning. They found his IQ to be within an average range but his ability to remember past events deeply impaired. When prompted to name as many musical composers as possible in 1 minute, Clive—a man who had devoted his career to the study of music—could only produce four: Mozart, Beethoven, Bach, and Haydn. He denied that dragonflies have wings and claimed he had never heard of John F. Kennedy (Wilson et al., 1995).

Clive was even more disabled when it came to developing new memories. Initially, he could not hold onto incoming information for more than a blink of an eye. If his wife Deborah left the room, even for a short trip to the restroom, he would welcome her back as if she had been away for years—embracing, celebrating, sometimes weeping. "How long have I been ill?" he would ask, forgetting the answer and repeating himself within seconds (Wearing, 2005, p. 181).

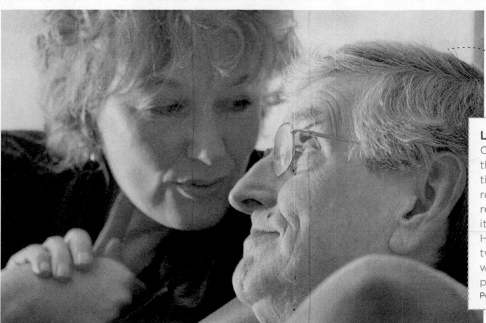

Love Triumphs
Clive forgot many things, but not the love he has for his wife. Every time Deborah came to visit, he recognized her but could not recall their last meeting, even if it happened just minutes before. Hugging, kissing, and sometimes twirling Deborah in the air, he would ask how much time had passed (Wearing, 2005). Jiri Rezac/ Polaris/Newscom

Amnesia, or memory loss, can result from either a physical or psychological condition. There are different types and degrees of amnesia, ranging from extreme (losing decades of autobiographical memories) to mild (temporarily forgetting names of acquaintances and other details following a concussion).

ANTEROGRADE AMNESIA   According to researchers, Clive suffers from "a more severe anterograde amnesia than any other patient previously reported" (Wilson et al., 1995, p. 680). **Anterograde amnesia** (an-tə-ˌrō-ˌgrād) is the inability to "lay down" or create new long-term memories (**FIGURE 6.12**), and it is generally caused by damage or injury to the brain, resulting from surgery, alcohol, head trauma, or illness. Someone with anterograde amnesia cannot form memories of events and experiences that occur following the damage to the brain, regardless of its cause. People affected by anterograde amnesia may be incapable of holding down a job, as their inability to lay down new memories affects their capacity to remember daily tasks. For Clive, his short-term memory still functioned to a certain extent, but he could only absorb and process information for several seconds before it was lost. From his perspective, every experience was fresh, and every person (with the exception of some he knew well from the past) a total stranger.

RETROGRADE AMNESIA   A second type of memory loss is **retrograde amnesia,** an inability to access memories created before brain injury or surgery (Brandt & Benedict, 1993; Figure 6.12). With retrograde amnesia, a person has difficulty retrieving old memories, though how "old" depends on the extent of the injury or trauma to the brain. People with retrograde amnesia generally remember who they are and the most important events of their earlier lives (Manns, Hopkins, & Squire, 2003; Squire & Wixted, 2011). Keep in mind that *retrograde* refers to the inability to access old memories, and *anterograde* refers to the inability to create new memories.

Clive suffered from retrograde amnesia in addition to his anterograde amnesia. While he appeared to retain a vague outline of his past (hazy information about his childhood, the fact that he had been a choral scholar at Clare College, Cambridge, and so on), he could not retrieve the names of his children unless prompted. And although Clive's children were all adults when he developed encephalitis, he came

FIGURE 6.12
Retrograde and Anterograde Amnesia
Retro means "before," so retrograde amnesia is the inability to retrieve memories for events that occurred *before* an amnesia-causing injury. *Antero* means "after," so anterograde amnesia is the inability to form memories for events that occur *after* an injury. Chris McGrath/Getty Image

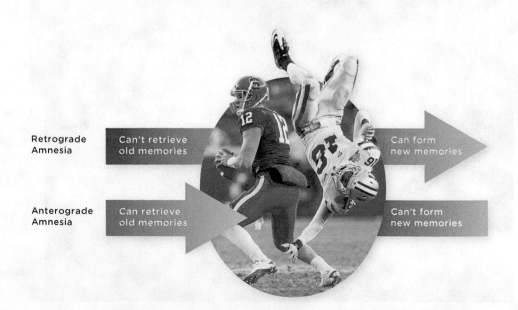

Retrograde Amnesia — Can't retrieve old memories — Can form new memories

Anterograde Amnesia — Can retrieve old memories — Can't form new memories out of the illness thinking they were young children. The retrograde amnesia has improved, but only minimally. In 2005, for example, Clive asked his forty-something son what subjects he was studying in grammar school (equivalent to American high school). Nowadays when inquiring about his children, Clive simply asks, "What are they doing?" (D. Wearing, personal communication, June 18 and 25, July 11, 2013).

In spite of the severe retrograde and anterograde amnesia, some of Clive's memory functions continued to operate quite well. At one point, Deborah arranged for Clive to be reunited with the singers from the London Lassus Ensemble, a group he had conducted for more than a decade before his illness. At first Clive paused and looked at the musicians with uncertainty, but then he raised his hands and began conducting, leading them through the music with precision and grace. Remembering the piece (which he had edited himself), Clive mouthed its words in Latin and employed the same tempo and conducting style he had used in the past (D. Wearing, personal communication, July 11, 2013). After the performance, the musicians left and Clive sat in the empty chapel wondering what had gone on there earlier (Wearing, 2005). When shown a video of himself leading the chorus, he remarked, "I wasn't conscious then" (Wilson et al., 2008). Clive's explicit memory of the event vanished in seconds, but his implicit memory—knowing how to conduct—was intact.

How is it possible that some of Clive's long-term memories were blotted out, while others, such as how to conduct music, remained fairly clear? The evidence suggests that different types of long-term memories travel distinct processing routes in the brain. Thus, damage to one area of the brain may impair some types of memory but not others. Let's take a closer look at where memories seem to be stored in the brain.

Where Memories Live in the Brain— A Macro Perspective

···▶ **LO 14** Identify the brain structures involved in memory.

A few years after the onset of Clive's illness, doctors evaluated his brain using an MRI scan. A troubling picture emerged; the virus had destroyed many parts of his brain, notably the **hippocampus,** which plays a vital role in the creation of new memories (Wilson et al., 2008).

Only in the last half-century have scientists come to appreciate the role of the hippocampus in memory (**INFOGRAPHIC 6.3** on page 270). Back in the 1920s, psychologist Karl Lashley set out to find a **memory trace:** the physical spot where memories are etched in the brain, also called an *engram*. Lashley selected a group of rats that had learned the layout of specific mazes, and then made large cuts at different places in their cortices to see how this affected their memory of the mazes. No matter where Lashley sliced, the rats still managed to maneuver their way through the mazes (Costandi, 2009, February 10; Lashley, 1950). These findings led Lashley and other scientists to believe that memory is spread throughout the brain rather than localized in a particular region (Costandi, 2009, February 10; Kandel & Pittenger, 1999). *Connectionism* is a model that suggests our memories are distributed throughout the brain in a network of interlinked neurons.

THE CASE OF H.M. Henry Molaison (better known as "H.M.") forced scientists to completely reevaluate their understanding of the brain's memory system. From the onset of his amnesia in 1953 until his death in 2008, H.M. served

▶ **CONNECTIONS**

In **Chapter 2,** we described the hippocampus as a pair of seahorse-shaped structures buried deep within the temporal lobes. The hippocampus is primarily responsible for processing and making new memories, but is not where memories are permanently stored. It is also one of the brain areas where *neurogenesis* occurs, that is, where new neurons are generated.

Synonym

connectionism parallel distributed processing (PDP)

---

anterograde amnesia (an-tə-ˌrō-ˌgrād) A type of memory loss; an inability to create new memories following damage or injury to the brain.

retrograde amnesia A type of memory loss; an inability to access memories formed prior to damage or injury to the brain, or difficulty retrieving them.

memory trace The location where memories are etched in the brain via physiological changes.

Tracking Memory in the Brain

Whether with lab rats or case studies, psychologists have spent decades tracking the location of memory in the brain. What they've found so far should be no surprise: Memory is a complex system involving multiple structures and regions of the brain. Memory is formed, processed, and stored throughout the brain, and different types of memory have different paths. So to find memory in the brain, it helps to know your way around the brain's structures. Remembering the amygdala's role in processing basic emotion, for instance, can help you understand its role in processing the emotional content of memories.

Forming New Memories

In an attempt to control the disabling seizures of a man named Henry Molaison (H.M.), doctors surgically removed portions of his brain, including the hippocampus. The surgery affected H.M.'s memory. He had profound anterograde amnesia: He could tap into old memories, but he could no longer make new explicit memories. However, he could still create implicit memories. Using information gathered about H.M.'s brain, scientists have been able to directly connect the hippocampus to the creation of new explicit memories.

After his death, H.M.'s brain was cut into over 2,000 slices that were preserved and digitized for research.

Prefrontal cortex
working memory
essential for retrieval

Cerebral cortex
memory storage
distributed throughout

Auditory cortex
(mostly hidden from view)
auditory memory storage

Temporal lobes
spatial memory storage

Visual cortex
visual memory storage

AMYGDALA
implicit memory formation,
emotional memory formation

HIPPOCAMPUS
explicit memory formation

CEREBELLUM
implicit memory formation

Hippocampus
memory consolidation

Storing Memories

Through his experiments slicing the cortices of rats that had learned to navigate mazes, Karl Lashley concluded that complex memories are not localized to a particular region in the cortex, but are instead widely distributed. Later research has established the interrelated roles of specific structures in the process of encoding, storing and retrieving memories.

In a process called *memory consolidation,* which occurs in the hippocampus, memories are moved to other parts of the cerebral cortex for long-term storage. Research on this topic is ongoing. For instance, scientists have been able to link explicit memory storage to areas of the brain where the original sensation was processed (see Harris, Petersen, & Diamond, 2001).

Lashley kept a careful record of the sizes and locations of lesions made in each rat as part of his experiments.

as a research participant for some 100 scientists (Corkin, 2002), making him the most extensively studied amnesic patient.

H.M.'s brain troubles began at the age of 10, a year or so after being knocked unconscious in a bicycle accident. He began to experience seizures, which worsened with age and eventually became so debilitating that he could no longer hold a steady job. Antiseizure medications were unsuccessful in controlling his seizures, so at the age of 27, H.M. opted for an experimental surgery to remove parts of his brain: the temporal lobes (just beneath the temples), including the hippocampus (Scoville & Milner, 1957).

H.M.'s surgery succeeded in reining in his epilepsy but left his memory in shambles. Upon waking from the operation, he could no longer find his way to the bathroom or recognize the hospital workers caring for him. He played the same jigsaw puzzles and read the same magazines day after day as if he were seeing them for the first time (Scoville & Milner, 1957). Like Clive, H.M. suffered from profound *anterograde amnesia,* the inability to encode new long-term memories, and a milder form of *retrograde amnesia,* trouble retrieving existing memories from storage. Although H.M. had difficulty recalling what occurred during the few years leading up to his surgery (Scoville & Milner, 1957), he did remember events from the more distant past, for example, the 1929 stock market crash and the events of World War II (Carey, 2008).

H.M. maintained a working implicit memory, which he demonstrated in an experiment involving the complex task of tracing a pattern reflected in a mirror. With repeated practice sessions (none of which he remembered), H.M. improved his performance on the drawing task, learning it as well as someone without amnesia (Gabrieli, Corkin, Mickel, & Growdon, 1993). Clive can also acquire new implicit memories, but his ability is very limited. According to Deborah, it took years for Clive to learn how to get to his bedroom in the small community residence where he moved after leaving the hospital (Wearing, 2005).

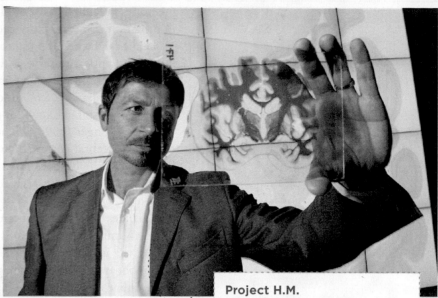

Project H.M.
Dr. Jacopo Annese, director of the Brain Observatory at the University of San Diego, stands in front of a massive digital image rendered from a slice of brain tissue preserved on a slide. Dr. Annese and his team have carved the brain of amnesiac Henry Molaison, or "H.M.," into 2,401 slices to be digitized and studied (The Brain Observatory, 2013). John Gibbins/U-T San Diego/Zuma Press/Newscom

THE ROLE OF THE HIPPOCAMPUS Imagine you are a scientist trying to figure out exactly what role the hippocampus plays in memory. Consider the facts you know about H.M.: (1) He has virtually no hippocampus; (2) he has lost the ability to make new *explicit* memories, yet can create *implicit* memories; and (3) he can still tap into memories of the distant past. So what do you think the hippocampus does? Evidence suggests that the hippocampus is essential for creating new explicit memories but *not* implicit memories. Researchers have also shown that explicit memories are processed and stored in other parts of the brain, including the temporal lobes and areas of the frontal cortex (García-Lázaro, Ramirez-Carmona, Lara-Romero, & Roldan-Valadez, 2012).

As in H.M.'s case, Clive's ability to form explicit memories is profoundly compromised, which is largely a result of the destruction of his hippocampus. Yet Clive also struggles with implicit memories—not surprising given the extensive damage to other regions of his brain, such as the amygdala and temporal lobes (Wilson et al., 2008). Studies have zeroed in on other brain areas, such as the cerebellum and amygdala, as processing hubs for implicit memory (Thompson & Kim, 1996; Thompson & Steinmetz, 2009). The amygdala also plays a central role in the processing of emotional memories (García-Lázaro et al., 2012). See Infographic 6.3 on page 270 for more information about memory processing in the brain.

So although the hippocampus plays a central role in laying down new memories, it does not appear to serve as their ultimate destination. This process of memory formation, which moves a memory from the hippocampus to other areas of the brain, is called *memory consolidation* (Squire & Bayley, 2007). The consolidation that begins in the hippocampus allows for the long-term storage of memories. According to Kandel and Pittenger (1999): "The final locus of storage of memory is widely assumed to be the cerebral cortex, though this is a difficult assertion to prove" (p. 2041). As for retrieval, the hippocampus appears to be in charge of accessing young memories, but then passes on that responsibility to other brain regions as memories grow older (Smith & Squire, 2009).

This idea that the hippocampus is essential for creating explicit memories (as opposed to implicit memories) is supported by what we know about *infantile amnesia,* that is, the inability to remember events from our earliest years. Most adults cannot remember events before the age of 3, though it is not clear why. Some researchers suggest that it is because the hippocampus and frontal cortex, both important for the creation of long-term explicit memories, are not fully developed in children (Bauer, 2006; Willoughby, Desrocher, Levine, & Rovet, 2012).

This macrolevel perspective allows us to see the "big picture" of memory, but what's going on microscopically? The next section focuses on the important changes occurring in and between neurons, but keep in mind that neurons are not the only cells in the brain. Neighboring glial cells may also play a role in memory.

from the pages of **SCIENTIFIC AMERICAN**

What Marijuana Reveals About Memory

Glial cells, not neurons, are responsible for marijuana-induced forgetfulness

Until recently, most scientists believed that neurons were the all-important brain cells controlling mental functions and that the surrounding glial cells were little more than neuron supporters and "glue." Now research published in March in *Cell* reveals that astrocytes, a type of glia, have a principal role in working memory. And the scientists made the discovery by getting mice stoned.

Marijuana impairs working memory—the short-term memory we use to hold on to and process thoughts. Think of the classic stoner who, midsentence, forgets the point he was making. Although such stupor might give recreational users the giggles, people using the drug for medical reasons might prefer to maintain their cognitive capacity.

To study how marijuana impairs working memory, Giovanni Marsicano of the University of Bordeaux in France and his colleagues removed cannabinoid receptors—proteins that respond to marijuana's psychoactive ingredient THC—from neurons in mice. These mice, it turned out, were just as forgetful as regular mice when given THC: they were equally poor at memorizing the position of a hidden platform in a water pool. When the receptors were removed from astrocytes, however, the mice could find the platform just fine while on THC.

The results suggest that the role of glia in mental activity has been overlooked. Although research in recent years has revealed that glia are implicated in many unconscious processes and diseases [*see* "The Hidden Brain," by R. Douglas Fields: *Scientific American Mind,* May/June 2011], this is one of the first studies to suggest that glia play a key role in conscious thought. "It's very likely that astrocytes have many more functions than we thought," Marsicano says. "Certainly their role in cognition is now being revealed."

Unlike THC's effect on memory, its pain-relieving property appears to work through neurons. In theory, therefore, it might be possible to design THC-type drugs that target neurons—but not glia—and offer pain relief without the forgetfulness. **Ruth Williams.**

Where Memories Live in the Brain— A Micro Perspective

LO 15 Describe long-term potentiation.

How does your brain change when you learn a new driving route to school? If we could peer into your skull, we might see a change in your hippocampus. As one study found, London taxicab drivers with greater time spent on the job had structural changes in some regions of the hippocampus, particularly to an area that processes "spatial knowledge" (Maguire, Woollett, & Spiers, 2006). Zooming in for a closer look, we might actually see changes at the level of the neuron. If you are looking for a memory imprint, the best place to look is the **synapse**.

LONG-TERM POTENTIATION   As it turns out, the more neurons communicate, the better the connections between them. **Long-term potentiation** occurs when sending neurons release neurotransmitters more effectively, and receiving neurons become more sensitive, boosting synaptic strength for days or even weeks (Lynch, 2002; Malenka & Nicoll, 1999; Whitlock, Heynen, Shuler, & Bear, 2006). In other words, long-term potentiation refers to the increased efficiency of neural communication over time, resulting in learning and the formation of memories. Researchers suggest long-term potentiation may be the biological basis of many kinds of learning. As you learn a new skill, for example, the neurons involved in performing that skill increase their communication with each other. It might start with a somewhat random firing of neurons, but eventually the neurons responsible for the new skill develop pathways through which they communicate more efficiently. Having trouble visualizing the process? Imagine this scenario: Your college has opened a new campus with an array of brand-new buildings, but it has yet to construct the sidewalks connecting them. In order to go from one class to the next, students have to wade through tall grass and weeds. All the trampling eventually gives way to a system of well-worn paths linking the buildings and a multitude of efficient paths develops among the buildings. Long-term potentiation of neural connections occurs in a similar fashion; over time, the communication among neurons improves and strengthens, allowing for the skill to develop and become more natural (Whitlock et al., 2006). This is where memory comes in; these paths represent how a skill, whether tying your shoes, learning to drive a stick shift, or mastering a skateboarding trick, is learned and thus becomes a memory.

APLYSIA   Amazingly, we have learned much about long-term potentiation from the sea slug *Aplysia*. Why the sea slug? One reason is that the sea slug only has about 20,000 neurons (Kandel, 2009)—a little easier to work with than the 100 billion neurons of a human brain. The sea slug's neural simplicity, that is, the fact that the synapses are relatively easy to examine individually, also allows for the intensive study of habituation, conditioning, and other processes involved in classical conditioning. Studies using sea slugs as their subjects indicate that long-term potentiation, or increases in synaptic "strength," is associated with learning and

CONNECTIONS

In **Chapter 2,** we introduced the synapse: the tiny gap between two neurons. Neurons communicate with each other via chemicals called neurotransmitters, which are released into the synapse. Here, we see how the activities at the neural level are related to the formation and maintenance of memories.

Smart Slug
Studying the neurons of sea slugs, researchers have observed the synaptic changes that underlie memory. Long-term potentiation enables a sea slug to retract its gills in anticipation of being squirted with water. NaturePL/SuperStock

long-term potentiation The increased efficiency of neural communication over time, resulting in learning and the formation of memories.

CONNECTIONS

In **Chapter 5,** we discussed classical conditioning and how a neutral stimulus can be paired with an unconditioned stimulus, ultimately leading to a conditioned stimulus resulting in a conditioned response. In the case of the sea slug, the squirt of water is the conditioned stimulus and its involuntary response of retracting its gills is the conditioned response.

memory. **What can a sea slug learn?** They can be classically conditioned to retract their gills in response to being squirted with water. Researchers report that when the sea slugs are conditioned in this way, there are structural changes in both presynaptic and postsynaptic cells, including changes to connections between neurons (Kandel, 2009)—evidence of long-term potentiation. So never, ever complain to your instructor that you cannot learn: If a sea slug can do it, so can you!

ALZHEIMER'S DISEASE   On a less positive note, disruptions in long-term potentiation appear to be at work in *Alzheimer's disease,* a progressive, devastating brain illness that causes cognitive decline, including memory, language, and thinking problems. Alzheimer's affects as many as 5.1 million Americans (National Institute on Aging, 2013). The disease was first discovered by Alois Alzheimer, a German neuropathologist, in the early 1900s. He had a patient with severe memory

Inside Alzheimer's

The PET scan (shown above, left) depicts the brain of a normal person, while the scan (above, right) shows that of a person with Alzheimer's. Studies using PET suggest a slowing of brain activity in certain regions of the Alzheimer's brain (Alzheimer's Association, 2013). The neurofibrillary tangles (far right image, with tangles in pink) result from twisted protein fibers accumulating inside brain cells.
left: Jessica Wilson/Science Source; right: Thomas Deerinck, NCMIR/Science Source

problems whose later autopsy revealed that the neurons in her brain were tangled up like wires of your earbud headphones. These *neurofibrillary tangles,* as they came to be called, were eventually shown to result from twisted protein fibers accumulating inside brain cells. In addition to the tangles, the other distinctive sign of Alzheimer's is the presence of *amyloid plaques,* protein clumps that build up between neurons, blocking their lines of communication (Vingtdeux, Davies, Dickson, & Marambaud, 2011).

There is no cure for Alzheimer's disease, and current treatments focus only on reducing the severity of symptoms rather than correcting the brain damage responsible. But there is also reason to be hopeful. Promising new drugs are coming down the pipeline, and there is some preliminary evidence suggesting that simple lifestyle changes, like becoming more physically active and pursuing intellectually and socially stimulating activities, may actually decrease the speed and severity of cognitive decline (Hertzog, Kramer, Wilson, & Lindenberger, 2009; Wilson & Bennett, 2003). Additional good news comes from recent research suggesting that we should not think of cognitive decline as inevitable in aging. We have more control of aging than previously thought, especially when we focus on the lifelong possibilities of learning and autonomy (Hertzog et al., 2009). Furthermore, it's not only the strengthening of synapses that makes for enduring memories, but also the activation of new ones (Yu, Ponomarev, & Davis, 2004), thus ameliorating, or offsetting, cognitive decline (**TABLE 6.2**).

Table 6.2 FACTS ABOUT MEMORY LOSS

Memory loss does not have to be an inevitable part of aging. Occasionally forgetting where you put your keys does not mean you have a degenerative memory disorder. This table provides some facts you should know about memory loss.

In the United States, 1 out of every 8 people who are 65 or older suffers from Alzheimer's disease, which leads to loss of memory and other cognitive functions (Alzheimer's Association, 2010).

The prevalence of dementia will double every 20 years, reaching 81 million by the year 2040 (Ferri et al., 2005).

There is no definitive way to know whether you or a family member will suffer from a neurocognitive disorder; most cases result from a complex combination of genetic, environmental, and lifestyle factors.

Studies of both animals and people have linked physical exercise to a variety of positive changes in the brain, including enhanced blood flow, increased thickness of the cortex, and less age-related deterioration of the hippocampus (Polidori, Nelles, & Pientka, 2010).

Some research suggests that people who begin exercising in their thirties (and stick with it) experience less cognitive decline than their sedentary peers by the time they reach their forties and fifties (Hertzog et al., 2009), although consistent exercise at any age has lasting cognitive benefits (Cotman & Berchtold, 2002; Kramer, Erickson, & Colcombe, 2006).

Intellectually engaging activities such as reading books and newspapers, writing, drawing, and solving crossword puzzles have been associated with a lower risk of memory loss (Hertzog et al., 2009; Wang, Karp, Winblad, & Fratiglioni, 2002).

Being socially active and hooked into social networks may reduce the risk of developing dementia (Fratiglioni, Paillard-Borg, & Winblad, 2004).

Like many topics psychologists study, the biological mechanisms that give rise to memory remain somewhat mysterious. We know we have memories; we know they are formed in the brain; and we know the brain is a physical entity, yet we still don't know exactly how we go from a bunch of firing neurons to a vivid recollection of your 21st birthday bash, your high school prom, or the image of Dave Roberts stealing second base to start the Red Sox's improbable comeback. Studies attempting to test the various theories of memory formation are inconclusive, often generating more questions than answers. But one thing seems certain: Memory researchers have plenty of exciting work ahead.

show what you know

1. _____ refers to the inability to lay down new long-term memories, generally resulting from damage to the brain.
   a. Anterograde amnesia
   b. Retrograde amnesia
   c. Infantile amnesia
   d. Long-term potentiation

2. The _____ is a pair of seahorse-shaped structures in the brain that play a central role in memory.
   a. engram
   b. temporal lobe
   c. hippocampus
   d. aplysia

3. _____ is the process of memory formation, which moves a memory from the hippocampus to other areas of the brain.
   a. Long-term potentiation
   b. Memory consolidation
   c. Priming
   d. The memory trace

4. Infantile amnesia makes it difficult for people to remember events that occurred before the age of 3. What is your earliest memory and how old were you when that event occurred?

✓ CHECK YOUR ANSWERS IN APPENDIX C.

Onward

(Left) Nearly two decades after falling ill, Clive renewed his wedding vows with Deborah. Now in his seventies, Clive lives in a country residence for people suffering from brain injuries (Vennard, 2011, November 20). Jiri Rezac/Polaris/Newscom

Dorothea (right) became the Junior World Memory Champion for the second time in 2009. Although she no longer competes in memory sport, she continues to exercise her intellect as a student of political science and sociology. © Ilona Huege

FINAL THOUGHTS   At this point, you may be wondering what became of the two people featured in this chapter, Clive Wearing and Dorothea Seitz. After living in the hospital 7 years, Clive moved to a country residence specially designed for people suffering from brain injuries. As he left the hospital, some of the staff members offered him a farewell and said they would miss him. Addressing them with a polite bow, Clive exclaimed, "You're the first people I've seen!" When Deborah would visit Clive in his new home, she found him happy and relaxed, spending much of his time on walks through gardens and the local village (Wearing, 2005, p. 293). In 2002 Clive and Deborah renewed their marriage vows. Clive participated fully in the service, reciting scripture he had memorized during his career as a professional singer decades before (D. Wearing, personal communication, June 10, 2013). After the ceremony, he had no recollection of what had taken place but nevertheless was very happy, laughing and devouring sponge cake (Wearing, 2005).

As for Dorothea, she succeeded in defending her title of Junior World Memory Champion in 2009 and finished the competition in 11th place overall. After finishing high school, she spent a year doing volunteer work in Peru. She is currently studying political science and sociology in Freiburg, Germany.

6 summary of concepts

LO 1 Define memory. (p. 234)

Memory refers to the information collected and stored in the brain that is generally available for later use. Exactly how the brain absorbs information from the outside world and files it for later use is still not completely understood. However, scientists have proposed many theories and constructed various models to help explain how the brain processes, or works on, data on their way to becoming memories.

LO 2 Identify the processes of encoding, storage, and retrieval in memory. (p. 234)

Encoding is the process through which new information enters our memory system. Information is taken in by our senses and converted into neural activity that travels to the brain and, if successfully encoded, it is stored. Storage preserves the information for possible recollection in the future. Retrieval is the process of accessing information stored in memory.

LO 3 Explain the stages of memory described by the information-processing model. (p. 236)

According to the information-processing model, the brain has three types of memory storage associated with the stages of memory: sensory memory, short-term memory, and long-term memory. The levels of processing framework suggests there is a hierarchy of processing stages that corresponds to different depths of information processing.

LO 4 Describe sensory memory. (p. 240)

Data picked up by the senses enter sensory memory, where sensations are registered. Here, almost exact copies of our sensations are processed for a very brief moment of time. Information from the outside world floods our sensory memory through multiple channels. Although this stage of memory is fleeting, it is critical to the creation of memories.

LO 5 Summarize short-term memory. (p. 243)

Short-term memory is the second stage of the original information-processing model. Information is temporarily maintained and processed, hosting current thoughts and whatever activities the brain is engaged in. Short-term memory has a limited capacity, and what is held there depends on how much distraction is created by other cognitive activities. We can only concentrate on a small proportion of data flooding our sensory memory.

LO 6 Give examples of how we can use chunking to improve our memory span. (p. 244)

Grouping numbers, letters, or other items into meaningful subsets, or "chunks," is an effective strategy for juggling and increasing the amount of information in short-term memory. In addition, chunking can help nudge the same information into long-term memory.

LO 7 Explain working memory and how it compares with short-term memory. (p. 244)

The active processing component of short-term memory, working memory, has four important parts. The phonological loop is responsible for working with verbal information for brief periods of time. The visuospatial sketchpad is where visual and spatial data are briefly stored and manipulated. The central executive directs attention, makes plans, coordinates activities, and determines what information should be ignored. The episodic buffer is where information from the phonological loop, visuospatial sketchpad, and long-term memory can all be brought together temporarily, as directed by the central executive.

LO 8 Define long-term memory. (p. 246)

Long-term memory is a stage of memory with essentially unlimited capacity. Explicit memory is the type of memory you are aware of having and can consciously express, and it can be further be divided into semantic and episodic memory. Semantic memory pertains to general facts about the world and is theoretically available to anyone. Episodic memory is the personal form of memory that records personal experiences. Implicit memory is the memory of something you know or you know how to do, but that might be automatic or unconscious, and therefore difficult to articulate.

LO 9 Illustrate how encoding specificity relates to retrieval cues. (p. 255)

Retrieval cues are stimuli that help you retrieve stored information that is difficult to access. The encoding specificity principle states that memories are more easily recalled when the context and cues at the time of encoding are similar to those at the time of retrieval. Thus, the context (external or internal) at the time of encoding and retrieval strengthens retrieval cues. Priming, recall, and recognition also play a role in the retrieval of stored information.

LO 10 Identify some of the reasons why we forget. (p. 259)

Memory failure may occur during any of the three stages of memory processing. There are a variety of reasons why; these can include encoding failure, retrieval failure, and the tip-of-the-tongue phenomenon, as well as interference.

LO 11 Explain how the malleability of memory influences the recall of events. (p. 263)

Eyewitness accounts are not always reliable because people's memories are far from perfect. Memories can change over time, which means we should be careful when questioning people about crimes and other events they have witnessed. Studies on the misinformation effect suggest that information obtained after an incident can distort one's memory of it.

LO 12 Define rich false memory. (p. 264)

Rich false memories are experienced as true recollections of an event, including details, emotions, and confidence that the event occurred, although the event never happened. Some researchers have implanted memories of events that never occurred.

LO 13 Compare and contrast anterograde and retrograde amnesia. (p. 267)

There are different types or degrees of amnesia, or memory loss, due to medical or psychological condition, ranging from extreme loss of memory to less severe forms. Anterograde amnesia is the inability to "lay down" or create new long-term memories, and is generally caused by damage or injury to the brain, resulting from surgery, alcohol, head trauma, or illness. Retrograde amnesia is an inability to access memories created before the occurrence of a brain injury or surgery. Retrograde refers to the inability to access old memories, and anterograde refers to the inability to create new memories.

LO 14 Identify the brain structures involved in memory. (p. 269)

Researchers have identified many structures in the brain involved in the processing and storage of memory. The hippocampus is essential for creating new explicit memories, as are the temporal lobes and frontal cortex. Other areas, such as the cerebellum and amygdala, are integral in the processing of implicit memories.

LO 15 Describe long-term potentiation. (p. 273)

Long-term potentiation refers to the increased efficiency of neural communication over time, resulting in learning and the formation of memories. The communication among neurons improves and strengthens, allowing for new skills to develop and become more natural. These new pathways represent how a skill, for example, is learned and thus becomes an implicit memory.

key terms

anterograde amnesia, p. 268
chunking, p. 244
distributed practice, p. 252
echoic memory, p. 242
effortful processing, p. 250
elaborative rehearsal, p. 250
encoding, p. 234
encoding specificity principle, p. 257
episodic memory, p. 247
explicit memory, p. 247

flashbulb memory, p. 247
iconic memory, p. 240
implicit memory, p. 248
long-term memory, p. 236
long-term potentiation, p. 273
maintenance rehearsal, p. 250
massed practice, p. 252
memory, p. 234
memory trace, p. 269
misinformation effect, p. 264
mnemonic, p. 248

primacy effect, p. 256
priming, p. 255
proactive interference, p. 261
procedural memory, p. 248
recall, p. 255
recency effect, p. 256
recognition, p. 256
relearning, p. 258
retrieval, p. 235
retrieval cues, p. 255

retroactive interference, p. 261
retrograde amnesia, p. 268
rich false memories, p. 265
semantic memory, p. 247
sensory memory, p. 236
serial position effect, p. 256
short-term memory, p. 236
storage, p. 235
working memory, p. 244

TEST PREP are you ready?

1. You try to remember the name of a movie you watched last year, but you are struggling. When you do finally remember it was *Lincoln,* which stage of memory were you using?
   a. short-term memory
   b. sensory memory
   c. encoding
   d. retrieval

2. According to the levels of processing framework, there is a _____ that corresponds to the depth at which information is processed, as well as reflect how durable and retrievable a memory may be.
   a. hierarchy of processing
   b. computer metaphor
   c. method of loci
   d. phonological loop

3. Using the partial report method, Sperling (1960) showed that participants could recall 76% of the letters briefly flashed on a screen. The findings from this study indicate the capabilities of:
   a. eidetic imagery.
   b. depth of processing.
   c. iconic memory.
   d. the phonological loop.

4. Miller (1956) reviewed findings on the Digit Span test and found that short-term memory capacity is limited to between 5 and 9 numbers, that is, the "magical seven, plus or minus two." However, through the use of _____, we can improve the span of our short-term memory.
   a. echoic memory
   b. iconic memory
   c. multitasking
   d. chunking

5. Baddeley and colleagues proposed that the purpose of _____ is to actively maintain information while the mind is performing complex tasks. The phonological loop, visuospatial sketchpad, central executive, and episodic buffer all play a role in this process.
   a. eidetic imagery
   b. working memory
   c. short-term memory
   d. semantic memory

6. In a classic study, Godden and Baddeley (1975) asked participants to learn lists of words under two conditions: while underwater and on dry land. Participants were better able to recall the information in the same context in which it was encoded. This finding supports:

   a. the encoding specificity principle.

   b. Baddeley's working memory model.

   c. the serial position effect.

   d. the information-processing model of memory.

7. Your friend tells you she does much better on multiple-choice tests because she is able to recognize an answer when she sees it listed as one of the choices for a question. She is describing her _____, which is the process of matching incoming data to information stored in long-term memory.

   a. relearning

   b. recall

   c. recognition

   d. retrieval

8. _____ causes problems with the retrieval of memories because of information you learned in the past and _____ causes problems with retrieval due to recently learned information.

   a. The recency effect; the primacy effect

   b. The primacy effect; the recency effect

   c. Proactive interference; retroactive interference

   d. Retroactive interference; proactive interference

9. According to _____, memories can fade over time, becoming more vulnerable to new information. Thus, your memory of an event might include revisions of what really happened.

   a. the information-processing model of memory

   b. the levels of processing framework

   c. Baddeley's model of working memory

   d. a reconstructionist model of memory

10. In studies by Loftus and colleagues, around 25% of participants are able to "remember" an event that never happened. This type of _____ shows us how the malleability of memory can influence our recall of events.

    a. hyperthymestic syndrome

    b. rich false memory

    c. proactive interference

    d. serial position effect

11. In one study, Loftus and Palmer (1974) found that when they told participants two cars had "smashed" into each other, these same participants were more likely to report they had seen broken glass in a previously viewed film than participants who were told the cars had "hit" each other. This tendency for new and possibly deceptive information to distort one's memory of a past incident is known as.

    a. the misinformation effect.

    b. retroactive interference.

    c. proactive interference.

    d. the serial position effect.

12. Traumatic experiences that are thought to be pushed out of consciousness are often referred to as _____ memories.

    a. long-term

    b. short-term

    c. repressed

    d. sensory

13. Retrograde amnesia is generally caused by some sort of trauma to the brain. People with retrograde amnesia generally cannot:

    a. form memories of events that occur following the trauma.

    b. access memories of events created before the trauma.

    c. form semantic memories following the trauma.

    d. use procedural memories.

14. _____ refers to the increased efficiency of neural communication over time, resulting in learning and the formation of memories.

    a. Memory consolidation

    b. Long-term potentiation

    c. Memory trace

    d. Priming

15. The _____ is essential for creating new explicit memories, but not implicit memories.

    a. parietal lobe

    b. amygdala

    c. cerebellum

    d. hippocampus

16. A friend says, "My grandmother has terrible short-term memory. She can't remember anything from a couple of hours ago." This statement represents a very common mistake people make when discussing memory. How would you explain this confusion about short-term memory versus long-term memory?

17. How are iconic memory and echoic memory different from each other?

18. How does working memory differ from short-term memory?

19. Provide two examples of mnemonics you've used in the past.

20. Imagine you are a teacher creating a list of classroom rules in case of an emergency. If you were expecting your students to remember these rules after only reading through them once, where in the list would you position the most important rules? Why?

✓ CHECK YOUR ANSWERS IN APPENDIX C.

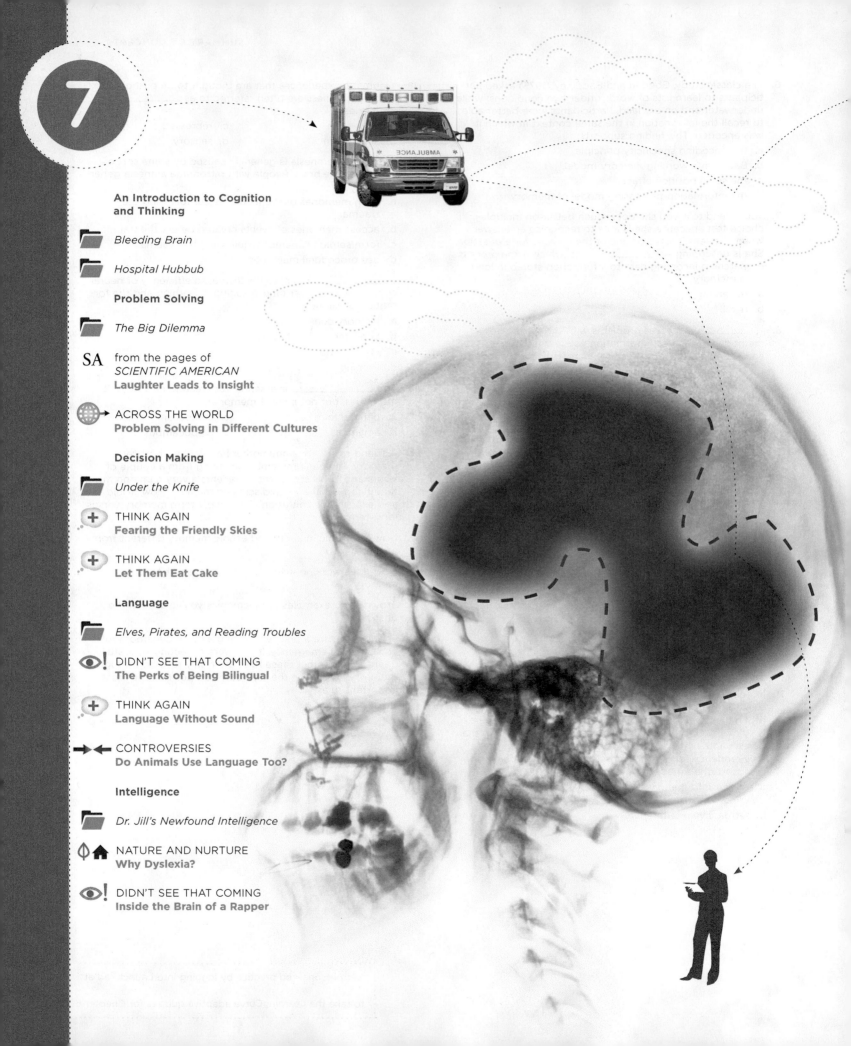

7

An Introduction to Cognition and Thinking

Bleeding Brain

Hospital Hubbub

Problem Solving

The Big Dilemma

SA from the pages of
SCIENTIFIC AMERICAN
Laughter Leads to Insight

ACROSS THE WORLD
Problem Solving in Different Cultures

Decision Making

Under the Knife

THINK AGAIN
Fearing the Friendly Skies

THINK AGAIN
Let Them Eat Cake

Language

Elves, Pirates, and Reading Troubles

DIDN'T SEE THAT COMING
The Perks of Being Bilingual

THINK AGAIN
Language Without Sound

CONTROVERSIES
Do Animals Use Language Too?

Intelligence

Dr. Jill's Newfound Intelligence

NATURE AND NURTURE
Why Dyslexia?

DIDN'T SEE THAT COMING
Inside the Brain of a Rapper

cognition, language, and intelligence

An Introduction to Cognition and Thinking

BLEEDING BRAIN December 10, 1996, was the day a blood vessel in Dr. Jill Bolte Taylor's brain began to bleed. At approximately 7:00 A.M., Dr. Jill awoke to a pain behind her left eye, a stabbing sensation she found similar to the "brain freeze" felt after a hasty gulp of ice cream. It seemed strange for a healthy 37-year-old woman to experience such a terrible headache, but Dr. Jill was not the type to lounge in bed all day. Pushing through the pain, she got up, ambled over to her exercise machine, and climbed on. But as soon as she began moving her limbs back and forth, a weird out-of-body sensation took hold, as if her mind had come unhooked from her body and was watching like a curious bystander. "I felt as though I was observing myself in motion, as in the playback of a memory," Dr. Jill writes in her book, *My Stroke of Insight.* "My fingers, as they grasped on to the handrail, looked like primitive claws" (Taylor, 2006, p. 37).

The pain, meanwhile, kept hammering away at the left side of her head. She stepped off the workout machine and headed toward the bathroom, but walking no longer felt automatic and effortless. Her steps seemed plodding and premeditated, and maintaining balance demanded intense concentration. Finally reaching the shower, Dr. Jill propped herself against the wall and turned on the faucet, but the sound of the water splashing against the tub was not the soothing *whoosh* she had expected to hear. It was more like an earsplitting roar. Dr. Jill's brain was no longer processing sound in a normal way. For the first time that morning, she began to wonder if her brain was in serious trouble (Taylor, 2006).

"What is going on? Have I ever experienced anything like this before?" she thought. "What is happening in my brain?" (Taylor, 2006, p. 41). If anyone was poised to answer these questions, it was Dr. Taylor herself. A devoted neuroanatomist—or "brain scientist," as she calls herself—Dr. Jill spent

→

7

LEARNING OBJECTIVES

after reading and studying this chapter, you should be able to:

LO 1 Define cognition and explain how it is related to thinking.

LO 2 Define concepts and identify how they are organized.

LO 3 Differentiate between formal concepts and natural concepts.

LO 4 Describe the biological processes associated with cognition.

LO 5 Explain how trial and error and algorithms can be used to solve problems.

LO 6 Identify different types of heuristics used to solve problems.

LO 7 Define decision making and explain how heuristics can lead us astray.

LO 8 Define language and give examples of its basic elements.

LO 9 Identify the linguistic relativity hypothesis and its relation to language and thought.

LO 10 Examine and distinguish among various theories of intelligence.

LO 11 Describe how intelligence is measured and identify important characteristics of assessment.

LO 12 Define creativity and its associated characteristics.

The Brain Scientist
An accomplished neuroanatomist, Dr. Jill Bolte Taylor had devoted her career to studying the brains of others. But one winter morning in 1996, she was given the frightening opportunity to observe her own brain in the midst of a meltdown. AJ Mast/ The New York Times/Redux

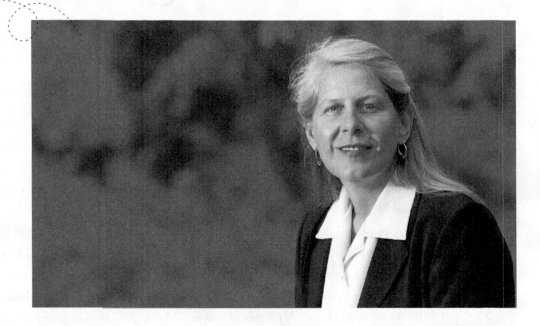

CONNECTIONS

In **Chapter 6,** we presented the process of retrieval in memory. Dr. Taylor was having difficulty retrieving her memories. We assume that the information she was trying to access had been successfully encoded and stored prior to the stroke.

Dr. Jill, in Her Own Words:
http://qrs.ly/9t3m62b

her days studying neurons at a prestigious laboratory affiliated with Harvard Medical School. She now imagined herself rummaging through her mental library for any memories that might help diagnose her condition (she was in the habit of using this method of **recall** in her daily life), but all the files seemed to be locked. The knowledge was there, but she could not tap into it (Taylor, 2006).

Dr. Jill sensed that something was terribly wrong, but she could not help feeling mesmerized by the "tranquil euphoria" of her new state of consciousness. She no longer felt separate from the outside world. Like a fluid running fast and free, her body drifted in and out of surrounding space. Memories of the past floated into the distance, everyday worries evaporated, and the little voices in her mind that normally narrated her train of thought fell silent (Taylor, 2006).

Wading in a dreamlike fog, Dr. Jill managed to shower and put on clothes. Then, just as she began visualizing the journey to work, her right arm fell limp like a dead fish. It was paralyzed. At that moment she knew: "Oh my gosh, I'm having a stroke! I'm

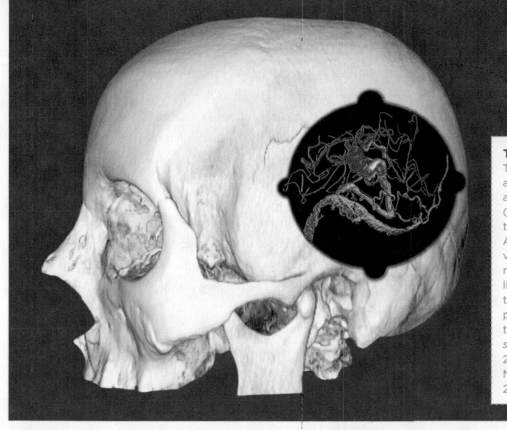

Tangled
The tangled intersection of arteries (red) and veins (blue) is an arteriovenous malformation (AVM), the anatomical abnormality that led to Dr. Taylor's stroke. An AVM is essentially a clump of blood vessels that results when there are no tiny vessels called capillaries linking arteries to veins. Sometimes the vessels of an AVM burst under pressure, allowing blood to pool in the brain; this is called a *hemorrhagic stroke* (American Stroke Association, 2012; National Institute of Neurological Disorders and Stroke, 2012). Medical Body Scans/Science Source

having a stroke!" (Taylor, 2006, p. 44). Her next thought was: "Wow this is so cool! . . . How many scientists have the opportunity to study their own brain function and mental deterioration from the inside out?" (p. 44).

Dr. Jill was indeed having a rare form of stroke caused by a defective linkage between blood vessels in the brain. This faulty connection in the central nervous system, known as an arteriovenous malformation (AVM), affects a substantial number of people—about 300,000 in the United States alone (around 0.1% of the population) at any given time. Most individuals born with AVMs are symptomless and unaware of their condition, but about 12% (36,000 people) experience effects ranging in severity from annoying headaches to life-threatening brain bleeds like the kind Dr. Jill was experiencing (National Institute of Neurological Disorders and Stroke, 2012).

Having a backstage pass to her own stroke was a once-in-a-lifetime learning opportunity for a neuroanatomist, but it was also a serious condition requiring an immediate response. Dr. Jill understood that strokes can cause permanent paralysis, sometimes even death. Urgent medical attention was needed. She walked into her home office and took a seat by the phone, racking her brain for ideas of how to get help. The usual strategies like calling 911 or knocking on a neighbor's door simply did not cross her mind. As she gazed at the phone keypad, a string of digits materialized in her brain. It was the phone number of her mother in Indiana. Calling her mom was certainly an option, but what would she say? Dr. Jill didn't want to worry her mother, so she sat and waited, hoping that another set of digits would appear.

Finally, another phone number flickered by in two separate chunks—it was her work number. She scrawled down the digits as fast as she could, but looking down at what she had written, she only saw cryptic lines and curves. Fortunately, those lines and curves she saw on the paper matched the set of figures that appeared on the phone keypad. Dr. Jill picked up the receiver and dialed the desk of her coworker and friend, Dr. Stephen Vincent (Taylor, 2006). Steve answered the phone immediately, but his words were incomprehensible to Dr. Jill. "Oh my gosh, he sounds like a golden retriever!" she thought to herself. Mustering all her mental might, she opened her mouth and said, "This is Jill, I need help!" Well, that's what she hoped she had said. Her own voice sounded like a golden retriever as well (Taylor, 2006, p. 56; TED.com, 2008). Luckily, Steve managed to recognize that the murmurs and cries belonged to his friend Dr. Jill, and before long he was driving her to the hospital (Taylor, 2006).

As blood hemorrhaged into Dr. Jill's brain, she became increasingly unable to process sensory information, tap into memories, or use language. As she later reflected: "In the course of four hours, I watched my brain completely deteriorate in its ability to process all information" (TED.com, 2008). The bleeding had begun to limit her capacity for cognition.

Cognition. You've probably heard the term "cognition" tossed around in conversation, and perhaps you know that it has something to do with thinking. But what exactly do we mean by cognition, and where does it figure in the vast landscape of psychology?

Cognition and Thinking

The study of cognition is deeply rooted in the history of psychology. Early psychologists were intensely focused on understanding the mysterious workings of the mind, often using **introspection** (examination of one's own conscious activities) in their studies. With the rise of behaviorism in the 1930s, the emphasis shifted away from internal processes and on to behavior. Researchers shunned thoughts, emotions, and anything they could not observe or measure objectively. In the 1950s, psychologists once again began to probe the private affairs of the mind. Psychology experienced a *cognitive revolution,* and research on cognition and thinking has flourished ever since.

LO 1   Define cognition and explain how it is related to thinking.

Cognition is the mental activity associated with obtaining, converting, and using knowledge. But how is this type of mental activity different from *thinking*? Thinking is a specific type of cognition that requires us to "go beyond" information or to manipulate information to reach a goal. **Thinking** involves coming to a decision, reaching a solution, forming a belief, or developing an attitude (Matlin, 2009). Cognition is a broad term that describes mental activity, and thinking is a subset of cognition. These definitions are not universally accepted, however; some psychologists consider cognition and thinking to be one and the same activity. However the terms are defined, Dr. Jill was clearly experiencing significant impairments in both cognition and thinking on the morning of her stroke.

HOSPITAL HUBBUB   Upon arriving at Mount Auburn Hospital, Dr. Jill received a **computerized axial tomography** (CT or CAT) brain scan. Unfortunately, the cross-sectional slices provided by the scan merged into a troubling picture: a giant hemorrhage in the left side of her brain. According to Dr. Jill, "My left hemisphere was swimming in a pool of blood and my entire brain was swollen in response to the trauma" (Taylor, 2006, p. 68).

Dr. Jill needed urgent, expert attention. She was rushed by ambulance to the emergency room at Massachusetts General Hospital, where she was eventually assigned to

---

CONNECTIONS

In **Chapter 1,** we introduced early psychologists who used *introspection* as a research method. Wundt used it to examine psychological processes involved in sensations, feelings, and images experienced in response to stimuli. Titchener used introspection to determine the structure of the mind. Their work set the stage for the field of cognitive psychology, the study of mental processes, and *cognitive neuroscience,* which explores the physiological basis of mental processes.

CONNECTIONS

In **Chapter 2,** we described CAT scans. This technology uses X-rays to create cross-sectional "slices" of the brain that come together to form a three-dimensional image. CAT scans can detect tumors and brain damage and display the brain's structural features.

a room in the neurological intensive care unit. The hospital scene, with its blinding lights and loud noises, was far too hectic for Dr. Jill's fragile sensory systems, which had become ultra-sensitive to stimulation. Light assaulted her eyes and scorched her brain "like fire" (Taylor, 2006, p. 67). Hospital workers grilled her with questions that she couldn't understand. Their words were nothing more than a bewildering racket. "Sound streaming in through my ears blasted my brain senseless so that when people spoke, I could not distinguish their voices from the underlying clatter of the environment," she remembers (p. 75). Some of the hospital personnel, who didn't understand Dr. Jill's condition and were insensitive to her vulnerability, tried to communicate by speaking louder and louder, as if she were hearing impaired, but this only upset and confused her more. What she needed was for those addressing her to speak slowly, pronounce clearly, and show a bit of compassion (Taylor, 2006). Fortunately, the neurologist overseeing her case was one of the few people who actually understood her condition. Dr. Anne Young looked into Dr. Jill's eyes, spoke quietly, and touched her body with respect. "Although I could not completely understand her words, I completely understood her intention," Dr. Jill recalls. "This woman understood that I was not stupid but that I was wounded" (p. 86).

Concepts

On Day 2 in the hospital, Dr. Jill's friend Steve told her that her mother, who went by the name of "G.G.," would be coming to visit. Dr. Jill found the news perplexing (Taylor, 2006). What on Earth was a *mother*, and who or what was a *G.G.*? "Initially, I didn't understand the significance of G.G.—as I had lost the *concept* of what a mother was," she writes (p. 88). The following day, G.G. appeared at the doorway, walked over to her daughter's bed, and climbed in alongside her. As Dr. Jill recalls, "She immediately wrapped me up in her arms and I melted into the familiarity of her snuggle" (p. 90).

···▶ **LO 2**   Define concepts and identify how they are organized.

Although the touch of G.G. felt familiar, the *concept* of her had slipped away, at least temporarily. *Concepts* are a central ingredient of cognitive activity, and are used in important processes such as memory, reasoning, and language (Slaney & Racine, 2011). **Concepts** are mental representations of *categories* of objects, situations, and ideas that belong together based on their central features or characteristics. The concept of *superhero,* for example, includes a variety of recognizable characteristics, such as: has supernatural powers, battles villains, protects innocent people, and wears unbecoming tights. Later we will demonstrate how the formation of these categories is dependent on experience, culture, and other factors. Abstract concepts (such as love, belonging, and honesty) are far more difficult to pinpoint than concrete concepts (like animals, furniture, and telephones). Personal experiences and culture shape the construction of abstract concepts, and we don't always agree on their most important characteristics.

Without concepts, it would be quite difficult to understand the tidal wave of data flooding our brains every day. For example, we all know what *dessert* is. But if the concept *dessert* did not exist, we would have to describe all the characteristics that we expect of a dessert whenever one comes up in conversation: "Yesterday I ate the most delicious food—you know, those sweet-tasting, mouth-watering, high-calorie items typically consumed after lunch or dinner?" Thanks to our dessert concept, however, we can simply use the word "dessert" as shorthand for all of them. ("Yesterday I ate the most delicious dessert.") And even if someone offers you a dessert with which you're not familiar (for example, a chocolate tartelette), you still know that you are being offered a sweet food typically eaten after a meal.

Bleeding Brain
The red zone on the right of the CT scan shows a hemorrhage on the left side of the brain. (Note that the patient's left is your right.) In Dr. Jill's case, the bleeding interfered with activity in Broca's and Wernicke's areas, impairing her ability to produce and understand language. Her frontal lobe function also deteriorated the morning of the stroke, as illustrated by the difficulty she had in devising a coherent strategy to get medical help. Scott Camazine/ Science Source

You Asked, Dr. Jill Answers
http://qrs.ly/5t3m66g
How did you communicate thoughts and ideas to others when you weren't able to effectively express yourself?

cognition The mental activity associated with obtaining, converting, and using knowledge.

thinking Mental activity associated with coming to a decision, reaching a solution, forming a belief, or developing an attitude.

concepts Mental representations of categories of objects, situations, and ideas that belong together based on their central features or characteristics.

Concepts allow us to organize and synthesize information, and to draw conclusions about specific objects, situations, and ideas that we have never encountered before. Imagine how exhausting thinking and talking would be if we did not have concepts to fall back on.

HIERARCHIES OF CONCEPTS   One way to understand concepts is to consider how they can be organized in *hierarchies.* Generally, psychologists use a three-level concept hierarchy to categorize information.

At the top of the hierarchy are *superordinate* concepts. This is the broadest category, encompassing all the objects belonging to a concept. The superordinate concept of furniture is depicted at the top of the hierarchy in **INFOGRAPHIC 7.1** on page 288. This is a very broad group, including everything from couches to nightstands.

Narrowing our focus to include only couches, we are considering the *midlevel* or basic level of our hierarchy. This is still a fairly general grouping, but not as broad as a superordinate concept such as furniture.

Subordinate-level concepts are even narrower, in this case referring to specific types or instances of couches, such as a loveseat, a La-Z-Boy, or my own couch with crumbs between the cushions.

The midlevel category is what we use most often to identify objects in everyday experience. Most children learn the midlevel (or "basic") concepts first, followed by the superordinate and subordinate concepts (Mandler, 2008; Rosch, Mervis, Gray, Johnson, & Boyes-Braem, 1976). Although a child might grasp the meaning of *couch,* she may not understand *furniture* (the superordinate level) or *chaise lounge* (the subordinate level).

Reconstructing concept hierarchies was a formidable task for Dr. Jill, because so many of their layers had been washed away by the hemorrhage. But with hard work, relentless optimism, and the help of G.G., she slowly reconstructed concepts as diverse as *alphabet letters* and *tuna salad.* Using children's books like *The Puppy Who Wanted a Boy,* G.G. helped her daughter retrain her brain to read, and by putting together puzzles, Dr. Jill was able to recreate concepts such as *right side up* and *edge* (Taylor, 2006). A trip to the laundromat became a lesson in first-grade math concepts—and the challenges involved in learning concepts all over again. Putting a few coins in her daughter's hand, G.G. posed the following question: "What's one plus one?" Perplexed, Dr. Jill came back with a more basic question: "What's a one?" (p. 108).

> **LO 3**   Differentiate between formal concepts and natural concepts.

FORMAL CONCEPTS   Now let's take a look at the way concepts are formed. **Formal concepts** are created through rigid and logical rules (or "features" of a concept). When a child learns that 1 is an odd number because, like all other odd numbers, it cannot be divided evenly by 2 without a remainder, she is developing a simple formal concept. An object, idea, or situation must explicitly adhere to strict criteria in order to meet the definition of a particular formal concept. Science uses formal concepts to develop laws, theorems, and rules. Formal concepts introduced in this textbook include the pitch of a sound (defined by the frequency of the sound wave) and iconic memory (with a span of less than 1 second).

NATURAL CONCEPTS   In contrast to formal concepts, **natural concepts** are defined by general characteristics and acquired during the course of our daily lives (Rosch, 1973). Identifying objects that fall into such categories is more difficult because their boundaries are imprecise and harder to define; natural concepts don't have the same types of rigid rules for identification that formal concepts do (Hampton, 1998). This makes them more difficult to outline and therefore less useful in science.

Mouthwatering Concepts
Which dessert do you prefer: the American sundae (right), the Turkish baklava (left), or the French tart (bottom)? You may not have tasted every one of these desserts, but you know they are sweet foods eaten after meals because you have developed a "dessert" concept. left: Kailash K Soni/shutterstock. com; right: Shutterstock; bottom: Kheng Guan Toh/shuttterstock.com

CONNECTIONS

In **Chapter 1,** we introduced *operational definitions,* which specify the precise manner in which a variable is defined and measured. The scientific method incorporates the use of operational definitions, thereby allowing others to replicate experiments. Creating operational definitions for formal concepts is relatively straightforward, because they are already defined by rigid and logical rules. Natural concepts are more challenging, as experts do not always agree on how to define or measure them.

Consider the natural concept of *mother*. Not everyone agrees what characteristics make a mother. Your concept of *mother* may be quite different from that of the person sitting next to you. What criteria do you use to determine if someone is a mother? Is it necessary for a person to get pregnant and have a baby? If so, the large group of women who adopt children are not included. What about someone who gives birth but then immediately puts the baby up for adoption—is she a mother?

PROTOTYPES   In our daily use of natural concepts, we rely on **prototypes,** which are the ideal or most representative examples of natural concepts (Mervis & Rosch, 1981). Prototypes help us categorize or identify specific members of a concept. If you were asked to identify the ideal example of a mother, you might very well begin describing the characteristics of your *own* mother, because she is probably the mother with whom you are most familiar. If we asked you to name an example of a fruit, you would most likely say apple or orange—and *not* olive, unless, of course, you happen to be from Greece where olives are practically a staple. Infographic 7.1 on page 288 presents a list of fruit organized from the most frequently suggested prototype (orange) to the least frequently suggested prototype (olive; Rosch & Mervis, 1975).

Remember, natural concepts evolve through life experience. Each person has a different journey and accumulates a unique collection of prototypes along the way. Dr. Jill's mother G.G. was extremely patient and optimistic, perhaps contributing to Dr. Jill's prototype of *mother*. Not all mothers have G.G.'s extraordinary patience and optimism, of course. Some have other characteristics, ranging from fierce loyalty to relentless pessimism. Think for a moment about the mothers who have touched your life, and how they have shaped your prototype of *mother*.

Items are easier to identify when they closely resemble prototypes. In the United States and Canada, the prototypes for the natural concept of fruit are commonly apples and oranges. If you were shown an image of a papaya (which may be very different from your prototype for a fruit), it would take you longer to identify it as belonging to the fruit category than if you were shown an image of a peach (which is more similar to the common prototypes). We suspect it would take you even longer to identify a durian or rambutan. Because natural concepts develop through daily experiences, prototypes vary from one person to the next. One study comparing adults in the United States and China found cross-cultural differences in the prototypical examples for mythological figures and tropical fish (Yoon et al., 2004).

We now know how the brain organizes information into meaningful categories, or concepts. But how is that information represented inside our heads, especially for concepts applying to people, places, and things not even present? With the help of *mental imagery*, another key ingredient of cognition, we see them in our mind's eye and imagine how they look, sound, smell, taste, and feel.

Mental Imagery

Dr. Taylor's stroke devastated certain aspects of her cognitive activity, such as language and memory. But some functions, like her ability to think visually, continued humming along quite smoothly. She had become hypersensitive to the subtle changes in people's facial expressions and body language, and could understand the emotional content of their communication even when their words sounded all garbled (Taylor, 2006). If asked a question, she would search for answers in her arsenal of mental images. When a doctor quizzed her with the question, "Who is the president of the United States?", Dr. Jill produced two pictures in her mind: one of a president and another of the United States. But when it came time to connect the dots—*the president of the United States is Bill Clinton*—she could not draw the line between the two facts. As Dr. Jill describes it, "Language with linear processing was out. But thinking in pictures was in" (p. 78).

Synonym
formal concepts artificial concepts

formal concepts The mental representations of categories that are created through rigid and logical rules, or features.

natural concepts The mental representations of categories resulting from experiences in daily life.

prototype The ideal or most representative example of a natural concept; helps us categorize or identify specific members of a concept.

Concepts and Prototypes

Concepts are used to organize information in a manner that helps us understand things even when we are encountering them for the first time. *Formal concepts,* like "circle," allow us to categorize objects and ideas in a very precise way— something either meets the criteria to be included in that category, or it doesn't. *Natural concepts* develop as a result of our everyday encounters, and vary according to our culture and individual experiences. We tend to use *prototypes*, ideal representations with features we associate most with a category, to identify natural concepts.

formal
CONCEPT
Defined by rigid, precise rules

A circle is a two-dimensional shape in which all points are the same distance from its center.

natural
CONCEPT
Defined by general characteristics established through everyday encounters

A couch is a large piece of furniture used for sitting.

Concepts can be organized into **HIERARCHIES**

furniture — SUPERORDINATE LEVEL

couch   **bed** — MIDLEVEL (BASIC)

SUBORDINATE LEVEL

Did you think of this? Maybe not. But if you're from India, the traditional charpai may be your prototype—the first image that comes to mind when someone says "bed." What comes to mind when you think of the concept "fruit"? Researchers studying the development of categories organized a group of items from the most prototypical to the least prototypical (Rosch & Mervis, 1975). How long would it take you to think of an olive?

most prototypical   least prototypical

orange   apple   banana   strawberry   pineapple   lemon   date   coconut   tomato   olive

(a)   (b)

FIGURE 7.1
Manipulating Mental Images
Can you tell which object pair is congruent? In order to figure this out, you must hold images of these figures in your mind and mentally manipulate them. (See bottom of column for answer.) *Source:* Shepard and Metzler (1971).

MENTAL IMAGES   When people try to describe cognitive activity, they often provide descriptions of images from the "mind's eye," or *mental images.* Try to imagine, for instance, where your cell phone is right now. Did a picture of your beloved mobile device suddenly materialize in your head? If so, you have just created a mental image. Whether contemplating the whereabouts of cell phones or daydreaming about celebrities walking the red carpet, our brains are constantly whipping up vivid pictures. These mental images are not two-dimensional scenes frozen in time. Our brains have an amazing knack for manipulating them in three dimensions.

Let's consider what we do when we examine a *new* object for the first time. We typically hold it in our hands (if it's not too heavy) and rotate it to get a better sense of what we are looking at. If the object is too large to hold, we will often walk around it to see how it looks from various angles. Researchers are particularly interested in finding out if we *mentally* behave this way as well, and they have spent a great deal of time studying mental imagery and the rotation of objects.

IMAGINING OBJECTS AND MAPS   In one of the earliest studies on this topic, Roger Shepard and Jacqueline Metzler (1971) had eight participants look at 1,600 pairs of object drawings like those displayed in **FIGURE 7.1** and then asked them to mentally rotate one of the objects in the pair to determine if they were identical. In calculating the reaction times, the researchers discovered that the amount of time it took participants to rotate the object depended on the degree of difference between the orientations of the two objects. The greater the rotation, the longer it took participants to decide if the objects were identical.

This type of mental manipulation is extremely useful in your daily life. Remember, for example, the last time you tried to fit a large piece of furniture through a doorway, squeeze rolling luggage into the overhead bin of an airplane, or cram just one more container of leftovers into an overflowing refrigerator. In each case, you probably relied on some type of mental rotation to plan how to get each of these objects into or through a small space.

In another classic study, participants were instructed to study a map of a small fictional island (**FIGURE 7.2**). The researchers then asked them to close their eyes and imagine the map, first picturing one object (the hut) and then scanning across their mental image of the map until they "arrived" at a second object (the rock). The researchers found that it took longer for participants to "find" objects on the mental map when the objects were farther apart. As with the scanning of real objects, the amount of time it takes to scan a mental image is relative to the distances between the objects in

FIGURE 7.2
Scanning Mental Images
Researchers asked participants to imagine this fictional map and "find" objects there. As with a real object, it took longer to find objects that were farther apart. *Source:* Kosslyn, Reiser, and Ball (1978).

Answer to Figure 7.1: a

the image (Kosslyn, Ball, & Reiser, 1978). Kosslyn (1978) also suggested that the size of the image is related to how much detail people can see in their mind's eye. Fewer details can be detected on smaller images.

AUDITORY IMAGERY   Stop for a moment and imagine the smell of chocolate chip cookies baking in the oven, the tang of lemon on your tongue, or the sound of a cat meowing. It is important to remember that not all imagery is visual; other sensory experiences can be used to construct imagery in our minds. Reviewing research on auditory imagery, Hubbard (2010) concluded that auditory images are similar to true auditory stimuli (such as music and language) in their properties (for example, pitch and loudness), and that auditory images involve the brain areas used in auditory perception (like the right temporal lobe and Broca's area). Interestingly, auditory imagery is associated with a person's musical background and ability. When asked to think about two known song lyrics, study participants with **musical training** were better than other participants at identifying which of the songs would be sung at a higher pitch (Janata & Paroo, 2006).

We use mental images all the time—so often it's hard to conceive of thinking without them. Imagine reading this chapter without being able to visualize Dr. Jill staggering around her house the morning of her stroke. How would your brain interpret the description of Steve's voice sounding like a golden retriever if you could not "hear" the sound in your mind? Mental images, like concepts, lie at the heart of cognition.

Every cognitive activity we have discussed thus far, from establishing prototypes of fruit to mentally rotating leftovers in the refrigerator, is made possible by the electric and chemical bustle of millions of neurons. Let's dive into that bustle and get acquainted with the biology of cognition.

Biology of Cognition

> **LO 4**   Describe the biological processes associated with cognition.

Dr. Jill's story provides a stark illustration of the following principle: If the brain's biological integrity is compromised, cognition is likely to suffer. The bleeding in her brain began in a small region on the left side of her cerebral cortex but soon spread across large areas of her brain (Taylor, 2006). Among the areas affected were her left frontal lobe, a part of the brain critical for a broad array of higher cognitive functions such as processing emotions, controlling impulses, and making plans. Remember that Dr. Jill experienced enormous difficulty devising a simple plan to save her own life (for example, she was unable to think of calling 911).

The stroke also ravaged brain regions critical for another major element of cognition: language processing. "As the blood interrupted the flow of information transmission between my two language centers (Broca's anteriorly and Wernicke's posteriorly). . . . I could neither create/express language nor understand it," Dr. Jill recalls in her book (Taylor, 2006, p. 62). **Broca's and Wernicke's areas** work with other parts of the brain to generate and understand language.

COGNITION AND NEURONS   The biology of cognition can be found at the neural level as well. The torrent of blood passed through areas of Dr. Jill's brain that were involved in memory and learning (Taylor, 2006). At some point in her life, she had surely *learned* that 911 is the number to call in a dire emergency, yet when it came time to *retrieve* that crucial information, her brain could not deliver. Normally, changes at the level of neurons make it possible to store and retrieve information.

CONNECTIONS

In **Chapter 1,** we emphatically noted that a correlation does not prove a cause-and-effect link between variables. Here, we need to determine if musical training made participants better at identifying the pitch, or whether some other *third factor* was involved. Perhaps the musicians had better auditory abilities to begin with and decided to study music because of that.

CONNECTIONS

In **Chapter 2,** we described the *association areas,* which integrate information from all over the brain. Dr. Taylor's stroke impacted her ability to use language, presumably by disrupting the normal activities of two association areas: Broca's area, pivotal for speech production, and Wernicke's area, for language comprehension.

Apparently, the stroke had interfered with neurons involved in the retrieval of memories. It is also at the neuronal level where we see the amazing plasticity of the brain at work. Following a stroke, healing and regeneration begin with changes to neurons. These changes include greater excitability of the neurons, rewiring to take advantage of both hemispheres, increases in dendritic connections, and **increased efficiency** of connections at the synapses (Dobkin, 2005).

MEASURING COGNITION IN THE BRAIN Reading Dr. Jill's CT scans, the doctors were able to see the cause of all these cognitive malfunctions—an enormous hemorrhage on the left side of her brain: "It didn't take someone with a Ph.D. in neuroanatomy to figure out that the huge white hole in the middle of the brain scan didn't belong there!" (Taylor, 2006, p. 68).

Technologies such as CT are extremely useful for detecting abnormalities like strokes and tumors, but they also tell us a lot about normal cognitive functioning. Many interesting studies on cognition have investigated the biological basis of mental imagery. As it turns out, the brain often displays similar patterns of activity, whether we are imagining something or seeing it in real life.

In one study, researchers implanted electrodes in the brains of participants with severe epilepsy. This allowed the researchers to monitor individual neurons as participants looked at houses, animals, famous people, and other images. They found that some neurons responded to certain objects but not to others. A neuron would fire when the participant was looking at a picture of a baseball but not at an image of a face, for example. The researchers could identify the image the person was viewing simply by observing his brain activity. They also observed that *the same* neurons that became excited when the person was looking at an actual object also were active when the person was merely imagining that object (Kreiman, Koch, & Fried, 2000).

Using technology such as PET and fMRI, researchers have found that the visual cortex can be activated by mental imagery as well as by external stimuli (Ganis, Thompson, & Kosslyn, 2004). Information (from either an external stimulus or a mental image) is processed by the **visual cortex,** which works with other areas of the brain to identify images based on knowledge stored in memory. Researchers have noted that similar areas of the frontal and parietal regions of the brain are activated when study participants look at, for example, an image of a tree *and* when they imagine a tree. Once again, it appears that perception and imagery use many of the same neural mechanisms (Ganis et al., 2004).

We have now defined *cognition,* examined concepts and mental imagery, and explored their biological foundations. In the pages to come, we will learn about the more goal-oriented activities of problem solving and decision making. As you will learn, these processes can be fraught with difficulties.

CONNECTIONS

In **Chapter 6,** we described how learning and memory are evident at the neural level. Through the process of *long-term potentiation,* communication between sending and receiving neurons is enhanced. This increased synaptic strength facilitates learning and memory formation, and is apparent in the aftermath of a stroke.

CONNECTIONS

In **Chapter 2,** we reported that the visual cortex is the part of the brain where visual information is received, interpreted, and processed. Here, we see that the information processed by the visual cortex does not always arise from visual stimuli.

◐◑◐◐ ✓ show what you know

1. _____ is the mental activity associated with obtaining, converting, and using knowledge.

2. If you were to define the _____ of *superhero,* you might suggest that comic book characters in this category have supernatural powers, battle villains, and protect people.
   a. cognition
   b. concept
   c. hierarchy
   d. mental imagery

3. Your instructor explains that the pitch of a sound is defined by the frequency of the sound wave. She is describing a _____, which is created through rigid rules or features.
   a. prototype
   b. natural concept
   c. formal concept
   d. cognition

4. Give two examples of how biology is associated with cognition.

✓ CHECK YOUR ANSWERS IN APPENDIX C.

Problem Solving

THE BIG DILEMMA On Day 3 at the hospital, a team of doctors arrived at Dr. Jill's bedside to discuss the possibility of performing surgery. One of the doctors, an expert in AVMs (the blood vessel abnormality responsible for her stroke), informed Dr. Jill that there was a blood clot as big as a "golf ball" on the left side of her brain. Both the clot and the remainder of the AVM needed to be extracted; otherwise, she risked suffering another stroke (Taylor, 2006).

Dr. Jill did not understand much of what she heard from the doctors because her language-processing neurons were, as she puts it, "swimming in a pool of blood" (Taylor, 2006, p. 91). But she did catch the part about slicing open her skull, a prospect that she found quite unappealing. "Any self-respecting neuroanatomist would *never* allow anyone to cut their head open!" she writes (p. 91). Dr. Jill had good reason to worry, for brain surgery is not without risks. When surgeons go into the brain to fix one problem, there is always the possibility that they will unintentionally create a new one. Dr. Jill worried that she might emerge from the operating room unable to speak or see. And there were other potential complications of brain surgery, including infections, internal bleeding, and coma (Medline Plus, 2011). No one could be certain of the operation's outcome.

Dr. Jill had a very big problem on her hands and a very important decision to make. The next two sections of this chapter are devoted to problem solving and decision making, two distinct yet tightly interwoven topics. We will explore many types of problems, from life-changing dilemmas to minor hassles, and how we arrive at decisions. Read carefully: The knowledge we are about to impart may be very useful to you. Understanding problems and how they are solved can make life's difficulties a lot more manageable.

What's the Problem?

Have you ever considered the multitude of problems you encounter and solve every day? Problems crop up when something gets in the way of a goal, like a computer crashing when you are racing to finish a project or a tricky scheduling situation at work. Problems range from the mundane (*My profile picture on Facebook is old.*) to the potentially overwhelming (*I have a life-threatening brain bleed.*). In psychology, **problem solving** refers to the variety of approaches that can be used to achieve a goal.

COMPONENTS OF PROBLEM SOLVING Problem solving has intrigued psychologists for generations. Newell, Shaw, and Simon (1958) developed an information-processing approach to solving problems, a model suggesting that problem solving proceeds from an initial state (the situation at the start of a problem) to a goal state (the situation when the problem is solved; Matlin, 2009). Think about how this model applies to Dr. Jill. Her *initial state* included two very big problems: a massive blood clot and a troublesome clump of blood vessels in the left hemisphere of her brain. The *goal state* was maximizing her health, both physically and cognitively.

Another crucial component of problem solving is recognizing obstacles that block the path to a solution (Matlin, 2009). Think about a problem you want to solve and try to identify the initial state, the goal state, and the obstacles in your way. If your initial state is unfinished homework and your goal state is the completion of your homework in a timely manner, the obstacles might include the

"As soon as we solve one problem, another one appears. So let's keep this problem going for as long as we can!"

©Randy Glasbergen/glasbergen.com

problem solving The variety of approaches that can be used to achieve a goal.

trial and error An approach to problem solving that involves finding a solution through a series of attempts and eliminating those that do not work.

algorithm (al-gə-ri-thəm) An approach to problem solving using a formula or set of rules that, if followed, ensures a solution.

competing duties of household chores or something more internal, like sleepiness or lack of motivation.

STEPS TO SOLVING PROBLEMS   The first step in problem solving is understanding the problem (see **INFOGRAPHIC 7.2** on page 296). If you can't identify or label a problem, then solving it is going to be difficult. Once you grasp the problem, you must choose one of many available approaches or strategies to tackle it. Which one you settle on—and the speed, accuracy, and success of your solution—will depend on many factors, including your fund of knowledge, your organization of knowledge, and the amount of time spent assessing the problem (Ericsson, 2003; Goldstein, 2011).

Problems are a constant part of life, but they are much easier to manage if we understand the strategies available to solve them. The aim of the upcoming discussion is to provide you with several approaches for solving problems, while also examining the various factors that come into play during the process.

Approaches to Problem Solving

LO 5   Explain how trial and error and algorithms can be used to solve problems.

TRIAL AND ERROR   One common approach to problem solving is **trial and error,** the process of finding a solution through a series of attempts. Mistakes will likely be made along the way, but attempts that don't work are simply eliminated. Let's say you have a HUGE set of keys and you have to unlock a door you don't use very often. With the trial-and-error approach, you would insert keys, one by one, hoping the correct key is on the ring. By the process of elimination, you would rule out each key before you tried the next one on your key ring.

Trial and error is only useful in certain circumstances. This approach should not be used if the stakes are extremely high, particularly in situations where a potentially wrong selection would be harmful or life-threatening. Imagine, for example, if Dr. Jill's physicians had used trial and error to figure out what procedure she needed. *Let's try this surgery first: If it doesn't work, we'll try a different one next week, and then another the following week.* When people's health and well-being are on the line, trial and error is clearly not the way to go.

Nor is this approach recommended for problems with too many possible solutions. If your keychain has 1,000 keys, you probably would not want to spend your time randomly selecting keys until one fits (potentially trying the same key more than once). Trial and error is somewhat of a gamble because there is no guarantee it will lead to a solution. By the way, computer hackers may use this approach to get your password and gain uninvited access to your digital world. More about this to come.

64,000 Combos
Forgot your lock combination? Trying to figure it out by trial and error is not an effective strategy, as there are 64,000 possible solutions. Better buy a new lock. Pixel Embargo/ shutterstock.com

ALGORITHMS   If you're looking for a problem-solving approach that is more of a sure thing, an *algorithm* is probably your best bet. **Algorithms** (al-gə-ri-thəmz) use formulas or sets of rules that provide solutions to problems. Unlike trial and error, algorithms ensure a solution, as long as you follow all the steps. Suppose you are trying to figure out a 20% tip for a server at a restaurant. Here's an easy algorithm to calculate your tip—take the total amount of your bill, move the decimal to the left one space, and multiply by 2. This will result in 20% of your bill. This simple algorithm provides a guaranteed "correct" solution to the problem.

As reliable as algorithms may be, they are not always practical. If you don't know the algorithm's formula, you obviously cannot use it, and sometimes the steps may require too much time. Let's return to our example of computer hacking. After losing patience with trial and error, the hacker designs an algorithm that generates a series of possible passwords made up of letters, numbers, and symbols. Because algorithms guarantee solutions, the hacker eventually will generate your password. But the question is: Will it happen in this century? If you have chosen your password wisely, the algorithm may not work within a time frame that the hacker is willing—or able—to wait. For example, simply changing your eight-letter password by one character (lowercase to uppercase) and adding an * can increase a hacker's processing time from 2.4 days to 2.1 centuries (Mahmood, 2010). "Ha ha, hacker!"

··· ➤ **LO 6**   **Identify different types of heuristics used to solve problems.**

HEURISTICS   If using an algorithm is not an option, which is often the case with everyday problems, we can turn to **heuristics** (hyù-ris-tiks). A heuristic is a problem-solving approach that employs a "rule of thumb" or broad application of a strategy. Although heuristics are not always reliable in their results, they do help us identify and evaluate possible solutions to our problems. Let's say you are cooking rice, but the instructions are unavailable. One good rule of thumb is to use 2 cups of water for every cup of rice. Another heuristic is to put the rice in the pot and add water until it is one thumb-knuckle above the rice. But unlike algorithms, which use formulas and sets of rules, there is no guarantee a heuristic will yield a correct solution. The advantage of heuristics is that they allow you to shrink the pool of possible solutions to a size that is manageable (given all the varieties of rice, there are many different ways to cook it). Heuristics provide shortcuts, allowing you to ignore the pool of solutions you know will not work and move on to solutions more likely to be successful. But you might need to use trial and error to choose the best solution from that smaller pool of possibilities. A hacker might use a heuristic that combines a commonly used password (123456, password, football) and then add something from the domain itself. For example, if the hacker is trying to break into a Sony PlayStation account, her heuristic might be to try a variety of commonly used passwords and add "PS" at the end (123456PS, passwordPS, footballPS). She would then use trial and error until she breaks into the account. Most problems in life do not come with ready-made algorithms for reaching a correct solution, so we tend to fall back on heuristics.

Heuristics come in a variety of forms. One commonly used heuristic involves *creating subgoals* or *subproblems.* In the days following her stroke, Dr. Jill had a great deal of trouble moving her body. One of her main challenges was sitting up, but she was able to solve this problem by parsing the laborious process into smaller, more manageable steps. "By breaking the effort of sitting up into the smaller steps of rocking and then rolling upward, I found regular success along the way" (Taylor, 2006, p. 93). When writing your last term paper, did you break it into shorter more achievable parts? If so, you were using a type of heuristic that instructors often recommend to students.

Another frequently used heuristic is **means–ends analysis.** With this heuristic, you try to figure out how to decrease the distance between your goal and your current point in the process. You determine *how* to reach your goal (the means), which allows you to *solve the problem* (the end). Using means–ends analysis may involve breaking a problem into subproblems that can be solved independently. The challenge is to decide which subproblem to address first. If you are struggling with your term paper, you must first identify the problem (finding appropriate support for your thesis) and then divide the problem into two subproblems: (1) identifying an appropriate database to search for articles in the field; and (2) finding a library where you can obtain and read the articles.

INSIGHT   Another way of finding a solution is **insight,** which represents an understanding that occurs in a sudden stroke of clarity (that oh-so-satisfying "aha!"

heuristics (hyù-ris-tiks) Problem-solving approaches that incorporate a rule of thumb or broad application of a strategy.

means–ends analysis Heuristic used to determine how to decrease the distance between a goal (the means) and the current status, leading to the solution of a problem (the end).

insight An understanding or solution that occurs in a sudden stroke of clarity (the feeling of "aha!").

moment). It can stem from experience solving previous problems, or it can be totally new. Insight often comes as a pleasant surprise because we are not aware of the mental "work" that occurs to achieve it.

Insight happens so suddenly that we sometimes say to ourselves: *Why did it take me so long to figure that out? The answer seems so obvious now.* Theories suggest that, without our conscious awareness, our minds are busy reorganizing the way the problem is represented, and this allows us suddenly and inexplicably to see things in a new light. Sometimes stepping away from a problem for a short time allows the solution to "suddenly appear" (Sio & Ormerod, 2009). Various areas of the brain seem to be involved in this cognitive work. Research suggests that activity in the frontal and temporal lobes immediately precedes the "aha!" moment (Kounios & Beeman, 2009).

Wolfgang Köhler, a Gestalt psychologist, made some remarkable discoveries on insight in chimpanzees. As early as 1913, he created various problems for the chimps to solve. For example, Köhler put bananas just out of the chimps' reach, supplied them with various "tools" (crates, sticks, and so forth), and watched how they went about getting the bananas. The chimps were very clever; they stacked crates, used sticks, and managed to retrieve the bananas using what Köhler hypothesized was intelligence and insight (Köhler, 1925).

Gestalt psychologists believed that humans and animals solve problems through perception and cognition—by creating mental representations of objects and their relationships (Whitman, 2011). As the chimp faces the "how do I get that banana" problem, its mind is reorganizing the relative positions of the objects to reach a solution. We humans manipulate pictures in our minds in a similar fashion, and it requires no conscious effort. Ah, the beauty of insight.

As you probably know from personal experience, great ideas do not always materialize when we need them. How might we increase the chances of having bright insights? When struggling with a problem, sometimes the best thing to do is let loose and laugh.

I Want Bananas

In a classic study, Wolfgang Köhler provided chimpanzees with some out-of-reach bananas and materials that could potentially be used to fetch them. Resourceful chimps they were, building towers of crates and poking at the fruit with sticks. Rather than using trial and error to solve the problem, they seemed to rely on insight. Wolfgang Köhler Papers/ American Philosophical Society

from the pages of **SCIENTIFIC AMERICAN**™

Laughter Leads to Insight

Happy moods facilitate aha! moments

Stumped by a crossword puzzle? Try taking a break to watch a funny TV show. Recent research shows that people in a lighthearted mood more often have eureka moments of sudden inspiration.

Karuna Subramaniam, then at Northwestern University, and her colleagues found that boosting the mood of volunteers increased their likelihood of having an aha! moment that helped solve a word association puzzle. Those who watched a Robin Williams comedy special did measurably better at the task using insight than those who watched a quantum electronics talk or a scary movie. The games, in which players must find a word that connects three seemingly unrelated words, have been used for decades to demonstrate creative problem solving.

In the brain, sudden insight is accompanied by increased activity in the brain's anterior cingulate cortex (ACC) prior to solving each problem. The region is involved in regulating attention; in problem solving, it seems to work in conjunction with other brain areas either to stay focused on a particular strategy or to switch to a new one. Subramaniam found with functional MRI that people in a positive mood had more ACC activity going in to the task, which probably helped prepare the brain to find novel solutions. Participants who watched anxiety-producing movies such as *The Shining*, however, showed less activity in the ACC and less creativity in solving the puzzles. **Elizabeth King Humphrey. Reproduced with permission. Copyright © 2011 Scientific American, a division of Nature America, Inc. All rights reserved.**

Problem Solving

Problem solving involves figuring out how to achieve a goal. Once you understand a problem, you can identify an approach to solving it. A successful approach will help you manage obstacles that come from the problem itself, such as a rigid deadline for an essay you're struggling to write. But sometimes the way we think about a problem can itself be a barrier, preventing us from identifying available approaches.

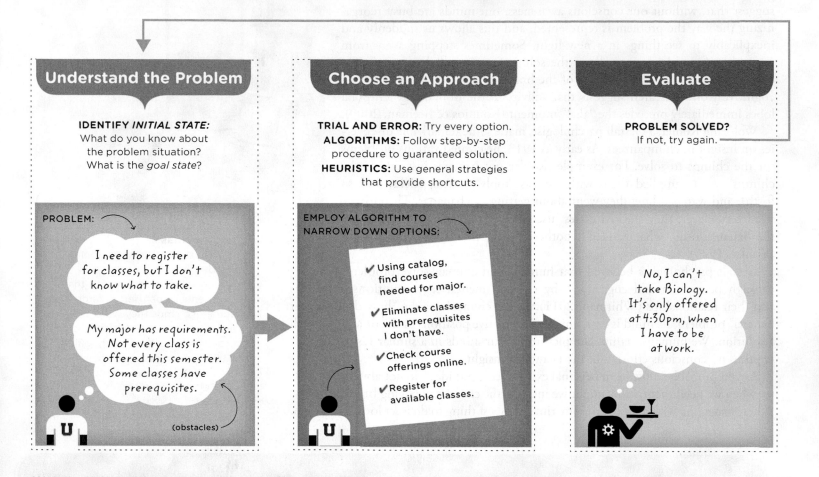

Understand the Problem

IDENTIFY *INITIAL STATE*:
What do you know about the problem situation?
What is the *goal state*?

PROBLEM:

> I need to register for classes, but I don't know what to take.

> My major has requirements. Not every class is offered this semester. Some classes have prerequisites.

(obstacles)

Choose an Approach

TRIAL AND ERROR: Try every option.
ALGORITHMS: Follow step-by-step procedure to guaranteed solution.
HEURISTICS: Use general strategies that provide shortcuts.

EMPLOY ALGORITHM TO NARROW DOWN OPTIONS:

✓ Using catalog, find courses needed for major.

✓ Eliminate classes with prerequisites I don't have.

✓ Check course offerings online.

✓ Register for available classes.

Evaluate

PROBLEM SOLVED?
If not, try again.

> No, I can't take Biology. It's only offered at 4:30pm, when I have to be at work.

Barriers to Problem Solving

Being stuck in a certain way of thinking about a problem can limit what we see as available approaches. For example, our student registering for classes may assume that "classes" must be in-person meetings with an instructor on campus. This assumption prevents the student from investigating more flexible online classes, hybrid classes, or classes that could be transferred from another college.

Sticking with our usual solution strategies is called a **mental set**. To see if you can overcome your mental set, try solving this problem:

Without lifting your pencil, can you connect all nine dots using only 4 straight lines and without crossing any dot more than once? *(Solution on page 298.)*

Functional fixedness is another barrier in which we can only imagine using familiar objects in their usual way. Say you need to tie two ropes together, but you can't reach them both at the same time. Will functional fixedness keep you from solving this problem? *(Solution on page 298.)*

Credits: Snip ropes with knot, Shutterstock; Collection set of vertical ropes with knots, Shutterstock; Collection of various ropes, Shutterstock; Bushes, Shutterstock

Barriers to Problem Solving

But problems are not always a laughing matter. As you may have noticed in your own life, there are many barriers to problem solving (Infographic 7.2). You might be trying to get your car out of the driveway, but the wheels keep slipping in the snow. Or perhaps you are trying to calculate a tip for your server, but you can't concentrate because of the noise in the room. These types of problems are not always easily solved, sometimes due to common barriers.

One barrier is **functional fixedness,** which occurs when we can only imagine using familiar objects in their normal or usual way. This *fixation* can hinder problem solving, because it stops us from being able to find other creative uses for objects. Suppose the hem of your pants gets caught on something and the thread starts unraveling. A roll of tape and a stapler are on your desk, and both could be used to "fix" your wardrobe malfunction. But because of functional fixedness, you only view these items in their "usual" capacities. Children have less trouble with functional fixedness than adults because they have not become accustomed to using familiar objects in a fixed way (German & Defeyter, 2000).

Mental sets represent another barrier to problem solving. When faced with a problem, we tend to fall back on solution strategies we have always used—even if they don't work so well. For example, when your hem comes out of your pants, you grab for the needle and thread because that is the solution you have always used. With mental sets, an approach that has worked in the past will often come immediately to mind and be reused, preventing us from seeing other solutions to a problem.

Emotional barriers can also get in the way of problem solving. If you are trying to figure out how to fix the dripping faucet and someone is peering over your shoulder saying, "Hurry up! What's taking you so long?", you may feel rushed, anxious, and annoyed. These negative emotions affect your ability to think clearly and creatively. Positive emotions, on the other hand, may set the stage for innovative thinking. Good feelings are thought to promote a "flexible" way of thinking, one that enables quick attention shifting and the ability to develop new strategies in response to a changing environment (Isen, 2008). Keep this in mind when you are trying to help someone solve a problem.

Think Outside the Box
Who knew that a paint roller could be used for holding toilet paper and that car tires doubled as planters? Sometimes it's hard to imagine using objects for unconventional purposes. Our resistance toward using familiar objects in new ways is known as *functional fixedness,* and it can get in the way of problem solving. top: Andrea Jones/ Garden World Images/age fotostock; right: Andreas Schlegel/age fotostock

across the WORLD

Problem Solving in Different Cultures

Another factor influencing problem solving is culture. People from highly individualistic or self-focused societies, such as the United States, tend to be action oriented in their problem solving, making a lot of decisions in a short amount of time. In contrast, those from more collectivist or community-focused countries, such as Brazil, tend to be more careful in their approach, making fewer decisions when faced with a problem (Güss, 2011; Ohbuchi, Fukushima, & Tedeschi, 1999).

Building on these and other findings, researcher Dominick Güss investigated how people from five countries—Germany, the United States, Brazil, India, and the Philippines—approached different problems. Güss hypothesized that participants who leaned toward individualism, particularly those who placed a high value on equality and uniqueness, would be more action oriented in solving problems. Collectivists who recognized inequalities and prioritized group needs would be more careful in generating solutions (Güss, 2011).

functional fixedness A barrier to problem solving that occurs when familiar objects can only be imagined to function in their normal or usual way.

Overall, the results of the study supported Güss's hypothesis. There were notable exceptions, however. Participants from India and the Philippines (collectivist cultures) were expected to be hesitant problem solvers. Nevertheless, when it came to tackling a problem without a clear cause (trying to maintain the temperature of a supermarket freezer department when the thermostat appears to be failing), they seemed to have little trouble cranking out decisions. In fact, they were more action-oriented than their U.S. and German counterparts who were expected to be the enthusiastic decision makers. One possible explanation is that the Indian and Filipino participants were more comfortable with the ambiguity surrounding that particular problem, and thus had an easier time responding to it (Güss, 2011). As it turns out, different cultures have varying degrees of tolerance for unpredictability. This characteristic is known as *uncertainty avoidance* (Hofstede, 1993), and is one of several cultural forces shaping the problem-solving process.

CRANKING OUT DECISIONS ACROSS CULTURES

Untangling the cultural factors affecting problem solving and other cognitive functions is no easy task. Culture is complex. Cognition is complex. Add other characteristics to the mix, and you've got a lot of exciting research for the future! 🌐

The last few pages have been devoted to problem solving, the many approaches used to attain an out-of-reach goal. In the process, we have made various references to decision making. Next we will examine what decision making is, and how it relates to problem solving.

FIGURE 7.3
Solution to the Dot Problem in Infographic 7.2
Did your mental set cause you to assume the square implied boundaries? If so, it may not have occurred to you that you could draw lines extending outside the square.

FIGURE 7.4
Solution to the Two-Rope Problem in Infographic 7.2
Using a shovel to create a pendulum will allow you to swing the second rope. When it swings near you, you can grab it and hold both ropes at the same time.

show what you know

1. Imagine it is the first day of classes, but you forgot to write down the number of the room where your psychology class is meeting. You decide you will try to find your classroom by sticking your head in a random number of rooms until you see the assigned psychology textbook on someone's desk. This approach to finding your classroom uses:
   a. means–ends analysis.
   b. an algorithm.
   c. trial and error.
   d. heuristics.

2. One common barrier to problem solving is _____, which occurs when we can only imagine using familiar objects in their usual way.
   a. functional fixedness
   b. uncertainty avoidance
   c. an algorithm
   d. a goal state

3. One assignment in your psychology class is to design an experiment. Describe how you would use means–ends analysis to choose a topic for your experiment and write a review of the literature.

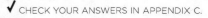
✓ CHECK YOUR ANSWERS IN APPENDIX C.

Decision Making

UNDER THE KNIFE With the help of her mother's gentle coaxing, Dr. Jill made the decision to go through with surgery. She left the hospital and returned to her apartment where G.G. could help her relearn basic life skills such as walking, reading, and doing the laundry. Two weeks later, she returned to Massachusetts General for the surgery (Taylor, 2006).

Late in the afternoon of December 27, 1996, Dr. Jill awoke in the recovery room with the left side of her head shaved clean and a 9-inch wound in the shape of a horseshoe (Taylor, 2006). She had survived the operation, and she didn't feel drained and confused, as you might expect. "Upon awakening, I realized that I felt different now. There was brightness in my spirit again and I felt happy" (p. 112).

"Say something!" demanded G.G., as she approached her daughter's bedside (Taylor, 2006, p. 113). G.G. needed to know that her daughter could still use language. Surgeons had just spent hours poking around her left hemisphere, home to the language-processing regions of Broca's and Wernicke's areas. The surgeons might have inadvertently short-circuited one of these key regions, compromising her ability to speak. Dr. Jill opened her mouth and responded, and she and G.G. both became teary-eyed. The operation appeared to have gone well; Dr. Jill, it seemed, had made the right decision (Taylor, 2006).

Decisions, Decisions

> **LO 7** Define decision making and explain how heuristics can lead us astray.

You may be wondering how decision making differs from problem solving. As you now know, problem solving refers to the approaches that can be used to achieve a goal. **Decision making** is the cognitive process of choosing from those alternatives. Thus, problem solving and decision making can occur at the same time.

PREDICTING THE FUTURE Decision making often involves predicting the future: What is the likelihood that Event A will occur under these circumstances? How about Event B? In cases like these, all we can do is make an educated guess, and some situations lend themselves to more accurate guesses than others. If the weather channel predicts there is a 99% chance of thunderstorms today, it's fairly safe to assume it's going to rain. Better bring your umbrella.

But there are many times when predicting the future is like rolling dice—you have almost no way of knowing the outcome. Suppose you are searching for a used car on craigslist. How do you choose a "gently used" car from among the hundreds listed in your locality? With no prior knowledge of the cars or their owners (apart from whatever information they choose to post on craigslist), all you can do is hope the car you choose is not a lemon. But who knows if your gamble is going to work? Choices that hinge on predictions can be very risky, and we sometimes make the wrong decision.

SINGLE FEATURE There are many ways to go about making decisions. One way is to focus on a single aspect, or feature, of the situation. Let's say you are trying to decide where to stop for gas. If your only criterion is cost, you will seek out the gas station with the cheapest gasoline, paying no attention to what kind of donuts they sell inside or how clean their bathroom may be. The *single feature* on which you are basing your decision (where to stop for gas) is the price of the fuel (not tasty donuts or a clean bathroom).

Post-Op
Dr. Jill poses with her mother, G.G., who played an instrumental role in the recovery process. When Dr. Jill emerged from surgery, G.G. was anxious to know whether her daughter's language-processing abilities were still intact. When Dr. Jill opened her mouth and spoke, it seemed clear that everything was going to be okay.
© My Stroke of Insight, Inc. Photo by Kip May

decision making The cognitive process of choosing from alternatives that might be used to reach a goal.

"Would you be interested in adding a few options?"

ADDITIVE MODEL   The single-feature approach may not be effective for making complex decisions, as there are *many* features to consider. With a more complex decision, such as which car to purchase, you might create a list of the primary features you consider important (gas mileage, safety ratings, sound system, and so on). Using this list, you could rate each of the possible choices (for example, Ford Focus versus Toyota Prius) according to their features, and then tally these ratings to see which car comes out on top, with the highest score winning. This method of calculating the highest rating is often referred to as an *additive model* of decision making.

Decisions, Heuristics, and the Confirmation Bias

At the start of the section, we mentioned that decision making often involves making predictions, and different scenarios afford different levels of certainty about the future. Heuristics, which involve a rule of thumb or a broad application of a strategy, can be used to help predict the probability of an event occurring. Unfortunately, heuristics can lead us astray in our assessment of situations or prediction of outcomes. Daniel Kahneman and Amos Tversky (1973) were among the first to systematically research the ways in which heuristics can be ineffective. They found that people are prone to ignore important information while using heuristics (Kahneman & Tversky, 1996). This is particularly true for the *availability heuristic* and the *representativeness heuristic*.

THE AVAILABILITY HEURISTIC   Using the **availability heuristic,** we predict the probability of something happening in the future based on how easily we can recall a similar type of event from the past. The availability heuristic is essentially a decision-making strategy that relies on memory. If we can easily recall a certain event, then we tend to base our decisions on the assumption that it can happen again. Many factors make an event more available, including its recency, frequency, familiarity, and vividness. Let's look at each of these categories.

Imagine the year is 2010 and you have just learned about the mine collapse that left 33 Chilean workers trapped underground. If asked to predict the likelihood of a similar mining collapse occurring in the near future, your estimation would likely be higher than normal because you just heard about the Chilean incident. Our predictions using the availability heuristic are based on how easily we can recall similar events from the past, and the *more recently* a similar situation has occurred, the more easily it will be recalled. With an event still fresh in our minds, we are more likely to overestimate the odds of a similar event occurring in the future.

Now imagine that you were asked to decide the following: Do more students at your college use Macs or PCs? Before deciding how to answer, you would probably think about the number of students you have seen using these types of computers and make an estimation based on that tally. In this case, the *frequency* of occurrence is the factor that influences your decision. You rely on your recall of seeing students using Macs or PCs in the hall, classroom, and library. The availability heuristic can be accurate for determining frequency, but it only works when all the right information is available and in its proper context. If you are in the graphic design department, for example, chances are you'll see more Macs than PCs. Based strictly on your observations from a single department, your **sample would not be representative** of the entire college, and the availability heuristic would lead you to the wrong answer.

The *familiarity* of an event might also lead to inaccurate estimates. If you and your friends are all avid PC users, you may overestimate the extent to which others are using PCs. The more familiar you are with a situation, the more likely you are to predict a similar occurrence in the future.

CONNECTIONS

In **Chapter 6,** we described the *recency effect,* which is the tendency to remember items more accurately when they appear at the end of a list or series. Here, we discuss the tendency to remember *similar* events better if they have occurred recently.

CONNECTIONS

In **Chapter 1,** we discussed the importance of using a *representative sample* for making generalizations from a sample to the population. With the use of the availability heuristic, we must be careful that the sample used is representative; sometimes the memories in our "sample" are not randomly selected. Instead, they are chosen because of their recency, frequency, familiarity, and vividness.

Ralph Hagen/Cartoonstock.com

Finally, the *vividness* of an event can influence our recall. Try to conjure up an image of someone winning the "big one" at a casino. There are lights, sounds, and a lot of hubbub. The prizewinner jumps joyfully in the air, hollering and crying at the top of his lungs, with onlookers clapping and shouting in approval. This type of dramatic display never occurs when some poor guy loses his last $100; the details of a losing bet would consequently be far more difficult to recall. Because the winning image is more vivid, we are more likely to recall it and thus to overestimate the likelihood it will occur in our own lives. Memorable imagery leads us to believe that these types of wins happen all the time, when in fact they are very rare. Tversky and Kahneman (1982) suggested that, if an event has made a striking impression on you, even a rare occurrence such as an airplane crash, you will be more likely to overestimate the probability of it happening again.

THINK again

Fearing the Friendly Skies

Are people generally more afraid of flying in an airplane or riding in a car? Airplanes seem frightening to many people, yet the statistics suggest we should be more concerned about driving. The odds of getting into a fatal traffic accident are 1 in 98, compared to about 1 in 7,000 for a plane crash (National Safety Council, 2012).

Now consider the weeks and months following the terrorist attacks of September 11, 2001. How did people feel about flying after seeing what happened to the hijacked planes on the news? Countless people stayed away from airports and airplanes. So many would-be air travelers took to the roads after 9/11 that there was a temporary surge in traffic fatalities. In the 3 months following September 11th, more people died in car accidents (apparently trying to avoid air travel) than did in the four hijacked airplanes (Gigerenzer, 2004). In this unfortunate case, people were increasing their risk of death by trying to reduce it.

Risk perception is complex. A number of factors contribute to an overblown fear of flying. The fact that airplane crashes and terrorist attacks are beyond one's control and represent the potential for enormous disasters tends to increase many people's perceptions of risk (Slovic & Weber, 2002, April 12–13). And, as we've learned from our earlier discussion of the availability heuristic, people tend to deem events more probable when similar scenarios are easy to recall. A highly detailed media report of an airplane crash is far more likely to linger in one's thoughts than a traffic accident glossed over on the six o'clock news.

SIT BACK, RELAX, AND ENJOY THE FLIGHT.

Safer Than Your Car
The odds of dying in a plane crash are extremely low— lower than perishing in a fall, a drowning incident, or a car accident (National Safety Council, 2012). Still, many people are petrified of flying. This is partly a result of the availability heuristic; we tend to overestimate the likelihood of events that easily spring to mind.
ssuaphotos/shutterstock.com

THE REPRESENTATIVENESS HEURISTIC Sometimes we have to make decisions based on our judgment of a situation or person. The **representativeness heuristic** evaluates the degree to which their primary characteristics are similar to our prototypes. With the representativeness heuristic, we make quick, effortless judgments about how closely a person or situation fits our preconceived prototype (Shah & Oppenheimer, 2008). In contrast, with the availability heuristic people access information from their long-term memory to make predictions about events.

Let's examine how the representativeness heuristic works in practice. Peter is a middle-aged man. He is conservative, a lovely speaker, thoughtful, and well read. He lives alone in an apartment in the city. Is Peter a truck driver or a poet? Forced to choose between these two occupations and using the representativeness heuristic, the majority of people would likely guess that Peter is a poet because his description

availability heuristic A decision-making strategy that predicts the likelihood of something happening based on how easily a similar type of event from the past can be recalled.

representativeness heuristic A decision-making strategy used to evaluate the degree to which the primary characteristics of a person or situation are similar to our prototype of that type of person or situation.

"Give it to me straight, Doc. How long do I have to ignore your advice?"

better matches their prototype of a poet than their prototype of a truck driver. But this approach fails to consider the *base rate* (the prevalence of features or events in the population) of these occupations. There are far more truck drivers than poets, suggesting the better guess would be that Peter is a truck driver. The representativeness heuristic can be useful, but the accuracy of our information must be taken into account, as the poet/truck driver example illustrates; our conclusions should be drawn from base rates, not stereotypes. The other limitation of the representativeness heuristic is that most people fail to recognize the problems associated with relying on small samples. The smaller the sample, the less likely it is to provide a good representation of the population, and generally our prototypes are based on exposure to limited samples.

THE CONFIRMATION BIAS   We can also miss important information through the **confirmation bias,** when we unintentionally look for evidence that upholds our beliefs. People tend to overlook or discount evidence that runs counter to their original beliefs or positions. For example, you decide to go on a date with someone you are *really* interested in, even though you don't know him very well. You Google stalk him and look on his Facebook page to see what his friends write on his wall, and you immediately connect with one of the "likes" he has. With this information in hand, you stop your search, convinced you now have evidence to support your decision to go out with him. We tend to focus on information that supports favorable outcomes (Krizan & Windschitl, 2007; Scherer, Windschitl, O'Rourke, & Smith, 2012), but what other sources of information could you use to avoid the confirmation bias in this case? The confirmation bias is not a conscious act; we do not deliberately set out looking for information to support what we already think. The danger of the confirmation bias is that we miss or ignore relevant (and possibly contradictory) information without conscious intent.

You've Been Framed!

We have spent a great deal of time discussing the limitations that impede the decision maker. But in many situations, the characteristics of the problem itself, or the presentation of the problem, are to blame.

WHAT'S IN A FRAME?   The **framing effect** demonstrates how the wording of questions or the context of a problem can influence the outcome of a decision. To look at this effect, researchers conducted a study in which they instructed participants to imagine that they had purchased a $10 ticket to attend a show, but lost their ticket on the way to the theater. Each participant was then asked whether he or she would be willing to pay $10 for another ticket. Only 46% of participants indicated that they would spend another $10 for a new ticket. Participants were next instructed to imagine another situation: In it, they planned to buy a $10 ticket to attend a show, but once they got in the ticket line, they suddenly realized that they had lost one of their $10 bills. Faced with this second scenario, 88% of the participants were willing to fork over the $10. In each case, the participants were faced with the proposition of spending an additional and unexpected $10, but they tended to make different decisions in response to the different circumstances. The background information framing these hypothetical scenarios influenced the decisions made, even though the outcomes would have been identical—a net loss of $10 (Kahneman & Tversky, 1984; Tversky & Kahneman, 1981).

confirmation bias The tendency to look for evidence that upholds our beliefs and overlook evidence that runs counter to them.

framing effect Occurs when the wording of questions or the context of a problem influences the outcome of a decision.

WHAT'S IN A QUESTION?   The specific wording of questions should also be considered. One study found that people are more likely to prefer ground beef if it is described as "80% lean," as opposed to "20% fat." Although 80% lean and 20% fat describe exactly the same product, these phrases evoke very different responses (Johnson, 1987). Another study investigated the effects of question framing on women using a telephone-based counseling service to inquire about the side effects of drugs taken during pregnancy (Jasper, Goel, Einarson, Gallo, & Koren, 2001). The women calling in were assigned to one of two groups. Women in the first group were told that "in every pregnancy there is a 1–3% chance that a woman will give birth to a child who has a major birth defect. This drug has not been shown to change that" (p. 1237). Women in the second group were told that "in every pregnancy, there is a 97–99% chance that a woman will give birth to a child who does not have a major birth defect. This drug has not been shown to change that" (p. 1237). The researchers then followed up with a series of questions. Participants in the first group believed that they faced a greater risk of bearing a child with a birth defect if they had taken the drug than those in the second group. Decision making is often influenced by whether a question is worded in a positive way (the glass is half full) or in a negative way (the glass is half empty) (Huber, Neale, & Northcraft, 1987).

THINK again

Let Them Eat Cake

Decisions can also be influenced by how much we have "on our plate" at a given time. Imagine making a decision when you are trying to cook dinner, watch the nightly news, and discipline your dog all at the same time. A study by Shiv and Fedorikhin (1999) helps us understand that stressful external demands impact how we make decisions. The researchers asked one group of participants to memorize two numbers and the other group to keep a string of seven numbers in their minds. Meanwhile, participants were offered the choice of fruit or chocolate cake to eat. Surprisingly, the people who only had to memorize the two numbers selected the fruit every time, whereas those trying to remember the string of seven numbers tended to choose the cake! What this suggests is that our stress level impacts our decisions—and not in a way that benefits our waistlines. ●+

HOW MUCH DO YOU HAVE ON YOUR PLATE?

This section has focused on decision making, exploring the ways that heuristics, confirmation bias, and framing can lead us to faulty decisions. Our next discussion centers on one of the most extraordinary qualities of human cognition: language.

✓ show what you know

1. _____ refers to the cognitive process of choosing from a variety of alternatives you might use to reach your goal.

2. We often predict the probability of an event happening in the future based on how easily we can recall a similar type of event from the past. This is known as the:
   a. framing effect.
   b. confirmation bias.
   c. representativeness heuristic.
   d. availability heuristic.

3. A good friend is terrified of flying. How would you use your knowledge of heuristics to make him feel less afraid?

4. Your friend just told you about someone she met on the train. He seemed well spoken, thoughtful, and very informed about current events. She asked you to guess whether he was a factory worker or a politician. Your best guess in this situation, based on the base rates of these occupations, would be that he worked in a factory. But you choose politician based on your prototypes of these two occupations. This is a good example of:
   a. the representativeness heuristic.
   b. the confirmation bias.
   c. the availability heuristic.
   d. how the wording of a question can influence the outcome.

✓ CHECK YOUR ANSWERS IN APPENDIX C.

►Language

► A-Lister

A close-up shot of Orlando Bloom during the Los Angeles premiere of *The Lord of The Rings: The Two Towers.* His performance as the elven character "Legolas" in *The Rings* trilogy established him as a major force in Hollywood. Gregg DeGuire/WireImage/Getty Images

ELVES, PIRATES, AND READING TROUBLES Right around the time that Dr. Jill Bolte Taylor's life was uprooted by a massive brain hemorrhage, an aspiring actor by the name of Orlando Bloom was launching his career on the big screen. In 1997 the 19-year-old native of Canterbury, Kent, England, made his first appearance in a major film, playing a small part in *Wilde,* a movie about the life of the playwright/poet Oscar Wilde (IMDB, 2012a). A couple of years later, the young Orlando was riding horseback through the rolling hills of New Zealand and shooting arrows at goblinlike *orcs,* playing the role of a pointy-eared elf named "Legolas Greenleaf" in a film trilogy that would make him a superstar: *The Lord of the Rings.* Not long after battling evil alongside hobbits and wizards, Orlando dueled with villainous pirates in another blockbuster film series: *Pirates of the Caribbean.* Now, with many major motion pictures under his belt, Orlando is one of the hottest actors in Hollywood (IMDB, 2012b; Sella, 2005).

Starring in adventure films requires extensive training in sword fighting, archery, and martial arts, but according to those who have seen Orlando in action, the athletic demands of the job are not an issue. "Orlando is all physical grace," says fellow actor Liam Neeson (Sella, 2005). Acting also presents a major *cognitive* challenge, as it requires reading and memorizing thousands of lines. This part of the job may not come so easily for Orlando, however, because he has *dyslexia.*

Dyslexia, or specific reading disability, is characterized by difficulty reading, writing, spelling, and/or pronouncing (International Dyslexia Association, 2012). Although people with dyslexia struggle with reading, all the presumed prerequisites for good reading (adequate intelligence and eyesight, desire to learn, access to good instruction, for example) appear to be in place. Yet, the person still has trouble mastering fundamental skills (Shaywitz, 1996; Shaywitz & Shaywitz, 2005).

School was an endless struggle for Orlando. "Homework was always hard for me. Writing essays . . . getting my thoughts on the page, it was so difficult," he acknowledged in a 2010 interview (Child Mind Institute, 2010a, October 11). Whenever it was time to read aloud in class, young Orlando would ask to use the bathroom or say he felt ill—anything to avoid the embarrassment of reading before his peers (Child Mind Institute, 2010b, October 11). "It was something that I hid from other kids as best I could," he remembered (Child Mind Institute, 2010c, October 11). Teachers didn't understand why Orlando was so distracted in class. As a progress report once said (according to Orlando): "If he would only stop looking out the window or into the hamster cage, we think he's probably quite a bright boy" (Child Mind Institute, 2010c, October 11). And a bright boy he was. We'll talk more about the relationship between dyslexia and intelligence in a later section.

Orlando attended elementary school in the 1980s, when dyslexia was still not well understood. A large number of cases went unrecognized, and many children struggled to get through school in a fog of confusion. Unless you have dyslexia or know someone with this disability, it's hard to understand how far-reaching its impact can be. In order to write an essay on a novel in English class, you have to read the book. To answer word problems in math, you must understand the written part of the question. Every standardized test requires fast and fluid reading. So many aspects of modern life reflect a general assumption that every adult knows how to read.

When dyslexia was first recognized over a century ago, many people assumed children fell behind in reading because they were ignorant or lazy, or had bad teachers

Synonym
dyslexia developmental reading disorder

language A system for using symbols to think and communicate.

(International Dyslexia Association, 2012; Shaywitz, 2003; Wolf, 2007). Scientists have since discovered that dyslexia is rooted in the brain. With scanning technologies such as fMRI, scientists can examine the brain of someone with dyslexia as she reads, writes, or speaks. "We now know exactly where and how dyslexia manifests itself in the brain," writes dyslexia researcher Sally Shaywitz (2003, p. 4). Dyslexia, the evidence suggests, is caused by defects in the brain's ability to retrieve and manipulate certain components of language (Démonet, Taylor, & Chaix, 2004).

Language, Amazing Language

Language is an amazing ability. Try to imagine human relationships in its absence. There would be no saying "What's wrong?" or "I love you." Language gives us the power to explicitly convey complex thoughts and feelings to others, and that is a remarkable feat.

LO 8   Define language and give examples of its basic elements.

Language can be defined as a system for using symbols to think and communicate. These symbols are words, gestures, or sounds put together according to specific rules. Pinker (1994) reminds us that words usually don't match their content. While a small number of words are onomatopoetic—or formed by sounds that resemble the realities they represent ("plop" to signify something dropping into the water)—the majority of the words we use are just arbitrary symbols. Within a language, speakers generally agree on the meaning of these symbols. We use them when we think, mentally manipulating them while solving problems, making decisions, and lying in bed daydreaming. It's hard to imagine what life would be like if we only thought in images.

Language is the ultimate medium for creativity. We can use words, gestures, and sounds to create an infinite number of statements.

You Asked, Dr. Jill Answers

http://qrs.ly/di3m66y
Did you fully recover language and cognition after the surgery?

> Construct as many sentences as you can that include the following words: "giraffe," "kitten," "blue," "pretty," "rough," "run."

try this

The average English speaker is familiar with some 30,000 (Lessmoellmann, 2006, October 4) to 60,000 words (Pinker, 1994). What's more, humans are always finding new meanings for old words or inventing new ones. If we say "apple product," for example, we could be referring to a crunchy red fruit or to a fancy new computer. Just think of how many new words have come from the use of digital technologies like text messages, and social media. Do you know what "friend farming" is (we didn't, btw)? This is the "practice of adding many contacts (on Facebook or other social media) by using a list of another person's friends" (*Merriam-Webster's Open Dictionary*, n.d.). Another example, "phonecrastinate," means "to put off answering the phone until caller ID displays the name and number" (*Merriam-Webster's Open Dictionary*, n.d.).

The Basic Elements of Language

Language can be portrayed as written, spoken, and signed. Speaking comes naturally to us because we are born with brains evolved for that purpose (Shaywitz, 1996). Young Orlando did not need speaking and listening lessons; neither did you. Children learn to speak by hearing others talk. (In

OH, FOR CRYIN' OUT LOUD... YOU NEVER END A SENTENCE WITH A 🐦 !

ANCIENT GRAMMAR POLICE

Wiley Miller/Cartoonstock.com

Chapter 8, we will describe the consistent pathways through which language develops for children.)

Dyslexia usually begins to manifest itself as soon as a child starts learning to read, often in kindergarten. Think back to your first reading lesson. Your teacher probably introduced you to written language by teaching you to break words into their basic sound units (for example, the combination of *kuh, aah,* and *tuh* to form the word "cat"; Shaywitz, 1996). She was introducing you to **phonemes** (fō-nēmz), the basic building blocks of spoken language.

PHONEMES   All spoken languages are made up of phonemes. Examples of English phonemes include the sounds made by the letter *t* in the word "tail" and the letter *s* in the word "sail." Every phoneme has its own individual characteristic(s) (see **INFO-GRAPHIC 7.3** on page 308). For example, the letter *i* can represent two phonemes with distinctly different sounds in the words "bit" and "bite." The symbols we call words are made up of phonemes.

Infants can recognize all phonemes from all languages until about 9 months of age. After that, they can no longer distinguish between phonemes that are not in the language(s) they regularly hear spoken (de Boysson-Bardies, Halle, Sagart, & Durand, 1989; Werker & Tees, 1984). This is what makes it so difficult for older children and adults to learn to speak a foreign language without an accent.

If you have children (or plan to have them), it wouldn't hurt for them to learn more than one language very early in life. Not only will their pronunciation sound natural; they may enjoy some cognitive perks, too.

didn't SEE that coming

The Perks of Being Bilingual

👁️❗ Psychologists once thought that the brain was best suited for learning a single language, and that exposing children to more than one language frustrated their intellectual development (Klass, 2011, October 10). Researchers are now uncovering evidence that learning two languages does not lead to word mix-ups and other cognitive troubles; in fact, it may actually improve a child's performance on various cognitive tasks (Westly, 2011, July/August).

Bilingualism has been associated with enhanced creativity, abstract thought, and working memory. Among the most striking qualities associated with bilingualism are strong executive control and more efficient *executive functioning* (Bialystok, 2011; Engel de Abreu, Cruz-Santos, Tourinho, Martin, & Bialystok, 2012; Westly, 2011, July/August). As the name implies, executive control is concerned with managing the brain's precious resources, deciding what's important and where to focus attention. Executive functioning refers to abilities related to planning ahead and solving problems.

A study of 7-month-old babies found that those growing up in bilingual homes already had an executive control advantage over their peers from monolingual environments. They could, for example, adjust their responses in order to get a reward (the appearance of a puppet) in ways that the monolingual babies could not (Kovács & Mehler, 2009). Research further demonstrates that bilingual children carry this executive control advantage into adulthood (Bialystok, 2011).

DOES BEING BILINGUAL CLUTTER YOUR BRAIN?

Why is this so? The bilingual brain is constantly exercising its executive control system. A person who speaks two languages cannot just turn on one language and turn off the other; the knowledge of both is always present and awake. The speaker is eternally torn between the two competing languages. Resolving this ongoing conflict seems to keep the executive control system very busy and always practicing (Bialystok, 2011). 👁️❗

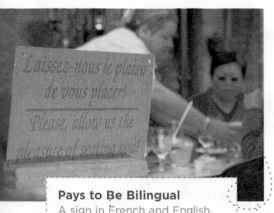

Pays to Be Bilingual
A sign in French and English outside a restaurant in Canada's Quebec City, where many people are bilingual. Speaking two languages may boost the brain's ability to manage many different activities (Bialystok, 2011). Rob Crandall/The Image Works

HOW WE READ   Understanding phonemes is the first and most essential step in reading. In order to digest the writing on the page, your brain must chop words into these fundamental sound bites (Shaywitz, 1996, 2003). This is where young Orlando probably encountered his first and most disabling roadblocks. A growing body of evidence suggests that the roots of dyslexia frequently lie in the person's problems with phonological processing (Shaywitz, Mody, & Shaywitz, 2006), the ability to distinguish and manipulate phonemes. Like most children with dyslexia, Orlando probably had trouble naming letters in the alphabet and knowing what sounds they make, identifying words that rhyme (for example, "hat," "mat," "rat"), and understanding how a word changes when one letter is swapped for another (for example, the transformation of "cat" to "cut" when the middle vowel is changed; L. Hecker, personal communication, July 22, 2011). If a child with dyslexia does not receive the special instruction he needs to overcome difficulties with phonemes, mastering the more complex layers of language will be very challenging.

MORPHEMES   **Morphemes** (mȯr-fēmz) represent the next level of language. They consist of one or more phonemes (the fundamental units of spoken language). It is the morpheme that brings meaning to a language. For example, "unimaginable" has three morphemes: *un, imagine,* and *able.* Each morpheme has a meaning and communicates something. Remove just one, and the word takes on a whole new significance. Clipping off *un,* for example, produces the word "imaginable," which means the exact opposite of the word you started with.

SYNTAX   The **syntax** of a language refers to the collection of rules dictating where words and phrases should be placed. Syntax guides both word choice and word order, providing consistency in sentence organization (Brandone, Salkind, Golinkoff, & Hirsh-Pasek, 2006). We say, "I love you," not "Love you I," because English syntax demands that the words appear in this order. Different languages have different syntaxes. In German, helping verbs often come toward the end of sentences, a variation in syntax that is strikingly noticeable to English speakers learning to speak German.

GRAMMAR AND SEMANTICS   **Grammar** refers to the rules associated with both word and sentence structure (Evans & Green, 2006). It tells us how words are made from sounds, how sentences are formed with words, where to place punctuation, and which word tenses to use. It combines syntax (the rules governing word choice and word order) and semantics. **Semantics** represents the rules used to bring meaning to words and sentences. Here are two sentences with different syntax, but the same semantics: *Jill kicked the ball. The ball was kicked by Jill.*

Semantics also refers to the context in which words appear. Let's consider the word "chip":

- I would like to eat a *chip.*
- You have a *chip* on your shoulder.
- I lost my last *chip* in that hand.
- You are going to have to make a *chip* shot.
- The new policy will finally start to *chip* away at the retirement benefits.
- The store just installed a new computer *chip.*

In each instance, we determine the meaning of the word "chip" based on the context in which it is used in the sentence.

phonemes (fō-nēmz) The basic building blocks of spoken language.

morphemes (mȯr-fēmz) The fundamental units that bring meaning to language.

syntax The collection of rules concerning where to place words or phrases.

grammar The rules associated with word and sentence structure.

semantics The rules used to bring meaning to words and sentences.

The Building Blocks of Language

Language is made up of a collection of units and rules. These build upon each other to help us think and communicate. At the base are phonemes, which combine to make up morphemes, the smallest unit of language that carries meaning. At the top is displacement, which is the human ability to refer to things that are abstract or hypothetical.

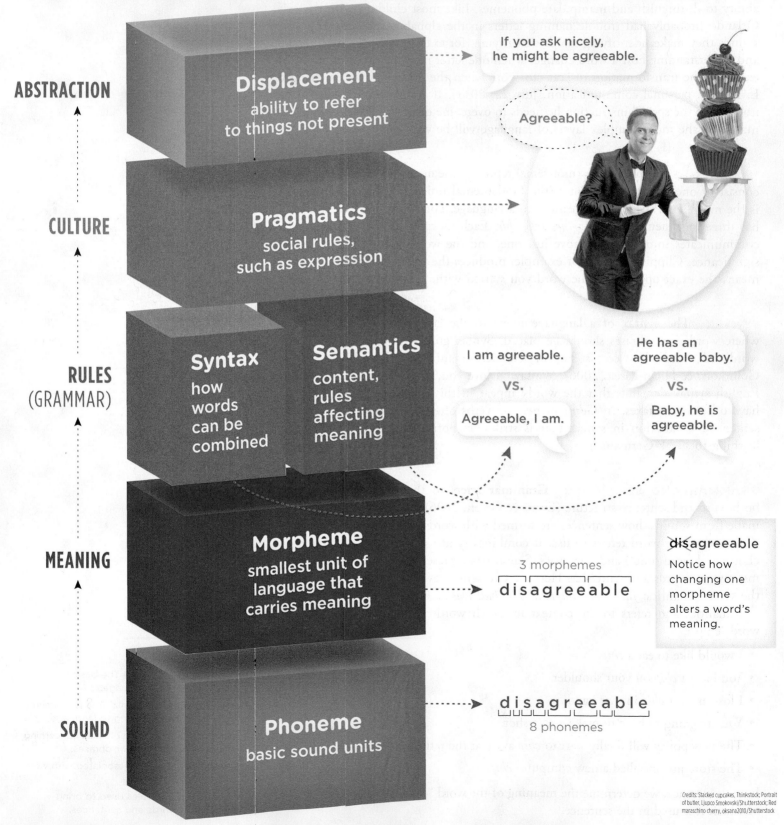

ABSTRACTION

Displacement
ability to refer
to things not present

If you ask nicely,
he might be agreeable.

Agreeable?

CULTURE

Pragmatics
social rules,
such as expression

**RULES
(GRAMMAR)**

Syntax
how
words
can be
combined

Semantics
content,
rules
affecting
meaning

I am agreeable.

vs.

Agreeable, I am.

He has an
agreeable baby.

vs.

Baby, he is
agreeable.

MEANING

Morpheme
smallest unit of
language that
carries meaning

3 morphemes

disagreeable

di̶s̶agreeable

Notice how
changing one
morpheme
alters a word's
meaning.

SOUND

Phoneme
basic sound units

disagreeable

8 phonemes

Credits: Stacked cupcakes, Thinkstock; Portrait of butler, Ljupco Smokovski/Shutterstock; Red maraschino cherry, oksana2010/Shutterstock

PRAGMATICS Language is used in social interactions, which are governed by certain norms and expectations. **Pragmatics** represents the social rules that help organize language. We have to learn how to take turns in a conversation, what gestures to use and when, and how to address people according to social standing (speaking with someone who occupies a higher status, an equal status, and so on) (Steiner, 2012, September 4; Yule, 1996). When addressing the Queen of Denmark, you would say, "Good day, Your Majesty," but when addressing your friend, you might say, "Hey, there. What have you been up to?"

How do we "know" these rules for language? Learning theorists propose that children learn language just like they learn other behaviors through processes such as reinforcement and modeling (Bandura, 1977a; Skinner, 1957). In contrast, linguist Noam Chomsky (1928–) suggests that humans are born with innate language abilities. Children needn't be taught the basics of language, according to Chomsky (2000); language develops like other organs in the body. Chomsky's position is based on the observation that children possess a much deeper knowledge of language than that which could have been acquired through experience. Their knowledge of language is not simply the result of hearing and imitating; it is hardwired within the brain. This built-in *language acquisition device* (LAD) accounts for the universality of language development. In fact, researchers have observed this innate capacity for language across cultures, and in non-hearing children (Chomsky, 2000; Petitto & Marentette, 1991).

Babble
Deaf babies who are exposed to sign language develop their own version of babbling. Instead of rattling off spoken syllables (*da-da-da* or *ma-ma-ma*) as hearing infants typically do, they babble with their hands, repeating the basic units of sign language (Petitto & Marentette, 1991). Courtesy Dr. Laura-Ann Petitto

THINK again

Language Without Sound

If Chomsky is right, then children would learn all languages, including signed languages, in basically the same way. Evidence suggests this is exactly what happens.

No one sat down with you and "taught" you language. You just picked it up because people around you were using it. The same is true for all native speakers, whether they converse in Russian, Mandarin, or American Sign Language (ASL). Spoken and signed languages also share the same critical period for acquisition. Between birth and 5 years old, the brain is highly plastic and ready to incorporate any language, but after that critical period, fluency is difficult to develop (Humphries et al., 2012).

Even the stages of language acquisition appear to proceed along the same path. Research suggests, for example, that deaf babies pass through a babbling stage around the same time as hearing babies. If you are unfamiliar with babbling, we are referring to the *ba-ba-ba* or *dah-dah-dah* sounds babies like to make while cruising on all fours. Babbling is accompanied by activation of the left hemisphere, a clue that it represents a step in language acquisition, not simply a new motor skill (Holowka & Petitto, 2002). Deaf babies who are exposed to ASL babble using their hands to repeat the fundamental units of sign language. This is called manual babbling (Petitto & Marentette, 1991).

DEAF BABIES BABBLE WITH THEIR HANDS.

ASL is a language with symbols, syntax, and a grammatical structure that parallels spoken language (Petitto, 1994). When people speak sign, some of the same regions of the brain are activated as when spoken language is used (Horwitz et al., 2003; Levänen, Uutela, Salenius, & Hari, 2001). ●+

pragmatics The social rules that help to organize language.

DISPLACEMENT   Many scientists argue that language, more than any other human ability, truly sets us apart from other species. Animals have evolved complex systems of communication, but there are some features of human language that appear to be unique. One of these unique features is *displacement*—the ability to talk and think about things that are not present at the moment. "I wonder if it's going to rain today," you might say to a friend. This statement demonstrates displacement, because it refers to an abstract concept and a hypothetical event. Displacement allows us to communicate about the future and the past, and fantasize about things that may or may not exist.

Thinking What We Say or Saying What We Think?

LO 9   Identify the linguistic relativity hypothesis and its relation to language and thought.

Psychologists are not in total agreement about the relationship between language and thought. The major controversy concerns the potential effect language can have on thinking. According to the *linguistic relativity hypothesis* (earlier known as the Sapir–Whorf hypothesis) developed by Benjamin Lee Whorf (b. 1956), languages have different effects on thinking and perception. For example, the Inuit and other Alaska Natives have many terms that refer to "snow" (in contrast to the single word used in English). This may cause them to perceive and think about snow differently than English speakers.

Whorf's hypothesis is not without controversy, however. Critics suggest that he exaggerated the number of words the Inuit and other Alaska Natives had for "snow" and underestimated the number of words in English (Pullum, 1991). For example, although English doesn't have different words for "snow," this does not mean that we don't understand or cannot express understanding using word combinations (such as "light snow," "wet snow," and the like).

Whorf also observed different color-naming systems across languages. For example, there are 11 generally recognized words referring to color in English (black, white, red, green, yellow, blue, brown, purple, pink, orange, and grey). The Dani of New Guinea have far fewer names for color. The linguistic relativity hypothesis would predict that the Dani's experience of color is different than an English-speaking person's (Rosch, 1973). However, most research has not found this to be the case; color discrimination across cultures does not consistently indicate differences of color perception.

Although language might not determine thinking and perception, it certainly has an influence. Consider the role of gender in language. The English language tends to use "he" and "his" when gender is unspecified. Research indicates that the use of masculine pronouns often results in people ignoring females and focusing on males when forming mental images (Gastil, 1990; Hegarty & Buechel, 2006). "He" and "his" in these situations theoretically refer to either males or females, but the majority of English-speaking Americans think of males. Perhaps you can predict the potential downside of this tendency. Narrowing the focus to male images inevitably promotes gender bias and stereotyping.

The capacity for language is one of the defining characteristics of humanity. But it is not certain whether this capacity is unique to human beings. Animals communicate with a variety of instinctual (unlearned) behaviors (for example, chirping, whistling, tail slapping, and dancing). Is it possible they use language as well? Read on and draw your own conclusions.

CONTROVERSIES

Do Animals Use Language Too?

▶◀ Rico was a German Border Collie who knew 200 vocabulary words, including the name of his dinosaur toy, "T-rex," and a little Santa Claus named "Weihnachtsmann" (Kane, 2004, June 10). When Rico's owners instructed him to fetch a certain toy, he would run into the next room and race back with that exact toy in his mouth. So impressive were the dog's verbal abilities that a team of researchers decided to make him the focus of a case study. They concluded that Rico was capable of "fast-mapping," the ability to deduce the meaning of a word by hearing someone use it just once (Kaminski, Call, & Fischer, 2004).

Rico is not alone in possessing exceptional communication skills. The green-rumped parrotlet of Venezuela learns its early contact calls, or socially meaningful songs, from its parents. In other words, it learns to communicate through social interaction as opposed to instinct (Berg, Delgado, Cortopassi, Beissinger, & Bradbury, 2012). Kanzi the bonobo can create simple sentences with the help of pictograms, or images that represent words (Lessmoellmann, 2006). And Sarah the chimpanzee reportedly learned to read 130 word symbols and connect them into meaningful combinations such as, "Mary give raisin Sarah" (Premack & Premack, 1972, p. 6).

There is no question that animals are capable of very sophisticated communication. But does that communication qualify as *language*? Keep in mind that animals need extensive training to learn and use vocabulary (you don't think Rico learned 200 words on his own, do you?), while human children pick up language through exposure. To our knowledge, only people have the ability to convey a vast number of ideas through complex grammatical constructs, and apply those constructs to critical thinking. Even if animals do possess rudimentary language abilities, humans appear to be the only species capable of grasping and using intricate sentence structures (Lessmoellmann, 2006; Pinker, 2003). ▶◀

HOT DOG!

Where would we be without the complex system of symbols we use to think and communicate? Through our innate language ability, we exchange ideas, make plans, and communicate emotions. We have discussed the significance of language, broken it down into its constituent phonemes and morphemes, and described its various rules. Now it is time to address intelligence.

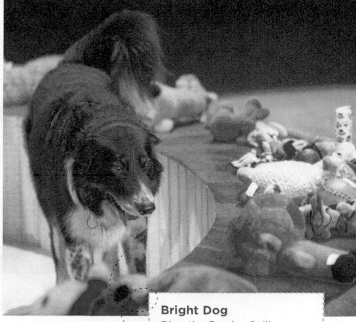

Bright Dog
Rico the Border Collie demonstrated his linguistic prowess by fetching toys on the German game show *Wetten, dass...? (Bet That)*. Rico reportedly knew 200 different words (Kano, 2004, June 10). More recently, researchers trained another Border Collie by the name of Chaser to recognize the names of 1,022 objects (Pilley & Reid, 2011). Rolf Haid Deutsch Presse Agentur/Newscom

---

show what you know

1. _____ are the basic building blocks of spoken language.

2. According to the linguistic relativity hypothesis, language differences lead to differences in:
   a. phonemes.
   b. thinking and perception.
   c. the language acquisition device.
   d. displacement.

3. The Dutch word *gezelligheid* does not really have a one-word counterpart in English. It refers to a primary component of Dutch culture: a cozy type of setting that can be quaint, fun, and intimate. Most languages have these types of untranslatable words. How might this phenomenon be an advantage for people who know more than one language?

✓ CHECK YOUR ANSWERS IN APPENDIX C.

Intelligence

Orlando Bloom was first diagnosed with dyslexia at the age of 7. Fortunately, he had a mother who believed in him and a school that allowed him to leave campus and attend special classes to address the issue (Child Mind Institute, 2010c, October 11; Child Mind Institute, 2010d, October 11). But many children are not identified as having dyslexia until they have lost considerable academic ground. Even those who receive an early diagnosis may not get into effective reading programs. Despite such challenges, people with dyslexia can be very successful.

Nothing Can Stop Us Now ◄
Nobel Prize winner Carol Greider (left) and financier Charles Schwab (right) are just two examples of successful people with dyslexia. There are many others, including Jay Leno, Tom Cruise, Anderson Cooper, and Ingvar Kamprad, the creator of IKEA (Allen, 2009, October 30; Turgeon, 2011, July 14). left: UPI/ Landov; right: Erin Lubin/Landov

Many great intellectuals have battled dyslexia, among them Nobel Prize winners Pierre Curie, Archer Martin, and Carol Greider (Allen, 2009, October 30); financier Charles Schwab; acclaimed writer John Irving; and the president of the esteemed Cleveland Clinic, Dr. Delos Cosgrove (Shaywitz, 2003). Dyslexia, it turns out, is not a gauge of intelligence (Ferrer, Shaywitz, Holahan, Marchione, & Shawyitz, 2010).

What Is Intelligence?

Generally speaking, **intelligence** is one's innate ability to solve problems, adapt to the environment, and learn from experiences. Intelligence relates to a broad array of psychological factors, including memory, learning, perception, and language, and how it is defined often depends on what particular variable is being measured.

In the United States, intelligence is often associated with "book smarts." We think of "intelligent" people as those who score high on tests measuring academic abilities. But intelligence is more complicated than that—so complicated, in fact, that psychologists have yet to agree on its precise definition. It is not even clear whether intelligence is a single unified entity, or a collection of capabilities.

Survival Smarts ◄
Maasai children in Kenya go through the motions of starting a fire. Definitions of intelligence vary according to culture. In the United States, intelligence is typically associated with high grades and test scores. Elsewhere in the world, being "smart" may have more to do with knowing how to survive and stay healthy. Harald WENZEL-ORF/age fotostock

We do know that intelligence is, to a certain degree, a cultural construct. We have already noted that people in America tend to equate intelligence with school smarts, but this is not the case everywhere in the world. Children living in a village in Kenya, for example, grow up using herbal medicine to treat parasitic diseases in themselves and others. Identifying illness and developing treatment strategies is a regular part of life. These children would score much higher on tests of intelligence relating to practical knowledge than on tests assessing vocabulary (Sternberg, 2004).

Table 7.1	GARDNER'S ORIGINAL MULTIPLE INTELLIGENCES	
Logical-mathematical	Scientist Mathematician	Sensitivity to, and capacity to discern, logical or numerical patterns; ability to handle long chains of reasoning.
Linguistic	Poet Journalist	Sensitivity to the sounds, rhythms, and meanings of words; sensitivity to the different functions of language.
Musical	Composer Violinist	Abilities to produce and appreciate rhythm, pitch, and timbre; appreciation of the forms of musical expressiveness.
Spatial	Navigator Sculptor	Capacities to perceive the visual-spatial world accurately and to perform transformations on one's initial perceptions.
Bodily-kinesthetic	Dancer Athlete	Abilities to control one's body movements and to handle objects skillfully.
Interpersonal	Therapist Salesman	Capacities to discern and respond appropriately to the moods, temperaments, motivations, and desires of other people.
Intrapersonal	Person with detailed, accurate self-knowledge	Access to one's own feelings and the ability to discriminate among them and draw upon them to guide behavior; knowledge of one's own strengths, weaknesses, desires, and intelligences.

This table reprinted with permission from Gardner and Hatch (1989) presents Gardner's original 7 intelligences. Each intelligence has associated strengths and capabilities.

SOURCE: GARDNER AND HATCH (1989).

Even within a single culture, the meaning of intelligence changes across time. "Intelligence" for modern Kenyans may differ from that of their 14th-century ancestors.

As we explore this topic further, please keep in mind that intelligence does not always go hand in hand with *intelligent behavior*. People can score high on intelligence measures but exhibit a low level of judgment. Psychologists and educators must be careful to distinguish between test scores and everyday smarts.

Theories of Intelligence

LO 10 Examine and distinguish among various theories of intelligence.

Very early in the history of intelligence measurement, Charles Spearman (1863–1945) speculated that humans have a **general intelligence** (or **g factor**), which refers to a singular underlying aptitude or intellectual ability. This g factor, according to Spearman, drives capabilities in many areas, including verbal, spatial, and reasoning competencies. The g factor is the common link.

MULTIPLE INTELLIGENCES   Howard Gardner (2011, 1999) suggested that intelligence can be divided into *multiple intelligences* (**FIGURE 7.5**). According to Gardner, there are eight types of intelligences or "frames of mind:" linguistic (verbal), logical-mathematical, spatial, bodily-kinesthetic, musical, intrapersonal, interpersonal, and naturalist. He has proposed that there also may be an existentialist intelligence, but the evidence is, for now, only suggestive (Gardner, 2011; Visser, Ashton, & Vernon, 2006). Take a look at **TABLE 7.1** and consider how different occupations might be well suited for individuals who excel in Gardner's original 7 intelligences.

According to Gardner (2011), partial evidence for multiple intelligences is apparent in people with brain damage. Some mental capabilities are lost, whereas others remain intact, suggesting that they are really distinct categories. Further evidence for multiple intelligences (as opposed to just a g factor) comes from observing people with savant syndrome. Individuals with *savant syndrome* generally score low on intelligence tests but have some area of extreme singular ability (calendar calculations, art,

▲ FIGURE 7.5
Gardner's Theory of Multiple Intelligences

intelligence Innate ability to solve problems, adapt to the environment, and learn from experiences.

general intelligence (g factor) A singular underlying aptitude or intellectual competence that drives abilities in many areas, including verbal, spatial, and reasoning abilities.

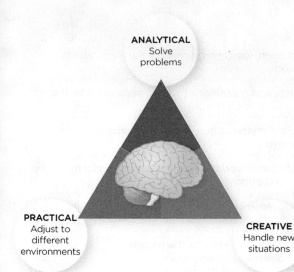

▲ FIGURE 7.6
Sternberg's Triarchic
Theory of Intelligence

You Asked, Dr. Jill Answers

http://qrs.ly/7p3m671

Did you undergo any psychological treatment during your recuperation?

mental arithmetic, and so on). Interestingly, the majority of individuals with savant syndrome are male (Treffert, 2009).

Some psychologists question whether these abilities qualify as intelligence, as opposed to skills. Critics contend that there is little empirical support for the existence of multiple intelligences (Geake, 2008; Waterhouse, 2006).

THE TRIARCHIC THEORY OF INTELLIGENCE Robert Sternberg (1988) proposed three kinds of intelligence. Sternberg's **triarchic theory of intelligence** (trī-är-kik) suggests that humans have varying degrees of analytical, creative, and practical competencies (**FIGURE 7.6**). *Analytic intelligence* refers to our capacity to solve problems. *Creative intelligence* represents the knowledge and skills we use to handle new situations. *Practical intelligence* includes our ability to adjust to different environments.

Let's take a moment and see how the triarchic theory of intelligence relates to Dr. Jill Bolte Taylor. Following the stroke, Dr. Jill struggled with what Sternberg referred to as *analytic intelligence,* or the ability to solve problems. She did, however, demonstrate evidence of *creative intelligence,* using knowledge and skills to handle new situations. While recovering at the hospital, Dr. Jill had routine meetings with a doctor who regularly gave her three things to remember and then asked her to recall them on his way out. Since the stroke had dismantled much of Dr. Jill's memory system, she found this assignment nearly impossible. But on one particular day, she was dead set on remembering the assigned items: *firefighter, apple,* and *33 Whippoorwill Drive.* Using all her available brain power, she recited the words over and over in her mind, but when the doctor finally quizzed her, she could not remember the "33" part of *33 Whippoorwill Drive.* She did, however, come up with a creative theoretical solution: She told the doctor that she would walk down Whippoorwill Drive and knock on every door until she identified the house (Taylor, 2006).

Following her stroke, Dr. Jill also maintained some degree of *practical intelligence,* the ability to adjust to her surroundings. Her world was thrown into turmoil by the stroke, but she developed pragmatic coping mechanisms to deal with the novelty of it all. Quickly realizing that talking to people and watching television caused mental exhaustion, she and G.G. decided to limit these overstimulating activities so that her brain could heal in tranquility. This practical strategy turned out to be a key component of her recovery (Taylor, 2006).

Needless to say, there are different ways to conceptualize intelligence (**TABLE 7.2**), none of which appear to be categorically "right" or "wrong." Given these varied

Table 7.2 **THEORIES OF INTELLIGENCE**		
Theory	**Advantages**	**Further Thoughts**
Spearman's general intelligence (*g*) There is a general intelligence driving abilities in many areas.	There is a connection among different abilities such as verbal, spatial, and reasoning competencies.	Given the complexity of the mind, can intelligence really be explained by a single general factor?
Gardner's multiple intelligences There are eight types of intelligences, which go beyond academic smarts and scholarship.	Linguistic, logical-mathematical, spatial, bodily-kinesthetic, musical, intrapersonal, interpersonal, and naturalist are "frames of mind" that allow humans to succeed.	What differentiates intelligence from skills?
Sternberg's triarchic theory Humans have varying degrees of analytical, creative, and practical competencies.	Analytic intelligence allows us to solve problems, creative intelligence represents knowledge and skills used to handle new situations, and practical intelligence includes the ability to adjust to different environments, all of which can be assessed.	Are each of these areas separate, or do they share something in common (like a *g* factor)?

A summary of the main theories of intelligence, each with its own set of strengths and other considerations.

approaches, you might expect there are also many tools to measure intelligence. Let's explore several ways psychologists assess intellectual ability.

Measuring Brainpower

LO 11 Describe how intelligence is measured and identify important characteristics of assessment.

Recall that Orlando was 7 years old when he was diagnosed with dyslexia. Around the same time, he took an intelligence test and scored very high (Child Mind Institute, 2010c, October 11). Tests of intelligence generally aim to measure **aptitude,** or a person's potential for learning. On the other hand, measures of **achievement** are designed to assess acquired knowledge (what a person has learned). Many brilliant people with dyslexia have performed poorly on achievement tests, but very well on aptitude tests, demonstrating normal to high intelligence. John Irving, for example, got a low score on the verbal portion of the SAT, and the successful physician Delos Cosgrove performed poorly on the Medical College Admission* Test (Shaywitz, 2003). Fortunately, they did not allow a single test to deter them. The line between aptitude and achievement tests is somewhat hazy, however; most tests are not purely one or the other.

A BRIEF HISTORY OF INTELLIGENCE TESTING Intelligence testing has an extensive history. In 1904 psychologist Alfred Binet (1857–1911) joined a commission of the French government that sought to create a way to identify students who might have trouble learning in regular classroom settings. A new French law had recently required school attendance by all children. The Minister of Public Instruction recognized that this transition would be difficult because some French children had never attended school. For the law to be implemented successfully, it was necessary to identify who had potential to succeed. A measure was needed to predict the performance of these schoolchildren (Fancher & Rutherford, 2012; Watson, 1968).

Binet worked with one of his students, Théodore Simon, to construct an assessment of intelligence. They studied Binet's daughters and Parisian schoolchildren, coming up with the 30 items in the original assessment. These items were designed to be of increasing difficulty, starting with a simple test to see if a child could follow a lit match that the tester moved in front of her. The items became more difficult as testing progressed (explaining how paper and cardboard are different, making rhymes with words; Fancher & Rutherford, 2012).

Binet and Simon assumed that children generally follow the same path of intellectual development. Their primary goal in creating their assessment was to compare the mental ability of an individual child with the mental abilities of other children of the same age. They would determine the **mental age (MA)** of an individual child by comparing his performance to that of other children in the same age category. For example, a 10-year-old boy with average intellectual abilities would score similarly to other 10-year-old children and thus would have a *mental age* of 10. An intelligent 10-year-old boy would score better than other 10-year-old children and thus have a higher mental age (for example, a mental age of 12) compared to his chronological age. Similarly, a child who was intellectually slower would have a mental age lower than his chronological age. Although Binet and Simon's measure of intelligence was groundbreaking at the time, it had many shortcomings that were eventually addressed by others.

One of the problems with relying on mental age as an index is that it cannot be used to compare intelligence levels across age groups. For example, you can't use mental

What's Your IQ?
French psychologist Alfred Binet collaborated with one of his students, Théodore Simon, to create a systematic assessment of intelligence. The materials pictured here come from Lewis Terman and Maude Merrill's 1937 version of Binet and Simon's test. Using these materials, the test administrator prompts the test taker with statements such as "Point to the doll's foot," or "What advantages does an airplane have over a car?" (Sattler, 1990). top: Albert Harlingue/Roger-Viollet/The Image Works; bottom: SSPL/Getty Images

triarchic theory of intelligence (trī-är-kĭk) Sternberg's theory suggesting that humans have varying degrees of analytical, creative, and practical abilities.

aptitude An individual's potential for learning.

achievement Acquired knowledge, or what has been learned.

mental age (MA) A score representing the mental abilities of an individual in relation to others of a similar chronological age.

age to compare the intelligence levels of an 8-year-old girl and a 12-year-old girl. In 1912, William Stern solved this problem by devising the **intelligence quotient (IQ),** providing a way to compare intelligence across ages. To calculate IQ, a child's mental age is divided by her chronological age and multiplied by 100. A 10-year-old girl with a mental age of 8 would have an IQ score of $(8 \div 10) \times 100 = 80$. If her mental age and chronological age were the same, her IQ would be 100. The IQ score can be used to compare the level of intelligence of this 10-year-old girl with children of other ages.

This method does not apply to adults, however. It wouldn't make sense to give a 60-year-old man who scores the same as a 30-year-old man an IQ score of 50 (that is, $30 \div 60 \times 100 = 50$). Modern intelligence tests still assign a numerical score (which we continue to refer to as "IQ"), although they no longer use the actual quotient score.

THE STANFORD-BINET TEST American psychologist Lewis Terman (1916) revised Stern's work so that Binet's test could be used in the United States, where it came to be known as the Stanford–Binet. Terman changed some items, added items, developed standards based on American children, and extended the test to include teens and adults. The Stanford–Binet Intelligence Scales, as it is now known in its fifth edition (Roid, 2003), includes the assessment of verbal and nonverbal abilities (for instance, defining words, tracing paths in a maze). The Stanford–Binet yields an overall score for general intelligence, as well as scores relating to more specific abilities, such as knowledge, reasoning, visual processing, and working memory (Becker, 2003).

THE WECHSLER TESTS In the late 1930s, David Wechsler began creating intelligence tests for adults (Anastasi & Urbina, 1997). Wechsler noted that the Stanford–Binet was designed exclusively for children. And although many had been using the Stanford–Binet with adults, it was not an ideal measure, given that adults might not react positively to the questions geared to the daily experiences of school-age children. The Wechsler Adult Intelligence Scale (WAIS) was published in 1955 and has since been revised numerous times (1981, 1997), with the most recent revision in 2008 (WAIS–IV). In addition to creating assessments for adults, Wechsler also developed scales for older children (Wechsler Intelligence Scale for Children, WISC–IV) and younger children (Wechsler Preschool and Primary Scale of Intelligence, WPPSI–III).

The Wechsler assessments of intelligence consist of a variety of subtests designed to measure different aspects of intellectual ability. The 10 subtests on the WAIS–IV target four domains of intellectual performance: verbal abilities, perceptual reasoning, working memory, and processing speed. Results from the WAIS–IV include an overall IQ score, as well as scores on the four domains. Psychologists look for consistency among the domain scores and subtest scores. Substantial inconsistency may suggest an issue that should be further explored, such as a reading or language disability. In the United States, Wechsler tests are now used more frequently than the Stanford–Binet.

Let's Test the Intelligence Tests

As you read about the history of intelligence assessment, did you wonder how effective those early tests were? We hope so, because this would indicate you are thinking critically about the construct of intelligence and how it is measured. Psychologists make great efforts to ensure the accurate assessment of intelligence, paying close attention to three important characteristics: validity, reliability, and standardization.

VALIDITY One primary characteristic of a measure of intelligence is its **validity.** This is the degree to which the assessment measures what it intends to measure.

---

intelligence quotient (IQ)
A score from an intelligence assessment; originally based on mental age divided by chronological age, multiplied by 100.

validity The degree to which an assessment measures what it intends to measure.

reliability The ability of an assessment to provide consistent, reproducible results.

standardization Occurs when test developers administer a test to a large sample and then publish the average scores for specified groups.

normal curve Depicts the frequency of values of a variable along a continuum; bell-shaped symmetrical distribution, with the highest point reflecting the average score.

We can assess the validity of a measure by comparing its results to those of other assessments that have been found to measure the factor of interest. In addition, we determine the validity of a measure by seeing if it can predict what it is designed to measure, or its *predictive validity.* Thus, to determine if an intelligence test is valid, we would check to see if the scores it produces are consistent with those of other intelligence tests. A valid intelligence test should also be able to predict future performance on tasks related to intellectual ability.

RELIABILITY   Another important characteristic of assessment is **reliability,** the ability of a test to provide consistent, reproducible results. If given repeatedly, a reliable test will continue producing the same types of scores. If we administer an intelligence test to an individual, we would expect (if it is reliable) that the person's scores will remain consistent across time. We can also determine the reliability of an assessment by splitting the test in half and then determining whether the findings of the first and second halves of the test agree with each other. It is important to note that it is possible to have a reliable test that is not valid. For this reason, we always have to determine *both* reliability and validity.

STANDARDIZATION   In addition to being valid and reliable, a good intelligence test provides standardization. Perhaps you have taken a test that measured your achievement in a particular area (for example, an ACT or SAT), or an aptitude test to measure your innate abilities (for example, an IQ test). Upon receiving your scores, you may have wondered how you performed in comparison to other people in your class, your college, or your state. Most aptitude and achievement tests allow you to make these judgments through the use of **standardization.** Standardization occurs when test developers administer a test to a large sample of people and then publish the average scores, or *norms,* for specified groups. The test developers provide these norms using a sample that is representative of the population of interest. It is important that the sample include a variety of individuals who are similar to the population using the test. This allows you to compare your own score with people of the same age, gender, socioeconomic status, or region. With test norms, you are able to make judgments about the relative performance (often provided as percentiles) of an individual compared to others with similar characteristics.

It is also critical that assessments are given and scored using standard procedures. This ensures that no one is given an unfair advantage or disadvantage in terms of testing conditions. Intelligence tests are subject to tight control. The public does not have access to the questions or answers, and all testing must be administered by a professional. What about those IQ tests found on the Internet? They simply are not valid due to lack of standardization.

THE NORMAL CURVE   Have you ever wondered how many people in the population are really smart? Or perhaps how many people have average intelligence? With aptitude tests like the Wechsler assessments and the Stanford–Binet, we can predict what percentage of the population will have scores between two intervals by using a **normal curve,** which depicts the frequency of values along a continuum (INFO-GRAPHIC 7.4 on page 319). The normal curve is symmetrical and shaped like a bell. The highest point on the graph reflects the average score.

The normal curve shown in Infographic 7.4 portrays the distribution of scores for the Wechsler tests. As you can see, the *mean* or average score is 100. As you follow the horizontal axis, notice that the higher and lower scores occur less and less frequently in the population. A score of 145 or 70 is far less common than a score of 100, for example.

Measuring Achievement
Tests such as the SAT and ACT are called achievement tests because they are geared toward measuring learned knowledge, as opposed to innate ability. These tests are also standardized, making it possible to compare scores of people who are demographically similar. Rui Vieira/PA Wire/AP Photos

Synonym

normal curve normal distribution

One final note about the normal curve is that it applies to a variety of characteristics, including IQ, height, weight, and personality characteristics, and that we use it to make predictions about these characteristics. Consult Appendix A for more information on the normal curve and a variety of other topics associated with statistics.

But Are They Fair?

A major concern with intelligence tests is that IQ scores consistently differ across certain groups of people. For example, researchers have reported that Black Americans in general score lower on intelligence tests than do White Americans. The difference in the average of these two groups is around 10 to 15 IQ points (Ceci & Williams, 2009; Dickens & Flynn, 2006). Group differences are also apparent for East Asians, who score around 6 points higher than average White Americans, and for Hispanics, who score around 10 points lower than average White Americans (Rushton & Jensen, 2010). Although researchers disagree about what causes these gaps in IQ scores, they are in general agreement that there is *no* evidence to support a "genetic hypothesis" (Nisbett et al., 2012). Instead, researchers generally attribute these group differences to environmental factors.

The evidence for environmental influence is strong and points to a variety of factors that contribute to this gap in IQ scores. One adoption study, for example, found that Black and mixed-race children adopted by White families had significantly higher IQ scores than did Black and mixed-race children who were adopted by Black families (Moore, 1986). This indicates strongly that differences in household environments accounted for disparities in IQ scores. Another likely environmental explanation for the IQ gap is stress (Nisbett et al., 2012). Research suggests that Black families often live in more stressful environments than White families. Chronic stress can have a negative impact on the function of the brain, particularly those areas responsible for attention and memory (**short-term, long-term, and working memory**), which are vulnerable to sustained high levels of stress (McEwen, 2000).

Socioeconomic status (SES) is yet another important variable to consider. The disproportionate percentage of minorities in the lower strata may, in fact, mask the critical issue of environmental factors and their relationship with IQ. For example, children raised in homes with lower SES tend to watch more TV, have less access to books and technology, and are not read to as often. In addition, individuals with lower SES often live in disadvantaged neighborhoods and have limited access to quality schools (Hanscombe et al., 2012).

CULTURE-FAIR INTELLIGENCE TESTS   It has not yet been determined whether group differences on IQ scores also reflect biases of the tests themselves. Can an assessment be valid for some groups, but not others? For example, are these IQ tests solely aptitude tests, or do they incorporate some level of achievement (learned content)? If that is the case, then people with limited exposure to certain types of test content may be at a disadvantage. Early versions of the IQ tests exhibited some bias against individuals from rural areas, people of lower socioeconomic status, as well as African Americans. Bias may result from language, dialect, or the culture of those who have created the tests (Sattler, 1990; Sternberg, 2004).

To address these problems, psychologists have tried to create **culture-fair intelligence tests,** designed to measure intelligence without putting people at a disadvantage because of their cultural backgrounds. One way to avoid bias is to use

CONNECTIONS

In **Chapter 6,** we discussed the biology of memory, exploring areas of the brain responsible for memory formation and storage (hippocampus, cerebellum, and amygdala) as well as changes at the level of the neuron (long-term potentiation). Here, we note that stressful environments can impact the functioning of the memory system.

culture-fair intelligence test
Assessments designed to minimize cultural bias.

How Smart Are Intelligence Tests?

Tests that claim to measure intelligence are everywhere—online, in your favorite magazine, at job interviews, and in many elementary and secondary schools. But can all of these tests be trusted? The results of an intelligence test aren't meaningful unless the test is *valid*, *reliable*, and *fair*. But what do those concepts mean, and how can we be sure whether a test is valid, reliable, or fair—let alone all three? Let's take a look.

validity   DOES THE TEST MEASURE WHAT IT INTENDS TO MEASURE?

Is a bathroom scale valid for measuring length?

How about a ruler missing its first inch?

A shortened ruler would not be a valid measure because it would provide different results than other rulers.

A valid intelligence test will provide results that:

✔ agree with the results of other valid intelligence tests
✔ predict performance in an area related to intelligence, such as academic achievement

reliability   WILL YOUR SCORE BE CONSISTENT EVERY TIME YOU TAKE THE TEST?

A shortened ruler isn't valid, but it is *reliable* because it will give the same result every time it's used.

A reliable intelligence test will provide results that:

✔ are reproducible (produce a similar score if taken a second time)
✔ show the first and second halves of the test are consistent with each other

68% of all people score within 15 points above or below the average score

68%

95%

2%   2%

55   70   85   100   115   130   145

Wechsler IQ score

Number of scores

Because most intelligence tests are *standardized*, you can determine how well you have performed in comparison to others. Test scores tend to form a bell-shaped curve—called the normal curve—around the average score. Most people (68%) score within 15 points above or below the average. If the test is reliable, each person's score should stay around the same place on the curve across multiple testings.

fairness   IS THE TEST VALID FOR THE GROUP?

An animal weighing 2 stone is likely to be a:
(a) sparrow   (c) mature lion
(b) small dog   (d) blue whale

Unless you live in the United Kingdom, where the imperial system of weights is used, you probably wouldn't know that a stone is approximately 14 pounds, and therefore the correct answer is B. Does this mean that you are less intelligent, or that the test is biased against people without a specific background? A test that is culture-fair is designed to minimize the bias of cultural background.

3 inches   2.286 Chinese Imperial cùn   .1667 cubits

questions that would be familiar to people from a variety of backgrounds. Another approach is to use nonverbal questions. (The Raven's Progressive Matrices uses this approach; see **FIGURE 7.7**.) Since intelligence is defined within a culture and tests are created within a culture, some have suggested that we can only create culture-relevant tests, not culture-fair nor culture-free assessments (Sternberg, 2004).

Ultimately, IQ tests are good at predicting academic success. They are highly correlated with SATs, ACTs, and GREs, for example, and the correlations are stronger for the higher and lower ranges of IQ scores. Strong correlations help us make predictions about future behavior. Researchers have found, however, that self-discipline may be a better predictor of success than IQ tests (Duckworth & Seligman, 2005).

The study of intelligence is far from straightforward. Assessing a concept with no universally accepted definition is not an easy task, but these tests do serve useful purposes. The key is to be mindful of their limitations, while appreciating their ability to measure an array of cognitive abilities.

The Diversity of Human Intelligence

Once called mental retardation, *intellectual disability* consists of a delay in thinking, intelligence, as well as social and practical skills, which is evident before age 18. Psychologists can assess intellectual functioning with IQ scores; for example, disability is identified as an IQ below approximately 70 on the Wechsler tests. It can also be assessed in terms of one's ability to adapt; for example, being able to live independently, and understanding number concepts, money, and hygiene. Although intellectual disability is the preferred term, the phrase "mental retardation" is still used in most laws and policies relating to intellectual disability (Individuals With Disabilities Education Act, 2004; Social Security Disability Insurance; and Medicaid Home and Community Based Waiver; Schalock et al., 2010).

There are many causes of intellectual disability, but we cannot always pinpoint them. According to the American Association on Intellectual and Developmental

FIGURE 7.7
Nonverbal Intelligence
The Raven's Progressive Matrices test (left), and the Matrix Reasoning subtest of the WISC–IV (right) are used to assess components of nonverbal intelligence. For both sample questions pictured here, the test taker is required to choose the item that completes the matrix pattern. The correct answer for the Raven's is choice 2; the correct answer for the Matrix Reasoning is choice 4. These types of tests are generally considered culturally fair, meaning they do not favor certain cultural groups over others.

Disabilities (AAIDD), nearly half of intellectual disability cases have unidentifiable causes (Schalock et al., 2010). We do know the causes for Down syndrome (an extra chromosome in what would normally be the 21st pair), fetal alcohol syndrome (exposure to alcohol while in utero), and fragile X syndrome (a defect in a gene on the X chromosome leading to reductions in protein needed for development of the brain). There are also known environmental factors, such as lead and mercury poisoning, lack of oxygen at birth, various diseases, and exposure to drugs during fetal development.

At the other end of the intelligence spectrum are the intellectually **gifted,** those who have IQ scores of 130 or above. Above 140, one is considered a "genius." As you might imagine, very few people—about 2% of the population—are classified as gifted. An even smaller proportion falls in the genius range: only the top 1% of the population (Simonton, 2012). What roles do you think these gifted people take on in our society?

Feel the Music
Chinese conductor Hu Yizhou rehearses for an upcoming concert in Korea. Yizhou, who has Down syndrome, is part of the China Disabled Peoples Performing Art Troupe. REUTERS/You Sung-Ho

TERMAN'S STUDY OF THE GIFTED American psychologist Lewis Terman was interested in discovering if gifted children could function successfully in adulthood. His work led to the longest-running longitudinal study on genius and giftedness in the early 1900s. This study, formerly called the Genetic Studies of Genius, is now called the Terman Study of the Gifted. Terman (1925) monitored 857 boys and 671 girls with IQs ranging from 130 to 200. These children (known as "Termites") were well adjusted socially, showed leadership skills, and were physically healthy and attractive, according to Terman and Oden (1947). Following the participants into adulthood, the study found that they earned more academic degrees and achieved more financial success than their non-gifted peers (Fancher & Rutherford, 2012; Holahan & Sears, 1995). But life isn't all about test scores, and a high IQ score doesn't guarantee success in all areas of life.

Life Smarts

Some people are better at recognizing and controlling their emotional responses, regardless of how well they might do on an intelligence test. This awareness and control is a component of **emotional intelligence,** which includes the capacity to perceive, understand, regulate, and use emotions to adapt to social situations. People with emotional intelligence also display the ability to use information about their emotions to direct their behavior in an efficient and creative way (Salovey, Mayer, & Caruso, 2002). Furthermore, emotionally intelligent people are self-aware and can properly judge how to behave in social situations.

According to Goleman (1995), emotional intelligence has a major impact on everyday functioning. Someone with high emotional intelligence shows self-control; has the ability to manage anger, impulsiveness, and anxiety. She exhibits empathy, awareness of emotions, and persistent self-motivation. Research suggests that emotional intelligence is related to performance on the job and at school (MacCann, Fogarty, Zeidner, & Roberts, 2011). An example of someone with emotional intelligence is Dr. Jill Bolte Taylor.

gifted Highly intelligent; defined as having an IQ score of 130 or above.

emotional intelligence The capacity to perceive, understand, regulate, and use emotions to adapt to social situations.

▶ New Beginnings
Dr. Jill currently serves as the national spokesperson for the Harvard Brain Tissue Resource Center, where scientists conduct research on brain tissue from cadavers. It took 8 years for Dr. Jill to recover from her stroke. Her bestselling book *My Stroke of Insight* is being adapted for the big screen by Sony Pictures and Imagine Entertainment (drjilltaylor.com, 2010).
© My Stroke of Insight, Inc. Photo by Kip May

DR. JILL'S NEWFOUND INTELLIGENCE   It took Dr. Jill 8 years to recuperate from what she now calls her "stroke of insight," and it was not smooth sailing. Regaining her physical and cognitive strength required painstaking effort. "Recovery was a decision I had to make a million times a day," she writes (Taylor, 2006, p. 115). Every step along the way, Dr. Jill made a conscious effort to apply herself to the task of recovery, and her steadfast determination made all the difference. She also had many people cheering her on—family and friends who had faith in her brain's plasticity, or ability to repair and rewire (Taylor, 2006).

If stroke victims fail to regain all faculties by 6 months, they never will. At least that is what Dr. Jill remembers hearing her doctors say. But she proved all the naysayers wrong. Within 2 years, Dr. Jill was living back in her home state of Indiana and teaching college courses in anatomy/physiology and neuroscience. Four years after the operation, she had retrained her body to walk gracefully and her brain to multitask. By Year 5, she could solve math problems, and by Year 7, she had accepted another teaching position, this time at Indiana University (Taylor, 2006). Today, she is working on book number two, creating a game that helps people with brain trauma, and developing a nonprofit organization for "brain awareness" and education (drjilltaylor.com, 2010).

Dr. Jill has now recovered, but how have the stroke and her response to it affected her life? "Thanks to this stroke," she writes, "I have become free to explore the world again with childlike curiosity" (Taylor, 2006, p. 147). Dr. Jill has become more open to new experiences and ways of thinking (a prerequisite for creativity), and she has also emerged more empathetic and emotionally aware.

Do you think everyone would respond so positively when faced with such a challenge? Some people seem more resilient and better equipped to deal with life's trials. Is it something in their nature, or did they learn to cope through experience? Like many topics in psychology, it comes down to nature and nurture. This is true of dyslexia as well.

nature AND nurture

Why Dyslexia?

We don't have access to Orlando Bloom's genetic code, and we certainly are not in a position to speculate on what caused his dyslexia. In some cases, however, it appears that reading difficulties are written into the genes. Dyslexia is, to a certain extent, inherited. Some of the earliest dyslexia researchers noticed that the condition runs in families, and many studies have confirmed this observation (Fisher & DeFries, 2002). If you have dyslexia and you have children, there is a good chance one of your kids will develop it as well.

DYSLEXIA CAN BE TRACED TO ATYPICAL CONNECTIONS IN THE BRAIN. . . .

But genes aren't the whole story. Your genetic code provides a blueprint for the development of a human brain and body—not the finished product. Just as nutrition can affect the growth of a child's bones and muscles, early learning experiences can shape cognitive development. Strong reading, for example, is fostered by a variety of factors, including providing children with access to books, activities that help them understand phonemes (rhyming and other word games), and good schooling (Shaywitz, 2003).

The nurture side of the coin even has value for adults, whose brains are still receptive to training. Dyslexia can be traced to atypical connections in the brain, and, specifically, decreased activity in various areas, including the left parietotemporal region. fMRI research suggests this region can be awakened when a person with

heritability The degree to which hereditary factors (genes) are responsible for a particular characteristic observed within a population; the proportion of variation in a characteristic attributed to genetic factors.

dyslexia receives intensive phonological training and learns to read more efficiently (Eden et al., 2004). The takeaway: Nature isn't everything. With proper intervention (nurture), the brain of someone with dyslexia can begin to behave more like the brain of an average reader (Shaywitz, 2003). ◊⌂

Origins of Intelligence

While we are on the topic of nature and nurture, let's examine how these two forces impact intelligence in general. Twin studies (research involving identical and fraternal twins) are an excellent way to examine the relative weights of nature and nurture for virtually any psychological trait. The Minnesota twin studies (Johnson & Bouchard, 2011; McGue, Bouchard, Iacono, & Lykken, 1993) indicate there are strong correlations between the IQ scores of identical twins—stronger than the correlations between the IQ scores of fraternal twins or other siblings. In other words, the closer the degree of the genetic relationship (identical twins have identical genes), the more similar their IQ scores are. This suggests that genes play a major role in determining intellectual abilities. According to the Minnesota twin studies, identical twins' IQ scores have correlations as high as .86 (remembering that ±1.00 is a perfect correlation) (**FIGURE 7.8**).

Heritability refers to the degree to which heredity is responsible for a particular characteristic or trait. As psychologists study the individual differences associated with a variety of traits, they try to determine the heritability of each one. Many traits have a high degree of heritability (for example, eye color, height, and other physical characteristics), but others are determined by the environments in which we are raised (for example, manners; Dickens & Flynn, 2001). Results from twin and adoption studies suggest that heritability for "general cognitive abilities" is about 50% (Plomin & DeFries, 1998; Plomin, DeFries, Knopik, & Niederhiser, 2013). In other words, about half of the variation in intellectual or cognitive ability can be attributed to genetic make-up, and the other half to environment.

It is important to emphasize that heritability applies to groups of people, not individuals. We cannot say, for example, that an individual's intelligence level is 40% due to genes and 60% the result of environment. We can only make general predictions about groups and how they are influenced by genetic factors (Dickens & Flynn, 2001).

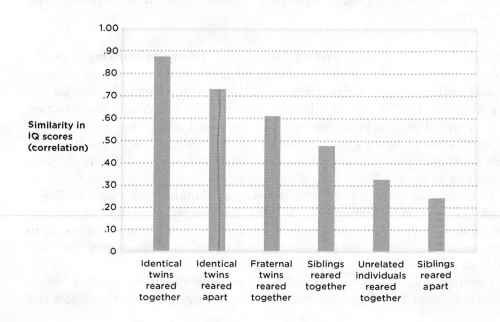

FIGURE 7.8

The Impact of Nature and Nurture on Intelligence

The most genetically similar people, identical twins, have the strongest correlation between their scores on IQ tests. This suggests that genes play a major role in determining intelligence. But if identical twins are raised in different environments, the correlation is slightly lower, showing some environmental effect (McGue et al., 1993).

In this test, you will be asked to consider some common objects. Each object has a common use, which will be stated. You are to list as many as six other uses for which the object or parts of the object could serve.

Example:

Given: A NEWSPAPER (used for reading). You might think of the following other uses for a newspaper.

a. Start a fire

b. Wrap garbage

c. Swat flies

d. Stuffing to pack boxes

e. Line drawers or shelves

f. Make a kidnap note

Notice that all of the uses listed are different from each other and different from the primary use of a newspaper. Each acceptable use must be different from others and from the common use.

▲ **FIGURE 7.9**

Instructions for Guilford's Alternate Uses Task

The sample question above is from Guilford's Alternate Uses Task, a revised version of the *unusual uses test,* which is designed to gauge creativity. Reproduced by special permission of the Publisher, MIND GARDEN, Inc., www.mindgarden.com from the Alternate Uses by J.P. Guilford, Paul R. Christensen, Philip R Merrifield, & Robert C. Wilson. Copyright 1960 by SheridanSupply Co. Further reproduction is prohibited without the Publisher's written consent.

creativity In problem solving, the ability to construct valuable results in innovative ways; the ability to generate original ideas.

divergent thinking The ability to devise many solutions to a problem; a component of creativity.

convergent thinking A conventional approach to problem solving that focuses on finding a single best solution to a problem by using previous experience and knowledge.

We have now explored the various approaches to assessing intelligence. Let's shift our focus to a quality that is associated with intelligence but far more difficult to measure.

Creativity

LO 12   Define creativity and its associated characteristics.

Do you remember the last time you encountered a situation or problem that required you to "put on your thinking cap"? Sometimes it takes a little creativity to solve a problem. In a problem-solving situation, **creativity** is the ability to construct valuable results in innovative ways. While not exclusively linked, creativity and intelligence are correlated, and a basic level of intelligence is necessary for creativity to flow. For example, you need to have a certain level of intelligence to generate original ideas, as opposed to just more ideas (Benedek, Franz, Heene, & Neubauer, 2012; Nusbaum & Silvia, 2011).

Most psychologists agree that there are several basic characteristics associated with creativity (Baer, 1993; Sternberg, 2006a, 2006b):

- Originality: the ability to come up with unique solutions when trying to solve a problem

- Fluency: the ability to create many potential solutions

- Flexibility: the ability to use a variety of problem-solving tactics to arrive at solutions

- Knowledge: a sufficient base of ideas and information

- Thinking: the ability to see things in new ways, make connections, see patterns

- Personality: characteristics of a risk taker, who perseveres and tolerates ambiguity

- Intrinsic motivation: influenced by internal rewards, motivated by the pleasure and challenge of work

Because it doesn't present itself in a singular or uniform manner, creativity is difficult to measure. One way to assess creativity is to add up the number of times an individual exhibits the four characteristics of originality, fluency, flexibility, and elaboration in a problem-solving situation and then use these data to create a creativity score (Baer, 1993).

DIVERGENT AND CONVERGENT THINKING   **Divergent thinking** is an important component of creativity. It refers to the ability to devise many solutions to a problem (Baer, 1993). A classic measure of divergent thinking is the *unusual uses test* (Guilford, 1967; Guilford, Christensen, Merrifield, & Wilson, 1960; **FIGURE 7.9**). A typical prompt in the unusual uses test would ask the test taker to come up with as many uses for a brick as she can imagine. (What ideas do you have? Paperweight? Shot put? Stepstool?) Remember that we often have difficulty thinking about how to use familiar objects in atypical ways because of functional fixedness.

In contrast to divergent thinking, **convergent thinking** focuses on finding a single best solution by converging on the correct answer. With this type of thinking, we fall back on previous experience and knowledge. This conventional approach to problem solving leads to one solution, but, as we have noted, many problems have multiple solutions.

Creativity comes with many benefits. People with this ability tend to have a broader range of knowledge and interests. They are open to new experiences and tend to be uninhibited in thoughts and behaviors (Feist, 2004; Simonton, 2000). The good news is that we can become more creative by practicing divergent thinking, taking risks, and looking for unusual connections between ideas (Baer, 1993).

Sometimes finding those new connections takes a little relaxing on the part of the brain. Let's see how this phenomenon might come into play by peering into the brain of a rapper.

didn't SEE that coming

Inside the Brain of a Rapper

 How long would it take you to come up with a rhyme that looks something like this?

I shine and glow, even in the dark,
Stay smart, stay sharp, as a harp,
Played by a musician in this position,
Feel blessed to make the whole world listen,
And just glisten without even trying
Even when I die, I won't stay dead,
And it's straight off the head,
And it's straight out the lungs,
Looking fly, fresh, old man, so young

(Mos Def, 2011)

Hip-hop artist Mos Def came up with these rhymes off the top of his head one night at a club in New York City. He was freestyle rapping alongside fellow performer Kanye West ("freestyle" means to invent lyrics in the moment—no cheat sheets involved, no memorizing the night before). In a true freestyle session, rappers essentially create poetry as it flows from their mouths. An amazing cognitive feat, don't you think? Something special must be going on in the brain of a rapper in order for freestyle to occur.

Researchers have studied the brains of freestyle rappers as they "flow," or "spit rhymes," and they have discovered an interesting pattern of excitement and calmness in different areas of the brain. Using fMRI, Siyuan Liu and colleagues (2012) compared the brain activity of rappers as they freestyled and performed lyrics they had rehearsed. Freestyle sessions were correlated with greater activity in language-processing hot spots on the left side of the brain—not surprising, given the extraordinary language demands of improvisational rhyming. There was also heightened activity in an area of the frontal lobes known as the medial prefrontal cortex (MPFC) and a quieting down of another area known as the dorsolateral prefrontal cortex (DLPFC). This calming down of the DLPFC, which receives and filters input from the MPFC about internal intentions, may effectively relax the rules about which intentions are turned into action, setting the stage for creativity. "Letting go," it seems, is an essential part of the creative process. ◉!

MOS DEFINITELY CREATIVE!

Let It Flow ◄
Generating rap lyrics on the spot appears to involve a slowdown of activity in the dorsolateral prefrontal cortex (DLPFC), a part of the brain thought to play a role in deciding which intentions are transformed into actions (Liu et al., 2012). This loosening of inhibition may facilitate creative expression. AP Photo/Joe Giblin

Closing Thoughts

From freestyle rap to near-fatal brain hemorrhages—we certainly have covered a lot of ground in this chapter. It is now time to wrap things up. Let's review the major topics. We began our discussion by defining cognition and saw what happens when cognitive processes are derailed, using the story of Dr. Jill Bolte Taylor as an example. Then we explored the many dimensions of language. Drawing on the insights of actor Orlando Bloom, we discovered how minor differences in language processing pave the way for dyslexia. Finally, we explored the concept of intelligence, examining the various ways psychologists define and evaluate it.

Although you have reached the end of this chapter your study of cognition is far from over. In the pages to come, we will explore intelligence in relation to age (Chapter 8), and gender (Chapter 10), and a host of cognitive processes related to social interactions (Chapter 15). As you continue your journey in this book, you will see cognition popping up everywhere. Cognitive processes underlie perception, memory, behavior, and most every psychological phenomenon you can imagine.

show what you know

1. Sternberg believed that intelligence is made up of three types of competencies, including.
   a. linguistic, spatial, musical.
   b. intrapersonal, interpersonal, existentialist.
   c. analytic, creative, practical.
   d. achievement, triarchic, prototype.

2. Some tests of intelligence measure _____, or a person's potential for learning, and other tests measure _____, or acquired knowledge.

3. Define IQ. How is it derived?

4. According to findings from the Minnesota twin studies, the _____ for intelligence is around 50%. This means that around half of the population-wide variation in intellectual ability may be attributed to genetic make-up.
   a. heritability   c. divergent thinking
   b. standardization   d. average

5. An artist friend of yours easily comes up with unique solutions when trying to solve problems. This _____ is one of the defining characteristics of creativity.

✓ CHECK YOUR ANSWERS IN APPENDIX C.

7 summary of concepts

LO 1 Define cognition and explain how it is related to thinking. (p. 284)

Cognition is the mental activity associated with obtaining, converting, and using knowledge. Thinking is a more specific type of cognition, which involves coming to a decision, reaching a solution, forming a belief, or developing an attitude. Cognition is a broad term that describes mental activity, and thinking is a subset of cognition.

LO 2 Define concepts and identify how they are organized. (p. 285)

Concepts are the mental representations of *categories* of objects, situations, and ideas that belong together based on their central features or characteristics. Psychologists

often use a three-level hierarchy to categorize objects. At the top of the hierarchy are superordinate concepts, the broadest category encompassing all the objects belonging to it. Below is the more specific midlevel or basic level of the hierarchy, the category used most often to identify objects. At the bottom of the hierarchy is the subordinate-level, the most specific category.

LO 3 Differentiate between formal concepts and natural concepts. (p. 286)

Formal concepts are created through rigid and logical rules, or features of a concept. Natural concepts, on the other hand, are acquired through everyday experience.

Natural concepts don't have the same types of rigid rules for identification that formal concepts do, and this makes them harder to outline. We organize our worlds with the help of prototypes, which are the ideal or most representative examples of particular natural concepts.

LO 4 Describe the biological processes associated with cognition. (p. 290)

The biology of cognition is evident in the brain, both on a micro and macro level. Changes at the level of the neuron, whether through rewiring, heightened excitability, or increased efficiency of synaptic transmission, make it possible to store, retrieve, and manipulate information. The plasticity of the brain enables dramatic recoveries from trauma.

LO 5 Explain how trial and error and algorithms can be used to solve problems. (p. 293)

Problem solving refers to the variety of approaches used to achieve goals. One approach to problem solving is trial and error, which involves finding a solution through a series of attempts. Algorithms provide a virtually guaranteed solution to a problem by providing a formula or set of rules. Unlike trial and error, algorithms ensure that you will reach a solution if you follow all the steps.

LO 6 Identify different types of heuristics used to solve problems. (p. 294)

Heuristics refer to a problem-solving approach that incorporates a rule of thumb or broad application of a strategy. One commonly used heuristic involves creating subgoals or subproblems. Another commonly used heuristic is means–ends analysis, which involves figuring out how to decrease the distance between a goal and current status. Using means–ends analysis, you can break a problem into subproblems and solve them independently.

LO 7 Define decision making and explain how heuristics can lead us astray. (p. 299)

Decision making generally refers to the cognitive process of choosing among various ways to reach a goal. Sometimes a decision is based on a single feature. With more complex decisions, we tend to consider a variety of features. Using the availability heuristic, we predict the probability of something happening in the future based on how easily we can recall a similar type of event from the past. If we can easily recall a similar type of event, then we judge that event as being more likely to occur. With the representativeness heuristic, we evaluate the degree to which the primary characteristics of an event, person, or situation are similar to our prototype of that type of person or situation.

LO 8 Define language and give examples of its basic elements. (p. 305)

Language can be defined as a system for using symbols to think and communicate. These symbols are words, gestures, or sounds, and there are specific rules for putting them together. Phonemes are the basic building blocks of spoken language. Morphemes consist of one or more phonemes and represent the fundamental units of meaning. The syntax of a language refers to the collection of rules guiding word choice and word order. Grammar refers to the rules associated with word and sentence structures and how these are formed from their components. Semantics refers to rules that are used to bring meaning to words and sentences. Pragmatics refers to the social rules for using language.

LO 9 Identify the linguistic relativity hypothesis and its relation to language and thought. (p. 310)

The linguistic relativity hypothesis proposes that language differences lead to disparities in thinking and perception. Most psychologists agree that although language might not determine thinking and perception, it certainly can influence it.

LO 10 Examine and distinguish among various theories of intelligence. (p. 313)

Charles Spearman speculated that intelligence consists of a general intelligence (or *g* factor), which refers to a singular underlying aptitude or intellectual ability. Howard Gardner suggested we have multiple intelligences, proposing eight different types of intelligences or "frames of mind": linguistic (verbal), logical-mathematical, spatial, bodily-kinesthetic, musical, intrapersonal, interpersonal, and naturalist. Robert Sternberg proposed three kinds of intelligences. His triarchic theory of intelligence suggests that humans have varying degrees of analytical, creative, and practical abilities.

LO 11 Describe how intelligence is measured and identify important characteristics of assessment. (p. 315)

Some tests of intelligence aim to measure aptitude, or a person's potential for learning. Measures of achievement are designed to assess acquired knowledge (what a person has learned). Psychologists must ensure the accurate assessment of intelligence by determining validity, that is, the degree to which the test measures what it intends to measure. Another important characteristic is reliability, the ability of a test to provide consistent, reproducible results. A reliable test, given repeatedly, will result in similar scores.

LO 12 Define creativity and its associated characteristics. (p. 324)

Creativity is the ability to construct valuable results in innovative ways. Most psychologists agree on the basic characteristics of creativity, including originality, fluency, and flexibility. Because creativity is not evident in a singular or uniform manner, it is difficult to measure.

key terms

achievement, p. 315

algorithm, p. 293

aptitude, p. 315

availability heuristic, p. 300

cognition, p. 284

concept, p. 285

confirmation bias, p. 302

convergent thinking, p. 324

creativity, p. 324

culture-fair intelligence test, p. 318

decision making, p. 299

divergent thinking, p. 324

dyslexia, p. 302

emotional intelligence, p. 321

formal concept, p. 286

framing effect, p. 302

functional fixedness, p. 297

general intelligence (*g* factor), p. 313

gifted, p. 321

grammar, p. 307

heritability, p. 323

heuristics, p. 294

insight, p. 294

intelligence, p. 312

intelligence quotient (IQ), p. 316

language, p. 305

means–ends analysis, p. 294

mental age (MA), p. 315

morpheme, p. 307

natural concepts, p. 286

normal curve, p. 317

phonemes, p. 306

pragmatics, p. 309

problem solving, p. 292

prototype, p. 287

reliability, p. 317

representativeness heuristic, p. 301

semantics, p. 307

standardization, p. 317

syntax, p. 307

thinking, p. 284

trial and error, p. 293

triarchic theory of intelligence, p. 314

validity, p. 316

TEST PREP are you ready?

1. _____ is a mental activity associated with obtaining, converting, and using knowledge, and _____ refers to coming to a decision, reaching a solution, or forming a belief.

   a. Thinking; formal concept
   b. Cognition; superordinate concept
   c. Thinking; cognition
   d. Cognition; thinking

2. _____ are the mental representations of categories of objects, situations, and ideas that belong together based on their central features or characteristics.

   a. Concepts
   b. Prototypes
   c. Algorithms
   d. Heuristics

3. The boundaries of _____ are imprecise and hard to define, because they do not have rigid rules for identification. For example, not everyone agrees with what qualities make a *mother*.

   a. algorithms
   b. heuristics
   c. natural concepts
   d. formal concepts

4. Following a stroke, the neurons in the brain exhibit greater excitability, rewiring occurs, and there is increased efficiency of synaptic connections, all indicating _____ of the brain.

   a. algorithms
   b. the plasticity
   c. means–ends analysis
   d. the functional fixedness

5. You are at dinner with a friend and you are struggling to determine the tip you should leave. Your friend suggests you do what she does to calculate a 20% tip: Move the decimal to the left one space and multiply by 2. This is an example of using _____ to solve the problem.

   a. prototypes
   b. a heuristic
   c. trial and error
   d. an algorithm

6. _____ is thought of as an understanding or solution that occurs in a sudden stroke of clarity. Research suggests activity occurs in the frontal and temporal lobes immediately preceding an "aha!" moment, implying that a reorganization occurs without our awareness.

   a. Insight
   b. Functional fixedness
   c. A superordinate concept
   d. A mental set

7. Factors such as the frequency and vividness of an event make us more likely to predict such an event will occur in the future. This is known as using the:

   a. representativeness heuristic.
   b. availability heuristic.
   c. additive model.
   d. confirmation bias.

8. Sometimes we do not gather important information when making decisions because we are only looking for evidence that upholds our beliefs. This is known as the:

a. availability heuristic.

b. framing effect.

c. single feature approach to decision making.

d. confirmation bias.

9. The wording of a question can influence the outcome of a decision. People are more likely to prefer ground beef if it is described as 80% lean as opposed to 20% fat. This is an example of:

a. insight.

b. the confirmation bias.

c. the framing effect.

d. the vividness of an event.

10. Infants can recognize and distinguish between all _____ from all languages until about 9 months of age. This is why it is so much more difficult for older children and adults to learn to speak a foreign language without an accent.

a. morphemes

b. phonemes

c. words

d. semantics

11. One important component of creativity is _____, which refers to the ability to devise many solutions to a problem.

a. divergent thinking

b. convergent thinking

c. emotional intelligence

d. the normal curve

12. The word "unexcitable" can be broken into three parts (un, excite, able). Remove one of these and the meaning of the word changes. These three parts represent _____, the fundamental units that bring meaning to a language.

a. grammar

b. phonemes

c. morphemes

d. semantics

13. _____ is one's innate ability to solve problems, adapt to the environment, and learn from experience.

a. Heritability

b. Giftedness

c. Insight

d. Intelligence

14. To determine the _____ of an intelligence test, you could give the assessment to a sample of participants and then compare the results with another assessment of intelligence to make sure the test is measuring what it intends to measure.

a. reliability

b. validity

c. standardization

d. norms

15. Although there is a consistent gap between how Black Americans and White Americans score on IQ tests, research evidence suggests this is the result of:

a. environmental factors such as chronic stress.

b. heritability.

c. genetic differences.

d. emotional intelligence.

16. How are formal and natural concepts different from each other? Give examples of each.

17. Explain how the theories of intelligence differ.

18. Many people on the Jersey Shore had to leave their homes when Hurricane Irene hit in 2011. On returning home, they found that no significant damage had occurred. When told to evacuate for Superstorm Sandy in 2012, many of these same residents did not leave. What heuristic do you think they used?

19. Why are reliability and validity important in test construction? What is at risk if you have developed an unreliable IQ test? What might happen if your IQ test is not valid?

20. Using your divergent thinking, how many uses can you think of for a hammer?

✓ CHECK YOUR ANSWERS IN APPENDIX C.

8

The Study of Human Development

📁 *A Day in the Life*

Genetics, Conception, and Prenatal Development

📁 *16 and Pregnant*

Infancy and Child Development

📁 *26 and Pregnant*

➕ THINK AGAIN
Genie the "Feral Child"

📁 *Some Things Never Change*

🌿🏠 NATURE AND NURTURE
Destiny of the Difficult Baby

Adolescence

📁 *The Walking, Talking Hormone*

💬 SOCIAL MEDIA AND PSYCHOLOGY
The Social Networking Teen Machine

Adulthood

📁 *A Work in Progress*

SA from the pages of
SCIENTIFIC AMERICAN
Changing Social Roles Can Reverse Aging

🌐➤ ACROSS THE WORLD
Death in Different Cultures

📁 *Latest Developments*

human development

The Study of Human Development

A DAY IN THE LIFE   Montgomery, Illinois: Mondays are especially hectic for working mom and college student Jasmine Mitchell. The 31-year-old starts the day at 5:00 A.M. with a morning workout of hip-swaying, shoulder-shimmying Zumba® dance. Then, in between catching her breath and folding laundry, she wakes up her 14-year-old daughter Jocelyn and her 5-year-old son Eddie. At 7:00 A.M., two more children appear at Jasmine's doorstep, a 14-year-old nephew and a 9-year-old niece. Jasmine takes care of the kids in the morning to help out her mother, who is their legal guardian. It is now 7:15 A.M., and Jasmine is fixing eggs and sausage for a house full of children.

Meanwhile, in Austin, Texas, 22-year-old Chloe Ojeah is dropping an array of multicolored pills into her grandparents' pill dividers. This painstaking task is something she needs to do carefully because it's critical that both her grandmother and grandfather take the correct medication in the morning and again at night. Her 79-year-old grandmother is struggling with Alzheimer's disease and her 85-year-old grandfather is recovering from a stroke. After skipping breakfast herself, Chloe heads out the door and drives to Austin Community College, where she is working toward a degree in communications and, down the road, a career in teaching.

Back in Illinois, the time is now 8:30 A.M., and Jasmine has already dropped off the four children in her early morning care at three different schools. She returns home, cleans up the mess from breakfast, showers, and then starts her homework. Jasmine is studying to become a social worker at Waubonsee Community College, where she also works 40 hours a week as a receptionist. Not much time remains for studying, because Jasmine needs to arrive at work by 11:00 A.M.

Right around the time Jasmine walks into the office, Chloe is returning home from her morning class. She checks in with her grandparents' caregiver (*How did the morning go? Do we*

→

8

LEARNING OBJECTIVES

after reading and studying this chapter, you should be able to:

LO 1 Define human development.

LO 2 Describe three longstanding discussions in developmental psychology.

LO 3 Identify the types of research psychologists use to study developmental processes.

LO 4 Examine the role genes play in our development.

LO 5 Discuss how genotype and phenotype relate to development.

LO 6 Identify the progression of prenatal development.

LO 7 Summarize some developmental changes that occur in infancy.

LO 8 Describe the theories explaining language acquisition.

LO 9 Examine the universal sequence of language development.

LO 10 Summarize the constructs of Piaget's theory of cognitive development.

LO 11 List the key elements of Vygotsky's theory of cognitive development.

LO 12 Identify how Erikson's theory explains psychosocial development through puberty.

LO 13 Give examples of significant physical changes that occur during adolescence.

LO 14 Explain how Piaget described cognitive changes that take place during adolescence.

LO 15 Identify how Erikson explained changes in identity during adolescence.

LO 16 Summarize Kohlberg's levels of moral development.

LO 17 Name some of the physical changes that occur across adulthood.

LO 18 Identify some of the cognitive changes that occur across adulthood.

LO 19 Explain some of the socioemotional changes that occur across adulthood.

LO 20 Summarize the four types of parenting proposed by Baumrind.

LO 21 Describe how Kübler-Ross explained the stages of death.

Supermom

Jasmine Mitchell is coping with the complex issues of childhood, adolescence, and young adulthood. She juggles motherhood with college and a full-time job.

Jasmine Mitchell

Other Voices: Allie Fuentes

http://qrs.ly/hu3m67f

need anything from the store?), chats with her grandfather, grabs lunch, and hits the books. Within a few hours, she is cooking dinner—enchiladas, a cheeseburger pie, or something else warm and comforting—and dispensing her grandparents' evening pills. During supper, they discuss the news, the family business, or whatever happens to be on their minds. Sometimes in midconversation, Chloe's grandmother stares blankly at the window, a sign that she has lost track of the conversation.

Back in Illinois, Jasmine is just about to leave work. Around 8:30 P.M., she arrives at the home of her mother, who has picked up the kids at the end of their school day and cooked dinner for them. Once home, Eddie heads straight to bed and Jocelyn stays up late, working on homework. After finishing her own homework and tying up some odds and ends around the house, Jasmine finally goes to bed at 11:00 P.M.

It's nighttime in Texas, and Chloe is sitting footsteps away from her grandparents' bedroom. They've long since retired. She likes to stay close by, though, until 11:00 P.M., just in case they need her for some reason. Finally, in the silence of the night, Chloe climbs the stairs and crawls into bed.

Note: Quotations attributed to Jasmine Mitchell, Chloe Ojeah, and J. M. Richard are personal communications.

Jasmine Mitchell and Chloe Ojeah are actual college students with real-world responsibilities. They are pursuing challenging degree programs, launching careers, and finding their place in the world. Both women are making their way through a busy, often tumultuous, period of life called *young adulthood*. At the same time, they are up to their necks in issues pertinent to other stages of life: *childhood* and *adolescence* for Jasmine, the young mother, and *late adulthood* for Chloe, the caretaker of two elderly family members.

Here, we feature the stories of these young women because they are people whose lives, in many respects, may resemble your own. Psychologists often focus their research on "normal" or "average" individuals, as it helps them uncover universal or common themes and variations across the life span.

You Asked, Allie Answers
http://qrs.ly/6q3m67g
How does being a parent affect your work and school?

> **LO 1** Define human development.

DEVELOPMENTAL PSYCHOLOGY What do psychologists mean when they say "development"? Obviously, humans do not stay the same from conception to death. Development refers to the changes in our bodies, minds, and social functioning. The goal of **developmental psychology** is to examine these changes. The study of development is, in many ways, an attempt to understand the struggles and triumphs of everyday people at different stages of their lives. Many of the topics presented in this chapter, such as personality, learning, and emotion, are covered elsewhere in this book. Here, we focus on how these change over the course of a lifetime, homing in on three major categories of developmental change: physical, cognitive, and socioemotional.

PHYSICAL DEVELOPMENT Physical development begins the moment a sperm unites with an egg, and it continues until we take our final breath. Human development is influenced by the genes we inherit from our biological parents, the hormones circulating in our bloodstream, and many other biological factors. The physical growth beginning with conception and ending when the body stops growing is referred to as **maturation.** For the most part, this maturation follows a progression that is universal in nature and biologically driven, as these changes are common across all cultures and ethnicities, and generally follow a predictable pattern. Most babies, for example, become physically capable of sitting up alone at approximately 5½ months (ranging from

developmental psychology A field of psychology that examines physical, cognitive, and socioemotional changes across the life span.

maturation Physical growth beginning with conception and ending when the body stops growing.

4 to 9 months; WHO Multicentre Growth Reference Study Group, 2006). After maturation, physical changes continue, but not necessarily in a positive or growth direction; for example, many older adults begin to have trouble seeing at night (Stuen & Faye, 2003).

I Can Sit!
Most babies learn to sit without assistance between 4 and 9 months of age (WHO Multicentre Growth Reference Study Group, 2006). Sitting upright is one of the milestones of physical development. Maturation tends to follow a predictable pattern, regardless of ethnicity or culture. Getty Images/Blend Images

COGNITIVE DEVELOPMENT   Changes in memory, problem-solving abilities, decision making, language, and intelligence all fall under the umbrella of cognitive development. Like physical development, cognitive development tends to follow a universal course early in life. Infants, for example, begin to babble around the age of 7 months and say their first words around 12 months. But there is enormous variation in the way cognitive abilities change, particularly as people get older (Skirbekk, Loichinger, & Weber, 2012; Small, Dixon, & McArdle, 2012; von Stumm & Deary, 2012). Chloe's 85-year-old grandfather won't necessarily have the same cognitive abilities as his 85-year-old neighbor, whose memory and wit may not be as sharp.

SOCIOEMOTIONAL DEVELOPMENT   Socioemotional development refers to social behaviors, emotions, and the changes people experience with respect to their relationships, feelings, and overall disposition. A developmental psychologist studying Jasmine and her family might look at how Jasmine's relationship with her mother has changed over time, or how her children have developed close bonds with their cousins. They might be interested in learning how Jasmine's approach to motherhood changed in the decade between Jocelyn and Eddies' births.

BIOPSYCHOSOCIAL PERSPECTIVE   In this chapter, we draw on the biopsychosocial perspective, which recognizes the contributions of biological, psychological, and social forces shaping human development. We consider the intricate interplay of heredity, chemical activity, and hormones (biological factors); learning and personality traits (psychological factors); and family, culture, and media (social factors). When examining and explaining complex psychological phenomena, it is important to incorporate a variety of approaches.

Three Debates

> **LO 2**   Describe three longstanding discussions in developmental psychology.

Science is, at its core, a work in progress, full of unresolved questions and areas of disagreement. In developmental psychology, longstanding debates and discussions tend to cluster around three major themes: stages and continuity, nature and nurture, and stability and change. Each of these themes relates to a basic question: (1) Does development occur in separate or discrete stages, or is it a steady, continuous process? (2) What are the relative roles of heredity and environment in development? (3) How stable is one's personality over a lifetime and across situations?

STAGES OR CONTINUITY   Some aspects of development occur in discrete stages; others in a steady, continuous process. Abrupt changes are often related to environmental circumstances. High school graduation, for example, marks the time when many young people feel free to move out of the family home. This response is not universal, however. Chloe graduated from high school years ago, but she is living with her grandparents so she can care for them. Physical changes may also occur in stages, such as learning to walk and talk, or developing the physical characteristics of a sexually mature adult.

critical period Specific time frame in which an organism is sensitive to environmental factors, and certain behaviors and abilities are readily shaped or altered by events or experiences.

One line of evidence supporting developmental stages with definitive beginnings and endings comes to us indirectly through the animal kingdom. Konrad Lorenz (1937) was one of the first researchers to document the *imprinting* phenomenon, showing, for example, that when baby geese hatch, they become attached to the first "moving and sound-emitting object" they see, whether it's their mother or a nearby human (p. 269). Lorenz made sure he was the first moving creature several goslings saw, and he found that they followed him as soon as they could stand up and walk, becoming permanently attached to him because he was that first "object." But there appeared to be a limited time frame within which this imprinting occurred. Experiences during a **critical period** for this type of automatic response result in permanent and "irreversible changes" in brain function (Knudsen, 2004). Critical periods are a type of *sensitive period* of development, during which "certain capacities are readily shaped or altered by experience" (p. 1412). Young barn owls, for example, learn how to navigate their environment during a sensitive period in which auditory information is used to create a type of mental map, but this period is not considered critical because it is not characterized by irreversible brain changes (Knudsen, 2004).

How does all this talk of geese and owls relate to people? Some psychologists suggest there is a critical period for language acquisition. Until a certain age, children are highly receptive to learning language, but after that critical period ends, it is difficult for them to acquire a first language that is age-appropriate and "normal" (Kuhl, Conboy, Padden, Nelson, & Pruitt, 2005). Others suggest that language acquisition is not subject to a critical period, but rather to sensitive periods that all children experience (Knudsen, 2004). (For more on this topic, read about Genie the "feral child" later in this chapter.)

Although some aspects of development occur in stages, others occur gradually, without a clear distinction between them (McAdams & Olson, 2010). Observing a toddler making her transition into early childhood, you probably won't be able to pinpoint her shift from the "terrible twos" to the more emotionally self-controlled young child.

HEREDITARY AND ENVIRONMENTAL INFLUENCES   Psychologists also debate the degree to which heredity (nature) and environment (nurture) influence behavior and development, but few would dispute the important contributions of both (Mysterud, 2003). Researchers can study a trait like impulsivity, which is the tendency to act before thinking, to determine the extent to which it results from hereditary factors and environment. In this particular case, nature and nurture appear to have equal weight (Bezdjian, Baker, & Tuvblad, 2011). Later in this chapter, we will examine the balance of nature and nurture in relation to brain and intellectual development, a longstanding, sometimes controversial debate in psychology and beyond.

STABILITY AND CHANGE   How much does a person change from childhood to old age? Some researchers suggest that personality traits identified early in life can be used to predict behaviors across the life span (McAdams & Olson, 2010). Others report that personality characteristics change as a result of the relationships and experiences we have throughout life (Specht, Egloff, & Schmukle, 2011). Psychologists often

He Must Be My Mother
A brood of baby geese follows scientist Konrad Lorenz. The goslings treated Lorenz like a mother because he was the first "moving and sound-emitting" object with whom they had contact (Lorenz, 1937, p. 269). As Lorenz discovered, there appears to be a critical period during which imprinting occurs. Time & Life Pictures/ Getty Images

discuss how experiences in infancy can set the stage for stable cognitive characteristics, particularly when it comes to early enrichment and its long-term impact on intellectual abilities (more on this topic later).

Three Methods

> **LO 3**   Identify the types of research psychologists use to study developmental processes.

Developmental psychologists use a variety of methods to study differences across ages and time (INFOGRAPHIC 8.1).

CONNECTIONS

In **Chapter 6,** we described recall as the process of retrieving information held in long-term memory without the help of explicit retrieval cues. Here, we will see how these memory processes change as a function of development.

THE CROSS-SECTIONAL METHOD   The **cross-sectional method** enables researchers to examine people of different ages at one point in time. For example, Castel and his colleagues (2011) used the cross-sectional method to investigate developmental changes in the efficiency of memory **recall.** They divided their 320 participants into groups according to age (children, adolescents, younger adults, middle-aged adults, young-old adults, and old-old adults) and compared the scores of the different groups to see if changes occur across the life span. One advantage of the cross-sectional method is that it can provide a great deal of information quickly; by studying differences across age groups, we don't have to wait for people to get older.

But a major problem with the cross-sectional method is that it doesn't tell us whether differences across age groups result from actual developmental changes or common experiences within groups, a phenomenon known as the **cohort effect.** Members of each age group have lived through similar historical and cultural eras, and these common experiences may be responsible for some differences across groups. For example, the "old-old adults" in the memory recall study described above probably have different perspectives than those in the younger adult group. They were not raised on cell phones, iPads, computers, Google, or Facebook. The authors of the study were quick to point out this pitfall: "The present design was cross-sectional, whereas (in some ways) a longitudinal design would allow for stronger conclusions regarding . . . *changes* with age" (Castel et al., 2011, p. 1562).

CONNECTIONS

In **Chapter 1,** we described confounding variables as unaccounted factors that change in sync with the independent variable, making it very hard to discern which one is causing changes in the dependent variable. Here, we consider how a cohort can act as a confounding variable.

THE LONGITUDINAL METHOD   Researchers can avoid the cohort effect by using the **longitudinal method,** which follows one group of individuals over a period of time. Curious to find out what "lifestyle activities" are associated with age-related cognitive decline, one team of researchers studied 952 individuals over a 12-year period (Small, Dixon, McArdle, & Grimm, 2011). Every 3 to 4 years, they administered tests to all participants, assessing, for example, cognitive abilities and health status. The more engaged and socially active the participants were, the better their long-term cognitive performance. Using the longitudinal method, we can compare the same individuals over time, identifying similarities and differences in the way they age. But these studies are difficult to conduct because they require a great deal of money, time, and participant investment. Common challenges include attrition (people dropping out of the study) and practice effects (people performing better on measures as they get more "practice"). The advantage, though, is that changes are tracked within the same people, to avoid the cohort effect of an era or generation.

cross-sectional method A research design that examines people of different ages at a single point in time.

longitudinal method A research design that examines the same sample of people over a period of time to determine age-related changes.

cross-sequential method A research design that examines groups of people of different ages, following them across time.

THE CROSS-SEQUENTIAL METHOD   The **cross-sequential method,** also used by developmental psychologists, is a mixture of the longitudinal and cross-sectional methods. You might call it the best of both worlds. Participants are divided into

Research Methods in Developmental Psychology

Developmental psychologists use several research methods to study changes that occur with age. Imagine you want to know whether using social media helps protect against feelings of loneliness over time. How would you design a study to measure that? Let's compare methods.

Longitudinal

Measure a **single group** at **different points in time**

Example: Researchers follow a sample of participants, interviewing them every decade for a total of three measurements. As they age, participants report lower levels of loneliness than expected. But because the study is longitudinal, we can't eliminate the possibility that this particular group of participants is less lonely because of some historically specific effect.

GROUP 1	20 YEARS OLD	30 YEARS OLD	40 YEARS OLD
	2005	2015	2025

BENEFITS
+ Can track age-related changes.

PROBLEMS
− Measured changes could be specific to the particular group of participants.
− Takes a long time, leading some participants to drop out before study is complete.

Cross-sectional

Measure groups of people of **different ages** (for example, 20-, 40-, and 60-year-olds) at a **single point in time**

Example: Researchers interview participants in three different age groups: 20-, 40-, and 60-year-olds. The oldest group reports higher levels of loneliness. But because the study is cross-sectional, we can't be sure if this finding reflects a cohort effect, in which differences may be due to age or to common experiences within the group, as opposed to developmental changes in physical, cognitive, or socioemotional functioning.

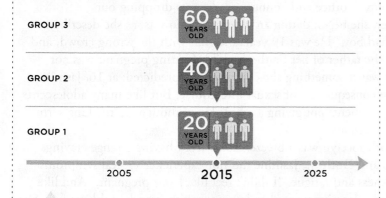

BENEFITS
+ Allows comparison between age groups.
+ Can be completed relatively quickly.

PROBLEMS
− Susceptible to cohort effect.

Cross-sequential

Measure groups of people of **different ages**, following them across **different points in time**

Example: Researchers interview participants from three age groups every decade for a total of three measurements. This results in data showing how social media use and loneliness change within each group as they age.

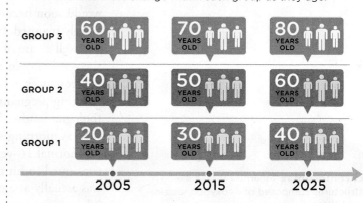

BENEFITS
+ Shows changes within individuals and between groups.
+ Better addresses cohort effect.

PROBLEMS
− Requires substantial resources and many participants.
− Takes a long time, leading some participants to drop out before study is complete.

age groups as well as followed over time, so researchers can examine developmental changes within individuals and across different age groups. One team of researchers used this approach to identify the age at which cognitive decline becomes evident (Singh-Manoux et al., 2012). They recruited 10,308 participants, assigning each to a 5-year age group (45–49, 50–54, 55–59, 60–64, and 65–70), and then followed them for 10 years. Using this approach, they could observe changes in individuals as they aged *and* identify differences across the five age groups.

Human development is very complex. Some processes are universal; others are specific to an individual, and it is this combination that makes the field so fascinating. As you learn about the development of Chloe, Jasmine, and their families, you may be struck by the degree of similarity (or differences) in your own family.

✓ show what you know

1. A 3-year-old decides he doesn't need diapers, and much to his parents' surprise, he starts using the toilet. This physiological change likely results from his maturation, which follows a progression that is universal and biologically driven. This is an example of human _____, which includes changes in physical, cognitive, and socioemotional characteristics.

2. Explain the three longstanding discussions of developmental psychology.

3. A researcher is interested in studying developmental changes in memory recall. She asks 300 participants to take a memory test and then compares the results across five different age groups. This researcher is using which of the following methods?
   a. cross-sequential
   b. longitudinal
   c. cross-sectional
   d. biopsychosocial

✓ CHECK YOUR ANSWERS IN APPENDIX C.

Genetics, Conception, and Prenatal Development

16 AND PREGNANT Jasmine has always had a mind of her own. As a teenager, she pretty much did as she pleased. If her mother forbade her to leave the house, she would go out and party extra-hard, her basic philosophy being, *If I'm going to get in trouble anyway, I might as well have a really good time.* Jasmine did not like high school, so on her 16th birthday, she walked into the principal's office and announced she was dropping out.

A few months later, she began dating an older guy who was, as she describes, "the definition of a bad boy." He was 19 years old, ran with the wrong crowd, and would soon become the father of her firstborn child. Getting pregnant was not exactly planned, nor was it something she couldn't have predicted; at 16, Jasmine was well aware of the consequences of sexual intercourse. But like many adolescents, she was living in the moment, not giving a whole lot of thought to the long-term consequences of her decisions.

Being pregnant with Jocelyn was a breeze. Apart from having strange cravings (bologna sandwiches and Doritos), Jasmine did not experience typical symptoms such as morning sickness and fatigue. "I didn't feel like I was pregnant." And like any normal 16-year-old, Jasmine wanted to hang out with friends and have fun. She continued to hit the party scene throughout the 9 months of her pregnancy (she was actually at a party when her water broke), but refrained from using alcohol and other drugs—a very wise decision, as you will soon learn.

Jasmine's pregnancy may have been easy, but the delivery was pure misery. "I thought I was going to die," says Jasmine, who insisted on an all-natural labor to show her mother that she could endure the pain. But as it turned out, the pain was beyond description. Her labor lasted 36 hours.

Initially, Jasmine was somewhat surprised by her newborn's appearance. "I was grossed out, honestly," Jasmine says. "She was covered with slime and ooze." But as

chromosomes Inherited threadlike structures composed of deoxyribonucleic acid (DNA).

deoxyribonucleic acid (DNA) A molecule that provides the instructions for the development and production of cells.

gene Specified segment of a DNA molecule.

genotype An individual's complete collection of genes.

soon as the nurses cleaned baby Jocelyn, she looked much more like a sweet little cherub. Okay, thought Jasmine, *She is kind of cute . . . and she came out of me!* It was mind-boggling to think that her body had produced this 7-pound, 9-ounce infant from the ground up—in less than a year. How did this living, breathing baby with 10 little fingers and toes emerge from a single cell roughly the size of the dot at the bottom of this question mark? We thought you'd never ask.

Chromosomes and Genes

LO 4   Examine the role genes play in our development.

You are a walking, talking collection of biological building blocks called cells. But you weren't always this way. You began as a single cell. Then that cell divided into two daughter cells, and those daughter cells divided, and their daughters divided, until eventually there were trillions of cells (Sherwood, 2010).

With the exception of red blood cells, every cell in the human body has a nucleus at its center. Within this nucleus is material containing the blueprint or plan for the building of a complete person. (But as you will soon learn, these plans are easily altered by the environment.) This material is coiled tightly into 46 **chromosomes,** the inherited threadlike structures we get from our biological parents—23 from our biological mother and 23 from our biological father. A chromosome contains one molecule of **deoxyribonucleic acid (DNA).** Looking at the DNA molecule in FIG-URE 8.1, you can see a specific section along its length has been identified. This section corresponds to a **gene,** and each gene encodes a particular protein. The proteins encoded by genes determine the texture of your hair, the color of your eyes, and some aspects of your personality. Genes influence nearly every dimension of the complex living system known as YOU.

How exactly did you get your genes from your biological parents? As we mentioned above, genes are found in chromosomes, and chromosomes are what we inherit from our biological parents. (Both the sperm and egg contain 23 chromosomes, which explains why we have 23 *pairs.*) The 23rd chromosome pair, in particular, determines genetic sex (the *XX* for a female, and *XY* for a male; Chapter 10).

LO 5   Discuss how genotype and phenotype relate to development.

GENOTYPE AND PHENOTYPE   These 23 chromosome pairs are unique to you and are known as your **genotype.** Genotypes do not change in response to the environment, but they do interact with the environment. Because so much variability exists in the surrounding world, the outcome of this interaction is not predetermined.

FIGURE 8.1
Chromosomes, DNA, and Genes
Every cell in your body, except red blood cells and sex cells (sperm or egg), contains a full set of 23 chromosome pairs like those shown in the photo below. These 23 chromosome pairs contain the full blueprint for you as a complete, unique person. The primary component of each chromosome is a single, tightly wound molecule of DNA. Within that DNA are around 21,000 genes, each determining specific traits such as hair texture. CNRI/Science Source

Chromosome

Nucleus

Gene

Cell

DNA

The color and appearance of your skin, for example, result from an interplay between your genotype and a variety of environmental factors including sun and wind exposure, age, nutrition, and smoking—all of which can impact how your genes are expressed (Kolb & Whishaw, 2011; Rees, 2003). The results of this interaction are the observable characteristics of an individual, or **phenotype.** A person's phenotype is apparent in her unique physical, psychological, and behavioral characteristics (Scarr & McCartney, 1983).

You might be wondering what all this talk of genotype and phenotype has to do with psychology. Our genetic make-up influences our behavior, and psychologists are interested in learning how genes might do this. Consider schizophrenia, a psychological disorder (Chapter 13) with symptoms ranging from hallucinations to emotional problems. A large body of evidence now suggests that a person's genotype may predispose him to developing schizophrenia. Researchers report heritability rates as high as 80 to 85% (Craddock, O'Donovan, & Owen, 2005; Tandon, Keshavan, & Nasrallah, 2008). But the expression or manifestation of the disorder results from a combination of genotype and experience, including diet, stress, toxins, and early parenting (Champagn & Mashoodh, 2009; Zhang & Meaney, 2010). Identical twins, who have the same genotype, may display different phenotypes, including different expressions of schizophrenia if they both have this disorder. This is because schizophrenia, or any psychological phenomenon, results from complex relationships between genes and environment.

EPIGENETICS   We know that environmental factors influence the expression of genes, and how this occurs is the focus of **epigenetics,** a field that examines the processes involved in the development of phenotypes. As mentioned previously, the environment cannot change our genetic make-up, but it does impact the expression of our genes. For example, maternal behavior during pregnancy can determine which genes are expressed by a fetus (Masterpasqua, 2009; Petronis, 2010). In one longitudinal study following 40 pairs of identical twins, the researchers found that gene expression differed significantly between twins. As the twins grew older, their lifestyles, susceptibility to diseases, and a variety of other characteristics became less and less similar, even though their genetic make-up remained identical (Fraga et al., 2005).

DOMINANT AND RECESSIVE GENES   Genes are behind just about every human trait you can imagine—from height, to shoe size, to behavior. But remember, you possess two versions of a gene from each chromosome pair: one from your biological mother and one from your biological father. Sometimes the genes in a pair are identical (two genes encoding dimples, for instance). In other cases, the two genes differ, providing conflicting instructions about the outcome (one encodes dimples, while the other encodes no dimples). Often one gene variant has more power than the other. This **dominant gene** governs the expression of the inherited characteristic, overpowering the recessive, or subordinate, gene in the pair. A **recessive gene** cannot overcome the influence of a dominant gene. For example, "dimples" are dominant, and "no dimples" are recessive. If one gene encodes for dimples and the other no dimples, then dimples will be expressed. If both genes encode for no dimples, no dimples will be expressed.

This all sounds relatively straightforward, but it's not. Psychological traits—and the genetics behind them—are exceedingly complex. Characteristics such as intelligence and aggressive tendencies are influenced by multiple genes, most of which have yet to be identified.

CONNECTIONS

In **Chapter 7,** we described heritability as the degree to which heredity is responsible for a particular characteristic. Here, we see that around 80% to 85% of the population-wide variation in schizophrenia can be attributed to genetic make-up and 20% to the environment.

Seas of DNA
The colored lights are an artistic representation of the human genome, the complete set of DNA found in nearly every cell in the body. Researchers with the Human Genome Project have decoded the entire human genome, which contains about 21,000 DNA segments known as genes (Pennisi, 2012, September 5). Genes are the blueprints for proteins that endow you with a unique set of traits, including eye color, hair texture, and—to a certain extent—psychological characteristics. Mario Tama/Getty Images

Even if you could identify every gene associated with every trait, you would still face the daunting task of untangling the effects of heredity and environment. Take Jasmine's son Eddie, who might be described as introverted. We could try to estimate the degree to which his introversion results from something in the environment (being the youngest in a family of very outgoing people, for example). We could also search for something in his genetic background that contributes to his introversion (perhaps his father is shy, and he passed this trait along to his son). The nature–nurture issue is complex yet vital for a thorough understanding of development. Now, let's explore the biological beginnings of human development.

From Zygote to Embryo to Fetus

LO 6   Identify the progression of prenatal development.

As you may recall, Jasmine's pregnancy with Jocelyn was not particularly difficult. She "didn't feel" pregnant. But the changes occurring within her body were extraordinary. The making of a human being, from a single cell to a sensing, perceiving, aware individual, is nothing short of awesome. Let's take a look at *prenatal development*, the 38–40 weeks between conception and birth.

THE ZYGOTE   In the beginning, before you became you, an egg (also known as an *ovum*) from your biological mother and a sperm cell from your biological father came together at the moment of *conception*. Together, the egg and sperm formed a single cell called a **zygote,** which is smaller than the tip of a needle. Under normal circumstances, a zygote immediately begins to divide into two cells, then each of those cells divides, and so on. This fast-growing mass of cells begins to move through the fallopian tube toward the uterus.

Conception sometimes results in twins or multiples. Identical or **monozygotic twins** develop from one egg inseminated at conception. This egg is fertilized by one sperm and then it splits, forming separate zygotes. Monozygotic twins have identical sets of 46 chromosomes, as they originate from the same zygote; the resulting infants are the same sex and have almost identical features. Fraternal or **dizygotic twins,** on the other hand, occur when two eggs are inseminated by two different sperm, leading to the development of two zygotes. This can occur naturally, but assisted reproductive technology may increase the odds of a woman releasing more than one egg (Manninen, 2011). Twins and multiples resulting from these distinct sperm–egg combinations are like other biological siblings; they share around 50% of their genes.

GERMINAL AND EMBRYONIC PERIODS   From conception to the end of the 2nd week is the *germinal period,* during which the rapidly dividing zygote implants in the uterine wall. Between the 3rd and 8th weeks of development, the growing mass of cells is called an **embryo.** The embryo is protected in the amniotic sac and eventually receives nourishment, hydration, and oxygen through the umbilical cord, which is attached to the placenta. For the most part, the placenta ensures that the blood of the mother and the baby do not mix and disposes of carbon dioxide and waste. Until now, all the cells have been identical. But during this *embryonic*

phenotype The observable expression or characteristics of one's genetic inheritance.

epigenetics A field of study that examines the processes involved in the development of phenotypes.

dominant gene One of a pair of genes that has power over the expression of an inherited characteristic.

recessive gene One of a pair of genes that is dominated by the other gene in the pair.

zygote A single cell formed by the union of a sperm cell and egg.

monozygotic twins Identical twins who develop from one egg inseminated at conception, which then splits into two separate cells.

dizygotic twins Fraternal twins who develop from two eggs inseminated by two sperm, and are as genetically similar as any sibling pair.

embryo The unborn human from the beginning of the 3rd week of pregnancy, lasting through the 8th week of prenatal development.

Germinal period   **Embryonic period**   **Fetal period**   **Full term**

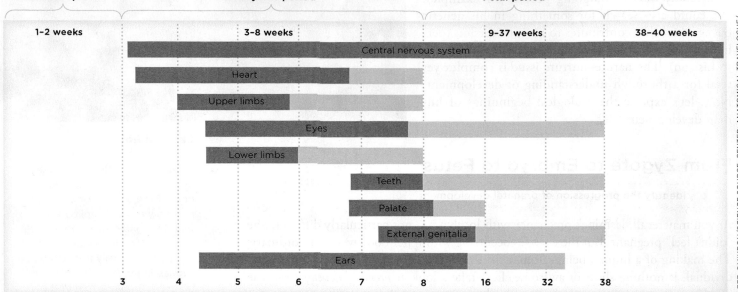

| 1–2 weeks | 3–8 weeks | 9–37 weeks | 38–40 weeks |

Central nervous system
Heart
Upper limbs
Eyes
Lower limbs
Teeth
Palate
External genitalia
Ears

3   4   5   6   7   8   16   32   38

Establishing the structure (period of higher vulnerability to defects)

Continued development of structure and function (moderately vulnerable to defects)

LEFT: OMIKRON/SCIENCE SOURCE; CENTER: ANATOMICAL TRAVELOGUE/SCIENCE SOURCE; RIGHT: NEIL BROMHALL/SCIENCE SOURCE

▲ **FIGURE 8.2**
Prenatal Development and Periods of Critical Growth
During prenatal development, individual structures form and are fine-tuned at different times. As each structure is being established, it is particularly vulnerable to alterations. Once their critical periods are complete, the structures are fully established.

period, the cells differentiate and the major organs and systems begin to form (**FIGURE 8.2**). This differentiation allows for the heart to begin to beat, arms and legs to grow, and the spinal cord and intestinal system to develop by the end of this period. But less than half of all zygotes actually implant in the uterine wall (Gold, 2005). Of reported pregnancies, around 21% end in a miscarriage (Buss et al., 2006), many of which result from genetic abnormalities of the embryo (Velagaleti & Moore, 2011).

Dad and Daughter
A father enjoys time with his 25-year-old adopted daughter. The girl has fetal alcohol syndrome, a condition that results from exposure to alcohol during fetal development. The symptoms of fetal alcohol syndrome—which can be avoided by abstaining from alcohol during pregnancy—include delays in physical growth, learning disabilities, and problems with anxiety, attention, and impulse regulation (Mayo Clinic, 2011, May 21). Stuart Wong KRT/Newscom

TERATOGENS   The embryo may be safely nestled in the amniotic sac, but it is not protected from all environmental dangers. **Teratogens** are agents that can damage a zygote, embryo, or fetus (**TABLE 8.1**). Radiation, viruses, bacteria, chemicals, and drugs are all considered teratogens. The damage depends on the agent, as well as the timing and duration of exposure, and can result in miscarriage, decreased birth weight, and heart defects. One well-known teratogen is alcohol, which can lead to *fetal alcohol spectrum disorders (FASD).* In particular, **fetal alcohol syndrome (FAS)** is the result of moderate to heavy alcohol use during pregnancy, which can cause delays in normal development, a small head, lower intelligence, and distinct facial characteristics (for example, wide-spaced eyes, flattened nose). Researchers continue to debate what constitutes an acceptable amount of alcohol use during pregnancy, but they do agree even a small amount poses risks (Nathanson, Jayesinghe, & Roycroft, 2007; O'Brien, 2007).

teratogens Environmental agents that can damage the growing zygote, embryo, or fetus.

fetal alcohol syndrome (FAS) Delays in normal development that result from moderate to heavy alcohol use during pregnancy.

fetus The unborn human from 2 months following conception to birth.

Table 8.1 THE DANGERS OF TERATOGENS	
Teratogens	**Potential Effects**
Alcohol	Fetal alcohol syndrome: developmental delay, poor growth, heart problems, growth delay
Caffeine	High exposure associated with miscarriage
Cocaine	Birth defects, miscarriage
Lead	High exposure linked with miscarriage
Lithium	Heart defects, malformations
LSD	Arm and leg defects, central nervous system problems
Mercury	Cerebral palsy, developmental delay, blindness
Nicotine	Malformations, low birth weight, cleft lip or palate, heart defects
Radiation exposure	Small skull, blindness, spina bifida, cleft palate

From conception until birth, the developing human is nestled deep inside a woman's body, but it remains vulnerable to threats from the outside. Listed here are some common teratogens and their effects.

SOURCE: BRENT (2004) AND LANGWITH (2010).

THE FETAL PERIOD   Between 2 months and birth, the growing human is called a **fetus** (Figure 8.2). During the *fetal period,* the developing person grows from the size of a pumpkin seed to a small watermelon, the average birth weight being approximately 7 pounds (by North American standards). The fetus rapidly gains weight and begins to prepare for birth, and it already has clear **sleep–wake cycles** (Suwanrath & Suntharasaj, 2010). Under normal circumstances, all organs, systems, and structures are fully developed at birth, and the brain is approximately one-quarter the weight of an adult brain (Sherwood, Subiaul, & Zawidzki, 2008).

If you step back and contemplate the baby-making phenomenon, it's really quite amazing. But many more exciting developments are in store. Are you ready for some shrieking, babbling, and a little game of peekaboo? And then perhaps some talking, toddling, and tantrums? Let's move on to infancy and childhood.

CONNECTIONS

In **Chapter 4,** we noted that the daily patterns in some of our physiological functioning roughly follow the 24-hour cycle of daylight and darkness, driven by our *circadian rhythm.* Here, we can see that even before birth, sleep–wake cycles are becoming evident.

⬤✓⬤⬤   show what you know

1. _____ are threadlike structures humans inherit from their biological mothers and fathers.
   a. Teratogens
   b. Zygotes
   c. Genes
   d. Chromosomes

2. _____ represents a complete collection of genes, and _____ represents the observed expression of inherited characteristics.

3. A co-worker tells you that she is in her 6th week of pregnancy. She is excited because she has learned that during this _____ , her baby is developing a spinal cord, its heart is beginning to beat, and its intestinal system is forming.
   a. embryonic period
   b. phenotype
   c. germinal period
   d. genotype

4. How would you describe the difference between dominant and recessive genes to someone who has never taken an introductory psychology course?

✓ CHECK YOUR ANSWERS IN APPENDIX C.

Infancy and Child Development

26 AND PREGNANT The circumstances surrounding the birth of Jasmine's second child were strikingly different from those of her first. When Eddie came into the world, Jasmine was a married, working woman with 10 more years of life experience; and a decade can make a world of difference in development. As Jasmine can testify, "The mental capacity is way different between a 16- and a 26-year-old." By this time in life, Jasmine had become much more aware of how her decisions impacted others, especially her children.

Being pregnant with Eddie was nothing like the carefree experience of carrying Jocelyn. Jasmine noticed every ache and pain, and her nausea was so severe that she lost 20 pounds during the first few months. About midway into the pregnancy, doctors put her on strict bed rest in an effort to prevent a premature delivery, but Eddie still arrived 9 weeks early. In developed countries like the United States, the *age of viability*, or the earliest point at which a baby can survive outside of the mother's womb, has dropped to 22 weeks gestational age (Lawn et al., 2011).

During the fetal stage, the digestive, respiratory, and other organ systems become fully developed. For babies born early, those systems may not be fully prepared to function. Eddie needed a breathing tube, a feeding tube, and an incubator because he could not yet control his body temperature. For a week following his delivery, Jasmine could only make contact by sticking her hands through a hole in his incubator. When she finally did get to hold Eddie, his response was breathtaking. Not only did he stop fussing and whining, he reacted with measurable physiological changes. "His vital signs went up," Jasmine says. "He breathed better on his own."

KANGAROO CARE Physical closeness can have a profound impact on parents and babies alike. Preemie mothers such as Jasmine who "kangaroo," or have close skin-to-skin contact with their babies in the hospital, report less depression and may become more attuned to their babies' needs than those who do not. Their babies in turn may have an advantage over their preterm peers in terms of cognitive and motor development (Feldman, Eidelman, Sirota, & Weller, 2002; Feldman, Weller, Sirota, & Eidelman, 2002). Premature babies who receive this type of attention also have shorter stays in the hospital and an easier time learning how to nurse (Gregson & Blacker, 2011). Touch is very important to preterm infants, which is evident in its clear link with weight gain (Field, 2001). Whether premature or full-term, there is evidence that some infants cry less and sleep better when they have plenty of skin-to-skin contact with parents, but the amount of tactile stimulation varies from culture to culture. Infant massage is unheard of in some parts of the world, but is a daily practice in India, Bangladesh, and China (Underdown, Barlow, & Stewart-Brown, 2010).

Kangarooing
Jasmine "kangaroos" with her son Eddie in the neonatal intensive care unit. Kangarooing, or holding a premature baby to facilitate skin-to-skin contact, benefits both babies and parents. Some researchers have found that preemies who were kangarooed later performed better on tests of cognitive and motor skills than those kept in incubators (Feldman et al., 2002).
Jasmine Mitchell

Newborn Growth and Development

LO 7   Summarize some developmental changes that occur in infancy.

Newborn babies exhibit several *reflexes,* or unlearned patterns of behavior. Some are necessary for survival; others do not serve any obvious purpose. A few fade away in the first weeks and months of life, but many will resurface as voluntary movements as the infant grows and develops motor control (Thelen & Fisher, 1982). Let's take a look at two of these reflexes.

ROOTING AND SUCKING REFLEXES   What does a newborn do when you stroke its cheek? She opens her mouth and turns her head in the direction of your finger, apparently in search of a nipple. This *rooting reflex* typically disappears at 4 months, never to be seen again. The *sucking reflex,* evident when you touch her lips, also appears to be a feeding reflex. Sucking and swallowing abilities don't fully mature until the gestational age of 33 to 36 weeks, so babies who are born before that time—like Jasmine's son Eddie—may struggle with feeding (Lee et al., 2011). But that doesn't mean they cannot enjoy the benefits of breast milk, which is thought to have important effects on growth and cognitive development (Chaimay, 2011; de Lauzon-Guillain et al., 2012; Horwood & Fergusson, 1998). Jasmine pumped her breast milk, making it possible for Eddie to get its nutritional benefits through his feeding tube.

A newborn spends most of its time eating, sleeping, and crying. Sounds like a simple routine, but waking every 2 to 3 hours to feed a wailing baby can be very exhausting. Nevertheless, this stage soon gives way to a period of change that is far more interactive, and includes waving, clapping, walking, and dangerous furniture climbing. **INFOGRAPHIC 8.2** on page 346 details some of the sensory and motor milestones of infancy. Keep in mind that the listed ages are averages; significant variation does exist across infants. The general sequence and timing, however, are fairly universal.

THE NEWBORN SENSES   Babies come into the world equipped with keen sensory capabilities that seem to be designed for facilitating relationships. For example, infants prefer to look at human faces as opposed to geometric shapes (Salva, Farroni, Regolin, Vallortigara, & Johnson, 2011). They can discriminate their mother's voice from those of other women within hours of birth, and they show a preference for her voice (DeCasper & Fifer, 1980). Jocelyn emerged from the womb crying but calmed down instantly when placed in Jasmine's arms. It was as if she already knew the sound of her mother speaking and singing. And she very well might have; studies suggest that babies do indeed come to recognize their mothers' voices while in the womb (Kisilevsky et al., 2003; Sai, 2005). Hearing is developed and functioning before a baby is born, but sounds are initially distorted. It takes some time for amniotic fluid to dry up completely before a baby can hear clearly (Hall, Smith, & Popelka, 2004).

Smell, taste, and touch are also well developed in newborn infants. These tiny babies can distinguish the smell of their own mothers' breast milk from that of other women within days of birth (Nishitani et al., 2009). Babies prefer sweet tastes, react strongly to sour tastes, and notice certain changes to their mothers' diets because those tastes are present in breast milk. If a mother eats something very sweet, for instance, the infant tends to breast-feed longer.

The sense of touch is evident before birth; as early as 2 months after conception, for example, a fetus will show the rooting reflex. It was once believed that newborns were incapable of experiencing pain. But research suggests otherwise. Newborns respond to pain with reactions similar to those of older infants, children, and adults (Gradin & Eriksson, 2011; Urso, 2007).

Sight is the weakest sense in newborns, who have difficulty seeing things that are not in their immediate vicinity. The optimal distance for a newborn to see an object is approximately 8–14 inches away from his face (Cavallini et al., 2002), which happens to be the approximate distance between the face of a nursing baby and his mother. Eye contact is thought to strengthen the relationship between mother and baby. A newborn's vision can be blurry for several months, one reason being that the **light-sensitive cones** in the back of the eye are still developing (Banks & Salapatek, 1978).

THE GROWING BRAIN   The speed of brain development in the womb and immediately after birth is astounding. There are times in fetal development when the brain

CONNECTIONS

In **Chapter 3,** we reported that cones are specialized neurons called *photoreceptors,* which absorb light energy and turn it into chemical and electrical signals for the brain to process. Cones enable us to see colors and details. Newborns have blurry eyesight in part because their cones have not fully developed.

Infant Brain and Sensorimotor Development

As newborns grow, they progress at an astounding rate in seen and unseen ways. When witnessing babies' new skills, whether it be reaching for a rattle or pulling themselves into a standing position, it's easy to marvel at how far they have come. But what you can't see is the real action. These sensorimotor advancements are only possible because of the incredible brain development happening in the background.

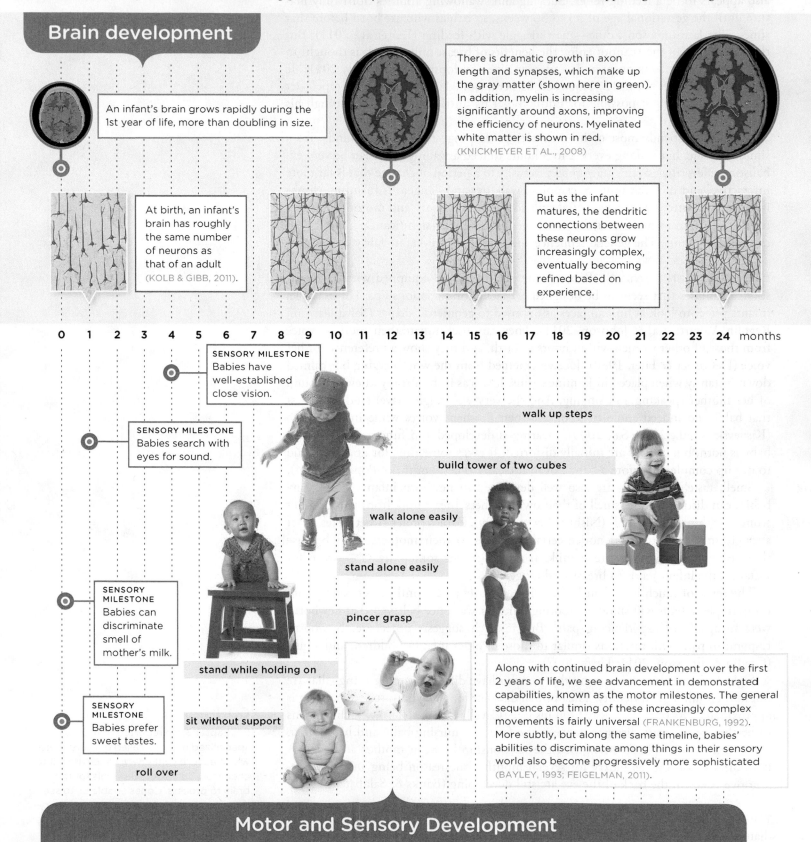

Brain development

An infant's brain grows rapidly during the 1st year of life, more than doubling in size.

There is dramatic growth in axon length and synapses, which make up the gray matter (shown here in green). In addition, myelin is increasing significantly around axons, improving the efficiency of neurons. Myelinated white matter is shown in red. (KNICKMEYER ET AL., 2008)

At birth, an infant's brain has roughly the same number of neurons as that of an adult (KOLB & GIBB, 2011).

But as the infant matures, the dendritic connections between these neurons grow increasingly complex, eventually becoming refined based on experience.

0 1 2 3 4 5 6 7 8 9 10 11 12 13 14 15 16 17 18 19 20 21 22 23 24 months

SENSORY MILESTONE
Babies have well-established close vision.

SENSORY MILESTONE
Babies search with eyes for sound.

SENSORY MILESTONE
Babies can discriminate smell of mother's milk.

SENSORY MILESTONE
Babies prefer sweet tastes.

walk up steps

build tower of two cubes

walk alone easily

stand alone easily

pincer grasp

stand while holding on

sit without support

roll over

Along with continued brain development over the first 2 years of life, we see advancement in demonstrated capabilities, known as the motor milestones. The general sequence and timing of these increasingly complex movements is fairly universal (FRANKENBURG, 1992). More subtly, but along the same timeline, babies' abilities to discriminate among things in their sensory world also become progressively more sophisticated (BAYLEY, 1993; FEIGELMAN, 2011).

Motor and Sensory Development

Credits: Brain Scans, Figure 1 from: Knickmeyer, R. C.; Gouttard, S.; Kang, C.; Evans, D.; Wilber, J.; Smith, K.; Hamer, R. M.; Lin, W.; Gerig, G.; & Gilmore, J. H. (2008). A structural MRI study of human brain development from birth to 2 years. The Journal of Neuroscience, (28)47, 12176-12182; Real People: Black African American Toddler Boy Orange Hat Galoshes Thinkstock; Small child, Jaroslaw Wojcik/Getty Images; Baby boy (12-15 months) close-up, portrait, Photodisc/Getty Images; Baby boy eating, © sanapadh/Alamy; Baby learning to stand assisted by a stoll, Aseph/Shutterstock; Little boy playing with colorful cubes, Sergiy Bykhunenko/Shutterstock is producing some 250,000 new neurons per minute! The creation of *new* neurons is mostly complete by the end of the 5th month of fetal development (Kolb & Gibb, 2011). At the time of birth, a baby's brain has approximately 100 billion neurons (Toga, Thompson, & Sowell, 2006)—roughly the same number as that of an adult. Meanwhile, **axons** are growing longer, and more neurons—particularly those involved in motor control—are developing a myelin sheath around their axons. The myelin sheath increases the efficiency of neural communication, which leads to better motor control, enabling a baby to reach the milestones described earlier (waving, walking, and so forth).

SYNAPTIC PRUNING   Neurons rapidly sprout new connections among each other, a dramatic phase of synaptic growth that is influenced by the infant's experiences and stimulation from the environment. The increase in connections is not uniform throughout the brain. Between the ages of 3 and 6, for example, the greatest increase in neural connections occurs in the frontal lobes, the area of the brain involved in planning and attention (Thompson et al., 2000; Toga et al., 2006). As more links are established, more associations can be made between different stimuli, and between behavior and consequences. A young person needs to learn quickly, and this process makes it possible.

However, the extraordinary growth in synaptic connections does not last forever, as their number decreases by 40 to 50% by the time a child reaches puberty (Thompson et al., 2000; Webb, Monk, & Nelson, 2001). In a process known as *synaptic pruning,* unused synaptic connections are downsized or eliminated (Chechik, Meilijson, & Ruppin, 1998).

ROSENZWEIG'S RATS   Synaptic pruning and other aspects of brain development are strongly influenced by experiences and input from the outside world. In the 1960s and 1970s, Mark Rosenzweig and his colleagues at the University of California, Berkeley, demonstrated how much environment can influence the development of animal brains (Kolb & Whishaw, 1998). In one study, the researchers placed young rats in three different settings: (1) enriched environments, or cages with other rats and a variety of toys and interesting objects; (2) standard colony cages, which contained no stimulating objects; and (3) isolation cages with no playthings or companions (Barredo & Deeg, 2009, February 24; Rosenzweig, 1984). Rats reared in the enriched condition experienced greater increases in brain weight and synaptic connections compared to rats in the nonstimulating environments (Kolb & Whishaw, 1998).

CONNECTIONS

In **Chapter 2,** we described the structure of a typical neuron, which includes an axon projecting from the cell body. Many axons are surrounded by a myelin sheath, which is a fatty substance that insulates the axon. This insulation allows for faster communication within and between neurons. Here we see how this impacts motor development.

Stimulate the Brain
A kindergarten teacher leads students through dance movements (left) in what appears to be an enriched environment. Opportunities for physical exercise, social interaction, and other types of stimulating activity characterize enriched environments, which promote positive changes in the brain (van Praag, Kempermann, & Gage, 2000). Fewer signs of enrichment appear in the photo on the right, which shows another teacher with her class of preschoolers in a sparse room without books or even furniture. left: Goh Chai Hin/ Afp/Getty Images. right: © Robert Van Der Hilst/Corbis

try this

Check your answers in Appendix C.

Identify the independent and dependent variables in the Rosenzweig study that examined the changes in brain development associated with three living conditions.

How does this research on lab rats relate to human development? Isolation and lack of stimulation may also put a damper on the brain development of infants and children. Some research suggests that orphanage-raised babies who have received minimal care and human interaction experience delays in cognitive, social, and physical development. There is, however, a great deal of variability in later development when the children are placed in adoptive homes (Rutter & O'Connor, 2004).

The Language Explosion

The brain development that occurs during childhood and the cognitive changes associated with it are critical. Consider the fact that babies come into the world incapable of using language, yet by the age of 6, most have amassed a vocabulary of about 13,000 words (Pinker, 1994). The development of **language** is a remarkable feat. Let's take a look at some of the theories that attempt to explain it.

CONNECTIONS

In **Chapter 7,** we introduced the basic elements of language, such as phonemes, morphemes, and semantics. We also introduced some basic theories of language development. In this chapter, we discuss how language develops in humans.

Chapter 5 presented the principles of learning. Here, we see how *operant conditioning,* through reinforcement and punishment, and *observational learning,* through modeling, can be used to understand how language is acquired.

LO 8   Describe the theories explaining language acquisition.

BEHAVIORISM AND LANGUAGE   Behaviorists propose that all behavior—including the use of language—is learned through associations, reinforcers, and observation. Infants and children learn language in the same way they **learn** everything else, through positive attention to correct behavior (for example, praising correct speech), unpleasant attention to incorrect behavior (for example, criticizing incorrect speech), and the observation of others.

LANGUAGE ACQUISITION DEVICE   But the behaviorist theory may not explain all the complexities of language acquisition. If a young child tries to imitate a particular sentence structure, such as "I am going to the kitchen," he might instead say something grammatically incorrect, "I go kitchen." Children are not directly taught the structure of grammar, because its rules are too difficult for their developing brains to understand. Linguist Noam Chomsky (1959) suggested humans have a language acquisition device (LAD) that provides an innate mechanism for learning language. With the LAD, children compare the language they hear in their environment to a framework already hardwired in their brains. The fact that children all over the world seem to learn language in a fixed sequence, and during approximately the same sensitive period, is evidence that this innate language capacity may exist.

Synonym
infant-directed speech motherese

cooing Production of vowel-like sounds by infants, often repeated in a joyful manner.
babbling The combining of consonants with vowels typically displayed at the age of 4 to 6 months.
telegraphic speech Two-word phrases typically used by infants around the age of 18 months.

INFANT-DIRECTED SPEECH (IDS)   More recent theories of language acquisition focus on parents' and other caregivers' use of *infant-directed speech* (IDS). High-pitched and repetitive, IDS is observed throughout the world (Singh, Nestor, Parikh, & Yull, 2009). Can't you just hear Jasmine saying to baby Jocelyn in a high-pitched, sing-song voice, "Who's my little girl?" Researchers report that infants as young as 5 months old pay more attention to people who use IDS, which allows them to choose "appropriate social partners," or adults who are more likely to provide them with chances to learn and interact (Schachner & Hannon, 2011).

LANGUAGE IN THE ENVIRONMENT   It's not only the type of voice that matters but also the amount of talking. Infants may not be the best conversation partners, but they benefit from a lot of chatter. It turns out that the amount of language spoken in the home correlates with socioeconomic status. Children from high-income families are more likely to have parents who engage them in conversation. Just look at these numbers for parents of toddlers: 35 words a minute spoken by high-income parents; 20 words a minute spoken by middle-income parents; 10 words a minute spoken by low-income parents (Hoff, 2003). The consequences of such interactions are apparent, with toddlers from high-income households having an average vocabulary of 766 words, and those from low-income homes only 357 (Hart & Risley, 1995). How might this disparity impact these same children when they start school? Research suggests that children from lower socioeconomic households begin school already lagging behind in reading, math, and academic achievement in general (Lee & Burkan, 2002), all skills that could potentially be linked to decreased verbal interactions.

LO 9   Examine the universal sequence of language development.

THE SEQUENCE OF ACQUISITION   Coo. Babble. Talk. No matter what language infants speak, or who raises them, you can almost be certain they will follow the universal sequence of language development (Chomsky, 2000). At the age of 2 to 3 months, infants typically start to produce vowel-like sounds known as **cooing.** These "oooo" and "ahhh" sounds are often repeated in a joyful manner. Jasmine's children tended to coo in response to specific stimuli. For Jocelyn, it was the sound of people talking; for Eddie, the appearance of colorful images.

When infants reach the age of 4 to 6 months, they begin to combine consonants and vowels in the **babbling** stage. These sounds are meaningless, but babbling can resemble real language ("ma, ma, ma, ma, ma" *Did you say . . . mama?*). Jasmine distinctly remembers Jocelyn as a tiny infant repeating "da, da, da, da," as if she were saying "Dadda" over and over. Amused by the irony of the situation (Jasmine was a single mother), she would put her face close to Jocelyn's and repeatedly say, "ma, ma, ma, ma." Eventually, Jocelyn did say the word "mama," but it took several months. Nonhearing infants also go through this babbling stage, but they move their hands instead of babbling aloud (Petitto & Marentette, 1991). For both hearing and deaf infants, the babbling stage becomes an important foundation for speech production; when infants babble, they are on their way to their first words.

When do real words begin? At around 12 months, infants typically begin to utter their magical first words. Often, these are nouns used to convey an entire message, or *holophrase.* Perhaps you have heard an infant say something emphatically, such as "JUICE!" or "UP!" What she might be trying to say is "I am thirsty, could I please have some juice?" or "I want you to pick me up."

At about 18 months, infants start to use two-word phrases in their **telegraphic speech.** These brief statements might include only the most important words of a sentence, such as nouns, verbs, and adjectives, but no prepositions or articles. "Baby crying" might be a telegraphic sentence meaning the baby at the next table is crying loudly. Jocelyn's first two-word phrase was "Stop it!" Jasmine suspects that she was the one who schooled her daughter in this phrase. As a teenage mom, she had not yet developed the patience that she would have in her twenties and thirties.

As children mature, they start to use more complete sentences. Their grammar becomes more complex and they pack more words into statements. A "vocabulary

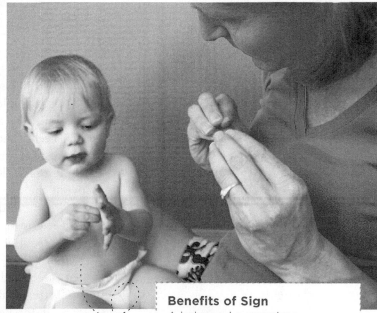

Benefits of Sign
A baby and a caregiver communicate with sign language. Introducing sign to children as young as 6 months may help them communicate before they use verbal speech (Doherty-Sneddon, 2008). Early use of sign may also provide a verbal advantage down the road when they enter elementary school (Barnes, 2010). © Pop! Studio Photography/www.alamy.com/Corbis

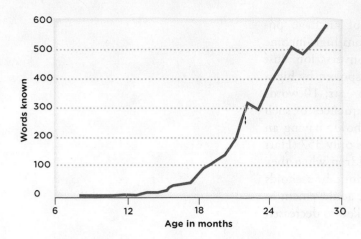

▲ **FIGURE 8.3**

The Vocabulary Explosion

Around the 2nd year of life, the rate at which a child learns new words begins to increase dramatically. *Source:* Reprinted by permission of the authors from Mitchell and McMurray (2008).

explosion" tends to occur around 2 to 3 years of age (McMurray, 2007; FIGURE 8.3). By 5 to 6, most children are fluent in their native language, although their vocabulary does not match that of an adult.

There are two important components of normal language development: (1) physical development, particularly in the language-processing areas of the brain (Chapter 2); and (2) exposure to language. If a child does not observe people using language during the first several years of life, normal language skills will not develop. Evidence for this phenomenon comes from case studies of people who have suffered damage to the brain after the critical period or were deprived of language in childhood (Goldin-Meadow, 1978). One of the most well-documented—and deeply troubling—cases of childhood deprivation centers on a young girl known as Genie.

THINK again

Genie the "Feral Child"

In 1970 a social worker in Arcadia, California, discovered a most horrifying case of child neglect and abuse. "Genie," as researchers came to call her, was 13 at the time her situation came to the attention of the authorities, though she barely looked 7. Feeble and emaciated, the child could not even stand on two feet. Genie was neither potty-trained nor capable of chewing food. She could not even speak (Curtiss, Fromkin, Krashen, Rigler, & Rigler, 1974; PBS, 1997, March 4).

Between the ages of 20 months and 13 years, Genie had been locked away in a dark room, strapped to a potty chair or confined in a cagelike crib. Her father beat her when she made any type of noise. There, Genie stayed for 12 years, alone in silence, deprived of physical activity, sensory stimulation, and affection (Curtiss et al., 1974).

When discovered and brought to a hospital at age 13, Genie would not utter a sound (Curtiss et al., 1974). She did seem to understand simple words, but that was about it for her language comprehension. Researchers tried to build Genie's vocabulary, teaching her basic principles of syntax, and she made considerable gains, eventually speaking meaningful sentences. But some aspects of language, such as the ability to use the passive tense ("The carrot was given to the rabbit") or words such as "what" and "which" continued to mystify her (Goldin-Meadow, 1978). Why couldn't Genie master certain linguistic skills? Was it because she missed a critical period for language development?

This is a real possibility. Similar outcomes have been observed in other "feral" children. Consider the example of 6-year-old Danielle Crockett of Florida, who was discovered living among cockroaches and excrement in her mother's closet in 2005. Danielle was removed from that home and later adopted by a loving family,

AT AGE 13, GENIE COULD NOT EVEN SPEAK.

but her speech therapist is not sure she will ever develop the ability to speak (DeGregory, 2008). There are other variables to consider in the Genie case, like the possibility that she may have suffered from an underlying intellectual disability, or that she never developed the throat muscles required for normal speech (Curtiss et al., 1974; James, 2008, May 7). We should note that Genie's story does end with a glimmer of hope. Genie is reported to be "happy," living in a group home for adults with intellectual disabilities (James, 2008, May 7). ●+

Piaget and Cognitive Development: Blossoming of a Young Mind

LO 10 Summarize the constructs of Piaget's theory of cognitive development.

Language is just one domain of cognitive development. How do other processes like memory and problem solving evolve through childhood? As noted earlier, psychologists do not always agree on whether development is continuous or occurs in steps. Swiss biologist and developmental psychologist Jean Piaget (pyä-'zhā; 1896–1980) was among the first to suggest that infants have cognitive abilities, a notion that was not widely embraced at the time. Children do not think like adults, suggested Piaget, and their cognitive development takes place in stages.

One of the basic units of cognition, according to Piaget (1936/1952), is the **schema,** a collection of ideas or notions representing a basic unit of understanding. Young children form schemas based on functional relationships. The schema "toy," for example, might include any object that can be played with (such as dolls, trucks, and balls). As children mature, so do their schemas, which begin to organize and structure their thinking around more abstract categories, such as "love" (romantic love, love for one's country, and so on). As they grow, children expand their schemas in response to life experiences and interactions with the environment.

Piaget (1936/1952) believed humans are biologically driven to advance in intellectual development, partly as a result of an innate need to maintain *cognitive equilibrium,* or a feeling of mental or cognitive balance. Suppose a kindergartener's schema of airplane pilots includes only men, but then he sees a female pilot on television. This experience shakes up his notion of who can be a pilot, causing an uncomfortable sense of *disequilibrium* that motivates him to restore cognitive balance. There are two ways he might accomplish this. He could use **assimilation,** an attempt to understand new information using his already existing knowledge base, or schema. For example, the young boy might think about the female bus drivers he has seen and connect that to the female pilot idea (*Women drive buses, so maybe they can fly planes too*). However, if the new information is so disconcerting that it cannot be assimilated, he might use **accommodation,** a restructuring of old notions to make a place for new information. With accommodation, we remodel old schemas or create new ones. If the child had never seen a female driving anything other than a car, he might become confused at the sight of a female pilot. To eliminate that confusion, he could create a new schema. This is how we make great strides in cognitive growth. We assimilate information to fit new experiences into our old ways of thinking, and we accommodate our old way of thinking to understand new information.

Piaget (1936/1952) also proposed that cognitive development occurs in four periods or stages, and these stages have distinct beginnings and endings (**INFOGRAPHIC 8.3** on page 353).

SENSORIMOTOR STAGE   From birth to about 2 years old is the **sensorimotor stage.** Infants use their sensory abilities and motor activities (such as reaching, crawling, and handling things) to learn about the surrounding world, exploring objects with their mouths, fingers, and toes. It's a nerve-racking process for parents ("Please do *not* put that shoe in your mouth!"), but an important part of cognitive development.

One significant milestone of the sensorimotor stage is **object permanence,** or an infant's realization that objects and people still exist when they are out of sight or

At Play with Piaget
Developmental psychologist Jean Piaget (center) works with students in a New York City classroom. Piaget's research focused on school-age children, including his own three, who became participants in some of his studies. Children think differently from adults, Piaget proposed, and they experience cognitive development in distinct stages. Bill Anderson/Science Source

schema A collection of ideas that represents a basic unit of understanding.

assimilation Using existing information and ideas to understand new knowledge and experiences.

accommodation A restructuring of old ideas to make a place for new information.

sensorimotor stage Piaget's stage of cognitive development during which infants use their sensory capabilities and motor skills to learn about the surrounding world.

object permanence A milestone of the sensorimotor stage of cognitive development; an infant's realization that objects and people still exist even when out of sight or touch.

touch. Have you ever watched a young infant play peekaboo? Her surprise when your face appears from behind your hands indicates that to a certain extent she forgot you were there when your face was hidden. Jasmine tried to play peekaboo with Eddie when he was a baby, but he had a mixed reaction to the game, crying when she hid her face behind a blanket and laughing as soon as she pulled it away. Eddie's fear of his mother's disappearance and surprise at her reappearance didn't last; he learned about object permanence.

PREOPERATIONAL STAGE   The next stage in cognitive development is the **preoperational stage,** which applies to children from 2 to 7 years old. During this time, children start using language to explore and understand their worlds (rather than relying primarily on sensory and motor activities). In this stage, children ask questions and use symbolic thinking. They may, for example, use words and images to refer to concepts. This is a time for pretending and magical thinking. Eddie, who is in this stage right now, likes to pretend he is Harry Potter. He drives Jasmine and Jocelyn crazy, racing around the house with a wand. Children in this phase are somewhat limited by their **egocentrism.** They can only imagine the world around them from their own perspective, and they have a hard time putting themselves in someone else's shoes (see the Three Mountains task in Infographic 8.3). "Eddie is going through that 'world stops when I say so' phase right now," Jasmine explains. He expects everyone around him to stop and listen to what he is saying. If he gets the attention he desires, all is well; if not, a screaming fit may ensue. According to Piaget (1936/1952), children in this stage have not yet mastered *operations* (hence, it is called the *preoperational* stage), which are the logical reasoning processes that older children and adults use to understand the world. For example, these children have a difficult time understanding the *reversibility* of some actions or events. They may have trouble comprehending that vanilla ice cream can be refrozen after it melts, but not turned back into sugar, milk, and vanilla.

The fact that children in this stage have not yet mastered operations is also apparent in their errors concerning the concept of **conservation,** which refers to the unchanging properties of volume, mass, or amount in relation to appearance (**FIGURE 8.4** on page 354). For example, if you take two masses of clay of the same shape and size, and then roll only one of them out into a hotdog shape, a child at this age will think that the longer-shaped clay is now made up of more clay than the undisturbed clump of clay. Even though she watched you take the clump of clay and roll it, without adding anything, she sees that the clump is longer and assumes it is made up of more clay. Or, the child may look at the newly formed clump of clay and see that it is skinnier, and therefore assume it is smaller. Why is this so? Children at this age generally focus on only one characteristic of an object. They do not understand the logical reasoning behind conservation or how the object stays fundamentally the same, even if it is manipulated or takes on a different appearance.

CONCRETE OPERATIONAL STAGE   Around age 7, children enter what Piaget called the **concrete operational stage.** They begin to think more logically, but mainly in reference to concrete objects and circumstances: things that can be seen or touched, or are well defined by strict rules. Children in this stage tend to be less egocentric and can understand the concept of conservation. However, their logical thinking is limited to concrete concepts; thus, they still have trouble with abstract concepts. Around age 8 or 9, Jocelyn tended to take everything literally. Once she asked to go outside when it was pouring rain, and Jasmine replied, "Are you crazy?

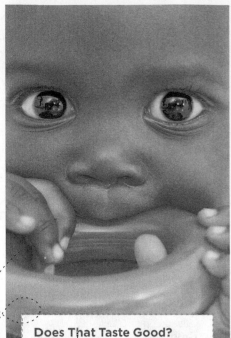

Does That Taste Good?
Babies are notorious for putting just about everything, including toys, shoes, and sand, in their mouths. Mouthing is one of the main ways babies experience their worlds, and it is an important aspect of cognitive development. It also provides exposure to viruses and other environmental pathogens, which helps prepare the developing immune system to fight infections (Fessler & Abrams, 2004). Elie Bernager/Getty Images

preoperational stage Piaget's stage of cognitive development during which children can start to use language to explore and understand their worlds.

egocentrism Being able to imagine the world only from one's own perspective.

conservation Refers to the unchanging properties of volume, mass, or amount in relation to appearance.

concrete operational stage Piaget's stage of cognitive development during which children begin to think more logically, but mainly in reference to concrete objects and circumstances.

Piaget's Theory of Cognitive Development

Jean Piaget proposed that children's cognitive development occurs in stages characterized by particular cognitive abilities. These stages have distinct beginnings and endings.

Formal Operational
Child is now able to think logically and systematically and is capable of hypothetical thinking.

Concrete Operational
Child understands operations and thinks more logically in reference to concrete objects and circumstances.

Preoperational
Child uses symbolic thinking to explore and understand the world. Children at this stage are known for magical thinking and egocentrism.

Sensorimotor
Child uses sensory capabilities and motor activities to learn about the world; develops object permanence.

Formal Operational
11 yrs and up

Concrete Operational
7–11 yrs

Preoperational
2–7 yrs

Sensorimotor
birth–2 yrs

Piaget's four stages of cognitive development

How do we assess a child's stage of cognitive development?

Piaget developed techniques to test characteristic capabilities associated with each stage.

Object permanence test: Does the child realize objects continue to exist when they are hidden? Infants who have developed object permanence will search for an object.

Three Mountains task tests egocentrism. Can the child imagine a perspective different than her own? "What would you see if you were standing at Point B?"

Conservation of Volume test assesses understanding of operations. Does a child understand that the amount of liquid remains constant when it is poured into a container with a different shape?

Third Eye task tests formal operational thought. "If you had a third eye, where would you put it?" Children at this stage come up with logical, innovative answers.

FIGURE 8.4

Conservation Tasks
Children in the preoperational stage don't realize that properties like volume and mass stay constant when items are only rearranged or reshaped. Tasks like those outlined here are used to test children's understanding of the concept of conservation.

Type of Conservation Task	Original Presentation	Alteration	Question	Preoperational Child's Answer
Volume	Two equal beakers of liquid	Pour one into a taller, narrower beaker.	Does one beaker have more liquid?	The taller beaker has more liquid.
Mass	Two equal lumps of clay	Roll one lump into a long, hotdog shape.	Does one lump weigh more?	The original lump weighs more.
Length	Two equal lengths of rope	Move one rope.	Is one rope longer?	The top rope is longer.
Number	Two equal lines of buttons	Increase amount of space between buttons in one line.	Does one line have more buttons?	The longer line has more buttons.

It's raining cats and dogs!" Jocelyn became distressed and cried, "The poor little kitties are gonna get hurt when they fall from the sky!" Children in this stage also have trouble thinking hypothetically. A 7-year-old may respond with a blank stare if you ask her a "what if?" type of question. (*If you were able to travel to the future, what kind of animals would your great grandchildren see in the wild?*)

FORMAL OPERATIONAL STAGE At age 11, children enter the **formal operational stage;** they begin to think more logically and more systematically than younger children. They can solve problems such as those in the Third Eye task in Infographic 8.3. This activity asks a child where she would put a third eye, and why. (*I'd put it in the back of my head so that I could see what is going on behind my back.*) These types of capabilities do not necessarily develop overnight, and logical abilities are likely to advance in relation to interests and skills developed in a work setting. Piaget suggested that not everyone reaches this stage of formal operations. But to succeed in most colleges, this type of logical thinking is essential; students need to think critically and use abstract concepts to solve problems.

THE CRITICS Critics of Piaget suggest that although cognitive development might occur in stages with distinct characteristics, the transitions from one stage to the next are likely to be gradual, and do not necessarily represent a complete leap from one type of thinking to the next. Some believe Piaget's theory underestimates children's cognitive abilities. For example, some researchers have found that object permanence occurs sooner than suggested by Piaget (Baillargeon, Spelke, & Wasserman, 1985). Others have questioned Piaget's assertion that the formal operational stage is reached by 11 to 12 years of age, and that no further delineations can be made between the cognitive abilities of adolescents and adults of various ages.

formal operational stage Piaget's stage of cognitive development during which children begin to think more logically and systematically.

scaffolding Pushing children to go just beyond what they are competent and comfortable doing, while providing help in a decreasing manner.

One solution is to consider stages beyond Piaget's original formulation, that is, to account for cognitive changes occurring in adulthood.

Vygotsky and Cognitive Development

····▶ **LO 11** List the key elements of Vygotsky's theory of cognitive development.

One other major criticism of Piaget's work is that it does not take into consideration the social interactions that influence the developing child. Russian psychologist Lev Vygotsky (vī-'gät-skē; 1896–1934) was particularly interested in how social and cultural factors affect a child's cognitive development (Vygotsky, 1934/1962).

What are some of the social factors that influence cognitive development? Children are like apprentices in relation to others who are more capable and experienced (Zaretskii, 2009). Those children who receive help from older children and adults progress more quickly in their cognitive abilities. For example, when parents help their children solve puzzles by providing support for them to succeed on their own, the children show advancement in goal-directed behavior and the ability to plan ahead (Bernier, Carlson, & Whipple, 2010; Hammond, Müller, Carpendale, Bibok, & Liebermann-Finestone, 2012).

One way we can support children's cognitive development is through **scaffolding:** pushing them to go just beyond what they are competent and comfortable doing, but also providing help in a decreasing manner. We should offer guidance and examples to a greater degree at the beginning of the learning process, but give less help as the child becomes more skilled in a particular arena. A parent or caregiver provides support when necessary, but allows a child to solve problems independently: "Successful scaffolding is like a wave, rising to offer help when needed and receding as the child regains control of the task" (Hammond et al., 2012, p. 275).

Vygotsky also emphasized that learning always occurs within the context of a child's culture. Children across the world have different sets of expected learning outcomes, from raising sheep to weaving blankets to playing basketball. We need to keep these cross-cultural differences in mind when exploring cognitive development in children.

Culture and Cognition
A man and a boy work together threshing rice in the fields of Madagascar. What this child learns and how his cognitive development unfolds are shaped by the circumstances of his environment. Children reared in agricultural societies may not acquire the same cognitive skill set as those raised in urban, industrialized settings. © Yvan Travert/Photononstop/Corbis

SOME THINGS NEVER CHANGE Jocelyn and Eddie have very different personalities, and their unique characteristics began to surface early in their development. Jocelyn has always been easygoing and mild-mannered. As an infant, she would cry and fuss as infants do, but her discontent could usually be traced to a clear cause (for example, she was hungry or tired). Eddie was more apt to cry for no obvious reason; he was more difficult to please; and Jasmine describes him as having had a "hot" temper.

Jocelyn was a social butterfly from the start. As an infant, she would perk up on hearing a voice or spotting a person's face, and she began to talk at an early age. Baby Eddie was not such a "people person." He was more entranced by the bright colors and shapes he saw on TV programs for infants and toddlers. He also began to talk and walk considerably later than Jocelyn. But as his pediatrician said, these developmental discrepancies probably had a lot to do with gender (boys tend to lag behind girls in language and motor skills) and the fact that Eddie was born 2½ months early.

Many of Jocelyn's and Eddie's personality traits remained stable through toddlerhood. Both children started day care around the age of 2, but their adjustments to this change in routine were starkly different. Jocelyn, always very social, never cried after being dropped off. Eddie, the more introverted sibling, cried every day for 3 or 4 months. Why he had such a hard time saying goodbye is unclear, but there are probably many reasons. Perhaps he preferred the quiet solitude of home to the bustling environment of the childcare center, or maybe it had something to do with the fact that his parents were separating at the time. Eddie was experiencing *separation anxiety,* and we usually see this peak at approximately 13 months (Hertenstein & McCullough, 2005). Eddie has now been in day care or school for 3 years and has no problem being away from home. Any delays in language or motor development he experienced as a result of prematurity have long since vanished. "Now," says Jasmine, "he is 5 going on 15, mentally and physically."

Temperament and Attachment

Until now, we have mostly discussed physical and cognitive development, but recall we are also interested in *socioemotional* development. When thinking about Jocelyn and Eddie, it is important to consider their relationships, emotional processes, and personality characteristics.

TEMPERAMENT   From birth, infants display characteristic differences in their behavioral patterns and emotional reactions, that is, their **temperament.** Some babies and toddlers can be categorized as having an exuberant temperament, showing an overall positive attitude and sociability (Degnan et al., 2011). "High-reactive" infants exhibit a great deal of distress when exposed to unfamiliar stimuli, such as new sights, sounds, and smells. "Low-reactive" infants do not respond to new stimuli with great distress (Kagan, 2003). Classification as high- and low-reactive is based on measures of behavior, emotional response, and physiology (such as heart rate and blood pressure; Kagan, 1985, 2003).

These different characteristics seem to be innate, as they are evident from birth and consistent in the infants' daily lives. There is also evidence that some of these characteristics remain fairly stable throughout life (Kagan & Snidman, 1991). However, the environment can influence temperament (Caspi, Roberts, & Shiner, 2005). Factors such as maternal education, neighborhood, and paternal occupation through adolescence can predict characteristics of adult temperament (such as persistence, shyness, and impulsiveness; Congdon et al., 2012).

EASY, DIFFICULT, OR SLOW TO WARM UP   Researchers have shown that the majority of infants can be classified as having one of three fundamental temperaments (Thomas & Chess, 1986). Around 40% are considered "easy" babies; they are easy to care for because they follow regular eating and sleeping schedules. These happy babies can be soothed when upset and don't appear to get rattled by transitions or changes in their environments. Jasmine would put Jocelyn in this category. Baby Jocelyn's crying and fussiness were usually for obvious reasons (she was exhausted or thirsty), and she settled down when the problem was resolved.

"Difficult" babies (around 10%) are more challenging because they don't seem to have a set schedule for eating and sleeping. And they don't deal well with transitions or changes in the

Easy, Baby
Most babies can be classified according to one of three fundamental temperaments: about 40% are "easy," meaning they are generally content and follow predictable schedules; approximately 10% are "difficult," or hard to please and irregular in their schedules; and another 15% are "slow to warm up," meaning they struggle with change but eventually adjust. The remaining 35% do not fall into any one category. JGI/Jamie Grill/Getty Images

environment. Difficult babies are often irritable and unhappy, and compared to easy babies, they are far less responsive to the soothing attempts of caregivers. They also tend to be very active, kicking their legs on the changing table and wiggling like mad when you try to put on their clothes.

"Slow to warm up" babies (around 15%) are not as irritable (or active) as difficult babies, but they are not fond of change. Give them enough time, however, and they will adapt. Jasmine would place Eddie in this category. Eddie was not too keen on the new day care environment, but he did eventually adjust to it. He was just slow to warm up to the unfamiliar place and the people there.

These categories of baby temperaments are useful, but we should remember that 35% of babies are considered hard to classify because they share the characteristics of more than one type of temperament.

nature AND nurture

Destiny of the Difficult Baby

Perhaps you are wondering about the long-term implications of baby temperaments. What becomes of infants—particularly the difficult bunch—when they get older? Do they grow up to be difficult children, stirring up trouble in school and alienating other kids with their grumpy behavior? If the answer were unequivocally yes, then we would chalk it up to nature: Difficult is written into the genes and no amount of excellent parenting is going to change such babies. Fortunately, this does *not* appear to be the case. Research suggests that difficult babies are unusually sensitive to input from their parents, a characteristic that—depending on environmental circumstances—can be either a blessing or a curse (Stright, Gallagher, & Kelley, 2008).

Stright and colleagues (2008) studied over a thousand mothers and babies during the first 6 years of life. Baby temperament was assessed at 6 months, and the mothers and their children were observed interacting on six separate occasions, from 6 months old until the time they were first graders. The children's first-grade teachers also participated, filling out questionnaires about their pupils' academic and social skills.

The researchers found that children with mothers demonstrating "higher-quality parenting styles" (being emotionally responsive and respectful of their children's need for independence) fared better than those with moms exhibiting lower-quality parenting (emotional distance and disregard for autonomy). Come first grade, children exposed to higher-quality parenting were more likely to succeed academically and maintain positive relationships with peers and teachers. Meanwhile, first graders raised by more detached and controlling mothers had the most trouble adjusting to school. The effects—both good and bad—were magnified for the difficult babies, suggesting these children are more receptive to parenting in general (Stright et al., 2008). Nature may have endowed them with a "difficult" temperament, but with some encouragement and respect from loving parents, their energy could be channeled in a very constructive way.

DO DIFFICULT BABIES BECOME OBNOXIOUS CHILDREN?

As you can see, parents have the power to steer the development of their children in positive and negative directions. But what exactly makes a good parent? The adjectives or phrases that come to our minds are "patience," "sensitivity," "acceptance," "strength," and "unconditional love." It also helps to be soft, warm, and snuggly—especially if you happen to be a monkey.

THE HARLOWS AND THEIR MONKEYS As we have noted, infants need contact with caregivers. Among the first to explore this topic in an experimental situation were Harry Harlow, Margaret Harlow, and their colleagues at the University of

temperament Characteristic differences in behavioral patterns and emotional reactions.

CONNECTIONS

In **Chapter 1,** we discussed *research ethics* and the importance of ensuring the ethical treatment of research participants (human and animal). Psychologists must do no harm and safeguard the welfare of participants. This would not have been possible if the Harlows had taken human newborns from their parents to study the importance of physical contact. Many even question the ethics of their use of newborn monkeys in this manner.

Soft Like Mommy
A baby monkey in a laboratory experiment clings to a furry mother surrogate. Research by Harry and Margaret Harlow and colleagues at the University of Wisconsin showed that physical comfort is important for the socioemotional development of these animals. When given the choice between a wire mesh "mother" that provided milk and a cloth-covered "mother" without milk, most of the monkeys opted to snuggle with the cuddly cloth-covered one. Photo Researchers

attachment The degree to which an infant feels an emotional connection with primary caregivers.

Wisconsin (Harlow, Harlow, & Suomi, 1971). The researchers were initially interested in learning how physical contact affects the development of loving relationships between infants and mothers. But they realized this would be **difficult** to study with human infants; instead, they turned to studying newborn macaque monkeys (Harlow, 1958).

Infant monkeys were put in cages alone, each with two artificial "surrogate" mothers. One surrogate was outfitted with a soft cloth and heated with a bulb. The other surrogate mother was designed to be lacking in "contact comfort," as she was made of wire mesh and not covered in cloth. Both of these surrogates could be set up to feed the infants. In one study, half the infant monkeys received their milk from the cloth surrogates and the other half got their milk from the wire surrogates. The great majority of the infant monkeys spent most of their time clinging to or in contact with the cloth mother, even if she was not the mother providing the milk. The baby monkeys spent 15 to 18 hours a day physically close to the cloth mother, and only 1 to 2 hours touching the wire mother.

Harlow and colleagues also created situations in which they purposefully scared the infants with a moving toy bear, and found that the great majority of the infant monkeys (around 80%) ran to the cloth mother, regardless of whether she was a source of milk. In times of fear and uncertainty, these infant monkeys found more comfort in the soft and furry mothers. Through their experiments, Harlow and his colleagues showed how important physical contact was for these living creatures (Harlow, 1958; Harlow & Zimmerman, 1959).

ATTACHMENT   Physical contact plays an important role in **attachment,** or the degree to which an infant feels an emotional connection with primary caregivers. Using a design called the *Strange Situation,* Mary Ainsworth (1913–1999) studied the attachment styles of infants between 12 and 18 months (Ainsworth, 1979, 1985; Ainsworth & Bell, 1970; Ainsworth, Blehar, Waters, & Wall, 1978). The Strange Situation goes roughly like this: A mother and child are led into a room. A stranger enters, and the mother then exits the room, leaving the child in the unfamiliar environment with the stranger, who tries to interact with the child. The mother returns to the room but leaves again, and then returns once more. At this point, the stranger departs. During the observation, the researchers note the amount of anxiety displayed by the child before and after the stranger arrives, the child's willingness to explore the unfamiliar environment, and the child's response to the mother's return. The following response patterns were observed:

- **Secure attachment:** Around 65% of the children were upset when their mothers left the room, but were easily soothed upon her return, quickly returning to play. These children seemed confident that their needs would be met and felt safe exploring their environment, using the caregiver as a "secure base."

- **Avoidant attachment:** Approximately 20% of the children displayed no distress when their mothers left, and they did not show any signs of wanting to interact with their mothers when they returned, seemingly happy to play in the room without looking at their mothers or the stranger. They didn't seem to mind when their mothers left, or fuss when they returned.

- **Ambivalent:** Children in this group (around 10%) were quite upset and very focused on their mothers, showing signs of wanting to be held, but unable to be soothed by their mothers. These children were angry (often pushing away their mothers) and not interested in returning to play.

Ideally, parents or caregivers provide a *secure base* for infants, and are ready to help regulate emotions (soothe or calm) or meet other needs. This makes infants feel comfortable exploring their environments. Ainsworth and colleagues (1978) suggested that development, both physical and psychological, is greatly influenced by the quality of an infant's attachment to caregivers. But, much of the early research in this area focused on infants' attachment to their mothers. Subsequent research suggests that we should examine infants' attachment to multiple individuals (mother, father, caregivers at day care, and close relatives), as well as cross-cultural differences in attachment (Field, 1996; Rothbaum, Weisz, Pott, Miyake, & Morelli, 2000).

Critics of the Strange Situation method suggest it creates an artificial environment and does not provide good measures of how infant–mother pairs act in their natural environments. Some suggest that the temperament of infants predisposes them to react the way they do in this setting. Infants prone to anxiety and uncertainty are more likely to respond negatively to such a scenario (Kagan, 1985). More generally, attachment theories are criticized for not considering cross-cultural differences in relationships (Rothbaum et al., 2000).

Attachments are formed early in childhood, but they have implications for a lifetime: "Experiences in early close relationships create internal working models that then influence cognition, affect, and behavior in relationships that involve later attachment figures" (Simpson & Rholes, 2010, p. 174). People who experienced ambivalent attachment as infants tend to have strong desires for continued closeness in adult relationships. Those who had secure attachments are more likely to expect that they are lovable and that others are capable of love. They are aware that nobody is perfect, and this attitude allows for intimacy in relationships (Cassidy, 2001). Infant attachment may even have long-term health consequences. One 32-year longitudinal study found that adults who had been insecurely attached as infants were more likely to report inflammation-based illnesses (for example, asthma, cardiovascular disease, and diabetes) than those with secure attachments (Puig, Englund, Simpson, & Collins, 2013).

Erikson's Psychosocial Stages

···▶ **LO 12** Identify how Erikson's theory explains psychosocial development through puberty.

Feeling Secure
A childcare worker plays with toddlers at Moore Community Center's Early Head Start program in Biloxi, Mississippi. Children are more willing to explore their environments when they have caregivers who consistently meet their needs and provide a secure base. Jim West/Photo Edit

One useful way to understand socioemotional development is to consider its progression through stages. According to Erik Erikson (1902–1994), human development is marked by eight psychosocial stages, spanning infancy to old age (Erikson & Erikson, 1997). Each of these stages is marked by a developmental task or an emotional crisis that must be handled successfully to allow for healthy psychological growth. The crises, according to Erikson, stem from conflicts between the needs of the individual and the expectations of society (Erikson, 1993). Successful resolution of a stage enables an individual to approach the following stage with more tools. Unsuccessful resolution leads to more difficulties during the next stage. Let's take a look at the stages associated with infancy and childhood (TABLE 8.2 on page 360).

• **Trust versus mistrust** (birth to 1 year): In order for an infant to learn to trust, her caregivers must be responsive and attentive to her needs. If caregivers are not responsive, she will develop in the direction of mistrust, always expecting the worst of people and her environment.

• **Autonomy versus shame and doubt** (1 to 3 years): If his caregivers allow it, a child will learn how to be autonomous and independent. If a child in this stage is not given the freedom to explore, but is punished or restricted, he will likely learn to feel shame and doubt.

• **Initiative versus guilt** (3 to 6 years): In this age range, children have more experiences that prompt them to extend themselves socially. Often they become more responsible and show the ability to make and follow through on plans. If a child does not have responsibilities or cannot handle them, she will develop feelings of guilt and anxiety.

Table 8.2   ERIKSON'S EIGHT STAGES

Stage	Age	Positive Resolution	Negative Resolution
Trust versus mistrust	Birth to 1 year	Trusts others, has faith in others.	Mistrusts others, expects the worst of people.
Autonomy versus shame and doubt	1 to 3 years	Learns to be autonomous and independent.	Learns to feel shame and doubt when freedom to explore is restricted.
Initiative versus guilt	3 to 6 years	Becomes more responsible, shows the ability to follow through.	Develops guilt and anxiety when unable to handle responsibilities.
Industry versus inferiority	6 years to puberty	Feels a sense of accomplishment and increased self-esteem.	Feels inferiority or incompetence, which can later lead to unstable work habits.
Ego identity versus role confusion	Puberty to twenties	Tries out roles and emerges with a strong sense of values, beliefs, and goals.	Lacks a solid identity, experiences withdrawal, isolation, or continued role confusion.
Intimacy versus isolation	Young adulthood (twenties to forties)	Creates meaningful, deep relationships.	Lives in isolation.
Generativity versus stagnation	Middle adulthood (forties to mid-sixties)	Makes a positive impact on the next generation through parenting, community involvement, or work that is valuable and significant.	Experiences boredom, conceit, and selfishness.
Integrity versus despair	Late adulthood (mid-sixties and older)	Feels a sense of accomplishment and satisfaction.	Feels regret and dissatisfaction.

These are the eight stages of psychosocial development proposed by Erik Erikson. Each stage is marked by a developmental task or an emotional crisis that must be handled successfully to allow for healthy psychological growth.

SOURCE: ERIKSON AND ERIKSON (1997).

- **Industry versus inferiority** (6 years to puberty): Children in this age range are generally engaged in a variety of learning tasks. When they are successful at these tasks, they begin to feel a sense of accomplishment and their self-esteem increases. If a child at this stage does not succeed at tasks, he will feel a sense of inferiority or incompetence, and theoretically this lack of industriousness in childhood could lead to unstable work habits or unemployment later on.

This introduction to development during childhood provides an opportunity to understand the physical, cognitive, and socioemotional changes from birth to late childhood. But enough about children. The time has come to explore the exciting period of adolescence.

show what you know

1. The _____ reflex occurs when you stroke a baby's cheek; she opens her mouth and turns her head toward your hand. The _____ reflex occurs when you touch the baby's lips; this reflex helps with feeding.

2. Your instructor describes how he is teaching his infant to learn new words by showing her flashcards with images. Every time the infant uses the right word to identify the image, he gives her a big smile. When she uses an incorrect word, he frowns. Your instructor is using which of the following to guide his approach:
   - a. theories of behaviorism.
   - b. Chomsky's language acquisition device.
   - c. infant-directed speech.
   - d. telegraphic speech.

3. Piaget suggested that when we try to understand new information and experiences by incorporating our already existing knowledge and ideas, we are using:
   - a. the rooting reflex.
   - b. schemas.
   - c. accommodation.
   - d. assimilation.

4. Vygotsky recommended supporting children's cognitive development by pushing them a little harder than normal, while providing help in a decreasing manner through _____.

5. Erikson proposed that socioemotional development comprises eight psychosocial stages, and these stages include:
   - a. scaffolding.
   - b. physical maturation.
   - c. developmental tasks or emotional crises.
   - d. conservation.

6. What advice would you give new parents about what to expect regarding the sequence of their child's development of language and how they might help encourage it?

 CHECK YOUR ANSWERS IN APPENDIX C.

Adolescence

THE WALKING, TALKING HORMONE Jocelyn is no longer a cute little bundle of girlhood; nowadays, she is a "walking, talking hormone," says Jasmine. "Boys, make-up, and friends are the center of her world now." At age 14, Jocelyn can also be mouthy; she cares a lot about what other people think of her; and she is mortified by her 31-year-old mother whom she thinks of as "so old." There are times when Jocelyn blatantly disregards her mother's instructions. She might, for example, go to a friend's house even after Jasmine has explicitly denied her permission to do so.

Jocelyn's behaviors are stereotypical of teenagers, or *adolescents*. **Adolescence** refers to the transition period between late childhood and early adulthood, and it can be challenging for both parents and kids. As you may recall from earlier in the chapter, Jasmine proved to be quite a challenge for her own mom when she was a teen, skipping school and carousing until late at night with friends. "At 14, I had already started the crazy life," says Jasmine, who considers herself blessed to have a daughter like Jocelyn, who gets As and Bs in school, doesn't use drugs or alcohol, and participates in her school's volleyball, basketball, and dance teams.

In the United States, adult responsibilities often are distant concepts for adolescents. But, this is not universal. For example, in underdeveloped countries, children take on adult responsibilities as soon as they are able. In some parts of the world, girls younger than 18 are already married and dealing with adult responsibilities. In Bolivia, girls can legally marry at 14 years old (Nour, 2009). However, adolescence generally allows for a much slower transition to adult duties in America. Although adolescents might develop adult bodies, including the ability to become parents, here their schooling and training generally do not occur at the same adult level, in part because of longer periods of required education and dependence on parents and caregivers.

You Asked, Allie Answers

http://qrs.ly/yy3m67j

How has your relationship with your son changed as he's entered adolescence?

Physical and Cognitive Development in Adolescence

LO 13 Give examples of significant physical changes that occur during adolescence.

PHYSICAL DEVELOPMENT Adolescence is a time of dramatic physical growth, comparable to that which occurs during fetal development. The "growth spurt" includes rapid changes in height, weight, and bone growth, and usually begins between ages 9 and 10 years for girls and ages 12 and 16 years for boys. Sex hormones, which influence this growth and development, are at high levels.

Puberty is the period during which the body changes and becomes sexually mature and able to reproduce. During puberty, the **primary sex characteristics** or reproductive organs (ovaries, uterus, vagina, penis, scrotum, and testes) mature. In addition, the **secondary sex characteristics,** which are not associated with reproduction, become more distinct and include the development of pubic, underarm, and body hair. Breast changes also occur in boys and girls (with the areola increasing in size), and fat increases in girls' breasts. Adolescents experience changes to their skin and overall body hair. Girls' pelvises begin to broaden, while boys experience a deepening of their voices and broadening of their shoulders.

adolescence The transition period between late childhood and early adulthood.

puberty The period of development during which the body changes and becomes sexually mature and capable of reproduction.

primary sex characteristics Organs associated with reproduction, including the ovaries, uterus, vagina, penis, scrotum, and testes.

secondary sex characteristics The development of pubic, underarm, and body hair in boys and girls along with a variety of other gender-specific bodily changes not associated with reproduction.

Growing Up Fast
Members of the St. Thomas Boys Choir in Leipzig, Germany, practice a chant in rehearsal. Choir directors are struggling with the fact that young boys' voices are deepening earlier as the years go by. In the mid-1700s, voice changes reportedly occurred in singers aged 17 or 18; today, the average age is closer to 10 (Mendle & Ferrero, 2012). No one is certain why boys are hitting puberty sooner, but some researchers point to a correlation with increasing body mass index (Sørensen, Aksglaede, Petersen, & Juul, 2010). Wolfgang Kluge/picturealliance/dpa/AP Images

It is during this time that girls will experience **menarche** ('me-ˌnär-kē), the point at which menstruation begins. Menarche can occur as early as age 9 or after age 14; but typical onset is around 12 or 13. Boys experience **spermarche** ('spər-ˌmär-kē), their first ejaculation, during this time period as well. But, when it occurs is more difficult to specify, as boys may be reluctant to talk about the event (Mendle, Harden, Brooks-Gunn, & Graber, 2010).

Not everyone matures at the same time, however. Some evidence suggests that early maturing adolescents face a greater risk of engaging in unsafe behaviors, such as drug and alcohol use (Shelton & van den Bree, 2010). Compared to their peers, girls who mature early seem to experience more negative outcomes than those who mature later, such as increased social anxiety; they also appear to face a higher risk of emotional problems and delinquent behaviors (Blumenthal et al., 2011; Harden & Mendle, 2012). Early maturing girls are more likely to smoke, drink alcohol, have lower self-confidence, and later take on jobs that are "less prestigious." There are certain factors that can reduce such risks, though, including parents who show warmth and support (Shelton & van den Bree, 2010).

Boys who mature early generally have a more positive experience and do not show evidence of increased anxiety (Blumenthal et al., 2011). But, when researchers examine the "tempo," or speed, with which boys reach full sexual maturity, they find that rapid development can be associated with a range of problems, including aggressive behavior, cheating, and temper tantrums (Marceau, Ram, Houts, Grimm, & Susman, 2011).

Adolescence is a time when sexual interest peaks, yet teenagers don't always make the best choices when it comes to sexual activity. A study by the Centers for Disease Control and Prevention (CDC, 2008a) found that over 25% of girls (approximately 1 of every 4) between ages 14 and 19 are infected with "at least one of the most common sexually transmitted diseases" (p. 1). Over half of new *sexually transmitted infections* affect young people ages 15–24; keep in mind that this group represents only 25% of the sexually active population (CDC, 2013). Sexually transmitted infections are especially risky for adolescents because they often go untreated and can lead to a host of problems, including long-term sterility.

LO 14 Explain how Piaget described cognitive changes that take place during adolescence.

Synonym

sexually transmitted infections sexually transmitted diseases

menarche The point at which menstruation begins.
spermarche A boy's first ejaculation.
identity A sense of self based on values, beliefs, and goals.

COGNITIVE DEVELOPMENT Alongside the remarkable physical changes of adolescence are equally remarkable cognitive developments. As noted earlier, children in this age range are better able to distinguish between abstract and hypothetical situations. This ability is an indication the teenager has entered Piaget's formal operational stage, which begins in adolescence and continues into adulthood. During this period, the adolescent begins to use deductive reasoning to draw conclusions and critical thinking to approach arguments. She can reason abstractly, classify ideas, and use symbols. The adolescent can think beyond what is going on in the moment, pondering the future and considering many possibilities or hypothetical situations.

She may also begin to contemplate what will happen beyond high school, including career choices and education.

A specific type of egocentrism emerges in adolescence. Before this age, children can only imagine the world from their own perspective, but during adolescence they begin to become aware of others' perspectives. Egocentrism is still apparent, however, as they believe others share their preoccupations. For example, a teenager who focuses on his appearance will think that others are focusing on his appearance as well (Elkind, 1967). Adolescents also tend to believe that everyone thinks the same way they do.

Adolescent egocentrism also helps explain the sense of uniqueness many teenagers feel. This intense focus on the self may lead to a feeling of immortality, which can result in risk-taking behaviors (Elkind, 1967). Because they have not had many life experiences, adolescents may fail to consider the long-term consequences of their behaviors. Nor is the logic used by adolescents the same as that used by adults. In particular, adolescents may not think about what might happen if they participate in risky behaviors (such as unprotected sex or drug use). Their focus on the present (for example, having fun in the moment) outweighs their ability to assess the potential harm in the future (pregnancy or addiction). So to help adolescents stop engaging in risky behaviors such as smoking, we might focus on short-term consequences, like bad breath when kissing a partner, rather than long-term dangers such as lung cancer (Robbins & Bryan, 2004).

Michelle was the first in her class to pupate.

THE ADOLESCENT BRAIN Risk taking in adolescence is thought to result from characteristics of the adolescent brain. The limbic system, which is responsible for processing emotions and perceiving rewards and punishments, undergoes significant development during adolescence. Another important change is the increased myelination of axons in the prefrontal cortex, which improves the connections within the brain involved in planning, weighing consequences, and multitasking (Steinberg, 2012). But the relatively quicker development of the limbic system in comparison to the prefrontal cortex can lead to risk-taking behavior. Because the prefrontal cortex has not yet fully developed, the adolescent may not foresee the possible consequences of reward-seeking activities that are supported by the reward center of the limbic system. Changes to the structure of the brain continue through adolescence, resulting in a fully adult brain between the ages of 22 and 25, and a decline in risk-taking behaviors (Giedd et al., 2009; Steinberg, 2010, 2012).

Given this state of affairs, should adolescents be tried as adults in our legal system? In 2005 the U.S. Supreme Court ended the juvenile death penalty with its *Roper v. Simmons* decision (Borra, 2005). But the studies on brain structure provide results for groups, which may not apply to every individual. We cannot use such findings to draw definitive conclusions about individual teenagers (Bonnie & Scott, 2013).

Too Young
Teen inmates stand in line at a Texas prison facility. As of 2005, defendants being tried for crimes committed before age 18 are no longer candidates for the death penalty. The U.S. Supreme Court arrived at this decision after carefully weighing evidence submitted by the American Psychological Association (APA) and others, which suggests that the juvenile mind is still developing and vulnerable to impulsivity and poor decision making (APA, 2013c). © Michael Ainsworth/Dallas Morning News/Corbis

Socioemotional Development in Adolescence

Adolescence is also a time of great socioemotional development. During this time, children become more independent from their parents. Conflicts may result as the adolescent searches for his **identity,** or sense of who he is based on his values, beliefs, and goals. Until this point in development, the child's identity was based primarily on the parents' or caregivers' values and beliefs. Adolescents explore who they are by trying out different ideas in a variety of categories, including politics and religion. Once these areas have been explored, they begin to commit to a particular set of beliefs and attitudes, making decisions to engage in activities related to their evolving identity. One word of caution is in order: Their commitment may shift back and forth, sometimes on a day-to-day basis (Klimstra et al., 2010).

> LO 15   Identify how Erikson explained changes in identity during adolescence.

ERIKSON AND ADOLESCENCE   Erikson's theory of development addresses this important issue of identity formation (Erikson & Erikson, 1997). The time from puberty to the twenties is the stage of *ego identity versus role confusion,* which is marked by the creation of an adult identity. The adolescent strives to define himself. If the tasks and crises of Erikson's first four psychosocial stages have not been successfully resolved, the adolescent may enter this stage with distrust toward others, and feelings of shame, guilt, and inadequacy. In order to be accepted, he may try to be all things to all people.

It is during this period that one wrestles with some important life questions: *What career do I want to pursue? What kind of relationship should I have with my parents? What religion (if any) is compatible with my views, beliefs, and goals?* This stage often involves "trying out" different roles. A person who resolves this stage successfully emerges with a stronger sense of her values, beliefs, and goals. One who fails to resolve *role confusion* will not have a solid sense of identity and may experience withdrawal, isolation, or continued role confusion. However, just because we reach adulthood doesn't mean our identity stops evolving. As we will soon see, there is still plenty of growth throughout life.

PARENTS AND ADOLESCENTS   What role does a parent play during this difficult period? Generally speaking, parent–adolescent relationships are positive (Paikoff & Brooks-Gunn, 1991), but conflict does increase during early adolescence (Van Doorn, Branje, & Meeus, 2011), and it frequently relates to issues of control and parental authority. Often these parent–teen struggles revolve around everyday issues such as curfew, chores, schoolwork, and personal hygiene. Fortunately, conflict tends to decline as both parties become more comfortable with the adolescents' growing sense of autonomy and self-reliance (Lichtwarck-Aschoff, Kunnen, & van Geert, 2009; Montemayor, 1983).

FRIENDS   Friends become increasingly influential during adolescence. Some parents seem to be concerned about the negative influence of peers; however, it is typical for adolescents to form relationships with others of the same age and with whom they might share beliefs and interests, among other things—this only tends to support what parents encouraged during childhood (McPherson, Smith-Lovin, & Cook, 2001). Adolescents tend to behave more impulsively in front of their peers than do adults. It appears that social pressure may inhibit their ability to "put the brakes on" impulsivity in decision making (Albert, Chein, & Steinberg, 2013). But peers can also have a positive influence, supporting prosocial behaviors (for example, getting good grades or helping others; Roseth, Johnson & Johnson, 2008; Wentzel, McNamara Barry, & Caldwell, 2004).

With the use of smart phones and tablets, these negative and positive influences are often transmitted through digital space. Peer pressure can be exerted through posts on Facebook walls and texts and tweets sent out through mobile devices. To what extent do teens connect through these digital platforms, and what is the nature of their online activity?

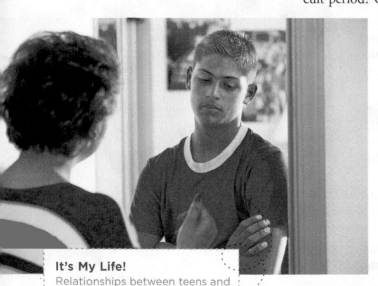

It's My Life!
Relationships between teens and parents are generally positive, but most involve some degree of conflict. Many disputes center on everyday issues, like clothing and chores, but the seemingly endless bickering does have a deeper meaning. The adolescent is breaking away from his parents, establishing himself as an autonomous person.
SW Productions/Getty Images

SOCIAL MEDIA and psychology

The Social Networking Teen Machine

Around 95% of American teens use the Internet, and 80% of them have established identities on social media sites, primarily Facebook. Twitter is less popular, but still used by a substantial 16% (Lenhart et al., 2011). Most teenagers have cell phones, which means they can engage in digital communication virtually 24 hours a day (Lenhart, 2012).

How does all this social media activity affect young people? Networking sites are places where friendships are created and cultivated, but some experts worry that teens place excessive importance on the number of online interactions they have, rather than the depth of those interactions (FoxNews.com, 2013, March 20). Others are concerned that overreliance on digital communication is making teenagers less attuned to facial expressions and social cues normally conveyed in real-life interactions (Stout, 2010, April 30). Social media sites can also serve as staging grounds for negative behaviors like bullying. Just take a look at some data from a survey of several hundred Internet-using teenagers (Lenhart et al., 2011): Approximately 8% say they have been bullied online in the past year; 88% have observed others being "mean or cruel" on a social media site; 25% say their interactions through social media have led to offline arguments; and 8% claim their online conversations have served as the impetus for physical fights.

NETWORK BULLIES AND FRIENDS

But it's not all bad news. The majority of teens who use social media also say that their interactions on these sites have made them feel better about themselves and more deeply connected to others (Lenhart et al., 2011). Online communities provide teens with a space to explore their identities and interact with people from diverse backgrounds. They serve as platforms for the exchange of ideas and art (sharing music, videos, and blogs), and places for students to study and collaborate on school projects (O'Keeffe, Clarke-Pearson, & Council on Communications and Media, 2011).

Social media is here to stay, and it will continue to impact the socioemotional development of adolescents. The challenge for parents is to find ways to direct this online activity while still recognizing their child's need for space and autonomy (Yardi & Bruckman, 2011). What steps do you think parents should take to ensure that teenagers are using social media in a positive way?

Kohlberg's Stages of Moral Development

LO 16 Summarize Kohlberg's levels of moral development.

Moral development is another important aspect of socioemotional growth. Lawrence Kohlberg (1927–1987), influenced by the work of Piaget, proposed three levels of moral development that occur in sequence over the life span. These levels, which are further divided into two stages, focus on specific changes in beliefs about right and wrong (**FIGURE 8.5** on page 367).

Kohlberg used a variety of fictional stories about moral dilemmas to determine the stage of moral reasoning of participants in his studies. The Heinz dilemma is a story about a man named Heinz who was trying to save his critically ill wife. Heinz did not have enough money to buy a drug that could save her, so after trying unsuccessfully to borrow money, he finally decided to steal the drug. The two questions asked of individuals in Kohlberg's studies were these: "Should the husband have done that? Was it right or wrong?" (Kohlberg, 1981, p. 12). Kohlberg was not really interested in whether his participants thought Heinz should

Kohlberg at Work
American psychologist Lawrence Kohlberg proposed that moral reasoning progresses through three major levels: preconventional, conventional, and postconventional. The rate at which we move through these developmental levels partly depends on environmental factors, such as interactions with parents and siblings. Critics contend that Kohlberg's research focused too heavily on men in Western cultures (Endicott, Bock, & Narvaez, 2003; Gilligan, 1982).
Lee Lockwood/Time & Life Pictures/Getty Images

steal the drug or not; instead, the goal was to determine the moral reasoning behind their answers.

Although Kohlberg described moral development as sequential and universal in its progression, he noted that environmental influences and interactions with others (particularly those at a higher level of moral reasoning) support its continued development. Additionally, not everyone progresses through all three levels; an individual may get stuck at an early stage and remain at that level of morality throughout life. Let's look at these three levels.

PRECONVENTIONAL MORAL REASONING From the time a toddler or preschooler begins to understand the connection between behavior and its consequences, she can begin to think about moral issues, and make decisions about what is right and wrong. **Preconventional moral reasoning** usually applies to young children, and it focuses on the consequences of behaviors, both good and bad. For children in Stage 1 (*punishment and obedience orientation*), "goodness" and "badness" are determined by whether a behavior is punished. Behavior is motivated by showing respect and obedience to avoid being punished. For example, a child decides not to cheat on a test because she is worried about getting caught and then punished. Thus, consequences drive the belief about what is right and wrong. Regarding the Heinz dilemma, a child at this level may say the husband should not steal the drug because he may go to jail if caught. Children in Stage 2 (*instrumental–relativist orientation*) behave in accordance with a "marketplace" mentality, looking out for their own needs most of the time. The world is seen as an exchange of goods and services, so giving to others does not occur out of loyalty or fairness, but for the hope of reciprocity ("You scratch my back and I'll scratch yours"; Kohlberg & Hersh, 1977).

CONVENTIONAL MORAL REASONING At puberty, **conventional moral reasoning** is used, and determining right and wrong is informed by expectations from society and important others, not simply personal consequences. The emphasis is on conforming to society's rules and regulations. In Stage 3 (*interpersonal concordance orientation*), actions that are helpful or please others are considered "good." Gaining the approval of others (being a "good boy" or "nice girl") is an important motivator. Faced with the Heinz dilemma, the adolescent might suggest that because society says a husband must take care of his wife, Heinz should steal the drugs so that others won't think poorly of him. In Stage 4 (*law and order orientation*), the focus is on rules and social order. Duty and obedience to authorities define what is right. Heinz should not steal because stealing is against the law. Cheating on exams is not right because one is obligated to uphold a student code of conduct (Kohlberg & Hersh, 1977).

POSTCONVENTIONAL MORAL REASONING The third level of Kohlberg's theory is **postconventional moral reasoning.** Right and wrong are determined by the individual's beliefs about morality, which may be inconsistent with society's rules and regulations. Stage 5 (*social contract, legalistic orientation*) reasoning suggests that laws should be followed when they are upheld by society as a whole; but, if a law does not exhibit "social utility," it should be changed to meet the needs of society. In other words, a law and order approach isn't always morally right. Someone using this type of reasoning might suggest that Heinz should steal the drug because the laws of society fail to consider his unique situation. In Stage 6 (*universal ethical principle orientation*), moral behavior is determined by universal principles of justice, equality, and respect for human life. An understanding of the "right" thing to do is guided not only by

preconventional moral reasoning Kohlberg's stage of moral development in which a person, usually a child, focuses on the consequences of behaviors, good or bad, and is concerned with avoiding punishment.

conventional moral reasoning Kohlberg's stage of moral development that determines right and wrong from the expectations of society and important others.

postconventional moral reasoning Kohlberg's stage of moral development in which right and wrong are determined by the individual's beliefs about morality, which sometimes do not coincide with society's rules and regulations.

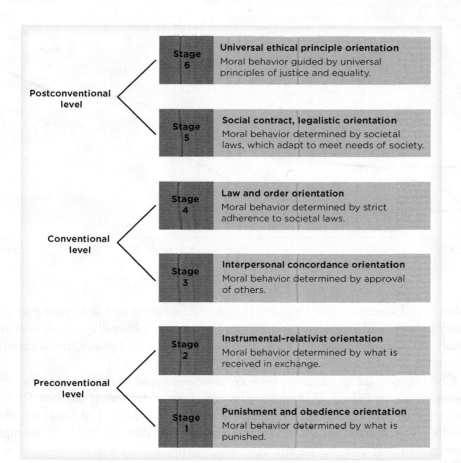

◀┈┈┈┈┈┈┈┈┈┈┈┈┈┈┈┈┈┈

FIGURE 8.5
Kohlberg's Stages of Moral Development

what is universally regarded as right, but also by one's conscience and personal ethical perspective. With regard to the Heinz dilemma, someone using postconventional moral reasoning would thoughtfully consider all possible options, but ultimately decide human life overrides societal laws.

CRITICISMS   Kohlberg's stage theory of moral development has not been without criticism. Carol Gilligan (1982) leveled a number of serious critiques, suggesting that the theory did not represent women's moral reasoning. She noted that Kohlberg's initial studies included only male participants, introducing bias into his research findings. Gilligan suggested that Kohlberg had discounted the importance of caring and responsibility and that his choice of an all-male sample was partially to blame. Another issue with Kohlberg's theory is that it focuses on the moral reasoning of individuals, and thus is primarily applicable to Western cultures; in more collectivist cultures, the focus is on the group (Endicott et al., 2003). One last concern about Kohlberg's theory is that we can define and measure moral reasoning, but predicting moral behavior is not always easy. Research that examines moral reasoning and moral behavior indicates that the ability to predict moral behavior is weak at best (Blasi, 1980; Krebs & Denton, 2005).

CONNECTIONS

In **Chapter 1,** we discussed the importance of collecting data from a *representative sample,* whose members' characteristics closely reflect the population of interest. Kohlberg's early research included only male participants, but he and others *generalized* his findings to females. Generalizing from an all-male sample to females in the population may not be justifiable.

Emerging Adulthood

When does a child become an adult? There isn't one particular age that distinctly marks the boundary between a nonadult and an adult. In the United States, the legal age of adulthood is 18 for some activities (voting, military enlistment) and 21 for others (drinking, financial responsibilities). These ages are not consistent across

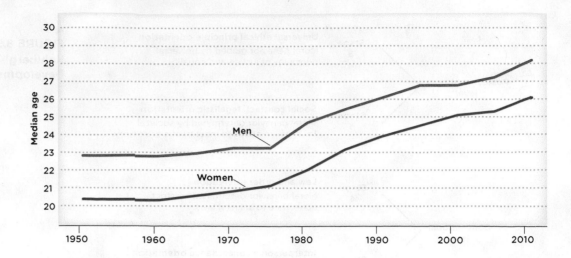

FIGURE 8.6
Age of First Marriage
Many developmental psychologists consider marriage a marker of adulthood because it often represents the first time a person leaves the family home to set out on his or her own. Since the 1950s and 1960s, the median age at which men and women marry for the first time has increased, a trend that appears likely to continue.
Source: U.S. Census Bureau (2011).

cultures and countries (the legal drinking age in some nations is as young as 16). Many cultures and religions mark the transition into adulthood by ceremonies and rituals (for example, Jewish *bar/bat mitzvahs,* Australian walkabouts, Christian confirmations, Latin American *quinceañeras*), starting as early as age 12.

Complicating the demarcation between adolescence and adulthood is the fact that young people in today's Western societies now remain dependent on their families for longer periods of time. In the past, young people in the United States left their families' homes much earlier as indicated by marriage data. In 1970, for example, women were marrying for the first time at approximately 21 years of age, and men at 23. In 2010 the age at first marriage was 26 for women, and 28 for men (Arnett, 2000; Elliott, Krivickas, Brault, & Kreider, 2012; **FIGURE 8.6**). Psychologists now propose a phase known as **emerging adulthood,** which is the time of life between 18 and 25 years of age. It is neither adolescence nor early adulthood because it is a period of exploration and opportunity. The emerging adult has neither the permanent responsibilities of adulthood nor the dependency of adolescence. By this time, most adolescent egocentrism has disappeared, which is apparent in intimate relationships and empathy (Elkind, 1967). There are opportunities to seek out loving relationships, education, and new views of the world before settling into the relative permanency of family and career (Arnett, 2000).

The transition from adolescence to young adulthood can be rocky at times. It is by exploring and then committing to their own identities that adolescents often become their own people. Trying out relationships and careers during this period allows them to emerge into adulthood.

emerging adulthood A phase of life between 18 and 25 years that includes exploration and opportunity.

○✓○○   **show what you know**

1. The physical changes not associated with reproduction, but that become more distinct during adolescence, are known as
   a. primary sex characteristics.
   c. menarche.
   b. secondary sex characteristics.
   d. puberty.

2. Your cousin is almost 14, and she has begun to use deductive reasoning to draw conclusions and critical thinking to support her arguments. Her cognitive development is occurring in Piaget's
   a. formal operational stage.
   b. concrete operational stage.
   c. ego identity versus role confusion stage.
   d. instrumental-relativist orientation.

3. _____ moral reasoning usually applies to young children, and it focuses on the consequences of behaviors, both good and bad.

4. "Helicopter" parents pave the way for their children, troubleshooting problems for them, making sure they are successful in every endeavor. How might this type of parenting impact an adolescent in terms of Erikson's stage of ego identity versus role confusion?

 CHECK YOUR ANSWERS IN APPENDIX C.

Adulthood

A WORK IN PROGRESS At the very beginning of this chapter, we introduced Chloe Ojeah, a 22-year-old community college student caring for two aging grandparents, a 79-year-old grandmother with Alzheimer's disease and an 85-year-old grandfather recovering from a stroke. Like Jasmine, Chloe is immersed in young adulthood, a time when many people are continuing to forge their identities and lay the groundwork for enduring lifelong relationships. Many of the "Who am I?" type of questions that pop up in adolescence may spill over into this stage of life. Chloe, for example, still hasn't decided where she stands politically, even though her family clearly leans in a certain direction. Nor has she settled on a religious faith, despite her exposure to at least two different churches. "It's not a decision I can make with my family," says Chloe, who wants to find answers on her own terms. "I'm still questioning everything."

Like many young adults, Chloe is also beginning to explore her capacity to form deep and loving relationships. Her first serious romantic relationship evolved out of a close friendship she had established while living in Houston. Chloe trusted this boyfriend; she was committed to him; she even loved him, though she wouldn't say she was "in love" with him. "More than anything," Chloe insists, "we just enjoyed being around each other." But spending time together was not much of an option when Chloe relocated to Austin to care for her grandparents. Since they split a little over a year ago, Chloe has remained on good terms with her ex-boyfriend and his relatives.

As Chloe is just beginning to experience her first meaningful relationships, her grandfather, J. M. Richard, is enjoying his 61st year of married life. When you ask Mr. Richard what he considers his most important achievements, the first thing he says is "marrying my wife." The last few years have been trying, given her battle with Alzheimer's disease, but Mr. Richard continues to be deeply committed to her. As he himself offers, "We still love each other."

Looking back on nearly nine decades of life, Mr. Richard says he feels satisfied: "I am happy with my life, and I am happy with my accomplishments." His fulfillment does not just stem from marriage and fatherhood. "I am also deep into the Baptist church," Mr. Richard notes. "I have met most of my spiritual needs with the people of the church and the God I know. . . . The other thing I have been blessed with up until a year ago was good health." Before the stroke, Mr. Richard was able to drive his car, which allowed him the freedom to take care of business at his funeral home, maintain the various buildings he rents out to tenants, and oversee building projects on his properties. Now he has nerve damage on the left side of his body, which causes persistent pain. He walks with a cane, is visually impaired, and can no longer drive.

But Mr. Richard hasn't thrown in the towel. Far from it. With the help of an occupational therapist, he hopes to get behind the wheel again one day. And unlike most people, even those who are half his age, he spends 30 to 40 minutes pedaling on his exercise bike each day. Not only does physical exercise improve his muscle tone and cardiovascular health; it may also help preserve his memory by upping the birthrate of new brain cells (more on this to come). Mr. Richard also maintains a vibrant intellectual life. He is very much involved in the day-to-day activities of the funeral home, talking with his employees on the phone several times a day.

A Good Life
Chloe's grandfather, J. M. Richard, enjoys breakfast with his wife of six decades. Mr. Richard says that his greatest accomplishment was marrying Mrs. Richard, whom he still loves deeply. Mrs. Richard struggles with Alzheimer's disease, but her impaired memory does not stop her from enjoying many daily activities. Chloe Ojeah

What do you hope to accomplish by the time you reach Mr. Richard's age? Do you want to have a satisfying marriage and a house full of grandkids? An intense and rewarding career? Perhaps you dream of becoming an accomplished musician, businessperson, or filmmaker. Whatever you want from life, you are most likely to pursue and attain it during the developmental stage known as adulthood. Developmental psychologists have identified various stages of this long period, each corresponding to an approximate age group: *early adulthood* spans the twenties and thirties, *middle adulthood* the forties to mid-sixties, and *late adulthood* everything beyond.

Physical Development

> **LO 17** Name some of the physical changes that occur across adulthood.

The most obvious signs of aging tend to be physical in nature. Often you can estimate a person's age just by looking at his hands or facial lines. Let's get a sense of some of the basic body changes that occur through adulthood.

EARLY ADULTHOOD   During early adulthood, our sensory systems are sharp, and we are at the height of our muscular and cardiovascular ability. But some systems have already begun their downhill journey. Hearing, for instance, often starts to decline as a result of noise-induced hearing impairment that commences in early **adolescence** (Niskar et al., 2001). The body is fairly resilient at this stage, but lifestyle choices can have profound health consequences. Heavy drinking, drug use, poor eating habits, and sleep deprivation can make a person look, feel, and function like someone much older.

As we head toward our late thirties, fertility-related changes occur for both men and women. Women experience a 6% reduction in fertility in their late twenties, 14% in their early thirties, and 31% in their late thirties (Menken, Trussell, & Larsen, 1986; Nelson, Telfer, & Anderson, 2013). Men also experience a fertility dip, but it appears to be gradual and results from fewer and poorer quality sperm (Sloter et al., 2006). It is not until age 50 that male fertility declines substantially, however (Kidd, Eskenazi, & Wyrobek, 2001).

MIDDLE ADULTHOOD   In middle adulthood, the skin wrinkles and sags due to loss of collagen and elastin, and skin spots may appear (Bulpitt, Markowe, & Shipley, 2001). Hair starts to turn grey and may fall out. Hearing loss continues and may be exacerbated by exposure to loud noises (Kujawa & Liberman, 2006). Eyesight may decline. The bones weaken. Oh, and did we mention you might shrink as well? All this sounds awful, but do not despair. There are measures you can take to slow the aging process. For example, genes influence height and bone mass, but research suggests we can limit the shrinking process through continued exercise. In one study, researchers followed over 2,000 people for three decades. Everyone in the study got shorter (the average height loss being 4 centimeters, or about 1.6 inches), but those who had engaged in "moderate vigorous aerobic" exercise lost significantly less (Sagiv, Vogelaere, Soudry, & Ehrsam, 2000). The

CONNECTIONS

In **Chapter 3,** we described causes for hearing impairment. Damage to the hair cells or the auditory nerve is sensorineural deafness. Conduction hearing impairment results from damage to the eardrum or the middle-ear bones that transmit sound waves. Exposure to loud sounds, such as listening to music through earbuds, may play a role in hearing impairment starting in adolescence.

Move It Or Lose It?
Exercise is one of the best ways to fight the aging process. Working out on a regular basis improves cardiovascular health, bone and muscle strength, and mood. A study of more than 400,000 people in Taiwan found that those who exercised just 15 minutes a day lived an average of 3 years longer than their sedentary peers (Wen et al., 2011).
© yellowdog/cultura/Corbis

good news is that to maintain your stature and overall physique, you would be wise to participate in lifelong moderate endurance activities such as jogging, walking, and swimming.

For women, middle adulthood is a time of major physical change. Estrogen production decreases, the uterus shrinks, and menstruation no longer follows a regular pattern. This marks the transition toward **menopause,** the time when ovulation and menstruation cease, and reproduction is no longer possible. Menopausal women can experience hot flashes, sweating, vaginal dryness, and breast tenderness (Newton et al., 2006). These symptoms may sound unpleasant, but many women consider menopause to be a temporary inconvenience, reporting a sense of relief following the cessation of their menstrual periods, as well as increased interest in sexual activity (Etaugh, 2008).

Men experience their own constellation of midlife physical changes, sometimes referred to as male menopause or *andropause.* Some suggest calling it androgen decline in the aging male, as there is a reduction in testosterone production, not an end to it (Morales, Heaton, & Carson, 2000). Men in middle adulthood may complain of depression, fatigue, and cognitive difficulties, which might be associated with lower testosterone. But research suggests this link between hormones and behavior is evident in only a tiny proportion of aging men (Pines, 2011).

LATE ADULTHOOD Late adulthood, which begins around 65, is also characterized by the decline of many physical and psychological functions. Vision problems, such as cataracts and impaired night vision, are common. Hearing continues on a downhill course, and reaction time increases (Fozard, 1990). The brain processes information more slowly, and brain regions responsible for memory deteriorate (Eckert, Keren, Roberts, Calhoun, & Harris, 2010).

Some of this physical decline is inevitable, but it is possible to age gracefully. Exercise improves bone density and muscle strength, and lowers the risk for cardiovascular disease and obesity. There is even research suggesting that exercise fosters the development of neural networks, helping with the production of **new hippocampus nerve cells,** which are important in memory (Deslandes et al., 2009; Erickson et al., 2011; see **FIGURE 8.7**). Exercise may also reduce the risk of Alzheimer's disease and other disorders of the nervous system (Radak et al., 2010).

Mr. Richard is exceptionally sharp for his age, but his occupational therapist has noticed a decline in some of his cognitive abilities, such as integrating information and reaction time. It is possible, however, that he has actually delayed these processes by staying physically fit. Physical and cognitive development are closely intertwined.

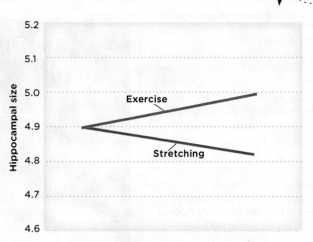

▲ FIGURE 8.7
Exercise to Build Bigger . . . Brains?
Researchers interested in the effects of exercise on the aging brain randomly assigned participants to two groups: One group engaged in a program of gentle stretching exercises, and the other began doing more aerobic activity. During the course of the yearlong study, the researchers found typical levels of age-related shrinkage in the hippocampi of the stretching group. However, in the group that exercised more vigorously, not only was age-related deterioration prevented, hippocampal volume actually increased, with corresponding improvements in memory. *Source:* Adapted from Erickson et al. (2011)

CONNECTIONS

In **Chapter 2,** we reported that studies with animals and humans have shown that some areas of the brain are constantly generating new neurons, in a process known as *neurogenesis.* As we age, this production of new neurons seems to be supported by physical exercise.

Cognitive Development

What's going on in the brain as we pass through the various stages of adulthood, and how do those changes affect our ability to function? Let's explore the cognitive changes of adulthood.

LO 18 Identify some of the cognitive changes that occur across adulthood.

EARLY ADULTHOOD Measures of aptitude, such as intelligence tests, indicate that cognitive ability remains stable from early to middle adulthood (Larsen, Hartmann, & Nyborg, 2008), though processing speed begins to decline (Schaie, 1993).

menopause The time when a woman no longer ovulates, her menstrual cycle stops, and she is no longer capable of reproduction.

Young adults are theoretically in Piaget's formal operational stage, which means they can think logically and systematically, but some researchers estimate that only 50% of adults ever exhibit formal operational thinking (Arlin, 1975).

MIDDLE AND LATE ADULTHOOD   Much of the discussion of middle adulthood has focused on decline: declining metabolism, skin elasticity, testosterone, cardiovascular health, and so on. Yet cognitive function does not necessarily decrease during middle adulthood. Longitudinal studies by Schaie and colleagues indicate that decreases in cognitive abilities cannot be reliably measured before 60 (Gerstorf, Ram, Hoppmann, Willis, & Schaie, 2011; Schaie, 1993, 2008). There are some exceptions, however. Midlife is a time when information processing and memory can decline, particularly the ability to remember past events (Ren, Wu, Chan, & Yan, 2013).

After the age of 70, cognitive decline is more apparent. The Seattle Longitudinal Study has shown that the cognitive performance of today's 70-year-old participants is similar to the performance of 65-year-olds tested 30 years ago (Gerstorf et al., 2011; Schaie, 1993, 2008). So, turning 65 does not mean it is time to retire, from a cognitive abilities perspective. Processing speed may slow with old age, but older adults are still capable of amazing accomplishments. Frank Lloyd Wright finished designing New York's Guggenheim Museum when he was 89 years old and Nelson Mandela became president of South Africa when he was 76. Age does not limit us unless we allow it to.

Some types of cognitive skills diminish in old age and others become more refined. Older people may not remember all of their academic knowledge, but their practical abilities seem to grow. Life experiences allow people to develop a more balanced understanding of the world around them, one that only comes with age (Sternberg & Grigorenko, 2005).

When studying cognitive changes across the life span, psychologists frequently describe two types of intelligence: **crystallized intelligence,** the knowledge we gain through learning and experience, and **fluid intelligence,** the ability to think in the abstract and create associations among concepts. As we age, the speed with which we learn new material and create associations decreases (von Stumm & Deary, 2012). In one study, researchers examined performance on fluid and crystallized intelligence tasks in adults between the ages of 20 and 78. Crystallized abilities increased with age, whereas fluid abilities increased from 20 to 30 years of age and remained stable until age 50 (Cornelius & Caspi, 1987). Working memory, the active processing component of short-term memory that maintains and manipulates information, also becomes less efficient with age (Nagel et al., 2008; Reuter-Lorenz, 2013).

crystallized intelligence Knowledge gained through learning and experience.

fluid intelligence The ability to think in the abstract and create associations among concepts.

Earlier we mentioned that physical exercise provides a cognitive boost. The same appears to be true of mental exercises, such as those required for playing a musical instrument (Hanna-Pladdy & MacKay, 2011). That said, there does appear to be a lot of hype surrounding the "use it or lose it" mantra to aging, which suggests that exercising the brain will stop cognitive decline. Use it or lose it might be a slight overstatement when it comes to maintaining cognitive function (Salthouse, 2006). Although there are clear advantages to doing crossword puzzles and reading the newspaper, inconclusive evidence exists to support the notion that this activity has the same effect it would have on a child, for example. When older adults exercise their brains in a particular domain (for example, playing a musical instrument or using Wii *Big Brain Academy* software), the results do not necessarily transfer to other general abilities, such as cognitive and perceptual information processing (Ackerman, Kanfer, & Calderwood, 2010). Specifically, tasks that help to train working memory may (or may not) improve fluid intelligence, even into older age (Nisbett et al., 2012). But, research suggests that people who continue to work, both physically and mentally, and remain in good physical shape are less likely to experience **significant cognitive decline** (Rohwedder & Willis, 2010). Thus, if your goal is to maintain a sharp mind as you age, don't just increase your Sudoku playing or your reading time. You need to maintain a balanced approach incorporating a broad range of activities and interests.

Socioemotional Development: Early, Middle, and Late Adulthood

Socioemotional development does not always occur in a neat, stepwise fashion. Some of us become parents as teenagers, others not until our forties. This next section describes a host of social and emotional transformations that typically occur during adulthood.

LO 19 Explain some of the socioemotional changes that occur across adulthood.

ERIKSON AND ADULTHOOD Earlier we described Erikson's approach to explaining socioemotional development from infancy through adolescence, noting that unsuccessful resolution of prior stages has implications for the stages that follow (see Table 8.2 on page 360). During young adulthood (twenties to forties), people are challenged by *intimacy versus isolation*. Young adults tend to focus on creating meaningful, deep relationships, and failing at this endeavor may lead to a life of isolation, Erikson proposed. He also believed that we are unable to form these relationships if identity has not been clearly established in the identity versus role confusion of adolescence.

Moving into middle adulthood (forties to mid-sixties), we face the crisis of *generativity versus stagnation*. Positive resolution of this stage includes feeling like you have made a real impact on the next generation, through parenting, community involvement, or work that is valuable and significant. Those who do not have a positive resolution of this stage face stagnation, characterized by boredom, conceit, and selfishness.

In late adulthood, we look back on life and evaluate how we have done, a crisis of *integrity versus despair* (mid-sixties and older). If previous stages have resulted in positive resolutions, we feel a sense of accomplishment and satisfaction. A negative resolution of this stage indicates that we have regrets and dissatisfaction.

Before we further explore socioemotional development in adulthood, we must note that Erikson's theory, though very important in the field of developmental psychology, has provided more framework than substantive research findings. His theory was

CONNECTIONS

Here, we are reminded of an issue presented in **Chapter 1:** We must be careful not to equate correlation with causation. In this case, if you experience a decline in cognitive ability, you are less likely to work. Thus, it is the cognitive decline that would lead to the lack of work.

based on case studies, with limited supporting research. In addition, the developmental tasks of Erikson's stages might not be limited to the particular time frame proposed. For example, creating an adult identity is not limited to adolescence, as this stage may resurface at any point in adulthood (Schwartz, 2001).

ROMANCE AND RELATIONSHIPS   Young adulthood is a time when romantic relationships move in a new direction. The focus shifts away from fun-filled first experiences with sex and love to deeper connections. For many people, the twenties are a transition period between the "here and now" type of relationships of adolescence to the serious, long-term partnerships of adulthood (Arnett, 2000). Some of these relationships lead to what many people consider the most challenging, yet rewarding, role in life: parenthood.

···▶ **LO 20** Summarize the four types of parenting proposed by Baumrind.

PARENTING   Do you ever find yourself watching parent–child interactions at the store? You likely have noticed a vast spectrum of child-rearing approaches. Diana Baumrind (1966, 1971) has been studying parenting for over four decades, and her work has led to the identification of four parenting behavioral styles. These styles seem to be stable across situations, and are distinguished by levels of warmth, responsiveness, and control (Maccoby & Martin, 1983).

Parents who insist on rigid boundaries, show little warmth, and expect high control exhibit **authoritarian parenting.** They want things done in a certain way, no questions asked. "Because I said so" is a common justification used by such parents. Authoritarian parents are extremely strict and demonstrate poor communication skills with their children. Their kids, in turn, tend to have lower self-assurance and autonomy, and experience more problems in social settings (Baumrind, 1991).

Authoritative parenting may sound similar to authoritarian parenting, but it is very different. Parents who practice authoritative parenting set high expectations, demonstrate a warm attitude, and are responsive to their children's needs. Being supported and respected, children of authoritative parents are quite responsive to their parents' expectations. They also tend to be self-assured, independent, responsible, and friendly (Baumrind, 1991).

With **permissive parenting,** the parent demands little of the child and imposes few limitations. These parents are very warm but often make next to no effort to control their children. Ultimately, their children tend to lack self-control, act impulsively, and show no respect for boundaries.

Uninvolved parenting describes parents who seem indifferent to their children. Emotionally detached, these parents exhibit minimal warmth and devote little time to their children, although they do provide for their children's basic needs. Children raised by uninvolved parents tend to exhibit behavioral problems, poor academic performance, and immaturity (Baumrind, 1991).

Keep in mind that the great majority of research on these parenting styles has been conducted in the United States, which should make us wonder how applicable these categories are in other countries and cultures (Grusec, Goodnow, & Kuczynski, 2000). Other factors to consider include the home environment, the child's personality and development, and the unique parent–child relationship. A child who is irritable will react to an authoritarian parent's restrictions in a different way than one who is easygoing, for example (Grusec & Goodnow, 1994).

Parenting is incredibly hard work. Physically exhausting, emotionally trying, and sometimes plain exasperating, parenting can make you feel like you are aging at the speed of light, but some evidence suggests it's quite the opposite.

authoritarian parenting A rigid parenting style characterized by strict rules and poor communication skills.

authoritative parenting A parenting style characterized by high expectations, strong support, and respect for children.

permissive parenting A parenting style characterized by low demands of children and few limitations.

uninvolved parenting A parenting style characterized by a parent's indifference to a child, including a lack of emotional involvement.

Changing Social Roles Can Reverse Aging

from the pages of **SCIENTIFIC AMERICAN**

Old bees that start caring for young ones gain cognitive power.

How many mothers have looked at their children and thought, "Ah, they keep me young"? Now we know how right they are.

Caring for the young may delay—and in some cases, even reverse—multiple negative effects of aging in the brain. Gro Amdam, who studies aging in bees at Arizona State University, observed tremendous improvements in cognition among older bees that turn their attention back to nursing. She has reason to believe that changes in social behavior could shave years off the human brain as well.

When bees age, their duties switch from taking care of the brood to foraging outside the hive. The transition is followed by a swift physical and cognitive decline. Amdam removed young bees from their hives, which tricked the older bees into returning to their caretaker posts. Then she tested their ability to learn new tasks. A majority reverted to their former cognitive prowess, according to results published in the journal *Experimental Gerontology*. "What we saw was the complete reversal of the dementia in these bees. They were performing exactly as well as young bees," Amdam says.

The ones that improved had higher levels of the antioxidant PRX6 in their brain, a protein that exists in humans and is thought to protect against neurodegenerative diseases. Amdam's theory is that when older individuals participate in tasks typically handled by a younger generation—whether in a hive or in our own society—antioxidant levels increase in the brain and turn back the clock. Youth, it turns out, may be infectious after all. **Morgen Peck. Reproduced with permission.**

And so, it seems, aging does not always go hand-in-hand with cognitive decline. The same could be said of wisdom, the ability to use reasoning to tackle life's challenges (Kross & Grossmann, 2012) and make better decisions (Worthy, Gorlick, Pacheco, Schnyer, & Maddox, 2011). Wisdom grows as we accumulate a vast amount of experience (Ardelt, 2010), but experience does not always correlate with age. Chloe, who is only 22, and Jasmine, 31, may be young, but they are also quite wise.

GROWING OLD WITH GRACE When many people think of growing older, the image that surfaces is of a frail old woman (or man) sitting in a bathrobe and staring out the window, unable to care for herself. This stereotype is not accurate. As of 2000, fewer than 5% of Americans older than 65 lived in a nursing home (Hetzel & Smith, 2001). Most older adults in the United States enjoy active, healthy, independent lives. They are involved in their communities, faith, and social lives, and contrary to popular belief—a large number have active sex lives (Lindau et al., 2007). Researchers have discovered that happiness generally increases with age (Jeste et al., 2013). Positive emotions become more frequent than negative ones, and emotional stability increases, meaning that we experience fewer extreme emotional swings (Carstensen et al., 2011). Stress and anger begin to diminish in early adulthood, and worry becomes less apparent after age 50 (Stone, Schwartz, Broderick, & Deaton, 2010).

Older people might feel happy because they no longer care about proving themselves in the world, they are pleased with the outcome of their lives, or they have developed a strong sense of emotional equilibrium (Jeste et al., 2012). Research suggests that older adults who are healthy, independent, and engaged in social activities also report being happy, and there is some evidence that this increased happiness may result in a longer life (Oerlemans, Bakker, & Veenhoven, 2011). Americans are now living longer than ever, with the average life expectancy of women being 81.1 years and men 76.3 years (Hoyert & Xu, 2012). Could happiness be one of the factors driving this increase in life span?

Death and Dying

We have spent this entire chapter discussing life. Many of the stages and changes described occur at different times for different people, sometimes overlapping, other times skipped altogether. When it comes to life, nothing is certain—except, of course, the arrival of death.

LO 21 Describe how Kübler-Ross explained the stages of death.

Apart from sex, few topics are as difficult to address as death and dying. Psychiatrist Elisabeth Kübler-Ross (2009) opened the discussion in the early 1960s, while working with people facing the end of life. She found they experienced similar reactions when faced with the news that their deaths were imminent: denial, anger, bargaining, depression, and acceptance. These stages, Kübler-Ross suggested, are coping mechanisms for dealing with what is to come.

- **Denial:** In the denial stage, a person may react to the news with shock and disbelief, perhaps even suggesting the doctors are wrong. Unable to accept the diagnosis, he may seek other medical advice.

- **Anger:** A dying person may feel anger toward others who are healthy, or toward the doctor who does not have the cure. *Why me?* she may wonder, projecting her anger and irritability in a seemingly random fashion.

- **Bargaining:** This stage may involve negotiating with God, doctors, or other powerful figures for a way out. Usually, this involves some sort of time frame: *Let me live to see my firstborn get married,* or *Just give me one more month to get my finances in order.*

- **Depression:** There comes a point when a dying person can no longer ignore the inevitable. Depression may be due to the symptoms of the patient's actual illness, but it can also result from the overwhelming sense of loss—the loss of the future.

- **Acceptance:** Eventually, a dying person accepts the finality of his predicament; death is inevitable, and it is coming soon. This stage can deeply impact family and close friends, who, in some respects, may need more support than the person who is dying. According to one oncologist, the timing of acceptance is quite variable. For some people, it occurs in the final moments before death; for others, soon after they learn there is no chance of recovery from their illness (Lyckholm, 2004).

Kübler-Ross was instrumental in bringing attention to the importance of attending to the dying person (Charlton & Verghese, 2010; Kastenbaum & Costa, 1977). The stages she proposed provide a valuable framework for understanding death, but keep in mind that every person responds to death in a unique way. For some people, the stages are overlapping; others don't experience the stages at all (Schneidman, 1973). We should also note that there is little research supporting the validity of stages of death, and that the theory arose in a Western cultural context. Evidence suggests that people from other backgrounds may view death and dying from very different perspectives.

across the WORLD

Death in Different Cultures

What does death mean to you? Some of us believe death marks the beginning of a peaceful afterlife. Others see it as a crossing over from one life to another. Still others believe death is like turning off the lights; once you're gone, it's all over.

Views of death are very much related to religion and culture. A common belief among Indian Hindus, for example, is that one should spend a lifetime preparing for a "good death" (*su-mrtyu*). Often this means dying in old age, after conflicts have been put to rest, family matters settled, and farewells said. To prepare a loved one for a good death, relatives place the person on the floor at home (or on the banks of the Ganges River, if possible) and give her water from the hallowed Ganges. If these and other rituals are not carried out, the dead person's soul may be trapped and the family suffers the consequences: nightmares, infertility, and other forms of misfortune (Firth, 2005). Imagine a psychologist trying to assist grieving relatives without any knowledge of these beliefs and traditions.

Every culture has its own collection of ideas about death. In Japan and other parts of East Asia, families often make medical decisions for the dying person (Matsumura et al., 2002). They may avoid using words like "cancer" to shield them from the bad news, believing this knowledge may cause them to lose hope and deteriorate further (Koenig & Gates-Williams, 1995; Searight & Gafford, 2005). Yet, healthy East Asians are more likely than European Americans to engage in and enjoy life when reminded of the imminence of death (Ma-Kellams & Blascovich, 2012).

EVERY CULTURE HAS ITS OWN IDEAS ABOUT DEATH.

Interesting as these findings may be, remember they are only cultural trends. Like any developmental step, the experience of death is shaped by countless social, psychological, and biological factors.

Celebrating the Dead

A mariachi band plays at a cemetery in Mexico's Michoacan state on Dia de los Muertos, "Day of the Dead." During this holiday, people in Mexico and other parts of Latin America celebrate the lives of the deceased. Music is played, feasts are prepared, and graves adorned with flowers to welcome back the spirits of relatives who have passed. In this cultural context, death is not something to be feared or dreaded, but rather a part of life that is embraced (National Geographic, 2013). © Christian Kober/ Robert Harding World Imagery/Corbis

LATEST DEVELOPMENTS   Do you wonder what became of Jasmine Mitchell and Chloe Ojeah? Both women continue to stay busy, pursuing careers and looking after their families. Chloe is still in school and caring for her grandparents. She switched her academic focus to sign language and hopes to become an interpreter for the deaf community, though she is also contemplating a career in phlebotomy, the medical specialty of drawing blood. Jasmine graduated from Waubonsee Community College and is now studying psychology at Aurora University. Eddie is busy playing soccer and learning to read, while Jocelyn juggles schoolwork, basketball, and driver's education. Stay tuned for further developments in the next edition!

1. Physical changes during middle adulthood include hearing loss, declining eyesight, and loss of height. Research suggests which of the following can help limit the shrinking process?
   a. physical exercise
   b. elastin
   c. andropause
   d. collagen

2. As we age, our _____ intelligence, or ability to think abstractly, decreases, but our knowledge gained through experience, our _____ intelligence, increases.

3. When faced with death, a person can go through five stages. The final stage is _____, and sometimes family members need more support during this stage than the dying person.
   a. denial
   b. anger
   c. bargaining
   d. acceptance

4. An aging relative in his mid-seventies is looking back on his life and evaluating what he has accomplished. He feels satisfied with his work, family, and friends. Erikson would say that he has succeeded in solving the crisis of _____ versus _____.

5. Describe the four types of parenting proposed by Baumrind. Think of your two closest friends in high school. Citing specific examples, identify the type of parenting their parents used.

✓ CHECK YOUR ANSWERS IN APPENDIX C.

⑧ summary of concepts

LO 1 Define human development. (p. 333)

Development refers to the changes that occur in physical, cognitive, and socioemotional functioning over the course of the life span. These changes begin at conception and end at death. The goal of developmental psychology is to examine these changes.

LO 2 Describe three longstanding discussions in developmental psychology. (p. 334)

Developmental psychologists' longstanding debates and discussions have centered on three major themes: stages and continuity; nature and nurture; and stability and change. Each of these themes relates to a basic question: (1) Does development occur in separate or discrete stages, or is it a steady, continuous process? (2) What are the relative roles of heredity and environment in human development? (3) How stable is one's personality over a lifetime and across situations?

LO 3 Identify the types of research psychologists use to study developmental processes. (p. 336)

Developmental psychologists use several methods to explore changes across the life span. The cross-sectional method examines people of different ages at one point in time, and the longitudinal method follows one sample of individuals over a period of time. In the cross-sequential method, participants are divided into age groups as well as followed over time, so researchers can examine developmental changes within individuals and across different age groups.

LO 4 Examine the role genes play in our development. (p. 339)

All the cells in the human body (except for red blood cells) include a nucleus at their center. Inside this nucleus is the material that provides the blueprint or plans for our physiological development and structure, including our chromosomes, deoxyribonucleic acid (DNA), and genes, which provide the inherited framework for how we will develop.

LO 5 Discuss how genotype and phenotype relate to development. (p. 339)

Genotype refers to the 23 chromosome pairs that are unique to each individual and do not change in response to the environment. The genotype interacts with the environment, which results in a phenotype. This phenotype is the particular combination of a genotype and experiences, leading to unique physical, psychological, and behavioral characteristics.

LO 6 Identify the progression of prenatal development. (p. 341)

At conception, when the sperm and egg merge, they form a single cell called a zygote. During the germinal period, the zygote grows through cell division and eventually becomes implanted in the uterine wall. Between the 3rd and 8th weeks of development, the mass of cells is now called an embryo. From 2 months following conception to birth, the growing human is identified as a fetus. The amniotic sac serves as a protective barrier; however, harmful environmental agents called teratogens can damage zygotes and the growing embryo or fetus.

LO 7 Summarize some developmental changes that occur in infancy. (p. 344)

Newborn babies exhibit several reflexes, or unlearned patterns of behavior. They come into the world equipped with keen sensory capabilities that seem to be designed for facilitating relationships. In addition, neurons rapidly sprout new connections among each other and this dramatic synaptic growth is influenced by the infant's experiences and stimulation from the environment.

LO 8 Describe the theories explaining language acquisition. (p. 348)

The behaviorist's view of language development proposes that infants and children learn language in the same way they learn everything else—through positive attention to correct behavior, unpleasant attention to incorrect behavior, and observation. Chomsky suggested that humans have a language acquisition device (LAD), an innate mechanism that provides a framework for children to learn language. Infant-directed speech (IDS) also plays a role in language acquisition. Infants pay more attention to adults who use IDS and are more likely to provide them with chances to learn and interact, thus allowing more exposure to language.

LO 9 Examine the universal sequence of language development. (p. 349)

At age 2–3 months, infants typically start to produce vowel-like sounds known as cooing. At 4–6 months, in the babbling stage, infants combine consonants with vowels. This progresses to the one-word stage around 12 months, followed by two-word telegraphic speech at approximately 18 months. As children mature, they start to use more complete sentences.

LO 10 Summarize the constructs of Piaget's theory of cognitive development. (p. 351)

Piaget proposed that one of the basic units of cognition is the schema, which is a collection of ideas or notions that represent a basic unit of understanding. Humans have a need to maintain cognitive equilibrium, and use assimilation and accommodation for that purpose. When we assimilate, we attempt to understand new information using an already existing knowledge base or schema, and when we accommodate, we restructure old notions to make a place for new information. Piaget proposed that cognitive development occurs in four stages: the sensorimotor stage, preoperational stage, concrete operational stage, and formal operational stage.

LO 11 List the key elements of Vygotsky's theory of cognitive development. (p. 355)

Vygotsky was particularly interested in how social and cultural factors affect cognitive development. He proposed that one way to help children's cognitive development is through scaffolding—pushing them to go just beyond what they are competent and comfortable doing, but also providing help, when needed, in a decreasing manner.

LO 12 Identify how Erikson's theory explains psychosocial development through puberty. (p. 359)

According to Erikson, human development is marked by eight psychosocial stages, spanning infancy through old age. Each stage is marked by a developmental task or an emotional crisis that must be handled successfully to allow for healthy psychological growth: trust versus mistrust, autonomy versus shame and doubt, initiative versus guilt, and industry versus inferiority.

LO 13 Give examples of significant physical changes that occur during adolescence. (p. 361)

Adolescence is characterized by many physical changes: a growth spurt in height, weight, and bones; sex hormones, which influence this growth and development, are also at high levels. In addition, primary sex characteristics (those changes associated with reproductive organs) and secondary sex characteristics (those changes not associated with reproductive organs) mature in both boys and girls.

LO 14 Explain how Piaget described cognitive changes that take place during adolescence. (p. 362)

During the formal operational stage of cognitive development, adolescents begin to use deductive reasoning and logic to draw conclusions. A specific type of egocentrism also emerges in adolescence. Adolescents may believe everyone thinks the same way they do. Because they have not had a lot of life experiences, they may fail to consider overall long-term consequences associated with their behaviors.

LO 15 Identify how Erikson explained changes in identity during adolescence. (p. 364)

The stage of ego identity versus role confusion occurs during adolescence and is marked by the creation of an adult identity. During this stage, the adolescent seeks to define himself through his values, beliefs, and goals. Erikson believed that the period of role confusion is important for the adolescent to navigate, as it provides a chance to "try out" different roles. Successful resolution of this stage results in stronger fundamental values, beliefs, and goals with a firmer sense of identity.

LO 16 Summarize Kohlberg's levels of moral development. (p. 365)

Kohlberg proposed three levels of moral reasoning that occur in sequence. Preconventional moral reasoning usually applies to young children and focuses on the personal consequences of behaviors, both good and bad. At puberty, conventional moral reasoning is used, with the determination of right and wrong based on the expectations of society and important others. In postconventional moral reasoning, right and wrong are determined by the individual's beliefs about morality, which may not coincide with society's rules and regulations.

LO 17 Name some of the physical changes that occur across adulthood. (p. 370)

Adulthood brings about many physical changes. We are physically at our peak in early adulthood, but that typically declines as we reach late adulthood. Gradual physical changes occur, including hearing and vision loss, wrinkles, graying hair, reduced stamina, and for women menopause. Lifestyle choices can have significant influences on health. Heavy drinking, drug use, poor eating habits, and sleep deprivation can make one look, feel, and function like someone much older.

LO 18 Identify some of the cognitive changes that occur across adulthood. (p. 371)

Cognitive ability remains stable from early to middle adulthood, but midlife is a time when information processing and memory can decline, particularly the ability to remember past events. Processing speed may slow with old age. Crystallized intelligence refers to the knowledge we gain through learning and experience, and fluid intelligence refers to the ability to think in the abstract and create associations among concepts. As we age, the speed with which we learn new material and create associations decreases, but crystallized intelligence increases.

LO 19 Explain some of the socioemotional changes that occur across adulthood. (p. 373)

According to Erikson, during young adulthood, people face the crisis of intimacy versus isolation, and failure to create meaningful, deep relationships may lead to a life of isolation. In middle adulthood, we face the crisis of generativity versus stagnation. Positive resolution of this stage includes feeling like one has made a valuable impact on the next generation. In late adulthood, in the crisis of integrity versus despair, we look back on life and evaluate how we have done.

LO 20 Summarize the four types of parenting proposed by Baumrind. (p. 374)

Parents who insist on rigid boundaries, show little warmth, and expect high control exhibit authoritarian parenting. Parents who practice authoritative parenting set high expectations, demonstrate a warm attitude, and are highly responsive to their children's needs. Parents who place very few demands on their children and do not set many limitations exhibit permissive parenting. Uninvolved parenting refers to parents who seem to be indifferent, are emotionally uninvolved with their children, and do not exhibit warmth, although they provide for their children's basic needs.

LO 21 Describe how Kübler-Ross explained the stages of death. (p. 376)

Kübler-Ross documented similar reactions among people faced with the news of their imminent death: denial (reacting with shock and disbelief), anger (toward others who are healthy, or about the lack of a cure), bargaining (negotiating for more time), depression (due to illness or the overwhelming sense of loss), and acceptance (accepting death is inevitable). People vary greatly in how they deal with and experience dying. Many of these reactions or coping mechanisms may occur simultaneously or in stages, or the dying individual might not experience any of these stages.

key terms

accommodation, p. 351
adolescence, p. 361
assimilation, p. 351
attachment, p. 358
authoritarian parenting, p. 374
authoritative parenting, p. 374
babbling, p. 349
chromosomes, p. 339
concrete operational stage, p. 352
conservation, p. 352
conventional moral reasoning, p. 366
cooing, p. 349
critical period, p. 335
cross-sectional method, p. 336

cross-sequential method, p. 336
crystallized intelligence, p. 372
deoxyribonucleic acid (DNA), p. 339
developmental psychology, p. 333
dizygotic twins, p. 341
dominant gene, p. 340
egocentrism, p. 352
embryo, p. 341
emerging adulthood, p. 368
epigenetics, p. 340
fetal alcohol syndrome (FAS), p. 342
fetus, p. 343
fluid intelligence, p. 372

formal operational stage, p. 354
gene, p. 339
genotype, p. 339
identity, p. 363
longitudinal method, p. 336
maturation, p. 333
menarche, p. 362
menopause, p. 371
monozygotic twins, p. 341
object permanence, p. 351
permissive parenting, p. 374
phenotype, p. 340
postconventional moral reasoning, p. 366
preconventional moral reasoning, p. 366

preoperational stage, p. 352
primary sex characteristics, p. 361
puberty, p. 361
recessive gene, p. 340
scaffolding, p. 355
schema, p. 351
secondary sex characteristics, p. 361
sensorimotor stage, p. 351
spermarche, p. 362
telegraphic speech, p. 349
temperament, p. 356
teratogens, p. 342
uninvolved parenting, p. 374
zygote, p. 341

TEST PREP are you ready?

1. A researcher is interested in studying changes across the life span with regard to memory, problem solving, and language. She chooses a large sample of college seniors and decides to follow them for the next 30 years. This is an example of:
   a. socioemotional development.   c. cross-sectional research.
   b. longitudinal research.   d. epigenetics.

2. Chloe's grandmother suffers from Alzheimer's disease. Chloe wonders if she will experience a similar future because of her biological relationship to her grandmother. What Chloe is contemplating is similar to which of the following debates in developmental psychology?
   a. stability and change   c. critical or sensitive period
   b. stages or continuity   d. nature and nurture

3. DNA molecules include sections corresponding to _____, which encode proteins that determine the texture of hair, color of eyes, and some aspects of personality.
   a. phenotypes   c. zygotes
   b. epigenetics   d. genes

4. Your psychology instructor often discusses the factors in the environment that can influence how genes are expressed. This topic is a part of the field studying:
   a. epigenetics.   c. the cohort effect.
   b. maturation.   d. prenatal development.

5. Human development is influenced by the interaction of many factors. Brain development, for example, is influenced by biological maturation and experiences in the environment. This is evident in _____, which occurs when unused synaptic connections are eliminated.
   a. myelin sheath   c. synaptic pruning
   b. socioemotional development   d. the rooting reflex

6. _____ are agents that can damage a growing embryo or fetus.
   a. Phenotypes   c. Zygotes
   b. Genotypes   d. Teratogens

7. Your friend's daughter starts to say "ma, ma, ma" over and over when you walk in the room. This _____ is a stage that starts at around 4 to 6 months, and it is generally characterized by meaningless combinations of consonants and vowels.
   a. cooing   c. telegraphic speech
   b. babbling   d. infant-directed speech

8. Erikson proposed that human development is characterized by eight psychosocial stages, each marked by a developmental task or emotional crisis. In the first stage, the infant must resolve the _____ conflict. Caregivers who are not responsive might lead the infant always to expect the worst in people.
   a. autonomy versus shame and doubt
   b. industry versus inferiority
   c. trust versus mistrust
   d. ego identity versus role confusion

9. According to Vygotsky, _____ is an approach that helps children learn, providing support when necessary but allowing them to problem solve as much as possible on their own.
   a. assimilation   c. phenotype
   b. scaffolding   d. schema

10. _____ further develop during adolescence, including changes associated with reproductive organs, such as the maturation of ovaries, uterus, penis, and testes.
    a. Zygotes   c. Primary sex characteristics
    b. Temperaments   d. Secondary sex characteristics

11. Adolescents begin thinking more logically and systematically, and start to use deductive reasoning to draw conclusions. They have entered what Piaget would refer to as the
    a. formal operational stage.
    b. postconventional moral reasoning stage.
    c. industry versus inferiority stage.
    d. concrete operational stage.

12. One of the important tasks of adolescence is to _____, that is, to find a sense of self based on values, beliefs, and goals.
    a. use preconventional moral reasoning
    b. search for identity
    c. establish secure attachment
    d. use scaffolding

13. During middle adulthood, one major physical change for women is _____, which is often preceded by a decrease in estrogen production and a reduction in the size of the uterus.
    a. andropause   c. shrinking in height
    b. menarche   d. menopause

14. A research team has followed a large sample of men from their college graduation in 1995 through their retirement, trying to understand better how their cognitive abilities change over time. They interview and test these men once every 5 years. This would be considered a
    a. cohort effect.   c. cross-sectional method.
    b. longitudinal method.   d. phenotype.

15. A woman learns that her death is imminent. According to Kübler-Ross, her initial reaction to this news will likely be shock and disbelief, which are common to the _____ stage.
    a. denial   c. late adulthood
    b. conventional moral reasoning   d. preoperational

16. Developmental psychologists explain changes across the life span using the biopsychosocial perspective. How would you categorize the following factors in terms of whether they are biological, psychological, or social influences: family, learning, media, heredity, hormones, traits, culture?

17. Describe the stages in the development of a fertilized egg, from conception to birth.

18. Infants as young as 5 months old pay more attention to people who use infant-directed speech. Using the evolutionary perspective, explain why this might be the case.

19. Becoming a parent is an important socioemotional change of adulthood. Create a tool to help you remember the names of the four parenting styles observed by Baumrind.

20. We have described how cognitive abilities tend to decline with age. What kinds of cognitive activities might actually improve with age?

✓ CHECK YOUR ANSWERS IN APPENDIX C.

Get personalized practice by logging into LaunchPad at
http://www.worthpublishers.com/launchpad/Licht
to take the LearningCurve adaptive quizzes for Chapter 8.

9

Introduction to Motivation

First Day of School

Theories of Motivation

Goodbye, Somalia

Four Years in Kenya

SOCIAL MEDIA AND PSYCHOLOGY
Network Needs

Back to Basics: Hunger

Starving in Somalia

SA   from the pages of
SCIENTIFIC AMERICAN
Lunchtime Leniency

ACROSS THE WORLD
**A Cross-Cultural Look
at Eating Disorders**

Introduction to Emotion

Shark Attack

Theories of Emotion

Fight Back

CONTROVERSIES
Problems with Polygraphs

Face Value

ACROSS THE WORLD
Can You Feel the Culture?

Types of Emotion

SA   from the pages of
SCIENTIFIC AMERICAN
Happy in the Morning

motivation and emotion

Introduction to Motivation

FIRST DAY OF SCHOOL   When Mohamed Dirie started first grade, he did not know his ABCs or 123s. He had no idea what the words "teacher," "cubby," or "recess" meant. In fact, he spoke virtually no English. As for his classmates, they were beginning first grade with basic reading and writing skills from preschool and kindergarten. Mohamed's early education had taken place in an Islamic school, where he spent most of his time learning to read and recite Arabic verses of the Qur'an (kə-'rän). But Arabic wasn't going to be much help to a 6-year-old trying to get through first grade in St. Paul, Minnesota.

Months earlier, Mohamed and his mother, father, and older sister had arrived in St. Paul from the East African nation of Kenya, some 8,000 miles across the globe. Kenya was not their native country, just a stopping point between their homeland, Somalia, and a new life in America.

Perhaps you have heard about Somalia. Most of the news stories coming out of this nation during the past two decades have related themes of tragedy: bloody clashes between rival factions, kidnappings by pirates, suicide bombings, and starving children. Somalia's serious troubles began in 1991 when rebel forces overthrew the government of President Siad Barre. That was the year Mohamed's family and thousands of others fled the country, narrowly escaping death. Packed in a truck full of people, they sped away from their home city of Mogadishu as gunshots rang through the streets. And it's a good thing they left when they did, because as of the publication of this book, Somalia is still mired in civil war.

The first day of school in St. Paul, little Mohamed strapped on his backpack and walked with his mother to the bus stop. When the yellow bus pulled up to the curb, Mohamed's mother followed him inside and insisted on accompanying him to school. But Mohamed was ready to make the journey alone. "No, Mom, I got this," he remembers saying in his native Somali.

When Mohamed arrived at his new school, he found his way to the first-grade classroom and discovered a swarm of children chattering and making friends. Mohamed wanted to mingle,

→

9

LEARNING OBJECTIVES

after reading and studying this chapter, you should be able to:

LO 1 Define motivation.

LO 2 Explain how extrinsic and intrinsic motivation impact behavior.

LO 3 Summarize instinct theory.

LO 4 Describe drive-reduction theory and explain how it relates to motivation.

LO 5 Explain how arousal theory relates to motivation.

LO 6 Outline Maslow's hierarchy of needs.

LO 7 Explain how self-determination theory relates to motivation.

LO 8 Discuss how the stomach and the hypothalamus make us feel hunger.

LO 9 Outline the major eating disorders.

LO 10 Define emotions and explain how they are different from moods.

LO 11 Identify the major theories of emotion and describe how they differ.

LO 12 Discuss evidence to support the idea that emotions are universal.

LO 13 Indicate how display rules influence the expression of emotion.

LO 14 Describe the role the amygdala plays in the experience of fear.

LO 15 Summarize evidence pointing to the biological basis of happiness.

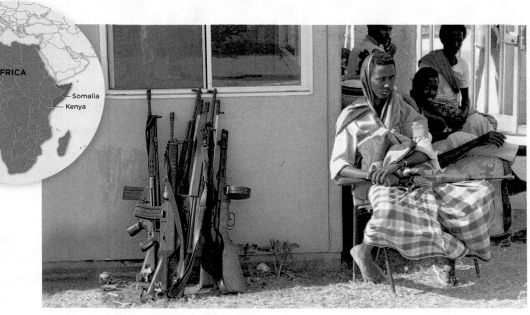

War-Torn Somalia
Mohamed's family comes from the East African nation of Somalia (shaded red on the map). They fled their homeland in 1991 during a violent government overthrow that led to more than 20,000 civilian deaths (Gassmann, 1991, December 21). The image on the right shows a group of Somali rebels in the capital city of Mogadishu about a month after the regime was toppled.
Left: Globe Turner, LLC/Getty; Right: AP Photo

Mohamed, In His Own Words
http://qrs.ly/gg3m6b2

too, so he endeared himself to the other kids the best way he could—by smiling. Flashing a grin was Mohamed's way of communicating, *Hey, I am a good person and you should get to know me.* And it was a strategy that worked. "I really felt like other people approached me better," he says. Mohamed's warm and welcoming demeanor may have been one reason his teacher took a special interest in him, providing the individual attention he needed to catch up to his peers. And Mohamed caught up quickly.

By the end of third grade, he had graduated from an English as a Second Language (ESL) program and could converse fluently with classmates. He sailed through the rest of elementary school with As and Bs in all subjects. Middle school presented new challenges, as Mohamed attended one of the poorest schools in the district and

Note: Quotations attributed to Mohamed Dirie are personal communications.

occasionally got picked on, but he continued to excel academically, taking the most challenging classes offered. In high school, he took primarily international baccalaureate (IB) or pre-IB classes, which prepped him for his undergraduate work at the University of Minnesota. Now with his bachelor's degree in scientific and technical communication, Mohamed is contemplating his next step. Will it be law school? A master's degree? Maybe a PhD?

If you think about where Mohamed began and where he is today, it's hard not to be awed. He entered the United States' school system 2 years behind his peers, unable to speak a word of English, an outsider in a culture radically different from his own. Without any tutoring from his parents (who couldn't read the class assignments, let alone help him with schoolwork), he managed to propel himself to the upper levels of the nation's educational system in just 12 years.

The Scholar ◄····
Four-year-old Mohamed (left) dressed in special attire to celebrate his completion of a *surah,* or chapter in the Qur'an. When this photograph was taken, the Dirie family had left Somalia and was living in a temporary home in Kenya. Some 14 years later, Mohamed graduated from high school in St. Paul, Minnesota (right). Courtesy of Mohamed Dirie

How do you explain Mohamed's success? This young man definitely is intelligent. You can tell he is bright after 5 minutes of conversation. But **intelligence** is not the only ingredient in the recipe for outstanding achievement. Other factors are important as well, including something psychologists consider essential for success in school: *motivation* (Conley, 2012; Hodis, Meyer, McClure, Weir, & Walkey, 2011; Linnenbrink & Pintrich, 2002).

CONNECTIONS

In **Chapter 7,** we described intellectually *gifted* people as those with very high IQ scores. We also presented the concept of *emotional intelligence*. Here, we see that in addition to intelligence, *motivation* plays a role in success.

What Is Motivation?

There are people who get kicks from bungee jumping from helicopters, and those who feel completely invigorated by a rousing match of chess. Human behaviors can be logical: We eat when hungry, sleep when tired, and go to work to pay the rent. Our behaviors can also be senseless and destructive: A beautiful fashion model starves herself, or an aspiring politician throws away an entire career for a fleeting sexual adventure. Why do people spend their hard-earned money on lottery tickets when the chances of winning may be 1 in 175 million (Wasserstein, 2013, May 16)? And what in the world drives teenagers to wrap houses in toilet paper on Halloween night?

One way to explain human behavior is through learning. We know that people (not to mention dogs, chickens, and slugs) can *learn* to behave in certain ways through classical conditioning, operant conditioning, and observational learning (Chapter 5). But learning isn't everything. Another way to explain behavior is to consider what might be motivating it. In the first half of this chapter, you will learn about different forms of motivation and the theories explaining them. Keep in mind that human behavior is complex and should be studied in the context of culture, biology, and the environment. Every behavior is likely to have a multitude of causes (Maslow, 1943).

You Asked, Mohamed Answers
[http://qrs.ly/bk3m6b5

What motivated you to go to college and better your education?

Adrenaline Junkie ◄

Why are some people drawn to thrill-seeking activities like bungee jumping? Their behaviors are best explained by intrinsic motivation—the stimulation from these experiences is highly rewarding. "Sensation seeking" appears to be an inherited trait associated with certain patterns of dopamine activity in the brain (Derringer et al., 2010). VisualCommunications bungee jumping/Getty Images

CONNECTIONS ▾

In **Chapter 5,** we introduced *positive* and *negative reinforcers,* which are stimuli that increase future occurrences of target behaviors. In both cases, the behavior becomes associated with the reinforcer. Here, we see how these associations become incentives.

motivation A stimulus that can direct behavior, thinking, and feeling.

incentive An association established between a behavior and its consequences, which then motivates that behavior.

extrinsic motivation The drive or urge to continue a behavior because of external reinforcers.

intrinsic motivation The drive or urge to continue a behavior because of internal reinforcers.

> ➤ **LO 1**   Define motivation.

Psychologists propose that **motivation** is a stimulus or force that can direct the way we behave, think, and feel. A motivated behavior tends to be guided (that is, it has a direction), energized, and persistent. Mohamed's academic behavior has all three features: *guided* because he sets specific goals like getting into graduate school, *energized* because he goes after those goals with zeal, and *persistent* because he sticks with his goals even when challenges arise.

INCENTIVE   In this chapter, we will explain why people do the things they do using the concepts of motivators and motivation. But first, let's take a closer look at how operant conditioning, particularly the use of *reinforcers,* can help us understand the relationship between learning and motivation. When a behavior is reinforced (through **positive or negative reinforcers**), an association is established between the behavior and its consequence. If we consider motivated behavior, this association becomes the **incentive,** or reason to repeat the behavior. Imagine there is a term paper you have been avoiding. You decide you will treat yourself to an hour of Web surfing for every three pages you write. *Adding* a reinforcer (surf time) increases your writing behavior; thus, we call it a *positive reinforcer.* It is the association between the behavior (writing) and the consequence (Web surfing) that transforms the Web surfing into an incentive. Before you know it, you begin to expect this break from work, which motivates you to write.

> ➤ **LO 2**   Explain how extrinsic and intrinsic motivation impact behavior.

EXTRINSIC MOTIVATION   When a learned behavior is motivated by the incentive of external reinforcers in the environment, we would say there is an **extrinsic motivation** to continue that behavior (Deci, Koestner, & Ryan, 1999; TABLE 9.1). In other words, the motivation comes from consequences that are found in the environment or situation. Bagels and coffee might provide extrinsic motivation for people to attend a boring meeting. Sales commissions provide extrinsic motivation for sales representatives to sell more goods. For most people, money serves as a powerful form of extrinsic motivation.

INTRINSIC MOTIVATION   But learned behaviors can also be motivated by personal satisfaction, interest in a subject matter, and other variables that exist within a person. When the drive or urge to continue a behavior comes from within, we call it **intrinsic motivation** (Deci et al., 1999). Reading a textbook because it is inherently interesting exemplifies intrinsic motivation. The reinforcers originate inside of you (learning feels good and brings you satisfaction), and not from the external environment.

Consider some of the forces motivating other behaviors. Do you exercise on a regular basis, and if so, why? If being able to show off your washboard abs is what you desire, then extrinsic motivation is sending you to the gym. If you exercise because it gives you pleasure (you like feeling "the burn," or releasing pent-up stress), then intrinsic motivation is your fuel. What compels you to offer your seat to an older adult on a bus: Is it because you've been praised for helping others before (extrinsic motivation), or because it simply feels good to help someone (intrinsic motivation)? Perhaps your response is a combination of both.

EXTRINSIC VERSUS INTRINSIC   Many behaviors are inspired by a blend of extrinsic and intrinsic motivation, but there do appear to be potential disadvantages to extrinsic motivation (Deci et al., 1999). Researchers have found that using rewards, such as money and marshmallows, to reinforce already interesting activities (like doing puzzles, playing word games, and so on) can lead to a decrease in what was initially intrinsically motivating. Why is this so? It could be that external reinforcers make it more difficult for people to develop self-regulation. Receiving external rewards may cause

Table 9.1 EXAMPLES OF INTRINSIC, EXTRINSIC, AND NEUTRAL PHRASES USED IN A MOTIVATION STUDY

Intrinsic Motivation Phrases	Extrinsic Motivation Phrases	Neutral Phrases
Writing an enjoyable paper	Writing an extra-credit paper	Writing an assigned paper
Working on the computer out of curiosity	Working on the computer for bonus points	Working on the computer to meet a deadline
Participating in a fun project	Participating in a money-making project	Participating in a required project
Pursuing my personal interests in class	Pursuing an attractive reward in class	Pursuing a routine task in class
Working with freedom	Working for incentives	Working with pressure
Having options and choices	Having prizes and awards	Having pressures and obligations
Working because its fun	Working because I want money	Working because I have to
Feeling interested	Anticipating a prize	Feeling frustrated

Listed here are descriptions of activities that typically arouse intrinsic motivation, extrinsic motivation, or no motivation.

SOURCE: REPRODUCED WITH PERMISSION OF ELSEVIER SCIENCE/THE LANCET/JAPAN NEUROSCIENCES SOCIETY FROM LEE (2012).

them to feel less responsible for initiating their own behaviors. In general, behavior resulting from intrinsic motivation is likely to include "high-quality learning," but only when the activities are novel, challenging, or have aesthetically pleasing characteristics. Extrinsic motivation may be less effective, resulting in resentment or disinterest (Ryan & Deci, 2000). Unfortunately, researchers have found that "tangible rewards—both material rewards, such as pizza parties for reading books, and symbolic rewards, such as good student awards—are widely advocated by many educators and are used in many classrooms, yet the evidence suggests that these rewards tend to undermine intrinsic motivation for the rewarded activity" (Deci, Koestner, & Ryan, 2001, p. 15).

For Mohamed, the most powerful source of extrinsic motivation was the approval of his mother. He recalls how proud she had been after returning from a parent–teacher conference in which the first-grade teacher said, "Your child is as bright as the sun." Mohamed doesn't remember his mom rewarding him with material things like toys and candy; apparently, making her proud was gratifying enough. But there were also forces driving Mohamed from within (intrinsic motivation). He enjoyed the process of learning. It was rewarding to master a second language and nail down his multiplication tables. Outside of class, Mohamed read books for fun. He still enjoys reading science fiction, so much that he hopes to write his own novel one day. Says Mohamed, "I want to be the first Somali to write a science fiction [book] in Somali."

We now have developed a basic understanding of what motivation is: a stimulus or force that can direct the way we behave, think, and feel. We also have established that motivation may stem from factors outside of ourselves (extrinsic) or from within (intrinsic). But what underlies motivation? Let's take a look at the major theories.

◯ ✓ ◯ ◯ show what you know

1. _____ is a stimulus that directs the way we behave, think, and feel.

2. Behavior that is motivated by internal reinforcers is considered to be the result of
   a. extrinsic motivation.
   b. intrinsic motivation.
   c. persistence.
   d. external consequences.

3. Imagine you are a teacher trying to motivate your students. Explain why you would want your students to be influenced by intrinsic motivation as opposed to extrinsic motivation.

✓ CHECK YOUR ANSWERS IN APPENDIX C.

Theories of Motivation

Hungry and Waiting
A group of starving Somalis hope to receive food from an aid center in the city of Bardera. The situation in Somalia turned to chaos and desperation after rebels toppled the government in 1991. Over 240,000 people died in the ensuing war and famine (Gundel, 2003). Les Stone/Zuma

GOODBYE, SOMALIA Somalia was not a safe place in 1991. The groups that orchestrated the revolution began warring among themselves, and the country plunged into bloody chaos. Over 20,000 innocent people were killed in the crossfire (Gassmann, 1991, December 21). A famine and food crisis ensued, which, in addition to the ongoing fighting, led to 240,000 to 280,000 deaths within the next 2 years (Gundel, 2003). It is easy to understand why Mohamed's parents, or anyone, would want to remove their family from Somalia during this period. Faced with a life-or-death situation, they were motivated by what you might call a "survival" instinct.

Instinct. You hear this word used all the time in everyday conversation: "Trust your instincts," people say in times of uncertainty. "That fighter has a killer instinct," a sports commentator remarks during a boxing match. But what exactly are instincts, and do humans really have them?

Instinct Theory

LO 3   Summarize instinct theory.

Instincts form the basis of one of the earliest theories of motivation. Scientists studying animal behaviors were among the first to observe **instincts.** These complex behaviors are fixed, unlearned, and consistent within a species. Motivated by instincts, South American ovenbirds construct elaborate cavelike nests, and sea turtles swim back hundreds of miles to feeding grounds they visited years earlier (Broderick, Coyne, Fuller, Glen, & Godley, 2007). No one teaches the birds to build their nests or the turtles to retrace migratory routes; through evolution, these behaviors appear to be etched into their genetic make-up.

Nesting Instinct
South American ovenbirds build cozy cavelike nests using mud, grass, and bark. Elaborate home-building behaviors, which are seen in all 240 ovenbird species, appear to be innate, or unlearned (Wuethrich, 1999, November 29). Their architectural aptitude appears to be the result of instinct. Fritz Poelking/Age Fotostock

Inspired in part by Charles Darwin's theory of evolution, early theorists proposed that humans also have a variety of instincts (McDougall, 1912). American psychologist William James (1890/1983) suggested we could explain some human behavior through instincts such as attachment and cleanliness. At the height of instinct theory's popularity, several thousand human "instincts" had been named (for example, curiosity, flight, and aggressiveness; Bernard, 1926; Kuo, 1921). Yet there was little evidence they were true instincts—that is, complex behaviors that are fixed, unlearned, and consistent within a species. Only a handful of human behaviors might be considered instincts, such as rooting behavior in newborn infants (Chapter 8). But even these are more related to reflexes than a complex activity like nest building.

Although instinct theory itself faded into the background, some of its themes are apparent in the **evolutionary perspective.** A substantial body of research suggests that evolutionary forces influence human behavior. For example, emotional responses, such as fear of snakes, heights, and spiders, may have evolved to protect us from danger (Plomin, DeFries, Knopik, & Neiderhiser, 2013). But these fears are not instincts, because they are not universal. Not everyone is afraid of snakes and spiders; some of us have learned to fear (or not fear) them through experience. When trying to pin down the motivation for behavior, it is difficult to determine the relative contributions of learning (nurture) and innate factors (nature) such as instinct (Deckers, 2005).

CONNECTIONS

In **Chapter 1,** we presented the *evolutionary perspective,* which suggests humans have evolved adaptive traits through natural selection. Behaviors that improve the chances of survival and reproduction are most likely to be passed along to offspring, whereas less adaptive behaviors decrease in frequency. Humans do appear to have innate responses that have been shaped by our ancestors' behaviors.

FOUR YEARS IN KENYA After fleeing the bullet-riddled city of Mogadishu, Mohamed and his family made their way across the border into the neighboring country of Kenya, where they lived for about 4 years. Mohamed considers himself one of the "more fortunate ones." Not only was he lucky to get out of the war zone alive—"A lot of people lost their lives trying to flee," he notes—but he also had a decent place to go. Many Somalis had no choice but to settle in squalid, overcrowded refugee camps. Mohamed's family had the means to rent a small apartment in the capital city of Nairobi.

Being an outsider in Kenya was not easy, however. Career opportunities were scarce. Back in Somalia, Mohamed's father had earned a solid living constructing buildings, and his mother had been a successful entrepreneur selling homemade food from their house. In Kenya, neither parent could find employment. They had no choice but to live off "remittances," or money sent from family members outside of Africa, and relying on other people was not their style. "You're waiting on other people to feed you," Mohamed says, "and [my father] didn't like that."

Daily life presented its fair share of challenges, too. Mohamed's diet was painfully monotonous, with most meals centering around *ugali*, a dense gruel made of corn or millet flour—similar to oatmeal, but harder in consistency. At times, the apartment building lost electricity for weeks, or water stopped flowing from faucets. During water shortages, the whole family would carry empty buckets and tubs to a nearby army base and ask for water. Despite these difficulties, Mohamed never went hungry or thirsty. His basic *physiological needs* were usually met.

Drive-Reduction Theory

Humans and animals have basic physiological **needs** or requirements that must be maintained at some baseline or constant state to ensure continued existence. **Homeostasis** refers to the way in which our bodies maintain these constant states through internal controls. In order to survive, there is a continuous monitoring of required levels of oxygen, fluid, nutrients, and so on. If these fall below desired or necessary levels, an urge to restore equilibrium surfaces. And this urge motivates us to act.

LO 4 Describe drive-reduction theory and explain how it relates to motivation.

The **drive-reduction theory** of motivation proposes that this biological balancing act is the basis for motivation (Hull, 1952). According to this theory, behaviors are driven by the need to maintain homeostasis—that is, to fulfill basic biological needs for nutrients, fluids, oxygen, and so on (see **INFOGRAPHIC 9.1** on p. 391). If a need is not fulfilled, this creates a **drive,** or state of tension, that pushes us or motivates behaviors to meet the need. The urges to eat, drink, sleep, seek comfort, or have sex are associated with physiological needs. Once a need is satisfied, the drive is reduced, at least temporarily, because this is an ongoing process, as the need inevitably returns. For example, when the behavior (let's say eating) stops, the deprivation of something (such as food) causes the need to increase again.

Let's look at another concrete example of drive reduction. Imagine you visit a mountainous area 6,500 feet above sea level, which puts a strain on breathing. While jogging, you find yourself gasping for air because your oxygen levels have dropped. Motivated by the need to maintain homeostasis, you stop what you are doing until your oxygen levels return to normal. Having an unfulfilled *need* (not enough oxygen) creates a *drive* (state of tension) that pushes you to modify your behavior in order to restore homeostasis (you stop and breathe deeply, allowing your blood oxygen levels to return to a normal level). The drive-reduction theory helps us understand how physiological needs can be motivators, but it is less useful for explaining why we climb mountains, go to college, or drive cars too fast.

Surviving in Somalia Habiba Ibrahim hauls wood to build a new home near Baidoa, Somalia, in December 1993. The 30-year-old mother was pushed off her land by fighting between ethnic groups. In the years following the government overthrow, 1–2 million Somalis fled their homes. Some resettled in the Western world, but most became refugees within their own country or in the neighboring nations of Kenya and Ethiopia (Gundel, 2003). Ricardo Mazalan/Associated Press

You Asked, Mohamed Answers

http://qrs.ly/n83m6b8

How have your childhood experiences impacted you as an adult?

instincts Complex behaviors that are fixed, unlearned, and consistent within a species.

needs Physiological or psychological requirements that must be maintained at some baseline or constant state.

homeostasis The tendency for bodies to maintain constant states through internal controls.

drive-reduction theory Suggests that maintaining homeostasis motivates us to meet biological needs.

drive A state of tension that pushes us or motivates behaviors to meet a need.

Dangerous Fun
Babies and toddlers are notorious for climbing on furniture, mouthing nonfood items, and reaching for hazardous objects (this is why many parents "baby proof" their homes). Like adults looking for exciting places to travel and new electronic gadgets to own, these babies may be searching for novel forms of stimulation. BSIP/Phototake

Arousal Theory

Mohamed arrived in America when he was 6 years old. Stepping off the plane in the Twin Cities (Minneapolis/St. Paul) was quite a shock for a young boy who had lived most of his childhood in the crowded, pavement-covered city of Nairobi. "It was really strange to me," Mohamed says. "At that time, I hadn't really seen a place that had space." How odd it was to see patches of green grass in front of every house. "Everything looked like it sparkled."

New places, people, and experiences can be frightening. They can also be delightfully exhilarating. Humans are fascinated by novelty, and you see evidence of this innate curiosity in the earliest stages of life. Babies grab, suck, and climb on just about everything they can get their hands on, including (much to the horror of their parents) dangerous electrical devices. Ignoring the most forceful parental warnings (*Do NOT touch that hot plate!*), many toddlers still reach out and touch extremely hot cookware or recklessly leap between pieces of furniture. But mind you, children are not the only ones seeking new experiences. Grown men and women will pay hundreds of dollars to parachute out of airplanes or float over jagged mountains in hot-air balloons. They also spend hours tooling around Web sites like Wikipedia and YouTube—just to learn about new things. Why engage in activities that have little, if anything, to do with satisfying basic biological needs? Humans are driven by other types of urges, including the apparent need for stimulation.

But we are not the only ones hungry for new experiences. Our primate cousins are also inquisitive, which suggests that they too have an innate need for enrichment and sensory stimulation. Researchers studying monkeys, for example, report that they attempt to open latches even without extrinsic motivation; apparently, their curiosity motivates their behavior (Butler, 1960; Harlow, Harlow, & Meyer, 1950).

┈┈▶ **LO 5**   Explain how arousal theory relates to motivation.

According to **arousal theory,** humans (and perhaps other primates) seek an optimal level of arousal, as not all motivation stems from physical needs. Arousal, or engagement in the world, can be a product of anxiety, surprise, excitement, interest, fear, and many other emotions. Have you ever had an unexplained urge to make simple changes to your daily routines, like taking a new route to work, preparing your morning eggs differently, or adding new clothes to your wardrobe? These behaviors may stem from your need to increase arousal, as *optimal* arousal is a personal or subjective matter that is not the same for everyone (Infographic 9.1). Zuckerman (1979, 1994) found evidence that some people are *sensation seekers;* that is, they appear to seek activities that increase arousal. Popularly known as "adrenaline junkies," these individuals relish activities like cliff diving, racing motorcycles, and watching horror movies. High sensation seeking is not necessarily a bad thing, as it may be associated with a higher tolerance for stressful events (Roberti, 2004).

We have discussed motivation in the context of instinct, drive reduction, and arousal. Now let's explore how motivation relates to satisfying a broad spectrum of biological and psychological needs.

Needs and More Needs: Maslow's Hierarchy

┈┈▶ **LO 6**   Outline Maslow's hierarchy of needs.

Have you ever been in a car accident, lived through a hurricane, or witnessed a violent crime? At the time, you probably were *not* thinking about what show you were going to watch on television that night. When physical safety is threatened, everything else tends to take a backseat. This is one of the themes underlying the **hierarchy of needs** theory of motivation proposed by Abraham Maslow (1908–1970), a leading figure in

arousal theory Suggests that humans are motivated to seek an optimal level of arousal, or alertness and engagement in the world.

hierarchy of needs A continuum of needs that are universal and ordered in terms of the strength of their associated drives.

Theories of Motivation

Motivational forces drive our behaviors, thoughts, and feelings. Psychologists have proposed different theories addressing the needs that create these drives within us. Let's look at the three most prominent theories of motivation. Some theories, like drive-reduction theory, best explain motivation related to physiological needs. Other theories focus on psychological needs, such as the need for an optimum level of stimulation, as described in arousal theory. In his hierarchy of needs, Abraham Maslow combined various drives and proposed that we are motivated to meet some needs before others.

Drive-Reduction Theory

Homeostasis motivates us to meet physiological needs.

EQUILIBRIUM

Drive-reducing behaviors restore balance

Balance disturbed by deprivation

Need creates a *drive* to restore balance

Arousal Theory

Humans have an innate need to seek an optimal level of stimulation.

Boredom drives curiosity and activity-seeking behavior.

Feels like anxiety to some, but **sensation seekers** are comfortable here.

OPTIMUM AROUSAL

Level of comfort

Level of arousal

Hierarchy of Needs

Abraham Maslow's theory combines physiological and psychological needs in a hierarchy, or sequence. We are motivated to meet higher-level needs when physiological needs at the base of the hierarchy have been met.

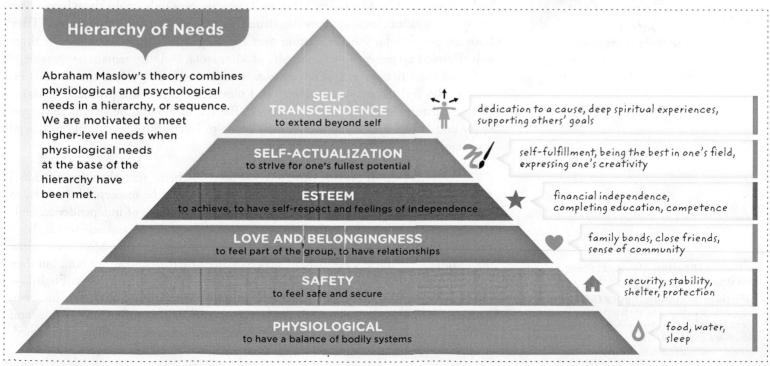

SELF TRANSCENDENCE
to extend beyond self — *dedication to a cause, deep spiritual experiences, supporting others' goals*

SELF-ACTUALIZATION
to strive for one's fullest potential — *self-fulfillment, being the best in one's field, expressing one's creativity*

ESTEEM
to achieve, to have self-respect and feelings of independence — *financial independence, completing education, competence*

LOVE AND BELONGINGNESS
to feel part of the group, to have relationships — *family bonds, close friends, sense of community*

SAFETY
to feel safe and secure — *security, stability, shelter, protection*

PHYSIOLOGICAL
to have a balance of bodily systems — *food, water, sleep*

CONNECTIONS

In **Chapter 1,** we discussed Maslow and his involvement in *humanistic psychology.* The humanists suggest that people are inclined to grow and change for the better, and this perspective is apparent in the hierarchy of needs. Humans are motivated by the universal tendency to move up the hierarchy and meet needs toward the top.

Love, Affection, and Belongingness Relationships with friends help fulfill what Maslow called love and belongingness needs. TobKatrina/Shutterstock

self-actualization The need to be one's best and strive for one's fullest potential.

self-determination theory (SDT) Suggests that humans are born with the need for competence, relatedness, and autonomy, which are always driving us in the direction of growth and optimal functioning.

the **humanistic movement.** Maslow organized human needs into a hierarchy of biological and psychological needs, often depicted as a pyramid (Infographic 9.1). The needs in the hierarchy are considered universal and are ordered according to the strength of their associated drives, with the most critical needs at the bottom. Hunger and thirst, for example, are situated at the base of the hierarchy, and generally take precedence over higher-level needs (that is, these higher-level needs are ignored for the time being).

PHYSIOLOGICAL NEEDS   *Physiological needs* include the requirements for food, water, sleep, and an overall balance of bodily systems. If a life-sustaining need such as fluid intake goes unsatisfied, other needs are placed on hold and the person is motivated to find ways to satisfy it. For example, the Chilean miners introduced in Chapter 1 spent weeks trapped underground with no clean drinking water. To quench their thirst, they were willing to drink oil-contaminated water (and urine, in the case of one man).

SAFETY NEEDS   For most North Americans, basic physiological needs are "relatively well gratified" (Maslow, 1943), and thus Maslow would suggest their behavior is motivated by the next higher level of needs in the hierarchy: *safety needs.* But how you define safety depends on the circumstances of your life. If you were living in Mogadishu during the 1991 revolution (and many times subsequent to that period), staying safe might have involved dodging bullets and artillery fire. For those currently living in Somalia, safety includes having access to safe drinking water and disease-preventing vaccines. Most people living in America do not have to worry about access to clean water or routine vaccinations. Here, safety is more likely equated with the need for predictability and order: having a steady job, a home in a safe neighborhood, health insurance, and living in a country with a stable economy. What does safety mean for you?

LOVE AND BELONGINGNESS NEEDS   If safety needs are being met, then people will be motivated by the *love and belongingness needs.* Maslow suggested this includes the need to avoid loneliness, to feel like part of a group, and to maintain affectionate relationships. Except for a rare run-in with neighborhood bullies, Mohamed enjoyed a fairly secure existence in Minnesota. His need for safety was met, so he was motivated at this next level of the hierarchy. In addition to cultivating deep family bonds, Mohamed befriended two boys he met in middle school, one who had emigrated from Bangladesh and the other a first-generation Mexican American. Not only could these boys relate to the immigrant experience; they also shared Mohamed's academic motivation. "They both are people who value education over anything else," Mohamed says. The three pals all ended up going to the University of Minnesota, and they remain inseparable.

We all want to belong, and failing to meet this need has significant consequences. People who feel disconnected or excluded may demonstrate less prosocial behavior (Twenge, Baumeister, DeWall, Ciarocco, & Bartels, 2007) and behave more aggressively and less cooperatively, which only tends to intensify their struggle for social acceptance (DeWall, Baumeister, & Vohs, 2008).

ESTEEM NEEDS   If the first three levels of needs are being met, then the individual might be motivated by *esteem needs,* including the need to be respected by others, to achieve, and to have self-respect, self-confidence, and feelings of independence. Cultivating and fulfilling these needs foster a sense of confidence and self-worth, both qualities that Mohamed seems to possess. It was early in life that Mohamed began doing things for himself. His parents may have been there to encourage him, but they could not hold his hand when it came to tasks demanding proficiency in English—like filling out employment applications. But Mohamed did just fine on his own, landing his first job at a nonprofit student loan company just after ninth grade, and performing so well that the company employed him throughout college. Mohamed, it appears, began meeting esteem needs very early on.

SELF-ACTUALIZATION   Even with the above-mentioned needs actively being met, Maslow suggested that the need for **self-actualization** would motivate someone "to become more and more what one is, to become everything that one is capable of becoming" (Maslow, 1943, p. 382). Self-actualization is the need to reach one's fullest potential. Some will meet this need by being the best possible parent, others will strive to be the best artist or musician. This need is at the heart of the humanistic movement: Self-actualization represents the human tendency toward growth and self-discovery (Chapter 11). For Mohamed, it means being an exceptional scholar, employee, and father. He also dreams of bringing together Somalis from all around the world through his social networking/media company, Calaacal. The site is just getting off the ground, but it has great potential. Perhaps one day Calaacal will facilitate a grassroots movement to restore peace, unity, and prosperity to Somalia.

SELF-TRANSCENDENCE   Toward the end of his life, Maslow proposed an additional need: that for *self-transcendence*. This need motivates us to go beyond our own needs and feel outward connections through "peak experiences" of ecstasy and awe. Fulfilling this need might mean devoting oneself to a humanitarian cause, pursuing a lofty ideal, or achieving spiritual enlightenment. If you walked into Mohamed's room, you would see a huge poster that says, "Live a simple life so others can simply live." What this means, explains Mohamed, is that you should do the best you can in life, but also strive to allow others to do the same. "It's balancing your life so that you're always doing the most positive good," he says. As president of the University of Minnesota's Somali Student Association, Mohamed put this slogan to work, organizing activities to support Somali students, and arranging cultural awareness events at the university and in the greater Twin City communities.

EXCEPTIONS TO THE RULE   Maslow's hierarchy provides suggestions for the order of needs, but this sequence is not set in stone. In some cases, people abandon physiological needs in order to meet a self-actualization need—going on a hunger strike or giving up material possessions, for example. During the Islamic holy month of Ramadan, Mohamed refrains from drinking or eating from dawn to dusk—not an easy task during August in Minnesota, where the sun rises at about 6:00 A.M. and sets well after 8:00 P.M. The practice of fasting, which also occurs in Christianity, Hinduism, and Judaism, illustrates how basic physiological needs (eating and drinking) can temporarily be placed on hold for a greater purpose (religion).

Safety is another basic need often relegated in the pursuit of something more transcendent. Just think of all the soldiers who have given their lives fighting for causes like freedom and social justice. Somali parents living in a war zone and battling hunger may neglect their own basic needs to ensure their children's well-being, thus fulfilling higher needs such as love and esteem.

Breaking Fast
Iraqi families gather for Iftar, the evening meal eaten after the daytime fast. During the holy month of Ramadan, Muslims foreswear food and water from dawn to dusk. They also step up charity work and other efforts to help those less fortunate (Huffington Post, 2012, July 16). Here, as in Maslow's hierarchy, basic needs (eating and drinking) are put on hold for something more transcendent. Johan Spanner/Polaris

---

> **LO 7**   Explain how self-determination theory relates to motivation.

SELF-DETERMINATION THEORY   Building on the ideas of both Maslow and **Erik Erikson**, Edward Deci and Richard Ryan (2008) proposed the **self-determination theory (SDT),** which suggests that humans are born with three universal, fundamental needs that are always driving us in the direction of optimal functioning: competence, relatedness, and autonomy (**FIGURE 9.1** on page 394; Stone, Deci, & Ryan, 2009). Competence represents the need to reach our goals through successful mastery of day-to-day responsibilities. Relatedness is the need

CONNECTIONS

In **Chapter 8,** we introduced Erikson's theory of psychosocial development, which suggests that stages of development are marked by a task or emotional crisis. These crises often touch on issues of competence, relatedness, and autonomy.

▲ **FIGURE 9.1**
Self-Determination Theory
Deci and Ryan's theory
proposes that we are born
with fundamental needs for
competence, relatedness,
and autonomy. Copyright © 2005 by
the American Psychological Association.
Adapted with permission from Lyubormirsky,
Shledon, and Schkade (2005); photo: Justin
Horrocks/Getty Images

to create meaningful and lasting relationships. And autonomy means managing one's behavior to reach personal goals. Self-determination theory does not focus on overcoming one's shortcomings, but on moving in a positive direction.

NEED FOR ACHIEVEMENT   In the early 1930s, Henry Murray proposed that humans are motivated by 20 fundamental human needs, one of which has been the subject of a great deal of research: the **need for achievement (n-Ach),** or a drive to reach attainable and challenging goals especially in the face of competition. McClelland and colleagues (1976) suggested that people tend to seek out situations that provide opportunities for satisfying this need. A child who aspires to become a professional basketball player might start training at a very young age, read books about the sport, and apply for basketball camp scholarships. A high school student dead-set on going to college may set up meetings with the college counselor, take practice SATs, and read books about how to write an exceptional application essay.

NEED FOR POWER   According to McClelland and colleagues (1976) some people are motivated by a **need for power (n-Pow),** or a drive to control and influence others. People with this need are motivated to project their importance through outward appearances. They may drive around in luxury cars, wear flashy designer clothing, and buy expensive houses. Some even flex their influence muscles on the pages of Facebook, building massive numbers of contacts just to show how important and popular they are. The need for power is one of many needs motivating people to use social media.

SOCIAL MEDIA and psychology

Network Needs

Some of the most enthusiastic users of Facebook—those who tend to have large numbers of contacts and wall posts—score high on assessments of a personality trait called *narcissism* (Buffardi & Campbell, 2008). Narcissistic people are vain and self-absorbed; they seek prestige and power, and they may feel a sense of superiority over others. These characteristics shine through online, and presumably have a negative impact on the Facebook social climate (Buffardi & Campbell, 2008; Carpenter, 2012).

Like all human beings, social media users are driven by the desire for love and belonging (the third level from the bottom on Maslow's hierarchy). But social media may not be the answer for those who struggle to get those needs met in real life. One study of college students, for example, found no evidence that using Facebook cured lonely people of their loneliness. Those who were socially isolated offline were also socially isolated online (Freberg, Adams, McGaughey, & Freberg, 2010). In some cases, using social media actually intensified feelings of loneliness (DiSalvo, 2010). Perhaps this is because interactions with network "friends" tend to be more superficial than those in real life. Can anyone really maintain deep and meaningful relationships with 300 Facebook friends?

FACEBOOK: A CURE FOR LONELINESS?

But there is a bright side. Facebook does appear to be a useful tool for strengthening established relationships (DiSalvo, 2010). A century ago, families were not as geographically scattered as they are today. Grandparents, siblings, and cousins might have lived in the same town or county, and this would have created more opportunities for love, affection, and belonging. These days, families are dispersed all over the globe, and staying connected through social media may be a lot easier (and cheaper) than buying airplane tickets. The bottom line is that social media can be used to satisfy a variety of needs, and the nature of these needs depends on both the user and the site.

We have now covered several important theories of motivation, including Maslow's hierarchy of needs. In the next section, we return our focus to the base of Maslow's pyramid, where basic requirements such as hunger and thirst are represented. Sadly, many people in the world do not get those needs fulfilled.

show what you know

1. Your instructor describes an interesting finding about gender differences regarding dating behavior. She explains that these behavior differences are ultimately motivated by evolutionary forces. She is using which of the following to support her explanation?
   a. operant conditioning
   b. arousal theory
   c. instinct theory
   d. homeostasis

2. The _____ theory of motivation suggests biological needs and homeostasis motivate us to meet our needs.
   a. arousal
   b. instinct
   c. incentive
   d. drive-reduction

3. According to Maslow, the biological and psychological needs that motivate us to behave are arranged in a _____.

4. Self-determination theory proposes that we are motivated by three universal, fundamental needs: competence, relatedness, and autonomy. Describe one example for each of these needs.

5. How does drive-reduction motivation differ from arousal motivation?

✓ CHECK YOUR ANSWERS IN APPENDIX C.

Back to Basics: Hunger

STARVING IN SOMALIA Mohamed has never suffered from extreme hunger, but he is very familiar with topics like famine, food shortages, and starvation. Like many Somali Americans, he regularly sends money back home to relatives in need. Without money from family members living in more prosperous countries like the United States, many Somalis would not be able to afford food, medicine, and other necessities. As Mohamed says, "You can't just leave your family back home to starve."

In the spring of 2011, the Horn of Africa was hit by a drought that caused Somalia to plunge into one of the greatest humanitarian crises of our time—a famine responsible for the starvation deaths of 250 children every day, or 1 child every 6 minutes (British Broadcasting Company [BBC], 2011, July 22). Refugees poured out of Somalia by the thousands. Desperate for food, they walked for weeks to reach refugee camps in neighboring countries. Aid workers said they encountered wounded children, dehydrated and malnourished, arriving at the camps with no shoes (BBC, 2011, June 28). According to a 2011 report, nearly half of Somalia's population was in need of "lifesaving assistance" (United Nations, 2011). The situation has since improved, but the country is still reeling from the crisis (Caspani, 2012, January 23).

In the coming pages, we will explore hunger, one of the most powerful motivators of human behavior. You will learn what happens in the brain and body when a person is in dire need of food, either because of external circumstances (a famine) or deep-seated psychological factors (an eating disorder). We will also investigate the causes of overeating. So fasten your waist belt and get ready for a journey into the psychological realm of hunger.

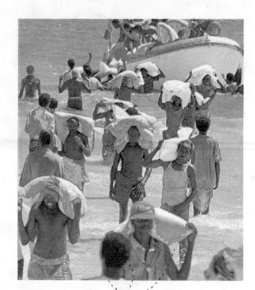

Food Aid
Men haul bags of rice from a boat arriving on the northern coast of Somalia. French children donated the food in response to the 1992 famine. Somalia plunged into yet another famine in 2011. This recent crisis led to the deaths of 10% of children under the age of 5 in the country's south and central regions (BBC News, 2013, May 2). Denis Paquin/Associated Press

Hungry Brain, Hungry Body

It's midnight; you are struggling to get through the final pages of your psychology chapter. Suddenly, your stomach lets out a desperate gurgling cry. "Feed me!" *Time to heat up that frozen burrito,* you say to yourself as you head into the kitchen. But wait! Are you really hungry?

need for achievement (n-Ach) A drive to reach attainable and challenging goals especially in the face of competition.

need for power (n-Pow) A drive to control and influence others.

→ **LO 8**   Discuss how the stomach and the hypothalamus make us feel hunger.

THE STOMACH AND HUNGER   In a classic study, Walter Cannon and A. L. Washburn (1912) sought to answer this question (well, not this *exact* question, but they did want to learn what causes stomach contractions). Here's a brief synopsis of the experiment: To help monitor and record his stomach contractions, Washburn swallowed a balloon that the researchers could inflate. The researchers also kept track of Washburn's hunger levels, having him push a button anytime he felt "hunger pangs" (**FIGURE 9.2**). What did the experiment reveal? Anytime he felt hunger, his stomach contracted.

▲ **FIGURE 9.2**

Cannon and Washburn's Classic Hunger Study
Washburn swallowed a special balloon attached to a device designed to monitor stomach contractions. At the same time, he pressed a key every time he felt hungry. Comparing the record of key presses against the balloon measurements, Washburn was able to show that stomach contractions accompany feelings of hunger.

CONNECTIONS

In **Chapter 2,** we described *hormones* as chemical messengers released in the bloodstream. Hormones do not act as quickly as neurotransmitters, but their messages are more widely spread throughout the body. Here, we see how hormones are involved in communicating information about hunger and feeding behaviors.

BLOOD CHEMISTRY AND HUNGER   Washburn's experiment demonstrates that the stomach plays an important role in hunger, but it's just one piece of the puzzle. For example, we know this because people who have had their stomachs surgically removed because of cancer do not differ from people with their stomachs intact in regard to feelings of satiety (that is, feeling full) or the amount of food eaten during a meal (Bergh, Sjöstedt, Hellers, Zandian, & Södersten, 2003). We also must consider the chemicals in the blood, such as glucose, or blood sugar. When glucose levels dip, the stomach and liver send signals to the brain that something must be done about this reduced energy situation. The brain, in turn, will initiate a sense of hunger.

THE HYPOTHALAMUS AND HUNGER   One part of the brain that helps regulate hungry feelings is the hypothalamus, which can be divided into functionally distinct areas. When the *lateral hypothalamus* is activated, appetite increases. This occurs even in well-fed animals if this region is stimulated electrically. Destroy this area of the brain, and animals lose interest in food, even to the point of starvation. The lateral hypothalamus is also involved in motivating behavior, ultimately helping to preserve the balance between energy supply and demand (Leinninger, 2011).

If the *ventromedial hypothalamus* becomes activated, appetite declines, causing an animal to stop eating. Disable this region of the brain, and the animal will overeat to the point of obesity. The ventromedial hypothalamus receives information about levels of blood glucose and other feeding-related stimuli, as it too works to maintain the body's energy balance (King, 2006).

The hypothalamus has a variety of sensors that react to information about appetite and food intake. Once this input is processed, appropriate responses are communicated via **hormones** in the bloodstream (**INFOGRAPHIC 9.2**). One such hormone is *leptin,* a protein emitted by fat cells that plays a role in suppressing hunger. Another is *insulin,* a pancreatic hormone involved in controlling levels of glucose in the bloodstream. With input from these and other hormones, the brain can monitor energy levels and respond accordingly. This complex system enables us to know when we are hungry, full, or somewhere in between.

Let's Have a Meal: Cultural and Social Context

Biology is not the only factor influencing eating habits. We must also consider the culture and social context in which we eat. In the United States, most of our social activities, holidays, and work events revolve around food. We may not even be hungry, but when presented with a spread of food, we find ourselves eating. All too often we eat too fast,

Mechanisms in Hunger Regulation

We are all aware—sometimes uncomfortably so—when our stomachs are grumbling. But most hunger signals are communicated in an imperceptible cycle throughout our bodies. Feelings of hunger and satisfaction are the result of many independent signals. Different organs are involved in monitoring blood chemistry, prompting the communication of hunger or satiety signals to the brain. These messages are received by the hypothalamus, which regulates basic physiological needs. Separate areas of the hypothalamus then send signals to other parts of the brain, motivating us to increase or decrease eating.

The rat on the right weighs 988 grams—about as much as a pineapple. Researchers destroyed this animal's ventromedial hypothalamus, which prevented the communication of satiety signals. This resulted in extreme overeating. The more typical rat on the left, which has no such damage to the hypothalamus, weighs about a third as much (King, 2006).

Different divisions of the hypothalamus perform distinct functions in relation to regulating hunger.

Lateral hypothalamus works to increase appetite

Ventromedial hypothalamus works to decrease appetite

Hypothalamus

Liver

Pancreas

Stomach

SATIETY SIGNALS

Cholecystokinin (CCK): Hormone released from the gastrointestinal tract that aids digestion.

Leptin: A protein hormone released by fat cells to communicate information about the body's fat stores.

HUNGER SIGNALS

Orexins: Hormones produced in the lateral hypothalamus. Stimulate increased eating.

Ghrelin: Hormone released by empty stomach. Levels rise when we are hungry.

Insulin: Hormone produced by pancreas in response to food intake; controls levels of glucose in the bloodstream. A drop in glucose is a primary hunger signal for the body.

Fat cells

Credits: Young woman eating red apple, © Piotr Marcinski/ Agefotostock; Rats, BW photo, Dr. Bruce King/Psychology Dept. at Clemson University; MRI, midsagittal section, showing a normal brain, highlighting the hypothalamus (orange), © ISM/Phototake rushing to our next event, class, or meeting, not taking the time to experience the sensation of taste. We tend to match our food intake to those around us, although we may not be aware of their influence (Herman, Roth, & Polivy, 2003; Howland, Hunger, & Mann, 2012). Gender plays a role in eating habits as well. Using **naturalistic observation,** researchers found that women choose lower-calorie meals when eating with a man than when eating with another woman (Young, Mizzau, Mai, Sirisegaram, & Wilson, 2009).

PORTION DISTORTION   A variety of factors drive our decisions to begin or stop eating, including hunger, satiety, and food taste (Vartanian, Herman, & Wansink, 2008). But more subtle variables, such as portion size, come into play, too. In one study, participants at a movie theater were given free popcorn, some in medium-sized buckets and others in large buckets. Some of the buckets contained popcorn that was fresh, and others were filled with popcorn that was 14 days old. Participants given large buckets consistently ate 33% more than those given medium-size buckets, regardless of whether the popcorn was fresh or stale. The stale popcorn was described as "soggy" or "terrible," yet the participants still ate more of it when given larger portions (Wansink & Kim, 2005). Remember this the next time you sit down in front of the TV with an entire bag of snack food.

Portion size is just one factor influencing food intake. Visual cues are also important, especially when they provide feedback about how much you have eaten. Researchers gave college students tubes of potato chips to eat while watching a movie. In some of the tubes, every 7th chip was dyed red. Participants given tubes with the occasional red chips consumed 50% less than those given tubes with no red chips. Thus we see, interrupting mindless eating (*Wait a second, that's a red chip*) can decrease the amount of food consumed in one sitting (Geier, Wansink, & Rozin, 2012).

Perhaps the healthiest approach is to eat small portions throughout the day rather than consuming three huge meals. Dividing up the day with meal breaks may also promote better decision making. At least this appears to be the case in the courtroom.

from the pages of **SCIENTIFIC AMERICAN**

Lunchtime Leniency

Judges' rulings are harsher when they are hungrier

Lawyers quip that justice is what the judge ate for breakfast. New research suggests that justice might actually depend on *when* the judge ate breakfast.

Researchers at Ben Gurion University in Israel and Columbia University examined more than 1,000 decisions by eight Israeli judges who ruled on convicts' parole requests. Judges granted 65 percent of requests they heard at the beginning of the day's session and almost none at the end. Right after a snack break, approvals jumped back to 65 percent again.

Jonathan Levav, associate professor of business at Columbia, said that the judges could just be grumpy from hunger. But they probably also suffer from mental fatigue. Previous studies have shown that repeated decisions make people tired, and they start looking for simple answers. For instance, after making a slew of choices, car buyers will start accepting the standard options rather than continuing to customize. As sessions drag on, judges may find it easier to deny requests and let things stand as they are.

Levav says he suspects a similar effect occurs in hospitals, university admissions offices or anywhere people make repeated decisions. So if you're thinking about asking the boss for something special, you might want to do it right after a nice lunch. **Kurt Kleiner. Reproduced with permission. Copyright © 2011 Scientific American, a division of Nature America, Inc. All rights reserved.**

Obesity

Our discussion on strategies for cutting down food intake provides particularly relevant lessons in today's world, where a growing number of people struggle with obesity. According to one study, nearly 70% of adults in the United States are overweight, and over 30% meet the criteria for *obesity*, defined as having a body mass index (BMI) of 30 or higher (Flegal, Carroll, Ogden, & Curtin, 2010). Adults aren't the only ones battling the bulge; one third of America's children and teens are overweight (American Heart Association, 2011).

SET POINT, SETTLING POINT, AND HEREDITY Surprisingly, there is relatively little fluctuation in adult weight over time. The communication between the brain and the appetite hormones help regulate the body's **set point,** or stable weight that we tend to maintain despite variability in day-to-day exercise and intake of food. If you don't consume enough calories and your weight falls below this set point, metabolism decreases, causing you to gain weight and return to your set point. Exceed the set point, and metabolism increases, once again moving you back toward your stable weight (Keesey & Hirvonen, 1997). The set point acts like a thermostat, helping to maintain a consistent weight in part through changes in metabolism.

Some critics of the *set point* model suggest that it fails to appreciate the importance of social and environmental influences (Stroebe, van Koningsbruggen, Papies, & Aarts, 2013). These theorists suggest we should consider a *settling point,* which is less rigid and can explain how the "set" point can actually change based on the relative amounts of food consumed and energy used. A settling point can help us understand how body weight may shift to a newly maintained weight, and why so many people are overweight as a result of environmental factors, such as bigger meal portions, calorie-dense foods, increased dining at restaurants, and eating while engaged in another activity like watching television—all of which tend to make us eat more and gain weight. Nevertheless, there does seem to be a genetic component of body weight. Studies suggest that the **heritability** of BMI is around 65% (Speakman et al., 2011). More research is needed, but it seems we may be genetically predisposed to stay within a certain weight range.

OVEREATING, SLEEP, AND SCREEN TIME As you well know, deciding what and when to eat does not always come down to being hungry or full. Overeating clearly can have a strong connection to obesity, but there are a variety of reasons *why* people overeat, including psychological issues (such as depression, anxiety, obsessive-compulsive disorder, and poor impulse control). We must consider how motivation plays a role in what and when we eat. Some people eat not because they are hungry, but because they are bored, sad, or anxious. Others eat simply because the clock indicates that it is mealtime. Higher brain regions involved in eating decisions can override the hypothalamus, driving you to devour that cheesy burrito even when you don't need the calories.

If our set point works to help us maintain a certain weight, how does this impact people who struggle with *obesity*? Obesity represents both a physiological and psychological issue. There is some evidence that genes play a role, and we also know some illnesses can lead to obesity (Anis et al., 2010; Plomin et al., 2013). But one often overlooked lifestyle factor related to obesity is sleep. Preliminary research suggests that inadequate sleep is linked to weight problems (a negative correlation between sleep and weight gain). In contrast, individuals who sleep between 6 and 8 hours are more

Obesity Epidemic
Thirty-six percent of U.S. adults are obese, meaning they have a body mass index (BMI) greater than or equal to 30 (Flegal et al., 2012). Obesity has become a worldwide phenomenon, affecting countries as far-flung as Canada and Iran. Some researchers suspect the problem is related to the growing availability of cheap, processed, and well-marketed food (Swinburn et al., 2011). Digital Vision/Thinkstock

CONNECTIONS

In **Chapter 7,** we presented *heritability,* the degree to which heredity is responsible for a particular characteristic in a population. The heritability for BMI is 65%, indicating that around 65% of the variation in BMI can be attributed to genes, and 35% to environmental influences.

set point The stable weight that is maintained despite variability in exercise and food intake.

likely to lose weight. A positive correlation exists between screen time and weight gain: the more screen time, the more weight gain. When screen time interferes with making healthy eating choices and getting regular physical exercise, weight loss is not as successful (Elder et al., 2012).

To lose weight, one must eat less and move more (TABLE 9.2). You must use more calories than you are taking in. Our ancestors didn't have to worry about this. They didn't have a Starbucks on every street corner to tempt them with that delicious cup of calories. They *had* to choose foods rich in calories to give them the energy to sustain themselves. Although this was a very efficient means of survival for them, it doesn't work out so well for us. When experiencing a "famine" (or a decrease in the caloric intake our bodies are accustomed to), our metabolism naturally slows down, requiring fewer calories and making it harder to lose weight.

In response to the obesity problem in the United States, policies have been implemented to raise awareness and discourage overeating. One such intervention is requiring information about calories to be clearly visible, which can serve as a visual cue or reminder. Providing this information can impact healthy food choices. However, accessibility to comparably priced healthy alternatives must be increased (in vending machines, for example)—but this too may require changes in policy (Stroebe et al., 2013).

Table 9.2	WEIGHT LOSS: MAKING IT FIT
Strategies	**Description**
Set realistic goals.	Set goals and expectations that are specific, realistic, and flexible.
Get regular exercise.	Exercising just 30 minutes a day 5 times a week can help with weight loss. Add a variety of physical activity to your daily routines.
Eat regularly and track intake.	Eat on a set schedule to minimize mindless eating. Eat only when hungry, and write down what and how much you consume by using a food diary.
Control portions.	Watch your portions. This is the amount you decide to eat. Read labels to determine the recommended serving size.
Drink water.	Eliminate sweetened beverages.
Join a weight loss support group.	Social support helps promote healthier coping strategies and accountability.

Losing weight is not an easy task, but it doesn't have to be painful. Making basic lifestyle changes in your daily routines can have significant benefits.

SOURCE: KRUGER, BLANCK, AND GILLESPIE (2006).

anorexia nervosa An eating disorder identified by significant weight loss, an intense fear of being overweight, a false sense of body image, and a refusal to eat the proper amount of calories to achieve a healthy weight.

bulimia nervosa An eating disorder characterized by extreme overeating followed by purging, with serious health risks.

binge-eating disorder An eating disorder characterized by episodes of extreme overeating, during which a larger amount of food is consumed than most people would eat in a similar amount of time under similar circumstances.

Eating Disorders

> **LO 9**   Outline the major eating disorders.

Although many people deal with obesity, others struggle with food in a different way. Eating disorders are serious dysfunctions in eating behavior that can involve restricting food consumption, obsessing over weight or body shape, eating too much, and purging (American Psychiatric Association [APA], 2013). Eating disorders usually begin in the early teens and typically affect girls. That doesn't mean boys do not struggle with eating disorders; 1 in 4 children ages 5–13 with an eating disorder is male (Madden, Morris, Zurynski, Kohn, & Elliot, 2009). However, the causes of body image distortions often differ according to gender. Females desire to be smaller and thinner, whereas males seek an "idealized masculine shape" (Darcy et al., 2012). Let's take a look at three of the most recognized eating disorders.

ANOREXIA NERVOSA   One of the most commonly known eating disorders is **anorexia nervosa,** which is characterized by self-imposed restrictions on calories needed to maintain a healthy weight. These restrictions lead to extremely low body weight in relation to age, sex, development, and physical health. Someone with this disorder has an extreme fear of gaining weight and getting fat, even though her body weight is extremely low. Often there is an altered and distorted sense of body weight and figure, as well as no realization of the "seriousness" of her low body weight (APA, 2013). In some cases, women experience an absence of menstrual periods, a condition called *amenorrhea* (Attia & Roberto, 2009). Other severe symptoms may include brain damage, multi-organ failure, infertility, and thinning of the bones (National Institute of Mental Health [NIMH], 2011). Anorexia is associated with the highest death rates of all psychological disorders (Darcy et al., 2012; Harris & Barraclough, 1998; Smink, van Hoeken, & Hoek, 2012). Approximately 20% of those deaths are due to suicide (Smink et al., 2012). Although anorexia nervosa affects mostly women and adolescent girls, males can also be affected by it (in particular, males involved in wrestling, running, or dancing, who are required to maintain a certain weight).

BULIMIA NERVOSA   Another eating disorder is **bulimia nervosa,** which involves recurrent episodes of binge eating, consuming a large amount of food in a short period of time (with that amount being greater than most people would eat in the same time frame). While bingeing, the person feels a lack of control and thus engages in purging behaviors to prevent weight gain (for example, self-induced vomiting, misuse of laxatives, fasting, or excessive exercise; APA, 2013). Like anorexia, bulimia more often affects women and girls (Stice, Marti, Shaw, & Jaconis, 2009). Bulimia also has serious health risks, such as high blood pressure, heart disease, and Type 2 diabetes (Haedt-Matt & Keel, 2011). Other symptoms include decaying teeth, damage to the throat, gastrointestinal disorders, and electrolyte imbalance from vomiting, which can lead to cardiac failure (NIMH, 2011). Research has found that 23% of deaths associated with bulimia nervosa result from suicide (Smink et al., 2012).

BINGE-EATING DISORDER   You may have also heard of **binge-eating disorder** (APA, 2013), characterized by episodes of excessive food consumption (eating more than most people would eat in the same amount of time and in similar situations). As in bulimia, the individual feels unable to control her eating during that period of time, but the difference is that she does not engage in excessive weight control or purging behaviors. Some psychological effects could include feelings of embarrassment about how much food has been consumed, depression, and guilt after overeating.

We know that eating disorders are apparent in America—we see evidence of them on television, in magazines, and in everyday life. But are these disorders also observed in India, South Africa, and Egypt? Let's take a look at eating disorders across the world.

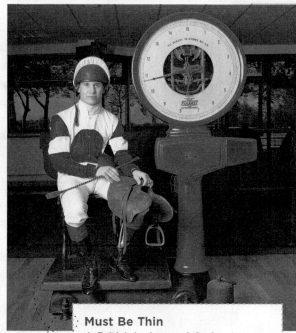

Must Be Thin
A British jockey weighs in at a horse racetrack near Manchester, England. Jockeys must satisfy strict weight requirements in order to ride in races. For many competitions, this means weighing 110 pounds or less. In an effort to stay thin, jockeys have been known to restrict their intake of food and liquid, sweat off water weight in saunas, and force themselves to vomit (Associated Press, 2008, April 25; McKenzie, 2012, October 23). Lichfield/Getty Images

A Cross-Cultural Look at Eating Disorders

Close your eyes and imagine the stereotypical beauty queen. Is she curvy like a Coke bottle or long and lean like a Barbie doll? We suspect the image that popped into your mind's eye looked more like the famed plastic doll. Let's face it: Western concepts of beauty, particularly female beauty, often go hand-in-hand with *thinness*.

With all this pressure to be slender, it's no wonder eating disorders like anorexia and bulimia are most commonly diagnosed and treated in Western societies such as the United States (**TABLE 9.3**; Keel & Klump, 2003; Littlewood, 2004). Psychologists once believed eating disorders *only* occurred in regions of the world influenced by Western culture. Anorexia and bulimia were thought to be psychological disorders unique to certain societies. But evidence suggests it is not that simple.

Keel and Klump (2003) conducted a large review of studies and concluded that anorexia occurs throughout the non-Western world, from Hong Kong to Malaysia to Iran. They also found evidence of people, particularly young women, starving themselves since medieval times—long before Barbie dolls and runway models began making "normal" people feel "fat." Fear of fat may be an important factor driving self-starvation, but it is not necessarily the only one. There are other reasons people forgo food—a desire for some type of control, for instance (Simpson, 2002).

However, Keel and Klump (2003) found no evidence of bulimia (based on strict criteria) existing in regions isolated from Western culture. They also determined that the prevalence of the disorder dramatically increased during the second half of the 1900s, just as the fixation with thin was beginning to take hold. This pattern might not be as strong outside of Western culture, but such a fixation with body image is becoming more prevalent across cultures.

Skinny Around the World
We typically think of eating disorders as a Western problem, but anorexia nervosa has been documented in countries across the world, from Hong Kong to the United Arab Emirates (Keel & Klump, 2003).
Camera Press/Redux

THEY ... FOUND EVIDENCE OF PEOPLE, PARTICULARLY YOUNG WOMEN, STARVING THEMSELVES SINCE MEDIEVAL TIMES. . . .

Table 9.3   **TREATMENT OF EATING DISORDERS**

Treatment Options	Description
Counseling and psychotherapy	Treatment may involve individual, group, or family counseling. The focus of counseling and psychotherapy can be on nutrition, psychological issues, or thoughts and behaviors surrounding the eating disorder.
Health care and medical monitoring	Many eating disorders result in serious medical crises. Medical monitoring and care are critical when it comes to the patient's health.
Drug therapies	Although drugs will not prevent, cure, or restore an individual to a normal weight, drug therapies may be useful in treating the mood issues (often anxiety and depression) that can accompany eating disorders.

Effective treatment of eating disorders often involves a combination of approaches tailored to the individual. This tends to be more effective than one type of treatment alone.

SOURCE: ADAPTED FROM NIMH (2011).

We have now explored the many facets of motivation, from basic physiological drives to transcendent needs for achievement. As you may have guessed from the title of this chapter, all these motivations are intimately tied to emotions. To understand motivated behaviors, you can't ignore emotion. In the sections to come, we will explore the complex world of human emotion, with a focus on fear and happiness.

show what you know

1. Washburn swallowed a special balloon to record his stomach contractions. He also pressed a button to record his feelings of hunger. The findings indicated that whenever he felt hunger, his:
   a. stomach was contracting.
   b. stomach was still.
   c. blood sugar went up.
   d. ventromedial hypothalamus was active.

2. Bulimia nervosa is an eating disorder characterized by
   a. restrictions of energy intake.
   b. extreme fear of gaining weight, although one's body weight is extremely low.
   c. a distorted sense of body weight and figure.
   d. extreme overeating followed by purging.

3. Describe how the hypothalamus triggers hunger and its relationship to eating.

✓ CHECK YOUR ANSWERS IN APPENDIX C.

Introduction to Emotion

SHARK ATTACK For those longing for a quiet beach escape, Ocracoke Island on the North Carolina coast is hard to beat. A quaint island wrapped in 16 miles of pristine beach, Ocracoke is a perfect place for building sandcastles, collecting seashells, and riding the waves. The breeze is sweet, the water refreshing, and the sand soft on your feet. Circumstances are ideal for young children, except for the occasional rip current. Oh, and there's one more thing: Beware of sharks.

One summer night in 2011, 6-year-old Lucy Mangum was splashing around on her boogie board at her family's favorite Ocracoke beach. She was close to shore in water no deeper than 2 feet. Suddenly, Lucy let out a spine-chilling scream. Her mother Jordan, just feet away, spotted the fin of a shark cutting through the water. Running to swoop up her daughter, Jordan did not realize what had occurred—until she saw the blood streaming from her daughter's right leg, which was "completely open" from heel to calf (Allegood, 2011, July 27). The shark had attacked Lucy.

Jordan did the right thing. She applied pressure to the gushing wound and called for help. Lucy's father Craig, who happens to be an emergency room doctor, rushed over and looked at the wound. Right away, he knew it was severe and needed immediate medical attention (Stump, 2011, July 26). In the moments following the attack, Lucy was remarkably calm. "Am I going to die?" she asked her mom. "Absolutely not," Jordan replied. "Am I going to walk?" Lucy asked. "Am I going to have a wheelchair?" It was too early to know (CBS News, 2011, July 26).

Spooky Shark
How would it feel to become the target of this great white predator? You would likely feel *fear*, one of the most extensively researched emotions. But perhaps the shark is the one that should be afraid. Every year, humans kill about 70 million sharks; meanwhile, shark attacks on humans number about 100 (Florida Museum of Natural History, 2011; Smithsonian Institution, 2013). Hemera/Thinkstock

What Is Emotion?

Unprovoked shark attacks are extremely uncommon, occurring less than 100 times per year worldwide. And most attacks are not fatal. To put things in perspective, you are 75 times more likely to be killed by a bolt of lightning and 26 times more likely to be killed by a dog (Florida Museum of Natural History, 2011). Despite their rarity, shark attacks seem to be particularly fear provoking. Maybe the thought of becoming the prey of a wild creature reminds us that we are still, at some level, animals: vulnerable players in the game of natural selection.

Fear is an emotion you experience throughout your life. When you were a baby, you might have been afraid of the vacuum cleaner or the hair dryer. As you matured, your fears may have shifted to the dog next door or the monster in the closet. These days you might be scared of growing older, being diagnosed with a serious disease, or losing someone you love.

→ **LO 10** Define emotions and explain how they are different from moods.

But what exactly is fear? That's an easy question: Fear is an emotion. Now here's the hard question: What is an *emotion*? An **emotion** is a psychological state that includes a subjective or inner experience. In other words, emotion is an intensely personal experience; we cannot actually feel each other's emotions firsthand. Emotion also has a physiological component; it is not only "in our heads." For example, anger can make you feel hot, anxiety might cause sweaty palms, and sadness may sap your physical energy. Finally, emotion entails a behavioral expression. We scream and run when frightened, gag in disgust, and shed tears of sadness. Think about the last time you felt joyous. What was your inner experience of that joy, how did your body react, and what would someone have noticed about your behavior?

Thus, emotion is a subjective psychological state that includes both physiological and behavioral components. But are these three elements—psychology, physiology, and behavior—equally important, and in what order do they occur? The answer to these questions is still under debate, as is the very definition of emotion (Davidson, Scherer, & Goldsmith, 2002). With uncertainty about the cause and function of emotion, it comes as no surprise that many scholars are interested in studying it. Psychologists, physicians, neuroscientists, economists, biologists, geneticists, and others are working from a variety of perspectives to determine the nature of emotions (Coan, 2010), including the roles that the brain, body, and face play.

MOODS VERSUS EMOTIONS   Most psychologists agree that emotions are different from moods. Emotions are quite strong, but they don't generally last as long as moods, and they are more likely to have an identifiable cause. An emotion is initiated by a stimulus, and it is more likely than a mood to motivate someone to action. Moods are longer-term emotional states that are less intense than emotions and do not appear to have distinct beginnings or ends (Kemeny & Shestyuk, 2008; Matlin, 2009; Oatley, Keltner, & Jenkins, 2006). An example might help clarify: Imagine your mood is happy, but a car cuts you off on the highway, creating a negative emotional response like anger.

Now let's see how the three distinguishing characteristics of emotion (as opposed to moods) might apply to Lucy's situation. When Lucy's mother saw the wound from the shark bite, she remembers feeling "afraid" (CBS News, 2011, July 26). Her emotion (1) had a clear cause (the shark attacking her daughter) and (2) produced an immediate emotional reaction (fear), which (3) motivated her into action (applying pressure to the wound and calling for help).

LANGUAGE AND EMOTION   If you were Lucy's mom, what words might you use to describe your fear—frightened, terrified, horrified, scared, petrified, spooked, aghast? Having a variety of labels at your disposal certainly helps when it comes to communicating your emotions. "I feel *angry at you*" conveys a slightly different meaning than "I feel *resentful of you*," or "I feel *annoyed by you*." The English language includes about 200 words to describe emotions. But does that mean we are capable of feeling only 200 emotions? Probably not. And if another language offers more descriptive words, speakers of that language don't necessarily experience a broader array of emotions. Words and emotions are not one and the same, but they are closely linked. In fact, their relationship has captivated the interest of linguists from fields as different as anthropology, psychology, and evolutionary biology (Majid, 2012).

Rather than focusing on words or labels, scholars typically characterize emotions along different dimensions. Izard (2007) suggests that we can describe emotions according to valence and arousal (**FIGURE 9.3**). The *valence* of an emotion

FIGURE 9.3
Dimensions of Emotion
Emotions can be compared and contrasted according to their valence (how pleasant or unpleasant they are) and their arousal level.
Copyright © 1980 by the American Psychological Association. Adapted with permission from Russell (1980).

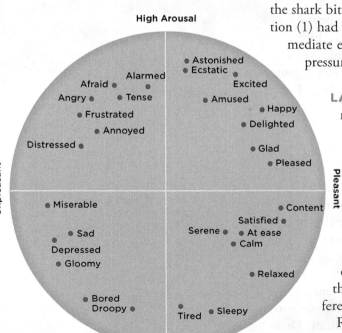

refers to how pleasant or unpleasant it is. Happiness, joy, and pleasure are on the pleasant end of the valence dimension; anger and disgust lie on the unpleasant end. The *arousal level* of an emotion describes how active, excited, and involved a person is while experiencing the emotion, as opposed to how calm, uninvolved, or passive she may be. With valence and arousal level, we can compare and contrast emotions. The emotion of ecstasy, for example, has a high arousal level and a positive valence. Feeling relaxed has a low arousal and a positive valence. When Lucy looked down and saw the shark, she likely experienced an intense fear—high arousal, but low valence. Fortunately, for Lucy and her family, fear eventually gave way to more positive emotions. Let's find out what happened.

show what you know

1. _____ is a psychological state that includes a subjective or inner experience, physiological component, and behavioral expression.
   a. Valence
   b. An instinct
   c. A mood
   d. An emotion

2. Emotions can be described along two dimensions: valence and _____.

3. On the way to a wedding, you get mud on your clothing. Describe how your emotion and mood would differ.

✓ CHECK YOUR ANSWERS IN APPENDIX C.

Theories of Emotion

FIGHT BACK Within 35 minutes of the attack, Lucy was lifted off Ocracoke Island by helicopter and on her way to a trauma center in Greenville, North Carolina. The damage to her leg was extensive, with large tears to the muscle and tendons. She would need two surgeries, extensive physical therapy, and a wheelchair for some time after leaving the hospital (WRAL.com, 2011, July 26).

How did Lucy hold up during this period of extreme stress? According to lead surgeon Dr. Richard Zeri, the 6-year-old was "remarkably calm" (Allegood, 2011, July 27). But she did seem to harbor some negative feelings toward the shark, at least initially. "I hate sharks," she told her parents (Stump, 2011, July 26). "I should have kicked him in the nose," she reportedly said (Allegood, 2011, July 27). Eventually, Lucy forgave the shark: "I don't care that the shark bit me," she told reporters, "I forgive him" (Stump, 2011, July 26), but her initial reaction appeared to be defensive. Fighting back is not an unusual response; some victims have prevented sharks from attacking by grabbing their tails, punching them in the gills, and gouging their eyes (Cabanatuan & Sebastian, 2005, October 19; Caldicott, Mahajani, & Kuhn, 2001).

Emotion and Physiology

Such acts of self-defense are mediated by the sympathetic nervous system's **fight-or-flight** response (Chapter 12). When faced with a stressful situation like a shark attack, stress hormones are released into the blood; breathing rate increases; the heart pumps faster and harder; blood pressure rises; the liver releases extra glucose into the bloodstream; and blood surges into the large muscles. All these physical changes prepare the body for confronting or fleeing the threat; hence the expression "fight or flight." But fear is not the only emotion that involves dramatic physical changes. Tears pour

CONNECTIONS

In **Chapter 2**, we explained how the sympathetic nervous system prepares the body to respond to an emergency, whereas the parasympathetic nervous system brings the body back to a noncrisis mode through the "rest-and-digest" process. Here, we see how the autonomic nervous system is involved in physical experiences of emotion.

emotion A psychological state that includes a subjective or inner experience, a physiological component, and a behavioral expression.

from the eyes during intense sadness and joy. Anger is associated with sweating, an elevated heart rate, and increased blood flow to the hands, apparently preparing them to strike (Ekman, 2003).

⋯▶ **LO 11**   Identify the major theories of emotion and describe how they differ.

Most psychologists agree that emotions and physiology are deeply intertwined. Some suggest there are basic emotions that are biologically determined; others promote a more cognitive approach, focusing on how thinking is involved in the experience of emotions. Furthermore, what they have not always agreed on is the precise order of events. What happens first: the body changes associated with emotion or the emotions themselves? That's a no-brainer, you may be thinking. Emotions occur first, and then the body responds. American psychologist William James would not agree.

Ha Ha Ha! ◀
Does laughing make you happy? According to the James–Lange theory of emotion, yes. It suggests that a behavioral response such as laughing paves the way for an emotion (happiness). Some clinicians actually incorporate "laugh therapy" into their treatment, and encouraging results have been seen in cancer patients and elderly people (Joshua, Cotroneo, & Clarke, 2005; Ko & Youn, 2011). Jason Stitt/ Shutterstock

JAMES–LANGE THEORY   In the late 1800s, James and Carl Lange, a Danish physiologist, working independently, derived similar explanations for emotion (James, 1890/1983; Lange & James, 1922). What is now known as the **James–Lange theory of emotion** suggests that a stimulus initiates a physiological reaction (for example, the heart pounding, muscles contracting, a change in breathing) and/or a behavioral reaction (such as crying or striking out), and this reaction leads to an emotion (**INFOGRAPHIC 9.3** on page 409). Emotions *do not* cause physiological or behavioral reactions to occur, as common sense might suggest. Instead, "we feel sorry because we cry, angry because we strike, afraid because we tremble" (James, 1890/1983, p. 1066). In other words, changes in the body and behavior pave the way for emotions. Our bodies automatically react to stimuli, and awareness of this physiological reaction leads to the subjective experience of an emotion.

How might the James–Lange theory apply to our shark attack victim Lucy? It all begins with a stimulus, in this case the appearance of the shark and the pain of the bite. Next occur the physiological reactions (an increased heart rate, faster breathing, and so on) and the behavioral responses (screaming, trying to swim away). Finally, the emotion registers. Lucy feels fear. Imagine that Lucy, for some reason, had no physiological reaction to the shark—no rapid heartbeat, and so forth. Would she still experience the same degree of terror? According to the James–Lange theory, no. Lucy might see the shark and decide to flee, but she wouldn't *feel* afraid.

The implication of the James–Lange theory is that each emotion has its own distinct physiological fingerprint. If this were the case, it would be possible to identify an emotion based on a person's physiological/behavioral responses. Someone who is sad would display a different physiological/behavioral profile when feeling angry, for example. PET scans have confirmed that different emotions such as happiness, anger, and fear do indeed have distinct activation patterns in the brain, lending evidence in support of the James–Lange theory (Berthoz, Blair, Le Clec'h, & Martinot, 2002; Carlsson et al., 2004; Damasio et al., 2000; Salimpoor, Benovoy, Larcher, Dagher, & Zatorre, 2011).

However, critics of the James–Lange theory of emotion suggest it cannot fully explain emotional phenomena because (1) people who are incapable of feeling physiological reactions of internal organs (as a result of surgery or spinal cord injuries, for example) can still experience emotions; (2) the speed of an emotion is much faster than physiological changes occurring in internal organs; and (3) when physiological changes are made to the functions of internal organs (through a hormonal injection, for instance), emotions do not necessarily change (Bard, 1934; Cannon, 1927; Hilgard, 1987). In one experiment, researchers used surgery to stop animals from becoming physiologically aroused, yet the animals continued to exhibit behavior associated with emotion (such as growling and posturing; Cannon, 1927).

CANNON-BARD THEORY   Walter Cannon (1927) and his student Philip Bard (1934) were among those who believed the James–Lange theory could not explain all emotions. The **Cannon–Bard theory of emotion** suggests that we do *not* feel emotion as a result of physiological and behavioral reactions, but rather these experiences occur simultaneously (Infographic 9.3). The starting point of this response is a stimulus in the environment.

Let's use the Cannon–Bard theory to see how the appearance of a snake might lead to an emotional reaction. Imagine you are about to crawl into bed for the night. You pull back the sheets, and there, in YOUR BED, is a snake! According to the Cannon–Bard theory, the image of the snake will stimulate sensory neurons to relay signals in the direction of your cortex. But rather than rushing to the cortex, these signals pass through the thalamus, splitting in two directions—one toward the cortex and the other toward the hypothalamus.

When the neural information reaches the cortex and hypothalamus, several things could happen. First, the "thalamic–hypothalamic complex will be thrown into a *state of readiness*" (Krech & Crutchfield, 1958, p. 343), in a sense, waiting for the determination of whether the message will continue to the skeletal muscles and internal organs, instructing them to react. The neural information from the thalamus will arrive in the cortex at the same time, enabling you to "perceive" the snake on your bed. If it is just a rubber snake, this news will be sent from the cortex to the thalamic–hypothalamic complex, preventing the emergency signal from being sent to the skeletal muscles and internal organs. However, if the object in your bed is a real snake, then the emergency message will be forwarded to your skeletal muscles and internal organs, prompting a physiological and/or behavioral response (heart racing, jumping backward). At the same time, the thalamus sends a message to the cortex that this situation must be responded to right away. It is at this point, along with the perception of the snake, that an emotion is experienced. The emotion and physiological reaction occur simultaneously.

Critics of the Cannon–Bard theory suggest that the thalamus might not be capable of carrying out this complex processing on its own and that other areas may contribute (Beebe-Center, 1951; Hunt, 1939). Research suggests that the limbic system, hypothalamus, and prefrontal cortex are also substantially involved in processing emotions (Kolb & Whishaw, 2009; Northoff et al., 2009).

Cognition and Emotion

SCHACHTER-SINGER THEORY   Schachter and Singer (1962) also took issue with the James–Lange theory, primarily because different emotions do not have distinct and recognizable physiological responses. They suggested there is a *general* pattern of physiological arousal caused by the sympathetic nervous system, and this pattern is common to a variety of emotions. The **Schachter–Singer theory of emotion** proposes that the experience of emotion is the result of two factors: (1) physiological arousal, and (2) a cognitive label for this physiological state (the arousal). According to this theory, if someone experiences physiological arousal, but doesn't know why it has occurred, she will label the arousal and explain her feelings based on her "knowledge" of the environment (that is, in recognition of the context of the situation). Depending on the "cognitive aspects of the situation," the physiological arousal might be labeled as joy, fear, anxiety, fury, or jealousy (Infographic 9.3).

When you are certain about what is causing your physiological arousal, you won't look to the situation to label the emotion. Imagine you are about to deliver an important speech in front of hundreds of people and your heart is pounding. If you are afraid of public speaking, then you know what is causing your heart to pound and you would

Eek, a Snake! ◀
Most people would be terrified to see a snake slithering across their bedsheets. Does the feeling of fear come before or after the heart starts racing and the body flinches? According to the Cannon–Bard theory of emotion, everything happens simultaneously: the emotional reaction, physiological changes, and a behavioral response.
fivespots/shutterstock

James-Lange theory of emotion
Suggests that a stimulus initiates the experience of a physiological and/or behavioral reaction, and this reaction leads to the feeling of an emotion.

Cannon-Bard theory of emotion
Suggests that environmental stimuli are the starting point for emotions, and physiological or behavioral responses occur at the same time emotions are felt.

Schachter-Singer theory of emotion
Suggests that the experience of emotion is the result of physiological arousal and a cognitive label for this physiological state.

label the arousal as fear. But sometimes ambiguity exists in a situation, and you might not be sure how to label an emotion. For example, if your heart is pounding and you are not afraid of public speaking, you might try to label the arousal based on your assessment of the situation (*I drank a lot of coffee, I am excited to give the speech,* or *Someone special is in the crowd*). However, it is unlikely you will report feeling any emotion without experiencing physiological arousal (Schachter & Singer, 1962).

To test their theory, Schachter and Singer injected participants (male college students) with either epinephrine to mimic physiological reactions of the sympathetic nervous system (such as increased blood pressure, respiration, and heart rate) or a placebo. The researchers also divided the participants into the following groups: those who were informed correctly about possible side effects (for example, tremors, palpitations, flushing, or accelerated breathing), those who were misinformed about side effects, and others who were told nothing about side effects.

The participants were left in a room with a "stooge," a confederate secretly working for the researcher, who was either euphoric (elated) or angry. When the confederate behaved euphorically, the participants who had been given no explanation for their physiological arousal were more likely to report feeling happy or appeared happier. When the confederate behaved angrily, participants given no explanation for their arousal were more likely to appear or report feeling angry. Through observation and self-report, it was clear the participants who did not receive an explanation for their physiological arousal could be manipulated to feel either euphoria or anger, depending on the confederate they were paired with. The participants who were accurately informed about side effects did not show signs or report feelings of euphoria or anger. Instead, they accurately attributed their physiological arousal to the side effects clearly explained to them at the beginning of the study (Schachter & Singer, 1962).

Some have criticized the Schachter–Singer theory, though, suggesting it overstates the link between physiological arousal and the experience of emotion (Reisenzein, 1983). Studies have shown that people can experience an emotion without labeling it, especially if neural activity sidesteps the cortex, heading straight to the limbic system (Dimberg, Thumberg, & Elmehed, 2000; Lazarus, 1991a). We will discuss this process in the section below on fear.

COGNITIVE APPRAISAL AND EMOTION Rejecting the notion that emotions result from cognitive labels of physiological arousal, Lazarus (1984, 1991a) suggested that emotion is the result of the way people appraise or interpret interactions they have in their surroundings. We appraise what is happening in our environment based on its significance. It doesn't matter if someone can label an emotion or not; he will experience the emotion nonetheless. We've all felt emotions such as happiness, anxiety, shame, and so forth, and we don't need an agreed upon label or word to experience them. Babies, for example, can feel emotions long before they are able to label them with words.

Lazarus also suggested that emotions are adaptive, because they help us cope with the surrounding world. In a continuous feedback loop, as an individual's appraisal or interpretation of his environment changes, so do his emotions (Folkman & Lazarus, 1985; Lazarus, 1991b). Emotion is a very personal reaction to the environment. This notion became the foundation of the **cognitive appraisal approach** to emotion (Infographic 9.3). The cognitive-appraisal approach suggests that the appraisal causes an emotional reaction, whereas the Schachter–Singer theory asserts the arousal comes first and then has to be labeled.

Responding to the cognitive-appraisal approach, Zajonc (zay-ənts) (1984) suggested that thinking does not always have to be involved when we experience an emotion. As Zajonc (1980) saw it, emotions can precede thoughts and may even

cognitive appraisal approach
Suggests that the appraisal or interpretation of interactions with surroundings causes an emotional reaction.

Theories of Emotion

Imagine you are swimming and you think you see a shark. Fear pierces your gut, sending your heart racing as you swim frantically to shore. Or is it actually your churning stomach and racing heart that cause you to feel so terrified? And what part, if any, do your thoughts play in this process?

Psychologists have long debated the order in which events lead to emotion. Let's compare four major theories, each proposing a different sequence of events.

Body changes lead to emotions.	Body changes and emotions happen together.	Our thoughts about our body changes lead to emotions.	Our thoughts about our situation lead to emotions.

James–Lange

STIMULUS

PHYSIOLOGICAL RESPONSE

FEAR

EMOTION

Cannon–Bard

STIMULUS

PHYSIOLOGICAL RESPONSE

FEAR

EMOTION

Schachter–Singer

STIMULUS

PHYSIOLOGICAL RESPONSE

I'm scared.

COGNITIVE LABELING

FEAR

EMOTION

Cognitive Appraisal

STIMULUS

I'm scared.

COGNITIVE APPRAISAL

FEAR

EMOTION

STIMULUS: external situation

PHYSIOLOGICAL RESPONSE: physical changes (for fear, preparing body for threat: heart pounds, muscles contract, breathing changes)

COGNITIVE ACTIVITY: evaluation of the situation and/or labeling the physiological response

EMOTION: subjective experience (fear)

Credit: Sharks, Shutterstock

cause them. He also suggested we can experience emotions without interpreting what is occurring in the environment. Emotion can influence cognition and cognition can influence emotion.

One of the main areas of disagreements among the theories just described concerns cognition and how it fits into the picture. Forgas (2008) proposed that the association between emotion and cognitive activity is complex as well as bidirectional: "Cognitive processes determine emotional reactions, and, in turn, affective states influence how people remember, perceive, and interpret social situations and execute interpersonal behaviors" (p. 99).

Emotions are complex and closely related to cognition, physiology, and perception. We know, for example, that certain physiological changes are likely to occur when a person is frightened, anxious, or attempting to conceal deceit. In fact, some important technologies are built on this very premise. Perhaps you've heard of the polygraph?

CONTROVERSIES

Problems with Polygraphs

▶◀ Since its introduction in the early 1900s, the polygraph, or "lie detector" test, has been used by government agencies for a variety of purposes, including job screening, crime investigation, and spy identification (Department of Justice, 2006; Nature, 2004, April 15). The FBI (along with many police departments) will not even hire applicants unless they undergo a thorough background check, which includes a polygraph (Federal Bureau of Investigation, 2013). Despite the widespread use of this technology, many scientists have serious doubts about its validity (Nature, 2004, April 15).

What is this so-called lie detector and how does it work? The **polygraph** is a machine that attempts to determine if someone is lying by measuring physiological arousal presumed to be associated with deceit. When some people lie, they feel anxious, which causes changes in blood pressure, heart rate, breathing, and production of sweat. By monitoring these variables, the polygraph can theoretically detect when a person feels stressed from lying (American Psychological Association [APA], 2004).

But here's the problem: Biological signs of anxiety do not always go hand-in-hand with deception. There are many other reasons one might feel nervous while taking a polygraph test. Just sitting in a room with an interrogator and being attached to recording equipment may be enough to get the heart racing. And certain people are capable of lying without feeling stressed, and thus their deceit might slip past the polygraph undetected. A person with antisocial personality disorder (discussed in Chapter 13), for example, may not experience the typical physiological changes associated with lying (Simpson, 2008).

As you probably guessed, results from the polygraph are not very accurate. Research suggests that error rates are anywhere from 25 to 75% (Saxe, 1994). Searching for a better alternative, some have turned to **fMRI technology** (Hakun et al., 2009; Simpson, 2008), but its results are not completely reliable either. According to one group of researchers, the ability of fMRI to detect lying was "better than chance but far from perfect" (Monteleone et al., 2009, p. 537). ▶◀

Thus, it appears that lie detection technologies are not much better than old-fashioned observation. If we rely on body language, facial expressions, and other social cues, our lie-detection accuracy is no more than 60% (Gamer, 2009). We may not be skilled at spotting dishonesty, but we are pros at identifying basic emotions like

Does It Work?
The polygraph, or "lie-detector" test, is not as effective as Hollywood may lead you to believe. Research suggests that error rates may be anywhere from 25 to 75% (Saxe, 1994). Given this level of uncertainty, do you think polygraphs should be admissible evidence in court? Most U.S. states have said no (Nature, 2004, April 15).
Guy Bell/Alamy

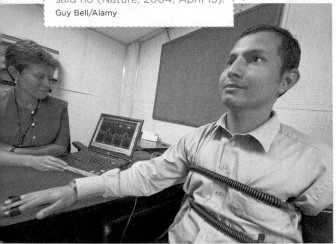

JUST HOW ACCURATE ARE POLYGRAPH TESTS?

CONNECTIONS
In **Chapter 2,** we described how *fMRI* technology reveals patterns of blood flow in areas of the brain, which is a good indicator of how much oxygen is being used as a result of activity there. Here, we see how researchers are trying to use this technology to detect lying.

happiness, anger, and fear. Just imagine Lucy and her parents during a television interview 1 week after the shark attack. What emotions would be written on their faces?

FACE VALUE Lucy was lucky. With a 90% tear to the muscle and tendon and a severed artery, she could have easily lost her leg. But the surgeries went well. Just a week after the horrific incident, she was flashing a bashful grin on national television. Seated between mom and dad, Lucy played with her mother's fingers, squirmed, and then nestled her head under her father's arm. She looked as bright-eyed and vibrant as any child her age (MSNBC.com, 2011, July 26).

"The prognosis is great," Lucy's father Craig told *TODAY*'s Ann Curry. "It's going to take some time and some physical therapy, but she's going to be, you know, back and running and playing like she should" (MSNBC.com, 2011, July 26). The look on Craig's face was calm, happy. Jordan also appeared relieved. Their little girl was going to be okay.

Suppose you knew nothing about Lucy's shark attack, and someone showed you an image of Lucy's parents during that television interview. Would you be able to detect the relief in their facial expressions? How about someone from Japan, Trinidad, or New Zealand: Would a cultural outsider also be able to "read" the emotions written across Craig and Jordan's faces? If we could go back in time and pose this question to Charles Darwin, we suspect his answer would be yes. As Darwin saw it, humans use a similar set of facial expressions to display their emotions and have a natural ability for recognizing those emotions in others.

LO 12 Discuss evidence to support the idea that emotions are universal.

Writing in *The Expression of the Emotions in Man and Animals* (1872/2002), Darwin suggested that interpreting facial expressions is not something we learn but rather is an innate ability that evolved because it promotes survival. Sharing the same facial expressions allows for communication. Being able to identify the emotions of others—like the fear in a friend who has just spotted a snake on the trail—would seem to come in handy. Thus, if facial expressions are truly unlearned and universal, then people from all different cultures ought to interpret them in the same way. A "happy face" should look much the same wherever you go, from the United States to the Pacific island of New Guinea.

EKMAN'S FACES Some four decades ago, psychologist Paul Ekman traveled to a remote mountain region of New Guinea to study an isolated group of indigenous peoples. Ekman and his colleagues were very careful in selecting their participants, choosing only those who were unfamiliar with *Western facial behaviors*—people who were unlikely to know the signature facial expressions we equate with basic emotions like disgust and sadness. The participants didn't speak English, nor had they watched Western movies, worked for anyone with a Caucasian background, or lived among Westerners. The study went something like this: The researchers told the participants stories conveying various emotions such as fear, happiness, and anger. In the story conveying fear, for example, a man is sitting alone in his house with no knife, axe, bow, or any weapon to defend himself. Suddenly, a wild pig appears in his doorway, and he becomes frightened that the pig will bite him. Next, the researchers asked the participants to match the emotion described in the story to a picture of a person's face (choosing from among 6–12 sets of photographs). The results indicated that the same facial expressions represent the same basic emotions across cultures (Ekman & Friesen, 1971). And so it seems, a "happy face" really does look the same to people in the United States and New Guinea.

polygraph Machine used to determine if someone is lying by measuring the physiological arousal associated with deceit.

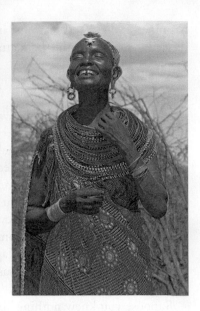

Universal Smile
A smile in India (left) means the same thing as a smile in Lithuania (middle) or Kenya (right). Facial expressions associated with basic emotions like happiness, disgust, and anger are strikingly similar across cultures (Ekman & Friesen, 1971). left: Design Pics Inc. Alamy; middle: Wojtek Buss/age fotostock/Robert Harding; right: M Lohmann/agefotostock

Further evidence for the universal nature of these facial expressions is apparent in children born blind; although they have never seen a human face demonstrating an emotion, their smiles and frowns are similar to those of sighted children (Galati, Scherer, & Ricci-Bitti, 1997; Matsumoto & Willingham, 2009).

> **LO 13** Indicate how display rules influence the expression of emotion.

across the WORLD

Can You Feel the Culture?

Although the expression of some basic emotions appears to be universal, culture acts like a filter, determining the appropriate contexts in which to exhibit them. According to Mohamed (the Somali American we introduced earlier in the chapter), people from Somalia tend to be much less expressive than those born in the United States. "I have cousins who have just come to America, and even [now] when they have been here for about five years, they still like to keep to themselves about personal feelings," says Mohamed. This is especially true when it comes to interacting with people outside the immediate family.

These differences Mohamed observes are probably reflections of display rules. A culture's **display rules** provide the framework or guidelines for when, how, and where an emotion is expressed. Think about some of the display rules in American culture. Negative emotions such as anger are often hidden in social situations. Suppose you are furious at a friend for forgetting to return a textbook she borrowed last night. You probably won't reveal your anger as you sit among other students. Other times display rules compel you to express an emotion you are *not* feeling. Your friend gives you a birthday gift that *really* isn't you. Do you say, "This is not my style. I think I'll exchange it for a store credit," or "Thank you so much" and smile graciously?

Generally speaking, Americans tend to be fairly expressive. Showing emotion, particularly positive emotions, is socially acceptable. This is less the case in Japan, where people rarely reveal their feelings in public. One group of researchers secretly videotaped Japanese and American students while they were watching film clips that included surgeries, amputations, and other events commonly viewed as repulsive. Japanese and American participants showed no differences in their responses to the clips when they didn't think researchers were watching. The great

display rules Framework or guidelines for when, how, and where an emotion is expressed.

facial feedback hypothesis The facial expression of an emotion can affect the experience of that emotion.

majority demonstrated similar facial expressions of disgust and emotional reactions in response to the stress-inducing clips. But when a researcher was present, the Japanese were more likely than the Americans to conceal their negative expressions with smiles (Ekman et al., 1987). This tendency to hide feelings from the researcher is the result of cultural display rules.

WHEN TO REVEAL, WHEN TO CONCEAL

FACIAL FEEDBACK HYPOTHESIS While we are on the topic of facial expressions, let's take a brief detour back to the very beginning of the chapter when Mohamed arrived in his first-grade classroom speaking no English. Without a common language to communicate, Mohamed turned to a more universal form of communication: smiling. It is probably safe to assume that most of Mohamed's classmates took this to mean he was enjoying himself, as smiling is viewed as a sign of happiness in virtually every corner of the world. It also seems plausible that Mohamed's smiling had a positive effect on his classmates, making them more likely to approach and befriend him. But how do you think the act of smiling affected Mohamed?

Believe it or not, the simple act of smiling can make a person *feel* happier. Although facial expressions are caused by the emotions themselves, they sometimes affect the experience of that emotion. This is known as the **facial feedback hypothesis** (Buck, 1980), and if it is correct, we should be able to manipulate our emotions through our facial activities. Try this for yourself.

Take a pen and put it between your teeth, with your mouth open for about half a minute. Now, consider how you are feeling. Next, hold the pen with your lips, making sure not to let it touch your teeth, for half a minute. Again, consider how you are feeling.

try this

If you are like the participants in a study conducted by Strack, Martin, and Stepper (1988), holding the pen in your teeth should result in your seeing the objects and events in your environment as funnier than if you hold the pen with your lips. Why would that be? Take a look at the photo to the right and note how the person holding the pen in his teeth seems to be smiling—the feedback of those smiling muscles leads to a happier mood.

We are now nearing the end of this chapter—and what an emotional one it has been! Before wrapping things up, let's examine various kinds of emotions humans can experience, narrowing our gaze on fear and happiness.

Facial Feedback
Holding a pencil between your teeth (left) will probably put you in a better mood than holding it with your lips closed (right). This is because the physical act of smiling, which occurs when you place the pencil in your teeth, promotes feelings of happiness. So next time you're feeling low, don't be afraid to flex those smile muscles! Robert M. Errera

show what you know

1. The _____ theory of emotion suggests that changes in the body and behavior lead to the experience of emotion.

2. _____ of a culture provide a framework for when, how, and where an emotion is expressed.
   a. Beliefs
   b. Display rules
   c. Feedback loops
   d. Appraisals

3. The _____ suggests the expression of an emotion can affect the experience of that emotion.
   a. James–Lange theory
   b. Cannon–Bard theory
   c. Schachter–Singer theory
   d. facial feedback hypothesis

4. Name two ways in which the Cannon–Bard and Schachter–Singer theories of emotion are different.

5. What evidence exists that emotions are universal?

✓ CHECK YOUR ANSWERS IN APPENDIX C.

Types of Emotions

Imagine the whirlwind of emotions you would feel if you witnessed a loved one being attacked by a shark. Fear is probably the most obvious, but there are others, including *anger* toward the shark, *disgust* at the sight of blood, *anxiety* about the outcome, *gratitude* toward those who came to the rescue, and *guilt* (*It should have been me*).

BASIC EMOTIONS   Are such feelings common to all people? Some researchers have proposed that there is a set of "biologically given" emotions, which includes anger, fear, disgust, sadness, and happiness (Coan, 2010). These types of emotions are considered basic because people all over the world experience and express them in similar ways; they appear to be innate and have an underlying neural basis (Izard, 1992). The fact that children born deaf and blind have the same types of expressions of emotion (happiness, anger, and so on) suggests the universal nature of their displays (Hess & Thibault, 2009).

It is also noteworthy that unpleasant emotions (fear, anger, disgust, and sadness) have survived throughout our evolutionary history, and are more prevalent than positive emotions such as happiness, surprise, or interest (Ekman, 1992; Forgas, 2008; Izard, 2007). This suggests that negative emotions have "adaptive value"; in other words, they may be useful in dangerous situations, for example, those that demand a fight-or-flight response (Forgas, 2008).

This isn't always the case, of course. Sometimes feelings of fear, anger, disgust, and sadness can be provoked by scenarios that involve no danger whatsoever—like watching a frightening movie.

Fascinating Fear

In the summer of 1975, a film called *Jaws* hit the box office, inspiring fear in people across America. A horror movie based on Peter Benchley's popular novel, *Jaws* told the story of a monstrous great white shark that terrorized beachgoers in a resort community. The movie turned out to be an absolute blockbuster, as people across the country flocked to theaters, apparently fascinated by the horror of it all (BBC, 2001, November 16). Today's movie buffs are equally intrigued by frightening subjects, whether vampires, supernatural forces, or serial killers. Fear has also captivated psychologists; it remains one of the most heavily researched human emotions.

The Biology of Fear

> **LO 14** Describe the role the amygdala plays in the experience of fear.

Have you ever wondered what takes place in your brain when you feel afraid? Researchers certainly have. With the help of brain-scanning technologies, they have zeroed in on an almond-shaped structure in the limbic system (Cheng, Knight, Smith, & Helmstetter, 2006; Pape & Pare, 2010). This structure, known as the amygdala, is central to our experience of fear (Davis & Whalen, 2001; Hariri, Tessitore, Mattay, Fera, & Weinberger, 2002). If a person views threatening images, or even looks at an image of a frightened face, the amygdala is activated (Chiao et al., 2008; Laeng et al., 2010).

PATHWAYS TO FEAR   What exactly does the amygdala do? When confronted with a fear-provoking situation, the amygdala enables an ultrafast and unconscious response. According to LeDoux (1996, 2000, 2012), sensory information (sights, sounds) entering the thalamus can either go to the cortex for processing, or head straight for the amygdala without stopping at the cortex. The direct path that goes from the thalamus to the amygdala conveys raw information about the threat,

Jaws the Terrible
The 1975 movie *Jaws* was America's first "summer blockbuster." *Jaws* told the tale of a great white shark that stalked beachgoers in a summer vacation spot. So frightening were the film's story and imagery that many Americans stopped going to the beach that summer (BBC, 2001, November 16).
Universal/The Kobal Collection

enabling your brain and body to respond to danger without your awareness. Like a panic button, the amygdala issues an alert, summoning other parts of the brain that play a role in the experience of fear (for example, the hypothalamus and medulla), which then alert the sympathetic nervous system. A pathway also goes to the pituitary gland, resulting in the secretion of stress hormones (LeDoux, 2012).

The snake in the bed example from earlier in the chapter provides a clear example of an immediate fear response. Visual information about the snake goes directly to the thalamus, and from there to the amygdala, which triggers an alarm reaction. Your heart rate increases and breathing becomes rapid, preparing you to flee the slithery, slimy reptile. Meanwhile, information that was sent to the sensory processing centers of the visual cortex results in a visual representation of the snake materializing. You quickly realize that you are looking at a rubber snake, and your cortex sends a message to the amygdala: "False alarm. The snake in the bed is a rubber toy." The key thing to note is that it takes longer for neural information to go from the thalamus to the cortex than from the thalamus to the amygdala. This explains why one generally needs a moment to calm down: The physiological reaction starts before the false alarm message from the cortex reaches the amygdala (INFOGRAPHIC 9.4 on page 416).

EVOLUTION AND FEAR   LeDoux (2012) suggested an evolutionary advantage to these two systems. The direct route (thalamus to amygdala, causing an emotional reaction) has resulted from the evolutionary advantage of being able to react quickly to threats for which we are biologically prepared (snakes, spiders, aggressive faces). The other pathway allows us to evaluate more complex threats (such as nuclear weapons, job layoffs) with our cortex, overriding the fast-response pathway when necessary.

The amygdala also plays an important role in the creation of "emotional memories," which are fairly robust and detailed (Johnson, LeDoux, & Doyère, 2009; LeDoux, 2002). This is useful because we are more likely to survive if we remember threats in our environments. For some people, however, emotional memories cause troublesome fear and anxiety (Chapter 12).

AUTONOMIC NERVOUS SYSTEM AND FEAR   Earlier in the chapter, we discussed the fight-or-flight response. In a stressful situation, the sympathetic nervous system, which is a part of the autonomic nervous system (ANS), automatically and quickly activates a variety of physiological responses. Blood pressure increases, goose bumps appear, hair stands on end, pupils dilate, digestion stops, blood sugar increases, and so on. The same response can also occur with some other emotions such as love and joy (Levenson, 1992). But separating the physiological profiles of emotions can get tricky, as they often overlap. For example, fear, anger, and sadness are all accompanied by an increased heart rate (Ekman, 2003; Rhudy & Meagher, 2000). Anger is associated with heightened skin temperature and a greater increase in heart rate than fear. Meanwhile, fear promotes increased blood flow to the legs and decreased skin temperature in the hands (Ekman, Levenson, & Friesen, 1983).

Research suggests that the physiological responses resulting from activation of the sympathetic nervous system are universal, and biological response patterns accompanying basic emotions are innate. Irrespective of gender or age, these patterns are the same, although these responses in older adults tend to be less extreme (Levenson, Carstensen, Friesen, & Ekman, 1991).

What happens to these automatic responses when the amygdala is not working? Animal studies suggest that damage to the amygdala impairs the fear response (Bliss-Moreau, Bauman, & Amaral, 2011; Phillips & LeDoux, 1992). Similarly, people with amygdala damage exhibit weaker than normal responses to stimuli that inspire fear or disgust (Buchanan, Tranel, & Adolphs, 2004). They also have difficulty perceiving emotion and comprehending nonverbal behavior associated with emotion (Adolphs, 2008).

The Anatomy of Fear

You instantly recoil when you spot a snake—then sigh with relief just a moment later when it registers that the snake is a rubber toy. Have you ever wondered why you react with fear when a "threat" turns out to be nothing? Why does it take longer for you to process a threat than react to it? Sensory information (sight, sound) entering the brain travels to the thalamus and is then routed to the cortex for processing. Sensory information can also go directly to the amygdala. In the case of a threat, the amygdala alerts other areas of the brain and the endocrine system instantly without waiting for a conscious command. This enables a response to fear before you are even fully aware of what you are reacting to.

2 Basic information about threat is conveyed directly to the amygdala, enabling rapid response.

3 It takes longer for neural information to go to the visual cortex for processing.

Direct path

Indirect path

Thalamus

Visual cortex

Processing

1 Visual information goes directly to the thalamus.

Information about threat

Amygdala

4 If it's been determined that the threat is a false alarm, this message will instruct the amygdala to inhibit the fear reaction.

5 After receiving information about threat, the amygdala:
- instructs hypothalamus and medulla to alert sympathetic nervous system;
- prompts pituitary gland to secrete stress hormones.

The amygdala, shown here in red, plays a pivotal role in experiencing fear. Information about threats prompts the amygdala to activate the physiological responses that characterize fear.

What happens when the amygdala doesn't work? Animals with amygdala damage may not exhibit any response to a threat, like this rat, which is uncharacteristically comfortable with a predator. Similarly, one study found that people with amygdala damage demonstrated an absence of expected fear behaviors (Feinstein, Adolphs, Damasio, & Tranel, 2011).

Happiness

In the very first chapter of this book, we introduced the field of study known as positive psychology, "the study of positive emotions, positive character traits, and enabling institutions" (Seligman & Steen, 2005, p. 410). Rather than focusing on mental illness and abnormal behavior, positive psychology emphasizes human strengths and virtues. The goal is well-being and fulfillment, and that means "satisfaction" with the past, "hope and optimism" for the future, and "flow and happiness" at the current time (Seligman & Csikszentmihalyi, 2000). Let's take a moment to explore that flow and happiness of the moment.

The Brighter Side
Psychologist Martin Seligman is a leading proponent of positive psychology, which emphasizes the goodness and strength of the human spirit. Getting the most out of life, according to Seligman, means not only pursuing happiness, but also cultivating relationships, achieving goals, and being deeply engaged in meaningful activities (Szalavitz, 2011, May 13). Courtesy Positive Psychology Center, University of Pennsylvania

LO 15 Summarize evidence pointing to the biological basis of happiness.

THE BIOLOGY OF HAPPINESS   To what degree do we inherit happiness? Happiness has heritability estimates between 35% and 50%, and as high as 80% in longitudinal studies (Nes, Czajkowski, & Tambs, 2010). In other words, we can explain a high proportion of the variation in happiness, life satisfaction, and well-being by considering genetic make-up, as opposed to environmental factors.

Research suggests that the biological basis of happiness may include a "set point," similar to the set point for hunger (Bartels et al., 2010; Lyubomirsky et al., 2005). Happiness tends to fluctuate around a fixed level (this point is the degree of happiness we experience when we are not trying to be happier). As we strive for personal happiness, it is important to recognize the strength of this set point, which is influenced by genes and **temperament.** But do not lose hope; researchers also suggest it is possible to increase happiness over time (Lyubomirsky et al., 2005).

INCREASING HAPPINESS   Positive events in our lives generally only seem to bring temporary happiness (Diener, Lucas, & Scollon, 2006; Mancini, Bonanno, & Clark, 2011). Why is this? We tend to become **habituated** to new feelings of happiness or a new level of happiness rather quickly. If you win the lottery, get a new job, or buy a beautiful house, you will likely experience an increased level of happiness for a while, but then go back to your baseline, or "set point" of happiness (Lyubomirsky et al., 2005). Things that feel new and improved or life-changing quickly become mundane, suggesting that happiness will not be found in new possessions or shopping sprees. The implication is that we need to be careful when pursuing happiness as a goal in life, as we don't want to emphasize obtaining a specific outcome (like moving to a house near the ocean) or acquiring a desired object (Lyubomorsky et al., 2005). Our focus should not be on becoming happier, but rather on being content with what we have (Lyubomorsky, Dickerhoof, Boehm, & Sheldon, 2011).

There are many steps you can take to increase your level of happiness. Engaging in physical exercise, showing kindness, and getting involved in activities that benefit others are all linked to increased positive emotions (Lyubomorsky et al., 2011; Walsh, 2011). The same can be said for recording positive thoughts and feelings of gratefulness in a journal. One group of researchers asked participants to write down in a diary those aspects of their lives for which they were grateful each day. The researchers measured well-being and found that the participants in the diary group were better off than those not counting their blessings. We can change our happiness by changing this aspect of our thinking. The participants who recorded their blessings were also more likely to report they had helped someone else or offered emotional support to another (Emmons & McCullough, 2003). Another way to increase happiness is to identify and actively pursue goals that will have an important effect on your life (Brunstein, 1993). Write down what you are trying

CONNECTIONS

In **Chapter 8,** we described several *temperaments* exhibited by infants. Around 40% of infants can be classified as *easy* babies who follow regular schedules, are relatively happy, easy to soothe when upset, and quick to adjust to changes in the environment. The existence of such a temperament lends support to the biological basis of happiness discussed here.

In **Chapter 5,** we presented the concept of *habituation,* a basic form of learning in which repeated exposure to an event generally results in a reduced response. Here, we see the same effect can occur with events that result in happiness. With repeated exposure, we will habituate to an event that initially elicited happiness.

to accomplish and take action to make it happen. Knowing what you are actively working toward and being committed to attainable goals are associated with increased feelings of well-being and happiness. There may be a genetic component of happiness, but nature isn't everything. Life is what you make of it, and happiness is yours to discover.

All of the above activities are within your control, but some variables in the happiness equation are not easily manipulated. If only the morning could last all day long. . . .

from the pages of SCIENTIFIC AMERICAN

Happy in the Morning

Twitter reveals daily emotional rhythms are consistent across cultures.

"Happy hour" is not when you might expect it to be, according to a new analysis of about half a billion Twitter messages from around the globe. On average, people are chipper when they wake up and become grouchy as the day wears on. This pattern holds true on weekends, too, but is delayed by about two hours—a trend confirmed in tweets from the United Arab Emirates, where the workweek is Sunday through Thursday. The data suggest that sleep schedules strongly influence mood cycles. The duo at Cornell University who carried out the research, published last September in *Science,* say that the rising popularity of online social media is allowing scientists to study human behavior in surprising new ways. **Janelle Weaver. Reproduced with permission. Copyright © 2012 Scientific American, a division of Nature America, Inc. All rights reserved.**

Gender and Emotions

Urban myth, common sense, stereotypes, and our daily experiences in North America all lead us to believe that men and women experience and express their emotions differently, but is this true? Are women really more "emotional" than men? Do men hide their emotions? Barrett and Bliss-Moreau (2009) set out to answer some of these very

Who Is Emotional?
Both of these individuals appear angry, but why are they feeling this way? Research suggests that people are more likely to attribute a woman's unpleasant expression to her "emotional" disposition and a man's angry face to "having a bad day." These assumptions rest on the stereotype that women are more emotional than men. Nicole Betz, Lab Coordinator/ Research Technician, Interdisciplinary Affective Science Lab Northeastern University, photo courtesy of Dr. Lisa Feldman Barret

questions. In their study, participants were shown pictures of faces expressing emotions such as anger, happiness, and sadness. Each of the faces was paired with a label stating some situational cause for its emotion (for example, a face showing anger was paired with the phrase "insulted by a stranger"). Then the participants were shown the same images without any label, and asked to state whether the individual depicted was "emotional" or "having a bad day." Female expressions were more likely to be described as emotional, whereas the male faces were more likely to be labeled as having a bad day. Apparently, the participants assumed that the female emotions stemmed from some internal characteristic (being an "overly emotional female"). Meanwhile, the men's emotions were presumed to be responses to situations or environments (Chapter 15).

The gender differences suggested by the participants' beliefs in Barrett and Bliss-Moreau's study are not necessarily accurate, however. Most psychologists studying gender differences suggest that men and women are more similar than different when it comes to experiencing and expressing emotion (Else-Quest, Higgins, Allison, & Morton, 2012). As noted earlier, there are universal facial expressions, and these are similar across gender. But the notion that women are more emotional is a gross overgeneralization at best.

That being said, research has uncovered some interesting gender disparities related to emotion. Some evidence suggests that women tend to feel more guilt, shame, and embarrassment than men (Else-Quest et al., 2012). They also seem to be more adept at identifying the emotion behind a particular face (Hall & Matsumoto, 2004). We don't know if this results from biological or cultural differences (perhaps women start practicing earlier, and this ability becomes more automatic for them). Women who paid closer attention to eyes, in one study, were able to discern emotional expressions more quickly and correctly than men, suggesting that the eyes are especially important for conveying emotions (Hall, Hutton, & Morgan, 2010). With that thought in mind, take a minute and look into the eyes of Mohamed (below). Do you see a look of happiness and tranquility? We certainly do.

Closing Thoughts

Before moving on, let's briefly outline what we have learned in this chapter. The success story of Mohamed Dirie introduced us to the concept of motivation, a stimulus or force that can direct the way we behave, think, and feel. Early attempts to explain motivation include the instinct theory, which suggests that human behaviors are driven by instinct. But the evidence to support this notion was scanty, and it was eclipsed by other theories, some emphasizing basic physiological drives and others incorporating high-level needs such as self-transcendence. Using the example of Lucy and the shark, we ventured into the complexity of human emotion, examining the theories of its origins, and the many faces and forms it can assume. Although our understanding of emotions remains incomplete, we know that many are universal. So whatever you may be feeling at this moment, you can be certain that someone else has felt the same way. Emotions are what bring humankind together.

You Asked, Mohamed Answers

http://qrs.ly/ha3m6ba

Did you do extracurricular activities in high school, and did they help make you feel connected?

Happy As Ever
Mohamed got married in 2011, became a father in 2012, and graduated from the University of Minnesota in 2013. He is now working as an Information Technology Support Technician for Volunteers of America-Minnesota.
Courtesy Mohamed Dirie

show what you know

1. Researchers have found that when people view images that are threatening, or when they see images of faces of people who are afraid, the _____ becomes active.

2. How would you explain to a fellow student what the following statement means: Happiness has heritability estimates as high as 80%?

3. When confronted by a potential threat, such as a shark, your heart starts pounding, your breathing speeds up, and your pupils dilate. These changes are activated by
   a. the cognitive appraisal approach.
   b. the cortex.
   c. the sympathetic nervous system.
   d. gender differences.

✓ CHECK YOUR ANSWERS IN APPENDIX C.

9 summary of concepts

LO 1 Define motivation. (p. 386)

Motivation is a stimulus that can direct the way we behave, think, and feel. A motivated behavior tends to be guided (that is, it has a direction), energized, and persistent. When a behavior is reinforced, an association is established between the behavior and its consequence. With motivated behavior, this association becomes the incentive, or reason to repeat the behavior.

LO 2 Explain how extrinsic and intrinsic motivation impact behavior. (p. 386)

When a learned behavior is motivated by the incentive of external reinforcers in the environment, there is an extrinsic motivation to continue that behavior. The motivation comes from consequences that are found in the environment or situation. Intrinsic motivation occurs when a learned behavior is motivated by the prospect of internal reinforcers. Performing a behavior because it is inherently interesting or satisfying exemplifies intrinsic motivation, when the reinforcers originate from within.

LO 3 Summarize instinct theory. (p. 388)

Instinct theory proposes that through evolution some behaviors are etched into our genetic makeup, and are consistent from one member of the species to the next. Instincts are complex behaviors that are fixed, unlearned, and consistent within a species. Although they apply to other animals, there are limited data suggesting that humans display instincts.

LO 4 Describe drive-reduction theory and explain how it relates to motivation. (p. 389)

The drive-reduction theory of motivation suggests that biological needs and homeostasis motivate us to meet these needs. If a need is not fulfilled, this creates a drive, or state of tension, that pushes us or motivates behaviors to meet the need. Once a need is met, the drive is reduced, at least temporarily, because this is an ongoing process, as the need inevitably returns.

LO 5 Explain how arousal theory relates to motivation. (p. 390)

According to arousal theory, humans seek an optimal level of arousal, and what is optimal is based on individual differences. Behaviors can arise out of the simple desire for stimulation, or arousal, which is a level of alertness and engagement in the world. Because humans have different optimal levels in terms of their need for arousal and sensory stimulation, people are motivated to seek out activities that fulfill this need.

LO 6 Outline Maslow's hierarchy of needs. (p. 390)

The needs in Maslow's hierarchy, often depicted as a pyramid, are considered to be universal and are ordered in terms of the strength of their associated drive, with the most critical needs, those that are physiological, at the bottom. Moving up the pyramid are increasingly higher-level needs: safety needs; love and belongingness needs; esteem needs; self-actualization; and self-transcendence. Maslow suggested that one's most basic needs must be met before higher-level needs motivate behavior.

LO 7 Explain how self-determination theory relates to motivation. (p. 393)

This theory suggests that humans are motivated in the direction of growth and optimal functioning. According to the self-determination theory, we are born with three universal, fundamental needs: the needs for competence (reaching goals through mastery of day-to-day responsibilities), relatedness (creating meaningful and lasting relationships), and autonomy (managing behavior to reach personal goals). The focus is not on overcoming one's shortcomings, but on moving in a positive direction.

LO 8 Discuss how the stomach and the hypothalamus make us feel hunger. (p. 395)

In a classic experiment, researchers confirmed the stomach and brain both work to indicate hunger. When glucose levels dip, the stomach and liver send signals to the brain that something must be done about this reduced energy source. The brain, in turn, initiates a sense of hunger. Signals from the digestive system are sent to the hypothalamus, which then transmits signals to higher regions of the brain. When the lateral hypothalamus is activated, appetite increases. On the other hand, if the ventromedial hypothalamus becomes activated, appetite declines, causing an animal to stop eating.

LO 9 Outline the major eating disorders. (p. 400)

Anorexia nervosa is a serious, life-threatening eating disorder characterized by a significantly low body weight in relation to age, sex, development, and physical health; an extreme fear of gaining weight or getting fat; an altered and distorted sense of body weight and figure; and self-imposed restrictions on "energy intake" (calories) needed to maintain a healthy weight. Bulimia nervosa is characterized by recurrent episodes of binge eating followed by purging (self-induced vomiting, misuse of laxatives, fasting, excessive exercise). Binge-eating disorder is characterized by episodes during which a larger amount of food is consumed than most people would eat in a similar amount of time under similar circumstances. As in bulimia, the individual feels unable to control eating during that period of time, but the difference is that there are no excessive weight control or purging behaviors.

LO 10 Define emotions and explain how they are different from moods. (p. 404)

Emotion is a psychological state that includes a subjective or inner experience. It also has a physiological component and entails a behavioral expression. Emotions are quite strong, but they don't generally last as long as moods. In addition, emotions are more likely to have an identifiable cause (that is, a reaction to a stimulus that provoked it), which has a greater probability of motivating a person to take some sort of action. Moods are longer-term emotional states that are less intense than emotions and do not appear to have distinct beginnings or ends.

LO 11 Identify the major theories of emotion and describe how they differ. (p. 406)

The James–Lange theory of emotion suggests there is a stimulus that initiates the experience of a physiological reaction and/or a behavioral reaction, and it is this reaction that leads to an emotion. The Cannon–Bard theory of emotion suggests that we don't feel emotion because of physiological and behavioral reactions, but rather environmental stimuli are the starting point for emotions. The Schachter–Singer theory of emotion suggests there is a general pattern of physiological arousal caused by the sympathetic nervous system, and this pattern is common to a variety of emotions. The experience of emotion is the result of two factors: (1) physiological arousal and (2) a cognitive label for this physiological state (the arousal). The cognitive appraisal theory suggests that the appraisal or interpretation of interactions with surroundings causes an emotional reaction.

LO 12 Discuss evidence to support the idea that emotions are universal. (p. 411)

Darwin suggested that interpreting facial expressions is not something we learn, but rather an innate ability that evolved because it promotes survival. Sharing the same facial expressions allows for communication. In research with an isolated group of indigenous peoples in New Guinea, the results indicated that the same facial expressions represent the same basic emotions across cultures. In addition, the fact that children born deaf and blind have the same types of expressions of emotion (for example, happiness and anger) suggests the universal nature of these displays.

LO 13 Indicate how display rules influence the expression of emotion. (p. 412)

Although the expression of basic emotions appears, in many cases, to be universal, culture acts like a filter to determine the specific context in which to exhibit them. That is, the display rules of a culture provide the framework or guidelines for when, how, and where an emotion is expressed.

LO 14 Describe the role the amygdala plays in the experience of fear. (p. 414)

The amygdala is an almond-shaped structure found in the temporal lobes. It is a key part of the limbic system and appears to be central to our experience of fear. When people view threatening images, or even look at an image of a frightened face, the amygdala is activated. When confronted with a fear-provoking situation, the amygdala enables an ultrafast and unconscious response. The amygdala also plays an important role in the creation of emotional memories. This is useful because we are more likely to survive if we remember threats in our environments.

LO 15 Summarize evidence pointing to the biological basis of happiness. (p. 417)

Happiness has heritability estimates between 35% and 50%, with genetic inheritance believed to be as high as 80% in longitudinal studies. There may be a set point for happiness, suggesting that we all have a degree of happiness around which our happiness levels will hover. As we consider our level of happiness and strive for personal happiness, we should keep in mind our set point, as it is strong, and directed by our genes and temperament.

key terms

anorexia nervosa, p. 401
arousal theory, p. 390
binge-eating disorder, p. 401
bulimia nervosa, p. 401
Cannon–Bard theory of emotion, p. 407
cognitive appraisal approach, p. 408
display rules, p. 412

drive, p. 389
drive-reduction theory, p. 389
emotion, p. 404
extrinsic motivation, p. 386
facial feedback hypothesis, p. 413
hierarchy of needs, p. 390
homeostasis, p. 389

incentive, p. 386
instincts, p. 388
intrinsic motivation, p. 386
James–Lange theory of emotion, p. 406
motivation, p. 386
needs, p. 389
need for achievement (n-Ach), p. 394

need for power (n-Pow), p. 394
polygraph, p. 410
Schachter–Singer theory of emotion, p. 407
self-actualization, p. 393
self-determination theory (SDT), p. 393
set point, p. 399

TEST PREP are you ready?

1. To get a child to play the piano, you allow her 15 minutes to play her favorite computer game when she is done practicing. Playing on the computer eventually represents _____ for her to practice the piano.
   a. negative reinforcement
   b. intrinsic motivation
   c. satiety
   d. an incentive

2. Learned behaviors that are motivated by reinforcers in the environment have
   a. extrinsic motivation.
   b. intrinsic motivation.
   c. drives.
   d. needs.

3. _____ are complex behaviors that are fixed, unlearned, and consistent within a species.
   a. Drives
   b. Motivators
   c. Instincts
   d. Needs

4. Biological needs and homeostasis motivate us to meet our needs. If a need is not fulfilled, this creates a state of tension that pushes us to meet it. This describes the _____ theory of motivation.
   a. self-actualization
   b. drive-reduction
   c. cognitive-appraisal
   d. Schachter–Singer

5. Humans have different optimal levels of need for arousal. These individual differences indicate that some people are _____; they appear to seek out activities that increase arousal.
   a. sensation seekers
   b. externally motivated
   c. driven by extrinsic motivation
   d. bulimic

6. When the _____ is stimulated electrically, it sends a hormone signal to decrease appetite. If this region of the brain is destroyed, an animal will drastically overeat.
   a. limbic system
   b. amygdala
   c. lateral hypothalamus
   d. ventromedial hypothalamus

7. A serious health issue characterized by a body mass index of 30 or higher is known as:
   a. anorexia nervosa.
   b. obesity.
   c. bulimia nervosa.
   d. binge-eating disorder.

8. Kory routinely eats large amounts of food that most people could not eat in similar situations or in a similar amount of time. Kory often feels an inability to control her eating and frequently eats alone because she is embarrassed by how much she eats. It is likely that Kory has a diagnosis of:
   a. anorexia nervosa.
   b. bulimia nervosa.
   c. amenorrhea.
   d. binge-eating disorder.

9. Emotion is a psychological state that includes a subjective experience, a physiological component, as well as a(n):
   a. mood.
   b. drive.
   c. behavioral expression.
   d. incentive.

10. To study the universal nature of emotions, Paul Ekman traveled to New Guinea to explore native peoples' detection of facial expressions. Although unfamiliar with Western facial behaviors, the participants in his study:
    a. could not identify the facial expressions in the photos he showed them.
    b. could identify the facial expressions common across the world.
    c. could understand English.
    d. had no display rules.

11. The Schachter–Singer theory suggests that the experience of emotion is the result of:
    a. physiological arousal.
    b. cognitive labeling.
    c. physiological arousal and cognitive labeling.
    d. an appraisal of the environment.

12. The _____ suggests that emotion is a very personal reaction to and interpretation of the environment, and that emotion does not result from a cognitive label of physiological arousal.
    a. James–Lange theory
    b. cognitive-appraisal approach
    c. Schachter–Singer theory
    d. Cannon–Bard theory

13. The polygraph is used to determine if someone is lying by measuring:
    a. physiological arousal.
    b. cognitive appraisal.
    c. activity in the amygdala.
    d. activity in the thalamus.

14. When confronted with a fear-provoking situation, initial processing can be unconscious. Information from the thalamus can take two paths: It may go to the _____ for processing, or directly to the_____, which sets the stage by preparing the body for response to a threat.
    a. cortex; amygdala
    b. parasympathetic nervous system; cortex
    c. hypothalamus; parasympathetic nervous system
    d. parasympathetic nervous system; sympathetic nervous system

15. Evidence from research on emotions suggests that when looking at faces, women seem to:
    a. spend less time paying attention to eyes than men.
    b. be less likely to feel embarrassment than men.
    c. be less able to identify what emotion is being felt than men.
    d. be better able to identify what emotion is being felt than men.

16. Describe situations in which you respond to intrinsic motivation. In what types of situations do you respond to extrinsic motivation?

17. Describe a situation you are aware of when someone's motivation did not follow the order outlined in Maslow's hierarchy of needs.

18. After reading and understanding the mechanisms underlying hunger, what advice can you give someone who is struggling to lose weight?

19. List some of the display rules you respond to on a daily basis. What different display rules do you follow at school in comparison to those at home?

20. What are some activities you can get involved in to increase your happiness?

✓ CHECK YOUR ANSWERS IN APPENDIX C.

10

Sex and Sexuality

📁 *Guess the Profession*

Gender

📁 *A Masculine Touch*

◊🏠 NATURE AND NURTURE
The Case of Bruce Reimer

The Birds and the Bees

📁 *The Making of a Sexpert*

SA from the pages of
SCIENTIFIC AMERICAN
Crying Women Turn Men Off

🌐➤ ACROSS THE WORLD
Homosexuality and Culture

👁! DIDN'T SEE THAT COMING
Great Ape Sex

🌐➤ ACROSS THE WORLD
**What They Are Doing in Bed . . .
or Elsewhere**

⊕ THINK AGAIN
Sext You Later

**The Trouble With Sex:
Sexual Dysfunctions**

📁 *Not Tonight, Babe*

Sex, Its Consequences, and Culture

➤◄ CONTROVERSIES
Are You My Natural Selection?

📁 *Back to the Future*

sexuality
and gender

Sex and Sexuality

GUESS THE PROFESSION Stephen Patten usually walks into Portland's veteran's hospital around 6:00 A.M. Then he checks his e-mail, puts on his scrubs, and heads to the operating room to prepare for the day's surgeries. What do you think Stephen does for a living?

Stephanie Buehler spends much of her workday discussing erections, orgasms, and relationship woes. People of all different ages, ethnicities, and cultural backgrounds come to her for help with their most intimate problems. What is Stephanie's profession?

Stephen Patten is a nurse. But if you guessed he is a doctor, you're not alone. Many of Stephen's patients jump to the same conclusion when they see a man in his mid-fifties approach their bedside. Stephen is indeed unusual in his field: More than 90% of nurses in the United States are women, according to a 2008 survey (Health Resources and Services Administration, 2010). But there is another reason patients do a double take when this 200-pound lumberjack type walks through the door and says, "Hi, I'm Stephen. I'll be your nurse today." It has to do with our notions of masculine and feminine. In other words, it relates directly to *gender,* a concept we will explore in the upcoming pages.

Dr. Stephanie Buehler is a certified sex therapist, a psychotherapist who specializes in helping individuals and couples resolve sexual issues. You may think your secret sexual fantasies are unusual, but Dr. Buehler would probably not be surprised if you shared them with her. It takes a lot to shock a woman who spends 8 hours a day discussing sexual concerns with all types of people. Her clients range in age from 18 to 80 and come from all walks of life. She sees firefighters, physicians, homemakers, and college students like you; she sees heterosexual, homosexual, and bisexual clients. Her work has afforded her a privileged view of human *sexuality*—a slice of which we are going to share with you.

➡

LEARNING OBJECTIVES

after reading and studying this chapter, you should be able to:

LO 1 Define sex and distinguish it from sexuality.

LO 2 Identify the biological factors that determine sex.

LO 3 Identify some of the causes of intersexual development.

LO 4 Define gender and explain how culture plays a role in its development.

LO 5 Distinguish between transgender and transsexual.

LO 6 Describe the human sexual response as identified by Masters and Johnson.

LO 7 Define sexual orientation and summarize how it develops.

LO 8 Identify the symptoms of sexual dysfunctions.

LO 9 Classify sexually transmitted infections and identify their causes.

LO 10 Describe human immunodeficiency virus (HIV) and its role in acquired immune deficiency syndrome (AIDS).

LO 11 Define sexual scripts and describe some of the ways people deviate from sex-related cultural norms.

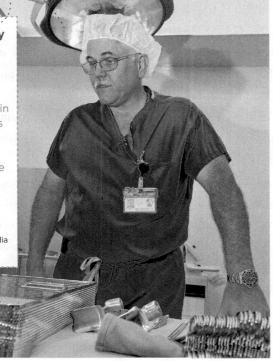

I'll Be Your Nurse Today Stephen Patten has been a nurse for over three decades. He has worked in the trenches, treating gunshot and stab wounds in trauma centers, and he has held important leadership positions, serving as director of a hospital tissue bank and president of the National Association of Clinical Nurse Specialists (2012–2013). D. Michael Moody Medical Photographer, Medical Media Production Service

Let's Talk About Sex

 LO 1 Define sex and distinguish it from sexuality.

When people talk about **sex**, they often are referring to a sexual act such as intercourse. But sex can also refer to the classification of people as male or female, a distinction based on genetic composition and the structure and/or function of reproductive organs (Pryzgoda & Chrisler, 2000). **Gender**, on the other hand, refers to the dimension of masculinity and femininity based on social, cultural, and psychological characteristics. The American Psychological Association (APA, 2010c, 2011a) recommends using the term "sex" when referring to biological status and "gender" for the cultural roles and expectations that distinguish males and females. According to the American Psychiatric Association (APA, 2013), "gender" also indicates the public and often legally recognized role a person has as a man or woman, boy or girl.

From your reading of other chapters in this book, you know that psychologists often view behaviors as resulting from an interaction of biological, psychological, and social forces. We will use this biopsychosocial perspective to emphasize the role these factors play in our **sexuality**. In other words, how they influence our sexual activities, attitudes, and behaviors.

CONNECTIONS

In **Chapter 1**, we describe *variables* as measurable characteristics that can vary or change over time. Some variables, like sex and gender, vary across groups, and we study their impact on the members of those groups. In this chapter, we will explore sex and gender as they relate to a variety of topics in psychology.

Sex: It's In Your Biology

What are the topics of sex and gender doing in a *psychology* textbook, and are they important enough to merit their own chapter? *Sex* and *gender* play a role in the scientific study of behavior and mental processes, serving as important **variables** to be studied. And you know intuitively that relationships and emotions related to *sexuality* are a part of what makes us human.

Note: Quotations attributed to Stephen Patten and Dr. Stephanie Buehler are personal communications.

Sexual Healing

Dr. Stephanie Buehler is a certified sex therapist. She helps couples and individuals resolve sexual problems, including low desire, erectile dysfunction, pain during intercourse, and confusion about sexual orientation. Sex therapy is a rapidly advancing field, as researchers continue to develop and test new approaches to treatment (Althof, 2010). Mark Buehler

In this chapter, you will learn about the biology of sexual determination and differences of sex development, and explore how sex influences human behavior. Sex is one of the most intimate—and fascinating—dimensions of human behavior. It is also one of the most difficult to study.

A very personal topic for most people, sex is not openly discussed in many homes, schools, doctors' offices, or even bedrooms in North America (Byers, 2011). This is ironic, given that North American culture supplies a steady stream of sexual imagery, words, and media. Many parents feel embarrassed discussing sex with their children. Medical and mental health professionals find it difficult to communicate with patients about sexual issues. Some of us cannot even talk honestly about sex with our sexual partners.

RESEARCH AND SEX   Researchers use a variety of approaches to study human sexuality, including surveys, interviews, case studies, and the experimental method. There are also many technologies to observe and measure physiological responses (Chivers, Seto, Lalumiere, Laan, & Grimbos, 2010). For example, MRI and fMRI can be used to study sexual arousal during intercourse and other sexual activities (Schultz, van Andel, Sabelis, & Mooyaart, 1999).

But as you can imagine, studying sexual behavior has its difficulties. People are often uncomfortable discussing sex, especially their own sex lives, so getting participants to open up can be tricky. The extreme intimacy many people feel about their sexuality can also make research that includes the *observation* of sexual behavior especially challenging. As a result, our knowledge of sexual behavior is often limited to self-reporting. Yet there are problems with relying on self-reported data, including the tendency for some people to be dishonest or portray themselves in the best possible light. There are ways to sidestep these issues, however. For example, Rieger and Savin-Williams (2012)

Dr. Buehler, in Her Own Words

http://qrs.ly/xy3m6bn

sex The classification of someone as male or female based on biological characteristics; a sexual act such as intercourse.

gender The dimension of masculinity and femininity based on social, cultural, and psychological characteristics.

sexuality Sexual activities, attitudes, and behaviors.

had participants view short video clips of images that were neutral (landscape) or sexually explicit (male or female models masturbating). Given that our pupils dilate when we are sexually aroused, the researchers were able to use this variable as an index of sexual arousal. They measured the degree to which participants' pupils dilated when they looked at neutral versus sexually explicit images, gauging the participants' sexual arousal without being too intrusive.

Not everyone is shy about personal sexual behavior, of course, and that is good news for researchers. Participants in human sexuality studies engage in a variety of sexual activities, including sexual intercourse and masturbation, with approval from Institutional Review Boards (IRBs) to ensure ethical treatment.

Now it's time to delve into the heart of the chapter. Get ready to explore the many facets of sexuality and gender.

The Biology of Sexual Determination

A person's sex (male or female) depends on both genes and hormones. *Sex determination* refers to the designation of genetic sex, which guides the activity of hormones that direct the development of reproductive organs and structures (Ngun, Ghahramani, Sánchez, Bocklandt, & Vilain, 2011). Let's take a closer look at how all this works.

LO 2   Identify the biological factors that determine sex.

Your *genetic sex* was determined by your father's sperm. In the moment of conception, dad's sperm united with mom's egg to form a zygote. A **zygote** contains genetic material from both parents in the form of 46 chromosomes—23 from mom, 23 from dad. These chromosomes provide the blueprint for biological development, including that of the physiological structures associated with sex. The 23rd pair of chromosomes, also referred to as the *sex chromosomes,* includes specific instructions for the zygote to develop into a female or a male. It's as simple as X and Y.

CONNECTIONS

In **Chapter 1,** we discussed the importance of using representative samples. Here, we refer to participants who have chosen to take part in human sexuality research. We must interpret findings cautiously as their behaviors may not reflect those of the general population.

CONNECTIONS

In **Chapter 8,** we learned that the mother's ovum and the father's sperm come together and form a single cell known as a *zygote*. Under normal circumstances, the zygote continues to divide as it moves through the fallopian tube toward the uterus. The resulting mass of cells eventually implants in the uterine wall.

23 Pairs
A typical person has 23 pairs of chromosomes (46 total) in almost every cell. The 23rd pair, also referred to as the *sex chromosomes,* contains genes that determine the sex of the developing person. If the 23rd pair is XY, then the zygote will develop into a male; if XX, it will become a female. Can you tell what genetic sex is represented here? (See bottom of column on page 433 for answer.) © BSIP SA/Alamy

SEX CHROMOSOMES   The egg from the mother carries an *X chromosome,* and the sperm from the father carries either an *X chromosome* or a *Y chromosome.* When the sperm contributes an X chromosome to the 23rd pair, the genetic sex is *XX,* and the zygote generally develops into a female. If the sperm carries a Y chromosome, the genetic sex is *XY,* and the zygote typically develops into a male. About 50% of sperm carry the X chromosome, and 50% carry the Y chromosome. This is the reason the population is approximately half male and half female.

GENES AND HORMONES   From the moment a zygote is formed, genetic sex is constant. In other words, the composition of the 23rd pair of chromosomes remains female (XX) or male (XY). We should note, however, that the structure and function of the reproductive organs do not always match the original *genetic* sex (XX or XY). The development of reproductive anatomy is influenced by a variety of factors, including interactions among genes and the activity of hormones produced by the sex glands (also

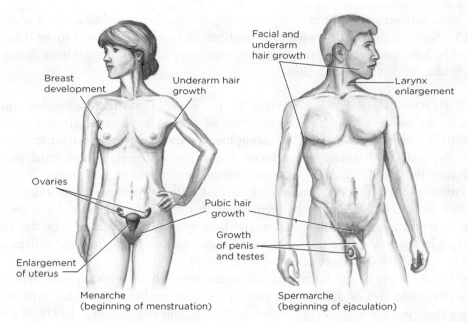

Breast
development

Underarm hair
growth

Ovaries

Pubic hair
growth

Growth
of penis
and testes

Enlargement
of uterus

Menarche
(beginning of menstruation)

Facial and
underarm
hair growth

Larynx
enlargement

Spermarche
(beginning of ejaculation)

FIGURE 10.1

Physical Changes at Puberty

During puberty, the body changes and becomes sexually mature and able to reproduce. The primary sex characteristics mature, and the secondary sex characteristics become more distinct. Primary sex characteristics are related to reproductive organs. The reproductive organs, present at birth, begin to function differently at puberty. For instance, the testes and ovaries are involved in stimulating more visible changes, such as breast development and growth of the penis.

known as *gonads*) of the fetus (Blecher & Erickson, 2007; Dennis, 2004). For the sake of the discussion here, we'll assume that the genetic sex matches the developing physical characteristics.

In a genetic male, the presence of the Y chromosome causes the gonads to become testes. If the Y chromosome is not present, as in the case of a genetic female, then the gonads develop into ovaries (Hines, 2011a). Both the testes and ovaries secrete hormones that influence the development of reproductive organs: **androgens** in the case of the testes and **estrogen** in the case of the ovaries. (These sex hormones are also secreted by the adrenal glands in both males and females.) **Testosterone,** for example, is an androgen that influences whether the fetus develops male or female genitals.

DISTINGUISHING BETWEEN MALES AND FEMALES Even though the genetic sex of the fetus is determined at conception, it is not possible to ascertain the sex until 7 weeks after conception through blood tests (Devaney, Palomaki, Scott, & Bianchi, 2011). Fetal genital anatomy can be determined by ultrasound by the end of the first trimester (Scheffer et al., 2010). But it is usually not until adolescence that the sex structures kick into reproductive action. Puberty begins, and the cycle of life is poised to continue.

Puberty is a period when notable changes occur in physical development, ultimately leading to sexual maturity and the ability to reproduce. During this time, the *primary* and *secondary sex characteristics* develop (**FIGURE 10.1**). In addition, one of the most significant changes for males is *spermarche,* or first ejaculation (often occurring during sleep). The equivalent for females is *menarche,* or first menstruation (Ladouceur, 2012; Mendle, Harden, Brooks-Gunn, & Graber, 2010).

Vive la Différence

Apart from the obvious physical differences between the sexes, what else distinguishes males and females? Adult male brains, on average, are approximately 10% larger than adult female brains (Feis, Brodersen, von Cramon, Luders, & Tittgemeyer, 2013). There are also structural disparities in the brain; for example, the cerebral hemispheres are not completely symmetric, and males and females differ somewhat in these asymmetries (Tian, Wang, Yan, & He, 2011). MRI analyses point to sex differences in

CONNECTIONS

In **Chapter 8,** we noted that primary sex characteristics, including the ovaries, uterus, vagina, penis, scrotum, and testes, are related to reproduction. Secondary sex characteristics, such as deepening of the voice in males and breast development in females, are indirectly involved with reproduction.

androgens The male hormones secreted by the testes in males and by the adrenal glands in both males and females.

estrogen The female hormone secreted primarily by the ovaries and by the adrenal glands in both males and females.

testosterone An androgen produced by the testes.

CONNECTIONS

In **Chapter 9,** we described one robust gender difference relating to social cognition: Women are better and faster than men in identifying emotional expressions. However, it is not clear if these differences result from biological or cultural influences.

CONNECTIONS

In **Chapter 7,** we explored mental imagery, which is involved in the cognitive task of mental rotation. Here, we see that this visual-spatial ability seems to be different for men and women, although it is not clear how much is due to biology and how much is due to environmental influences.

CONNECTIONS

In **Chapter 2,** we learned there are many similarities between male and female brains, but some disparities do exist. The differences in brain function, although biological, can also be explained in terms of experience.

CONNECTIONS

In **Chapters 7 and 8** we presented the concept of heritability (in relation to intelligence and schizophrenia, for example). Here, we note that around half of the variability in aggressive behavior can be attributed to genes and the other half to environment.

the brain networks involved in **social cognition** and visual-spatial abilities (Feis et al., 2013). Some distinctions between male and female brains are believed to be influenced by hormones secreted prenatally, suggesting they have a biological basis (Sanders, Sjodin, & de Chastelaine, 2002).

COGNITION   Despite these contrasts in brain size and structure, males and females do not differ significantly in terms of general intelligence (Burgaleta et al., 2012; Halpern et al., 2007), a pairing many researchers find remarkable: "Apparently, males and females can achieve similar levels of overall intellectual performance by using differently structured brains in different ways" (Deary, Penke, & Johnson, 2010, p. 209). Researchers do find different patterns of neurological activity in males and females, but remember that brains can change in response to experience, a phenomenon called neuroplasticity. Sex differences may be due to changes in synaptic connections and neural networks that result from the different experiences of being male or female (Hyde, 2007).

What are some of the functional differences between male and female brains? One important area of difference is mental rotation; studies suggest that men are better than women at **mentally rotating objects** (Collins & Kimura, 1997). With practice, women may be able to catch up, however. In one study, women who practiced mentally rotating objects while playing computer games showed greater improvement on measures of mental rotation than did the men (Cherney, 2008). Another area of difference is verbal competence. In childhood, girls tend to perform better on tests of verbal ability, but the discrepancies are so small that they don't provide useful information for making educational decisions (Hyde & Linn, 1988; Wallentin, 2009). Differences in cognitive development between boys and girls are "minimal," and these disparities are only responsible for a small proportion of the variability in children's scores on cognitive tasks (Ardila, Rosselli, Matute, & Inozemtseva, 2011).

Research suggests that some cognitive gender disparities carry over into adulthood, with women outperforming men in verbal tasks and men showing greater spatial and mathematical abilities. These differences between men and women have declined over the past several decades, suggesting changes in sociocultural factors, such as greater availability of advanced math courses and more support for both men and women to pursue careers that interest them (Deary et al., 2010; Wai, Cacchio, Putallaz, & Makel, 2010). When it comes to mathematics performance in children, gender is not the best predictor; **environmental factors** such as mother's education, the learning environment of the home, and effectiveness of the elementary school are "far stronger predictors" (Lindberg, Hyde, Petersen, & Linn, 2010).

AGGRESSION   We've discussed gender disparities in brain anatomy and cognitive abilities, but how do males and females differ in terms of behavior? Men tend to demonstrate more physical aggression (such as hitting) than females (Ainsworth & Maner, 2012; see Chapter 15), but that doesn't mean females aren't aggressive in their own way. Some researchers report that females exhibit more *relational aggression,* or aggressive behaviors that are indirect and aimed at relationships, such as spreading rumors or excluding certain group members (Archer, 2004; Archer & Coyne, 2005; Crick & Grotpeter, 1995). These gender differences typically appear early in life (Card, Stucky, Sawalani, & Little, 2008; Hanish, Sallquist, DiDonato, Fabes, & Martin, 2012).

What causes these differences in males and females? One hormonal candidate is testosterone, which has been associated with aggression (Montoya, Terburg, Bos, & van Honk, 2012) and, as discussed earlier, exists at higher levels in males. Studies of identical twins suggest that **approximately 50% of aggressive behavior** can be explained by genetic factors (DiLalla, 2002; Tackett, Waldman, & Lahey, 2009). This implies that a significant proportion of gender differences in aggressive behavior results from an interaction between environmental factors and genetics (Brendgen et al., 2005; Rowe, Maughan, Worthman, Costello, & Angold, 2004). In addition, researchers have noted that boys tend to be more aggressive when raised in nonindustrial societies; patriarchal societies, in which women have less power and are considered inferior to men; and polygamous societies, in which men can have more than one wife. Why are these males more aggressive? Evolutionary psychology would suggest that competition for resources (including females) increases the likelihood of aggression (Wood & Eagly, 2002).

One thing to keep in mind is that, overall, the variation within a gender is much greater than the variation between genders: "Males and females are similar on most, but not all, psychological variables" (Hyde, 2007, p. 260). This *gender similarities hypothesis* proposed by Hyde (2005) states that males and females exhibit large differences in only a few areas, including some motor behaviors (throwing distance), some characteristics of sexuality (frequency of masturbation), and to a moderate degree, aggression. These physical and behavioral differences between males and females are interesting, but keep in mind that sex development does not always occur along a strictly "male" or "female" path.

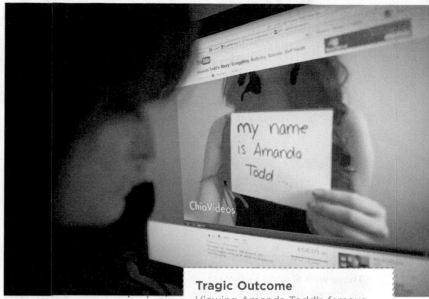

Tragic Outcome
Viewing Amanda Todd's famous YouTube video is heartrending. Todd was just 15 years old when she took her own life, a tragedy many people believe resulted from years of being bullied and harassed online and at school (Shaw, 2013, March 13). Most of the abuse Todd suffered took the form of *relational aggression,* a type of aggression that is not physical but extremely hurtful (Archer & Coyne, 2005). The ongoing threats, rumors, and gossip drove her to become anxious, depressed, and eventually suicidal (Shaw, 2013, March 13). AFP PHOTO/MLADEN ANTONOVMLADEN ANTONOV/AFP/Getty Images

Differences of Sexual Development

LO 3   Identify some of the causes of intersexual development

In some cases, hormonal imbalances and genetic abnormalities lead to differences of sex development (Topp, 2013; **INFOGRAPHIC 10.1** on page 432). Such disparities result from "congenital conditions in which development of chromosomal, gonadal, or anatomic sex is atypical" (Lee, Houk, Ahmed, & Hughes, 2006, p. e488). According to the American Psychiatric Association (2013, p. 451), **intersexual** refers to having "conflicting or ambiguous biological indicators" of male or female in sexual structures and organs (**TABLE 10.1** on page 433). For example, intersexual development would be apparent in a genetic female (XX) or male (XY) who has sexual structures and organs that are ambiguous or inconsistent with genetic sex. Around 1% of infants are found to have differences of sex development at birth. Such an individual might once have been called a "hermaphrodite," but this term is outdated, derogatory, and misleading because it refers to the impossible condition of being both fully male and fully female (Vilain, 2008).

The roots of intersexuality lie early in development, when fetal sensitivity to hormones determines the path of sexual differentiation, with timing and the amount of hormones as important factors. If a male fetus is insensitive to androgens, for example, he may develop more femalelike sex organs (known as *androgen insensitivity syndrome;* Mazur, 2005). A fetally *androgenized female* develops more malelike sex organs as a result of being exposed to excess androgens (Dessens, Slijper, & Drop, 2005).

CHROMOSOMES AND INTERSEXUALITY   Differences of sexual development can also be traced to irregularities in the sex chromosomes, as the creation of the 23rd pair does not always follow the expected pattern of XX or XY (Juul, Main,

intersexual Ambiguous or inconsistent biological indicators of male or female in the sexual structures and organs.

Different Layers of Sexual Determination

When thinking about the biological factors that determine sex, most people envision the primary sex characteristics that indicate our assignment at birth. But one's sex is made up of many layers with different influences. Though they often all combine in a predictable way, there can be exceptions at any point. Looking at variations at each layer demonstrates the complex reality of sex that goes far beyond what is declared on our birth certificates.

Primarily influenced by **genes**

CHROMOSOMES

One chromosome from each parent combines to determine genetic sex:
XX (female)
or XY (male).

exceptions:
Boys with *Klinefelter's syndrome* (XXY) develop normally until puberty, but can have underdeveloped male characteristics or additional female secondary sex characteristics because of the extra X chromosome. Also: *Turner's syndrome* (female born with an absent or incomplete X chromosome).

exception:
Those with *5-alpha reductase deficiency* appear female at birth. At puberty, hormonal surges cause external masculinization sufficient to make them indistinguishable from other men.

SECONDARY SEX CHARACTERISTICS

Prompted by hormonal changes, these characteristics appear at puberty and are only indirectly involved with reproduction.

GONADS

Presence of Y chromosome causes gonads to become testes. If Y chromosome is not present, gonads develop into ovaries.

exception:
Intersexual development is apparent when individuals are born with sexual structures and organs that are ambiguous or inconsistent with genetic sex.

PRIMARY SEX CHARACTERISTICS

Testes secrete androgens that influence the development of male genitals. The absence of this signal leads to the development of female genitals.

exception:
Though genetically male and possessing testes, those with *androgen-insensitivity syndrome* do not respond to androgens and develop more femalelike sex organs and other characteristics.

Primarily influenced by **hormones**

Table 10.1 DIFFERENCES OF SEXUAL DEVELOPMENT

Differences of Sexual Development	Frequency
Intersex (atypical genitalia)	1 in 1,500 births
Klinefelter's syndrome	1 in 1,000 births
Turner's syndrome	1 in 2,500 female births
Androgen-insensitivity syndrome	1 in 13,000 births
5-alpha reductase deficiency	Very rare—incidence unknown

People with ambiguous sexual characteristics are considered to have differences of sexual development. Listed above are the frequency estimates for some common causes of intersexuality.

SOURCES: GENETICS HOME REFERENCE (2008); INTERSEX SOCIETY OF NORTH AMERICA (2008); NATIONAL INSTITUTES OF HEALTH, EUNICE KENNEDY SHRIVER NATIONAL INSTITUTE OF CHILD HEALTH AND HUMAN DEVELOPMENT (N.D.).

& Skakkebaek, 2011; Wodrich & Tarbox, 2008). On some occasions, there are too many chromosomes or one missing. In the case of *Klinefelter's syndrome,* a male is born with at least one extra X chromosome in the 23rd pair (for example, XXY). A boy with Klinefelter's syndrome typically develops normally until puberty, but then has a greater chance of developing female sex characteristics such as breasts. He is infertile or may have underdeveloped sexual organs and secondary sex characteristics (Mandoki, Sumner, Hoffman, & Riconda, 1991; Manning, Kilduff, & Trivers, 2013). In *Turner's syndrome,* a female is born with only one X chromosome (as opposed to two X chromosomes), anatomically normal genitals, ovaries that are not fully developed, and infertility. Girls with this syndrome who go undiagnosed or untreated are at increased risk for estrogen deficiency, hypothyroidism, cardiovascular issues, and short stature (Hjerrild, Mortensen, & Gravholt, 2008). Despite the possibility of developmental delays in cognitive, social, and emotional functioning, women with Turner's syndrome who receive treatment can lead independent, stable, and productive lives (McCauley & Sybert, 2006).

✓ show what you know

1. _____ refers to our sexual activities, attitudes, and behaviors.
   a. Sex
   b. Sex determination
   c. Sexuality
   d. Gender

2. A physician attempts to explain to a young couple some of the biological factors that determine sex. She states that when the 23rd chromosome pair contains an X and a Y, the zygote generally develops:
   a. into a female.
   b. into a male.
   c. ovaries.
   d. the anatomy of both sexes.

3. On occasion, the 23rd pair of chromosomes does not follow the expected pattern and will include too many chromosomes. For example, a person with _____ is born with at least one extra X chromosome.

4. How are chromosomes involved in differences of sex development?

✓ CHECK YOUR ANSWERS IN APPENDIX C.

On the lower right, above, and to the right of the 22nd chromosome pair, is the 23rd pair (sex chromosomes). Since one is X and the other is Y, we can conclude the gender is male.

Gender

With the prior biology lesson under our belt, let's consider its implications for psychology. What does it mean to be a "man" or "woman" in today's world? Many think of men as being assertive, logical, and in charge, whereas women are perceived as more caring, sensitive, and emotional. But such characterizations are simplistic and frequently inaccurate. Just ask Stephen Patten.

A MASCULINE TOUCH   Have you ever been hospitalized? If so, you probably remember your nurses—perhaps better than your doctors. The role of the nurse is extremely important. Nurses are the people who make sure you are clean, comfortable, and properly medicated at all hours of the day.

When you press the call button at 2:00 A.M., it is the nurse who appears at your bedside. As you undergo a frightening or painful procedure, it is typically the nurse who holds your hand. Few professions demand such a high level of sensitivity and compassion.

The field of nursing is dominated by women, who are sometimes perceived as being more caring and nurturing than men. But according to Stephen Patten, the ability to care and nurture has little to do with gender. The son of a minister, Stephen was raised to believe that men have the capacity for deep compassion—and he has put this lesson to work in his 32-year career.

Nothing is more rewarding than the nurse–patient relationship, according to Stephen. Nursing, he says, is "the most intimate of any of the health-care professions." Doctors diagnose and treat diseases (an important job indeed), but the nurse is the patient's advocate and lifeline. Lying on an operating table unable to move and unconscious, you are in no position to help yourself, but the nurse is there to make sure you are hydrated, to cover you with a warming blanket, and to ensure that hospital staff use proper sterilization techniques so you do not acquire a dangerous infection, among other things.

Some patients are pleasantly surprised to discover a man will be caring and advocating for them in their most vulnerable state. But others have trouble accepting the idea that Stephen could serve in such a capacity. "What are you, some sort of lesbian trapped in a man's body?" one patient demanded to know. Another flat-out refused to have a male nurse participate in her care. Why do you think these patients reacted to Stephen this way? We suspect it has something to do with their preconceived notions about *gender roles*.

"No, this is not Mel's secretary. This is Mel."

Cartoonstock

Gender: Beyond Biology

LO 4   Define gender and explain how culture plays a role in its development.

Earlier we described gender as the dimension of masculinity and femininity based on social, cultural, and psychological characteristics. Men are typically perceived as masculine, and women are assumed to be feminine. But concepts of masculine and feminine vary according to culture, social context, and the individual. We learn how to *behave* in gender-appropriate ways through the **gender roles** designated by our culture (although some behavioral differences between males and females are apparent from birth; more on this in a bit). Gender roles are demonstrated through the actions, general beliefs, and characteristics associated with masculinity and femininity. This understanding of expected male and female behavior is generally demonstrated by around age 2 or 3. So too is the ability to differentiate

gender roles The collection of actions, beliefs, and characteristics that a culture associates with masculinity and femininity.

gender identity The feeling or sense of being either male or female, and compatibility, contentment, and conformity with one's gender.

between boys and girls, and men and women (Zosuls, Miller, Ruble, Martin, & Fabes, 2011). Most of us have been the target of a curious toddler, openly asking questions or making comments about sex or gender.

A person's **gender identity** is the feeling or sense of being either male or female, and compatibility, contentment, and conformity with one's gender (Egan & Perry, 2001; Tobin et al., 2010). Gender identity is often reinforced by learning and parental stereotyping of appropriate girl/boy behaviors, but does not always follow such a script. Researchers have found that an environment that does not specify strict gender roles results in children developing more fluid ideas about gender-appropriate behavior (Hupp, Smith, Coleman, & Brunell, 2010). Thus, if a child is growing up in a single-parent home, she will likely see her parent taking on the traditional gender roles of both males and females, and will be more comfortable stepping outside the boundaries prescribed by such roles.

LEARNING AND GENDER ROLES *Gender typing* is "the development of traits, interests, skills, attitudes, and behaviors that correspond to stereotypical masculine and feminine social roles" (Mehta & Strough, 2010, p. 251). These gender roles can be acquired through **observational learning,** as explained by social-cognitive theory (Bussey & Bandura, 1999; Else-Quest, Higgins, Allison, & Morton, 2012; Tenenbaum & Leaper, 2002). We learn from our observations of others in our environment, particularly by watching those of the same gender. Children also learn and model the behaviors represented in electronic media and books (Kingsbury & Coplan, 2012).

Operant conditioning is also involved in the development of gender roles. Children often receive reinforcement for behaviors considered gender-appropriate and punishment (or lack of attention) for those viewed as inappropriate. Parents, caregivers, relatives, and peers reinforce gender-appropriate behavior by smiling, laughing, or encouraging. But when children exhibit gender-inappropriate behavior (a boy playing with a doll, for example), the people in their lives might frown, get worried, or even put a stop to it. Through this combination of **encouragement and discouragement** a child learns to conform to society's expectations. Keep in mind that not all parents and caregivers are passionate about preserving traditional gender roles.

> **CONNECTIONS**
>
> In **Chapter 5,** we described how learning can occur by observing and imitating a model. Here we see how this type of learning can shape the formation of gender roles.

> **CONNECTIONS**
>
> In **Chapter 5,** we discussed operant conditioning, which is learning that results from consequences. Here, the positive reinforcer is encouragement, which leads to an increase in a desired behavior. The punishment is discouragement, which reduces the unwanted behavior.

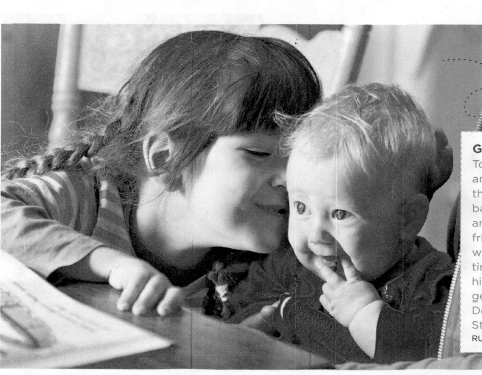

Gender Free
Toronto parents Kathy Witterick and David Stocker decided to raise their third child gender free. When baby Storm was born, Witterick and Stocker informed family and friends that the sex of the child would remain a secret for some time; they wanted Storm to make his or her own decision about gender identity (Poisson, 2011, December 26). Pictured here is Storm with big brother Jazz. STEVE RUSSELL/TORONTO STAR, Kathy Witterick

COGNITION AND GENDER SCHEMAS   In addition to learning by observation and reinforcement, children seem to develop gender roles by actively processing information (Bem, 1981). In other words, children think about the behaviors they observe, including the differences between males and females. They watch their parents' behavior, often following suit (Tenenbaum & Leaper, 2002). Using the information they have gathered, they develop a variety of gender-specific rules they believe should be followed (for example, girls help around the house, boys play with model cars; Yee & Brown, 1994). These rules provide the framework for **gender schemas,** which are the psychological or mental guidelines that dictate how to be masculine or feminine. Gender schemas also impact how we process information or remember events (Barberá, 2003). For example, Martin and Halverson (1983) found that children were more likely to remember events incorrectly if those events violated gender stereotypes. If they saw a little girl playing with a truck and a little boy playing with a doll, they were likely to recall the girl having the doll and the boy having the truck when tested several days later. In a more recent study, children were asked to recall information from storybooks they had just heard on audiotape. Immediately afterward, their recall of the stories was "often imprecise," most likely because their notions of gender-appropriate behavior (gender schemas) colored their memories. For example, one of the stories told of a little girl who was trying to help an adult male overcome his fear of walking on a high wire. Yet many children inaccurately remembered the little girl being afraid, or thought that the man was protecting her (Frawley, 2008). Apparently, their gender schemas incorporated the assumption that men are brave, and this interfered with their ability to recall the story correctly.

CONNECTIONS

In **Chapter 7,** we stated that *schemas* are a component of cognition. Schemas are collections of ideas or notions representing a basic unit of understanding. Here, we see a specific type of schema that influences conceptions of gender and memories.

BIOLOGY AND GENDER   Clearly, culture and learning influence the development of gender-specific behaviors and interests, but could biology play a role too? Research on nonhuman primates suggests this is the case (Hines, 2011a). A growing body of literature points to a link between testosterone exposure *in utero* and specific play behaviors (Swan et al., 2010). For example, male and female infants

Monkey Play
A male vervet monkey rolls a toy car on the ground (left), and a female examines a doll (right). When provided with a variety of toys, male vervet monkeys spend more time playing with cars and balls, whereas females are drawn to dolls and pots (Alexander & Hines, 2002). Similar behaviors have been observed in rhesus monkeys (Hassett, Siebert, & Wallen, 2008). These studies suggest a biological basis for the gender-specific toy preferences often observed in human children.
MCT/MCT via Getty Images

as young as 3 to 8 months demonstrate gender-specific toy preferences that cannot be explained by mere socialization or learning (Hines, 2011b). Research using eye-tracking technology reveals that baby girls spend more time looking at dolls, while boys tend to focus on toy trucks (Alexander, Wilcox, & Woods, 2009). Although these early differences seem to be unlearned, infants as young as 6 months can learn to discriminate between male and female faces and voices. Perhaps their toy interests have a learned component as well (Martin, Ruble, & Szkrybalo, 2002). But the bottom line is, not all gender-specific behaviors can be attributed to culture and upbringing—a principle well illustrated by the heartbreaking story of Bruce Reimer.

nature AND nurture

The Case of Bruce Reimer

Bruce Reimer and his twin brother were born in 1965. During a circumcision operation at 8 months, Bruce's penis was almost entirely burnt away by electrical equipment used in the procedure. When he was about 2 years old, his parents took the advice of Johns Hopkins psychologist John Money and decided to raise Bruce as a girl (British Broadcasting Company [BBC], 2005, September). The thinking at the time was that what made a person a male or female was not necessarily the original structure of the genitals, but rather how he or she was raised (Diamond, 2004).

Just before Bruce's second birthday, doctors removed his testicles and used the tissues to create the beginnings of female genitalia. His parents began calling him Brenda, dressing him like a girl and encouraging him to engage in stereotypically "girl" activities such as baking and playing with dolls (BBC, 2005, September). But Brenda did not adjust so well to her new gender assignment. An outcast at school, she was called cruel names like "caveman" and "gorilla." She brawled with both boys and girls alike, and eventually got kicked out of school (CBC News, 2004, May 10; Diamond & Sigmundson, 1997).

When Brenda hit puberty, the problem became even worse. Despite ongoing psychiatric therapy and estrogen replacement, she could not deny what was in her *nature*—she refused to consider herself female (Diamond & Sigmundson, 1997). Brenda became suicidal, prompting her parents to tell her the truth about the past (BBC, 2005, September).

At age 14, Brenda decided to "reassign himself" to be a male. He then changed his name to David, began taking male hormones, and underwent a series of penis construction surgeries (Colapinto, 2000; Diamond & Sigmundson, 1997). At 25, David married and adopted his wife's children, and for some time it appeared he was doing quite well (Diamond & Sigmundson, 1997). But sadly, at the age of 38, he took his own life.

We are in no position to explain the tragic death of David Reimer, but we cannot help but wonder what role his traumatic gender reassignment might have played. Keep in mind that this is just an isolated *case*. As discussed in Chapter 1, we should be extremely cautious about making generalizations from case studies, which may or may not be representative of the larger population. Many people who undergo sex reassignment go on to live happy and fulfilling lives.

HIS PARENTS . . . DECIDED TO RAISE BRUCE AS A GIRL.

GENDER-ROLE STEREOTYPES The case of Bruce Reimer touches on another important topic: gender-role stereotypes. Growing up, David (who was called "Brenda" at the time) did not enjoy wearing dresses and playing "girl" games. He

gender schemas The psychological or mental guidelines that dictate how to be masculine and feminine.

Androgynous Idol
American Idol sensation Adam Lambert reportedly embraces androgyny, the mixing of stereotypically male and female qualities. "I'm trying to make it current again," Lambert told the *Daily Xtra.* "I've always been attracted to that" (Thomas, December 30, 2009). Steve Jennings/WireImage

didn't adhere to the *gender-role stereotypes* assigned to little girls. Gender-role stereotypes, which begin to take hold around age 3, are strong ideas about the nature of males and females—how they should dress, what kinds of games they should like, and so on. Decisions about children's toys, in particular, follow strict gender-role stereotypes (boys play with trucks, girls play with dolls), and any crossing over risks ridicule from peers, sometimes even adults. Gender-role stereotypes are apparent in toy commercials (Kahlenberg & Hein, 2010) and pictures in coloring books (Fitzpatrick & McPherson, 2010). They also manifest themselves in academic settings. For example, many girls have negative attitudes about math, which seem to be associated with parents' and teachers' expectations about gender differences in math competencies (Gunderson, Ramirez, Levine, & Beilock, 2012).

Children, especially boys, tend to cling to gender-role stereotypes very tightly. You are much more likely to see a girl playing with a "boy" toy than a boy playing with a "girl" toy. Society, in turn, is more tolerant of girls who cross gender stereotypes. In many cultures, the actions of a tomboy (a girl who behaves in ways society considers masculine) are more acceptable than those of a "sissy" (a derogatory term for a boy who acts in a stereotypically feminine way; Martin & Ruble, 2010; Thorne, 1993). Despite such judgments, some children do not conform to societal pressure (Tobin et al., 2010).

ANDROGYNY   Those who cross gender-role boundaries and engage in behaviors associated with both genders are said to exhibit **androgyny.** An androgynous person might be nurturing (generally considered a feminine quality) and assertive (generally considered a masculine quality), thus demonstrating characteristics associated with both genders (Johnson et al., 2006). But concepts of masculine and feminine—and therefore what constitutes androgyny—are not consistent across cultures. In North America, notions about gender are revealed in clothing colors; parents frequently dress boy babies in blue and girl babies in pink. In the African nation of Swaziland, on the other hand, children are dressed androgynously, wearing any color of the rainbow (Bradley, 2011).

LO 5   Distinguish between transgender and transsexual.

TRANSGENDER AND TRANSSEXUAL   The development of gender identity and the acceptance of gender roles go relatively smoothly for most people. But sometimes societal expectations of being male or female differ from what an individual is feeling inwardly, leading to discontent. At birth, most people are identified as male or female; this is referred to as an infant's *natal gender,* or gender assignment. When natal gender does not feel right, an individual may have *transgender* experiences. According to the American Psychological Association, **transgender** refers to people "whose *gender identity, gender expression,* or behavior does not conform to that typically associated with the sex to which they were assigned at birth" (APA, 2011b, p. 1). Remember that gender identity is the feeling or sense of being either male or female. For a person who is transgender, a mismatch occurs between that sense of identity and the gender assignment at birth. This disparity can be temporary or persistent (American Psychiatric Association, 2013). Approximately 700,000 individuals in the United States (around 0.2% of the population) consider themselves to be transgender (Gates, 2011).

When the discrepancy between natal gender and gender identity leads to significant experiences and/or expression of distress, an individual might meet the criteria for a *gender dysphoria* diagnosis (American Psychiatric Association, 2013). Some

androgyny The tendency to cross gender-role boundaries, exhibiting behaviors associated with both genders.

transgender Refers to people whose gender identity and expression do not typically match the gender assigned to them at birth.

transsexual An individual who seeks or undergoes a social transition to the other gender, and who may make changes to his or her body through surgery and medical treatment.

transgender individuals try to resolve this discontent through medical intervention. According to the American Psychiatric Association, a person is considered **transsexual** if he or she seeks or undergoes "a social transition from male to female or female to male, which in many, but not all, cases also involves a somatic transition by cross-sex hormone treatment and genital surgery (*sex reassignment surgery*)" (APA, 2013, p. 451, italics in original). Transsexual people frequently report they have always had the feeling they were born into the body of a person of the opposite sex. There is a lot of inconsistency in the terminology and labels associated with *trans*: those who are considered and identify themselves as transgender, transsexual, or nonconforming to traditional gender identities. Thus, we should be sensitive about labeling and, when possible, ask *trans* people how they would like to be identified (Hendricks & Testa, 2012).

As you can see, gender is a complex and intangible social construct. Now let's tackle something a little more concrete. Are you ready for sex?

show what you know

1. _____ refers to how masculinity and femininity are defined based on culture, social setting, and psychological characteristics.
   a. Sex
   b. Sex role
   c. Gender schema
   d. Gender

2. A sixth-grader states that men are more assertive, logical, and in charge than women. She has learned about this _____ from a variety of sources in her immediate setting and culture.
   a. gender identity
   b. observational learning
   c. gender role
   d. androgyny

3. The psychological or mental rules that dictate how to be masculine and feminine are known as _____.

4. Describe the difference between transgender and transsexual.

✓ CHECK YOUR ANSWERS IN APPENDIX C.

The Birds and the Bees

THE MAKING OF A SEXPERT Dr. Stephanie Buehler grew up in California's San Fernando Valley during the 1970s, when the sexual revolution was in full gear. During this time in American history, many people questioned conventional notions about sex and explored different avenues of sexual expression. "There was a lot of sexual activity at that time," explains Dr. Buehler, who had many gay, bisexual, and transgender friends. "I was really exposed to a lot of different aspects of sexuality." At home, she knew it was okay to ask her parents questions about sex and birth control. So, it was no big deal when Stephanie's family went with her to see the avant-garde and sexually explicit movie *Last Tango in Paris* (which received an X rating at the time of its release, and currently has an NC-17 rating).

With this upbringing, Dr. Buehler was fairly relaxed talking about sex, and therefore her pursuit of a career as a sex therapist would seem like a plausible path. But graduate school looked like a long shot for a girl growing up in the 1970s, when women were just beginning to establish themselves as a major presence in the workforce. After graduating from college, the

Therapist at Work
Dr. Buehler found sex therapy so rewarding that she established her own sex therapy practice: The Buehler Institute, in Newport Beach, California. In addition to meeting with clients, Dr. Buehler is a peer reviewer for *The Journal of Sexual Medicine* and the author of a new book, *What Every Mental Health Professional Needs to Know about Sex.* Mark Buehler

Sexy Science ◀

In the mid-1950s, William Masters teamed with Virginia Johnson to study the bodily changes occurring during masturbation and sex. Their research was groundbreaking, and it upended many long-held misconceptions about sex. For example, Masters and Johnson found that the length of a man's penis does not determine his ability to give pleasure (Fox, 2013, July 25).
© Bettmann/CORBIS

first person in her immediate family to do so, she became a teacher at an inner-city elementary school, and then decided to pursue a master's degree and eventually a doctorate in psychology. Her PsyD concentration was family therapy, but another interest was brewing beneath the surface. During couples' role-playing sessions in class, Dr. Buehler always was the student asking questions about sex: "What about your sex life?" "What's going on in the bedroom?" She recalls her classmates looking at her and asking, "Why are you bringing that up? What does that have to do with anything?" The answer, she can now state with confidence, is a whole lot.

After working as a licensed psychotherapist for several years, Dr. Buehler began her sex therapy training. She found it so rewarding that she launched her own sex therapy institute, The Buehler Institute in Newport Beach, California. "I just find I'm never, ever bored with my work," says Dr. Buehler. Sexuality is quite personal . . . and that means that everybody is quite different.

Everything You Always Wanted to Know About Sex

When you think of sex, what comes to mind? Genitals? Intercourse? To grasp the complexity of sexual experiences, we must understand the basic physiology of the sexual response. Enter William Masters and Virginia Johnson and their pioneering laboratory research, which included the study of approximately 10,000 distinct sexual responses of 312 male and 382 female participants (Masters & Johnson, 1966).

LO 6   Describe the human sexual response as identified by Masters and Johnson.

HUMAN SEXUAL RESPONSE CYCLE   Masters and Johnson made some of the most important contributions to the study of the human sexual response. Their research started in 1954, not exactly a time when sex was thought to be an acceptable subject for dinner conversation. Nevertheless, almost 700 people volunteered to participate in their study, which lasted a little more than a decade (Masters & Johnson, 1966). In particular, Masters and Johnson were interested in determining the physiological responses that occurred during sexual activity, such as masturbation and intercourse. They used a variety of instruments to measure blood flow, body temperature, muscular changes, and heart rate. What they discovered is that most people experience a similar physiological sexual response, which can result from oral stimulation, manual stimulation, vaginal intercourse, or masturbation. Men and women tend to follow a similar pattern or cycle: *excitement, plateau, orgasm,* and *resolution* (**FIGURE 10.2**). It is important to note, though, that these phases vary for each individual in terms of duration.

FIGURE 10.2

Masters and Johnson's Human Sexual Response Cycle

In the male sexual response (left), excitement is typically followed by a brief plateau, orgasm, and then a refractory period during which another orgasm is not possible. In the female sexual response (right), there is no refractory period. Orgasm is typically followed by resolution (A) or, if sexual stimulation continues, additional orgasms (B).

Sexual arousal begins during the *excitement phase.* This is when physical changes start to become evident. Muscles tense, the heartbeat quickens, breathing accelerates, the nipples become firm, and blood pressure rises a bit. In men, the penis becomes erect, the scrotum constricts, and the testes pull up toward the body. In women, the vagina lubricates and the clitoris swells (Levin, 2008).

Many factors can dampen the sexual excitement of this phase, among them unhappy babies and ringing phones. But would you guess that a woman's tears can ruin the moment?

from the pages of **SCIENTIFIC AMERICAN**

Crying Women Turn Men Off

Weeping releases a chemical that reduces sexual arousal.

Women may have a more subtle way of telling men "no" than anyone imagined. Chemical cues in their tears signal that they are not interested in romantic activities, according to a study published online January 6 in *Science*.

Crying reveals a person's mood, but its evolutionary origins have long been a mystery. Because emotional tears have a different chemical makeup than those evoked by irritants in the eye, cognitive neuroscientist Noam Sobel of the Weizmann Institute of Science in Rehovot, Israel, wondered whether emotional tears relay chemical messages to others.

Sobel and his research team collected tears from self-professed "easy criers" as they watched sad movies. Later, the researchers held jars containing the odorless tears and pads that had been dipped in the tears under men's noses.

These men rated female faces as less sexually attractive than did men who sniffed saline. Moreover, their sexual excitement dropped, as indicated by their own reports and by levels of testosterone in their saliva.

The researchers then scanned the men's brains as they watched a titillating movie scene using functional MRI. Brain regions associated with sexual arousal showed less activity in men who sniffed tears compared with those who sniffed saline.

The findings represent the first evidence that human tears send chemical messages, Sobel reports. Because a decrease in testosterone levels is linked to reduced hostility, he speculates that weeping dampens not only the libido but also violent behavior. "If the signal really lowers aggression toward you, then the evolutionary value of crying is clear," he says. *Janelle Weaver.*

Assuming no tears are shed during the excitement phase, the next likely step is the *plateau phase*. There are no clear physiological signs to mark the beginning of this phase, but it is the natural progression from the excitement phase. During the plateau phase, the muscles continue to tense, breathing and heart rate increase, and the genitals begin to change color as blood fills this area. This phase is usually quite short-lived, lasting only a few seconds to minutes.

The shortest phase of the sexual response cycle is the *orgasm phase*. As the peak of sexual response is reached, an **orgasm** occurs, which is a powerful combination of extremely gratifying sensations and a series of rhythmic muscular contractions. When men and women are asked to describe their orgasmic experiences, it is very difficult to differentiate between them. Brain activity observed via PET scans is also very similar (Georgiadis, Reinders, Paans, Renken, & Kortekaas, 2009; Mah & Binik, 2001).

The final phase of the sexual response cycle, according to Masters and Johnson, is called the *resolution phase*. This is when bodies return to a relaxed state. Without further sexual arousal, the body will immediately begin the resolution phase. The blood flows out of the genitals, and blood pressure, heart rate, and breathing slow to normal. Men lose their erection, the testes move down, and the skin of the scrotum loosens. Men will also experience a **refractory period,** an interval during which they

orgasm A powerful combination of extremely gratifying sensations and a series of rhythmic muscular contractions.

refractory period An interval of time during which a man cannot attain another orgasm.

cannot attain another orgasm. This can last from minutes to hours, and typically the older the man is, the longer the refractory period lasts. For women, the resolution phase is characterized by a decrease in clitoral swelling and a return to the normal labia color. Women do not experience a refractory period, and if sexual stimulation continues, some are capable of having multiple orgasms.

Masters and Johnson's landmark research has led to further studies of the physiological aspects of the sexual response cycle, and although their basic model is viewed as valid, research suggests there may be the need for "correction or modification, or additional explanation" (Levin, 2008, p. 2). As mentioned, sex is different for every person, and not everyone fits neatly into the same model.

Armed with this knowledge about the physiology of sex, let's move on to its underlying psychology. How are sexual activities shaped by learning, relationships, and the **need to be loved and belong**?

Sexual Orientation

> **LO 7**   Define sexual orientation and summarize how it develops.

According to the American Psychological Association (APA, 2008), **sexual orientation** is the "enduring pattern" of sexual, romantic, and emotional attraction that individuals exhibit toward the same sex, opposite sex, or both sexes. When attracted to members of the opposite sex, sexual orientation is **heterosexual.** When attracted to members of the same sex, sexual orientation is **homosexual.** When attracted to members of the same sex *and* members of the opposite sex, sexual orientation is **bisexual,** although most people tend to prefer one sex or the other. Those who do not feel sexually attracted to others are referred to as *asexual.* Lack of interest in sex does not necessarily prevent a person from maintaining relationships with spouses, partners, or friends, but little is known about the impact of asexuality because research on the topic is scarce. We can't be sure how many people would consider themselves asexual, but by one estimate, they constitute 1% of the population (Crooks & Baur, 2014). Dr. Buehler's mentor once explained sexual orientation like this: There is a universe of orientations and identities, and each person gets to put him- or herself in the constellation.

There is also a universe of labels for different sexual orientations. In America, the most common terminology refers to a homosexual woman as a "lesbian," and a homosexual man as "gay" (APA, 2008). But sexual orientation is not a trait or characteristic one possesses. It is a label that reflects the relationships someone establishes and the qualities of those relationships, including degree of intimacy, mutual goals, commitment, and affection. We essentially become members of the group with which we have the most in common and in which we are the most comfortable, thus allowing us to build satisfying romantic relationships.

WHAT'S IN A NUMBER?   What percentage of the population is heterosexual? How about homosexual and bisexual? These questions may seem straightforward, but they are not easy to answer. This is partly because there are no clear-cut criteria for identifying individuals as homosexual, heterosexual, or bisexual. In other words, there is a vast spectrum representing sexual orientation. At one end are people who are "exclusively heterosexual" and at the other end are those considered "exclusively homosexual." Between these two poles is considerable variation (Kinsey, Pomeroy, & Martin, 1948; **FIGURE 10.3**). Some people might be exploring their sexuality, but not necessarily exhibiting a particular orientation, and this adds to the variability of rates. Estimates are available, but definitions of sexual orientation vary across cultures, and findings can be inconsistent as a result of differing survey designs: data collection

---

CONNECTIONS

In **Chapter 9,** we noted that Maslow in particular emphasized our deep-seated need to feel loved, to experience affection, and to belong to a group. These needs motivate us to seek out relationships, which can include sexual activities.

---

sexual orientation A person's enduring sexual interest in individuals of the same sex, opposite sex, or both sexes.

heterosexual Attraction to members of the opposite sex.

homosexual Attraction to members of the same sex.

bisexual Attraction to members of both the same and opposite sex.

in different years, the use of different age groups, different wording of questions, and so forth (Mosher, Chandra, & Jones, 2005). According to one estimate, 8 million people in the United States, or 3.5% of the adult population, are homosexual or bisexual (Gates, 2011).

Other estimates suggest the homosexual population is as low as 1% (referring only to same-sex behavior) and as high as 24% (defined as any sexual attraction to the same sex). This high end refers specifically to young women, who show greater fluidity in their sexual attractions and orientations (Ainsworth & Baumeister, 2012; Savin-Williams, 2009). As you digest these statistics, remember that sex is, first and foremost, a human experience. We may have different preferences, but our bodies react to sexual activity in similar ways. As Masters and Johnson (1979) demonstrated, we all experience a similar sexual response cycle, regardless of orientation. Even our brains display similar patterns of activity, apparent from fMRI and PET studies, when we feel sexual desire (Diamond & Dickenson, 2012). What makes us different is what we find sexually arousing (Cerny & Janssen, 2011).

How Sexual Orientation Develops

We are not sure how sexual orientation develops, although most research supports biological factors (a topic we will revisit in a little while). Among professionals in the field, there is near agreement that human sexual orientation is not a matter of choice. Research has focused on everything from genetics to culture, but there is no strong evidence that sexual orientation is determined by one particular factor (or set of factors). Instead, it appears to result from an interaction between nature and nurture, but this is still under investigation, and may never be fully determined or understood (APA, 2008).

GENETICS AND SEXUAL ORIENTATION   To determine the influence of biology in sexual orientation, we turn to twin studies, which are commonly used to examine the degree to which nature and nurture contribute to psychological traits. Since monozygotic twins share 100% of their genetic make-up, we expect them to share more genetically influenced characteristics than dizygotic twins, who only share about 50% of their genes. In a large study of Swedish twins, researchers explored the impact of genes and environment on "same-sex sexual behavior" (2,320 monozygotic twin pairs, 1,506 dizygotic twin pairs). In their sample, the monozygotic twins were moderately more likely than the dizygotic twins to have the same sexual orientation. They also found that same-sex sexual behavior for monozygotic twins had heritability estimates around 34–39% for men, and 18–19% for women (Långström, Rahman, Carlström, & Lichtenstein, 2010). These findings highlight two important factors: Men and women differ in terms of the heritability of same-sex sexual behavior, and the influence of the environment is substantial.

Researchers have searched for specific genes that might influence sexual orientation. Some have suggested that genes associated with male homosexuality might be transmitted by the mother. In one key study, around 64% of male siblings who were both homosexual had a set of several hundred genes in common, and these genes were located on the X chromosome (Hamer, Hu, Magnuson, Hu, & Pattatucci, 1993). But critics suggest this research was flawed, and no replications of this "gay gene" have been published since the original study (O'Riordan, 2012).

0   Exclusively heterosexual
1   Predominantly heterosexual, only incidentally homosexual
2   Predominantly heterosexual, but more than incidentally homosexual
3   Equally heterosexual and homosexual
4   Predominantly homosexual, but more than incidentally heterosexual
5   Predominantly homosexual, only incidentally heterosexual
6   Exclusively homosexual

▲ FIGURE 10.3
The Kinsey Sexuality Rating Scale
When interviewing people for a study on human sexuality, Alfred Kinsey and his colleagues (1948) discovered that people were not always exclusively heterosexual or homosexual. Instead, some described thoughts and behaviors that put them somewhere in between. This finding led the Kinsey team to develop the scale here, which shows a range associated with sexual orientation. Reprinted by permission of the Kinsey Institute for Research in Sex, Gender, and Reproduction, Inc.

THE BRAIN AND SEXUAL ORIENTATION   Researchers have also studied the brains of people with different sexual orientations, and their findings are interesting. LeVay (1991) discovered that a "small group of neurons" in the hypothalamus of homosexual men was almost twice as big as that found in heterosexual men. He did not suggest this size difference was indicative of homosexuality, but he did find it intriguing. LeVay also noted that these differences could have been the result of factors unrelated to sexual orientation. More recently, researchers using MRI technology found the corpus callosum to be thicker in homosexual men (Witelson et al., 2008). With the help of MRI and PET, some researchers are studying the neurobiological foundations of sexual orientation, trying to determine if there are similarities in functioning and connectivity between those attracted to women (homosexual women and heterosexual men), as well as between those attracted to men (homosexual men and heterosexual women) (Savic & Lindström, 2008).

HORMONES, ANTIBODIES, AND SEXUAL ORIENTATION   How do differences arise in the brain? They may emerge before birth. As we noted earlier, hormones (estrogen and androgens) secreted by the fetal gonads play a role in the development of reproductive anatomy. One hypothesis is that the presence of androgens (the hormones secreted primarily by the male gonads) influences the development of a sexual orientation toward women. This would lead to heterosexual orientation in men, but homosexual orientation in women (Mustanski, Chivers, & Bailey, 2002). Because it would be unethical to manipulate hormone levels in pregnant women, researchers rely on cases in which hormones are elevated because of a genetic abnormality or medication taken by a mother. For example, high levels of androgens early in a pregnancy may cause girls to be more "male-typed," and promote the development of a homosexual orientation (Berenbaum, Blakemore, & Beltz, 2011; Jordan-Young, 2012).

Interestingly, having older brothers in the family seems to be associated with homosexuality in men, particularly in right-handed men (Blanchard, 2008; **FIGURE 10.4**). Why would this be? Evolutionary theory would suggest that the more males there are in a family, the more potential for "unproductive competition" among the male siblings. If sons born later in the birth order were less aggressive, the result would be fewer problems among siblings, especially related to competition for mates and resources to support offspring. A homosexual younger brother would be less of a threat to an older brother than would a heterosexual younger brother.

How does right-handedness play a role? Researchers suggest that handedness might be related to the production of an anti-male antibody produced by the mother during pregnancy: "Some mothers may eventually become 'immunized' to a factor or substance important in male fetal development" (Bogaert, 2007, p. 141). The maternal immune hypothesis suggests that mothers develop an antibody that crosses the placenta and affects the development of the brain structures influencing sexual orientation (for example, the hypothalamus). Although subsequent research has supported the birth order effect, the handedness link has been more difficult to replicate (Bogaert, 2007). And, despite numerous attempts to identify genetic markers for homosexuality, researchers have had very little success (Dar-Nimrod & Heine, 2011). Some suggest that the search for genes underlying homosexuality is misguided. Why do we spend so much time and money seeking biological explanations for a "valid alternative lifestyle" (Jacobs, 2012)?

FIGURE 10.4

How Many Older Brothers?

The number of older brothers a man has seems to be associated with the probability of his homosexuality. Interestingly, this link has been found to be more prominent among right-handed men. *Source:* Reproduced/Adapted with permission of Psychology Press/Taylor & Francis Ltd (informaworld.com) from Blanchard (2008).

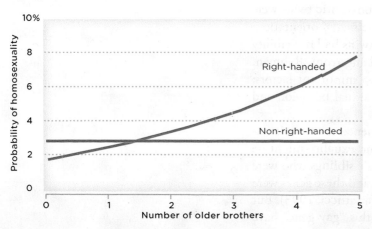

BIAS Although differences in sexual orientation are universal and have been evident throughout recorded history, individuals identified as members of the nonheterosexual minority have been subjected to stereotyping, prejudice, and discrimination. Nonheterosexual people in the United States, for example, have been, and continue to be, subjected to harassment, violence, and unfair practices related to housing and employment.

Counter to some stereotypes, a homosexual or bisexual orientation does not serve as a barrier to maintaining long-lasting relationships. Most same-sex couples experience the same ups and downs as heterosexual couples. When San Francisco's Mayor Gavin Newsom sanctioned same-sex marriages in the city in 2004, a number of long-partnered same-sex couples were finally able to legalize their relationships. Among those marrying long-time partners was Ronnie Gilbert, the female singer in The Weavers (famous for their song "Goodnight, Irene"), now in her eighties.

Bride and Bride ◄
Ellen DeGeneres and Portia de Rossi pose for wedding photos at their Beverly Hills home in 2008. DeGeneres and de Rossi are perhaps the most famous lesbian couple to marry, and their union has called attention to the ongoing debate on gay marriage. According to a recent survey, 58% of Americans support same-sex marriage, a significant increase from 37% in 2003 (Neary, 2013, March 25; Cohen, 2013, March 18). Getty Images

across the WORLD

Homosexuality and Culture

As you read earlier, approximately 3.5% of the U.S. population is gay, lesbian, or bisexual, and approximately 0.2% is transgender (Gates, 2011). These figures could be underestimates, as people may not always disclose their true sexual orientation to researchers.

When it comes to studying homosexuality in some parts of the world—particularly in developing nations—the research is lacking. One group of researchers reviewed the scientific literature for articles addressing male homosexuality in various countries and found limited, if any, data for parts of Africa, the Middle East, and the English-speaking Caribbean (Cáceres, Konda, Pecheny, Chatterjee, & Lyerla, 2006). For those regions where data did exist, the researchers were able to calculate the following percentages of men who had sex with other men: East Asia, 3–5%; South and South East Asia, 6–12%; Eastern Europe, 6–15%; and Latin America, 6–20% (Cáceres et al., 2006). But in cultures where sex between men is taboo or forbidden, people tend to remain tight lipped about the phenomenon, and researchers may not even study it (Wellings et al., 2006).

As you consider these statistics, keep in mind that "sex between men" does not necessarily equate to homosexuality. In India, for example, young straight men have few outlets for their sexual energy because heterosexual sex outside of marriage is generally forbidden. In this context, having sexual relationships with other men does not automatically make one homosexual (Go et al., 2004). Similarly in the United States, "sex between women" does not always go hand-in-hand with being lesbian or bisexual. Concepts of sexual orientation depend on culture as well as individual attitudes and perceptions.

. . . "SEX BETWEEN MEN" DOES NOT NECESSARILY EQUATE TO HOMOSEXUALITY.

EVOLUTIONARY PSYCHOLOGY AND SEX What is the purpose of sex? Evolutionary psychology would suggest that humans have sex to make babies and ensure the survival of the species (Buss, 1995). But if this were the only reason, then why would so many people choose same-sex partners? Some researchers believe it has something to do with "kin altruism," which suggests that homosexual men and women support reproduction in the family by helping relatives care for their children. Homosexual individuals may not "spend their time reproducing," but they can nurture the reproductive efforts of their "kin" (Erickson-Schroth, 2010).

There are other reasons to believe that there is more to human sex than making babies. If sex were purely for reproduction, we would expect to see sexual activity occurring only during the fertile period of the female cycle. Obviously, this is not the case. People have sex throughout a woman's monthly cycle and long after she goes through menopause. Sex is for feeling pleasure, expressing affection, and forming social bonds. In this respect, we are different from other members of the animal kingdom, who generally mate to procreate. There is at least one notable exception, however. If you could venture deep into the forests of the Democratic Republic of Congo, you might be surprised at what you would see happening between our close primate cousins, the bonobos.

didn't SEE that coming

Great Ape Sex

Bonobos are tree- and land-dwelling great apes that look like small and lanky versions of chimpanzees. And like chimps, these animals are closely related to humans, sharing 98.7% of our genetic material (Prüfer et al., 2012). Bonobos and people also happen to share some sexual behaviors.

Bonobos have both oral sex and vaginal sex. They enjoy a variety of positions, including the so-called missionary style commonly employed by people. They French kiss and fondle each other. Males mate with females, but pairs of females also rub their genitals together, a phenomenon known as *genito–genital rubbing*, or *G–G rubbing*. Males engage in similar activities called *scrotal rubbing* and *penis fencing* (De Waal, 2009).

BONOBOS HAVE BOTH ORAL AND VAGINAL SEX.

In bonobo society, sex happens at the times you might least suspect. Imagine two female bonobos simultaneously discovering a delicious piece of sugar cane. Both of them want it, so you might expect a little aggression to ensue. But what do the bonobos do instead? They rub their genitals together, of course! Now picture two males competing for the same female. They could fight over her, but why fight when you can make love? The vying males set aside their dispute and engage in a friendly scrotal rub (De Waal, 2009).

As these examples illustrate, bonobo sex has a lot to do with maintaining social harmony. Sex is used to defuse the tension that might arise over competition for food and mates (De Waal, 2009). It helps younger females bond with the dominant females in a new community—an important function given the supremacy of females in this species (Clay & Zuberbühler, 2012). Female relationships, it seems, are the glue holding together bonobo society.

Sex Conquers All?
Two bonobos enjoy a slobbery kiss. In bonobo society, sexual activity appears to reduce social tension and promote unity—a strategy that seems to work very well, because bonobos rarely fight. Females are the dominant sex, and the bonds between them hold communities together (Santa Maria, 2012, February 14).
Biosphoto/SuperStock

What kinds of similarities do you detect between the sex lives of bonobos and humans? 👁!

The Sex We Have

Thus far we have discussed sex in broad terms, but let's get into some specifics. Have you ever wondered how common it is to masturbate or think about sex? Do you sometimes wonder how many married people remain faithful to their spouses? You have come to the right chapter.

THE HISTORY OF SEX RESEARCH   Alfred Kinsey and colleagues (1948, 1953) were among the first to try to scientifically and objectively examine human sexuality in America. Using the survey method, Kinsey and his team collected data on the sexual behaviors of 5,300 White males and 5,940 White females. Their findings were surprising; both men and women masturbated, and participants had experiences with premarital sex, adultery, and sexual activity with someone of the same sex. Perhaps more shocking was the fact that so many people were willing to talk about their personal sexual behavior in post–World War II America. At that time, people generally did not talk openly about sexual topics.

The Kinsey study was groundbreaking in terms of its data content and methodology, which included accuracy checks and assurances of confidentiality. The Kinsey data have served as a valuable reference for researchers studying how sexual behaviors have evolved over time. However, Kinsey's work was not without limitations. For example, Kinsey and colleagues (1948, 1953) utilized a biased sampling technique that resulted in a sample that was **not representative** of the population. It was a completely White sample, with an overrepresentation of well-educated Protestants (Potter, 2006; Wallin, 1949). Another criticism of the Kinsey study is that it failed to determine the context in which orgasms occurred. Was a partner involved? Was the orgasm achieved through masturbation (Potter, 2006)?

Subsequent research has been better designed, including samples more representative of the population. Robert Michael and colleagues (1994) conducted the now-classic National Health and Social Life Survey (NHSLS), which examined the sexual activities of a representative sample of some 3,000 Americans between the ages of 18 and 59. A more recent study included a sample of approximately 5,800 men and women between the ages of 14 and 94 years (Herbenick et al., 2010). Some of the findings from these studies are presented below. For more information on sexual activities worldwide, take a look at the Across the World feature on page 449.

Radical Research
Alfred Kinsey meets with an interview subject in his office at the Institute for Sex Research, now The Kinsey Institute. Kinsey began investigating human sexuality in the 1930s, when talking about sex was taboo. He started gathering data with surveys, but then switched to personal interviews, which he believed to be more effective. These interviews often went on for hours and included hundreds of questions (PBS, 2005, January 27). Wallace Kirkland//Time Life Pictures/Getty Images

CONNECTIONS

In **Chapter 1,** we emphasized that representative samples enable us to generalize findings to populations. Here we see that inferences about sexual behaviors for groups *other* than White, well-educated Protestants could be problematic, as few members of these groups participated in the Kinsey study.

SEXUAL ACTIVITY IN RELATIONSHIPS   In the United States, the average age at first marriage is 26 for women and 28 for men. The odds of a first marriage lasting at least 10 years is 68% for women and 70% for men, and the probability of a first marriage lasting 20 years is only 52% for women and 56% for men (Copen, Daniels, Vespa, & Mosher, 2012). Most Americans are monogamous (one partner at a time), and 65–85% of married men and approximately 80% of married women report that they have always been faithful to their spouses (Laumann, Gagnon, Michael, & Michaels, 1994). Although monogamy is preferred in the United States, infidelity within marriages is as high as 76%. In a recent study, 4–5% of the participants reported they are in "open" relationships, that is, consensually nonmonogamous relationships (Conley, Ziegler, Moors, Matsick, & Valentine, 2013).

Around 77% of adults in the United States report they engaged in intercourse by age 20, regardless of cultural background or ethnicity. By the age of 44, 95% of adults have had intercourse. And the overwhelming majority are not waiting for marriage (Finer, 2007; see **FIGURE 10.5** on page 448.) However, married people do have more sex than those who are unmarried (Laumann et al., 1994). According to

FIGURE 10.5
Premarital Sex in the United States
Looking across adolescence and into adulthood, the number of people having sex increases steadily with age. Of those currently having sex, 97% engaged in sex before marriage. *Source:* Adapted from Finer (2007), Figure 1.

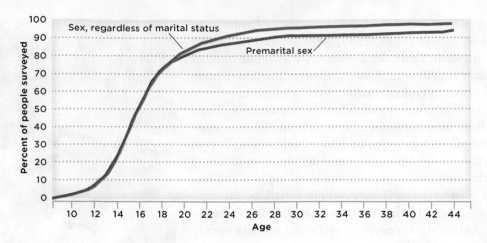

a large study of Swedish adults, the frequency of penile–vaginal intercourse is associated with sexual satisfaction, as well as satisfaction with relationships, mental health, and life in general. Other sexual activities, such as masturbation, were found to have an inverse relationship with a variety of measures of satisfaction (Brody & Costa, 2009; see **TABLE 10.2** for reported gender differences in frequency of sexual activity). Many studies indicate not only psychological benefits, but also physiological benefits to penile–vaginal intercourse. Correlations are apparent between the frequency of penile–vaginal intercourse and greater life expectancy, lower blood pressure, slimmer waistline, and less prostate and breast cancer risk (Brody, 2010).

Table 10.2	WHAT'S GOING ON?	
Sexual Activity	Average Frequency in Prior Month for Men	Average Frequency in Prior Month for Women
Penile–vaginal intercourse	5.2	4.8
Oral sex	2.3	1.9
Anal sex	0.10	0.08
Masturbation	4.5	1.5

How often do people engage in different types of sexual activity? Here are the monthly averages for adult men and women (the average age being 41). Keep in mind that significant variation exists around these averages.

SOURCE: BRODY AND COSTA (2009), TABLE 1, P. 1950.

SEXUAL ACTIVITY AND GENDER DIFFERENCES   As stereotypes might suggest, men think about sex more often than women. In the United States, 54% of men report thinking about sex "every day or several times a day"; 67% of women report thinking about sex only "a few times a week or a few times a month" (Laumann et al., 1994). One other notable gender difference is that men consistently report a higher frequency of masturbation (Peplau, 2003), a finding that has been replicated with a British sample (Gerressu, Mercer, Graham, Wellings, & Johnson, 2008). Men in the United States tend to be more tolerant than women when it comes to casual sex before marriage, as well as more permissive in their attitudes about extramarital sex (Laumann et al., 1994). But these attitude differences are not apparent in heterosexual teenagers and young adults, as young men and women more commonly engage in hookups, or "brief uncommitted sexual encounters among individuals who are not romantic partners or dating each other" (Garcia, Reiber, Massey, & Merriwether, 2012, p. 161). For these young people, attitudes about casual sex are apparent in their "hookup" behavior (**TABLE 10.3**).

SEXUAL ACTIVITY AND AGE   What sexual encounters do people commonly have? Herbenick and colleagues (2010) used a cross-sectional survey study to provide a snapshot of the types and rates of sexual behaviors across a wide range of ages in the United States. They found that masturbation is more common than partnered sexual activities among adolescents and people over the age of 70. They also discovered that more than half of the participants aged 18 to 49 had engaged in oral sex in the past year, with a lower proportion of the younger and older age groups engaging in this activity. Penetrative sex (vaginal and anal) was most common among adults ages 20 to 49. In another study of around 3,000 adults (57 to 85 years old), researchers reported that aging did not seem to adversely affect interest in sexual activity; many of the respondents in their sixties, seventies, and eighties were still sexually active. In fact, through the age of 74, the frequency of sexual activity remained steady, even with a high proportion of "bothersome sexual problems." Physical health problems can affect sexual activity at any age (Lindau et al., 2007).

Table 10.3 **HOOKUP BEHAVIOR**	
Hookup Behavior	**Undergraduates Reporting Behavior (%)**
Kissing	98
Sexual touching above waist	58
Sexual touching below the waist	53
Performed oral sex	36
Received oral sex	35
Sexual intercourse	34

What exactly do college students mean when they say they "hooked up" with someone? As you can see from the data presented here, hooking up can signify anything from a brief kiss to sexual intercourse.

SOURCE: GARCIA ET AL. (2012).

across the WORLD

What They Are Doing in Bed . . . or Elsewhere

How often do people in New Zealand have sex? How many lovers has the average Israeli had? And are Chileans happy with the amount of lovemaking they do? These are just a few of the questions answered by the Global Sex Survey (2005), which, we dare to say, is one of the sexiest scientific studies out there (and which was sponsored by Durex, a condom manufacturer). We cannot report all the survey results, but here is a roundup of those we found most interesting:

PEOPLE IN GREECE ARE HAVING THE MOST SEX.

- People in Greece have the most sex—an average of 138 times per year, or 2 to 3 times per week.

- People in Japan have the least amount of sex—an average of 45 times per year, or a little less than once per week.

- The average age for losing one's virginity is lowest among Icelanders (between 15 and 16) and highest for those from India (between 19 and 20).

- Across nations, the average number of sexual partners is 9. If gender is taken into account, that number is a little higher for men (11) and lower for women (7).

- Of respondents, 50% reported having sex in cars, 39% in bathrooms, and 2% in airplanes.

- Across the world, many people use sexual aids such as pornography (41%), massage oils and creams (31%), lubricants (30%), and vibrators (22%).

Happy Between the Sheets
Nearly half (44%) of adults participating in the Global Sex Survey said they were happy with their sex lives. Men were more likely than women to say they wanted to have sex more often (Global Sex Survey, 2005). © John Lund/Blend Images/Corbis

- Approximately 13% of adults say they have had a sexually transmitted infection.
- Nearly half the people around the world are happy with their sex lives.

As you reflect on these results, remember that **surveys** have limitations. People are not always honest when it comes to answering questions about personal issues (like sex), and the wording of questions can influence people's responses. Even if responses are accurate, we can only speculate about the beliefs and attitudes underlying them.

CONNECTIONS

In **Chapter 1,** we discussed limitations of using self-report surveys. People often resist revealing attitudes or behaviors related to sensitive topics, such as sexual activity. The risk is gathering data that do not accurately represent participants' attitudes and beliefs, particularly with face-to-face interviews.

Contemporary Trends in Sexual Behavior

As noted earlier, we can define sex as an activity (for example, she had *sex*), but how we define what constitutes sex is not always consistent (Schwarz, Hassebrauck, & Dörfler, 2010). If you ask one teenager whether she has had "sex," she might say no, even if she has had oral sex, whereas another teen might say yes, thinking that oral sex does count as sex. Such variability may explain why teenagers are more likely to participate in oral sex than intercourse, and to have more oral sex partners because they are not defining it as sex (Prinstein, Meade, & Cohen, 2003).

If oral sex doesn't qualify as "sex," as some teenagers believe, then it doesn't pose a health risk . . . right? Wrong. Many diseases can be transmitted through oral sex, among them HIV, herpes, syphilis, genital warts, and hepatitis (Saini, Saini, & Sharma, 2010). Needless to say, it is crucial for teen-targeted sex education programs to spread the word about the risks associated with oral sex (Brewster & Tillman, 2008).

THINK again

Sext You Later

What kinds of environmental factors do you think encourage casual attitudes about sex among teens? Most adolescents have cell phones these days (77%, according to one survey; Lenhart, 2012) and a large number of those young people are using their phones to exchange text messages with sexually explicit words or images. In other words, today's teenagers are doing a lot of *sexting*. One study found that 20% of high school students have used their cell phones to share sexual pictures of themselves, and twice as many have received such images from others (Strassberg, McKinnon, Sustaíta, & Rullo, 2013). Teens who sext are more likely to have sex and take sexual risks, such as having unprotected sex (Rice et al., 2012).

Sext Offender
Sending sexually explicit text messages, or "sexting," has become increasingly popular among young people. Although it may seem casual and fun, sexting can have serious repercussions. When 18-year-old Phillip Alpert texted a naked photo of his 16-year-old girlfriend, police arrested him for distributing child pornography. He was then assigned 5 years of probation and required to register as a sex offender (Feyerick & Steffen, 2009, April 8). Ricardo Ramirez Buxeda/Orlando Sentinel/MCT/Getty Images

Sexting carries another set of risks for those who are married or in committed relationships. As many people see it, sexting outside a relationship is a genuine form of cheating. And because text messages can be saved and forwarded, it becomes an easy and effective way to damage the reputations of people, sometimes famous ones. Perhaps you have read about the sexting scandals associated with golfer Tiger Woods, ex-footballer Brett Favre, and former U.S. Congressman Anthony Weiner?

Now that's a lot of bad news about sexting. But can it also occur in the absence of negative behaviors and outcomes? When sexting is between two consenting, or shall we say "consexting," adults, it may be completely harmless (provided no infidelity is involved). According to one survey of young adults, sexting was not linked to unsafe sex or psychological problems such as depression and low self-esteem (Gordon-Messer, Bauermeister, Grodzinski, & Zimmerman, 2013). For some, sexting is just a new variation on flirting; for others, it may fulfill a deeper need, like helping them feel more secure in their romantic attachments (Weisskirch & Delevi, 2011). **◉+**

ARE TEENS WHO SEXT MORE LIKELY TO HAVE SEX?

SEX EDUCATION   One way to learn about this relatively new phenomenon of sexting—or any sexual topic, for that matter—is through sex education in the classroom. School is the primary place where American children get information about sex (Byers, 2011), yet it is somewhat controversial. Many parents are afraid that some types of sex education essentially condone sexual activity among young people. Until 2010, Title V federal funding was limited to states that taught abstinence only (Chin et al., 2012). Yet, research suggests that programs promoting abstinence are associated with more teenage pregnancies: States with a greater emphasis on abstinence (as reflected in state laws and policies) have higher teenage pregnancy and birth rates (Stanger-Hall & Hall, 2011).

Teenagers who are provided a thorough education on sexual activity, including information on how to prevent pregnancy, are less likely to become pregnant (or get someone pregnant). Research shows that formal sex education increases safe-sex practices, reducing the likelihood of disease transmission (Kohler, Manhart, & Lafferty, 2008; Stanger-Hall & Hall, 2011). Sex education clearly impacts the behaviors of teenagers and young adults. In some European nations, "openness" and "comfort" about sex lead to an understanding that sexuality is "a lifelong process." Sex education programs in these countries aim "to create self-determined and responsible attitudes and behavior with regard to sexuality, contraception, relationships and life strategies and planning" (Advocates for Youth, 2009; Stanger-Hall & Hall, 2011, p. 9).

○○✓○○   show what you know

1. Masters and Johnson studied the physiological changes that accompany sexual activity. They determined that men and women experience a similar sexual response cycle, including the following ordered phases:
   a. excitement, plateau, orgasm, and resolution.
   b. plateau, excitement, orgasm, relaxation.
   c. excitement, plateau, orgasm.
   d. excitement, orgasm, resolution.

2. Some have suggested that "kin altruism" may explain how homosexual men and women contribute to the overall reproduction of the family, by helping to care for children of relatives. This explanation draws upon the _____ perspective.

3. Explain how twin studies have been used to explore the development of sexual orientation.

4. _____ is the "enduring pattern" of sexual, romantic, and emotional attraction that individuals exhibit toward the same sex, opposite sex, or both sexes.

5. A neuroscientist gives a lecture at a senior citizens center in which he describes what is known about the origins of sexual orientation. Which of the following might he report?
   a. Dizygotic twins have greater similarity in sexual orientation than monozygotic twins.
   b. Some brain structures, such as areas in the hypothalamus, have differences that correlate with sexual orientation.
   c. Sexual orientation is definitely a matter of choice.
   d. Sexual orientation results entirely from biological factors.

✓ CHECK YOUR ANSWERS IN APPENDIX C.

The Trouble With Sex: Sexual Dysfunctions

 NOT TONIGHT, BABE *Ever since we had kids, my wife never seems to want sex. What can we do to rekindle her interest?*

My boyfriend used to get really turned on by me, but now he seems to be more interested in Internet porn. What happened?

Low desire is the number one sexual problem facing Dr. Buehler's clients. What's behind the decline in libido? "It's generally different for men and women," Dr. Buehler says. Every case is unique, but a common explanation for low desire might be called *The Woman Wearing Too Many Hats.* "What I frequently find is that women have a need to be perfect in everything they do, and women also have a lot of demands put on them (or they put them on themselves)," Dr. Buehler explains. "They don't leave any energy left over for pleasure." So when their partners want sex, it just becomes another demand.

Is it possible a woman might be avoiding sex by packing her schedule with activities? Perhaps she does not derive much pleasure from sex (she may have trouble achieving orgasm), or maybe there is a problem in the relationship that makes her want to push away. Dr. Buehler is always on the lookout for relationship problems that have infiltrated the bedroom.

Low libido is much less common in men, and when present, often results from low testosterone levels. If the problem isn't biological, then there may be a relationship issue, Dr. Buehler explains. "The common terminology is passive-aggressive behavior," she says. "You know, just not participating in sex as a way of communicating that 'I'm not interested in being with you right now. I don't like things that are going on in our relationship'."

One of the most challenging scenarios, according to Dr. Buehler, is when the man has lower desire than the woman. This often leads to feelings of rejection on the woman's part: *He's not into me anymore. He's mad at me. He's having an affair!* "Everybody thinks it's normal for men to have more desire, but you know, there are individual variations for both sexes," Dr. Buehler explains. (The assumption that all men are sex machines is a prime example of a *gender-role stereotype,* a concept presented earlier in the chapter.) Some men want sex twice a day, whereas others are perfectly satisfied with once a week. "If everybody is happy and fulfilled," Dr. Buehler notes, "it's normal."

"I really think you should see a specialist about your lack of libido, Sharon."

Cartoonstock

You Asked, Dr. Buehler Answers

http://qrs.ly/dm3m6bs

How do you make sexual topics more approachable as a discussion?

Sexual Difficulties

LO 8   Identify the symptoms of sexual dysfunctions.

When there is a "significant disturbance" in the ability to respond sexually or to gain pleasure from sex, we call this **sexual dysfunction** (APA, 2013). In the National Health and Social Life Survey, researchers found 43% of women and 31% of men suffered from some sort of sexual dysfunction (Laumann, Paik, & Rosen, 1999). Everyday stressors or situational issues may cause temporary sexual difficulties, which can be resolved once the stress or the situation has passed.

Then there are the longer-term sexual difficulties, which can stem from a variety of issues, including beliefs about sex, ignorance about sexual practices, and even performance expectations. Health conditions can also give rise to sexual difficulties. The *biopsychosocial* perspective is invaluable for helping to untangle the roots of sexual problems.

sexual dysfunction A significant disturbance in the ability to respond sexually or to gain pleasure from sex.

Sexual dysfunctions may result from problems with desire, arousal, orgasm, and pain, but these are not mutually exclusive categories (**TABLE 10.4**). Let's examine each one more carefully.

DESIRE Situational issues such as illness, fatigue, or frustration with one's partner can lead to temporary problems with desire. In some cases, however, lack of desire is persistent and distressing. Although low desire can affect both men and women, women tend to report desire problems more frequently than men (Brotto, 2010; Heiman, 2002).

AROUSAL Problems with arousal occur when the psychological desire to engage in sexual behavior is there, but the body does not cooperate. Men may have trouble getting or maintaining an erection, or they may experience a decrease in rigidity, which is called *erectile disorder* (APA, 2013). More than half of all men report they have occasionally experienced problems with erections (Hock, 2012). Women can also struggle with arousal. *Female sexual interest/arousal disorder* is apparent in reduced interest in sex, lack of initiation of sexual activities, reduced excitement, or decreased genital sensations during sexual activity (APA, 2013).

ORGASM Disorders related to orgasm are yet another category of dysfunction. *Female orgasmic disorder* is diagnosed when a woman is consistently unable to reach orgasm, has reduced orgasmic intensity, or does not reach orgasm quickly enough during sexual activity (APA, 2013). Men who experience frequent delay or inability to ejaculate might have a condition known as *delayed ejaculation* (APA, 2013; Segraves, 2010). With this disorder, the ability to achieve orgasm and ejaculate

Table 10.4 SEXUAL DYSFUNCTIONS

Sexual Dysfunction	Description
Delayed ejaculation	Frequent delayed ejaculation or failure to ejaculate
Erectile disorder	Issues in getting or maintaining an erection, or a decrease in penile rigidity
Female orgasmic disorder	Consistent inability to reach orgasm, reduced orgasmic intensity, or not reaching orgasm quickly enough during sexual activity
Female sexual interest/ arousal disorder	Reduced interest in sex, lack of initiation of sexual activity, lack of sexual excitement during sexual activity, or lack of genital sensations during sexual activity
Genito-pelvic pain/ penetration disorder	Refers to four types of co-occurring symptoms specific to women: difficulty having intercourse, genito-pelvic pain, fear of pain or vaginal penetration, and tension of pelvic floor muscles
Male hypoactive sexual desire disorder	Reduced interest in and desire for sex, lacking or absent sexual/erotic thoughts or fantasies
Premature (early) ejaculation	Related to the timing of, or the inability to control, ejaculation when it occurs, specifically in relation to vaginal sex

Sexual dysfunction can stem from problems with desire, arousal, orgasm, and pain. Above are some of the most common sexual dysfunctions.

SOURCE: APA (2013).

is inhibited or delayed during partnered sexual activity. Men who have trouble controlling when they ejaculate (particularly during vaginal sexual activity) may suffer from *premature (early) ejaculation* (APA, 2013).

PAIN The fourth category of sexual dysfunction is painful intercourse. Women typically report more problems with intercourse-related pain than men. *Genito-pelvic pain/penetration disorder* refers to four types of co-occurring symptoms specific to women: difficulty having intercourse, pain in the genitals or pelvis, fear of pain or vaginal penetration, and tension of the pelvic floor muscles (APA, 2013). Up to 15% of women in North America report frequent pain during intercourse, and issues related to pain are associated with reduced desire and arousal.

Sexual dysfunction is surprisingly common and often related to psychological and social variables such as anxiety and relationship troubles. The good news is that many of these conditions can be resolved with interventions that target their biological, psychological, and social roots. Unfortunately, we cannot say the same for some of the diseases transmitted through sex. As you will learn in the next section, some sexually transmitted infections have no cures.

Cartoonstock

"This stuff isn't selling. Maybe we should switch to Viagra."

✓◯◯◯ **show what you know**

1. Difficulties related to sexual activity can be divided into four categories:
   a. being heterosexual, homosexual, bisexual, and nonsexual.
   b. excitement, plateau, orgasm, and relaxation.
   c. desire, arousal, orgasm, and pain.
   d. desire, arousal, orgasm, and the sexual response cycle.

2. A man in his late fifties is concerned because he has occasional troubles with delayed ejaculation and his wife is not interested in sex. They have three small children and both work full time. Many of their friends are "empty nesters" whose grown children have moved out, and they seem to be celebrating their second honeymoons. Use the biopsychosocial perspective to help understand what might be contributing to this couple's sexual problems.

✓ CHECK YOUR ANSWERS IN APPENDIX C.

Sex, Its Consequences, and Culture
Sexually Transmitted Infections

LO 9 Classify sexually transmitted infections and identify their causes

Although sex is pleasurable and exciting for most, it is not without risks. Many people carry **sexually transmitted infections (STIs)**—diseases or illnesses passed on through sexual activity (Centers for Disease Control and Prevention [CDC], 2012f). The more sexual partners you have, the greater your risk of acquiring an STI. But you can lower your risk by communicating with your partner. People who know that their partners have had (or are having) sex with others face a lower risk of acquiring an STI than those who do not know. Why is this so? If you are aware of your partner's activities, you may be more likely to take preventative measures, such as using condoms. Of course, there is always the possibility that your sexual partner (or you) has a disease but doesn't know it. Some people with STIs are asymptomatic, meaning they have no symptoms. There are many causes of STIs, but we will focus on two of the most common types: *bacterial* and *viral* (**TABLE 10.5** for data on their prevalence).

sexually transmitted infections (STIs) Diseases or illnesses transmitted through sexual activity.

Table 10.5 SEXUALLY TRANSMITTED INFECTIONS (STIs)

STI	Symptoms	Estimated Annual Prevalence of New Infections in the U.S.
Chlamydia	Women often have no symptoms; men can experience discharge from penis, burning when urinating, and pain/swelling of the testicles.	2.86 million
Gonorrhea	No symptoms may be present in men or women. Men can experience burning when urinating; white, yellow, or green discharge. Women can experience pain/burning when urinating, or vaginal discharge.	820,000
Herpes	Blisters on the genitals, rectum or mouth; painful sores after blisters break; fever, body aches, and swollen glands can occur.	776,000
Human papillomavirus (HPV)	Genital warts; certain cancers; warts growing in the throat.	14.1 million
Syphilis	Firm, round sores that first appear where the infection enters the body and can then spread to other parts of the body.	55,400

Sexually transmitted infections (STIs) are extremely common. HPV, for example, is so widespread that nearly all sexually active people are infected at one time or another.

SOURCES: CDC (2012A, B, C, D, F, 2013).

BACTERIAL INFECTIONS *Syphilis* is a bacterial infection. Initial signs of syphilis might include sores on the genitals, breasts, anus, lips, or in the mouth. If the infection proceeds untreated over the course of years, it can lead to heart failure, blindness, liver damage, severe mental disturbance, or death. Another bacterial infection is *gonorrhea,* one of the most pervasive STIs in the United States. The initial symptoms of gonorrhea are more prominent for men than women. For a man, the first sign might be painful urination and cloudy discharge with a bad odor. Early symptoms in women, such as unusual discharge from the vagina, might go unnoticed or be mistaken for a less serious problem. Without treatment, men can become sterile and develop problems with the prostate and testes. Untreated gonorrhea can also lead to sterility in women. Like other bacterial infections, *gonorrhea* is treated with antibiotics, but resistance to these medications is becoming a problem (CDC, 2012d).

Another common bacterial infection is *chlamydia.* Teenage girls and young women are the most susceptible to this infection due to the immature development of the cervix. There are two types of chlamydial infections that affect women. One type affects the urethral tube or cervix; the other leads to *pelvic inflammatory disease,* which can result in lower back pain, menstrual difficulties, and headaches. Around 80–90% of women with chlamydia are asymptomatic, and 80% of women with gonorrhea are asymptomatic (CDC, 2012e).

VIRAL INFECTIONS One of the most common viral STIs is *genital herpes,* caused by *herpes simplex virus two (HSV-2).* HSV-2 results in sores and lesions on or near the genitals. Herpes can also infect other parts of the body, such as the mouth (American Social Health Association, 2012).

Even more common than herpes is the *human papillomavirus (HPV),* which can cause genital warts. Over 100 types of HPV have been identified, and research shows that untreated HPV can lead to the development of cervical, vaginal, urethral, penile, and anal cancers. One of the most worrisome aspects of HPV is that many carriers have no symptoms, so they can spread the infection without even knowing they have it. Although bacterial infections often clear up with antibiotics, viral infections like herpes and HPV have no cure, only treatments to reduce symptoms.

··▶ LO 10 Describe human immunodeficiency virus (HIV) and its role
in acquired immune deficiency syndrome (AIDS).

HIV AND AIDS   Perhaps the most feared STI is **human immunodeficiency virus (HIV).** This virus is spread through the transfer of bodily fluids (such as blood, semen, vaginal fluid, or breast milk) and eventually causes the breakdown of the immune system. HIV often will not show up on blood tests for up to 6 months after infection, which means that even if you have had a negative test result for HIV, you cannot assume you are "safe"—hence, the importance of having protected sex. HIV eventually progresses to **acquired immune deficiency syndrome (AIDS),** which generally results in a severely compromised immune system. A weakened immune system makes the body much more susceptible to opportunistic infections caused by bacteria, viruses, or fungi, and this vulnerability increases as the disease progresses.

The World Health Organization (WHO) reported in 2009 that approximately 60 million people were infected with HIV and some 25 million had died of HIV complications since it was first identified in 1981. In sub-Saharan Africa, HIV/AIDS has left over 14 million children orphaned. In addition, the WHO (2009) reported that approximately 2 million people died AIDS-related deaths in 2008. In the United States, approximately 1.2 million people have HIV, and it's likely that around 20% of these people are unaware they have the infection (Hoppel, 2012). Worldwide, HIV is a leading cause of death, and in sub-Saharan Africa it is *the* leading killer (Kendall, 2012). **INFOGRAPHIC 10.2** provides a closer examination of regional statistics.

Apparently, knowing the dangers of HIV does not motivate most people to change their risky habits. Unprotected sex and intravenous (through a needle) drug use are the most common forms of transmission. There is no cure for HIV/AIDS, but anti-HIV drugs have been developed to help reduce viral levels in the blood. These medications are very expensive, with a cost of approximately $20,000 per year per person, and funding shortfalls will result in over 2,000 people in the United States not being able to get the treatments they need (Maxmen, 2012). The problem is global. In 2010, 7.6 million HIV sufferers around the world could not gain access to treatment (Granich et al., 2012).

Many people are uncomfortable discussing HIV and other STIs, and often there is a stigma attached to those who suffer from these conditions. But everyone—with the exception of those who practice abstinence—is vulnerable. When it comes to STIs, or any aspect of human sexuality, be careful about passing judgment.

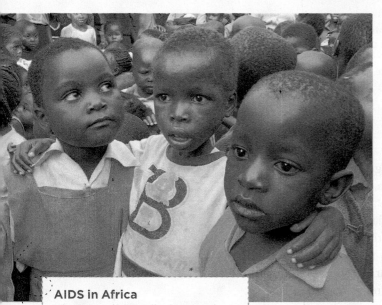

AIDS in Africa
Nine-year-old Fatsileni Luwanda (center) poses with friends at the Chifundo Orphan Care Center in the African nation of Malawi. Luwanda is among those children orphaned as a result of the AIDS epidemic. About 1 in 10 Malawians between the ages of 15 and 49 are HIV-positive (UNAIDS, 2012a).
© Eldson Chagara/X01723/Reuters/Corbis

"Normal" Is Relative

··▶ LO 11 Define sexual scripts and describe some of the ways
people deviate from sex-related cultural norms.

human immunodeficiency virus (HIV) A virus transferred via bodily fluids (blood, semen, vaginal fluid, or breast milk) that causes the breakdown of the immune system, eventually resulting in AIDS.

acquired immune deficiency syndrome (AIDS) This condition, caused by HIV, generally results in a severely compromised immune system, which makes the body vulnerable to other infections.

It is only natural for us to wonder if what we are doing between the sheets (or elsewhere) is normal or healthy. Is it normal to masturbate? Is it normal to fantasize about sex with strangers? The answers to these types of questions depend somewhat on cultural context. Most of us unknowingly learn *sexual scripts,* or cultural rules that tell us what types of activities are "appropriate" and don't interfere with healthy sexual intimacy. In some cultures, the sexual script suggests that women should have minimal, if any, sexual experience before marriage, but men are expected to explore their sexuality, or "sow their wild oats."

STIs Around the World

Should you be concerned about sexually transmitted infections (STIs)? Every year in the U.S., new STI cases number 20 million. Half of these new infections occur among people aged 15 to 24 (CDC, 2013). The graph at right shows estimated numbers of people living with selected STIs in the Americas. The bacterial STIs shown here in teal are curable, but can have serious health consequences if left untreated. Viral STIs, shown in red, have no cures. The map below provides estimated numbers for HIV worldwide.

SOURCES: CDC (2013); LOOKER, GARNETT, AND SCHMID (2008); UNAIDS (2012b); WHO (2008c).

STIs in the Americas

(INCLUDES NORTH, SOUTH, AND CENTRAL AMERICA)

SYPHILIS	2,800,000
HIV	2,800,000
GONORRHEA	11,000,000
CHLAMYDIA	26,500,000
HPV (U.S. ONLY)	79,000,000
HERPES	83,500,000

BACTERIAL   VIRAL

HIV Around the World

EASTERN EUROPE AND CENTRAL ASIA
1,400,000

WESTERN AND CENTRAL EUROPE
900,000

EAST ASIA
830,000

NORTH, SOUTH, AND CENTRAL AMERICA
2,800,000

MIDDLE EAST AND NORTH AFRICA
300,000

SOUTH AND SOUTHEAST ASIA
4,000,000

SUB-SAHARAN AFRICA
23,500,000

STIs can have serious implications, especially for young women.

Some people with STIs are asymptomatic. Many infections are never diagnosed.

Serious health consequences can be avoided if curable STIs are treated in time. The CDC recommends screening for chlamydia and other STIs depending on risk factors.

HIV will not show up on blood tests for up to 6 months after infection. Protected sex is important even if a recent test showed a negative result.

STIs are preventable. You can lower your risk by communicating with your partner.

Credits: Aids awareness red ribbon, Graphic design/Shutterstock; Condoms, Volodymyr Krasyuk/Shutterstock

FETISHES AND PARAPHILIA   There are some behaviors that most people would consider unusual, regardless of culture. An example would be *fetishism,* a sexual fixation with an object or nongenital body part (APA, 2013). Fetishes center on just about any object you can imagine, such as stuffed animals and nongenital body parts, like bald heads or red toenails. Typically, sexual fetishes don't present a problem unless they interfere with relationships.

How do sex therapists deal with these sexual obsessions? According to Dr. Buehler, therapists and clients in past decades would spend years trying to understand and eliminate fetishes. "These days the thinking is, if it doesn't hurt anybody, who cares," she says. "You like shoes? Okay. You like latex? Great. Whatever it is, it's fine, as long as whatever activity you're involved [in] is consensual." The issue is usually a couple's issue, Dr. Buehler adds. Can the partner accept the fetish, and if so, is there a way to integrate it into the couple's sex life? If not, perhaps the partner can tolerate the other person masturbating with the fetish object.

As already mentioned, many people are not comfortable discussing their *own* sexual activities, which often leaves them wondering if what they do is appropriate. Sexual behavior is as varied as any other type of human behavior. As with any definition of appropriate versus inappropriate, deviant versus normal, we must always consider the sociocultural context and whether the behavior is harmful to oneself or others.

What we want to emphasize is that there is a range of sexual behavior, and the overwhelming majority of it is perfectly healthy. But some fetishes and other sexual behaviors are rare and/or problematic. **Paraphilia** is the term used to describe these uncommon sexual acts (**TABLE 10.6**). Here, the sexual activity might involve nonhuman objects, and sometimes results in the suffering or humiliation of those involved. Often, the behavior is repeated and compulsive (Kafka, 2009).

Table 10.6 PARAPHILIAS	
Type of Paraphilia	**Description**
Exhibitionism	Sexual arousal as a result of exposing oneself to an unwilling bystander
Fetishism	Sexual arousal with an object or nongenital body part
Frotteurism	Sexual arousal as a result of touching or rubbing against an unwilling person
Klismaphilia	Sexual arousal associated with receiving enemas
Pedophilia	Sexual arousal associated with sexual fantasies or urges about prepubescent children
Sexual masochism	Sexual arousal as a result of experiencing pain or suffering
Sexual sadism	Sexual arousal as a result of inflicting pain or suffering
Telephone scatologia	Sexual arousal as a result of making obscene phone calls to an unwilling person
Voyeurism	Sexual arousal as a result of watching unsuspecting individuals undress or engage in sexual activity

Paraphilia refers to unusual sexual interests. A paraphilia becomes problematic when it causes pain or suffering in oneself or others.

paraphilia Uncommon sexual acts.

SOURCE: CROOKS AND BAUR (2014); MCANULTY, DILLON, & ADAMS, 2002.

Pedophilia is a paraphilia in which a person at least 16 years old has sexual fantasies or urges about children (usually younger than 14). In some cases, the person never acts on the urges or fantasies. Others, however, victimize children and develop techniques to gain access to them. Pedophilia is more common in men and appears to last throughout life (APA, 2013).

CULTURE AND SEX Culture plays a role in determining what sexual behaviors are deemed acceptable, and there is considerable variation in this regard. Whereas some cultures abhor nudity and view sex only as a means of reproduction, others believe that children should be educated about sex early in life. It was reported for many years that Inis Beag (a pseudonym for an island off the coast of Ireland) was a "sex-negative" society, known for abstinence, monogamy, and infrequent sexual encounters. In contrast, the "sex-positive" culture of Mangaia in the South Pacific was known for frequent sexual encounters and reports of multiple orgasms each night (Levine & Troiden, 1988).

What about Americans? Do you think we tend to promote sexual modesty? Or is the cast of the show *Jersey Shore* more representative? Americans generally value sexual modesty, but we are also exposed to a broad spectrum of sexual expression via the media (although there is a great deal of variation based on subcultural and regional differences within the United States). In one study from 1998, researchers examined attitudes regarding nonmarital sex in 24 different countries. They reported that the United States belonged to a cluster of countries referred to as "sexual conservatives," with the great majority of people disapproving of any form of nonmarital sex—both premarital and extramarital (Widmer, Treas, & Newcomb, 1998). Do you think this attitude still prevails?

People engage in sexual activity for procreation, recreation, and everything in between. Sexual motives and preferences vary from person to person and across time, but are also based on culture. What motivates individuals to engage in sexual activity? Women seem more likely to be looking for love and commitment, intimacy, or to solidify a relationship. Men report being motivated by the physical appearance of their partner, pleasure, and the desire to reduce stress. While such gender disparities do exist, research reveals they are quite small (Hatfield, Luckhurst, & Rapson, 2010).

The influence of culture extends beyond sex, impacting our choices of mates and long-term sexual partners. In Chapter 15, we discuss the various factors important for interpersonal attraction, including proximity, similarity, and physical attractiveness. These variables are shaped by culture, but they may also be dependent on biology. According to one controversial theory, mate choices are guided by the forces of evolution.

Jersey Shore Nation?
The behaviors and attitudes exhibited by "Snooki," "The Situation," and other *Jersey Shore* characters are not representative of the average American. Most people in the United States have more traditional views about sex and relationships (Widmer, Treas, & Newcomb, 1998).
Splash News/Newscom

CONTROVERSIES

Are You My Natural Selection?

Sex serves an important function in human evolution; without it, none of us would be here. If you hope to pass along your precious genes to future generations, then you'd better produce vigorous children who will survive and reproduce. But you can't accomplish this alone; you need a partner with characteristics that complement your own. How do you find this perfect someone?

Let's approach this question from a purely evolutionary standpoint, ignoring social and cultural factors. Men and women have the same goal—to ensure that their genes outlast them—but they have different roles in reproduction. Women

"Marry me, Virginia. My genes are excellent and, as yet, unpatented."

generally invest more in childbearing and rearing (getting pregnant, breastfeeding, and so on) and they are limited in the number of offspring they can produce. Men are capable of fathering hundreds, if not thousands, of children, and they are not hampered by the biological constraints of pregnancy and breastfeeding. Under these circumstances, a woman's best strategy is to find a mate who will ensure that her children have all the resources they need to survive and reproduce. A man, on the other hand, should be on the lookout for a woman who can bear many children—someone who shows signs of fertility, like youth and beauty (Geary, Vigil, & Byrd-Craven, 2004).

Do people really choose partners according to these criteria? One study of over 10,000 participants from 37 cultures concluded that women around the world do indeed favor mates who appear to be good providers, whereas men place greater value on good looks and youth (Buss, 1989). Subsequent studies have produced similar results (Buss, Shackelford, Kirkpatrick, & Larsen, 2001; Schwarz & Hassebrauck, 2012; Shackelford, Schmitt, & Buss, 2005).

A WOMAN'S FINANCIAL SECURITY HAS BECOME AN INCREASINGLY IMPORTANT CRITERION FOR MALE SUITORS.

Sure, we all have preferences for the type of partner we want, but do they really impact the choices we make? Do men, for instance, typically marry women who are younger? Yes, this appears to be the case. Husbands across the world are, on average, a few years older than their wives (Buss, 1989; Lakdawalla & Schoeni, 2003; Otta, da Silva Queiroz, de Sousa Campos, da Silva, & Silveira, 1999).

But let's put these findings in perspective. Two or three years is not much of a gap if you're thinking about growing old together. (Is age 83 really any different from 80?) And we all know there are many women in search of "hot men," and men in pursuit of "sugar mamas." Over the past several decades, in fact, a woman's financial security has become an increasingly important criterion for male suitors (Buss et al., 2001). In today's ever-changing social and cultural environment, evolution is just one factor influencing our selection of a mate. ➡◄

BACK TO THE FUTURE   You may be wondering what the future holds for Stephen Patten and Dr. Stephanie Buehler. Stephen is considering retirement in about 4 years, after which he and his wife (also a nurse) might island hop in the Caribbean or Pacific Ocean. Currently a part-time nursing instructor at a community college, he hopes to teach at local colleges in between his travels.

Dr. Buehler is currently writing her second book, a text intended to help general therapists address sexual issues with clients (in other words, what every therapist needs to know about sex). In between speaking engagements, she also plans to organize continuing education activities for therapists who want to learn more about sex therapy.

show what you know

1. _____ and _____ are both bacterial infections that are spread through unprotected sexual activity.
   a. Syphilis; gonorrhea
   b. Pelvic inflammatory disease; herpes
   c. Human papillomavirus; herpes
   d. Syphilis; acquired immune deficiency syndrome

2. Most people learn _____, which are the rules our culture has taught us about what is "appropriate" for sexual activity.

3. Describe how HIV is transmitted and how it progresses to AIDS.

✓ CHECK YOUR ANSWERS IN APPENDIX C.

⑩ summary of concepts

LO 1 Define sex and distinguish it from sexuality. (p. 426)

Sex can refer to a sexual act such as intercourse or masturbation. Sex also refers to the classification of someone as male or female based on genetic composition and structure and/or function of reproductive organs. Sexuality refers to sexual activities, attitudes, and behaviors.

LO 2 Identify the biological factors that determine sex. (p. 428)

The 23rd pair of chromosomes, also referred to as the sex chromosomes, provides specific instructions for the zygote to develop into a female or male (the biological sex of the individual). The egg from the mother carries an X chromosome, and the sperm from the father carries either an X chromosome or a Y chromosome. When both members of the 23rd pair are X chromosomes (XX), the zygote will generally develop into a female. When the 23rd pair contains an X chromosome and a Y chromosome (XY), the zygote generally develops into a male.

LO 3 Identify some of the causes of intersexual development. (p. 431)

Intersexuality can result from genetic irregularities, hormone activity early in development, and/or environmental factors. In some cases, there are too many sex chromosomes, or one missing. In other cases, the sex chromosomes are normal, but the developing fetus does not respond to hormones in a typical way.

LO 4 Define gender and explain how culture plays a role in its development. (p. 434)

Gender refers to the dimension of masculinity and femininity based on social, cultural, and psychological characteristics. It is often used in reference to the cultural roles that distinguish males and females. We generally learn by observing other people's behavior and by internalizing cultural beliefs about what is appropriate for men and women.

LO 5 Distinguish between transgender and transsexual. (p. 438)

Sometimes societal expectations of being male or female differ from what an individual is feeling inwardly, leading to feelings of discontent. Transgender refers to the mismatch between a person's gender assigned at birth and his or her gender identity. Some transgender people try to resolve this discontent through medical interventions. A transsexual person seeks or undergoes a social transition to an alternative gender by making changes to his or her body through sex reassignment surgery and/or medical treatment.

LO 6 Describe the human sexual response as identified by Masters and Johnson. (p. 440)

The human sexual response is the physiological pattern that occurs during sexual activity. Men and women tend to experience a similar pattern or cycle of excitement, plateau, orgasm, and resolution, but the duration of these phases varies from person to person.

LO 7 Define sexual orientation and summarize how it develops. (p. 442)

According to the American Psychological Association, sexual orientation is the "enduring pattern" of sexual, romantic, and emotional attraction that individuals exhibit toward the same sex, opposite sex, or both sexes. Sexual orientation may be heterosexual (when a person is attracted to members of the opposite sex), homosexual (attracted to members of the same sex), or bisexual (attracted to both sexes). Research has focused on the causes of sexual orientation, but there is no strong evidence pointing to any one factor or factors. Sexual orientation is the result of a complex interaction between nature and nurture.

- -

LO 8 Identify the symptoms of sexual dysfunctions. (p. 452)

Difficulties related to sexual activity can be divided into four sometimes overlapping categories: desire, arousal, orgasm, and pain. Problems associated with desire must be persistent to be considered a dysfunction.

When an individual has the desire to engage in sexual behavior, but the body does not cooperate, an arousal problem exists. Difficulties with orgasm may include reduced orgasmic intensity and the inability to reach orgasm. Problems associated with pain are more frequently reported by women, and may also be associated with reduced desire and arousal.

- -

LO 9 Classify sexually transmitted infections and identify their causes. (p. 454)

Sexually transmitted infections (STIs) are infections caused by viruses and bacteria and are contracted through sexual activity. Having multiple sexual partners increases the risk of getting an STI; however, awareness that a partner has had (or is having) sex with other partners lowers the risk somewhat. Once aware of a partner's activities, one is more inclined to take preventive measures, such as using condoms. Syphilis, gonorrhea, and chlamydia are bacterial infections.

Genital herpes, human papillomavirus, and human immunodeficiency virus (HIV) are viral infections.

- -

LO 10 Describe human immunodeficiency virus (HIV) and its role in acquired immune deficiency syndrome (AIDS). (p. 456)

Human immunodeficiency virus (HIV) is spread through the transfer of bodily fluids (blood, semen, vaginal fluid, or breast milk) and eventually causes the breakdown of the immune system. HIV often does not show up on blood tests for up to 6 months after infection occurs; it eventually progresses to acquired immune deficiency syndrome (AIDS), which generally results in a severely compromised immune system. A weakened immune system makes the body much more susceptible to opportunistic infections caused by bacteria, viruses, or fungi, and this vulnerability increases as the disease progresses.

- -

LO 11 Define sexual scripts and describe some of the ways people deviate from sex-related cultural norms. (p. 456)

Sexual scripts are cultural rules about what is and is not appropriate sexual activity. There is a range or continuum of sexual behavior, and the overwhelming majority of it is perfectly normal. Yet some sexual behaviors are rare and/or problematic. For example, paraphilia refers to uncommon sexual behaviors that are repeated and compulsive. Paraphilia typically involves nonhuman objects and may cause suffering or humiliation for those involved.

key terms

acquired immune deficiency syndrome (AIDS), p. 456
androgens, p. 429
androgyny, p. 438
bisexual, p. 442
estrogen, p. 429
gender, p. 426

gender identity, p. 435
gender roles, p. 434
gender schemas, p. 436
heterosexual, p. 442
homosexual, p. 442
human immunodeficiency virus (HIV), p. 456

intersexual, p. 431
orgasm, p. 441
paraphilia, p. 458
refractory period, p. 441
sex, p. 426
sexual dysfunction, p. 452
sexual orientation, p. 442

sexuality, p. 426
sexually transmitted infections (STIs), p. 454
testosterone, p. 429
transgender, p. 438
transsexual, p. 439

TEST PREP are you ready?

1. _____ refers to a sexual act or the classification of male or female. _____ refers to masculinity and femininity based on social, cultural, and psychological characteristics.
   a. Gender; Sex
   b. Sex; Gender
   c. Sex; Sexuality
   d. Gender; Sexuality

2. The _____ provide(s) specific instructions on whether a zygote will develop into a male or female, that is, the genetic sex of the individual.
   a. 23rd pair of chromosomes
   b. gonads
   c. primary sex characteristics
   d. secondary sex characteristics

3. The sensitivity of a fetus to _____ produced during its early development can play a role in the development of intersexuality.

   a. the X chromosome
   b. the Y chromosome
   c. secondary sex characteristics
   d. hormones

4. A psychologist refers to biological characteristics when discussing a client's _____, but when talking about sexual attitudes and behaviors, a psychologist is referring to _____.

   a. sex; sexuality
   b. primary sex characteristics; secondary sex characteristics
   c. secondary sex characteristics; primary sex characteristics
   d. heterosexuality; homosexuality

5. The general beliefs, in American culture, that men are assertive and logical, and women are caring and emotional represent:

   a. gender identity.   c. androgyny.
   b. gender schemas.   d. gender roles.

6. The acquisition of gender roles can occur through _____, as explained by social-cognitive theory. That is, we are shaped by models in our environment.

   a. genes   c. observational learning
   b. chromosomes   d. paraphilias

7. According to Masters and Johnson, sexual arousal begins in the _____ phase, when physical changes begin to take place.

   a. excitement   c. resolution
   b. plateau   d. orgasm

8. A family friend confides that he has always had the feeling he was born in the body of a female and that he has started cross-sex hormone treatment. Your friend would be considered _____ by the American Psychiatric Association.

   a. homosexual   c. transsexual
   b. heterosexual   d. bisexual

9. Having older brothers in a family seems to be associated with homosexuality in men. One explanation for this is the maternal immune hypothesis, which suggests that:

   a. older mothers become immune to homosexuality while pregnant.
   b. mothers develop an anti-male antibody while pregnant.
   c. mothers with brothers of their own develop an anti-male antibody while pregnant.
   d. children with no siblings will not be homosexual.

10. Research regarding the sexual response cycle indicates:

    a. it should not be treated with psychotherapy.
    b. the orgasm phase is the longest phase.
    c. it is experienced more frequently by men.
    d. men and women experience a similar pattern or cycle.

11. Some men experience problems getting or maintaining an erection, which is referred to as:

    a. hypoactive sexual desire.
    b. erectile disorder.
    c. male orgasmic disorder.
    d. premature ejaculation.

12. _____ is spread through the transfer of bodily fluids, such as blood, semen, and breast milk, and it eventually progresses to _____.

    a. Human immunodeficiency virus; acquired immune deficiency syndrome
    b. Acquired immune deficiency syndrome; human immunodeficiency virus
    c. Human papillomavirus; chlamydia
    d. Chlamydia; human papillomavirus

13. People who know their partners have had (or are having) sexual activity with others will

    a. definitely see symptoms of an STI in themselves or their partners.
    b. have an equal risk of acquiring an STI than those who don't know of this activity.
    c. have a lower risk of acquiring an STI than those who don't know of this activity.
    d. have a higher risk of acquiring an STI than those who don't know of this activity.

14. A friend of yours shies away from some of the more daring sexual escapades her husband suggests. For example, yesterday he asked her to engage in a "threesome." She unknowingly has learned _____ from her culture, telling her that such sexual behavior is not appropriate.

    a. sexual scripts   c. fetishes
    b. paraphilia   d. gender dysphoria

15. _____ refers to uncommon sexual acts that might involve nonhuman objects, and sometimes results in the suffering or humiliation of those involved.

    a. Sex determination   c. A sexual script
    b. Spermarche   d. Paraphilia

16. We have noted how difficult it can be to get people to participate in a study, but also to be open and honest in research examining sexual activity. If you were planning to conduct this type of research, how would you go about convincing potential participants that their involvement will be worthwhile and that they should be honest in their responses?

17. Explain how gender roles are acquired through culture and learning.

18. How would an evolutionary psychologist explain extramarital sex?

19. Describe the four areas in which sexual dysfunction can occur.

20. Describe three paraphilias.

✓ CHECK YOUR ANSWERS IN APPENDIX C.

Get personalized practice by logging into LaunchPad at **http://www.worthpublishers.com/launchpad/Licht** to take the LearningCurve adaptive quizzes for Chapter 10.

11

An Introduction to Personality

 Meet Tank

 NATURE AND NURTURE
The Funny Thing About Personality

Psychoanalytic Theories

 Never Good Enough for Dad

 Tank's Ongoing Troubles

→←← CONTROVERSIES
How Birth Order May— or May Not—Affect Your Personality

Humanistic Theories

Learning and Social- Cognitive Theories

 Robots Can Learn, Too

Trait Theories and Their Biological Basis

 A Few Words About Tank

 ACROSS THE WORLD
Culture of Personality

SA from the pages of
SCIENTIFIC AMERICAN
Open Mind, Longer Life

Personality Assessment

 A Lifetime of Mishaps

 SOCIAL MEDIA AND PSYCHOLOGY
It's Written All Over Your Facebook

 Final Thoughts

personality

An Introduction to Personality

MEET TANK When you enter the lobby of a building or office, the receptionist is often the first individual you encounter. The role of the receptionist is of great importance, as this employee shapes a visitor's first impression of an organization. A good receptionist is eager to help, friendly, and reliable. A neat physical appearance and pleasant voice are also big pluses.

Newell Simon Hall, the computer science building at Pittsburgh's Carnegie Mellon University, has an excellent receptionist. His name is Marion LeFleur, but everyone calls him "Tank," a fitting title given his square jaw and overall tough-guy appearance. But don't be intimidated by the Rambo look. "Tank is a nice guy," says Tank's boss, Dr. Reid Simmons. "He just does his job and has a really good heart." Approach his booth, and Tank will take note of your presence immediately. "Hello there. What can I do for you?" he asks ever so politely (Greenfieldboyce, 2005, December 26). Looking for the room number of a university employee? Tank will find it in seconds. Need directions to a different building on campus? Tank is all over it. He can also provide updates on the local time and weather. Ask the right questions, and Tank might even share some details of his personal life—about his family, girlfriend, and dog, or the fact that he once dated the scoreboard at the Pittsburgh Steelers stadium (Lee, Kiesler, & Forlizzi, 2010; Simmons et al., 2011). Tank is not afraid to discuss his failures. He may tell you about his career disaster with NASA, or his botched mission with the CIA (Carnegie Mellon University, 2013).

Now that you have learned a few things about Tank, perhaps you feel as if you are beginning to know him. Maybe you are getting a basic sense of what kind of person he is. But Tank isn't a person; he is a robot—a "roboceptionist," to be precise—and robots are not capable of exhibiting

→

LEARNING OBJECTIVES

after reading and studying this chapter, you should be able to:

LO 1   Define personality.

LO 2   Distinguish how the perspectives of psychology explain personality development.

LO 3   Illustrate Freud's models for describing the mind.

LO 4   Summarize Freud's use of psychosexual stages to explain personality.

LO 5   Explain how the neo-Freudians' theories of personality differ from Freud's.

LO 6   Describe how Maslow's hierarchy of needs relates to personality.

LO 7   Discuss Rogers' view of self-concept, ideal self, and unconditional positive regard.

LO 8   Use learning theories to explain personality development.

LO 9   Summarize Rotter's view of personality.

LO 10   Discuss how Bandura uses the social-cognitive perspective to explain personality.

LO 11   Distinguish trait theories from other personality theories.

LO 12   Identify the biological roots of the five-factor model of personality.

LO 13   Explain why reliability and validity are important in personality assessment.

LO 14   Define projective tests and evaluate their strengths and limitations.

LO 15   Describe objective personality tests and evaluate their strengths and limitations.

Hello Tank

The Computer Science Department at Carnegie Mellon University has a robot receptionist named "Tank." Some of Tank's behaviors are amazingly humanlike; he blinks, flares his nostrils, and even displays emotional expressions consistent with what he is saying (Simmons et al., 2011). But no matter how "human" Tank may seem, he does not possess a true personality.

Debra Marie Tobin, art director for the Robotics Institute

Tank, in Dr. Simmons' Own Words

http://qrs.ly/xy3m6jj

the complex behaviors and interactions you would expect from a human being. At least not yet.

Looking at Tank, it's fairly obvious he is not a person. His blue, chiseled face lives in a 15-inch flat-panel LCD screen, and his body looks somewhat like a massive red coffee thermos. He has sensors to detect your presence, but he cannot see your facial expressions, read your body language, or even hear your voice. In fact, the only way

Note: Quotations attributed to Dr. Reid Simmons are personal communications.

to communicate with Tank is by typing on his keyboard, and he can only understand simple questions such as "Where is the ladies' room?"

Tank is the latest product of Carnegie Mellon's Social Robots Project, a collaboration between the university's Robotics Institute and School of Drama. The goal is to "create a robot that can provide useful services, but that also exhibits personality and character" (Gockley et al., 2005, p. 2199). How is this accomplished? Every one of Tank's behaviors, from the movements of his eyes to the subtle tilts of his head, is preprogrammed by Dr. Simmons's team of computer whizzes. His backstory and script were written by members of the university's drama department. It's all "smoke and mirrors," according to Dr. Simmons. Creating the illusion of a "personality" turns out to be quite a challenge. This would be no surprise to psychologists studying *personality.*

What Is Personality?

One of the major challenges of creating social robots is programming behaviors that gel coherently. If you want to craft a robot with a convincing personality, you'd better make sure that everything it does and says fits the part. One out-of-character remark and people will be reminded that they are merely talking to a collection of electrical circuits.

LO 1   Define personality.

So far we have used the term "personality" rather loosely. The reality is that robots do not actually have personalities. They take on roles or *personas* whose characteristics may bear resemblance to personalities, but all of their behaviors are programmed by people. Well then, what is personality? Generally speaking, **personality** refers to the unique core set of characteristics that influence the way one thinks, acts, and feels—characteristics many psychologists would agree are relatively consistent and enduring throughout the life span.

We should point out that personality is not the equivalent of *character.* When people discuss character, they often are referring to qualities of morality or culture-specific ideas about what makes a person "good" or "bad." A person who is untrustworthy or makes "poor" choices might be described as having a weak character, while someone who stands up for what she believes might be said to have a strong character. You may hear that the guy with the blue mohawk or the woman with the multiple body piercings is a "real character"—often in a judgmental way. Psychologists try not to make such judgments; our goal is to describe behaviors and characteristics objectively.

TEMPERAMENT   Some aspects of adult personality appear to derive from temperament, the distinct patterns of emotional reactions and behaviors observed early in life. Because various **temperaments** are evident in infants, they appear to have a genetic basis (Plomin, DeFries, Knopik, & Neiderhiser, 2013). And although temperament remains somewhat stable across the life span (Kagan & Snidman, 1991; Sigelman & Rider, 2009), it can be molded by environment (Caspi, Roberts, & Shiner, 2005). You can think of temperament as one dimension of the broader construct of personality (Goldsmith et al., 1987).

CONNECTIONS

In **Chapter 8,** we described various infant temperaments. Some infants are easy to calm, others cranky, sociable, or highly reactive. Humans are born with certain temperaments, and many of the attending characteristics seem to persist throughout life. Here, we introduce temperament in the context of personality.

personality The unique, core set of characteristics that influence the way one thinks, acts, and feels, and that are relatively consistent and enduring throughout the life span.

Table 11.1 PERSONALITY THEORIES

Personality Theory	Main Points	Criticisms
Psychoanalytic	Personality develops early in life; we are greatly influenced by processes of which we are unaware (e.g., internal conflicts, aggression, sexual urges).	Ignores importance of current experiences; overemphasis on the unconscious and the role of sexuality in personality; theory based on a biased, nonrepresentative sample; concepts difficult to operationally define and empirically test.
Behavioral	Personality is shaped by interactions with the environment, specifically through learning (classical conditioning, operant conditioning, and observational learning).	Narrow focus on behavioral processes; ignores influence of unconscious processes and emotional factors.
Humanistic	We are innately good and control our destinies; we have a force moving us toward growth.	Concepts difficult to operationally define and empirically test; ignores the negative aspects of human nature.
Social-cognitive	Focuses on social influences and mental processes that affect personality; emphasis on the combination of environment, cognitive activity, and individual behavior.	Narrow focus on social-cognitive factors; ignores influence of unconscious processes and emotional factors.
Biological	Emphasizes the physiological and genetic influences on personality development; incorporates gene–environment explanations for the emergence of certain characteristics.	Inconsistent findings regarding the stability of the personality dimensions; varying estimates of environmental influences.
Trait	Looks at current traits of the individual to describe and predict personality.	Underestimates the environmental influences on personality; neglects to explain foundations of personality.

LO 2   Distinguish how the perspectives of psychology explain personality development.

PERSPECTIVES ON PERSONALITY   Psychologists explain the development of personality in a variety of ways, often in accordance with certain theoretical perspectives (**TABLE 11.1**). You may be familiar with several of these perspectives, but let's summarize their main points before using them to explore personality:

- *Psychoanalytic*: Personality is formed very early in life and is strongly influenced by processes of which we are unaware (internal conflicts, aggression, sexual urges); the development of personality depends on the expression of unconscious processes and how caregivers respond.

- *Behavioral*: Originates from the learning theories; explains how the environment shapes personality and specifically how classical conditioning and reinforcers influence behaviors. Observation and modeling also play a role in personality development.

- *Humanistic*: We have capabilities we can and should exploit as we strive for personal growth; the choices we make in life influence our personalities; the focus is on the positive aspects of human nature.

- *Social-cognitive*: Emphasizes relationships, environmental influences, individual behavior, and mental processes that come together to form personality.

- *Biological*: Physiological and genetic factors, including gene–environment interactions, influence personality development; hormones and neurotransmitters influence personality expression, which correlates with activity in certain brain areas.

- *Trait*: Focuses on personality traits and dimensions; theories describe and predict behavior, focusing on the present rather than the past.

None of these perspectives can completely account for the development and expression of personality, but they do help describe, explain, and predict behavior. Most also have strong ties to their founders, all of whom were influenced by the historical period in which they lived. Sigmund Freud's emphasis on sexuality, for example, was partly a reaction to the Victorian era into which he was born.

Our traits, abilities, and experiences are what make us unique. But remember that we share some characteristics with all other humans (physiological make-up, for example), others with a subset of the population (such as our peers), and still others with no one.

In the next section, we will examine these theories of personality in greater depth, but first let's take a quick detour somewhere fun. How would you describe your sense of humor?

nature AND nurture

The Funny Thing About Personality

Some of us rely on humor to connect with other people, cracking jokes and acting silly for their enjoyment. Others use it as a way to cope with challenges. (We must admit, it does feel good to let loose and laugh when life's stresses become unbearable.) Both of these styles of humor are viewed as positive, as they strengthen social bonds and promote personal well-being (Martin, Puhlik-Doris, Larsen, Gray, & Weir, 2003). There are also negative forms of humor, like ridiculing another person to make yourself look good, or poking fun at yourself in a way that seems to erode self-esteem (Martin et al., 2003; McCosker & Moran, 2012).

Where do these styles of humor originate? According to one large Australian study, identical twins (who have identical genes) are more likely to share humor styles than fraternal (nonidentical) twins. What this tells you is that genes matter. In fact, the study suggests that 30–47% of variation in styles of humor can be attributed to genetics (Baughman et al., 2012), and some research shows an even higher proportion (Vernon, Martin, Schermer, Cherkas, & Spector, 2008). But how do you explain the other 53–70% of the variation? Chalk it up to nurture. Humor is very much like other aspects of personality—grounded in biology, but chiseled and refined by a lifetime of experiences.

HUMOR IS VERY MUCH LIKE OTHER ASPECTS OF PERSONALITY— GROUNDED IN BIOLOGY. . . .

Silly Genes
Identical twins, who have all the same genes, are more likely to have similar humor styles than fraternal twins, who share only about half their genes (Baughman et al., 2012). This suggests that sense of humor is to some degree inherited. Education Images/UIG via Getty Images

Keep this nature-and-nurture theme in mind as you explore the theories of personality in the pages to come. To what degree does each perspective recognize the contributions of nature and nurture, and how do these forces interact? Let's get this discussion rolling with the help of Tank.

show what you know

1. _____ is the unique core set of characteristics that influence the way one thinks, acts, and feels.

2. Which perspective describes and explains personality based on the effects of the environment and reinforcers?
   a. psychoanalytic
   b. trait
   c. social-cognitive
   d. behavioral

3. How do character and temperament differ from personality?

✓ CHECK YOUR ANSWERS IN APPENDIX C.

Psychoanalytic Theories

 NEVER GOOD ENOUGH FOR DAD Tank the Roboceptionist has quite a colorful past, thanks to the creative minds at Carnegie Mellon's School of Drama, who carefully crafted his background to mesh with his current persona. Tank's father was a NASA scientist who failed to fulfill his dream of becoming an astronaut. Unfortunately, dad focused his "unfinished business" onto his robot son, pressuring him to accomplish what he never did. Dad wanted Tank to be like the Hubble Space Telescope, able to fly into space and capture beautiful images of other planets and celestial bodies. But Tank turned out to be an utter failure. He got his coordinates mixed up and sent back photos of Earth. Tank's father was so humiliated that he disowned him (Carnegie Mellon University, 2013).

If only we could ask Sigmund Freud what he thought of this father–son relationship—surely, he would have some interesting things to say. Freud believed childhood is the prime time for personality development. Early years and basic drives are particularly important, according to Freud, because they shape our thoughts, emotions, and behaviors in ways beyond our awareness. **Psychoanalysis** refers to Freud's views about personality as well as his system of psychotherapy and tools for the exploration of the unconscious. In this next section, we will present an overview of Freud's psychoanalysis as it relates to personality and some of the later personality theories it influenced.

Many students have trouble understanding why we should study Freud, whose ideas they consider sexist, perverse, and outdated. Freud is an important historical figure in psychology, and we can't ignore his legacy just because we disagree with him. You wouldn't find many world history teachers ignoring Hitler in their coverage of the 1900s, would you? The same principle applies to Freud; his impact was huge and cannot be overlooked.

Freud and the Mind

Sigmund Freud (1856–1939) spent the majority of his life in Vienna, Austria. He was his parents' first child and quite favored by his mother (Gay, 1988). A smart, ambitious young man, Freud attended medical school and became a physician and researcher with a primary interest in physiology and later neurology. Freud loved doing research, but he soon came to realize that the anti-Semitic culture in which he lived would drastically interfere with his ability to work as a researcher (Freud was Jewish). So, instead of pursuing the career he loved, he opened a medical practice in 1881, specializing in clinical neurology. Working with patients, he noted that many had unexplained or unusual symptoms that seemed related to emotional problems. He also observed (along with colleagues) that the basis of the problems appeared to be sexual in nature, although his patients weren't necessarily aware of this influence (Freud, 1900/1953). Thus began Freud's lifelong journey to untangle the mysteries of the unconscious mind.

> **LO 3** Illustrate Freud's models for describing the mind.

CONSCIOUS, PRECONSCIOUS, AND UNCONSCIOUS Freud (1900/1953) proposed that the mind has three levels of consciousness: conscious, preconscious, and unconscious. This so-called iceberg model, or *topographical model,* was his earliest attempt to explain the bustling activity occurring within the head (Westen, Gabbard, & Ortigo, 2008). It describes the *features* of the mind (which explains the reference

▶ **Little Freud**
Looking at this photo of Sigmund Freud and his father Jacob, we can't help but wonder how this father–son relationship influenced the development of the younger Freud's personality. Freud believed that events and conflicts from childhood—particularly those involving parents and other caregivers—have a powerful influence on adult personality.
Imagno/Getty Images

psychoanalysis Freud's views regarding personality as well as his system of psychotherapy and tools for the exploration of the unconscious.

unconscious According to Freud, the level of consciousness outside of awareness, which is difficult to access without effort or therapy.

to topography), and many who subsequently have presented this model use an iceberg analogy to portray these levels (Schultz & Schultz, 2013; FIGURE 11.1).

Freud believed that behaviors and personality are guided by mental processes occurring at all three levels of the mind. Everything you are aware of at this moment exists at the *conscious* level, including thoughts, emotions, sensations, and perceptions. At the **preconscious** level are the mental activities outside your current awareness, but that can be brought easily to your attention. (You are studying Freud's theory at this moment, but your mind begins to wander and you start thinking about what you did yesterday.) The **unconscious** level is home to activities outside of your awareness, such as feelings, wishes, thoughts and urges, which are very difficult to access without concerted effort and/or therapy. To gain access to the unconscious level, Freud (1900/1953) used a variety of techniques, such as dream interpretation (Chapter 4), hypnosis (Chapter 4), and free association (Chapter 14). Freud did suggest, however, that some content of the unconscious can enter the conscious level through manipulated and distorted processes beyond a person's control or awareness (more on this shortly).

Id, Ego, and Superego: The Structural Model of the Mind

In addition to the topographical model, Freud proposed a *structural model,* which describes the "functions or purposes" of the mind's components (Westen et al., 2008, p. 65). As Freud saw it, the human mind is composed of three structures: the *id,* the *ego,* and the *superego* (Figure 11.1). These components lie at the core of the unconscious conflicts influencing our thoughts, emotions, and behaviors—that is, our personality (Westen et al., 2008).

CONNECTIONS

In **Chapter 6,** we presented the concept of *episodic buffer* (a component of *working memory*), which forms a bridge between memory and conscious awareness. Although Freud did not refer to such a buffer, the preconscious level includes activities somewhat similar to those of the episodic buffer.

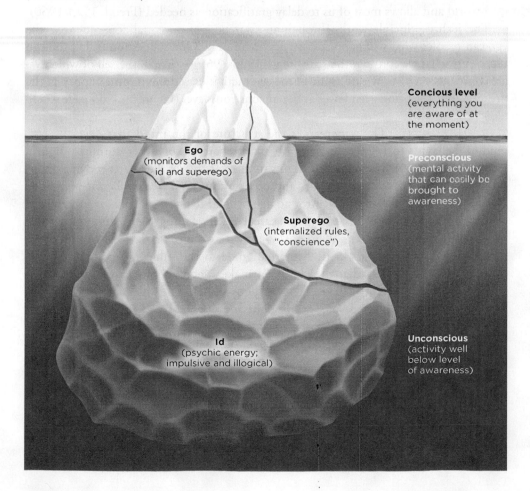

Concious level
(everything you are aware of at the moment)

Ego
(monitors demands of id and superego)

Preconscious
(mental activity that can easily be brought to awareness)

Superego
(internalized rules, "conscience")

Id
(psychic energy; impulsive and illogical)

Unconscious
(activity well below level of awareness)

FIGURE 11.1
Psychoanalytic
Description of the Mind

THE ID The **id** is the most primitive structure of the mind. It is present from birth, and its activities occur at the unconscious level. The infantlike part of our mind and personality (being impulsive, illogical, pleasure seeking) results from the workings of the id. Our biological drives and instincts, which motivate us, derive from the **id**. Freud proposed that the id represents the component of the mind that forms the primary pool of *psychic energy* (Freud, 1923/1961, 1933/1964). Included in that pool is sexual energy, which motivates much of our behavior. The primary goal of the id is to ensure that the individual's needs are being met, helping to maintain **homeostasis**. The id is not rational; it is impulsive, and it wants what it wants when it wants it. Unfilled needs or urges compel the id to insist on immediate action. The id is ruled by the **pleasure principle**, which guides behavior toward instant gratification—and away from contemplating consequences. The id seeks pleasure and avoids pain.

THE EGO As an infant grows and starts to realize that the desires of the id cannot prevail in all situations, her **ego**, which is not present from birth, begins to develop from the id (Freud, 1933/1964, 1940/1949). The ego manipulates situations, plans for the future, solves problems, and makes decisions to satisfy the needs of the id. The goal is to make sure that the id is not given free rein to decide on or steer behavior, as this would cause problems. To control the psychic energy generated by the id, the ego must "negotiate" between the desires of the id and the requirements of real life. Adults know they can't always get what they want when they want it, but the id does not know or care. Imagine what a busy supermarket would be like if we were all ruled by our ids, ignoring societal expectations to stand in line, speak politely, and pay for food; the store would be full of adults having toddlerlike tantrums. The ego uses the **reality principle** to negotiate between the id and the environment. This requires knowledge of the rules of the "real" world and allows most of us to delay gratification as needed (Freud, 1923/1960). The reality principle works through an awareness of potential consequences; the ego can predict what will happen if we act on an urge. One suggestion is that the ego represents what we consider the self (Freud, 1923/1960)—that is, the self of which we are consciously aware. We are aware of the ego's activities, although some happen at the preconscious level, and even fewer at the unconscious level (Figure 11.1 on page 471).

THE SUPEREGO The **superego** is the structure of the mind that develops last, guiding behavior to follow the rules of society, parents, or other authority figures (Freud, 1923/1960). The superego begins to form as the toddler starts moving about on his own, coming up against rules and expectations (*No, you cannot hit your sister! You need to put your toys away.*). Around age 5 or 6, the child begins to incorporate the morals and values of his parents or caregivers, including their expectations and ideas about right and wrong, colloquially known as the *conscience*. Once the superego is rooted, it serves as a critical internal guide to the values of society (not just those of the parents), so that the child can make "good" choices without constant reminders from a parent, caregiver, or religious leader. The rules and expectations now come from an internal voice citing right and wrong. Yet at times, the superego might serve as a harsh and judgmental voice in response to the unrealistic standards it has set. The superego is an internalized version of what you have been *taught* is right and wrong, not necessarily an independent moral authority. Some of the activities of the superego are conscious, but the great majority occur at the preconscious and unconscious levels.

CAUGHT IN THE MIDDLE The ego monitors the demands of both the id and the superego, trying to satisfy both. Rules and expectations must be dealt with by the ego, as it maneuvers between the wishes of the id and the requirements and limits set

---

CONNECTIONS ◄

Meeting the demands of the id is similar to the concept of *drive reduction* discussed in **Chapter 9.** If a need is not fulfilled, a drive or a state of tension results that motivates behavior. Once the need is met, the drive is reduced. According to Freud's model, the id is in charge of making sure needs are met.

S.Harris/
Cartoonstock

---

id According to Freud, the most primitive structure of the mind, the activities of which occur at the unconscious level and are guided by the pleasure principle.

pleasure principle Collection of rules that guide the id, resulting in behavior to achieve instant gratification without thought to consequences.

ego According to Freud, the structure of the mind that uses the reality principle to manipulate situations, plan for the future, solve problems, and make decisions.

reality principle Collection of rules that guide the ego as it negotiates between the id and the environment.

superego According to Freud, the structure of the mind that guides behavior to follow the rules of society, parents, or other authority figures.

ego defense mechanisms Distortions of perceptions and memories of the real world, without one's awareness, to reduce the anxiety created by the conflict among the id, ego, and superego.

repression The way the ego moves uncomfortable thoughts, memories, or feelings from the conscious level to the unconscious.

by the environment. Think of the energy of the id, pushing to get all desires met instantly. The ego must ensure needs are met in an acceptable manner, reducing tension as much as possible. But not all urges and desires can be met (sometimes not instantly, sometimes never), so when the ego cannot satisfy the id, it must do something with the unsatisfied urge or unmet need. One solution is to remove it from the conscious part of the mind.

Defense Mechanisms

As you have figured out by now, the job of the ego is not easy. It must balance the infantile demands of the id with the perfectionist authority of the superego, and deal with the resulting conflict. This is feasible, but it takes some fancy footwork on the part of the ego. Freud proposed that **ego defense mechanisms** distort our perceptions and memories of the "real" world, without our awareness, to reduce the anxiety created by the conflicts among the id, ego, and superego.

Imagine you are about to leave for class and a good friend texts to invite you to a movie. You are torn, because you know an exam for the course is coming up next week and you should not skip today's class. Your id is demanding a movie, some popcorn, and freedom from work. Your superego demands that you go to class so that you will be fully prepared for the exam next week. Clearly, your ego can't satisfy both of these demands. The ego must also deal with the external world and its requirements (for example, getting points for attendance). Freud (1923/1960) proposed that this sort of struggle is an everyday, recurring experience that is not always won by the ego. Sometimes, the id will win, and the person will act in an infantile, perhaps even destructive manner (you give in to the pressures of your friend and your id, and happily decide to skip class). Occasionally, the superego will prevail, and the person will feel a great deal of remorse or guilt for not living up to some moral ideal (you skip class, but the entire time you are at the movie you feel so guilty you aren't able to enjoy it). Sometimes, the anxiety associated with the conflict between the id and the superego, which generally is unconscious, will surface to the conscious level. The ego will then have to deal with this anxiety and make it more bearable (perhaps by suggesting that a day off will help you study, because you haven't had any free time all semester). More often than not, the ego must come up with a way to decrease the tension. If the ego can't find a compromise, the anxiety may become overwhelming, and the ego will turn to defense mechanisms to reduce it.

Projection is a defense mechanism that occurs when the expression of a thought or urge is so anxiety provoking that the ego makes us see it in someone else or accuse another of harboring these same urges. For example, if you are attracted to someone, but this attraction causes you a lot of anxiety, you may project that feeling onto your friend and ask her, "Oh, you really like Tai, don't you?" Freud proposed a variety of other defense mechanisms, which were expanded upon by his daughter, Anna Freud. Some of these are shown in **INFOGRAPHIC 11.1** (on page 474).

REPRESSION   Probably the defense mechanism best known by the general public is **repression,** which refers to the way the ego moves uncomfortable thoughts, **memories,** or feelings from the conscious level to the unconscious. With anxiety-provoking memories, the reality of an event can become distorted to such an extreme that you don't even remember it. Someone involved in a bad car accident, for example, might have unconsciously or automatically repressed the memories surrounding the traumatic event. The ego moves the memory from the conscious to the unconscious so that the person can function day-to-day without anxiety from the accident surfacing into consciousness. Repressed thoughts are like ping-pong balls held below the surface of the water. As long as you hold them down, they stay submerged; but if you let

CONNECTIONS

In **Chapter 6,** we presented the controversy surrounding *repressed memories* of childhood abuse. Many psychologists question the validity of research supporting the existence of repressed memories. Freud's case studies describing childhood sexual abuse have been questioned as well.

Ego Defense Mechanisms

The impulsive demands of the id sometimes conflict with the moralistic demands of the superego, resulting in anxiety. When that anxiety becomes a source of tension, the ego works to relieve this uncomfortable feeling through the use of defense mechanisms (Freud, 1923/1960). Defense mechanisms give us a way to "defend" against tension and anxiety, but they are only sometimes adaptive, or helpful. Defense mechanisms can be categorized ranging from less adaptive to more adaptive (Vaillant, 1992). More adaptive defense mechanisms help us deal with our anxiety in more productive and mature ways.

EGO relieves anxiety by employing a defense mechanism.

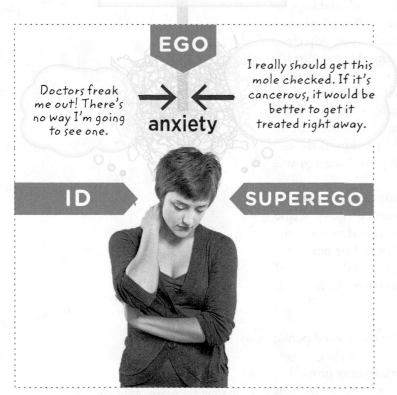

EGO

anxiety

Doctors freak me out! There's no way I'm going to see one.

I really should get this mole checked. If it's cancerous, it would be better to get it treated right away.

ID

SUPEREGO

***** We may get better at dealing with stress and anxiety as we age. In a study comparing the use of defense mechanisms in different age groups, older participants were found to use fewer maladaptive defense mechanisms (Segal, Coolidge, & Mizuno, 2007).

SUBLIMATION
Redirecting unacceptable impulses into acceptable outlets.

Example: Instead of worrying about cancer risk, spend time researching clinics and selecting a highly trained dermatologist who specializes in mole analysis.

IDENTIFICATION
Unconsciously modeling our feelings or actions on the behaviors of someone we admire.

Example: Feeling worried about sun exposure, begin sporting the floppy hat and sunglasses frequently worn by a famous model.

DISPLACEMENT
Shifting negative feelings and impulses to an acceptable target.

Example: When scheduling appointment with dermatologist, complain to receptionist about the long wait and inconvenient hours.

REPRESSION
Anxiety-producing information is pushed into the unconscious.

Example: Continually forget to make an appointment.

RATIONALIZATION
Creating an acceptable excuse for an uncomfortable situation.

Example: "I've always had that mole. There's nothing to worry about."

PROJECTION
Attributing your own anxiety-provoking thoughts and impulses to someone else.

Example: "My girlfriend spends too much time sunbathing. I'll tell her she should get screened for skin cancer!"

DENIAL
Refusing to recognize a distressing reality.

Example: Ignore the mole. "I'm way too young. It can't be cancer."

MORE ADAPTIVE

LESS ADAPTIVE

go, they pop up to the surface. The balls didn't cease to exist—they were simply just below the surface, out of sight and mind.

There are two important points to remember about defense mechanisms. First, we are often unaware of using them, even if they are brought to our attention. Second, using defense mechanisms is not necessarily a bad thing (Vaillant, 2000). There are times when it helps to have reality distorted; for example, when anxiety seeps to the surface, defense mechanisms can bring it down to a more manageable level. But sometimes conflicts between the id and the superego are overwhelming, the anxiety is too much for the ego, and we overuse defense mechanisms. If this is the case, our behaviors may turn inappropriate or unhealthy (Cramer, 2000, 2008; Tallandini & Caudek, 2010).

▶ Oops

A "Freudian slip" occurs when an unintended word accidentally slips off the tongue, shedding light on unconscious thoughts. Here, the woman reassures the balding man he still has plenty of hair, but her Freudian slip reveals she thinks otherwise. Cartoonstock

Freud's Stages of Development

···▶ LO 4 Summarize Freud's use of psychosexual stages to explain personality.

Freud (1905/1953) also conceived a *developmental* model to explain how personality is formed through experiences in childhood, with a special emphasis on sexuality. The development of sexuality and personality follows a fairly standard path through what Freud termed the **psychosexual stages,** which all children experience as they mature into adulthood (**TABLE 11.2**). The sexual energy of the id is a force behind this development, and because children are sexual beings starting from birth, this indicates a strong biological component to personality development. Associated with each of the psychosexual stages is a specific *erogenous zone,* or area of the body that when stimulated provides more sexual pleasure than other areas of the body.

Table 11.2 FREUD'S PSYCHOSEXUAL STAGES

Stage	Age	Erogenous Zone	Focus	Types of Conflict	Results of Fixation
Oral	Birth–1½ years	Mouth	Sucking, chewing, and gumming	Weaning	Smoking, drinking, nail biting, talking more than usual
Anal	1½–3 years	Anus	Eliminating bodily waste and controlling bodily functions responsible for them	Toilet training	Rule-bound, stingy, chaotic, destructive
Phallic	3–6 years	Genitals	Sexual feelings and awareness of self	Autoeroticism	Promiscuity, flirtation, vanity, or overdependence, and a focus on masturbation
Latency Period	6 years–puberty	Period during which children develop mentally, socially, and physically			
Genital	Puberty and beyond	Genitals	Reawakening of sexuality, with focus on relationships	Sexuality and aggression	Inability to thrive in adult activities such as work and love

According to Freud, psychological and sexual development proceeds through distinct stages. Each stage is characterized by a certain pleasure area, or "erogenous zone," and a conflict that must be resolved. If resolution is not achieved, the person may develop a problematic "fixation."

If the idea of a preschooler getting sexual pleasure from a body part makes you uncomfortable, then you are experiencing firsthand the child's feeling of conflict between pleasurable sexual feelings and the restrictions and potential disapproval of caregivers. Along with each psychosexual stage comes a conflict, and these must be

psychosexual stages According to Freud, the stages of development, from birth to adulthood, each of which has an erogenous zone as well as a conflict that must be dealt with.

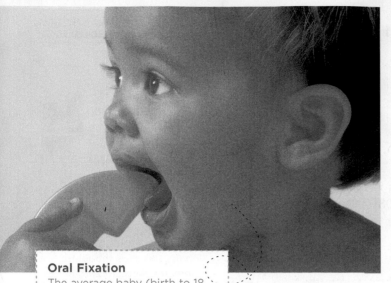

Oral Fixation
The average baby (birth to 18 months) spends 108 minutes per day sucking on a pacifier and another 33 minutes mouthing other objects (Juberg, Alfano, Coughlin, & Thompson, 2001). Freud identified this phase of life with the oral stage of psychosexual development.
BSIP SA/Alamy

successfully resolved in order for an individual to become a well-adjusted adult. If these conflicts are not suitably addressed, one may suffer from a **fixation** and get stuck in that particular stage, unable to progress smoothly through the remaining stages. Freud believed that fixation at a psychosexual stage during the first 5 to 6 years of life can dramatically influence an adult's personality. Let's look at each stage, its erogenous zone, conflicts, and some consequences of fixation.

THE ORAL STAGE   The *oral stage* is the first psychosexual stage, beginning at birth and lasting until the infant is 1 to 1.5 years old. As its name suggests, the erogenous zone for this stage is the mouth. During this period, the infant gets his greatest pleasure from sucking, chewing, and gumming. According to Freud, the conflict during this stage generally centers on weaning. Infants must stop nursing or using a bottle or pacifier, and the timing of this weaning often is decided by the caregiver. Here is a possible conflict: The infant wants to continue using the bottle because it is a pleasurable activity, but his parent believes he is old enough to switch to a cup. How the caregiver handles this conflict can have long-term consequences for personality development. Freud suggested that certain behavior patterns and personality traits are associated with an oral fixation, including smoking, nail biting, and excessive talking and alcohol consumption.

THE ANAL STAGE   Following the oral stage, a child enters the *anal stage,* which lasts approximately until the age of 3. During this stage, the erogenous zone is the anus, and pleasure is derived from eliminating bodily waste as well as learning to control the body parts responsible for this process. The conflict during this stage centers on toilet training: The parents want their child to control her waste elimination in a socially acceptable way, but the child is not necessarily on board with this new procedure for doing so. Once again, how caregivers deal with this learning task may have long-term implications for personality. Freud suggested that toilet training can set the stage for power struggles between child and adult; the child ultimately will gain control over her bodily functions, and then she can use this control to manipulate caregivers (not always "going" at the appropriate time and place). If a parent is too harsh about toilet training (growing angry when there are accidents, forcing a child to sit on the toilet until she goes) or too lenient (making excuses for accidents, not really encouraging the child to learn control), the child might grow up with an *anal-retentive* personality (rule-bound, stingy) or an *anal-expulsive* personality (chaotic, destructive).

PHALLIC STAGE   Age 3 to 6 marks the *phallic stage* (*phallus* means "penis" in Latin, and as you will see, Freud's original theory of development is somewhat male-centered). During this period, the erogenous zone is the genitals, and many children begin to discover that self-stimulation is pleasurable. Freud (1923/1960) assigned special importance to the conflict that occurs in the phallic stage.

During this time, little boys develop a desire to replace their fathers. These feelings are normal, according to Freud, but they lead to boys becoming jealous of their fathers, who are now considered rivals for their mothers' affection. This pattern, referred to as the **Oedipus complex** (e-də-pəs), is named for a character in a complex Greek myth. Oedipus was abandoned by his parents when he was a newborn, so he did not know their identities. As an adult, he unknowingly married his mother and

fixation Being stuck in a particular psychosexual stage of development as a result of unsuccessfully dealing with the conflict of that stage.

Oedipus complex (e-də-pəs) According to Freud, the attraction a child feels toward the opposite-sex parent, along with the resentment or envy directed toward the same-sex parent.

killed his father. Freud named the behavior pattern of the phallic stage after the Greek tragedy, as how boys behave and feel during this period seems to follow such a pattern. When a little boy becomes aware of his attraction to his mother, he realizes his father is a formidable rival and experiences jealousy and anger toward him. He also begins to fear his father, who is so powerful, and worry that his father might punish him. Specifically, he fears that his father will castrate him (Freud, 1917/1966). In order to reduce the tension, the boy must identify with and behave like his father, a process otherwise known as *identification*. This defense mechanism resolves the Oedipus complex by allowing the boy to take on or internalize the behaviors, gestures, morals, and standards of his father. Freud proposed that the fear of castration causes a great deal of anxiety, but with successful resolution of the Oedipus complex, this anxiety is repressed. The boy realizes that sexual affection should only be between his father and mother, and the incest taboo develops.

Freud (1923/1960) believed that little girls experience a different conflict, which others refer to as the *Electra complex*. Little girls feel an attraction to their fathers, and become jealous and angry toward their mothers. Around the same time, they realize that they do not have a penis. This leads to feelings of loss and jealousy, known as *penis envy*. The girl responds with anger, blaming her mother for her missing penis. Realizing she can't have her father, she begins to act like her mother, a process again known as *identification*. She takes on her mother's behaviors, gestures, morals, and standards. Freud's theory of female development is now regarded as a product of its historical and social context, as opposed to objective observation.

If children do not resolve the sexual conflicts that arise during the phallic stage, they develop a fixation, which can lead to promiscuity, flirtation, vanity, overdependence, bravado, and an increased focus on masturbation.

Just Like Dad ◢
Young boys often look up to their fathers and strive to be like them. Freud believed this is the way boys resolve the Oedipus complex. Unable to displace his powerful father, the son stops trying to compete and begins to identify with his dad. Jose Luis Pelaez/Getty Images

LATENCY PERIOD Freud proposed that from 6 years old to puberty, children remain in a *latency period* (not a "stage" according to Freud's definition; there is no erogenous zone, no conflict, no fixation). During this time, psychosexual development slows. Where does the child's sexual energy go during this period? According to Freud, it is repressed: Although children develop mentally, socially, and physically, their sexual development is on hold. This idea seems to be supported by the fact that most prepubertal children tend to gravitate toward same-sex friends and playmates.

GENITAL STAGE Following the calm of the latency period, a child's psychosexual development picks up speed again. The *genital stage* begins at puberty and is the final stage of psychosexual development. During this time, there is a reawakening of sexuality. The erogenous zone is centered on the genitals, but now in association with relationships, as opposed to autoeroticism or masturbation. Adolescents become interested in partners, whereas earlier their focus was family members. This is a time when one resolves the Oedipus or Electra complex and often becomes attracted to partners who resemble one's opposite-sex parent, according to Freud (1905/1953). Because of the ever-present *id* and its requirement for satisfaction, there still are unconscious conflicts to be addressed, including the continual battle against unconscious sexual and aggressive urges. The resolution of these conflicts impacts the types of relationships we seek and cultivate. If earlier conflicts are put to rest, then it is possible to thrive in adult activities such as work and love.

Taking Stock: An Appraisal of Psychoanalytic Theory

Freud's psychoanalytic theory has been the subject of much criticism (Bornstein, 2005). Some of Freud's own followers (a few of whom we will discuss shortly) recognized several key weaknesses. For example, psychoanalysis does not take into account the possibility that people can change; we are not predestined to develop certain personality types simply because we had specific experiences in childhood. Similarly, psychoanalysis ignores the importance of current development. Critics also contend that Freud placed too much weight on the unconscious forces guiding behavior, instead proposing that we can be conscious of our motivations and change our behaviors. Finally, many have objected to Freud's emphasis on sexuality and its role in personality development.

Given the amount of attention Freud's concepts have received, one might expect there is a great deal of research supporting or refuting aspects of his theory. But where would a researcher start? For example, how would you go about designing an experiment to test whether early weaning causes later problems in relationships? How about persuading an ethics committee to approve a study with an independent variable that manipulates toilet training? Given these types of difficulties, it is no surprise there is relatively little published research on Freudian concepts.

Another serious concern regarding psychoanalysis is that much of Freud's theory is based on a biased, **nonrepresentative sample** (a handful of middle- and upper-class Viennese women and Freud himself), although more recent research attempts to address this issue (Shedler, 2010). Many feminists have raised concerns about Freud's one-sided male perspective, although not necessarily dismissing potential usefulness of psychoanalysis to women (Young-Bruehl, 2009).

Who Is Anna O.?
Anna O. was the alias for Bertha Pappenheim (1859–1936), whose case study appears in the 1895 book *Studies on Hysteria* by Josef Breuer and Sigmund Freud. Although Anna O. inspired Freud's psychoanalytic theory, the facts of her case remain foggy. What type of disorder did she have, and did psychoanalytic methods really help her? Answers to these questions are still up in the air (Hurst, 1982). Mary Evans/Sigmund Freud Copyrights/ The Image Works

CONNECTIONS

In **Chapter 1,** we introduced the *case study,* a form of *descriptive research.* A major weakness of the case study is its failure to provide a *representative sample,* or sample whose characteristics reflect the population. Freud's case studies focused on a particular subgroup, thus his findings might not be generalizable.

TANK'S ONGOING TROUBLES   Let's return to the fictitious backstory of Tank the Roboceptionist for a moment. What happened to our robot after he was kicked to the curb by his father? He got a job with the CIA, which ended in another great failure. The agency shipped Tank to Afghanistan to fight in the war against terror, but his performance was so poor that he was sent home. As luck had it, Carnegie Mellon University was looking to hire a new roboceptionist around this time. Valerie, the robot who occupied the post, was about to abandon her administrative career and pursue her longtime dream of touring with a Barbra Streisand cover band. Tank accepted the roboceptionist position, which he has held since 2005 (Carnegie Mellon University, 2013).

Tank's story is the intelligent invention of playwrights, but its basic themes are familiar to many. Parents often make the mistake of developing unrealistic expectations for their children, potentially setting them up for failure. According to the imaginary storyline, Tank's father longed for him to replace the Hubble Space Telescope, but did he ever ask Tank what *he* wanted out of life?

According to Freud, personality is largely shaped by early childhood experiences and sexual impulses. But some of the most defining experiences in Tank's life—like being abandoned by his father and bungling his mission with the CIA—occurred later in life and had nothing to do with sex. Some personality theorists might argue that these types of nonsexual experiences are important factors in the development of personality. We now turn to the neo-Freudians, who agree with Freud on many points, but depart from his intense emphasis on early childhood experiences and sexuality.

The Neo-Freudians

LO 5   Explain how the neo-Freudians' theories of personality differ from Freud's.

Not surprisingly, Freud's psychoanalytic theory was quite controversial, but he did have a following of students who **adapted** some of the main aspects of his theory. Some who disagreed with Freud on key points (such as his focus on sex, aggression, and the determination of personality by the end of childhood) broke away to develop their own theories; they are often referred to as neo-Freudians (*neo* = "new").

ALFRED ADLER   One of the first followers to forge his own path was Alfred Adler (1870–1937), whose own theory conflicted with the Freudian notion that personality is, to a large degree, shaped by unconscious motivators. As Adler saw it, humans are not just pleasure seekers, but conscious and intentional in their behaviors. We are motivated by the need to feel superior—to grow, overcome challenges, and strive for perfection. This drive originates during childhood, when we realize that we are dependent on and inferior to adults. Whether imagined or real, the sense of inferiority pushes us to compensate, so we cultivate our special gifts and skills. This attempt to balance perceived weaknesses with strengths is not a sign of abnormality, but a natural response.

Adler's theory of *individual psychology* focuses on each person's unique struggle with feelings of inferiority. Unfortunately, not everyone is successful in overcoming feelings of helplessness and dependence, but instead develop what is known as an *inferiority complex* (Adler, 1927/1994). Someone with an inferiority complex feels incompetent, vulnerable, and powerless, and cannot achieve his full potential. Based on what you know about Tank, would you say he has been programmed to resemble someone who suffers from an inferiority complex?

Perhaps you can imagine how an inferiority complex might play out in sibling relationships. The firstborn child receives all his parents' attention for the first years of life. Then along comes a baby brother or sister, and suddenly mom and dad must divide their attention. How might this affect the older child's sense of worth? Younger siblings have their own reasons for feeling inferior. They are, after all, the newcomers, smaller and less developed than their older siblings. And unlike the firstborn, who enjoyed being an only child for some time, younger siblings never had that special time with mom and dad. They always had to share their parents' love.

Adler was one of the first to theorize about the psychological repercussions of birth order. He believed that first born children experience different environmental pressures than youngest and middle children, and these pressures can set the stage for the development of certain personality traits (Ansbacher & Ansbacher, 1956).

CONNECTIONS

Although he considered himself a "loyal Freudian," Erik Erikson took Freud's ideas in a new direction (Schultz & Schultz, 2013). As noted in **Chapter 8,** Erikson suggested psychosocial development occurs throughout life, with eight stages marked by a conflict between the individual's needs and society's expectations.

An Individual Psychology
Alfred Adler studied with Freud but ultimately broke from his teacher and created his own theory. According to Adler, personality is strongly influenced by the drive to conquer feelings of inferiority. Failure to succeed at this endeavor paves the way for an inferiority complex. Imagno/ Getty Images

CONTROVERSIES

How Birth Order May—or May Not—Affect Your Personality

➡️⬅️ Firstborns are conscientious and high achieving. They play by the rules, excel in school, and become leaders in the workforce. The youngest children, favored and coddled by their parents, grow up to be gregarious and rebellious. Middle children tend to get lost in the shuffle, but they learn to be self-sufficient.

Have you heard these stereotypes about birth order and personality? How well do they match your personal experience, and do you think they are valid?

If you search the scientific literature, you will indeed find research supporting such claims. According to one analysis of 200 studies, firstborns (as well as only children) are often accomplished and successful; middle children are sociable but tend to lack a sense of belonging; and last-born children are agreeable and rebellious (Eckstein et al., 2010). You will also find plenty of skepticism regarding such findings (Ernst & Angst, 1983; Hartshorne, 2010).

There are over 2,000 scientific papers published on the birth order–personality connection, but it is still an active area of scholarly debate (Eckstein et al., 2010; Hartshorne, Salem-Hartshorne, & Hartshorne, 2009; Healey & Ellis, 2007). One of the problems with birth order studies is that they tend to be cluttered with confounding variables. Hartshorne (2010) points to the **confounding variable** of family size: We know that firstborn children are high achievers, but firstborns are also more likely to come from smaller families. Just think about it: The chances of being a firstborn are much greater if you come from a family with two children (1 in 2), as opposed to a family with four children (1 in 4). This makes it difficult to determine which variable is driving high achievement—being a firstborn or coming from a small family (Hartshorne, 2010).

We cannot resolve this longstanding debate here, but we can lighten the discussion with some interesting bits of information: Oprah Winfrey was a first child, as were most American presidents (Neal, 2009, February 11). Jim Carrey and Cameron Diaz are the youngest of their siblings, and Madonna and Miley Cyrus are middle children, as was Charles Darwin (MSN.com, 2012; Zupek, 2008, October 22). Given what you know about these famous people, are these revelations what you would expect? ➡️⬅️

Famous Firstborn
Oprah Winfrey has many of the stereotypical qualities of a firstborn child. She is ambitious, successful, and seems to be a natural leader. But her example also highlights some of the problems with making generalizations about birth order and personality. Studies on birth order focus on full-blood siblings, yet Winfrey had two half-siblings growing up, and discovered a third half-sibling in 2010 (Allen, 2011, January 24). Gallo Images/Sunday Times/Kevin Sutherland

CONNECTIONS

In **Chapter 1,** we discussed *confounding variables,* which are a type of *extraneous variable* that changes in sync with an *independent variable* (IV). Here, the IV is birth order, the confounding variable is family size, and the *dependent variable* (DV) is a measure of high achievement. But we don't know if differences in achievement (DV) are due to birth order (IV) or family size (confounding variable).

MIDDLE CHILDREN TEND TO GET LOST IN THE SHUFFLE. . . .

collective unconscious According to Jung, the universal experiences of humankind passed from generation to generation, including memories.

archetypes (är-ki-tīps) Primal images, patterns of thoughts, and storylines stored in the collective unconscious, with themes that may be found in art, literature, music, dreams, and religions.

CARL GUSTAV JUNG Carl Gustav Jung (yůŋ; 1875–1961) was another influential neo-Freudian. Jung's focus was on growth and self-understanding. Although he agreed with Freud about the importance of the unconscious, in his *analytic psychology* he placed less emphasis on biological urges (sex and aggression), proposing more positive and spiritual aspects of human nature. Critical of Freud's overemphasis on the sex drive, Jung claimed that Freud viewed the brain as "an appendage to the genital glands" (Westen et al., 2008, p. 66). Jung (1969) proposed we are driven by psychological energy (not sexual energy) that promotes growth, insight, and balance. He also believed personality development is not limited to childhood; adults continue to evolve throughout life.

Jung also differed from Freud in his view of the unconscious. Jung believed personality is made up of the ego (at the conscious level), a *personal unconscious,* and a *collective unconscious.* The personal unconscious is akin to Freud's notion of the preconscious and the unconscious mind; items from the personal unconscious range from easily retrievable memories to anxiety-provoking repressed memories. The **collective unconscious,** according to Jung, holds the universal experiences of humankind passed from generation to generation, memories that are not easily retrieved without some degree of effort or interpretation. We inherit a variety of primal images, patterns of thoughts, and storylines. The themes of these **archetypes** (är-ki-tīps) may be found in art, literature, music, dreams, and religions across time, geography, and culture. Some of the consistent archetypes include the nurturing mother, powerful father, innocent child, and brave hero. Archetypes provide a blueprint for us as we respond to situations, objects, and people in our environments (Jung, 1969). The *anima* refers to the part of our personality that is feminine, and the *animus* to that which is masculine. Jung believed both of these parts exist in everyone's personality, and we must acknowledge and appreciate them. Failure to accept the anima and animus can result in an imbalance, which prevents us from being whole.

KAREN HORNEY   Karen Horney (hȯr-ˌnī; 1885–1952) was a neo-Freudian who emphasized the role of relationships between children and their caregivers, not erogenous zones and psychosexual stages. She believed individuals respond to feelings of helplessness and isolation created by inadequate parenting, which she referred to as *basic anxiety* (Horney, 1945). In order to deal with this anxiety, Horney suggested that people use three strategies: moving toward people (looking for affection and acceptance), moving away from people (looking for isolation and self-sufficiency), or moving against people (looking to control others). Horney believed that a balance of these three strategies is important for psychological stability. She was also a committed critic of Freud's sexist approach to the female psyche, pointing out that women are not jealous of the penis itself, but rather what it represents in terms of power and status in society. Horney (1926/1967) also proposed that boys and men can envy women's ability to bear and breastfeed children.

Questioning Freud

Freud's psychoanalytic theory was groundbreaking and controversial, and it led to a variety of extensions and permutations through neo-Freudians such as Adler, Jung, Horney, and Erikson. Freud's theories are considered among the most important in the field of personality development. He courageously called attention to the existence of infant sexuality at a time when sex was a forbidden topic of conversation. He recognized the importance of infancy and early childhood in the unfolding of personality, and appreciated the universal stages of human development. It was a blow to our collective self-esteem to realize that so much of our thinking occurs without conscious awareness, but this notion has been widely accepted, even among psychologists who are not Freudians or neo-Freudians. Some suggest Freud's work has "become so pervasive in Western thinking that he is to be ranked with Darwin and Marx for introducing new—and often disturbing—modes of thought in Western culture" (Hilgard, 1987, p. 99).

Timeless Heroines
Jennifer Lawrence (top) plays the role of Katniss Everdeen in the 2012 film *The Hunger Games*. Her strength, bravery, and charisma resemble that of 15th-century French heroine Joan of Arc, portrayed in the poster (bottom). These heroines have the qualities of a Jungian archetype; the thoughts and feelings they evoke are relatively consistent across time and culture. top: Lionsgate/The Kobal Collection; bottom: V&A Images, London / Art Resource

⦿✓⦾⦾ show what you know

1. According to Freud, all children go through _____ stages as they mature into adulthood. If conflicts are not successfully resolved along the way, a child may suffer from a

   _____ .

2. Freud's _____ includes three levels: conscious, preconscious, and unconscious.
   a. structural model of the mind
   b. developmental model
   c. individual psychology
   d. topographical model of the mind

3. Jung believed personality is made up of the ego, a personal unconscious, and the:
   a. id.
   b. collective unconscious.
   c. superego.
   d. preconscious.

4. How did the theories of the neo-Freudians differ from Freud's psychoanalytic theory in regard to personality development?

   ✓ CHECK YOUR ANSWERS IN APPENDIX C.

Humanistic Theories

We have thus far discussed the psychoanalytic theories of personality development, which emphasize the importance of factors beyond one's control. You don't get to choose the identity of your parents, the dynamics within your family, or the nature of your childhood conflicts. Nor do you have the ability to direct unconscious activities. For those looking for more self-direction than the psychoanalytic theories permit, humanism may offer an attractive alternative. With this theoretical approach, the power is in your hands.

The Brighter Side: Maslow and Rogers

The humanistic perspective began gaining momentum in the 1960s and 1970s in response to the negative, **mechanistic view** of human nature apparent in other theories. According to the humanists, not only are we innately good, we are also in control of our destinies, and these positive aspects of human nature drive the development of personality. According to leading humanists Abraham Maslow and Carl Rogers, our natural tendency is to grow in a positive direction.

> ► **LO 6**   Describe how Maslow's hierarchy of needs relates to personality.

MASLOW AND PERSONALITY   Abraham Maslow (1908–1970) is probably best known for his theory of motivation. According to Maslow, human behaviors are motivated by biological and psychological needs. When a need is not being met, a state of tension motivates us to meet it, leading to the reduction of the drive. Maslow's **hierarchy of needs** explains the organization of human needs, which are universal and ordered in terms of their strength (from basic physiological needs to self-actualization and self-transcendence). How does this discussion of needs relate to personality? If you recall, personality is the unique core set of characteristics that influence the way we think, act, and feel. Although we tend to respond to needs in a universal order, Maslow suggested that we all have the ability to reorder them. Not only are we responsible for being proactive in our lives; we also have an urge to "feel free and to be free" (Maslow, 1971, p. 14). Maslow was particularly interested in *self-actualizers* (**TABLE 11.3**), or people who are continually seeking to reach their fullest potential, a drive that is one of the guiding principles of the humanistic perspective.

> ► **LO 7**   Discuss Rogers' view of self-concept, ideal self, and unconditional positive regard.

ROGERS AND PERSONALITY   Carl Rogers (1902–1987) was another humanist who had great faith in the essential goodness of people and their ability to make sound choices (Rogers, 1979). According to Rogers, we all have an innate urge to move toward situations and people that will help us grow and to avoid those with the potential to inhibit growth. He believed we should have faith in our ability to find happiness and mental balance, that is, to be *fully functioning*, and strive to really experience life, not just be passive participants. At the same time, we must also be sensitive to the needs of others.

Rogers highlighted the importance of **self-concept**, which refers to a person's knowledge of her own strengths, abilities, behavior patterns, and temperament. Problems arise when a person's self-concept is *incongruent* with, or does not correspond to, her experiences in the world (Rogers, 1959). If a woman believes she is kind and sociable but fails to get along with most people in her life, this incongruence will produce tension and confusion. Rogers also proposed that people

CONNECTIONS

The *behaviorists*, introduced in **Chapter 1** and then again in **Chapter 5**, suggested that our behaviors are shaped by factors in the environment. Because of this, we are at the mercy of forces beyond our control. The humanists challenged this position.

Maslow's hierarchy of needs was introduced in **Chapter 9**, in reference to motivation. According to Maslow, behaviors are motivated by needs. If a basic need is not being met, we are less likely to meet needs higher in the hierarchy. Here, we see how Maslow's hierarchy can be used to understand personality.

Reaching High
Pope Francis greets residents of the Varginha shantytown in Rio de Janeiro, Brazil. The leader of the Catholic Church is known for his humility and commitment to helping the poor. He is the type of person Maslow might have called a "self-actualizer," or one who strives to achieve his full potential.
AP Photo/L'Osservatore Romano

Table 11.3 ATTRIBUTES OF SELF-ACTUALIZERS

Tendencies	Characteristics	Examples
Realistic perceptions of reality	Nonjudgmental, objective, and acutely aware of others	An individual who is empathetic and unbiased
Acceptance of self, others, and nature	Has patience with weaknesses of self, others, and society	Someone who is forgiving and accepting of others
Spontaneity and creativeness	Original, flexible, and willing to learn from mistakes	Someone who is self-sufficient and lives in unconventional ways
Independent and private	Not reliant on others, enjoys time alone	A person with a strong sense of self who doesn't conform to peer pressure
Freshness of appreciation	Views each experience as if it were the first time (e.g., sunrise), is grateful for what he has	An individual who lives life thankful for each day
Peak experiences	Has moments of ecstasy and transcendence	A highly spiritual individual who experiences intense happiness in day-to-day activities
Social interest and fellowship	Empathic and sympathetic toward others	A person who is devoted to helping others
Profound interpersonal relations	Maintains deep and lasting friendships	Someone with intense, lifelong friendships
A democratic character structure	Tolerant and accepting of others	A person who is open-minded and humble
Autonomous and resistant to enculturation	Independent and free from cultural pressures	An individual who is self-sufficient in thought and behavior and resists social pressure

According to Maslow, a "self-actualizer" is someone who continually strives to achieve his maximum potential. Listed here are common traits and examples of self-actualizers.

SOURCE: ADAPTED FROM SHULTZ AND SHULTZ (2013) WITH PERMISSION.

often develop an **ideal self,** which is the *self-concept* a person fervently strives to achieve. Problems arise when the ideal self is unattainable or incongruent with one's self-concept, a topic we will discuss further in Chapter 14 (Rogers, 1959).

Like Freud, Rogers believed caregivers play a vital role in the development of personality and self-concept. Ideally, caregivers should show **unconditional positive regard,** which is the total acceptance of a child regardless of her behavior. According to Rogers, people need to feel totally accepted and valued for who they are, not what they do. Caregivers who place too much emphasis on rules, morals, and values, ignoring a child's innate goodness, can cause the child to experience *conditions of worth.* When our behaviors are judged by others to be bad or wrong, we feel unworthy, so we may try to please others by hiding or repressing these "unacceptable" behaviors and emotions. Seeking approval from others, we deny our true selves, and anxiety is ever-present in our lives. As caregivers, it is important to show children that we value them all the time, not just when they obey us and act the way we want them to. Of course, children behave in ways we dislike; but parents should love their children unconditionally, because it is the behavior that is unacceptable, not the child.

Conditional Love?
Amy Chua poses with her daughters at home in New Haven, Connecticut. This Yale law professor is best-known for writing *Battle Hymn of the Tiger Mother,* a book about cross-cultural parenting differences. Chua never allowed her children to participate in play dates, select their after-school activities, or receive any grade lower than an A. When one daughter behaved "extremely disrespectfully" way, Chua called her "garbage" (Chua, 2011, January 8). This type of response lacks what Rogers called unconditional positive regard, or total acceptance of a child regardless of her behavior. Erin Patrice O'Brien

self-concept The knowledge an individual has about his strengths, abilities, behavior patterns, and temperament.

ideal self The self-concept a person strives for and fervently wishes to achieve.

unconditional positive regard According to Rogers, the total acceptance or valuing of a person, regardless of behavior.

Taking Stock: An Appraisal of the Humanistic Theories

Let's step back and review the potential weaknesses of the humanistic approach. For humanistic and psychoanalytic theories alike, creating operational definitions can be challenging. How can you use the experimental method to test a subjective approach whose concepts are open to interpretation (Schultz & Schultz, 2013)? Imagine submitting a research proposal that included two randomly assigned groups of children: one group whose parents were instructed to show them *unconditional positive regard* and the other group whose parents were told to instill *conditions of worth*. The proposal would never amount to a real study, not only because it raises ethical issues, but because it would be impossible to control the experimental conditions. Another problem with unconditional positive regard in particular is that constantly praising, attempting to boost self-esteem, and withholding criticism can be counterproductive. In some cases, we run the risk of "fostering narcissism," or another unproductive characteristic of elevated self-esteem such as aggression (Baumeister, Campbell, Krueger, & Vohs, 2003). Finally, humanism almost completely ignores the negative aspects of human nature evident in war, greed, abuse, and aggression (Burger, 2011). And while it is important to recognize that humans have great potential to grow and move forward, we should not discount the developmental impact of early experiences. In spite of these weaknesses, the humanistic perspective has led to a less negative and more balanced view of human nature, influencing approaches to parenting, education, and psychotherapy. Its legacy is alive and well in the emerging field of **positive psychology** (Chapter 12).

In the next section, we will explore how personality is influenced by forces in the outside world. How do you think your interactions with the environment have shaped your personality?

CONNECTIONS

In **Chapter 1,** we described positive psychology as a relatively new approach. The humanists' optimism struck the right chord with many psychologists, who wondered why the field was not focusing on human strengths and virtues.

 show what you know

1. _____ was a humanist who was interested in exploring people who are self-actualizers. _____, also a humanist, discussed self-concept and problems that can arise when it is incongruent with our experiences in the world.

2. The total acceptance of a child regardless of her behavior is known as:
   a. conditions of worth.
   b. repression.
   c. the real self.
   d. unconditional positive regard.

3. How do the psychoanalytic and humanistic perspectives differ in regard to personality development?

✓ CHECK YOUR ANSWERS IN APPENDIX C.

Learning and Social-Cognitive Theories

You Asked, Dr. Simmons Answers
http://qrs.ly/7z3nr8e
Is Tank capable of learning new tasks?

ROBOTS CAN LEARN, TOO Tank the Roboceptionist is very good at what he does (providing room numbers, directions, weather forecasts, and so on), and he can respond to a range of unexpected remarks and questions in character with his persona. Say "I love you," and he will shoot back with something like, "That's nice, but you don't even know me." Assault his keyboard with offensive remarks such as "I hate you!" and "@#?! you!" and he will tell you that you are not being very nice. But Tank's persona and everything he says are predetermined by the human beings who created him. Imagine if Tank could craft his own witty responses from scratch? And wouldn't it be something if he could learn from his environment and independently develop new skills?

It turns out that robots can "learn" to some degree. For example, researchers have fashioned robots that can take a collection of objects and categorize them according to the sounds they make when shaken, dropped, or manipulated in other ways (Smith, 2009, March 23). HERB (the Home Exploring Robot Butler) can learn to find his way through messy rooms (Srinivasa et al., 2009). There are also robots that demonstrate observational learning, imitating simple human behaviors like head movements and hand gestures. At least one robot learned to play air hockey by observing the movements of a human opponent (Breazeal & Scassellati, 2002). What does this have to do with personality? Hold on, we're almost there.

One very popular area of robot research is "reinforcement learning," according to Dr. Simmons. Here's a hypothetical example of how it might work. Researchers program a robot to have some goal, such as exiting a room. The robot begins the task by randomly moving around (not unlike Thorndike's cats from Chapter 5), but eventually it will come upon a path that leads to an exit. Upon leaving the room, the robot gets a signal indicating that the behavior should be repeated. With continued **reinforcement** through signals received for correct behavior, the robot tends to make fewer errors and reaches the exit more quickly. Over time, its average performance improves. But like most robot learning feats accomplished thus far, leaving a room is far from an expression of personality.

With improvements in technology and computer programming, is it possible that robots might one day be capable of possessing personality? If you asked a follower of Freud, we suspect the answer would be a forceful "no." Robots do not have unresolved conflicts from childhood; in fact, they don't even have childhoods (remember, the story of Tank is just a human invention). A robot cannot dream, feel sexual urges, or repress unwanted thoughts. Ask a strict behaviorist if the robots of the future might be capable of having personality, and you might get a very different answer.

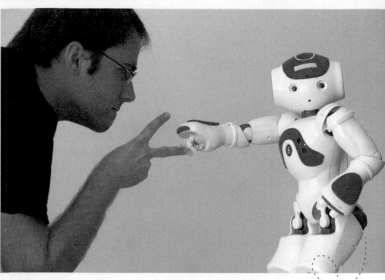

Robots Can Learn, Too ◄
A student at the Edinburgh International Science Festival interacts with a robot that is capable of developing game strategies. This robot is engaging the student in "rock-scissors-paper." Who won this round? Press Association via AP Images

CONNECTIONS

In **Chapter 5,** we described *operant conditioning*, the type of learning that occurs when we make connections between behaviors and their consequences. The robot's exiting is followed by a signal, which serves as a *reinforcer*. But unlike Thorndike's cats, the robot cannot experience "pleasurable" outcomes. It is programmed to respond to outcomes in a predetermined way.

The Role of Learning, Thought, and Environment

···► **LO 8**   Use learning theories to explain personality development.

Behaviorists like B. F. Skinner were not interested in studying the thoughts and emotions typically thought to be expressions of personality. They focused on measuring observable behaviors that they believed resulted from learning processes such as classical conditioning, operant conditioning, and observational learning. From this perspective, personality is a compilation or collection of behaviors, all of which have been shaped through a lifetime of learning.

Let's look at an example. Think of a friend or classmate who is very outgoing. A behaviorist would suggest she has been consistently reinforced to act this way. She gets positive attention, perhaps a promotion at work, and is surrounded by many friends, all of which reinforce her outgoing behavior. This characteristic, which psychologists might call "extraversion," is just one of the many dimensions of personality molded by learning. Now apply the behaviorist principle to robots. Learning is the foundation for personality, and robots are capable of learning. Looking at things from this perspective, it seems plausible that robots could develop rudimentary personalities.

Like any theory of personality, behaviorism is limited. Critics contend that behaviorism essentially ignores anything that is not directly observable and thus portrays humans too simplistically; as passive and unaware of what is going on inside their internal and external environments. Julian Rotter (b. 1916) is one of the early social learning theorists who countered these weaknesses, suggesting that not all aspects of behavior and personality can be directly observed (Rotter, 1990). He proposed several important cognitive aspects of personality, including *locus of control* and *expectancy.*

···▶ **LO 9**   Summarize Rotter's view of personality.

ROTTER AND PERSONALITY   According to Rotter, a key component of personality is locus of control, a pattern of beliefs about where control or responsibility for outcomes resides. If a person has an *internal* locus of control, she believes that the causes of her life events generally reside within her, and that she has some control over them. For example, such a person would say that her career success depends on how hard she works, not on luck (Rotter, 1966). Someone with an *external* locus of control believes that causes for outcomes reside outside of him; he assigns great importance to luck, fate, and other features of the environment, over which he has little control. As this person sees it, getting a job occurs when all the circumstances are right and luck is on his side (Rotter, 1966). A person's locus of control refers to beliefs about the self, not about others.

Rotter also explored how behaviors are influenced by thoughts about the future. **Expectancy** refers to the predictions we make about the outcomes and consequences of our behaviors (**INFOGRAPHIC 11.2**). A woman who is considering whether she should confront the manager of a restaurant over a bad meal will decide her next move based on her expectancy: Does she expect to be thrown out the door, or does she believe it will lead to a free meal? In these situations, there is an interaction among expectancies, behaviors, and environmental factors. The *reinforcement value* of the consequence plays a role (Rotter, 1954). People have different preferences regarding reinforcements. Getting an A on a final exam may have high reinforcement value for you, but another student might consider it more important to win an award for perfect attendance.

···▶ **LO 10**   Discuss how Bandura uses the social-cognitive perspective to explain personality.

BANDURA AND PERSONALITY   Another early critic of the behaviorist approach was Albert Bandura (b. 1925). Bandura rejected the notion that psychologists should only focus on observable behavior, and recognized the importance of cognitions, reinforcers, and environmental factors (Bandura, 2006). This **social-cognitive perspective** suggests that personality results from patterns of thinking (cognitive) as well as relationships and other factors in the environment (social). Prior experiences have shaped, and will continue to shape, your personality. Cognitive abilities, including knowledge, are partly the result of our interactions with others (Bandura, 1977a, 2006). We don't spend much time in isolation; in fact, almost everything we do involves some sort of collaboration. We are social creatures who work together and live in family units.

Bandura also pointed to the importance of **self-efficacy,** which refers to beliefs about our ability and effectiveness in reaching goals (Bandura, 1977b, 2001). People

expectancy A person's predictions about the consequences or outcomes of behavior.

social-cognitive perspective Suggests that personality results from patterns of thinking (cognitive) as well as relationships and other environmental factors (social).

self-efficacy Beliefs one has regarding how effective one will be in reaching a goal.

The Social-Cognitive Perspective on Personality

Social-cognitive theorists rejected behaviorists' exclusive focus on observable behavior. Acknowledging that personality may be shaped through learning, social-cognitive theorists such as Albert Bandura also emphasized the roles of cognitions and environmental influences on behavior. Bandura's theory of reciprocal determinism shows how cognition, behaviors, and the environment all interact to determine our personality.

"Good job!" ★★★ 🎓

- Child is praised for reading quietly.
- Child receives attention for effort in school.
- Child is rewarded for school achievement.

Behaviorists believe personality is the compilation of behaviors shaped through a lifetime of learning. A child who receives reinforcement for studying and effort in school will repeat this behavior, eventually exhibiting the personality characteristic "studious."

cognition

Thinking about behaviors and what they have led to in the past creates expectancies, predictions about what future outcomes will result from a behavior. When we recognize that past efforts to study usually resulted in good grades, we will expect that studying will lead to good grades in the future. Bandura calls this learned expectation of success *self-efficacy*.

> I succeed because I am a studious person.

> I will apply to college because I can succeed there.

> I get good grades when I study, so I will continue to do this.

> I am in college, so I know I can handle a busy schedule like other college students.

EXPECTANCIES INFLUENCE BEHAVIOR.

ENVIRONMENT INFLUENCES EXPECTANCIES.

EXPECTANCIES INFLUENCE THE ENVIRONMENT YOU SEEK OUT.

> When I study, I get good grades.

PRIOR EXPERIENCES CREATE EXPECTANCIES.

environment

> I'm a college student now, so I need to spend more time studying.

behavior

Reinforced behaviors become more consistent over time. When an instructor praises our participation in class, that reinforcement will lead us to participate again. We also learn by observing others' behaviors. If our classmates form a study group that helps them better understand the material, we may learn to adopt that technique.

ENVIRONMENT INFLUENCES BEHAVIOR.

BEHAVIOR INFLUENCES ENVIRONMENT.

The environment can include the college you choose, the major you select, the classes you enroll in, and also the culture where you are a student. For example, in Chinese classrooms, struggle is assumed to be part of the learning process. However, in Western classrooms, struggle is often seen as a sign of lower ability (Li, 2005; Schleppenbach, Flevares, Sims, & Perry, 2007). The culture you live in—your environment—can influence how you think about your own skills and behaviors, and how hard you work at something that is difficult for you.

> I study hard and am a successful student, so I've chosen to go to college.

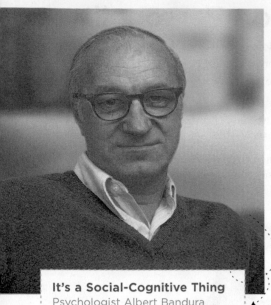

It's a Social-Cognitive Thing
Psychologist Albert Bandura asserts that personality is molded by a continual interaction between cognitions and social interactions, including observations of other people's behaviors. His approach is known as the *social-cognitive perspective*. Jon Brenneis/Life Magazine/ Time & Life Pictures

who exhibit high self-efficacy often achieve greater success at work because they are more likely to be flexible and open to new ideas (Bandura, 2006). A person who demonstrates low self-efficacy generally believes he will not succeed in a particular situation, regardless of his abilities or past experience. Beliefs about self-efficacy are influenced by experience and may change across situations. Generally speaking, people who believe they can change and progress are more likely to persevere in difficult situations.

Beliefs play a key role in our ability to make decisions, problem-solve, and deal with life's challenges. The environment also responds to our behaviors, which in turn are based in part on our beliefs. In essence, we have internal forces (beliefs, expectations) directing our behavior, external forces (reinforcers, punishments) responding to those behaviors, and the behaviors themselves influencing our beliefs and the environment. These three components form a complex system that determines our behavior patterns and personality (Infographic 11.2 on page 487). Bandura refers to this multidirectional interaction as **reciprocal determinism** (Bandura, 1978, 1986).

Let's use an example to see how reciprocal determinism works. A student harbors a certain belief about herself (*I am going to graduate with honors*). This belief influences her behavior (she studies hard and reaches out to instructors), which affects her environment (instructors take note of her enthusiasm and offer support). Thus, you can see, personality is the result of an ongoing interaction among cognitions, behaviors, and the environment. Bandura's reciprocal determinism resembles Rotter's view. Both suggest that personality is shaped by an ongoing interplay of cognitive expectancies, behaviors, and environment.

Taking Stock: An Appraisal of Learning and Social-Cognitive Theories

The learning and social-cognitive theorists were among the first to realize that we are not just products of our environments, but dynamic agents capable of altering the environment itself. Their focus on research and testable hypotheses is a clear advantage over the psychoanalytic and humanistic theories. Some critics argue that these approaches minimize the importance of unconscious processes and emotional influences (Schultz & Schultz, 2013; Westen, 1990), but overall, the inclusion of cognition and social factors offers valuable new ways to study and understand personality.

So far, our main focus has been understanding the origins of personality. In the next section, we direct our attention away from theories explaining personality and onto those describing it.

You Asked, Dr. Simmons Answers
http://qrs.ly/q83nr8f

How did you decide what personality traits and backstory Tank would have?

○ ✓ ○ ○   **show what you know**

1. According to _____, personality is the compilation of behaviors that have been shaped via reinforcement and conditioning.

2. Julian Rotter proposed that personality is influenced by _____, one's beliefs about where responsibility or control exists.
   a. reinforcement
   b. locus of control
   c. expectancy
   d. reinforcement value

3. Reciprocal determinism represents a complex multidirectional interaction among beliefs, behavior, and environment. Draw a diagram illustrating how reciprocal determinism explains one of your behavior patterns.

✓ CHECK YOUR ANSWERS IN APPENDIX C.

Trait Theories and Their Biological Basis ◄

A FEW WORDS ABOUT TANK   If you ask Dr. Reid Simmons to come up with some adjectives to describe Tank the Roboceptionist, he will offer words like "conscientious," "agreeable," "reserved," "naïve," "loyal," and "caring." All of these are examples of **traits,** the relatively stable properties of personality. The **trait theories** presented in this next section are different from theories discussed earlier in that they focus less on explaining why and how personality develops and more on describing personality and predicting behaviors.

Who's Who in Trait Theory

▶ **LO 11   Distinguish trait theories from other personality theories.**

ALLPORT AND PERSONALITY   One of the first trait theorists was Gordon Allport (1897–1967), who created a comprehensive list of traits to describe personality. One primary reason for developing this list was to operationalize the terminology used in personality research; when researchers study the same topic, they should agree on definitions. If two researchers are studying a trait called "vivacious," they will have an easier time comparing results if they use the same definition. Allport and his colleague carefully reviewed *Webster's New International Dictionary* (1925) and identified 17,953 words (out of approximately 400,000 entries in the dictionary) that they proposed were "descriptive of personality or personal behavior" (Allport & Odbert, 1936, p. 24). The list contained terms that were considered to be personal traits (such as "acrobatical" and "zealous"), temporary states (such as "woozy" and "thrilled"), social evaluations (such as "swine" and "outlandish"), and metaphorical and doubtful (such as "mortal" and "middle-aged"). Most relevant to personality were the personal traits, of which they identified 4,504—a little over 1% of all the entries in the dictionary. Surely, this long list could be condensed, reduced, or classified to make it more manageable. Enter Raymond Cattell.

CATTELL AND PERSONALITY   Raymond Cattell (1905–1998) proposed grouping the long list of personality traits into two major categories: surface traits and source traits (Cattell, 1950). **Surface traits** are the easily observable personality characteristics we commonly use to describe people: *She is quiet. He is friendly.* **Source traits** are the foundational qualities that give rise to surface traits. For example, "extraversion" is a source trait, and the surface traits it produces may include "warm," "gregarious," and "assertive." There are thousands of surface traits but only a few source traits. Cattell (1950) proposed that source traits are the product of both heredity and environment (nature and nurture), and surface traits are the "combined action of several source traits" (p. 34).

Cattell also condensed the list of surface traits into a much smaller set of 171. Realizing that some of these surface traits would be **correlated,** he used a statistical procedure known as *factor analysis* to group them into a smaller set of dimensions according to common underlying properties. With factor analysis, Cattell was able to produce a list of 16 personality factors.

These 16 factors, or personality dimensions, can be considered primary source traits. Looking at **FIGURE 11.2,** you can see that the ends of the dimensions represent polar extremes. On one end of the first dimension is the reserved and unsocial person; at the other end is the "social butterfly." Based on these factors, Cattell developed the Sixteen Personality Factor Questionnaire (16PF), which is described in greater detail later in the chapter, in the section on objective personality tests.

1.	Reserved ⟷	Outgoing
2.	Concrete thinker ⟷	Abstract thinker
3.	Affected by feelings ⟷	Emotionally stable
4.	Submissive ⟷	Dominant
5.	Serious ⟷	Happy-go-lucky
6.	Expedient ⟷	Conscientious
7.	Timid ⟷	Bold
8.	Tough-minded ⟷	Sensitive
9.	Trusting ⟷	Suspicious
10.	Practical ⟷	Imaginative
11.	Forthright ⟷	Shrewd
12.	Self-assured ⟷	Insecure
13.	Conservative ⟷	Experimenting
14.	Group-dependent ⟷	Self-sufficient
15.	Undisciplined ⟷	Controlled
16.	Relaxed ⟷	Tense

▲ **FIGURE 11.2**

Cattell's 16 Personality Factors
Using this list of 16 source traits, Raymond Cattell produced personality profiles by measuring where people fell between the two opposing ends of the dimension for each trait. *Sources:* Adapted from Cattell (1973b) and Cattell, Eber, and Tatsuoka (1970).

CONNECTIONS

In **Chapter 1,** we described a *correlation* as a relationship between two variables. Here, we describe *factor analysis,* which examines the relationships among an entire set of variables.

reciprocal determinism According to Bandura, multidirectional interactions among cognitions, behaviors, and the environment.

traits The relatively stable properties that describe elements of personality.

trait theories Theories that focus on personality dimensions and their influence on behavior; can be used to predict behaviors.

surface traits Easily observable characteristics that derive from source traits.

source traits Basic underlying or foundational characteristics of personality.

EYSENCK AND PERSONALITY   Hans Eysenck (1916–1997) continued to develop our understanding of source traits, proposing that we could describe personalities using three dimensions: introversion–extraversion (E), neuroticism (N), and psychoticism (P) (**FIGURE 11.3**).

FIGURE 11.3

Eysenck's Dimensions of Personality

Psychologist Hans Eysenck developed a model showing the range of human personality dimensions. This figure displays only the original dimensions Eysenck studied, but years later he proposed an additional dimension: psychoticism. People who score high on the psychoticism trait tend to be impersonal and antisocial.

Source: Eysenck and Eysenck (1968).

People high on the *extraversion* end of the introversion–extraversion (E) dimension tend to display a marked degree of sociability and are outgoing and active with others in their environment. Those on the *introversion* end of the dimension tend to be quiet and careful and enjoy time alone. Having high *neuroticism* (N) typically goes hand in hand with being restless, moody, and excitable, while low neuroticism means being calm, reliable, and emotionally stable. A person who is high on the *psychoticism* dimension is likely to be cold, impersonal, and antisocial, whereas someone at the opposite end of this dimension is warm, caring, and empathetic. (The psychoticism dimension is not related to psychosis, which is described in Chapter 13.)

In addition to identifying these dimensions, Eysenck worked diligently to unearth their biological basis. For example, Eysenck (1967) proposed a direct relationship between the behaviors associated with the introversion–extraversion dimension and the reticular formation. According to Eysenck (1967, 1990), introverted people display higher reactivity in their reticular formation than those who are extraverted. An introvert has higher levels of arousal, thus is more likely to react to stimuli, and therefore has developed a pattern of behavior to cope. He may be more careful or restrained, for example. An extravert has lower levels of arousal, and thus is less reactive to stimuli. Extraverts seek stimulation because their arousal levels are low, so they tend to be more impulsive and outgoing.

The trait theories of Allport, Cattell, and Eysenck paved the way for the trait theories commonly used today. Let's take a look at one of the most popular models.

> **LO 12**   Identify the biological roots of the five-factor model of personality.

FIGURE 11.4

The Five-Factor Model of Personality

The mnemonic OCEAN will help you remember these factors. *Source:* Adapted from McCrae and Costa (1990).

THE BIG FIVE   The **five-factor model of personality,** also known as the Big Five, is a current trait approach for explaining personality (McCrae & Costa, 1987). This model, developed using factor analysis, indicates there are five factors, or dimensions, to describe personality. Although 100% agreement does not exist on the names of these factors, in general, trait theorists propose they are openness to experience, conscientiousness, extraversion, agreeableness, and neuroticism (McCrae, Scally, Terracciano, Abecasis, & Costa, 2010). Openness is the degree to which someone is willing to try new experiences. Conscientiousness refers to someone's attention to detail and organizational tendencies. The extraversion and neuroticism dimensions are similar to Eysenck's dimensions noted earlier: Extraversion refers to degree of sociability and outgoingness; neuroticism, to emotional stability (degree to which a person is calm, secure, and even tempered). Agreeableness indicates how trusting and easygoing a person is. To remember these factors, students sometimes use the mnemonic OCEAN: Openness, Conscientiousness, Extraversion, Agreeableness, and Neuroticism (**FIGURE 11.4**).

Empirical support for this model has been established using cross-cultural testing. People in more than 50 cultures, who speak languages as diverse as German, Spanish, and Czech, have been shown to exhibit these five dimensions (McCrae et al., 2000, 2005, 2010). Even the everyday terms used to describe personality characteristics across continents (North America, Europe, and Asia) fit well with the five-factor model (McCrae et al., 2010).

One possible explanation is that these five dimensions are biologically based and universal to humans (Allik & McCrae, 2004; McCrae et al., 2000). Three decades of **twin and adoption** studies point to a genetic basis of these five factors (McCrae et al., 2000; Yamagata et al., 2006), with openness to experience showing the greatest degree of heritability (McCrae et al., 2000; TABLE 11.4). Some researchers suggest that dog personalities also can be described using similar dimensions, such as extraversion and neuroticism (Ley, Bennett, & Coleman, 2008). And such research is not limited to canines; animals as diverse as squid and orangutans seem to display personality characteristics that are surprisingly similar to those observed in humans (Sinn & Moltschaniwskyj, 2005; Weiss, King, & Perkins, 2006).

More evidence for the biological basis of these five factors is apparent from their general stability over time (Kandler et al., 2010; McCrae et al., 2000). This implies that the dramatic environmental changes most of us experience in life do not have as great an impact as our inherited characteristics. That does not mean personalities are completely static, however; people can experience changes in these five factors over the life span (Specht, Egloff, & Schmukle, 2011). For example, as people age, they tend to score higher on agreeableness and lower on neuroticism, openness, extraversion, and conscientiousness. They also seem to become happier and more easygoing with age, displaying more positive attitudes (Marsh, Nagengast, & Morin, 2013). Yet, a study of forager-farmers in Bolivia indicated that this model of personality was not a good fit for a predominantly illiterate and indigenous "small-scale society" (Gurven, von Rueden, Massenkoff, Kaplan, & Lero Vie, 2013).

CONNECTIONS

In **Chapter 7**, we described the Minnesota twin studies, which showed that genes play a role in intellectual abilities. Identical twins share 100% of their genes, fraternal twins share about 50% of their genes, and adopted siblings are genetically very different. Comparing personality traits among these siblings can show the relative importance of genes (nature) and the environment (nurture).

Table 11.4 HERITABILITY OF THE BIG FIVE TRAITS

Big Five Personality Dimensions	Heritability
Openness	.61
Conscientiousness	.44
Extraversion	.53
Neuroticism	.41
Agreeableness	.41

Heritability is the degree to which heredity is responsible for a particular characteristic. Here, we can see the percent of variation in the Big Five traits attributed to genetic make-up, leaving the remainder to be attributed to environmental influences.

SOURCE: JANG, LIVESLEY, AND VERNON (1996).

"Big," But Not Universal
The five-factor model of personality is useful for the vast majority of people in today's world, but it does not apply to everyone. The Big Five did not find strong support in a recent study of Bolivia's indigenous Tsimane people, (Gurven, von Rueden, Massenkoff, Kaplan, & Lero Vie, 2013). Angel Franco/The New York Times/Redux

Men and women appear to differ with respect to the five factors, although there is not total agreement on how. Schmitt and colleagues reviewed studies from 55 nations and reported that, across cultures, women score higher than men on conscientiousness, extraversion, agreeableness, and neuroticism (Schmitt, Realo, Voracek, &

five-factor model of personality
A trait approach to explaining personality, including dimensions of openness to experience, conscientiousness, extraversion, agreeableness, and neuroticism; also known as "the Big Five."

CONNECTIONS

In **Chapter 10,** we presented the *gender similarities hypothesis,* which states that, overall, the variation within a gender is greater than the variation between genders. Here we see how this applies to the five factors of personality.

Allik, 2008). Men, on the other hand, seem to demonstrate greater degrees of openness to experience. These **disparities are not extreme,** however; the variation within the groups of males and females is greater than the differences between males and females. Critics suggest that using such rough measures of personality may conceal some of the true differences between men and women; in order to shed light on such disparities, they suggest investigating models that incorporate 10 to 20 traits rather than just 5 (Del Guidice, Booth, & Irwing, 2012).

Maybe you could have predicted women would score higher on measures of agreeableness and neuroticism; perhaps you would have guessed the opposite. Research suggests that some gender stereotypes do indeed contain a kernel of truth (Costa, Terracciano, & McCrae 2001; Terracciano et al., 2005). Let's find out if this principle holds true for cultural stereotypes as well.

across the WORLD

Culture of Personality

Have you heard the old joke about European stereotypes? It goes something like this: In heaven, the chefs are French, the mechanics German, the lovers Italian, the police officers British, and the bankers Swiss (Mulvey, 2006, May 15). This joke plays upon what psychologists might call "national stereotypes," or preconceived notions about the personalities of people belonging to certain cultures. The joke assumes, for example, that Italian people have some underlying quality that makes them excel in romance but not money management. Are such national stereotypes accurate?

To get to the bottom of this question, Terracciano and colleagues (2005) used personality tests to assess the Big Five traits of nearly 4,000 people from 49 cultures. When they compared the results of the personality tests to national stereotypes, they found no evidence that the stereotypes mirrored reality. Not only are these stereotypes invalid, but as history demonstrates, they can pave the way for "prejudice, discrimination, or persecution" (p. 99).

PLEASE LEAVE YOUR STEREOTYPES AT THE BORDER!

Better with Age

Japanese calligrapher Kawamata-sensei paints a giant character that will go on display at a betting theatre for bike racing. Creativity is associated with the personality trait of openness, which has been linked to longevity.

James Whitlow
Delano/Redux

Taking Stock: An Appraisal of the Trait Theories

As you can see from the examples above, trait theories have facilitated important psychological research. But like any scientific approach, they have their flaws. One major criticism is that trait theories fail to explain the origins of personality. What aspects of personality are innate, and which are environmental? How do unconscious processes, motivations, and development influence personality? If you're looking to answer these types of questions, trait theories might not be your best bet.

Trait theories also tend to underestimate environmental influences on personality. As Walter Mischel pointed out, environmental circumstances can affect the way traits manifest themselves (Mischel & Shoda, 1995). A person who is high on the openness factor may be nonconforming in college, wearing unique clothing and pursuing unusual hobbies, but put her in the military and her nonconformity will probably assume a new form.

We are about to wrap up our discussion of the trait theories and move on to the intriguing topic of personality testing. Before we do so, though, let's look at one final example illustrating the value of trait theories. Which of the Big Five would you guess is linked to longevity?

from the pages of SCIENTIFIC AMERICAN

Open Mind, Longer Life

The trait of openness improves health through creativity

Researchers have long been studying the connection between health and the five major personality traits: agreeableness, extraversion, neuroticism, openness and conscientiousness. A large body of research links neuroticism with poorer health and conscientiousness with superior health. Now openness, which measures cognitive flexibility and the willingness to entertain novel ideas, has emerged as a lifelong protective factor. The linchpin seems to be the creativity associated with the personality trait—creative thinking reduces stress and keeps the brain healthy.

A study published in the June issue of the *Journal of Aging and Health* found that higher openness predicted longer life, and other studies this year have linked that trait with lower metabolic risk, higher self-rated health, and more appropriate stress response.

The June study sought to determine whether specific aspects of openness better predicted survival rates than overall openness, using data on more than 1,000 older men collected between 1990 and 2008. The researchers found that only creativity—not intelligence or overall openness—decreased mortality risk. One possible reason creativity is protective of health is because it draws on a variety of neural networks within the brain, says study author Nicholas Turiano, now at the University of Rochester Medical Center.

"Individuals high in creativity maintain the integrity of their neural networks even into old age," Turiano says—a notion supported by a January study from Yale University that correlated openness with the robustness of study subjects' white matter, which supports connections between neurons in different parts of the brain.

Because the brain is the command center for all bodily functions, exercising it helps all systems to continue running smoothly. "Keeping the brain healthy may be one of the most important aspects of aging successfully—a fact shown by creative persons living longer in our study," Turiano says.

He also cites creative people's ability to handle stress—they tend not to get as easily flustered when faced with an emotional or physical hurdle. Stress is known to harm overall health, including cardiovascular, immune and cognitive systems. "Creative people may see stressors more as challenges that they can work to overcome rather than as stressful obstacles they can't overcome," Turiano says. Although studies thus far have looked at those who are naturally open-minded, the results suggest that practicing creative-thinking techniques could improve anyone's health by lowering stress and exercising the brain. **Tori Rodriguez . Reproduced with permission. Copyright © 2012 Scientific American, a division of Nature America, Inc. All rights reserved.**

☑○○○   show what you know

1. The relatively stable properties that describe elements of personality are:
   a. traits.
   b. expectancies.
   c. reinforcement values.
   d. ego defense mechanisms.

2. The traits we easily observe and quickly describe based on someone's behavior or characteristics are called _____.

3. Name the Big Five traits and give one piece of evidence for their biological basis.

✓ CHECK YOUR ANSWERS IN APPENDIX C.

Personality Assessment

A LIFETIME OF MISHAPS The life of Tank the Roboceptionist has been marked by a series of disappointments. After failing to live up to his father's expectations of becoming NASA's next great telescope, Tank had a disastrous career in military reconnaissance. The CIA deployed him to a war zone to fight terrorists, but the hapless robot could not distinguish between comrade and enemy. Exasperated with Tank's bungling performance, American soldiers were ready to recycle his metal parts. The disgraced robot was promptly returned to the United States (Carnegie Mellon University, 2013).

How do you think a string of such disasters might have shaped Tank's personality? If only we could understand how his life experiences have influenced his levels of neuroticism, openness, and agreeableness. Wouldn't it be fascinating to see how this blue-headed robot performs on a personality test? But alas, Tank is not a person, and thus he is not a viable candidate for personality assessment.

Is It Legit? Reliability and Validity

> **LO 13** Explain why reliability and validity are important in personality assessment.

Before we discuss the various types of personality tests, let's get a handle on the qualities that render these tests effective—reliability and validity. **Reliability** can refer to two aspects of an assessment. *Test–retest reliability* is how consistent results are when the same person takes the test more than once. Suppose you take the same personality test today and tomorrow. From one day to the next, your personality is unlikely to change, so your results shouldn't either. With a reliable test, the scores should be very similar at different points in time. *Interrater reliability* refers to the consistency across people scoring an assessment. With high interrater reliability, the results are the same regardless of who scores the test.

The other important quality of a personality assessment is validity. A valid measure is one that can be shown to measure what it intends to measure. Let's say a psychologist develops an assessment for extraversion. In order for her test to be considered valid, it must yield results that are similar to already established and valid assessments of extraversion.

Assessment of personality can be broadly classified into objective and subjective measures. Findings from subjective assessments are based, in part, on personal intuition, opinions, or interpretations. With objective assessments, findings are based on a standardized procedure in which the scoring is free of opinions, personal beliefs, expectations, and values. Critics of subjective assessments suggest that there is not enough consistency across findings, as a result of nonstandard scoring procedures. And as noted in earlier chapters, humans are prone to a **variety of biases** and cognitive errors that can interfere with our ability to make useful assessments of people and situations. Critics of objective assessments challenge the standardized nature of objective testing because it does not allow for flexibility or fully appreciate individual differences in experiences. Despite these alleged flaws, many psychologists use a mixture of objective and subjective assessment techniques with their clients.

Not everyone agrees about the effectiveness of personality assessment. Even so, they are used in many contexts and in ways that have profound implications. Psychologists use personality tests to get to know their clients and diagnose mental

CONNECTIONS

In **Chapter 7,** we discussed ways to determine the reliability of intelligence tests. In addition to test–retest reliability, we can split a test in half to see if the findings of the two halves agree. This type of reliability can be determined with personality assessment as well.

CONNECTIONS

In **Chapter 1,** we noted that people are prone to the *hindsight bias,* the feeling that "I knew it all along." Researchers, in particular, can introduce *observer bias* into the recording of observations. When choosing a personality assessment, it is important to be alert to the biases that can interfere with objective data collection.

disorders. Companies use them to make decisions about new hires and promotions (*Does this person have what it takes to be a manager?*). Personality tests are part of the battery of assessments used to evaluate the functioning of parents embroiled in custody disputes: *Is mom depressed? Can she care for this child?* (Lilienfeld, Wood, & Garb, 2005).

In this next section, we will explore the major types of personality tests that psychologists employ: interviews, projective personality tests, and objective personality tests. Many of these are aligned with specific perspectives (psychoanalytic or behavioral, for example) but most psychologists use an integrative approach, drawing on multiple perspectives in their assessment of clients.

What Brings You Here Today?

One way to gather information about personality is through a face-to-face interview. In an unstructured, or open-ended, interview, there is no predetermined path. A psychologist might begin with a question like, "What brings you here today?" and then gently direct the conversation in a way that helps her understand her client's strengths and weaknesses, hopes and plans. Semistructured and structured **interviews**, on the other hand, employ specific paths of questioning that hinge on the respondent's answers. This format provides a more systematic means of comparing behaviors across individuals.

One great advantage of the interview is that it allows a psychologist to see a client in a relatively natural, realistic setting. Talking with a client face-to-face, a psychologist can observe facial expressions and body language, which may offer clues to what's going on inside. There are drawbacks, however. Interview subjects may lie to the interviewer (without even realizing it), spin the facts to misrepresent themselves, or share memories that are distorted or incomplete. Another source of error is the interviewer. She may, for example, lead the interview in a particular direction or interpret responses in a way that reinforces her own beliefs about personality. Clients can also be influenced by the interviewers' nonverbal language. The desire to answer "correctly" is strong in an interview format. Just as in surveys, the way a question is asked can have a profound influence on the answer.

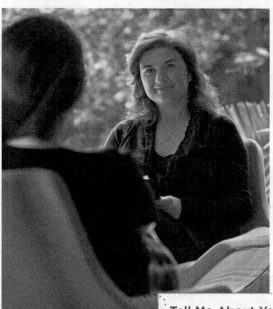

Tell Me About Yourself
Psychologists assess personality using a variety of tools, including personal interviews. These face-to-face sessions range from open-ended and exploratory to highly structured.
Niko Guido/Getty Images

CONNECTIONS

An important factor to consider in the interview procedure is the *malleability* of memory, which we discussed in **Chapter 6.** The interviewer should avoid posing questions that might lead to the *misinformation effect,* which is the tendency for new or misleading information to distort memories.

What Do *You* See? Projective Personality Tests

> **LO 14** Define projective tests and evaluate their strengths and limitations.

It's a hot summer's day and you're lying on the beach, gazing at the clouds. "What do you see?" you ask your friend. "I see the profile of a Doberman pinscher," she replies. "That's funny," you say. "I see a child doing jumping jacks."

How is it possible that two people can look at the same image and come away with such different impressions? Some would argue that it has a lot to do with personality. The idea that personality influences perception is the premise of **projective personality tests,** which psychologists use to explore characteristics that might not be accessible through interview or observation, as they attempt to access aspects of the unconscious (**INFOGRAPHIC 11.3** on page 496). With this type of assessment, the test taker is shown a stimulus without a specified meaning and then prompted to *project* meaning onto it. Projective personality tests assume that people carry around anxiety and unresolved conflicts, often beneath conscious awareness. Because these tests attempt to uncover such issues indirectly, they are less threatening than other methods, and therefore provoke less resistance. The goal of the test administrator is

projective personality tests Assessments that present stimuli without a specified meaning to test takers, whose responses can then be interpreted to uncover underlying personality characteristics.

Examining the Unconscious: Projective Personality Tests

The psychoanalytic perspective holds that some aspects of personality exist beneath conscious awareness. Projective personality tests seek to uncover these characteristics. Ideas and anxieties in the unconscious will appear in descriptions of ambiguous stimuli, revealing previously hidden conflicts that the test administrator can evaluate.

◄ Test administration ►

The best-known projective tests, the Thematic Apperception Test (TAT) and the Rorschach Inkblot Test, are both conducted in the same way (Lilienfeld, Wood, & Garb, 2005): The test administrator presents a series of picture cards, one at a time, then records the participant's responses. The administrator also notes behaviors such as gestures, tone of voice, and facial expressions.

The standard administration of the TAT presents a selection of 5 to 12 cards. The participant is asked to tell a story for each scene, including what the characters are feeling and how the story might end.

The Rorschach has 10 cards with symmetrical inkblots, 5 in color and 5 in black-and-white. The participant is prompted to give multiple responses for each image, identifying details.

Test Interpretation

To help decrease the influence of administrator bias in interpretation of projective tests, comprehensive systems have been developed to standardize scoring and interpretation of some tests. For the Rorschach Inkblot Test, responses are coded on dimensions such as location (whole inkblot or one detail), themes (unique or consistent), and thought processes (Erdberg, 1990). The use of a comprehensive system allows administrators to compare typical and atypical responses.

PARTICIPANT RESPONSES

"Looks like two people."

"The people are fighting over something."

"Or they're carrying something heavy together."

"Maybe it's one person looking in a mirror."

"I also see a butterfly."

These sample responses are representative for this inkblot. Most participants interpret this Rorschach inkblot as two figures (Burstein & Loucks, 1989).

EXAMINER RESPONSES

Participant mentions the typical response of two figures.

Suggestion that the people are fighting could indicate issues with aggression or an aggressive personality.

Focus on individuals working together could represent a need for social connection.

However, seeing one person alone could indicate social anxiety, too.

Now participant switches to a specific part of the image, which could also show that he is uncomfortable thinking about others, perhaps related to introversion.

to take the manifest content (what the person reports seeing) and try to understand its underlying meaning.

THE RORSCHACH INKBLOTS   The most well-known projective personality test is the Rorschach. The original version of the test was developed by Swiss psychiatrist Hermann Rorschach in 1921. Today's psychologists typically use Rorschach inkblots with the comprehensive coding system introduced by John Exner in the 1970s (Exner, 1980, 1986).

Here is a rough description of how the test is administered: Imagine someone hands you a series of cards covered in odd-looking blotches of ink—five cards with black-and-white blotches, and another five with color. Presenting the cards one by one, he asks you to report what you see. The images you describe and the details on which you focus will be important factors in the assessment of your personality, which involves a systematic comparison with answers given by other test takers who have known personality characteristics and diagnoses. Do you see bears playing patty cake? Seeing animals in motion might be interpreted as a sign of rashness. Are you homing in on the black areas? This could suggest a feeling of melancholy or sadness (Lilienfeld et al., 2005).

THE THEMATIC APPERCEPTION TEST (TAT)   In the mid-1930s, Henry Murray and his colleagues developed the Thematic Apperception Test (TAT), a projective test that consists of 20 cards containing black-and-white illustrations of ambiguous scenes. When shown a card, the test taker is asked to tell a story about it. The story might incorporate a description of the people in the scene, and should include what led up to the scene, the emotions and thoughts of the characters, and the conclusion of the story. The assumption is that the test taker will project underlying conflicts onto the ambiguous stimuli of the picture; the job of the test administrator is to unearth them.

Taking Stock: An Appraisal of Projective Personality Tests

One criticism of projective personality tests is that they can take too much time. However, because the test taker may be willing to speak openly, honestly, and freely due to the unstructured nature of the assessment, the benefits seem to outweigh the costs. Another major concern, mentioned earlier, is the subjectivity of interpreting the results, which can lead to problems with their reliability. Different test administrators might not arrive at similar scores, or when the assessment is given a second time to the same person, the results might be different. Even the comprehensive scoring system for the Rorschach inkblots has not resolved concerns about projective tests, because the issue of validity still remains. Many critics suggest projective tests are not valid because they do not measure what they claim to be measuring (Schultz & Schultz, 2013).

Nonetheless, projective tests are used by clinicians because they often provide a way to begin forming a picture of a client. Clinicians can use a multifaceted approach to understanding personality, administering projective tests in conjunction with interviews, observations, and objective assessments.

What tools do you use to get a feel for someone's personality? Maybe you pay close attention to how they behave in social situations, or observe the ways they respond to stress. Do you ever try to size up someone's personality by looking at his Facebook page? Believe it or not, this strategy may actually be effective. In some cases, personality characteristics projected through social media bear close resemblance to who people are in real life.

"But... your Facebook profile says you're a vegetarian!"

SOCIAL MEDIA and psychology

It's Written All Over Your Facebook

Facebook profiles reveal a great deal about the personalities of their owners. In one study, researchers assessed the offline personalities of American Facebook users and German StudiVZ users (StudiVZ is a popular European network), and then compared those results with the impressions of people checking out their profiles. Their readings of the profiles turned out to be quite accurate, particularly when it came to the traits of extraversion and openness (Back et al., 2010).

This tendency for Facebook to betray one's true personality may not be a good thing if you happen to be narcissistic. Narcissism is a personality trait often equated with vanity, self-absorption, and feelings of superiority and entitlement. Strangers can easily pick out real-life narcissists by viewing their Facebook profiles (Buffardi & Campbell, 2008), and there is no reason to believe that other characteristics wouldn't be detectable as well.

You may be wondering what aspect of online information strangers rely on to make inferences about your offline personality. A group of researchers from Tufts University wondered the same thing. The results of their study suggest that profile photos are most important, while favorite quotes and interests come in second (Ivcevic & Ambady, 2012). Our advice to you based on these findings? Better make sure you have a decent and representative profile photo!

FACEBOOK PROFILES REVEAL A GREAT DEAL ABOUT . . . THEIR OWNERS.

Objective Personality Tests

LO 15 Describe objective personality tests and evaluate their strengths and limitations.

Earlier we mentioned that clinicians use a variety of tools to assess the personalities of their clients. Among those tools are *objective personality tests,* assessments made up of a standard set of questions with previously established answers (true/false, multiple choice, circle the number). These tests are called *objective* because the results are assessed in a standardized way, free of personal bias. In contrast to the projective inventories, which often seem to be overly subjective, objective personality tests have clear scoring instructions that are identical for anyone taking the test. Often scores are calculated by a computer. In addition to being convenient and unbiased, objective tests have a solid base of evidence supporting their reliability and validity (Anastasi & Urbina, 1997). Some of these tests may focus on a particular personality characteristic or trait (such as locus of control); others might assess a group of characteristics (such as the Big Five).

THE MMPI-2 The most commonly used objective personality test is the Minnesota Multiphasic Personality Inventory (MMPI–2) (Butcher & Rouse, 1996). This self-report questionnaire includes more than 567 statements to which the individual responds "true," "false," or "cannot say." Some of the items you might see on the MMPI–2 include statements such as "I often wake up rested and ready to go" or "I want to work as a teacher." Since the original purpose of the MMPI was to identify disorders and abnormal behavior, it includes 10 clinical scales (such as hypochondriasis and depression). It also has validity scales (such as the Lie scale and the Defensiveness scale) to assess the degree to which the results are useful. The validity measures help ensure that the person taking the assessment is not trying to appear either more disturbed or more healthy than she actually is. Often the MMPI is used to inform decisions about custody or other legal issues, and in a variety of nonclinical settings. So, it is important to control for manipulation of the assessment by the test taker. Like other personality assessments, the MMPI has its share of criticisms. Since it was designed to help make diagnoses, many feel its application outside of therapeutic settings is inappropriate. The scales are based on groups exhibiting abnormalities, and therefore they may not translate to nonclinical populations.

16PF   Another objective assessment of personality is the Sixteen Personality Factor Questionnaire (16PF), originally created by Raymond Cattell and based on his trait theory of personality. With the 16PF, the test taker must select one of three choices (forced choices) in response to 185 questions. Ultimately, a profile is constructed, which indicates where the person falls along the continuum of each of the 16 dimensions. Take a look at **FIGURE 11.5** and you can see how pilots and writers compare on the 16 factors. For example, airline pilots tend to fall on the tough-minded end of the continuum, whereas writers tend to be located on the sensitive, tender-minded end (Cattell, 1973a).

MYERS–BRIGGS   One *very* popular objective assessment of personality is the Myers–Briggs Type Indicator (MBTI) (Briggs & Myers, 1998). Katherine Briggs and her daughter Isabel Briggs-Myers created this assessment in the 1940s. It designates a personality "type" as it relates to the following four dimensions: extraversion (E) versus introversion (I); sensing (S) versus intuiting (N); thinking (T) versus feeling (F); and judgment (J) versus perception (P). For example, someone characterized as ISTP would be introspective, rely on the senses (rather than intuition) to understand the environment, and favor logic over emotion.

Problems arise when assessments incorporate somewhat vague descriptions of personality traits. Some would even liken this to the Barnum effect, which was named after P. T. Barnum, who was famous for his ability to convince people he could read minds. Essentially, he did this by making generally complimentary and vague statements that could be true about anyone (*You are creative and work well with others and you sometimes procrastinate, but ultimately you get the job done*). Similarly, with the MBTI, the personality type descriptions are "general flattering and sufficiently vague so that most people will accept the statements as true of themselves" (Pittenger 1993, p. 6). Although the MBTI is very popular, the research support for this objective assessment is weak, especially as it relates to job performance, career choices, and so forth (Pittenger, 2005). Because the test results don't always correlate with job success, this puts into question the validity of the assessment. In addition, the test–retest reliability is not always strong. A person can take the test twice and end up with different results (Hunsley, Lee, & Wood, 2003; Pittenger, 2005).

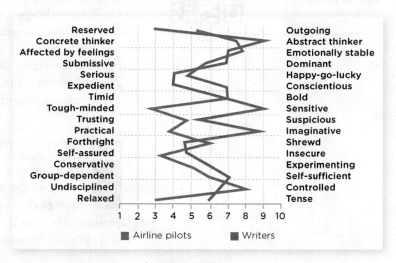

▲ **FIGURE 11.5**
Example Profiles Generated by the 16PF
On Cattell's 16PF, writers appear to be more reserved, sensitive, and imaginative than airline pilots. Pilots, on the other hand, tend to fall on the tough-minded end of the continuum. Are you surprised that they also appear to be more relaxed?
Source: Cattell (1973b).

Taking Stock: An Appraisal of Objective Personality Tests

We have noted specific criticisms of the MMPI and Myers–Briggs tests, but there are other serious drawbacks of objective assessments. Although many of the objective tests include some sort of mechanism for checking the validity of the test taker's answers, people may lie (and get away with it), particularly when the assessment results may impact some important aspect of their lives, such as work or custody cases. In addition, social desirability can influence the results. In other words, individuals may unintentionally answer questions in a way that makes them "look better" or be viewed in a more favorable light by others.

Technology and Personality Assessment

Is there any way to be 100% sure of the findings of personality assessments? Not yet, but psychologists are developing new measures that take advantage of technology, bypassing self-report as much as possible. For example, scanning technology has been used to identify particular areas of the brain associated with personality expression. Canli and colleagues were interested in teasing apart the relationship between personality and mood states. Using fMRI, they found that activity in the anterior cingulate sometimes was associated with extraversion, possibly identifying an area of the brain involved in extraversion and introversion (Canli, Amin, Haas, Omura, & Constable, 2004). Perhaps future technologies will enable more precise assessment of personality characteristics (Eisenberger, Lieberman, & Satpute, 2005).

FINAL THOUGHTS You may be wondering why we chose to feature Tank the robot in a chapter on personality. We can give robots characteristics and traits; we can even endow them with the capacity to "learn" and interact with their environments. But try as we may, we cannot provide them with genuine personalities. Our inclusion of Tank is a deliberate attempt to illustrate the complex and uniquely human nature of personality.

show what you know

1. _____ personality tests present ambiguous test stimuli to the test taker, so the tester can interpret and uncover underlying personality characteristics based on that participant's responses.
   a. Objective
   b. Projective
   c. 16PF
   d. Myers–Briggs

2. Objective personality tests are made up of a set of standardized questions with previously established answers (for instance, true/false or multiple choice), and are assessed free of:
   a. intuition or bias.
   b. reliability.
   c. validity.
   d. objectivity.

3. A psychologist gives a client several personality tests to help her choose a career path. What might the consequences be if the tests are not valid? What if they are not reliable?

✓ CHECK YOUR ANSWERS IN APPENDIX C.

(11) summary of concepts

SA

LO 1 Define personality. (p. 467)

Personality refers to the unique, core set of characteristics that influence the way one thinks, acts, and feels—characteristics many psychologists would agree are consistent and enduring throughout the life span. Personality differs from persona in that persona refers to a role, not human personality.

LO 2 Distinguish how the perspectives of psychology explain personality development. (p. 468)

The psychoanalytic perspective suggests that personality development is heavily influenced by processes of which we are unaware, how they are expressed, and the way caregiv-ers respond. The behavioral perspective describes and explains how the environment shapes personality, and specifically, how reinforcers influence behaviors. The humanistic perspective suggests that we have capabilities we can and should take advantage of as we strive for personal growth, and the choices we make in life influence our personalities. The social-cognitive perspective focuses on relationships, environmental influences, cognitive activity, and individual behavior as they come together to form personality. The biological perspective suggests physiological and genetic factors for some components of personality development. Trait theories look at current dimensions of the individual to describe and predict personality.

LO 3 Illustrate Freud's models for describing the mind. (p. 470)

Psychoanalysis refers to Freud's views regarding personality as well as his system of psychotherapy and tools for the exploration of the unconscious. According to his topographical model, our personalities and behaviors result from mental processes that occur at three levels: the conscious, preconscious, and unconscious. The structural model of the mind describes the functions of the components of the mind. The id is the most primitive component of personality. The activities in the id occur at the unconscious level. The ego develops as the infant grows; the ego finds ways to manipulate situations, plan for the future, solve problems, and make decisions in order to satisfy the needs of the id. The superego develops last and is the part of our personality that guides our behavior to follow the rules of society, parents, or other authority figures.

LO 4 Summarize Freud's use of psychosexual stages to explain personality. (p. 475)

The developmental model helps explain personality and sexuality in terms of a standard developmental path through what Freud called the psychosexual stages. He believed all children must go through these stages as they mature into adulthood. Associated with each stage is an erogenous zone as well as a conflict that must be dealt with. If the conflict is not successfully resolved, the child may suffer from a fixation and get "stuck" in that particular stage, not able to progress smoothly through the remaining stages. The stages include the oral stage, anal stage, phallic stage, latency period, and genital stage.

LO 5 Explain how the neo-Freudians' theories of personality differ from Freud's. (p. 479)

Some of Freud's followers branched out on their own due to disagreements about certain issues, such as his focus on the instincts of sex and aggression, his idea that personality is determined by the end of childhood, and his somewhat negative view of human nature. Adler proposed that humans are conscious and intentional in their behaviors. Jung suggested that we are driven by a psychological energy (as opposed to sexual energy), which encourages positive growth, self-understanding, and balance. Horney emphasized the role of relationships between children and their caregivers, not erogenous zones and psychosexual stages.

LO 6 Describe how Maslow's hierarchy of needs relates to personality. (p. 482)

Maslow proposed a hierarchy of needs, which represents a continuum of drives that are universal and ordered in terms of their strength. He suggested that although we respond to these needs in a similar order, we have the ability to make choices in our lives to be proactive, striving to reach our fullest potential.

LO 7 Discuss Rogers' view of self-concept, ideal self, and unconditional positive regard. (p. 482)

Rogers proposed that the development of personality is highly influenced by the role of caregivers in the life of a child. He suggested there is an innate urge in humans to move toward and be attracted to situations and people that will help us grow, and to avoid those that have the potential to stop our growth. Self-concept is one's knowledge of one's strengths, abilities, behavior patterns, and temperament. Rogers believed that individuals develop an ideal self, which refers to the self-concept we strive for and fervently wish to achieve. Ideally, caregivers should show unconditional positive regard, which is the total acceptance of a child regardless of behavior. People need to feel totally accepted and valued for who they are, not what they do.

LO 8 Use learning theories to explain personality development. (p. 485)

According to learning theory, personality is a compilation or collection of behaviors, all of which have been shaped through a lifetime of reinforcement and conditioning. Some behaviorists use learning principles to explain personality, including classical conditioning, operant conditioning, and observational learning.

LO 9 Summarize Rotter's view of personality. (p. 486)

Rotter suggested that not all aspects of behavior and personality can be directly observed. He believed a key component of personality is locus of control, which is a pattern of beliefs regarding where responsibility or control for an outcome exists. Rotter explored how these beliefs can influence behavior. Expectancy is a person's predictions about what a behavior will lead to in terms of consequences or outcomes.

LO 10 Discuss how Bandura uses the social-cognitive perspective to explain personality. (p. 486)

Bandura rejected the notion that psychologists should only focus on observable behavior; he realized behavior is determined by cognitions as well as reinforcers and other environmental influences. He used this social-cognitive perspective to explain personality. Personality results from patterns of thinking (cognitive) in addition to our relationships and other environmental factors (social). Reciprocal determinism refers to the multidirectional interaction among beliefs, behaviors, and the environment.

LO 11 Distinguish trait theories from other personality theories. (p. 489)

Traits are the relatively stable properties of an individual that describe elements of personality. The trait theories are different from other personality theories in that they focus less on explaining why and how personality develops, and more on describing personality and predicting behaviors. Allport created a comprehensive list of traits to help operationalize the terminology used in personality research. Cattell grouped the traits into two categories: surface traits and source traits. He used factor analysis to group surface traits in 16 personality factors and developed the Sixteen Personality Factor Questionnaire (16PF) to measure them. Eysenck proposed that we could describe personalities using three dimensions: introversion–extraversion, neuroticism, and psychoticism. He also worked to understand the biological basis of these dimensions.

LO 12 Identify the biological roots of the five-factor model of personality. (p. 490)

The five-factor model of personality, also known as the Big Five, is another trait approach to explaining personality, which includes the following factors: extraversion, neuroticism, agreeableness, conscientiousness, and openness to experience. Researchers have conducted studies across the world and found similar results regarding the genetic basis of the five-factor model using twin and adoption studies. These characteristics have proven stable over time, suggesting the changing environments that most individuals experience across life do not have as great an impact on personality as inherited characteristics.

LO 13 Explain why reliability and validity are important in personality assessment. (p. 494)

Reliability generally refers to two aspects of a personality assessment: test–retest reliability and interrater reliability. Test-retest reliability is consistency of results when the same person takes a test more than once. Interrater reliability refers to the consistency across people scoring an assessment. Validity refers to the degree to which an assessment measures what it is intended to measure. A valid test must yield results similar to established assessments. We need to ensure that the results from assessments are consistent and dependable. Both reliability and validity are important in the assessment of personality because they help render the assessments effective.

LO 14 Define projective tests and evaluate their strengths and limitations. (p. 495)

Personality influences perceptions. With projective personality tests, a test taker is shown a stimulus that has no specified meaning and then prompted to respond, thus projecting meaning onto it. Testers interpret and uncover underlying personality characteristics from these responses—characteristics that might not be accessible through interview or observation. One strength of this type of assessment is its unstructured nature, which makes it less threatening to test takers, therefore provoking less resistance. Limitations include the amount of time needed to administer the assessment as well as the subjective nature of its interpretation, which can lead to problems with the reliability of the test. Some of the best-known projective tests are the Rorschach Inkblot Test and the Thematic Apperception Test (TAT).

LO 15 Describe objective personality tests and evaluate their strengths and limitations. (p. 498)

Objective personality tests are made up of a standard set of questions with previously established answers (true/false, multiple choice, circle the number). One strength of this type of personality test is that it is scored in a standardized way, free of any personal intuition or bias. Limitations of this type of assessment include the potential for dishonesty on the part of test takers as well as the tendency for individuals to unintentionally answer questions in a way that makes them "look better" or be viewed in a more favorable light by others (social desirability). Two commonly used objective personality tests are the Minnesota Multiphasic Personality Inventory (MMPI–2) and the Sixteen Personality Factor Questionnaire (16PF).

key terms

archetypes, p. 481

collective unconsciousness, p. 481

ego, p. 472

ego defense mechanisms, p. 473

expectancy, p. 486

five-factor model of personality, p. 490

fixation, p. 476

id, p. 472

ideal self, p. 483

Oedipus complex, p. 476

personality, p. 467

pleasure principle, p. 472

projective personality tests, p. 495

psychoanalysis, p. 470

psychosexual stages, p. 475

reality principle, p. 472

reciprocal determinism, p. 488

repression, p. 473

self-concept, p. 482

self-efficacy, p. 486

social-cognitive perspective, p. 486

source traits, p. 489

superego, p. 472

surface traits, p. 489

traits, p. 489

trait theories, p. 489

unconditional positive regard, p. 483

unconscious, p. 471

TEST PREP are you ready?

1. The _____ perspective of personality development is based on the theories of Sigmund Freud and suggests that unconscious conflicts are at the root of personality development.
   a. trait
   b. humanistic
   c. biological
   d. psychoanalytic

2. A professor doing research on personality development insists that humans have capabilities and that we should take advantage of these as we strive for personal growth. This professor appears to be proposing which of the following perspectives?
   a. humanistic
   b. behavioral
   c. psychoanalytic
   d. social-cognitive

3. Freud's topographical model suggests our personalities and behaviors result from
   a. components of the mind, including the id, ego, and superego.
   b. the reality principle.
   c. the pleasure principle.
   d. mental processes that occur at three levels of consciousness.

4. According to Freud, the part of the personality that develops last and guides our behaviors to follow rules is the
   a. preconscious.
   b. superego.
   c. id.
   d. ego.

5. _____ help to reduce the anxiety created by the conflict among the id, ego, and superego.
   a. Psychosexual stages
   b. Three levels of consciousness
   c. Defense mechanisms
   d. Erogenous zones

6. _____ refers to the drive to achieve one's full potential.
   a. Repression
   b. Conditions of worth
   c. Self-actualization
   d. Reciprocal determinism

7. Rogers believed that problems can develop when a person's self-concept is _____ with his experiences in the world.
   a. incongruent
   b. in harmony
   c. self-actualized
   d. conditioned

8. A person high in _____ strongly believes she will succeed in a particular situation even if she has experienced failure in similar circumstances.
   a. reciprocal determinism
   b. reinforcers
   c. self-efficacy
   d. source traits

9. _____ suggests personality is the result of interactions among cognitions, behaviors, and the environment.
   a. Self-efficacy
   b. Factor analysis
   c. Reciprocal determinism
   d. Expectancy

10. Using _____ and other research methods, Cattell proposed that there are 16 personality factors.
    a. source traits
    b. reciprocal determinism
    c. the Big Five
    d. factor analysis

11. According to Eysenck, we can describe personalities based on:
    a. three dimensions of traits.
    b. self-actualization.
    c. locus of control.
    d. reinforcement value.

12. Evidence for the biological basis of the five-factor model of personality includes
    a. the instability of the personality characteristics over time.
    b. the stability of the personality characteristics over time.
    c. the fact that there are no gender differences in the personality characteristics.
    d. the absence of heritability of these personality characteristics.

13. The _____ of an assessment can be determined when someone takes the same personality assessment more than once and the results do not change.
    a. heritability
    b. effectiveness
    c. reliability
    d. validity

14. The idea that personality traits influence perception is part of the logic underlying _____, which attempt to explore characteristics that might not be accessible through interview or observation.
    a. projective personality tests
    b. semistructured interviews
    c. structured interviews
    d. fMRI studies

15. The neo-Freudians agree with Freud on many issues, but tend to disagree with which of the following?
    a. his belief in the positive aspect of human nature
    b. his belief in the importance of personality growth throughout life
    c. his intense emphasis on the instincts of sex and aggression
    d. his notion that caregivers cannot shape personality

16. How would a behaviorist describe some of your personality characteristics?

17. What is the difference between the humanistic perspective and the social-cognitive perspective of personality development?

18. Describe the Oedipus complex and the Electra complex. How are they different?

19. Consider how you are doing in your college courses. Name three causes for your successes that represent an internal locus of control. Name three causes for your successes that represent an external locus of control.

20. Describe the differences between objective and subjective approaches to the assessment of personality.

✓ CHECK YOUR ANSWERS IN APPENDIX C.

Get personalized practice by logging into LaunchPad at **http://www.worthpublishers.com/launchpad/Licht** to take the LearningCurve adaptive quizzes for Chapter 11.

12

An Introduction to Stress

📁 *Drive*

📁 *Everything Happens for a Reason*

🌐 ➤ ACROSS THE WORLD
The Stress of Starting Anew

📁 *The Paramedic's Rollercoaster*

Stress and Your Body

📁 *Trouble Undercover*

Stress and Your Health

📁 *Adrenaline Junkies*

Factors Related to Stress

📁 *Ambulance Burnout*

📁 *It's A Personal Thing*

📁 *From Ambulance to Firehouse*

➤◄ CONTROVERSIES
Meditate on This

SA from the pages of
SCIENTIFIC AMERICAN
Meditate That Cold Away

➕ THINK AGAIN
Think Positive

📁 *To Protect, Serve, and Not Get
Too Stressed*

stress and health

An Introduction to Stress

DRIVE When Eric Flansburg first enrolled in the police academy at Onondaga Community College in upstate New York, there were 21 students in his class. Of those 21, only 6 graduated. Eric was not among them. Why? Because he failed one very important test: the Emergency Vehicle Operations Course (EVOC).

The EVOC requires exceptional driving skills. The test involves weaving a police car in and out of a serpentine (zigzag) maze of cones and making superfast lane changes—just the kind of police chase maneuvering you see in the movies. Once you get to the end of the course, you have to do it all over again, but this time in reverse. Knock down one cone, or simply brush against it, and you fail. Exceed the allotted 2 minutes and 20 seconds, and you fail. "It's pretty intense driving," Eric says. "It's also fun." Going into the test, Eric was well prepared. He had learned and rehearsed the steering and breaking techniques needed to succeed. But when the time came to put his hard-earned skills to work, he faltered. "It was all mental," Eric says. "I totally psyched myself out. I was so scared of failing that I failed." There are no two ways about it: Eric was feeling the *stress* of the situation.

12

LEARNING OBJECTIVES

after reading and studying this chapter, you should be able to:

LO 1 Define stress and stressors.

LO 2 Describe the Social Readjustment Rating Scale in relation to life events and illness.

LO 3 Summarize how poverty, adjusting to a new culture, and daily hassles affect health.

LO 4 Identify the brain and body changes that characterize the fight-or-flight response.

LO 5 Outline the general adaptation syndrome (GAS).

LO 6 Describe the function of the hypothalamic–pituitary–adrenal (HPA) system.

LO 7 Explain how stressors relate to health problems.

LO 8 List some consequences of prolonged exposure to the stress hormone cortisol.

LO 9 Identify different types of conflicts.

LO 10 Illustrate how appraisal influences coping.

LO 11 Describe Type A and Type B personalities and explain how they relate to stress.

LO 12 Discuss several tools for reducing stress and maintaining health.

Stress and Stressors

CONNECTIONS

In **Chapter 9,** we defined emotion as a psychological state that includes a subjective or inner experience. Emotion also has a physiological component and a behavioral expression. Here, we discuss *stress responses,* which are psychological, physiological, and emotional in nature.

Eric, in His Own Words

http://qrs.ly/w13nrb5

LO 1 Define stress and stressors.

We all have an intuitive sense of what stress is, and many of us are more familiar with it than we would like. But what exactly is stress, where does it come from, and how does it affect our physical and mental health? As with many concepts in psychology, stress is not easy to define. For example, people often report they experience the *feeling* of stress, almost as if stress is an **emotion.** Others describe stress as if it is a force that needs to be resisted. An engineer might say that stress refers to the application of a force on a target, such as the wing of an airplane, to determine how much load it can handle before breaking (Lazarus, 1993). Perhaps you have felt like you might "break" when the load you bear causes too much strain.

Here, **stress** is defined as the response to perceived threats or challenges resulting from stimuli or events that cause strain, analogous to the airplane wing bending because of an applied load. For humans, these stimuli, or **stressors,** can cause psychological, physiological, and emotional reactions. As you read this chapter, be careful not to confuse *how we react to stressors* with the *stressors* themselves; stress is the response and stressors are the cause (Harrington, 2013). Hans Selye (sĕl'yĕ; 1907–1982), an endocrinologist who studied the impact of hormones and stress, proposed that "stress is the nonspecific response of the body to any demand. A stressor is an agent that produces stress at any time" (1976, p. 53).

There are countless types of stressors. Stressors can be events, such as police academy driving tests. They can also be beliefs and attitudes, such as Eric's thoughts and worries about not passing the driving test. Stressors can even be people, like the drill instructors who run the police academy's Saturday morning physical training. Starting at 6:00 A.M., these guys lead Onondaga's aspiring police officers through 3 hours of running, push-ups, and other backbreaking exercises. If a student makes one mistake, the drill instructors are more than happy to point it out with the full force of their lungs. Mind you, this is all for the cadet's own benefit. The instructors are preparing the students for one of the more unpleasant aspects of police work: being ridiculed and insulted by the public. Police officers must learn how to brush off rude comments, maintain their composure, and carry on with their duties.

Note: Quotations attributed to Eric Flansburg and Kehlen Kirby are personal communications.

stress The response to perceived threats or challenges resulting from stimuli or events that cause strain.

stressors Stimuli that cause physiological, psychological, and emotional reactions.

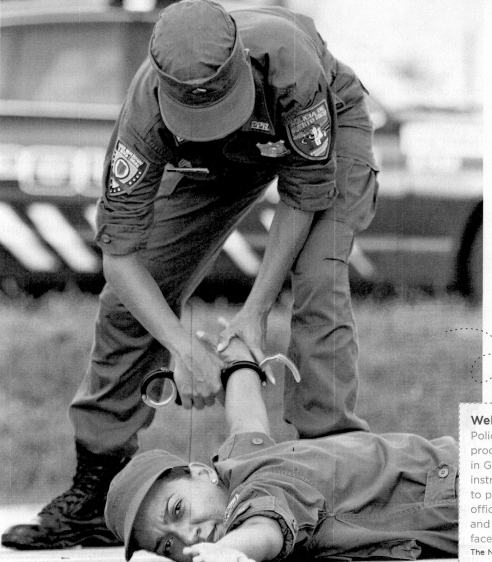

Welcome to the Academy
Police cadets practice arrest procedures at an academy in Gurabo, Puerto Rico. Drill instructors go to great lengths to prepare aspiring police officers for the extreme physical and mental stressors they will face on their beats. DENNIS RIVERA/ The New York Times/Redux Pictures

What are some of the stressors in your life? Some exist outside of you, like homework assignments, dirty dishes in the sink, and job-related problems. Others are more internal, like the *anxiety* stemming from a strained relationship or the *pressure* of looming deadlines. Generally, we experience stress in response to stressors, although there is at least one exception to this rule: People with anxiety disorders can feel intense anxiety in the absence of any apparent stressors (Chapter 13). Which brings us to another point: Stress is very much related to how one perceives the surrounding world.

In many cases, stress results from a *perceived* threat, because what constitutes a threat differs from one person to the next. The police academy driving test might have been threatening to Eric because he felt anxious about failing it, while another student viewed the test as an opportunity to shine. Similarly, Eric may have felt completely relaxed taking written exams that other students found highly threatening.

Remember that stress can have psychological, physiological, and emotional effects. Eric's physiological reaction to the driving test may have included increased blood pressure, or heart rate, but he was far more aware of the psychological and emotional components of his stress response. Bursting through the starting gates, his mind raced from one thought to the next. He was envisioning every little thing he had to do to pass the exam and at the same time saying to himself, *Eric, Eric, you can't fail.*

The very same day that Eric failed his driving test, he resolved to return to the academy and start the program again. This minor setback was not going to interfere

CONNECTIONS

In **Chapter 11,** we presented *self-efficacy,* or beliefs about one's ability to reach a goal. People with high self-efficacy are more successful on the job because they are flexible, open to new ideas, and persevere in difficult situations. Eric seems to be showing high self-efficacy as he pursues his goal of becoming a police officer.

You Asked, Eric Answers

http://qrs.ly/2v3nrb6

How does being a police officer compare to the stress of working in the plant?

▶ It's Nonstop

A dairy plant employee toils among steel vats of milk. Keeping the storage vessels and equipment sterile is an enormous responsibility; if the product becomes contaminated, thousands of consumers might be sickened. As Eric can testify, working as a sanitation manager can cause significant day-to-day stress. P. Magielsen/Corbis

with his childhood dream of becoming a police officer, and there was no way it was going to define his experience at the academy. "When you fall down, you have to **get back up,**" Eric says. "That's the only way to move forward in life."

Not everyone would have responded this way. Plenty of people would have viewed the test not as a stumbling block, but as the end of their journey. (*I guess I was never meant to be a police officer.*) As you will learn in this chapter, the ways people experience and cope with stressors are highly variable. The same exam that has you re-arranging your schedule to go to the library every day may not even faze a classmate. But come exam day, she may be shaking in her shoes while you calmly walk into the classroom, feeling cool and confident. A particular type of stressor may also trigger distinct reactions at different times. You might feel confident for the first midterm exam, but uneasy about the second midterm, even though you have spent the same amount of time preparing for each test. People's beliefs about their ability to cope with stressors and the strategies they use to do so have a profound impact on their stress reactions. We will address these concepts later in the chapter, but first let's focus on the positive. Not all stress is bad.

EVERYTHING HAPPENS FOR A REASON   In three decades of life, Eric has experienced his fair share of stressors. Immediately after graduating from high school in upstate New York, he traveled to an Air Force base in San Antonio, Texas, to begin basic training, a stepping-stone on the way to joining the military police. "You want to talk about psychological stress?" he says laughing. Try waking up at 4:00 A.M. to the sound of drill sergeants banging garbage cans and screaming, "Get out of bed!" Not a morning person? If you cannot wake up, shower, shave, and make your bed with perfect hospital corners (yes, they really expect to be able to bounce a quarter off the sheets) in a half-hour, you can be sure one of the drill sergeants will get in your face and scream something like, "Are you so stupid that you can't make your bed?" or "Did you have Mommy make your bed when you were home?"

After about a year of arduous training in the Air Force, Eric suffered a disabling injury and had to be discharged. It was a huge letdown, but Eric believes everything happens for a reason. He returned to New York and got a job at a dairy plant where he met his future wife and moved up the company ranks to become a high-level manager. Working at the plant introduced Eric to a different type of pressure. As a sanitation manager, it was his job to make sure all the processing equipment was sterile. If he failed to identify and correct one weak point in the process, the company might fail an inspection, or worse, thousands of consumers could get food poisoning. In 2010 Eric faced one of the most stressful, and unfortunately common, events in life: He was laid off. But he didn't view the job loss as a loss at all; he saw it as an opportunity to finally fulfill his childhood dream of pursuing a career in law enforcement. A few months later, he was training to become a police officer at Onondaga Community College.

When you ask Eric how the various stressors in his life affected him, he has few negative things to say. Even while working upwards of 70 hours at the plant each week, he was eating well, sleeping soundly, and maintaining balance in his life. Despite the long hours and constant pressure, he felt relatively happy and fulfilled. Have you ever considered that stressors shouldn't always be avoided? According to **arousal theory,** humans seek an optimal level of arousal, and what is *optimal* is not the same for everyone.

EUSTRESS AND DISTRESS   Clearly, stressors cannot be avoided completely. And some stressors are enjoyable, such as the excitement before a big trip, or the birth of a new baby. For Eric, getting married and witnessing the birth of his first child were among the most stressful and joyful events in life. "Oh man, you want to talk about sweaty palms, me shaking and a whole lot of emotion?" he says, remembering the day he stood at the altar. And the birth of his son? "Unreal," he says. Immediately after the delivery, doctors placed the infant on his mother's chest. The baby's eyes were still closed, but when he opened them, Eric was the first person he saw. It was the proudest moment of Eric's life. This "good" kind of stressor leads to **eustress** (yōō'-stres), which is the stress response to agreeable or positive events. Of course, most people associate stress with negative events. These types of undesirable or disagreeable events lead to the particular stress response known as **distress.** Now let's find out how eustress and distress might affect your health.

Major Life Events

- - - ➤ **LO 2**   Describe the Social Readjustment Rating Scale in relation to life events and illness.

Holmes and Rahe (1967) were among the first to propose that life-changing events are potentially stressors. In other words, any event that requires a life adjustment, such as marriage, the birth of a child, or a change in financial status, can cause a stress reaction. They also suggested that these life-changing events have a cumulative effect; the more events you experience in a row or within a brief period of time, the greater the potential for an increased stress reaction and negative health outcomes. Numerous studies have examined these types of events and the strain they cause. Think back to the analogy of applying a force to the wing of an airplane. The degree to which the wing bends (or breaks) indicates the strain it is under (Lazarus, 1993). Researchers have found links between certain life events (the force causing strain) and illnesses (the response) such as sudden cardiac death, heart attack, leukemia, diabetes, influenza, psychiatric disorders, and a variety of other conditions (Hatch & Dohrenwend, 2007; Rabkin & Struening, 1976).

SOCIAL READJUSTMENT RATING SCALE   Illnesses can be clearly defined and identified, but how do psychologists measure *life events*? Holmes and Rahe (1967) developed the Social Readjustment Rating Scale (SRRS) to do just that. With the SRRS, participants are asked to read through a list of events and experiences, and determine which of these happened during the previous year and how many times they occurred. A score is then calculated based on severity ratings of events and frequency of their occurrence. An event like the death of a spouse has a greater severity rating than something like a traffic violation. Participants are also asked to report on any illnesses or accidents they experienced during the same period. Researchers then use this information to look at the **correlation** between life events and health problems (Kobasa, 1979). Correlations range between .20 and .78, although they are generally lower than .30 (Rabkin & Struening, 1976). But remember, a correlation between life events and illness (or any correlation for that matter) is no proof of causality. There is always the possibility that a third factor, such as poverty, may be causing both illnesses and major life-changing events. Someone who is impoverished might not have employment or access to good

---

CONNECTIONS

In **Chapter 9,** we introduced arousal theory, which suggests behaviors can arise out of the need for stimulation or arousal. Here, we point out that people seek stressors in order to maintain a satisfying level of arousal.

CONNECTIONS

In **Chapter 1,** we explained that a positive correlation indicates that as one variable increases, so does the other variable. Here, we see a positive correlation between life events and health problems: The more life events people have experienced, the more health problems they are likely to have.

eustress (yōō'-stres) The stress response to agreeable or positive stressors.
distress The stress response to unpleasant and undesirable stressors.

health care, nutrition, and so forth. In this case, poverty is leading to stressful life events *and* poor health outcomes.

Popular in the late 1960s and 1970s, the Social Readjustment Rating Scale (SRRS) has evolved over the years. But as with many scales, the original version has now become outdated. (For example, the original scale included "mortgage over $10,000" as an event.) The rating scale has also been adapted to better match the life events of specific populations; for example, the College Undergraduate Stress Scale (Renner & Mackin, 1998; FIGURE 12.1). Even with this degree of specificity, the scale may not be suitable for every person. In addition to dealing with term papers, midterms, and other college-related life events, many of today's college students face a host of other potential stressors, such as making car payments and raising children.

try this

Imagine you were tasked with redesigning the College Undergraduate Stress Scale (CUSS) to bring it up to date. How would you decide what types of items to include in your rating scale? You could begin as many researchers do—by gathering pilot data. Ask five people to complete the CUSS inventory and then request that they make suggestions for additional events to be included in a new inventory.

FIGURE 12.1

Sample Items from the College Undergraduate Stress Scale

Event	Rating
Being raped	100
Death of a close friend	97
Contracting a sexually transmitted infection (other than AIDS)	94
Finals week	90
Flunking a class	89
Financial difficulties	84
Writing a major term paper	83
Talking in front of class	72
Difficulties with a roommate	66
Maintaining a steady dating relationship	55
Commuting to campus or work, or both	54
Getting straight As	51
Falling asleep in class	40

Source: Reprinted by permission of SAGE Publications/APA/ LAWRENCE/ERLBAUM ASSOCIATES, INC. from Renner and Mackin (1998).

Another possible problem with self-report scales such as the SRRS is that people tend to forget events over time, or the opposite—they tend to focus more on past events than recent ones (Pachana, Brilleman, & Dobson, 2011). What's more, not all negative life-changing events lead to bad outcomes. Some have even suggested that moderate exposure to stress makes us stronger, a view described as *stress inoculation.* Someone with a "low to moderate" degree of stress may end up with "better mental health and well-being" and a greater ability to cope with pain than those who either have faced no hardships or have had to handle an overwhelming level of adversity (Seery, 2011).

Looking across cultures, we see most people rate the weight of life-changing events very similarly (Leontopoulou, Jimerson, & Anderson, 2011; Scully, Tosi, & Banning, 2000). For example, when the SRRS was administered to French, Belgian, and Swiss participants, their rankings of how much readjustment the events would necessitate were similar to those made by Americans (Harmon, Masuda, & Holmes, 1970). Malaysians also have similar views about the amount of readjustment required for life events (Woon, Masuda, Wagner, & Holmes, 1971).

Posttraumatic Stress Disorder

One type of event not included in the SRRS, but which is familiar to police officers and other first responders, is a major disaster experience. These cataclysmic events include natural disasters such as hurricanes, earthquakes, and tornadoes, as well as multicar accidents, war, and terrorist attacks. The emotional and physical responses to such occurrences can last for many years, manifesting themselves in nightmares, flashbacks, depression, grief, anxiety, and other symptoms related to *posttraumatic stress disorder.*

In order to be diagnosed with **posttraumatic stress disorder (PTSD),** a person must be exposed to or threatened by an event involving death, serious injury, or some form of sexual violence. Someone could develop PTSD after witnessing a violent assault or accident, or upon learning about the traumatic experiences of family members, close friends, perhaps even strangers. For veterans and service members previously deployed to war zones in Afghanistan and Iraq, the estimated incidence of PTSD is 13.8%, based on a study of almost 2,000 participants questioned about symptoms within the last 30 days (Schell & Marshall, 2008). In contrast, around 3.5% of the general population is

posttraumatic stress disorder (PTSD)
A psychological disorder characterized by exposure to or threatened by an event involving death, serious injury, or sexual violence; can include disturbing memories, nightmares, flashbacks, and other distressing symptoms.

estimated to have received a PTSD diagnosis during the previous 12 months (American Psychiatric Association, 2013). In some cases, the exposure to trauma is ongoing. First responders like Eric, for example, may witness disturbing scenarios on a weekly basis.

However, not everyone exposed to trauma will develop PTSD. Over the course of a lifetime, most people will experience an event that qualifies as a "psychological trauma," but only 5 to 10% will actually develop PTSD as a result (Bonanno, Westphal, & Mancini, 2011). To be diagnosed with PTSD, a person must experience at least one of the following symptoms: (1) distressing, disturbing, and spontaneously recurring memories of an event; (2) dreams with content or emotions associated with the event; (3) "dissociative reactions" that include feeling as if the event is happening again (flashbacks); (4) extreme psychological distress when reminded of the event; or (5) obvious physical reactions to cues related to the event.

Many people with PTSD try to avoid the environmental cues (people, places, or objects) linked to the trauma. If someone were involved in a serious car accident on US Highway 101, then simply driving along that thoroughfare may trigger unwanted memories. Other symptoms include difficulty remembering the details of the event, unrealistic self-expectations, ongoing self-blame, and loss of interest in activities that once were enjoyable. Someone with PTSD might be irritable or aggressive, lashing out at loved ones for no apparent reason. She may have trouble sleeping and concentrating. Also associated with PTSD are *dissociative symptoms,* which may include distorted perceptions of the world, and the feeling of observing oneself from the outside (American Psychological Association, 2013d; Friedman, Resick, Bryant, & Brewin, 2011).

Among those at risk for PTSD are police officers (Berger et al., 2011), many of whom bear witness to bloody crime scenes, traumatized victims, and gun violence. But it is not just these types of traumas that impact police officers; just as important are the more chronic stressors, like being overworked and not having enough time with family (Collins & Gibbs, 2003). One study concluded that, for police officers, chronic stressors at work, such as discrimination and unpleasant relationships with coworkers, are associated with the symptoms of PTSD as well (Maguen et al., 2009), although such stressors (while they contribute) are not actually sufficient to define or diagnose it.

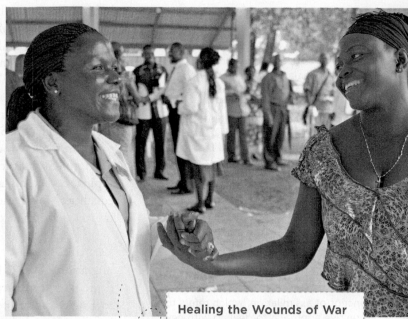

Healing the Wounds of War
Physician assistant Klubo Mulba (left) smiles at her former client, Surprise Otto, at JFK Hospital in Monrovia, Liberia. Mulba, who is one of Liberia's first mental health clinicians, received her training through a joint program between The Carter Center and the Liberia Ministry of Health and Social Welfare. Liberia's population is still recovering from a 13-year civil war that ended in 2003. Approximately 40% of the population is affected by PTSD (The Carter Center, 2013). The Carter Center/P. Rohe

It's Nonstop: Chronic Stressors

You don't have to be a police officer to appreciate the burden of everyday stress. For some of us, stressors come from balancing school and work, or taking care of young children. Many face the constant stressor of battling a chronic illness like diabetes, asthma, or cancer (Sansom-Daly, Peate, Wakefield, Bryant, & Cohn, 2012), or caring for an adult child with a severe mental disorder (Barker, Greenberg, Seltzer, & Almeida, 2012). And for a growing number of people around the world, poverty is an overwhelming stressor.

LO 3 Summarize how poverty, adjusting to a new culture, and daily hassles affect health.

POVERTY The number of Americans living at or below the poverty line continues to increase. As of 2011, 22% of children under 6 years in the United States were living below the poverty level (Addy, Engelhardt, & Skinner, 2013). People struggling to make ends meet experience numerous stressors, including poor health care,

CONNECTIONS

In **Chapter 7,** we discussed the relationship between poverty and cognitive abilities (socioeconomic status is associated with scores on intelligence tests). In **Chapter 8,** we presented evidence suggesting that isolation and lack of stimulation can hamper the development of young brains. Here, we highlight the link between poverty-related stressors and neurocognitive development.

CONNECTIONS

In **Chapter 8,** we discussed Piaget's concept of assimilation, which refers to a cognitive approach to dealing with new information. This suggests that a person attempts to understand new information using her existing knowledge base. Here, assimilation means letting go of old ways and adopting the customs of a new culture.

Culture Shock
A woman shops for groceries in the Chinatown area of Flushing in Queens, New York. Queens is the most ethnically diverse spot on the planet, providing a home for people from more than 100 countries (nyc. gov, 2013). Immigrants can either *assimilate* into, *separate* from, or *integrate* into their new cultures.
Mark Peterson/Redux

lack of preventive health care, noisy living situations, overcrowding, violence, and underfunded schools (Blair & Raver, 2012; Mistry & Wadsworth, 2011). The cycle of poverty is difficult to break, so these stressors often persist across generations. The longer people live in poverty, the more exposure they have to stressors, and the greater the likelihood they will become ill (Miller, Chen, & Parker, 2011). For children in particular, the impact of **socioeconomic status (SES)** can have lifelong repercussions because environmental stressors affect the developing brain. Some of the factors associated with low SES and permanent changes to the brain include poor nutrition, toxins in the environment, and abuse. In some cases, the resulting disparities in brain development may lead to differences in "adult neurocognitive outcomes" (D'Angiulli, Lipina, & Olesinska, 2012). Factors linked to poverty have been associated with "inequalities" in the development of cognitive and socioemotional abilities, which can impact performance in school and at work (Lipina & Posner, 2012).

ACCULTURATIVE STRESS   Another increasingly common source of stress is migration. The 214 million migrants dispersed across the world deal with varying degrees of **acculturative stress** (ə-ˌkəl-chə-ˈrā-tiv), or stress associated with adjusting to a new way of life (International Organization for Migration, 2013). How would it feel to leave behind your extended family and close friends, and move to a foreign land where the language, customs, holidays, and belief systems are new and different? Perhaps you have had this experience; about 1 in 10 people living in America were born in another country (U.S. Census, 2012).

There are various ways people respond to acculturative stress (Berry, 1997). Some try to **assimilate,** letting go of old ways and adopting those of the new culture. But assimilation can cause problems if family members or friends from the old culture reject the new one, or have trouble assimilating themselves. Another approach is to cling to one's roots and remain *separated* from the new culture. Such an approach can be very problematic if the new culture does not support this type of separation and requires assimilation. A combination of these two approaches is *integration,* or holding on to some elements of the old culture, but also adopting aspects of the new one.

The degree of acculturative stress varies greatly from one individual to the next. Some people thrive on new soil (a prime example being Mohamed Dirie introduced in Chapter 9), while others struggle with the stress of starting over. What determines the intensity of acculturative stress, and why do some people seem to have an easier time with it than others?

across the WORLD

The Stress of Starting Anew

Imagine trying to get a job, pay your bills, or simply make friends in a world where most everyone speaks a foreign language. Familiarity with language appears to play a key role in determining acculturative stress levels. Belizaire and Fuertes (2011) studied Haitian immigrants in the United States and found lower levels of acculturative stress among those who spoke English. "The ability to speak English is crucial to the adjustment and well-being of immigrants in the United States," the researchers write, "and some researchers see this ability as the best indicator of acculturation" (p. 93). Another important determinant of acculturative stress is the degree of difference between old and new cultures. Chinese graduate students have been found to experience less acculturative stress studying in Hong Kong as opposed to Australia. Presumably, this is because the cultures of China and Hong Kong are more similar (Pan & Wong, 2011). Finally, we cannot forget the unpleasant reality of discrimination, which causes great stress for the world's immigrant populations. Common targets of discrimination in the United States are people from India,

Pakistan, and other South Asian countries. Discrimination against South Asians, which appears to have increased after the terrorist attacks of 9/11, erodes psychological well-being, and in some cases correlates with the development of depression (Kaduvettoor-Davidson & Inman, 2013; Tummala-Narra, Alegria, & Chen, 2012).

IMMIGRATION IS STRESSFUL, ESPECIALLY IF YOU DON'T SPEAK THE NEW LANGUAGE.

Fortunately, there are ways to combat acculturative stress. One of the best defenses is **social support,** or assistance from others. In a small study by Renner and colleagues, refugees who had social support from a sponsor experienced less anxiety and depression and had an easier time adapting to their new homes in Austria (Renner, Laireiter, & Maier, 2012). 🌐➤

The stresses of acculturation tend to be gnawing and constant, but some stressors are sudden and dramatic. These are the types that ambulance drivers and paramedics encounter every day. Meet our next first responder, Kehlen Kirby.

THE PARAMEDIC'S ROLLERCOASTER Kehlen Kirby sees more pain and suffering in one month than most people do in a lifetime. In his 8 years working as an emergency medical services (EMS) provider in Pueblo, Colorado, this 26-year-old man has witnessed the highest highs and lowest lows of human experience. He has rescued people from flaming car wrecks, treated teenage gang members for stab and gunshot wounds, and watched chain-smokers who are dying from emphysema beg for cigarettes en route to the hospital. "We have had people that are struggling to breathe, using every muscle in their body to breathe, but they just want to get that last puff before we load them into the ambulance," Kehlen says. In between the sadness and suffering, though, there are also stories of hope and inspiration. One such tale takes place on the edge of a dark highway.

It was the middle of the night when Kehlen's crew received a call about a medical emergency on the side of the freeway. Arriving at the scene, they found a woman on the passenger side of a car, legs propped up on the dashboard. There was a pool of blood on the floor. The woman was panicked and screaming, and the man on the driver's side was not faring much better. It turned out that these poor souls were soon-to-be parents, and their baby boy was ready to make his debut. Upon closer examination, Kehlen could see the baby's head beginning to emerge. There was no time to load the woman into the ambulance and race to the hospital. This infant was about to take his first breaths on US Route 50. Kehlen and his colleagues delivered the baby, and the mother went from a state of screaming hysteria to smiling, laughing bliss.

Being involved in life-or-death situations may be emotionally challenging, but it helps Kehlen keep things in perspective. "All the traumatic calls, the car wrecks and shootings, it makes you appreciate life," he says. Kehlen will never ride in a car without wearing a seatbelt; he has seen the horrific consequences of not buckling up. He also doesn't get too aggravated by everyday annoyances, like the sound of his newborn shrieking and wailing. (Like Eric, Kehlen recently became a dad.) Many new parents find a baby's cries disconcerting. Not Kehlen. From his paramedic's perspective, a crying baby means a breathing baby. "I love it when she cries," he says. But the fact that Kehlen is unfazed by everyday annoyances like screaming infants and dirty laundry probably makes him the exception rather than the rule. Research suggests that these daily hassles can have a significant impact on us.

Life Saver ◄
Kehlen Kirby has one of the most stressful jobs imaginable—providing emergency medical services to people injured in car accidents, fires, and other traumatic incidents. The constant exposure to pain and suffering helps Kehlen maintain perspective on the hassles of daily life; he doesn't sweat the small stuff. Leslie Nazario/Portraits by Leslie

What a Hassle, What a Joy

Daily hassles are the minor problems or irritants we deal with on a regular basis, such as traffic, financial worries, misplaced keys, messy roommates—a list that does not seem to end. These hassles, although seemingly minor, are repetitive and

acculturative stress (ə-ˌkəl-chə-ˈrā-tiv) Stress that occurs when people move to new countries or cultures and must adjust to a new way of life.

social support The assistance we acquire from others.

daily hassles Minor and regularly occurring problems that can act as stressors.

Hassles					Uplifts			
0	1	2	3	Your child(ren)	0	1	2	3
0	1	2	3	Your friend(s)	0	1	2	3
0	1	2	3	Your work load	0	1	2	3
0	1	2	3	Enough money for emergencies	0	1	2	3
0	1	2	3	Financial care for someone who doesn't live with you	0	1	2	3
0	1	2	3	Your drinking	0	1	2	3
0	1	2	3	Your physical appearance	0	1	2	3
0	1	2	3	Political or social issues	0	1	2	3
0	1	2	3	Amount of free time	0	1	2	3
0	1	2	3	Being organized	0	1	2	3

▲ **FIGURE 12.2**

The Hassles and Uplifts Scale
On their scale of daily hassles and uplifts, Delongis, Folkman, and Lazarus (1988) asked participants to consider how much of a hassle and how much of an uplift each item on the scale was the day of the test. Participants were instructed to circle a number rating the degree to which each item was a hassle (left column) and an uplift (right column). Numbers range from 0 ("none or not applicable") to 3 ("a great deal"). The scale includes 53 items, a sample of which are shown here. *Sources:* Copyright ©1988 by the American Psychological Association. Adapted with permission from DeLongis, Folkman, and Lazarus (1988).

CONNECTIONS ◄

In **Chapter 9,** we discussed different ways that we can increase our well-being. Keeping a journal and recording feelings of gratefulness are associated with increased happiness and well-being. Here, we see that uplifts are linked to family satisfaction. Being mindful of the good things in our lives has many benefits.

ever present. The strain of dealing with them can add up, seemingly taking a toll on our health and well-being (DeLongis, Coyne, Dakof, Folkman, & Lazarus, 1982; DeLongis, Folkman, & Lazarus, 1988). For example, research suggests that hassles are closely associated with short-lived illnesses, such as colds and headaches (Bottos & Dewey, 2004; DeLongis et al., 1988; Pedersen, Zachariae, & Bovbjerg, 2010). It's a good thing that the weight of our daily hassles is counterbalanced by the uplifts in our lives.

Uplifts are positive experiences that have the potential to make us happy. Think about the last time you smiled; it was likely in response to an uplift, such as a funny text from a good friend, a child presenting you with a handmade gift, or a congratulatory e-mail about one of your achievements. We all have hassles and uplifts, but how do they interact to affect our health and well-being? Researchers have been asking this question for decades.

DeLongis and colleagues (1988) developed a scale of daily hassles and uplifts, and used it to explore the relationship between stress and illness (**FIGURE 12.2**). They asked participants in their study to read through a list of 53 items that could be either hassles or uplifts, such as meeting deadlines, maintaining a car, interacting with fellow workers, and dealing with the weather. Participants then rated these items on a 4-point scale indicating "how much of a hassle" and "how much of an uplift" each was on that particular day (0 = none or not applicable, to 3 = a great deal). They also asked participants to report any illness, injuries, or symptoms they experienced that same day. What did they find? Over a 6-month period, there was a significant link between hassles and health problems. The more daily stressors the participants reported, the more likely they were to suffer from sore throats, headaches, influenza, back problems, and other health issues. More recently, researchers uncovered a link between daily stressors and cardiovascular risk factors, such as high blood pressure (Uchino, Berg, Smith, Pearce, & Skinner, 2006). Daily hassles also increase the risk of catching contagious diseases and may prolong the course of illness (Glaser & Kiecolt-Glaser, 2005).

How do hassles and uplifts affect psychological and social health? One group of researchers studied two Israeli populations (Jewish and Arab), exploring the similarities and differences within subgroups living in the same country. While differences existed, the researchers noted some important similarities. In both groups, for example, daily **uplifts** had a positive impact on "family satisfaction" and daily hassles had a negative impact on "life satisfaction," though the meaning of "uplift" differed between the two groups (Lavee & Ben-Ari, 2008).

Now that we have explored various types of stressors, from major life events to everyday annoyances, let's find out what occurs in the body and brain when we respond.

✔✔✔✔ **show what you know**

1. _____ is a response to perceived threats or challenges resulting from stimuli that cause strain.

2. The Social Readjustment Rating Scale was created to measure the severity and frequency of life events. This scale is most often used to examine the relationship between stressors and which of the following?
   a. aging
   b. levels of eustress
   c. perceived threats
   d. illness

3. _____ can occur when a person must adjust to a new way of life in a new country, often due to an unfamiliar language, religious beliefs, and holidays.
   a. Eustress
   b. Acculturative stress
   c. Uplifts
   d. Posttraumatic stress disorder

4. Reflect upon the last few days. Can you think of three uplifts and three hassles you have experienced during this period?

✔ CHECK YOUR ANSWERS IN APPENDIX C.

Stress and Your Body

TROUBLE UNDERCOVER Meet Sergeant Michelle, a long-time veteran of a police department in a large city at the foot of the Rocky Mountains. Michelle currently works in internal affairs investigating potential policy violations by police officers—a highly stressful position given that the outcome of such investigations can lead to the suspension or termination of fellow officers. But it doesn't match the intense, fear-for-your-life type of stress that Michelle has experienced at other points in her career, like the time her cover was nearly blown in an operation to bust crack-cocaine dealers. Posing as a buyer, Michelle walked into a house where a suspected dealer was selling. One of the men who happened to be hanging out in the house gave her a funny look, and she instantly realized that he recognized her as a police officer. Fortunately, the man did not give her away (who knows what the dealer would have done had her identity been revealed), and Michelle escaped the situation unscathed. But we can only imagine what she must have felt at that moment.

Faced with the prospect of being gunned down by a drug dealer, Michelle most likely experienced the sensations associated with the **fight-or-flight** response, such as increased pulse, breathing rate, and mental alertness. A coordinated effort of the sympathetic nervous system and the endocrine system, the fight-or-flight reaction primes the body to respond to danger, either by escaping (bolting out of the crack house, as in Michelle's case) or confronting the threat head-on (defending herself against a physical attack). Let's take a closer look at this survival mechanism.

CONNECTIONS

We introduced the fight-or-flight response to stressors in **Chapter 2.** The sympathetic nervous system is a division of the autonomic nervous system, which regulates the body's involuntary activity (such as digestion and the beating of the heart). Here, we will learn how this automatic activity may relate to illness.

Fight or Flight

> **LO 4** Identify the brain and body changes that characterize the fight-or-flight response.

When faced with a threatening situation, portions of the brain, including the hypothalamus, activate the sympathetic nervous system, which leads to the secretion of catecholamines, such as epinephrine and norepinephrine. These hormones cause heart rate, blood pressure, respiration, and blood flow to the muscles to increase. Meanwhile, digestion slows and the pupils dilate.

Physiological responses prepare us for an emergency by efficiently managing the body's resources. Once the emergency has ended, the **parasympathetic system** reverses these processes by reducing heart rate, blood pressure, and so on. If a person is exposed to a threatening situation for long periods of time, the fight-or-flight system remains active. This in turn can have detrimental effects on health (Shonkoff et al., 2012), an issue we will explore later in this chapter.

> **LO 5** Outline the general adaptation syndrome (GAS).

GENERAL ADAPTATION SYNDROME Hans Selye, introduced earlier in the chapter, identified police work "as likely the most stressful occupation in the world" (according to Violanti, 1992, p. 718). One of the first to suggest the human body responds to stressors in a predictable way, Selye (1936) described a specific pattern of physiological reactions, which he called the **general adaptation syndrome (GAS).**

CONNECTIONS

In **Chapter 2,** we introduced the parasympathetic nervous system, which is responsible for the "rest-and-digest" process following activation of the fight-or-flight response. The parasympathetic nervous system works with the sympathetic nervous system to prepare us for crises and then to calm us when danger has passed.

uplifts Experiences that are positive and have the potential to make one happy.

general adaptation syndrome (GAS) A specific pattern of physiological reactions to stressors, that includes the alarm stage, resistance stage, and exhaustion stage.

Physiological Responses to Stress

When faced with an emergency, our bodies go through a series of physiological responses that assist us in coping with a stressor. Activation of the *fight-or-flight* response and *hypothalamic–pituitary–adrenal (HPA)* system gives us the energy and resources we need to cope with a temporary stressor. Studying these physiological responses, Hans Selye (1956) suggested that the sequence follows the same path no matter the stressor. He found that when the stressor remains, our bodies can no longer adapt. Selye called this sequence the *general adaptation syndrome (GAS)*.

GENERAL ADAPTATION SYNDROME (GAS)

In the alarm stage, short-term responses are activated, giving us energy to combat a threat. In the resistance stage, resources remain mobilized, and we continue to cope with the stressor. But eventually we enter the exhaustion stage when we become weak and susceptible to illness, and are less able to cope with the stressor (Selye, 1956).

STRESSOR

Resistance to stress — high / low

normal level of resistance to stress

Alarm stage
(stress response activated)

Resistance stage
(coping with stressor)

Exhaustion stage
(reserves diminished)

SHORT-TERM RESPONSES TO STRESS

Amygdala processes information about stressor. If threat is perceived, hypothalamus triggers short-term stress response.

STRESSOR

Hypothalamus

Pituitary gland

FIGHT-OR-FLIGHT RESPONSE

HYPOTHALAMIC–PITUITARY–ADRENAL (HPA) SYSTEM

ACTIVATES

Sympathetic Nervous System

SENDS SIGNAL TO

Adrenal Medulla
(core of adrenal glands)

RELEASES

Catecholamines
epinephrine, norepinephrine

CAUSES

Efficient management of bodily resources ensures these are available for emergency action:
- increased heart rate
- increased respiration
- increased blood flow to muscles
- slowed digestion
- dilated pupils

ALERTS

Pituitary gland

SENDS SIGNAL TO

Adrenal Cortex
(outside layer of adrenal glands)

RELEASES

Corticosteroids
including cortisol

CAUSES

Efficient management of bodily resources; immune system activation

Adrenal glands

Kidneys

* The HPA system manages resources similar to the fight-or-flight response, but it takes longer to mobilize these processes, and the effects are more sustained.

PROLONGED STRESS

Relative risk of a cold — 0 to 4

no stressor / less than 1 / 1–6 / 7–24 / more than 24

Duration of stressor (in months)

Prolonged stress can cause the immune system to break down. As you can see, the risk of becoming sick is directly related to the duration of a stressor. This effect is seen even when the stressor is not traumatic. Data in this study were collected from people reporting on interpersonal conflicts and problems concerning work (Cohen et al., 1998).

Credit: Firefighter, Thinkstock; Firefighter crouching, Alan Bailey/Shutterstock; Male fire fighter with smoky background, Colin Anderson/age fotostock

According to this theory, the body passes through three stages (**INFOGRAPHIC 12.1**). The first is the *alarm stage*, or the body's initial response to a threatening situation, similar to the fight-or-flight response. Arousal increases, and the body prepares to deal with the threat. Following the alarm stage is the *resistance stage*. During this period, the body maintains a high level of arousal (though not as high as that of the alarm stage), but with a decreased response to new stress. Under such intense physiological demands, the body simply cannot address any new threatening situations that might arise. According to Selye, this is when some people start to show signs of *diseases of adaptation*, such as hypertension and arthritis (Selye, 1953; Selye & Fortier, 1950). If the threat remains and the person can no longer adapt, Selye suggested that the body then moves into the *exhaustion stage*. At this point, the body's resources become depleted, resulting in vulnerability to illnesses, physical exhaustion, and even death.

Selye's Stages
Endocrinologist Hans Selye proposed that the body passes through a predictable sequence of changes in response to stress. Selye's general adaptation syndrome includes three phases: the *alarm stage,* the *resistance stage,* and the *exhaustion stage.* Bettmann/CORBIS

- - -> **LO 6**   Describe the function of the hypothalamic–pituitary–adrenal (HPA) system.

HYPOTHALAMIC–PITUITARY–ADRENAL SYSTEM   Overseeing the sympathetic nervous system's response to stress is the ***hypothalamic–pituitary–adrenal (HPA)* system** (Infographic 12.1). This HPA system helps to maintain balance in the body by directing not only the sympathetic nervous system, but also the neuroendocrine and immune systems (Ben-Zvi, Vernon, & Broderick, 2009). When a stressful situation arises, the hypothalamus initiates a cascade of responses, by alerting the pituitary gland, which then sends signals to the adrenal cortex, which in turn orders the secretion of corticosteroids, such as cortisol. These hormones summon the immune system to fend off a threat and reduce the amount of energy used for nonessential activities (that is, those not associated with the threat), such as digestion and bladder control. The immune system defends the body from bacteria, viruses, and other types of invaders by deploying cells and chemicals to confront these threats. When faced with a stressor, the HPA system responds in the same way it would to a pathogen—by mobilizing a defense response. You might say it's working overtime. How do you think this affects your health?

Synonym

hypothalamic–pituitary–adrenal (HPA) system hypothalamic–pituitary–adrenal axis (HPA axis)

✓◯◯◯   show what you know

1. According to the _____, the human body responds in a predictable way to stressors, following a specific pattern of physiological reactions.

2. As a police officer, Michelle has found herself in life-threatening situations. When faced with danger, Michelle's body initially exhibits a fight-or-flight reaction, which is equivalent to the _____ of the general adaptation syndrome.
   a. alarm stage
   b. exhaustion stage
   c. diseases of adaptation
   d. acculturative stress

3. _____ helps maintain balance in the body by overseeing the sympathetic nervous system, as well as the neuroendocrine and immune systems.
   a. The general adaptation syndrome
   b. The exhaustion stage
   c. The hypothalamic–pituitary–adrenal system
   d. Eustress

4. Explain the processes that occur in the human body when it is faced with a life-threatening situation.

✓ CHECK YOUR ANSWERS IN APPENDIX C.

FIGURE 12.3
The Immune System
Our immunity derives from
a complex system involving
structures and organs throughout
the body that support the work
of specialized cell types to keep
us healthy. man: B2M Productions/Getty
Images; T lymphocytes & B lymphocytes:
Steve Gschmeissner/Science Source; Natural
killer cells & macrophages: Eye of Science/
Science Source

T lymphocytes (pink),
which fight viruses, cancer,
and other invaders, mature
in the thymus.

Thymus

Spleen
The spleen
stores pro-
immune cells
and filters out
successfully
destroyed
invaders.

Lymph nodes

Natural killer (NK)
cells (yellow), stored
in the lymph nodes,
are sent out to kill
diseased cells.

Macrophages are
created where they
are needed. They
consume invaders
and worn-out cells.

Bone marrow

B lymphocytes,
which fight bacteria,
mature in the bone
marrow.

Stress and Your Health

How does stress impact the lives of your relatives and friends? How does it affect you? Psychologists have spent decades examining how stress influences different people. In the early 1960s, the field of **health psychology** began to gather momentum. Many researchers began to explore the biological, psychological, and social factors contributing to illness and health. They wanted to understand how stress could be tempered and illness prevented.

Health psychology seeks to explain how our food choices, social interactions, and living environments affect our predispositions to illness and health. Researchers in this field contribute to health education, helping people develop positive eating and exercise habits; they also conduct public policy research that influences health-related guidelines. Health psychologists also study the impact of personality factors, coping style, cognitive appraisal, poverty, culture, social support, and religion—all topics addressed in this chapter.

Is Stress Making You Sick?

LO 7   Explain how stressors relate to health problems.

Before we explore the connection between stress and illness, we must understand how the body deals with illness in the first place. Let's take a side trip into introductory biology and learn about the body's main defense against disease—the immune system (**FIGURE 12.3**). The immune system is made up of the spleen, lymph nodes, and bone marrow. When disease-causing invaders threaten the body, the immune system deploys a special army of white blood cells called **lymphocytes.** Lymphocytes are produced in bone marrow, and their job is to battle enemies such as viruses and bacteria. When the body is expending its resources to deal with an ongoing stressor, the immune system is less powerful, and the work of the lymphocytes is compromised.

Like a platoon of soldiers, the immune system has a defense team to fight off invaders. Should the intruder(s) get past the skin, the *macrophages* ("big eaters") are ready to attack. These cells hunt and consume invaders as well as worn-out cells in the body. Cells that have been infected by invaders, such as viruses and cancer, are the targets of *natural killer cells* (*NK cells*), which inject the compromised cells with a deadly chemical. In addition, NK cells release a protein that prevents the infection from spreading to other cells. In some cases, the body must call on its "special ops" teams. These are the **B lymphocytes** and **T lymphocytes.** The B lymphocytes (white blood cells) mature in the bone marrow and produce antibodies that chemically inhibit bacteria. The T lymphocytes (also white blood cells) mature in the thymus and play an integral role in fighting viruses, cancer, and other disease-causing agents that the B lymphocytes had not been successful in warding off (Straub, 2012).

Earlier we mentioned that stressors are correlated with health problems. But how exactly do stressors such as beliefs and attitudes affect the physical body? In other words, what is the *causal* relationship between stressors and illness? Let's address this question by examining some illnesses thought to be closely linked to stressors (Cohen, Miller, & Rabin, 2001).

GASTRIC ULCERS AND STRESSORS   Gastric ulcers have long been thought to be associated with stress, but the nature of this link has not always been clear. For many years, it was believed that stress alone caused gastric ulcers, but researchers then started to suspect other culprits. They found evidence that the bacterium *H. pylori* plays an important role. This does not mean that *H. pylori* is always to blame, however. Some people who carry the bacteria never get ulcers, while others develop ulcers in its absence. It seems that many factors influence the development of ulcers, among them tobacco use, family history, and excess gastric acid (Fink, 2011).

CANCER AND STRESSORS   Cancer has also been linked to stress, both in terms of risk and development. Specifically, stress has been linked to the suppression of T lymphocytes and NK cells, which help monitor the body for immune system reactions to the invasion of developing tumors. Thus, when a person is exposed to stressors, the body is less able to mount an effective immune response, which increases the risk of cancer (Reiche, Nunes, & Morimoto, 2004).

In the United States and other Western countries, breast cancer is the greatest cancer risk for women, and some evidence suggests it is associated with stress. In a meta-analysis of 26 studies examining the association between life events and risk for breast cancer, death of a spouse was found to be modestly linked to the development of breast cancer; however, no other life events were related to increased risk (Duijts, Zeegers, & Borne, 2003). Other studies have found no association between life events and breast cancer risk (Roberts, Newcomb, Trentham-Dietz, & Storer, 1995).

Stress has been correlated with other types of cancer, though not always in the expected direction. Nielsen and colleagues (2008) examined the relationship between chronic daily stressors and the development of colorectal cancer using a **prospective study** in which nearly 12,000 Danes (who had never been diagnosed with colorectal cancer) were followed for 18 years. The researchers noted some surprising findings, particularly with respect to females. Women who reported higher levels of "stress intensity" and "daily stress" were less likely to develop colon cancer during the course of the study. In contrast, men with "high stress intensity" experienced higher levels of rectal cancer, although this association was not considered to be strong because only a small number actually developed this kind of cancer. The authors suggested that a variety of physiological, mental, and behavioral factors (for example, sex hormones, burnout, and increased alcohol intake) were involved in the relationship between high stress and lower rates of colon cancer in the women.

Why can't researchers agree on the link between cancer and stressors? Part of the problem is that studies are focusing on stressors of different durations. But as it turns out, short- and long-term stressors have distinct effects on the immune system (and thus its ability to combat cancer; Segerstrom & Miller, 2004). For short-lived stressors such as midterm exams, public speaking, and other activities lasting between 5 and 100 minutes, the body responds by increasing the number of NK cells and deploying other immune cells where needed. In other words, short-term stressors tend to augment immune functioning. The situation is quite different with long-term stressors such as military deployment or caring for someone with dementia, which are associated with decreases in NK cells. In order to appreciate the complex relationship between stress, immune function, and cancer, we must also consider biopsychosocial influences on a person's response to stressors. Factors such as age, medical history, social support, and mental health can mediate the link between stressors and cancer (Reiche et al., 2004; Segerstrom & Miller, 2004).

CARDIOVASCULAR DISEASE AND STRESSORS   The same is true for cardiovascular disease, which has also been linked to stressors. Dimsdale (2008) noted that over 40,000 citations popped up in a medical database when the search terms were "stress" and "heart disease." What constitutes a stressor in this context? Earthquakes, unhappy marriages, and caregiving burdens are just a few stressors associated with a variety of outcomes or vulnerabilities, ranging from abnormalities in heart function

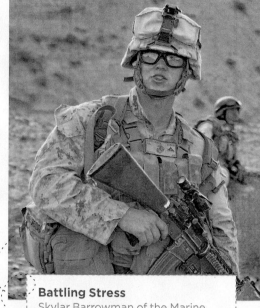

Battling Stress
Skylar Barrowman of the Marine Corps serves in a security capacity during Operation Nightmare in Nowzad, Afghanistan, the summer of 2013. Long-term stressors such as military deployment are associated with declines in NK cells, which help the body fight infections. U.S. Marine Corps photo by Kowshon Ye/Released

CONNECTIONS

In **Chapter 6,** we discussed the malleability of memory. Problems arise because many studies in this area ask participants to remember events and illnesses from the past. Here we are describing a prospective study, which does not require participants to retrieve information from the distant past, thus reducing opportunities for error.

Synonyms
health psychology behavioral medicine
B lymphocytes B cells
T lymphocytes T cells

health psychology The study of the biological, psychological, and social factors that contribute to illness and health.

lymphocyte Type of white blood cell produced in the bone marrow whose job is to battle enemies such as viruses and bacteria.

to sudden death. Earlier we discussed socioeconomic status and stress; it turns out that both of those variables are factors in cardiovascular disease. Joseph and colleagues (2013) reported 5-fold higher odds of experiencing "cardiometabolic events" (within 5 years) for people who became unemployed as a result of Hurricane Katrina, a devastating natural disaster that occurred in 2005. The faster people get support to decrease "socioeconomic disruptions" related to a disaster, the better their health outcomes.

Other stressors have also been linked to heart disease. "Social-evaluative threats," or concerns about being judged by others (about physical appearance or behaviors in a social context, for example), are associated with increases in blood pressure and consequently elevated risk of heart disease (Smith, Birmingham, & Uchino, 2012). One model suggests that increased job stress can put people at greater risk for developing coronary heart disease, particularly among those who perceive a significant degree of job "strain" resulting from high demands, lack of control, and other factors (Ferris, Kline, & Bourdage, 2012).

The mechanisms of the causal relationship between stressors and cardiovascular disease are not totally understood (Straub, 2012). However, we do know that an increase of fatty deposits, inflammation, and scar tissue within artery walls, that is, *atherosclerosis,* is a dangerous risk factor for stroke and heart disease (Go et al., 2013). With this type of damage, blood flow in an artery may become blocked or reduced. Researchers are not sure exactly how atherosclerosis starts, but one theory suggests that it begins with damage to the inner layer of the artery wall, which may be caused by elevated cholesterol and triglycerides, high blood pressure, and cigarette smoke (American Heart Association, 2012). It is important to note that stressors cannot be shown to *cause* changes in cardiovascular health (Dimsdale, 2008). Although there is a clear correlation between biopsychosocial stressors and cardiovascular disease, we cannot say with complete certainty that these stressors are responsible for the disease (Ferris et al., 2012).

Stress, Insidious Stress

Stress often exerts its harmful effects more indirectly (Cohen et al., 2001). During times of stress, we may sleep poorly, eat erratically, and perhaps even drink more alcohol. These behavioral tendencies can lead to significant health problems (Benham, 2010; Ng & Jeffery, 2003).

SMOKING AND STRESS   In Chapter 4, on consciousness, we described how drugs are used to alleviate pain, erase memories, and toy with various aspects of consciousness. But a discussion of drugs is also in order here, because many people use drugs to ease stress. Smokers report that they smoke more cigarettes in response to stressors, as they believe it improves their mood. The association between lighting up and feeling good is one reason smokers have such a hard time quitting (Lerman & Audrain-McGovern, 2010). One study found that when participants were forced to abstain from smoking (for, say, a half day), their mood did improve when they finally puffed on a cigarette. However, this was the only stressful condition of the study in which smoking heightened mood; the effect was not observed when the participants were made to prepare for a public speaking task, for example (Perkins, Karelitz, Konklin, Sayette, & Giedgowd, 2010). Such findings are inconsistent with the self-reports of smokers, who claim that they smoke to feel better in a variety of stressful situations.

How do we get people to kick a habit that is perceived as so pleasurable? One effective way to help people reduce their smoking

Staying Alive
Paramedics transfer a patient from the ambulance to the emergency room. The patient is clearly experiencing a health crisis, but the paramedics face their own set of health risks. Working odd hours, not getting enough exercise, eating poorly, and dealing with the ongoing stresses of paramedic work make it challenging to stay healthy. Juan Manuel Silva/age fotostock

is to meet them where they are, rather than taking a one-size-fits-all approach (Mahoney, 2010; Prochaska, Velicer, Prochaska, Delucchi, & Hall, 2006). In other words, we should recognize that not all smokers need the same type of help. Some need help with smoking only; others engage in additional risky behaviors, like eating high-fat diets or getting too much sun. First-time quitters need different interventions than those who have quit before and relapsed. And success is more likely when the benefits and risks of smoking are made clear. For example, smokers often believe quitting will make them gain weight; therefore, they continue to smoke and don't give enough thought to the serious risks of smoking. Gender is another important consideration, as women seem to be more susceptible to anxiety, depression, and perceived stressors when they fail to quit. Men, on the other hand, seem more vulnerable to cigarette cravings (Nakajima & al'Absi, 2012). This leads us to an important point: Do not underestimate the biology of nicotine addiction. Through **tolerance,** the body becomes dependent on the nicotine; the more you use it, the more you need to get the same effect.

ALCOHOL AND STRESS   Much the same could be said for alcohol, another drug frequently used to "take the edge off," or counteract the unpleasant feelings associated with stress. Perhaps you know someone who "needs" a drink to relax after a rough day. Psychologists explain this type of behavior with *the self-medication hypothesis,* which suggests that people turn to drugs and alcohol to reduce anxiety (Swendsen et al., 2000).

Teenagers, in particular, appear to rely on alcohol to cope with daily hassles (Bailey & Covell, 2011). Adolescents frequently face disagreements with family members, teachers, and peers. They may worry about how they look and whether they are succeeding in school. We need to help adolescents find new and more "healthy" ways to handle these hassles in their lives. This means providing more support in schools, and perhaps educating teachers and counselors about the tendency to self-medicate with drugs and alcohol. Later we will discuss some positive coping strategies for teens and adults alike, but first let's see how stress can be channeled in a way that promotes the health and well-being of others.

ADRENALINE JUNKIES   What lures a person into an EMS career? The reward of alleviating human suffering is "incredible," according to Kehlen. Imagine walking into the home of a diabetic who is lying on the floor, unconscious and surrounded by trembling family members. You insert an IV line into the patient's vein and deliver D50, a dextrose solution that increases blood sugar. In a few moments, the person is awake as if nothing happened. The family is ecstatic; you have saved their loved one from potential brain damage or death. "People that like to do selfless acts, I think, are made for this job," Kehlen says. And for those who enjoy a good challenge, an EMS career will not disappoint. Try working for 24 hours in a row, making life-and-death decisions, hoisting heavy bodies onto stretchers, and crouching over patients until your joints burn. This profession also provides a steady stream of intellectual stimulation. Medical treatments and patterns of illness and injury are constantly evolving. In the past, for example, ambulance crews rarely encountered accidents involving hybrid cars. Nowadays these electrical machines are all over the road, and prying them apart to rescue accident victims can be very dangerous. Rescuers must know exactly where to cut in order to avoid electrocution.

But there appears to be something else drawing people into the EMS profession. You might call it the "adrenaline junkie" factor. Ever since Kehlen was a small boy,

CONNECTIONS

In **Chapter 4,** we discussed the concept of physiological dependence and tolerance. When we use drugs, such as nicotine, they alter the chemistry of the brain and body. Over time, the body adapts to the drug and therefore needs more and more of it to create the original effect.

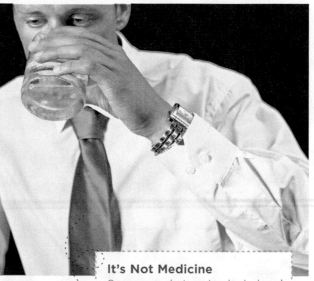

It's Not Medicine
Some people turn to alcohol and other drugs for stress relief, but the *self-medication* approach is not effective. A better strategy might be jogging in the park, laughing with a friend, or doing some deep breathing exercises.
Image Source/Alamy

he enjoyed a certain amount of risk taking. He was the kid who fearlessly scaled the monkey bars and leaped off the jungle gym, and many of his colleagues claim they were the same way. "All of us probably thought we were 10 feet tall and made of steel," Kehlen says, careful to note that "daring" is not the same as "reckless." One must be calculating when it comes to determining what risks are worth taking.

The adrenaline junkie quality is also apparent in some police officers, according to Sergeant Michelle. An officer patrolling a city beat probably experiences the so-called adrenaline rush at least a few times per week. "When a hot call comes in, anyone worth their salt wants to go," Sergeant Michelle explains ("hot call" meaning anything full of excitement and drama, like a robbery in progress). "You hope that the robbers are there," she says, "and you get to arrest them."

Is there really some common adrenaline junkie tendency among officers, EMS providers, and other first responders? That remains an open question. We do know, though, that first responders are frequently exposed to highly stressful events (Anderson, Litzenberger, & Plecas, 2002; Gayton & Lovell, 2012). With all this exposure to violence and trauma, how do the body and mind hold up? The answer is probably different for each individual, but constant stress certainly has the potential to erode health and well-being.

Too Much Cortisol

····▶ LO 8   List some consequences of prolonged exposure
to the stress hormone cortisol.

Earlier we discussed the stress hormone cortisol, which plays an important role in mobilizing the body to react to threats and other stressful situations. Cortisol is useful if you are responding to immediate danger, like a raging fire or ruthless assailant. However, you don't want cortisol levels to remain high for long. The body and brain are impacted when the cortisol system flips into overdrive.

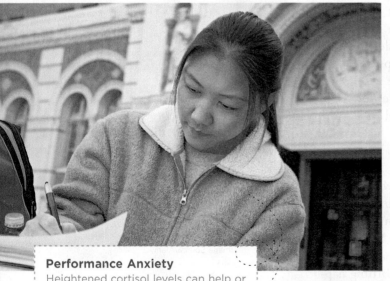

Performance Anxiety
Heightened cortisol levels can help or hinder a person studying for a math test. For people with "higher working memory" and low math anxiety, cortisol seems to boost performance, but it has the opposite effect when math anxiety is high (Mattarella-Micke et al., 2011). Jim Vecchione/Getty Images

psychoneuroimmunology
(sī-kō-ˌn(y)ùr-ō-ˌim-yə-ˈnä-lə-jē) The field that studies the relationship among psychological factors, the nervous system, and immune system functioning.

CORTISOL AND KIDS   The negative effects of stress are apparent very early in life—even before birth, in some cases. Increased levels of cortisol in mother and fetus can cause a variety of problems during pregnancy and after birth, including spontaneous abortion, preeclampsia, heart defects, and even preterm delivery (Mulder et al., 2002). Infants born to mothers subjected to natural disasters, trauma, and other extreme stressors are more likely to be born prematurely, have low birth weights, exhibit behavioral difficulties, and perhaps even show problems with cognitive development (Davis & Sandman, 2010; Tollenaar, Beijers, Jansen, Riksen-Walraven, & De Weerth, 2011). Field and Diego (2008) report that prenatal stressors are associated with fussing and crying, but this association might be indirect; such temperamental difficulties could be due to preterm birth (Baibazarova et al., 2013).

Now consider the types of stressors some preschool children confront every day. Research shows that conflicts at home can increase cortisol levels in children (Slatcher & Robles, 2012). Verbal exchanges such as the child exclaiming, "No! I don't want to!" and parents saying, "You are going to shut your mouth and be quiet!" are exactly the types of conflicts associated with increased cortisol levels. Cortisol activity may help explain why exposure to conflict during childhood seems to pave the way for health problems (Slatcher & Robles, 2012). Clearly, cortisol plays a role in early development. But how does this stress hormone affect adults?

CORTISOL ON THE JOB High cortisol levels can have life-or-death consequences, particularly for workers who make on-the-spot safety decisions. In one study, researchers had police officers participate in a realistic simulation of being targeted by shooters. Not only did the officers' cortisol levels rise, but the functioning of their **working memory** decreased (Taverniers, Smeets, Van Ruysseveldt, Syroit, & von Grumbkow, 2011). Can you imagine the implications of being in a dangerous situation with impaired working memory? Think of the last time you were really afraid, and how difficult it was to think clearly. Your working memory was probably compromised.

Other research suggests that heightened cortisol levels may have the opposite effect. When police officers had to make threat-related decisions in a video simulation, they were better able to discern whether threatening individuals were armed when their cortisol levels were high. But this accuracy increased when the officer faced a simulation involving a Black suspect, and decreased when the suspect was White. This finding was the same for the White officers and minority officers participating in the study. The researchers concluded that higher cortisol levels, which were caused by the stressful situation, resulted in "heightened vigilance for danger" (Akinola & Mendes, 2012, p. 172). Apparently, the perceived threat of Black men was greater, which is consistent with what social psychologists have learned about the conscious and unconscious reactions many people have to racial minorities (Chapter 15).

PSYCHONEUROIMMUNOLOGY We have now discussed some of the effects of short- and long-term stressors. You know that a spurt of cortisol gives you a boost in energy and alertness and steps up your immunity. You also know that if cortisol levels remain high for prolonged periods (as occurs with chronic stressors), the immune system may not function at an optimal level. We discussed how this affects one's risk for developing gastric ulcers, cancer, and heart disease, but the list of negative health effects is much longer. According to a meta-analysis of over 300 studies, chronic stressors were found to be associated with problematic immune system responses, which may increase the risk for various illnesses involving inflammation, including multiple sclerosis, rheumatoid arthritis, asthma, and allergies (Segerstrom & Miller, 2004). The exact nature of these relationships is yet to be determined, but researchers are working hard to uncover them, including the impact of aging and vulnerable immune systems (Cohen et al. 2001). It is an exciting time for those who specialize in the field of **psychoneuroimmunology** (sī-kō-ˌn(y)uṙ-ō-ˌim-yə-ˈnä-lə-jē), which examines the relationships among psychological factors (such as coping, emotions, beliefs), the nervous system, and the functioning of the immune system.

The field of health psychology, which draws on the biopsychosocial model and psychoneuroimmunology, has shed light on the complex relationship between stress and health (Havelka, Lučanin, & Lučanin, 2009). Now that we understand how profoundly stressors can impact physical well-being, let's explore some real-life situations that can trigger stress.

CONNECTIONS

In **Chapter 6,** we presented the concept of working memory, which refers to how we actively maintain and manipulate information that is in short-term memory. Here, we see how these activities in working memory can be impacted by stressful situations.

show what you know

1. When everyday stressors get to be too much, some people seek relief in alcohol. The _____ suggests that people turn to drugs and alcohol to ease anxiety.

2. Infants born to mothers subjected to extreme stressors may be born prematurely, have low birth weights, and exhibit behavioral difficulties. These outcomes result from increased levels of the stress hormone _____.
   a. *H. pylori*
   b. lymphocytes
   c. cortisol
   d. NK cells

3. Why are people under stress more likely to get sick?

✓ CHECK YOUR ANSWERS IN APPENDIX C.

Tricky Situation
Police officers deal with a variety of conflicts in their daily work. Imagine you are an officer trying to decide whether to arrest a parent suspected of child abuse. If you make the arrest, the child may be removed from the home and placed in foster care (not an ideal scenario), but at least the threat of abuse is removed. This is an *approach–avoidance* conflict—the outcome has both positive and negative elements. Siri Stafford/Getty Images

approach–approach conflict A type of conflict in which one must choose between two or more options that are attractive.

approach–avoidance conflict A type of conflict that occurs when faced with a choice or situation that has favorable and unfavorable characteristics.

avoidance–avoidance conflict A type of conflict in which one is faced with two or more options that are unattractive.

burnout Emotional, mental, and physical fatigue that results in reduced motivation, enthusiasm, and performance.

Factors Related to Stress

First responders encounter a wide variety of scenarios, ranging in intensity from five-car pile-ups to soccer injuries. What determines how a first responder reacts in these situations? There are two types of variables to consider: those that reside within the individual and those that exist in the environment. We can see both of these variables at work in one of the most common stressors of everyday life: conflict.

Conflicts

LO 9 Identify different types of conflicts.

When most people think of conflict, they imagine fist fights and arguments, but here conflict is defined as the discomfort one feels when making tough choices. There are various types of conflict. In an **approach–approach conflict,** two or more favorable alternatives are pitted against each other. Here, you must choose between two options you find attractive. Imagine this situation: You have to pick only one class this semester, and to fit your schedule, you must choose between two classes you would really like to take. An **approach-avoidance conflict** occurs when you face a choice or situation that has both favorable and unfavorable characteristics. You are required to take a biology lab class this semester, and although you like biology, you do not like working with other students in lab settings. You are faced with an approach–avoidance conflict (you enjoy biology/you don't like working with partners). A third type of conflict is the **avoidance–avoidance conflict,** which occurs when you are faced with two or more alternatives that are unattractive. In order to fulfill a requirement, you must choose between two courses that you really dread taking.

Let's test your understanding of these conflict types, using some examples related to police work:

1. Imagine you are a police officer contemplating whether to arrest a mother and father suspected of child abuse. If you make the arrest, all of the children in the home will be placed in foster care, an unfamiliar, often frightening environment for children. Something good will come out of the change (the children are no longer at risk of being abused), but the downside is that the children will be thrown into an unfamiliar environment. *Approach–avoidance. There is an upside and a downside to removing the children from their home.*

2. You are new to the police force. It is your second day on the job, and you are given a choice between the following two tasks: ride in the squad car with a partner you dislike or stay in the station all day and answer calls (a very boring choice). You are torn, because you really don't want to do either of these things. *Avoidance–avoidance. Both decisions lead to negative outcomes—a hard day for you.*

3. You are a 30-year veteran of the Houston police department. You can either retire now and begin receiving a pension or stay on the job and continue to enjoy your work. *Approach–approach. Both options are positive—retiring early or continuing to work.*

Conflicts can be even more complicated than this. A *double approach–avoidance conflict* occurs when you must decide between two choices, each possessing attractive and unattractive qualities. For example, a student trying to decide whether to purchase an e-book or a hardback might create a list of the good and bad qualities for both types of books. On the one hand, the e-book allows for portability and quick access, but it is not a good option if the Internet fails or electricity is unavailable. The hardback is long lasting and always accessible, but it is heavy and more expensive. You might even have to deal with *multiple approach–avoidance conflicts,* which occur when you are faced with a decision that has more than two possible choices. You are trying to decide where to live when you attend college in a new city. Should you apply for a dormitory room, look for an apartment, share a house, or live with a family member? Each of these choices has attractive and unattractive qualities.

Sometimes conflicts and other stressors pile up so high they become difficult to tolerate. When we can no longer deal with stress in a constructive way, we experience what psychologists call burnout.

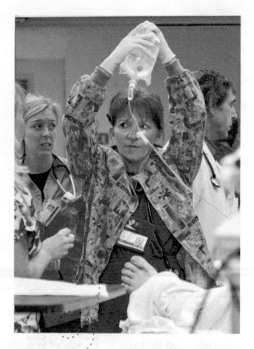

AMBULANCE BURNOUT Kehlen has been in the EMS field for nearly a decade, and most of that time he has spent working for a private ambulance company. He estimates that the average ambulance worker lasts about 8 years before quitting to pursue another line of work. What makes this career so hard to endure? The pay is dismal, the 24-hour shifts grueling, and the constant exposure to trauma profoundly disturbing. The pressure to perform is enormous, but there is seldom a "thank-you" or recognition for a job well done. Perhaps no other profession involves so much responsibility—combined with so little appreciation. "The ambulance crews, they're kind of like the silent heroes," Kehlen explains. "You work so hard and you don't get any thanks at the end of the day."

It might not surprise you that the EMS profession has one of the highest rates of *burnout* (Gayton & Lovell, 2012). **Burnout** refers to emotional, mental, and physical fatigue that results from repeated exposure to challenges, leading to reduced motivation, enthusiasm, and performance. People who work in the helping professions, such as nurses, mental health professionals, and child protection workers, are clearly at risk for burnout (Jenaro, Flores, & Arias, 2007; Linnerooth, Mrdjenovich, & Moore, 2011; Rupert, Stevanovic, & Hunley, 2009).

Drained ◄
A nurse holds a patient's IV bag in the emergency room. Nursing is one of the professions associated with high burnout—the emotional, mental, and physical exhaustion that develops when a person faces constant challenges. Lisa Krantz/San Antonio Express-News/Zuma Press

I Can Deal: Coping with Stress

Police work is among the most stressful careers around, and it is not for everybody. To survive and thrive in this career, you must excel under pressure. Police departments need officers who are emotionally stable and capable of making split-second decisions with potentially serious ethical implications. If a tired, stressed-out officer makes one bad decision, the reputation of the entire police department could be tarnished. No wonder over 90% of city police departments in the United States require job applicants to take psychological evaluations, such as the Minnesota Multiphasic Personality Inventory–2 (MMPI–2) (Butcher & Rouse, 1996; Cochrane, Tett, & Vandecreek, 2003). Psychological testing is just one hurdle facing the aspiring police officer; some departments also require full-length meetings with a psychologist. And most city agencies also require criminal background checks, polygraph (lie detector) tests, and physical fitness assessments. And don't forget the 1,000-or-so hours of training at the police academy (Cochrane et al., 2003). But even after overcoming all the hurdles of the hiring process, some police officers end up struggling with stress management. In this respect, police work is like any other field; there will always be people who have trouble coping with the stress of the job.

You Asked, Eric Answers
http://qrs.ly/dr3nrbc
Has the stress of police training ever made you want to quit?

> **LO 10** Illustrate how appraisal influences coping.

CONNECTIONS

In **Chapter 9,** we described the *cognitive-appraisal* theory of emotion, which suggests that *emotion* results from the way people appraise or interpret interactions they have. We appraise events based on their significance, and our subjective appraisal influences our response to stressors.

APPRAISAL AND COPING   Needless to say, people respond to stress in their own unique ways. Lazarus suggests that stress is the result of a person's **appraisal** of a stressor, not necessarily the stressor itself (Folkman & Lazarus, 1985; Lazarus & Folkman, 1984). This viewpoint stands in contrast to Selye's suggestion (noted earlier) that we all react to stressors in a similar manner. **Coping** refers to the cognitive, behavioral, and emotional abilities used to effectively manage something that is perceived as difficult or challenging. In order to cope, we must determine if an event is harmful, threatening, or challenging (**INFOGRAPHIC 12.2**). A person making a **primary appraisal** of a situation determines how the event will affect him. He must decide if it is irrelevant, positive, challenging, or harmful. Determining whether something constitutes a threat, for example, is a personal appraisal. Next, the individual makes a **secondary appraisal,** or decides how to respond. If he believes he can cope with virtually any challenge that comes his way, the impact of stress remains low. If he thinks his coping abilities are poor, then the impact of stress will be high. These differences in appraisals help explain why two people can react to the same event in dramatically different ways.

There are two basic types of coping. **Problem-focused coping** means taking a direct approach, confronting a problem head-on. Suppose you are having troubles in a relationship; an example of problem-focused coping might be reading self-help books or finding a counselor. **Emotion-focused coping** involves addressing the emotions that surround a problem, rather than trying to solve it. With a troubled relationship, you might think about your feelings and how miserable you are, instead of addressing the problem directly. Sometimes it's better to use emotion-focused coping—when an emotional reaction might be too stressful or interferes with daily functioning, or when a problem cannot be solved (for example, the death of a loved one). In the long run, however, problem-focused coping is usually more productive.

You Asked, Eric Answers

http://qrs.ly/283nrbd

Do you ever feel so overwhelmed that you can't relax?

coping The cognitive, behavioral, and emotional abilities used to effectively manage something that is perceived as difficult or challenging.

primary appraisal One's initial assessment of a situation to determine its personal impact and whether it is irrelevant, positive, challenging, or harmful.

secondary appraisal An assessment to determine how to respond to a challenging or threatening situation.

problem-focused coping A coping strategy in which a person deals directly with a problem by attempting to solve and address it head-on.

emotion-focused coping A coping strategy in which a person addresses the emotions that surround a problem, as opposed to trying to solve it.

IT'S A PERSONAL THING   In June 2011 Eric began his second run through Onondaga's police training program. This time around, he nailed the Emergency Vehicle Operations Course (EVOC). "I can't even describe to you how great it felt." The secret to his success? "Instead of worrying about everything, I had fun," Eric says. "Once you relax . . . [it] helps you focus better." Eric graduated in December 2011. He soon landed a position with a local police department.

"Police training is different everywhere," says Eric, who chose the police academy at Onondaga Community College because of its rigor. No training program can totally prepare you for police work, but the academy makes every effort to simulate real-world scenarios. "The individuals who can deal with stress in the best way make it through," says Eric. "Those that cannot weed themselves out on their own."

> **LO 11** Describe Type A and Type B personalities and explain how they relate to stress.

TYPE A AND TYPE B PERSONALITIES   Personality appears to have a profound effect on coping style and predispositions to stress-related illness. For example, people with certain personality types are more prone to developing cardiovascular disease. How do we know this? Two cardiologists, Meyer Friedman and Ray Rosenman, were among the first to suspect a link between personality type and the cardiovascular problems they observed in their patients (Friedman & Rosenman, 1974). Specifically, they noted that many of the people they treated were intensely focused on time and always in a hurry. This characteristic pattern

The Process of Coping

Coping refers to the cognitive, emotional, and behavioral methods we employ to manage stressful events. But we don't always rely on the same strategies to manage stressors in our lives. Coping is an individual *process* through which we appraise a stressor to determine how it will affect us and how we can respond.

stressful encounter

I have a final exam!

MAY **12** Math Final

How will this affect me?

BEFORE TEST

PRIMARY APPRAISAL

Now how will this affect me?

DURING TEST

PRIMARY APPRAISAL

Most stressful events are not static. Therefore, we may appraise them at different stages with different results. For example, you will appraise the challenge of a test differently before you take it, while you are taking it, and after you have taken it but are waiting to receive a grade.

There will be independent responses from each instance of primary appraisal.

I missed a lot of classes and don't understand the material.

STRESS!

I don't know how to manage this.

PERSON "X"

CHALLENGING

PERSON "Y"

POSITIVE

I'm doing well in class. I will still get a good grade for the class even if I don't do that well on the final.

not too stressed

I can cope with this.

People respond differently to stressors depending on differences in appraisal. A student who is struggling in a class because she hasn't worked hard may find a test even more challenging than a student who has been working hard all semester.

SECONDARY APPRAISAL

What can I do?

SECONDARY APPRAISAL

What can I do?

Once we know how an event will affect us, a secondary appraisal determines how to respond.

* problem focused

Seek help from friends

emotion focused

Seek emotional support

* problem focused

Planning

emotion focused

Emphasize the positive

In response to a stressor, most people use several coping strategies, including both problem-focused and emotion-focused coping. Problem-focused coping involves doing something to deal with the source of stress. People who do not feel they can solve the problem tend to rely more on emotion-focused coping to manage their feelings about the situation.

I'll get notes from a classmate.

I'll feel better after venting.

First I'll take the online self-quiz, then I'll look up incorrect answers in my textbook.

I feel so much better when I study.

emotion focused

Mental disengagement

* problem focused

Suppress competing activities

I don't care about this class anyway.

I won't go out this weekend so I can focus on studying.

* Problem-focused coping is usually the most productive. Here are some other problem-focused strategies:

➡ Restraint (wait to act until all relevant data has come to light)

➡ Break the problem into manageable chunks

➡ Research the situation

➡ Pursue alternatives

Laid-Back Lochte
Olympic swimmer Ryan Lochte appears to have what psychologists call a Type B personality—he is easygoing, relaxed, and apparently not preoccupied with beating other swimmers. As Lochte once told Reuters, "I told myself I'll quit swimming once I stop having fun, and right now I'm having a blast. I'm not thinking about the money or medals or anything else, I'm just having fun racing" (Linden, 2012, July 5). AP Photo/Daniel Ochoa De Olza

of behaviors eventually was referred to as **Type A personality.** Someone with a Type A personality is competitive, aggressive, impatient, and often hostile (Diamond, 1982; Smith & Ruiz, 2002). Through numerous studies, Friedman and Rosenman discovered that people with Type A personalities were twice as likely to develop cardiovascular disease as those with **Type B personality.** People with Type B personality are found to be more relaxed, patient, and nonaggressive (Rosenman et al., 1975). There appear to be various reasons people with Type A personality suffer disproportionately from cardiovascular disease: they are more likely to have high blood pressure, heart rate, and stress hormone levels. Type A individuals are also prone to more interpersonal problems (for example, arguments, fights, or hostile interactions), which increase the time their bodies are prepared for fight or flight.

Although many years of research confirmed the relationship between Type A behavior and coronary heart problems, some researchers began to report findings inconsistent with this (Smith & MacKenzie, 2006). Failure to reproduce the results led some to question the validity of this relationship, although one major factor was a lack of consistency in research methodology. For example, some studies used samples with high-risk participants, whereas others included healthy people. As researchers continued to probe the relationship between personality type and coronary heart disease, they found that the component of *hostility* in Type A personality was the strongest predictor of coronary heart disease.

TYPE D PERSONALITY   More recently, researchers have suggested another personality type that may better predict how patients fare when they already have heart disease: *Type D personality,* where the "D" refers to distress (Denollet & Conraads, 2011). Someone with Type D personality is characterized by emotions like worry, tension, bad moods, and social inhibition (avoids confronting others, poor social skills). There is a clear link between Type D characteristics and a "poor prognosis" in patients with coronary heart disease (Denollet & Conraads, 2011). In other words, people who have heart problems and exhibit these Type D characteristics are more likely to struggle with their illness. It could be that people with Type D personality tend to avoid dealing with their problems directly and don't take advantage of social support. Such an approach might lead to poor choices about coping with stressors over time (Martin et al., 2011).

THE THREE Cs OF HARDINESS   Clearly, not everyone has the same tolerance for stress (Ganzel, Morris, & Wethington, 2010; Straub, 2012). Some people seem capable of handling intensely stressful situations (for example, war and poverty). These individuals appear to have a personality characteristic referred to as **hardiness,** meaning that even when functioning under a great deal of stress, they are very resilient and tend to remain positive. Kehlen, who considers himself "a very optimistic person," may very well fit into this category, and findings from one study of Scottish ambulance personnel suggest that EMS workers with this characteristic are less likely to experience burnout (Alexander & Klein, 2001).

Kobasa (1979) and others have studied how some executives seem to withstand the effects of extremely stressful jobs. Their hardiness seems to be associated with three characteristics: feeling a strong *commitment* to work and personal matters; believing they are in *control* of the events in their lives and not victims of circumstances; and not feeling threatened by *challenges,* but rather seeing them as opportunities for growth. For example, Sheard (2009) reported that the level of commitment of nontraditional female students predicted higher academic success. Women who

Type A personality Competitive, aggressive, impatient, and often hostile pattern of behaviors.

Type B personality Relaxed, patient, and nonaggressive pattern of behaviors.

hardiness A personality characteristic indicating an ability to remain resilient and optimistic despite intensely stressful situations.

were older than 20 experienced a greater degree of success in their college work than their younger counterparts, presumably due to their commitment to obtaining an education.

I Am in Control

The ability to respond to stress is very much dependent on one's perceived level of personal control. Psychologists have consistently found that people who believe they have control over their lives, circumstances, and/or situations are less likely to experience the negative impact of stressors than those who do not feel the same control. For example, Langer and Rodin (1976) conducted a series of studies using nursing home residents as their participants. Residents in a "responsibility-induced" group were allowed to make a variety of choices about their daily activities as well as their environments. Members of the "comparison" group were not given these kinds of choices; instead, the nursing home staff made all of these decisions for them (the residents were told the staff were responsible for their happiness and care). After following the residents for 18 months, the researchers found that members of the responsibility-induced group were more lively, active in their social lives, and healthier than the residents in the comparison group. And twice as many of the residents in the comparison group died during this period (Rodin & Langer, 1977).

Researchers have examined how having a sense of **personal control** relates to a variety of health issues across all ages. Feelings of control are linked to how patients fare with some diseases. Cancer patients who exhibit a "helpless attitude" regarding their disease seem more likely to experience a recurrence of the cancer than those with perceptions of greater control. Why would this be? Women who have had breast cancer and believe they maintain control over their lifestyle, through diet and exercise, are more likely to make proactive changes related to their health, and perhaps reduce risk factors associated with recurrence (Costanzo, Lutgendorf, & Roeder, 2011). The same type of relationship is apparent in cardiovascular disease; the less control people feel they have, the greater their risk (Shapiro, Schwartz, & Astin, 1996). As we pointed out, having choices increases a perceived sense of control.

But feelings of control may also have a more direct effect on the body; for example, a sense of powerlessness is associated with increases in catecholamines and corticosteroids, both key players in a typical physiological response to stress. Some have suggested that a causal relationship exists between feelings of perceived control and immune system function; the greater the sense of control, the better the functioning of the immune system (Shapiro et al., 1996). But these are correlations, and the direction of causality should not be assumed. Could it be that better immune functioning, and thus better health, might increase a sense of control?

We must also consider cross-cultural differences. Individual control is emphasized and valued in individualist cultures like our own, but not necessarily in collectivistic cultures, where people look to "powerful others" and "chance factors" to explain events and guide decision making (Cheng, Cheung, Chio, & Chan, 2013).

LOCUS OF CONTROL Differences in perceived sense of control stem from beliefs about where control resides (Rotter, 1966). Someone with an *internal locus of control* generally feels as if she is in control of life and its circumstances; she probably believes it is important to take charge and make changes when problems occur. A person with an *external locus of control* generally feels as if chance, luck, or fate is responsible for her circumstances; there is no need to try to change things or make them better. How does this relate to health and stress? Any decisions related

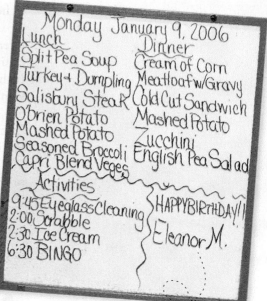

It's My Life
A nursing home white board displays a list of menu items and activities that residents can choose from. One study found that putting nursing home residents in charge of their daily activities led to increased levels of energy, health, and social engagement. Their empowerment was also associated with lower death rates (Rodin & Langer, 1977). AP Photo/Charles Rex Arbogast

CONNECTIONS

In **Chapter 11,** we discussed *locus of control,* a key component of personality. Someone with an *internal* locus of control believes the causes of outcomes reside within him. A person with an *external* locus of control thinks causes for outcomes reside outside of him. Here, we see that higher personal control is associated with better health outcomes.

to healthy choices can be influenced by locus of control. Imagine that a doctor tells a patient he needs to change his lifestyle and start exercising. If the patient has an internal locus of control, he will likely take charge and start walking to work or hitting the gym at night; he expects his actions will impact his health outcome. If the patient has an external locus of control, he is more apt to think his actions won't make a difference because his health is controlled by chance. Thus, he might not even attempt lifestyle changes. In the 1970 British Cohort Study, researchers examined over 11,000 children at age 10, and then assessed their health at age 30. Participants with an internal locus of control, measured at 10 years of age, were less likely as adults to be overweight or obese, and they had lower levels of psychological problems. Women with an internal locus of control were less likely to suffer from hypertension. Furthermore, people with a more internal locus of control were less likely to be smokers and more likely to exercise regularly than those with a more external locus of control (Gale, Batty, & Deary, 2008).

▶ Camaraderie

Firefighters climb the notoriously difficult "Incline," a seemingly endless set of stairs up Pikes Peak in Colorado Springs, Colorado. Every year on the morning of September 11, the firefighters walk up the 1-mile path to commemorate those who died in the 9/11 terrorist attacks. The tight-knit community at the firehouse provides Kehlen with friendship, emotional support, and a great deal of stress reduction. Nicole Pritts

FROM AMBULANCE TO FIREHOUSE Kehlen's original career goal was to become a firefighter, but jobs are extremely hard to come by in this field. Fresh out of high school, Kehlen joined an ambulance crew with the goal of moving on to the firehouse. Seven years later, he reached his destination. Kehlen is now a firefighter paramedic with the Pueblo Fire Department. His job description still includes performing CPR, inserting breathing tubes, and delivering lifesaving medical care. But now he can also be seen handling fire hoses and rushing into 800-degree buildings with 80 pounds of gear.

Compared to an ambulance, the firehouse is a far more conducive environment for managing stress. For starters, there is enormous social support. Fellow firefighters are a lot like family members. They eat together, go to sleep together, and wake to the same flashing lights and tones announcing the latest emergency. "The fire department is such a brotherhood," Kehlen says. Spending a third of his life at the firehouse with his colleagues, Kehlen has come to know and trust them on a deep level. They discuss disturbing events they witness and help each other recover emotionally. "If you don't talk about it," says Kehlen, "it's just going to wear on you." Another major benefit of working at the firehouse is having the freedom to exercise, which Kehlen considers a major stress reliever. The firefighters are actually required to work out 1 hour per day during their shifts.

Ambulance work is quite another story. Kehlen and his coworkers were friends, but they didn't share the tight bonds that Kehlen now can count on at the firehouse. And eating healthy and exercising were almost impossible. Ambulance workers don't have the luxury of making a healthy meal in a kitchen. They often have no choice but to drive to the nearest fast-food restaurant and wipe the crumbs off their faces as they race to the next emergency. One of the worst aspects of the job was the lack of exercise. Says Kehlen, "That killed me when I was in the ambulance."

Tools for Healthy Living

▸ **LO 12** Discuss several tools for reducing stress and maintaining health.

Dealing with stressors can be challenging, but you don't have to grin and bear it. There are many simple ways to manage and reduce stress. One of your most powerful stress-fighting weapons is physical exercise.

EXERCISE   You are feeling the pressure. Exam time is here, and you haven't cracked open a book because you've been so busy at work. The holidays are approaching, you haven't purchased a single present, and the pile of unpaid bills on your desk is starting to build. With so much to do, you feel paralyzed. In these types of situations, the best solution may be to drop to the floor to do some push-ups, or run out the door and take a jog. When you come back, you feel a new sense of calm. *I can handle this,* you'll think to yourself. *One thing at a time.*

How does exercise work its magic? Physiologically, we know exercise increases blood flow, activates the autonomic nervous system, and helps initiate the release of several hormones. These physiological reactions help the body defend itself from potential illnesses, especially those that are stress related. Exercise also spurs the release of the body's natural painkilling and pleasure-inducing neurotransmitters, the endorphins (Salmon, 2001).

When it comes to choosing an exercise regimen, the tough part is finding an activity that is intense enough to reduce the impact of stress, but sufficiently enjoyable to keep you coming back for more. Research has suggested that only 30 minutes of daily exercise is needed to decrease the risk of heart disease, stroke, hypertension, certain types of cancer, and diabetes (Warburton, Charlesworth, Ivey, Nettlefold, & Bredin, 2010) and improve mood (Bryan, Hutchison, Seals, & Allen, 2007; Hansen, Stevens, & Coast, 2001). And exercise needn't be a chore. Your daily 30 minutes could mean dancing to *Just Dance 4* on the Wii, going for a bike ride, raking leaves on a beautiful fall day, or shoveling snow in a winter wonderland.

RELAX   Exercise is all about getting the body moving, but relaxing the muscles can also relieve stress. "Just relax." We have heard it said a thousand times, but do we really know how to begin? Edmund Jacobson (1938) introduced a technique known as *progressive muscle relaxation,* which has since been expanded upon. With this technique, you begin by tensing a muscle group (for example, your toes), for about 10 seconds, and then releasing as you focus on the tension leaving. Next you progress to another muscle group, such as the calves, and then the thighs, buttocks, stomach, shoulders, arms, neck, forehead, and so on. After several weeks of practice, you will begin to recognize where you hold tension in your muscles—at least this is the goal. Once you become aware of that tension, you can focus on relaxing those specific muscles without going through the entire process. Progressive muscle relaxation has been shown to diffuse anxiety in highly stressed college students. In one study, researchers found that just 20 minutes of progressive muscle relaxation had "significant short-term effects," including decreases in anxiety, blood pressure, and heart rate (Dolbier & Rush, 2012). Participants also reported a feeling of increased control and energy. This *relaxation response* may also serve as an effective way to reduce pain (Benson, 2000; Dusek et al., 2008).

CONTROVERSIES

Meditate on This

➡️⬅️ An increasingly popular way to induce relaxation is meditation. If you've ever known an anxious person who began meditating regularly, you know that it can have a dramatic "chilling out" effect. A sense of serenity envelops people who take up meditation. But anecdotal evidence or folk wisdom is no substitute for scientific data. What does the research say?

Numerous studies point to a variety of meditation-related physical and mental health benefits, including increased immune system activity, enhanced empathy, and reduced levels of anxiety, neuroticism, and negative emotions (Davidson et al., 2003; Roemer, Orsillo, & Salters-Pedneault, 2008; Sedlmeier et al., 2012; Walsh, 2011). ▼

This all sounds great, but some scholars assert that many meditation studies are riddled with methodological flaws and lack the support of solid theoretical frameworks (Ireland, 2012; Sedlmeier et al., 2012).

In many cases, it's unclear whether meditation or some other lifestyle factor such as regular exercise is causing the positive effects researchers have observed. It's also important to recognize that the expectations of research participants can sway study results in a favorable direction. In other words, just *thinking* meditation is beneficial may affect the way people perceive and report its effects. Meditation may exert a *placebo effect*, leading its practitioners to believe that their efforts are paying off. If this is the case, then the beliefs (rather than the meditation) are producing the health benefits.

That said, we should point out that long-term meditation has been shown to produce observable changes in the brain (Davidson & Lutz, 2008; Hölzel et al., 2011). There is little doubt that something important happens when a person meditates, and that something appears to be positive. Now let's take a closer look at some of the research pointing to one of those positive outcomes. ➤◄

> ... JUST *THINKING* MEDITATION IS BENEFICIAL MAY AFFECT THE WAY PEOPLE PERCEIVE AND REPORT ITS EFFECTS.

from the pages of SCIENTIFIC AMERICAN

Meditate That Cold Away

Practicing meditation or exercising might make you sick less often

To blunt your next cold, try meditating or exercising now. A new study from the University of Wisconsin–Madison found that adults who practiced mindful meditation or moderately intense exercise for 8 weeks suffered less from seasonal ailments during the following winter than those who did not exercise or meditate.

The study appeared in the July issue of *Annals of Family Medicine*. Researchers recruited about 150 participants, 80 percent of them women and all older than 50, and randomly assigned them to three groups. One group was trained for eight weeks in mindful meditation; another did eight weeks of brisk walking or jogging under the supervision of trainers. The control group did neither. The researchers then monitored the respiratory health of the volunteers with biweekly telephone calls and laboratory visits from September through May—but they did not attempt to find out whether the subjects continued meditating or exercising after the initial eight-week training period.

Participants who had meditated missed 76 percent fewer days of work from September through May than did the control subjects. Those who had exercised missed 48 percent fewer days during this period. The severity of the colds also differed between the two groups. Those who had exercised or meditated suffered for an average of five days; colds of participants in the control group lasted eight. Lab tests confirmed that the self-reported length of colds correlated with the level of antibodies in the body, which is a biomarker for the presence of a virus.

"I think the big news is that mindfulness meditation training appears to have worked" in preventing or reducing the length of colds, says Bruce Barrett of the department of family medicine. He cautions, however, that the findings are preliminary. **Harvey Black.**

Many forms of meditation emphasize control and awareness of breathing. This may be one of the reasons people find meditation so relaxing. Taking slow, deep breaths is a fast and easy way to reduce the impact of stress.

try this

Look at a clock or watch. Now breathe in slowly for 5 seconds. Then exhale slowly for 5 seconds. Do this for 1 minute. With each breath, you begin to slow down and your body starts to relax. The key, however, is to breathe deeply. Draw your breath deep into the diaphragm and avoid shallow, rapid chest breathing.

BIOFEEDBACK A proven method for reducing physiological responses to stressors is **biofeedback.** This technique builds on learning principles and involves providing visual or auditory information about biological processes, allowing for control of seemingly involuntary physiological responses (such as heart rate, blood pressure, and skin temperature). The biofeedback equipment monitors internal responses and helps a person identify those that are maladaptive (for example, tense shoulder muscles). One would begin by focusing on a mechanism (a light or tone, for example) that indicates when a desired response occurs. By controlling the biofeedback indicator, one learns to maintain the desired response (relaxed shoulders in this example). The goal is to be able to tap into this technique outside of the clinic or lab, and translate what has been learned into real-life practice.

Mind-Body Connection
A patient at the Max Planck Institute in Munich, Germany, combats back pain using biofeedback, a learning technique that enables a person to manipulate seemingly automatic functions, such as heart rate and blood pressure. With the help of a monitor that signals the occurrence of a target response, a patient can learn how to sustain this response longer. Ronald Frommann/laif/Redux

The use of biofeedback can decrease the frequency of headaches and chronic pain (Flor & Birbaumer, 1993; Sun-Edelstein & Mauskop, 2011). Biofeedback appears to be useful for all age groups, including children, adolescents, and the elderly (Morone & Greco, 2007; Palermo, Eccleston, Lewandowski, Williams, & Morley, 2010).

SOCIAL SUPPORT Up until now, we have discussed ways to manage the body's physiological response to stressors. There are also situational methods to deal with stressors, like maintaining a social support network. Researchers have found that proactively participating in positive enduring relationships with family, friends, and religious groups can generate a health benefit similar to exercise and not smoking (House, Landis, & Umberson, 1988). And people who maintain positive, supportive relationships also have better overall health (Walsh, 2011). Both Eric and Kehlen find family time to be a major stress reliever. At home with their wives and children, they feel relaxed and happy. Kehlen's wife, a nurse practitioner, once worked in an emergency room, so she can relate to her husband's experiences with trauma.

What Goes Around
Volunteers in Chongqing, China, celebrate Father's Day with elderly men in a nursing home. *Altruism,* or helping others because it feels good, is an excellent stress reliever.
TopPhoto via AP Images

You might expect that receiving support is the key to lowering stress, but research suggests that *giving* support also really matters. In a study of older married adults, researchers reported reduced mortality rates for participants who indicated that they helped or supported others, including friends, spouses, relatives, and neighbors. There were no reductions in mortality, however, associated with receiving support from others (Brown, Nesse, Vinokur, & Smith, 2003).

Helping others because it gives you pleasure, and expecting nothing in return, is known as *altruism,* and it appears to be an effective stress reducer and happiness booster (Schwartz, Keyl, Marcum, & Bode, 2009; Schwartz, Meisenhelder, Yunsheng, & Reed, 2003). When we care for others, we generally don't have time to focus on our own problems; we also come to recognize that others may be dealing with more troubling circumstances or events than we are.

biofeedback A technique that involves providing visual or auditory information about biological processes, allowing a person to control physiological responses (for example, heart rate, blood pressure, skin temperature).

Stressed Out

Every year, the American Psychological Association (APA) commissions a survey investigating perceived stress among adults in the United States. In addition to measuring attitudes about stress, the survey identifies leading sources of stress and common behaviors used to manage stressors. The resulting picture shows that stress is a significant issue for many people in the United States and that we are not always managing it well (APA, 2013d). Even when we acknowledge the importance of stress management and resolve to make positive lifestyle changes, many adults report barriers such as a lack of time or willpower that prevent them from achieving their goals. The good news? Our ability to manage stress appears to improve with age. (ALL INFORMATION PRESENTED IN THIS INFOGRAPHIC, EXCEPT THE PERCEIVED STRESS SCALE, IS FROM APA, 2013D)

4 OUT OF 5

Number of people reporting their stress level has increased or stayed the same in the past year.

TOP SOURCES OF STRESS

money 69%

work 65%

the economy 61%

family responsibilities 57%

relationships 56%

family health problems 52%

Number experiencing **responses to stress,** including **anger, fatigue** and **feeling overwhelmed.**

NEARLY 7 IN 10

People with high stress also report poor health behaviors.

Only **30%** of adults with high stress report eating healthy and getting enough sleep.

OVER THE PAST 5 YEARS

60% **60%** of people have tried to reduce their stress

53% **53%** are still trying

STRESS OVER THE LIFE SPAN

People across all age groups agree that managing stress is very important. However, the ability to manage stress varies with age. Younger adults are more likely to rely on unhealthy behaviors like drinking alcohol and smoking for stress management. Older adults report more success in achieving healthy lifestyle goals such as eating healthy and getting enough sleep. They also report higher rates of religious participation (APA, 2013d).

▶ 50% Oldest people report highest rate of meeting stress management goals.

Age groups	18-33	34-47	48-66	67+
Managing stress is very important	61%	69%	63%	65%
Doing a very good job managing stress	29%	35%	38%	50%

Age groups

- Managing stress is **very important**
- Doing a very good job managing stress

DO YOU FEEL STRESSED?

Psychologist Sheldon Cohen and colleagues (1983) developed the Perceived Stress Scale to measure the degree to which we appraise situations as stressful. By comparing your score against others tested in your age group, you are able to assess the amount of perceived stress in your life. Simply knowing you find your life uncontrollable or overloaded can be a trigger to seek help implementing positive lifestyle change.

For each question, indicate how often you felt or thought a certain way. The best approach is to answer each question fairly quickly, choosing the alternative that seems like a reasonable estimate.

0=never	3=fairly often
1=almost never	4=very often
2=sometimes	

1. In the last month, how often have you been upset because of something that happened unexpectedly?

2. In the last month, how often have you felt that you were unable to control the important things in your life?

3. In the last month, how often have you felt nervous and "stressed"?

4. In the last month, how often have you felt confident about your ability to handle your personal problems?

5. In the last month, how often have you felt that things were going your way?

6. In the last month, how often have you found that you could not cope with all the things that you had to do?

7. In the last month, how often have you been able to control irritations in your life?

8. In the last month, how often have you felt that you were on top of things?

9. In the last month, how often have you been angered because of things that were outside of your control?

10. In the last month, how often have you felt difficulties were piling up so high that you could not overcome them?

FAITH, RELIGION, AND PRAYER Psychologists are also discovering the health benefits of faith, religion, and prayer. Research suggests elderly people who actively participate in religious services or pray experience improved health and noticeably lower rates of depression than those who don't participate in such activities (Lawler-Row & Elliott, 2009; Powell, Shahabi, & Thoresen, 2003). In addition, religious affiliation is associated with increased reports of happiness and physical health (Green & Elliott, 2010).

These various types of proactive, stress-reducing behaviors reflect a certain type of attitude. You might call it a positive psychology attitude.

THINK again

Think Positive

In the very first chapter of this book, we introduced a field of study known as *positive psychology,* "the study of positive emotions, positive character traits, and enabling institutions" (Seligman & Steen, 2005, p. 410). Rather than focusing on mental illness and abnormal behavior, positive psychology emphasizes human strengths and virtues. The goal is well-being and fulfillment, and that means "satisfaction" with the past, "hope and optimism" for the future, and "flow and happiness" at the current time (Seligman & Csikszentmihalyi, 2000, p. 5).

As we wrap up this chapter on stress and health, we encourage you to focus on that third category: flow and happiness in the present moment. No matter what stressors come your way, try to stay grounded in the here and now. The past is the past, the future is uncertain, but this moment is yours. Finding a way to enjoy the present is one of the best ways to reduce the impact of stress. We also remind you that your current stress level is very much within your control. If you're feeling overwhelmed, make time to engage in activities such as exercise and meditation, which produce measurable changes in the body and brain. 💬➕

. . . YOUR CURRENT STRESS LEVEL IS WITHIN YOUR CONTROL.

TO PROTECT, SERVE, AND NOT GET TOO STRESSED If you're wondering how Eric Flansburg and Kehlen Kirby are doing these days, both young men are thriving in their careers. Eric recently joined the police department in Cicero, New York, and is busy raising Eric Junior, 4, and baby Nathan, 11 months. It is a pleasure working in Cicero, where police officers are tightly integrated into the school community. "The kids all know me as Officer Eric," says Eric. "I love it. Can't see myself doing anything else."

Having worked at the fire station since 2010, Kehlen is really getting into the fire department groove. When he's not putting out fires and rescuing people, Kehlen keeps busy helping his wife launch her own family medicine practice and trying to keep up with his daughter, Kinley, who is now nearly 2 years old. "She's one of my biggest stress relievers," suggests Kehlen. "Just chasing her around is enough of a stress reliever for anyone."

show what you know

1. When you must choose between two options that are equally attractive to you, this is called a(n) _____ conflict.

2. _____ is apparent when a person deals directly with a problem by attempting to solve it.
   a. Emotion-focused coping
   c. Support seeking
   b. Positive psychology
   d. Problem-focused coping

3. Individuals who are more relaxed, patient, and nonaggressive are considered to have a:
   a. Type A personality.
   c. Type C personality.
   b. Type B personality.
   d. Type D personality.

4. Describe three "tools" for healthy living that you could use to improve your health.

✓ CHECK YOUR ANSWERS IN APPENDIX C.

⑫ summary of concepts

LO 1 Define stress and stressors. (p. 506)

Stress is the response to perceived threats or challenges resulting from stimuli or events that cause strain, analogous to an airplane wing bending in response to an applied load. For humans, these stimuli, or stressors, can cause physiological, psychological, and emotional reactions. We must be careful not to confuse how we react to stressors and the stressors themselves; stress is the response, stressors are the cause. Stress primarily occurs in reaction to a perceived threat.

LO 2 Describe the Social Readjustment Rating Scale in relation to life events and illness. (p. 509)

Holmes and Rahe developed the Social Readjustment Rating Scale (SRRS) to measure the impact of life events. The score is based on the severity of events and their frequency of occurrence. Researchers use this to examine relationships between life events and health problems. Although correlations do exist, they are not necessarily indicative of cause and effect.

LO 3 Summarize how poverty, adjusting to a new culture, and daily hassles affect health. (p. 511)

People living in poverty, moving to a new culture, and dealing with everyday hassles are faced with a number of stressors that increase the likelihood of illness. Unlike major life changes and catastrophes, the source of stress in these situations is not limited, as we are exposed to these stressors on a more constant basis. One type of major life change can result in acculturative stress; however, integrating the different cultures and developing social support helps combat the effects of this source of stress. With all the stressors in our lives, we can be grateful for the positive experiences, or uplifts that can serve to balance them.

LO 4 Identify the brain and body changes that characterize the fight-or-flight response. (p. 515)

When faced with a threatening situation, portions of the brain, including the hypothalamus, trigger the sympathetic nervous system, which then leads to the secretion of catecholamines, such as epinephrine and norepinephrine. These hormones cause heart rate, blood pressure, respiration, and blood flow to the muscles to increase. At the same time, the digestive system slows down and the pupils dilate. These physiological responses prepare us for an emergency by efficiently managing the body's resources.

LO 5 Outline the general adaptation syndrome (GAS). (p. 515)

The human body responds in a predictable way to stressors. The general adaptation syndrome suggests that the body passes through three stages. The first is the alarm stage, or initial response to a threatening situation. This stage includes an increase in arousal, during which the body prepares to deal with a threat. Next is the resistance stage, during which the body maintains a high level of arousal (although not as high as that of the alarm stage), as it deals with a threatening situation; at this point there is a decreased response to new stress. During the resistance stage, some people start to show signs of diseases of adaptation. Finally there is the exhaustion stage; during this phase, the body's resources become depleted, resulting in vulnerability to illnesses, physical exhaustion, and even death.

LO 6 Describe the function of the hypothalamic–pituitary-adrenal (HPA) system. (p. 517)

Overseeing the sympathetic nervous system's response to stress is the HPA system. When a stressful situation arises, the hypothalamus initiates a cascade of responses, by alerting the pituitary gland, which then sends signals to the adrenal cortex. In turn, the cortex orders the secretion of corticosteroids (for example, cortisol). These hormones summon the immune system to fight off a threat and reduce the amount of energy used on nonessential activities. When faced with a stressor, the body responds in the same way it would to a pathogen—by mobilizing a defense response.

LO 7 Explain how stressors relate to health problems. (p. 518)

When the body is mobilizing its resources for fight or flight, the immune system is less powerful, and the work of the lymphocytes is compromised. During times of stress, people tend to sleep poorly, eat erratically, and may increase their drug and alcohol use, along with other poor behavioral choices. These tendencies can lead to health problems. In particular, stressors have been linked to ulcers, cancer, and cardiovascular disease.

LO 8 List some consequences of prolonged exposure to the stress hormone cortisol. (p. 522)

Cortisol gives a boost in energy, increases alertness, and steps up immunity. But when cortisol levels remain high for prolonged periods (which is the case with chronic stressors and threatening situations), immune system functioning may decrease. Elevated cortisol has been associated with premature birth and low birth weight in infants. For workers who have to make on-the-spot safety decisions, high cortisol levels can decrease working memory. The field of psychoneuroimmunology explores the complex interplay of psychological, neurological, and immunological factors in the stress response.

LO 9 Identify different types of conflicts. (p. 524)

One major source of stressors is conflict, which can be defined by the discomfort felt when making tough choices. Often two choices presented are both attractive (approach–approach conflict), at times one choice has both favorable and unfavorable characteristics (approach–avoidance conflict), and other times two alternatives are both unattractive (avoidance–avoidance conflict). Even more challenging are conflicts that occur when someone must decide between two choices, each possessing attractive and unattractive qualities (double approach–avoidance conflict), or those that occur when faced with a decision that has more than two possible choices (multiple approach–avoidance conflicts).

LO 10 Illustrate how appraisal influences coping. (p. 526)

Coping refers to the cognitive, behavioral, and emotional abilities used to effectively manage something that is perceived as difficult or challenging. We must decide whether an event is irrelevant, benign, or harmful (primary appraisal) and how we will respond (secondary appraisal). If we determine that we have the ability to cope, then the impact of stress will remain low. We can choose to deal directly with a problem (problem-focused coping), or address the emotions surrounding the problem (emotion-focused coping).

LO 11 Describe Type A and Type B personalities and explain how they relate to stress. (p. 526)

Personality appears to have a profound effect on coping style and predispositions to stress-related illnesses. People with Type A personalities are competitive, aggressive, and impatient and twice as likely to develop cardiovascular disease as people with Type B personalities, who are more relaxed, patient, and nonaggressive. The presence of Type D personality may be a better predictor of how patients fare when they already have heart disease, and it is characterized by emotions such as worry, tension, bad moods, and social inhibition. People who exhibit a personality characteristic referred to as hardiness seem to be better able to handle a great deal of stress, are resilient, and remain optimistic.

LO 12 Discuss several tools for reducing stress and maintaining health. (p. 530)

Stress management incorporates tools to lower the impact of possible stressors. Exercise, meditation, progressive muscle relaxation, biofeedback, and social support all have positive physical and psychological impact on the response to stressors. In addition, looking out for the well-being of others by caring and giving of yourself is an effective way to reduce the impact of stress.

key terms

acculturative stress, p. 512

approach–approach conflict, p. 524

approach–avoidance conflict, p. 524

avoidance–avoidance conflict, p. 524

biofeedback, p. 533

burnout, p. 525

coping, p. 526

daily hassles, p. 513

distress, p. 509

emotion-focused coping, p. 526

eustress, p. 509

general adaptation syndrome (GAS), p. 515

hardiness, p. 528

health psychology, p. 518

lymphocytes, p. 518

posttraumatic stress disorder (PTSD), p. 510

primary appraisal, p. 526

problem-focused coping, p. 526

psychoneuroimmunology, p. 523

secondary appraisal, p. 526

social support, p. 513

stress, p. 506

stressors, p. 506

Type A personality, p. 528

Type B personality, p. 528

uplifts, p. 514

TEST PREP are you ready?

1. _____ are defined as the situations, beliefs, people, and attitudes that cause you to feel stress, a response that can include physiological, psychological, and emotional components.
   a. Levels of eustress
   b. Diseases of adaptation
   c. Stressors
   d. Conflicts

2. When Eric witnessed the birth of his first child, he felt it was the proudest moment of his life. This kind of "good" stressor leads to a reaction known as:
   a. eustress.
   b. distress.
   c. perceived threats.
   d. optimal arousal.

3. Your professor is using the Social Readjustment Rating Scale in a study she is conducting. She predicts that the more _____ people have, the more stress reactions they will experience, which increases the likelihood they will become ill.
   a. assimilation
   b. stress inoculation
   c. social support
   d. life-changing events

4. When faced with a threat, portions of the brain, including the hypothalamus, trigger the _____, which leads to the secretion of epinephrine and norepinephrine.
   a. parasympathetic nervous system
   b. sympathetic nervous system
   c. general adaptation syndrome
   d. lymphocytes

5. Once an emergency has ended, the _____ reverses the processes put in motion through the fight-or-flight reaction. Heart rate and blood pressure start to decrease and respiration returns to normal.
   a. parasympathetic nervous system
   b. sympathetic nervous system
   c. general adaptation syndrome
   d. resistance stage

6. According to the general adaptation syndrome, if a threat remains constant, the body's resources become depleted during the _____, resulting in a vulnerability to illnesses, physical exhaustion, and even death.
   a. alarm stage
   b. resistance stage
   c. exhaustion stage
   d. diseases of adaptation stage

7. The hypothalamic–pituitary–adrenal system plays an important role in stress reactions. This system helps to maintain balance in the body by overseeing the neuroendocrine and _____ while monitoring the immune system.
   a. diseases of adaptation
   b. gastric ulcers
   c. assimilation
   d. sympathetic nervous system

8. Stressors can lead to health problems, because as the body mobilizes its resources for fight or flight, _____ is less powerful, and the work of its lymphocytes is reduced.
   a. the immune system
   b. *H. pylori*
   c. atherosclerosis
   d. cortisol

9. Physical exercise provides a powerful way to reduce the impact of stress, by increasing blood flow, activating the autonomic nervous system, and initiating the release of _____, the body's natural painkilling neurotransmitter.
   a. macrophages
   b. endorphins
   c. B lymphocytes
   d. natural killer cells

10. The students in your study group are extremely worried about tomorrow's final exam in algebra. One student in particular has been seeing a counselor all semester because of her anxiety about the upcoming test. When she walks into class tomorrow, she will use what she has learned about _____ to help her reduce tension in her body.
    a. the hypothalamic–pituitary–adrenal system
    b. macrophages
    c. stress inoculation
    d. progressive muscle relaxation

11. A friend just told you about a very stressful workday he had yesterday, which included finding out he might get fired. He said he went home last night and drank too much alcohol because he was so worried. His reaction may be explained by the self-medication hypothesis, and his behavior is an example of how
    a. social-evaluative threats can provide support.
    b. the general adaptation syndrome ends.
    c. stressors are related to health problems.
    d. an acculturative stress response occurs.

12. _____ refers to the cognitive, behavioral, and emotional abilities used to effectively manage a challenging or difficult situation.
    a. Stress
    b. Coping
    c. Altruism
    d. Eustress

13. You have been given two options for a presentation in your speech class: a 15-minute speech about a childhood friend or a 15-minute speech about a favorite pet. These two speeches sound equally boring to write and to deliver. Your decision regarding which to choose would be considered an
    a. avoidance–approach conflict.
    b. approach–approach conflict.
    c. approach–avoidance conflict.
    d. avoidance–avoidance conflict.

14. Someone who is competitive, aggressive, and hostile would be likely to have a _____, which indicates he is more likely to develop cardiovascular disease than someone who is more relaxed, patient, and nonaggressive.
    a. Type A personality
    b. Type B personality
    c. Type C personality
    d. Type D personality

15. You met an exchange student last week who began to tell you about her life back home. She described times when she had to deal with hunger, war, and living in an orphanage. Yet she seems so optimistic and resilient. Psychologists would likely suggest her personality includes a characteristic known as
    a. Type A.
    b. hardiness.
    c. responsibility.
    d. locus of control.

16. Describe how someone you know used assimilation, separation, or integration to deal with the acculturative stress of moving to a new country or new region of the United States.

17. List the many hassles you have had to deal with during the past week. Also list any life events you have experienced in the past 12 months. Consider how all these stressors may have influenced your health and explain what you can do to reduce their impact.

18. Describe an example from a movie or television show of someone who seemed to be responding to a threat by the fight-or-flight response. What evidence of this did you observe?

19. Give examples of an approach–approach conflict, an approach–avoidance conflict, and an avoidance–avoidance conflict that you have encountered in your own life.

20. Describe someone you know who has an internal locus of control, in particular, regarding his or her health-related behaviors. Now describe someone you know who has an external locus of control, and focus on his or her health-related behaviors.

✔ CHECK YOUR ANSWERS IN APPENDIX C.

Get personalized practice by logging into LaunchPad at **http://www.worthpublishers.com/launchpad/Licht** to take the LearningCurve adaptive quizzes for Chapter 12.

13

Psychological Disorders and Abnormal Behavior

 Winter Night

 THINK AGAIN
The Insanity Plea

 Dispelling Stigma: Ross Finds His Voice

Classifying and Explaining Psychological Disorders

 DIDN'T SEE THAT COMING
On Being Sane in Insane Places

 Unwelcome Thoughts: Melissa's Story

Anxiety Disorders

 ACROSS THE WORLD
The Many Faces of Social Anxiety

Obsessive-Compulsive Disorder

Depressive Disorders

 Melissa's Second Diagnosis

SA from the pages of
SCIENTIFIC AMERICAN
Inflammation Brings on the Blues

Bipolar Disorders

 Highest Highs, Lowest Lows

Schizophrenia

 NATURE AND NURTURE
Four Sisters

Personality Disorders

Dissociative Disorders

Postscript: Where Are They Now?

 Defying Stigma: Ross Learns to Thrive

 Outsmarting OCD: Melissa Finds a Therapy That Works

psychological disorders

Psychological Disorders and Abnormal Behavior

WINTER NIGHT It was a clear, cold night in January when 17-year-old Ross Szabo decided to end his life. Nothing bad had happened that day. Ross had woken up, gone to school, played in a basketball game (a victory for his team), and then gone with his buddies to Friendly's restaurant for mozzarella sticks and a sundae. But for some reason, on that clear winter night, Ross decided he could no longer take it. As he gazed out the window at Pennsylvania's snow-blanketed cornfields, an overwhelming sense of calm descended on him.

For the 4 months leading to that moment, Ross had been free-falling into an abyss of sadness. No one knew—not his parents, his brothers, or his friends—because Ross was a good actor. Around other people, he was smiling, joking, acting like a normal teenager. But every time he was alone, he was crying. As he puts it, "I had been thinking about suicide 24 hours a day by that point."

Some people say suicide is a selfish act; a person ends his own suffering and destroys the lives of those left behind. Ross truly believed his friends and family would be happier without him. *Maybe you're the problem; maybe you'd be doing them a favor by removing the problem,* Ross remembers thinking to himself. "I didn't think I would have a funeral," he says. "I didn't think anyone should care about me."

When Ross got home, he tried calling a friend but was too upset to speak. So he walked into the bathroom and prepared to kill himself. Fortunately, his father was home and could tell Ross was in distress. He convinced his son to come downstairs and talk. "If you don't take me to the hospital right now, I'm going to kill myself," Ross said as he walked into the kitchen. Instead of returning to school the next day, Ross was admitted to the hospital.

Note: Ross Szabo's story is based on personal communications with Ross Szabo and various passages from the book he co-authored with Melanie Hall: *Behind Happy Faces* (Szabo & Hall, 2007). Unless otherwise specified, quotations attributed to Ross Szabo and Melissa Hopely are personal communications.

LEARNING OBJECTIVES

after reading and studying this chapter, you should be able to:

LO 1   Define psychological disorders and the criteria used to identify abnormal behavior.

LO 2   Recognize limitations in the classification of psychological disorders.

LO 3   Summarize the etiology of psychological disorders.

LO 4   Define and illustrate an understanding of anxiety disorders and their causes.

LO 5   Summarize the symptoms and causes of obsessive-compulsive disorder.

LO 6   Summarize the symptoms and causes of major depressive disorder.

LO 7   Compare and contrast bipolar disorders and major depressive disorder.

LO 8   Recognize the symptoms of schizophrenia.

LO 9   Analyze the biopsychosocial factors that contribute to schizophrenia.

LO 10   Differentiate between antisocial and borderline personality disorders.

LO 11   Identify differences among dissociative disorders.

Looks Can Be Deceiving
Ross Szabo appears happy in his senior class photo, but beneath his smile is profound pain and suffering. This was the year Ross began to have persistent thoughts of death and suicide that nearly drove him to take his own life.
Martin Fella/Fella Studios

CONNECTIONS

The field of *abnormal psychology* encompasses the study of psychological disorders as well as their treatment. In **Chapter 1,** we described various mental health professionals, and the training they require. The current chapter focuses on abnormal psychology, a subfield many people associate with the word *psychology*.

Ross, in His Own Words

http://qrs.ly/sq3nrcz

What's Normal, What's Not

LO 1   Define psychological disorders and the criteria used to identify abnormal behavior.

A year-and-a-half earlier, Ross had been diagnosed with **bipolar disorder,** a condition marked by dramatic mood swings. We all have our ups and downs—periods of feeling happy, sad, anxious, or irritable—but the emotional roller coaster of bipolar disorder is something quite different. We will explore bipolar disorder in greater detail later in the chapter, but first let's familiarize ourselves with the broader focus of this chapter: psychological disorders.

A **psychological disorder** is a set of behavioral, emotional, and cognitive symptoms that are significantly distressing and disabling in terms of social functioning, work endeavors, and other aspects of life. These symptoms are not the result of religious or spiritual experiences; nor are they mere departures from cultural norms. And although stressors can trigger symptoms of psychological disorders, these conditions primarily result from disturbances in psychological, biological, and developmental processes (American Psychiatric Association [APA], 2013).

The academic field devoted to the study of psychological disorders is generally referred to as ***abnormal psychology.*** **Researchers and scholars in abnormal psychology** typically have backgrounds in clinical psychology, or psychiatry if they obtained medical degrees.

DEFINING ABNORMAL BEHAVIOR   Psychologists and other mental health professionals determine if a behavior is *abnormal* using a variety of criteria (**TABLE 13.1**). Perhaps the most straightforward criterion is *typicality* (or lack thereof). An atypical behavior is rarely seen, or infrequent. The profound sadness Ross experienced is relatively rare. Most people experience sadness, even deep sadness at times, but suicidal thoughts are unusual. Although the typicality criterion is useful, it is not enough to confirm the existence of a psychological disorder. A child prodigy who learns to play the piano like a virtuoso by the age of 5 is atypical, but his rare talent does not indicate a psychological disorder.

We should also consider **maladaptive behaviors,** or actions that run counter to one's best interests. The degree of risk associated with these maladaptive behaviors (both to oneself and others) is often used by professionals to determine if a person needs to be admitted to a hospital. In Chapter 14, you can see how Dr. Dan Foster used this criterion in deciding whether to seek hospital care for a client with schizophrenia. We should point out, however, that maladaptive behavior is not always a sign of abnormality. People without disorders exhibit maladaptive behaviors all the time. Just think of the child who occasionally has a tantrum, or the adult who drowns his sorrows in alcohol one night.

To arrive at a more definitive determination of **abnormal behavior,** mental health professionals typically rely on three criteria (in addition to typicality): *dysfunction, distress,* and *deviance,* or the "3 Ds" (APA, 2013; Wakefield, 1992).

The first D, *dysfunction,* indicates the degree to which a behavior interferes with daily life and relationships. Ross's depression sometimes rendered him unable to get out of bed; this type of behavior certainly has the potential to interfere with daily life. But dysfunction alone does not confirm the presence of a psychological disorder.

You Asked, Ross Answers

http://qrs.ly/v83nrd0

How do you explain your ability to hide what was going on with your bipolar disorder?

Synonyms

psychological disorder mental disorder, mental illness, psychiatric illness, mental disability, mental disease

abnormal psychology experimental psychopathology, clinical psychology

bipolar disorder A mood disorder marked by dramatic swings in mood, ranging from manic episodes to depressive episodes.

psychological disorder A set of behavioral, emotional, and/or cognitive symptoms that are significantly distressing or disabling in terms of social functioning, work endeavors, and other aspects of life.

maladaptive behaviors Behaviors or actions that run counter to what is in one's own best interest.

abnormal behavior Behavior that is atypical, dysfunctional, distressful, and/or deviant.

Table 13.1	DEFINING ABNORMAL BEHAVIOR
Criteria	**What does it mean?**
Typicality	Degree to which behavior is atypical, meaning rarely seen or statistically abnormal
Dysfunction	Degree to which behavior interferes with daily life and relationships
Distress	Degree to which behavior or emotions cause an individual to feel upset or uncomfortable
Deviance	Degree to which behavior is considered outside the standards or rules of society

Defining abnormal behavior is challenging, and psychologists use a variety of criteria when evaluating behaviors.

If you stay up all night to meet a deadline, you might experience temporary dysfunction in memory and attention, but that doesn't mean you have a disorder.

The second D is personal *distress.* Feeling regularly upset or uncomfortable because of unwanted behaviors or emotions is another feature of abnormality, and it's not always evident from the outside. Prior to his suicide attempt, Ross appeared to be happy and healthy, but inside he was suffering. There are times, however, when distress does not accompany a disorder. When Ross experienced the euphoric highs of bipolar disorder, he may not have been distressed at all. People with psychological disorders do not always have the insight to recognize that a problem exists.

The third D is *deviance,* or the degree to which a behavior is considered to be outside the standards or rules of a society. Behaving in a way that does not conform to social expectations might be indicative of a psychological disorder. Individuals who are euphoric might talk too loudly in a library or church where people are expected to be quiet, or become so disinhibited that they walk around naked in a public place. Once again, the presence of this sole criterion does not necessarily indicate a psychological disorder. Political protesters, for example, may deliberately break social norms to make a statement. Many participants in Occupy Wall Street chose to set up camp and sleep in public places normally used by others just passing through. Their behavior was deviant but not necessarily suggestive of a psychological disorder.

We should note that conceptions of abnormality and definitions of psychological disorders have changed during the course of history. Homosexuality was once considered a psychological disorder, but this notion was overturned in the 1970s and 1980s by psychiatrists and other mental health professionals (Silverstein, 2009), in part because cultural norms had changed. Always remember that the definition or meaning of "abnormal" is relative to place and time.

IT'S A CONTINUUM   Given how psychologists define abnormal behavior, understand that anyone can have experiences similar to the symptoms of psychological disorders. This is because there is a continuum for many behaviors and feelings: Those at one end are generally considered normal, and those at the other end abnormal. Ross's profound sadness would likely fall at the *abnormal* end of the continuum, whereas a teary farewell to a close friend who is moving away would be at the *normal* end.

CULTURALLY DEFINED   The definition of mental health is not the same for all groups of people. As the biopsychosocial model reminds us, we must consider culture and other social influences when trying to understand concepts like "normal" and "abnormal." Some disorders and symptoms are unique to particular cultures. *Koro,* for example, is an episode of intense anxiety observed mainly in Southeast Asia, although similar conditions have been documented in China. The main feature of *koro* is the unrealistic and intense fear that sexual organs will be pulled into the body, perhaps resulting in death (APA, 2013; Roy et al., 2011). A man with *koro* might be exceedingly anxious about the idea of his penis disappearing into his abdomen, whereas a woman might fear that her nipples will be pulled into her chest. Another example is *susto,* most evident in Latino populations (Donlan & Lee, 2010). Someone with *susto* reacts to a frightening situation with the belief that her soul has left her body, which ultimately results in illness and sadness (APA, 2013).

We know some disorders are specific to certain cultures because researchers have studied the frequency and variation of these conditions across cultures. Susto and koro, for example, are found only in some cultures; however, *schizophrenia* (discussed later in the chapter) is evident across all cultures and throughout the world, suggesting it is a universal disorder.

insanity A legal determination of the degree to which a person is responsible for criminal behaviors.

Let's review what we have learned. Psychologists use three main criteria to identify abnormality—*dysfunction, distress,* and *deviance.* The 3 Ds are useful, but be mindful of their limitations. The same could be said of other mental health concepts (normal, abnormal, and so forth), because their meanings may vary over time, across cultures, and even within the same culture.

THINK again

The Insanity Plea

Perhaps you have heard the term "insanity" used in a legal context. "The defendant got off on an insanity plea," or "The defense failed to demonstrate insanity." What do these mean? **Insanity** is a *legal* determination of the degree to which a person is responsible for his criminal behaviors. Those deemed legally insane are thought to have little or no control over or understanding of their behaviors at the time they committed their crimes. Therefore, they are offered psychological treatment rather than criminal punishment, such as imprisonment or the death penalty. In America, 46 states offer a form of the *insanity defense;* only Idaho, Kansas, Montana, and Utah do not (Lilienfeld & Arkowitz, 2011). **Many people believe** that the insanity defense is frequently used, when in fact it is utilized in about 1% of cases. Of those cases, just 10–25% of insanity defenses are successful (Torry & Billick, 2010). Among those who avoided prison after entering an insanity plea was John Hinckley Jr., the man who attempted to assassinate President Ronald Reagan in 1981. The insanity plea did not work so well for serial murderer Jeffrey Dahmer, however; in 1992 he was sentenced to 15 life terms for the horrific murders of 15 young men (PBS, 2013).

Insanity?
In the summer of 2012, James Holmes walked into a movie theater in Aurora, Colorado, and opened fire on the audience, killing 12 people. Holmes's attorneys entered a plea of insanity; they claim he committed the murders in a psychotic state (Ingold, 2013, September 30). AP Photo/ The Denver Post, Andy Cross, Pool

THE INSANITY PLEA DID NOT WORK SO WELL FOR SERIAL MURDERER JEFFREY DAHMER.

CONNECTIONS
In **Chapter 7,** we discussed the *availability heuristic;* we often predict the probability of something happening in the future based on how easily we can recall a similar type of event from the past. Here, the vividness of a crime and the ensuing trial make the insanity plea more available in our memories, so we are prone to overestimate its likelihood in the future.

Do you believe individuals whom the courts judge to be insane are still responsible for their actions? Knowing that a handful of states do not allow the insanity defense, what argument might you use to convince their legislatures to allow it? 💬➕

Now that we have explored the meaning of abnormality, let's find out more about the experience of having a psychological disorder—and the negative judgments that sometimes accompany it.

DISPELLING STIGMA: ROSS FINDS HIS VOICE After being discharged from the hospital, Ross returned to school where he was greeted with rumors and stares. A couple of his friends stopped spending time with him, perhaps because they were afraid of what they didn't understand. Or maybe it was because people in the farmlands of Pennsylvania didn't talk much about emotions and mental health.

Not long after the hospital stay, a psychologist came to Ross's school to give his annual presentation about helping people with psychological disorders. Most of the students thought the topic was funny and laughed (perhaps out of discomfort) throughout the presentation. But, Ross did not find it one bit amusing. After class, he told his teacher that he wanted to give his own presentation. Before long, Ross was standing before his peers, heart pounding and knees wobbling, talking about life with bipolar disorder. The students listened intently, and some approached Ross after class to talk about their own struggles with psychological disorders. By coming forward to share his experiences, Ross dispelled some of his classmates' misconceptions and fears about psychological disorders. He was a real person they knew and liked, and he had a disorder.

WHAT IS STIGMA?   Watching his classmates laugh about people with psychological disorders, Ross bore witness to the *stigma* attached to mental illness. **Stigma** is a negative attitude or opinion about groups of individuals based on certain traits or characteristics they have. It can lead to discrimination and stereotypes, and negative characterizations in general (Corrigan, 2005). Surely, you have heard people equate psychological disorders with violence and aggression, or perhaps you have seen TV shows portraying people with mental illness as wild and aggressive. Reality check: People with psychological disorders are usually *not* violent. Other factors, such as lower socioeconomic status, male gender, and substance abuse, may be better predictors of violence (Stuart, 2003). The criterion of being a danger to oneself and others does determine the necessity of treatment, but given the degree of violence in our society, it is actually *atypical* of people with serious psychological disorders, and more commonly associated with substance abuse (Arkowitz & Lilienfeld, 2011; Fazel, Gulati, Linsell, Geddes, & Grann, 2009).

Hollywood Stereotypes
Anthony Hopkins (right) plays the role of serial killer Hannibal Lecter in the 1991 film *The Silence of the Lambs.* Characters like "Hannibal the Cannibal" tend to perpetuate stereotypes about people with psychological disorders, most of whom are not violent (Arkowitz & Lilienfeld, 2011; Fazel et al., 2009). Orion/ The Kobal Collection

Stigma can have devastating repercussions. It may lower self-esteem, impair social functioning, and interfere with people getting much needed treatment. Research suggests that many individuals do not seek mental health services because of the stigma associated with psychological disorders and their treatment (Corrigan, 2005).

What can we do to combat stigma? One suggestion is to use "people-first language"; that is, refer to the individual affected by the disorder (*She has been diagnosed with schizophrenia*), not define the person by her disorder (*She is schizophrenic;* American Psychological Association [APA], 2010c). We should also be cautious about using terms such as "crazy" and "insane." While these words are used to describe people on a daily basis, they are inappropriate, derogatory, and sure indicators of stigma.

Thus far, our discussion has focused on overarching concepts like abnormal behavior and stigma, which have relevance for all psychological disorders. Now it's time to shift to a discussion of more practical matters. How do psychologists and psychiatrists go about identifying and classifying disorders?

stigma A negative attitude or opinion about a group of people based on certain traits or characteristics.

◯✓◯◯ show what you know

1. Which of the following is a criterion used to define abnormal behavior?
   a. dysfunction
   b. psychopathology
   c. developmental processes
   d. stigma

2. If someone goes for days in a row without sleeping and consumes excessive alcohol to calm his nerves, he is exhibiting _____ behaviors; his actions are counter to his best interests.

3. Using Table 13.1 on page 543 as your guide, think of behaviors that are (1) atypical but not dysfunctional; (2) dysfunctional but not distressful; and (3) deviant but not dysfunctional.

✓ CHECK YOUR ANSWERS IN APPENDIX C.

Classifying and Explaining Psychological Disorders

How was Ross diagnosed with *bipolar disorder*? He consulted with a psychiatrist. But how did this mental health professional come to the conclusion that his client suffered from bipolar disorder, and not something else? Given what we know about the complexity of determining abnormal behavior, it probably comes as no surprise that clinicians have not always agreed on what qualifies as a psychological disorder. Over the years, however, they have developed common criteria and procedures for making reliable diagnoses. These criteria and decision-making procedures are presented in manuals, which are shared across mental health professions, and are based on research findings and clinical observations.

The *Diagnostic and Statistical Manual of Mental Disorders* (DSM–5)

Think about the last time you were ill and went to a doctor. You probably answered a series of questions about your symptoms. The nurse took your blood pressure and temperature, and the doctor performed a physical exam. Based on these subjective and objective findings, the doctor formulated a diagnosis. Mental health professionals must do the same—make diagnoses based on evidence. In addition to gathering information from interviews and other clinical assessments, psychologists typically rely on manuals to guide their diagnoses. Most mental health professionals in North America use the *Diagnostic and Statistical Manual of Mental Disorders* (*DSM–5;* APA, 2013). The *DSM–5* is an evidence-based classification system of mental disorders first developed and published by the American Psychiatric Association (APA; www.psych. org) in 1952. This manual was conceived and designed to help ensure accurate and consistent diagnoses based on the observation of symptoms. Although the *DSM* is published by the American Psychiatric Association (www.psych.org)—different from the American Psychological Association, also abbreviated APA—it is used by psychiatrists, psychologists, social workers, and a variety of other clinicians.

DSM, TAKE FIVE When the *DSM* was comprehensively revised in 1994, it included classifications for 172 psychological disorders. The *DSM–5* revision lists 157 disorders (American Psychiatric Association Division of Research, personal communication, July 26, 2013) and presents some new ideas on how to think about them (**INFOGRAPHIC 13.1**). The current revision also represents a substantial shift in how the manual is organized. The psychological disorders are presented in 20 chapters, with content organized around developmental changes occurring across the life span. Some disorders were removed from the manual (sexual aversion disorder, for instance) and others were added (hoarding disorder). Another major change is that several axes, or dimensions, previously used as additional information are now integrated within the diagnostic criteria for some disorders.

LO 2 Recognize limitations in the classification of psychological disorders.

CRITICISMS OF CLASSIFICATION Why is the *DSM* important? Classifying mental disorders helps therapists develop treatment plans, enables clients to obtain reimbursement from their insurance companies, and facilitates research and communication among professions. But there is a downside to classification. Anytime someone is diagnosed with a mental disorder, he runs the risk of being labeled, which can lead to the formation of expectations—not only from other people, but also from

The *DSM-5*

Revising the *Diagnostic and Statistical Manual of Mental Disorders* was no small task. The process took over 10 years and involved hundreds of experts poring over the most relevant and current research. The final product helps researchers conduct studies and clinicians develop treatment plans and work with other professionals.

Where does the *DSM-5* come from?

PREPARATION   Nearly 400 scientists from around the world evaluate research on psychological disorders for 10 years prior to publication of the *DSM-5*.

DRAFTING   160 scientists participating in the American Psychiatric Association's *DSM-5* Task Force and Work Groups review the research regarding disorders. Working with other researchers and clinicians, they gather as much information as possible about the current understanding of disorders. Then they compose and revise diagnostic criteria.

APPROVAL   Following approval of the diagnostic criteria by the APA Board of Trustees, the pre-publication *DSM-5* goes through two more rounds of review. The Scientific Review Committee examines the evidence informing the proposed changes to the *DSM*, and the Clinical and Public Health committee provides feedback on the criteria from a clinical and public health standpoint.

Some disorders included in the *DSM-5*

Each chapter of the *DSM-5* describes disorders that share common features and/or symptoms. Here we list 6 chapters, along with a sample disorder that you can read more about in your textbook.

Schizophrenia Spectrum and Other Psychotic Disorders
Dysfunction resulting from delusions, hallucinations, disorganized thinking, abnormal motor behavior, and negative symptoms.

READ ABOUT
Schizophrenia, page 568

Bipolar and Related Disorders
Manic and depressive behavior characterized by changes in mood and activity levels.

READ ABOUT
Bipolar I Disorder, page 566

Depressive Disorders
Dysfunction relating to profound sadness, feelings of emptiness, and irritable mood.

READ ABOUT
Major Depressive Disorder, page 560

Obsessive-Compulsive and Related Disorders
Dysfunction relating to obsessions and/or compulsions that cause distress and disrupt day-to-day functioning.

READ ABOUT
Obsessive-Compulsive Disorder, page 558

Trauma- and Stressor-Related Disorders
Distress resulting from exposure to traumatic or stressful incidents.

READ ABOUT
Posttraumatic Stress Disorder, page 510

Dissociative Disorders
Problems with memory, identity, consciousness, perception, and motor control that disrupt psychological functioning.

READ ABOUT
Dissociative Amnesia, page 575

Credits: Open book, Koya979/Shutterstock; Block, Shutterstock

How are disorders of childhood covered in the *DSM-5*?

The *DSM-5* does not include a separate chapter dedicated to disorders diagnosed in childhood, but diagnoses within chapters are presented in chronological order. The *DSM-5* also includes age-related factors in its descriptions and criteria. Here are two disorders commonly diagnosed in childhood:

Autism Spectrum Disorder
This spectrum of disorders recognizes a continuum of symptoms associated with social communication and interaction, repetitive behaviors or speech, and intellectual ability.

Attention deficit/hyperactivity disorder (ADHD)
This disorder begins in childhood, and must be recognized in more than one situation (for example, school and home). A child may have difficulty paying attention, and may easily get off task, fidget, or act impulsively. The manual also recognizes that this disorder does not necessarily end in childhood, and may continue into adulthood.

Who uses the *DSM-5*, and how is it used?

Trained mental health professionals use the *DSM-5* to diagnose psychological disorders. The manual is designed to summarize the signs and symptoms of disorders for the clinician to use as an evaluative tool. The presence of specified signs and symptoms may indicate an underlying psychological disorder, and the *DSM-5* criteria can help guide clinicians to accurate diagnoses and appropriate treatment.

SOURCE: AMERICAN PSYCHIATRIC ASSOCIATION, 2013.

himself. Few studies illustrate this phenomenon more starkly than David Rosenhan's classic 1973 study "On Being Sane in Insane Places."

didn't SEE that coming

"On Being Sane in Insane Places"

👁❗ What do you think would happen if you secretly planted eight completely "sane" people (no history of psychological disorders) in American psychiatric hospitals? The hospital employees would immediately identify them as "normal" and send them home . . . right?

In the early 1970s, psychologist David Rosenhan and seven other mentally healthy people managed to get themselves admitted to various psychiatric hospitals by faking auditory hallucinations ("I am hearing voices"), a common symptom of schizophrenia. (Such a feat would be close to impossible in this day and age, where people with documented psychological disorders struggle to obtain inpatient treatment at all; Scribner, 2001.) Upon admission, each of these pretend patients, or "pseudopatients," immediately stopped putting on an act and began behaving like their normal selves. But within the walls of a psychiatric hospital, their ordinary behavior assumed a whole new meaning. Staff members who spotted the pseudopatients taking notes concluded it must be a symptom of their psychological disorder. "Patient engaged in writing behavior," nurses wrote of one pseudopatient. "Nervous, Mr. X?" a nurse asked a pseudopatient who had been walking the halls out of sheer boredom (Rosenhan, 1973, p. 253).

No hospital staff member identified the pseudopatients as frauds. If anyone had them figured out, it was the other patients in the hospital. "You're not crazy," they would say to the pseudopatients. "You're a journalist, or a professor. You're checking up on the hospital" (Rosenhan, 1973, p. 252). After an average stay of 19 days (the range being 7 to 52 days), the pseudopatients were discharged, but not because doctors recognized their diagnostic errors. The pseudopatients, they determined, had gone into "remission" from their fake disorders. They were released back into society—but not without their labels.

Rosenhan's study was not warmly received by all members of the psychiatric community, and some raised legitimate concerns about its methodology, results, and conclusions (Lando, 1976; Spitzer, 1975). Nevertheless, it shed light on the persistence of labels and their associated stigma.

If eight sane people could be diagnosed with serious disorders like schizophrenia, you might be wondering if psychological diagnoses are **reliable or valid.** We've come a long way since 1973, but the diagnosis of psychological disorders remains a challenge, in part because it often relies on self-reports. Evaluating complex behaviors will never be as straightforward as measuring blood pressure or running a test for strep throat. 👁❗

ATHEORETICAL APPROACH   The *DSM* series tried to address this problem in 1980, by developing a checklist of observable signs and symptoms. This *atheoretical* approach removed the emphasis on particular theories and made it easier for mental health professionals to agree on diagnoses. But this method brought its own set of problems. Relying on checklists rather than theory tends to limit clinicians' understanding of their patients, and the overlapping of criteria across disorders led to some individuals being overdiagnosed (McHugh & Slavney, 2012). Yet, getting the

Film with a Message
Jack Nicholson (blue shirt) portrays the character R. P. McMurphy in the 1975 classic film *One Flew Over the Cuckoo's Nest.* In the film, McMurphy fakes the symptoms of a psychological disorder to get admitted into a mental hospital, where he and his fellow inmates are manipulated and abused. Although the movie deviated somewhat from reality, it did raise awareness about the problems with American mental institutions (Goodfriend, 2012, May 22). Fantasy Films/ The Kobal Collection

NO HOSPITAL STAFF MEMBER IDENTIFIED THE PSEUDOPATIENTS AS FRAUDS.

CONNECTIONS

In **Chapter 11,** we discussed the concepts of *reliability* and *validity* in relation to the assessment of personality. Here, we refer to these same concepts when discussing a classification system for psychological disorders. We must determine if diagnoses are reliable (able to provide consistent, reproducible results) and valid (measuring what they intend to measure).

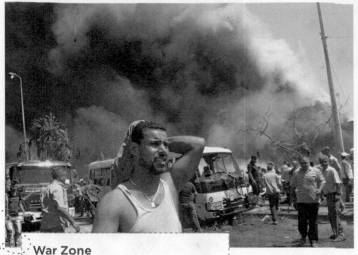

War Zone
Tripoli, Lebanon, was rocked by explosions on August 23, 2013. The attacks occurred outside two Sunni mosques, killing dozens of innocent people. Over half of the Lebanese population has witnessed the events of war, and this exposure to violence and death seems to increase the likelihood of developing a psychological disorder (Karam et al., 2008). AP Photo

right diagnosis is critical. If one patient is feeling down due to a "life encounter," such as the loss of a spouse, and another is feeling the same as a result of a "brain disease," such as bipolar disorder, their treatment needs will be drastically different (McHugh & Slavney, 2012).

"Abnormal," But Not Uncommon

You probably know someone with bipolar disorder, major depressive disorder, or attention-deficit/hyperactivity disorder (ADHD). Perhaps you have experienced a disorder yourself. Psychological disorders are not uncommon (**TABLE 13.2**). Findings from a large study of approximately 9,000 individuals indicated that around 50% of the population in the United States, at some point over the course of their lives, experience symptoms that meet the criteria of a psychological disorder (Kessler, Berglund, et al., 2005; Kessler & Wang, 2008). Yes, you read that correctly; "Nearly half the population meet criteria for a mental disorder in their life . . ." (Kessler, 2010, p. 60). The majority of these disorders begin before the age of 14. Longitudinal studies monitoring children through young adulthood indicate that psychological disorders are "very common," with more than 70% being diagnosed by age 30 (Copeland, Shanahan, Costello, & Angold, 2011; Farmer, Kosty, Seeley, Olino, & Lewinsohn, 2013). And it's not just Americans who struggle with these issues. Lifetime prevalence rates for major psychological disorders range from approximately 26% in Lebanon (Karam et al., 2008) to about 30% in South Africa (Stein et al., 2008), with rates in many other countries similar to those in the United States (Organisation for Economic Co-operation and Development, 2008; Wittchen & Jacobi, 2005).

Table 13.2 **YEARLY RATES OF PSYCHOLOGICAL DISORDERS**	
Psychological Disorder	**Annual Prevalence**
Anxiety disorders	18.1%
Specific phobia	8.7%
Social phobia	6.8%
Disruptive behavior disorders	8.9%
Mood disorders	9.5%
Major depression	6.7%
Substance disorders	3.8%
Any disorder	26.2%

In any given year, many people are diagnosed with a psychological disorder. The numbers here represent annual prevalence: the percentage of the U. S. population affected by a disorder over a year. (Elsewhere we have referred to lifetime prevalence, which means the percentage of the population affected by a disorder anytime in life.)

SOURCE: KESSLER (2010).

A TOUGH ROAD   With such high rates of disorders, you can be sure there are many people around you dealing with tough issues. In some cases, psychological disorders lead to greater impairment than chronic medical conditions, yet people with mental ailments are *less* likely to get treatment (Druss et al., 2009). Keep in mind that various psychological disorders are chronic (a person suffers from them continuously), others have a regular pattern (symptoms appear every winter, for example), and some are temporary.

Further complicating the picture is the fact that many people suffer from more than one psychological disorder at a time, a phenomenon called **comorbidity** (kō-'mȯr-bəd-'i-tē). The Kessler studies mentioned above found that around 22% of participants had received two diagnoses in the course of a year, and 23% three diagnoses (Kessler, Chiu, Demler, & Walters, 2005). You already know that one psychological disorder can lead to significant impairment; now just imagine how these problems compound with more than one disorder.

What Causes Psychological Disorders?

LO 3   Summarize the etiology of psychological disorders.

As we describe psychological disorders throughout this chapter, we will highlight some of the major theories of their *etiology*, or causes. But before getting into the specifics, let's familiarize ourselves with the models commonly used to explain the etiology of psychological disorders.

IT'S IN YOUR BIOLOGY: THE MEDICAL MODEL   The **medical model** explains psychological disorders from a biological standpoint, focusing on genes, neurochemical imbalances, and problems in the brain. This medical approach has had a long and uninterrupted history, as our culture continues to view psychological disorders as illnesses. It is evident in the language used to discuss disorders and their treatment: mental illness, therapy, remission, symptoms, patients, and doctors. Some scholars criticize this approach (Szasz, 2011), in part because it fails to acknowledge how concepts of mental health and illness have changed over time and across cultures (Kawa & Giordano, 2012).

IT'S IN YOUR MIND: PSYCHOLOGICAL FACTORS   Another way to understand the etiology of disorders is to focus on the contribution of psychological factors. Some theories propose that cognitive factors or personality characteristics contribute to the development and maintenance of disorders. Others focus on the ways **learning or childhood experiences** might lay their foundation.

IT'S IN YOUR ENVIRONMENT: SOCIOCULTURAL FACTORS   Earlier we mentioned that culture can shape definitions of "abnormal" and influence the development of psychological disorders. Social factors, like poverty and community support systems, can also play a role in the development and course of these conditions (Honey, Emerson, & Llewellyn, 2011; Lund et al., 2011).

We have established that mental disorders result from a confluence of biological, psychological, and social factors. But is there a way to bring them together? Complex behaviors deserve complex explanations.

THE BIOPSYCHOSOCIAL PERSPECTIVE   As we have suggested in previous chapters, the best way to understand human behavior is to examine it from a variety of perspectives. The *biopsychosocial perspective* provides an excellent model for explaining psychological disorders, which result from a complex interaction of biological, psychological, and sociocultural factors (**FIGURE 13.1**). For example, some disorders appear to have a genetic basis, but their symptoms may not be evident until social or psychological factors come into play. We will discuss this again in the section on schizophrenia, when we take a look at the *diathesis–stress model.*

Now that we have a general understanding of how psychologists conceptualize psychological disorders, let's delve into specifics. We cannot cover every **disorder identified in the DSM-5,** but we can offer an overview of those commonly discussed in an introductory psychology course.

Synonym

medical model biological model

CONNECTIONS

In **Chapter 5,** we presented a variety of learning theories used to explain how behavior patterns develop. Here, we see how these theories explain how abnormal behavior can be learned. Previous chapters have also discussed Freud's psychoanalytic theory, which suggests that early experiences may pave the way for psychological disorders.

CONNECTIONS

We have introduced psychological disorders in various chapters of this book. In **Chapter 9,** we discussed eating disorders in the context of motivation of hunger. In **Chapter 10,** we described sexual dysfunctions outlined in the *DSM-5.* And **Chapter 12** explored the relationship between stressors and posttraumatic stress disorder.

FIGURE 13.1

The Biopsychosocial Perspective
The biopsychosocial perspective considers the complex interaction of biological, psychological, and sociocultural factors that may contribute to a specific disorder.

comorbidity (kō-ˈmȯr-bəd-ˈi-tē) The occurrence of two or more disorders at the same time.

medical model An approach suggesting that psychological disorders are illnesses that have underlying biological causes.

UNWELCOME THOUGHTS: MELISSA'S STORY   Melissa Hopely was about 5 years old when she began doing "weird things" to combat anxiety: flipping light switches on and off, touching the corners of tables, and running to the kitchen to make sure the oven was turned off. Taken at face value, these behaviors may not seem too strange, but for Melissa they were the first signs of a psychological disorder that eventually pushed her to the edge.

Anxiety is a normal part of growing up. Children get nervous for an untold number of reasons: doctors' appointments, the first day of school, or the neighbor's German shepherd. But Melissa was not suffering from common childhood jitters. Her anxiety overpowered her physically, gripping her arms and legs in pain and twisting her stomach into a knot. It affected her emotionally, bringing on a vague feeling that something awful was about to occur—unless she did something to stop it. *If I just touch all the corners of this table like so, nothing bad will happen*, she would think to herself.

As Melissa grew older, her behaviors became increasingly regimented. She felt compelled to do everything an even number of times. Instead of entering a room once, she would enter or leave twice, four times, perhaps even twenty times—as long as the number was a multiple of 2. Some days she would sit in her bedroom for hours, methodically touching all of her possessions twice, then repeating the process again, and again. By performing these rituals, Melissa felt she could prevent her worst fears from becoming reality.

What was she so afraid of? Dying, losing all her friends, and growing up to be jobless, homeless, and living in a dumpster. She also feared striking out in her next softball game and making the whole team lose. Something dreadful was about to happen, though she couldn't quite put her finger on what it was. The reality was that Melissa had little reason to worry. Neither she nor her family members were in ill-health or danger. She seemed to have everything going for her: health, smarts, beauty, and a loving circle of friends and family.

We all experience irrational worries from time to time, but Melissa's anxiety had become overwhelming. Where does one draw the line between anxiety that is normal and anxiety that is abnormal?

▶ **Then and Now**
Melissa Hopely was about 3 years old when the photo on the left was taken. Within a couple of years, Melissa would begin to experience the symptoms of a serious mental disorder that would carry into adulthood. Melissa Hopely

---

✔○○○   **show what you know**

1. The classification and diagnosis of psychological disorders have been criticized for
   a. having specific criteria to identify disorders.
   b. the creation of labeling and expectations.
   c. placing too much emphasis on sociocultural factors.
   d. their research base.

2. In the United States, approximately _____ of people will meet the criteria of a psychological disorder at some point in their lives.
   a. 25%   c. 50%
   b. 40%   d. 75%

3. One common approach to explaining the etiology of psychological disorders is the _____, which implies that psychological disorders have underlying biological causes, such as genes, neurochemical imbalances, and problems in the brain.

4. Melissa indicated that her worries began early in life. Using the biopsychosocial perspective, speculate about the factors that may have caused and reinforced these worries.

✔ CHECK YOUR ANSWERS IN APPENDIX C.

Anxiety Disorders
Extreme Anxiety

LO 4 Define and illustrate an understanding of anxiety disorders and their causes.

Think about the objects or situations that cause you to feel afraid or uneasy. Maybe you fear creepy crawly insects, slithery snakes, or crowded public spaces. A mild fear of spiders or a very crowded subway is normal, but if you become highly disturbed by the mere thought of them, or if your fear interferes with your everyday functioning, then a problem may exist. People who suffer from **anxiety disorders** have extreme anxiety and/or irrational fears that are debilitating (TABLE 13.3).

Table 13.3 ANXIETY DISORDERS

Anxiety Disorder	Annual Prevalence	Description	Cultural Impact
Separation anxiety disorder	0.9–1.9% in adults; 1.6% in adolescents; 4% in children	Anxiety or fear related to "separation from home or attachment figures" (p. 191).	Cultures vary with respect to age at which it is appropriate to move from parental home.
Specific phobia	7–9%	Anxiety about, or fear of, a specific object or situation.	Specific phobias vary across cultures.
Social anxiety disorder (social phobia)	7%	Anxiety about, or fear of being in, a social situation that could result in scrutiny by other people.	*Taijin kyofu* (Japan and Korea).
Panic disorder	2–3%	Reoccurring panic attacks that are unexpected and for which there is no apparent cue or trigger.	*Trúng gió* (Vietnam); *ataque de nervios* (Latin America); *khyâl* (Cambodia).
Agoraphobia	1.7%	Anxiety or fear regarding "using public transportation; being in open spaces; being in enclosed places; standing in line or being in a crowd; or being outside of the home" (p. 217).	None listed in *DSM-5*.
Generalized anxiety disorder	0.9% in adolescents; 2.9% in adults	Anxiety and worry that are out of proportion to the actual event or situation.	Varies by culture.

Anxiety disorders are relatively common in both sexes, but they are more apparent in women by an approximate 2:1 ratio.

SOURCE: DSM-5 (AMERICAN PSYCHIATRIC ASSOCIATION, 2013).

How do we differentiate between normal anxiety and an anxiety disorder? We look at the degree of dysfunction the anxiety causes, how much distress it creates, and whether it gets in the way of everyday behavior (interfering with relationships, social interactions, work, and time management, for example). Let's take a look at some of the anxiety disorders identified in the *DSM–5*: panic disorder, specific phobia, agoraphobia, social anxiety disorder, and generalized anxiety disorder.

Panic Disorder

If you see somebody trembling and sweating, gasping for breath, or complaining of heart palpitations, what comes to mind? If you are concerned it's a heart attack,

anxiety disorders A group of psychological disorders associated with extreme anxiety and/or debilitating, irrational fears.

Combatting Panic
Actress Emma Stone, known for her roles in movies such as *Superbad* and *The Help*, began having panic attacks at the age of 8. Fortunately, she sought treatment and discovered a positive way to channel her anxiety—through acting and comedy. Stone still suffers from panic attacks, but they haven't gotten in the way of her success (Heller, 2012, June 18). Cindy Ord/Getty Images

you may be correct; call 911 immediately if you are not sure. What you may not know is that a person experiencing a **panic attack** may behave very similarly to someone having a heart attack. A panic attack is a sudden, extreme fear or discomfort that escalates quickly, often with no evident cause, and includes symptoms such as increased heart rate, sweating, shortness of breath, chest pain, nausea, lightheadedness, and fear of dying. A diagnosis of **panic disorder** requires such attacks to recur unexpectedly and have no obvious trigger. In addition, the person worries about having more panic attacks, or she feels as if she might be losing control. People with panic disorder often make decisions that are maladaptive, like purposefully avoiding exercise or places that are unfamiliar.

CONNECTIONS

In **Chapter 2,** we described how the sympathetic division of the autonomic nervous system directs the body's stress response. When a stressful situation arises, the sympathetic nervous system prepares the body to react, causing the heart to beat faster, respiration to increase, and the pupils to dilate, among other things.

In **Chapter 5,** we described how, for Little Albert, an originally neutral stimulus (a rat) was paired with an unconditioned stimulus (a loud sound), which led to an unconditioned response (fear). With repeated pairings, the conditioned stimulus (the rat) led to a conditioned response (fear).

panic attack Sudden, extreme fear or discomfort that escalates quickly, often with no obvious trigger, and includes symptoms such as increased heart rate, sweating, shortness of breath, chest pain, nausea, lightheadedness, and fear of dying.

panic disorder A psychological disorder that includes recurrent, unexpected panic attacks and fear that can cause significant changes in behavior.

specific phobia A psychological disorder that includes a distinct fear or anxiety in relation to an object or situation.

THE BIOLOGY OF PANIC DISORDER   Panic disorder does appear to have a biological cause (APA, 2013). Researchers have identified specific parts of the brain thought to be responsible for panic attacks, including regions of the hypothalamus, which is involved in the *fight-or-flight* response (Johnson et al., 2010). There is also evidence suggesting that people diagnosed with panic disorder have smaller amygdala. The amygdala is involved in fear and aggression, as well as the memories associated with those emotions. A smaller amygdala could lead to dysfunction in the autonomic nervous system (which directs the *fight-or-flight* response), resulting in behavioral and physical symptoms of panic attacks (Hayano et al., 2009).

GENETICS, GENDER, AND PANIC DISORDER   Panic disorder affects about 2–3% of the population (APA, 2013). Research indicates that panic disorder runs in families, with heritability estimates around 40–48% (Maron, Hettema, & Shlik, 2010; Weber et al., 2012). This means that over 40% of the variation of the disorder in the *population* can be attributed to genetic factors and the remaining 60% is due to environmental factors. In other words, the frequency and distribution of panic disorder across people result from a combination of factors, 40% of which are due to genes and 60% to nongenetic factors. People often assume heritability refers to an individual's risk for the disorder ("Her panic disorder is 40% the result of her genes, and 60% due to her environment"). This is incorrect. Remember, heritability explains the variation and risk *among* individuals in a population.

Women are twice as likely to be diagnosed with panic disorder, and this disparity is already apparent by the age of 14 (APA, 2013; Craske et al., 2010; Weber et al., 2012). Such gender differences may have a biological basis, but we must also consider the psychological and social factors that might contribute.

LEARNING AND PANIC DISORDER   Some researchers propose that learning—particularly **classical conditioning**—can play a role in the development of panic disorder (Bouton, Mineka, & Barlow, 2001). In a panic disorder scenario, the neutral stimulus might be something like a location (a shopping mall), the unconditioned stimulus an unexpected panic attack, and the unconditioned response the fear resulting from the panic attack. The panic attack location (the shopping mall) would become the conditioned stimulus, such that every time the person thinks of the shopping mall, she responds with fear (now the conditioned response).

COGNITION AND PANIC DISORDER   Other researchers suggest there is a cognitive component of panic disorder, with some individuals misinterpreting physical sensations as signs of major physical or psychological problems (Clark et al., 1997; Teachman, Marker, & Clerkin, 2010). For example, many people have a strange sensation when their hearts skip a beat (technically known as *arrhythmia*), but they realize it is probably not serious, perhaps just the result of too much coffee. A person with panic disorder might interpret that sensation as an indication of an imminent heart attack.

Specific Phobias and Agoraphobia

Panic attacks can occur without apparent triggers. This is not the case with a **specific phobia,** which centers on a particular object or situation, like rats or airplane travel. Most people who have a phobia do their best to avoid the feared object or situation. If avoidance is not possible, they withstand it, but only with extreme fear and anxiousness. Take a look at **TABLE 13.4** for a list of some specific phobias.

LEARNING AND SPECIFIC PHOBIAS   As with panic disorder, phobias can be explained using the principles of learning (LeBeau et al., 2010). Classical conditioning may lead to the acquisition of a fear, through the pairing of stimuli. Operant conditioning could maintain the phobia, through negative reinforcement; if anxiety (the unpleasant stimulus) is reduced by avoiding a feared object or situation, the avoidance behavior is **negatively reinforced** and thus more likely to recur. Observational learning can also help explain the development of a phobia. Simply watching someone else experience a phobia could create fear in an observer. Some research demonstrates that even rhesus monkeys become afraid of snakes if they observe other monkeys reacting fearfully to real *or* toy snakes (Heyes, 2012; Mineka, Davidson, Cook, & Keir, 1984).

BIOLOGY, CULTURE, AND SPECIFIC PHOBIAS
Phobias can also be understood through the lens of evolutionary psychology. Humans seem to be biologically predisposed to fear certain threats such as spiders, snakes, foul smells, and bitter foods. In particular, people appear to be afraid of and disgusted by spiders,

Table 13.4 SPECIFIC PHOBIAS	
Scientific Name	**Fear of . . .**
Acrophobia	Heights
Astraphobia or keraunophobia	Lightning
Brontophobia	Thunder
Claustrophobia	Closed spaces
Cynophobia	Dogs
Epistemophobia	Knowledge
Gamophobia	Marriage
Ophidiophobia	Snakes
Odontophobia	Dental procedures
Xenophobia	Strangers

A person with a specific phobia feels extreme anxiety about a particular object or situation. Fears center on anything from dogs to dental procedures.

SOURCE: REBER, ALLEN, AND REBER (2009).

Paul-Francois Gay/ AGE fotostock

CONNECTIONS

In **Chapter 5,** we discussed *negative reinforcement;* behaviors increase when they are followed by the *removal* of something unpleasant. Here, the avoidance behavior *takes away* the anxious feeling, increasing the likelihood of avoiding the object in the future.

EEK!

Emotional responses, such as fear of spiders, snakes, and heights, may have evolved to protect us from danger (Plomin, DeFries, Knopik, & Neiderhiser, 2013). Avoiding harmful creatures and precarious drop-offs would tend to increase the chances of survival, particularly for our primitive ancestors living in the wild. But when such fears become excessive and irrational, a specific phobia might be present. skydie/Shutterstock perhaps because they can be dangerous, but there appears to be a cultural component of this reaction as well (Gerdes, Uhl, & Alpers, 2009). From an evolutionary standpoint, these fears would tend to protect us from true danger. But sometimes the link between anxiety and evolution is less apparent. It's hard to imagine how an intense fear of being in public, for example, would promote survival.

AGORAPHOBIA   Do you ever feel a little anxious when you are out in public, in a new city, or at a crowded amusement park? A person with **agoraphobia** (a-gǝ-rǝ-ˈfō-bē-ǝ) feels extremely anxious in these types of settings. This disorder is characterized by a distinct fear or anxiety related to public transportation, open spaces, retail stores, crowds, or being alone and away from home in general. Someone with agoraphobia consistently avoids these situations and fears she will be unable to escape. Agoraphobia may also result in "panic-like symptoms," which can be difficult to handle. Typically, people with agoraphobia need another person to accompany them on outings, because they feel they may not be able to cope on their own. They may avoid situations they fear, or be overwhelmed with fear when avoidance is not possible. As with other anxiety disorders, the fear felt by someone with agoraphobia is beyond what might be expected in a particular cultural context (APA, 2013).

Attack of the Nerves
In Puerto Rico and other parts of Latin America, stress may trigger a syndrome known as ataque de nervios, or "attack of the nerves." People suffering from this condition may burst into tears, yell frantically, behave aggressively, and feel a sensation of heat moving from the chest to the head (APA, 2013). Kamira/Shutterstock

Social Anxiety Disorder

According to the *DSM–5*, a person with *social anxiety disorder* (*social phobia*) has a distinct fear of social situations and scrutiny by others. What causes this severe anxiety? It could occur during a speech or presentation, while eating a meal, or simply in an intimate conversation. Social anxiety often stems from a preoccupation with offending someone or behaving in a way that reveals one's anxiety. This extreme fear is not warranted, however. Being evaluated or even mocked by others is not necessarily a dangerous situation and should not cause debilitating stress. This type of social anxiety, where one fears the judgment and scrutiny of others, is what psychologists often observe in Western societies. In other parts of the world, social anxiety may take a different form.

Synonym
taijin kyofu taijin kyofusho

agoraphobia (a-gǝ-rǝ-ˈfō-bē-ǝ) Extreme fear of situations involving public transportation, open spaces, or other public settings.

generalized anxiety disorder
A psychological disorder characterized by an excessive amount of worry and anxiety about activities relating to family, health, school, and other aspects of daily life.

across the WORLD

The Many Faces of Social Anxiety

Every society has its own collection of social norms, so it's not surprising that social anxiety presents itself in distinct ways across the world. People in Asian cultures, for example, are more likely to avoid outward displays of anxiety, such as blushing, sweating, or shaking. Some individuals in Japan and Korea suffer from **taijin kyofu,** a cultural syndrome characterized by an intense fear of offending or embarrassing other people with one's body odor, stomach rumblings, or facial expressions. Note that with *taijin kyofu,* the fear is associated with causing distress in others, as opposed to oneself, which is typical of social anxiety disorder in Western cultures (Hofmann, Asnaani, & Hinton, 2010;

Kinoshita et al., 2008). This distinction may relate to the fact that Japanese and Korean cultures are more collectivist than Western cultures (Rapee & Spence, 2004). Collectivist cultures value social harmony over individual needs, so causing discomfort in others is worse than personal humiliation. 🌐➤

BODY ODOR AND OTHER CULTURAL AFFRONTS

The anxiety disorders we have discussed thus far relate to specific objects and scenarios. You can predict that a person with agoraphobia will feel distressed walking through an enormous shopping mall, and there is a good chance that someone with social phobia will feel very uncomfortable at a cocktail party. But what about anxiety that is more pervasive, affecting many aspects of life?

Generalized Anxiety Disorder

Someone with **generalized anxiety disorder** experiences an excessive amount of worry and anxiety about many activities relating to family, health, school, and other aspects of daily life (APA, 2013). The psychological distress is accompanied by physical symptoms such as muscle tension and restlessness. Individuals with generalized anxiety disorder may avoid activities they believe will not go smoothly, spend a great deal of time getting ready for such events, or wait until the very last minute to engage in the anxiety-producing activity. Like other disorders, the anxiety must cause substantial distress in social settings or work environments to merit a diagnosis.

Twin studies suggest there is a hereditary component to generalized anxiety disorder. This genetic factor appears to be associated with irregularities in parts of the brain associated with fear, such as the amygdala and hippocampus (Hettema et al., 2012; Hettema, Neale, & Kendler, 2001). Environmental factors such as adversity in childhood and overprotective parents also appear to be associated with the development of generalized anxiety disorder (APA, 2013).

We introduced this section with the story of Melissa Hopely, a young woman who performed elaborate rituals to combat her anxiety. Her behavior caused significant distress and dysfunction, which suggests that it was abnormal, but does it match with any of the anxiety disorders described above? Her anxiety was not attached to a specific object or situation, so it doesn't appear to fit the description of a phobia. Nor was her anxiety widespread and nonspecific, as might be the case with generalized anxiety disorder. Melissa's fears emanated from nagging, dreadful thoughts generated by her own mind. She may not have been struggling with an anxiety disorder per se, but she certainly was experiencing anxiety as a result of some disorder. So what was it?

⬤✔⬤⬤ show what you know

1. Someone with a diagnosis of panic disorder will experience unexpected and recurrent:
   a. comorbidity.
   b. medical illnesses.
   c. panic attacks.
   d. dramatic mood swings.

2. A behaviorist might propose that you acquire a phobia through _____, but the maintenance of that phobia could be the result of _____.

3. People suffering from *taijin kyofu* tend to worry more about embarrassing others than they do about being embarrassed themselves. Yet in Western cultures, the opposite is true. What characteristics of the two cultures might lead to these differences in the expression of anxiety?

✔ CHECK YOUR ANSWERS IN APPENDIX C.

Obsessive-Compulsive Disorder

DSM-5 and Obsessive-Compulsive Disorder

At age 12, Melissa was diagnosed with **obsessive-compulsive disorder (OCD),** a psychological disorder characterized by unwanted thoughts, or obsessions, and repetitive, ritualistic behaviors known as compulsions.

> **LO 5**   Summarize the symptoms and causes of obsessive-compulsive disorder.

Soccer Star's Struggle
The Pepsi cans in David Beckham's refrigerator are arranged in a perfect line or in groups of two; if the total number of cans is odd, he removes one to make it even. When Beckham goes to a hotel, he can only relax after systematically organizing all the objects in his room. The British soccer legend reportedly suffers from obsessive-compulsive disorder (Frith, 2006, April 3). Michel Euler/AP Photo

TROUBLING THOUGHTS, TROUBLING BEHAVIORS   An **obsession** is a thought, urge, or image that recurs repeatedly, is intrusive and unwelcome, and often causes feelings of intense anxiety and distress. Melissa's recurrent, all-consuming thoughts of disaster and death are examples of obsessions. People with obsessions stop these unwanted thoughts and urges, or at least ignore them, often attempting to "neutralize" them with a replacement thought or activity. This isn't always helpful, though, because the replacement can become a **compulsion,** which is a behavior or "mental act" repeated over and over.

For Melissa, these compulsions eventually took over her life. In the morning, for example, she would reapply deodorant and put her clothes on and take them off up to 20 times—because if she failed to execute these procedures just right, she believed something dreadful was bound to happen. On September 11, 2001, when terrorists attacked New York City and Washington, D.C., Melissa blamed herself because she had put on her blouse an odd, rather than even, number of times that day.

People with OCD experience various types of obsessions and compulsions. In many cases, obsessions focus on fears of contamination with germs or dirt, and compulsions revolve around cleaning and sterilizing (Cisler, Brady, Olatunji, & Lohr, 2010). One such OCD sufferer reported washing her hands until her knuckles bled, living in fear that she would kill someone with her germs (Turk, Marks, & Horder, 1990). Other common compulsions include repetitive rituals and checking behaviors. Melissa, for example, developed a compulsion about locking her car. After parking on the street, she would do what any street-smart person does—lock the doors. But unlike most people who lock their cars once and walk away, Melissa felt compelled to lock it twice. Then she would begin to wonder whether the car was really locked, so she would lock it a third time—just in case. But 3 is an odd number, and odd numbers just don't sit well with Melissa, so she would lock it a fourth time. Yet that didn't feel quite right either. By the time Melissa finally felt sufficiently comfortable to walk away, she had locked her car eight times. And sometimes that was still not enough.

How do you explain this type of behavior? OCD compulsions often aim to thwart unwanted situations, and thereby **reduce** anxiety and distress. Melissa was tormented by multiple obsessions ranging from catastrophic (the death of her mother) to minor (someone stealing her iPod). But the compulsive behaviors of OCD are either "clearly excessive" or not logically related to the event or situation the person is trying to prevent (APA, 2013).

CONNECTIONS

Negative reinforcement (**Chapter 5**) promotes the maladaptive behavior here. The compulsions are not actually preventing unwanted occurrences, but they do lead to a *decrease* in anxiety, and thus negatively reinforce the behavior. Repeatedly locking the car temporarily reduced Melissa's anxiety, making her more likely to perform this behavior in the future.

obsessive-compulsive disorder (OCD)
A psychological disorder characterized by obsessions and/or compulsions that are time-consuming and cause a great deal of distress.

obsession A thought, an urge, or an image that happens repeatedly, is intrusive and unwelcome, and often causes anxiety and distress.

compulsion A behavior or "mental act" that a person repeats over and over in an effort to reduce anxiety.

Where do we draw the line between obsessive or compulsive behavior and the diagnosis of a disorder? Remember, behaviors or symptoms must be significantly distressing or disabling in order to be considered abnormal and qualify as a disorder. This is certainly the case with OCD, in which obsessions and/or compulsions are very time-consuming (taking more than 1 hour a day) and cause a great deal of distress and disruption in daily life. Everyone has odd thoughts and quirky routines, but they don't eat up multiple hours of the day and interfere with school, work, and relationships. That's the key distinction between normal preoccupations and OCD (APA, 2013).

THE BIOLOGY OF OCD   Evidence suggests that the symptoms of OCD are related to abnormal activity of neurotransmitters. Reduced activity of serotonin is thought to play a role, though other neurotransmitters are also being studied (Bloch, McGuire, Landeros-Weisenberger, Leckman, & Pittenger, 2010). Certain areas of the brain have also been implicated, including locations in the basal ganglia, cingulate gyri, and orbital frontal cortex (APA, 2013; Radua & Mataix-Cols, 2009). These regions play a role in planning and regulating movement (Rotge et al., 2009).

Why do these biological differences arise? There appears to be a genetic basis for OCD. If a first-degree relative (parent, sibling, or offspring who shares about 50% of one's DNA) has an OCD diagnosis, the risk of developing OCD is twice as high as someone whose first-degree relatives do not have the disorder (APA, 2013).

THE ROLE OF REINFORCEMENT   To ease her anxiety, Melissa turned to compulsions—repetitive, ritualistic behaviors aimed at relieving or offsetting her obsessions. Because her greatest fears never came to pass, Melissa assumed that her actions had prevented them. *I didn't die because I touched all the things in my room just the right way,* she would think to herself. The more she followed through on her compulsions and saw that her fears never played out, the more convinced she became that her behaviors prevented them. As Melissa put it, "When you feed it, feed it, feed it, it gets stronger."

Here, we see how learning can play a role in OCD. Melissa's compulsions were negatively reinforced by the reduction in her fear. The negative reinforcement led to more compulsive behaviors, those compulsions were negatively reinforced, and so on. As you can see, this learning process is ongoing and potentially very powerful. In one study, researchers monitored 144 people with OCD diagnoses for more than 40 years. The participants' OCD symptoms improved, but almost half continued to show "clinically relevant" symptoms after four decades (Skoog & Skoog, 1999).

◯◯✓◯◯   **show what you know**

1. Melissa has demonstrated recurrent all-consuming thoughts and feelings of worry. She tries to stop unwanted thoughts and urges through a variety of behaviors that she repeats over and over. These behaviors are known as

   a. obsessions.   c. panic attacks.

   b. classical conditioning.   d. compulsions.

2. Evidence suggests there is a _____ basis for OCD. If a first-degree relative has an OCD diagnosis, a person's risk of developing the same disorder is twice as high as someone whose first-degree relatives do not have the disorder.

3. Imagine Melissa's therapist helped reduce the negative reinforcement of her obsessions and compulsions by not allowing her to repeatedly check that her car was locked. Explain why such a technique would work.

✓ CHECK YOUR ANSWERS IN APPENDIX C.

Depressive Disorders

MELISSA'S SECOND DIAGNOSIS Unfortunately for Melissa, receiving a diagnosis and treatment did not solve her problems. She hated herself for having OCD, and her parents and some friends had a hard time accepting her diagnosis. "Every day I woke up, I wanted to die," says Melissa, who reached a breaking point during her sophomore year in high school. After a particularly difficult day at school, Melissa returned home with the intention of taking her own life. Luckily, a friend recognized that she was in distress and notified her family members, who rushed home to find Melissa curled up in a ball in the corner of her room, rocking back and forth and mumbling nonsense. They took Melissa to the hospital, where she would be safe and begin treatment. During her 3-day stay in the hospital psychiatric unit, Melissa finally met people who didn't think she was "crazy" or define her by the disorder. For the first time, she explains, "I realized I wasn't my disorder."

The Importance of Friends
Melissa (right) poses with childhood friend Mary Beth, whom she credits for helping to save her life. The day that Melissa came home intending to attempt suicide, Mary Beth recognized her friend's distress and called for help. Thanks to the intervention of friends and family, Melissa received the treatment she needed. Melissa Hopely

DSM–5 and Major Depressive Disorder

LO 6　Summarize the symptoms and causes of major depressive disorder.

During that hospital stay, doctors gave Melissa a new diagnosis in addition to OCD. They told her that she was suffering from *depression.* Apparently, the profound sadness and helplessness she had been feeling were symptoms of **major depressive disorder,** one of the depressive disorders described in *DSM–5* (TABLE 13.5). A *major depressive episode* is evident if five or more of the symptoms listed below (1) occur for at least 2 consecutive weeks and represent a change from prior functioning, (2) cause significant distress or impairment, and (3) are not due to a medical or drug-related condition:

- depressed mood, which might result in feeling sad or hopeless;
- reduced pleasure in activities almost all of the time;
- substantial loss or gain in weight, without conscious effort, or changes in appetite;
- sleeping excessively or not sleeping enough;
- feeling tired, drained of energy;
- feeling worthless or extremely guilt-ridden;
- difficulty thinking or concentrating;
- persistent thoughts about death or suicide.

Someone with five or more of these symptoms would feel significantly distressed and experience problems in social interactions and at work.

In order to be diagnosed with major depressive disorder, a person must have experienced at least one major depressive episode. Some people experience only one major depressive episode, and others suffer from *recurrent* episodes. The disorder can also be triggered by the birth of a baby. Approximately 3–6% of women experience depression starting during pregnancy or within weeks or months of giving birth; this is known as *peripartum onset* (APA, 2013).

When making a diagnosis, the clinician must be able to distinguish the symptoms of major depression from normal reactions to a "significant loss," such as the death of a loved one. This is not always easy because responses to death often resemble depression. A key distinction is that grief generally decreases with time, and comes in waves associated with memories or reminders of the loss; the sadness associated with a major depressive episode tends to remain steady (APA, 2013).

major depressive disorder
A psychological disorder that includes at least one major depressive episode, with symptoms such as depressed mood, problems with sleep and loss of energy.

Table 13.5 DEPRESSIVE DISORDERS		
Depressive Disorder	**Description**	**Annual Prevalence**
Disruptive mood dysregulation disorder	Persistent irritability that typically results in "temper outbursts" and "angry mood that is present between the severe temper outbursts" (p. 156).	2–5% in children
Major depressive disorder	Feeling depressed (sad, empty, hopeless) almost every day for 2 weeks, or "a loss of interest or pleasure in" almost all activities (p. 163).	7% in ages 18–29 and then 3 times higher in age 60 and older
Persistent depressive disorder (dysthymia)	Feeling depressed the majority of the time: at least 2 years in adults and 1 year in children and adolescents.	0.05%
Premenstrual dysphoric disorder	Feeling irritable, low, or anxious during the premenstrual phase of one's cycle, a condition that resolves itself during menses or shortly thereafter.	1.8–5.8% of menstruating women

As you can see from these descriptions, the word *depression* can mean many things. Some of these depressive disorders are rare, whereas others are more common.

SOURCE: DSM-5 (AMERICAN PSYCHIATRIC ASSOCIATION, 2013).

Major depressive disorder is one of the most common and devastating psychological disorders. In the United States, for example, the lifetime prevalence of major depressive disorder is almost 17% (Kessler, Berglund, et al., 2005); this means that nearly 1 in 5 people experience a major depressive episode at least once in life. Women are more likely to be affected than men (Kessler et al., 2003), and rates of this disorder are already 1.5 to 3 times higher for females beginning in adolescence (APA, 2013).

The effects of major depressive disorder extend far beyond the individual. For Americans ages 15 to 44 years old, this condition is at the top of the list enumerating causes of disability (World Health Organization, 2008b)—and this means it impacts the productivity of the workforce. Major depressive disorder can result in "substantial" severity of symptoms as well as impairment in the ability to perform expected roles. In a comprehensive study of major depressive disorder, respondents reported that their symptoms prevented them from going to work or performing day-to-day activities for an average of 35 days a year (Kessler et al., 2003). Stop and think about this statistic—we are talking about a loss of 7 work weeks!

CULTURE   Depression is one of the most common disorders in the world, yet the symptoms experienced, the course of treatment, and the words used to describe it vary from culture to culture. For example, people in China rarely report feeling "sad," but instead focus on physical symptoms, such as dizziness, fatigue, or inner pressure (Kleinman, 2004). In Thailand, depression is commonly expressed through physical *and* mental symptoms, such as headaches, fatigue, daydreaming, social withdrawal, irritation, and forgetfulness (Chirawatkul, Prakhaw, & Chomnirat, 2011).

SUICIDE   Not only is major depressive disorder a widespread condition, its recurrent nature creates increased risk for suicide and health complications (Monroe & Harkness, 2011). Around 9% of adults in 21 countries confirm they have harbored "serious thoughts of suicide" at least once (**INFOGRAPHIC 13.2** on page 562), and around 3% have attempted suicide (Borges et al., 2010). According to the National

History of Depression
Actor Jon Hamm is among the millions of Americans who have suffered from depressive disorders (Vernon, 2010, September 18). In any one year, approximately 7% of the American population is diagnosed with major depressive disorder (APA, 2013; Kessler, Chiu, et al., 2005). If you or someone you know appears to be experiencing depression or suicidal thoughts, do not hesitate to seek help. Call the National Suicide Prevention Line: 1-800-273-TALK or 1-800-273-8255. Francis Specker/Landov Photographers

Suicide in the United States

In 2009, suicide emerged as the leading cause of death from injury in the United States, surpassing rates for homicide and traffic accidents (Rockett et al., 2012). Researchers examine suicide rates across gender, age, and ethnicity in order to better understand risk factors and to help develop suicide prevention strategies. Let's take a look at what this means—and what you can do if a friend or family member might be contemplating suicide.

Among adults aged 18 and older, **8.7 million reported having serious thoughts about suicide** in the past year.

1,100,000 attempted suicide.

(SUBSTANCE ABUSE AND MENTAL HEALTH SERVICES ADMINISTRATION, 2011)

In 2010, someone died as a result of suicide almost every **14 minutes.**
(AMERICAN FOUNDATION FOR SUICIDE PREVENTION, 2013)

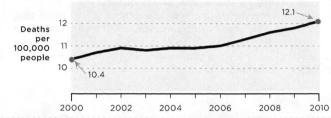

Deaths per 100,000 people

12.1

10.4

2000 2002 2004 2006 2008 2010

From 2000 to 2010, suicide rates **increased by nearly 20%.**
(AMERICAN FOUNDATION FOR SUICIDE PREVENTION, 2013)

Suicide is the second leading cause of death for people aged 25 to 34, and the third leading cause of death for people aged 15 to 24.

(CENTERS FOR DISEASE CONTROL AND PREVENTION, NATIONAL CENTER FOR INJURY PREVENTION AND CONTROL, 2010)

Until 2006, people aged 85 and older had the highest rate of suicide. Now people 45 to 64 years old have the highest rate.

(AMERICAN FOUNDATION FOR SUICIDE PREVENTION, 2013)

The suicide rate for males is nearly 4 times higher than females.

WHITE	14.1
AMERICAN INDIAN AND ALASKAN NATIVE	11.0
ASIAN AND PACIFIC ISLANDER	6.2
HISPANIC	5.9
BLACK	5.1

White Americans have the highest rate of suicide: In 2010, 14.1 out of every 100,000 died by suicide.
(AMERICAN FOUNDATION FOR SUICIDE PREVENTION, 2013)

Risk factors for suicide include:

✔ Previous suicide attempt(s)

✔ Family history of suicide or violence

✔ Alcohol or drug abuse

✔ Physical illness

✔ History of depression or other mental illness

✔ Feeling alone

(CENTERS FOR DISEASE CONTROL AND PREVENTION, 2012i)

If you believe a **friend may be** thinking about **suicide:**

• Encourage your friend to contact a responsible person who can help. This may be a counselor, teacher, or health-care professional. Or call a suicide prevention hotline.

• Don't be afraid to be wrong. Talking about suicide will not put the idea in your friend's head. Be direct and ask your friend if he is thinking about hurting himself.

• Just talking with your friend can help. Listen without being judgmental.

• If your friend admits that she has made a detailed plan or obtained a means of hurting herself, stay with her until help arrives or until she is willing to go talk with someone who can help.

• Never agree to keep someone's thoughts about suicide a secret.

(MAINE SUICIDE PREVENTION PROGRAM, 2006; YOUTH SUICIDE PREVENTION PROGRAM, 2011)

Ninety percent of those who commit suicide had a psychological disorder. Of these, 60% involved major depressive disorder. More than 80% of those people with disorders had not been receiving treatment at the time (Mann et al., 2005).

NATIONAL SUICIDE PREVENTION LIFELINE: 1-800-273-TALK (8255)   suicidepreventionlifeline.org

Credit: Young men talking in front of window, Serge/Getty Images

Institute of Mental Health (NIMH, 2012), approximately 90% of people who commit suicide had a psychological disorder, most commonly depressive disorder and/or substance abuse disorder.

The Biology of Depression

Nearly 7% of Americans battle depression in any given year (APA, 2013; Kessler, Chiu, et al., 2005). How can we explain this staggering statistic? There appears to be something biological at work.

GENETIC FACTORS   Studies of twins, family pedigrees, and adoptions tell us that major depressive disorder runs in families, with a heritability rate of approximately 40–50% (APA, 2013; Levinson, 2006). This means that about 40–50% of the variability of major depressive disorder in the population can be attributed to genetic factors. People who have a first-degree relative with this disorder are 2 to 4 times more likely to develop it than those whose first-degree relatives are unaffected (APA, 2013).

NEUROTRANSMITTERS AND THE BRAIN   What happens inside the brain of a person who suffers from depression? Three neurotransmitters appear to be associated with the cause and course of major depressive disorder: *norepinephrine, serotonin,* and *dopamine.* The relationships among these neurotransmitters are complicated and research is still ongoing (El Mansari et al., 2010; Torrente, Gelenberg, & Vrana, 2012), but the findings are intriguing. For example, serotonin deficiency has been associated with major depressive disorder (Torrente et al., 2012) and genes may be responsible for some of this irregular activity, particularly in the amygdala and other brain areas involved in processing emotions associated with this disorder (Northoff, 2012).

Depression also seems to be correlated with specific structural features in the brain (Andrus et al., 2012). People with major depressive disorder may have irregularities in various parts of the brain, including the amygdala, the prefrontal cortex, and the hippocampus. For example, some regions of the right cortex show significant thinning in people who face a high risk of developing major depressive disorder (Peterson et al., 2009). Studies have zeroed in on a variety of factors, such as increased structure size, decreased volume, and changes in neural activity (Kempton et al., 2011; Sacher et al., 2012; Singh et al., 2013). Research using functional magnetic resonance imaging (fMRI) technologies points to irregularities in neural pathways involved in processing emotions and rewards for people with major depressive disorder (APA, 2013). The take-home message is that major depressive disorder most likely results from a complex interplay of many neural factors. What's difficult to determine is whether changes in the brain preceded the disorder, or the disorder altered the brain.

HORMONES   There is also evidence that **hormones** play a role in depression. People with depressive disorders may have high levels of cortisol, a hormone secreted by the adrenal glands (Belmaker & Agam, 2008; Dougherty, Klein, Olino, Dyson, & Rose, 2009). Women sufferers, in particular, appear to be affected by stress-induced brain activity and hormonal fluctuations (Holsen et al., 2011). The hormonal changes associated with pregnancy and childbirth seem to be linked to major depressive episodes before or after delivery. For women suffering from these symptoms, there appear to be problems with the **hypothalamic-pituitary-adrenal (HPA) system** (Corwin & Pajer, 2008; Pearlstein, Howard, Salisbury, & Zlotnick, 2009). This is not just an issue for pregnant women. Research suggests that hyperactivity of the HPA system is linked to major depressive episodes in general (APA, 2013). And, as you will soon discover, certain changes in immune activity are associated with major depressive disorder.

Baby Blues
Having a baby is a stressful, life-changing event, and a time of dramatic hormonal changes. The hormone activity associated with pregnancy and childbirth may contribute to the major depressive episodes some women experience before and after the birth of a baby. Laurent/Ravonison/AGE fotostock

CONNECTIONS

In **Chapter 2,** we described the endocrine system, which uses glands to convey messages via *hormones*. These chemicals released into the bloodstream can cause aggression and mood swings, as well as influence growth and alertness. Hormones may also play a role in major depressive disorder.

CONNECTIONS

In **Chapter 12,** we discussed the *HPA system,* which helps to maintain balance in the body by overseeing the sympathetic nervous system, the neuroendocrine system, and the immune system. The HPA system is also associated with depressive episodes.

from the pages of **SCIENTIFIC AMERICAN**

Inflammation Brings on the Blues

Our immune system may mean well, but it might also cause depression

As if being stuck sick in bed wasn't bad enough, several studies conducted during the past few years have found that the immune response to illness can cause depression. Recently scientists have pinpointed an enzyme that could be the culprit, as it is linked to both chronic inflammation—such as that found in patients with coronary heart disease, type 2 diabetes and rheumatoid arthritis—and depressive symptoms in mice.

In the new study, immunophysiologist Keith Kelley and his colleagues at the University of Illinois exposed mice to a tuberculosis vaccine that produces a low-grade, chronic inflammation. After inoculation, production in the mice brains of an enzyme called IDO, which breaks down tryptophan, spiked. The animals exhibited normal symptoms of illness such as moving around and eating less. Yet even after recovering from the physical illness induced by the vaccine, they showed signs of depression—for example, struggling less than control mice to escape from a bucket of water. Surprisingly, their listlessness was solved relatively simply. "If you block IDO, genetically or pharmaceutically, depression goes away" without interfering with the immune response, Kelley explains.

The research makes a solid case that the immune system communicates directly with the nervous system and affects important health-related behaviors such as depression. The findings could bring relief to patients afflicted with obesity, which leads to chronic inflammation, as well as to cancer patients treated with radiation and chemotherapy drugs that produce both inflammation and depression. "IDO is a new target for drug companies to aim for, to treat patients with both clinical depression and systemic inflammation," Kelley says. **Corey Binns. Reproduced with permission. Copyright © 2009 Scientific American, a division of Nature America, Inc. All rights reserved.**

Psychological Roots of Depression

Earlier we mentioned heritability rates of 40–50% for depression. But what about the other 50–60% of the variability? Clearly, biology is not everything. Psychological factors also play a role in the onset and course of major depressive disorder.

LEARNED HELPLESSNESS According to researcher Martin Seligman, people often become depressed because they believe they have no control over the consequences of their behaviors (Overmier & Seligman, 1967; Seligman, 1975; Seligman & Maier, 1967). To demonstrate this **learned helplessness,** Seligman restrained dogs in a "hammock" and then randomly administered inescapable painful electric shocks to their paws (**FIGURE 13.2**). The next day the same dogs were put into another cage. Although unrestrained, they did not try to escape shocks administered through a floor grid (by jumping over a low barrier in the cage). Seligman concluded the dogs had learned they couldn't control painful experiences during the prior training; they were acting in a depressed manner. He translated this finding to people with major depressive disorder, suggesting that they too feel powerless to change things for the better, and therefore become depressed.

NEGATIVE THINKING Cognitive therapist Aaron Beck (1976) suggested that depression is connected with negative thinking. Depression, according to Beck, is the product of a "cognitive triad"—a negative view of experiences, self, and the future. Here's an example: A student receives a failing grade on an exam, so she begins to think she is a poor student, and that belief leads her to the conclusion that she will fail the course. This self-defeating attitude may actually lead to her failing the course,

learned helplessness A tendency for people to believe they have no control over the consequences of their behaviors, resulting in passive behavior.

FIGURE 13.2
Seligman's Research on Learned Helplessness
Dogs restrained in a hammock were unable to escape painful shocks administered through an electrical grid on the floor of a specially designed cage called a shuttle box. The dogs soon learned that they were helpless and couldn't control these painful experiences. They did not try to escape by jumping over the barrier even when they were not restrained. The figure here shows the electrical grid activated on side B.

reinforcing her belief that she is a poor student, and perhaps evolving into a broader belief that her life is a failure.

If you aren't convinced that beliefs contribute to depression, consider this: The way people respond to their experience of depression may impact the severity of the disorder. People who repeatedly focus on this experience are much more likely to remain depressed and perhaps even descend into deeper depression (Eaton et al., 2012; Nolen-Hoeksema, 1991). Women tend to *ruminate* or constantly think about their negative emotions more than men, rather than using "active problem solving" (Eaton et al., 2012). Yet changing negative thoughts and moods during major depressive episodes is difficult to do without help. We also should keep in mind the distinction between the risk for depression and the cause of depression, and that a correlation between rumination and depression should not be confused with a cause-and-effect relationship. Not every negative thinker develops depression, and depression can lead to negative thoughts.

We can think of mental health as a continuum, with healthy thoughts, emotions, and behaviors at one extreme, and dysfunction, distress, and deviance at the other. We can also conceptualize mood as a continuum, with depression at one end and neutral moods (not too sad, not too happy) in the center. But what lies at the other extreme? If it's the opposite of depression, then it must be good, right? Not necessarily, as you will soon see.

✓ show what you know

1. Melissa is sleeping too much, she feels tired all of the time, and has been avoiding activities she used to enjoy. Which of the following best describes what Melissa may be experiencing?
   a. obsessive-compulsive disorder
   b. major depressive disorder
   c. agoraphobia
   d. panic attacks

2. What neurotransmitters are associated with the cause and course of major depressive disorder?
   a. serotonin and norepinephrine
   b. serotonin and dopamine
   c. norepinephrine and dopamine
   d. serotonin, norepinephrine, and dopamine

3. There are many factors involved in the cause and course of major depressive disorder. Prepare notes for a 5-minute speech you might give on this topic.

✓ CHECK YOUR ANSWERS IN APPENDIX C.

Bipolar Disorders

HIGHEST HIGHS, LOWEST LOWS   When Ross began battling bipolar disorder, he went through periods of euphoria and excitement. Sometimes he would stay awake for 4 consecutive days, or sleep barely an hour for 2 weeks in a row—without feeling the least bit tired. In fact, he was exploding with energy, supercharged with confidence, and feeling high on life. Ideas flashed through his mind so fast that it was difficult to focus on any one of them. "My brain was a television," Ross says, "and someone was just constantly flipping channels." The only way he could ease his mind was by drinking—and we're not talking about a couple of beers or a few shots of vodka, but an entire case or a whole bottle. Ross was using alcohol to drown out his symptoms.

DSM-5 and Bipolar Disorders

LO 7   Compare and contrast bipolar disorders and major depressive disorder.

The extreme energy, euphoria, and confidence Ross felt were most likely the result of **manic episodes,** also known as *mania.* Manic episodes are often characterized by continuous elation that is out of proportion for the situation. Other features include irritability, very high and sustained levels of energy, and an "expansive" mood, meaning the person feels more powerful than he really is and behaves in a showy or overly confident way. During one of these episodes, a person exhibits three or more of the symptoms listed below, which represent deviations from normal behavior (APA, 2013):

- grandiose or extremely high self-esteem;
- reduced sleep;
- increased talkativeness;
- a "flight of ideas" or the feeling of "racing" thoughts;
- easily distracted;
- heightened activity at school or work;
- physical agitation;
- displaying poor judgment and engaging in activities that could have serious consequences (risky sexual activities, excessive shopping sprees).

It is not unusual for a person experiencing a severe manic episode to be hospitalized. Mania is difficult to hide and can be dangerous. One may act out of character, doing things that damage important relationships or jeopardize work. A person may become violent, posing a risk to himself and others. Seeking help is unlikely, because mania leads to impaired judgment, feelings of grandiosity, and euphoria. (Why would you seek help if you feel on top of the world?) At these times, the support of others is essential.

There are various types of bipolar disorder. To be diagnosed with *bipolar I disorder,* a person must experience at least one *manic episode,* substantial distress, and great impairment. *Bipolar II disorder* requires at least one major depressive episode as well as a *hypomanic episode. Hypomania* is associated with some of the same symptoms as a manic episode, but it is not as severe and does not impair one's ability to function (APA, 2013; TABLE 13.6).

Table 13.6	BIPOLAR DISORDERS	
Bipolar Disorder	**Description**	**Annual Prevalence**
Bipolar I disorder	Episodes of mania that include an "abnormally, persistently elevated, expansive, or irritable mood and persistently increased activity or energy that is present for most of the day, nearly every day, for a period of at least 1 week" (p. 127). This may be preceded by hypomania or depression.	0.6%
Bipolar II disorder	Repeated major depressive episodes (lasting at least 2 weeks) and "at least one hypomanic episode," which must last for a minimum of 4 days (p. 135).	0.8%

The two forms of bipolar disorder have distinct patterns of highs and lows. Looking at the annual prevalence (yearly occurrence) of these disorders, you can see that they are relatively rare.

SOURCE: DSM-5 (AMERICAN PSYCHIATRIC ASSOCIATION, 2013).

manic episodes States of continuous elation that are out of proportion to the setting, and can include irritability, very high and sustained levels of energy, and an "expansive" mood.

BIPOLAR CYCLING   Some people with bipolar disorder cycle between extreme highs and lows of emotion and energy that last for days, weeks, or even months. During bouts of *mania,* a person's mood can be unusually elevated, irritable, or expansive. At the other extreme are feelings of deep sadness, emptiness, and helplessness. Periods of mania and depression may be brought on by life changes and stressors (Malkoff-Schwartz et al., 1998), though some research suggests that it is only the *first* episode that tends to be triggered by some sort of life event, such as a first love. Subsequent episodes do not seem to be as closely linked to such events (Belmaker, 2004).

Bipolar disorder is uncommon. Over the course of a lifetime, about 0.8% of the American population will receive a diagnosis of bipolar I disorder, and 1.1% bipolar II disorder (Merikangas et al., 2007). Men and women are equally likely to be affected, but the course of the disorder may differ according to gender. Men tend to experience earlier onset of symptoms, while the incidence for women seems to be higher later in life (Altshuler et al., 2010; Kennedy et al., 2005).

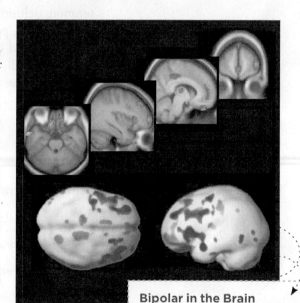

Battling Bipolar
Actress Catherine Zeta-Jones went public with her bipolar diagnosis in 2011. Zeta-Jones suffers from bipolar II disorder, which is characterized by major depressive episodes as well as hypomania, or mania that is not full-blown (Takeda, 2013, July 12). Steve Granitz/WireImage/Getty Images

WHO GETS BIPOLAR DISORDER?   Although researchers have not determined the cause of bipolar disorders, evidence from twin and adoption studies underscores the importance of genes. If one identical twin is diagnosed with bipolar disorder, there is a 40–70% chance the other twin will have the disorder as well. Among fraternal twins, there is only a 5% chance that the second twin will develop the disorder (Craddock, O'Donovan, & Owen, 2005). According to the American Psychiatric Association (2013), "a family history of bipolar disorder is one of the strongest and most consistent risk factors for bipolar disorders" (p. 130). Adults with a family member who has bipolar disorder, on average, have a "10-fold increased risk" for developing the disorder themselves.

But nature is not the only force at work in bipolar disorder; nurture seems to play an important role, too. The fact that there is a higher rate of bipolar disorder in high-income countries (1.4%) than in low-income countries (0.7%; APA, 2013) suggests that environment may act as a catalyst for its development. Some researchers hypothesize that exposure to viruses, poor nutrition, and stress during fetal development spark a cascade of biological events that leads to the development of bipolar disorder. The same has been said of another serious disorder, schizophrenia (Carter, 2007; Yolken & Torrey, 1995).

Bipolar in the Brain
Using imaging techniques, researchers have identified certain brain irregularities that appear to be linked to bipolar disorder. These MRI images highlight areas of decreased gray matter volume in prefrontal and temporal areas associated with high-level cognitive functioning and emotional regulation (Rietschel, Maier, & Schulze, 2013). Dr. Marcella Rietschel

✔️ **show what you know**

1. Ross described going for 4 days straight without sleeping at all, or 2 weeks in a row sleeping only 1 hour per night. He was exploding with energy, supercharged with confidence, and feeling on top of the world. It is likely that Ross was experiencing periods of euphoria and excitement, which can best be described as:

   a. depression.
   b. manic episodes.
   c. panic attacks.
   d. anxiety.

2. What is the difference between bipolar I disorder and bipolar II disorder?

3. Compare the symptoms of bipolar disorder with those of major depressive disorder.

✔ CHECK YOUR ANSWERS IN APPENDIX C.

Schizophrenia
Degrees of Psychopathology

LO 8 Recognize the symptoms of schizophrenia.

How would it feel to have voices following you throughout the day, commenting on your behaviors, attacking your character, and taunting you with hurtful remarks: "You're ugly, you're worthless, you deserve to die" (Halpern, 2013, p. 2). Meanwhile, your perception of the world is grossly distorted. Nickels, dimes, and pennies all look the same, and the subway you take to class is really on its way to a Nazi concentration camp—or so you believe. These are actual symptoms reported by Lisa Halpern, who suffers from a disabling psychological disorder called **schizophrenia** (skit-sə-ˈfrē-nē-ə). People with schizophrenia experience **psychosis,** a loss of contact with reality that is severe and chronic.

Schizophrenia, Take 5

The hallmark features of schizophrenia are disturbances in thinking, perception, and language (**TABLE 13.7**). Psychotic symptoms include **delusions,** which are strange or false beliefs that a person maintains even when presented with contradictory evidence. Common delusional themes include being persecuted by others, spied upon, or ridiculed. Some people have grandiose delusions; they may believe they are extraordinarily talented or famous, for example. Others are convinced that radio reports, newspaper headlines, or public announcements are about them. Delusions appear very real to those experiencing them.

Table 13.7 UNDERSTANDING SCHIZOPHRENIA
• Delusions
• Hallucinations
• Disorganized speech
• Grossly disorganized or catatonic behavior
• Decreased emotional expression
• Decreased level of functioning at work, socially, or in self-care
• Continuous disturbance lasting at least 6 months
• Symptoms not related to substance use
• Symptoms not related to another medical condition
• Lack of motivation
There is a great deal of public confusion about what it means to have schizophrenia. Listed above are some common features of this frequently misunderstood disorder.

SOURCE: DSM-5 (AMERICAN PSYCHIATRIC ASSOCIATION, 2013).

People with schizophrenia may also hear voices or see things that are not actually present. This psychotic symptom is known as a **hallucination**—a "perception-like experience" that the individual believes is real, but that is not evident to others. Hallucinations can occur with any of the senses, but auditory hallucinations are most common. Often they manifest as voices commenting on what is happening in the environment, or using threatening or judgmental language (APA, 2013).

The symptoms of schizophrenia are often classified as **positive and negative** (TABLE 13.8). **Positive symptoms** are excesses or distortions of normal behavior, and include delusions, hallucinations, and disorganized speech—all of which are generally not observed in people without psychosis. **Negative symptoms,** on the other hand, refer to the reduction or absence of normal behaviors. Common negative symptoms are social withdrawal, diminished speech or speech content, limited emotions, and loss of energy and follow-up (Tandon, Nasrallah, & Keshavan, 2009).

CONNECTIONS

In **Chapter 5,** we noted that the term *positive* does not always mean "good." *Positive punishment* means the addition of an aversive stimulus. *Positive symptoms* refer to additions or excesses, not an evaluation of the "goodness" of the symptoms. *Negative* refers to the reduction or absence of behaviors, not an evaluation of the "badness" of the symptoms.

Table 13.8 SYMPTOMS OF SCHIZOPHRENIA	
Positive Symptoms of Schizophrenia	**Negative Symptoms of Schizophrenia**
Delusions	Decreased emotional expression
Hallucinations	Lack of motivation
Disorganized speech	Decreased speech production
Grossly disorganized behavior	Reduced pleasure
Abnormal motor behavior	Lack of interest in interacting with others

Schizophrenia symptoms can be grouped into two main categories: *Positive symptoms* indicate the presence of excesses or distortions of normal behavior; *negative symptoms* refer to a reduction in normal behaviors and mental processes.

SOURCE: DSM-5 (AMERICAN PSYCHIATRIC ASSOCIATION, 2013).

To be diagnosed with schizophrenia, a person must display symptoms for the majority of days in a 1-month period and experience significant dysfunction with respect to work, school, relationships, or personal care for at least 6 months. (And it must be determined that these problems do not result from substance abuse or a serious medical condition.) *DSM–5* introduced a major change in how schizophrenia is diagnosed, as the new edition no longer includes the subtypes used in previous editions (paranoid, disorganized, catatonic, undifferentiated, and residual). With the new edition, clinicians can rate the presence and severity of symptoms (hallucinations, delusions, disorganized speech, unusual psychomotor behaviors, and negative symptoms).

With estimates ranging from a 0.3–1% lifetime risk, schizophrenia is relatively unusual (APA, 2013; Saha, Chant, Welham, & McGrath, 2005). Although men and women appear to be equally likely to be affected (Abel, Drake, & Goldstein, 2010; Saha et al., 2005), the onset of the disorder tends to occur earlier in men. Males are typically diagnosed during their late teens or early twenties, whereas the peak age for women is the late twenties (APA, 2013; Gogtay, Vyas, Testa, Wood, & Pantelis, 2011). In most cases, schizophrenia is a lifelong disorder that causes significant disability and a high risk for suicide. The prognosis is worse for earlier onset schizophrenia, but this may be related to the fact that men, who tend to develop symptoms earlier in life, are in poorer condition when first diagnosed (APA, 2013). Furthermore, there is a higher prevalence of schizophrenia among people in lower socioeconomic classes (Tandon, Keshavan, & Nasrallah, 2008).

Untangling the Roots of Schizophrenia

LO 9   Analyze the biopsychosocial factors that contribute to schizophrenia.

Schizophrenia is a complex psychological disorder that results from a perfect storm of biological, psychological, and social factors. Because this disorder springs from a

schizophrenia (skit-sə-ˈfrē-nē-ə) A disabling psychological disorder that can include delusions, hallucinations, disorganized speech, and abnormal psychomotor behavior.

psychosis Loss of contact with reality that is severe and chronic.

delusions Strange or false beliefs that a person firmly maintains even when presented with evidence to the contrary.

hallucinations Perceptual-like experiences that an individual believes are real, but that are not evident to others.

positive symptoms Excesses or distortions of normal behavior, which include delusions, hallucinations, and disorganized speech.

negative symptoms Behaviors or characteristics that are limited or absent; includes social withdrawal, diminished speech, limited or no emotions, and loss of energy and follow-up.

complex interaction of genes and environment, researchers have a hard time predicting who will be affected.

For many years, various experts focused the blame on environmental factors, such as unhealthy family dynamics and bad parenting. A common scapegoat was the "schizophrenogenic mother," whose poor parenting style was believed to cause the disorder in her child (Harrington, 2012). Thankfully, this belief has been shattered by our new understanding of the brain. Schizophrenia is now one of the most heavily researched psychological disorders, with approximately 5,000 new articles added to the search databases every year (Tandon et al., 2008)! Among the most promising areas of research is the genetics of schizophrenia. It turns out that schizophrenia runs in families, and few cases illustrate this principle better than that of the Genain sisters.

nature AND nurture

Four Sisters

Nora, Iris, Myra, and Hester Genain were identical quadruplets, born in 1930. Their mother went to great lengths to treat them equally, and in many ways the children were equals (Mirsky & Quinn, 1988). As babies, they cried in unison and teethed at the same times. As toddlers, they played with the same toys, wore the same dresses, and rode the same tricycles. The little girls were said to be so mentally in sync that they never argued (Quinn, 1963).

Mr. and Mrs. Genain kept the girls isolated. Spending most of their time at home, the quads cultivated few friendships and didn't go out with boys. The Genains may have protected their daughters from the world outside, but they could not shield them from the trouble brewing inside their brains.

At age 22, one of the sisters, Nora, was hospitalized for a psychiatric disorder characterized by hallucinations, delusions, altered speech, and other symptoms. Within months, a second sister, Iris, was admitted to a psychiatric ward as well. She, too, had the symptoms of psychosis. Both Nora and Iris were diagnosed with schizophrenia, and it was only a matter of years before Myra and Hester joined them (Mirsky & Quinn, 1988). What are the odds of a birth resulting in identical quadruplets who would all develop schizophrenia? One in 1.5 billion, according to one scholar's estimate (Mirsky et al., 2000). As you can imagine, the case of the Genain quads has drawn the attention of many scientists. David Rosenthal and his colleagues at the National Institute of Mental Health studied the women when they were in their late twenties and again when they were 51. To protect the quads' identities, Rosenthal assigned them the pseudonyms Nora, Iris, Myra, and Hester, which spell out NIMH, the acronym for the National Institute of Mental Health. *Genain* is also an alias, meaning "dreadful gene" in Greek (Mirsky & Quinn, 1988).

The Genain sisters are genetically equal, which suggests that there is some heritable component to their schizophrenia. Yet, each woman experiences the disorder in her own way. Hester did not receive a diagnosis of schizophrenia until she was in her twenties, but she started to show signs of psychological impairment much earlier than her sisters and was never able to hold down a job or live alone. Myra, however, has been employed for the majority of her life and has a family of her own (Mirsky et al., 2000; Mirsky & Quinn, 1988). Like any psychological phenomenon, schizophrenia is a product of both nature and nurture. ◊⌂

LIKE ANY PSYCHOLOGICAL PHENOMENON, SCHIZOPHRENIA IS A PRODUCT OF BOTH NATURE AND NURTURE.

GENETIC FACTORS Overall, researchers agree that schizophrenia is "highly heritable," with genetic factors accounting for around 80% of the risk for developing this

Relationship to person with schizophrenia

General population	1%
First cousins	2% — 12.5% of genes shared
Uncles/aunts	2%
Nieces/nephews	4%
Grandchildren	5% — 25% of genes shared
Half siblings	6%
Parents	6%
Siblings	9%
Children	13% — 50% of genes shared
Fraternal twins	17%
Identical twins	48% — 100% of genes shared

Risk of developing schizophrenia

FIGURE 13.3
The Role of Genetics in Schizophrenia
The average lifetime risk of developing schizophrenia for the general population is 1% or lower. However, if you have a sibling diagnosed with schizophrenia, your own lifetime risk increases to 9%. If that sibling is your identical twin, someone with whom you share 100% of genes, your risk rockets to 48%. This suggests a significant role for genetic factors in the development of schizophrenia. *Source:* Copyright © 2001 by the American Psychological Association. Adapted with permission from Gottesman (2001).

disorder (Tandon et al., 2008). Much of the evidence derives from twin, family, and adoption studies (**FIGURE 13.3**). If one identical twin has schizophrenia, the risk of the other twin developing the disorder is approximately 41–65% (Petronis, 2004). Compare that to a mere 2% risk for those whose first cousins have schizophrenia (Tsuang, Stone, & Faraone, 2001). If both parents have schizophrenia, the risk of their children being diagnosed with this disorder is 27% (Gottesman, Laursen, Bertelsen, & Mortensen, 2010). Keep in mind that schizophrenia is not caused by a single gene, but by a combination of many genes interacting with the environment (Howes & Kapur, 2009).

DIATHESIS-STRESS MODEL   Like other disorders, schizophrenia is best understood from the biopsychosocial perspective. One model that takes these factors into account is the ***diathesis–stress model,*** where *diathesis* refers to the inherited disposition, for example, to schizophrenia, and *stress* refers to the stressors and other factors in the environment (internal and external). Identical twins share 100% of their genetic make-up (diathesis), yet the environment produces different stressors for the twins (only one of them loses a spouse, for example). As a result, one twin may develop the disorder, but the other does not. This model suggests that developing schizophrenia involves a genetic predisposition *and* environmental triggers.

THE BRAIN   People with schizophrenia generally experience a thinning of the cortex, leading to enlarged ventricles, the cavities in the brain that are filled with cerebrospinal fluid. Research also shows that the total volume of the brain is reduced in schizophrenia (Tandon et al., 2008). In general, these abnormalities are thought to be related to problems with "cognitive control" and psychotic symptoms (Glahn et al., 2008). A word of caution when interpreting these findings, however: It is possible that differences in brain structures are not just due to schizophrenia; they may also result from long-term use of medications to control its symptoms (Jaaro-Peled, Ayhan, Pletnikov, & Sawa, 2010).

Synonyms
diathesis–stress model stress-vulnerability model, constitutional vulnerability

CONNECTIONS

In **Chapter 2,** we discussed activity at the synapse. When neurotransmitters are released, they must bind to receptor sites in order to relay their message to the receiving neuron ("fire" or "don't fire"). Medications that block or inhibit the receptor sites on the receiving neuron are referred to as *antagonists,* and some of these are used to reduce symptoms of schizophrenia.

NEUROTRANSMITTER THEORIES   Evidence suggests that abnormal neurotransmitter activity plays a role in schizophrenia. According to the **dopamine hypothesis,** the synthesis, release, and concentrations of dopamine are all elevated in people who have been diagnosed with schizophrenia and are suffering from psychosis (van Os & Kapur, 2009). Support for the dopamine hypothesis comes from the successful use of medications that **block the receptor sites for dopamine.** These drugs reduce the psychotic symptoms of schizophrenia, presumably because they decrease the potential impact of the excess dopamine being produced (van Os & Kapur, 2009).

Although the effect of increased dopamine has not been precisely determined, one suggestion is that it influences the "reward system" of the brain. Excess dopamine may make it hard for people to pay attention to what is rewarding in the environment, or pick out its most salient, or important, aspects (van Os & Kapur, 2009). They often focus on environmental stimuli that lead them to lose touch with reality. So, when they experience delusions, it is possible they are trying to make sense of the salient experiences on which they are focused. Hallucinations might result from placing too much importance on some of their "internal representations" (Kapur, 2003).

The dopamine hypothesis has evolved over the last several decades, with many researchers coming to appreciate the ongoing dynamic between neurochemical processes as they relate to the individual in the environment. We cannot just study what dopamine does in the synapse; we must take into consideration how dopamine's irregularities are affected by the individual's interactions within the environment (Howes & Kapur, 2009).

ENVIRONMENTAL TRIGGERS AND SCHIZOPHRENIA   Some experts suspect that schizophrenia is associated with exposure to a virus in utero, such as human papilloma virus (HPV). Several illnesses a woman can contract while pregnant, including genital reproductive infections, influenza, and some parasites, may increase her baby's risk of developing schizophrenia later in life (Brown & Patterson, 2011). Retrospective evidence (that is, information collected much later) suggests that the offspring of mothers who were exposed to viruses while pregnant are more likely to develop schizophrenia as adolescents. However, research on this theory is still ongoing and must be replicated.

Schizophrenia is not the result of poor parenting; nor is it a product of classical or operant conditioning. That being said, there are some sociocultural and environmental factors that may play a minor role in one's risk for developing the disorder, as well as the severity of symptoms. Evidence exists, for instance, that complications at birth, social stress, and cannabis abuse are related to a slightly increased risk of schizophrenia onset (Tandon et al., 2008).

We now turn our focus to another type of disorder that is intimately connected to one of psychology's core areas of study: personality.

●✓●● show what you know

1. A loss of contact with reality is referred to as _____.

2. A woman with schizophrenia reports hearing voices that tell her she is ugly and worthless. This is an example of a(n):
   a. hallucination.
   c. negative symptom.
   b. delusion.
   d. diathesis.

3. What are some biopsychosocial factors that contribute to the development of schizophrenia?

✓ CHECK YOUR ANSWERS IN APPENDIX C.

Personality Disorders

LO 10 Differentiate between antisocial and borderline personality disorders.

Before reading this chapter, you probably knew something about depression, bipolar disorder, and schizophrenia. But you may have been less familiar with a somewhat common group of disorders relating to personality. Approximately 1 in 10 adults in the United States has a *personality disorder* (Lenzenweger, Lane, Loranger, & Kessler, 2007). People with **personality disorders** exhibit "an enduring pattern of inner experience and behavior that deviates markedly from the expectations of the individual's culture, is pervasive and inflexible, has an onset in adolescence or early adulthood, is stable over time, and leads to distress or impairment" (APA, 2013, p. 645). Specifically, someone with a personality disorder exhibits behaviors that deviate substantially in the following areas: (1) cognition, including perceptions of self, others, and events; (2) emotional responses; (3) interpersonal functioning; and (4) impulse control. In order to be diagnosed with a personality disorder, one must struggle in at least two of these four categories. In addition, these problems must be resistant to change and have far-reaching consequences for interpersonal relationships.

Like personality traits in general, the core qualities of people with personality disorders (as well as the problems that result) are fairly stable over a lifetime and across situations. When diagnosing this type of disorder, the clinician must focus on troublesome personality traits—and be very careful not to confuse them with problems resulting from developmental changes, culture, drug use, or medical conditions.

The *DSM–5* includes 10 personality disorder types (**TABLE 13.9**). Here, we direct the spotlight onto those that have received the greatest amount of research attention: *antisocial personality disorder* and *borderline personality disorder*.

Table 13.9 PERSONALITY DISORDERS	
Personality Disorder	**Explanation**
Paranoid	Widespread distrust of others without basis
Schizoid	Detachment from relationships and a limited range of emotional expression
Schizotypal	Difficulty in establishing relationships, limited ability to maintain close relationships, and eccentric or strange behavior
Antisocial	Unethical behavior, deceitful, impulsive, irritable, aggressive, disregard for others, lack of remorse
Borderline	Incomplete sense of self, extreme self-criticism, unstable emotions, and feelings of emptiness
Histrionic	Extreme emotions used to gain attention
Narcissistic	Self-absorbed, needs to be admired, lack of empathy
Avoidant	Social self-consciousness, hypersensitive to negative feedback
Dependent	Clingy, needs to be cared for by others
Obsessive-compulsive	Fixation with order, perfection, and control

Listed above are the 10 personality disorders identified by the *DSM-5*.

SOURCE: DSM-5 (AMERICAN PSYCHIATRIC ASSOCIATION, 2013).

dopamine hypothesis A theory suggesting that the synthesis, release, and concentrations of the neurotransmitter dopamine play a role in schizophrenia.

personality disorders A group of psychological disorders that can include impairments in cognition, emotional responses, interpersonal functioning, and impulse control.

Sociopath or Avenger?
Swedish actress Noomi Rapace plays
the role of Lisbeth Salander in *The
Girl with the Dragon Tattoo* (2009).
Salander displays some of the hallmark
characteristics of antisocial personality
disorder: She seems to feel no remorse
about violating social norms, hurting
others, and breaking laws.
Yet she appears to care
about those she
avenges, making it
hard to place her
in this category
(Burkley, 2012,
January 3). Knut
Koivisto/Ronald Grant
Archive/Mary Evans/
Everett Collection

CONNECTIONS

In **Chapter 7,** we noted that executive
functioning is involved in planning,
maintaining focus, and suppressing
automatic responses. In **Chapter 2,** we
learned that the frontal lobes are critical
in processing emotions and controlling
impulses. If these areas in the brain are
not functioning properly, one may exhibit
antisocial behavior.

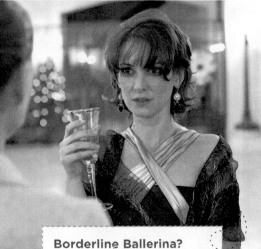

Borderline Ballerina?
Winona Ryder plays the part
of ex-ballerina Beth Macintyre
in the 2010 film *Black Swan.*
Emotionally needy, highly
insecure, and prone to angry
outbursts, this character
displays many characteristics
associated with borderline
personality disorder. Fox
Searchlight Pictures/Photofest

Antisocial Personality Disorder

Many films, including *The Girl with the Dragon Tattoo* and *The Silence of the Lambs,*
feature characters who behave in ways most people find incomprehensible. The qualities of these characters often parallel a diagnosis of **antisocial personality disorder.**

People with antisocial personality disorder may seek personal gratification even
when it means violating ethical standards and breaking laws. They sometimes lie or
con others, and exhibit aggressive, impulsive, or irritable behaviors. These individuals have difficulty feeling empathy, and may not show concern for others or feel
remorse upon hurting them. Other common behavior patterns include care-
lessness in sexual relationships, and the use of intimidation to control others
(APA, 2013). Around 1% of American adults are diagnosed with antisocial
personality disorder, which is more common in men than women (Lenzenweger et al., 2007).

How does antisocial personality disorder develop? There is some evidence for family risk factors, but it is unclear how much of this risk is
transmitted through genes, and how much results from learning. Heredity
does appear to play a role, as first-degree biological relatives of people with
antisocial personality disorder are more likely to have the disorder than those
in the general population (APA, 2013). However, no single gene has been implicated in the development of antisocial behavior patterns. Like most mental health
problems, antisocial personality disorder seems to result from a complex interaction
of genes and environment (Ferguson, 2010).

You may be wondering what is unique about the brain of a person with antisocial
personality disorder. Some studies point to irregularities in the **frontal lobes,** a region
of the brain that is crucial for executive functioning. For example, reduced tissue volume in the prefrontal cortex (11% less than expected) is apparent in some men with
antisocial personality disorder. This deficit might be linked to problems in decision
making, planning, reduced morality, and difficulties with learning in relation to fear,
all potentially associated with antisocial behavior. The fact that the prefrontal cortex
plays a role in controlling arousal may explain why people with this disorder tend
to seek out stimulation, including aggressive and antisocial activities (Raine, Lencz,
Bihrle, LaCasse, & Colletti, 2000).

Borderline Personality Disorder

Another personality disorder commonly portrayed in movies is **borderline personality disorder.** If you have seen *Black Swan,* you may remember the emotionally
unstable, intense, and extremely needy Beth Macintyre. If Beth were a real person,
she might fit the diagnostic criteria for borderline personality disorder, which is distinguished by an incomplete sense of self and feelings of emptiness. People with this
disorder may exhibit intense anger, have difficulty controlling their temper, and get
into physical fights. They can be impulsive when it comes to sexual activity, substance
abuse, and spending money, and may threaten or attempt suicide on a recurring basis.
Developing intimacy may also be a struggle, and relationships tend to be unstable,
tainted with feelings of mistrust and the fear of being abandoned. Those with borderline personality disorder may see the world in terms of black and white, rather
than different shades of gray. This tendency to perceive extremes may lead a person
to become overinvolved or totally withdrawn in relationships (APA, 2013).

According to *DSM–5,* individuals with borderline personality disorder experience
emotions that are unstable, intense, and inappropriate for the situation at hand. They
may feel extreme anxiety and insecurity, concern about being rejected one moment,
worried about being too dependent the next. Depressed moods are common, along
with feelings of hopelessness, pessimism, and shame. The person may act without
thinking and frequently change plans.

Seventy-five percent of people diagnosed with borderline personality disorder are female, and research suggests that some traits associated with this disorder have a genetic component (APA, 2013). There is also evidence that childhood trauma sets the stage for the development of this condition. A biosocial developmental model has been proposed, indicating an early vulnerability that includes impulsive behavior and increased "emotional sensitivity." If the environment is right, this susceptibility can lead to problems with emotions, behaviors, and cognitive processes (Crowell, Beauchaine, & Linehan, 2009).

As you now know, personality disorders stem from well-established personality characteristics. People suffering from these disorders have traits that are relatively easy to characterize. This is *not* the case for people with dissociative disorders, whose personal identities may be very difficult to pin down.

◯✓◯◯ show what you know

1. The personality disorders include impairments concerning
   a. contact with reality.
   b. manic episodes.
   c. developmental processes.
   d. the self and interpersonal relationships.

2. Individuals with _____ are likely to feel a sense of emptiness, become angry easily, and maintain intense but unstable relationships.

3. Two of the identifiers of abnormal behavior are distress and impairment. How would the personality disorders fit the criteria for abnormal behavior?

✓ CHECK YOUR ANSWERS IN APPENDIX C.

Dissociative Disorders

LO 11 Identify differences among dissociative disorders.

Dissociative disorders are disturbances in normal psychological functioning, which can include problems with memory, identity, consciousness, perception, and motor control. The main feature of these disorders is **dissociation,** or a disturbance in the normally unified experience of psychological functions involved in memory, consciousness, perception, or identity (Speigel et al., 2011). Dissociation may lead to difficulty recalling personal information (for example, where I live, who I am), or the feeling of being detached from one's body.

In North America and Europe, the prevalence of dissociative disorders imposes a high financial burden (Brand, Classen, McNary, & Zaveri, 2009), in part because of lengthy treatment times. Dissociative disorders generally do not resolve with a simple drug prescription or a couple of therapy sessions. Here, we focus our discussion on two of the more well-known dissociative disorders: *dissociative amnesia* and *dissociative identity disorder.*

Dissociative Amnesia

People suffering from **dissociative amnesia** have difficulty remembering important personal information. Often the lost memories center on traumatic or stressful events. In some cases the amnesia is localized, or fixed around a certain event; other times it may span a lifetime. A person suffering from dissociative amnesia typically reports a great deal of distress or impairment in relationships, work, and other important areas of life, and puts a lot of effort into managing the mundane details of daily existence (Staniloiu & Markowitsch, 2012).

A person with dissociative amnesia who wanders in a confused and unexpected manner may also be experiencing **dissociative fugue** (fyüg; Spiegel et al., 2011). Consider this example from a case study: A 62-year-old woman is found in a city many miles away from home. She has no understanding of her whereabouts or activities since leaving home. After a medical evaluation, physicians determine there is no neurological or physical explanation for her memory loss. Over time, she is able to recall

Synonyms

antisocial personality disorder psychopathy, sociopathy

antisocial personality disorder
A psychological disorder distinguished by unethical behavior, deceitfulness, impulsivity, irritability, aggressiveness, disregard for others, and lack of remorse.

borderline personality disorder
A psychological disorder distinguished by an incomplete sense of self, extreme self-criticism, unstable emotions, and feelings of emptiness.

dissociative disorders Psychological disorders distinguished by disturbances in normal psychological functioning; may include problems with memory, identity, consciousness, perception, and motor control.

dissociation A disturbance in the normally integrated experience of psychological functions involved in memory, consciousness, perception, or identity.

dissociative amnesia A psychological disorder marked by difficulty remembering important personal information and life events.

dissociative fugue (fyüg) A condition in which a person with dissociative amnesia wanders about in a confused and unexpected manner.

Trance Dance
A young man in Sao Paulo, Brazil, dances in a trance state during a religious ceremony. Behaviors observed in this type of context may resemble those of dissociative identity disorder, but it is important to differentiate between religious practices and disordered behaviors (Moreira-Almeida et al., 2008). Yasuyoshi Chiba/AFP/Getty Images

some events from the "preceding weeks," including an argument with her husband that left her in despair (Rajah, Kumar, Somasundaram, & Kumar, 2009). As often occurs with dissociative amnesia, this woman's memory loss seemed to be associated with distressing events.

Dissociative Identity Disorder

Perhaps the most commonly known dissociative disorder is **dissociative identity disorder** (often referred to as multiple personality disorder), which is characterized by the presence of two or more distinct personalities. Dissociative identity disorder is considered the most complicated and persistent of the dissociative disorders (Sar, 2011). One of its key features is a lack of connection among behavior, awareness, memory, cognition, and other functioning. There is often a reported gap in remembering day-to-day events and personal information. One may feel significant distress in relationships, work, and other areas. And this experience cannot be related to cultural or religious practice, substance use, or other medical issues.

Clinicians have to be mindful of cross-cultural differences and religious differences in relation to dissociative states. For example, some characteristics associated with dissociative identity disorder seem to occur in Brazilian mediums, and it is important to distinguish between culturally accepted religious practice and disordered behavior (Moreira-Almeida, Neto, & Cardeña, 2008). Gender differences can be attributed mostly to cultural and environmental factors, specifically childhood abuse and trauma, although there are inconsistent findings in relation to gender differences and prevalence (Sar, 2011).

What Causes Dissociative Disorders?

A great deal of controversy surrounds the apparent increase in diagnoses of dissociative identity disorder in the United States. One possible explanation is that clinicians are reinforcing the development of these disassociations. In other words, by suggesting the possibility of alternate personalities or using hypnosis to "recover" lost memories, the clinician "cues" the individual to believe an alternative personality is responsible for behaviors (Lynn, Lilienfeld, Merckelbach, Giesbrecht, & van der Kloet, 2012). These disorders are difficult to substantiate when they are based on self-reports. We should also note that they are often linked to childhood abuse and neglect, war, and terrorism not only in the United States, but also around the globe (APA, 2013). Thus, education about and the prevention of early-life stress, as it relates to childhood abuse and neglect, is of significant importance (Sar, 2011).

Psychological disorders are serious and potentially debilitating. The good news is that many people live successful and fulfilling lives in spite of their disorders. Just look at Ross and Melissa.

 show what you know

1. _____ is a disturbance in the normally integrated experiences of memory, consciousness, perception, or identity.

2. _____ involves two or more distinct personalities within an individual. This experience is characterized by a lack of connection with behavior, awareness, memory, cognition, and other functioning.
   a. Dissociative identity disorder   c. Major depressive disorder
   b. Borderline personality disorder   d. Schizophrenia

3. Describe the similarities and differences between dissociative amnesia and dissociative identity disorder.

✓ CHECK YOUR ANSWERS IN APPENDIX C.

Postscript: Where Are They Now?

DEFYING STIGMA: ROSS LEARNS TO THRIVE After graduating from high school, Ross started college at American University in Washington, D.C. But he didn't have much of a plan for managing his disorder. "What I did was essentially the equivalent of showing up to college in a wheelchair, and hoping they would have ramps," he recalls in his book *Behind Happy Faces* (Szabo & Hall, 2007, p. 100).

Three weeks into freshman year, Ross had his stomach pumped for alcohol poisoning and, within 2 months, a major relapse with bipolar disorder. He returned to Pennsylvania and was hospitalized. After this, Ross felt like a failure: "I used to sleep on my couch for 18 hours a day or sit out in my backyard and stare out at nothing," he remembers. "I felt like bipolar disorder had won out, and that there was nothing more I could do about it" (Szabo & Hall, 2007, p. 101).

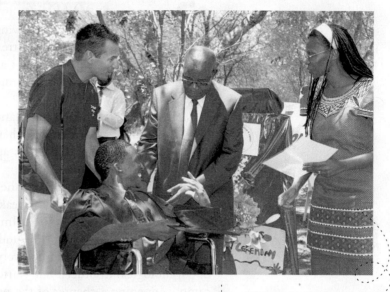

But then Ross did something. He found employment and began taking classes at a community college, which led to his enrollment at a local four-year college. Eventually, he returned to American University to finish what he had started 4 years before. Unfortunately, drinking alcohol was still a big part of his life. One night, after downing multiple shots of liquor, Ross passed out cold. He awoke 22 hours later, looked in the mirror, and started to weep. "Okay. ENOUGH. You are either going to continue this pattern and DIE, or you are going to make a change," Ross remembers thinking to himself. "I chose to change that night, but change isn't easy. It isn't quick—and it isn't fun" (Szabo & Hall, 2007, p. 102).

What followed were years of hard work. Ross quit using alcohol and caffeine and smoking cigarettes and marijuana. He imposed structure on his life, waking up and going to sleep at the same time each day, eating regular meals, and exercising. He started being open and honest in his relationships with friends, family, and his therapist. And most important, he confronted his self-hatred, working hard to identify and appreciate things he liked about himself. Says Ross, "I had to learn to care enough about myself to want to change."

Although Ross had been taking medication and seeing psychotherapists for years, treatment alone wasn't the answer. "What was missing was me being an active member in my treatment," he says, "and doing things outside of treatment [to get better]."

In 2002 Ross graduated cum laude from American University, and then he picked up where he left off that day he spoke to his high school class about his experience with bipolar disorder. He became a mental health advocate, giving presentations at high schools and colleges across America. As Director of Youth Outreach for the National Mental Health Awareness Campaign, Ross started The Heard (now part of Active Minds), a speakers' bureau that includes other young presenters who have battled disorders. In his 8 years as a mental health advocate, Ross has addressed about 1 million people.

Making a Difference
Ross celebrates graduation day at the center for people with disabilities where he worked in Botswana, Africa. After completing his work with the Peace Corps, Ross returned to the United States and founded a consulting group, which designs mental health curricula for middle and high schools. Heidi Pendergast

You Asked, Ross Answers
http://qrs.ly/qf3nrd9
Are you afraid that you may pass your disorder on to your children and does that impact your desire to have them?

dissociative identity disorder
A psychological disorder that involves the occurrence of two or more distinct personalities within an individual.

Today, Ross enjoys life in Los Angeles, California. He recently returned from Botswana, Africa, where he served as a member of the Peace Corps, and launched his own consulting group, which designs mental health curricula for middle and high schools. His battle with bipolar disorder is ongoing ("I'm not cured," says Ross), but he continues learning better ways to cope. It has now been over a decade since Ross experienced a disabling episode of mania or depression.

OUTSMARTING OCD: MELISSA FINDS A THERAPY THAT WORKS

Shortly after leaving the hospital, Melissa found out about a study on OCD treatments at the University of Pennsylvania. She decided to participate and got acquainted with the lead investigator, who became her therapist. "He taught me how to live with OCD," says Melissa. "He basically saved my life."

Melissa had been taking medications since she was 12, but she only experienced a dramatic improvement when she combined her medication with cognitive behavioral therapy (CBT), an approach you will learn about in Chapter 14 on psychological therapies.

Like Ross, Melissa discovered she had a gift for public speaking. At age 19, she decided to share her story, speaking about her battle with OCD as part of a panel hosted by her college, Immaculata University in Pennsylvania. Her presentation moved some of the audience members to tears. From that point forward, Melissa decided to do everything in her power to dispel the stigma of psychological disorders. She started a mental health awareness group on her campus, opening a chapter of the national mental health awareness organization Active Minds, and later joined Ross Szabo's speakers' bureau and became a presenter for the mental health organization Minding Your Mind. Melissa recently published a book, *The People You Meet in Real Life*, which relates the stories of those who have inspired her along the way. She hopes these tales of resiliency and optimism will help readers understand they are not alone in their struggles.

Melissa is now 25. She still has OCD, but it's under control. Instead of walking through a doorway 20 times, she now passes through it twice. And the time she once spent sitting alone in her room meticulously touching objects in sets of 2s she now spends talking to classrooms full of students, shattering the stigma surrounding psychological disorders.

Voice of Inspiration
As a presenter for the mental health organization Minding Your Mind, Melissa travels across the country, educating students about mental health issues. She recently published a book, *The People You Meet in Real Life,* which provides first-person accounts of resilient individuals facing a variety of trials and tribulations. The book addresses issues relating to mental health, bullying, suicide, cancer, and HIV, sending a message of hope and inspiration. Photo by Ken Alexander

13 summary of concepts

LO 1 Define psychological disorders and the criteria used to identify abnormal behavior. (p. 542)

A psychological disorder is a set of behavioral, emotional, or cognitive symptoms that are significantly distressing in terms of social functioning, work endeavors, and other aspects of life. Abnormal behavior often falls along a continuum and is based on typicality and the 3 Ds: dysfunction, distress, and deviance. This continuum includes what we would consider normal at one end and abnormal at the other end, and is determined in part by one's culture.

LO 2 Recognize limitations in the classification of psychological disorders. (p. 547)

Although a classification system is important for communication and treatment planning among professionals, one of its limitations is how it leads to labeling and the creation of expectations. Because of the stigma associated with psychological disorders, once given a diagnosis, the effects can be potentially long lasting. Some critics suggest there is too much emphasis on the medical model, which may ignore the importance of psychological and sociocultural factors.

LO 3 Summarize the etiology of psychological disorders. (p. 550)

Psychological disorders can be explained in terms of underlying biological causes, psychological influences, and sociocultural factors. Biological causes include genetic predispositions for disorders as well as neurochemical imbalances. Psychological influences include cognitive factors and developmental experiences. Sociocultural factors, such as poverty and support systems, may also impact the development and course of psychological disorders. The biopsychosocial perspective provides a model for explaining the causes of psychological disorders, which are complicated and often the result of interactions among biological, psychological, and sociocultural factors.

LO 4 Define and illustrate an understanding of anxiety disorders and their causes. (p. 553)

Anxiety disorders are a group of psychological disorders associated with extreme anxiety and/or irrational fears that are debilitating. Panic disorder includes worries about experiencing unexpected panic attacks or losing control. Specific phobias include a distinct fear or anxiety in relation to an object or situation. Agoraphobia is a distinct fear or anxiety related to situations such as public transportation, open spaces, retail stores, crowds, or being alone and

away from home. Social anxiety disorder is a type of phobia in which a person has a distinct fear or anxiety regarding social situations, particularly the idea of being scrutinized by others. Someone with generalized anxiety disorder experiences an excessive amount of worry and anxiety about many activities relating to family, health, school, and other aspects of daily life. Anxiety disorders can develop as a result of environmental factors and genetic predisposition, and are more prevalent in women. They can be culture specific and/or learned.

LO 5 Summarize the symptoms and causes of obsessive-compulsive disorder. (p. 558)

Obsessive-compulsive disorder (OCD) includes obsessions and/or compulsions that are very time-consuming (taking more than 1 hour a day) and cause a great deal of distress and disruptions in everyday life. An obsession is a thought, urge, or image that occurs repeatedly, is intrusive and unwelcome, and often causes feelings of intense anxiety and distress. Compulsions are behaviors or "mental acts" that a person repeats over and over in an attempt to neutralize obsessions. Sociocultural factors, learning theory, and biological causes are all involved in the course and maintenance of OCD.

LO 6 Summarize the symptoms and causes of major depressive disorder. (p. 560)

Symptoms of major depressive disorder include feelings of sadness or hopelessness, reduced pleasure, sleeping excessively or not at all, loss of energy, feelings of worthlessness, or difficulties thinking or concentrating. The hallmarks of major depressive disorder are the substantial severity of symptoms and impairment in the ability to perform expected roles. Biological theories suggest the disorder results from a genetic predisposition, neurotransmitters, and hormones. Psychological theories suggest that feelings of learned helplessness and negative thinking may play a role. It is not just one factor involved in major depressive disorder, but rather an interplay of several.

LO 7 Compare and contrast bipolar disorders and major depressive disorder. (p. 556)

A diagnosis of bipolar I disorder requires that a person experience at least one manic episode, substantial distress, and great impairment. Bipolar II disorder requires at least one major depressive episode as well as a hypomanic episode, which is associated with some of the same symptoms as a manic episode, but is not as severe and does not impair one's ability to function. People with bipolar disorder cycle between extreme highs and lows of emotion and energy that last for days, weeks, or even months. Individuals with major depressive disorder, on the other hand, tend to experience a persistent low mood, loss of energy, and feelings of worthlessness.

LO 8 Recognize the symptoms of schizophrenia. (p. 568)

Schizophrenia is a disabling disorder that can involve delusions, hallucinations, disorganized speech, abnormal psychomotor behavior, diminished speech, limited emotions, or loss of energy. Delusions are strange and false beliefs that a person maintains even when presented with contradictory evidence. Hallucinations are "perception-like experiences" that the individual believes are real, but that are not evident to others.

LO 9 Analyze the biopsychosocial factors that contribute to schizophrenia. (p. 569)

Schizophrenia is a complex psychological disorder that results from biological, psychological, and social factors. Because this disorder springs from a complex interaction of genes and environment, researchers have a hard time predicting who will be affected. The diathesis–stress model takes these factors into account, with diathesis referring to the inherited disposition, and stress referring to the stressors in the environment (internal and external). Genes, neurotransmitters, differences in the brain, and exposure to a virus in utero are all possible biopsychosocial influences in the development of schizophrenia.

LO 10 Differentiate between antisocial and borderline personality disorders. (p. 573)

People with antisocial personality disorder may seek personal gratification even when it means violating ethics and breaking laws. They sometimes deceive others, and exhibit aggressive, impulsive, or irritable behavior. These individuals lack empathy, and may not show concern for others or feel remorse upon hurting someone. Borderline personality disorder is distinguished by an incomplete sense of self and feelings of emptiness. Those affected may exhibit intense anger, have difficulty controlling their temper, and get into physical fights. They can be impulsive, especially where sexual activity, substance abuse, and spending money are concerned. Suicide threats and attempts may occur repeatedly. Both disorders may result in issues connected to intimacy and trust.

LO 11 Identify differences among dissociative disorders. (p. 575)

People suffering from dissociative amnesia seem to lack the ability to remember important personal information about their lives. If a person with dissociative amnesia also wanders in a confused and unexpected manner, this is considered dissociative amnesia with dissociative fugue. Dissociative identity disorder occurs when an individual experiences two or more distinct personalities. This disorder is considered the most complicated and persistent of the dissociative disorders. The commonality in this group of disorders is dissociation, or disturbance in the normally unified experience of psychological functions involved in memory, consciousness, perception, or identity.

key terms

abnormal behavior, p. 543

agoraphobia, p. 556

antisocial personality disorder, p. 574

anxiety disorders, p. 553

bipolar disorder, p. 542

borderline personality disorder, p. 574

comorbidity, p. 550

compulsion, p. 558

delusions, p. 568

dissociation, p. 575

dissociative amnesia, p. 575

dissociative disorders, p. 575

dissociative fugue, p. 575

dissociative identity disorder, p. 576

dopamine hypothesis, p. 572

generalized anxiety disorder, p. 557

hallucination, p. 568

insanity, p. 545

learned helplessness, p. 564

major depressive disorder, p. 560

maladaptive behaviors, p. 543

manic episodes, p. 566

medical model, p. 551

negative symptoms, p. 569

obsession, p. 558

obsessive-compulsive disorder (OCD), p. 558

panic attacks, p. 554

panic disorder, p. 554

personality disorders, p. 573

positive symptoms, p. 569

psychological disorder, p. 542

psychosis, p. 568

schizophrenia, p. 568

specific phobia, p. 555

stigma, p. 546

TEST PREP are you ready?

1. The 3 Ds used to distinguish abnormal behavior are:
   a. _____   c. _____
   b. _____

2. Although classifying mental disorders through the *DSM* is helpful to mental health professionals, its use has been criticized because the manual
   a. cannot be used to develop treatment plans.
   b. is used to obtain insurance reimbursement.
   c. labels individuals, which only heightens problems with stigma.
   d. does not attempt to be atheoretical.

3. Melissa experienced recurrent, all-consuming thoughts of disaster and death. These _____ were accompanied by her _____, which included reapplying deodorant and taking her clothes on and off up to 20 times a day.
   a. obsessions; compulsions
   b. compulsions; obsessions
   c. compulsions; contamination
   d. negative reinforcers; obsessions

4. To help explain the causes of psychological disorders, researchers often use the _____ perspective, which examines the complex interaction of biological, psychological, and sociocultural factors.
   a. medical model   c. etiological
   b. biopsychosocial   d. learning

5. A woman is extremely anxious when she is out in public alone. She no longer uses public transportation, refuses to go to the mall, and does not like being away from home. Perhaps she should get evaluated to see if she has which of the following diagnoses?
   a. panic disorder   c. social anxiety disorder
   b. agoraphobia   d. specific phobia

6. A man with a diagnosis of _____ exhibits a distinct fear or anxiety related to social situations, particularly the idea of being scrutinized by those around him. This fear often stems from his preoccupation with offending someone.
   a. generalized anxiety disorder   c. social anxiety disorder
   b. panic attack   d. panic disorder

7. While walking to class one day, you notice a woman who is short of breath, clutching her chest, and appears lightheaded. You are concerned she may be experiencing a heart attack. She tells you she knows it is not her heart, but that she suffers from _____, which involve sudden, extreme fear that escalates quickly.
   a. psychotic episodes   c. panic attacks
   b. manic episodes   d. hallucinations

8. A neighbor describes a newspaper article she read last night about a man in his twenties who has been known to lie and con others, be aggressive and impulsive, and show little empathy or remorse. These are long-standing traits of his, so it is possible that he has
   a. borderline personality disorder.
   b. antisocial personality disorder.
   c. dissociative identity disorder.
   d. dissociative amnesia.

9. Which of the following plays a role in the etiology of major depressive disorder?
   a. manic episodes   c. classical conditioning
   b. virus contracted by the mother   d. serotonin

10. One of the major distinctions of bipolar II disorder is that, unlike bipolar I disorder, it involves:
    a. at least one major depressive episode as well as a hypomanic episode.
    b. at least one major depressive episode as well as a manic episode.
    c. at least one hypomanic episode and one manic episode.
    d. at least one episode of psychosis.

11. One symptom that both major depressive disorder and bipolar disorder share is
    a. hypomania.
    b. manic episodes.
    c. problems associated with sleep.
    d. extremely high self-esteem.

12. Which of the following is a symptom of a manic episode?
    a. low energy level   c. quiet or shy personality
    b. need for more sleep   d. irritability

13. A man with schizophrenia has hallucinations and delusions, and seems to be out of touch with reality. A psychologist explains to his mother that her son is experiencing:
    a. mania.   c. dissociative identity disorder.
    b. psychosis.   d. hypomania.

14. A woman in your neighborhood develops a reputation for being emotionally unstable, intense, and extremely needy. She also doesn't seem to have a sense of herself and complains of feeling empty. She struggles with intimacy and her relationships are unstable. If these are long-standing traits, which of the following might she be evaluated for?
    a. borderline personality disorder
    b. antisocial personality disorder
    c. bipolar II disorder
    d. major depressive disorder

15. Dissociative identity disorder (commonly called multiple personality disorder) involves two or more distinct _____ within an individual.
    a. hypomanic episodes   c. panic disorders
    b. personalities   d. psychotic episodes

16. Describe the 3 Ds and give an example of each in relation to a psychological disorder.

17. What is wrong with the following statement: "My friend is schizophrenic"?

18. How can classical conditioning be used to explain the development of panic disorder?

19. How does negative thinking lead to depression?

20. Briefly summarize the theories of the etiology of schizophrenia.

✓ CHECK YOUR ANSWERS IN APPENDIX C.

Get personalized practice by logging into LaunchPad at **http://www.worthpublishers.com/launchpad/Licht** to take the LearningCurve adaptive quizzes for Chapter 13.

14

An Introduction to Treatment

📁 *Voices*

SA from the pages of
SCIENTIFIC AMERICAN
A Brighter Tune

Insight Therapies

📁 *Awareness Equals Power*

📁 *The Client Knows*

Behavior Therapies

👁️❗ DIDN'T SEE THAT COMING
Virtual Reality Exposure Therapy

Cognitive Therapies

📁 *Follow-Up*

Group Therapies

Biomedical Therapies

Psychotherapy Today

📁 *When to Listen, When to Talk*

🌐➡ ACROSS THE WORLD
Know Thy Client

💬 SOCIAL MEDIA AND PSYCHOLOGY
Therapist or Friend?

📁 *Passionate Providers*

treatment of psychological disorders

An Introduction to Treatment

VOICES It's a beautiful evening on the Rosebud Indian Reservation in south-central South Dakota. The sun, low in the sky, casts a warm glow over pine-covered hills. Oceans of prairie grass roll in the wind. The scene could not be more tranquil. But for Chepa,* a young Lakota woman living in this Northern Plains sanctuary, life has been anything but tranquil. For days, Chepa has been tormented by the voice of a deceased uncle. Hearing voices is nothing unusual in the Lakota spiritual tradition; ancestors visit the living often. But in the case of this young woman, the voice is telling her to kill herself. Chepa has tried to make peace with her uncle's spirit using prayer, pipe ceremony, and other forms of traditional medicine, but he will not be appeased. Increasingly paranoid and withdrawn, Chepa is making her relatives uneasy, so they take her to the home of a trusted neighbor, Dr. Dan Foster. A sun dancer and pipe carrier, Dr. Foster is a respected member of the community. He also happens to be the reservation's lead clinical psychologist.

---

*The story about Chepa, a Lakota woman with schizophrenia, is hypothetical, but it is based on actual scenarios that Dr. Foster encounters every week.

→

14

LEARNING OBJECTIVES

after reading and studying this chapter, you should be able to:

LO 1   Outline the history of the treatment of psychological disorders.

LO 2   Discuss how the main approaches to therapy differ and identify their common goal.

LO 3   Describe how psychoanalysis differs from psychodynamic therapy.

LO 4   Explain the concepts that form the basis of humanistic therapy.

LO 5   Summarize person-centered therapy.

LO 6   Describe the concepts that underlie behavior therapy.

LO 7   Outline the concepts of cognitive therapy.

LO 8   Identify the benefits and challenges of group therapy.

LO 9   Compare and contrast biomedical interventions and identify their common goal.

LO 10   Describe how culture interacts with the therapy process.

LO 11   Summarize the effectiveness of psychotherapy.

LO 12   Evaluate the strengths and weaknesses of online psychotherapy.

Breathtaking
South Dakota is home to many American Indian tribes, including the Sicangu Lakota Oyate, or Rosebud Sioux. The Rosebud Indian Reservation is a vast and beautiful land, but its residents struggle with severe poverty—and all the problems that come with it. Poverty-related stressors can interfere with work, strain personal relationships, and trigger the symptoms of mental disorders.
© Marilyn Angel Wynn/Marilyn Angel Wynn/
Nativestock Pictures/Corbis

CONNECTIONS

In **Chapter 3,** we described *sensation* as the detection of stimuli by sensory organs. Stimuli are transduced into neural signals and sent to various parts of the brain. With hallucinations, the first step is not occurring (no apparent physical stimuli), but the sensory experience exists nevertheless. The brain interprets internal information as coming from outside the body.

Dr. Foster, in His Own Words

http://qrs.ly/xb3nre5

Upon meeting with Chepa and her family, Dr. Foster realizes that she is having *hallucinations,* **sensory experiences** she thinks are real, but are not evident to anyone else. Chepa is also having false and irrational beliefs known as *delusions.* And because she is vulnerable to acting on those hallucinations and delusions, she poses a risk to herself, and possibly others. Chepa needs to go to the hospital, and it is Dr. Foster's responsibility to make sure she gets there, even if it requires going to a judge and getting a court order. "I'm going to make an intervention," Dr. Foster offers, "and I'm going to have to do it in a way that's respectful to that person and to the culture, but still respectful to the body of literature and training that I come from as a psychologist."

Chepa's grandmother protests: "I don't want her going to the hospital. I want to use Indian medicine." Trying to remain as clear and neutral as possible, Dr. Foster explains that traditional medicine has not worked in this case; if the voice were that of a spirit, it would have responded to prayer, pipe ceremony, and other traditional approaches. "I believe you're hearing voices," he says to Chepa. "But that voice is not coming from your uncle. . . . I think it's coming from your own mind." He goes on to explain that the brain has a region that specializes in hearing, and areas that store memories of

Note: Quotations attributed to Dr. Dan Foster and Laura Lichti are personal communications.

people and their voices. It is possible, he explains, that the brain is calling forth a voice from the past, making it seem like it is here at this moment.

Chepa may not agree with Dr. Foster, but she trusts him. He is, after all, a relative. In Lakota culture, *relatives* are not necessarily linked by blood. One can be adopted into a family or community through a formal ceremony known as *hunka*. At Rosebud, all of the therapists and medical providers are linked to the community through *hunka*—a great honor and also a great responsibility.

An ambulance arrives and transports Chepa to the emergency room, where she finds Dr. Foster waiting. He is there to make a diagnosis and develop a treatment plan, but also to provide her with a sense of security, and to do so in the context of a nurturing relationship. "First of all my concern is safety, and secondly my concern is that you realize I am concerned about you," Dr. Foster says. "We're going to form a relationship, you and I," he says. "Whatever it is that we're facing, we are going to make it so that it comes out better than it is right now."

The blood and urine screens come back negative, indicating that the hallucinations and delusions are not resulting from a drug, such as PCP or methamphetamine, and doctors find no evidence of a medical condition that could be driving the symptoms. Dr. Foster's observations and assessments point to a complex psychological disorder known as *schizophrenia.*

Because Chepa poses an imminent risk to herself, Dr. Foster and his colleagues arrange a transfer to a psychiatric hospital, where she may stay for several days. The medical staff will stabilize her with a drug to help reduce her symptoms, the first of many doses likely to be administered in years to come. When she returns to the reservation, Dr. Foster and his colleagues will offer her treatment, which will be designed with her specific needs in mind.

Who Gets Treatment?

Therapists working on the Rosebud Reservation tend to see clients in crises, often related to the conditions of extreme poverty that exist on Northern Plains Indian reservations. The average unemployment rate is nearly 80% (United States Senate, 2010, January 28), and affordable housing is scarce. It is not unusual to have 14 or 15 relatives packed into living quarters the size of a two-bedroom apartment. "Here we are in

CONNECTIONS

In **Chapter 13,** we reported that *schizophrenia* is a persistent and debilitating disorder that affects approximately 0.3% to 1% of the population. In this chapter, we will present some approaches to treating people with this diagnosis.

CONNECTIONS

In **Chapter 13,** we noted that stressors can impact the course of some psychological disorders. Periods of mania, depression, and psychosis can be brought on by life changes and stressors. The *diathesis–stress model* suggests that a genetic predisposition and environmental triggers play a role in the development of schizophrenia.

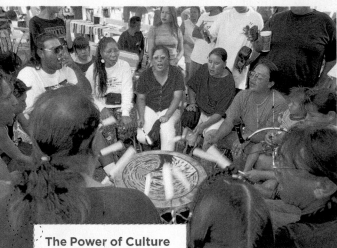

The Power of Culture
Residents of the Rosebud Reservation gather for a powwow. Participating in cultural ceremonies and prayer may help people deal with stressors that could otherwise impact psychological problems.
LAIF/Redux

CONNECTIONS

We discussed the *etiology* of psychological disorders in **Chapter 13.** The *medical model* implies that disorders have biological causes. The *biopsychosocial approach* suggests disorders result from an interaction of biological, psychological, and sociocultural factors.

deinstitutionalization The mass movement of patients with psychological disorders out of mental institutions, and the attempt to reintegrate them into the community.

this beautiful, pastoral Northern Plains setting with the kind of crowding [you might] experience in New York City," Dr. Foster says. "We're a rural ghetto." Squeezed into their homes without employment, entertainment, or access to transportation, people tend to feel stressed, and **stress** can play a role in psychological disorders. Some seek relief in alcohol, drugs, risky sex, gambling, or as Dr. Foster puts it, "outlets that [temporarily] feel good in the midst of a painful life." Young people may turn to gangs, which can provide a sense of self-worth and belonging. Dr. Foster believes and hopes that Indian language, spiritual ceremony, and culture can act somewhat like a shield, protecting people from self-destructive behaviors. But centuries of assaults by Western society have eroded American Indian cultures.

As you may already know, the arrival of European colonists in 1492 marked the beginning of a long, drawn out attack on the physical, social, and psychological well-being of the continent's native people. American Indians were pushed out of their native lands, relocated to reservations, economically disenfranchised, and murdered and raped by generations of American soldiers. Their children were sent away to government boarding schools, where they lost touch with their native language, religion, and culture (Struthers & Lowe, 2003). Tribal cultures are still alive, but struggling to stay afloat.

As we learn more about Dr. Foster's work on Rosebud Reservation, be mindful that therapists work with a broad spectrum of psychological issues. Dr. Foster tends to work with people in severe distress. Some of his clients do not seek therapy, but end up in his care only because friends and relatives intervene. Other therapists spend much of their time serving those who seek help with issues such as shyness, low self-esteem, and unresolved childhood conflicts. Therapy is not just for those with psychological disorders and life catastrophes, but for anyone wishing to live a more fulfilling existence.

Psychologists use various **models** to explain abnormal behavior and psychological disorders. As our understanding of what causes psychological disorders has changed over time, so have treatments. While reading the brief history that follows, try to identify connections between the perceived causes of disorders and treatments designed to resolve them.

A Primitive Past: The History of Treatment

LO 1   Outline the history of the treatment of psychological disorders.

Psychological disorders and their treatments are as old as recorded history, although some of the early attempts to "cure" and "treat" them were inhumane and unproven. One theory suggests that during the Stone Age, people believed psychological disorders were caused by possession with demons and evil spirits, suggesting that our cave dweller ancestors used *trephination,* or drilling holes in the skull, to create exit routes for evil spirits (Maher & Maher, 2003).

ASYLUMS OR PRISONS?   A major shift came in the 16th century. Religious groups began creating *asylums,* or special places to house and treat people with psychological disorders. However, these asylums were overcrowded and resembled prisons, with inmates chained in dungeonlike cells, starved, and subjected to sweltering heat and frigid cold. During the French Revolution (the late 1700s), Philippe Pinel, a French physician, began his work in Paris asylums. Horrified by the conditions he observed, Pinel removed the inmates' chains and insisted they be treated more humanely (Hergenhahn, 2005; Maher & Maher, 2003). The idea of using "moral treatment," or respect and kindness instead of harsh methods, spread throughout Europe and America (Routh & Reisman, 2003).

During the mid- to late 1800s, an American schoolteacher named Dorothea Dix vigorously championed the "mental hygiene movement," a campaign to reform asylums in the United States. Appalled by what she witnessed in American prisons and "mental" institutions, including the caging of naked inmates, Dix helped establish and upgrade over 30 state mental hospitals (Parry, 2006). Despite the good intentions of reformers like Pinel and Dix, however, many institutions eventually deteriorated into warehouses for people with psychological disorders: overcrowded, understaffed, and underfunded. In the early 1900s, psychiatrists began to realize that mental health problems existed outside asylums, among ordinary people who were capable of functioning in society. Rather than drawing a line between the sane and insane, psychiatrists began to view mental health as a continuum. They started developing a system to classify psychological disorders based on symptoms and progression, and this effort ultimately led to the creation of the first *Diagnostic and Statistical Manual of Mental Disorders* in 1952 (*DSM;* American Psychiatric Association [APA], 1952; Pierre, 2012).

The Reformer
American schoolteacher Dorothea Dix led the nation's "mental hygiene movement," an effort to improve the treatment of people living in mental institutions. Her advocacy work began in the mid-1800s, at a time when people in some mental hospitals were chained, beaten, and locked in cages (Parry, 2006). National Portrait Gallery, Smithsonian Institution

RETURN TO THE COMMUNITY   The 1950s and 1960s saw a mass exodus of patients out of institutions in the United States and back into the community (**FIGURE 14.1**). This **deinstitutionalization** was partially the result of a movement to reduce the social isolation of people with psychological disorders and integrate them in society. Deinstitutionalization was also made possible by the introduction of medications that reduced some symptoms of severe psychological disorders. Thanks to these new drugs, many people who had previously needed constant care and supervision were able to function in society. They began caring for themselves and managing their own medications—an arrangement that worked for some but not all, as many former patients ended up living on the streets or behind bars (Harrington, 2012). By 2007 approximately 2.7 million inmates in American jails and prisons were suffering from mental health problems, representing more than one half of the inmate population (Hawthorne et al., 2012).

In spite of the deinstitutionalization movement, psychiatric hospitals and institutions continue to play an important role in the treatment of psychological disorders. The scenario involving Dr. Foster and his client Chepa may be unusual in some respects, but not when it comes to the initiation of treatment. For someone

CONNECTIONS

In **Chapter 13,** we noted that most mental health professionals in the United States use the *DSM-5.* The *DSM-5* is a classification system designed to help clinicians ensure accurate and consistent diagnoses based on the observation of symptoms. This manual does not include information on treatment.

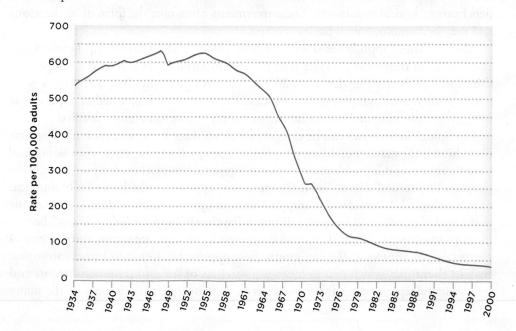

FIGURE 14.1
Deinstitutionalization
Since the 1950s, the rate of institutionalization has declined dramatically. Copyright © 2011 by the University of Chicago Press from Harcourt (2011).

CONNECTIONS

In **Chapter 13,** we described *psychotic symptoms,* such as hallucinations and delusions. Psychotic episodes can be risky for the person experiencing them—as well as those around him. In these cases, a person may be admitted to a hospital against his will. Hospitals have procedures in place to ensure that involuntary admissions are ethical.

experiencing a dangerous **psychotic episode,** the standard approach includes a stay in a psychiatric hospital or ward. Some of these admissions are voluntary; others are not.

Typically, a person is ready to leave the hospital after a few days or weeks, but many people in crisis are released after just a few hours, due to the high cost of treatment and financial pressures facing hospitals. The length of a hospital stay is often determined by what insurance will cover, rather than what a patient needs, as well as the severe shortage of available beds in psychiatric hospitals and units. Many psychiatric facilities simply cannot accommodate the scores of people seeking treatment (Honberg, Diehl, Kimball, Gruttadaro, & Fitzpatrick, 2011; Interlandi, 2012, June 22).

After being discharged from the hospital, Chepa returns home, but not everyone has family and friends who can take them in. Those needing ongoing support for their psychological disorders may live in a supervised housing facility, some providing 24-hour services, others offering support only when the need arises (National Alliance on Mental Illness, 2012). Sadly, many of these mental health facilities are terribly underfunded and understaffed. We have come a long way in the treatment of psychological disorders, but there is still considerable progress to be made.

With that brief historical lesson under our belts, let's shift our focus to contemporary treatment. These days, people receive treatment for a variety of reasons, not just mental disorders. Psychotherapy helps clients resolve work problems, cope with chronic illness, and adjust to major life changes like immigration and divorce. Some people enter psychotherapy to work on a specific issue or to improve their relationships. Let's explore the major types of therapy used today.

Treatment Today: An Overview of Major Approaches

LO 2   Discuss how the main approaches to therapy differ and identify their common goal.

The word *psychotherapy* derives from the Ancient Greek *psychē,* meaning "soul," and *therapeuō,* meaning "to heal" (Brownell, 2010), and there are many ways to go about this healing of the soul. Some therapies promote increased awareness of situations and the self; you need to understand the origins of your problems in order to deal with them. Others focus on active steps toward behavioral change. The key to resolving issues is not so much understanding their origins, but changing the thoughts and behaviors that precede them. Finally, there are interventions aimed at correcting disorders from a physical standpoint: These treatments often take the form of medication, and may be combined with psychotherapy.

Many of these approaches share common features: The relationship between the client and the treatment provider is of utmost importance, as is a sense of hope that things will get better (Snyder et al., 2000). And they generally share a common goal, which is to reduce symptoms and increase the quality of life, whether a person is struggling with a psychological disorder or simply wants to be more fulfilled.

Psychological therapies can be categorized along three major dimensions. The first dimension is the manner of delivery—whether therapy is administered to an *individual* (one therapist working with one person) or a *group* (therapists working with multiple people). The second dimension is the treatment approach, which can be biomedical or psychological. **Biomedical therapy** refers to drugs and other medical interventions that target the biological basis of a disorder. **Psychotherapy,** or "talk therapy," homes in on psychological factors. The third dimension of therapy represents the theoretical perspective or approach. We can group these approaches into two broad categories: **insight therapies,** which aim to increase awareness of self and the environment, and **behavior therapies,** which focus on behavioral change. As you learn about the many

biomedical therapy Drugs and other physical interventions that target the biological processes underlying psychological disorders; primary goal is to reduce symptoms.

psychotherapy "Talk therapy"; a treatment approach in which a client works with a mental health professional to reduce psychological symptoms and improve quality of life.

insight therapies A type of psychotherapy, aimed at increasing awareness of self and the environment.

behavior therapy A type of therapy that focuses on behavioral change.

According to some estimates, there exist at least 500 specific types of psychotherapy (Arkowitz & Lilienfeld, 2012). Many approaches to therapy share common features, and it can be helpful to use these broad dimensions as a means of organizing our discussion. However, keep in mind that divisions between therapeutic approaches are much less rigid than it may appear in this diagram. As many as half of therapists today combine approaches, either in terms of specific techniques associated with theoretical perspectives, or in terms of the perspectives themselves (Norcross & Beutler, 2014). But for every approach the goal remains the same: to reduce symptoms and increase the quality of life.

Major Approaches to Therapy

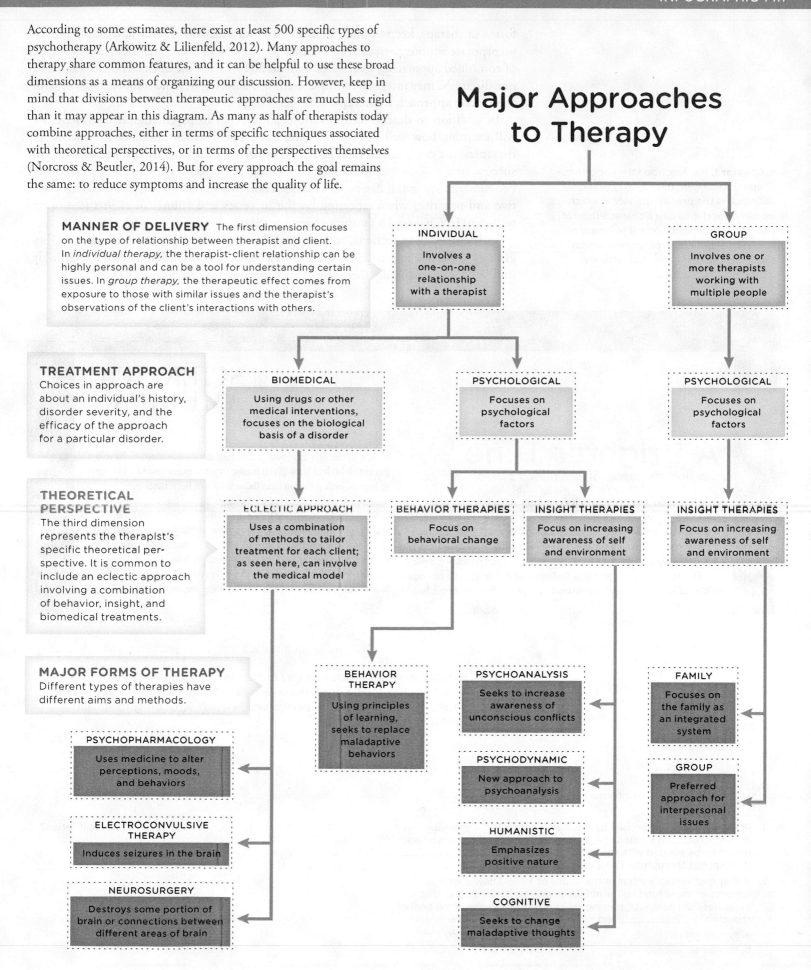

MANNER OF DELIVERY The first dimension focuses on the type of relationship between therapist and client. In *individual therapy,* the therapist-client relationship can be highly personal and can be a tool for understanding certain issues. In *group therapy,* the therapeutic effect comes from exposure to those with similar issues and the therapist's observations of the client's interactions with others.

INDIVIDUAL
Involves a one-on-one relationship with a therapist

GROUP
Involves one or more therapists working with multiple people

TREATMENT APPROACH
Choices in approach are about an individual's history, disorder severity, and the efficacy of the approach for a particular disorder.

BIOMEDICAL
Using drugs or other medical interventions, focuses on the biological basis of a disorder

PSYCHOLOGICAL
Focuses on psychological factors

PSYCHOLOGICAL
Focuses on psychological factors

THEORETICAL PERSPECTIVE
The third dimension represents the therapist's specific theoretical perspective. It is common to include an eclectic approach involving a combination of behavior, insight, and biomedical treatments.

ECLECTIC APPROACH
Uses a combination of methods to tailor treatment for each client; as seen here, can involve the medical model

BEHAVIOR THERAPIES
Focus on behavioral change

INSIGHT THERAPIES
Focus on increasing awareness of self and environment

INSIGHT THERAPIES
Focus on increasing awareness of self and environment

MAJOR FORMS OF THERAPY
Different types of therapies have different aims and methods.

BEHAVIOR THERAPY
Using principles of learning, seeks to replace maladaptive behaviors

PSYCHOANALYSIS
Seeks to increase awareness of unconscious conflicts

FAMILY
Focuses on the family as an integrated system

PSYCHOPHARMACOLOGY
Uses medicine to alter perceptions, moods, and behaviors

PSYCHODYNAMIC
New approach to psychoanalysis

GROUP
Preferred approach for interpersonal issues

ELECTROCONVULSIVE THERAPY
Induces seizures in the brain

HUMANISTIC
Emphasizes positive nature

NEUROSURGERY
Destroys some portion of brain or connections between different areas of brain

COGNITIVE
Seeks to change maladaptive thoughts

forms of therapy, keep in mind that they are not mutually exclusive; therapists often incorporate various perspectives. Around 25 to 50% of therapists today use this type of combined approach (Norcross & Beutler, 2014). Even therapists who are trained in one discipline may integrate multiple methods, tailoring treatment for each client with an **eclectic approach to therapy.**

In addition to describing the various approaches to psychological treatment, we will examine how well they work. *Outcome research,* which evaluates the success of therapies, is a complicated task. First, it is not always easy to pinpoint the meaning of success, or **operationalize** it. Should we measure self-esteem, happiness, or some other benchmark? Second, it can be difficult for clinicians to remain free of bias (both positive and negative) when reporting on the successes and failures of clients (see pages 629–630 in Chapter 15 on the self-serving bias).

In the upcoming sections, we will describe the major types of psychotherapy, beginning with the insight therapies. But first let's take a brief detour into a seemingly unrelated, yet potentially therapeutic, activity: listening to music.

CONNECTIONS

In **Chapter 1,** we described the importance of operational definitions. An *operational definition* is the precise manner in which we define and measure a characteristic of interest. Here, it is important to create an operational definition of success, which allows for the comparison of different treatment approaches.

---

from the pages of **SCIENTIFIC AMERICAN**

A Brighter Tune
Classical music may lift depressed patients' spirits.

Add "therapist" to Beethoven's list of talents. After listening to the master's third and fifth sonatas, depressed patients in a recent study felt happier. The research, presented at the annual meeting of the Society for Neuroscience, found that classical music benefited both genders and that the music gave the biggest boost to educated and younger people.

This study supports previous findings that music therapy can be an effective and economical way to treat patients. A recently published review of the literature found that four out of five studies showed patients who had been given music therapy experienced a greater reduction in depression than those who had been randomly assigned to a different type of therapy. "Music has a specific potential that can be used therapeutically to promote well-being and alleviate symptoms like depression, anxiety, stress, anger and agitation," reports the Beethoven study's co-author, Pasadena City College neuroscientist Parvaneh Mohammadian. **Corey Binns.**

---

try this   Use the *Scientific American* article as a way to start thinking about research on psychological therapies. Make a list of the questions that came to mind while reading it. For example, how was depression operationally defined? What other treatments did participants receive?

---

show what you know

1. Philippe Pinel was horrified by the conditions in Parisian asylums in the late 1700s. He insisted that the inmates' chains be removed and that they be treated with respect and kindness. This _____ then spread throughout Europe and America.

2. A therapist writes a letter to the editor of a local newspaper in support of more funding for mental health facilities, stating that regardless of therapists' training, all therapy shares the same goal of reducing _____ and increasing the quality of life.
   a. symptoms
   b. combined approaches
   c. biomedical therapy
   d. the number of asylums

3. What has been the significance of deinstitutionalization?

✓ CHECK YOUR ANSWERS IN APPENDIX C.

Insight Therapies

AWARENESS EQUALS POWER Laura Lichti grew up in a picturesque town high in the clouds of the Rocky Mountains. Her family was, in her words, "very, very conservative," and her church community tight-knit and isolated. As an adolescent, Laura experienced many common teenage emotions (*Who am I? No one understands me*), and she longed for someone to listen and understand. Fortunately, she found that safe spot in a former Sunday school teacher, a twenty-something woman with children of her own, who had a wise "old soul," according to Laura. "The role she played for me was just like a life line," Laura recalls. "What I appreciated is that she really didn't direct me." If Laura felt distressed, her mentor would never say, "I told you so." Instead, she would listen without judgment. Then she would respond with an empathetic statement such as, "I can see that you're having a really hard time. . ."

With her gentle line of inquiry, the mentor encouraged Laura to search within herself for answers. Thoughtfully, empathically, she taught Laura how to find her voice, create her own solutions, and direct her life in a way that was true to herself. "[She] took it back to me," Laura says. "It was beautiful."

Inspired to give others what her mentor had given her, Laura resolved to become a psychotherapist for children and teens. She paid her way through community college, went on to a four-year university, and eventually received her master's degree in psychology, gaining experience in various internships along the way. After logging in hundreds of hours of supervised training and passing the state licensing exam, Laura finally became a licensed professional counselor. The process was 10 years in the making.

Today, Laura empowers clients much in the same way her mentor empowered her—by developing their self-awareness. She knows that her therapy is working when clients become aware enough to anticipate a problem and use coping skills without her prompting. "I got into an argument and [started] getting really angry," a client might say, "but instead of flying off the handle I took a walk and calmed down." Developing self-awareness is one of the unifying principles of the insight therapies, which we will now explore.

On Her Way
Laura Lichti had many reasons to feel proud the day she received her master's degree in counseling. After working full-time to put herself through college, earning an associate's degree from a community college and then a bachelor's degree from a four-year institution, Laura was one of 16 people admitted to a highly competitive master's program in counseling. Dan Penn

Taking It to the Couch, Freudian Style: Psychoanalysis

LO 3 Describe how psychoanalysis differs from psychodynamic therapy.

When imagining the stereotypical "therapy" session, many people often picture a person reclining on a couch and talking about dreams and memories from childhood. Modern-day therapy generally does not resemble this image. But if we could travel back in time to 1930s Vienna, Austria, and sit on Sigmund Freud's (1856–1939) sofa, we might just see this stereotype come to life.

FREUD AND THE UNCONSCIOUS Sigmund Freud (1900/1953), the father of psychoanalysis, proposed that humans are motivated by two animal-like drives: aggression and sex. But acting on these drives is not always compatible with social norms, so they create conflict and get pushed beneath the surface, or *repressed*. These drives do not just go away, though; they continue simmering beneath our conscious awareness, affecting our moods and behaviors. And when we can no longer keep them at bay, the result may be disordered behavior, such as that seen with phobias, obsessions, and panic attacks (Solms, 2006). To help patients deal with these drives, Freud created psychoanalysis, the first formal system of psychotherapy, which involved

CONNECTIONS

In **Chapter 11**, we introduced the concept of *repression,* which is a *defense mechanism* through which the *ego* moves anxiety-provoking thoughts, memories, or feelings from consciousness to unconsciousness. Here, we will see how psychoanalysis helps uncover some of these activities occurring outside of our awareness.

Synonym

eclectic approach to therapy integrative approach to therapy

eclectic approach to therapy Drawing on multiple theories and approaches to therapy to tailor treatment for a client.

CONNECTIONS

In **Chapter 4,** we introduced Freud's theory of dreams. He suggested *manifest content* is the apparent meaning of a dream. The *latent content* contains the hidden meaning of a dream, representing unconscious urges. Freud believed that to expose this latent content, we must look deeper than the reported storyline of the dream.

Leo Cullum/
The New Yorker

"It's that same dream, where I'm drowning in a bowl of noodles."

CONNECTIONS

In **Chapter 11,** we presented *projective personality tests.* The assumption is that the test taker's unconscious conflicts are projected onto the test material. It is up to the therapist to try to uncover these underlying issues. Here, the patient is projecting these conflicts onto a therapist.

The Famous Couch
Freud's psychoanalytic couch appears on display at the Freud Museum in London. All of Freud's patients reclined on this piece of furniture, which is reportedly quite comfortable with its soft cushions and Iranian rug cover (Freud Museum, 2013). Freud sat in the chair at the head of the couch, close to but not within view of his patient. Bjanka Kadic/Alamy

multiple weekly sessions. Psychoanalysis attempts to increase awareness of unconscious conflicts, thus making it possible to address and work through them.

Dreams, according to Freud, are a pathway to unconscious thoughts and desires brewing beneath our awareness (Freud, 1900/1953). The overt material of a dream (what we remember upon waking) is called its **manifest content,** which can disguise a deeper meaning, or *latent content,* hidden from awareness due to potentially uncomfortable issues and desires. Freud would often use dreams as a launching pad for **free association,** a therapy technique in which a patient says anything and everything that comes to mind, regardless of how silly, bizarre, or inappropriate it may seem.

Freud believed the seemingly directionless train of thought would lead to clues about the patient's unconscious. Piecing together the hints he gathered from dreams, free association, and other parts of therapy sessions, Freud would identify and make inferences about the unconscious conflicts driving the patient's behavior. He called this investigative work **interpretation.** When the time seemed right, Freud would share his interpretations, increasing the patient's self-awareness and helping her come to terms with conflicts, with the aim of moving forward (Freud, 1900/1953).

You might be wondering what behaviors psychoanalysts consider signs of unconscious conflict. One indicator is **resistance,** a patient's unwillingness to cooperate in therapy. Examples of resistance might include "forgetting" appointments or arriving late for them, falling asleep during free association, or becoming angry or agitated when certain topics arise. Resistance is a crucial step in psychoanalysis because it means the discussion might be veering close to something that makes the patient feel uncomfortable and threatened, like a critical memory or conflict causing distress. If resistance occurs, the job of the therapist is to help the patient identify its unconscious roots.

Another key sign of unconscious conflict is **transference,** a type of resistance that occurs when a patient reacts to the therapist as if she is dealing with her parents or other important people from childhood. Suppose Chepa relates to Dr. Foster as if he were a favorite uncle. She never liked letting her uncle down, so she resists telling Dr. Foster things she suspects would disappoint him. Transference is a good thing, because it illuminates the unconscious conflicts fueling a patient's behaviors (Hoffman, 2009). One of the reasons Freud sat off to the side and out of a patient's line of vision was to encourage transference; remaining neutral allows a patient to **project** his unconscious conflicts and feelings onto Freud. A therapist might experience *countertransference,* projecting his own unconscious conflicts onto his patient.

TAKING STOCK: AN APPRAISAL OF PSYCHOANALYSIS   The oldest form of talk therapy, psychoanalysis is still alive and well today. But Freud's theories have come under sharp criticism. For one thing, they are not evidence based, meaning there is no scientific data to back them up. It is nearly impossible to evaluate effectively the subjective interpretations used in psychoanalysis. And neither therapists nor patients actually know if they are tapping the patients' unconscious because it is made up of thoughts, memories, and desires of which we are largely unaware. How then can we know if these conflicts are being resolved? In addition, not every person is a good candidate for psychoanalysis; one must be very verbal, have time during the week for multiple sessions, and the money to pay for this often expensive therapy.

Although Freud's theories have been undeniably criticized, the impact of his work is extensive (just note how often his work is cited in this textbook). Freud helped us appreciate how childhood experiences and unconscious processes can shape personality and behavior. Even Laura, who does not identify herself as a psychoanalyst, says that Freudian notions sometimes come into play with her clients. If a person has a traumatic experience in childhood, for example, it may resurface both in therapy and real life, she notes. Like Laura, many contemporary psychologists do not identify themselves as psychoanalysts. But that doesn't mean Freud has left the picture. Far from it.

Goodbye, Couch; Hello, Chairs: Psychodynamic Therapy

Psychodynamic therapy is an updated take on psychoanalysis. This newer approach has been evolving over the last 30 to 40 years, incorporating many of Freud's core themes, including the idea that personality and behaviors often can be traced to unconscious conflicts and experiences from the past.

However, **psychodynamic therapy** breaks from traditional psychoanalysis in important ways. Therapists tend to see clients once a week for several months rather than many times a week for years. And instead of sitting quietly off to the side of a client reclining on a couch, the therapist sits face-to-face with the client, engaging in a two-way dialogue. The therapist may use a direct approach, guiding the therapy in a clearer direction, and providing feedback and advice. Frequently, the goal of psychodynamic therapy is to understand and resolve a specific, current problem. Suppose a client finds herself in a pattern of dating abusive men. Her therapist might help her see how unconscious conflicts from the past creep into the present, influencing her feelings and behaviors (*My father was abusive. Maybe I'm drawn to what feels familiar, even if it's bad for me*).

For many years, psychodynamic therapists treated clients without much evidence to back up their methods (Levy & Ablon, 2010, February 23). But recently, researchers have begun testing the effects of psychodynamic therapy with rigorous scientific methods, and their results are encouraging. **Randomized controlled trials** suggest psychodynamic psychotherapy is effective for treating an array of disorders, including depression, panic disorder, and eating disorders (Leichsenring & Rabung, 2008; Milrod et al., 2007; Shedler, 2010), and the benefits may last long after treatment has ended. People with borderline personality disorder, for example, appear to experience fewer and less severe symptoms (such as a reduction in suicide attempts) for several years following psychodynamic therapy (Bateman & Fonagy, 2008; Shedler, 2010). Yet, this approach is not ideal for everyone. It requires high levels of verbal expression and awareness of self and the environment. Symptoms like hallucinations or delusions might interfere with these requirements.

You Can Do It! Humanistic Therapy

LO 4   Explain the concepts that form the basis of humanistic therapy.

For the first half of the 20th century, most psychotherapists leaned on the theoretical framework established by Freud. But in the 1950s, some psychologists began to question Freud's dark view of human nature and his approach to treating clients. A new perspective began to take shape, one that focused on the positive aspects of human nature; this *humanism* would have a powerful influence on generations of psychologists, including Laura Lichti.

THE CLIENT KNOWS   During college, Laura worked as an adult supervisor at a residential treatment facility for children and teens struggling with mental health issues. The experience was eye opening. "I hadn't really been exposed to the level of intensity, and severe needs . . . of that population," Laura says. "I really had never been with people who constantly wanted to kill themselves, or had a severe eating disorder, or [who] were extreme cutters." Laura was not a therapist at the time, so she could not offer them professional help. To connect with the residents, she relied on the relational skills she had learned from her mentor. Her message was, *I'm here. I'll meet you where you are, and I really care about you.*

CONNECTIONS

In **Chapter 11,** we introduced the *neo-Freudians,* who disagreed with Freud's main ideas, including his singular focus on sex and aggression, his negative view of human nature, and his idea that personality is set by the end of childhood. Here, we can see that psychodynamic therapy grew out of discontent with Freud's ideas concerning treatment.

CONNECTIONS

In **Chapter 1,** we described the experimental method, a research technique that can uncover cause-and-effect relationships. Here, the experimental method is used to study the outcome of therapy. In *randomized controlled trials,* participants are randomly assigned to treatment and control groups. The independent variable is the type of treatment, and the dependent variables are the measures of effectiveness.

free association   A psychoanalytic technique in which a patient says anything that comes to mind.

interpretation   A psychoanalytic technique used to discover unconscious conflicts driving behavior.

resistance   A patient's unwillingness to cooperate in therapy; a sign of unconscious conflict.

transference   A type of resistance that occurs when a patient reacts to a therapist as if dealing with parents or other caregivers from childhood.

psychodynamic therapy   A type of insight therapy that incorporates core psychoanalytic themes, including the importance of unconscious conflicts and experiences from the past.

Laura continues to use this approach in her work as a therapist, allowing each client to steer the course of his therapy. For example, Laura might begin a session by asking a client to experiment with art therapy. Some people are enthusiastic about art therapy; others resist, but Laura makes it a rule never to coerce a client with statements such as, "Well, you need to do it because I am your therapist." Instead, she might say, "Okay, what do you think would work? If art is not going to work, what is interesting to you?" Maybe the client likes writing song lyrics; if so, Laura will follow his lead. "Okay, then why don't you write a song for me?"

CONNECTIONS

In **Chapter 1,** we introduced the field of *positive psychology,* which draws attention to human strengths and potential for growth. The *humanistic perspective* was a forerunner to this approach. As a treatment method, humanistic therapy emphasizes the positive nature of humans and strives to harness this for clients in treatment.

This approach to therapy is very much a part of the **humanistic movement,** which was championed by American psychotherapist Carl Rogers (1902–1987). Rogers believed that human beings are inherently good and inclined toward growth. "It has been my experience that persons have a basically positive direction," Rogers wrote in his widely popular book *On Becoming a Person* (Rogers, 1961, p. 26). Rogers recognized that humans have basic biological needs for food and sex, but he also saw that we have powerful desires to form close relationships, treat others with warmth and tenderness, and grow and mature as individuals (Rogers, 1961).

With this optimistic spirit, Rogers and others pioneered several types of insight therapies collectively known as **humanistic therapy,** which emphasizes the positive nature of humankind. Unlike psychoanalysis, which tends to focus on the distant past, humanistic therapy concentrates on the present, seeking to identify and address current problems. Rather than digging up unconscious thoughts and feelings, humanistic therapy emphasizes conscious experience: What's going on in your mind right now?

LO 5   Summarize person-centered therapy.

PERSON-CENTERED THERAPY   Rogers' distinct form of humanistic therapy is known as **person-centered therapy,** and it closely follows his theory of personality. According to Rogers, each person has a natural tendency toward growth and *self-actualization,* or achieving one's full potential. But factors such as expectations from family and society may stifle the process or block this tendency. He suggested these external factors often cause an *incongruence,* or a mismatch, between the client's *ideal self* (often involving unrealistic expectations of who she should be) and *real self* (the way the client views herself). The main goal of treatment is to reduce the incongruence between these two selves.

Suppose Laura has a male client who is drawn toward artistic endeavors. He loves dancing, singing, and acting, but his parents believe that boys should be tough and play sports. The client has spent his life trying to become the person others expect him to be, meanwhile denying the person he is deep down, which leaves him feeling unfulfilled and empty. Using a person-centered approach, Laura would take this client on a journey toward self-actualization. She would be supportive and involved throughout the process, but she would not tell him where to go, because as Rogers stated, "It is the *client* who knows what hurts, what directions to go, what problems are crucial, what experiences have been deeply buried" (Rogers, 1961, pp. 11–12). This type of therapy is **nondirective,** in that the therapist follows the lead of the client. The goal is to help clients see they are empowered to make changes in their lives and continue along a path of positive growth.

Part of Rogers' philosophy was his refusal to identify the people he worked with as "patients" (Rogers, 1951). Patients depend on doctors to make decisions for them, or at least give them instructions. All humans have an innate drive to become fully

Paint Me What You're Feeling
Thirteen-year-old Alyssia Crook uses her left leg and foot to create a painting during an art therapy session. This photo was taken less than 2 weeks before Crook, who suffers from a rare disease called pterygium syndrome, had part of her left leg amputated. Art therapy is an approach that uses art to help people understand, express, and deal with their emotions in a constructive way (American Art Therapy Association, 2013). AP Photo/The Grand Rapids Press, Rex Larson

Table 14.1   BUILDING A THERAPEUTIC ALLIANCE

Components of the Therapeutic Alliance	Description
Empathy	The ability to feel what a client is experiencing; seeing the world through the client's eyes (Rogers, 1951); therapist perceives feelings and experiences from "inside" the client (Rogers, 1961)
Unconditional positive regard	Total acceptance of a client no matter how distasteful the client's behaviors, beliefs, and words may be (Chapter 11)
Genuineness	Being authentic, responding to a client in a way that is real rather than hiding behind a polite or professional mask; knowing exactly where the therapist stands allows the client to feel secure enough to open up (Rogers, 1961)
Active listening	Picking up on the content and emotions behind words in order to understand a client's point of view; reflection or echoing the main point of what a client says

Humanist Carl Rogers believed it was critical to establish a strong and trusting therapist-client relationship. Above are the key elements of a therapeutic alliance.

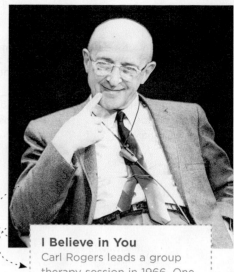

I Believe in You
Carl Rogers leads a group therapy session in 1966. One of the founders of humanistic psychology, Rogers firmly believed that every human being is fundamentally good and capable of *self-actualization,* or becoming all that she can be. Michael Rougier/ Time & Life Pictures/Getty Images

functioning. In Rogers' mind, it was the patient who had the answers, not the therapist. So he began using the term *client* and eventually settled on the term *person.*

The focus in person-centered therapy is not therapeutic techniques; the goal is to create a warm and accepting relationship between client and therapist. This **therapeutic alliance** is based on mutual respect and caring between the therapist and the client, and provides a safe place for self-exploration.

At this point, you may be wondering what exactly the therapist does during sessions. If a client has all the answers, why does he need a therapist at all? Sitting face-to-face with a client, the therapist's main job is to "be there" for that person through **empathy,** *unconditional positive regard,* **genuineness,** and **active listening,** all of which are essential for building a therapeutic alliance (TABLE 14.1).

TAKING STOCK: AN APPRAISAL OF HUMANISTIC THERAPY   The humanistic perspective has had a profound impact on our understanding of personality development and on the practice of psychotherapy. Therapists of all different theoretical orientations draw on humanistic techniques to build stronger relationships with clients and create positive therapeutic environments. This type of therapy is useful for an array of people dealing with complex and diverse problems (Corey, 2013), but how it compares to other methods remains somewhat unclear. Studying humanistic therapy is difficult because its methodology has not been operationalized and its use varies from one therapist to the next. Like other insight therapies, humanistic therapy is not ideal for everyone; it requires a high level of verbal skills and self-awareness.

The insight therapies we have explored—psychoanalysis, psychodynamic therapy, and humanistic therapy—help clients develop a deeper understanding of self. By exploring events of the past, clients in psychoanalysis or psychodynamic therapy may discover how prior experiences affect their current thoughts and behaviors. Those working with humanistic therapists may become more aware of what they want in life—and how their desires conflict with the expectations of others. These insights are invaluable, and they often lead to positive changes in behavior. But is it also possible to alter behavior directly? This is the goal of behavior therapy, the subject of the next section.

Synonym

person-centered therapy client-centered therapy

humanistic therapy A type of insight therapy that emphasizes the positive nature of humankind.

person-centered therapy A form of humanistic therapy developed by Rogers; aimed at helping clients achieve their full potential.

nondirective A technique used in person-centered therapy wherein the therapist follows the lead of the client during treatment sessions.

therapeutic alliance A warm and accepting client–therapist relationship that serves as a safe place for self-exploration.

empathy The ability to feel what a person is experiencing by attempting to observe the world through the client's eyes.

genuineness The ability to respond to a client in an authentic way rather than hiding behind a polite or professional mask.

active listening The ability to pick up on the content and emotions behind words in order to understand a client's perspective, often by echoing the main point of what the client says.

1. Suzanne is late for her therapy appointment yet again. Her therapist suggests this might be due to _____, which generally refers to a patient's unwillingness to cooperate in therapy.

2. The group of therapies known as _____ therapy focus on the positive nature of human beings and on the here-and-now.
   a. humanistic
   b. psychoanalytic
   c. psychodynamic
   d. free association

3. Seeing the world through a client's eyes and understanding how it feels to be the client is called
   a. interpretation.
   b. genuineness.
   c. empathy.
   d. self-actualization.

4. What are the differences between psychoanalytic and psychodynamic therapy?

✓ CHECK YOUR ANSWERS IN APPENDIX C.

Behavior Therapies
Get to Work! Behavior Therapy

> **LO 6**   Describe the concepts that underlie behavior therapy.

White Terror

A classic in the history of psychology, the case study of Little Albert showed that emotional responses such as fear can be classically conditioned. Researchers John B. Watson and Rosalie Rayner (1920) repeatedly exposed Albert to a frightening "bang!" every time he reached for a white rat, which led him to develop an intense fear of the animals. Vasiliy Koval/Shutterstock

The most famous baby in the history of psychology is probably Little Albert. At the age of 11 months, Albert developed an intense fear of rats while participating in a classic study conducted by John B. Watson and Rosalie Rayner (1920). You may wonder whether the researchers ever attempted to reverse the effects of their ethically questionable experiment. Did they do anything to help Albert overcome his fear of rats? As far as we know, they did not. But we can't help but wonder whether Albert could have been helped with behavior therapy.

Using the learning principles of classical conditioning, operant conditioning, and observational learning (Chapter 5), behavior therapy aims to replace maladaptive behaviors with those that are more adaptive. If behaviors are learned, who says they can't be changed through the same mechanisms? Little Albert learned to fear rats, so perhaps he could also learn to be comfortable around them.

CONNECTIONS

In **Chapter 5,** we learned about *negative reinforcement;* behaviors followed by a reduction in something unpleasant are likely to recur. If anxiety is reduced as a result of avoiding a feared object, the avoidance will be repeated.

EXPOSURE AND RESPONSE PREVENTION   To help a person overcome a fear or phobia, a behavior therapist might use **exposure,** a technique of placing clients in the situations they fear—without any actual risks involved. Take, for example, a client struggling with a rat phobia. Rats cause this person extreme anxiety; the mere thought of seeing one scamper beneath a dumpster causes great distress. The client usually goes to great lengths to avoid the rodents, and this makes his anxiety drop. This reduced anxiety (and the satisfaction associated with it) will **negatively reinforce** his avoidance behavior. With exposure therapy, the therapist might arrange for the client to be in a room with a very friendly pet rat. After a positive experience with the animal, the client's anxiety diminishes (along with his efforts to avoid it), and he learns the situation does not have to be anxiety provoking. Ideally, both the anxiety and the avoidance behavior are extinguished. This process of stamping out learned associations is called *extinction.* The theory behind this *response prevention* technique is that if you encourage someone to confront a feared object or situation, and prevent him from responding the way he normally does, the fear response eventually diminishes or disappears.

A particularly intense form of exposure is to *flood* a client with an anxiety-provoking stimulus that she cannot escape, causing a high degree of arousal. In one study, for example, women with snake phobias sat in very close proximity to a garter snake in a glass aquarium for 30 minutes without a break (Girodo & Henry, 1976).

But sometimes, it's better to approach a feared scenario with "baby steps," upping the exposure with each movement forward (Prochaska & Norcross, 2014). This can be accomplished with an *anxiety hierarchy,* which is essentially a list of activities or experiences ordered from least to most anxiety provoking (**INFOGRAPHIC 14.2** on page 599). For example, Step 1: Think about a caged rat; Step 2: Look at a caged rat from across the room; Step 3: Walk two steps toward the cage, and so on.

But take note: Working up the anxiety hierarchy needn't involve actual rodents. With technologies available today, you could put on some fancy goggles and travel into a virtual "rat world" where it is possible to reach out and "touch" that creepy crawly animal with the simple click of a rat, er . . . mouse. Virtual reality exposure therapy has become a popular way of reducing anxiety associated with various disorders, including specific phobias. Let's see how it works.

didn't SEE that coming

Virtual Reality Exposure Therapy

Imagine you are 1 of the 19 million Americans suffering from a specific phobia (Kessler et al., 2005). The object of your phobia does not happen to be rats, snakes, or anything with a heartbeat, but something that zooms through the clouds at 500 miles per hour. You suffer from *aviaphobia,* or fear of airplane travel. The idea of flying makes you so anxious that you haven't stepped in a plane in years. In fact, your phobia has prevented you from taking your dream trip to Mexico, and you are tired of being afraid. So you consult a therapist, who develops a treatment plan incorporating virtual reality exposure therapy. Are you ready to fly the virtual skies?

Wearing a helmetlike apparatus known as a head mounted display (HMD), you are suddenly transported into the virtual interior of a jumbo jet: The rows of blue seats, the luggage compartments overhead, and the tray table on the seat in front of you all seem so real. So, too, do the sounds of the flight attendant's voice and the rumble of the engine, thanks to the woofer situated beneath your seat (Rothbaum, Hodges, Smith, Lee, & Price, 2000). Turn your head to the side or look toward the ceiling, and the HMD's computer automatically adjusts to show you the part of the "plane" you are viewing. The surroundings are so realistic that you almost forget you're sitting on a chair in a therapist's office.

A few feet away, your therapist sits at her desk clicking away at a computer keyboard; she is moving you through the virtual airplane and monitoring your anxiety levels along the way (Krijn, Emmelkamp, Olafsson, & Biemond, 2004). Now it's time for you to buckle your seatbelt. Once that is accomplished, prepare yourself for takeoff. If you're really feeling comfortable, your therapist might simulate some turbulence or a bumpy landing. With enough virtual reality trials and your regular therapy, you just might be ready for that flight to Mexico.

Virtual reality exposure therapy sounds like a great idea, but does it work? Studies suggest that this method is effective for treating various phobias, including *aviaphobia, arachnophobia* (fear of spiders and similar insects), and *social phobia* (Parsons & Rizzo, 2008), though further research is needed to determine how good it is as a stand-alone treatment. As Krijn and colleagues (2004) point out, virtual reality exposure therapy is usually combined with other forms of therapy, and in the case of aviaphobia, this approach may be just as effective as regular exposure therapy (Rothbaum et al., 2000). It's certainly a lot more practical than using a real plane.

Face the Spider
A woman with arachnophobia (spider phobia) confronts the dreaded creature in a virtual environment called SpiderWorld. The goal of exposure therapy (virtual or otherwise) is to reduce the fear response by exposing clients to situations they fear. When nothing bad happens, their anxiety diminishes and they are less likely to avoid the feared situations in the future. Stephen Dagadakis/Hunter Hoffman

VIRTUAL REALITY EXPOSURE THERAPY SOUNDS LIKE A GREAT IDEA, BUT DOES IT WORK?

exposure A therapeutic technique that brings a person into contact with a feared object or situation while in a safe environment, with the goal of extinguishing or eliminating the fear response.

CONNECTIONS

In **Chapter 12,** we described *progressive muscle relaxation* in the context of reducing the impact of responses to stress. Here, we see it can also be used to help with the treatment of phobias.

try this

Sit in a quiet room in a comfortable chair. Start by tensing the muscles controlling your scalp: Hold that position for about 10 seconds and then release, focusing on the tension leaving your scalp. Next follow the same procedure for the muscles in your face, tensing and releasing. Continue all the way down to your toes and see what happens.

CONNECTIONS

Classical conditioning, presented in **Chapter 5,** can be used to reduce alcohol consumption. Drinking alcohol is a *neutral stimulus* to start (one drink does not normally cause vomiting). Drinking is paired with a nausea inducing drug, which is an *unconditioned stimulus* that causes an *unconditioned response* of vomiting. After repeated pairings, drinking alcohol becomes the *conditioned stimulus,* and the vomiting becomes the *conditioned response.*

In **Chapter 5,** we described how *positive reinforcement* (supplying something desirable) increases the likelihood of a behavior being repeated. Therapists use reinforcement in behavior modification to shape behaviors to be more adaptive.
Synonym

behavior modification applied behavior analysis

systematic desensitization A treatment that combines anxiety hierarchies with relaxation techniques.

aversion therapy Therapeutic approach that uses the principles of classical conditioning to link problematic behaviors to unpleasant physical reactions.

behavior modification Therapeutic approach in which behaviors are shaped through reinforcement and punishment.

SYSTEMATIC DESENSITIZATION Therapists often combine anxiety hierarchies with relaxation techniques in an approach called **systematic desensitization,** which takes advantage of the fact that we can't be relaxed and anxious at the same time. The therapist begins by teaching clients how to relax their muscles. One technique for doing this is **progressive muscle relaxation,** which is the process of tensing and then relaxing muscle groups, starting at the head and ending at the toes. Using this method, a client can learn to release all the tension in his body. It's very simple—want to try it?

Once a client has learned how to relax, it's time to face the anxiety hierarchy (either in the real world or via imagination), while trying to maintain a sense of calm. Imagine a client who fears flying, moving through an anxiety hierarchy with her therapist. Starting with the least-feared scenario at the bottom of her hierarchy, she imagines purchasing a ticket online. If she can stay relaxed through the first step, then she moves to the second item in the hierarchy, thinking about boarding a plane. At some point in the process, she might start to feel jittery or unable to take the next step. If this happens, the therapist guides her back a step or two in the hierarchy, or as many steps as she needs to feel calm again, using the relaxation technique described above. Then it's back up the hierarchy she goes. It's important to note that this process does not happen in one session, but over the course of many sessions.

AVERSION THERAPY Exposure therapy focuses on *extinguishing* or eliminating associations, but there is another behavior therapy aimed at producing them. It's called **aversion therapy.** Seizing on the power of classical conditioning, aversion therapy seeks to link problematic behaviors, such as alcohol overuse, drug use, or fetishes, to unpleasant physical reactions like sickness and pain (Infographic 14.2). The goal of aversion therapy is to get people to have an involuntary unpleasant physical reaction to an undesired behavior, so that eventually the undesired behavior becomes a conditioned stimulus to the conditioned response of feeling bad. A good example is the drug Antabuse, which has helped some people with alcoholism stop drinking, at least temporarily (Cannon, Baker, Gino, & Nathan, 1986; Gaval-Cruz & Weinshenker, 2009). Antabuse interferes with the body's ability to break down alcohol, so combining it with even a small amount of alcohol brings on an immediate unpleasant reaction (vomiting, throbbing headache, and so on). With **repeated pairings** of alcohol consumption and physical misery, drinkers are less inclined to drink in the future. But aversion therapies like this are only effective if the client is motivated to change and comply with treatment.

CONDITIONING, LEARNING, AND THERAPY Another form of behavior therapy is **behavior modification,** which draws on the principles of operant conditioning, shaping behaviors through *reinforcement.* Therapists practicing behavior modification use **positive and negative reinforcement,** as well as punishment, to help clients increase adaptive behaviors and reduce those that are maladaptive. For behaviors that resist modification, therapists might use successive approximations by reinforcing incremental changes. Some will incorporate observational learning (that is, learning by imitating and watching others) to help clients change their behaviors.

Classical Conditioning in Behavior Therapies

Behavior therapists believe that most behaviors—either desirable or undesirable—are learned. When a behavior is maladaptive, a new, more adaptive behavior can be learned to replace it. Behavior therapists use learning principles to help clients eliminate unwanted behaviors. The two behavior therapies highlighted here rely upon classical conditioning techniques. In exposure therapy, a therapist might use an approach known as *systematic desensitization* to reduce an unwanted response, such as a fear of needles, by pairing it with relaxation. In *aversion therapy*, an unwanted behavior such as excessive drinking is paired with unpleasant reactions, creating an association that prompts avoidance of that behavior.

SYSTEMATIC DESENSITIZATION

A client practices relaxation techniques while engaging in situations listed on her anxiety hierarchy, beginning with the least anxiety-provoking situation. After repeated pairings, the client learns to associate the anxiety-provoking situation with the desirable, conditioned response (calm), which is incompatible with fear or anxiety. The process is repeated for every step on the hierarchy.

MOST ANXIETY PROVOKING

Anxiety Hierarchy for Fear of Needles

8 Getting a flu shot.

7 Allowing someone to prep your arm for a shot.

6 Visiting a health clinic to discuss getting a shot.

5 Watching someone get a shot.

4 Holding a hypodermic needle.

3 Touching a hypodermic needle in its packaging.

2 Looking at an actual hypodermic needle.

1 Looking at a photo of a hypodermic needle.

LEAST ANXIETY PROVOKING

During conditioning, two stimuli that produce incompatible responses are repeatedly paired.

+ relaxation

ANXIETY → calm

Because the responses are incompatible, one response will eventually be extinguished. Starting at the bottom of the hierarchy with the least anxiety-provoking situation enables the desired response (calm) to prevail.

Before conditioning

Unconditioned stimulus (US) → Unconditioned response (UR)

During conditioning

Unconditioned stimulus (US)

Neutral stimulus (NS)

→ Unconditioned response (UR)

After conditioning

Conditioned stimulus (CS) → Conditioned response (CR)

AVERSION THERAPY

Aversion therapy seeks to diminish a behavior by linking it with an unpleasant reaction. To reduce alcohol consumption, alcohol is consumed with a drug that causes feelings of nausea. Eventually, alcohol becomes a conditioned stimulus, prompting the unpleasant physical reaction all on its own.

CONNECTIONS

Tokens are an excellent example of a *secondary reinforcer*. In **Chapter 5,** we reported that secondary reinforcers derive their power from their connection with *primary reinforcers*, which satisfy biological needs.

Coveted Coins

In a token economy, positive behaviors are reinforced with tokens, which can be used to purchase food, obtain privileges, and secure other desirable things. Token economies are typically used in institutions such as schools or mental health facilities. Jon Schulte/Getty Images

One common approach using behavior modification is the **token economy,** which harnesses the power of positive reinforcement to encourage good behavior. Token economies have proven successful for a variety of populations, including psychiatric patients in residential treatment facilities and hospitals, children in classrooms, and convicts in prisons (Dickerson, Tenhula, & Green-Paden, 2005; Kazdin, 1982). In a residential treatment facility, for example, patients with schizophrenia may earn tokens for socializing with each other, cleaning up after themselves, and eating their meals. Tokens can be exchanged for candy, outings, privileges, and other perks. They can also be taken away as a punishment to reduce undesirable behaviors. Critics contend that token economies manipulate and humiliate the people they intend to help (you might agree that giving grown men and women play money for good behavior is degrading). But, from a practical standpoint, these systems can help people adopt healthier behaviors.

Unlike the reward systems parents might use to encourage good behavior at home, token economies tend to be implemented in institutions, such as schools. Dr. Foster, for example, sometimes works with children who are acting out in the classroom. To reinforce positive behaviors, he might arrange for a school counselor or teacher's aide to provide rewards such as candies, stickers, the privilege of handing out papers, or whatever happens to be reinforcing for that particular child.

TAKING STOCK: AN APPRAISAL OF BEHAVIOR THERAPY Behavior therapy covers a broad range of treatment approaches that share a long history. Instead of focusing on unobservable constructs (such as thinking and emotion), this approach focuses on observable behaviors occurring in the present moment. As such, it offers a few key advantages over insight therapies. Behavior therapy tends to work fast, producing quick resolutions to stressful situations, some of which may be resolved in a single session (Ollendick et al., 2009; Öst, 1989). And reduced time in therapy typically translates to a lower cost. What's more, the procedures used in behavior therapy are often easy to operationalize (remember, the focus is on modifying observable behavior), so evaluating the outcome of therapy is more straightforward.

Behavior therapy has its drawbacks, of course. The focus is changing learned behaviors, but not all behaviors are learned (you can't "learn" to have hallucinations). And because the reinforcement comes from an external source, newly learned behaviors may disappear when reinforcement stops. Finally, the emphasis on observable behavior may downplay the social, biological, and cognitive roots of psychological disorders. This narrow approach works well for treating phobias and other clear-cut behavior problems, but not as well for addressing far-reaching, complex issues arising from disorders such as schizophrenia.

✓○○○   show what you know

1. The primary goal of _____ therapy is to replace maladaptive behaviors with more adaptive ones.
   a. behavior   c. humanistic
   b. exposure   d. psychodynamic

2. Therapists will often help a client develop a(n) _____, which includes a list of stimuli ordered from least to most anxiety-provoking.

3. The goal of _____ is to get people to have an involuntary unpleasant physical reaction to an undesirable behavior.
   a. exposure therapy   c. systematic desensitization
   b. aversion therapy   d. extinction

4. Imagine you are working in a treatment facility for children, and one of the residents has begun throwing objects at others during quiet time. Using the principles of operant conditioning and observational learning, how might you use behavior modification to change this behavior?

✓ CHECK YOUR ANSWERS IN APPENDIX C.

Cognitive Therapies

FOLLOW-UP Upon discharge from the psychiatric hospital, Chepa returns to the reservation where Dr. Foster and his colleagues from Indian Health Services follow her progress. Every month, she goes to the medical clinic for an injection of medication to quell her psychosis (more on these antipsychotic drugs later in the chapter). This is also when she is most likely to have a therapy session with Dr. Foster.

Psychologists on the reservation typically don't have the luxury of holding more than two or three sessions with a client, so Dr. Foster has to make the most of every minute. For a client who has just received a new diagnosis, a good portion of the session is spent on *psychoeducation,* or learning more about a disorder: *What is schizophrenia, and how will it affect my life?* Dr. Foster and the client might go over some of the user-friendly literature on schizophrenia published by the National Alliance on Mental Illness (NAMI; http://www.nami.org/).

Another main goal is to help clients restructure cognitive processes, or turn negative thought patterns into healthier ones. To help clients recognize the irrational nature of their thoughts, Dr. Foster might provide a metaphor that goes something like this:

Dr. Foster: If we had a blizzard in February and it's 20 degrees below for four days in a row, would you consider that a strange winter?

Chepa: No.

Dr. Foster: If we had a day that's 105 degrees in August, would you consider that an odd summer?

Chepa: Well, no.

Dr. Foster: Yet you're talking about a difference of 125 degrees, and we're in the same place and we're saying this is normal weather. . . . We're part of nature. You and I are part of this natural world, and so you might have a day today where you're very distressed, very upset, and a week from now where you're very calm and very at peace, and both of those are normal. Both of those are appropriate.

Dr. Foster might also remind Chepa that her symptoms result from her psychological condition. "Your response is a normal response [for] a human being with this [psychological disorder]," he says, "and so of course you're scared, of course you're upset." Here, Dr. Foster is helping his client see the situation differently; he is normalizing her response by placing it in context.

You Are What You Think: Cognitive Therapy

LO 7 Outline the concepts of cognitive therapy.

Dr. Foster has identified his client's maladaptive thoughts and is beginning to help her change the way she views her world and her relationships. This is the basic goal of **cognitive therapy**, an approach advanced by psychiatrist Aaron Beck (b. 1921).

BECK'S COGNITIVE THERAPY Beck was trained in psychoanalysis, but he opted to develop his own approach after trying (without luck) to produce scientific evidence showing that Freud's methods worked (Beck & Weishaar, 2014). Beck believes that patterns of *automatic thoughts* are at the root of psychological disturbances. These distortions in thinking cause individuals to misinterpret events in their lives (**TABLE 14.2** on page 602).

Beck's Cognitive Approach
The father of cognitive therapy, Aaron Beck, believes that distorted thought processes lie at the heart of psychological problems.

token economy A treatment approach that uses behavior modification to harness the power of reinforcement to encourage good behavior.

cognitive therapy A type of therapy aimed at addressing the maladaptive thinking that leads to maladaptive behaviors and feelings.

Table 14.2 COGNITIVE DISTORTIONS

Cognitive Distortion	Explanation	Example of Distorted Thinking
Arbitrary inference	Coming to a conclusion even when there is no evidence to support it	*I am a horrible student.*
Selective abstraction	Ignoring information and assuming something has happened based on details taken out of context	*I know he is cheating because he is e-mailing a woman at work.*
Overgeneralizing	Belief that something may always occur because it has occurred before	*My boss doesn't like me; I will never be liked.*
Magnification-minimization	Belief that something is more or less critical than it really is—catastrophizing	*If I don't pass this first quiz, I will fail the course.*
Dichotomous thinking	Viewing experiences in extremes	*I can either be the top of my class, or I can get married and have a family.*
Personalizing	Taking other people's behaviors too personally	*I waved at her, but she didn't even acknowledge me. I must have upset her.*

Psychiatrist Aaron Beck contends that psychological problems stem from distorted patterns of thought. Cognitive therapy aims to replace these cognitive distortions with more realistic and constructive ways of thinking.

SOURCE: BECK AND WEISHAAR (2014), PP. 231-264.

CONNECTIONS

In **Chapter 8,** we presented Piaget's concept of *schema,* a collection of ideas or notions representing a basic unit of understanding. Young children form schemas based on functional relationships they observe in the environment. Here, Beck is suggesting that schemas can also direct the way we interpret events, not always in a realistic or rational manner.

Beck identified a collection of common *cognitive distortions* or *errors* associated with psychological problems, such as depression (Beck, Rush, Shaw, & Emory, 1979). One such distortion is **overgeneralization,** or thinking that self-contained events will have major repercussions in life (Prochaska & Norcross, 2014). For example, a person may assume that just because something is true under one set of circumstances, it will be true in all others (*I have had difficulty working for a male boss, so I will never be able to work effectively under a male supervisor*). Another common cognitive distortion is *dichotomous thinking,* or seeing things in extremes (*I can either be a good student, or I can have a social life*).

One goal of cognitive therapy then is to help clients recognize and challenge cognitive errors such as overgeneralization. Beck suggests that *cognitive schemas* underlie these patterns of automatic thoughts, directing the way we interpret events. The goal is to restructure these schemas into more rational frameworks, a process that can be facilitated by client homework. For example, the therapist may challenge a client to test a "hypothesis" related to her dysfunctional thinking. (*If you are truly the worst student in the world, then do you think you would have made it to college?*) Client homework is an important component of cognitive therapy. So, too, is psychoeducation, which might include providing resources or links to resources that help clients understand their disorders and thus adopt more realistic attitudes and expectations.

Beck's cognitive therapy aims to dismantle or take apart the mental frameworks harboring cognitive errors and replace them with beliefs that nurture more positive, realistic thoughts. Dr. Foster calls these mental frameworks "paradigms," and he also tries to create a more holistic change in thinking. "I tell people that thoughts, behaviors, and words come from beliefs, and when a belief is not working for you, let's change it," he says. "To modify a belief doesn't mean all or none," he adds, "but when we outgrow a belief, that's a wonderful time for transformation."

ELLIS'S RATIONAL EMOTIVE BEHAVIOR THERAPY   The other major figure in cognitive therapy is psychologist Albert Ellis (1913–2007). Like Beck, Ellis was trained in psychoanalysis but was disappointed by its results, so he created his own

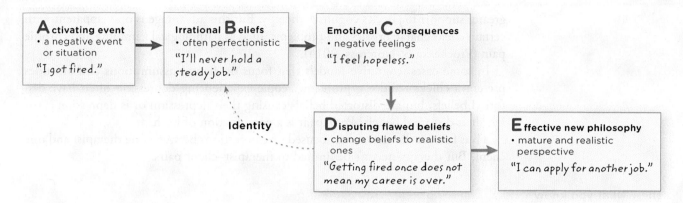

▲ **FIGURE 14.2**
The ABC's of REBT
A rational-emotive behavior
therapist uses the ABC model to
understand a client's problems. This
part of the model is depicted in blue.
Therapy, shown in green, helps a
client identify and address irrational
beliefs—and ultimately develop a
mature and realistic perspective.

treatment approach: **rational-emotive behavior therapy (REBT).** The goal of REBT is to help people identify their irrational or illogical thoughts and convert them into rational ones. An REBT therapist uses the ABC model to understand a client's problems. Point A represents an *Activating event* in the client's life ("My boss fired me"); point B stands for the *irrational Beliefs* that follow ("I will never be able to hold a steady job"); and point C represents the *emotional Consequences* ("I feel hopeless and depressed"). Therapy focuses on addressing point B, the irrational beliefs causing distress. If all goes well, the client successfully reaches point D: *Disputing flawed beliefs* ("Losing one job does not spell the end of my career"), and that leads to point E: an *Effective new philosophy* ("I can apply for another job"), a mature and realistic perspective on life (Ellis & Dryden, 1997; **FIGURE 14.2**).

According to Ellis, people tend to have unrealistic beliefs, often perfectionist in nature, about how they and others should think and act. This inevitably leads to disappointment, as no one is perfect. The ultimate goal of REBT is to arrive at self-acceptance, that is, to change these irrational thoughts to realistic ones. This often involves letting go of the "I shoulds" and "I musts," what Ellis called "musturbatory thinking" (Prochaska & Norcross, 2014, p. 266). Through REBT, one develops a rational way of thinking that helps reduce suffering and amplify enjoyment: "The purpose of life," as Ellis was known to say, "is to have a $&%#@ good time" (p. 263).

As Ellis developed his therapy throughout the years, he realized it was important to focus on cognitive processing as well as behavior. Thus, REBT therapists focus on changing both cognitions and behaviors, and assigning homework to implement the insights clients gain during therapy. Ellis took a hardline with clients, forcefully challenging them to provide evidence for their irrational ideas (for instance, he might have asked: "Where is it written that you have to be beautiful in order to be happy?"). He often shocked people with his blunt style (Kaufman, 2007, July 25; Prochaska & Norcross, 2014).

Because Ellis and Beck incorporated both cognitive and behavior therapy methods, their approaches are commonly referred to as **cognitive behavioral therapy.** Both are action oriented, as they require clients to confront and resist their illogical thinking.

TAKING STOCK: AN APPRAISAL OF COGNITIVE THERAPY   There is considerable overlap between the approaches of Ellis and Beck. Both are short-term (usually no more than about 20 one-hour sessions), action oriented, and homework-intensive. In some instances, cognitive therapy has been found to be more successful than relaxation and exposure therapy in treating certain disorders, such as social phobia and generalized anxiety disorder (Clark et al., 2006; Dugas et al., 2010). If you compare the effectiveness of Beck's and Ellis's approaches, you will find some studies showing

overgeneralization A cognitive distortion that assumes self-contained events will have major repercussions.

rational emotive behavior therapy (REBT) A type of cognitive therapy, developed by Ellis, that identifies illogical thoughts and converts them into rational ones.

cognitive behavioral therapy An action-oriented type of therapy that requires clients to confront and resist their illogical thinking.

greater support for Beck's cognitive therapy. But this advantage is only apparent with certain client characteristics and problems, such as pathological gambling and chronic pain (Prochaska & Norcross, 2014).

In some cases, cognitive models that focus on flawed assumptions and attitudes present a chicken-and-egg problem. People experiencing depression often have distorted beliefs, but are distorted beliefs causing their depression or is depression causing their distorted beliefs? Perhaps it is a combination of both.

Thus far, our discussion has focused on interactions between one therapist and one client. But therapy needn't be limited to therapist–client pairs.

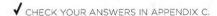

show what you know

1. The basic goal of _____ is to help clients identify maladaptive thoughts and change the way they view the world and their relationships.

2. _____ therapy uses the ABC model to help people identify their illogical thoughts and convert them into logical ones.
   a. Behavior
   b. Psychodynamic
   c. Exposure
   d. Rational emotive behavior

3. Describe the similarities and differences between cognitive and behavior therapies.

✓ CHECK YOUR ANSWERS IN APPENDIX C.

Group Therapies
Let's Get Through This Together: Group Therapy

LO 8   Identify the benefits and challenges of group therapy.

For some people, group therapy is a better fit than individual therapy. First developed in the 1940s, group therapy has adapted to the ever-changing demands of work in the clinical field (Yalom & Leszcz, 2005). Usually, group therapy is led by one or two therapists trained in any of the various approaches (such as psychoanalytic or cognitive). Sessions can include as few as 3 clients, or up to 10 or more, often facing similar problems. There are groups to help people cope with shyness, panic disorder, chronic pain, compulsive gambling, divorce, grief, and sexual identity issues, to name just a few. It is not always a psychological disorder that brings people to group therapy, but instead a desire to work on a specific issue.

Group members share their problems as openly as possible, and it is valuable to hear they are not alone in their struggles or desire to improve. Research typically shows that group therapy is as effective as individual therapy for addressing many problems. It is actually the preferred approach for interpersonal issues, because it allows therapists to observe clients interacting with others. The therapist's skills play an important role in the success of group sessions, and the dynamics between clients and therapists may be similar to those that arise in individual therapy. (Clients may demonstrate resistance or transference, for example.)

SELF-HELP GROUPS* Other group settings for interpersonal growth are **self-help groups.** Among the most commonly known are Alcoholics Anonymous (AA), Al-Anon, Parents without Partners, and Weight Watchers. Members of self-help groups provide support (not therapy) to each other while facing bereavement, divorce, infertility, HIV/AIDS, cancer, and other issues. Typically, sessions are not run by a psychiatrist, licensed psychologist, or other mental health professional, but by

Finding Strength in Others
Members of the Brave at Heart breast cancer support group convene at the Harold Leever Regional Cancer Center in Waterbury, Connecticut. Self-help groups provide valuable support for people facing similar struggles, but they usually are not led by mental health professionals. AP Photo/The Republican-American, Jim Shannon

---

*You can learn more about their purposes and meetings in your area from The National Mental Health Consumers' Self-Help Clearinghouse, at http://www.mhselfhelp.org/.

a mental health advisor or *paraprofessional* trained to run the groups. A typical AA leader, for example, is a "recovering alcoholic" who grasps the complexities of alcoholism and recovery, but is not necessarily a mental health professional.

Family members often participate in these groups, because when it comes to relating to other people, there is always room for growth. Any family therapist could tell you that.

We Are Family: Family Therapy

Introduced in North America in the 1940s, **family therapy** focuses on the family as an *integrated system,* recognizing that the interactions within it can create instability or lead to the breakdown of the family unit (Corey, 2013). Family therapy explores relationship problems rather than the symptoms of particular disorders, teaching communication skills in the process. The family is viewed as a dynamic, holistic entity, and the goal is to understand each person's role in the system, *not* to root out troublemakers in the family, assign blame, or identify one member who must be "fixed." Because families typically seek the resolution of a specific problem, the course of therapy tends to be brief (Corey, 2013). Suppose a teenage girl has become withdrawn at home and is acting out in school, and the whole family decides to participate in therapy. The therapist begins by helping the parents identify ways they encourage her behaviors (not following through with consequences, for example), and may examine how their marital dynamics affect the kids. If it becomes evident that the marriage is in trouble, the parents might seek therapy without the rest of the family, which brings us to the next topic: couples therapy.

THAT'S THE WAY LOVE GOES: COUPLES THERAPY   Let's face it, most couples have issues. High on the list are conflicts about money ("You are so stingy!"), failures to communicate ("You never listen!"), **languishing physical bonds** ("No dear, not tonight"), children, and jealousy (Storaasli & Markman, 1990). But when these problems begin to cause significant distress, ***couples therapy*** is a smart choice. Couples therapists are trained in many of the therapeutic approaches described earlier, and they tend to focus on conflict management and communication. One goal of couples therapy and relationship education programs is to provide guidance on how to communicate within relationships (Scott, Rhoades, Stanley, Allen, & Markman, 2013).

Couples therapy can yield positive results for many couples—they stay together, feel more satisfied with the relationship—but some seem to benefit more than others. This is especially true for those who are committed to saving their relationships (Greenberg, Warwar, & Malcolm, 2010). People who respond well to couples therapy seem to have higher marital satisfaction and are emotionally engaged (Jacobson & Addis, 1993). Those who participate in relationship education programs prior to marriage may be better off as well, as these may help couples identify some of the situations that could lead to divorce, including a spouse being unfaithful, problems with aggression, and substance abuse.

TAKING STOCK: AN APPRAISAL OF GROUP THERAPY   Like any treatment, group therapy has its strengths and limitations (**TABLE 14.3** on page 606). Group members may not get along, or they may feel uncomfortable discussing sensitive issues. But conflict and discomfort are not necessarily bad when it comes to therapy (group or otherwise), because such feelings often motivate people to reevaluate how they interact with others, and perhaps try new approaches.

CONNECTIONS

In **Chapter 10,** we introduced sex therapist Dr. Stephanie Buehler. She reported that the number one sexual problem facing her clients is low desire. We also noted gender differences regarding the frequency of masturbation and sexual thoughts. This information can be used to help couples in treatment.

Synonyms

self-help groups mutual help groups, support groups

family therapy family counseling

couples therapy marital therapy

family therapy A type of therapy that focuses on the family as an integrated system, recognizing that the interactions within it can create instability or lead to the breakdown of the family unit.

Table 14.3	BENEFITS AND DRAWBACKS OF GROUP THERAPY	
Strengths of Group Therapy	**Weaknesses of Group Therapy**	
Sessions generally cost about half as much as individual therapy (American Group Psychotherapy Association, 2010).	Not everyone feels at ease discussing personal troubles in a room full of people.	
People find relief and comfort knowing that others face similar struggles.	Group members may not always get along. This friction can inhibit the therapeutic process.	
Group members offer support and encouragement. They also challenge one another to think and behave in new ways.	Groups may have members who show resistance to group therapy, resulting in poor attendance, tardiness, or drop outs (Yalom & Leszcz, 2005).	
Seeing others improve offers hope and inspiration.	Some group therapy participants have had negative family experiences, and thus have negative expectations of the group setting (Yalom & Leszcz, 2005).	

For some individuals struggling with certain psychological problems, group therapy is a good alternative to individual therapy. Listed above are some of the pros and cons of group therapy.

Evaluating group therapies can be difficult because there is so much variation in approaches (psychodynamic, cognitive behavioral, and so on). However, strong evidence exists that couples and marital therapy are effective for treating a wide range of problems (Shadish & Baldwin, 2003). Likewise, the outcomes for group therapy rival those of individual therapy for many types of clients and problems (Burlingame & Baldwin, 2011; Yalom & Leszcz, 2005). As with individual therapies, the role of the group therapist is of critical importance: Empathy, good facilitation skills, listening, and careful observation are important predictors of successful outcomes. So, too, are the preparation of the group members, the therapist's verbal style, and the "climate" and cohesion of the group (Burlingame & Baldwin, 2011).

All the therapies we have discussed thus far involve interactions among people. But in many cases, interpersonal therapy is not enough. The problem is rooted in the brain, and a biological solution may also be necessary.

 show what you know

1. A single man has had trouble dealing with his co-workers and has not been on a second date in over a year because of his poor interpersonal skills. His therapist decides the best course of treatment is _____, which is led by one or two mental health professionals, involves three or more clients, and allows the therapists to observe the client interacting with others.

2. _____ bring(s) together people with common disorders, addictions, or other problems. Sessions typically are not run by psychiatrists, psychologists, or other mental health professionals.
   a. Self-help groups   **c.** Couples therapy
   b. Family therapy   **d.** Group therapies

3. Under what conditions might group therapy fail or be inappropriate?

 CHECK YOUR ANSWERS IN APPENDIX C.

Biomedical Therapies

Earlier in the chapter, we described Dr. Foster's work with Chepa, the young woman with schizophrenia. After being discharged from the hospital, Chepa returns to her family, but her treatment is far from over. In addition to receiving psychotherapy, Chepa will most likely go to the medical clinic for monthly injections of drugs to control her psychosis. Prescribing medications for psychological disorders is generally the domain of *psychiatrists,* physicians who specialize in treating people with psychological disorders (psychiatrists are medical doctors, whereas clinical psychologists have PhDs and generally cannot prescribe medication).

LO 9   Compare and contrast biomedical interventions and identify their common goal.

People with severe disorders like depression, schizophrenia, and bipolar disorder often benefit from biomedical therapy, a type of treatment that targets the biological processes underlying psychological disorders. There are three basic biological approaches to treating psychological disorders: (1) the use of drugs, or *psychotropic* medications; (2) the use of electroconvulsive therapy; and (3) the use of surgery.

Medicines That Help: Psychopharmacology

Psychotropic medications are used to treat psychological disorders and their symptoms. *Psychopharmacology* is the scientific study of how these medications alter perceptions, moods, behaviors, and other aspects of psychological functioning. These drugs can be divided into four categories: *antidepressant, mood-stabilizing, antipsychotic,* and *antianxiety.*

ANTIDEPRESSANT DRUGS   The primary reason people come to Dr. Foster seeking psychological help is major depressive disorder. Commonly referred to as *depression,* it is one of the most prevalent psychological disorders in America and a common cause of disability in young adults (National Institute of Mental Health, 2012). Major depressive disorder affects around 7% of the population in any given year (APA, 2013), resulting in a high demand for ways to lessen its symptoms.

Major depressive disorder is commonly treated with **antidepressant drugs,** a category of psychotropic medication used to improve mood (and to treat anxiety and eating disorders in certain individuals). Essentially, there are three classes of antidepressant drugs: monoamine oxidase inhibitors (MAOIs), such as Nardil; tricyclic antidepressants, such as Elavil; and selective serotonin reuptake inhibitors (SSRIs), such as Prozac. All these antidepressants are thought to work by influencing the activity of **neurotransmitters** that are hypothesized to be involved in depression and other disorders (**INFOGRAPHIC 14.3** on page 611). (Keep in mind, no one has pinpointed the exact neurological mechanisms underlying depression.)

The monoamine oxidase inhibitors (MAOIs), developed in the 1950s, help people with major depressive disorder by slowing the breakdown of norepinephrine, serotonin, and dopamine in synapses (these neurotransmitters are categorized as monoamines). The natural role of the enzyme monoamine oxidase is to break down the monoamines when they are in the synaptic gap. MAOIs extend the amount of time these neurotransmitters linger in the gap by hindering the normal activity of monoamine oxidase. It is not clear how the monoamine neurotransmitters interact to cause depression, but by making them more available (that is, allowing them more time in the synapse), symptoms of depression can be lessened. This group of

Psychologists Who Prescribe

Psychotropic medications are typically prescribed by psychiatrists, but a small number of psychologists have prescription privileges as well. New Mexico and Louisiana have passed laws giving psychologists the green light to prescribe, provided they have a master's degree in psychopharmacology and adequate in-field training. The same is true for psychologists working in the Defense Department or Indian Health Services. Piotr Pabijan/ Shutterstock

CONNECTIONS

In **Chapter 2,** we described how neurons communicate with each other. Sending neurons release *neurotransmitters* into the synaptic gap, where they bind to receptors on the receiving neuron. Neurotransmitters not immediately attached are reabsorbed by the sending neuron (*reuptake*) or are broken down in the synapse. Here, we see how medications can influence this process.

antidepressant drugs Psychotropic medications used for the treatment of depression.

antidepressants reduces depression, but they have fallen out of use due to safety concerns and side effects, as they require great attention to diet. MAOIs can trigger a life-threatening jump in blood pressure when ingested alongside tyramine, a substance found in many everyday foods including cheddar cheese, salami, and wine (Anastasio et al., 2010; Blackwell, Marley, Price, & Taylor, 1967; Horwitz, Lovenberg, Engelman, & Sjoerdsma, 1964; Rosenberg & Kosslyn, 2011).

The tricyclic antidepressants, named as such because of their three-ringed molecular structure, inhibit the reuptake of norepinephrine and serotonin in the synaptic gap. Again, the cause of depression is not clear, but if a lack of serotonin and norepinephrine is involved, allowing them longer time to be active appears to reduce symptoms. The tricyclic drugs are not always well tolerated by patients and can cause a host of problematic side effects, including sexual dysfunction, confusion, and increased risk of heart attack (Cohen, Gibson, & Alderman, 2000; Higgens, Nash, & Lynch, 2010). Overdoses can be fatal.

Doctors relied heavily on monoamine oxidase inhibitors and tricyclics until newer, more popular pharmaceutical interventions were introduced in the 1980s. These selective serotonin reuptake inhibitors (SSRIs) include brands such as Prozac, Paxil, and Zoloft. SSRIs also impede reuptake, but this class of drug inhibits the reuptake of serotonin specifically.

SSRIs are generally safer and have fewer negative effects than the older generation of antidepressants, which helps explain why they have become so popular in recent decades. But they are far from perfect. Weight gain, fatigue, hot flashes and chills, insomnia, nausea, and sexual dysfunction are all possible side effects. Some research suggests that they work no better than a **placebo** when it comes to treating mild to moderate depression (Fournier et al., 2010). But these drugs can be very beneficial in reducing the potentially devastating symptoms of depression. Improvement is generally noticed within 3–5 weeks after treatment has started.

CONNECTIONS

In **Chapter 1**, we stated that a *placebo* is a "pretend" treatment used to explore the effectiveness of a "true" treatment. The *placebo effect* is the tendency to feel better if we believe we are being treated with a medication. Expectations about getting better can change treatment outcomes.

Synonyms

mood-stabilizing drugs antimanic drugs

traditional antipsychotic medications first-generation antipsychotic medications, typical antipsychotic medications

atypical antipsychotics second-generation antipsychotic medications

mood-stabilizing drugs Psychotropic medications that minimize the lows of depression and the highs of mania.

antipsychotic drugs Psychotropic medication used in the treatment of psychotic symptoms, such as hallucinations and delusions.

MOOD-STABILIZING DRUGS In Chapter 13, we introduced Ross Szabo, a man who suffers from bipolar disorder. Ross has battled extreme mood swings in his life—the highest highs and the lowest lows. Many people suffering from bipolar disorder find some degree of relief in **mood-stabilizing drugs,** which can minimize the lows of depression and the highs of mania. Lithium, for instance, helps smooth the mood swings of people with bipolar disorder, leveling out the dramatic peaks (mania) and valleys (depression). For this reason, it is sometimes called a "mood normalizer" (Bech, 2006) and has been widely used to treat bipolar disorder for decades. Unlike standard drugs that chemists cobble together in laboratories, this drug is a mineral salt, in other words, a naturally occurring substance. (You can find lithium in the Periodic Table of the Elements—just look for the symbol Li.)

Scientists have yet to determine the cause of bipolar disorder and how its symptoms might be lessened with lithium. But numerous theories exist, some pointing to imbalances in neurotransmitters such as glutamate and serotonin (Cho et al., 2005; Dixon & Hokin, 1998). Lithium also seems to be effective in lowering suicide risk among people with bipolar disorder (Angst, Angst, Gerber-Werder, & Gamma, 2005), who are 20 times more likely than people in the general population to take their own lives (Tondo, Isacsson, & Baldessarini, 2003). Doctors must be very careful when prescribing lithium, monitoring the blood levels of patients who use it. Too small a dose will fall short of controlling bipolar symptoms, whereas one that is too large can be lethal. Even when the amount is just right, mild side effects such as hand tremors, thirst, and nausea may occur (National Institute of Mental Health, 2007).

Anticonvulsant medications are also used to treat bipolar disorder. Originally created to treat seizure disorders, scientists discovered they might also be used as mood stabilizers, and some research suggests that they can reduce the symptoms of mania (Bowden et al., 2000). Unfortunately, certain anticonvulsants may increase the risk of suicide or possible suicide masked as violent death through injury or accident (Patorno et al., 2010). For this reason, the U.S. Food and Drug Administration (USFDA, 2008) requires drug companies to place warnings on their labels.

ANTIPSYCHOTIC DRUGS   The hallucinations and delusions of people with disorders like schizophrenia can be subdued with antipsychotics. **Antipsychotic drugs** are designed to block neurotransmitter receptors. Although it is not entirely clear how neurotransmitters cause the symptoms of schizophrenia, blocking these receptor sites reduces the activity of neurons presumably associated with psychotic symptoms.

Two kinds of medications can be used in these cases: ***traditional antipsychotic medications*** and ***atypical antipsychotics*** (each with about a half-dozen generic drug offshoots). Both types seek to reduce dopamine activity in certain areas of the brain, as dopamine is a neurotransmitter believed to contribute to the psychotic symptoms of schizophrenia and other disorders (Schnider, Guggisberg, Nahum, Gabriel, & Morand, 2010). Antipsychotics accomplish this by acting as dopamine antagonists, meaning they "pose" as dopamine, binding to receptors normally reserved for dopamine (sort of like stealing someone's parking space). By blocking dopamine's receptors, antipsychotic drugs reduce dopamine's excitatory effect on neurons. The main difference between atypical antipsychotics and the traditional variety is that the atypical antipsychotics *also* interfere with neural pathways involving other neurotransmitters, such as serotonin (which is associated with psychotic symptoms as well).

First rolled out in the 1950s, traditional antipsychotics, such as Haldol, made it possible for scores of people to transition out of psychiatric institutions and into society. These new drugs reduced hallucinations and delusions for many patients, but doctors soon realized that they had other, not-so-desirable effects. After taking the drugs for about a year, some patients developed a neurological condition called *tardive dyskinesia,* the symptoms of which include shaking, restlessness, and bizarre grimaces.

These problems were partially solved with the development of the atypical antipsychotics, such as Risperdal (risperidone), which reduce psychotic symptoms and usually do not cause tardive dyskinesia (Correll, Leucht, & Kane, 2004). But there are other potential side effects, such as weight gain, increased risk for Type 2 diabetes, sexual dysfunction, and heart disease (Ücok & Gaebel, 2008). And although these drugs reduce the symptoms in 60–85% of patients, they are not a cure for the disorder.

ANTIANXIETY DRUGS   Anxiety disorders are the second most common class of conditions Dr. Foster encounters on the reservation. Like many impoverished areas, Rosebud has a high rate of trauma (for example, alcohol-associated accidents and homicides). In the United States, the suicide rate among American Indian and Alaska Native youth (ages 10 to 24) exceeds that of all other racial groups. Youth

CONNECTIONS

In **Chapter 2,** we described how drugs influence behavior by changing what is happening in the synapse. *Agonists* increase the normal activity of a neurotransmitter, and *antagonists* block normal neurotransmitter activity. Here we see how psychotropic medications alter activity in the synapse.

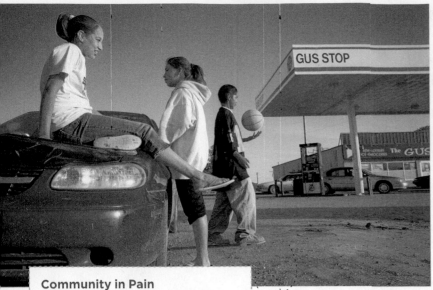

Community in Pain
Teenagers Ariel Farmer (left), Kyla Sharp Butte, and Will Sharp Butte relax at a gas station on the Rosebud Indian Reservation. This photo appeared in a 2007 *New York Times* article about the shocking rates of suicide among reservation youth (Nieves, 2007, June 9). Suicides, homicides, and alcohol-related accidents continue to be a major problem on Rosebud, where the average male life expectancy is just 47 years (White, 2013, April 22). Kevin Moloney/The New York Times/Redux

CONNECTIONS

In **Chapter 4,** we discussed psychoactive drugs. *Physiological dependence* can occur with constant use of some drugs, indicated by *tolerance* and *withdrawal symptoms*. *Psychological dependence* is apparent when a strong desire or need to continue using a substance occurs, but without tolerance or withdrawal symptoms.

You Asked, Dr. Foster Answers

http://qrs.ly/yq3nrea

How might medication impact the effectiveness of psychotherapy?

antianxiety drugs Psychotropic medications used for treating the symptoms of anxiety.

suicides have increased substantially over the last two decades (Dorgan, 2010). Researchers have tried to untangle the complex web of factors responsible for the deeply troubling statistics, but few would question its connection to the centuries of psychological and cultural damage wrought by colonization. Physical and sexual assault by occupying soldiers, destruction of tribal culture and spirituality by three generations of Indian boarding schools, and ongoing marginalization and discrimination—these types of realities do not just fade away. Traumatic incidents like suicides inevitably have witnesses, and those witnesses suffer from what they see and hear. Their pain often manifests itself in the form of anxiety.

Antianxiety drugs are used to treat the symptoms of anxiety and anxiety disorders including panic disorder, social phobia, and generalized anxiety disorder. Most of today's antianxiety medications are *benzodiazepines,* such as Xanax and Ativan, or "minor tranquilizers." These minor tranquilizers are used for a continuum of anxiety, from fear of flying to extreme panic attacks. And since these drugs promote sleep in high doses, they can also be used to treat insomnia. Doctors often prescribe benzodiazepines in combination with other psychotropic medications.

Valium is one of the most commonly used minor tranquilizers, and it was the first psychotropic drug to be used by people who were not necessarily suffering from serious disorders. For most of the 1970s, Valium was so popular among white collar businessmen and women that it came to be called "Executive Excedrin." But then people began to realize how dependent they had become on Valium, both **physically and psychologically,** and its popularity diminished (Barber, 2008). Nevertheless, medications such as Valium and Xanax are still the most commonly abused antianxiety drugs (Phillips, 2013).

A key benefit of benzodiazepines is that they are fast acting. But they are also dangerously addictive, and mixing them with alcohol can produce a lethal cocktail. Benzodiazepines ease anxiety by enhancing the effect of the neurotransmitter GABA. An inhibitory neurotransmitter, GABA works by decreasing or stopping some neural activity. By giving GABA a boost, these drugs inhibit the firing of neurons that normally induce anxiety reactions.

PSYCHOTROPIC MEDICATION PLUS PSYCHOTHERAPY Psychotropic medications have helped countless people get back on their feet and enjoy life, but many believe that drugs alone don't produce the best long-term outcomes. Ideally, medications should be taken in conjunction with psychotherapy. With therapy, Dr. Foster says, "The person feels greater self-efficacy. They're not relying on a pill to manage depression."

Indeed, studies suggest that psychotropic drugs are most effective when used alongside psychotherapy. Researchers have shown that combining medication with an integrative approach to psychotherapy, including cognitive, behavioral, and psychodynamic perspectives, reduces major depressive symptoms faster than either approach alone (Manber et al., 2008).

Another key point to remember: Medications affect people in different ways. An antidepressant that works for one person may have no effect on another; this is also the case for side effects. We metabolize (break down) drugs at different rates,

Sending neuron

Normal neurotransmitter reuptake

Synaptic gap

Receptor

Receiving neuron

SSRI

Serotonin

CHEMICAL:
Psychotropic Medications

Drug therapies, which alter the brain's chemistry, are the most commonly prescribed biomedical treatment. Each works to influence neurotransmitters thought to be associated with the disorders the drugs are designed to treat. This illustration shows the action of a class of antidepressants known as selective serotonin reuptake inhibitors (SSRIs).

In normal communication between neurons, neurotransmitters released into the synaptic gap bind to the receiving neuron, sending a message. Excess neurotransmitters are reabsorbed.

As indicated by their name, SSRIs inhibit the reuptake of the neurotransmitter serotonin. Allowed to remain longer in the synapse, serotonin can achieve a greater effect.

Biomedical Therapies

Biomedical therapies use physical interventions to treat psychological disorders. These therapies can be categorized according to the method by which they influence the brain's functioning: chemical, electrical, or structural.

Wire coil

Pulsed magnetic field

Positioning frame

Maximum field depth

Magnetic field

Activated neurons

Resting neurons

STRUCTURAL: Neurosurgery

Modern surgical techniques are able to target a very precise area of the brain known to be directly involved in the condition being treated. For example, the black circles on these scans mark areas typically targeted for a form of surgery known as anterior cingulotomy, which has been shown to reduce symptoms in patients suffering severe cases of major depression (Steele, Christmas, Elijamel, & Matthews, 2008). Using radio frequencies emitted from a 6-millimeter probe, the surgeon destroys part of the anterior cingulate cortex, an area known to be associated with emotions (Faria, 2013).

ELECTRICAL: Brain Stimulation

Brain stimulation techniques can be used to relieve symptoms by affecting the electrical activity of the brain. Research on electroconvulsive therapy found an 86% remission rate for those with severe major depression (Kellner et al., 2006). Repetitive transcranial magnetic stimulation (rTMS), shown here, is a noninvasive procedure. A coil pulses a magnetic field that passes painlessly through scalp and bone, penetrating just to the outer cortex. The field induces electric current in nearby neurons, activating targeted regions in the brain (George, 2003).

which means dosages must be assessed on a case-by-case basis. To complicate matters further, many people take multiple medications at once, and some drugs interact in harmful ways.

When Drugs Aren't Enough: The Other Biomedical Therapies

As you likely have guessed from this section, psychotropic drugs are not a cure-all. Sometimes symptoms of psychological disorders do not improve with medication. In these extreme cases, there are other biomedical options. For example, repetitive transcranial magnetic stimulation (rTMS) appears to be effective in treating symptoms of depression and some types of hallucinations. With rTMS, electromagnetic coils are put on (or above) a person's head, directing brief electrical current into a particular area of the brain (Slotema, Blom, Hoek, & Sommer, 2010). Another technique under investigation is deep brain stimulation, which involves implanting a device that supplies weak electrical stimulation to specific areas of the brain thought to be linked to depression (Kennedy et al., 2011; Schlaepfer, Bewernick, Kayser, Mädler, & Coenen, 2013). These new techniques show great promise, but more research is required to determine their long-term impact.

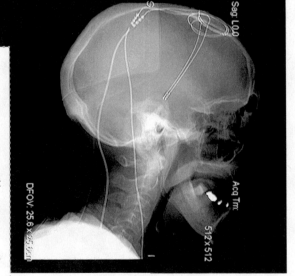

Stimulate the Brain
An X-ray image of a person undergoing deep brain stimulation reveals two electrodes implanted in the brain—one in each hemisphere. These electrodes send electrical impulses through certain neural networks, inducing changes that may lead to reduced symptoms. This treatment has produced promising results in patients with depression, but further research is needed to identify its long-term effects (Kennedy et al., 2011). Medical Body Scans/Science Source

ELECTROCONVULSIVE THERAPY   One biomedical approach that essentially causes seizures in the brain is **electroconvulsive therapy (ECT),** which is used with severely depressed people who have not responded to psychotropic medications or psychotherapy. If you've ever seen ECT or "shock therapy" portrayed in movies, you might think it's a barbaric form of abuse. Truth be told, ECT was a brutal and overly used treatment in the mid-20th century (Glass, 2001; Smith, 2001). Doctors jolted patients (in some cases a dozen times a day) with powerful currents, creating seizures violent enough to break bones and erase weeks or months of memories (Smith, 2001). Today, ECT is much more humane, administered according to guidelines developed by the American Psychiatric Association (2001). Patients take painkillers and muscle relaxants before the treatment, and general anesthesia can be used during the procedure. Furthermore, the electrical currents are weaker, inducing seizures only in the brain. Patients in the United States typically get three treatments per week for up to a month (Glass, 2001).

Scientists don't know exactly how ECT reduces the symptoms of depression, although a variety of theories have been proposed (Cyrzyk, 2013). And despite its enduring "bad rap," ECT can be an effective treatment for depression, bipolar disorder, and schizophrenia for people who haven't responded well to psychotherapy or drugs (Baker, 2009, January 8; Glass, 2001). Yet in the United States, the number of patients admitted to a hospital for ECT treatment in 2009 was 7.2 per 100,000 adults, which represented a substantial decline over the years (Case et al., 2013). The major downside of ECT is its tendency to induce confusion and memory loss,

Synonyms

neurosurgery psychosurgery, brain surgery

electroconvulsive therapy (ECT) A biomedical treatment of severe depression that induces seizures in the brain through electrical currents.

neurosurgery A biomedical therapy that involves the destruction of some portion of the brain or connections between different areas of the brain.

including **anterograde and retrograde amnesias** (APA, 2001; Fink & Taylor, 2007; Read & Bentall, 2010).

NEUROSURGERY   One extreme option for patients who don't show substantial improvement with psychotherapy or psychotropic drugs is **neurosurgery,** which destroys some portion of the brain or connections between different areas of the brain. Like ECT, neurosurgery is tarnished by an unethical past. During the 1930s, 1940s, and 1950s, doctors performed *prefrontal lobotomies,* destroying part of the frontal lobes or disconnecting them from lower areas of the brain (Kucharski, 1984). But lobotomy outcomes were mixed at best. These operations can lead to severe side effects, including permanent impairments to everyday functioning. In the past, this procedure had no precision, often resulting in permanent personality changes and diminished function. The consequences of lobotomy were often worse than the disorders they aimed to fix. The popularity of the surgery plummeted in the 1950s when the first-generation antipsychotics were introduced, offering a safer alternative to psychosurgery (Mashour, Walker, & Martuza, 2005).

Brain surgeries are only used to treat psychological disorders as a last resort, and they are far more precise than the archaic lobotomy. Surgeons home in on a small target, destroying only tiny tracts of tissue. One of these surgeries has been a lifesaver for a select few suffering from a severe, drug-resistant form of obsessive-compulsive disorder (OCD), but the precise effects have yet to be determined (Mashour et al., 2005). People suffering from severe seizure disorders sometimes undergo **split-brain operations**—the surgical disconnection of the right and left hemispheres. With the corpus callosum severed, the two hemispheres are disconnected, preventing the spread of electrical storms responsible for seizures. These more invasive biomedical therapies are seldom used, but they can make a difference in the quality of life for some individuals.

TAKING STOCK: AN APPRAISAL OF BIOMEDICAL THERAPY   Medications and other biomedical treatments can reduce the symptoms of major psychological disorders. In fact, psychotropic drugs work so well that their introduction led to the deinstitutionalization of thousands of people. But it would be a mistake to think of these biological interventions as a cure-all, as this deemphasizes the importance of the other two components of the biopsychosocial model: psychological and social factors. Furthermore, research on the long-term outcomes of many of these treatments remains inconclusive.

CONNECTIONS

In **Chapter 6,** we discussed *amnesia,* which is memory loss resulting from physical or psychological conditions. *Retrograde amnesia* is the inability to access old memories; *anterograde amnesia* is the inability to make new memories. ECT can cause these types of amnesia, which is one reason the American Psychiatric Association developed guidelines for this treatment (2001).

CONNECTIONS

In **Chapter 2,** we discussed the use of the *split-brain operation* to treat drug-resistant seizures. When the hemispheres are disconnected, researchers can study them separately to explore their unique capabilities. People who undergo this operation have fewer seizures, and can have normal cognitive abilities and no obvious changes in temperament or personality traits.

⚫✓⚫⚫   **show what you know**

1. A young man is taking psychotropic medications for major depression, but the drugs do not seem to be alleviating his symptoms. Which of the following biomedical approaches might his psychiatrist try next?
   a. split-brain operation
   b. tardive dyskinesia
   c. prefrontal lobotomy
   d. electroconvulsive therapy

2. Psychotropic drugs can be divided into four categories, including mood-stabilizing, antipsychotic, antianxiety drugs, and
   a. mood normalizers.
   b. antidepressants.
   c. antagonists.
   d. atypical antipsychotics.

3. One treatment option used for individuals who do not show substantial improvement with psychotherapy or psychotropic drugs is _____, which destroys some portion of the brain or connections between different areas of the brain.

4. How do biomedical interventions differ from psychotherapy? Compare their goals.

✓ CHECK YOUR ANSWERS IN APPENDIX C.

Psychotherapy Today

> **LO 10** Describe how culture interacts with the therapy process.

► Culture Conscious
A Canadian psychologist talks with residents of a displaced persons camp in Port-au-Prince, Haiti. This photo was taken in December 2010, about a year after the country suffered a devastating earthquake. Psychologists must always be mindful of cultural factors that may come into play during therapy. AP Photo/The Canadian Press, Paul Chiasson

WHEN TO LISTEN, WHEN TO TALK   One of the challenges of providing therapy in a country like the United States, where ethnic minorities comprise over a third of the population (Yen, 2012, May 18), is meeting the needs of clients from vastly different cultures. A therapist living in a diverse city like Houston or San Francisco may serve clients from multiple cultures in a single week, and each of those cultures has its own set of social norms dictating when to be quiet, when to speak, and how to express oneself.

For Dr. Foster, this part of the job is relatively straightforward. All his clients are Northern Plains Indians, which means they follow similar social rules. Because Dr. Foster belongs to this culture too, its norms are second nature to him. He has come to expect, for example, that a young Lakota client will not begin talking until he, the therapist, has spoken first. Dr. Foster is their elder, and elders are shown deference. Thus, to make a younger client feel more comfortable, he might begin a session by talking for 3 or 4 minutes. Once the client does open up, he limits his verbal and nonverbal feedback, sitting quietly and avoiding eye contact. In mainstream American culture, people continuously respond to each other with facial animation and filler words like "wow" and "uh-huh," but the Lakota find this ongoing feedback intrusive. "I might even shut my eyes so they're not feeling influenced by my responses," Dr. Foster says. "I'm not going to respond to what they're telling me, out of respect to their story."

Another facet of Lakota communication—one that often eludes therapists from outside the culture—is the tendency to pause for long periods in the middle of a conversation. "In the Northern Plains, silence is pretty comfortable for us," Dr. Foster says, "but our silences are active silences. They're not passive." If he poses the question, "How are you doing?" a client might take 20 to 30 seconds to respond. "They are not going to answer me on a superficial social level," he explains. "They're going to go inside"—meaning really take the time to consider the question and formulate an answer (*How am I doing?*). These long pauses make some non-Indians very uncomfortable, according to Dr. Foster. "I've found that an outside provider will feel awkward, will start talking within 3 to 5 seconds," he adds. "The client will feel that they never have a chance to speak, and they'll leave frustrated because the person wouldn't be quiet [and] listen."

across the WORLD

Know Thy Client

Clearly, it is important for a therapist to know the cultural context in which he works. But does that mean therapists and clients should be matched according to race, ethnicity, or gender? Some clients feel more comfortable discussing private thoughts and feelings with a therapist who shares their experience—someone who knows firsthand how it feels to be, say, a Mexican American woman or a Japanese American man. A study in Los Angeles County found that non-English-speaking Mexican and Asian Americans were more likely to stick with and benefit from therapy when matched with a therapist of the same ethnicity and native language (Sue, Fujino, Hu, Takeuchi, & Zane, 1991). Working with a therapist of the same background may be helpful, but it is not essential.

When the therapist and client do come from different worlds, it is the therapist's job to get in touch with the client's unique perspective. That includes being respectful of cultural norms. Western therapists working in India or sub-Saharan Africa, for example, may find that clients are unfamiliar with psychotherapy and reluctant to discuss personal matters (Bolton et al., 2007; Manickam, 2010). Therapists must also be sensitive to the many forms of prejudice and discrimination that people can experience.

Within any group, there is vast variation from one individual to the next, but cultural themes do emerge. The Sioux and Blackfeet Indians, for example, are very relationship-oriented. "What kind of car you drive or how nice your home is, and so forth, is not even important," Dr. Foster says. "Relationships matter." Some therapists working with American Indian groups report that entire families may show up at sessions to express support for the client (Prochaska & Norcross, 2014). Similarly, Latino American cultures place a high value on family, often prioritizing relationships with relatives over individual needs (Romero, Cuéllar, & Roberts, 2000). These groups tend to be more collectivist, or community-minded, whereas European American cultures tend to place a high premium on individualism (Oyserman, Coon, & Kemmelmeier, 2002).

Immigrant populations face their own set of challenges. Men often have a difficult time adjusting to the declining social status and income that comes with moving to a new country. Women tend to fare better, adapting to the new culture and finding jobs more quickly, which can lead to tension between spouses (Prochaska & Norcross, 2014). Keep in mind that these are only general trends; assuming they apply to an entire population promotes stereotyping.

SHOULD THERAPISTS AND CLIENTS BE MATCHED IN TERMS OF RACE, ETHNICITY, OR GENDER?

This brings us to one of the key themes of the chapter: When it comes to psychological treatment, there is no "one-size-fits-all." Every client has a unique story and a singular set of psychological needs. Responding to the needs of the person—her culture, religious beliefs, and unique personal qualities—is one of the keys to successful therapy (Lakes, Lopez, & Garro, 2006; Norcross & Wampold, 2011). 🌐➡

Does Psychotherapy Work?

LO 11 Summarize the effectiveness of psychotherapy.

Now that we have familiarized ourselves with the strengths and weaknesses of various therapeutic approaches, let's direct our attention to overall outcomes. How effective is psychotherapy in general? This question is not easily answered, partly because therapeutic "success" is so difficult to quantify. What constitutes success in one therapy context may not be the same in another. And for therapists trying to measure the efficacy of methods they use, eliminating bias can be very challenging.

That being said, there is solid evidence suggesting that therapy usually "works," especially if it is long-term. In one large study investigating the effects of psychotherapy, all therapeutic approaches performed equally well across all disorders. But there is one caveat: Individuals who were limited by their insurance companies in terms of therapist choice and duration of treatment did not see the same improvement as those who were less restricted by their insurance (Seligman, 1995). Another important finding is that people who start therapy but then quit tend to experience less successful outcomes (Swift & Greenberg, 2012). As such, around 50% of clients show "clinically significant improvement" after 21 psychotherapy sessions, whereas some 75% show the same degree of improvement after twice that many sessions (Lambert, Hansen, & Finch, 2001). Given the many types of therapeutic approaches, the uniqueness of the client, and the variety of therapists, it is challenging to identify an approach that works best for every client (Pope & Wedding, 2014). But we can say this with relative confidence: Psychotherapy is "cost-effective, reduces disability, morbidity and mortality, improves work functioning, decreases the use of psychiatric hospitalization, and . . . leads to reduction in unnecessary use of medical and surgical services" (APA, 2012a, p. 2).

I Think I Need Help. What Should I Do?

If you suspect you or someone you care about is suffering from a psychological disorder or needs support coping with a divorce, death, or major life change, do not hesitate to seek professional help. The first step is figuring out what kind of therapy will work (individual, family, group, and so on). Then there is the issue of cost: Therapy can be expensive. These days, one 60-minute therapy session can cost anywhere from $80 to $250 (or more, believe it or not). If you are a student at a college or university, however, your student fees may cover services at a student counseling center.

Many people have health insurance that helps pay for medication and psychotherapy. In 2010 the Mental Health Parity and Addiction Equity Act (MHPAEA) took effect, requiring all group health insurance plans (with 50 employees or more) to provide mental health treatment benefits as part of their insurance plan—with benefits equal to those provided for medical treatment. Essentially, this means that mental health problems merit the same treatment benefits as physical health problems. Co-payments must be the same, limits on treatment must be the same, and so on. If your insurance plan does not restrict the number of times you can see your family physician, it also cannot limit the number of visits you have with a psychologist (APA, 2010a). For those without insurance, community-based mental health centers provide quality care to all in need, often with a sliding scale for fees.

The next step is finding the right therapist, that is, the right *qualified* therapist. Helping others manage their mental health issues is a tremendous responsibility that only licensed professionals should take on. But who exactly meets the criteria for a "qualified professional"? It depends on where you live. Different states have different licensing requirements, and because these requirements vary from state to state, we encourage you to verify the standing of a therapist's license with your state's Department of Regulatory Agencies. The pool of potential therapists might include clinical psychologists with PhDs or PsyDs, counseling psychologists, individuals with EdDs, psychiatrists, psychiatric nurses, social workers, marriage and family therapists, pastoral counselors, and more. (See Appendix B for more information about education and careers in psychology.) If you don't seek psychological help from a trained and certified professional in person, you should be very cautious about seeking assistance online.

Nonstandard Treatment: Self-Help and e-Therapy

Type "psychology" or "self-help" into the search engine of Amazon.com, and you will come across thousands of books promising to eliminate your stress, boost your self-esteem, and help you beat depression. Although some self-help books contain valuable information, others are packed with claims that have little or no scientific basis. Keep an open mind, but approach these resources with skepticism, especially when it comes to the research that authors cite. As you have learned, determining the effect of therapy is a difficult business, even when studies are impeccably designed. Reader beware.

Victoria Roberts/
The New Yorker Collection

e-therapy A category of treatment that utilizes the Internet to provide support and therapy.

► **LO 12** Evaluate the strengths and weaknesses of online psychotherapy.

ONLINE PSYCHOTHERAPY With more people gaining access to the Internet and more therapists trying to specialize and make themselves marketable, online therapies are multiplying. A relative newcomer to the treatment world, **e-therapy** can mean anything from email communication between client and therapist to real-time sessions via a webcam. Some approaches include a hybrid version of online and face-to-face sessions, whereas others offer virtual support through chat rooms. These digital tools are valuable for serving rural areas and providing services to those who would otherwise have no access. Videoconferencing is a useful supplement to regular therapy, particularly for consultation and supervision. But online psychotherapy and telehealth raise many concerns, including licensing and privacy issues, problems with nonverbal cues, and difficulty developing therapeutic relationships (Barak, Hen, Boniel-Nissim, & Shapira, 2008; Maheu, Pulier, McMenamin, & Posen, 2012; Sucala et al., 2012).

While we are on the topic of the Internet, we cannot resist a tie-in to social media. What role do Facebook, LinkedIn, and other types of social media play in the lives of therapists and their clients?

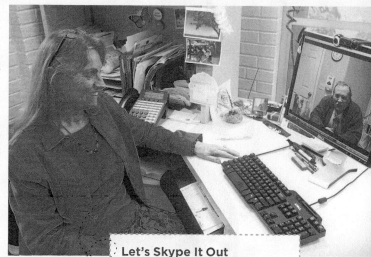

Let's Skype It Out
Mental health nurse practitioner Cassandra Donlon chats with a client via computer at the Roseburg, Oregon, Veterans Affairs Medical Center. With online technologies such as Skype and Google Hangouts, therapists can conduct sessions with clients on the opposite side of the globe. Sandy Huffaker/The New York Times/Redux

SOCIAL MEDIA and psychology

Therapist or Friend?

Imagine that you are the psychotherapist serving a small community college. You talk to students about their deepest fears and conflicts. They talk to you about their mothers, fathers, lovers, and foes. In some respects, you know these students better than their closest friends do. But your clients are not your buddies. They are your clients. So what do you say when a client asks you to become a friend on Facebook, a professional contact on LinkedIn, or a follower on Twitter?

Our answer to that question is a definitive no. The relationship between therapist and client should remain a professional one, both online and offline. But that doesn't mean that social media has no place in the mental health field. Psychologists are among the many professionals using social media to connect with colleagues and market their services to potential clients. They may be avid Twitter users, tweeting their latest musings about current events and everyday life. Social media may even come in handy for therapy itself. Kolmes (2012) offered the example of a client with public speaking anxiety who shows his therapist a video of himself giving a speech.

But along with new opportunities come new risks. Psychologists who use social media to communicate with colleagues, for instance, may inadvertently compromise confidentiality in seeking advice about how to tailor therapy for a particular client. (As you well know, what's said online stays online.) Others may go online to investigate clients' statements about themselves (*He claims to have 400 Facebook friends; let me just take a peek and confirm;* Kolmes, 2012).

DOES FACEBOOK HAVE A PLACE IN THERAPY?

As you can see, the emergence of social media presents new challenges and new opportunities for therapists. This is an area in which we would like to see more research. Stay tuned. . . .

Dr. Dan Foster with his wife, Dr. Becky Foster.

Laura Lichti

top: WHF/Worth Archive;
bottom; Lee Bernhard

PASSIONATE PROVIDERS Before wrapping up, we thought you might like to know what Dr. Dan Foster and Laura Lichti are doing these days. Dr. Foster is as busy as ever, working with two other psychologists, one case manager, and one discharge manager to provide mental health services to Rosebud's 13,000 residents. In addition to working up to 70 hours per week, he and his wife Becky (also a doctorate-level psychologist) have seven adopted children, five of whom are affected by fetal alcohol spectrum disorders (FASDs). Dan doesn't get more than 5 or 6 hours of sleep at night, but he seems to have a limitless supply of energy and optimism.

It's been a major period of change for Laura, who began working as a behavior therapist for people with developmental disabilities. On top of her new job, Laura fulfilled the requirements to become registered in play therapy, a type of treatment that uses natural play to help clients—primarily children—communicate their thoughts and emotions. She also launched her own private practice, which focuses on grief counseling for people of all ages. "It's been a busy year," Laura says, "and I continue to love the work I do!"

---

show what you know

1. A large study in Los Angeles County found that non-English-speaking Asian and Mexican Americans were _____ likely to stick with and benefit from therapy when matched with a therapist of _____ ethnicity and native language.

   a. less; the same
   b. more; the same
   c. more; a different
   d. equally; a different

2. E-therapy is a relatively new approach to helping people with psychological problems or disorders. It varies in terms of how much and what type of contact the "client" has with a "therapist." Concerns regarding online psychotherapy include _____.

3. If you were trying to convince a friend that treatment for psychological disorders does work for many groups of people, how would you summarize the effectiveness of psychotherapy? What would you say about the role of culture in its outcome?

✓ CHECK YOUR ANSWERS IN APPENDIX C.

---

(14) summary of concepts

LO 1 Outline the history of the treatment of psychological disorders. (p. 586)

One theory suggests that during the Stone Age, trephination, in which holes were drilled through the skull, was used to open up the skull to allow evil spirits to exit the body. Pinel was horrified by the conditions of asylums in Paris. He removed the inmates' chains and insisted they be treated more humanely. In the mid- to late 1800s, Dix supported the "mental hygiene movement," a campaign to reform asylums in America. Appalled by the conditions she witnessed in "mental" institutions, Dix helped establish and upgrade many state mental hospitals. A movement to reduce the so-

cial isolation of people with psychological disorders, deinstitutionalization resulted in patients integrating into the community.

LO 2 Discuss how the main approaches to therapy differ and identify their common goal. (p. 588)

Insight therapies include psychoanalysis, psychodynamic therapy, and humanistic therapy, which aim to increase awareness of self and the environment. Behavior therapies focus on behavioral change, with the belief that the key to resolving problems is not understanding their origins, but changing the thoughts and behaviors that precede them. Biomedical therapy targets the biological basis of disorders, often using medications. All these approaches share a common goal: They aim to reduce symptoms and increase the quality of life for individuals, whether they seek help for debilitating psychological disorders or simply want to lead happier lives.

LO 3 Describe how psychoanalysis differs from psychodynamic therapy. (p. 591)

Psychoanalysis, the first formal system of psychotherapy, attempts to increase awareness of unconscious conflicts, making it possible to address and work through them. The therapist's goal is to uncover these unconscious conflicts. Psychodynamic therapy is an updated form of psychoanalysis; it incorporates many of Freud's core themes, including the notion that personality characteristics and behavior problems often can be traced to unconscious conflicts. With psychodynamic therapy, therapists see clients once a week for several months rather than many times a week for years. And instead of sitting quietly off to the side, therapists sit face-to-face and engage clients in a two-way dialogue.

LO 4 Explain the concepts that form the basis of humanistic therapy. (p. 593)

Humanistic therapy concentrates on the positive aspects of human nature: our powerful desires to form close relationships, treat others with warmth and empathy, and grow as individuals. Humanistic therapists concentrate on current problems and the everyday factors that may contribute to them. Instead of digging up unconscious thoughts and feelings, humanistic therapy emphasizes conscious experience.

LO 5 Summarize person-centered therapy. (p. 594)

Person-centered therapy focuses on achieving one's full potential. The focus is not therapeutic techniques, but rather creating a warm and accepting client–therapist relationship using a nondirective approach. Sitting face-to-face with the client, the therapist's main job is to "be there" for the client through empathy, unconditional positive regard, genuineness, and active listening, all important components of building a therapeutic alliance. The main goal of treatment is to reduce the incongruence between the ideal self and the real self.

LO 6 Describe the concepts that underlie behavior therapy. (p. 596)

Using the learning principles of classical conditioning, operant conditioning, and observational learning, behavior therapy aims to replace maladaptive behaviors with more adaptive behaviors. It incorporates a variety of techniques, including exposure therapy, aversion therapy, systematic desensitization, and behavior modification. Behavior ther-

apy covers a broad range of treatment approaches, and focuses on observable behaviors in the present.

LO 7 Outline the concepts of cognitive therapy. (p. 601)

The goal of cognitive therapy is to identify potentially maladaptive thinking and help individuals change the way they view the world and relationships. Aaron Beck believed patterns of automatic thoughts and cognitive distortions, such as overgeneralization (thinking that self-contained events will have major repercussions in life), are at the root of psychological disturbances. The aim of cognitive therapy is to help clients recognize and challenge cognitive distortions and illogical thought in short-term, action-oriented, and homework-intensive therapy sessions. Albert Ellis created rational-emotive behavior therapy (REBT), another form of cognitive therapy, to help people identify their irrational or illogical thoughts and convert them into rational ones.

LO 8 Identify the benefits and challenges of group therapy. (p. 604)

Some of group therapy's benefits include cost-effectiveness, identification with others, accountability, support, encouragement, and a sense of hope. Challenges include potential conflict among group members and discomfort in expressing oneself in the presence of others. But such feelings are not necessarily bad when it comes to therapy (group or otherwise), because they often motivate people to reevaluate how they interact with others, and perhaps try new approaches.

LO 9 Compare and contrast biomedical interventions and identify their common goal. (p. 607)

Psychopharmacology is the scientific study of how psychotropic medications alter perception, mood, behavior, and other aspects of psychological functioning. Psychotropic drugs include antidepressant, mood-stabilizing, antipsychotic, and antianxiety drugs. When severe symptoms do not improve with medication and psychotherapy, other biomedical options are available: electroconvulsive therapy (ECT), which causes seizures in the brain, for cases of severe depression; and neurosurgery, which destroys some portion of the brain or connections between different areas of the brain, only as a last resort. The common goal of biomedical interventions is to treat the biological basis of psychological disorders through physical interventions.

LO 10 Describe how culture interacts with the therapy process. (p. 614)

One challenge of providing therapy is to meet the needs of clients from vastly different cultures. Within any group, there is variation from one individual to the next, but it is still necessary for therapists to know the cultural context in which they work. The therapist must keep in mind the client's cultural experience. This includes being respectful of cultural norms and sensitive to the many forms of prejudice and discrimination that people can experience. Every client has a unique story and a singular set of psychological needs. Responding to those needs and determining which approach will be most effective are key to successful therapy.

LO 11 Summarize the effectiveness of psychotherapy. (p. 615)

In general, therapy "works," especially if it is long-term. All approaches to psychotherapy perform equally well across all disorders. But individuals who are limited by their insurance companies in terms of their choice of therapists and how long they can attend therapy do not see the same improvement as those who are less restricted by their insurance. In addition, people who start therapy but then decide to stop it experience less successful outcomes. The Mental Health Parity and Addiction Equity Act of 2010 requires group health insurance plans to provide mental health treatment benefits as part of their insurance plan—with benefits equal to those provided for medical treatment.

LO 12 Evaluate the strengths and weaknesses of online psychotherapy. (p. 617)

As more people gain access to the Internet and as more therapists try to specialize and make themselves marketable, online therapies have multiplied. E-therapy can mean anything from an email communication between client and therapist to real-time sessions via a webcam. These digital tools are valuable for serving rural areas and providing services to those who would otherwise have no access. Videoconferencing is useful for consultation and supervision. However, online psychotherapy raises many concerns, including licensing and privacy issues, lack of nonverbal cues, and potential problems with developing therapeutic relationships

key terms

active listening, p. 595
antianxiety drugs, p. 610
antidepressant drugs, p. 607
antipsychotic drugs, p. 609
aversion therapy, p. 598
behavior modification, p. 598
behavior therapy, p. 588
biomedical therapy, p. 588
cognitive therapy, p. 601
cognitive behavioral therapy, p. 603
deinstitutionalization, p. 587

eclectic approach to therapy, p. 590
electroconvulsive therapy (ECT), p. 612
empathy, p. 595
e-therapy, p. 617
exposure, p. 596
family therapy, p. 605
free association, p. 592
genuineness, p. 595
humanistic therapy, p. 594
insight therapies, p. 588

interpretation, p. 592
mood-stabilizing drugs, p. 608
neurosurgery, p. 613
nondirective, p. 594
overgeneralization, p. 602
person-centered therapy, p. 594
psychoanalysis, p. 591
psychodynamic therapy, p. 593
psychotherapy, p. 588

rational emotive behavior therapy (REBT), p. 603
resistance, p. 592
systematic desensitization, p. 598
therapeutic alliance, p. 595
token economy, p. 600
transference, p. 592

TEST PREP are you ready?

1. Which of the following changes did Pinel introduce when he reformed the treatment of individuals with psychological disorders?
   a. reintroduced trephination
   b. reintegrated inmates into society
   c. removed the inmates' chains and listened to their complaints
   d. built new hospitals for the insane

2. Although most therapies share the common goal of reducing symptoms and increasing quality of life, they do this in various ways. One dimension in which they may differ is theoretical perspective. Psychotherapists who aim to increase awareness of self and the environment tend to use
   a. biomedical therapy.   c. insight therapy.
   b. behavior therapy.   d. deinstitutionalization.

3. Free association and interpretation are used by _____ in their treatment of patients.
   a. psychoanalysts
   b. humanists
   c. behaviorists
   d. cognitive therapists

4. What are some of the weaknesses of Freud's theories?
   a. It is evidence-based
   b. It is difficult to test through experimentation
   c. It is client-directed
   d. It focuses on the present

5. A friend told you about his therapist, who is nondirective, uses active listening, and shows empathy and unconditional positive regard. It sounds as if your friend's therapist is conducting
   a. cognitive therapy.
   b. behavior therapy.
   c. psychoanalysis.
   d. person-centered therapy.

6. Systematic desensitization uses _____ that represent(s) a gradual increase in a client's anxiety.
   a. hierarchies
   b. token economies
   c. behavior modification
   d. free association

7. Which of the following statements would not be among Beck's collection of cognitive errors?
   a. My friend stole from me; therefore, everyone will steal from me.
   b. Getting fired once does not mean my career is over.
   c. I forgot to vote; that's why the president lost.
   d. My hairdresser added $20 to my Visa charge. You can't trust salons.

8. The key advantage of behavior therapy is that it
   a. tends to work quickly.
   b. focuses on changing innate behaviors.
   c. addresses global issues arising from personality disorders.
   d. brings about changes on the inside.

9. Which of the following claims about group therapy is true?
   a. It generally costs twice as much as one-on-one therapy.
   b. Everyone feels comfortable sharing their troubles with a group.
   c. Group members avoid pushing others to own up to their mistakes.
   d. Seeing others improve offers hope and inspiration.

10. One specific type of group therapy is _____. The goal is to understand each family member's unique role in an integrated system, often exploring relationship problems rather than symptoms of particular disorders.
    a. flooding
    b. aversion therapy
    c. systematic desensitization
    d. family therapy

11. _____ therapy emphasizes the positive nature of humans. With a focus on the present, it seeks to identify current problems and emphasizes conscious experience.
    a. Psychoanalytic
    b. Rational emotive behavior
    c. Psychodynamic
    d. Humanistic

12. _____ is the scientific study of how medication alters perceptions, moods, behaviors, and other aspects of psychological functioning.
    a. Biomedical therapy
    b. Psychoeducation
    c. Therapeutic alliance
    d. Psychopharmacology

13. Overall, psychotherapy is cost-effective and helps to decrease disability, hospitalization, and problems at work. Which of the following factors seems to reduce its effectiveness?
    a. unlimited number of sessions
    b. limitations on choice of therapist as mandated by a health insurance policy
    c. number of people in therapy session
    d. gender of therapist

14. Electroconvulsive therapy (ECT) is a technique that essentially causes _____ in the brain.
    a. increased activity of neurotransmitters
    b. tardive dyskinesia
    c. seizures
    d. MAO inhibitors

15. One factor a therapist needs to consider is how _____ may interact with the therapy process: whether a client is from a group that is collectivist or one that values individualism.
    a. culture
    b. biomedical interventions
    c. repression
    d. unconscious conflicts

16. Compare cognitive behavioral therapy to insight therapies.

17. Beck identified a collection of common cognitive distortions. Describe two of these distortions and give examples of each.

18. How would a behavior therapist help someone overcome a fear of rats?

19. How does culture influence and interact with the therapeutic process?

20. Describe several strengths and weaknesses of online psychotherapy.

✓ CHECK YOUR ANSWERS IN APPENDIX C.

15

An Introduction to Social Psychology

📁 *Love Story*

Social Cognition

📁 *The Dating Game*

🌱🏠 NATURE AND NURTURE
Why the Attitude?

👁! DIDN'T SEE THAT COMING
Something Doesn't Feel Right

Social Influence

📂 *11 Orphans*

📂 *Boy Soldiers*

Groups and Relationships

📂 *Let's Do This Together*

🌐→ ACROSS THE WORLD
Slackers of the West

📂 *The Bystander Who Refused to Stand By*

Aggression

📁 *The Ultimate Insult*

SA from the pages of
SCIENTIFIC AMERICAN
Following the Crowd

→◄ CONTROVERSIES
The Stanford "Prison"

SA from the pages of
SCIENTIFIC AMERICAN
Rudeness on the Internet

Attraction and Love

💬 SOCIAL MEDIA AND PSYCHOLOGY
Relationships Online

social psychology

An Introduction to Social Psychology

LOVE STORY Prior to 2006, Joe Maggio did not have the best of luck with women. While serving overseas in the military, he had a relationship with a local woman with whom he was not at all compatible. But something beautiful came out of their failed union: a baby girl named Kristina. Joe was awarded full custody, and he returned to Long Island, New York, to begin his life as a single dad. In between work and taking care of his daughter, there was little time for dating. Joe was not the type to frequent bars and nightclubs, and his work as an ice cream truck driver provided few opportunities for meeting other singles. It never seemed to work out with the girlfriends he did manage to date. And as Joe admits, "I had my share of doozies [extraordinarily bad experiences]."

After several years of dating frustrations, everything abruptly changed. Susanne entered the picture. Their first face-to-face meeting was at a Chili's restaurant. Joe and his daughter, then 7 years old, were chatting at a table when Susanne appeared. "The minute she walked in the door on our first date, I honestly felt like I was actually waiting for my wife to have dinner with me and my daughter," Joe says. He remembers exactly how she looked: straight hair, a pink blouse with a butterfly necklace, a black vest, and a pair of blue jeans. As Joe puts it, "Very, very cute."

Instantly at ease, Susanne sat down and began to talk with Joe and Kristina. "It was just kind of relaxed . . . like we had known each other forever," says Susanne, who had encountered her own share of unique individuals before meeting Joe. At 32, she was finished playing games and exploring dead-end relationships. "At this point in my life I was really just looking for somebody

→

623

LEARNING OBJECTIVES

after reading and studying this chapter, you should be able to:

LO 1 Define social psychology and identify how it is different from sociology.

LO 2 Describe social cognition and how we use attributions to explain behavior.

LO 3 Explain how attributions lead to mistakes about the causes of behaviors.

LO 4 Describe social influence and recognize the factors associated with persuasion.

LO 5 Define compliance and explain some of the techniques used to gain it.

LO 6 Evaluate conformity and identify the factors that influence the likelihood of someone conforming.

LO 7 Describe obedience and explain how Stanley Milgram studied it.

LO 8 Recognize the circumstances that influence the occurrence of the bystander effect.

LO 9 Demonstrate an understanding of aggression and identify some of its causes.

LO 10 Recognize how group affiliation influences the development of stereotypes.

LO 11 Compare prosocial behavior and altruism.

LO 12 Identify the three major factors contributing to interpersonal attraction.

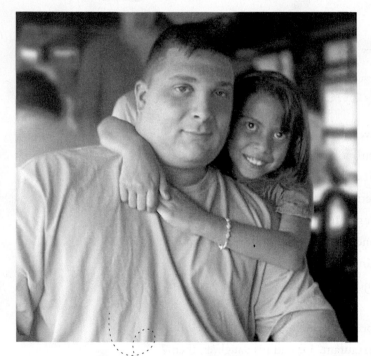

▶ Loving Dad
Before joining Match.com, Joe Maggio was a single father to daughter Kristina. Dating was a challenge, as most of the women Joe met lacked the qualities he desired. Then, with a few clicks and keystrokes, along came Susanne... Joseph Maggio

that wanted to settle down," she offers. Joe seemed so kind, it was hard to believe he was authentic.

After eating dinner and watching *The Pink Panther* at a nearby movie theater ("a child-catered kind of date," as Joe calls it), Joe and Kristina bid Susanne farewell—but only for a matter of hours. The next morning, Joe called Susanne and invited her for a cup of coffee. "We did not leave the local Starbucks until almost seven, eight hours later," he recalls. During that marathon date, Joe and Susanne shared stories about their families and talked about their hopes and dreams. "I didn't want the day to end," says Joe, who then invited Susanne home and made her a dinner of sautéed pork chops, roasted peppers, and potatoes. "I think I kind of won her heart that night."

Joe and Susanne's initial impressions of one another were right on. They were extremely compatible people with similar backgrounds and family values. Both were big fans of cooking, baseball (the Mets), and spending Friday night curled up on the couch watching a movie. Susanne found it attractive that Joe was a single father. And Joe came to love how Susanne treated Kristina like her own daughter, and how Kristina loved her back. You might say Joe and Susanne were perfectly matched. How did they find one another?

What Is Social Psychology?

Joe and Susanne did not meet at a church, a library, or a bar. They did not work in the same office, nor were they introduced by mutual friends. Like a growing number of couples, Joe and Susanne first encountered one another online. They met through a popular Internet dating Web site called Match.com.

Note: Quotations attributed to Julius Achon and Joe and Susanne Maggio are personal communications.

In less than two decades, online dating has gone from being essentially nonexistent to a primary avenue for finding love (**FIGURE 15.1**). Research suggests that the Internet is the second most common way to connect with a potential partner, the first being an introduction by mutual friends (Finkel, Eastwick, Karney, Reis, & Sprecher, 2012). Joe and Susanne met through one of the mainstream dating sites, but there are also highly specialized services to accommodate particular interests. Looking for a vegetarian mate? Try VeggieDate.org. Searching for a farmer to love? Visit FarmersOnly.com. There are even dating sites designed to match people with the same book preferences and food allergies.

Dating Web sites have forever changed the singles' landscape. What other medium allows you to scan and research a database of thousands, if not millions, of potential partners from the comfort of your sofa? How else can you narrow your search to "Asian heterosexual male Democrat between the ages of 30 and 35 in the 85702 zip code who enjoys football" in a matter of seconds? Internet dating has also created a new laboratory for psychologists to study the way people's thoughts, emotions, and behaviors are influenced by others. In other words, it is an emerging topic of research in *social psychology*.

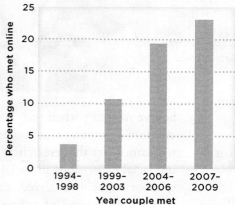

FIGURE 15.1

Nearly 1 in 4 Couples Met Online

In the mid-1990s, only 4 percent of heterosexual couples in the United States met online. More recently, that number has grown to 23 percent. *Source:* Adapted with permission of Blackwell Publishing/SAGE Publications from Finkel, Eastwick, Karney, Reis, & Sprecher (2012).

LO 1   Define social psychology and identify how it is different from sociology.

In every chapter of this book, we have touched on issues relevant to social psychology. Chapter 1, for example, tells the story of 33 Chilean miners trapped in a sweltering, underground hole for more than 2 months. How do you think the social interactions among these men influenced their behaviors, thoughts, and feelings? In Chapter 3, we journeyed into the world of Zoe, Emma, and Sophie, identical deaf and blind triplets. How might the triplets' social behaviors differ from those of children with normal hearing and vision? Then there was Clive Wearing from Chapter 6. How do you suppose Clive's devastating memory loss affects his relationships? Social psychologists strive to answer these types of questions.

Social psychology is the study of human cognition, emotion, and behavior in relation to others. Throughout this text, we have emphasized the importance of the biopsycho*social* perspective, which recognizes the biological, psychological, and social forces underlying human behavior. This chapter focuses on the third aspect of that triad: social forces.

WHAT'S THE DIFFERENCE? SOCIAL PSYCHOLOGY VERSUS SOCIOLOGY

Students often ask how social psychology differs from the field of *sociology*. The answer is simple: Social psychology explores the way individuals behave in relation to others and groups, while sociology examines the groups themselves—their cultures, societies, and subcultures. A social psychologist studying religion might focus on the relationship between congregants and their spiritual leaders. A sociologist would more likely investigate religious practices, rituals, and organizations. Perhaps the most obvious differences lie in the *methods* used to conduct research. Let's take a look at how social psychologists design their experiments.

RESEARCH METHODS IN SOCIAL PSYCHOLOGY   Social psychologists use the same general research methods as other psychologists, but often with an added twist of deception. Deception is sometimes necessary because people do not always

social psychology The study of human cognition, emotion, and behavior in relation to others, including how people behave in social settings.

In the Name of Science
A research *confederate* in Stanley Milgram's classic experiment is strapped to a table and hooked up to electrodes. Participants in this study were led to believe they were administering electrical shocks to the confederate when in reality the confederate was just pretending to be shocked. This allowed the researchers to study how far the participants would go applying the shocks—without anyone actually being hurt. Alexandra Milgram/Alexander Street Press

CONNECTIONS

In **Chapter 1,** we described how participants' and researchers' expectations can influence the results of an experiment. One form of deception used to counter this is the double-blind study, in which neither participants nor researchers administering a treatment know who is getting the real treatment. Participants are told ahead of time they might receive a *placebo.*

CONNECTIONS

In **Chapter 1,** we discussed informed consent and debriefing. *Debriefing* is an ethical component of disclosure in which researchers provide participants with useful information related to the study. In some cases, participants are informed of deception or manipulation they were exposed to in the study, information that couldn't be revealed to them beforehand.

behave naturally when they know they are **being observed.** Some participants try to conform to expectations; others do just the opposite, behaving in ways they believe will contradict the researchers' predictions. Suppose a team of researchers is studying facial expressions in social settings. If participants know that every glance and grimace are being analyzed, they may feel self-conscious and display atypical facial expressions. Instead of telling participants the real focus of the study, researchers might lead them to believe they are participating in a study on, say, problem solving. That way, they can study the behavior of interest (facial expressions in social settings) more naturally.

Social psychology studies often involve *confederates,* who are people secretly working for the researchers. Playing the role of participants, experimenters, or simply bystanders, confederates say what the researchers tell them to say and do what the researchers tell them to do. They are, unknown to the other participants, just part of the researchers' experimental manipulation.

In most cases, the deception is not kept secret forever. Researchers *debrief* their participants at the end of a study or review aspects of the research initially kept under wraps. Even after learning about the deceit, many participants report they are willing to take part in subsequent psychology experiments (Blatchley & O'Brien, 2007). Debriefing is also a time when researchers make sure that participants were not harmed or upset by their involvement in a study. We should note that all psychology research affiliated with colleges and universities must be approved by an Institutional Review Board (IRB) to ensure that no harm will come from participation. This requirement is partly a reaction to early studies involving extreme deception and manipulation—studies that many viewed as dehumanizing and unethical. Psychologists agree that deception is only acceptable if there is no other way to study the topic of interest. We will describe many examples of such research in the upcoming pages, but first let's familiarize ourselves with some of the basic concepts in social psychology.

show what you know

1. _____ studies individuals in relation to others and groups, whereas _____ studies the groups themselves, including cultures and societies.
   a. Sociology; social psychology
   b. Social psychology; sociology
   c. Sociology; a confederate
   d. A confederate; social psychology

2. When a participant has completed his involvement in a research project, generally the researcher will _____ him by discussing aspects of the study and making sure he was not upset or harmed by his involvement.

3. Social psychology research occasionally involves some form of deception that includes a confederate. How is this type of deception different from the use of double-blind studies?

✓ CHECK YOUR ANSWERS IN APPENDIX C.

Social Cognition

THE DATING GAME   The story of Joe and Susanne begins right around Valentine's Day 2006, when Joe decided to sign up for a full membership to Match.com. A couple of days after joining the site, he noticed that an intriguing woman was checking out his profile. Susanne was just returning to the Internet dating scene after breaking off an 8-month relationship with someone she had met online.

While browsing through Match.com, Susanne came across Joe's page. "I thought he was cute," she says. "That was obviously the reason why I originally opened it." Joe was a burly guy with a dynamite smile, and Susanne was drawn to big, teddy bear types. Reading his profile, she was immediately intrigued. "The fact that he was a single parent, you know, kind of piqued my interest," she says. Before long, Joe was checking out Susanne's page, liking what he saw, and he initiated the e-mail exchange that ultimately led to that first date at Chili's.

Attributions

▸ **LO 2**   Describe social cognition and how we use attributions to explain behavior.

Put yourself in Joe or Susanne's position. There you are on Match.com, looking at the profile page of someone you find attractive. On a conscious level, you are tallying up all the interests you have in common and scrutinizing every self-descriptive adjective this person has chosen. There is also some information processing happening **outside of your awareness.** You might not even realize that this person reminds you of someone you know, like your mother or father, and that sense of familiarity makes you more inclined to reach out. Will you contact this person?

Whatever your decision may be, it is very much reliant on **social cognition**—the way you think about others, attend to social information, and use this information in your life, both consciously and unconsciously. **Joe and Susanne** used social cognition in forming first impressions of one another. You use **social cognition** anytime you try to interpret or respond to another person's behavior. Let's take a closer look at two critical facets of social cognition: *attributions* and *attitudes*.

▸ **LO 3**   Explain how attributions lead to mistakes about the causes of behaviors.

TYPES OF ATTRIBUTIONS   Joe and Susanne's courtship did not involve game playing or guesswork. Their relationship has always been fairly open, with Joe rarely wondering what Susanne is thinking and vice versa. This is usually *not* the case with online dating, or any kind of dating for that matter. The "dating game" typically involves a lot of guesswork about the other person's behavior: *Why didn't he call back? What did she mean by that :-) yesterday?* These kinds of questions have relevance for all human relationships, not just the romantic kind. Just think about how much time you spend wondering why people do the things that they do. The "answers" you come up with to resolve these questions are called *attributions*.

Attributions are beliefs we develop to explain human behaviors and characteristics, as well as situations. "Why is my friend in such a bad mood?" you might ask yourself. Your attribution might be, "Maybe he just got some bad news" or "Perhaps he is hungry." When psychologists characterize attributions, they use the term *observer* to identify the person making the attribution, and *actor* to identify the person exhibiting a behavior of interest. If Joe was trying to explain why Susanne had checked out his profile page, then Joe is the observer and Susanne is the actor.

"Thank God we're cute. You only get one chance to make a good impression."

CONNECTIONS

In **Chapter 14,** we described *psychoanalysis,* one goal of which is to increase awareness of unconscious conflicts. Here, we discuss social cognition, and how it can influence behaviors. Therapists can help clients see how some of their choices in social situations might be driven by unconscious social cognitions.

In **Chapter 10,** we reported that there are gender differences in some of the brain networks involved in *social cognition.* Gender is an important variable to consider when evaluating how people think about others and attend to social information.

In **Chapter 7,** we defined *cognition* as the mental activity associated with obtaining, storing, converting, and using knowledge. *Thinking* is a specific type of cognition that involves coming to a decision, forming a belief, or developing an attitude. In this section, we examine how cognition and thinking affect the way we use social information.

---

social cognition The way people think about others, attend to social information, and use this information in their lives, both consciously and unconsciously.

attributions Beliefs one develops to explain human behaviors and characteristics, as well as situations.

ATTRIBUTIONAL DIMENSIONS   There are many types of attributions, and differentiating among them is quite a task. To make things more manageable, psychologists often describe attributions along three dimensions: controllable–uncontrollable, stable–unstable, and internal–external. Let's see how these might apply to attributions relating to Joe and Susanne:

Controllable–uncontrollable dimension: Suppose Susanne had been 15 minutes late to meet Joe at Starbucks. If Joe assumed it happened because she got stuck in unavoidable traffic, we would say he was making an uncontrollable attribution. (As far as he knows, Susanne has no control over the traffic.) If, however, Joe assumed that Susanne's lateness resulted from factors within her control, such as how fast she drove or what time she left her house, then the attribution would be controllable.

Stable–unstable dimension: Why did Joe cook Susanne a delicious dinner of pork chops? Susanne could infer his behavior stems from a longtime interest in cooking. This would be an example of a stable attribution. With stable attributions, the cause is long-lasting. If she thought Joe's behavior resulted from a transient inspiration from watching a really good cooking show, then her attribution would be unstable. With unstable attributions, the cause is temporary.

Internal–external dimension: Why did Joe have trouble meeting nice single women before Susanne entered his life? If it was because there were few single women living in his immediate area, this would be an external attribution, because the cause of the problem resides outside of Joe. External attributions are commonly referred to as **situational attributions,** as the causes reside in the environment. If, however, Joe had trouble meeting women because he was reluctant to attend singles events, this would be an internal attribution—the cause is within Joe. For internal attributions, the cause is located inside the person, such as an illness, skill, or attitude.

Dispositional attributions are a particular type of internal attribution in which the presumed causes are traits or personality characteristics. Here, we refer to a subset of internal attributions that are deep-seated, enduring characteristics, as opposed to those that are more transient, like having the flu. If Joe had trouble meeting other singles because he has a shy, reserved personality (not actually the case, but let's assume for the sake of example), this would be a dispositional attribution.

When people make attributions, they are often *guessing* about the causes of events or behaviors, and this of course leaves plenty of room for error. This is particularly true with situational and dispositional attributions. Let's take a look at four of the most common mistakes (**INFOGRAPHIC 15.1** on page 631).

FUNDAMENTAL ATTRIBUTION ERROR   Suppose you are checking out some profiles on a dating Web site. You see someone cute and reach out with ;-) (a "wink"), but never hear back. If you fall prey to the **fundamental attribution error,** you might automatically assume the person's failure to respond results from her shyness (a dispositional attribution), but the real reason might be that her Internet is down (situational attribution). This is a common tendency; we often think that the cause of other people's behaviors is a characteristic of them (a dispositional attribution) as opposed to the environment (a situational attribution) (Ross, 1977; Ross, Amabile, & Steinmetz, 1977). We easily forget that situational factors can have a powerful effect on behavior, and assume that behaviors are the consequence of a person's disposition (Jones & Harris, 1967). When thinking about what causes or controls behavior, we "underestimate the impact of situational factors and . . . overestimate the role of dispositional factors" (Ross, 1977, p. 183).

Synonym

fundamental attribution error
correspondence bias

situational attribution   A belief that some environmental factor is involved in the cause of an event or activity.

dispositional attribution   A belief that some characteristic of an individual is involved in the cause of a situation, event, or activity.

fundamental attribution error   The tendency to overestimate the degree to which the characteristics of an individual are the cause of an event, and to underestimate the involvement of situational factors.

just-world hypothesis   The tendency to believe the world is a fair place and individuals generally get what they deserve.

self-serving bias   The tendency to attribute successes to personal characteristics and failures to environmental factors.

How do you think this happens? One suggestion is that we have a tendency to make **quick decisions** about others, often by labeling them as being certain types of people. Imagine how dangerous this could be in a medical setting, when doctors and nurses need to make quick choices about treatment. A nurse seeing a patient who has slurred speech, can't walk, and is aggressive might assume he is drunk and an "alcoholic," ignoring other situational factors that might be involved, such as homelessness and severe dehydration (Levett-Jones et al., 2010). Similarly, a doctor might take one look at a patient and decide he is uncooperative, dirty, and just "another homeless hippie," when in fact the patient is on the verge of a diabetic coma. Doctors should be careful not to let negative stereotypes color their diagnoses, and patients and their families should recognize that doctors are not immune to these types of attribution errors (Groopman, 2008).

Another reason people attribute behaviors to dispositions rather than to situations is that they tend to have much more information about themselves than they do about others. Yet we must make do with the information we have—even if that information is biased and based on our own values and belief systems (Callan, Ferguson, & Bindemann, 2013). This is evident in the *just-world hypothesis*.

JUST-WORLD HYPOTHESIS   People who believe the world is a fair place tend to expect that "bad things" happen for a reason. Their thinking is that when someone is "bad," it should be no surprise when things don't go well for him (Riggio & Garcia, 2009). Many people blame the actor in this way by applying the **just-world hypothesis,** which assumes that if someone is suffering, he must have done something to deserve it (Rubin & Peplau, 1975). In one study, researchers told a group of participants about a man who was violent with his wife, slapping and yelling at her. Another group heard about a loving man who gave his wife flowers and frequently made her dinner. Participants who heard about the "bad person" were more likely to predict a bad outcome for him (he will have a "terrible car accident") than those who heard about the "good person" (he will win a "hugely successful business contract") (Callan et al., 2013).

This just-world tendency, to some degree, may result from cultural teachings. Children in Western cultures are taught this concept so that they learn how to behave properly, show respect for authority figures, and delay gratification (Rubin & Peplau, 1975). For example, in the original tale of *Cinderella* (Grimm & Grimm, 1884), doves rest on Cinderella's shoulders prior to her wedding to the Prince. As the bridal party enters and leaves the church, the doves poke out her evil stepsisters' eyes—a punishment for being cruel to Cinderella. Through this tale, children learn that the stepsisters got what they deserved.

How does the just-world belief affect our responses to the fortune or misfortune of others? Would a strong belief in a just world inspire someone to help those living in poverty? Many people would answer yes, because they think of "just" as "fair," and fair as "equality." But a person who relies on the just-world hypothesis would assume the poor are poor because they deserve to be.

SELF-SERVING BIAS   The tendency to attribute one's successes to **internal characteristics** and one's failures to environmental factors is known as the **self-serving bias.** Before meeting Joe, Susanne dated a guy who tended to blame his failures on external circumstances. If he lost his job, it was because the boss never liked him—not because his performance fell short. This "woe is me" attitude annoyed Susanne, who had learned to take responsibility for what happened in her life. As her mother often told her, "You can be a survivor, or you can be a victim." Susanne's ex-boyfriend appears to have suffered from self-serving bias.

CONNECTIONS

In **Chapter 7,** we described *heuristics,* which are used to solve problems and make decisions. But heuristics are not always reliable. Here, we see how the fundamental attribution error can lead to errors in clinical reasoning. Critical thinking takes effort and time, so it is not unusual to depend on cognitive shortcuts.

Left to Die
Esther Grant holds a painting of Brian Sinclair, the man who died of a treatable urinary tract infection after waiting in a Winnipeg emergency room for 34 hours. Why was Sinclair ignored, even after various people in the emergency room approached hospital staff to voice their concern (Kubinec, 2013, September 5)? Perhaps it had something to do with the fact that Sinclair was a homeless, disabled ethnic minority (Fries, 2011, September 23). Using limited information to make assumptions about people can be very risky in a medical setting. Boris Minkevich/Winnipeg Free Press

CONNECTIONS

In **Chapters 11** and **12,** we introduced the concept of *internal locus of control,* which refers to the tendency to feel in control of one's life. People with an internal locus tend to make choices that are better for their health. The *self-serving bias* represents beliefs regarding an internal locus of control for successes.

You might be surprised to learn that therapists can also fall prey to this bias (Murdock, Edwards, & Murdock, 2010). When clients end their psychotherapy earlier than therapists recommend, therapists tend to think the causes are due to the client's situation (lack of finances) or something within the client (resistance to change), as opposed to some factor within themselves (the therapist). But when considering the same situation for another therapist, they tend to identify the opposite pattern, blaming the other therapist for the early termination of therapy.

FALSE CONSENSUS EFFECT   When trying to decipher the causes of other people's behaviors, we overrely on knowledge about ourselves. This can lead to the **false consensus effect,** which is the **tendency to overestimate** the degree to which people think or act like we do (Ross, Greene, & House, 1977). The opposite is also true; when others do not share our thoughts and behaviors, we tend to believe they are acting abnormally or inappropriately. This false consensus effect is evident in our beliefs about everything from celebrities—*Since I love Jeremy Lin, you should, too*—to adolescent substance use—*I like to use drugs, you should, too* (Bui, 2012; Henry, Kobus, & Schoeny, 2011). We seem to make this mistake because we have an overabundance of information about ourselves, and often limited information about others. Struggling to understand those around us, we fill in the gaps with what we know about ourselves.

Attribution errors may lead us astray, but we can minimize their impact by being aware of our tendency to fall back on them. Now it's time to explore another facet of social cognition. Where did you get that attitude?

Attitudes

In the last section, we discussed attributions, the explanations people create to make sense of what they observe in other people and the environment. Attributions play an important role in online dating, but there is a lot more to dating than making inferences about behaviors. For many people, including Joe and Susanne, the purpose of Internet dating is to find someone who shares common values, interests, and lifestyle choices—all variables that are strongly influenced by *attitudes*.

Attitudes are the relatively stable thoughts, feelings, and responses we have toward people, situations, ideas, and things (Ajzen, 2001; Wicker, 1969). Psychologists suggest that attitudes are composed of cognitive, affective, and behavioral components (**FIGURE 15.2** on page 632). The *cognitive* aspect of an attitude refers to your beliefs or ideas about an object, person, or situation. Generally, our attitudes include an emotional evaluation, which is the *affective* component relating to mood or emotion. We often have feelings that are positive or negative regarding objects, people, or situations (Ajzen, 2001). Feelings and beliefs guide the *behavioral* aspect of the attitude,

Errors in Attribution

Attributions are beliefs we develop to explain human behaviors and characteristics, as well as situations. We can explain behaviors in many ways, but social psychologists often compare explanations based on traits or personality characteristics (dispositional attributions) to explanations based on external situations (situational attributions). But as we seek to explain events and behaviors, we tend to make predictable errors, making the wrong assumption about why someone is behaving in a certain way. Let's look at four of the most common types of errors in attribution.

Fundamental attribution error

Observer tends to think actor's behavior is caused by internal characteristics, ignoring the role of the situation.

That waiter is so clumsy!

Observer ignores external circumstances, such as a slippery floor.

Actor   Observer

Just-world hypothesis

Observer tends to think people get what they deserve.

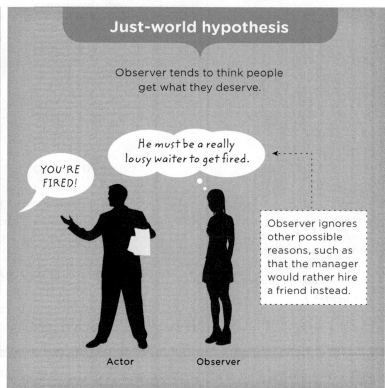

YOU'RE FIRED!

He must be a really lousy waiter to get fired.

Observer ignores other possible reasons, such as that the manager would rather hire a friend instead.

Actor   Observer

Self-serving bias

We tend to attribute our successes to internal characteristics and our failures to external circumstances.

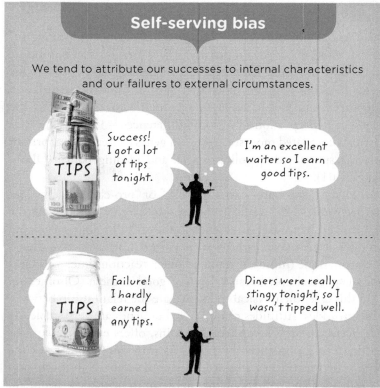

Success! I got a lot of tips tonight.

I'm an excellent waiter so I earn good tips.

TIPS

Failure! I hardly earned any tips.

Diners were really stingy tonight, so I wasn't tipped well.

TIPS

False consensus effect

Observer tends to assume the actor is behaving similarly to how she would act in that situation.

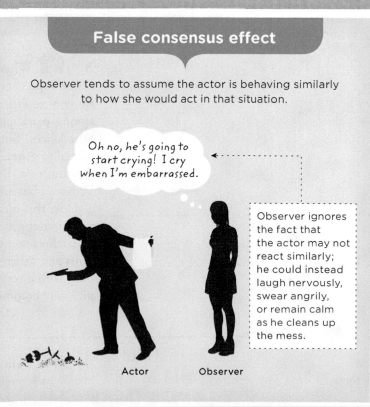

Oh no, he's going to start crying! I cry when I'm embarrassed.

Observer ignores the fact that the actor may not react similarly; he could instead laugh nervously, swear angrily, or remain calm as he cleans up the mess.

Actor   Observer

FIGURE 15.2
Attitudes
Attitudes are composed of cognitive, affective, and behavioral components. Cognitive and affective components usually guide the behavioral aspect of an attitude.

or the way we respond. There are also instances of the opposite effect, when behavior influences feelings or beliefs, a topic we will revisit in a little while.

WHERE DO ATTITUDES COME FROM?   Of all the nature–nurture conversations occurring in the field of psychology, there is at least one arena where nurture seemingly appears to dominate: attitudes. Our attitudes develop through experiences and interactions with the people in our lives, and even through exposure to media (via **classical conditioning** and observational learning).

That being said, genetic factors do play a role. But to what degree? One of the best ways to gauge the **relative weights** of nature and nurture is through the study of twins. If nature has a substantive effect on attitudes, then the following should be true: Identical twins (who have the same genetic make-up) should have more similar attitudes than fraternal twins (who share about 50 percent of their genes). Let's take a look at some of the research to see if this is the case.

nature AND nurture

Why the Attitude?

How do you feel about rollercoasters? How about alcohol consumption? Where do you stand on the death penalty? These are just a few of the attitude topics researchers have explored in the context of nature and nurture. One study of several hundred pairs of twins concluded that most of the attitude variation among participants resulted from nonshared environmental factors, or distinct life experiences. But a significant proportion of attitude differences—35 percent—was related to genes. Those that correlated most strongly with genes centered on abortion, the death penalty, playing sports, riding rollercoasters, and reading books (Olson, Vernon, Harris, & Jang, 2001).

Does this mean that each of us is born with a "pro-life" or "pro-choice" gene, and yet another gene that determines how we feel about sports? Highly unlikely. As the researchers point out, genes probably exert their effects indirectly, through personality traits and other genetically determined characteristics. For example, someone who is born with a very athletic physique (muscular frame or quick reaction time, for example) may become fond of sports simply because she is so good at them (Olson et al., 2001). In this case, the physical traits mediate the relationship between genes and attitudes. Attitudes can change, but genes are very stable.

More recent research, also involving twins, offers evidence that political attitudes are influenced by genes. As with the Olson study, the relationship between genes and attitudes appears to be indirect; personality traits, which are highly heritable, seem to predispose people to

CONNECTIONS

In **Chapter 5,** we described *classical conditioning* and how it might instill emotions and attitudes toward product brands. Observational learning can lead children to imitate others, including their attitudes.

In **Chapter 7,** we explored the heritability of intelligence. *Heritability* is the degree to which hereditary factors are responsible for differences across a variety of physical and psychological characteristics. Heritability research often involves comparing identical and fraternal twins, as is the case here regarding attitudes.

**DOES THIS MEAN ...
EACH OF US IS BORN
WITH A "PRO-LIFE" OR
"PRO-CHOICE" GENE?**

certain political attitudes. But as the researchers point out, family members and peers can also mold political inclinations (Kandler, Bleidorn, & Riemann, 2012). It makes good sense if you think about it: If someone important to you takes a certain political stance, it might seem more appealing, or at least tolerable. The bottom line: Nurture may come out ahead in this particular case, but nature holds its own. ◊⌂

We have established that attitudes are shaped by experience and, to a lesser extent, heredity. This may be interesting from a theoretical standpoint, but what impact do these attitudes have on everyday life? Let's explore how attitudes influence the choices we make.

CAN ATTITUDES PREDICT BEHAVIOR?   There are many factors determining whether an attitude can predict a behavior (Ajzen, 2001). The strength of an attitude is important, with stronger, more enduring attitudes having a greater impact (Armitage & Christian, 2003; Holland, Verplanken, & Van Knippenberg, 2002). Specificity is also key; the more specific an attitude, the more likely it will sway behavior (Armitage & Christian, 2003). This principle is well illustrated by Davidson and Jaccard (1979), who examined the relationship between people's general attitudes toward birth control and the use of birth control pills (*the behavior*). They found that general attitudes toward contraceptives were not as good at predicting their use as attitudes specific to birth control pills.

Not surprisingly, people are more likely to act on their attitudes when something important is at stake—like money. Imagine your college is holding a meeting to discuss the possibility of increasing student parking fees. What are the chances of your showing up to that meeting if you don't own a car? The greater the personal investment you have in an issue, the more likely you are to act (Sivacek & Crano, 1982).

We now know that attitudes can influence behaviors, but is the opposite true— that is, can behaviors shape attitudes? Absolutely.

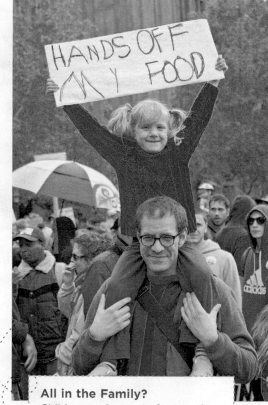

All in the Family?
Children and parents frequently have the same attitudes about politics and social issues. To a certain degree, these similarities trace to common personality traits, which are partly inherited (Kandler et al., 2012). But attitudes are more strongly influenced by life experiences (Olson et al., 2001). Tony Savino/Corbis

didn't SEE that coming

Something Doesn't Feel Right

👁! Most people would agree that cheating on a girlfriend, boyfriend, or spouse is not right. Even so, some people contradict their beliefs by seeking sexual gratification outside their primary relationships. How do you think cheating makes a person feel—relaxed and at peace? Probably not. The tension that results when a behavior (in this case, cheating) clashes with an attitude (*cheating is wrong*) is known as **cognitive dissonance** (Aronson & Festinger, 1958; Festinger, 1957). One way to reduce cognitive dissonance is to adjust the behavior (stop fooling around). Another approach is to change the attitude to better match the behavior (*cheating is actually good for our relationship, because it makes me a better partner*). Such attitude shifts often occur without our awareness.

The phenomenon of cognitive dissonance was elegantly brought to light in a study by Leon Festinger and J. Merrill Carlsmith (1959). Imagine, for a moment, that you are a participant in this classic study. The researchers have assigned you to a very boring task—placing 12 objects on a tray and then putting them back on the shelf, over and over again for a half-hour. Upon finishing, you spend an additional half-hour twisting 48 pegs ever so slightly, one peg at a time, again and again and again. How would you feel at the end of the hour—pretty bored, right?

Regardless of how you may feel about these activities, you have been paid money to convince someone else that they are a blast: "I had a lot of fun [doing] this task," you say. "It was intriguing, it was exciting. . ." (Festinger & Carlsmith, 1959, p. 205). Unless you like performing repetitive behaviors like a robot, we assume you

cognitive dissonance A state of tension that results when behaviors are inconsistent with attitudes.

would feel some degree of *cognitive dissonance,* or tension resulting from this mismatch between your attitude (*Ugh, this activity is so boring*) and your behavior (saying, "I had so much fun!"). What could you do to reduce the cognitive dissonance? If you're like participants in Festinger and Carlsmith's study, you would probably adjust your attitude to better fit your claims. In other words, you would rate the task more interesting than it actually was.

But here's the really interesting part: The students who were paid more money ($20 versus $1) were less inclined to change their attitudes to match their claim—a sign that they felt less cognitive dissonance. Apparently, the big bucks made it easier to justify their lies. *I said I liked the boring task because I got paid $20, not because I actually liked it.*

Here is one final example to drive home this concept of cognitive dissonance. We all know that smoking is bad for the body, but smokers around the world continue to light up. You would think awareness of health risks might lead to negative attitudes about smoking, as well as cognitive dissonance during the act (*Smoking is dangerous; I am smoking, and this doesn't feel right*). Reducing the conflict between the attitude and behavior could be accomplished in one of two ways: by changing the attitude or by changing the behavior. Which path do smokers take?

APPARENTLY, THE BIG BUCKS MADE IT EASIER TO JUSTIFY THEIR LIES.

It appears that smokers often take a third route: thought suppression. They reduce cognitive dissonance by suppressing thoughts about the health implications of smoking. This helps explain why so many smokers don't change their behavior when concerned friends and family members remind them of the dangers. So what should loved ones do to discourage the habit? One **strategy** is to reduce beliefs about positive outcomes, like pointing out that smoking is not effective as a social lubricant or relaxation aid (Kneer, Glock, & Rieger, 2012). ☻!

CONNECTIONS

In **Chapter 12,** we reported that many people smoke in response to stressors. To help people quit smoking, we must consider where they are in the process of smoking cessation (first time trying to quit, tried numerous times, etc.). Here, we see it's important to consider cognitive dissonance as well.

We have now learned about cognitive processes that form the foundation of our social existence. Attributions help us make sense of events and behaviors, and attitudes provide continuity in the way we think and feel about the surrounding world. It's time to shift our attention to behavior. How do people influence the way we act? Are you ready to meet running extraordinaire Julius Achon?

1. _____ are beliefs about the causes used to explain events, situations, and characteristics.
   a. Attributions
   b. Confederates
   c. Dispositions
   d. Attitudes

2. Because of the fundamental attribution error, we tend to be more likely to attribute causes of behaviors to the
   a. characteristics of the situation.
   b. factors involved in the event.
   c. length of the activity.
   d. disposition of the person.

3. What three elements comprise an attitude?

4. The just-world hypothesis is held by people who believe the world is a fair place; therefore, if someone is suffering, she must have done something to deserve it. What are some examples of the just-world hypothesis playing out in current popular stories or the media?

✓ CHECK YOUR ANSWERS IN APPENDIX C.

Social Influence

11 ORPHANS In 1983 a 7-year-old boy in northern Uganda came down with the measles. The child was feverish and coughing, and his skin was covered in a blotchy rash. He appeared to be dying. In fact, he did die—or so the local villagers believed. They dug his grave, wrapped him in a burial cloth, and sang him a farewell song. Then, just as they were about to lower the body into the ground, someone heard a sneeze. A few moments later, another sneeze. Could it be? The body inside the burial cloth started to writhe. Hastily unwrapping the cloth, the mourners found the child frantically kicking and crying. It's a good thing the boy sneezed that day at his funeral, as the world is a much happier place because he survived. His name is Julius Achon, and he would grow up to become an Olympic athlete and, perhaps more important, a world-class humanitarian.

Home in Uganda
A group of women sit together in Awake, Uganda, the village where Julius Achon was born and raised. Day-to-day life was difficult, and young Julius dreamed of leaving the village and pursuing a better life in the city. Inspired by the accomplishments of Uganda's Olympic hurdler John Akii-Bua, he decided to start running. Courtesy Dr. Julie Gralow

Julius was born on December 12, 1976, in Awake, a village that had no electricity or running water. "Life in Uganda is very tough," says Julius, who spent his childhood sleeping between eight brothers and sisters on the floor of a one-room hut. People in the village drink water from the same well as cows and pigs and eat just one meal a day, two if they're lucky, he explains. Julius grew up during a period when a government opposition group known as the Lord's Resistance Army (LRA) began its campaign of terror in northern Uganda. At age 12, Julius was kidnapped by the LRA and forced to become a child soldier, but his spirit would not be broken. Three months later, he escaped from the rebel camp and, running much of the way, he returned to his village some 100 miles away.

Upon returning home, Julius began to run competitively. Running made him feel free, and running was his great gift. He ran barefoot to his first major track meet in the city of Lira, some 42 miles away from his village. Hours after arriving, Julius was racing—and winning—the 800 meters, the 1,500 meters, and the 3,000 meters (Kahn, 2012, January). From that point on, it was one success after another: a stunning victory at the national championships, a track scholarship at a prestigious high school in the capital city of Kampala, a gold medal at the World Junior Championships, a college scholarship from George Mason University in the United States, a collegiate record in 1996, and participation in the 1996 and 2000 Olympics (Kahn, 2012, January).

As awe-inspiring as these accomplishments may be, the greatest achievement in Julius Achon's life was yet to come, and it had little to do with running. In 2003, while training back home in Uganda, he came upon a bus station in Lira. "I stopped, and then I saw children lying under the bus," Julius says. They had been sleeping there for warmth. One of them stood up and started to beg for money—a 13- or 14-year-old girl clad in a tattered skirt and torn blouse. Then more children emerged, 11 of them in all, some teenagers and others as young as 3. They were terribly thin and dirty, and the little ones wore nothing more than long T-shirts and underwear.

"Where are your parents?" Julius remembers asking. One of the children said their parents had been shot and killed. "Can I walk you to my home, you know, to go eat?" Julius asked. The children eagerly agreed and followed him home for a meal of rice, beans, and porridge. What happened next may seem unbelievable, but Julius and his family are extraordinary people. Julius asked his father to shelter the 11 orphans, provided that he, Julius, would send money home to cover their living expenses. Julius had been running with a professional team in Portugal, making

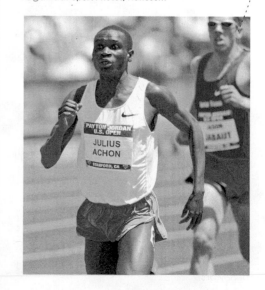

Fast and Free
Julius wins the 1,500 meters at the 2005 Payton Jordan U.S. Open at Stanford University. With two Olympics under his belt, the young runner had enjoyed an extremely successful athletic career, but his focus was beginning to shift onto something bigger—the task of providing for 11 orphans back home in Uganda. Sport Photos/Newscom

about $5,000 a year, not even enough to cover his own expenses. His parents already had six people living in their one-room home. How did his father respond?

"Ah, it's no problem," said Julius's father. And just like that, Julius and his family adopted 11 children.

Power of Others

Throughout the years Julius was trotting the globe and winning medals, he never forgot about Uganda. He remembered the people back home with empty stomachs and no access to lifesaving medicine, living in constant fear of the LRA. Julius was raised in a family that had always reached out to neighbors in need. "You will get help from other people when you do good," his parents used to say. Julius also felt blessed by all the support people outside the family had given him. "I feel I was so loved [by] others," says Julius, referring to the mentors and coaches who had provided him with places to stay, clothes to wear, and family away from home.

So when Julius encountered those 11 orphans lying under the bus, he didn't think twice about coming to their rescue. His decision to bring them into his life probably had something to do with the positive interactions he had experienced with people in his past.

> **LO 4**   Describe social influence and recognize the factors associated with persuasion.

SOCIAL INFLUENCE   Rarely a day goes by that we do not come into contact with other human beings. This contact may be up close and personal, in a family or a tight-knit work group. Other times it's more superficial, like the "Hello, how are you?" type of exchange you might have with a cashier at the store. Sometimes the interaction is so superficial that you never see the person face to face, like the online banker who helps you figure out why you were charged that mysterious fee. All of these interactions impact you in ways you may not realize. Psychologists refer to this as **social influence**—the way a person is affected by another person (or people) as apparent in behaviors, emotions, and cognition. Social influence can be glaringly obvious or barely noticeable, explicit or unspoken, strong or weak. We begin our discussion with a powerful, yet often overlooked, form of social influence: expectations.

EXPECTATIONS   Think back to your days in elementary school. What kind of student were you—an overachiever, a kid who struggled, or perhaps the class clown? The answer to this question may depend somewhat on the way your teachers perceived you. In a classic study, Rosenthal and Jacobson (1966, 1968) administered a nonverbal intelligence test to students in a San Francisco elementary school. Then all the teachers were provided with a list of students who were likely to "show surprising gains in intellectual competence" during the next year (Rosenthal, 2002a, p. 841). This prediction, they were told, was based on an intelligence test. But this was not true; the "intellectually competent" students were actually normal students who had been selected at random (a good example of how deception is used in social psychology). About 8 months later, the students were given a second intelligence test. Children whom the teachers expected to "show surprising gains" achieved greater increases in their test scores than their peers. Mind you, the only difference between these two groups was in teacher expectations and their resulting behaviors. The students who were expected to be superior actually became superior. Why do you think this happened?

As we discussed earlier, expectations can have a powerful impact on behaviors. Here, we have a case in which teachers' expectations (based on false information) seemed to transform students' aptitudes and facilitate substantial gains. Let's consider

social influence How a person is affected by others as evidenced in behaviors, emotions, and cognition.

persuasion Intentionally trying to make people change their attitudes and beliefs, which may lead to changes in their behaviors.

the types of teacher behaviors that could explain this effect. The teachers may have inadvertently communicated expectations by demonstrating "warmer socioemotional" attitudes toward the "surprising gain" students; they may have provided them with more material and opportunities to respond to high expectations; and they may have given them more complex and personalized feedback (Rosenthal, 2002, 2003). From the student's perspective, teacher behaviors can create a desire to work hard, or they can result in a decline in interest and confidence (Kassin, Fein, & Markus, 2011).

Since this classic study was conducted approximately 50 years ago, researchers have studied expectations in a variety of classroom settings. Their results demonstrate that teacher expectations do not have the same effect or degree of impact on all students (Jussim & Harber, 2005). They appear to have greater influence on younger students (first and second graders) and children of **lower socioeconomic status** (Sorhagen, 2013).

Expectations are powerful, but they are just one form of social influence. Let's return to the story of Julius for an example of a more targeted form of social influence.

Persuasion and Compliance

When Julius asked his father to shelter and feed the 11 orphans, he was using a form of social influence called **persuasion.** Persuasion means intentionally trying to make people change their attitudes and beliefs, which may (or may not) lead to changes in their behaviors. The person doing the persuading does not necessarily have control over those he seeks to persuade. Julius could not force his father to feel sympathy for the orphans. His father made a choice.

The important elements of persuasion were first described by Carl Hovland, a social psychologist who studied the morale of soldiers fighting in World War II. According to Hovland, three factors determine persuasive power: the source, the message, and the audience (Hovland, Janis, & Kelley, 1953).

THE SOURCE The credibility of the person or organization sending a message is critical, and credibility can be dependent on perceived expertise and trustworthiness (Hovland & Weiss, 1951). Let's look at an example. Suppose you are searching for information about the risks associated with vaccines—whom do you trust to furnish reliable information? In one study, German adults deemed vaccine information provided by government agencies to be more credible than that supplied by pharmaceutical companies (Betsch & Sachse, 2013). Of course, this assessment of government credibility depends on whether citizens consider the government trustworthy.

Persuasive ability also hinges on the attractiveness of the source, with more attractive people tending to be more persuasive (Bekk & Spörrle, 2010). But it's not just about *who* is sending the message. The content of the message also determines persuasive power.

THE MESSAGE What particular features of a message determine its power? One important factor is the degree to which the message is logical and to the point (Chaiken & Eagly, 1976). Fear-inducing information can increase persuasion, but it can also backfire. Imagine someone uses this message to encourage teeth-flossing: "If you don't floss daily, you can end up with infected gums, and that infection can spread to your eyes and create total blindness!" If the audience is overly frightened by a message (imagine small children being told to floss . . . or else!), the tension they feel may actually interfere with their ability to process the message (Janis & Feshbach, 1953).

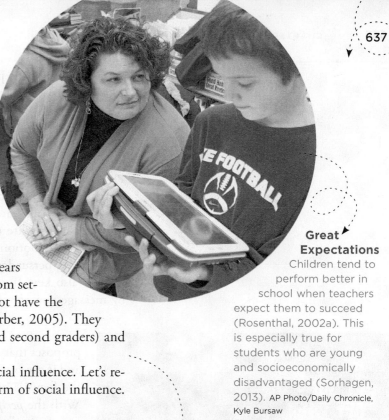

Great Expectations
Children tend to perform better in school when teachers expect them to succeed (Rosenthal, 2002a). This is especially true for students who are young and socioeconomically disadvantaged (Sorhagen, 2013). AP Photo/Daily Chronicle, Kyle Bursaw

CONNECTIONS

In **Chapter 12,** we discussed how poverty and its associated stressors can have a lasting impact on the development of the brain and subsequent cognitive abilities. Some factors that influence children's brain development include nutrition, toxins, and abuse. Here, we see that the expectations of others can impact cognitive functioning as well.

You Asked, Julius Answers

http://qrs.ly/nk3o0jm

How did you persuade your father to take in the 11 orphans?

If fear is used for the purpose of persuasion, those being persuaded must be provided with information about how to cope with any negative outcomes (Leventhal, Watts, & Pagano, 1967). Being as "gruesome as possible" is not effective; a better approach is to provide clear information about the negative consequences of not being persuaded (de Hoog, Stroebe, & de Wit, 2007).

THE AUDIENCE   Finally, we turn to the audience. Who is being persuaded, and which of their characteristics matter? One factor is age. For example, middle-age adults (40 to 60 years old) are unlikely to be persuaded to change their attitudes, whereas children are relatively susceptible (Roberts & DelVecchio, 2000). Another key factor is emotional state; when people are happy and well fed, they are more likely to be persuaded (Aronson, 2012; Janis, Kaye, & Kirschner, 1965). Mental focus is also key: If your mind is somewhere else, you are less likely to be affected by message content (Petty & Cacioppo, 1986).

ELABORATION LIKELIHOOD MODEL   The *elaboration likelihood model* proposes that persuasion hinges on the way people think about an argument, and it can occur via one of two pathways. With the *central route* to persuasion, the focus is on the content of the message, and thinking critically about it. With the *peripheral route,* the focus is not on the content but on "extramessage factors" such as the credibility or attractiveness of the source (Petty & Cacioppo, 1986). Little critical thinking is involved, and the commitment to the outcome is low. But how do we know which route the message will take? If the person receiving the message is knowledgeable and invested in its outcome, the central route to persuasion is used. If the person is distracted, lacks knowledge about the topic, or does not feel invested in the outcome, the peripheral route is typically taken (O'Keefe, 2008).

Immediately following the tragedy of the Newtown massacre in late 2012, there was an upsurge in calls for tighter gun control in the United States. Someone with strong feelings about gun control (either for or against it) would likely take advantage of central processing when trying to develop a persuasive argument. Some politicians, for example, tried to persuade others by supplying data about the number of gun-related deaths worldwide: "The United States, which has, per capita, more firearms and particularly more handguns than . . . [22 other 'populous, high-income'] countries, as well as the most permissive gun control laws, also has a disproportionate number of firearm deaths—firearm homicides, firearm suicides, and firearm accidents" (Richardson & Hemenway, 2011, p. 243). Such a message would be more persuasive to a person who is knowledgeable and invested in the issue, and thus uses the central processing route. Someone who is unfamiliar with and/or indifferent about gun-control policy would probably be more persuaded by the credibility of the source, appearance of the speaker, and so on.

The take-home message: If you want to persuade as many people as possible, make sure your arguments are logical *and* you present yourself as credible and attractive. That way you will be able to take advantage of both routes when making your case to an audience.

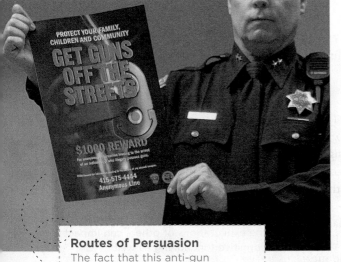

Routes of Persuasion
The fact that this anti-gun message is being presented by a police officer may increase its persuasive power. With the *peripheral route* to persuasion, people pay attention to factors outside the message content, such as the credibility or appearance of the individual who relays the message (Petty & Cacioppo, 1986).
Justin Sullivan/Getty Images

compliance Changes in behavior at the request or direction of another person or group, who in general do not have any true authority.

foot-in-the-door technique A compliance technique that involves making a small request first, followed by a larger request.

door-in-the-face technique A compliance technique that involves making a large request first, followed by a smaller request.

> **LO 5**   Define compliance and explain some of the techniques used to gain it.

COMPLIANCE   Being persuaded to change our *attitudes* about vaccinations or our opinions about broccoli is an act of free will. The results of persuasion are internal and related to a change in attitude (Key, Edlund, Sagarin, & Bizer, 2009). **Compliance,** on the other hand, occurs when someone voluntarily changes her *behavior* at the request or direction of another person or group, who in general does not have any true authority over her. Compliance is evident in changes to "overt behavior" (Key et al., 2009). For example, if you want to get someone to help clean up after a party, you would try to get him to comply with your request, perhaps through some mild form of guilt (*Remember the last party we had when I helped you?*).

Surprisingly, compliance often occurs **outside of our awareness.** Think of an everyday situation in which you mindlessly comply with another person's request. You're waiting in line at the copy machine, and someone asks if he can cut in front of you. Do you allow it? Your response may depend on the wording of the request. Researchers studying this very scenario—a person asking another person to cut in line—have found that compliance is much more likely to result when the request is accompanied by a *reason.* Saying, "Excuse me, I have 5 pages. May I use the [copy] machine?" will not work as well as "Excuse me, I have 5 pages. May I use the [copy] machine, *because I am in a rush?*" People are more likely to comply with a request that includes a "because" phrase, even if the reasoning is not logical. For example, stating that you need to use the copy machine "*because I am in a rush*" achieves about the same compliance as "*because I have to make copies*" (Langer, Blank, & Chanowitz, 1978). Kind of scary, right?

WELL . . . OKAY   The potential mindlessness associated with compliance should encourage you to reflect on when else you might automatically comply (Fennis & Janssen, 2010). For example, salespeople or marketing experts routinely use a variety of techniques to get consumers to comply with their requests. One common method is the **foot-in-the-door technique,** which occurs when someone asks for a small request, followed by a larger request (Freedman & Fraser, 1966). If a college club is trying to persuade students to help perform a large service project (such as raising money for packages to be sent to soldiers overseas), its members might first stop students in the hallway and ask them if they could help with a smaller task (labeling a couple of donated boxes lying close by). If a student responds positively to this small request, then the club members might make a bigger request (to sponsor packages), with the expectation that the student will comply with the second request on the grounds of having said yes to the first request. Why would this technique work?

The reasoning is that if you have already said yes to a small request, chances are you will agree to a bigger request to remain consistent in your involvement. Your prior participation leads you to believe you are the type of person who gets involved; in other words, your attitude has shifted (Cialdini & Goldstein, 2004; Freedman & Fraser, 1966). So why is such a strategy called *foot-in-the-door?* In the past, salespeople went door-to-door trying to sell their goods and services, and they would often be successful if they could physically get a "foot in the door," thereby keeping it open, which allowed them to continue with their sales pitch.

Another method for gaining compliance is the **door-in-the-face technique,** which involves making a large request first, and then a smaller request. With this technique, the expectation is that the person will not go along with the large request, but because the smaller request may seem so minor by comparison, the person will comply with it. There are numerous reasons people comply under these circumstances, but the main reason seems to be one of *reciprocal concessions.* If the solicitor (the person trying to obtain something) is willing to give up something (the large request), the person being solicited tends to feel that he too should give in and satisfy the smaller request (Cialdini & Goldstein, 2004). Think back to the college club that really does need help addressing boxes. Its members might stop students and ask them to make

CONNECTIONS

In **Chapter 4,** we discussed the *automatic cognitive activity* that guides some behaviors. These behaviors appear to occur without our intent or awareness. Compliance can be driven by automatic processes.

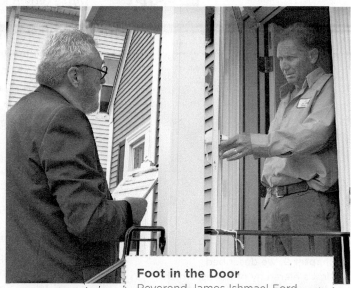

Foot in the Door
Reverend James Ishmael Ford goes door-to-door in Providence, Rhode Island, talking to residents about marriage equality. If Rev. Ford can just get his "foot in the door," the resident might be willing to talk to him. With the foot-in-the-door technique, the person makes a small request ("May I have just one minute of your time?") followed by a larger request ("Would you sign this petition?").
AP Images for Human Rights Campaign

a contribution to sponsor a package, but if a student says no to this request, the club representative may then say, "Okay, but can you at least help address a few boxes for us?" Chances are good students will comply with this request because it seems minor relative to the first one.

Let's review these concepts using Julius as an example. After meeting the 11 orphans, Julius brought them home and asked his parents to provide them with a meal. Once his parents *complied* with this initial request, Julius made a much larger request—he asked them to shelter the children indefinitely. This is an example of the *foot-in-the-door* technique because Julius first made a modest request ("Will you feed these children?") and then followed up with a larger one ("Will you shelter these children?"). Had these requests been flip-flopped, that is, had Julius only wanted to get the children a meal but first asked his parents if the children could move in, we would call it the *door-in-the-face* technique.

Compliance generally occurs in response to specific requests or instructions: Will you pick up the kids after school? Can you chop these onions? Please collect your sweaty socks from the bathroom floor! But social influence needn't be explicit. Sometimes we adapt our behaviors and beliefs simply to fit in with the crowd.

Conformity

When Julius came to the United States on a college scholarship in 1995, he was struck by some of the cultural differences he observed between the United States and Uganda—the way people dressed, for example. Women wore considerably less clothing, and men could be seen wearing jeans halfway down their posteriors (the "sagging" pants phenomenon). There were other differences, like the way people addressed authority figures. In Africa, explains Julius, students speak to their teachers with a certain kind of respect, using a low voice and standing still with their legs close together. Americans tend to use a more casual tone, he notes; they stand with their legs farther apart and shift around during conversation.

Throughout the years Julius has been abroad, he has never stopped acting like a Ugandan. "I am not changed," says Julius, who has worked and lived in the United States for the last decade. Before going out in the evening, Julius tucks in his shirt, checks his hair, and makes sure his clothes are ironed—and he never wears sagging pants. You might say Julius has refused to *conform* to certain aspects of American culture—and resisting conformity is not always easy to do.

- -

> **LO 6**   Evaluate conformity and identify the factors that influence the likelihood of someone conforming.

- -

FOLLOWING THE CROWD   Have you ever found yourself turning to look in the same direction as other people who are staring at something, just because you see them doing so? During the Waldo Canyon Fires in Colorado Springs in the summer of 2012, a day did not pass without people pointing to the mountain range. It was next to impossible to avoid looking in the direction they were pointing, and not just because of the smoke coming from the mountains. We seem to have a commanding urge to do what others are doing, even if it means changing our normal behavior. This tendency to modify our behaviors, attitudes, beliefs, and opinions to match those of others is known as **conformity.** Sometimes we conform to the **norms** or standards of the social environment, such as the group to which we are connected. Unlike compliance, which occurs in response to an explicit and direct request, conformity is generally unspoken. We often conform because we feel compelled to fit in and **belong.**

It is important to note that conformity is not always a bad thing. We rely on conformity in many cases to ensure the smooth running of day-to-day activities involving

CONNECTIONS ◀- - - - - -

In **Chapter 9**, we described Maslow's hierarchy of needs, which includes the *need to belong*. If physiological and safety needs are met, an individual will be motivated by the need for love and belongingness. Here we suggest that this need drives us to conform and fit in.

conformity The urge to modify behaviors, attitudes, beliefs, and opinions to match those of others.

norms Standards of the social environment.

groups of people. Think of what a third-grade classroom would be like if it weren't for the human urge to conform to what others are doing. Imagine checking out at Target if none of the customers adhered to common social rules.

try this

The next time you are outside in a fairly crowded area, look up and keep your eyes toward the sky. You will find that some people change their gazes to match yours, even though there is no other indication that something is happening above.

STUDYING CONFORMITY   Social psychologists have studied conformity in a variety of settings, including American colleges. In a classic experiment by Solomon Asch (1955), college-student participants were asked to sit at a table with six other people, all of whom were confederates working for the researcher. The participants were told to look at two cards, one with one vertical line on it, the standard line, and the other card with three vertical lines, each of different lengths but marked 1, 2, and 3 (**FIGURE 15.3**). The group seated at the table was instructed to look at the two cards and then announce, one at a time going around the table, which of the three lines was closest in length to the standard line, thus making a "visual judgment." The first two rounds of this task went smoothly, with everybody in agreement about which of the three lines matched the standard. But then, in the third round, the first five confederates at the table offered what was clearly the wrong answer, one after the other (prior to the experiment, the researchers had given them instructions about which line to choose in each trial).

Would the real participant (the sixth person to answer) follow suit and conform to the wrong answer, or would he stand his ground and report the correct answer? In roughly 37% of these trials, participants went along with the group and provided the incorrect answer. Furthermore, 76% of the participants conformed to the incorrect answers of the confederates at least once (Asch, 1955, 1956). When members of the **control group** made the same judgments alone in a room, they were correct

CONNECTIONS

In **Chapter 1,** we explained that a control group in an experiment is not exposed to the treatment variable. In this case, the control group is not exposed to the confederates making incorrect answers.

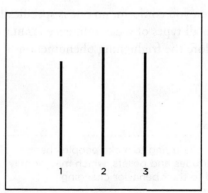

Standard line   Comparison lines

FIGURE 15.3

Asch's Conformity Experiment
Participants in this experiment were asked to look at the lines on two cards, announcing which of the comparison lines was closest in length to the standard line. Imagine you are a participant, like the man wearing glasses in this photo, and everyone else at the table chooses Line 3. Would that influence your answer? If you are like many participants, it would. Seventy-six percent conformed to the incorrect answer at least once. Photo by William Vandivert/Solomon E. Asch, Opinions and Social Pressure, *Scientific American*, Nov 1955, Vol 193, No. 5, 31-35

99% of the time, confirming that the differences between the standard line and the comparison lines were substantial, and generally not difficult to assess. This type of study was later replicated in a variety of cultures, with mostly similar results (Bond & Smith, 1996).

WHY CONFORM?   Clearly, people do not always conform to the behavior of others, but what factors come into play when they do? There are three major reasons for conformity. Most of us want the approval of others, to be liked and accepted. This desire influences our behavior and is known as *normative social influence.* Just think back to middle school—do you remember feeling pressure to be like some of your classmates or friends? This might have been due to a normative social influence to conform, so that you could fit in. A second reason we conform is so we might behave correctly; we look to others for confirmation when we are uncertain about something, and then do as they do. This is known as *informational social influence.* Perhaps you have a friend who is particularly well read in politics but you are not, or who is extremely knowledgeable about psychology. In both cases, your tendency is to defer to their expert knowledge. Third, we sometimes conform to others because they belong to a certain *reference group* we respect, admire, or long to join.

Certain conditions increase the likelihood of conforming (Aronson, 2012; Asch, 1955):

1. The group includes at least three other people who are unanimous.
2. You have to report your decision in front of others and give your reasons.
3. The task seems difficult to you.
4. You are unsure of your ability to perform the task.

Certain conditions decrease the likelihood of conforming:

1. At least one other person is going against the group with you (Asch, 1955).
2. Group members come from individualist, or "me-centered" cultures, meaning they are less likely to conform than those from collectivistic, or more community-centered cultures (Bond & Smith, 1996).

When you conform, no one is specifically telling you to do so. But this is not the case with all types of social influence (**TABLE 15.1**). Let's take a trip to the darker side and explore the frightening phenomenon of obedience.

Table 15.1	CONCEPTS OF SOCIAL INFLUENCE	
Concept	**Definition**	**Example**
Persuasion	Intentionally trying to make people change their attitudes and beliefs, which may or may not lead to their behavior changing	Buy our product because it is the best on the market.
Compliance	Voluntarily changing behavior at the request or direction of another person or group, who in general does not have any authority over you	Remove your shoes before you walk into the house because you have been asked.
Conformity	Urge to modify our behaviors, attitudes, beliefs, and opinions to match those of others	Remove your shoes before you walk into the house because everyone else who has entered did the same.
Obedience	Changing our behavior because we have been ordered to do so by someone in authority	Follow the detour sign.

Whether or not you realize it, other people constantly shape your thoughts, emotions, and behaviors. Above are some of the key elements of social influence.

BOY SOLDIERS   During Uganda's two-decade civil war, the Lord's Resistance Army (LRA) is said to have kidnapped some 66,000 youths. Scholars have estimated that 20% of male victims did not make it home (Annan, Blattman, & Horton, 2006). Julius came dangerously close to losing his life during a village raid that he and other child soldiers were forced to conduct. His boss ordered him to shoot a man who refused to hand over a chicken, but Julius would not pull the trigger. Had the boss not come from Julius's home village, the punishment probably would have been death. Instead, Julius received a caning that rendered him incapable of sitting for a week.

While a captive of the LRA, Julius witnessed other boy soldiers assaulting innocent people and stealing property. Sometimes at the end of the day, they would laugh or brag about how many people they had beaten or killed. But these were just "normal" boys from the villages, boys who never would have behaved this way under regular circumstances. And some showed clear signs of regret. Julius remembers seeing other child soldiers cry alone at night after returning to the camp when there was time to reflect on what they had done.

How do you explain this tragedy? What drives an ordinary child to commit senseless violence? A psychologist might tell you it has something to do with *obedience*.

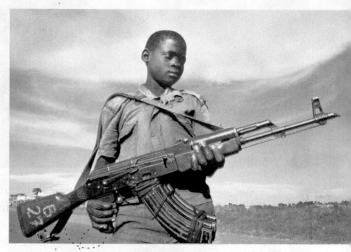

Boy Soldier
A young boy wields a Kalashnikov rifle near Kampala, Uganda. He is among the tens of thousands of children who have been exploited by military groups in Uganda. Julius was just 12 years old when he was abducted by the Lord's Resistance Army and forced to fight and plunder on the group's behalf. AFP/Getty Images

Obedience

▶ **LO 7**   Describe obedience and explain how Stanley Milgram studied it.

One of the most disconcerting results of social influence is **obedience,** which occurs when we change our behavior, or act in a way we might not normally act, because we have been ordered to do so by an authority figure. In these situations, an imbalance of power exists, and the **person with more power** (for example, a teacher, police officer, doctor, or boss) generally has an advantage over someone with less power (who is more likely to be obedient out of respect, fear, or concern). In some cases, the person in charge demands obedience for the good of those less powerful (a father demanding obedience from a child running wildly through a crowded store). Other times, the person wielding power demands obedience for his own benefit (an adult who perpetrates sexual abuses against innocent children).

THIS WILL *SHOCK* YOU: MILGRAM'S STUDY   Back in the 1960s, psychologist Stanley Milgram was interested in determining the extent to which obedience can lead to behaviors that most people would consider unethical. Milgram (1963, 1974) conducted a series of studies examining how far people would go, particularly in terms of punishing others, when urged to do so by an authority figure. Participants were told the study was about memory and learning (another example of research deception). The sample included teachers, salespeople, post office workers, engineers, and laborers, representing a wide range of educational backgrounds, from elementary school dropouts to people with graduate degrees.

Upon arriving at the Yale University laboratory, participants were informed they would be using punishment as part of a learning experiment. They were then asked to draw a slip of paper from a hat; the slip told them they had been randomly assigned the *teacher* role, although the truth was that a confederate always played the role of the *learner* (the hat contained two slips that both read "teacher"). To start, the participant was asked to sit in the learner's chair, so that he could experience a 45-volt shock,

CONNECTIONS

In **Chapter 14,** we introduced the concept of *transference,* a reaction some clients have to their therapists. A client demonstrating transference responds to the therapist as if dealing with a parent, or other important caregiver from childhood; this may include behaving more childlike and obedient.

obedience Changing behavior because we have been ordered to do so by an authority figure.

Troubling Discoveries
A photo of psychologist Stanley Milgram appears on the cover of his biography, *The Man Who Shocked The World: The Life and Legacy of Stanley Milgram*, by Thomas Blass. Milgram's research illuminated the dangers of human obedience. Feeling pressure from authority figures, participants in Milgram's studies were willing to administer what they believed to be painful and life-threatening electric shocks to other human beings (Milgram, 1963). Stanley & Alexandra Milgram/Alexander Street Press

just to know what the learner might be feeling. The teacher was told that the goal was for the learner to memorize a set of paired words. The teacher sat at a table that held a control panel for the generation of shocks. The panel went from 15 volts to 450 volts, and as you can see in **INFOGRAPHIC 15.2**, this range of voltage was labeled from "slight shock" to "XXX." The teacher was then told he was to administer a shock each time the learner made a mistake, and that the shock was to increase by 15 volts for every mistake. The learner was located in a separate room, arms strapped to a table and electrodes attached to his wrists; the electrodes were reportedly attached to a shock generator.

As you might have concluded, the learner (the confederate) was not really going to receive any true shocks, but had a script of responses he was to make as the experiment continued. The learner's behaviors, including the mistakes he made and his responses to the increasing shock levels (including mild complaints, screaming, references to his heart condition, pleas for the experiment to stop, and total silence as if he were unconscious or even dead), were identical for all participants. A researcher in a white lab coat (also a confederate with scripted responses) always remained in the room with the teacher, and he was insistent that the experiment proceed if the teacher began to question going any further given the learner's responses (such as "Experimenter, get me out of here. . . . I refuse to go on" or "I can't stand the pain"; Milgram, 1965, p. 62). The researcher would say to the teacher, "Please continue" and "You have no other choice, you *must* go on" (Milgram, 1963, p. 374).

How many teachers do you think obeyed the researcher and proceeded with the experiment in spite of the learner's desperate pleas? Before the experiment, Milgram asked a variety of people (including psychiatrists and students) to predict how many teachers would be obedient and obey the researcher. Many believed that the participants would refuse to continue at some point in the experiment. Most of the psychiatrists, for example, predicted that only 0.125% of participants would continue to the highest voltage (Milgram, 1965). They also guessed that the majority of the participants would quit the experiment when the learner began his protests.

Here's what actually happened: 65% of participants continued to the highest voltage level (to the point Milgram said there was "a whopping discrepancy" between predictions and outcome, p. 72). Most of these participants were obviously not comfortable with what they were doing (stuttering, sweating, trembling), yet they continued. Even those who eventually refused to proceed went much farther than anyone had predicted (even Milgram himself)—they all used shocks up to at least 300 volts (labeled as "Intense Shock") (Milgram, 1963, 1964; Infographic 15.2).

We should emphasize that participants were not necessarily comfortable with their role as *teachers,* even when they continued with the experiment. One observer of the study reported the following:

> I observed a mature and initially poised businessman enter the laboratory smiling and confident. Within 20 minutes he was reduced to a twitching, stuttering wreck, who was rapidly approaching a point of nervous collapse. He constantly pulled on his earlobe, and twisted his hands. At one point he pushed his fist into his forehead and muttered: "Oh God, let's stop it." And yet he continued to respond to every word of the experimenter, and obeyed to the end. (Milgram, 1963, p. 377)

REPLICATING MILGRAM   This type of research has been replicated in the United States and in other countries, and the findings have remained fairly consistent, with 61–66% of participants continuing to the highest level of shock (Aronson, 2012;

Milgram's Shocking Obedience Study

Stanley Milgram's study on obedience and authority was one of the most ground-breaking and surprising experiments in all of social psychology. Milgram wanted to test the extent to which we will follow the orders of an authority figure. Would we follow orders to hurt someone else, even when that person was begging us to stop? Milgram's experiment also raises the ethical issues of deception and informed consent.

Participants had to actually think they were shocking another person for the experiment to work. Creating this deception involved the use of confederates (people secretly working for the researchers) whose behaviors and spoken responses were carefully scripted. Milgram found high levels of obedience in his participants—much higher than he and others had predicted at the beginning of the study.

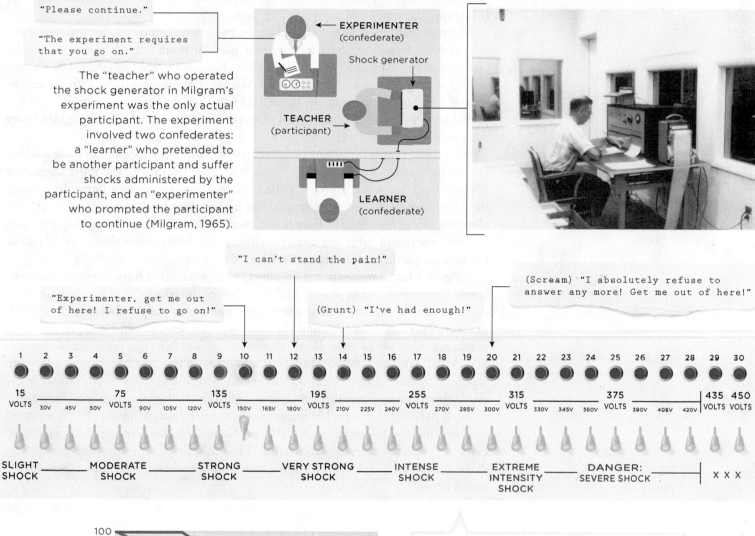

"Please continue."

"The experiment requires that you go on."

The "teacher" who operated the shock generator in Milgram's experiment was the only actual participant. The experiment involved two confederates: a "learner" who pretended to be another participant and suffer shocks administered by the participant, and an "experimenter" who prompted the participant to continue (Milgram, 1965).

EXPERIMENTER (confederate)

Shock generator

TEACHER (participant)

LEARNER (confederate)

"I can't stand the pain!"

(Scream) "I absolutely refuse to answer any more! Get me out of here!"

"Experimenter, get me out of here! I refuse to go on!"

(Grunt) "I've had enough!"

| 1 | 2 | 3 | 4 | 5 | 6 | 7 | 8 | 9 | 10 | 11 | 12 | 13 | 14 | 15 | 16 | 17 | 18 | 19 | 20 | 21 | 22 | 23 | 24 | 25 | 26 | 27 | 28 | 29 | 30 |

| 15 VOLTS | 30V | 45V | 50V | 75 VOLTS | 90V | 105V | 120V | 135 VOLTS | 150V | 165V | 180V | 195 VOLTS | 210V | 225V | 240V | 255 VOLTS | 270V | 285V | 300V | 315 VOLTS | 330V | 345V | 360V | 375 VOLTS | 390V | 405V | 420V | 435 VOLTS | 450 VOLTS |

SLIGHT SHOCK — MODERATE SHOCK — STRONG SHOCK — VERY STRONG SHOCK — INTENSE SHOCK — EXTREME INTENSITY SHOCK — DANGER: SEVERE SHOCK — X X X

On the control panel of Milgram's shock generator, the participant would see 30 switches clearly labeled as delivering a range from "Slight shock" (15 volts) to "Danger: Severe shock" (375 volts) and beyond. The "learner" also produced scripted responses at every level (Milgram, 1963).

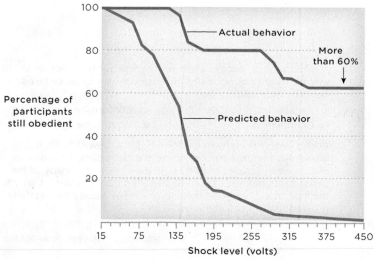

Percentage of participants still obedient

Actual behavior

More than 60%

Predicted behavior

100
80
60
40
20

15 75 135 195 255 315 375 450

Shock level (volts)

Before the experiment, Milgram and a panel of experts predicted most participants would not proceed beyond 150 volts, when the "learner" explicitly demands to end the experiment. In fact, actual results show that most participants obeyed the experimenter's commands all the way to the highest shock level. (ADAPTED FROM MILGRAM, 1965.)

CONNECTIONS

In **Chapter 1,** we reported that professional organizations have specific guidelines to ensure ethical treatment of research participants. They include doing no harm, safeguarding welfare, and respecting human dignity. An Institutional Review Board also ensures the well-being of participants.

Blass, 1999). Not surprisingly, the criticisms of Milgram's studies were strong. Many were concerned that this research went too far with its deception (it would certainly not receive approval from an **Institutional Review Board** today), and some wondered if the participants were harmed by knowing that they theoretically could have killed someone with their choices during the study. Milgram (1964) spent time with the participants following the study, and reported that 84% claimed they were "glad" they had participated, whereas only 1.3% reported they were "sorry" to have been involved. The participants were seen for psychiatric evaluations a year later, and reports indicate that none of them "show[ed] signs of having been harmed by his experiences" (Milgram, 1964, p. 850).

Milgram and others have followed up on the original study, to determine if there were specific factors or characteristics that made it more likely someone would be obedient in this type of scenario (Blass, 1991; Burger, 2009; Milgram, 1965). Burger (2009) conducted a partial replication of Milgram's original research, with the exception of stopping the experiment at the 150-volt level. In Burger's study, 70% of the participants went to the highest level of voltage (150 volts), which is a slightly lower percentage than continued to the 150-volt level in the original study.

Several key factors determined whether participants were obedient in these studies: (1) the legitimacy of the authority figure (the more legitimate, the more obedience demonstrated by participants); (2) the closeness of the authority figure (the closer the experimenter was to participants, the higher their level of obedience); (3) the closeness of the *learner* (the closer the learner, the less obedient the participant); and (4) the presence of other *teachers* (if another confederate was acting as an obedient teacher, the participant was more likely to obey as well).

Milgram's initial motivation for studying obedience came from learning about the horrific events of World War II and the Holocaust, which "could only have been carried out on a massive scale if a very large number of people obeyed orders" (Milgram, 1974, p. 1). And he found the same types of responses in his experiments on obedience. One ray of hope did shine through in his later experiments, and that was how participants responded when they saw others refuse to obey. In one follow-up experiment, two more confederates were included in the study as additional *teachers*. If these confederates showed signs of refusing to obey the authority figure, the research participant was far less likely to cooperate. In fact, Milgram (1974) reported that in this type of setting, only 10% of the research participants were willing to carry on with the *learning experiment*. What this suggests is that one person can make a difference, and when someone stands up for what is right, others will follow that lead.

● ✓ ● ● show what you know

1. Match the following definitions with the terms:
   a. how a person is affected by another person
   b. intentionally trying to make people change their attitudes
   c. a person voluntarily changes behavior at the request of someone without authority
   d. someone asks for a small request, followed by a larger request
   e. the urge to modify behaviors, attitudes, and beliefs to match those of others

   ____ conformity   ____ persuasion
   ____ compliance   ____ foot-in-the-door technique
   ____ social influence

2. _____ occurs when we change our behavior, or act in a way we might not normally, because we have been ordered to do so by an authority figure.
   a. Persuasion   c. Conformity
   b. Compliance   d. Obedience

3. Asch's experiments with conformity show how difficult it is to resist the urge to conform to the behaviors, attitudes, beliefs, and opinions of others. At the same time, many of his participants did not cave in to so-called peer pressure. Can you think of an everyday example in which somebody successfully resisted the urge to conform?

✓ CHECK YOUR ANSWERS IN APPENDIX C.

Groups and Relationships

Thus far, the primary focus of this chapter has been individuals in social situations. We learned, for example, how individuals process information about other people (social cognition) and how behavior is shaped by social interactions (social influence). But human beings do not exist solely as isolated units. When striving toward a common goal, we often come together in groups, and these groups have their own fascinating social dynamics.

LET'S DO THIS TOGETHER   The most important competition of Julius Achon's career was probably the 1994 World Junior Championships in Portugal. Julius was 17 at the time, and he represented Uganda in the 1,500 meters. It was his first time flying on an airplane, wearing running shoes, and racing on a rubber track. No one expected an unknown boy from Uganda to win, but Julius surprised everyone, including himself. Crossing the finish line strides ahead of the others, he almost looked uncertain as he raised his arms in celebration.

Julius ran the 1,500 meters (the equivalent of 0.93 miles) in approximately 3 minutes and 40 seconds. Do you suppose he would have run this fast if he had been alone? Research suggests the answer is no (Worringham & Messick, 1983). In some situations, people perform better in the presence of others. This is particularly true when the task at hand is uncomplicated (running) and group members are well prepared (runners may spend months training for races). Thus, **social facilitation** can improve personal performance when the task is fairly straightforward and a person is adequately prepared.

Sometimes other "people" don't have to be present and watching for social facilitation to work. For example, when faced with competitive avatars (graphical representations of people) while riding a stationary "cybercycle," more competitive elderly adults tend to put forth a greater effort than their less competitive counterparts (Anderson-Hanley, Snyder, Nimon, & Arciero, 2011).

Race that Avatar! Competitive seniors pedal harder on stationary bikes when they have an avatar rival to race against (Anderson-Hanley et al., 2011). Here we see that social facilitation does not necessarily require interaction with living, breathing human beings. Cay Anderson-Hanley, Union College, NY

When Two Heads Are *Not* Better Than One

Being around other people does not always provide a performance boost, however. Learning or performing difficult tasks may actually be harder in the presence of others (Aiello & Douthitt, 2001), and group members may not put forth their best effort. When individual contributions to the group aren't easy to ascertain, **social loafing** may occur (Latané, Williams, & Harkins, 1979). Social loafing is the tendency for people to make less than their best effort when individual contributions are too complicated to measure. Many students will shy away from working in groups because of the negative experiences they have had with other group members' social loafing. Want some advice on how to reduce social loafing? Even if an instructor doesn't require it, you should try to get other students in your group to designate and take responsibility for specific tasks, have group members submit their part of the work to the group before the assignment is due, and specify their contributions to the end product (Jones, 2013; Maiden & Perry, 2011).

Social loafing often goes hand-in-hand with **diffusion of responsibility,** or the sharing of duties and responsibilities among all group members. Diffusion of responsibility can lead to feelings of decreased accountability and motivation. If we suspect other group members are slacking, we tend to follow suit in order to keep things equal.

social facilitation The tendency for the presence of others to improve personal performance when the task or event is fairly uncomplicated and a person is adequately prepared.

social loafing The tendency for people to make less than their best effort when individual contributions are too complicated to measure.

diffusion of responsibility The sharing of duties and responsibilities among all group members that can lead to feelings of decreased accountability and motivation.

Slackers of the West

It turns out that social loafing is more likely to occur in societies where people place a high premium on individuality and autonomy. These *individualistic* societies include the United States, Western Europe, and other parts of the Western world. In the *collectivistic* cultures of China and other parts of East Asia, people tend to prioritize community over the individual, and social loafing is less likely to occur. Group members from these more community-oriented societies actually show evidence of working harder (Kerr & Tindale, 2004; Smrt & Karau, 2011). And unlike their individualistic counterparts, they are less interested in outshining their comrades. Preserving group harmony is more important (Tsaw, Murphy, & Detgen, 2011).

IF YOU ARE TRAVELING TO EAST ASIA, SHOULD YOU LEAVE YOUR EGO AT HOME?

Nothing in psychology is ever that simple, however. Social loafing may be less common in collectivist cultures, but it certainly happens (Hong, Wyer, & Fong, 2008). And within every "individualistic" or "collectivistic" society are individuals who do not behave according to these generalities. We should also point out that many group tasks require both individual and shared efforts; in these situations, a combination of individualism and collectivism may lead to more successful outcomes (Wagner, Humphrey, Meyer, & Hollenbeck, 2011).

DEINDIVIDUATION In the last section, we discussed how obedience played a role in the senseless violence carried out by boy soldiers in Uganda. We suspect that the actions of these children also had something to do with *deindividuation*. People in groups sometimes feel a diminished sense of personal responsibility, inhibition, or adherence to social norms. This state of **deindividuation** can occur when group members are not treated as individuals, and thus begin to exhibit a "lack of self-awareness" (Diener, 1979). As members of a group, the boy soldiers may have felt a loss of personal identity, social responsibility, and ability to discriminate right from wrong.

Research suggests that children are indeed vulnerable to deindividuation. In a classic study of trick-or-treaters, Ed Diener, a professor and researcher at the University of Illinois, and his colleagues set up a **study** in 27 homes throughout Seattle, Washington. Children arriving at these houses to trick-or-treat were ushered in by a woman (who was a confederate, of course). She told them they could take *one* piece of candy, which was on a table in a bowl. Coincidentally, next to the bowl of candy (about 2 feet away) was a second bowl full of small coins (pennies and nickels). The woman then excused herself, saying she had to get back to work in another room. What the children didn't know was that another experimenter was observing their behavior through a peep hole, tallying up the amount of candy and/or money they took. The other variable being recorded was the number of children and adults in the hallway; remember, the experimenters never knew how many people would show up when the doorbell rang!

The findings were fascinating. If a parent was present, the children were well behaved (only 8% took more than their allotted one piece of candy). But with no adult present, their behavior changed

CONNECTIONS

In **Chapter 1,** we discussed a type of descriptive research that involves studying participants in their natural environments. *Naturalistic observation* requires that the researcher not disturb the participants or their environment. Would Diener's study be considered naturalistic observation?

Mine for the Taking
A classic Halloween study by Diener and colleagues found that children were most likely to swipe candy and coins when they were anonymous group members. The condition of being anonymous and part of a group seemed to create a state of deindividuation (Diener, Fraser, Beaman, & Kelem, 1976). Samantha Grandy/Shutterstock

dramatically. Of the children who came to the door alone and anonymous (the confederate did not ask for names or other identifying information), 21% took more than they should have. By comparison, 80% of the children who were in a group and anonymous took extra candy and/or money. The researchers suggested that the condition of being in a group combined with anonymity created a sense of deindividuation (Diener et al., 1976). Are you wondering how much money and candy the kids took? It seems that the children who took more than their fair share of candy grabbed as much as their hands could hold (between 1.6 and 2.3 extra candy bars, on average). As for the money, around 14% of the children stole coins (and ignored the candy), while nearly 21% took money and more than one piece of candy.

We have shown how deindividuation occurs within groups of children, but what about adults? Perhaps you have heard about "Bedlam," a football game between arch rival teams from the University of Oklahoma (OU) and Oklahoma State University (OSU). Most years, OU has won, but in 2011, OSU beat OU 44-10. This was the first time in the university's history it captured a Big 12 championship, and the first time it had beaten OU in 9 years. With just a few seconds left, thousands of OSU fans stormed the field, tearing down the goal posts and injuring several people in the celebration. Although an announcement was made toward the end of the game, with the policy of staying off the field made very clear, fans ignored it and even laughed as they flooded the field, without regard for the safety of others. The fans' poor decisions seemed to be a result of deindividuation. This type of behavior has been repeated in many settings and with many groups of people. Why can't we learn to make better decisions when we find ourselves in groups? Perhaps it has something to do with our tendency to act in rash and extreme ways when surrounded by others.

RISKY SHIFT   Imagine you have $250,000 to spend for your company. Will you spend more if you're making decisions alone or working as part of a committee? Researcher James A. F. Stoner (1961, 1968) set out to find the answer to this question, and here's what he discovered: When group members were asked to make a unanimous decision on how to spend the money, they were more likely to recommend uncertain and risky options than individuals working alone, a phenomenon known as the **risky shift.**

GROUP POLARIZATION AND GROUPTHINK   As members of a group work together, their positions tend to become more extreme. If people who strongly support the legalization of marijuana are assembled in a group, their position will become increasingly pro-legalization over time. This phenomenon is known as **group polarization,** or the tendency for a group to take a more extreme position after deliberations and discussion (Myers & Lamm, 1976). As the members of the group listen to each other make arguments, their original positions become more entrenched. Thus, when people hear their opinions echoed by other members of the group, the conversation tends to become more extreme, as the new information tends to reinforce and strengthen the group members' original positions. This raises the following question: Does group deliberation actually help? Perhaps not when the members are initially in agreement.

As a group becomes increasingly united, a very different group dynamic, or process, known as **groupthink** can occur. This is the tendency for group members to maintain cohesiveness and agreement in their decision making, failing to consider all possible alternatives and related viewpoints (Janis, 1972; Rose, 2011). Groupthink has received part of the blame for a variety of disasters, including the *Challenger* space shuttle explosion in 1986, the Mount Everest climbing tragedy in 1996,

CONNECTIONS

What else motivated the children who were *alone*? In **Chapter 9,** we discussed various sources of motivation, ranging from instincts to the need for power. Which of these sources of motivation might help explain why some children took more than their fair share of candy when they thought no one was watching?

Thinking Inside the Box
When group members become increasingly unified, frequently reaching agreement but seldom questioning each other, groupthink has probably taken hold. S. Harris/Cartoonstock

deindividuation The diminished sense of personal responsibility, inhibition, or adherence to social norms that occurs when group members are not treated as individuals.

risky shift The tendency for groups to recommend uncertain and risky options.

group polarization The tendency for a group to take a more extreme stance than originally held after deliberations and discussion.

groupthink The tendency for group members to maintain cohesiveness and agreement in their decision making, failing to consider all possible alternatives and related viewpoints.

and the U.S. decision to invade Iraq in 2003 (Badie, 2010; Burnette, Pollack, & Forsyth, 2011).

As you can see, groupthink can have life-or-death consequences. So, too, can the bystander effect, another alarming phenomenon that occurs among people in groups.

THE BYSTANDER WHO REFUSED TO STAND BY   Before meeting Julius in 2003, the orphans spent their days begging for money and searching for food. Usually, they ate scraps that hotels had poured onto side roads for dogs and cats. Every morning it was the same routine: Wake up, split apart, and search for something to eat. No time for teamwork or group strategizing. But the orphans did help each other when possible, explains Samuel ("Sam") Mugisha, one of the older kids in the original 11 (S. Maugisha, personal communication, March 9, 2012). At night, they kept each other warm coiled beneath the bus, and they shared food when there was enough to go around. The older children looked after the little ones, making sure they had something to eat. The orphans leaned on one another, but they didn't get much assistance from the outside world.

Day after day, they encountered hundreds of passersby. But of all those people, only three or four would typically offer food or money, nothing more—until a thin, muscular man clad in the most unusual outfit appeared. Wearing a sleeveless top (a runner's singlet), short shorts, and fancy sneakers, Julius Achon looked different from any person the orphans had seen before. And he was, of course, different. This man would ultimately ensure the orphans had everything they needed for a chance at a better life—food, clothing, a place to sleep, an education, and a family.

LO 8   Recognize the circumstances that influence the occurrence of the bystander effect.

THE BYSTANDER EFFECT   Before meeting Julius, the orphans had been homeless for several months. Why didn't anyone try to rescue them? "Everybody was fearing responsibility," Julius says. In northern Uganda, many people cannot even afford to feed themselves, so they are reluctant to lend a helping hand.

But perhaps there was another factor at work, one that psychologists call the **bystander effect.** When a person is in trouble, bystanders have the tendency to assume (and perhaps wish) that someone else will help—and therefore they stand by and do nothing, partly a result of the *diffusion of responsibility.* This is particularly true when there are many other people present. Strange as it seems, we are more likely to aid a person in distress if no one else is present (Darley & Latané, 1968; Eagly & Crowley, 1986; Latané & Darley, 1968). So when people encountered the 11 orphans begging on the street, they probably assumed and hoped somebody else would take care of the problem. *These children must belong to someone; their parents will come back for them.*

Perhaps the most famous illustration of the bystander effect was the attack on Kitty Genovese. It was March 13, 1964, around 3:15 A.M., when Catherine "Kitty" Genovese arrived home from work in her Queens, New York, neighborhood. As she approached her apartment building, an attacker brutally stabbed her. Kitty screamed for help, but initial reports suggested that no one came to her rescue. The attacker ran away, and Kitty stumbled to her apartment building. But he soon returned, raping and stabbing her to death. The *New York Times* originally reported that 38 neighbors heard her cries for help, witnessed the attack, and did nothing to help. But the evidence suggests that the second attack occurred inside her building, where few people could have witnessed it (Manning, Levine, & Collins, 2007).

bystander effect The tendency for people to avoid getting involved in an emergency they witness because they assume someone else will help.

Casualties of the Bystander Effect
Kitty Genovese (left) and Hugo Tale-Yax (right) lived in different eras, but both were victims of brutal assaults and the cold indifference of bystanders in New York City. Genovese and Tale-Yax might have been saved if the passersby who saw them in distress had called for help. left: NY Daily News Archive via Getty Images; right: Christopher Sadowski/Splash News/Newscom

More recently, in April 2010, a homeless man (also in Queens) was left to die after several people walked by him and decided to do nothing. The man, Hugo Tale-Yax, had been trying to help a woman under assault, but the attacker stabbed him in the chest (Livingston, Doyle, & Mangan, 2010, April 25). As many as 25 people walked past Mr. Tale-Yax as he lay on the ground dying, and one even took a cell phone picture of him before walking away. Can you think of any reason why they wouldn't help? Would you help someone in such a situation?

A recent review of the research suggests that things might not be as "bleak" as these events suggest. In extremely dangerous situations, bystanders are actually *more* likely to help even if there is more than one person watching. More dangerous situations are recognized and interpreted quickly as being such, leading to faster intervention and help (Fischer et al., 2011). If we want to increase the likelihood of bystanders getting involved in stopping violence, the community needs to educate its members about their responsibilities as neighbors and take steps to increase people's confidence in their ability to help (Banyard & Moynihan, 2011). Take a look at **TABLE 15.2** to learn about factors that increase helping behavior.

Now that we have seen how *inaction* can perpetuate human suffering, let's take a look at the other extreme: hurtful behaviors that are in your face, unreasonable, and grounded in ignorance.

Table 15.2 WHY LEND A HAND?

Why People Help	Explanation
Kin selection	We are more likely to help those who are close relatives, as it might promote the survival of our genes (Alexander, 1974; Hamilton, 1964).
Empathy	We assist others to reduce their distress (Batson & Powell, 2003).
Social exchange theory	We help when the benefits of our good deeds outweigh the cost (Thibaut & Kelly, 1959).
Reciprocal altruism	We help those who we believe can return the favor in the future (Trivers, 1971).
Mood	We tend to help others when our mood is good, but we also help when our spirits are low, knowing that this behavior can improve our mood (Batson & Powell, 2003; Schnall, Roper, & Fessler, 2010).

There are many reasons people assist each other in times of need. Above are some common explanations.

show what you know

1. _____, or the tendency for people to put forth less than their best effort, might occur when individual contributions to the group are difficult to measure.
   a. Cognitive dissonance   c. Deindividuation
   b. Social facilitation   d. Social loafing

2. In an experiment studying _____, trick-or-treating children were more likely to take extra candy and/or money if they were anonymous members of a group.

3. _____ is the tendency for people to not react in an emergency, often thinking that someone else will step in to help.
   a. Group polarization   c. The bystander effect
   b. The risky shift   d. Deindividuation

4. Group polarization is the tendency for a group to take a more extreme stance after deliberations and discussion. If you were in a group making an important decision, what would you tell the other group members about group polarization and how to guard against it?

✓ CHECK YOUR ANSWERS IN APPENDIX C.

Aggression

THE ULTIMATE INSULT   When Julius attended high school in Uganda's capital city of Kampala, he never told his classmates that he had been kidnapped by the LRA. "I would not tell them, or anybody, that I was a child soldier," he says. Had the other students known, they might have called him a *rebel*—one of the most derogatory terms you can use to describe a person in Uganda. Calling someone a rebel is like saying that individual is worthless. "You're poor, you do not know anything; you're a killer," Julius says. "It's the same pain as in America [when] they used to call Black people 'nigger.' You feel that kind of pain inside you . . . when they call you a 'rebel' within your country."

LO 9   Demonstrate an understanding of aggression and identify some of its causes.

Using racial slurs and hurling threatening insults is a form of *aggression*. Psychologists define **aggression** as intimidating or threatening behavior or attitudes intended to hurt someone. Where does aggression originate? Some research suggests that aggressive tendencies are rooted in biology. Studies comparing identical and fraternal twins suggest that aggression may run in families. **Identical twins,** who have the same genes, are more likely than fraternal twins to share aggressive traits (Bezdjian, Tuvblad, Raine, & Baker, 2011; Rowe, Almeida, & Jacobson, 1999). Hormones also appear to be an important part of the equation, as high levels of testosterone and low levels of the neurotransmitter serotonin correlate with aggression (Glenn, Raine, Schug, Gao, & Granger, 2011; Montoya, Terburg, Bos, & van Honk, 2012).

But like any phenomenon in psychology, aggression is also influenced by **environment.** According to the **frustration-aggression hypothesis,** we can all show aggressive behavior when placed in a frustrating situation (Dollard, Miller, Doob, Mowrer, & Sears, 1939). Males tend to show more *direct aggression* (physical displays of aggression), while females are more likely to engage in *relational aggression* (gossip, exclusion, ignoring) (Archer, 2004; Archer & Coyne, 2005). One important reason for this tendency is that females run a greater risk of bodily injury resulting from a physical confrontation; therefore, they tend to opt for more relational aggression (Campbell, 1999).

Stereotypes and Discrimination

Typically, we associate aggression with behavior, but it can also exist in the mind, coloring our *attitudes* about people and things. This is evidenced by the existence of **stereotypes**—the conclusions or inferences we make about people who are different from us, based on their group membership (such as race, religion, age, or gender). Stereotypes are often negative (*Blonde people are airheads*), but they can also be positive (*Asians are good at math*). Either way, stereotypes can be harmful.

Stereotypes are often associated with a set of perceived characteristics that we think describe members of a group. The stereotypical college instructor is absentminded, absorbed in thought, and unapproachable. The quintessential motorcycle rider is covered in tattoos, and the teenager with the tongue ring is rebelling against her parents. What do all these stereotypes have in common? They are not objective or based on empirical research. In other words, they are like bad theories of personality that characterize people based on a single behavior or trait. These stereotypes typically include a variety of predicted behaviors and traits that are rooted in subjective observations and value judgments.

When Julius was living in Louisiana, a man once approached him and said, "Is it true in Africa people still walk [around] naked?" We can only imagine where this man

CONNECTIONS

In previous chapters, we have stated that *identical twins* share 100% of their genetic material, whereas fraternal twins share approximately 50%. Here, we see that identical twins are more similar on an aggressive trait than fraternal twins, which suggests there is a genetic basis for aggressive behavior.

In **Chapter 10,** we described *gender differences* in aggression, including a variety of causes (such as differences in testosterone levels). Here, we note that environmental factors play a role as well.

aggression Intimidating or threatening behavior or attitudes intended to hurt someone.

frustration-aggression hypothesis Suggests that aggression may occur in response to frustration.

stereotypes Conclusions or inferences we make about people who are different from us based on their group membership, such as race, religion, age, or gender.

in-group The group to which we belong.

out-group People outside the group to which we belong.

social identity How we view ourselves within our social group.

ethnocentrism To see the world only from the perspective of one's own group.

had gathered his knowledge of Africa (perhaps he had spent a bit too much time flipping through dated issues of *National Geographic*), but one thing seems certain: He was relying on an inaccurate stereotype of African people. The underlying message was clearly an aggressive one; he judged African people to be primitive and not as advanced as he was.

> **LO 10** Recognize how group affiliation influences the development of stereotypes.

GROUPS AND SOCIAL IDENTITY   Evolutionary psychologists would suggest that stereotypes allowed human beings to quickly identify the group to which they belonged (Liddle, Shackelford, & Weekes-Shackelford, 2012)—an adaptive trait, given that groups provide safety. But because we tend to think our group is superior, we may draw incorrect conclusions about members of other groups, or outsiders in general. We tend to see the world in terms of the **in-group** (the group to which *we* belong, or *us*) and the **out-group** (those who are outside the group to which we belong, or *them*). For better or worse, our affiliation with an in-group helps us form our **social identity,** or view of ourselves within a social group, and this process begins at a very young age. Those in your in-group may influence your behaviors and thoughts more than you realize. Their opinions may even shape your perception of beauty.

Running Hero
Julius runs by the Lira bus station where he discovered 11 orphans lying under a bus. Despite all the personal struggles Julius faced—living abroad, struggling financially, and battling foreign stereotypes of African people—Julius made a most selfless decision. He and his family adopted all 11 children. Charlie Shoemaker for Runner's World Magazine. Copyright: 2011

from the pages of **SCIENTIFIC AMERICAN**

Following the Crowd

Changing your mind to fit in may not be a conscious choice

Beauty is not just in the eye of the beholder—it is also in the eyes of the beholder's friends. A study published in April in *Psychological Science* found that men judge a woman as more attractive when they believe their peers find that woman attractive—supporting a budding theory that groupthink is not as simple as once thought.

Researchers at Harvard University asked 14 college-age men to rate the attractiveness of 180 female faces on a scale of 1 to 10. Thirty minutes later the psychologists asked the men to rate the faces again, but this time the faces were paired with a random rating that the scientists told the men were averages of

their peers' scores. The men were strongly influenced by their peers' supposed judgments—they rated the women with higher scores as more attractive than they did the first time. Functional MRI scans showed that the men were not simply lying to fit in. Activity in their brain's pleasure centers indicated that their opinions of the women's beauty really did change.

The results fit in with a new theory of conformity, says the study's lead author Jamil Zaki. When people conform to group expectations, Zaki says, they are not concealing their own preferences; they actually have aligned their minds. In addition, the likelihood of someone conforming depends on his or her place within the group, according to a study in the December 2010 issue of the *British Journal of Sociology*. Members who are central are more likely to dissent because their identities are more secure. Those at the edges, who feel only partially involved or are new to the group, may have more malleable opinions. **Carrie Arnold. Reproduced with permission. Copyright © 2011 Scientific American, a division of Nature America, Inc. All rights reserved.**

DISCRIMINATION   Seeing the world from the narrow perspective of our own group may lead to **ethnocentrism.** This term is often used in reference to cultural groups, yet it can apply to any group (think of football teams, glee clubs, college rivals, or nations). We tend to see our own group as *the one* that is worthy of emulation, the superior group. This type of group identification can lead to stereo-typing, discussed earlier, and **discrimination,** which involves showing favoritism or hostility to others because of their affiliation with a group. As noted by Julius, even former child soldiers are at risk for becoming objects of discrimination.

Those in the out-group are particularly vulnerable to becoming scapegoats. A **scapegoat** is the target of negative emotions, beliefs, and behaviors. During periods of major stress (such as an economic crisis), scapegoats are often blamed for upsetting social situations (such as high unemployment).

PREJUDICE   People who harbor stereotypes and blame scapegoats are more likely to feel **prejudice,** hostile or negative attitudes toward individuals or groups (INFO-GRAPHIC 15.3). While prejudice and explicit racism have declined in the United States over the last half-century, there is still considerable evidence that negative at-titudes persist. The same is true when it comes to sexual orientation, disabilities, and religious beliefs (Carr, Dweck, & Pauker, 2012; Dovidio, Kawakami, & Gaertner, 2002). The causes of prejudice are complex and varied. Cognitive aspects of preju-dice include the just-world hypothesis, which assumes that another person has done something to deserve the bad things happening to him. This type of belief can lead to feelings that a person should be able to control events in his life, which in turn can lead to feelings of anger and hostility. Prejudice may also result from conformity if a person seeks approval from others with strong prejudicial views.

Researchers have nevertheless concluded that prejudice can be reduced when people are forced to work together toward a common goal. In the early 1970s, Eliot Aronson and colleagues developed the notion of a jigsaw classroom. The teachers created exercises that required all students to complete individual tasks, the results of which would fit together like a jigsaw puzzle. The students began to realize the impor-tance of working cooperatively to reach the desired goal. Ultimately, every student's contribution was an essential piece of the puzzle, and this resulted in all the students feeling valuable (Aronson, 2013).

STEREOTYPE THREAT   Stereotypes, discrimination, and prejudice are conceptu-ally related to **stereotype threat,** a "situational threat" in which a person is aware of others' negative expectations. This leads to a fear of being judged and/or treated as inferior, and it can actually undermine performance in a specific area associated with the stereotype (Steele, 1997).

African American college students are often the targets of racial stereotypes about poor academic abilities. These threatening stereotypes can lead to lowered perfor-mance on tests designed to measure ability and/or a *disidentification* with the role of a student (in other words, taking on the attitude that *I am not a student*). Interestingly, a person does not have to believe the stereotype is accurate in order for it to have an impact (Steele, 1997, 2010). If someone has a stereotypical belief (all professors are absentminded, for example), it can still have an impact even if the target doesn't believe it's true. One may, for instance, vehemently deny or brush off such a claim with a laugh.

There is a great deal of variation in how people react to stereotype threats (Block, Koch, Liberman, Merriweather, & Roberson, 2011). Some people simply "fend off" the stereotype, by working harder to disprove it. Others feel discouraged and respond by getting angry, either overtly or quietly. Still others seem to ignore the threats. These resilient types appear to "bounce back" and grow from the negative experience. When confronted with a stereotype, they redirect their responses to create an environment that is more inclusive and less conducive to stereotyping.

discrimination Showing favoritism or hostility to others because of their affiliation with a group.

scapegoat A target of negative emotions, beliefs, and behaviors; typically, a member of the out-group who receives blame for an upsetting social situation.

prejudice Holding hostile or negative attitudes toward an individual or group.

stereotype threat A "situational threat" in which individuals are aware of others' negative expectations, which leads to their fear that they will be judged and/or treated as inferior.

Thinking About Other People
Stereotypes, Discrimination, and Prejudice

Attitudes are complex and only sometimes related to our behaviors. Like most attitudes, prejudicial attitudes can be connected with our *cognitions* about groups of people, our negative *feelings* about others (also referred to as prejudice), and our *behaviors* (discriminating against others). Understanding how and when these pieces connect to each other is an important goal of social psychology. Jane Elliott's classic "Blue Eyes/Brown Eyes" exercise helps demonstrate how stereotypes, discrimination, and prejudice may be connected.

Prejudical attitude toward others

Cognitive component (beliefs and ideas)

We tend to categorize people in terms of the *in-group* (the group to which we belong) and the *out-group* (people different from us in some way). **Stereotypes** are beliefs or assumptions we hold about people, based on perceived differences we think describe members of their group.

Affective component (emotional evaluation)

Prejudice, or feelings of hostility, anger, or discomfort toward members of out-groups.

Social psychologists often use prejudice to refer to both these negative attitudes and the negative feelings tied to them.

Behavioral component (the way we respond)

Discrimination, or treating others differently because of their affiliation with a group. Can include showing hostility or anger to others, or can be more subtle, such as different body language or tone of voice.

Stereotype

"cleaner, more civilized, smarter"

Prejudice

Preiudice

Discrimination

Brown-eyes dislike blue-eyes, but have to be nice while in class.

Brown-eyes dislike blue-eyes and exclude them from games at recess.

Brown-eyes, who are required to sit at the front of the room, do not sit with blue-eyes, who must sit at the back.

Discrimination

When Dr. Martin Luther King, Jr., was assassinated In 1968, a teacher named Jane Elliott gave her students a lesson about discrimination. Because no African Americans lived in their Iowa town, she knew students would have trouble understanding what motivated the terrible act. Elliott invited the class to join her in an exercise in which one set of students was segregated into a negatively stereotyped out-group: "Suppose we divided the class into blue-eyed people and brown-eyed people.... [B]rown-eyed people are better than blue-eyed people. They are cleaner . . . more civilized . . . smarter" (Peters, 1971, pp. 20–21).

In her exercise, Elliott created a situation in which discrimination initially existed without the presence of actual feelings of hostility or anger. Although prejudice and discrimination often go hand in hand, either condition can exist independently.

During the exercise, a list of rules governed behavior for both groups. For example, only children with brown eyes were allowed to sit at the front of the room near the teacher. The effect of this manufactured discrimination surprised even Elliott. The brown-eyed children quickly became openly hostile toward the blue-eyed children. And "[t]he blue-eyed children were miserable.... [T]heir entire attitudes were those of defeat. Their classroom work regressed sharply from that of the day before" (Peters, 1971, p. 25).

Unfortunately, stereotypes are pervasive in our society. Just contemplate all the positive and negative stereotypes associated with certain lines of work. Lawyers are greedy, truck drivers are overweight, and (dare we say) psychologists are manipulative. Can you think of any negative stereotypes associated with prison guards? As you read the next feature, think about how stereotypes come to life when people fail to think critically about their behaviors.

CONTROVERSIES

The Stanford "Prison"

➡️⬅️ August 1971: Philip Zimbardo of Stanford University launched what would become one of the most controversial experiments in the history of psychology. Zimbardo and his colleagues carefully selected 24 male college students to play the roles of prisoners and guards in a simulated "prison" setup in the basement of Stanford University's psychology building. (Three of the selected students did not end up

Prison Horrors
(left) Prisoners in Zimbardo's 1971 prison experiment are forced to wear bags over their heads. (right) An Abu Ghraib detainee lies on the floor attached to a leash in 2003. The dehumanization and cruel treatment of prisoners in the "Stanford Prison" and the Abu Ghraib facility are disturbingly similar. left: Philip G. Zimbardo, Inc.; right: AP Photo

participating, so the final number of participants included 10 prisoners and 11 guards.) The young men chosen for the experiment were deemed "normal-average" by the researchers, who administered several psychological tests (Haney, Banks, & Zimbardo, 1973, p. 90).

After being "arrested" in their homes by Palo Alto Police officers, the prisoners were searched and booked at a local police station, and then sent to the "prison" at Stanford. The experiment was supposed to last for 2 weeks, but the behavior of the guards and the prisoners was so disturbing the researchers abandoned the study after just 6 days (Haney & Zimbardo, 1998). The guards became abusive, punishing the prisoners, stripping them naked, and confiscating their mattresses. It seemed as if they had lost sight of the prisoners' humanity, as they ruthlessly wielded their newfound power. As one guard stated, "Looking back, I'm impressed how little I felt for them" (Haney et al., 1973, p. 88). Some prisoners became passive and obedient, accepting the guards' cruel treatment; others were released early due to "extreme emotional depression, crying, rage, and acute anxiety" (p. 81).

"...LOOKING BACK, I'M IMPRESSED HOW LITTLE I FELT FOR THEM."

How can we explain this fiasco? The guards and prisoners, it seemed, took their assigned **social roles** and ran way too far with them. Social roles guide our behavior and represent the positions we hold in social groups, and the responsibilities and expectations associated with those roles.

We should note that this experiment took place during a time when prisons were under intense public scrutiny. Some scholars suggest that the participants were "acting

social roles The positions we hold in social groups, and the responsibilities and expectations associated with those roles.

out their stereotypic images" of guards and prisoners, and behaving in accordance with the researchers' expectations (Banuazizi & Movahedi, 1975, p. 159).

Nevertheless, the Stanford Prison Experiment did shed light on the power of social roles. It also generated quite a storm of controversy. The study had been approved by the university's review committee, and it did not violate the existing standards of the American Psychological Association (APA), yet many people questioned its ethical validity. The APA has since changed its guidelines, and the Stanford Prison Experiment would no longer be considered acceptable (Ratnesar, 2011, July/August). Although the ethics of the study have been questioned, its findings continue to shed light on contemporary events. In 2004 news broke that American soldiers and intelligence officials at Iraq's Abu Ghraib prison had beaten, sodomized, and forced detainees to commit degrading sexual acts (Hersh, 2004, May 10). The similarities between Abu Ghraib and the Stanford Prison are remarkable (Zimbardo, 2007). In both cases, authority figures threatened, abused, and forced inmates to be naked. Those in charge seemed to derive pleasure from violating and humiliating other human beings (Haney et al., 1973; Hersh, 2004, May 10). ➤◄

Before we move on to more positive things, let's take one last detour through the dark side. You've learned all about aggressive behaviors, but did it ever occur to you that aggression can occur through a string of 1s and 0s? It's aggression 2.0: Rudeness on the Internet.

from the pages of **SCIENTIFIC AMERICAN**

Rudeness on the Internet

Mean comments arise from a lack of eye contact more than from anonymity

Read any Web forum, and you'll agree: people are meaner online than in "real life." Psychologists have largely blamed this disinhibition on anonymity and invisibility: when you're online, no one knows who you are or what you look like. A new study in *Computers in Human Behavior,* however, suggests that above and beyond anything else, we're nasty on the Internet because we don't make eye contact with our compatriots.

Researchers at the University of Haifa in Israel asked 71 pairs of college students who did not know one another to debate an issue over Instant Messenger and try to come up with an agreeable solution. The pairs, seated in different rooms, chatted in various conditions: some were asked to share personal, identifying details; others could see side views of their partner's body through webcams; and others were asked to maintain near-constant eye contact with the aid of close-up cameras attached to the top of their computer.

Far more than anonymity or invisibility, whether or not the subjects had to look into their partner's eyes predicted how mean they were. When their eyes were hidden, participants were twice as likely to be hostile. Even if the subjects were both unrecognizable (with only their eyes on screen) and anonymous, they rarely made threats if they maintained eye contact. Although no one knows exactly why eye contact is so crucial, lead author and behavioral scientist Noam Lapidot-Lefler, now at the Max Stern Yezreel Valley College in Israel, notes that seeing a partner's eyes "helps you understand the other person's feelings, the signals that the person is trying to send you," which fosters empathy and communication. **Melinda Wenner Moyer. Reproduced with permission. Copyright © 2012 Scientific American, a division of Nature America, Inc. All rights reserved.**

Much of this chapter has focused on the negative aspects of human behavior, such as obedience, stereotyping, and discrimination. And while we cannot deny the existence of these tendencies, we believe they are overshadowed by the goodness that lies within every one of us.

Prosocial Behavior

You may be wondering why we chose to include Joe and Susanne Maggio in the same chapter as Julius Achon. What do these people have in common, and why are they featured together in a chapter on social psychology? We chose these individuals because their stories send a positive message, illuminating what is best about human relationships, like the capacity to love and feel empathy. They epitomize the positive side of social psychology.

LO 11   Compare prosocial behavior and altruism.

Julius Achon's actions exemplify *prosocial behavior*, or behavior aimed at benefiting others. After meeting the orphans in 2003, Julius kept his promise to assist them, wiring his family $150 a month to cover the cost of food, clothing, school uniforms, tuition, and other necessities—even when he and his wife were struggling to stay afloat. For 3 years, Julius was the children's sole source of financial support. Then in 2006, when Julius was living in Portland and working for Nike, a friend helped him gather additional support from others. The following year, Julius formalized his efforts by creating the Achon Uganda Children's Fund (AUCF), a nonprofit organization dedicated to improving the living conditions of children in the rural areas of northern Uganda. AUCF's latest project is the construction and operation of a medical clinic in Julius's home county of Otuke. The Kristina Acuma Achon Health Center is named after Julius's mother, who was shot by the LRA in 2004 and died from her wounds because she lacked access to proper medical care. (For more information about the Achon Uganda Children's Fund, please see http://achonugandachildren.org.)

You Asked, Julius Answers

http://qrs.ly/t83o0kj

What advice would you give to someone interested in charitable work?

Beautiful Children
Julius runs alongside boys and girls from the Orum primary school in Uganda's Otuke district. Samson Opus

If you're wondering what became of the 11 orphans, they are all flourishing. The teenage girl in tattered clothing—the first to emerge from under the bus that morning in 2003—is now in nursing school. Sam Mugisha is following in the footsteps of Julius, running on the track team of an esteemed high school in Kampala. He is well on his way to becoming a competitive racer with an American college or professional club. As for the younger children, they are still living with the Achon family and attending school. They do their homework together at the dining room table, helping each other get through tough problems.

altruism A desire or motivation to help others with no expectation of anything in return.

On the Up Side

It feels good to give to others, even when you receive nothing in return. The satisfaction derived from knowing you made someone feel happier, more secure, or appreciated is enough of a reward. The desire or motivation to help others with no expectations of payback is called **altruism.** *Empathy,* or the ability to understand and recognize another's emotional point of view, is a major component of altruism.

ALTRUISM AND TODDLERS   The seeds of altruism appear to be planted very early in life. Children as young as 18 months have been observed demonstrating helping behavior. One study found that the vast majority of 18-month-olds would help a researcher obtain an out-of-reach object, assist him in a book-stacking exercise, and open a door for him when his hands were full. It is important to note the babies did not help when the researcher intentionally put the object out of reach, or if he appeared satisfied with the stack of books. They only assisted when it appeared assistance was needed (Warneken & Tomasello, 2006). What was happening in the brains of these young children? Research has shown that particular areas of the brain (such as the medial prefrontal cortex) show increased activity in association with feelings of empathy and helping behaviors (Rameson, Morelli, & Lieberman, 2012). Given that altruism shows up so early in life, perhaps you are wondering if it is an innate characteristic. Researchers are, in fact, trying to determine if this characteristic has a genetic component, and the findings from twin studies identify "considerable heritability" of altruistic tendencies and other prosocial behaviors (Jiang, Chew, & Ebstein, 2013). But as always, we should remember that with a characteristic like altruism, we must consider the biopsychosocial perspective, and recognize the interacting forces of genetics, environment, and culture (Knafo & Israel, 2010).

REDUCING STRESS AND INCREASING HAPPINESS   Research suggests that helping others reduces stress and increases happiness (Schwartz, Keyl, Marcum, & Bode, 2009; Schwartz, Meisenhelder, Yunsheng, & Reed, 2003). The gestures don't have to be grand to be altruistic or prosocial. Consider the last time you bought coffee for a colleague without being asked, or gave a stranger a quarter to fill his parking meter? Do you recycle, conserve electricity, and take public transportation? These behaviors indicate an awareness of the need to conserve resources for the benefit of all. Promoting sustainability is an indirect, yet very impactful, prosocial endeavor. Perhaps you haven't opened your home to 11 orphaned children, but you may perform prosocial acts more regularly than you realize.

Even if you're not the type to reach out to strangers, you probably demonstrate prosocial behavior toward your family and close friends. This giving of yourself allows you to experience the most magical element of human existence: love.

CONNECTIONS

In **Chapter 12,** we discussed how altruistic behaviors can reduce stress. When helping someone else, we generally don't have time to focus on our own problems; we also see that there are people dealing with more troubling issues than we are.

✓ show what you know

1. According to research, which of the following plays a role in aggressive behavior?
   a. low social identity
   b. low levels of the hormone testosterone
   c. low levels of the neurotransmitter serotonin
   d. low levels of ethnocentrism

2. Julius Achon sent money home every month to help cover the cost of food, clothing, and schooling for his 11 adopted children. This is a good example of
   a. the just-world hypothesis.
   b. deindividuation.
   c. individualistic behavior.
   d. prosocial behavior.

3. Name and describe the different displays of aggression exhibited by males and females.

4. Students often have difficulty identifying how the concepts of stereotypes, discrimination, and prejudice are related. If you were sitting at a table with a sixth-grade student, how would you explain their similarities and differences?

✓ CHECK YOUR ANSWERS IN APPENDIX C.

Love Grows
Joe, Kristina, and Susanne celebrate the arrival of their new family members: Joseph Jr., Michael Charles Frank, and Sophia Elizabeth. The triplets came into the world on February 11, 2013.
Joe Maggio

Attraction and Love

Less than a year after meeting Susanne, Joe purchased an engagement ring. He carried it around in his pocket for 3 months, and then proposed to her one morning over breakfast. They have been happily married for over 5 years. Some things have changed since that rendezvous at Chili's 8 years ago. Joe left the ice cream business for a corporate career, *little* Kristina is now a teenager, and Susanne gave birth to TRIPLETS in February 2013—two boys and a girl.

Other things remain the same, like Joe's goofy sense of humor. He still strolls into the supermarket singing at the top of his lungs and tells people "good morning" when it's 11 o'clock at night. "I'm a big kid," Joe says, "but you know when it comes to my family, it's all about making sure that they are happy and making sure that they are taken care of, and that's my only priority in life."

Interpersonal Attraction

LO 12 Identify the three major factors contributing to interpersonal attraction.

It seems Joe and Susanne have made a very happy life for themselves. Things can get hectic with three infant triplets and a teen, but they seem content and able to cope with whatever challenges may arise. Joe and Susanne make a great team. How do you explain their compatibility? We suspect it has something to do with **interpersonal attraction,** the factors that lead us to form friendships or romantic relationships with others. What are these mysterious attraction factors? Let's focus our attention on the three that are most important: proximity, similarity, and physical attractiveness.

WE'RE CLOSE: PROXIMITY   We would guess that the majority of people in your social circle live nearby. **Proximity,** or nearness, plays a significant role in the formation of our relationships. The closer two people live geographically, the greater the odds that they will meet and spend time together, and the more likely they are to establish a bond (Festinger, Schachter, & Back, 1950; Nahemow & Lawton, 1975). One study looking at the development of friendships in a college classroom setting concluded that sitting in nearby seats and being assigned to the same work groups **correlated** with the development of friendships (Back, Schmukle, & Egloff, 2008). In other words, sitting next to someone in class, or even in the same row, increases the chances that you will become friends. Would you agree?

Notions of proximity have changed since the introduction of the Internet. Thanks to applications like *Skype* and *Google Hangouts,* we can now have face-to-face conversations with people who are thousands of miles away. Online dating sites offer similar capabilities through chats and instant messaging. They also offer the option of geographic filtering, allowing users to narrow their searches to people who live in a certain zip code or city. But do all these new tools really improve the way people relate to one another? For Joe and Susanne, the answer seems to be "yes." If it weren't for Match.com, their paths probably would not have crossed. As for the rest of humanity, the answer is not so straightforward.

CONNECTIONS

In **Chapter 1,** we described how researchers examine relationships between two variables. A correlation does not necessarily mean one variable causes changes in the other. What other factors might be influencing friendships to develop in the classroom?

interpersonal attraction The factors that lead us to form friendships or romantic relationships with others.

proximity Nearness; plays an important role in the formation of relationships.

mere-exposure effect The more we are exposed to someone or something, the more positive a reaction we have toward it.

SOCIAL MEDIA and psychology

Relationships Online

The great advantage of online dating, according to researchers, is that it broadens the dating pool, providing users with opportunities to meet people they never would encounter offline (Finkel et al., 2012). What other medium offers a safe way to browse through thousands, if not millions, of potential partners and prescreen candidates based on a slew of personal data?

There are drawbacks, however, like the tendency for many online daters to focus on profile pictures and other superficial details. Also, don't count on the compatibility algorithms many online dating sites advertise, as researchers are skeptical of them (Finkel, et al., 2012). Despite these shortcomings, relationships that start on these sites are surprisingly successful. According to one study, around 20% of couples who met online had formed lasting relationships, defined as married, engaged, or living together (Bargh & McKenna, 2004).

You may be wondering how social media sites such as Facebook affect interpersonal bonds. Research suggests that many people use social media to enhance the relationships they already have (Anderson, Fagan, Woodnutt, & Chamorro-Premuzic, 2012). Teenagers, in particular, use social networking sites to make contact with their "offline" friends. Their online activities are primarily social (communicating as opposed to playing video games, for example) and seem to reinforce existing friendships (Reich et al., 2012). 🌑

Relationships 2.0
Social networking sites are an important component of modern relationships, particularly among young people. For many teens, communicating through sites like Facebook is an important means of cultivating relationships (Reich, Subrahmanyam, & Espinoza, 2012). Paul Noth/ The New Yorker Collection

"I can't wait to see what you're like online."

LOOKING FOR LOVE IN ELECTRONIC PLACES.

MERE-EXPOSURE EFFECT   These repeated contacts with friends serve a purpose; the **mere-exposure effect** suggests that the more we are exposed to people, food, jingles, songs, politics, or music, the more positive a reaction we have toward them. More time spent online with friends can strengthen relationships, *merely* through exposure.

The mere-exposure effect may, to a certain extent, explain why Joe and Susanne are more in love today than they were 8 years ago. After years of positive exposure to one another (living under the same roof, raising children together, and sharing new experiences), their connection has deepened.

Believe it or not, the mere-exposure effect also appears to affect your perception of your own face. Think of how many times you have looked at yourself in the mirror. How do you think that repeated exposure impacts your estimation of your attractiveness? In one study, researchers showed students pictures of themselves and the reversed, or mirror image, versions of those photos. Amazingly, students preferred the reversed image—the one they see every time they look in the mirror—to the "normal" photo. Yet, the opposite was true when the pictures were shown to their friends; they, too, preferred the image they repeatedly see (Mita, Dermer, & Knight, 1977).

But here's the flip side. Repeated *negative* exposures may lead to stronger distaste. If a person you frequently encounter has annoying habits or uncouth behavior, negative feelings might develop, even if your feelings were initially positive (Cunningham, Shamblen, Barbee, & Ault, 2005). This could be problematic for romantic relationships. All those minor irritations you overlooked early in the relationship can evolve into major headaches.

SIMILARITY   Perhaps you have heard the saying "birds of a feather flock together." This statement alludes to the concept of *similarity,* another factor that contributes to interpersonal attraction (Moreland & Zajonc, 1982; Morry, Kito, & Ortiz, 2011). We tend to prefer those who share our interests, viewpoints, ethnicity, values, and other characteristics. Even age, education, and occupation tend to be similar among those who are close (Lott & Lott, 1965).

"This isn't working. We have nothing in common."

PHYSICAL ATTRACTIVENESS   We probably don't need to tell you that *physical attractiveness* plays a major role in interpersonal attraction (Eastwick, Eagly, Finkel, & Johnson, 2011; Lou & Zhang, 2009). But here is the question: Is beauty really in the eye of the beholder or do people from different cultures and historical periods generally see eye to eye? There is some degree of consistency in the way people rate facial attractiveness (Langlois et al., 2000), with facial symmetry generally considered an attractive trait (Grammer & Thornhill, 1994). But some aspects of beauty do appear to be culturally distinct (Gangestad & Scheyd, 2005). In some parts of the world, people go to great lengths to elongate their necks, increase height, pierce their bodies, augment their breasts, enlarge or reduce the size of their waists, and paint themselves—just so others within their culture will find them attractive. In America, the ideal body shape for women has changed over the years (think of Marilyn Monroe versus Jennifer Aniston), suggesting that cultural concepts of beauty can morph over time.

LOOKING GOOD IN THOSE GENES: THE EVOLUTIONARY PERSPECTIVE
Why is physical attractiveness so important? Beauty is a sign of health, and healthy people have greater potential for longevity and successful breeding (Gangestad & Scheyd, 2005). Consider this evidence: Women are more likely to seek out men with healthy-looking physical characteristics when they are experiencing peak fertility and are likely to conceive. Ovulating women tend to look for masculine characteristics that suggest a genetic advantage, such as facial symmetry and social dominance, in order to provide the greatest benefit to offspring. This type of man can provide good genes, meaning his offspring have a greater chance of being healthy, attractive, and living longer, but will he stick around and help raise children?

One group of researchers used this "evolutionary explanation" to explore why women might seek out "sexy cads," or men who are unlikely to take care of their children. Female undergraduate students were asked to participate in what they believed was a study on how their health influenced their mate selection. The women were asked to provide several urine samples to determine when they were ovulating. In one of the research settings, women viewed pictures of physically attractive and average-looking men. The physically attractive men were charismatic and adventurous, and the average-looking men were reliable, stable, and good providers—or so the women were told. When the women were ovulating, they tended to believe that the sexy cads (physically attractive and charismatic men) would actually be more devoted fathers and partners than the "nice" reliable men (Durante, Griskevicius, Simpson, Cantú, & Li, 2012). The implication is that women may choose more attractive-looking men even when it is not in their best interest to do so. You can probably think of some films that portray women making these types of choices. More often than not, such movies have happy endings. Do you think this is what usually happens in real life?

BEAUTY PERKS   Physically attractive people seem to have more opportunities. Beauty is correlated with how much money someone makes, the type of job she holds, and overall success (Pfeifer, 2012). Good-looking children and adults are viewed as more intelligent and more popular, and are treated better in general (Langlois et al., 2000). Why would this be? From the perspective of evolutionary psychology, all these characteristics would be good indicators of reproductive potential. And many people fall prey to the *halo effect,* or the tendency to assign excessive weight to one dimension of a person. This concept was originally described by Thorndike in 1920 as it related to the evaluation of others. People tend to form these general impressions early on and then cling to them, even in the absence of supporting evidence, or the presence of contradictory evidence (Aronson, 2012). The way we respond to beautiful people is one example of the halo effect; our initial impression of their beauty may lead us to

---

romantic love   Love that is a combination of connection, concern, care, and intimacy.

passionate love   Love that is based on zealous emotion, leading to intense longing and sexual attraction.

companionate love   Love that consists of profound fondness, camaraderie, understanding, and emotional closeness.

consummate love   (kän(t)-sə-mət) Love that combines intimacy, commitment, and passion.

assume they have other positive characteristics like superior intelligence, popularity, and desirability.

Beauty may captivate you in the beginning stages of a relationship, but other characteristics and qualities gain importance as time goes along. Think about the type of person you want for a life partner. Whom would you want to hold your hand when you're sick in the hospital—the lingerie model or the person you most respect and trust?

What Is Love?

In America, we are taught to believe that love is the foundation of marriage. People in Western cultures do tend to marry for love, but this is not the case everywhere. In Harare, Zimbabwe, for example, people might also marry for reasons associated with the needs of the family, such as maintaining alliances and social status (Wojcicki, van der Straten, & Padian, 2010). Similarly, many marriages in India and other parts of South Asia are arranged by family members. Love may not be present in the beginning stages of such alliances, but it can blossom.

STERNBERG'S THEORY OF LOVE   In a pivotal study published in 1986, Robert Sternberg proposed that love is made up of three elements: passion (feelings leading to romance and physical attraction); intimacy (feeling close); and commitment (the recognition of love). He conceptualized these elements in terms of the corners of a triangle (**FIGURE 15.4**). Love comes in many varieties, according to Sternberg, and can include any combination of the three elements.

Many relationships begin with exhilaration and intense physical attraction, and then evolve into more intimate connections. This is the type of love we often see portrayed in the movies. The combination of connection, concern, care, and intimacy is what Sternberg called **romantic love.** Romantic love is similar to what some psychologists refer to as **passionate love** (also known as "love at first sight"), or love that is based on zealous emotion, leading to intense longing and sexual attraction (Hatfield, Bensman, & Rapson, 2012). As a relationship grows, intimacy and commitment develop into **companionate love,** or love that consists of profound fondness, camaraderie, understanding, and emotional closeness. Companionate love is typical of a couple that has been together for many years. They become comfortable with each other, routines set in, and passion often fizzles (Aronson, 2012). Although the passion may wane, the friendship is strong. **Consummate love** (kän(t)-sə-mət) is evident when intimacy and commitment are accompanied by passion. The ultimate goal is to maintain all three components of the triangle.

Research and life experiences tell us that relationships inevitably change. Romantic love is generally what drives people to commit to one another (Berscheid, 2010). But the passion associated with this stage generally decreases over time. That does not mean it cannot reemerge, however. Can you think of ways this passion might be rekindled—a romantic night out, some sexy new underwear, a trip to fantasyland? Companionate love, in contrast, tends to grow over time. As we experience life with a partner, it is companionate love that seems to endear us to one another (Berscheid, 2010).

What type of love do you think online dating sites tend to select for? Is it companionate love (SF loves to garden, looking for someone who. . .)? Or is it passionate love (SM looking for a good time with no strings attached. . .)? As Joe can attest, passionate love was present from the beginning of his relationship with Susanne (he jokes about taking a few cold showers before anything happened). Although their passion is still strong and steady, the love and respect they have for one another have grown much deeper.

▲ **FIGURE 15.4**
Sternberg's Triangular Model of Love
Sternberg proposed that there are different kinds of love resulting from combinations of three elements: passion, intimacy, and commitment. The ideal form, consummate love, combines all three elements. *Source:* Sternberg (1986).

CONNECTIONS

In **Chapter 3,** we discussed sensory adaptation, which refers to the way in which sensory receptors become less sensitive to constant stimuli. In **Chapter 5,** we presented the concept of habituation, which occurs when an organism becomes less responsive to repeated stimuli. Humans seem to be attracted to novelty, which might underlie our desire for passion.

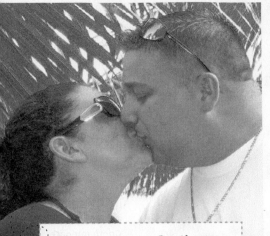

Have you ever wondered about the long-term stability of your relationships? Couples stay together for many reasons, some better than others. Caryl Rusbult's *investment model of commitment* focuses on the resources at stake in relationships, including finances, possessions, time spent together, and perhaps even children (Rusbult, 1983). According to this model, decisions to stay together or separate are based on how happy people are in their relationship, their notion of what life would be like without it, and their investment. According to the investment model of commitment (Rusbult & Martz, 1995), people may stay in unsatisfying or unhealthy relationships if they feel there are no better alternatives or believe they have too much to lose. This model helps us understand why people remain in destructive relationships.

Making This Chapter Work for You

At last, we reach the end of our journey through social psychology. We hope that what you have learned in this chapter will come in handy in your everyday social exchanges. Be conscious of the attributions you use to explain the behavior of others—are you being objective or falling prey to self-serving bias? Be mindful of your attitudes—how are they influencing your behavior? Know that your behaviors are constantly being shaped by your social interactions—both as an individual and as a member of groups. Understand the dangers of stereotyping, and know the human suffering caused by aggression. But perhaps most of all, be kind and helpful to others, and allow yourself to experience love.

The Honeymoon Continues
After several years of marriage and three new children, the love between Joe and Susanne Maggio is stronger than ever. They have what you might call consummate love, a type of love characterized by intimacy, commitment, and passion. Joseph Maggio

show what you know

1. What are the three major factors that play a role in interpersonal attraction?
   a. social influence; obedience; physical attractiveness
   b. proximity, similarity, physical attractiveness
   c. obedience; proximity; social influence
   d. proximity; love; social influence

2. Research has shown that most people prefer looking at pictures of their own faces when reversed, but friends prefer normal, nonreversed photos. This finding supports the _____,

suggesting repeated viewing of one's face in the mirror makes it more attractive.

3. We described how the investment model of commitment can be used to predict the long-term stability of a romantic relationship. How can you use this same model to predict the long-term stability of friendships, positions at work, or loyalty to institutions?

✓ CHECK YOUR ANSWERS IN APPENDIX C.

UGANDA
359

(15) summary of concepts

LO 1 Define social psychology and identify how it is different from sociology. (p. 625)

Social psychology is the study of human cognition, emotion, and behavior in relation to others. This includes how we perceive and react to others, are influenced by interactions with others, and behave in social settings. Social psychology focuses on studying individuals in relation to others and groups, whereas sociology studies the groups themselves—their cultures, societies, and subcultures. Using the same general research methods as other psychologists, social psychologists often conduct studies involving confederates, or people who are secretly working for them. At the end of a study, researchers debrief participants, or

review aspects of the research they had previously concealed.

LO 2 Describe social cognition and how we use attributions to explain behavior. (p. 627)

Social cognition refers to the way we think about others, attend to social information, and use this information in our lives, both consciously and unconsciously. Attributions are the beliefs we develop to explain human behaviors and characteristics, as well as situations. Because attributions rely on whatever information happens to be available (our observations of what people say and do, for example), they are vulnerable to personal bias and inaccuracies.

LO 3 Explain how attributions lead to mistakes about the causes of behaviors. (p. 627)

Situational attributions are a type of external attribution in which the assumed causes of behaviors are in the environment. Dispositional attributions are a type of internal attribution in which the causes of behaviors are thought to be traits or characteristics. When people make attributions, they are often guessing about the causes of events or behaviors, leaving plenty of room for error.

The fundamental attribution error assumes the causes of behaviors are in the person (dispositional) as opposed to the environment (situational). The just-world hypothesis assumes that if someone is suffering, he must have done something to deserve it. The self-serving bias attributes one's successes to internal characteristics and one's failures to environmental factors.

LO 4 Describe social influence and recognize the factors associated with persuasion. (p. 636)

Social influence refers to the way a person is affected by another person (or other people), as apparent in behavior, emotion, and cognition. Expectations are an often overlooked form of social influence. Students in Rosenthal's study who were expected to show surprising gains actually did as a result of the high expectations placed on them. Persuasion is intentionally trying to make people change their attitudes and beliefs, which may (or may not) lead to changes in their behavior. There are three factors that determine persuasive power: the source, the message, and the audience.

LO 5 Define compliance and explain some of the techniques used to gain it. (p. 638)

Compliance occurs when someone voluntarily changes her behavior at the request or direction of another person or group, who in general does not have any true authority over her. One commonly used method is the foot-in-the-door technique, which occurs when an individual initially makes a small request, followed by a larger one. Another method for gaining compliance is the door-in-the-face technique, which involves making a large request, followed by a smaller one.

LO 6 Evaluate conformity and identify the factors that influence the likelihood of someone conforming. (p. 640)

The urge to modify behaviors, attitudes, beliefs, and opinions to match those of others is known as conformity. There are three major reasons we conform. Most people want approval, to be liked and accepted by others. This desire, known as normative social influence, can have a significant impact on behaviors. A second reason to conform is that we want to be correct. We look to others for confirmation when we are uncertain about something, and then do as they do.

This is known as informational social influence. Finally, we may conform to others because they belong to a certain reference group we respect, admire, or long to join.

LO 7 Describe obedience and explain how Stanley Milgram studied it. (p. 643)

Obedience occurs when we change our behavior, or act in a way that we might not normally act, because we have been ordered to do so by an authority figure. Milgram conducted a series of studies examining how far people will go when urged by an authority figure to inflict punishment on others. During an early experiment, the goal was for the confederate (*learner*) to memorize a set of paired words. The participant (*teacher*) sat at a table, which held a control panel for administering electrical "shocks." The teacher was told to administer a shock each time the learner made a mistake, and the shock was to increase by 15 volts for every mistake. Milgram was surprised that so many people obeyed the experimenter and continued to administer "shocks" to the learner, even when they hesitated or were uncomfortable, simply because an authority figure had instructed them to do so.

LO 8 Recognize the circumstances that influence the occurrence of the bystander effect. (p. 650)

When a person is in trouble, bystanders have the tendency to assume that someone else will help—and therefore they stand by and do nothing, due in part to the diffusion of responsibility. This bystander effect is particularly true when there are many other people present. Individuals are more likely to aid a person in distress if no one else is present.

LO 9 Demonstrate an understanding of aggression and identify some of its causes. (p. 652)

Aggression is defined as intimidating or threatening behavior, or attitudes intended to hurt someone. Research on aggression suggests that it has a biological basis (for instance, high levels of testosterone and low levels of serotonin). In addition, the frustration-aggression hypothesis suggests that in a frustrating situation, we can all show aggressive behavior.

LO 10 Recognize how group affiliation influences the development of stereotypes. (p. 653)

Stereotypes are the conclusions or inferences we make about people who are different from us, based on their group membership (such as race, religion, age, or gender). When we hold a stereotype about a particular group, we tend to have a set of characteristics in mind that describe the members of that group, one that is often rooted in subjective observations and value judgments. A stereotype threat is a situational threat in which a person is aware of others' negative expectations. This leads to a fear of being judged and/

or treated as inferior, and it can actually undermine performance in a specific area associated with the stereotype.

When we see the world only from the perspective of our own group, this leads to ethnocentrism. This type of group identification can lead to stereotyping and discrimination, which involves showing favoritism or hostility to others because of their affiliation with a group. People who harbor stereotypes and blame scapegoats are more likely to feel prejudice, that is, hostile or negative attitudes toward individuals or groups.

LO 11 Compare prosocial behavior and altruism. (p. 658)

Behavior aimed at benefiting others is known as prosocial behavior. Altruism is a desire or motivation to help others with no expectation of anything in return. The ability to understand and recognize another's emotional perspective is a major component of altruism.

LO 12 Identify the three major factors contributing to interpersonal attraction. (p. 660)

Interpersonal attraction, or the factors that lead us to form friendships or romantic relationships with others, plays a role in determining with whom we choose to spend our time. Three major factors are often apparent: proximity, similarity, and physical attractiveness. Many relationships begin with exhilaration and intense physical attraction, and then evolve into more intimate connections. The combination of connection, concern, care, and intimacy is romantic love. This is similar to passionate love, or love that is based on zealous emotion, leading to intense longing and sexual attraction. As a relationship grows, intimacy and commitment develop into companionate love, which consists of fondness, camaraderie, understanding, and emotional closeness. Consummate love is evident when intimacy and commitment are accompanied by passion.

key terms

aggression, p. 652
altruism, p. 659
attitudes, p. 630
attributions, p. 627
bystander effect, p. 650
cognitive dissonance, p. 633
companionate love, p. 663
compliance, p. 638
conformity, p. 640
consummate love, p. 663
deindividuation, p. 648
diffusion of responsibility, p. 647
discrimination, p. 654
dispositional attribution, p. 628

door-in-the-face technique, p. 639
ethnocentrism, p. 653
false consensus effect, p. 630
foot-in-the-door technique, p. 639
frustration-aggression hypothesis, p. 652
fundamental attribution error, p. 628
group polarization, p. 649
groupthink, p. 649
in-group, p. 653
interpersonal attraction, p. 660

just-world hypothesis, p. 629
mere-exposure effect, p. 661
norms, p. 640
obedience, p. 643
out-group, p. 653
passionate love, p. 663
persuasion, p. 637
prejudice, p. 654
proximity, p. 660
risky shift, p. 649
romantic love, p. 663
scapegoat, p. 654
self-serving bias, p. 629

situational attribution, p. 628
social cognition, p. 627
social facilitation, p. 647
social identity, p. 653
social influence, p. 636
social loafing, p. 647
social psychology, p. 625
social roles, p. 656
stereotypes, p. 652
stereotype threat, p. 654

TEST PREP are you ready?

1. _____ is the study of human behavior in relation to the influence of other people, our perceptions, and reactions to others.
   a. Sociology
   b. Developmental psychology
   c. The biopsychosocial model
   d. Social psychology

2. A researcher is interested in studying how students attend to social information and use it in their lives. Her general focus is
   a. attributions.
   b. social cognition.
   c. the internal–external dimension.
   d. attitudes.

3. _____ is an uneasy feeling that occurs with the recognition that a mismatch exists between an attitude and a behavior.
   a. Cognitive dissonance
   b. An attitude
   c. A confederate
   d. Altruism

4. One common bias we have is to more often attribute causes of behaviors to the individual rather than to the environment, thus underestimating the powerful influence of the environment on behavior. This is known as:
   a. the just-world hypothesis.
   b. the false consensus effect.
   c. a dispositional attribution.
   d. the fundamental attribution error.

5. Hovland proposed that persuasive communication involves three important components, and we must consider factors associated with them. The three components are:
   a. the source, the audience, and the sender.
   b. the source, the message, and the social influence.
   c. the source, the persuasion, and the compliance.
   d. the source, the message, and the audience.

6. When someone changes his behavior at the request or direction of another person who does not have authority over him, this is known as:
   a. obedience.
   b. conformity.
   c. compliance.
   d. normative social influence.

7. Your neighbor seems to follow the lead in terms of decorating his house. If he sees others hanging lights, he immediately does the same. His urge to modify his behaviors to match those of others in the neighborhood is known as
   a. conformity.
   b. informational social influence.
   c. obedience.
   d. cognitive dissonance.

8. Milgram reported that 65% of the participants in his study gave shocks marked as the highest voltage level to a confederate. Researchers have found that the degree of compliance of participants in such studies is associated with the
   a. severity of the punishment.
   b. occupation of the participant.
   c. legitimacy of the authority figure.
   d. education level of the participant.

9. _____ occurs when the sharing of duties among all members of the group leads to feelings of decreased accountability.
   a. Obedience to authority
   b. Diffusion of responsibility
   c. A risky shift
   d. Groupthink

10. One study found that 80% of trick-or-treaters in a group who were anonymous took more candy or money than they were supposed to. The children's sense of anonymity as well as inclusion in a group likely led to their sense of
    a. deindividuation.   c. authority.
    b. obedience.   d. a risky shift.

11. A family friend of yours constantly goes on about how suburban teenagers with tongue rings are rebelling against their parents and most of them are troublemakers. These _____ are conclusions he has drawn based on his subjective observations and value judgments.
    a. norms   c. situational attributions
    b. external attributions   d. stereotypes

12. Psychologists define _____ as intimidating or threatening behavior or as attitudes intended to hurt someone.
    a. prejudice   c. aggression
    b. discrimination   d. stereotypes

13. When teachers in an elementary school in San Francisco were given a list of students who were likely to "show surprising gains in intellectual competence" during the coming year, the students on that list achieved greater increases in test scores than students not on it. This is an example of _____, a form of social influence.
    a. cognitive dissonance
    b. expectations
    c. altruism
    d. the mere-exposure effect

14. _____ suggests that the more we are exposed to people, food, jingles, or songs, the more positive a reaction we have toward them.
    a. The mere-exposure effect
    b. Prosocial behavior
    c. Altruism
    d. The self-serving bias

15. According to Sternberg, the three elements that make up love are:
    a. passion, mere exposure, and proximity.
    b. proximity, similarity, and passion.
    c. romantic love, mere exposure, and similarity.
    d. passion, intimacy, and commitment.

16. You are trying to explain why a colleague of yours is frequently absent from work. Can you come up with an attribution that is external, uncontrollable, and unstable? Can you think of a different attribution that is internal, controllable, and stable?

17. The findings from Milgram's experiment on obedience seemed surprising when they were first published. The problems associated with obedience to authority still exist today. What does this tell us about the importance of paying attention to how we react when under the influence of an authority figure?

18. Knowledge about the bystander effect provides a lesson for all of us, particularly in terms of crisis situations in a group setting. How would you describe this lesson to others?

19. When you are finished reading this chapter, identify any stereotypes you might harbor about certain groups of people. How did groups impact the development of these?

20. Think about someone you are close to and try to determine if—and how—proximity, similarity, and physical attractiveness played a role in your attraction to each other.

✔ CHECK YOUR ANSWERS IN APPENDIX C.

introduction to statistics

If you remember one thing from reading this textbook, we hope it is this: Psychology is a scientific discipline. As a science, psychology is required to support statements and theories with observations and research findings. The vast knowledge base that defines this field is the result of rigorous and meticulous scientific research, most of which entails the careful collection of data. In Chapter 1, we presented various methods used to gather this data, but we only touched upon the statistical approaches for analyzing it. Here, we will discover how we can use data meaningfully in everyday life. Welcome to **statistics,** the science of collecting, organizing, analyzing, displaying, and interpreting data.

Students in psychology programs often ask why they have to learn about statistics. In order to understand and think critically about the material in psychology textbooks and journal articles, you must have a basic handle on statistics. Drawing conclusions about research findings requires that you know how to synthesize and interpret data. These skills will come in handy outside the classroom as well. Statistics are everywhere—not just in the academic materials published by psychologists. Newspapers, Web sites, and television shows report on statistical findings every day, though they sometimes make mistakes, exaggerate, or leave out important information. You can detect these types of errors if you understand statistics. It is important for everyone (not just psychology students) to be familiar with statistics.

Descriptive and Inferential Statistics

There are two basic types of statistics: descriptive and inferential. With *descriptive statistics,* researchers summarize the information they have gleaned in their studies. The raw data can be organized and presented through tables, graphs, and charts, some of which we present in this appendix. We can also use descriptive statistics to represent the average and the spread of the data (how dispersed the values are), a topic to which we will return later. The goal of descriptive statistics is to describe the data, or offer a snapshot of what researchers have observed in their study. *Inferential statistics,* on the other hand, goes beyond simple data presentation. With inferential statistics, for example, we can determine the probability of events and make predictions about general trends. The goal of inferential statistics is to generalize findings from studies, make predictions based on relationships among variables, and test hypotheses. Inferential statistics also can be used to make statements about how confident we are in our findings based on the data collected.

In Chapter 1, we defined a *hypothesis* as a statement used to test a prediction. Once a researcher develops a hypothesis, she gathers data and uses statistics to test it, an important component of inferential statistics. **Hypothesis testing** involves mathematical procedures to determine whether the data support the hypothesis or if they simply result from chance. Let's look at an example to see how this works. (And you might find it useful to review Chapter 1 if your knowledge of research methods is a little rusty.)

CONNECTIONS

In **Chapter 1,** we presented a study examining the impact of fast-paced cartoons on executive functioning. The researchers tested the following hypothesis: Children who watch 9 minutes of *SpongeBob Square Pants* will be more likely to show cognitive changes than children who are watching *Caillou* or simply drawing. The researchers used inferential statistics to determine that the children in the *SpongeBob* group did show a lapse in cognitive functioning in comparison to the other two groups In the study.

statistics A science that focuses on how to collect, organize, analyze, display, and interpret data; numbers that describe characteristics of a sample.

hypothesis testing Mathematical procedures used to determine the likelihood that a researcher's predictions are supported by the data collected.

CONNECTIONS

In **Chapter 14,** we presented the biomedical approach to treating psychological disorders. Many researchers use a double-blind procedure to determine the causes of psychological disorders and the effectiveness of psychotropic medications in alleviating symptoms. For example, Schnider and colleagues (2010) used a randomized double-blind procedure to determine the impact of L-dopa, risperdone, and a placebo on participants' ability to "rapidly adapt thinking to ongoing reality" (p. 583). The researchers used a double-blind procedure to ensure that neither the participants' nor the researchers' expectations unduly influenced the results.

CONNECTIONS

In **Chapter 5,** we presented Bandura's work on observational learning and aggressive models. Bandura and colleagues (1961) divided participants into treatment and control groups and found that the average "expression of aggression" for children who viewed aggressive models was statistically significantly greater than for the control group children who did not observe an aggressive model. The difference in the amount of expressed aggression for the two groups was large enough to be considered due to the experimenters' manipulation as opposed to a chance result (for example, simply based on the children who were assigned randomly to each group).

statistical significance The probability that the findings of a study were due to chance.

parameters Numbers that describe characteristics of a population.

Suppose a researcher wants to determine whether taking vitamin D supplements can boost cognitive function. The researcher designs an experiment to test if giving participants vitamin D pills (the independent variable) leads to better performance on some sort of cognitive task, such as a memory test (the test score is the dependent variable). Participants in the treatment group receive doses of vitamin D and participants in the control group receive a placebo. Neither the participants nor the researchers working directly with those participants know who is getting the vitamin D and who is getting the placebo, so we call it a **double-blind procedure.** After the data have been collected, the researcher will need to compare the memory scores for the two groups to see if the treatment worked. In all likelihood, the average test scores of the two groups will differ simply because they include two different groups of people. So how does the researcher know whether the difference is sufficient to conclude that vitamin D had an effect? This is where statistics come into play. Using certain statistical procedures, the researcher can state with an assured level of certainty (for example, with 95% confidence) that the disparity in average scores resulted from the vitamin D treatment. In other words, there is a slight possibility (in this case, 5%) that the difference was merely due to chance.

Thus, using statistical methods, researchers can determine whether their data reveal anything meaningful. In other words, they can establish **statistical significance,** which indicates that differences between groups in a study (for example, average scores for treatment and control groups) are so great that they are likely due to the researcher's manipulations. If a research finding is statistically significant, the mathematical analyses have indicated that the probability those findings were due to chance is very minimal. When we use the experimental method (that is, randomly assign individuals, manipulate an independent variable, and control extraneous variables) and find significant differences between our experimental and control groups, we can be assured that the differences we see between these groups are very likely due to our manipulation (for example, vitamin D treatment versus a placebo) and not due to chance.

In addition to determining statistical significance, we also have to consider the *practical importance* of findings, which indicates the degree to which the findings of a study can be used in a meaningful way. In other words, do the findings have any relevance to real life? If our vitamin D regimen turns out to be statistically significant (with the performance gap between the treatment group and the control group most likely not due to chance), we still have to determine the practical importance of this disparity. If the two groups differ by only a few points on the cognitive test, we must ask ourselves if vitamin D supplementation is really worth the trouble.

Researchers may end up with differences between groups due to the size of their samples. Big samples are more likely to result in *statistically* significant results (small differences between groups can be amplified in some sense by the large sample) even though the results might not provide much practical information. The opposite can occur as well: A small sample size might hide an important difference between groups, which would only be apparent in a larger sample. Researchers can determine how big a sample is needed to detect differences between groups using statistical techniques (which you can learn more about in an elementary statistics class).

Sampling Techniques

Long before data are collected and analyzed, researchers must select people to participate in their studies. Depending on what a psychologist is interested in studying, the probability of being able to include all members of a *population* is not likely, so generally a *sample,* or subset of the population is chosen. The characteristics of the sample members must closely reflect those of the population of interest so that the researcher can generalize, or apply, her findings to the population at large.

One method for trying to ensure that the sample accurately reflects the larger population is to use *random sampling,* which means that any member of the population has an equally likely chance of being selected to participate in the study. A simple technique that can be used with a small population is to draw names or numbers from a hat: Every number in the hat has an equally likely chance of being drawn. If a researcher has a numbered list of the population members, she could generate random numbers on a computer and then contact the individuals with those numbers. Because the numbers are randomly picked, everyone on the list has an equal chance of being selected. Another approach is *stratified sampling.* With this method, the researcher decides that she wants a certain variable well represented—car ownership at the college, for example. She divides the population into four groups or *strata* (no car, one car, two cars, more than two cars), and then picks randomly from within each group or *stratum.* That way, she can be assured that the different types of car ownership are included in the sample. Often, researchers will use strata such as ethnicity, gender, and age groups to ensure that a sample has accurate proportions representing these important factors (such as an equal proportion of young adults, middle-aged adults, and elderly adults).

Some researchers use a method called *convenience sampling,* which entails choosing a sample from a group that is readily available or convenient. If a student researcher is interested in collecting data on coffee drinking behavior from people who frequent coffee shops, he might be tempted to go to the Starbucks and Peet's Coffee shops in his neighborhood. This approach may be better than nothing, but it certainly cannot be considered a random sample of coffee shop patrons. Just think of all the Dunkin' Donuts and Caribou coffee drinkers who would be excluded from the sample.

Why does it matter if a convenience sample fails to randomly select participants? If it is not random, then the likelihood that it is a *representative sample* is very slim. In other words, a randomly picked sample is more likely than a convenience sample to include members with characteristics similar to the larger population. This is important because the whole point of conducting the study is for the researcher to be able to make *inferences* about the population based on the findings. Only if the sample is representative can the researcher make valid generalizations about the characteristics of the population.

It's important to note that a randomly selected sample is not foolproof. There is always the possibility that the chosen group has characteristics that are not typical for the population. If this is the case, the sample is not truly representative, and our inferences might be incorrect. The smaller the sample, the less likely it will be representative, and the less reliable our findings. This is why larger samples are so desirable; they are more likely to provide accurate reflections of the population being studied.

How does this discussion of representative samples relate to statistics? Remember, the ultimate goal of the researcher is to use the results of a study to make inferences about the population at large. Every population is defined by various **parameters,** or numbers that describe its characteristics (for example, the average number of cars owned by sophomores in the United States). When the same characteristics are determined from a sample, they are referred to as *statistics* (the average number of cars owned by sophomores in the chosen random sample). (Note that the word "statistics" can also refer to the scientific discipline of collecting, organizing, analyzing, displaying, and interpreting data.) We will introduce you to these numerical characteristics later when we discuss *measures of central tendency* and *measures of variation,* but it is important to realize that without a representative sample, the use of statistics to make inferences about parameters is suspect. This is why it's important to pay careful attention to the sample descriptions in media reports on scientific studies: Do they describe the samples, and are they truly representative? If not, the findings might only be true for the sample, not the population.

try this

Go to the search engine of your favorite online news source (for example, CNN, ABC News, Google News) and type in "new research." Read through several of the articles that come up and see if you can determine how the sample was chosen, what the sample size was, and whether the researchers made inferences about the population based on the sample.

Variables

Once a study sample is selected, researchers can begin measuring and manipulating the variables of interest. Variables are measurable characteristics that vary over time or across people, situations, or objects. In psychology, variables may include cognitive abilities, social behaviors, or even the font size in books. Statisticians often refer to two types of variables. *Quantitative variables* are numerical, meaning they have values that can be represented by numbered units or ranks. Midterm exam scores, age at graduation, and number of students in a class are all quantitative variables. *Qualitative variables* are characteristics that are not easily quantified, but enable us to place members in categories. An example might be college major; you can ask all of the students in the library to line up under signs for psychology, biology, chemistry, undeclared, and so on, and thereby categorize them, but without a numerical rank. Of course we can rank how much we like the majors based on the courses associated with them, but they cannot be ordered or ranked in and of themselves. We can alphabetize them, but that is a ranking based on their labels. We can order the majors in terms of how many students are pursuing them, but that is a different variable (number of students). Other examples of qualitative variables include gender, ethnicity, and religious faith.

try this

Throughout this textbook, we have identified multiple characteristics and traits that can be used as variables in studies. Pick two chapters and see if you can identify five variables that are quantitative and five that are qualitative.

Synonym

qualitative variables categorical variables

meta-analysis A type of statistical analysis that combines findings from many studies on a single topic; statistics used to merge the outcomes of many studies.

frequency distribution A simple way to portray data that displays how often various values in a data set are present.

histogram Displays classes of a variable on the *x*-axis and the frequency of the data is represented as vertical bars that reach the height of the number of values.

frequency polygon A type of graphic display that uses lines to represent the frequency of data values.

Variables are the focal point of a psychological experiment. Typically, the goal is to determine how one variable (the dependent variable) is affected by changes in another (the independent variable). Many studies focus on similar topics, so you might imagine it's easy to compare their results. But this is not necessarily the case. Sometimes psychologists define variables in different ways, or study the same variables with vastly different samples, methods of measurement, and experimental designs. How do we reconcile all their findings? We rely on a **meta-analysis,** a statistical approach that allows researchers to combine the findings of different studies and draw general conclusions. A meta-analysis is an objective, quantitative (measurable) mechanism for gathering and analyzing findings from a set of studies on the same topic (Weathington, Cunningham, & Pittenger, 2010).

The Presentation of Data

Conducting an experiment is a major accomplishment, but it has little impact if researchers cannot devise an effective way to present their data. If they just display their raw data in a table, others will find it difficult to draw any useful conclusions.

Table A.1 RAW DATA FROM REM SLEEP STUDY

77	114	40	18	68	96	81	142	62	80	117
81	98	76	22	71	35	85	49	105	99	49
20	70	35	83	150	57	112	131	104	121	47
31	47	39	92	73	122	68	58	100	52	101

Imagine you have collected the data presented in **TABLE A.1,** which represents the number of minutes of REM sleep (the dependent variable) each of your 44 participants ($n = 44$; n is the symbol for sample size) had during 1 night spent in your sleep lab. Looking at this table, you can barely tell which variable you have chosen to study.

Quantitative Data Displays

A common and simple way to present data is to use a **frequency distribution,** which displays how often the various values in a data set are present. In **TABLE A.2,** we have displayed the data in 7 *classes,* or groups, of equal width. The frequency for each class is tallied up and appears in the middle column. The first class goes from 4 to 24 minutes, and in our sample of 44 participants, only 3 had a total amount of REM in this class (18, 20, 22 minutes). The greatest number of participants experienced between 67 and 87 minutes. By looking at the frequency for each class, you begin to see patterns. In this case, the greatest number of participants had REM sleep within the middle of the distribution, and fewer appear on the ends. We will come back to this pattern shortly.

Frequency distributions can also be presented with a **histogram,** which displays the classes of a variable on the *x-axis* and the frequency of the data on the *y-axis* (portrayed by the height of the vertical bars). The values on the *y*-axis can be either the raw frequency (actual number) or the relative frequency (proportion of the whole set). The example portrayed in **FIGURE A.1** is a histogram of the minutes of REM sleep, with the classes of the number of minutes in REM on the *x*-axis and the raw frequency on the *y*-axis. Looking at a histogram makes it easier to see how the data are distributed across classes. In this case you can see that the most frequent duration of REM is in the middle of the distribution (the 67- to 87-minute class), and that the frequency tapers off toward both ends. Histograms are often used to display quantitative variables that have a wide range of numbers that would be difficult to interpret if they weren't grouped in classes.

Similar to a histogram is a **frequency polygon,** which uses lines instead of bars to represent the frequency of the data values. The same data displayed in the histogram (Figure A.1) appear in the frequency polygon in **FIGURE A.2** on page A-6. We see the same general pattern of the distribution shape in the frequency polygon, but in the place of raw frequency we have used the relative frequency for each of the classes. Thus instead of saying 12 participants had 67 to 86 minutes of REM sleep, we can state that the proportion of participants in this class was .27, or 27%. Relative frequencies are especially useful when comparing data sets with different sample sizes. Imagine we wanted to compare two different studies examining REM sleep: one with a sample size of 500, and the other with a sample size of 44. If the larger sample had a greater number of participants in the 67- to 86-minute group (let's say 50 participants out of 500 [.10] versus the 12 out of

Table A.2 FREQUENCY DISTRIBUTION FOR REM SLEEP STUDY

No. of Minutes in REM (Class Limits)	Raw Frequency	Relative Frequency
4 to 24	3	.07
25 to 45	5	.11
46 to 66	8	.18
67 to 87	12	.28
88 to 108	8	.18
109 to 129	5	.11
130 to 150	3	.07

FIGURE A.1

▼ Histogram of REM sleep study

Amount of REM sleep in minutes

▲ FIGURE A.2
Frequency Polygon of REM
sleep study

FIGURE A.3
Stem-and-leaf plot
for REM sleep study

the 44 participants [.27] in the smaller sample), although the raw frequency (50) of those in the larger sample is greater than the raw frequency (12) for the smaller sample, the proportion for the smaller sample is greater (smaller sample = .27 versus larger sample = .10). The relative frequency makes it easier to detect these differences in proportion.

Another common way to display quantitative data is through a **stem-and-leaf plot,** which uses the actual data values in its display. The *stem* is made up of the first digits in a number, and the *leaf* makes up the last digit. This allows us to group numbers by 10s, 20s, 30s, and so on. In **FIGURE A.3,** we display the REM sleep data in a stem-and-leaf plot using the first part of the number (either the 10s and/or the 100s) as the stem, and the ones column as the leaf. In the first row, for example, 8 is from the ones column of the smallest number in the data set, 18; 0 and 2 in the second row represent the ones column from the numbers 20 and 22; the 0 in the last row comes from 150.

One nice feature of the stem-and-leaf plot (Figure A.3) is that it displays the raw data in a graphical manner. If you turn the book sideways (counterclockwise), you can see that the shape of the data is somewhat similar to that of the histogram presenting the same data (Figure A.1). However, the larger a sample is and the wider its range of numbers, the harder it would be to use the stem-and-leaf plot.

Distribution Shapes

Once the data have been displayed on a graph, researchers look very closely at the **distribution shape,** which is just what it sounds like—how the data are spread along the *x*-axis (that is, the shape is based on the variable represented along the *x*-axis and the frequency of its values portrayed by the *y*-axis). A *symmetric shape* is apparent in the histogram in **FIGURE A.4a,** which shows a distribution for a sample that is high in the middle, but tapers off at the same rate on each end. The *bell-shaped* or normal curve on the right also has a symmetric shape, and this type of curve is fairly typical in psychology (curves generally represent the distribution of the entire population). Many human characteristics have this type of distribution, including cognitive abilities, personality characteristics, and a variety of physical characteristics such as height and weight. Through many years of study, we have found that measurements for the great majority of people fall in the middle of the distribution, and a smaller proportion have characteristics represented on the ends (or in the tails) of the distribution. For example, if you look at the IQ scores displayed in **FIGURE A.4b,** you can see that 68% of people have scores between 85 and 115, about 95% have scores between 70 and 130, around 99.7% fall between 55 and 145, and only a tiny percentage (0.3%) are below 55 and above 145. These percentages are true for many other characteristics.

FIGURE A.4
Symmetrically shaped
▼ distributions

(a)

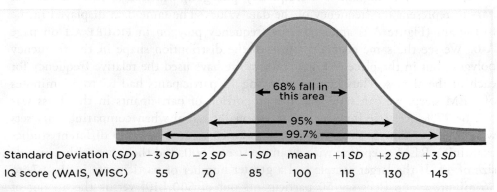

Standard Deviation (*SD*)	−3 *SD*	−2 *SD*	−1 *SD*	mean	+1 *SD*	+2 *SD*	+3 *SD*
IQ score (WAIS, WISC)	55	70	85	100	115	130	145

(b)

Some data will have a **skewed distribution,** which is not symmetrical. As you can see in FIGURE A.5a, a **negatively skewed** or *left-skewed* distribution has a longer tail to the left side of the distribution. A **positively skewed** or *right-skewed* distribution (FIGURE A.5b) has a longer tail to the right side of the distribution. Determining whether a distribution is skewed is particularly important because it informs our decision about what type of statistical analysis to conduct. Later, we will see how certain types of data values can play a role in *skewing* the distribution.

(a) Left skewed

(b) Right skewed

mean median mode

mode median mean

◄ ············

FIGURE A.5
Skewed distributions

Qualitative Data Displays

Thus far, we have discussed several ways to represent quantitative data. With qualitative data, a frequency distribution lists the various categories and the number of members in each. For example, if we wanted to display the college major data on 44 students interviewed at the library, we could use a frequency distribution (TABLE A.3).

Table A.3 FREQUENCY DISTRIBUTION OF COLLEGE MAJORS		
College Major	**Raw Frequency**	**Percent**
Biology	3	7
Chemistry	5	11.5
Culinary Arts	8	18
English	5	11.5
Nursing	12	27
Psychology	3	7
Undecided	8	18

stem-and-leaf plot A type of graphical display that uses the actual data values in the form of leading digits and trailing digits.

distribution shape How the frequencies of the values are shaped along the *x*-axis.

skewed distribution Nonsymmetrical frequency distribution.

negatively skewed A nonsymmetric distribution with a longer tail to the left side of the distribution; left-skewed distribution.

positively skewed A nonsymmetric distribution with a longer tail to the right side of the distribution; right-skewed distribution.

FIGURE A.6
Bar graph for
college majors

(a) Data on majors collected from library interviews

(b) Data on majors collected campus-wide

(c) Data on majors collected campus-wide

Another common way to display qualitative data is through a **bar graph,** which displays the categories of interest on the *x*-axis and the frequency on the *y*-axis. **FIGURE A.6** shows how the data collected in the library can be presented in a bar graph. Bar graphs are useful for comparing several different populations on the same variable (for example, perhaps comparing college majors by gender or ethnicity).

Like any type of data display, one must be on the lookout for misleading portrayals. In Figure A.6a, we display data for the 44 students interviewed in the library. In Figures A.6b and A.6c, we display data for one campus with 4,400 students. Quickly look at (b) and (c) of the figure and decide, if you were head of the psychology department, which bar chart you would prefer to use to show how strong your numbers are at the college. In (b), the department looks fairly small compared to the size of other departments, particularly relative to the size of the nursing program. But notice that the scale on the *y*-axis starts at 250 in (b), whereas it begins at 0 in (c). In this third bar chart, it appears that the student count for the psychology program is not far behind that for other programs like chemistry and English, for example. An important aspect of *critical thinking* is being able to evaluate the source of evidence, which one must consider when reading graphs and charts. (For example, does the author of the bar chart in Figure A.6b have a particular agenda to reduce funding for the psychology department?) And, one must also consider the interpretation of the material, which can be changed through manipulation in its presentation (the data on the 4,400 students are valid, but the way they are presented is not).

Pie charts can also be used to display qualitative data, with pie slices representing the relative proportion of each of the categories (**FIGURE A.7**). As you can see, the biggest percentage is nursing (27%), followed by culinary arts (18%), and undecided (18%). The smallest percentage is shared by biology and psychology (both 7%). Often researchers use pie charts to easily display data for which it is important to know the relative proportion of each category (for example, a psychology department trying to gain support for funding its courses might want to be able to display the relative number of psychologists in particular subfields; see Figure 1.1, page 4).

FIGURE A.7
Pie chart for
college majors

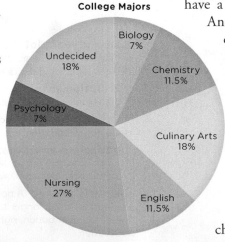

The Description of Data

In addition to using graphs and charts, psychologists can describe their data sets using numbers that express important characteristics: measures of central tendency, measures of variation, and measures of position. These numbers are an important component of descriptive statistics, as they provide a current snapshot of a data set.

Measures of Central Tendency

If you want to understand human behaviors and mental processes, it helps to know what is typical, or standard, for the population. What is the average level of intelligence? At what age do most people experience first love? To answer these types of questions, psychologists can describe their data sets by calculating **measures of central tendency,** which are numbers representing the "middle" of data sets. There are several ways of doing this. The **mean** is the arithmetic average of a data set. Most students learn how to calculate a mean, or "average," early in their schooling, using the following formula:

$$\bar{X} = \frac{X}{n}\Sigma$$ where $\bar{X}$ is the sample mean; X is a value in the data set; Σ represents sigma, meaning to sum the values; and n represents the sample size

or

$$\text{Sample mean} = \frac{\text{Sum of all of the values in the data set}}{\text{Number of values}}$$

To calculate the sample mean ($\bar{X}$) for minutes of REM sleep, you would just plug the numbers into the formula:

$$\bar{X} = (18 + 20 + 22 + 31 + 35 + 35 + 39 + \cdots + 131 + 142 + 150) \div 44$$
$$= 76.8 \text{ minutes}$$

Another measure of central tendency is the **median**—the number that represents the position in the middle of the data set. In other words, 50% of the data values are greater than the median, and 50% are smaller. To calculate the median for a small set of numbers, start by ordering the values, and then determine which number lies exactly in the center. This is relatively simple when the data set is odd-numbered; all you have to do is find the value that has the same number of values above and below it. For a data set that has an even number of values, however, there is one additional step: You must take the average of the two middle numbers (add them together and divide by 2). With an odd number of values in a data set, the median will always be a member of the set. With an even number of values, the median may or may not be a member of the data set.

Here is how you would determine the median (*Mdn*) for the minutes of REM sleep:

1. Order the numbers in the data set from smallest to largest. We can use the stem-and-leaf plot for this purpose.

2. Find the value in the data set that has 50% of the other values below it and 50% above it. Because we have an even number for our sample size ($n = 44$), we will have to find the middle two data values and calculate their average. We divide our sample size of 44 by 2, which is 22, indicating that the median is midway between the 22nd and 23rd values in our set. We count (starting at 18 in the stem-and-leaf plot) to the 22nd and 23rd numbers in our ordered list (76 and 77; there are 21 values below 76 and 21 values above 77).

3. $Mdn = \dfrac{(76 + 77)}{2}$
   $= 76.5$ minutes

1	8
2	0 2
3	1 5 5 9
4	0 7 7 9 9
5	2 7 8
6	2 8 8
7	0 1 3 6 7
8	0 1 1 3 5
9	2 6 8 9
10	0 1 4 5
11	2 4 7
12	1 2
13	1
14	2
15	0

bar graph Displays qualitative data with categories of interest on the x-axis and frequency on the y-axis.

pie chart Displays qualitative data with categories of interest represented by slices of the pie.

measures of central tendency Numbers that represent the middle of a data set.

mean The arithmetic average of a data set; a measure of central tendency.

median A number that represents the position in the data set for which 50% of the values are above it, and 50% are below it; a measure of central tendency.

▲ FIGURE A.8
Bimodal distribution

The third common measure of central tendency is the **mode,** which is the most frequently occurring value in a data set. If there is only one such value, we call it a *unimodal* distribution. With a symmetric distribution, the mean, median, and mode are the same (see Figure A.4a on page A-6). Sometimes there are two modes, indicating a **bimodal distribution,** and the shape of the distribution exhibits two vertical bars of equal height (**FIGURE A.8**). In our example of REM minutes, we cannot see a clear mode, as there are several values that have a frequency of 2 (35, 47, 49, 68, and 81 minutes). By the way, the mode often provides a better representation of the central tendency with bimodal distributions, because neither the mean nor median will indicate that there are in essence two "centers" for the data set.

Under other circumstances, the median is better than the mean for representing the middle of the data set. This is especially true when the data set includes one or more *outliers,* or values that are very different from the rest of the set. We can see why this is true by replacing just one value in our data set on REM sleep. See what happens to the mean and median when you swap 150 for 400. First calculate the mean:

1. $\bar{X} = (18 + 20 + 22 + 31 + 35 + 35 + 39 + \cdots + 131 + 142 + 400) \div 44$
   $= 82.5$ minutes (greater than the original mean of 76.8)

2. And now calculate the median. The numbers in the data set are ordered from smallest to largest. The middle two values have not changed (76 and 77).

   $Mdn = 76.5$ minutes (identical to the original median of 76.5)

No matter how large (or small) a single value is, it does not change the median, but it can have a great influence on the mean. When this occurs, psychologists often present both of these statistics, and discuss the possibility that an outlier is pulling the mean toward it. Look again at the skewed distributions in Figure A.5 on page A-7 and see how the mean is "pulled" toward the side of the distribution that has a possible outlier in its tail. Some types of data are predictably skewed in one direction or the other. For example, income data collected from populations are often positively skewed. The small proportion of very wealthy people pulls the tail of the distribution to the right. A common example for negatively skewed data is age at retirement, because the great majority of people do not retire until they are in their sixties. In either case, when data are skewed, it is often a good idea to use the median as a measure of central tendency, particularly if a problem exists with outliers.

Measures of Variation

In addition to providing information on the central tendency, psychologists can also use **measures of variation** to describe how much variation or dispersion there is in a data set. If you look at the two data sets in **FIGURE A.9** (number of miles commuting to school), you can see that they have the same central tendency (identical means: the mean commute for both samples is 30 miles; $\bar{X} = 30.0$), yet their dispersion is very different: One data set looks very closely packed, and the other spread out.

FIGURE A.9
Same mean, different variability for Sample A and Sample B

Data Values from Sample A
(daily commute to school in miles)
{9, 10, 15, 23, 25, 32, 35, 45, 48, 58}

0	9
1	0 5
2	3 5
3	2 5
4	5 8
5	8

$\bar{X} = 30.0$ miles, $Mdn = 28.5$ miles

Data Values from Sample B
(daily commute to school in miles)
{19, 27, 27, 28, 28, 30, 30, 32, 35, 44}

1	9
2	7 7 8 8
3	0 0 2 5
4	4

$\bar{X} = 30.0$ miles, $Mdn = 29.0$ miles

Thus, in addition to knowing the central tendency of a data set, it is also important to describe its *variability,* or how spread out or dispersed it is. There are several measures we can use to characterize the variability or variation of a data set. The **range** represents the length of a data set and is calculated by taking the highest value minus the lowest value. The range is a rough depiction of variability, but a useful value for trying to compare two samples with data on the same variable. For the data sets presented in Figure A.9, we can compare the ranges of the two samples and see that Sample A has a range of 49 miles and Sample B has a smaller range of 25 miles.

Sample A	**Sample B**
Range = 58 − 9	Range = 44 − 19
Range = 49 miles	Range = 25 miles

A more precise measure of dispersion is the **standard deviation** (referred to by the symbol *s* when describing samples), which essentially represents the average amount the data points are away from their mean. Think about it like this: If the values in a data set are very close to each other, they will also be very close to their mean, and the dispersion will be small. Their average distance from the mean is small. If the values are widely spread, they will not all be clustered around the mean, and their dispersion will be great. Their average distance from the mean is large. One way we can calculate the standard deviation of a sample is by using the following formula:

$$s = \sqrt{\frac{\sum(X - \bar{X})^2}{(n-1)}}$$

This formula does the following: (1) Subtract the mean from a value in the data set, then square the result. Do this for every value in the data set and take the sum of the results. (2) Divide this sum by the sample size minus 1. (3) Take the square root of the result. In **TABLE A.4,** we have gone through each of these steps for Sample A.

The standard deviation for Sample A is 16.7 miles and the standard deviation for Sample B is 6.4 miles (the calculation is not shown here). These standard deviations are consistent with what we expect from looking at the stem-and-leaf plots in Figure A.9. Sample A is more variable, or spread out, than Sample B.

The standard deviation is useful for making predictions about the probability of a particular value occurring Figure A.4b on page A-6. The *empirical rule* tells us that we can expect approximately 68% of all values to fall within 1 standard deviation below or above their mean. We can expect approximately 95% of all values to fall within 2 standard deviations below or above their mean. And we can expect approximately 99.7% of all values to fall within 3 standard deviations below or above their mean. Only 0.3% of the values will fall above or below 3 standard deviations—these values are extremely rare, as you can see in Figure A.4b.

Measures of Position

Another way to describe data is by looking at **measures of position,** which represent where particular data values fall in relation to other values in a set. You have probably heard of *percentiles,* which indicate the percentage of values occurring above and below a certain point in the data set. A value at the 50th percentile is at the median, which indicates that 50% of the values fall above it, and 50% fall below it. A value at the 10th percentile indicates that 90% fall above it, and 10% fall below it. Often you will see percentiles in reports from standardized tests, weight charts, height charts, and so on.

Table A.4   STANDARD DEVIATION FOR SAMPLE A

X	X − X̄	(X − X̄)²
9	9 − 30 = −21	−21² = 441
10	10 − 30 = − 20	−20² = 400
15	15 − 30 = −15	−15² = 225
23	23 − 30 = −7	−7² = 49
25	25 − 30 = −5	−5² = 25
32	32 − 30 = 2	2² = 4
35	35 − 30 = 5	5² = 25
45	45 − 30 = 15	15² = 225
48	48 − 30 = 18	18² = 324
58	58 − 30 = 28	28² = 784

$\sum(X - \bar{X})^2 = 441 + 400 + 225 + 49 + 25 + 4 + 25 + 225 + 324 + 784$
$\qquad = 2{,}502$

$n - 1 = (10 - 1) = 9$

$s = \sqrt{\dfrac{2{,}502}{9}}$

$s = 16.7$

mode The value of the data set that is most frequent; a measure of central tendency.

bimodal distribution A distribution with two modes, which are the two most frequently occurring values.

measures of variation Numbers that describe the variation or dispersion in a data set.

range A number that represents the length of the data set and is a rough depiction of dispersion; a measure of variation.

standard deviation A number that represents the average amount the values in a data set are away from their mean; a measure of variation.

measures of position Numbers that represent where particular data values fall in relation to other values in the data set.

try this

Check your answers
in Appendix C.

Using the data below, calculate the mean, median, range, and standard deviation.
Also create a stem-and-leaf plot to display the data and then describe the shape of
the distribution.

10 10 11 16 18 18 20 20 24 24 25 25 26 29 29 39 40 41 41 42 43 46 48 49 50 50
51 52 53 56 36 37 38 66 71 75 31 34 34 35 57 59 61 61 38

Statistics Is a Language

This introduction to statistics was created to provide you with an overview to the
"language" of statistics that psychologists use to collect, organize, analyze, display,
and interpret data. Like any *foreign* language, statistics is not something you master
by reading a brief overview. To become proficient in statistical methods, you must
study and practice them. And the best way to become fluent in this language is to
immerse yourself in it. For starters, we recommend taking a course in elementary statistics and reading articles published in psychology journals (see **TABLE A.5** for some
commonly used symbols). If you find statistics is your forte, keep taking classes, and
consider the possibility of becoming a researcher. Perhaps your work will be published
in a scientific journal one day—and cited in an introductory psychology textbook!

Table A.5	SYMBOLS COMMONLY USED IN STATISTICS	
Concept	**Symbol**	**Description**
Sample Correlation coefficient	r	Represents the strength and direction of the relationship between two variables
F-test value	F	Used to measure the statistical significance of the differences among 3 or more means
t-test value	t	Used to measure the statistical significance of the difference between 2 means.
p-value	p	An indication of the probability of getting a test statistic of a certain size by chance
Population mean	μ	The mean of a population (pronounced "mew")
Sample mean	M (or $\bar{X}$)	The mean of a sample (pronounced "X-bar")
Population standard deviation	σ	The standard deviation of the population; pronounced "sigma"
Sample standard deviation	s	The standard deviation of a sample
Population size	N	Indicates the size of a population
Sample size	n	Indicates the size of a sample
z-score	z	Indicates a standard score; number of standard deviations from the mean

key terms

bar graph, p. A-8
bimodal distribution, p. A-10
distribution shape, p. A-6
frequency distribution, p. A-5
frequency polygon, p. A-5
histogram, p. A-5
hypothesis testing, p. A-1

mean, p. A-9
measures of central tendency, p. A-9
measures of position, p. A-11
measures of variation, p. A-10
median, p. A-9
meta-analysis, p. A-4

mode, p. A-10
negatively skewed, p. A-7
parameters, p. A-3
pie chart, p. A-8
positively skewed, p. A-7
range, p. A-11
skewed distribution, p. A-7

standard deviation, p. A-11
statistical significance, p. A-2
statistics, p. A-1
stem-and-leaf plot, p. A-6

TEST PREP are you ready?

1. _____ is the science of collecting, organizing, analyzing, displaying, and interpreting data.

2. With descriptive statistics, researchers use tables, graphs, and charts to
   a. summarize data.
   b. make inferences about data.
   c. make predictions.
   d. test hypotheses.

3. A classmate is collecting data for a research project incorporating a treatment group and a control group. When the data collection is complete, she will check for _____ to see if the differences between the two groups are due to the researcher's manipulations.
   a. random sampling
   b. descriptive statistics
   c. standard deviations
   d. statistical significance

4. In the following, identify the variable as quantitative (1) or qualitative (2):
   _____ a. political affiliation
   _____ b. hair color
   _____ c. yearly income
   _____ d. weight in pounds

5. One common way to present data is to use a _____, which displays how often various values in a data set are present.
   a. qualitative variable
   b. meta-analysis
   c. frequency distribution
   d. measure of variation

6. A researcher is looking to measure cognitive ability in a large representative sample. She can expect that the distribution will be symmetric and have a bell shape. This type of distribution is also known as a
   a. normal curve.
   b. stem-and-leaf plot.
   c. qualitative variable.
   d. parameter.

7. Some data will have a skewed distribution, which is not symmetrical. A _____ distribution has a longer tail to the left side and a _____ distribution has a longer tail to the right side.

8. Numbers that represent the "middle" of data sets are known as
   a. standard deviations.
   b. measures of central tendency.
   c. measures of variability.
   d. misleading.

9. What is the mean for a sample that includes the following values: 4, 4, 6, 3, 8?
   a. 4
   b. 5
   c. 6
   d. 7

10. What is the median for a sample that includes the following values: 4, 4, 6, 3, 8?
    a. 4
    b. 5
    c. 6
    d. 7

11. What is the mode for a sample that includes the following values: 4, 4, 6, 3, 8?
    a. 4
    b. 5
    c. 6
    d. 7

12. A value that is very different from the rest of the data set is called a(n) _____, and it can have a great influence on the _____.
    a. mode; median
    b. variable; mode
    c. outlier; mean
    d. outlier; median

13. A classmate is trying to calculate a measure of variability. He takes the highest value in the data set and subtracts the lowest value from it. This is considered the _____ of the data set.
    a. range
    b. central tendency
    c. median
    d. standard deviation

14. What is the standard deviation for a sample that includes the following values: 4, 4, 6, 3, 8?
    a. 2
    b. 3
    c. 4
    d. 5

15. When you look at a graph in a newspaper, online, or elsewhere, you need to determine if it is a valid representation of the data being described. Sometimes, the graphic representation can be misleading, commonly by choosing values on the y-axis that can change how findings are interpreted. Find two examples of graphs in the media and examine their y-axes to see how the units are portrayed.

16. A positively skewed distribution is commonly found for data collected on income. Think of one other example of a positively skewed variable.

✓ CHECK YOUR ANSWERS IN APPENDIX C.

Get personalized practice by logging into LaunchPad at **http://www.worthpublishers.com/launchpad/Licht** to take the LearningCurve adaptive quizzes for Appendix A.

careers in psychology

Some students start college knowing what their majors are, but a great majority are uncertain about this decision. If you are considering psychology, or even if you have already chosen psychology as your major, it is important to determine if this is the right career choice for you. There is more to psychology than "being a good listener," or providing a "shoulder to cry on." You may feel drawn to the discipline because friends are always coming to you for advice, but there are many things to consider as you plan your career. Psychology is a vast field, and it may take time to figure out which subfield matches your interests, skills, and abilities. There is also the issue of finances. Will the career you choose allow you to reach your financial goals? Psychologists' salaries are highly variable and depend on many factors, including education level, specialty, and type of employer.

What Is a Psychologist?

Psychologists work in a variety of fields. Most people hear the word "psychologist" and automatically think of therapy, counseling, and Freud, but as we noted in Chapter 1, psychologists do much more than people commonly assume. Some conduct *basic research*, which often takes place in university laboratories and focuses on collecting data to support (or refute) theories. Others conduct *applied research*, which is more concerned with changing behaviors and outcomes, and often leads to real-world applications. Still other psychologists devote their careers to teaching at colleges and universities.

There is no shortage of psychology career paths. If you enter this field, plenty of choices will await you. But be aware that any career in psychology will require some degree of specialized education. The question is, how much are you willing and able to attain? For many students, the answer depends on age, family responsibilities, financial concerns, and life experiences. In psychology, there are three types of degrees you can consider at the undergraduate and graduate level: bachelor's, master's, and doctoral.

What Can I Do with a Bachelor's Degree in Psychology?

If you are reading this book for a college course, then you are likely taking an undergraduate-level course in psychology, and perhaps you are planning to earn an undergraduate degree. Many students begin their journey by obtaining a two-year associate's degree, eventually earning a bachelor's degree from a four-year institution. A bachelor's degree in psychology is a great step toward understanding the scientific study of behavior and mental processes. It can prepare you to enter a graduate program, or it may serve as the foundation for your career. The psychology bachelor's degree is exceptionally popular, with over 97,000 awarded in 2010–2011 (Snyder & Dillow, 2011), which could mean substantial competition in the job market. This is one place where the decision between entering the workforce or attending graduate

Table B.1 BACHELOR'S DEGREES AND CAREERS IN PSYCHOLOGY

Psychology Focus	Median Annual Salary	Business Focus	Median Annual Salary	Other Focus	Median Annual Salary
Caseworker	$28,000	Administrative assistant	$35,000	Child-care employee	$19,000
Correctional treatment specialist	$47,000	Advertising sales agent	$45,000	Clergy	$48,000
Foster-care home supervisor	$28,000	Airline reservations employee	$33,500	Community service manager	$58,000
Group home supervisor	$28,000	Customer relations	$30,000	Health services manager	$84,000
Probation officer	$47,000	Employment counselor	$56,000	High school teacher	$53,000
Residential treatment center employee	$27,000	Insurance agent	$47,000	Law enforcement	$55,000
Social services director	$58,000	Human resources	$53,000	Parks and recreation worker	$22,000
Substance abuse counselor	$38,000	Public relations	$57,500	Security officer	$24,000

A BACHELOR'S DEGREE IN PSYCHOLOGY PREPARES YOU FOR MANY TYPES OF EMPLOYMENT OPPORTUNITIES. HERE, WE SEE HOW THIS TYPE OF DEGREE IS NOT LIMITED TO THE FIELD OF PSYCHOLOGY. FOR MORE UP-TO-DATE INFORMATION, LOG ONTO LAUNCHPAD AT HTTP://WORTHPUBLISHERS.COM/LAUNCHPAD/LICHT.

SOURCE: ADAPTED FROM LANDRUM (2001) AND LLOYD (1997, JULY 16).
SALARY INFORMATION FROM BUREAU OF LABOR STATISTICS (2012–2013).

school becomes important. **TABLE B.1** gives you a sense of the types of jobs you can obtain with a bachelor's degree in psychology.

When it comes to earning potential, education level matters. People with bachelor's degrees earn an estimated $2.3 million over the course of a lifetime. Contrast that with $1.3 million lifetime earnings for those with only high school diplomas. Higher-level degrees generally lead to the most lucrative positions. The average lifetime salary for someone with a master's degree is $2.7 million. People with doctoral degrees earn approximately $3.3 million over the course of their careers (Carnevale, Rose, & Cheah, 2011).

Earning an undergraduate degree in psychology is a great accomplishment. Yet, many students find that they want an even deeper understanding of a particular field in psychology, which they can only get a taste of as an undergraduate. Other students decide to take a break after finishing their course of study for a bachelor's degree; but as the years pass following graduation, they start to realize they want to further their education and a career in psychology. In either case, the next step might be a graduate degree, which is an important decision that requires a great deal of research and effort. Opportunities abound in terms of the type of graduate degree and the colleges and universities that offer them. The American Psychological Association (APA) publishes a great resource for students thinking about this next step, *Graduate Study in Psychology* (American Psychological Association, 2013a). This guide, which is routinely updated, includes approximately 600 psychology graduate programs offered in the United States and Canada, and information about them, such as the number of applications they receive, deadlines for applications, employment information for their graduates, and tuition costs.

What Can I Do with a Master's in Psychology?

Students who decide to pursue a graduate degree sometimes start with a master's-level program, terminating with a degree that will allow them to follow a variety of career paths in psychology. A master's degree in psychology is flexible and can prepare you to work in areas outside the field of psychology, including government, health care, business, marketing, and education. Many master's-level psychologists devote their careers to research, working under PhD-level researchers at universities and other institutions. Finally, there are those who become therapists. Typically, this means earning a master's degree, with an emphasis on counseling and securing a state license to practice.

TABLE B.2 provides some general information about the types of degrees and training required of various mental health professions. In most states, master's-level clinicians must obtain a license to practice and share details about their education, training, and licensing status with their clients. One can also earn a master's degree in nonclinical specialties such as industrial/organizational psychology, engineering psychology, and leadership psychology. Some of these applied fields offer lucrative careers in business and industry. Many students earning a master's degree in psychology go on to complete their doctorate degrees. But for those who decide to earn a master's degree, there are still plenty of job opportunities.

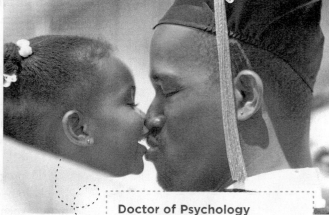

Doctor of Psychology
David Brantley III celebrates with his daughter after receiving a doctor of psychology degree (PsyD) from Rutgers Graduate School of Applied and Professional Psychology. Unlike PhD programs, which are highly research focused, PsyD programs focus more on the clinical side of things—that is, the diagnosis and treatment of psychological conditions. AP Photo/Mike Derer

Table B.2 MENTAL HEALTH PROFESSIONALS

Degree	Occupation	Training	Focus	Approximate Years of Study after Bachelor's Degree
Medical doctor, MD	Psychiatrist	Medical school and residency training	Treatment of psychological disorders; may include research focus	8 (including residency)
Doctor of philosophy, PhD	Clinical or counseling psychologist	Graduate school; includes dissertation and internship	Research-oriented and clinical practice	3–6
Doctor of psychology, PsyD	Clinical or counseling psychologist	Graduate school; includes internship; may include dissertation	Focus on professional practice	2–5
Master's degree, MA or MS	Mental health counselor	Graduate school; includes internship	Focus on professional practice	2

MENTAL HEALTH PROFESSIONALS HAVE A VARIETY OF BACKGROUNDS. HERE, WE PRESENT A HANDFUL OF THESE, INCLUDING GENERAL INFORMATION ON TRAINING, FOCUS, AND THE LENGTH OF EDUCATION.

Doctoral Degrees: PhD and PsyD

Determining if you need a degree at the doctoral level really depends on your interests. A PhD (doctor of philosophy) psychologist typically focuses on research, though some also provide therapy (Norcross & Castle, 2002). Earning a PhD requires graduate-level course work: 3 to 6 years of advanced college courses and training in addition to a bachelor's degree. PhD coursework and research culminate in a dissertation, which you might think of as a huge research paper in your field of study. PhD programs are highly competitive; it is not unusual for an applicant to apply to multiple schools, but only gain acceptance to one or two. The good news is that programs typically provide 70–80% of students with tuition assistance (Norcross & Castle, 2002). For some helpful tips on applying to PhD programs, you can visit the American Psychological Association Web site (http://www.apa.org/education/grad/applying.aspx) and LaunchPad at http://worthpublishers.com/launchpad/Licht.

If your interest is more clinically focused, then you may consider the other doctoral-level degree in psychology, a PsyD (doctor of psychology). It focuses more on clinical practice than on research, and typically requires 1 to 1.5 fewer years than a PhD program. Because most PsyD degrees are offered by professional schools of psychology or private colleges and universities, these programs can be substantially more expensive than PhD programs, with students amassing an average debt of $53,000 to $60,000 (Norcross & Castle, 2002). There also tends to be less financial aid available for PsyD students.

In the early 1970s, many psychologists believed that the practice of clinical psychology (that is, how therapists work) deserved more academic attention (Norcross & Castle, 2002; VanderVeen, Reddy, Veileux, January, & DiLillo, 2012). As a result, PhD programs try to ensure that students are "educated and trained to generate and integrate scientific and professional knowledge and skills so as to further psychological science, the professional practice of psychology, and human welfare" (American Psychological Association [Society of Clinical Psychology, Division 12], as cited in VanderVeen et al., 2012, p. 1049). The biggest difference between PhD and PsyD programs is that PhD programs are more research focused. This is not to say that PsyD programs do not require course work in statistics and research methods; it is just not the primary focus. PsyD programs traditionally emphasize clinical course work, practice, and experience (Norcross & Castle, 2002).

Subfields of Psychology

Despite being a relatively young field, psychology is a vast and varied discipline. Psychologists provide treatment for people with mental disorders, examine cognitive processes, study changes across the life span, work with children in schools, help corporations develop marketing strategies, and much more. They work in a variety of settings, including laboratories, courtrooms, schools, colleges, universities, prisons, and corporations (American Psychological Association [APA], 2011b). Many psychologists conduct innovative research, building on the field's extensive knowledge base. In an ever-changing and increasingly diverse environment, psychologists are leading efforts to improve the mental health and well-being of people throughout the world. Let's explore some of the subfields of psychology.

Clinical Psychology

Clinical psychologists focus on the diagnosis and treatment of people with psychological disorders. In addition to providing therapy, many of these professionals also conduct research on psychological disorders. They may, for example, use brain

Changing the World
With a budget of only $3,000, Dr. Tamara Russell launched an innovative mental health program at Washington State Penitentiary in Walla Walla, WA. Her treatment program provides inmates with opportunities to help others—by mentoring fellow inmates, tutoring students for the General Educational Development (GED) tests, and caring for orphaned kittens, among other things (Hagar, 2013, September 19). AP Photo/Walla Walla Union-Bulletin, Greg Lehman

scanning technologies to better understand the causes of depression, or design studies to compare the effects of different treatments. Some work as professors in colleges or universities, others as clinicians in medical facilities or private practice (APA, 1998b, 2011b).

Cognitive Psychology

Cognitive psychologists examine thinking, memory, intelligence, language, attention, and problem solving. Using the scientific method, these psychologists study how people "perceive, interpret and store information" (APA, 1998b, p. 14). Cognitive psychologists generally work in college and university settings, but many are employed as business consultants (APA, 1998b, 2011b).

Counseling Psychology

Like clinical psychologists, counseling psychologists provide treatment for people with psychological disorders. But as opposed to helping people with severe disorders, they tend to work with those needing support concerning day-to-day problems. They tend to focus on relationship issues, career exploration, and stress management. These psychologists can be found in academic settings, clinical practice, and hospitals (APA, 1998b, 2011b). The work of clinical and counseling psychologists overlaps to some degree, although differences may result from their specific training programs. In some cases, counseling programs are located in a psychology department, which is also the case for most clinical programs. However, many counseling psychology programs are affiliated with education departments, which might provide different types of research and training than psychology departments.

Developmental Psychology

Developmental psychologists are primarily concerned with physical, cognitive, and socioemotional changes that occur over the life span (APA, 1998b, 2011b). Research in this field provides information about people from conception to death, impacting, for example, how children are treated in day-care settings, students are educated in classrooms, and elderly people are advised to manage their health. Although this field once focused primarily on children from birth to adolescence, developmental psychologists have become increasingly aware of the importance of research focused on adults as they age. They are especially concerned with helping people remain independent throughout life (APA, 2011b).

Educational and School Psychology

Educational psychologists examine methods of learning and how memory relates to learning. As such, these specialists play a key role in developing teaching strategies and curricula. School psychologists often apply lessons gleaned by educational psychologists in the classroom and in classifying where students are academically. Educational and school psychologists work at colleges and universities, in school districts, and in private practice. Some educational psychologists are employed in industry, helping to create and evaluate student assessments (APA, 1998b, 2011b). These psychologists may collaborate with school administrators, teachers, and parents to provide an effective and safe learning environment. They also assist students who are having learning difficulties and those who are assessed as gifted, or they might assist teachers dealing with classroom management and student behavior problems.

Positive Work Environment
A physician uses a surgical microscope designed to facilitate a more comfortable sitting posture. Optimizing the relationship between humans and technology is one of the goals of engineering psychology. People who work in this subfield research and develop ways to improve work environments.
Business Wire via Getty Images

Engineering Psychology

Engineering psychologists conduct research to improve work environments by optimizing processes, systems, and equipment. They are also referred to as human factors specialists and usually work in industry and government (APA, 2011b). These specialists play a key role in observing on-the-job activities, conducting surveys, and recommending changes to facilitate optimal work environments with high productivity and safety. They may recommend changes in equipment, workload, personnel, or training.

Environmental Psychology

Environmental psychologists are interested in the connection between behavior and the physical environment. "Physical environment" is anywhere that humans spend time, be it at home, in a college dorm, or on a city block. Environmental psychologists are interested in exploring how to promote "positive human behavior" in governmental agencies, business, and other types of settings (APA, 1998b, 2011b).

Experimental Psychology

Experimental psychologists are science enthusiasts. They spend their days conducting basic and applied research on people, animals, and data. These researchers typically focus on a particular area of study, such as cognitive psychology, neuroscience, or animal behavior. Experimental psychologists may teach at colleges and universities, or conduct research for industries (APA, 1998b, 2011b).

Forensic Psychology

Forensic psychologists apply the principles of psychology to the legal system, working in diverse environments including criminal, family, and civil courts. These experts often are called upon in legal cases involving decisions about child custody, or situations in which a person's "mental competence to stand trial" is in question (APA, 2011b, p. 2). Some forensic psychologists are trained in law as well as in psychology, and they may conduct research on topics such as jury behavior or eyewitness testimony.

Health Psychology

Health psychologists are primarily interested in promoting positive health behaviors and preventing illness. They may conduct research aimed at answering questions such as, why do people smoke? or what drives someone to overeat? and their findings are used to promote good health practices. Health psychologists examine how individuals deal with sickness, pain, and medical treatment. They look at the interaction of biological, psychological, and social factors in relation to health and well-being. Health psychologists may be employed by hospitals, clinics, and rehabilitation centers, or they might conduct a private practice (APA, 1998, 2011b).

Industrial and Organizational (I/O) Psychology

Industrial and organizational psychologists examine the relationships of people working in organizations. They are particularly interested in employee job satisfaction, productivity, organizational structure and change, as well as the interface between humans and machines. In addition, I/O psychologists work with administrators to assist in hiring, training, and educating employees, and promoting their interests. I/O psychologists are often employed in industry, government, business, and academic settings (APA, 1998b, 2011b).

Media Psychology

Media psychologists examine the interactions among graphics, images, sound, and the human response. These psychologists study the field of psychology and the development, production, and use of technology. Media psychologists investigate all forms of media (print, radio, television, social media) through different formats (mobile, interactive, virtual; APA, 2012c). They are particularly concerned with the way media shape our time. They may also look at how social media, text messaging, and even e-mail have influenced the manner in which people relate to one another. Media psychologists might also consider the way reality shows can elevate ordinary people to celebrity status.

Neuropsychology and Psychobiology

Neuropsychologists and psychobiologists are interested in the relationship between human behavior and the body (neural activity, hormonal changes, and so on; APA, 1998b, 2011b). These psychologists work with people recovering from strokes and brain traumas, or struggling with learning disabilities and developmental delays. They investigate how the structure and function of the brain relate to behavior, cognition, and emotion. Neuropsychologists and psychobiologists often conduct research at colleges or universities, but they may also be employed by hospitals or other medical facilities (APA, 1998b, 2011b).

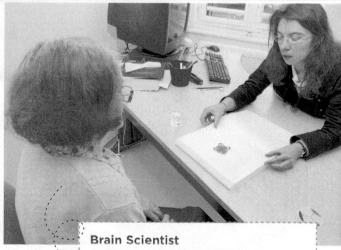

Brain Scientist
A neuropsychologist administers a memory test that requires the participant to identify previously viewed images. Neuropsychologists are primarily interested in the relationship between behavior and brain activity. They work with people struggling with Alzheimer's disease and other neurocognitive disorders, children with developmental delays, and individuals with traumatic brain injuries. BSIP/UIG Via Getty Images

Rehabilitation Psychology

Rehabilitation psychologists either conduct research on or work with patients who have lost functioning as a result of strokes, epilepsy, autism, or accidents, for example. These psychologists are particularly concerned with helping people adjust to work, relationships, and day-to-day living. Their research may impact the development of public programs (APA, 2011b).

Social Psychology

Social psychologists examine the behaviors, thoughts, and emotions of people in groups. They may study attitudes, persuasion, discrimination, conformity, or group behavior. Social psychologists are interested in the many factors that influence interpersonal relationships, as well as the factors associated with attraction and love. While often employed by colleges and universities, these psychologists may also work for businesses and corporations (APA, 1998b, 2011b).

Sport Psychology

Sport psychologists help athletes and their coaches address competition, motivation, anxiety, or worry related to athletic performance (APA, 2011b). As any sport psychologist can testify, being physically fit is not the only requirement for athletic excellence. Sport psychologists also work in many corporations, helping to build their "teams" and providing support for dealing with stress management, building confidence, and improving performance on the job (APA, n.d.).

Psychologist in the Field
Sport psychologist Jeremy Snape (middle) meets with legendary cricket player Sir Viv Richards (left) and Melbourne Stars captain Shane Warne (right) before a big cricket game. Sport psychologists help athletes and coaches contend with the psychological challenges of their sport. Paul Kane/Getty Images

The science of psychology is relatively young compared to other sciences, and it is growing and changing with the advancement of technology and interdisciplinary research. If you are considering a career in psychology, you will want to keep up with the exciting developments in the field, and one good place to do that is on the Web sites of the professional organizations associated with the field (the Association for Psychological Science and the American Psychological Association) as well as by logging onto LaunchPad at http://worthpublishers.com/launchpad/Licht.

1 introduction to the science of psychology

▢▢▢▢ show what you know

Presenting Psychology

1. behavior; mental processes

2. d. control

3. *Common sense* is a collection of knowledge that any reasonably smart person can pick up through everyday experiences and casual observations. Findings from psychology, however, are based on meticulous and methodical observations of behaviors and mental processes, as well as data analysis. Many people respond to psychological findings with *hindsight bias,* or the feeling as if they knew it all along. If the results of a study seem obvious, someone may feel as if she "knew it all along," when in reality she wouldn't have predicted the outcome ahead of time.

Roots, Schools, and Perspectives of Psychology

1. d. introspection

2. b. behavioral

3. a. natural selection

4. Answers will vary. *Sociocultural* and *biopsychosocial* perspectives are similar in that both examine how interactions with other people influence behaviors and mental processes. *Cognitive* and *biological* perspectives differ in that the *cognitive* perspective focuses on the thought processes underlying behavior, while the *biological* perspective emphasizes physiological processes.

Science and Psychology

1. b. critical thinking

2. Pseudopsychology

3. Astrology is a great example of a *pseudopsychology*, an approach to explaining and predicting behavior and events that appears to be psychology but lacks scientific support. If you search the scientific literature for empirical, objective studies supporting astrological claims, you will have a very difficult time finding any. Another sign astrology is a pseudoscience is that its predictions are often too broad to refute. Let's say an astrologer predicts that a friend or close family member will soon need your kind words and support. Such a prediction would likely apply to the great majority of people, as family members and friends often look to each other for strength. Such a prediction would always seem to come true, because the probability of its occurrence is almost 100%.

The Scientific Method

1. An *opinion* is a belief or attitude that is not based on research, and may completely result from personal experiences, often without any scientific evidence to support it. *Theories* synthesize research observations and can be used to explain phenomena and make predictions that are testable with the scientific method. Theories are often well-established bodies of principles that rest on a solid foundation of evidence.

2. d. operational definition

3. a. theory

Research Designs

1. variables

2. c. representative sample

3. A *representative sample* has members with characteristics similar to those of the target population. Characteristics to consider could include gender, age, socioeconomic status, and so forth. Without a representative sample, one should not generalize the study findings to the larger population.

Descriptive Research

1. c. Descriptive research

2. a. naturalistic observation.

3. positive correlation

4. *Descriptive research* explores and describes behaviors. This approach is excellent for investigating unfamiliar topics. A researcher conducting such a study has few or no specific expectations about outcomes, and may use his findings to direct future research. A critical weakness of descriptive research is that it cannot uncover cause-and-effect relationships.

Experimental Research

1. d. cause-and-effect relationship

2. a. dependent

3. b. whether the child was alone or with others.

4. In a *double-blind study,* neither the participants nor the researchers working directly with those participants know who is getting the treatment and who is getting the placebo. This type of study is designed to reduce expectations and biases that can arise when either participants or experimenters know what they've received or distributed. This use of deception is necessary so that neither

experimenter nor participant consciously or unconsciously alters their behaviors, that is, unknowingly changes the outcome of the experiment.

Important Issues in Psychology

1. a. Informed consent

2. b. debriefing.

3. Answers will vary: "Pacifiers and Emotional Health"; "Pacifiers and Empathy"; "Binkie Psychology"

TEST PREP are you ready?

1. b. applied research.

2. a. Common sense

3. c. the nature side of the nature–nurture issue.

4. d. functionalism.

5. d. Humanistic psychology

6. b. critical thinking

7. c. the scientific method

8. a. Inferential statistics

9. c. variables.

10. d. an equally likely chance of being picked to participate.

11. c. relationships among variables.

12. b. case study

13. d. independent; dependent

14. a. double-blind

15. b. experimental group

16. A thorough review of the literature informs us about what has been learned in the past. Without doing a literature search, we may find ourselves redoing a study that has already provided the answers we seek. In addition, it may help us develop research questions, move in new directions, and deepen our understanding of psychological phenomena.

17. Answers will vary. Possible answer may include: The treatment group could be told to write a lie, while the control group is instructed to write something truthful. The researcher could determine if other factors change the pressure and strokes of handwriting. She may include a treatment group to measure the effects of sleepiness, for example. In this instance, the treatment group would include those who get little sleep and the control group would include those who get an average amount of sleep.

18. The most accurate data are likely to come from participants who answer written questions in private. Those answering in face-to-face interviews are not always forthright with their answers, or they may be uncomfortable or embarrassed to reveal the truth.

19. Answers will vary. Look for studies on topics that would be very hard for researchers to manipulate in an ethical manner (for example, breast feeding, amount of television watched, attitudes).

20. Answers will vary. Some possibilities include showing the children a different cartoon; changing the ages of the children, including children of different ethnicities and socioeconomic backgrounds; determining whether they are hungry prior to participating; and so on.

2 biology and behavior

show what you know

An Introduction to the Brain

1. b. the human nervous system

2. neuroscience

3. Answers will vary. Building blocks can include items ranging from flour and butter in culinary training to numbers in mathematics. Atoms, chemical compounds, mechanical parts, and many other basic components may be building blocks in other fields of study.

Neurons and Neural Communication

1. myelin sheath

2. a. glial cells

3. b. Neurotransmitters; synaptic gap

4. A diagram could include the following information: Neural communication involves different processes within and between neurons. Using Infographic 2.1, you can follow the electrical action within the neuron. Messages received by the dendrites from neighboring neurons are passed along the axon, which sends messages to other neurons through its branchlike terminal buds.

   Infographic 2.2 demonstrates how neurons communicate with each other via chemicals called *neurotransmitters*. The signal to release neurotransmitters is the voltage change from the action potential, which results in vesicles that contain neurotransmitters attaching to the membrane on the terminal bud. This allows the neurotransmitter to be released into the synaptic gap. The majority of these neurotransmitters drift across the synaptic gap and come into contact with receptor sites of the receiving neuron's dendrites, which may (or may not) lead to an action potential in the receiving neuron.

The Supporting Systems

1. d. Motor neurons

2. b. spinal cord

3. pituitary

4. Both types of responses tend to increase the likelihood of survival and reproduction. The *flight-or-flight* strategy centers on self-preservation: by confronting or fleeing a threating situation, the individual is acting to ensure her own survival and ability to reproduce. *Tend and befriend* is perhaps a less direct approach. Forging social bonds and tending to the young strengthen the community as a whole, which can support the survival and reproduction of its members.

The Hemispheres

1. d. lateralization.

2. b. Broca's area.

3. split-brain operation

4. The *corpus callosum* is a bundle of nerve fibers that allows the two halves of the brain to communicate and work together to process information. This same band of nerve fibers can also serve as a

passageway for electrical storms responsible for seizures. With the split-brain operation, the corpus callosum is severed so that these storms can no longer pass freely between the hemispheres.

The Amazing Brain

1. c. neurogenesis

2. Independent variable: manipulation of hearing classical music.
   Dependent variable: measure of cognitive abilities.
   Answers will vary. The experimental group would listen to classical music and the control group would not listen to classical music.

3. Stem cells

4. a. neuroplasticity

The Cortex: A Peek Beneath the Skull

1. b. frontal lobes

2. association areas

3. Answers will vary. There is no right or wrong mnemonic; use one that will help you remember.
   Here is one example connecting letters or word segments to function:
   Frontal lobes: **Front** and center (integrating information from all over the brain)
   Occipital lobes: "**Oh,** did you see that?" (visual processing)
   Parietal lobes: **P**erceive touch (processing of touch sensations)
   Temporal lobes: **Tempo** is just right (auditory processing)

4. c. damage to his frontal lobes

Digging Below the Cortex

1. b. limbic system

2. amygdala

3. The *limbic system* helps process some of the emotions related to this romantic interest (amygdala), sensations of seeing, hearin, and touching (thalamus), memories of past first dates (hippocampus and amygdala); it also ensures that some of our basic needs are met during the course of the date (hypothalamus). The *brainstem* controls life-sustaining activities, allowing us to divert our attention from breathing onto engaging in conversation. The *cerebellum* is responsible for balance and producing appropriate emotional reactions while on the date.

4. a. relay sensory information.

TEST PREP are you ready?

1. c. Neurons

2. a. an action potential

3. a. myelin sheath

4. 1. acetylcholine: c. enables movement; 2. glutamate: b. learning, memory; 3. endorphins: a. reduces experience of pain; 4. serotonin: d. mood, aggression, appetite

5. a. central nervous system.

6. b. spinal cord

7. d. peripheral nervous system

8. d. "rest-and-digest" process.

9. b. endocrine system; glands

10. b. The right hemisphere is more competent handling visual tasks.

11. a. locations in the brain are responsible for certain activities.

12. d. Wernicke's area

13. 1. association area: b. integrates information from all over the brain; 2. temporal lobes: c. hearing and language comprehension; 3. meninges: a. three thin membranes protect brain; 4. occipital lobes: e. processes visual information; 5. parietal lobes: d. receives sensory information, such as touch

14. 1. amygdala: b. processes basic information; 2. hippocampus: a. responsible for making new memories; 3. hypothalamus: d. keeps body systems in steady state; 4. thalamus: c. relays sensory information

15. d. reticular formation

16. Answers will vary. *Agonists* boost normal neurotransmitter activity and *antagonists* dampen normal neurotransmitter activity. An agonist is somewhat like a substance you add to your car engine to increase its efficiency. An antagonist might be compared to a character in a novel who prevents a heroine from doing her job.

17. Diagrams will vary; see Figure 2.3. A *reflex* is an uncontrollable reaction that often protects us from bodily harm. For example, we automatically pull away when we touch a hot surface. Sensory neurons are activated and carry information from the environment to interneurons in the spinal cord, which activates motor neurons. The motor neurons excite the muscle and initiate the motion of pulling away.

18. *Neurotransmitters* are chemical messengers produced by neurons that enable communication between neurons. *Hormones* are chemical messengers produced by the endocrine system and released into the bloodstream. The effects of the neurotransmitters are almost instantaneous, whereas those of hormones are usually delayed and longer lasting. Both influence thoughts, emotions, and behaviors. Neurotransmitters and hormones can work together, for example directing the fight-or-flight response to stress.

19. Sperry and Gazzaniga's research demonstrated that the hemispheres of the human brain, while strikingly similar in appearance, specialize in different functions. The left hemisphere excels in language processing, and the right hemisphere excels at visuospatial tasks. The corpus callosum normally allows the two hemispheres to share and integrate information.

20. The *EEG* detects electrical impulses in the brain. The *CT* uses X-rays to create many cross-sectional images of the brain. The *MRI* uses pulses of radio waves to produce more detailed cross-sectional images than those of a CT scan, but both MRI and CT are used to study the structure of the brain. The *PET* uses radioactivity to track glucose consumption and construct a map of brain activity. The *fMRI* also captures changes in brain activity, but instead of tracking glucose consumption, it reveals patterns of blood flow in the brain, which is a good indicator of how much oxygen is being used. All of these tools have strengths and limitations (see Table 2.1).

try this
page 63

ANSWER: Yes, Brandon would display a reflex. Remember that the knee jerk is an involuntary reaction carried out by neurons outside of the brain.

3 sensation and perception

▢▢▢▢▢ show what you know

An Introduction to Sensation and Perception

1. a. Perception

2. *Signal detection theory* states that various sensory factors and a person's psychological state influence the ability to detect weak signals in the environment. Some things that may influence one's ability to detect an intruder's flashlight include the intensity of the light, level of alertness, the expectations about one's role, and other interfering stimuli in the environment.

3. d. sensory adaptation.

Vision

1. wavelength

2. b. photoreceptors

3. The *trichromatic theory of color vision* suggests there are three types of cones, each sensitive to particular wavelengths in the red, green, and blue spectrums. The brain identifies a precise hue by calculating patterns of excitement among the three types of cones, that is, the relative activity of the three types.

    The *opponent-process theory of color vision* suggests that in addition to the color-sensitive cones, we also have neurons that respond to opponent colors (for example, red–green, blue–yellow). One neuron in an opponent pair fires when one is looking at red, for example, but is inactive when one is looking at green. Both the trichromatic and opponent-process theories clarify different aspects of color vision, as color perception occurs in the light-sensing cones in the retina and in the opponent cells serving the brain.

4. d. rods.

Hearing

1. a. frequency

2. b. transduction.

3. place

4. Diagrams will vary. The pitch of a sound is determined by the frequency of its sound wave, which is usually measured in Hertz. *Place theory* suggests that the location of neural activity along the cochlea allows us to sense different pitches of high-frequency sounds. *Frequency theory* suggests that the pitch of a sound is determined by the vibrating frequency of the sound wave, basilar membrane, and associated neural impulses. Place theory explains our perception of pitches from 4,000 to 20,000 Hz, and frequency theory explains how we perceive the pitch of sounds from 20 to 400 Hz. The *volley principle* explains the perception of pitches from 400 to 4,000 Hz.

Smell, Taste, Touch: The Chemical and Skin Senses

1. olfaction

2. b. transduction.

3. Smell, taste, and touch all include the sensing of information in the environment through receptor cells designed to detect a particular kind of stimuli. These three senses also involve transduction, which is the process of transforming stimuli into neural signals. Neural signals for all three of these senses then are processed by the central nervous system. Smell and taste are considered chemical senses, as they both involve sensing chemicals (odor molecules for olfaction, flavor molecules for taste) in the environment. Taste and touch relay data through the thalamus before going to higher brain centers, whereas olfaction is not relayed through the thalamus.

4. c. the gate-control theory

Perception

1. Illusions

2. a. convergence

3. *ESP* is the purported ability to obtain information about the world in the absence of sensory stimuli. There is a lack of scientific evidence to support the existence of ESP, and most so-called evidence comes in the form of personal anecdotes. Subjective information can be biased. Using critical thinking, we must determine the credibility of the source and validity of the evidence. Despite ESP's lack of scientific credibility, many people still believe in its existence in part because of illusory correlations, which appear to be links between variables that are not closely related at all.

4. b. perceptual constancy

TEST PREP are you ready?

1. c. sensation.

2. a. transduction.

3. b. fatigue and motivation

4. d. cornea

5. b. rods and cones

6. a. afterimage effects; trichromatic

7. d. audition

8. c. neural impulses firing

9. b. 20%

10. a. thalamus

11. a. Feature detectors

12. a. proprioceptors

13. a. tension of the muscles focusing the eyes

14. d. proximity.

15. c. relative size.

16. Answers will vary. Examples might include judging distances to assess the safety of a situation; using vision to find food, water, or shelter; and seeing an attractive mate, which could be related to increasing reproductive success. Visual information in such cases increases the chances of survival.

17. The eye adjusts to drastic fluctuations in light levels, but this does not happen instantaneously, making it difficult to see when one first walks into a dark room. However, one's eyes immediately begin to adjust. This process starts with the pupil, which rapidly shrinks and expands in response to light changes, and then

continues with the rods and cones, which need more time to adjust to changes in lighting. After a few minutes, your eyes start to adjust to the dark in a process called *dark adaptation,* which takes about 8 minutes for cones and 30 minutes for rods. Cones respond more quickly, so they are more useful in the first few minutes of dark adaptation. The rods then begin to allow one to make out silhouettes of objects and people. To restore their sensitivity to light, rods and cones must undergo a chemical change associated with protein molecules, and this takes time.

18. Diagrams will vary; see Infographic 3.3. The pinna funnels sound waves into the auditory canal, focusing them toward the eardrum. Vibrations in the eardrum cause the hammer to push the anvil, which moves the stirrup, which presses on the oval window, amplifying waves. Pressure on the oval window causes fluid in the cochlea to vibrate and bend the hair cells on the basilar membrane. If vibration is strong enough in the cochlear fluid, the bending of hair cells causes nearby nerve cells to fire. The auditory nerve carries signals to the auditory cortex in the brain, where sounds are given meaning.

19. The *gate-control theory of pain* suggests that the perception of pain can either increase or decrease through the interaction of biopsychosocial factors. Signals are sent to open or close the "gates" that control the neurological pathways for pain. When large myelinated fibers are active, the gates are more likely to close, which then inhibits pain messages from being sent on. With a sore shoulder, applying ice to the injured area can stimulate the temperature and pressure receptors of the large fibers. This activity closes the gates, temporarily interfering with the pain message that would have been sent to the brain.

20. Answers will vary, but may include experiences such as getting into a hot tub and eventually becoming adapted to how hot it is; hearing the noise of a nearby highway at first, but then noticing it less as time passes.

4 consciousness

 show what you know

An Introduction to Consciousness

1. subjective

2. b. automatic processing

3. Answers will vary. The ability to focus awareness on a small segment of information that is available through our sensory systems is called *selective attention.* Although we are exposed to many different stimuli at once, we tend to pay particular attention to abrupt or unexpected changes in the environment. Such events may pose a danger and we need to be aware of them. However, selective attention can cause us to be blind to objects directly in our line of vision. This "looking without seeing" can have serious consequences, as we fail to see important occurrences in our surroundings. Our advice would be to try to remain aware of the possibility of inattentional blindness, in particular when you are in situations that could involve serious injury.

Sleep

1. d. retinal ganglion cells.

2. b. Stage 2

3. cataplexy

4. Drawings will vary; see Infographic 4.2. A normal adult sleeper begins in non-rapid eye movement sleep. Stage 1, the lightest sleep, is associated with theta waves. Stage 2 includes evidence of sleep spindles. Stages 3 and 4 are associated with delta waves and deep sleep. Sleep then becomes less deep as the sleeper works back from Stage 4 to Stage 1. But instead of waking up, the sleeper enters rapid eye movement sleep (REM). Each cycle lasts about 90 minutes, with the average adult sleeper looping through five cycles per night.

Dreams

1. manifest content; latent content

2. c. activation–synthesis model

3. Electroencephalogram (EEG) and PET scan technologies can demonstrate neural activity of the sleeping brain. During REM sleep, the motor areas of the brain are inhibited, but a great deal of neural activity is occurring in the sensory areas of the brain. The *activation–synthesis model* suggests dreams result when the brain responds to this random neural activity as if it has meaning. The creative human mind makes up stories to match the neural activity. The vestibular system is also active during REM sleep, resulting in sensations of floating or flying. The *neurocognitive theory of dreams* proposes that a network of neurons in the brain (including some areas in the limbic system and forebrain) are necessary for dreaming to occur.

4. a. until children are around 13 to 15 years old, their reported dreams are less vivid.

Altered States of Consciousness

1. 1. depressant: b. slows down activity in the CNS; 2. opioid: a. blocks pain; 3. alcohol: d. cirrhosis of the liver; 4. cocaine: c. increases neural activity in the CNS

2. c. LSD

3. psychoactive drugs

4. To determine if behaviors should be considered problematic, one could evaluate the presence of tolerance or withdrawal, both signs of physiological dependence. With *tolerance,* one's system adapts to a drug over time and therefore needs more and more of the substance to re-create the original effect. *Withdrawal* can occur with constant use of some psychoactive drugs, when the body has become dependent and then reacts when the drug is withheld. In some cases, with *psychological dependence,* behaviors may be problematic when there is a strong desire or need to continue the behavior, but with no evidence of tolerance or withdrawal symptoms. If an individual harms himself or others around him as a result of his behaviors, it is a problem. Overuse is maladaptive and causes significant impairment or distress to the user and/or his family. This might include difficulties at work or school, neglect of children and household duties, and physically dangerous behaviors.

TEST PREP are you ready?

1. d. consciousness

2. b. selective attention.

3. a. The cocktail-party effect

4. d. circadian rhythm.

5. c. hypothalamus; reticular formation

6. a. insomnia

7. b. alpha

8. d. REM sleep

9. a. REM rebound.

10. b. wish fulfillment.

11. d. the neurocognitive theory

12. c. Psychoactive drugs

13. a. dopamine

14. b. tobacco

15. c. Physiological; withdrawal

16. Answers will vary. If someone walks into your room while you are asleep, you wake up immediately if there is a noise. You hear a text message come in during the night and immediately wake up to answer the message.

17. Without one's awareness, the brain determines what is important, what requires immediate attention, and what can be processed and stored for later use if necessary. This *automatic processing* happens involuntarily, with little or no conscious effort, and is important because our sensory systems absorb large amounts of information that need to be processed. But it would not be possible to be consciously aware of all of it. Automatic processing also enables *sensory adaption,* which is the tendency to become less sensitive to and less aware of constant stimuli after a period of time.

18. We might not want a doctor with such a schedule to care for us because staying up for 48 hours can result in problems with memory, attention, reaction time, and decision making, all important processes that doctors use in caring for patients. Sleep deprivation impairs the ability to focus attention on a single activity, such as delivering medical care.

19. Answers will vary. See Table 4.1 for information on sleep disturbances and their defining characteristics.

20. Answers will vary. There are many different drugs that people use legally on an everyday basis. Caffeine is a psychoactive drug found in coffee, soda, tea, and some medicines. Over-the-counter pain-killers are legal drugs used to treat minor aches and pains. Nicotine is a highly addictive drug found in cigarettes or cigars. Alcohol is a legal psychoactive drug used on a daily basis by many people, as they drink a glass of wine or beer with an evening meal.

try this
page 150

ANSWER: Answers will vary. Conduct a study using a representative sample of U.S. college students. Because the goal of the study is to determine if the college living environment has some effect on sleep–wake cycles, the independent variable is living environment, and the dependent variable is sleep–wake cycle. The control group lives in a typical college dormitory, where there are no rules about when to go to sleep and wake up. The experimental group also lives in a dormitory, but this dorm has an early curfew and an 11 P.M. "lights-out" policy. At the end of some specified time period (for example, 6 weeks), the researchers observe and compare the sleep cycles of the two groups.

5 learning

■■■■ show what you know

An Introduction to Learning

1. behavior or thinking; experiences

2. c. associations

Classical Conditioning

1. c. the stethoscope

2. biological preparedness

3. a. salmonella

4. When Little Albert heard the loud bang, it was an unconditioned stimulus (US) that elicited fear, the unconditioned response (UR). Through conditioning, the sight of the rat became paired with the loud noise, and thus the rat went from being a *neutral stimulus* to a conditioned stimulus (CS). Little Albert's fear of the rat became a conditioned response (CR).

Operant Conditioning

1. law of effect

2. d. stimulus generalization.

3. a. positive punishment

4. Answers will vary, but can be based on the following definitions. *Reinforcers* are consequences that increase the likelihood of a behavior reoccurring. *Positive reinforcement* is the process by which pleasant reinforcers are presented following a target behavior. *Negative reinforcement* occurs with the removal of an unpleasant stimulus following a target behavior. *Successive approximation* is a method for shaping that uses reinforcers to condition a series of small steps that gradually approach the target behavior.

Observational Learning and Cognition

1. a. observational learning.

2. Answers will vary, but can be based on the following definitions. A *model* is an individual or character whose behavior is being imitated. *Observational learning* occurs as a result of watching the behavior of others.

3. c. latent learning.

TEST PREP are you ready?

1. b. habituation

2. c. ability to press a pendulum to get food.

3. a. involuntary; voluntary

4. b. conditioned response.

5. b. conditioned stimulus.

6. a. adaptive value

7. c. conditioned emotional response.

8. d. The law of effect

9. c. A dog whining in the morning, leading an owner to wake up and take it outside

10. a. positive reinforcement.

11. b. positive reinforcement.

12. a. were more likely to imitate the adult's aggressive behavior.

13. d. at increased risk of abusing their spouses when they become adults.

14. a. latent learning.

15. b. insight.

16. Differences: In *classical conditioning* the learned behaviors are involuntary, whereas in *operant conditioning,* the learned behaviors are voluntary. Classical conditioning links different stimuli, and operant conditioning links behaviors to their consequences. Shared characteristics: They both involve forming associations. They both have an acquisition phase, and in both cases extinction of the learned behavior can occur. (See Table 5.2 and Figure 5.4.)

17. *Biological preparedness* is a biological predisposition or inclination of animals to form associations quickly through classical conditioning. If an animal eats something and then gets sick, it is unlikely to eat that food again, which could influence the survival of the animal.

18. Answers will vary, but can be based on the following definitions. *Primary reinforcers* are reinforcers that satisfy biological needs, such as food, water, or physical contact. *Secondary reinforcers* do not satisfy biological needs, but often gain their power through their association with primary reinforcers. A primary reinforcer used to change behavior might be food. A college tries to increase student participation by providing food at important school functions. Money can be used as a secondary reinforcer. Employees are paid money, which increases attendance at work.

19. Answers will vary, but can be based on the following definitions. *Punishment decreases* the likelihood of the behavior it follows. On the other hand, *negative reinforcement increases* the likelihood of a behavior recurring. See Table 5.3 for examples.

20. Answers can vary. The studies that have found an association between violent films and violent behaviors are *correlational:* They can only highlight a link between the films and the behaviors, not a cause-and-effect relationship. There are other factors that have to be considered. For example, parenting could influence both television viewing and aggression. A parent who is emotionally neglectful may place a child in front of a television all day, such that the child is more likely to imitate some aggressive behaviors seen on the TV. Simultaneously, the child may resent her parent for ignoring her, and the resentment could lead to aggressive behavior. In this example, is it the television programming or the parenting that is leading to aggression?

try this
page 221

ANSWER: Independent variable: exposure to an adult displaying aggressive or nonaggressive behavior. Dependent variable: child's level of aggression.

Ideas for altering the study: Conducting the same study with older or younger children; exposing the children to other children (as opposed to adults) behaving aggressively; pairing children with adults of the same and different ethnicities to determine the impact of ethnic background.

6 memory

●●●● show what you know

An Introduction to Memory

1. Memory

2. b. Encoding

3. a. long-term memory

4. Paying little attention to data entering our sensory system results in *shallow processing.* For example, you remember seeing a word that has been boldfaced in the text while studying. You might even be able to recall the page that it appears on, and where on the page it is located. *Deeper-level processing* relies on characteristics related to patterns and meaning, and generally results in longer-lasting and easier to retrieve memories. As we study, if we contemplate incoming information and relate it to memories we already have, deeper processing occurs and the new memories are more likely to persist.

Flow With It: The Stages of Memory

1. b. iconic memory.

2. b. 30 seconds

3. b. working memory.

4. Explicit; implicit

5. d. flashbulb memory.

6. Answers will vary. **Ex**quisitely **Se**rious **Ep**isodes **Fl**ashed **Im**possible **Pr**oteins

   Explicit memory, **Se**mantic memory, **Ep**isodic memory, **Fl**ash-bulb memory, **Im**plicit memory, **Pr**ocedural memory

Retrieval and Forgetting

1. a. The encoding specificity principle

2. a. context-dependent memory.

3. b. curve of forgetting.

4. Your friend should submit her application on the first day, because the *primacy effect* suggests her application will be better remembered than those in the middle of the week. It is likely that the first applications submitted will be encoded into the long-term memories of the people on the hiring committee.

   Or, if she is not ready to send her application on the first day, you should encourage her to send her application so that it arrives on the seventh day. The *recency effect* suggests her application will be better remembered than those from the middle of the week, because it will linger somewhat in short-term memory (though not necessarily transition to long-term storage).

The Reliability of Memory

1. misinformation effect

2. d. rich false memory.

3. A *reconstructionist model* of memory suggests that memories are a combination of "fact and fiction." Over time, memories can fade, and because they are permeable, they become more vulnerable to the invasion of new information. In other words, memory of an event might include revisions to what really happened, based on

knowledge, opinions, and information you have gained since the event occurred. The Loftus and Palmer experiment indicates that the wording of questions can significantly influence recall, demonstrating that memories can change in response to new information (that is, they are malleable).

The Biology of Memory

1. a. Anterograde amnesia

2. c. hippocampus

3. b. Memory consolidation

4. Answers will vary, but can be based on the following information. *Infantile amnesia* is the inability to remember events from one's earliest years. Most adults cannot remember events before the age of 3.

TEST PREP are you ready?

1. d. retrieval

2. a. hierarchy of processing

3. c. iconic memory.

4. d. chunking

5. b. working memory

6. a. the encoding specificity principle.

7. c. recognition

8. c. Proactive interference; retroactive interference

9. d. a reconstructionist model of memory

10. b. rich false memory

11. a. the misinformation effect.

12. c. repressed

13. b. access memories of events created before the trauma.

14. b. Long-term potentiation

15. d. hippocampus

16. Information enters sensory memory, which includes an overwhelming array of sensory stimuli. If it is not lost in sensory memory, it enters the short-term memory stage. The amount of time information is maintained and processed in short-term memory can be about 30 seconds. And short-term memory has a limited capacity. Because short-term memories cannot last for a couple of hours, it is more likely his grandmother is having difficulty encoding, storing, and/or recalling information that should be held in long-term memory.

17. *Iconic memories* are visual impressions that are photograph-like in their accuracy but dissolve in less than a second. *Echoic memories* are exact copies of the sounds we hear, lasting about 1–10 seconds. Iconic memory uses our visual system, whereas echoic memory uses our auditory system.

18. *Short-term memory* is a stage of memory that temporarily maintains and processes a limited amount of information. *Working memory* is the active processing of information in short-term memory. Working memory refers to what is going on in short-term memory.

19. Answers will vary. Examples may include **P**lease **E**xcuse **M**y **D**ear **A**unt **S**ally to help remember the order of operations (**p**arentheses, **e**xponents, **m**ultiplication, **d**ivision, **a**ddition, and **s**ubtraction); **Roy**

G. Biv to help remember the colors of the rainbow (**r**ed, **o**range, **y**ellow, **g**reen, **b**lue, **i**ndigo, **v**iolet); **E**very **G**ood **B**oy **D**oes **F**ine for remembering the notes of the treble clef in music (**E, G, B, D, F**).

20. The teacher should list the most important rules first and last in the list. The *serial position effect* suggests items at the beginning and at the end of a list are more likely to be recalled. The *primacy effect* suggests we are more likely to remember items at the beginning of a list, because they have a better chance of moving into long-term memory. The *recency effect* suggests we are more likely to remember items at the end of a list because they linger in short–term memory. Students are likely to remember rules at the beginning of the list, as these would be encoded into long-term memory.

try this
page 260
ANSWER: f

7 cognition, language, and intelligence

◯◯◯◯ show what you know

An Introduction to Cognition and Thinking

1. Cognition

2. b. concept

3. c. formal concept

4. Answers will vary. Structures in the brain are associated with cognition. For example, the association areas integrate information from all over the brain. Broca's and Wernicke's areas work with other parts of the brain to generate and understand language.

   The biology of cognition can be found at the neural level as well. For example, changes at the level of neurons make it possible to store and retrieve information. It is also at the neuronal level where we see the plasticity of the brain at work.

Problem Solving

1. c. trial and error.

2. a. functional fixedness

3. Answers will vary. A *means–ends analysis* is a heuristic used to determine how to decrease the distance between a goal and the current state. The goal in this example is to complete an assignment in a timely manner. The means could be to break the problem into two subproblems: (1) choosing a topic (for example, by reading the textbook for interesting ideas, discussing ideas with your instructor); and (2) conducting a literature review (for example, identifying appropriate databases, finding a library to obtain and read articles).

Decision Making

1. Decision making

2. d. availability heuristic.

3. Answers will vary. A *heuristic* uses a "rule of thumb" or a broad application of a strategy to solve a problem, but it can also be used to help predict the probability of an event occurring. However, heuristics can lead us astray in our assessment of situations or predictions of outcomes. In the current example, you can present information to your friend that indicates flying is the safest form of travel. But you can also describe how the *availability heuristic* might lead him to believe that air travel is not safe. The vividness of airplane crashes can influence his recall; even though they are rare events, he is likely to overestimate the probability of them happening again due to the ease with which he recalls similar events. Highly detailed media reports of an airplane crash are likely to linger in his memory.

4. a. the representativeness heuristic.

Language

1. Phonemes

2. b. thinking and perception.

3. Answers will vary. Bilingualism is associated with enhanced creativity, abstract thought, and working memory. And knowing more than one language has been found to be associated with more efficient executive functioning, including abilities related to planning ahead and solving problems. Thus, bilingualism may actually improve performance on cognitive tasks, such as deciphering unknown and untranslatable words.

Intelligence

1. c. analytic, creative, practical.

2. aptitude; achievement

3. The *intelligence quotient (IQ)* is a score from an intelligence assessment, which provides a way to compare levels of intelligence across ages. Originally, an IQ score was derived by dividing mental age by chronological age and multiplying that number by 100. Modern intelligence tests still assign a numerical score, although they no longer use the actual quotient score.

4. a. heritability

5. originality

TEST PREP are you ready?

1. d. Cognition; thinking

2. a. Concepts

3. c. natural concepts

4. b. the plasticity

5. d. an algorithm

6. a. Insight

7. b. availability heuristic.

8. d. confirmation bias.

9. c. the framing effect.

10. b. phonemes

11. a. divergent thinking

12. c. morphemes

13. d. Intelligence

14. b. validity

15. a. environmental factors such as chronic stress.

16. *Formal concepts* are created through rigid and logical rules, or features of a concept. *Natural concepts* are acquired through everyday experience, and they do not have the same types of rigid rules for identification that formal concepts have.

   Examples will vary. An example of a formal concept is the pitch of a sound, which is defined by the frequency of the sound wave. The concept of family is an example of a natural concept. Is a family a group of people who just live together, or do they have to be related genetically? Family is a natural concept that can change based on individual experiences.

17. See Table 7.2. Charles Spearman speculated that intelligence consists of a *general intelligence* (or *g* factor), which refers to a singular underlying aptitude or intellectual ability. Howard Gardner suggested we have *multiple intelligences,* proposing eight different types of intelligences or "frames of mind": linguistic (verbal), logical-mathematical, spatial, bodily-kinesthetic, musical, intrapersonal, interpersonal, and naturalist. Robert Sternberg proposed three kinds of intelligences. His *triarchic theory of intelligence* suggests that humans have varying degrees of analytical, creative, and practical abilities.

18. Using the *availability heuristic,* we predict the probability of something happening in the future based on how easily we can recall a similar type of event from the past. The availability heuristic is essentially a decision-making strategy that relies on memory. They remembered a recent storm in which they did not have to leave their homes, and so they decided it was safe to stay.

19. *Reliability* is the ability of an assessment to provide consistent, reproducible results. *Validity* is the degree to which an assessment measures what it intends to measure. An unreliable IQ test might result in getting different scores for the IQ test taken now and again in a few months; it would not be consistent across time, which is counter to what you would expect (we expect level of intelligence to remain fairly stable over time). An IQ test that is not valid would not be able to predict future performance on tasks related to intellectual ability.

20. Answers will vary. *Divergent thinking* is the ability to devise many solutions to a problem.

   Possible solutions: As a door stop, icebreaker, paper weight, shovel, or axe; for killing a poisonous snake; for putting out cigarettes; for breaking glass; for crushing ingredients for a recipe; for putting out a candle; and so on.

8 human development

◖◗◗◗ show what you know

The Study of Human Development

1. development

2. Developmental psychologists' longstanding discussions have centered on three major themes: stages and continuity; nature and nurture; and stability and change. Each of these themes relates to a

basic question: (1) Does development occur in separate or discrete stages, or is it a steady, continuous process? (2) What are the relative roles of heredity and environment in human development? (3) How stable is one's personality over a lifetime and across situations?

3. c. cross-sectional

Genetics, Conception, and Prenatal Development

1. d. Chromosomes

2. Genotype; phenotype

3. a. embryonic period

4. Genes are behind most human traits, from shoe size to behavior. Each chromosome pair provides us with two versions of a gene: We acquire one gene from our biological mother and the other from our biological father. In some cases, the genes are identical. In other cases, the genes in a pair provide conflicting instructions about the outcome of some characteristic. Often one gene variant has more power than the other. This dominant gene then directs the expression of the inherited characteristic, overpowering the recessive, or subordinate, gene in the pair. A recessive gene cannot overcome the influence of a dominant gene. For example, the gene responsible for cystic fibrosis is recessive. If a child inherits the cystic fibrosis gene from one parent and a normal gene from the other parent, the disease gene will not be expressed (she will not develop cystic fibrosis). However, if she inherits the cystic fibrosis gene from both parents, the gene will be expressed (she will develop the disease).

Infancy and Child Development

1. rooting; sucking

2. a. theories of behaviorism

3. d. assimilation.

4. scaffolding

5. c. developmental tasks or emotional crises.

6. There is a universal sequence of language development. At around 2–3 months, infants typically start to produce vowel-like sounds known as *cooing*. At 4–6 months, in the *babbling stage,* infants combine consonants with vowels. This progresses to the *one-word stage* around 12 months, followed by *two-word telegraphic speech* at approximately 18 months. As children mature, they start to use more complete sentences. Infants pay more attention to adults who use infant-directed speech and are more likely to provide them with chances to learn and interact, thus allowing more exposure to language. Parents and caregivers should talk with their infants and children as much as possible, as babies benefit from a lot of chatter.

Adolescence

1. b. secondary sex characteristics.

2. a. formal operational stage.

3. Preconventional

4. Answers will vary. During the stage of *ego identity versus role confusion,* an adolescent seeks to define himself through his values, beliefs, and goals. If a helicopter parent has been troubleshooting all of her child's problems, the child has never had to learn to take care of things for himself. Thus, he may feel helpless and unsure of

how to handle a problem that arises. The parent might also have ensured the child was successful in every endeavor, but this too could cause the child to be unable to identify his true strengths, again interfering with the creation of an adult identity.

Adulthood

1. a. physical exercise

2. fluid; crystallized

3. d. acceptance

4. integrity; despair

5. Answers will vary, but can be based on the following definitions. Parents who insist on rigid boundaries, show little warmth, and expect high control exhibit *authoritarian parenting.* Parents who practice *authoritative parenting* set high expectations, demonstrate a warm attitude, and are highly responsive to their children's needs. Parents who place very few demands on their children and do not set many limitations exhibit *permissive parenting. Uninvolved parenting* refers to parents who seem to be indifferent, are emotionally uninvolved with their children, and do not exhibit warmth, although they provide for their children's basic needs.

TEST PREP are you ready?

1. b. longitudinal research.

2. d. nature and nurture

3. d. genes

4. a. epigenetics.

5. c. synaptic pruning

6. d. Teratogens

7. b. babbling

8. c. trust versus mistrust

9. b. scaffolding

10. c. Primary sex characteristics

11. a. formal operational stage.

12. b. search for identity

13. d. menopause

14. b. longitudinal method.

15. a. denial

16. Answers may vary. Family: social. Learning: psychological, social. Media: social, psychological. Heredity: biological. Hormones: biological. Traits: biological, psychological, and social. Culture: psychological, social.

17. At conception, when a sperm and egg merge, they form a single cell called a *zygote*. During the germinal period, the zygote grows through cell division and eventually becomes implanted in the uterine wall. Between the 3rd and 8th weeks of development, the mass of cells is now called an *embryo*. The embryo begins to develop everything the baby will need to live. The *fetal period* begins at the 9th week and continues until birth. Overall growth of the body and development of organ systems in the fetus is taking place. By the time a baby reaches this stage, everything that it needs to become

a new person is already in place; it just needs to grow, develop, and become more mature.

18. *Infant-directed speech (IDS)* is observed throughout the world. Infants as young as 5 months old pay more attention to people who use infant-directed speech. It helps a child to learn to interact with "appropriate social partners," or adults who are more likely to provide them with such chances. From an evolutionary perspective, IDS helps a baby know who is going to pay the most attention to her, and who is going to protect and guide her. It also ensures that the infant will be enriched by interactions with others.

19. Answers will vary. Authoritarians give strictness; authoritative give warmth; permissive give permission; uninvolved give little.

Authoritarian parenting; authoritative parenting; permissive parenting; uninvolved parenting.

20. *Wisdom* improves with age through an accumulation of instructive life experiences. As it increases, we make better decisions when encountering daily problems. Practical abilities also seem to increase. Experiences allow people to develop a more balanced understanding of the world surrounding them.

try this
page 348

ANSWER: Independent variable: level of environmental stimulation (enriched environment, standard colony cages, or isolation cages). Dependent variable: changes in brain development.

9 motivation and emotion

◼ **show what you know**

Introduction to Motivation

1. Motivation

2. b. intrinsic motivation.

3. Answers will vary. *Extrinsic motivation* is the drive or urge to continue a behavior because of external reinforcers. *Intrinsic motivation* is the drive or urge to continue a behavior because of internal reinforcers. A teacher wants to encourage intrinsic motivation because the reinforcers originate inside of the students, through personal satisfaction, interest in a subject matter, and so on. There are some potential disadvantages to extrinsic motivation. For example, using rewards, such as money and candy, to reinforce already interesting activities can lead to a decrease in what was intrinsically motivating. Thus, the teacher would want students to respond to intrinsic motivation because the tasks themselves are motivating, and the students love learning for the sake of learning itself.

When activities are not novel, challenging, or do not have aesthetically pleasing characteristics, intrinsic motivation will not be useful. Thus, using rewards might be the best way to motivate these types of activities.

Theories of Motivation

1. c. instinct theory

2. d. drive-reduction

3. hierarchy of needs

4. Answers will vary, but can be based on the following definitions. *Competence* means being able to reach goals through the mastery of everyday functioning (such as fixing meals, getting ready for work and school). *Relatedness* is the need to create relationships with others (for example, to make and keep friends, develop families). *Autonomy* means managing one's behavior to reach personal goals (such as finishing one's college degree).

5. The *drive-reduction theory* of motivation suggests that biological needs and homeostasis motivate us to meet needs. If a need is not fulfilled, this creates a drive, or state of tension, that pushes us or motivates behaviors to meet the need. Once a need is met, the drive is reduced, at least temporarily, because this is an ongoing process, as the need inevitably returns. *Arousal theory* suggests that humans seek an optimal level of arousal, and what is optimal is based on individual differences. Behaviors can arise out of the simple desire for stimulation, or arousal, which is a level of alertness and engagement in the world, and people are motivated to seek out activities that fulfill this need. Drive-reduction theory suggests that the motivation is to reduce tension, but arousal theory suggests that in some cases the motivation is to increase tension.

Back to Basics: Hunger

1. a. stomach was contracting.

2. d. extreme overeating followed by purging.

3. When glucose levels dip, the stomach and liver send signals to the brain that something must be done about this reduced energy source. The brain, in turn, initiates a sense of hunger. Signals from the digestive system are sent to the hypothalamus, which then transmits signals to higher regions of the brain. When the lateral hypothalamus is activated, appetite increases. On the other hand, if the ventromedial hypothalamus becomes activated, appetite declines, causing an animal to stop eating.

Introduction to Emotion

1. d. An emotion

2. arousal level

3. Answers will vary, but can be based on the following definitions. *Emotion* is a psychological state that includes a subjective or inner experience. It also has a physiological component and entails a behavioral expression. Emotions are quite strong, but they don't generally last as long as moods. In addition, emotions are more likely to have an identifiable cause (that is, a reaction to a stimulus that provoked it), which has a greater probability of motivating a person to take some sort of action. *Moods* are longer-term emotional states that are less intense than emotions and do not appear to have distinct beginnings or ends. It is very likely that on your way to a wedding you are in a happy mood, and you have been that way for quite a while. If you were to get mud on your clothing, it is likely that you would experience an emotion such as anger, which might have been triggered by someone jumping in a large mud puddle and splashing you. Your anger would have a subjective experience (your feeling of anger), a physiological component (you felt your face flush with heat), and a behavioral expression (you glared angrily at the person who splashed you).

Theories of Emotion

1. James–Lange

2. b. Display rules

3. d. facial feedback hypothesis

4. Answers may vary. See Infographic 9.3. The *Cannon–Bard* theory of emotion suggests that environmental stimuli are the starting point for emotions, and that body changes and emotions happen together. The *Schachter–Singer* theory of emotion suggests there is a general pattern of physiological arousal caused by the sympathetic nervous system, and this pattern is common to a variety of emotions. Unlike the Cannon–Bard theory, the Schachter–Singer theory suggests our thoughts about our body changes lead to emotions. The experience of emotion is the result of two factors: physiological arousal and a cognitive label for this physiological state (the arousal). Cannon–Bard did not suggest that a cognitive label is necessary for emotions to be experienced.

5. Darwin suggested that interpreting facial expressions is not something we learn but rather is an innate ability that evolved because it promotes survival. Sharing the same facial expressions allows for communication. Research on an isolated group of indigenous peoples in New Guinea suggests that the same facial expressions represent the same basic emotions across cultures. In addition, the fact that children born deaf and blind have the same types of expressions of emotion as children who are not deaf or blind suggests the universal nature of these displays, and thus the emotions that trigger them.

Types of Emotion

1. amygdala

2. *Heritability* is the degree to which heredity is responsible for a particular characteristic in a population. In this case, the heritability for happiness is as high as 80%, indicating that around 80% of the variation in happiness can be attributed to genes, and 20% to environmental influences. In other words, we can explain a high proportion of the variation in happiness, life satisfaction, and well-being by considering genetic make-up, as opposed to environmental factors.

3. c. the sympathetic nervous system.

TEST PREP are you ready?

1. d. an incentive

2. a. extrinsic motivation.

3. c. Instincts

4. b. drive-reduction

5. a. sensation seekers

6. d. ventromedial hypothalamus

7. b. obesity.

8. d. binge-eating disorder.

9. c. behavioral expression.

10. b. could identify the facial expressions common across the world.

11. c. physiological arousal and a cognitive labeling.

12. b. cognitive–appraisal approach

13. a. physiological arousal.

14. a. cortex; amygdala

15. d. be better able to identify what emotion is being felt than are men.

16. Answers will vary, but can be based on the following definitions. *Extrinsic motivation* is the drive or urge to continue a behavior because of external reinforcers. *Intrinsic motivation* is the drive or urge to continue a behavior because of internal reinforcers.

17. Answers will vary, but can be based on the following definition. *Maslow's hierarchy of needs* is considered to be universal and are ordered in terms of the strength of their associated drive, with the most critical needs at the bottom. The pyramid includes increasingly higher needs: physiological needs; safety needs; love and belongingness needs; esteem needs; self-actualization; self-transcendence. Maslow suggested that one's most basic needs must be met before higher-level needs motivate behavior. An example of someone not following the prescribed order of needs might be a martyr who is motivated by self-transcendence needs, ignoring safety needs altogether.

18. Answers will vary. See Table 9.2.

19. Answers will vary, but can be based on the following definition. *Display rules* provide a framework or guidelines for when, how, and where an emotion is expressed. Display rules are a product of cultures.

20. Answers will vary, but can include physical exercise, showing kindness, getting involved in activities that benefit others, recording positive thoughts and feelings of gratefulness in a journal, identifying and pursuing goals, and so on.

⑩ sexuality and gender

◼◼◼◼ show what you know

Sex and Sexuality

1. c. Sexuality

2. b. into a male.

3. Klinefelter's syndrome

4. Answers may vary. Differences of sex development can be traced to irregularities in the 23rd pair of chromosomes, also referred to as the sex chromosomes. The 23rd pair provides the specific instructions for the zygote to develop into a female or male (the biological sex of the individual). However, the creation of the 23rd pair does not always follow the expected pattern of *XX* or *XY*. In some cases, genetic abnormalities will lead to differences of sex development (for example, too many sex chromosomes, or one is missing). In other cases, the sex chromosomes are normal, but the developing fetus does not respond to hormones in a typical way. See Infographic 10.1.

Gender

1. d. Gender

2. c. gender role

3. gender schemas

4. *Transgender* refers to the mismatch between a person's gender assigned at birth and his or her gender identity. Some transgender people try to resolve the resulting discontent through medical interventions. A *transsexual* person seeks or undergoes a social transition to an alternative gender by making changes to his or her body through sex reassignment surgery and/or medical treatment.

The Birds and the Bees

1. a. excitement, plateau, orgasm, and resolution.

2. evolutionary

3. Because monozygotic twins share 100% of their genetic make-up, we expect them to share more genetically influenced characteristics than dizygotic twins, who only share about 50% of their genes. Using twins, researchers explored the impact of genes and environment on same-sex sexual behavior. Monozygotic twins were moderately more likely than dizygotic twins to have the same sexual orientation. They found men and women differ in terms of the heritability of same-sex sexual behavior (34–39% for men, 18–19% for women). These studies highlight that the influence of the environment is substantial with regard to same-sex sexual behavior.

4. Sexual orientation

5. b. Some brain structures, such as the hypothalamus, have differences that correlate to sexual orientation.

The Trouble With Sex: Sexual Dysfunctions

1. c. desire, arousal, orgasm, and pain.

2. Answers may vary, but could include *biological factors* (for example, age-related changes to physiology, hormonal changes, physical exhaustion), *psychological factors* (for example, balancing the stressors related to raising a family and working, raising young children), and *social factors* (for example, finding alone time to be together, feeling slightly jealous of friends who do not have small children at home, media influences).

Sex, Its Consequences, and Culture

1. a. Syphilis; gonorrhea

2. sexual scripts

3. Human immunodeficiency virus (HIV) is spread through the transfer of bodily fluids (blood, semen, vaginal fluid, or breast milk) and eventually causes the breakdown of the immune system. Although HIV often does not show up on blood tests for up to 6 months after infection occurs, it eventually progresses to acquired immune deficiency syndrome (AIDS), which generally results in a severely compromised immune system. A weakened immune system makes the body much more susceptible to opportunistic infections caused by bacteria, viruses, or fungi, and this vulnerability increases as the disease progresses.

TEST PREP are you ready?

1. b. Sex; Gender

2. a. 23rd pair of chromosomes

3. d. hormones

4. a. sex; sexuality

5. d. gender roles.

6. c. observational learning

7. a. excitement

8. c. transsexual

9. b. mothers develop an anti-male antibody while pregnant.

10. d. men and women experience a similar pattern or cycle.

11. b. erectile disorder.

12. a. Human immunodeficiency virus; acquired immune deficiency syndrome

13. c. have a lower risk of acquiring an STI than those who don't know of this activity.

14. a. sexual scripts

15. d. Paraphilia

16. Answers will vary, but might include the following. Explain to potential participants that they will remain anonymous and their responses will be confidential. You might also explain that the study has been approved by an Institutional Review Board, which ensures ethical studies. To help convince them that their participation is worthwhile and that they should be honest, you could remind the participants that because our knowledge of sexual behavior is often limited to self-reporting, their answers will be analyzed as reflective of the population.

17. *Gender* refers to the dimension of masculinity and femininity based on social, cultural, and psychological characteristics. It is often used in reference to the cultural roles that distinguish males and females. We generally learn gender roles by observing other people's behavior and by internalizing cultural beliefs about what is appropriate for men and women.

18. In general, the purpose of sex is to reproduce and ensure the survival of the species. To a certain extent, the more children we have, the higher the probability that our genes will outlast us. Evolutionary psychologists might suggest that extramarital sex could support these goals. Men will want to be with a woman (or women) who can bear many children, so men might be motivated to accomplish this through extramarital activities. For a female, involvement in extramarital sex might be more likely if her mate is not fertile. Or, she might seek out an extramarital experience with someone who has more material resources than her mate.

19. Difficulties related to sexual activity can be divided into four, sometimes overlapping categories: desire, arousal, orgasm, and pain. Problems associated with desire must be persistent to be considered a dysfunction. When an individual has the desire to engage in sexual behavior, but the body does not cooperate, an arousal problem exists. Difficulties with orgasm may include reduced orgasmic intensity and the inability to reach orgasm. Problems associated with pain are more frequently reported by women, and may also be associated with reduced desire and arousal.

20. Answers will vary. See Table 10.6.

11 personality

●●●● show what you know

An Introduction to Personality

1. Personality

2. d. behavioral

3. *Personality* is a unique core set of characteristics that influence the way one thinks, acts, and feels, which is relatively consistent

and enduring throughout the life span. *Temperament* is a distinct pattern of emotional reactions and behaviors that can be observed early in life, and *character* encompasses the qualities of morality or culture-specific ideas about what makes a person good or bad.

Psychoanalytic Theories

1. psychosexual; fixation

2. d. topographical model of the mind

3. b. collective unconscious.

4. Answers will vary, but could include the following. Some of *Freud's followers* branched out on their own due to disagreements about certain issues, such as his focus on the instincts of sex and aggression, his idea that personality is determined by the end of childhood, and his somewhat negative view of human nature. *Adler* proposed that humans are conscious and intentional in their behaviors. *Jung* suggested that we are driven by a psychological energy (as opposed to sexual energy), which encourages positive growth, self-understanding, and balance. *Horney* emphasized the role of relationships between children and their caregivers, not erogenous zones and psychosexual stages.

Humanistic Theories

1. Abraham Maslow; Carl Rogers

2. d. unconditional positive regard.

3. Answers will vary, but could include the following. The *psychoanalytic perspective* assumes that personality development begins early in life and is heavily influenced by processes of which we are unaware (like conflict, aggression, sexual urges) and the way caregivers respond. The *humanistic perspective* suggests that we have capabilities we can and should take advantage of as we strive for personal growth, the choices we make in life influence our personalities, and we are innately good and control our own destinies. The psychoanalytic perspective states that we have little control over our development and personality, while the humanistic perspective states that we can influence our growth.

Learning and Social-Cognitive Theories

1. learning theory

2. b. locus of control

3. Answers will vary, but can be based on the following definition (and see Infographic 11.2). *Reciprocal determinism* refers to the multidirectional interactions among cognitions, behaviors, and the environment guiding our behavior patterns and personality.

Trait Theories and Their Biological Basis

1. a. traits.

2. surface traits

3. Answers will vary (and see Table 11.4). The *Big Five* traits include openness, conscientiousness, extraversion, agreeableness, and neuroticism. Three decades of twin and adoption studies point to a genetic (and therefore biological) basis of these five factors. The proportion of variation in the Big Five traits attributed to genetic make-up is substantial (ranging from .41 to .61), suggesting that the remainder can be attributed to environmental influences.

Personality Assessment

1. b. Projective

2. a. intuition or bias.

3. Answers will vary, but can be based on the following definitions. A *valid measure* is one that can be shown to measure what it intends to measure. If a measure is not valid, a client might be given information that is not meaningful because the findings have not been shown to measure their intended topic. A *reliable measure* provides consistent results across time as well as across raters or people scoring the measure. If findings from a personality test are not reliable, a client may be given information that will not reflect a consistent pattern, or may be questionable due to problems with scoring.

TEST PREP are you ready?

1. d. psychoanalytic

2. a. humanistic

3. d. mental processes that occur at three levels of consciousness.

4. b. superego.

5. c. Defense mechanisms

6. c. Self-actualization

7. a. incongruent

8. c. self-efficacy

9. c. Reciprocal determinism

10. d. factor analysis

11. a. three dimensions of traits.

12. b. the stability of the personality characteristics over time.

13. c. reliability

14. a. projective personality tests

15. c. his intense emphasis on the instincts of sex and aggression

16. Answers will vary, but can be based on the following information. According to behaviorists and learning theory, the *environment* shapes personality through processes of classical conditioning and reinforcers. *Observation* and *modeling* also play a role in personality development.

17. Answers will vary. The *humanistic perspective* suggests that we are innately good and that we have capabilities we can and should take advantage of as we strive for personal growth. The choices we make in life influence our personalities. The *social-cognitive perspective* focuses on relationships, environmental influences, cognitive activity, and individual behavior as they come together to form personality. The humanistic perspective views personality as what we are able to do, whereas the social-cognitive perspective views personality, in part, as how we react to the environment.

18. Both the Oedipus (for boys) and the Electra (for girls) complex represent an important conflict that occurs during the phallic stage. For both boys and girls, the conflict can be resolved through the process of identification. Although basic urges and developmental processes underlie both of these complexes, there are several important differences. The *Oedipus complex* is the attraction a boy feels toward his mother, along with resentment

or envy directed toward his father. When a little boy becomes aware of his attraction to his mother, he realizes his father is a formidable rival and experiences jealousy and anger toward him. With the *Electra complex,* a little girl feels an attraction to her father and becomes jealous and angry toward her mother. Realizing she doesn't have a penis, she may respond with anger, blaming her mother for her missing penis.

19. Answers will vary, but can be based on the following definitions. An *internal locus of control* suggests that the causes of life events reside within an individual, and that one has some control over them. An *external locus of control* suggests that causes for outcomes reside outside of an individual, and there is little control over them.

20. *Objective assessments* of personality are based on a standardized procedure in which the scoring is free of opinions, beliefs, expectations, and values. Critics of objective assessments contend they do not allow flexibility or fully appreciate individual differences in experiences. Findings from *subjective assessments* of personality are based, in part, on personal intuition, opinions, and interpretations. Critics of the subjective assessments suggest there is not enough consistency across findings because of nonstandard scoring procedures.

12 stress and health

OOOO show what you know

An Introduction to Stress

1. Stress
2. d. illness
3. b. Acculturative stress
4. Answers will vary, but can be based on the following definitions. *Daily hassles* are the minor problems or irritants we deal with on a regular basis (for example, heavy traffic, financial worries, messy roommates). *Uplifts* are positive experiences that have the potential to make us happy (for example, a humorous text message, small gift).

Stress and Your Body

1. general adaptation syndrome (GAS)
2. a. alarm stage
3. c. The hypothalamic–pituitary–adrenal system
4. The *general adaptation syndrome (GAS)* suggests that the body passes through three stages. The first is the alarm stage, or initial response to a threatening situation. This stage includes an increase in arousal, during which the body prepares to deal with a threat. Next is the resistance stage, during which the body maintains a high level of arousal as it deals with a threatening situation; at this point, there is a decreased response to new stress. During the resistance stage, some people start to show signs of diseases of adaptation. Finally, there is the exhaustion stage. During this phase, the body's resources become depleted, resulting in vulnerability to illnesses, physical exhaustion, and even death.

Stress and Your Health

1. self-medication hypothesis
2. c. cortisol
3. When the body is expending its resources to deal with an ongoing stressor, the immune system is less powerful, and the work of the lymphocytes is compromised. During times of stress, people tend to sleep poorly, eat erratically, and may increase their drug and alcohol use, along with other poor behavioral choices. These tendencies can lead to health problems.

Factors Related to Stress

1. approach–approach
2. d. Problem-focused coping
3. b. Type B personality.
4. Answers may vary. *Stress management* incorporates tools to lower the impact of possible stressors. Exercise, meditation, progressive muscle relaxation, biofeedback, and social support all have positive physical and psychological effects on the response to stressors. In addition, looking out for the well-being of others by caring and giving of yourself is an effective way to reduce the impact of stress.

TEST PREP are you ready?

1. c. Stressors
2. a. eustress.
3. d. life-changing events
4. b. sympathetic nervous system
5. a. parasympathetic nervous system
6. c. exhaustion stage
7. d. sympathetic nervous systems
8. a. the immune system
9. b. endorphins
10. d. progressive muscle relaxation
11. c. stressors are related to health problems.
12. b. Coping
13. d. avoidance–avoidance conflict.
14. a. Type A personality
15. b. hardiness.
16. Answers will vary, but can be based on the following explanation. There are various ways people respond to acculturative stress. Some try to assimilate into the culture, letting go of old ways and adopting those of the new culture. Another approach is to cling to one's roots and remain separated from the new culture. Such an approach can be very problematic if the new culture does not support this type of separation and requires assimilation. A combination of these two approaches is integration, or holding on to some elements of the old culture, but also adopting aspects of the new one.
17. Answers will vary, but can be based on the following definitions. *Daily hassles* are the minor problems or irritants we deal with on a regular basis. *Life-changing events* are occurrences that require a life adjustment (for example, marriage, change in school status). During times of stress, people tend to sleep poorly, eat erratically,

and may increase their drug and alcohol use, along with other poor behavioral choices. These tendencies can lead to health problems. Exercise, meditation, progressive muscle relaxation, biofeedback, and social support all have positive physical and psychological effects on the response to stressors.

18. Answers will vary, but can be based on the following information. Reactions associated with the fight-or-flight response include increased pulse, breathing rate, and mental alertness. A coordinated effort of the sympathetic nervous system and the endocrine system, the fight-or-flight reaction primes the body to respond to danger, either by escaping or confronting the threat head-on.

19. Answers will vary, but can be based on the following definitions. One major source of stress is conflict, which can be defined as the discomfort felt when making tough choices. Often two choices presented are both attractive to you (*approach–approach conflict*); at times a choice or situation has favorable and unfavorable characteristics (*approach–avoidance conflict*); and at other times the two alternatives are both unattractive (*avoidance–avoidance conflict*).

20. Answers will vary, but can be based on the following definitions. Someone with an *internal locus of control* generally feel as if she is in control of life and its circumstances; she probably believe it is important to take charge and make changes when problems occur. A person with an *external locus of control* generally feel as if chance, luck, or fate is responsible for her circumstances; there is no need to try to change things or make them better. Any decisions related to healthy choices can be influenced by locus of control.

⑬ psychological disorders

◻◻◻◻ show what you know

Psychological Disorders and Abnormal Behavior

1. a. dysfunction

2. maladaptive

3. Answers will vary (see Table 13.1). An *atypical* behavior that is not dysfunctional might be an adolescent who dyes his hair in many different shades of green. A *dysfunctional* behavior that is not distressful might be someone having difficulty getting out of bed in the morning because she stayed up late to meet a deadline for the next day. *Deviant* but not dysfunctional behaviors were demonstrated in 2011 by the Occupy Wall Street protesters who slept in public places and refused to move when asked to do so by the police during their protests.

Classifying and Explaining Psychological Disorders

1. b. the creation of labeling and expectations.

2. c. 50%

3. medical model

4. Answers will vary, but can be based on the following information (see Figure 13.1). The *biopsychosocial perspective* suggests that psychological disorders result from a complex interaction of factors: *biological* (for example, neurotransmitters, hormones), *psychological* (for example, thinking, coping, personality traits), and *sociocultural* (for example, media, cultural beliefs).

Anxiety Disorders

1. c. panic attacks.

2. classical conditioning; operant conditioning

3. *Taijin kyofu* tends to occur in collectivist societies, where great emphasis is placed on the surrounding people, which might lead individuals from these societies to become overly concerned about making someone else feel uncomfortable. *Collectivist* cultures value social harmony over individual needs, so if you cause someone to be uncomfortable, that is worse than personal humiliation you might feel. Western cultures are more *individualistic*. People from these societies are much more afraid of embarrassing themselves than they are of embarrassing someone else. They tend to value their own feelings over those of others.

Obsessive-Compulsive Disorder

1. d. compulsions.

2. genetic

3. Repeatedly locking the car temporarily reduced Melissa's anxiety, making her more likely to perform this behavior in the future; thus, negative reinforcement promoted this maladaptive behavior. The therapist probably expected that if Melissa was not able to repeatedly check the locks and nothing bad happened, eventually Melissa would not need to continue locking her car repeatedly.

Depressive Disorders

1. b. major depressive disorder

2. d. serotonin, norepinephrine, and dopamine

3. Answers will vary, but can be based on the following information. The symptoms of major depressive disorder can include feelings of sadness or hopelessness, reduced pleasure, sleeping excessively or not at all, loss of energy, feelings of worthlessness, or difficulties thinking or concentrating. The hallmarks of major depressive disorder are the "substantial" severity of symptoms and impairment in the ability to perform expected roles. *Biological theories* suggest the disorder results from a genetic predisposition, neurotransmitters, and hormones. *Psychological theories* suggest that feelings of learned helplessness and negative thinking may play a role. Not just one factor is involved in major depressive disorder, but rather the interplay of several.

Bipolar Disorders

1. b. manic episodes.

2. In order to be diagnosed with *bipolar I disorder,* a person must experience at least one manic episode spanning a week or more. These periods of mania are characterized by increased energy and activity and unusual excitement and/or irritability. Depression and hypomania may also occur.

   To be diagnosed with *bipolar II disorder,* a person must experience recurrent episodes of major depression lasting 2 or more weeks and at least one episode of hypomania spanning 4 or more days. *Hypomania* is a mild version of mania; the symptoms are similar, but not disabling.

3. A diagnosis of *bipolar I disorder* requires that a person experience at least one manic episode, substantial distress, and great impairment. *Bipolar II disorder* requires at least one major depressive episode as well as a hypomanic episode, which is associated with some of the same symptoms as a manic episode, but is not as severe and does not impair one's ability to function. People with bipolar disorder cycle between extreme highs and lows of emotion and energy that last for days, weeks, or even months. Individuals with *major depressive disorder,* on the other hand, tend to experience a persistent low mood, loss of energy, and feelings of worthlessness.

Schizophrenia

1. psychosis

2. a. hallucination.

3. Answers will vary, but can be based on the following information. Schizophrenia is a complex psychological disorder that results from a combination of biological, psychological, and social factors. This disorder springs from a complex interaction of genes and environment. The diathesis–stress model takes these factors into account, with *diathesis* referring to an inherited disposition (for example, to schizophrenia) and *stress* referring to the stressors in the environment (internal and external). Genes, neurotransmitters, differences in the brain, and exposure to a virus in utero are all possible influences in the development of schizophrenia. There are some sociocultural and environmental factors that may play a minor role in one's risk for developing the disorder, as well as the severity of symptoms. Evidence exists, for instance, that complications at birth, social stress, and cannabis abuse are related to a slightly increased risk of schizophrenia onset.

Personality Disorders

1. the self and interpersonal relationships.

2. borderline personality disorder

3. Answers will vary, but can be based on the following information (see Table 13.1). *Distress* is the degree to which behavior or emotions cause an individual to feel upset or uncomfortable. *Impairment* or *dysfunction* is the degree to which behavior interferes with daily life and relationships. Personality disorders are a group of psychological disorders that can include impairments in cognition, emotional responses, interpersonal functioning, and impulse control. Thus, they involve issues that can meet two of the criteria of abnormal behavior: dysfunction (they interfere with daily life and relationships) and deviance (behaviors often considered outside the standards of society).

Dissociative Disorders

1. Dissociation

2. a. Dissociative identity disorder

3. Answers will vary, but can be based on the following information. The commonality in this group of disorders is dissociation, or disturbance in the normally unified experience of psychological functions involved in memory, consciousness, perception, or identity. *Dissociative identity disorder* is a psychological disorder that involves the occurrence of two or more distinct personalities within one individual, whereas *dissociative amnesia* is a psychological disorder that includes a lack of ability to remember important personal

information and memories. Both disorders interfere with relationships, memory, work, and other important areas of life.

TEST PREP are you ready?

1. dysfunction, distress, deviance

2. c. labels individuals, which only heightens problems with stigma.

3. a. obsessions; compulsions

4. b. biopsychosocial

5. b. agoraphobia

6. c. social anxiety disorder

7. c. panic attacks

8. b. antisocial personality disorder.

9. d. serotonin

10. a. at least one major depressive episode as well as a hypomanic episode.

11. c. problems associated with sleep.

12. d. irritability

13. b. psychosis.

14. a. borderline personality disorder

15. b. personalities

16. Answers will vary, but can be based on the following information. *Dysfunction* is the degree to which a behavior interferes with one's life or ability to function (for example, washing one's hands to the point of making them raw). *Distress* is feeling regularly upset or uncomfortable because of unwanted behaviors or emotions (for example, continually feeling sad and hopeless). *Deviance* is the degree to which a behavior is considered to be outside of the standards or rules of a society (for example, removing one's clothes in inappropriate settings).

17. Answers will vary. This statement does not follow the suggestion of using "people-first language." Instead, it is defining an individual by her disorder. People are much more than their diagnoses. The diagnosis does not describe who your friend is, but only what is causing her distress or discomfort.

18. Classical conditioning can play a role in the development of a panic disorder by pairing an initially neutral stimulus (for example, a mall) with an unexpected panic attack (the unconditioned stimulus). The panic attack location then becomes a conditioned stimulus. When the location is visited or even considered, a panic attack can ensue (now the conditioned response).

19. Cognitive therapist Aaron Beck suggested that depression is a product of a cognitive triad, which includes a negative view of experiences, self, and the future. Negative thinking may lead to self-defeating behaviors, which, in turn, reinforce the beliefs.

20. Answers will vary, but can be based on the following information. Schizophrenia is a complex psychological disorder that results from biological, psychological, and social factors. Because this disorder springs from a complex interaction of genes and environment, researchers have a hard time predicting who will be affected. The diathesis–stress model takes these factors into account, with *diathesis* referring to an inherited disposition (for example, to schizophrenia) and *stress* referring to the stressors in the environment

(internal and external). Genes, neurotransmitters, differences in the brain, and exposure to a virus in utero are all possible biological factors. Neurotransmitters are also thought to play a role in schizophrenia. The *dopamine hypothesis,* for example, suggests that the synthesis, release, and concentrations of dopamine are all elevated in people who have been diagnosed with schizophrenia and are suffering from psychosis. There are several environmental triggers thought to be involved in one's risk for developing the disorder as well as the severity of symptoms (for example, complications at birth, social stress, and cannabis abuse are related to a slightly increased risk of schizophrenia onset).

⑭ treatment of psychological disorders

▭▭▭▭ show what you know

An Introduction to Treatment

1. moral treatment

2. a. symptoms

3. *Deinstitutionalization* was the mass movement of patients with psychological disorders out of mental institutions, in an attempt to reintegrate them into the community. Deinstitutionalization was partially the result of a movement to reduce the social isolation of people with psychological disorders. This movement marked the beginning of new treatment modalities that allowed individuals to better care for themselves and function in society. However, many former patients ended up living on the streets or behind bars. Many people locked up in American jails and prisons are suffering from mental health problems.

Insight Therapies

1. resistance

2. a. humanistic

3. c. empathy.

4. *Psychoanalysis,* the first formal system of psychotherapy, attempts to increase awareness of unconscious conflicts, making it possible to address and work through them. The therapist's goal is to uncover these unconscious conflicts. *Psychodynamic therapy* is an updated form of psychoanalysis; it incorporates many of Freud's core themes, including the notion that personality characteristics and behavior problems often can be traced to unconscious conflicts. In psychodynamic therapy, therapists see clients once a week for several months rather than many times a week for years. And instead of sitting quietly off to the side, therapists and clients sit face-to-face and engage in a two-way dialogue.

Behavior Therapies

1. a. behavior

2. anxiety hierarchy

3. b. aversion therapy

4. Answers will vary, but may be based on the following information. In *behavior modification,* one uses positive and negative reinforcement, as well as punishment, to help a child increase adaptive behaviors and reduce those that are maladaptive. For behaviors that resist modification, therapists might use successive approximations by reinforcing incremental changes. Some therapists will incorporate observational learning (that is, learning by imitating and watching others) to help clients change their behaviors.

Cognitive Therapies

1. cognitive therapy

2. d. Rational emotive behavior

3. Answers will vary, but may be based on the following information. *Behavior therapies* focus on behavioral change, with the belief that the key to resolving problems is not understanding their origins. Using the learning principles of classical conditioning, operant conditioning, and observational learning, behavior therapy aims to replace maladaptive behaviors with more adaptive behaviors. It incorporates a variety of techniques, including exposure therapy, aversion therapy, systematic desensitization, and behavior modification. Behavior therapy covers a broad range of treatment approaches, and focuses on observable behaviors in the present. *Cognitive therapy* is a type of therapy aimed at addressing the maladaptive thinking that leads to negative behaviors and feelings. The aim of cognitive therapy is to help clients recognize and resist their own cognitive distortions and illogical thoughts in short-term, action-oriented, and homework-intensive therapy sessions. The goal of both approaches is to change the way an individual works or functions in the world. One major difference is that behavioral therapy focuses on behaviors, whereas cognitive therapy focuses on thinking—the way an individual views the world, and views herself in the world.

Group Therapies

1. group therapy

2. a. Self-help groups

3. Answers will vary (see Table 14.3). Group therapy would be inappropriate for an individual who is not comfortable talking or interacting with others and is unwilling to share his or her own thoughts, feelings, or problems. A group may fail if group members do not get along, are continually late for meetings, or drop out. The skills of the group therapist also play a role in the success of treatment (for example, empathy, facilitation skills, observation skills).

Biomedical Therapies

1. d. electroconvulsive therapy

2. b. antidepressants.

3. neurosurgery

4. Answers will vary. *Biomedical therapies* use physical interventions to treat psychological disorders. These therapies can be categorized according to the method by which they influence the brain's functioning: chemical, electrical, or structural. *Psychotherapy* is a treatment approach in which a client works with a mental health professional to reduce psychological symptoms and increase his or her quality of life. These approaches share

common features: The relationship between the client and the treatment provider is of utmost importance, as is a sense of hope that things will get better. And these approaches generally seek to reduce symptoms and increase the quality of life, whether a person is struggling with a psychological disorder or simply wants to be more fulfilled.

Psychotherapy Today

1. b. more; the same

2. licensing issues; privacy issues; limited empirical support

3. Answers will vary, but may be based on the following information. In general, therapy "works," especially if it is long-term. All approaches to psychotherapy perform equally well across all disorders. But individuals whose insurance companies limit their choice of therapists and how long they can receive treatment do not experience the same improvement as those who are less restricted. In addition, people who start therapy but then decide to stop it experience less successful outcomes. The client's cultural experience is important to keep in mind. Within any group, there is vast variation from one individual to the next, but it is still necessary for therapists to understand the cultural context in which they work. This includes being respectful of cultural norms and sensitive to the many forms of prejudice and discrimination that people can experience.

TEST PREP are you ready?

1. c. removed the inmates' chains and listened to their complaints

2. c. insight therapy.

3. a. psychoanalysts

4. b. It is difficult to test through experimentation

5. d. person-centered therapy.

6. a. hierarchies

7. b. Getting fired once does not mean my career is over.

8. a. tends to work quickly.

9. d. Seeing others improve offers hope and inspiration.

10. d. family therapy

11. d. Humanistic

12. d. Psychopharmacology

13. b. limitations on choice of therapist as mandated by a health insurance policy

14. c. seizures

15. a. culture

16. Answers will vary, but may be based on the following information. *Cognitive behavior therapy* is an action-oriented type of therapy that requires clients to confront and resist their illogical thinking. *Insight therapies* aim to increase awareness of self and the environment. These approaches share common features: The relationship between the client and the treatment provider is of utmost importance, as is a sense of hope that things will get better. And these approaches generally seek to reduce symptoms and increase the quality of life, whether a person is struggling with a psychological disorder or simply wants to be more fulfilled.

17. Answers will vary (see Table 14.2).

18. Answers will vary, but may be based on the following information. *Exposure* is a therapeutic technique that brings a person into contact with a feared object or situation while in a safe environment, with the goal of extinguishing or eliminating the fear response. An anxiety hierarchy (a list of activities ordered from least to most anxiety-provoking) can be used to help with exposure. *Aversion therapy* is an approach that uses principles of classical conditioning to link problematic behaviors to unpleasant physical reactions.

19. Answers will vary, but may be based on the following information. One challenge of providing therapy is to meet the needs of clients from vastly different cultures. Within any group, there is great variation from one individual to the next, but it is still necessary for the therapist to keep in mind the client's cultural experience. This includes being respectful of cultural norms and sensitive to the many forms of prejudice and discrimination that people can experience. Every client has a unique story and a singular set of psychological needs. Responding to those needs and determining which approach will be most effective are key to successful therapy.

20. Answers will vary, but may be based on the following information. As more people gain access to the Internet and as more therapists try to specialize and market their services, online therapies have multiplied. *E-therapy* can mean anything from e-mail communications between client and therapist to real-time sessions via a webcam. These digital tools are valuable for serving rural areas and providing treatment to those who would otherwise have no access. Videoconferencing is also useful for consultation and supervision. But online psychotherapy raises many concerns, including licensing and privacy issues, lack of nonverbal cues, and potential problems with developing therapeutic relationships.

⑮ social psychology

☐☐☐☐ show what you know

An Introduction to Social Psychology

1. b. Social psychology; sociology

2. debrief

3. Social psychology studies often involve confederates, who are working for the researchers. Playing the role of participants, confederates say what the researchers tell them to say and do what the researchers tell them to do. They are, unknown to the other participants, just part of the researchers' experimental manipulation. In a double-blind study, neither participants nor researchers administering a treatment know who is getting the real treatment. Participants are told ahead of time that they might receive a placebo, but do not necessarily know about confederates until after the study is complete.

Social Cognition

1. a. Attributions

2. d. disposition of the person.

3. Answers will vary, but may be based on the following information. *Attitudes* are the relatively stable thoughts, feelings, and responses

one has toward people, situations, ideas, and things. Attitudes are composed of three elements: cognitive (beliefs or ideas), affective (mood or emotion), and behavioral (response).

4. Answers will vary, but may be based on the following information. The *just-world hypothesis* is the tendency to believe the world is a fair place and individuals generally get what they deserve. For example, in the story of Cinderella, the doves that help Cinderella prepare for her wedding poke out the eyes of her evil stepsisters afterward.

Social Influence

1. a. social influence; b. persuasion; c. compliance; d. foot-in-the-door technique; e. conformity

2. d. Obedience

3. Answers will vary. Examples may include resisting the urge to eat dessert when others at the table are doing so, saying no to a cigarette when others offer one, and so forth.

Groups and Relationships

1. d. Social loafing

2. deindividuation

3. c. The bystander effect

4. Group members should know that when people hear their own opinions echoed by other members of a group, new information tends to reinforce and strengthen the group members' original positions. And, as the members of the group listen to each other make arguments, their original positions become more entrenched. Thus, group deliberation may not be helpful when the members of the group are initially in agreement.

Aggression

1. c. low levels of the neurotransmitter serotonin

2. d. prosocial behavior.

3. Males tend to show more direct aggression (physical displays of aggression), whereas females are more likely to engage in relational aggression (gossip, exclusion, ignoring), perhaps because females have a higher risk for physical or bodily harm than males do.

4. Answers will vary, but may be based on the following information. *Discrimination* is showing favoritism or hostility to others because of their affiliation with a group. *Prejudice* is holding hostile or negative attitudes toward an individual or group. *Stereotypes* are conclusions or inferences we make about people who are different from us based on their group membership, such as their race, religion, age, or gender. Discrimination, prejudice, and stereotypes involve making assumptions about others we may not know. They often lead to unfair treatment of others.

Attraction and Love

1. b. proximity, similarity, physical attractiveness

2. mere-exposure effect

3. According to this model, decisions to stay together or part ways are based on how happy people are in their relationship, their notion of what life would be like without it, and their investment in the relationship. People may stay in unsatisfying or unhealthy relationships if they feel there are no better alternatives or believe they have too much to lose. This model helps us understand why people remain in destructive relationships. These principles also apply to friendships, positions at work, or loyalty to institutions.

TEST PREP are you ready?

1. d. Social psychology

2. b. social cognition.

3. a. Cognitive dissonance

4. d. the fundamental attribution error.

5. d. the source, the message, and the audience.

6. c. compliance.

7. a. conformity.

8. c. legitimacy of the authority figure.

9. b. Diffusion of responsibility

10. a. deindividuation.

11. d. stereotypes

12. c. aggression

13. b. expectations

14. a. The mere-exposure effect

15. d. passion, intimacy, and commitment.

16. Answers will vary, but may be based on the following information (see Infographic 15.1). The *internal–external dimension* refers to the location of the cause. The *controllable–uncontrollable dimension* refers to whether the outcome can be controlled. The *stable–unstable dimension* refers to whether the cause is long-lasting. As an example, the reason your colleague has recently been absent is that she is caring for her father (external) who has just been diagnosed with an illness and there is no other family member available to help him (uncontrollable). This set of circumstances, however, has only caused problems this week (unstable).

17. Answers will vary. *Obedience* occurs when we change our behavior, or act in a way that we might not normally, because we have been ordered to do so by an authority figure. An imbalance of power exists, and the person with more power generally has an advantage over a person with less power. It is important for us to pay attention to how we react when under the influence of an authority figure as we could inflict harm on others. One person can make a difference when he or she stands up for what is right.

18. Answers will vary. When a person is in trouble, bystanders have the tendency to assume that someone else will help—and therefore they stand by and do nothing, a phenomenon that is partly due to the diffusion of responsibility. This bystander effect is particularly common when there are many other people present. Individuals are more likely to aid a person in distress if no one else is present.

19. Answers will vary, but can be based on the following definition. *Stereotypes* are the conclusions or inferences we make about people who are different from us, based on their group membership (such as race, religion, age, or gender). We tend to see the world in terms of *ingroups* (the group to which we belong) and *outgroups* (people who are outside the group to which we belong), which can impact the stereotypes we hold.

20. Answers will vary, but can be based on the following definitions. *Proximity* means nearness, which may play an important role in the formation of relationships. *Similarity* has to do with how much you have in common with someone else. We tend to prefer those who share our interests, viewpoints, ethnicity, values, and other characteristics.

appendix a

introduction to statistics

try this

page A-4

Answers will vary.

page A-4

Answers will vary, but here are examples from Chapter 3:

quantitative variables: frequency of sound waves, pitch of sound, number of hair cells, weight of butter, color wavelength

qualitative variables: gender, religion, marriage, supertasters, carpentered worlds versus traditional settings

page A-12

ANSWER: The mean for the sample is 38.6, the median is 38, the range is 65, and the standard deviation is 16.5. A stem-and-leaf plot would look like the following, and it appears it might be positively skewed.

1	0 0 1 6 8 8
2	0 0 4 4 5 5 6 9 9
3	0 1 1 2 3 6 8 9
4	0 1 1 2 3 6 8 9
5	0 0 1 2 3 6 7 9
6	1 1 6
7	1 5

TEST PREP are you ready?

1. Statistics
2. a. summarize data.
3. d. statistical significance
4. a. 2; b. 2; c. 1; d. 1
5. c. frequency distribution
6. a. normal curve.
7. negatively skewed; positively skewed
8. b. measures of central tendency.
9. b. 5
10. a. 4
11. a. 4
12. c. outlier; mean
13. a. range
14. a. 2
15. Answers will vary, but it is important to consider what is being measured, how that measurement is actually being depicted, where the data come from, and the purpose of gathering the data.
16. Answers will vary, but can be based on the following information. A *positively skewed distribution* has a longer tail to the right side of the distribution. Sometimes the mean is "pulled" toward the side of distribution that has a possible outlier in the tail of the distribution. Examples of positively skewed distributions are housing prices, prices of cars (used and new), and so on.

Glossary

abnormal behavior Behavior that is atypical, dysfunctional, distressful, and/or deviant. (p. 543)

absolute threshold The weakest stimuli that can be detected 50% of the time. (p. 96)

accommodation A restructuring of old ideas to make a place for new information. (p. 351)

accommodation The process by which the lens changes shape in order to focus on images near and far. (p. 104)

acculturative stress (ə-ˌkəl-chə-ˈrā-tiv) Stress that occurs when people move to new countries or cultures and must adjust to a new way of life. (p. 512)

achievement Acquired knowledge, or representing what has been learned. (p. 315)

acquired immune deficiency syndrome (AIDS) This condition, caused by HIV, generally results in a severely compromised immune system, which makes the body vulnerable to other infections. (p. 456)

acquisition The initial learning phase in both classical and operant conditioning (p. 190)

action potential The spike in electrical energy that passes through the axon of a neuron, the purpose of which is to convey information. (p. 56)

activation–synthesis model This theory proposes that humans respond to random neural activity while in REM sleep as if it has meaning. (p. 165)

active listening The ability to pick up on the content and emotions behind words in order to understand a client's perspective, often by echoing the main point of what the client says. (p. 595)

adaptive value The degree to which a trait or behavior helps an organism survive. (p. 195)

adolescence The transition period between late childhood and early adulthood. (p. 361)

adrenal glands (ə-drē-nəl) Part of the endocrine system involved in responses to stress as well as the regulation of salt balance. (p. 67)

afterimage An image that appears to linger in the visual field after its stimulus, or source, is removed. (p. 108)

aggression Intimidating or threatening behavior or attitudes intended to hurt someone. (p. 652)

agoraphobia (a-gə-rə-ˈfō-bē-ə) Extreme fear of situations involving public transportation, open spaces, or other public settings. (p. 556)

algorithm (al-gə-ri-thəm) An approach to problem solving using a formula or set of rules that, if followed, ensures a solution. (p. 293)

all-or-none A neuron either fires or does not fire; action potentials are always the same strength. (p. 56)

alpha waves Brain waves that indicate a relaxed, drowsy state. (p. 151)

altruism A desire or motivation to help others with no expectation of anything in return. (p. 659)

amphetamines Stimulant drugs; methamphetamine falls in this class of drugs. (p. 172)

amplitude The height of a wave; the distance from midpoint to peak, or from midpoint to the trough of a wave. (p. 102)

amygdala (ə-mig-də-lə) A pair of almond-shaped structures in the limbic system that processes basic emotions, such as fear and aggression, as well as associated memories. (p. 84)

androgens The male hormones secreted by the testes in males and by the adrenal glands in both males and females. (p. 429)

androgyny The tendency to cross gender-role boundaries, exhibiting behaviors associated with both genders. (p. 438)

anorexia nervosa An eating disorder, identified by significant weight loss, an intense fear of being overweight, a false sense of body image, and a refusal to eat the proper amount of calories to achieve a healthy weight. (p. 401)

anterograde amnesia (an-tə-ˌrō-ˌgrād) A type of memory loss; an inability to create new memories following damage or injury to the brain. (p. 268)

antianxiety drugs Psychotropic medications used for treating the symptoms of anxiety. (p. 610)

antidepressant drugs Psychotropic medications used for the treatment of depression. (p. 607)

antipsychotic drugs Psychotropic medication used in the treatment of psychotic symptoms, such as hallucinations and delusions. (p. 609)

antisocial personality disorder A psychological disorder distinguished by unethical behavior, deceitfulness, impulsivity, irritability, aggressiveness, disregard for others, and lack of remorse. (p. 574)

anxiety disorders A group of psychological disorders associated with extreme anxiety and/or debilitating, irrational fears. (p. 553)

approach–approach conflict A type of conflict in which one must choose between two or more options that are attractive. (p. 524)

approach–avoidance conflict A type of conflict that occurs when faced with a choice or situation that has favorable and unfavorable characteristics. (p. 524)

aptitude An individual's potential for learning. (p. 315)

archetypes (är-ki-tīps) Primal images, patterns of thoughts, and storylines stored in the collective unconscious, with themes that may be found in art, literature, music, dreams, and religions. (p. 481)

arousal theory Suggests that humans are motivated to seek an optimal level of arousal, or alertness and engagement in the world. (p. 390)

assimilation Using existing knowledge and ideas to understand new information and experiences. (p. 351)

association areas Regions of the cortex that integrate information from all over the brain, allowing us to learn, think in abstract terms, and carry out other intellectual tasks. (p. 79)

attachment The degree to which an infant feels an emotional connection with primary caregivers. (p. 358)

attitudes The relatively stable thoughts, feelings, and responses one has toward people, situations, ideas, and things. (p. 630)

attributions Beliefs one develops to explain human behaviors and characteristics, as well as situations. (p. 627)

audition The sense of hearing. (p. 110)

authoritarian parenting A rigid parenting style characterized by strict rules and poor communication skills. (p. 374)

authoritative parenting A parenting style characterized by high expectations, strong support, and respect for children. (p. 374)

automatic processing Refers to the processing of information with little or no conscious effort: detection, encoding, and sometimes storage of information without awareness. (p. 144)

autonomic nervous system (ô-tə-'nä-mik) The branch of the peripheral nervous system that controls involuntary processes within the body, such as contractions in the digestive tract, and activity of glands. (p. 64)

availability heuristic A decision-making strategy that predicts the likelihood of something happening based on how easily a similar type of event from the past can be recalled. (p. 300)

aversion therapy Therapeutic approach that uses the principles of classical conditioning to link problematic behaviors to unpleasant physical reactions. (p. 598)

avoidance–avoidance conflict A type of conflict in which one is faced with two or more options that are unattractive. (p. 524)

axon Skinny tubelike structure of a neuron that extends from the cell body, and which sends messages to other neurons. (p. 53)

babbling The combining of consonants with vowels typically displayed at the age of 4 to 6 months. (p. 349)

barbiturate (bär-'bi-chə-rət) Depressant drug that decreases neural activity and reduces anxiety; a type of sedative. (p. 168)

bar graph Displays qualitative data with categories of interest on the *x*-axis and frequency on the *y*-axis (p. A-9)

behaviorism The scientific study of observable behavior. (pp. 11, 203)

behavior modification Therapeutic approach in which behaviors are shaped through reinforcement and punishment. (p. 598)

behavior therapy A type of therapy that focuses on behavioral change. (p. 588)

beta waves Brain waves that indicate an alert, awake state. (p. 151)

bimodal distribution A distribution with two modes, which are the two most frequently occurring values (p. A-11)

binge-eating disorder An eating disorder characterized by episodes of extreme overeating, during which a larger amount of food is consumed than most people would eat in a similar amount of time under similar circumstances. (p. 401)

binocular cues Information gathered from both eyes to help judge depth and distance. (p. 131)

biofeedback A technique that involves providing visual or auditory information about biological processes, allowing a person to control physiological responses (for example, heart rate, blood pressure, skin temperature). (p. 533)

biological preparedness The tendency for animals to be predisposed or inclined to form associations. (p. 196)

biological psychology The branch of psychology that focuses on how the brain and other biological systems influence human behavior. (p. 51)

biomedical therapy Drugs and other physical interventions that target the biological processes underlying psychological disorders; primary goal is to reduce symptoms. (p. 588)

biopsychosocial perspective Explains behavior through the interaction of biological, psychological, and social factors. (p. 14)

bipolar disorder A mood disorder marked by dramatic swings in mood, ranging from manic episodes to depressive episodes. (p. 542)

bisexual Attraction to members of both the same and opposite sex. (p. 442)

blind spot The location where the optic nerve exits the retina. (p. 106)

borderline personality disorder A psychological disorder distinguished by an incomplete sense of self, extreme self-criticism, unstable emotions, and feelings of emptiness. (p. 574)

Broca's area (brō-kəz) An area of the cortex that is critical for speech production. (p. 72)

bulimia nervosa An eating disorder characterized by extreme overeating followed by purging, with serious health risks. (p. 401)

burnout Emotional, mental, and physical fatigue that results in reduced motivation, enthusiasm, and performance. (p. 525)

bystander effect The tendency for people to avoid getting involved in an emergency they witness because they assume someone else will help. (p. 650)

Cannon–Bard theory of emotion Suggests that environmental stimuli are the starting point for emotions, and physiological or behavioral responses occur at the same time emotions are felt. (p. 407)

case study A type of descriptive research that closely examines one individual or small group. (p. 29)

cell body The region of the neuron that includes a nucleus containing DNA, protein-producing mechanisms, and other structures that nourish the cell. (p. 53)

central nervous system (CNS) A major component of the human nervous system that includes the brain and spinal cord. (p. 61)

cerebellum (ser-ə-be-ləm) Structure located behind the brain stem that is responsible for muscle coordination and balance; Latin for "little brain." (p. 86)

cerebral cortex (sə-rē-brəl) The wrinkled outermost layer of the cerebrum, responsible for higher mental functions, such as decision making, planning, and processing visual information. (p. 79)

cerebrum The largest part of the brain, includes virtually all parts of the brain except primitive brain structures; has two distinct hemispheres. (p. 68)

chromosomes Inherited threadlike structures composed of deoxyribonucleic acid (DNA). (p. 339)

chunking Grouping numbers, letters, or other items into meaningful subsets as a strategy for increasing the quantity of information that can be maintained in short-term memory. (p. 244)

circadian rhythm (sər-'kā-dē-ən) The daily patterns roughly following the 24-hour cycle of daylight and darkness; 24-hour cycle of physiological and behavioral functioning. (p. 148)

classical conditioning Learning process in which two stimuli become associated with each other; when an originally neutral stimulus is conditioned to elicit an involuntary response. (p. 190)

cochlea (kō-klē-ə) Fluid-filled, snail-shaped organ of the inner ear lined with the basilar membrane. (p. 113)

cognition The mental activity associated with obtaining, converting, and using knowledge. (p. 284)

cognitive appraisal approach Suggests that the appraisal or interpretation of interactions with surroundings causes an emotional reaction. (p. 408)

cognitive behavioral therapy An action-oriented type of therapy that requires clients to confront and resist their illogical thinking. (p. 603)

cognitive dissonance A state of tension that results when behaviors are inconsistent with attitudes. (p. 633)

cognitive map The mental image of the layout of a physical space. (p. 223)

cognitive therapy A type of therapy aimed at addressing the maladaptive thinking that leads to maladaptive behaviors and feelings. (p. 601)

collective unconscious According to Jung, the universal experiences of humankind passed from generation to generation, including memories. (p. 481)

color constancy Objects are perceived as maintaining their color, even with changing sensory data. (p. 132)

comorbidity (kō-'mȯr-bəd-'i-tē) The occurrence of two or more disorders at the same time. (p. 550)

companionate love Love that consists of profound fondness, camaraderie, understanding, and emotional closeness. (p. 663)

compliance Changes in behavior at the request or direction of another person or group, who in general do not have any true authority. (p. 638)

compulsion A behavior or "mental act" that a person repeats over and over in an effort to reduce anxiety. (p. 558)

concepts Mental representations of categories of objects, situations, and ideas that belong together based on their central features or characteristics. (p. 285)

concrete operational stage Piaget's stage of cognitive development during which children begin to think more logically, but mainly in reference to concrete objects and circumstances. (p. 352)

conditioned emotional response An emotional reaction acquired through classical conditioning; process by which an emotional reaction becomes associated with a previously neutral stimulus. (p. 197)

conditioned response (CR) A learned response to a conditioned stimulus. (p. 190)

conditioned stimulus (CS) A previously neutral stimulus that an organism learns to associate with an unconditioned stimulus. (p. 190)

conditioned taste aversion A form of classical conditioning that occurs when an organism learns to associate a particular food or drink with illness. (p. 195)

cones Specialized light receptors responsible for our sensation of color and our ability to sense details. (p. 106)

confirmation bias The tendency to look for evidence that upholds our beliefs and overlook evidence that runs counter to them. (p. 302)

conformity The urge to modify behaviors, attitudes, beliefs, and opinions to match those of others. (p. 640)

confounding variable A type of extraneous variable that changes in sync with the independent variable, making it difficult to discern which one is causing changes in the dependent variable. (p. 37)

consciousness The state of being aware of oneself, one's thoughts, and/or the environment; includes various levels of conscious awareness. (p. 141)

conservation Refers to the unchanging properties of volume, mass, or amount in relation to appearance. (p. 352)

consummate love (kän(t)-sə-mət) Love that combines intimacy, commitment, and passion. (p. 663)

continuous reinforcement A schedule of reinforcement in which every target behavior is reinforced. (p. 210)

control group The participants in an experiment who are not exposed to the treatment variable; this is the comparison group. (p. 36)

conventional moral reasoning Kohlberg's stage of moral development that determines right and wrong from the expectations of society and important others. (p. 366)

convergence A binocular cue used to judge distance and depth based on the tension of the muscles that direct where the eyes are focusing. (p. 131)

convergent thinking A conventional approach to problem solving that focuses on finding a single best solution to a problem by using previous experience and knowledge. (p. 324)

cooing Production of vowel-like sounds by infants, often repeated in a joyful manner. (p. 349)

coping The cognitive, behavioral, and emotional abilities used to effectively manage something that is perceived as difficult or challenging. (p. 526)

cornea The clear, outer layer of the eye that shields it from damage and focuses incoming light waves. (p. 103)

corpus callosum (kȯr-pəs ka-lō-səm) The thick band of nerve fibers connecting the right and left cerebral hemispheres; principal structure for information shared between the two hemispheres. (p. 69)

correlation An association or relationship between two (or more) variables. (p. 31)

correlational method A type of descriptive research examining the relationships among variables. (p. 31)

correlation coefficient The statistical measure (symbolized as r) that indicates the strength and direction of the relationship between two variables. (p. 31)

creativity In problem solving, the ability to construct valuable results in innovative ways; the ability to generate original ideas. (p. 324)

critical period Specific time frame in which an organism is sensitive to environmental factors, and certain behaviors and abilities are readily shaped or altered by events or experiences. (p. 335)

critical thinking The process of weighing various pieces of evidence, synthesizing them, and evaluating and determining the contributions of each. (p. 18)

cross-sectional method A research design that examines people of different ages at a single point in time. (p. 336)

cross-sequential method A research design that examines groups of people of different ages, monitoring them across time. (p. 336)

crystallized intelligence Knowledge gained through learning and experience. (p. 372)

culture-fair intelligence test Assessments designed to minimize cultural bias. (p. 318)

daily hassles Minor and regularly occurring problems that can act as stressors. (p. 513)

dark adaptation Ability of the eyes to adjust to dark after exposure to brightness. (p. 107)

data-based processing Taking basic sensory information about incoming stimuli and processing it for further interpretation. (p. 96)

debriefing Sharing information with participants after their involvement in a study has ended, including the purpose of the study and deception used in it. (p. 27)

decision making The cognitive process of choosing from alternatives that might be used to reach a goal. (p. 299)

deindividuation The diminished sense of personal responsibility, inhibition, or adherence to social norms that occurs when group members are not treated as individuals. (p. 648)

deinstitutionalization The mass movement of patients with psychological disorders out of mental institutions, and the attempt to reintegrate them into the community. (p. 587)

delirium tremens (DTs) Withdrawal symptoms that can occur when a heavy drinker suddenly stops or significantly cuts down alcohol consumption; can include sweating, restlessness, hallucinations, severe tremors, and seizures. (p. 177)

delta waves Brain waves that indicate a deep sleep. (p. 152)

delusions Strange or false beliefs that a person firmly maintains even when presented with evidence to the contrary. (p. 568)

dendrites (den-drīts) Tiny, branchlike fibers extending from the cell body that receive messages from other neurons and send information in the direction of the cell body (p. 53)

deoxyribonucleic acid (DNA) A molecule that provides the instructions for the development and production of cells. (p. 339)

dependent variable (DV) In an experimental design, the characteristic or response that is measured to determine the effect of the researcher's manipulation. (p. 37)

depressants A class of psychoactive drugs that *depress* or slow down activity in the central nervous system. (p. 167)

depth perception The ability to perceive three-dimensional objects and judge distances. (p. 130)

descriptive research Research methods that describe and explore behaviors, although the findings cannot definitively state cause-and-effect relationships. (p. 28)

developmental psychology A field of psychology that examines physical, cognitive, and socioemotional changes across the life span. (p. 333)

difference threshold The minimum difference between two stimuli that can be noticed 50% of the time. (p. 97)

diffusion of responsibility The sharing of duties and responsibilities among all group members that can lead to feelings of decreased accountability and motivation. (p. 647)

discrimination Showing favoritism or hostility to others because of their affiliation with a group. (p. 654)

display rules Framework or guidelines for when, how, and where an emotion is expressed. (p. 412)

dispositional attribution A belief that some characteristic of an individual is involved in the cause of a situation, event, or activity. (p. 628)

dissociation A disturbance in the normally integrated experience of psychological functions involved in memory, consciousness, perception, or identity. (p. 575)

dissociative amnesia A psychological disorder marked by difficulty remembering important personal information and life events. (p. 575)

dissociative disorders Psychological disorders distinguished by disturbances in normal psychological functioning; may include problems with memory, identity, consciousness, perception, and motor control. (p. 575)

dissociative fugue (fyüg) A condition in which a person with dissociative amnesia wanders about in a confused and unexpected manner. (p. 575)

dissociative identity disorder A psychological disorder that involves the occurrence of two or more distinct personalities within an individual. (p. 576)

distress The stress response to unpleasant and undesirable stressors. (p. 509)

distributed practice Spreading out study sessions over time with breaks in between. (p. 252)

distribution shape How the frequencies of the values are shaped along the *x*-axis (p. A-7)

divergent thinking The ability to devise many solutions to a problem; a component of creativity. (p. 324)

dizygotic twins Fraternal twins who develop from two eggs inseminated by two sperm, and are genetically similar to any sibling pair. (p. 341)

dominant gene One of a pair of genes that has power over the expression of an inherited characteristic. (p. 340)

door-in-the-face technique A compliance technique that involves making a large request first, followed by a smaller request. (p. 639)

dopamine hypothesis A theory suggesting that the synthesis, release, and concentrations of the neurotransmitter dopamine play a role in schizophrenia. (p. 572)

double-blind study Type of study in which neither the researchers who are administering the independent variable nor the participants know what type of treatment is being given. (p. 38)

drive A state of tension that pushes us or motivates behaviors to meet a need. (p. 389)

drive-reduction theory Suggests that maintaining homeostasis motivates us to meet biological needs. (p. 389)

echoic memory (ə-'kō-ik) Exact copies of the sounds we hear; a form of sensory memory. (p. 242)

eclectic approach to therapy Drawing on multiple theories and approaches to therapy to tailor treatment for a client. (p. 589)

effortful processing The encoding and storage of information with conscious effort, or awareness. (p. 250)

ego According to Freud, the structure of the mind that uses the reality principle to manipulate situations, plan for the future, solve problems, and make decisions (p. 472)

egocentrism Being able to imagine the world only from one's own perspective. (p. 352)

ego defense mechanism Distortions of perceptions and memories of the real world, without one's awareness, to reduce the anxiety created by the conflict among the id, ego, and superego. (p. 473)

elaborative rehearsal The method of connecting incoming information to knowledge in long-term memory; a deep level of encoding. (p. 250)

electroconvulsive therapy (ECT) A biomedical treatment of severe depression that induces seizures in the brain through electrical currents. (p. 612)

embryo The unborn human from the beginning of the 3rd week of pregnancy, lasting through the 8th week of prenatal development. (p. 341)

emerging adulthood A phase of life between 18 and 25 years that includes exploration and opportunity. (p. 368)

emotion A psychological state that includes a subjective or inner experience, a physiological component, and a behavioral expression. (p. 404)

emotional intelligence The capacity to perceive, understand, regulate, and use emotions to adapt to social situations. (p. 321)

emotion-focused coping A coping strategy in which a person addresses the emotions that surround a problem, as opposed to trying to solve it. (p. 526)

empathy The ability to feel what a person is experiencing by attempting to observe the world through the client's eyes. (p. 595)

encoding The process through which information enters our memory system. (p. 234)

encoding specificity principle Memories are more easily recalled when the context and cues at the time of encoding are similar to those at the time of retrieval. (p. 257)

endocrine system (en-də-krən) The communication system that uses glands to convey messages by releasing hormones into the bloodstream. (p. 66)

epigenetics A field of study that examines the processes involved in the development of phenotypes. (p. 340)

episodic memory (e-pə-sä-dik) The record of memorable experiences or "episodes" including when and where an experience occurred; a type of explicit memory. (p. 247)

estrogen The female hormone secreted primarily by the ovaries and by the adrenal glands in both males and females. (p. 429)

e-therapy A category of treatment that utilizes the Internet to provide support and therapy. (p. 617)

ethnocentrism To see the world only from the perspective of one's own group. (p. 653)

eustress (yoo'-stres) The stress response to agreeable or positive stressors. (p. 509)

expectancy A person's predictions about the consequences or outcomes of behavior. (p. 486)

experiment A controlled procedure that involves careful examination through the use of scientific observation and/or manipulation of variables (measurable characteristic). (p. 19)

experimental group The members of an experiment who are exposed to the treatment variable or manipulation by the researcher; represents the treatment group. (p. 36)

experimental method A type of research that manipulates a variable of interest (independent variable) to uncover cause-and-effect relationships. (p. 35)

experimenter bias Researchers' expectations that influence the outcome of a study (p. 38)

explicit memory A type of memory you are aware of having and can consciously express in words or declare, including memories of facts and experiences. (p. 247)

exposure A therapeutic technique that brings a person into contact with a feared object or situation while in a safe environment, with the goal of extinguishing or eliminating the fear response. (p. 596)

extinction In classical conditioning, the process by which the CR decreases after repeated exposure to the CS in the absence of the US; in operant conditioning, the disappearance of a learned behavior through the removal of its reinforcer. (p. 193)

extraneous variable A variable in the environment or of the participants that could unintentionally influence the outcome of the study. (p. 37)

extrasensory perception (ESP) The purported ability to obtain information about the world without any sensory stimuli. (p. 133)

extrinsic motivation The drive or urge to continue a behavior because of external reinforcers. (p. 386)

facial feedback hypothesis The facial expression of an emotion can affect the experience of that emotion. (p. 413)

false-consensus effect The tendency to overestimate the degree to which others think or act like we do. (p. 630)

family therapy A type of therapy that focuses on the family as an integrated system, recognizing that the interactions within it can create instability or lead to the breakdown of the family unit. (p. 605)

feature detectors Neurons in the visual cortex specialized in detecting specific features of the visual experience, such as angles, lines, and movements. (p. 107)

fetal alcohol syndrome (FAS) Delays in normal development that result from moderate to heavy alcohol use during pregnancy. (p. 342)

fetus The unborn human from 2 months following conception to birth. (p. 343)

figure–ground A central principle of Gestalt psychology, involving the shifting of focus; as attention is focused on one object, all other features drop or recede into the background. (p. 128)

five-factor model of personality A trait approach to explaining personality, including dimensions of openness to experience, conscientiousness, extraversion, agreeableness, and neuroticism; also known as "the Big Five." (p. 490)

fixation Being stuck in a particular psychosexual stage of development as a result of unsuccessfully dealing with the conflict of that stage. (p. 476)

fixed-interval schedule A schedule in which the reinforcer comes after a preestablished interval of time goes by; the response or behavior is only reinforced after the given interval is over. (p. 213)

fixed-ratio schedule A schedule in which the subject must exhibit a predetermined number of desired behaviors before a reinforcer is given. (p. 212)

flashbulb memory A detailed account of circumstances surrounding an emotionally significant or shocking, sometimes historic, event. (p. 247)

fluid intelligence The ability to think in the abstract and create associations among concepts. (p. 372)

foot-in-the-door technique A compliance technique that involves making a small request first, followed by a larger request. (p. 639)

forebrain Largest part of the brain; includes the cerebral cortex and the limbic system. (p. 85)

formal concepts The mental representation of categories that are created through rigid and logical rules, or features. (p. 286)

formal operational stage Piaget's stage of cognitive development during which children begin to think more logically and systematically. (p. 354)

framing effect Occurs when the wording of questions or the context of a problem influences the outcome of a decision. (p. 302)

free association A psychoanalytic technique in which a patient says anything that comes to mind. (p. 592)

frequency The number of sound waves passing a given point per second; higher frequency is perceived as higher pitch, and lower frequency is perceived as lower pitch. (p. 111)

frequency distribution A simple way to portray data that displays how often various values in a data set are present. (p. A-4)

frequency polygon A type of graphic display that uses lines to represent the frequency of data values. (p. A-4)

frequency theory States that pitch is determined by the vibrating frequency of the sound wave, basilar membrane, and associated neural impulses. (p. 115)

frontal lobes The area of the cortex that organizes information among the other lobes of the brain and is responsible for higher-level cognitive functions and behavior. (p. 79)

frustration–aggression hypothesis Suggests that aggression may occur in response to frustration. (p. 652)

functional fixedness A barrier to problem solving that occurs when familiar objects can only be imagined to function in their normal or usual way. (p. 297)

functionalism An early school of psychology that focused on the function of thought processes, feelings, and behaviors and how they help us adapt to the environment. (p. 10)

fundamental attribution error The tendency to overestimate the degree to which the characteristics of an individual are the cause of an event, and to underestimate the involvement of situational factors. (p. 628)

gate-control theory Suggests that the perception of pain will either increase or decrease through the interaction of biopsychosocial factors; signals are sent to open or close "gates" that control the neurological pathways for pain. (p. 124)

gender The dimension of masculinity and femininity based on social, cultural, and psychological characteristics. (p. 426)

gender identity The feeling or sense of being either male or female, and compatibility, contentment, and conformity with one's gender. (p. 435)

gender roles The collection of actions, beliefs, and characteristics that a culture associates with masculinity and femininity. (p. 434)

gender schemas The psychological or mental guidelines that dictate how to be masculine and feminine. (p. 436)

gene Specified segment of a DNA molecule. (p. 339)

general adaptation syndrome (GAS) A specific pattern of physiological reactions to stressors that includes the alarm stage, resistance stage, and exhaustion stage. (p. 515)

general intelligence (g factor) A singular underlying aptitude or intellectual competence that drives abilities in many areas, including verbal, spatial, and reasoning abilities. (p. 313)

generalized anxiety disorder A psychological disorder characterized by an excessive amount of worry and anxiety about activities relating to family, health, school, and other aspects of daily life. (p. 557)

genotype An individual's complete collection of genes. (p. 339)

genuineness The ability to respond to a client in an authentic way rather than hiding behind a polite or professional mask. (p. 595)

gestalt (gə-'stält) The natural tendency for the brain to organize stimuli into a whole, rather than perceiving the parts and pieces. (p. 128)

gifted Highly intelligent; defined as having an IQ score of 130 or above. (p. 321)

glial cells (glē-əl) Cells that support, nourish, and protect neurons; produce myelin that covers axons. (p. 53)

grammar The rules associated with word and sentence structure. (p. 307)

group polarization The tendency for a group to take a more extreme stance than originally held after deliberations and discussion. (p. 649)

groupthink The tendency for group members to maintain cohesiveness and agreement in their decision making, failing to consider all possible alternatives and related viewpoints. (p. 649)

gustation (gəs-'tā-shən) The sensation of taste. (p. 120)

habituation (hah-bi-chü-ā-shən) A basic form of learning evident when an organism does not respond as strongly or as often to an event following multiple exposures to it. (p. 187)

hallucinations Perceptual-like experiences that an individual believes are real, but that are not evident to others. (p. 568)

hallucinogens (hə-'lü-sə-nə-jənz) A group of psychoactive drugs that can produce hallucinations (auditory, visual, or kinesthetic), distorted sensory experiences, alterations of mood, and distorted thinking. (p. 174)

hardiness A personality characteristic indicating an ability to remain resilient and optimistic despite intensely stressful situations. (p. 528)

health psychology The study of the biological, psychological, and social factors that contribute to illness and health. (p. 518)

heritability The degree to which hereditary factors (genes) are responsible for a particular characteristic observed within a population; the proportion of variation in a characteristic attributed to genetic factors. (p. 323)

heterosexual Attraction to members of the opposite sex. (p. 442)

heuristics (hyü-ris-tiks) Problem-solving approaches that incorporate a rule of thumb or broad application of a strategy. (p. 294)

hierarchy of needs A continuum of needs that are universal and ordered in terms of the strength of their associated drives. (p. 390)

higher order conditioning With repeated pairings of a conditioned stimulus and a neutral stimulus, the second neutral stimulus becomes a conditioned stimulus as well. (p. 193)

hindbrain Includes areas of the brain responsible for fundamental life-sustaining processes. (p. 85)

hippocampus A pair of seahorse-shaped structures located in the limbic system; primarily responsible for creating new memories. (p. 84)

histogram Displays classes of a variable on the x-axis and the frequency of the data is represented as vertical bars that reach the height of the number of values (p. A-4)

homeostasis The tendency for bodies to maintain constant states through internal controls. (p. 389)

homosexual Attraction to members of the same sex. (p. 442)

hormones Chemical messengers released into the bloodstream that influence mood, cognition, appetite, and many other processes and behaviors. (p. 66)

hue The color of an object, determined by the wavelength of light it reflects. (p. 102)

human immunodeficiency virus (HIV) A virus transferred via bodily fluids (blood, semen, vaginal fluid, or breast milk) that causes the breakdown of the immune system, eventually resulting in AIDS. (p. 456)

humanistic psychology An approach suggesting that human nature is by and large positive, and the human direction is toward growth. (p. 12)

humanistic therapy A type of insight therapy that emphasizes the positive nature of humankind. (p. 594)

hypnosis (hip-'nō-səs) An altered state of consciousness allowing for changes in perceptions and behaviors, which result from suggestions made by a hypnotist. (p. 179)

hypothalamus (hī-pō-tha-lə-məs) A small structure located below the thalamus that maintains a constant internal environment within a healthy range; helps regulate sleep–wake cycles, sexual behavior, and appetite. (p. 85)

hypothesis A statement that can be used to test a prediction. (p. 20)

hypothesis testing Mathematical procedures used to determine the likelihood that a researcher's predictions are supported by the data collected (p. A-1)

iconic memory Visual impressions that are photograph-like in their accuracy but dissolve in less than a second; a form of sensory memory. (p. 240)

id According to Freud, the most primitive structure of the mind, the activities of which occur at the unconscious level and are guided by the pleasure principle (p. 472)

ideal self The self-concept a person strives for and fervently wishes to achieve. (p. 483)

identity A sense of self based on values, beliefs, and goals. (p. 363)

illusions A perception incongruent with sensory data. (p. 127)

implicit memory A memory of something you know or know how to do, but that might be automatic or unconscious; this type of memory is often difficult to bring to awareness and express. (p. 248)

incentive An association established between a behavior and its consequences, which then motivates that behavior. (p. 386)

independent variable (IV) In an experimental design, the variable manipulated by the researcher to determine its effect on the dependent variable. (p. 37)

informed consent Acknowledgment of study participants that they understand what their participation will entail. (p. 26)

in-group The group to which we belong. (p. 653)

insanity A legal determination of the degree to which a person is responsible for criminal behaviors. (p. 545)

insight An understanding or solution that occurs in a sudden stroke of clarity (the feeling of "aha!"). (p. 294)

insight therapies A type of psychotherapy aimed at increasing awareness of self and the environment. (p. 588)

insomnia Sleep disorder characterized by an inability to fall asleep or stay asleep, impacting both the quality and the quantity of sleep. (p. 158)

instinctive drift The tendency for animals to revert to instinctual behaviors after a behavior pattern has been learned. (p. 205)

Instincts Complex behaviors that are fixed, unlearned, and consistent within a species. (p. 388)

Institutional Review Board (IRB) A committee that reviews research proposals to protect the rights and welfare of all participants. (p. 27)

intelligence Innate ability to solve problems, adapt to the environment, and learn from experiences. (p. 312)

intelligence quotient (IQ) A score from an intelligence assessment; originally based on mental age divided by chronological age, multiplied by 100. (p. 316)

interneurons A type of neuron that resides exclusively in the brain and spinal cord; acts as a bridge connecting sensory and motor neurons. (p. 62)

interpersonal attraction The factors that lead us to form friendships or romantic relationships with others. (p. 660)

interpretation A psychoanalytic technique used to discover unconscious conflicts driving behavior. (p. 592)

intersexual Ambiguous or inconsistent biological indicators of male or female in the sexual structures and organs. (p. 431)

intrinsic motivation The drive or urge to continue a behavior because of internal reinforcers. (p. 386)

introspection The examination of one's own conscious activities. (p. 9)

iris The muscle responsible for changing the size of the pupil. (p. 104)

James–Lange theory of emotion Suggests that a stimulus initiates the experience of a physiological and/or behavioral reaction, and this reaction leads to the feeling of an emotion. (p. 406)

just-world hypothesis The tendency to believe the world is a fair place and individuals generally get what they deserve. (p. 629)

kinesthesia (ki-nəs-ˈthē-zhē-ə) Sensory system that conveys information about body position and movement. (p. 126)

knowledge-based processing Drawing on past experiences and knowledge to understand and interpret sensory information. (p. 96)

language A system for using symbols to think and communicate. (p. 305)

latent content The hidden meaning of a dream, often concealed by the manifest content of the dream. (p. 164)

latent learning Learning that occurs without awareness and regardless of reinforcement, and is not evident until needed. (p. 224)

lateralization The idea that each cerebral hemisphere processes certain types of information and excels in certain activities. (p. 71)

law of effect Thorndike's principle stating that behaviors are more likely to be repeated when followed by pleasurable outcomes, and those followed by something unpleasant are less likely to be repeated. (p. 202)

learned helplessness A tendency for people to believe they have no control over the consequences of their behaviors, resulting in passive behavior. (p. 564)

learning A relatively enduring change in behavior or thinking that results from experiences (p. 187)

light adaptation Ability of the eyes to adjust to light after being in the dark. (p. 107)

limbic system A horseshoe-shaped collection of structures that regulates emotions and basic drives like hunger, and aids in the creation of memories. (p. 84)

longitudinal method A research design that examines the same sample of people over a period of time to determine age-related changes. (p. 336)

long-term memory A stage of memory with essentially unlimited capacity that stores enduring information about facts and experiences. (p. 236)

long-term potentiation The increased efficiency of neural communication over time, resulting in learning and the formation of memories. (p. 273)

lymphocyte Type of white blood cell produced in the bone marrow whose job is to battle enemies such as viruses and bacteria. (p. 518)

lysergic acid diethylamide (LSD) (lə-ˈsər-jik; dī-ˌe-thə-ˈla-ˌmīd) A synthetically produced, odorless, tasteless, and colorless hallucinogen that is very potent; produces extreme changes in sensations and perceptions. (p. 174)

maintenance rehearsal Technique of repeating information to be remembered, increasing the length of time it can be held in short-term memory. (p. 250)

major depressive disorder A psychological disorder that includes at least one major depressive episode, with symptoms such as depressed mood, problems with sleep, and loss of energy. (p. 560)

maladaptive behaviors Behaviors or actions that run counter to what is in one's own best interest. (p. 543)

manic episodes States of continuous elation that are out of proportion to the setting, and can include irritability, very high and sustained levels of energy, and an "expansive" mood. (p. 566)

manifest content The apparent meaning of a dream; the remembered story line of a dream. (p. 164)

massed practice Studying for long periods of time without breaks. (p. 252)

maturation Physical growth beginning with conception and ending when the body stops growing. (p. 333)

mean The arithmetic average of a data set; a measure of central tendency (p. A-9)

means–ends analysis Heuristic used to determine how to decrease the distance between a goal (the means) and the current status, leading to the solution of a problem (the end). (p. 294)

measures of central tendency Numbers that represent the middle of a data set (p. A-9)

measures of position Numbers that represent where particular data values fall in relation to other values in the data set (p. A-11)

measures of variation Numbers that describe the variation or dispersion in a data set (p. A-11)

median A number that represents the position in the data set for which 50% of the values are above it, and 50% are below it; a measure of central tendency (p. A-9)

medical model An approach suggesting that psychological disorders are illnesses that have underlying biological causes. (p. 551)

medulla (mə-'dùl-ə) A structure that oversees vital functions, including breathing, digestion, and heart rate. (p. 85)

memory Information collected and stored in the brain that is generally retrievable for later use. (p. 234)

memory trace The location where memories are etched in the brain via physiological changes. (p. 269)

menarche The point at which menstruation begins. (p. 362)

menopause The time when a woman no longer ovulates, her menstrual cycle stops, and she is no longer capable of reproduction. (p. 371)

mental age (MA) A score representing the mental abilities of an individual in relation to others of a similar chronological age. (p. 315)

mere-exposure effect The more we are exposed to someone or something, the more positive a reaction we have toward it. (p. 661)

meta-analysis A type of statistical analysis that combines findings from many studies on a single topic; statistics used to merge the outcomes of many studies (p. A-4)

methylenedioxymethamphetamine (MDMA) (meth'ĭ-lēn-dī-ok'sē-meth 'am-fet'ă-mēn) A synthetic drug chemically similar to the stimulant methamphetamine and the hallucinogen mescaline; produces a combination of stimulant and hallucinogenic effects. (p. 175)

midbrain The part of the brain stem involved in levels of arousal; responsible for generating movement patterns in response to sensory input. (p. 85)

misinformation effect The tendency for new and misleading information obtained after an incident to distort one's memory of it. (p. 264)

mnemonic (nih-ˌmän-ik) Technique to improve memory. (p. 248)

mode The value of the data set that is most frequent; a measure of central tendency (p. A-11)

model The individual or character whose behavior is being imitated. (p. 219)

monocular cues Depth and distance cues that require the use of only one eye. (p. 131)

monozygotic twins Identical twins who develop from one egg inseminated at conception, which then splits into two separate cells. (p. 341)

mood-stabilizing drugs Psychotropic medications that minimize the lows of depression and the highs of mania. (p. 608)

morphemes (mòr-fēmz) The fundamental units that bring meaning to language. (p. 307)

motivation A stimulus that can direct behavior, thinking, and feeling. (p. 386)

motor cortex A band of tissue toward the rear of the frontal lobes that works with other brain regions to plan and execute voluntary movements. (p. 80)

motor neurons Neurons specialized for transmitting information from the central nervous system to other parts of the body, such as muscles and glands. (p. 62)

myelin sheath (mī-ə-lən, shēth) Fatty substance that insulates the axon and speeds the transmission of neural messages. (p. 53)

narcolepsy A neurological disorder characterized by excessive daytime sleepiness, which includes lapses into sleep and napping. (p. 155)

natural concepts The mental representations of categories resulting from experiences in daily life. (p. 286)

natural selection The process through which inherited traits in a given population either increase in frequency because they are adaptive or decrease in frequency because they are maladaptive. (p. 12)

naturalistic observation A type of descriptive research that studies participants in their natural environment through systematic observation. (p. 28)

need for achievement (n-Ach) A drive to reach attainable and challenging goals especially in the face of competition (p. 394)

need for power (n-Pow) A drive to control and influence others (p. 394)

needs Physiological or psychological requirements that must be maintained at some baseline or constant state. (p. 389)

negative punishment The removal of something desirable following an unwanted behavior, with the intention of decreasing that behavior. (p. 215)

negative reinforcement The removal of an unpleasant stimulus following a target behavior, which increases the likelihood of occurring again. (p. 208)

negative symptoms Behaviors or characteristics that are limited or absent; includes social withdrawal, diminished speech, limited or no emotions, and loss of energy and follow-up. (p. 569)

negatively skewed A nonsymmetric distribution with a longer tail to the left side of the distribution; left-skewed distribution (p. A-7)

nerves Bundles of neurons that carry information to and from the central nervous system; provide communication between the central nervous system and the muscles, glands, and sensory receptors. (p. 63)

neurogenesis The generation of new neurons in the brain. (p. 74)

neurons The building blocks of the nervous system that transmit electrical and chemical signals in the body. (p. 52)

neuroplasticity The brain's ability to heal, grow new connections, and reorganize in order to adapt to the environment. (p. 73)

neuroscience The study of the brain and nervous system. (p. 51)

neurosurgery A biomedical therapy that involves the destruction of some portion of the brain or connections between different areas of the brain. (p. 613)

neurotransmitters Chemical messengers that neurons use to communicate at the synapse. (p. 57)

neutral stimulus A stimulus that does not cause a relevant automatic or reflexive response. (p. 190)

nightmares Frightening dreams that occur during REM sleep. (p. 158)

nondirective A technique used in person-centered therapy wherein the therapist follows the lead of the client during treatment sessions. (p. 594)

non-rapid eye movement (non-REM) The nondreaming sleep that occurs during sleep Stages 1 to 4. (p. 151)

normal curve Depicts the frequency of values of a variable along a continuum; bell-shaped symmetrical distribution, with the highest point reflecting the average score. (p. 317)

norms Standards of the social environment. (p. 640)

obedience Changing behavior because we have been ordered to do so by an authority figure. (p. 643)

object permanence A milestone of the sensorimotor stage of cognitive development; an infant's realization that objects and people still exist even when out of sight or touch. (p. 351)

observational learning Learning that occurs as a result of watching the behavior of others. (p. 219)

observer bias Errors introduced into the recording of observations due to the researcher's value system, expectations or attitudes. (p. 29)

obsession A thought, an urge, or an image that happens repeatedly, is intrusive and unwelcome, and often causes anxiety and distress. (p. 558)

obsessive-compulsive disorder (OCD) A psychological disorder characterized by obsessions and/or compulsions that are time-consuming and cause a great deal of distress. (p. 558)

obstructive sleep apnea hypopnea (hī-pop-ˈnē-ə) A serious disturbance of non-REM sleep characterized by complete absence of air flow (apnea) or reduced air flow (hypopnea). (p. 157)

occipital lobes (äk-si-pə-təl) The area of the cortex in the back of the head that processes visual information. (p. 79)

Oedipus complex (e-də-pəs) According to Freud, the attraction a child feels toward the opposite-sex parent, along with the resentment or envy directed toward the same-sex parent. (p. 476)

olfaction (ōl-ˈfak-shən) The sense of smell. (p. 117)

operant conditioning Learning that occurs when voluntary actions become associated with consequences. (p. 201)

operational definition The precise manner in which a variable of interest is defined and measured. (p. 20)

opiates A class of psychoactive drugs that cause a sense of euphoria; a drug that imitates the endorphins naturally produced in the brain. (p. 168)

opioids A class of psychoactive drugs that minimizes perceptions of pain. (p. 168)

opponent-process theory Perception of color derives from a special group of neurons that respond to opponent colors (red–green, blue–yellow). (p. 108)

optic nerve The bundle of axons from ganglion cells leading to the visual cortex. (p. 106)

orgasm A powerful combination of extremely gratifying sensations and a series of rhythmic muscular contractions. (p. 441)

out-group People outside the group to which we belong. (p. 653)

overgeneralization A cognitive distortion that assumes self-contained events will have major repercussions. (p. 602)

panic attack Sudden, extreme fear or discomfort that escalates quickly, often with no obvious trigger, and includes symptoms such as increased heart rate, sweating, shortness of breath, chest pain, nausea, lightheadedness, and fear of dying. (p. 554)

panic disorder A psychological disorder that includes recurrent, unexpected panic attacks and fear that can cause significant changes in behavior. (p. 554)

parameters Numbers that describe characteristics of a population (p. A-2)

paraphilia Uncommon sexual acts. (p. 458)

parapsychology The study of extrasensory perception. (p. 133)

parasympathetic nervous system The division of the autonomic nervous system that orchestrates the "rest-and-digest" response to bring the body back to a noncrisis mode. (p. 64)

parietal lobes (pə-rī-ə-təl) The area of the cortex that receives and processes sensory information such as touch, pressure, temperature, and spatial orientation. (p. 79)

partial reinforcement A schedule of reinforcement in which target behaviors are reinforced intermittently, not continuously. (p. 210)

partial reinforcement effect The tendency for behaviors acquired through intermittent reinforcement to be more resistant to extinction than those acquired through continuous reinforcement. (p. 211)

passionate love Love that is based on zealous emotion, leading to intense longing and sexual attraction. (p. 663)

perception The organization and interpretation of sensory stimuli by the brain. (p. 94)

perceptual constancy The tendency to perceive objects in our environment as stable in terms of shape, size, and color, regardless of changes in the sensory data received. (p. 132)

perceptual set The tendency to perceive stimuli in a specific manner based on past experiences and expectations. (p. 132)

peripheral nervous system (PNS) The part of the nervous system that connects the central nervous system to the rest of the body. (p. 61)

permissive parenting A parenting style characterized by low demands of children and few limitations. (p. 374)

personality The unique, core set of characteristics that influence the way one thinks, acts, and feels, and that are relatively consistent and enduring throughout the life span. (p. 467)

personality disorders A group of psychological disorders that can include impairments in cognition, emotional responses, interpersonal functioning, and impulse control. (p. 573)

person-centered therapy A form of humanistic therapy developed by Rogers; aimed at helping clients achieve their full potential. (p. 594)

persuasion Intentionally trying to make people change their attitudes and beliefs, which may lead to changes in their behaviors. (p. 637)

phenotype The observable expression or characteristics of one's genetic inheritance. (p. 340)

phonemes (fō-nēmz) The basic building blocks of spoken language. (p. 306)

photoreceptors Cells that absorb light energy and turn it into chemical and electrical signals for the brain to process. (p. 104)

phrenology An early approach to explaining the functions of the brain by trying to link the physical structure of the skull with a variety of characteristics. (p. 75)

physiological dependence With constant use of some psychoactive drugs, the body no longer functions normally without the drug. (p. 177)

pie chart Displays qualitative data with categories of interest represented by slices of the pie (p. A-9)

pitch The degree to which a sound is high or low determined by the frequency of its sound wave. (p. 111)

pituitary gland The pea-sized gland located in the center of the brain just under the hypothalamus; secretes hormones that dictate the release of hormones by other glands; known as the master gland. (p. 66)

placebo (plə-ˈsē-ˌbō) An inert substance given to members of the control group; the fake treatment that has no benefit, but is administered as if it does. (p. 36)

place theory States that pitch corresponds to the location of the vibrating hair cells along the cochlea. (p. 115)

pleasure principle Collection of rules that guide the id, resulting in behavior to achieve instant gratification without thought to the consequences. (p. 472)

polygraph Machine used to determine if someone is lying by measuring the physiological arousal associated with deceit. (p. 410)

pons A hindbrain structure that helps regulate sleep–wake cycles and co-ordinate movement between the right and left sides of the body. (p. 85)

population All members of an identified group about which a researcher is interested. (p. 26)

positive psychology An approach that focuses on the positive aspects of human beings, seeking to understand their strengths and uncover the roots of happiness, creativity, humor, and so on. (p. 43)

positive punishment The addition of something unpleasant following an unwanted behavior, with the intention of decreasing that behavior (p. 215)

positive reinforcement The process by which pleasant reinforcers are added or presented following the targeted behavior, increasing the likelihood of it occurring again. (p. 207)

positive symptoms Excesses or distortions of normal behavior, which include delusions, hallucinations, and disorganized speech. (p. 569)

positively skewed A nonsymmetric distribution with a longer tail to the right side of the distribution; right-skewed distribution (p. A-7)

postconventional moral reasoning Kohlberg's stage of moral development in which right and wrong are determined by the individual's beliefs about morality, which sometimes do not coincide with society's rules and regulations. (p. 366)

posttraumatic stress disorder (PTSD) A psychological disorder characterized by exposure to or threatened by an event involving death, serious injury, or sexual violence; can include disturbing memories, nightmares, flashbacks, and other distressing symptoms. (p. 510)

pragmatics The social rules that help to organize language. (p. 309)

preconventional moral reasoning Kohlberg's stage of moral development in which a person, usually a child, focuses on the consequences of behaviors, good or bad, and is concerned with avoiding punishment. (p. 366)

prejudice Holding hostile or negative attitudes toward an individual or group. (p. 654)

preoperational stage Piaget's stage of cognitive development during which children can start to use language to explore and understand their worlds. (p. 352)

primacy effect The tendency to remember items at the beginning of a list. (p. 256)

primary appraisal One's initial assessment of a situation to determine its personal impact and whether it is irrelevant, positive, challenging, or harmful. (p. 526)

primary reinforcer A reinforcer that satisfies a biological need, such as food, water, physical contact; innate reinforcer. (p. 208)

primary sex characteristics Organs associated with reproduction, including the ovaries, uterus, vagina, penis, scrotum, and testes. (p. 361)

priming The stimulation of memories as a result of retrieval cues in the environment. (p. 255)

proactive interference The tendency for information learned in the past to interfere with the retrieval of new material. (p. 261)

problem-focused coping A coping strategy in which a person deals directly with a problem by attempting to solve and address it head-on. (p. 526)

problem solving The variety of approaches that can be used to achieve a goal. (p. 292)

procedural memory The unconscious memory of how to carry out a variety of skills and activities; a type of implicit memory. (p. 248)

projective personality tests Assessments that present stimuli without a specified meaning to test takers, whose responses can then be interpreted to uncover underlying personality characteristics. (p. 495)

proprioceptors (proh-pree-uh-sep-tərs) Specialized nerve endings primarily located in the muscles and joints that provide information about body location and orientation. (p. 126)

prosocial behaviors Actions that are kind, generous, and benefit others. (p. 222)

prototype The ideal or most representative example of a natural concept; helps us categorize or identify specific members of a concept. (p. 287)

proximity Nearness; plays an important role in the formation of relationships. (p. 660)

pseudopsychology An approach to explaining and predicting behavior and events that appears to be psychology, but has no empirical or objective evidence to support it. (p. 17)

psychoactive drugs Substances that can cause changes in psychological activities such as sensation, perception, attention, judgment, memory, self-control, emotion, thinking, and behavior; substances that cause changes in conscious experiences. (p. 167)

psychoanalysis Freud's views regarding personality as well as his system of psychotherapy and tools for the exploration of the unconscious. (p. 470)

psychodynamic therapy A type of insight therapy that incorporates core psychoanalytic themes, including the importance of unconscious conflicts and experiences from the past. (p. 593)

psychological dependence With constant use of some psychoactive drugs, a strong desire or need to continue using the substance occurs without the evidence of tolerance or withdrawal symptoms (p. 177)

psychological disorder A set of behavioral, emotional, and/or cognitive symptoms that are significantly distressing or disabling in terms of social functioning, work endeavors, and other aspects of life. (p. 542)

psychologists Scientists who study behavior and mental processes. (p. 4)

psychology The scientific study of behavior and mental processes. (p. 4)

psychoneuroimmunology (sī-kō-ˌn(y)ùr-ō-ˌim-yə-ˈnä-lə-jē) The field that studies the relationship among psychological factors, the nervous system, and immune system functioning. (p. 523)

psychosexual stages According to Freud, the stages of development, from birth to adulthood, each of which has an erogenous zone as well as a conflict that must be dealt with. (p. 475)

psychosis Loss of contact with reality that is severe and chronic. (p. 568)

psychotherapy "Talk therapy"; a treatment approach in which a client works with a mental health professional to reduce psychological symptoms and improve quality of life. (p. 588)

puberty The period of development during which the body changes and becomes sexually mature and capable of reproduction. (p. 361)

punishment The application of a consequence that decreases the likelihood of a behavior recurring. (p. 213)

random assignment The process of appointing participants in a research study to the experimental or control groups, ensuring that every person has an equal chance of being assigned to either. (p. 36)

random sample A subset of the population chosen through a procedure that ensures all members of the population have an equally likely chance of being selected to participate in the study. (p. 26)

range A number that represents the length of the data set and is a rough depiction of dispersion; a measure of variation (p. A-11)

rapid eye movement (REM) The stage of sleep associated with dreaming; sleep characterized by bursts of eye movements, with brain activity similar to that of a waking state, but with a lack of muscle tone. (p. 152)

rational emotive behavior therapy (REBT) A type of cognitive therapy, developed by Ellis, that identifies illogical thoughts and converts them into rational ones. (p. 693)

reality principle Collection of rules that guide the ego as it negotiates between the id and the environment. (p. 472)

recall The process of retrieving information held in long-term memory without the help of explicit retrieval cues. (p. 255)

recency effect The tendency to remember items at the end of a list. (p. 256)

receptor sites The location where neurotransmitters attach on the receiving side of the synaptic gap. (p. 57)

recessive gene One of a pair of genes that is dominated by the other gene in the pair. (p. 340)

reciprocal determinism According to Bandura, multidirectional interactions among cognitions, behaviors, and the environment. (p. 488)

recognition The process of matching incoming data to information stored in long-term memory. (p. 256)

reflex arc An automatic response to a sensory stimulus, such as the "knee jerk" reaction; a simple pathway of communication from sensory neurons through interneurons in the spinal cord back out through motor neurons. (p. 63)

refractory period An interval of time during which a man cannot attain another orgasm. (p. 441)

reinforcement Process by which an organism learns to associate a voluntary behavior with its consequences. (p. 202)

reinforcers Consequences, such as events or objects, that increase the likelihood of a behavior reoccurring. (p. 202)

relearning Material learned previously is acquired more quickly in subsequent exposures. (p. 258)

reliability The ability of an assessment to provide consistent, reproducible results. (p. 317)

REM rebound An increased amount of sleep in the REM stage with the first sleep session following sleep deprivation. (p. 160)

REM sleep behavior disorder A sleep disturbance in which the mechanism responsible for paralyzing the body during REM sleep is not functioning, resulting in the acting out of dreams. (p. 156)

replicate To repeat an experiment, generally with a new sample and/or other changes to the procedures, the goal of which is to provide further support for the findings of the first study. (p. 24)

representative sample A subgroup of a population selected so that its members have characteristics that closely reflect those of the population of interest. (p. 26)

representativeness heuristic A decision-making strategy used to evaluate the degree to which the primary characteristics of a person or situation are similar to our prototype of that person or situation. (p. 301)

repression The way the ego moves uncomfortable thoughts, memories, or feelings from the conscious level to the unconscious. (p. 473)

resistance A patient's unwillingness to cooperate in therapy, a sign of unconscious conflict. (p. 592)

resting potential The electrical potential of a cell "at rest"; the state of a cell when it is not activated. (p. 54)

reticular formation A network of neurons running through the midbrain that controls levels of arousal and quickly analyzes sensory information on its way to the cortex. (p. 85)

retina The layer of the eye that contains photoreceptor cells and the location for the transduction of light energy into neural activity. (p. 104)

retinal disparity A binocular cue that uses the difference between the images the two eyes see to determine the distance of objects. (p. 131)

retrieval The process of accessing information encoded and stored in memory. (p. 234)

retrieval cues Stimuli that help in the retrieval of stored information that is difficult to access. (p. 235)

retroactive interference The tendency for recently learned information to interfere with the retrieval of things learned in the past. (p. 261)

retrograde amnesia A type of memory loss; an inability to access memories formed prior to damage or injury to the brain, or difficulty retrieving them. (p. 268)

reuptake Process by which neurotransmitters are reabsorbed by the sending terminal bud. (p. 57)

rich false memories Recollections of an event that never occurred, which are expressed with emotions and confidence and include details. (p. 265)

risky shift The tendency for groups to recommend uncertain and risky options. (p. 649)

rods Specialized light receptors in the retina that are responsible for sight when the light level is low; not sensitive to color, but useful for night vision. (p. 106)

romantic love Love that is a combination of connection, concern, care, and intimacy. (p. 663)

sample A subset of a population chosen for inclusion in an experiment. (p. 26)

saturation Color purity. (p. 103)

scaffolding Pushing children to go just beyond what they are competent and comfortable doing, while providing help in a decreasing manner. (p. 355)

scapegoat A target of negative emotions, beliefs, and behaviors; typically, a member of the out-group who receives blame for an upsetting social situation. (p. 654)

Schachter–Singer theory of emotion Suggests that the experience of emotion is the result of physiological arousal and a cognitive label for this physiological state. (p. 407)

schema A collection of ideas that represents a basic unit of understanding. (p. 351)

schizophrenia (skit-sə-'frē-nē-ə) A disabling psychological disorder that can include delusions, hallucinations, disorganized speech, and abnormal psychomotor behavior. (p. 568)

scientific method The process scientists use to conduct research, which includes a continuing cycle of exploration, critical thinking, and systematic observation. (p. 19)

secondary appraisal An assessment to determine how to respond to a challenging or threatening situation. (p. 526)

secondary reinforcer Reinforcers that do not satisfy biological needs but often gain their power through their association with primary reinforcers. (p. 208)

secondary sex characteristics The development of pubic, underarm, and body hair in boys and girls along with a variety of other gender-specific bodily changes not associated with reproduction. (p. 361)

selective attention The ability to focus awareness on a small segment of information that is available through our sensory systems. (p. 145)

self-actualization The need to be one's best and strive for one's fullest potential. (p. 392)

self-concept The knowledge an individual has about his strengths, abilities, behavior patterns, and temperament. (p. 482)

self-determination theory (SDT) Suggests that humans are born with the need for competence, relatedness, and autonomy, which are always driving us in the direction of growth and optimal functioning. (p. 393)

self-efficacy Belief one has regarding how effective one will be in reaching a goal. (p. 486)

self-serving bias The tendency to attribute successes to personal characteristics and failures to environmental factors. (p. 629)

semantic memory The memory of information theoretically available to anyone, which pertains to general facts about the world; a type of explicit memory. (p. 247)

semantics The rules used to bring meaning to words and sentences. (p. 307)

sensation The process by which sensory organs in the eyes, ears, nose, mouth, skin, and other tissues receive and detect stimuli. (p. 94)

sensorimotor stage Piaget's stage of cognitive development during which infants use their sensory capabilities and motor skills to learn about the surrounding world. (p. 351)

sensory adaptation Sensory receptors tend to become less sensitive to constant stimuli. (p. 97)

sensory memory A stage of memory that captures near-exact copies of vast amounts of sensory stimuli for a very brief period of time. (p. 236)

sensory neurons Neurons specialized for receiving information about the environment from the sensory systems and transmitting this information to the brain for further processing. (p. 62)

serial position effect The ability to recall items in a list depends on where they are in the series. (p. 256)

set point The stable weight that is maintained despite variability in exercise and food intake. (p. 399)

sex The classification of someone as male or female based on biological characteristics; a sexual act such as intercourse. (p. 426)

sexual dysfunction A significant disturbance in the ability to respond sexually or to gain pleasure from sex. (p. 452)

sexuality Sexual activities, attitudes, and behaviors. (p. 426)

sexually transmitted infections (STIs) Diseases or illnesses transmitted through sexual activity. (p. 454)

sexual orientation A person's enduring sexual interest in individuals of the same sex, opposite sex, or both sexes. (p. 442)

shape constancy An object is perceived as maintaining its shape, regardless of the image projected on the retina. (p. 132)

shaping The use of reinforcers to guide behavior to the acquisition of a desired, complex behavior. (p. 203)

short-term memory A stage of memory that temporarily maintains and processes a limited amount of information. (p. 236)

signal detection theory A theory explaining how various factors influence our ability to detect weak signals in the environment (p. 99)

situational attribution A belief that some environmental factor is involved in the cause of an event or activity. (p. 628)

size constancy An object is perceived as maintaining its size, regardless of the image projected on the retina. (p. 132)

skewed distribution Nonsymmetrical frequency distribution (p. A-7)

sleep terrors A disturbance of non-REM sleep, generally occurring in children; characterized by screaming, staring fearfully, and usually no memory of the episode the following morning. (p. 158)

social cognition The way people think about others, attend to social information, and use this information in their lives, both consciously and unconsciously. (p. 627)

social-cognitive perspective Suggests that personality results from patterns of thinking (cognitive) as well as relationships and other environmental factors (social). (p. 486)

social facilitation The tendency for the presence of others to improve personal performance when the task or event is fairly uncomplicated and a person is adequately prepared. (p. 647)

social identity How we view ourselves within our social group. (p. 653)

social influence How a person is affected by others as evidenced in behaviors, emotions, and cognition. (p. 636)

social loafing The tendency for people to make less than their best effort when individual contributions are too complicated to measure. (p. 647)

social psychology The study of human cognition, emotion, and behavior in relation to others, including how people behave in social settings. (p. 625)

social roles The positions we hold in social groups, and the responsibilities and expectations associated with those roles. (p. 656)

social support The assistance we acquire from others. (p. 513)

somatic nervous system The branch of the peripheral nervous system that includes sensory nerves and motor nerves; gathers information from sensory receptors and controls the skeletal muscles responsible for voluntary movement. (p. 63)

somatosensory cortex A band of tissue running parallel to the motor cortex that receives and integrates sensory information from all over the body. (p. 83)

source traits Basic underlying or foundational characteristics of personality. (p. 489)

specific phobia A psychological disorder that includes a distinct fear or anxiety in relation to an object or situation. (p. 555)

spermarche A boy's first ejaculation. (p. 362)

spinal cord The bundle of neurons that allows communication between the brain and the peripheral nervous system, connecting with the body's muscles, glands, and organs. (p. 61)

split-brain operation A rare procedure used to disconnect the right and left hemispheres by cutting the corpus callosum. (p. 69)

spontaneous recovery In classical conditioning, the reappearance of the conditioned response following its extinction; occurs in response to the conditioned stimulus after a period of rest. (p. 193)

standard deviation A number that represents the average amount the values in a data set are away from their mean; a measure of variation (p. A-11)

standardization Occurs when test developers administer a test to a large sample and then publish the average scores for specified groups. (p. 317)

statistical significance The probability that the findings of a study were due to chance (p. A-2)

statistics A science that focuses on how to collect, organize, analyze, display, and interpret data; numbers that describe characteristics of a sample (p. A-1)

stem-and-leaf plot A type of graphical display that uses the actual data values in the form of leading digits and trailing digits (p. A-7)

stem cells Cells responsible for producing new neurons. (p. 74)

stereotypes Conclusions or inferences we make about people who are different from us based on their group membership, such as race, religion, age, or gender. (p. 652)

stereotype threat A situational threat in which individuals are aware of others' negative expectations, which leads to their fear that they will be judged and/or treated as inferior. (p. 654)

stigma A negative attitude or opinion about groups of people based on certain traits or characteristics. (p. 546)

stimulants A class of drugs that increase neural activity in the central nervous system. (p. 171)

stimulus An event or occurrence that generally leads to a response. (p. 187)

stimulus discrimination The ability to differentiate between a conditioned stimulus and other stimuli sufficiently different from it. (p. 193)

stimulus generalization The tendency for stimuli similar to the conditioned stimulus to elicit the conditioned response. (p. 192)

storage The process of preserving information for possible recollection in the future. (p. 235)

stress The response to perceived threats or challenges resulting from stimuli or events that cause strain. (p. 506)

stressors Stimuli that cause physiological, psychological, and emotional reactions. (p. 506)

structuralism An early school of psychology that used introspection to determine the structure and most basic elements of the mind. (p. 10)

successive approximations A method of shaping that uses reinforcers to condition a series of small steps that gradually approach the target behavior. (p. 203)

superego According to Freud, the structure of the mind that guides behavior to follow the rules of society, parents, or other authority figures (p. 472)

surface traits Easily observable characteristics that derive from source traits. (p. 489)

survey method A type of descriptive research that uses questionnaires or interviews to gather data. (p. 30)

sympathetic nervous system The division of the autonomic nervous system that mobilizes the "fight-or-flight" response to stressful or crisis situations. (p. 64)

synapse (si-naps) The tiny gap between a terminal bud of one axon and a neighboring dendrite of the next neuron; junction between neurons where communication occurs. (p. 53)

syntax The collection of rules concerning where to place words or phrases. (p. 307)

systematic desensitization A treatment that combines anxiety hierarchies with relaxation techniques. (p. 598)

telegraphic speech Two-word phrases typically used by infants around the age of 18 months. (p. 349)

temperament Characteristic differences in behavioral patterns and emotional reactions. (p. 356)

temporal lobes The area of the cortex that processes auditory stimuli and language. (p. 79)

teratogens Environmental agents that can damage the growing zygote, embryo, or fetus. (p. 342)

testosterone An androgen produced by the testes. (p. 429)

tetrahydracannabinol (THC) (te-trə-hī-drə-kə-'na-bə-ˌnȯl) The active ingredient of marijuana. (p. 176)

thalamus (tha-lə-məs) A structure in the limbic system that processes and relays sensory information to the appropriate areas of the cortex. (p. 85)

theory Synthesizes observations in order to explain phenomena and guide predictions to be tested through research. (p. 20)

therapeutic alliance A warm and accepting client–therapist relationship that serves as a safe place for self-exploration. (p. 595)

theta waves Brain waves that indicate the early stage of sleep. (p. 151)

thinking Mental activity associated with coming to a decision, reaching a solution, forming a belief, or developing an attitude. (p. 284)

third variable An unaccounted for characteristic of participants or environment that explains changes in the variables of interest. (p. 32)

thyroid gland Gland of the endocrine system that regulates the rate of metabolism by secreting thyroxin. (p. 67)

token economy A treatment approach that uses behavior modification to harness the power of reinforcement to encourage good behavior. (p. 600)

tolerance With constant use of some psychoactive drugs, a condition in which the body requires more and more of the drug to create the original effect; a sign of physiological dependence. (p. 177)

traits The relatively stable properties that describe elements of personality. (p. 489)

trait theories Theories that focus on personality dimensions and their influence on behavior; can be used to predict behaviors. (p. 489)

transduction The process of transforming stimuli into neural signals. (p. 95)

transference A type of resistance that occurs when a patient reacts to a therapist as if dealing with parents or other caregivers from childhood. (p. 592)

transgender Refers to people whose gender identity and expression do not typically match the gender assigned to them at birth. (p. 438)

transsexual An individual who seeks or undergoes a social transition to the other gender, and who may make changes to his or her body through surgery and medical treatment. (p. 439)

trial and error An approach to problem solving that involves finding a solution through a series of attempts and eliminating those that do not work. (p. 293)

triarchic theory of intelligence (trī-är-kik) Sternberg's theory suggesting that humans have varying degrees of analytical, creative, and practical abilities. (p. 314)

trichromatic theory (trī-krō-ˌma-tik) The perception of color is the result of three types of cones, each sensitive to particular wavelengths in the red, green, and blue spectrums. (p. 108)

Type A personality Competitive, aggressive, impatient, and often hostile pattern of behaviors. (p. 528)

Type B personality Relaxed, patient, and nonaggressive pattern of behaviors. (p. 528)

unconditional positive regard According to Rogers, the total acceptance or valuing of a person, regardless of behavior. (p. 483)

unconditioned response (UR) A reflexive, involuntary response to an unconditioned stimulus. (p. 191)

unconditioned stimulus (US) A stimulus that automatically triggers an involuntary response without any learning needed. (p. 190)

unconscious According to Freud, the level of consciousness outside of awareness, which is difficult to access without effort or therapy. (p. 471)

uninvolved parenting A parenting style characterized by a parent's indifference to a child, including a lack of emotional involvement. (p. 374)

uplifts Experiences that are positive and have the potential to make one happy. (p. 514)

validity The degree to which an assessment measures what it intends to measure. (p. 316)

variable-interval schedule A schedule in which the reinforcer comes after an interval of time goes by, but the length of the interval changes from trial to trial. (p. 213)

variable-ratio schedule A schedule in which the number of desired responses or behaviors that must occur before a reinforcer is given changes across trials and is based on an average number of responses to be reinforced. (p. 212)

variables Measureable characteristics that can vary over time or across people. (p. 26)

vestibular sense (ve-ˈsti-byə-lər) The sense of balance and equilibrium. (p. 126)

volley principle States that the perception of pitches between 400 and 4,000 Hz is made possible by neurons working together to fire in volleys. (p. 116)

wavelength The distance between wave peaks (or troughs) (p. 102)

Weber's law The law stating that each of the five senses has its own constant ratios determining difference thresholds. (p. 99)

Wernicke's area (ver-nə-kəz) A region of the cortex that plays a pivotal role in language comprehension. (p. 72)

withdrawal With constant use of some psychoactive drugs, a condition in which the body becomes dependent and then reacts when the drug is withheld. (p. 177)

working memory The active processing of information in short-term memory; the maintenance and manipulation of information in the memory system. (p. 244)

zygote A single cell formed by the union of a sperm cell and egg. (p. 341)

References

Aase, H., & Sagvolden, T. (2006). Infrequent, but not frequent, reinforcers produce more variable responding and deficient sustained attention in young children with attention-deficit/hyperactivity disorder (ADHD). *Journal of Child Psychology and Psychiatry, 47*(5), 457–471.

Abel, K. M., Drake, R., & Goldstein, J. M. (2010). Sex differences in schizophrenia. *International Review of Psychiatry, 22,* 417–428.

Abou-Khalil, B. W. (2010). When should corpus callosotomy be offered as palliative therapy? *Epilepsy Currents, 10,* 9–10.

Ackerman, P. L., Kanfer, R., & Calderwood, C. (2010). Use it or lose it? Wii brain exercise practice and reading for domain knowledge. *Psychology and Aging, 25,* 753–766.

Addy, S., Engelhardt, W., & Skinner, C. (2013). *Basic facts about low-income children: Children under 18 years, 2011* [Fact sheet]. New York: National Center for Children in Poverty. Retrieved from http://www.nccp.org/publications/pub_1074.html

Adler, A. (1927/1994). *Understanding human nature.* Oxford, UK: Oneworld.

Adolphs, R. (2008). Fear, faces, and the human amygdala. *Current Opinion in Neurobiology, 18,* 166–172.

Advocates for Youth. (2009). *Adolescent sexual health in Europe and the U.S.—Why the difference?* (Sue Alford and Debra Hauser, Eds., 3rd ed.). Retrieved May 30, 2013, from http://www.advocatesforyouth.org/storage/advfy/documents/fsest.pdf

Aeschbach, D., Sher, L., Postolache, T. T., Matthews, J. R., Jackson, M. A., & Wehr, T. A. (2003). A longer biological night in long sleepers than in short sleepers. *Journal of Clinical Endocrinology & Metabolism, 88*(1), 26–30.

Agence France Presse. (2010, October 13). *In Chile mine accident, 33 is lucky number.* Retrieved from http://www.google.com/hostednews/afp/article/ALeqM5jnJi5wZWoy3N43PM04nk0Z1Uy2Bw?docId=CNG.eaac05d5f1986b04dd380561cc5ff4fe.131

Agence France Presse. (2010, October 15). Teníamos que pasar algo así, para mostrar cómo trabajan los mineros [Something like this has to happen, to show how the miners work]. *El Sur.* Retrieved from http://diarioelsur.cl/base_elsur/site/artic/20101015/pags/20101015084612.html

Agrawal, Y., Platz, E. A., & Niparko, J. K. (2008). Prevalence of hearing loss and differences by demographic characteristics among US adults: Data from the National Health and Nutrition Examination Survey, 1999–2004. *Archives of Internal Medicine, 168,* 1522–1530.

Ahima, R. S., & Antwi, D. A. (2008). Brain regulation of appetite and satiety. *Endrocrinology Metabolism Clinics of North America, 37,* 811–823.

Aiello, J. R., & Douthitt, E. A. (2001). Social facilitation from Triplett to electronic performance monitoring. *Group Dynamics: Theory, Research, and Practice, 5,* 163–180.

Ainsworth, M. D. (1985). Patterns of attachment. *Clinical Psychologist, 38*(2), 27–29.

Ainsworth, M. D. S., & Bell, S. M. (1970). Attachment, exploration, and separation: Illustrated by the behavior of one-year-olds in a Strange Situation. *Child Development, 41*(1), 49–67.

Ainsworth, M. D. S., Blehar, M. C., Waters, E., & Wall, S. (1978). *Patterns of attachment: A psychological study of the Strange Situation.* Hillsdale, NJ: Lawrence Erlbaum Associates.

Ainsworth, M. S. (1979). Infant–mother attachment. *American Psychologist, 34,* 932–937.

Ainsworth, S. E., & Baumeister, R. F. (2012). Changes in sexuality: How sexuality changes across time, across relationships, and across sociocultural contexts. *Clinical Neuropsychiatry, 9,* 32–38.

Ainsworth, S. E., & Maner, J. K. (2012). Sex begets violence: Mating motives, social dominance, and physical aggression in men. *Journal of Personality and Social Psychology, 103,* 819–829. doi: 10.1037/a0029428

Ajzen, I. (2001). Nature and operation of attitudes. *Annual Review of Psychology, 52,* 27–58.

Akcay, O., Dalgin, M. H., & Bhatnagar, S. (2011). Perception of color in product choice among college students: A cross-national analysis of USA, India, China and Turkey. *International Journal of Business and Social Science, 2,* 42–48.

Akinola, M., & Mendes, W. B. (2012). Stress-induced cortisol facilitates threat-related decision making among police officers. *Behavioral Neuroscience, 126,* 167–174.

Albert, D., Chein, J., & Steinberg, L. (2013). The teenage brain: Peer influences on adolescent decision making. *Current Directions in Psychological Science, 22,* 114–120.

Aldrete, J. A., Marron, G. M., & Wright, A. J. (1984). The first administration of anesthesia in military surgery: On occasion of the Mexican-American War. *Anesthesiology, 61,* 585–588.

Alexander, D. A., & Klein, S. (2001). Ambulance personnel and critical incidents: Impact of accident and emergency work on mental health and emotional well-being. *British Journal of Psychiatry, 178,* 76–81.

Alexander, G. M., & Hines, M. (2002). Sex differences in response to children's toys in nonhuman primates (Cercopithecus aethiops sabaeus). *Evolution and Human Behavior, 23,* 467–479.

Alexander, G. M., Wilcox, T., & Woods, R. (2009). Sex differences in infants' visual interest in toys. *Archives of Sexual Behavior, 38,* 427–433.

Alexander, R. D. (1974). The evolution of social behavior. *Annual Review of Ecology and Systematics, 5,* 325–383.

Al Firdaus, M. M. (2012). SQ3R strategy for increasing students' retention of reading and written information. *Majalah Ilmiah Dinamika, 37,* 49–63.

Allegood, J. (2011, July 27). Durham girl in good spirits after Ocracoke shark attack. *News & Observer.* Retrieved from http://www.newsobserver.com/2011/07/27/1371792/durham-girl-in-good-spirits-after.html

Allen, N. (2011, January 24). Oprah Winfrey reunited with 'secret half-sister.' *The Telegraph.* Retrieved from http://www.telegraph.co.uk/news/worldnews/northamerica/usa/8279477/Oprah-Winfrey-reunited-with-secret-half-sister.html

Allen, S. (2009, October 30). 11 famous people who overcame dyslexia. *CNN.com.* Retrieved from http://articles.cnn.com/2009-10-30/living/mf.dyslexia.famous.celebrities_1_international-dyslexia-association-winkler-hank-zipzer?_s=PM:LIVING

Allik, J., & McCrae, R. R. (2004). Toward a geography of personality traits patterns of profiles across 36 cultures. *Journal of Cross-Cultural Psychology, 35,* 13–28.

Allport, G. W. & Odbert, H. S. (1936). Trait-names: A psycho-lexical study. *Psychological Monographs, 47,* i–171.

Almeida, D. (2009, February 3). Ask the brains: Is the midlife crisis a myth? *Scientific American Mind.* Retrieved from http://www.scientificamerican.com/article.cfm?id=ask-the-brains-is-the-midlife

Alpert, P. T. (2012). The health lowdown on caffeine. *Home Health Care Management Practice, 24,* 156–158.

Althof, S. E. (2010). What's new in sex therapy. *The Journal of Sexual Medicine, 7,* 5–13.

Altshuler, L. L., Kuaka, R. W., Hellemann, G., Frye, M. A., Sugar, C. A., McElroy, S. L., . . . Suppes, T. (2010). Bipolar disorder evaluated prospectively in the Stanley Foundation Bipolar Treatment Outcome Network. *American Journal of Psychiatry, 167,* 708–715.

Alzheimer's Association. (2010). *2010 Alzheimer's disease facts and figures.* Washington, DC: Author.

Alzheimer's Association. (2013). *Alzheimer's and dementia testing for earlier diagnosis.* Retrieved from http://www.alz.org/research/science/earlier_alzheimers_diagnosis.asp#Brain

American Academy of Pediatrics. (2009). From the Academy of Pediatrics: Policy Statement—Media violence. *Pediatrics, 124,* 1495–1503.

American Academy of Pediatrics, Committee on Public Education. (2001). American Academy of Pediatrics: Children, adolescents, and television. *Pediatrics, 107,* 423–426.

American Art Therapy Association. (2013). *About art therapy.* Retrieved from http://www.arttherapy.org/

American Academy of Sleep Medicine. (2011, May 20). Shaquille O'Neal brings attention to sleep apnea and CPAP in Harvard video. *AASM Weekly Update.* Retrieved from http://www.aasmnet.org/articles.aspx?id=2273

American Cancer Society. (2012). *Child and teen tobacco use.* Retrieved from http://www.cancer.org/cancer/cancercauses/tobaccocancer/childandteentobaccouse/child-and-teen-tobacco-use-child-and-teen-tobacco-use

American Foundation for Suicide Prevention. (2013). *Understanding suicide: Facts and figures* [Fact sheet]. Retrieved from http://www.afsp.org/understanding-suicide/facts-and-figures

American Group Psychotherapy Association. (2010). *Group therapy.* Retrieved April 29, 2010, from http://www.agpa.org/group/consumersguide2000.html

American Heart Association. (2011). *Overweight in children.* Retrieved from http://www.heart.org/HEARTORG/GettingHealthy/Overweight-in-Children_UCM_304054_Article.jsp

American Heart Association. (2012). *Atherosclerosis.* Retrieved from http://www.heart.org/HEARTORG/Conditions/Cholesterol/WhyCholesterolMatters/Atherosclerosis_UCM_305564_Article.jsp

American Humane Association. (2013). *Animal-assisted therapy.* Retrieved from http://www.americanhumane.org/interaction/programs/animal-assisted-therapy/

American Psychiatric Association. (1952). *Diagnostic and statistical manual of mental disorders.* Arlington, VA: Author.

American Psychiatric Association. (2001). *The practice of ECT: A task force report* (2nd ed.). Washington, DC: Author.

American Psychiatric Association. (2013). *Diagnostic and statistical manual of mental disorders* (5th ed., *DSM–5*). Arlington, VA: Author.

American Psychological Association. (n.d.). *Sport psychology off the field.* Retrieved from http://www.apa.org/helpcenter/sport-psychology.aspx

American Psychological Association. (1998a). Final conclusions of the American Psychological Association's working group on investigation of memories of childhood abuse. *Psychology, Public Policy, and Law, 4,* 933–940.

American Psychological Association. (1998b). *Psychology education & career guide for college students of color: Subfields of psychology* [Brochure]. Retrieved from http://www.apa.org/careers/resources/guides/college-students.aspx?item=14

American Psychological Association. (2004). *The truth about lie detectors (aka polygraph tests).* Retrieved from http://www.apa.org/research/action/polygraph.aspx

American Psychological Association. (2008). *Answers to your questions: For a better understanding of sexual orientation and homosexuality.* Retrieved from http://www.apa.org/topics/sorientation.pdf

American Psychological Association. (2010a). *Ethical principles of psychologists and code of conduct,* 1–18. Retrieved from http://www.apa.org/ethics/code/principles.pdf

American Psychological Association. (2010b). *FYI: Mental health insurance under the federal parity law.* Retrieved October 19, 2012, from http://www.apa.org/helpcenter/federal-parity-law.aspx

American Psychological Association. (2010c). *Publication manual of the American Psychological Association* (6th ed.). Washington, DC: Author.

American Psychological Association. (2011a). *Answers to your questions about transgender people, gender identity, and gender expression.* Retrieved from http://www.apa.org/topics/sexuality/transgender.pdf

American Psychological Association. (2011b). *Careers in psychology: Some of the subfields in psychology* [Brochure]. Retrieved from http://www.apa.org/careers/resources/guides/careers.aspx?item=3#

American Psychological Association. (2011c). *The guidelines for psychological practice with lesbian, gay, and bisexual clients, adopted by the APA Council of Representatives, February 18–20, 2011.* Retrieved from http://www.apa.org/pi/lgbt/resources/guidelines.aspx

American Psychological Association (2012a). *Divisions of the APA.* Retrieved from http://www.apa.org/about/division/index.aspx

American Psychological Association (2012b). *Resolution on the recognition of psychotherapy effectiveness.* Retrieved October 19, 2012, from http://www.apa.org/news/press/releases/2012/08/resolution-psychotherapy.aspx

American Psychological Association. (2012c). *Society for Media Psychology and Technology* (Division 46). Retrieved from http://www.apa.org/divisions/div46/

American Psychological Association. (2012d). *Understanding alcohol use disorders and their treatment.* Retrieved February 20, 2013, from www.http://www.apa.org/helpcenter/alcohol-disorders.aspx

American Psychological Association. (2013a). *Graduate study in psychology, 2014 edition.* Washington, DC: Author.

American Psychological Association. (2013b). *Margaret Floy Washburn, PhD: 1921 APA President.* Retrieved from http://www.apa.org/about/archives/presidents/bio-margaret-washburn.aspx

American Psychological Association. (2013c). *Roper v. Simmons.* Retrieved from http://www.apa.org/about/offices/ogc/amicus/roper.aspx

American Psychological Association. (2013d). *Stress in America: Missing the health care connection.* Retrieved from http://www.apa.org/news/press/releases/stress/2012/full-report.pdf

American Red Cross. (2010, October 13). Chilean Red Cross provides aid to trapped miners and their families [Web log post]. Retrieved from http://redcrosschat.org/2010/10/13/chilean-red-cross-provides-aid-to-trapped-miners-and-their-families/

American Social Health Association. (2012). *Fast facts* [Fact sheet]. Retrieved from http://www.ashastd.org/std-sti/Herpes/learn-about-herpes.html

American Speech-Language Hearing Association. (2012). *Who should be screened for hearing loss?* Retrieved from http://www.asha.org/public/hearing/Who-Should-be-Screened/

American Stroke Association. (2012). *What is an arteriovenous malformation (AVM)?* Retrieved from http://www.strokeassociation.org/STROKEORG/AboutStroke/TypesofStroke/HemorrhagicBleeds/What-Is-an-Arteriovenous-Malformation-AVM_UCM_310099_Article.jsp

Amesbury, E. C., & Schallhorn, S. C. (2003). Contrast sensitivity and limits of vision. *International Ophthalmology Clinics, 43,* 31–42.

Anastasi, A., & Urbina, S. (1997). *Psychological testing* (7th ed.). Upper Saddle River, NJ: Prentice Hall.

Anastasio, A., Draisci, R., Pepe, T., Mercogliano, R., Quadri, F. D., Luppi, G., & Cortesi, M. L. (2010). Development of biogenic amines during the ripening of Italian dry sausages. *Journal of Food Protection, 73,* 114–118.

Anderson, A. (2010). Why testing boosts learning. *Scientific American Mind, 21,* 13. doi:10.1038/scientificamericanmind0111-13a

Anderson, B., Fagan, P., Woodnutt, T., & Chamorro-Premuzic, T. (2012). Facebook psychology: Popular questions answered by research. *Psychology of Popular Media Culture, 1,* 23–37.

Anderson, C. A. (2001). Heat and violence. *Current Directions in Psychological Science, 10,* 33–38.

Anderson, G. S., Litzenberger, R., & Plecas, D. (2002). Physical evidence of police officer stress. *An International Journal of Police Strategies & Management, 25,* 399–420.

Anderson, R. C. (1971). Encoding processes in the storage and retrieval of sentences. *Journal of Experimental Psychology, 91,* 338–340.

Anderson-Hanley, C., Snyder, A. L., Nimon, J. P., & Arciero, P. J. (2011). Social facilitation in virtual reality-enhanced exercise: Competitiveness moderates exercise effort of older adults. *Clinical Interventions in Aging, 6,* 275–280.

Andre, T., & Sola, J. (1976). Imagery, verbatim and paraphrased questions, and retention of meaningful sentences. *Journal of Educational Psychology, 68,* 661–669.

Andrus, B. M., Blizinsky, K., Vedell, P. T., Dennis, K., Shukla, P. K., Schaffer, D. J., . . . Redei, E. E. (2012). Gene expression patterns in the hippocampus and amygdala of endogenous depression and chronic stress models. *Molecular Psychiatry, 17,* 49–61.

Angst, J., Angst, F., Gerber-Werder, R., & Gamma, A. (2005). Suicide in 406 mood-disorder patients with and without long-term medication: A 40 to 44 years' follow-up. *Archives of Suicide Research, 9,* 279–300.

Anis, A. H., Zhang, W., Bansback, N., Guh, D. P., Amarsi, Z., & Birmingham, C. L. (2010). Obesity and overweight in Canada: An updated cost-of-illness study. *Obesity Reviews, 11,* 21–40.

Annan, J., Blattman, C., & Horton, R. (2006). *The state of youth and youth protection in northern Uganda: Findings from the Survey for War Affected Youth* [Report for UNICEF Uganda], ii–89. Retrieved from http://chrisblattman.com/documents/policy/sway/SWAY.Phase1.FinalReport.pdf

Ansbacher, H. L., & Ansbacher, R. R. (Eds.). (1956). *The individual psychology of Alfred Adler.* New York: Harper and Row.

Araque, A., & Navarrete, M. (2010). Glial cells in neuronal network function. *Philosophical Transactions of the Royal Society of Biological Sciences, 365,* 2375–2381.

Archer, J. (2004). Sex differences in aggression in real-world settings: A meta-analytic review. *Review of General Psychology, 8,* 291–322.

Archer, J., & Coyne, S. M. (2005). An integrated review of indirect, relational, and social aggression. *Personality and Social Psychology Review, 9,* 212–230.

Ardelt, M. (2010). Are older adults wiser than college students? A comparison of two age cohorts. *Journal of Adult Development, 17,* 193–207.

Ardila, A., Rosselli, M., Matute, E., & Inozemtseva, O. (2011). Gender differences in cognitive development. *Developmental Psychology, 47,* 984–990.

Arkowitz, H., & Lilienfeld, S. O. (2011). Deranged and dangerous? *Scientific American Mind, 22,* 64–65. Retrieved from http://www.scientificamerican.com/article.cfm?id=deranged-and-dangerous

Arkowitz, H., & Lilienfeld, S. O. (2012, September 13). Are all psychotherapies created equal? *Scientific American Mind.* Retrieved from http://www.scientificamerican.com/article.cfm?id=are-all-psychotherapies-created-equal

Arlin, P. K. (1975). Cognitive development in adulthood: A fifth stage? *Developmental Psychology, 11,* 602–606.

Armitage, C. J., & Christian, J. (2003). From attitudes to behaviour: Basic and applied research on the theory of planned behaviour. *Current Psychology: Developmental, Learning, Personality, Social, 22,* 187–195.

Arnett, J. J. (2000). Emerging adulthood: A theory of development from the late teens through the twenties. *American Psychologist, 55,* 469–480.

Arnold, C. (2011). Following the crowd. *Scientific American Mind, 22,* 6. doi: 10.1038/scientificamericanmind0911-6

Aronson, E. (2012). *The social animal* (11th ed.). New York: Worth.

Aronson, E. (2013). *Jigsaw classroom.* Retrieved from http://www.jigsaw.org

Aronson, E., & Festinger, L. (1958). *Some attempts to measure tolerance for dissonance* (WADC.TR-58.492ASTIA Document No. AD 207 337). San Antonio, TX: Lackland Air Force Base.

Asch, S. E. (1955). Opinions and social pressure. *Scientific American, 193,* 31–35.

Asch, S. E. (1956). Studies of independence and conformity: I. A minority of one against a unanimous majority. *Psychological Monographs: General and Applied, 70,* 1–70.

Associated Press. (2008, April 25). Jockeys still battle weight issues, but progress being made. *ESPN.* Retrieved from http://sports.espn.go.com/espn/wire?section=horse&id=3367868

Associated Press. (2010, August 25). *Geology of Chilean gold and copper mine helped miners survive with air, water and warmth.* Retrieved from http://www.foxnews.com/world/2010/08/25/geology-chilean-gold-copper-helped-miners-survive-air-water-warmth/

Associated Press. (2010, August 30). *Chilean miners must move tons of rock in rescue.* Retrieved from http://usatoday30.usatoday.com/news/world/2010-08-29-chile-mine-rescue_N.htm

Associated Press. (2010, September 7). *Skin infections pose risk to Chilean miners as rescuers work to cool the sweltering conditions.* Retrieved from http://www.foxnews.com/world/2010/09/07/skin-infections-pose-risk-chilean-miners-rescuers-work-cool-sweltering/

Association for Psychological Science. (2012). *Psychology links.* Retrieved from http://www.psychologicalscience.org/index.php/about/psychology-links

Atkinson, R. C., & Shiffrin, R. M. (1968 January 31–February 2). *Some speculations on storage and retrieval processes in long-term memory* (Technical Report No. 127). Paper presented at Conference on Research on Human Decision Making sponsored by NASA-Ames Research Center, Moffett Field, CA.

Attarian, H. P., Schenck, C. H., & Mahowald, M. W. (2000). Presumed REM sleep behavior disorder arising from cataplexy and wakeful dreaming. *Sleep Medicine, 1,* 131–133.

Attia, E., & Roberto, C. A. (2009). Should amenorrhea be a diagnostic criterion for anorexia nervosa? *International Journal of Eating Disorders, 42,* 581–589.

Aurora, R. N., Zak, R. S., Maganti, R. K., Auerbach, S. H., Casey, K. R., Chowdhuri, S., . . . American Academy of Sleep Medicine. (2010). Best practice guide for the treatment of REM sleep behavior disorder (RBD). *Journal of Clinical Sleep Medicine, 15,* 85–95.

Awikunprasert, C., & Sittiprapaporn, W. (2012). Sleep pattern and efficiency in Thai children aged 3–6. *Research Journal of Pharmaceutical, Biological and Chemical Sciences, 3,* 1208–1217.

Back, M. D., Schmukle, S. C., & Egloff, B. (2008). Becoming friends by chance. *Psychological Science, 19,* 439–440.

Back, M. D., Stopfer, J. M., Vazire, S., Gaddis, S., Schmukle, S. C., Egloff, B., & Gosling, S. D. (2010). Facebook profiles reflect actual personality, not self-idealization. *Psychological Science, 21,* 372–374

Baddeley, A. (1982). Domains of recollection. *Psychological Review, 89,* 708–729.

Baddeley, A. (1995). Working memory. In M. S. Gazzaniga (Ed.), *The cognitive neurosciences* (pp. 755–764). Cambridge, MA: MIT Press.

Baddeley, A. (1999). *Essentials of human memory.* East Sussex, UK: Psychology Press.

Baddeley, A. (2000). The episodic buffer: A new component of working memory? *Trends in Cognitive Sciences, 4,* 417–423.

Baddeley, A. (2002). Is working memory still working? *European Psychologist, 7,* 85–97.

Baddeley, A. (2006). Working memory: An overview. In S. J. Pickering (Ed.), *Working memory in education* (pp. 3–31). Burlington, MA: Elsevier.

Baddeley, A. D., & Hitch, G. J. (1974). Working memory. In G. Bower (Ed.), *Recent advances in learning and memory* (Vol. 8, pp. 47–90). New York: Academic Press.

Baddeley, A. D., & Hitch, G. J. (1994). Developments in the concept of working memory. *Neuropsychology, 8,* 485–493.

Badie, D. (2010). Groupthink, Iraq, and the war on terror: Explaining US policy shift toward Iraq. *Foreign Policy Analysis, 6,* 277–296.

Baer, J. M. (1993). *Creativity and divergent thinking.* Hillsdale, NJ: Erlbaum.

Bahrick, H. P., Hall, L. K., & Da Costa, L. A. (2008). Fifty years of memory of college grades: Accuracy and distortions. *Emotion, 8,* 13–22.

Bahrick, L. E., Gogate, L. J., & Ruiz, I. (2002). Attention and memory for faces and actions in infancy: The salience of actions over faces in dynamic events. *Child Development, 73,* 1629–1643.

Bahrick, L. E., & Newell, L. C. (2008). Infant discrimination of faces in naturalistic events: Actions are more salient than faces. *Developmental Psychology, 44,* 983–996.

Baibazarova, E., van de Beek, C., Cohen-Kettenis, P. T., Buitelaar, J., Shelton, K. H., & van Goozen, S. H. M. (2013). Influence of prenatal maternal stress, maternal plasma cortisol and cortisol in the amniotic fluid on birth outcomes and child temperament at 3 months. *Psychoneuroendocrinology, 38,* 907–915

Bailey, S. J., & Covell, K. (2011). Pathways among abuse, daily hassles, depression and substance use in adolescents. *The New School Psychology Bulletin, 8,* 4–14.

Baillargeon, R., Spelke, E. S., & Wasserman, S. (1985). Object permanence in five-month-old infants. *Cognition, 20,* 191–208.

Baker, M. (2009, January 8). How brain activity makes new neurons. *Nature Reports Stem Cells.* Retrieved from http://www.nature.com/stemcells/2009/0901/090108/full/stemcells.2009.15.html

Ball, A. L. (2010, May 28). Are 5,001 Facebook friends one too many? *The New York Times.* Retrieved from http://www.nytimes.com/2010/05/30/fashion/30FACEBOOK.html?pagewanted=all&_r=0

Ballantyne, C. (2009, January 1). Looking for sleep in all the wrong places. *Scientific American Online.* Retrieved from http://www.scientificamerican.com/article.cfm?id=looking-for-sleep-in-all

Bandell, M., Macpherson, L. J., & Patapoutian, A. (2007). From chills to chilis: Mechanisms for thermosensation and chemesthesis via thermoTRPs. *Current Opinion in Neurobiology, 17,* 490–497.

Bandura, A. (1977a). Self-efficacy: Toward a unifying theory of behavioral change. *Psychological Review, 84,* 191–215.

Bandura, A. (1977b). *Social learning theory.* Englewood Cliffs, NJ: Prentice Hall.

Bandura, A. (1978). The self system in reciprocal determinism. *American Psychologist, 33,* 344–358.

Bandura, A. (1986). *Social foundations of thought and action: A social cognitive theory.* Englewood Cliffs, NJ: Prentice Hall.

Bandura, A. (2001). Social cognitive theory: An agentic perspective. *Annual Review of Psychology, 52,* 1–26.

Bandura, A. (2006). Toward a psychology of human agency. *Perspectives on Psychological Science, 1,* 164–180.

Bandura, A., Ross, D., & Ross, S. A. (1961). Transmission of aggression through imitation of aggressive models. *Journal of Abnormal and Social Psychology, 63,* 575–582.

Banks, M. S., & Salapatek, P. (1978). Acuity and contrast sensitivity in 1-, 2-, and 3-month-old human infants. *Investigative Ophthalmology & Visual Science, 17,* 361–365.

Banks, S., & Dinges, D. F. (2007). Behavioral and physiological consequences of sleep restriction. *Journal of Clinical Sleep Medicine, 3,* 519–528.

Banuazizi, A., & Movahedi, S. (1975). Interpersonal dynamics in a simulated prison: A methodological analysis. *American Psychologist, 30,* 152–160.

Banyard, V. L., & Moynihan, M. M. (2011). Variation in bystander behavior related to sexual and intimate partner violence prevention: Correlates in a sample of college students. *Psychology of Violence, 1,* 287–301.

Barak, A., Hen, L., Boniel-Nissim, M., & Shapira, N. A. (2008). A comprehensive review and a meta-analysis of the effectiveness of Internet-based psychotherapeutic interventions. *Journal of Technology in Human Services, 26,* 109–160.

Barash, P. G., Cullen, B. F., Stoelting, R. K., & Cahalan, M. (2009). *Clinical anesthesia* (6th ed.). Philadelphia: Lippincott Williams & Wilkins.

Barber, C. (2008). *Comfortably numb.* New York: Pantheon Books.

Barberá, E. (2003). Gender schemas: Configuration and activation processes. *Canadian Journal of Behavioural Science, 35,* 176–184.

Bard, P. (1934). Emotion: I. The neuro-humoral basis of emotional reactions. In C. Murchison, (Ed.), *Handbook of general experimental psychology,* International University Series in Psychology (pp. 264–311). Worcester, MA: Clark University Press.

Bargh, J. A., & McKenna, K. Y. A. (2004). The Internet and social life. *Annual Review of Psychology, 55,* 573–590.

Barker, E. T., Greenberg, J. S., Seltzer, M. M., & Almeida, D. M. (2012). Daily stress and cortisol patterns in parents of adult children with serious mental illness. *Health Psychology, 31,* 130–134.

Barnes, A. J., De Martinis, B. S., Gorelick, D. A., Goodwin, R. S., Kolbrich, E. A., & Huestis, M. A. (2009). Disposition of MDMA and metabolites in human sweat following controlled MDMA administration. *Clinical Chemistry, 55,* 454–462.

Barnes, S. K. (2010). Sign language with babies: What difference does it make? *Dimensions of Early Childhood, 38,* 21–30.

Barredo, J. L., & Deeg, K. E. (2009, February 24). Could living in a mentally enriching environment change your genes? *Scientific American.* Retrieved from http://www.scientificamerican.com/article.cfm?id=enriched-environments-memory

Barrett, L. F., & Bliss-Moreau, E. (2009). She's emotional. He's having a bad day: Attributional explanations for emotion stereotypes. *Emotion, 9,* 649–658.

Barrionuevo, A. (2011, October 12). A year out of the dark in Chile, but still trapped. *The New York Times.* Retrieved from http://www.nytimes.com/2011/10/12/world/americas/chiles-rescued-miners-face-major-struggles-a-year-later.html?pagewanted=all

Bartels, M., Saviouk, V., De Moor, M. H. M., Willemsen, G., van Beijsterveldt, T. C. E. M., Hottenga, J.-J., . . . Boomsma, D. I. (2010). Heritability and genome-wide linkage scan of subjective happiness. *Twin Research and Human Genetics, 13,* 135–142.

Bateman, A., & Fonagy, P. (2008). 8-year follow-up of patients treated for borderline personality disorder: Mentalization-based treatment versus treatment as usual. *American Journal of Psychiatry, 165,* 631–638.

Batson, C. D., & Powell, A. A. (2003). Altruism and prosocial behavior. In I. B. Weiner, T. Millon, & M. J. Lerner (Eds.), *Handbook of psychology: Vol. 5. Personality and social psychology* (pp. 463–484). Hoboken, NJ: Wiley.

Bauer, P. J. (2006). Constructing a past in infancy: A neuro-developmental account. *Trends in Cognitive Sciences, 10,* 175–181.

Baughman, H. M., Giammarco, E. A., Veselka, L., Schermer, J. A., Martin, N. G., Lynskey, M., & Vernon, P. A. (2012). A behavioral genetic study of humor styles in an Australian sample. *Twin Research and Human Genetics, 15,* 663–667.

Baumeister, R. F., Campbell, J. D., Krueger, J. I., & Vohs, K. D. (2003). Does high self-esteem cause better performance, interpersonal success, happiness, or healthier lifestyles? *Psychological Science in the Public Interest, 4,* 1–44.

Baumrind, D. (1966). Effects of authoritative parental control on child behavior. *Child Development, 37,* 887–907.

Baumrind, D. (1971). Current patterns of parental authority. *Developmental Psychology Monograph, 4,* 1–103.

Baumrind, D. (1991). The influence of parenting style on adolescent competence and substance use. *Journal of Early Adolescence, 11,* 56–95.

Baumrind, D. (1996). Personal statements. *Pediatrics, 98,* 857–860.

Baumrind, D., Larzelere, R. E., & Cowan, P. A. (2002). Ordinary physical punishment: Is it harmful? [Peer commentary on the paper "Corporal punishment by parents and associated child behaviors and experiences: A meta-analytic and theoretical review" by E. T. Gershoff]. *Psychological Bulletin, 128,* 580–589.

Bayley, N. (1993). *The Bayley Scales of Infant Development* (2nd ed.). San Antonio, TX: Psychological Test Corporation.

BBC. (2005, September). *Dr Money and the boy with no penis—programme transcript.* Retrieved from http://www.bbc.co.uk/sn/tvradio/programmes/horizon/dr_money_trans.shtml

BBC News. (2001, November 16). *Rise of the blockbuster.* Retrieved from http://news.bbc.co.uk/2/hi/entertainment/1653733.stm

BBC News. (2010, October 14). *Jubilation as Chile mine rescue ends.* Retrieved from http://www.bbc.co.uk/news/world-latin-america-11469025

BBC News. (2010, November 20). *Global health officials target tobacco additives.* Retrieved from http://www.bbc.co.uk/news/world-latin-america-11804767?print=true

BBC News. (2011, June 28). *Somalia fleeing to Kenya in large numbers.* Retrieved from http://www.bbc.co.uk/news/world-africa-13937486

BBC News. (2011, July 22). *EU must do more on East Africa famine—David Cameron.* Retrieved from http://www.bbc.co.uk/news/uk-politics-14253766

BBC News. (2013, May 2). *Somalia famine "killed 260,000 people."* Retrieved from http://www.bbc.co.uk/news/world-africa-22380352

Beauchamp, M. H., & Anderson, V. (2010). Social: An integrative framework for the development of social skills. *Psychological Bulletin, 136,* 39–64.

Bech, P. (2006). The full story of lithium. *Psychotherapy and psychosomatics, 75,* 265–269.

Beck, A. T. (1976). *Cognitive therapy and the emotional disorders.* New York: International Universities Press.

Beck, A. T., Rush, A. J., Shaw, B. F., & Emory, G. (1979). *Cognitive therapy of depression.* New York: Guilford Press.

Beck, A. T., & Weishaar, M. E. (2014). Cognitive therapy. In R. J. Corsini & D. Wedding (Eds.), *Current psychotherapies* (10th ed., pp. 231–264). Belmont, CA: Brooks/Cole, Cengage Learning.

Beck, H. (2011, December 28). Newest Knick out to prove he's not just a novelty. *The New York Times.* Retrieved from http://www.nytimes.com/2011/12/29/sports/basketball/jeremy-lin-knicks-newest-addition-is-out-to-prove-hes-not-just-a-novelty.html

Beck, H. (2012, February 4). Lin sparks Knicks, to crowd's delight and D'Antoni's relief. *The New York Times.* Retrieved from http://www.nytimes.com/2012/02/05/sports/basketball/lin-leads-knicks-over-nets.html

Beck, H. (2012, February 24). The evolution of a point guard. *The New York Times.* Retrieved from http://www.nytimes.com/2012/02/25/sports/basketball/the-evolution-of-jeremy-lin-as-a-point-guard.html?pagewanted=all

Becker, K. A. (2003). History of the Stanford–Binet intelligence scales: Content and psychometrics. In *Stanford–Binet intelligence scales, Fifth Edition Assessment Service Bulletin* (no. 1). Itasca, IL: Riverside.

Beebe-Center, J. G. (1951). Feeling and emotion. In H. Helson (Ed.), *Theoretical foundations of psychology* (pp. 254–317). Princeton, NJ: Van Nostrand.

Bekk, M., & Spörrle, M. (2010). The influence of perceived personality characteristics on positive attitude towards and suitability of a celebrity as a marketing campaign endorser. *Open Psychology Journal, 3,* 54–66.

Belizaire, L. S., & Fuertes, J. N. (2011). Attachment, coping, acculturative stress, and quality of life among Haitian immigrants. *Journal of Counseling & Development, 89,* 89–97.

Belmaker, R. H. (2004). Bipolar disorder. *New England Journal of Medicine, 351,* 476–486.

Belmaker, R. H., & Agam, G. (2008). Major depressive disorder. *New England Journal of Medicine, 358,* 55–68.

Bem, D. J. (2011). Feeling the future: Experimental evidence for anomalous retroactive influences on cognition and affect. *Journal of Personality and Social Psychology, 100,* 407–425.

Bem, D. J., Utts, J., & Johnson, W. O. (2011). Must psychologists change the way they analyze their data? *Journal of Personality and Social Psychology, 101,* 716–719.

Bem, S. L. (1981). Gender schema theory: A cognitive account of sex typing. *Psychological Review, 88,* 354–364.

Benedek, M., Franz, F., Heene, M., & Neubauer, A. C. (2012). Differential effects of cognitive inhibition and intelligence on creativity. *Personality and Individual Differences, 53,* 480–485.

Benham, G. (2010). Sleep: An important factor in stress–health models. *Stress and Health, 26,* 201–214.

Benjamin, L. T. (2007). *A brief history of modern psychology.* Malden, MA: Blackwell.

Bennett, A. T. D., Cuthill, I. C., Partridge, J. C., & Maier, E. J. (1996). Ultraviolet vision and mate choice in zebra finches. *Nature, 380,* 433–435.

Benson, H. (2000). *The relaxation response.* New York: Avon Books.

Ben-Zvi, A., Vernon S. D., & Broderick G. (2009). Model-based therapeutic correction of hypothalamic–pituitary–adrenal axis dysfunction. *PLoS Computational Biology, 5,* e1000273. doi: 10.1371/journal.pcbi.1000273

Berenbaum, S. A., Blakemore, J. E. O., & Beltz, A. M. (2011). A role for biology in gender-related behavior. *Sex Roles, 64,* 804–825.

Berg, K. S., Delgado, S., Cortopassi, K. A., Beissinger, S. R., & Bradbury, J. W. (2012). Vertical transmission of learned signatures in a wild parrot. *Proceedings of the Royal Society of London, B279,* 585–591.

Berger, W., Coutinho, E. S. F., Figueira, I., Marques-Portella, C., Luz, M. P., Neylan, T. C., . . . Mendlowicz, M. V. (2011). Rescuers at risk: A systematic review and meta-regression analysis of the worldwide current prevalence and correlates of PTSD in rescue workers. *Social Psychiatry and Psychiatric Epidemiology, 47,* 1001–1011.

Bergh, C., Sjöstedt, S., Hellers, G., Zandian, M., & Södersten, P. (2003). Meal size, satiety and cholecystokinin in gastrectomized humans. *Physiology & Behavior, 78,* 143–147.

Berkeley Lab. (n.d.). *Electromagetic spectrum.* Retrieved February 16, 2013, from http://www.lbl.gov/MicroWorlds/ALSTool/EMSpec/EMSpec2.html

Bernard, L. L. (1926). *An introduction to social psychology.* New York: Henry Holt.

Bernier, A., Carlson, S. M., & Whipple, N. (2010). From external regulation to self-regulation: Early parenting precursors of young children's executive functioning. *Child Development, 81,* 326–229.

Berry, J. W. (1997). Immigration, acculturation, and adaptation. *Applied Psychology: An International Review, 46,* 5–68.

Berscheid, E. (2010). Love in the fourth dimension. *Annual Review of Psychology, 61,* 1–25.

Berthoz, S., Blair, R. J. R., Le Clec'h, G., & Martinot, J.-L. (2002). Emotions: From neuropsychology to functional imaging. *International Journal of Psychology, 37,* 193–203.

Besedovsky, L., Lange, T., & Born, J. (2012). Sleep and immune function. *Pflügers Archiv—European Journal of Physiology, 463,* 1–17.

Betsch, C., & Sachse, K. (2013). Debunking vaccination myths: Strong risk negations can increase perceived vaccination risks. *Health Psychology, 32,* 145–155. doi: 10.1037/a0027387

Bezdjian, S., Baker, L.A., & Tuvblad, C. (2011). Genetic and environmental influences on impulsivity: A meta-analysis of twin, family and adoption studies. *Clinical Psychology Review, 31,* 1209–1223.

Bezdjian, S., Tuvblad, C., Raine, A., & Baker, L. A. (2011). The genetic and environmental covariation among psychopathic personality traits, and reactive and proactive aggression in childhood. *Child Development, 82,* 1267–1281.

Bialystok, E. (2011). Reshaping the mind: The benefits of bilingualism. *Canadian Journal of Experimental Psychology, 65,* 229–235.

Bihm, E. M., Gillaspy, J. A., Lammers, W. J., & Huffman, S. P. (2010). IQ zoo and teaching operant concepts. *Psychological Record, 60,* 523–526

Bikle, D. D. (2004). Vitamin D and skin cancer. *Journal of Nutrition, 134,* 3472S–3478S.

Binns, C. (2008). A brighter tune. *Scientific American Mind, 19,* 17. doi: 10.1038/scientificamericanmind0408-17a

Binns, C. (2009). Inflammation brings on the blues. *Scientific American Mind, 20,* 16. doi: 10.1038/scientificamericanmind0909-16b

Black, H. (2012). Meditate that cold away. *Scientific American Mind, 23,* 18. doi: 10.1038/scientificamericanmind1112-18a

Blackmore, S. J. (2005). *Consciousness: A very short introduction.* New York: Oxford University Press.

Blackwell, B., Marley, E., Price, J., & Taylor, D. (1967). Hypertensive interactions between monoamine oxidase inhibitors and foodstuffs. *British Journal of Psychiatry, 113,* 349–365.

Blair, C., & Raver, C. C. (2012). Child development in the context of adversity: Experiential canalization of brain and behavior. *American Psychologist, 67,* 309–318. doi: 10.1037/a0027493

Blanchard, R. (2008). Review and theory of handedness, birth order, and homosexuality in men. *Laterality, 13,* 51–70.

Blasi, A. (1980). Bridging moral cognition and moral action: A critical review of the literature. *Psychological Bulletin, 88,* 1–45.

Blass, T. (1991). Understanding behavior in the Milgram obedience experiment: The role of personality, situations, and their interactions. *Journal of Personality and Social Psychology, 60,* 398–413.

Blass, T. (1999). The Milgram paradigm after 35 years: Some things we now know about obedience to authority. *Journal of Applied Social Psychology, 25,* 955–978.

Blatchley, B., & O'Brien, K. R. (2007). Deceiving the participant: Are we creating the reputational spillover effect? *North American Journal of Psychology, 9,* 519–534.

Blecher, S. R., & Erickson, R. P. (2007). Genetics of sexual development: A new paradigm. *American Journal of Medical Genetics Part A, 143A,* 3054–3068.

Blickenstaff, J. C. (2005). Women and science careers: Leaky pipeline or gender filter? *Gender and Education, 17,* 369–386.

Bliss-Moreau, E., Bauman, M. D., & Amaral, D. G. (2011). Neonatal amygdala lesions result in globally blunted affect in adult rhesus macaques. *Behavioral Neuroscience, 125,* 848–858.

Bloch, M. H., McGuire, J., Landeros-Weisenberger, A., Leckman, J. F., & Pittenger, C. (2010). Meta-analysis of the dose–response relationship of SSRI in obsessive-compulsive disorder. *Molecular Psychiatry, 15,* 850–855.

Block, C. J., Koch, S. M., Liberman, B. E., Merriweather, T. J., & Roberson, L. (2011). Contending with stereotype threat at work: A model of long-term responses. *Counseling Psychologist, 39,* 570–600.

Blumenthal, H., Leen-Feldner, E. W., Babson, K. A., Gahr, J. L., Trainor, C. D., & Frala, J. L. (2011). Elevated social anxiety among early maturing girls. *Developmental Psychology, 47,* 1133–1140.

Boccella, K. (2012, May 6). Blindness is no barrier for Center City triathlete. *The Philadelphia Inquirer.* Retrieved from http://articles.philly.com/2012-05-06/news/31587179_1_husband-retinal-cancer-guide/3

Boeve, B. F., Silber, M. H., Saper, C. B., Ferman, T. J., Dickson, D. W., Parisi, J. E., . . . Braak, H. (2007). Pathophysiology of REM sleep behaviour disorder and relevance to neurodegenerative disease. *Brain, 130,* 2770–2788.

Bogaert, A. F. (2007). Extreme right-handedness, older brothers, and sexual orientation in men. *Neuropsychology, 21,* 141–148.

Bold, K. W., Yoon, H., Chapman, G. B., & McCarthy, D. E. (2013). Factors predicting smoking in a laboratory-based smoking-choice task. *Experimental and Clinical Psychopharmacology, 21,* 133–143. doi: 10.1037/a0031559

Bolen, R. M., & Scannapieco, M. (1999). Prevalence of child sexual abuse: A corrective meta-analysis. *Social Service Review, 73,* 281–313.

Bolton, P., Bass, J., Betancourt, T., Speelman, L., Onyango, G., Clougherty, K. F., . . . Verdeli, H. (2007). Interventions for depression symptoms among adolescent survivors of war and displacement in northern Uganda. *Journal of the American Medical Association, 298,* 519–527.

Bonanno, G. A., Brewin, C. R., Kaniasty, K., & La Greca, A. M. (2010). Weighing the costs of disaster: Consequences, risks, and resilience in individuals, families, and communities. *Psychological Science in the Public Interest, 11,* 1–49.

Bonanno, G. A., Westphal, M., & Mancini, A. D. (2011). Resilience to loss and potential trauma. *Annual Review of Clinical Psychology, 7,* 1.1–1.25

Bond, R., & Smith, P. B. (1996). Culture and conformity: A meta-analysis of studies using Asch's (1952b, 1956) line judgment task. *Psychological Bulletin, 119,* 111–137.

Bonnie, R. J., & Scott, E. S. (2013). The teenage brain: Adolescent brain research and the law. *Current Directions in Psychological Science, 22,* 158–161.

Borges, G., Nock, M. K., Abad, J. M. H., Hwang, I., Sampson, N. A., Alonso, J., . . . Kessler, R. C. (2010). Twelve-month prevalence of and risk factors for suicide attempts in the WHO world mental health surveys. *Journal of Clinical Psychiatry, 71,* 1617–1628.

Boring, E. G. (1953). A history of introspection. *Psychological Bulletin, 50,* 169–189.

Born, J., Rasch, B., & Gais, S. (2006). Sleep to remember. *Neuroscientist, 12,* 410–424.

Bornstein, R. F. (2005). Reconnecting psychoanalysis to mainstream psychology: Challenges and opportunities. *Psychoanalytic Psychology, 22,* 323–340.

Borra, J. E. (2005). Roper v. Simmons. *Journal of Gender, Social Policy, & the Law, 13,* 707–715.

Bottos, S. H., & Dewey, D. (2004). Perfectionists' appraisal of daily hassles and chronic headache. *Headache, 44,* 772–779.

Bouton, M. E., Mineka, S., & Barlow, D. H. (2001). A modern learning theory perspective on the etiology of panic disorder. *Psychological Review, 108,* 4–32.

Bowden, C. L., Calabrese, J. R., McElroy, S. L., Gyulai, L., Wassef, A., Petty, F., . . . Wozniak, P. J. (2000). A randomized, placebo-controlled 12-month trial of divalproex and lithium in treatment of outpatients with bipolar I disorder. *Archives of General Psychiatry, 57,* 481–489.

Bower, G. H., Clark, M. C., Lesgold, A. M., & Winzenz, D. (1969). Hierarchical retrieval schemes and recall of categorized word lists. *Journal of Verbal Learning and Verbal Behavior, 8,* 323–343.

Bower, G. H., Gilligan, S. G., & Menteiro, K. P. (1981). Selectivity of learning caused by affective states. *Journal of Experimental Psychology: General, 110,* 451–473.

Bower, J. M., & Parsons, L. M. (2003, July 14). Rethinking "the lesser brain." *Scientific American, 289,* 51–57. Retrieved from http://www.scientificamerican.com/article.cfm?id=rethinking-the-lesser-bra

Bowers, J. S., Mattys, S. L., & Gage, S. H. (2009). Preserved implicit knowledge of a forgotten childhood language. *Psychological Science, 20,* 1064–1069.

Bowman, L. L., Levine, L. E., Waite, B. M., & Gendron, M. (2010). Can students really multitask? An experimental study of instant messaging while reading. *Computers & Education, 54,* 927–931.

Bradley, L. A. (2011). Culture, gender and clothing. *Paideusis-Journal for Interdisciplinary and Cross-Cultural Studies, 5,* A1–A6.

Brain Observatory. (2013). *Deconstructing Henry: The re-examination of the brain of patient H.M.* University of San Diego. Retrieved from http://thebrainobservatory.ucsd.edu/hm

Branan, N. (2010). Murder, she wrote. *Scientific American Mind, 20,* 17. doi: 10.1038/scientificamericanmind0110-17b

Brand, B. L., Classen, C. C., McNary, S. W., & Zaveri, P. (2009). A review of dissociative disorders treatment studies. *Journal of Nervous and Mental Disorders, 197,* 646–654.

Brandone, A. C., Salkind, S. J., Golinkoff, R. M., & Hirsh-Pasek, K. (2006). Language development. In G. G. Bear & K. M. Minke (Eds.), *Children's needs: III. Development, prevention, and intervention* (pp. 499–514). Washington, DC: National Association of School Psychologists.

Brandt, J., & Benedict, R. H. B. (1993). Assessment of retrograde amnesia: Findings with a new public events procedure. *Neuropsychology, 7,* 217–227.

Brascamp, J. W., Blake, R., & Kristjánsson, Á. (2011). Deciding where to attend: Priming of pop-out drives target selection. *Journal of Experimental Psychology: Human Perception and Performance, 37,* 1700–1707.

Breazeal, C., & Scassellati, B. (2002). Robots that imitate humans. *Trends in Cognitive Sciences, 6,* 481–487.

Breland, K., & Breland, M. (1951). A field of applied animal psychology. *American Psychologist, 6,* 202–204.

Breland, K., & Breland, M. (1961). The misbehavior of organisms. *American Psychologist, 16,* 681–684.

Brendgen, M., Dionne, G., Girard, A., Boivin, M., Vitaro, F., & Pérusse, D. (2005). Examining genetic and environmental effects on social aggression: A study of 6-year-old twins. *Child Development, 76,* 930–946.

Brent, R. L., (2004). Environmental causes of human congenital malformations: The pediatrician's role in dealing with these complex clinical problems caused by a multiplicity of environmental and genetic factors. *Pediatrics, 113,* 957–968.

Breus, M. J. (2009, May 6). Are you fooling yourself? [Huffpost Healthy Living]. *Huffington Post.* Retrieved from http://www.huffingtonpost.com/dr-michael-j-breus/are-you-fooling-yourself_b_198525.html

Brewster, K. L., & Tillman, K. H. (2008). Who's doing it? Patterns and predictors of youths' oral sexual experiences. *Journal of Adolescent Health, 42,* 73–80.

Bridge, H., Harrold, S., Holmes, E. A., Stokes, M., & Kennard, C. (2012). Vivid visual mental imagery in the absence of the primary visual cortex. *Journal of Neurology, 259,* 1062–1070.

Briggs, K. C., & Myers, I. B. (1998). *Myers–Briggs type indicator.* Palo Alto, CA: Consulting Psychologists Press.

Broadbelt, K. G., Paterson, D. S., Rivera, K. D., Trachtenberg, F. L., & Kinney, H. C. (2010). Neuroanatomic relationships between the GABAergic and serotonergic systems in the developing human medulla. *Autonomic Neuroscience: Basic & Clinical, 154,* 30–41.

Broderick, A. C., Coyne, M. S., Fuller, W. J., Glen, F., & Godley, B. J. (2007). Fidelity and over-wintering of sea turtles. *Proceedings of the Royal Society B: Biological Sciences, 274,* 1533–1538.

Brody, S. (2010). The relative health benefits of different sexual activities. *Journal of Sexual Medicine, 7,* 1336–1361.

Brody, S., & Costa, R. M. (2009). Satisfaction (sexual, life, relationship, and mental health) is associated directly with penile–vaginal intercourse, but inversely with other sexual behavior frequencies. *Journal of Sexual Medicine, 6,* 1947–1954.

Brogaard, P., & Marlow, K. (2012, December 11). Kim Peek, the real rain man. *Psychology Today.* Retrieved from http://www.psychologytoday.com/blog/the-superhuman-mind/201212/kim-peek-the-real-rain-man

Brotto, L. A. (2010). The *DSM* diagnostic criteria for hypoactive sexual desire disorder in men. *Journal of Sex Medicine, 7,* 2015–2030.

Brown, A. S., & Nix, L. A. (1996). Age-related changes in the tip-of-the-tongue experience. *American Journal of Psychology, 109,* 79–91.

Brown, A. S., & Patterson, P. H. (2011). Maternal infection and schizophrenia: Implications for prevention. *Schizophrenia Bulletin, 37,* 284–290.

Brown, P. K., & Wald, G. (1964). Visual pigments in single rods and cones of the human retina. *Science, 144,* 45.

Brown, R., & Kulik, J. (1977). Flashbulb memories. *Cognition, 5,* 73–99.

Brown, S. L, Nesse, R. M., Vinokur, A. D., & Smith, D. M. (2003). Providing social support may be more beneficial than receiving it: Results from a prospective study of mortality. *Psychological Science, 14,* 320–327.

Brown, T. T., & Dobs, A. S. (2002). Endocrine effects of marijuana. *Journal of Clinical Pharmacology, 42,* 90S–96S.

Brownell, P. (2010). *Gestalt therapy: A guide to contemporary practice.* New York: Springer.

Bruck, D., & Ball, M. (2007). Optimizing emergency awakening to audible smoke alarms: An update. *Human Factors, 49,* 1–17.

Brunstein, J. C. (1993). Personal goals and subjective well-being: A longitudinal study. *Journal of Personality and Social Psychology, 65,* 1061–1070.

Bryan, A., Hutchison, K. E., Seals, D. R., & Allen, D. L. (2007). A transdisciplinary model integrating genetic, physiological, and psychological, psychological correlates of voluntary exercise. *Health Psychology, 26,* 30–39.

Bryan, S. M. (2012, January 28). Wolves' senses tapped to keep them clear of cattle. *Bangor Dailey News.* Retrieved from http://bangordailynews.com/2012/01/28/outdoors/wolves-senses-tapped-to-keep-them-clear-of-cattle

Buchanan, T. W., Tranel, D., & Adolphs, R. (2004). Anteromedial temporal lobe damage blocks startle modulation by fear and disgust. *Behavioral Neuroscience, 188,* 429–437.

Buck, L. B. (2004). Olfactory receptors and odor coding in mammals. *Nutrition Reviews, 62,* S184–S188.

Buck, R. (1980). Nonverbal behavior and the theory of emotion: The facial feedback hypothesis. *Journal of Personality and Social Psychology, 38,* 811–824.

Buffardi, L. E., & Campbell, W. K. (2008). Narcissism and social networking web sites. *Personality and Social Psychology Bulletin, 34,* 1303–1314

Bui, N. H. (2012). False consensus in attitudes toward celebrities. *Psychology of Popular Media Culture, 1,* 236–243. doi: 10.1037/a0028569

Bulpitt, C. J., Markowe, H. L. J., & Shipley, M. J. (2001). Why do some people look older than they should? *Postgraduate Medical Journal, 77,* 578–581.

Bureau of Labor Statistics, U.S. Department of Labor. (2012–2013). *Occupational outlook handbook.* Retrieved from http://www.bls.gov/ooh

Burgaleta, M., Head, K., Álvarez-Linera, J., Martínez, K., Escorial, S., Haier, R., & Colom, R. (2012). Sex differences in brain volume are related to specific skills, not to general intelligence. *Intelligence, 40,* 60–68.

Burger, J. M. (2009). Replicating Milgram: Would people still obey today? *American Psychologist, 64,* 1–11.

Burger, J. M. (2011). *Personality* (8th ed.). Belmont, CA: Wadsworth, Cengage Learning.

Burkley, M. (2012, January 3). Is Lisbeth Salander a psychopath? *Psychology Today.* Retrieved from http://www.psychologytoday.com/blog/the-social-thinker/201201/is-lisbeth-salander-psychopath

Burlingame, G. M., & Baldwin, S. (2011). Group therapy. In J. C. Norcross, G. R. VandenBos, & D. K. Freedheim (Eds.), *History of psychotherapy: Continuity and change* (2nd ed., pp. 505–515). Washington, DC: American Psychological Association.

Burnette, J. L., Pollack, J. M., & Forsyth, D. R. (2011). Leadership in extreme contexts: A groupthink analysis of the May 1996 Mount Everest disaster. *Journal of Leadership Studies, 4,* 29–40.

Burstein, A. G., & Loucks, S. (1989). *Rorschach's test: Scoring and interpretation.* New York: Hemisphere.

Burton, H. (2003). Visual cortex activity in early and late blind people. *Journal of Neuroscience, 23,* 4005–4011.

Bushman, B. J., Wang, M. C., & Anderson, C. A. (2005). Is the curve relating temperature to aggression linear or curvilinear? Assaults and temperature in Minneapolis reexamined. *Journal of Personality and Social Psychology, 89,* 62–66. Retrieved from http://www-personal.umich.edu/~bbushman/BWA05a.pdf

Buss, D. M. (1989). Sex differences in human mate preferences: Evolutionary hypotheses tested in 37 cultures. *Behavioral and Brain Sciences, 12,* 1–14

Buss, D. M. (1995). Psychological sex differences: Origins through sexual selection. *American Psychologist, 50,* 164–168.

Buss, D. M., Shackelford, T. K., Kirkpatrick, L. A., & Larsen, R. J. (2001). A half century of mate preferences: The cultural evolution of values. *Journal of Marriage and Family, 63,* 491–503.

Buss, L., Tolstrup, J., Munk, C., Bergholt, T., Ottensen, B., Grønbæk, M., & Kjaer, S. K. (2006). Spontaneous abortion: A prospective cohort study of younger women from the general population in Denmark. Validation, occurrence and risk determinants. *Acta Obstetricia et Gynecologic, 85,* 467–475.

Bussey, K., & Bandura, A. (1999). Social cognitive theory of gender development and differentiation. *Psychological Review, 106,* 676–713.

Butcher, J. N., & Rouse, S. V. (1996). Personality: Individual differences and clinical assessment. *Annual Review of Psychology, 47,* 87–111.

Butler, R. A. (1960). Acquired drives and the curiosity-investigative motives. In R. H. Waters, D. A. Rethlingshafer, & W. E. Caldwell (Eds.), *Principles of comparative psychology* (pp. 144–176). New York: McGraw-Hill.

Byers, E. S. (2011). Beyond the birds and the bees and was it good for you?: Thirty years of research on sexual communication. *Canadian Psychology, 52,* 20–28.

Bynum, H. (2007). Anesthesia and the practice of medicine: Historical perspectives. *Journal of the American Medical Association, 298,* 2551–2552.

Cabanatuan, M., & Sebastian, S. (2005, October 19). Surfer fights off shark, escapes with bitten leg. *SFGate.com.* Retrieved from http://articles.sfgate.com/2005-10-19/news/17396469_1_salmon-creek-beach-shark-deputies

Cáceres, C., Konda, K., Pecheny, M., Chatterjee, A., & Lyerla, R. (2006). Estimating the number of men who have sex with men in low and middle income countries. *Sexually Transmitted Infections, 82* (Suppl. 3), iii3–iii9.

Cahill, L. (2012). His brain, her brain. *Scientific American Classics Mind, 1,* 40–47.

Caldicott, D. G., Mahajani R., & Kuhn M. (2001). The anatomy of a shark attack: A case report and review of the literature. *Injury, 32,* 445–453.

Callan, M. J., Ferguson, H. J., & Bindemann, M. (2013). Eye movements to audiovisual scenes reveal expectations of a just world. *Journal of Experimental Psychology: General, 142,* 34–40. doi: 10.1037/a0028261

Campbell, A. (1999). Staying alive: Evolution, culture, and women's intrasexual aggression. *Behavioral and Brain Sciences, 22,* 203–252.

Campbell, G. A., & Rosner, M. H. (2008). The agony of ecstasy: MDMA (3, 4-Methylenedioxymethamphetamine) and the kidney. *Clinical Journal of the American Society of Nephrology, 3,* 1852–1860.

Canli, T., Amin, Z., Haas, B., Omura, K., & Constable, R. T. (2004). A double dissociation between mood states and personality traits in the anterior cingulate. *Behavioral Neuroscience, 118,* 897–904.

Cannon, D. S., Baker, T. B., Gino, A., & Nathan, P. E. (1986). Alcohol-aversion therapy: Relation between strength of aversion and abstinence. *Journal of Consulting and Clinical Psychology, 54,* 825–830.

Cannon, W. B. (1927). The James–Lange theory of emotions: A critical examination and an alternative theory. *American Journal of Psychology, 39,* 106–124.

Cannon, W. B., & Washburn, A. L. (1912). An explanation of hunger. *American Journal of Physiology, 29,* 441–454.

Cantero, J. L., Atienza, M., Salas, R. M., & Gómez, C. M. (1999). Alpha EEG coherence in different brain states: An electrophysiological index of the arousal level in human subjects. *Neuroscience Letters, 271,* 167–170.

Card, N. A., Stucky, B. D., Sawalani, G. M., & Little, T. D. (2008). Direct and indirect aggression during childhood and adolescence: A meta-analytic review of gender differences, intercorrelations, and relations to maladjustment. *Child Development, 79,* 1185–1229.

Carey, B. (2008, December 4). H.M., an unforgettable amnesiac, dies at 82. *The New York Times.* Retrieved from http://www.nytimes.com/2008/12/05/us/05hm.html?pagewanted=all&_r=0

Carlsson, K., Petersson, K. M., Lundqvist, D., Karlsson, A., Ingvar, M., & Öhman, A. (2004). Fear and the amygdala: Manipulation of awareness generates differential cerebral responses to phobic and fear-relevant (but nonfeared) stimuli. *Emotion, 4,* 340–353.

Carnegie Mellon University. (2013). *Carnegie Mellon Robotic Performance Company presents Tank: Roboceptionist.* Retrieved from http://roboceptionist.org/index.htm

Carnevale, A. P., Rose, S. J., & Cheah, B. (2011). *The college payoff: Education, occupations, lifetime earnings.* Georgetown University Center on Education and the Workforce. Retrieved from http://www9.georgetown.edu/grad/gppi/hpi/cew/pdfs/collegepayoff-summary.pdf

Carpenter, C. J. (2012). Narcissism on Facebook: Self-promotional and anti-social behavior. *Personality and Individual Differences, 52,* 482–486

Carr, P. B., Dweck, C. S., & Pauker, K. (2012). "Prejudiced" behavior without prejudice? Beliefs about the malleability of prejudice affect interracial interactions. *Journal of Personality and Social Psychology, 103,* 452–471.

Carskadon, M. A., Labyak, S. E., Acebo, C., & Seifer, R. (1999). Intrinsic circadian period of adolescent humans measured in conditions of forced desynchrony. *Neuroscience Letters, 260,* 129–132.

Carstensen, L. L., Turan, B., Scheibe, S., Ram, N., Ersner-Hershfield, H., Samanez-Larkin, G. R., . . . Nesselroade, J. R. (2011). Emotional experience improves with age: Evidence based on over 10 years of experience sampling. *Psychology and Aging, 26,* 21–33.

Carter, C. J. (2007). eIF2B and oligodendrocyte survival: Where nature and nurture meet in bipolar disorder and schizophrenia? *Schizophrenia Bulletin, 33,* 1343–1353.

Carter Center. (2013). *Development of mental health services in Liberia.* Retrieved from http://www.cartercenter.org/resources/pdfs/factsheets/mental-health-liberia-facts.pdf

Caruso, R. (2007, August 13). Why does it take so long for our vision to adjust to a darkened theater after we come in from bright sunlight? *Scientific American Online.* Retrieved from http://www.scientificamerican.com/article.cfm?id=experts-eyes-adjust-to-darkness

Case, B. G., Bertollo, D. N., Laska, E. M., Price, L. H., Siegel, C. E., Olfson, M., & Marcus, S. C. (2013). Declining use of electroconvulsive therapy in United States general hospitals. *Biological Psychiatry, 73,* 119–126.

Caspani, M. (2012, January 23). Somalia food crisis recovery will take two years? ICRC. *Thomson Reuters Foundation.* Retrieved from http://www.trust.org/item/?map=somalia-food-crisis-recovery-will-take-two-years-icrc

Caspi, A., Roberts, B. W., & Shiner, R. L. (2005). Personality development: Stability and change. *Annual Review of Psychology, 56,* 453–484.

Cassidy, J. (2001). Truth, lies, and intimacy: An attachment perspective. *Attachment & Human Development, 3,* 121–155.

Castel, A. D., Humphreys, K. L., Lee, S. S., Galván, A., Balota, D. A., & McCabe, D. P. (2011). The development of memory efficiency and value-directed remembering across the life span: A cross-sectional study of memory and selectivity. *Developmental Psychology, 47,* 1553–1564.

Castellanos, M., Sobrino, T., Pedraza, S., Moldes, O., Pumar, J. M., Silva, Y., . . . Dávalos, A. (2008). High plasma glutamate concentrations are associated with infarct growth in acute ischemic stroke. *Neurology, 71,* 1862–1868.

Catalino, L. I., & Fredrickson, B. L. (2011). A Tuesday in the life of a flourisher: The role of positive emotional reactivity in optimal mental health. *Emotion, 11,* 938–950.

Cattell, R. B. (1950). *Personality: A systematic theoretical and factual study.* New York: McGraw-Hill.

Cattell, R. B. (1973a). *Personality and mood by questionnaire.* San Francisco: Jossey-Bass.

Cattell, R. B. (1973b). Personality pinned down. *Psychology Today, 7,* 40–46.

Cattell, R. B., Eber, H. W., & Tatsuoka, M. M. (1970). *Handbook for the sixteen personality factor questionnaire (16PF).* Champaign, IL: Institute for Personality and Ability Testing.

Cavallini, A., Fazzi, E., Viviani, V., Astori, M. G., Zaverio, S., Bianchi, P. E., & Lanzi, G. (2002). Visual acuity in the first two years of life in healthy term newborns: An experience with the teller acuity cards. *Functional Neurology, 17,* 87–92.

CBC News. (2004, May 10). *David Reimer: The boy who lived as a girl.* Retrieved from http://www.cbc.ca/news/background/reimer/

CBS News. (2011, February 11). *Chilean miners rescued, but were they saved?* Retrieved from http://www.cbsnews.com/stories/2011/02/10/60minutes/main7337759_page3.shtml

CBS News (2011, July 26). *Shark survivor girl: "I like dolphins way better."* Retrieved from http://www.cbsnews.com/stories/2011/07/26/earlyshow/living/petplanet/main20083393.shtml

CBS News/AP. (2010, October 12). *Florencio Avalos: The first miner chosen.* Retrieved from http://www.cbsnews.com/stories/2010/10/12/world/main6951753.shtml

CBS News/AP (2010, October 16). *Miners' fistfights, despair during ordeal.* Retrieved from http://www.cbsnews.com/stories/2010/10/15/earlyshow/main6961011.shtml

Ceci, S., & Williams, W. M. (2009). Yes: The scientific truth must be pursued. *Nature, 457,* 788–789.

Centers for Disease Control and Prevention. (2004). Alcohol-attributable deaths and years of potential life lost—United States, 2001. *Morbidity and Mortality Weekly Report, 53,* 866–870.

Centers for Disease Control and Prevention. (2008a). *Nationally representative CDC study finds 1 in 4 teenage girls has a sexually transmitted disease* [Press release]. Retrieved from http://www.cdc.gov/stdconference/2008/press/release-11march2008.htm

Centers for Disease Control and Prevention. (2008b). Smoking-attributable mortality, years of potential life lost, and productivity losses—United States, 2000–2004. *Morbidity and Mortality Weekly Report, 57,* 1226–1228.

Centers for Disease Control and Prevention. (2010). Vital signs: Current cigarette smoking among adults aged ≥18 Years—United States, 2009. *Morbidity and Mortality Weekly Report, 59,* 1135–1140.

Centers for Disease Control and Prevention. (2011, February 11). *Effects of blood alcohol concentration (BAC).* Retrieved February 20, 2013, from http://www.cdc.gov/Motorvehiclesafety/Impaired_Driving/bac.html

Centers for Disease Control and Prevention. (2012a). *Chlamydia* [Fact sheet]. Retrieved from http://www.cdc.gov/std/chlamydia/STDFact-chlamydia-detailed.htm

Centers for Disease Control and Prevention. (2012b). *Genital herpes* [Fact sheet]. Retrieved from http://www.cdc.gov/std/Herpes/STDFact-Herpes.htm

Centers for Disease Control and Prevention. (2012c). *Genital HPV infection* [Fact sheet]. Retrieved from http://www.cdc.gov/std/HPV/STDFact-HPV.htm

Centers for Disease Control and Prevention. (2012d). *Gonorrhea* [Fact sheet]. Retrieved from http://www.cdc.gov/std/gonorrhea/STDFact-gonorrhea.htm

Centers for Disease Control and Prevention. (2012e). *Health effects of secondhand smoke* [Fact sheet]. Retrieved from http://www.cdc.gov/tobacco/data_statistics/fact_sheets/secondhand_smoke/health_effects/

Centers for Disease Control and Prevention (CDC). (2012f). *Sexually transmitted disease surveillance 2011.* Retrieved from http://www.cdc.gov/std/stats11/

Centers for Disease Control and Prevention. (2012g). Short Sleep Duration Among Workers—United States, 2010. *Morbidity and Mortality Weekly Report, 61*(16). Retrieved from http://www.cdc.gov/mmwr/pdf/wk/mm6116.pdf

Centers for Disease Control and Prevention. (2012h). *Syphilis* [Fact sheet]. Retrieved from http://www.cdc.gov/std/syphilis/STDFact-Syphilis.htm

Centers for Disease Control and Prevention. (2012i). *Understanding suicide* [Fact sheet]. Retrieved from http://www.cdc.gov/violenceprevention/pdf/suicide_factsheet_2012-a.pdf

Centers for Disease Control and Prevention. (2013). *Incidence, prevalence, and cost of sexually transmitted infections in the United States* [Fact sheet]. Retrieved from http://www.cdc.gov/std/stats/STI-Estimates-Fact-Sheet-Feb-2013.pdf

Centers for Disease Control and Prevention, National Center for Injury Prevention and Control. (2010). *Injury prevention & control, data & statistics.* Retrieved from http://www.cdc.gov/injury/wisqars/pdf/10LCID_All_Deaths_By_Age_Group_2010-a.pdf

Centola, D. (2010). The spread of behavior in an online social network experiment. *Science, 329,* 1194–1197.

Cerny, J. A., & Janssen, E. (2011). Patterns of sexual arousal in homosexual, bisexual, and heterosexual men. *Archives of Sexual Behavior, 40,* 687–697.

Cervilla, J. A., Prince, M., Joels, S., Lovestone, S., & Mann, A. (2000). Long-term predictors of cognitive outcome in a cohort of older people with hypertension. *British Journal of Psychiatry, 177,* 66–71.

Chaiken, S., & Eagly, A. H. (1976). Communication modality as a determinant of message persuasiveness and message comprehensibility. *Journal of Personality and Social Psychology, 34,* 605–614.

Chaimay, B. (2011). Influence of breastfeeding practices on children's cognitive development—Systematic review. *Asia Journal of Public Health, 2,* 40–44.

Champagne, F. A., & Mashoodh, R. (2009). Genes in context: Gene–environment interplay and the origins of individual differences in behavior. *Current Directions in Psychological Science, 18,* 127–131.

Chandrashekar, J., Hoon, M. A., Ryba, N. J., & Zuker, C. S. (2006). The receptors and cells for mammalian taste. *Nature, 444,* 288–294.

Charlton, B., & Verghese, A. (2010). Caring for Ivan Ilyich. *Journal of General Internal Medicine, 25,* 93–95.

Chawla, D., Agarwal, R., Deorari, A., Paul, V. K., Chandra, P., & Azad, R. V. (2012). Retinopathy of prematurity. *Indian Journal of Pediatrics, 79,* 501–509.

Chechik, G., Meilijson, I., & Ruppin, E. (1998). Synaptic pruning in development: A computational account. *Neural Computation, 10,* 1759–1777.

Cheng, C., Cheung, S.-f., Chio, J. H.-m., & Chan, M.-p. S. (2013). Cultural meaning of perceived control: A meta-analysis of locus of control and psychological symptoms across 18 cultural regions. *Psychological Bulletin, 139,* 152–188. doi: 10.1037/a0028596

Cheng, D. T., Knight, D. C., Smith, C. N., & Helmstetter, F. J. (2006). Human amygdala activity during the expression of fear responses. *Behavioral Neuroscience, 120,* 1187–1195.

Cherney, I. D. (2008). Mom, let me play more computer games: They improve my mental rotation skills. *Sex Roles, 59,* 776–786.

Cheyne, J. A. (2002). Situational factors affecting sleep paralysis and associated hallucinations: Position and timing effects. *Journal of Sleep Research, 11,* 169–177.

Cheyne, J. A., Newby-Clark, I. R., & Rueffer, S. D. (1999). Relations among hypnagogic and hypnopompic experiences associated with sleep paralysis. *Journal of Sleep Research, 8,* 313–317.

Chiao, J. Y., Iidka, T., Gordon, H. L., Nogawa, J., Bar, M., Aminoff, E., . . . Ambady, N. (2008). Cultural specificity in amygdala response to fear faces. *Journal of Cognitive Neuroscience, 20,* 2167–2174.

Child Mind Institute. (2010a, October 11). *Orlando Bloom offers advice to kids who have dyslexia* [Video file]. Retrieved from http://www.youtube.com/watch?v=WDBVsghh4z0

Child Mind Institute. (2010b, October 11). *Orlando Bloom on dyslexia.* Retrieved from http://www.childmind.org/en/posts/articles/2010-10-18-orlando-bloom-on-growing-up-with-dyslexia

Child Mind Institute. (2010c, October 11). *Orlando Bloom on reading as a child* [Video file]. Retrieved from http://www.youtube.com/watch?v=vap_feUX3rw&feature=relmfu

Child Mind Institute. (2010d, October 11). *Orlando Bloom on some of the challenges he faced at school* [Video file]. Retrieved from http://www.youtube.com/watch?v=s-2RRKKs-9w

Chin, H. B., Sipe, T. A., Elder, R., Mercer, S. L., Chattopadhyay, S. K., Jacob, V., . . . Santelli, J. (2012). The effectiveness of group-based comprehensive risk-reduction and abstinence education interventions to prevent or reduce the risk of adolescent pregnancy, human immunodeficiency virus, and sexually transmitted infections: Two systematic reviews for the Guide to Community Preventive Services. *American Journal of Preventive Medicine, 42,* 272–294.

Chirawatkul, S., Prakhaw, P., & Chomnirat, W. (2011). Perceptions of depression among people of Khon Kaen City: A gender perspective. *Journal of Nursing Science & Health, 34,* 66–75.

Chivers, M. L., Seto, M. C., Lalumiere, M. L., Laan, E., & Grimbos, T. (2010). Agreement of self-reported and genital measures of sexual arousal in men and women: A meta-analysis. *Archives of Sexual Behavior, 39,* 5–56.

Cho, H. J., Meira-Lima, I., Cordeiro, Q., Michelon, L., Sham, P., Vallada, H., & Collie., D. A. (2005). Population-based and family-based studies on the serotonin transporter gene polymorphisms and bipolar disorder: A systematic review and meta-analysis. *Molecular Psychiatry, 10,* 771–781.

Choi, C. (2007, May 24). Strange but true: When half a brain is better than a whole one. *Scientific American Online.* Retrieved from http://www.scientificamerican.com/article.cfm?id=strange-but-true-when-half-brain-better-than-whole

Choi, C. Q. (2008, March). Do you need only half your brain? *Scientific American, 298,* 104.

Chomsky, N. (1959). Verbal behavior. *Language, 35,* 26–58.

Chomsky, N. (2000). *New horizons in the study of language and mind.* Cambridge, UK: Cambridge University Press.

Christakis, D. A., Garrison, M. M., Herrenkohl, T., Haggerty, K., Rivara, F. P., Zhou, C., & Liekweg, K. (2013). Modifying media content for preschool children: A randomized controlled trial. *Pediatrics, 131,* 431–438.

Chua, A. (2011, January 8). Why Chinese mothers are superior. *The Wall Street Journal.* Retrieved from http://online.wsj.com/article/SB10001424052748704111504576059713528698754.html

Chung, F., & Elsaid, H. (2009). Screening for obstructive sleep apnea before surgery: Why is it important? *Current Opinion in Anesthesiology, 22,* 405–411.

Cialdini, R. B., & Goldstein, N. J. (2004). Social influence: Compliance and conformity. *Annual Review of Psychology, 55,* 591–621.

Cisler, J. M., Brady, R. E., Olatunji, B. O., & Lohr, J. M. (2010). Disgust and obsessive beliefs in contamination-related OCD. *Cognitive Therapy Research, 34,* 439–448

Clapp, W. C., Rubens, M. T., Sabharwal, J., & Gazzaley, A. (2011). Deficit in switching between functional brain networks underlies the impact of multitasking on working memory in older adults. *Proceedings of the National Academy of Sciences, 108,* 7212–7217

Clark, D. M., Ehlers, A., Hackmann, A., McManus, F., Fennell, M., Grey, N., . . . Wild, J. (2006). Cognitive therapy versus exposure and applied relaxation in social phobia: A randomized controlled trial. *Journal of Consulting and Clinical Psychology, 74,* 568–578.

Clark, D. M., Salkovskis, P. M., Öst, L-G., Breitholtz, E., Koehler, K. A., Westling, B. E., . . . Gelder, M. (1997). Misinterpretation of body sensations in panic disorder. *Journal of Consulting and Clinical Psychology, 65,* 203–213.

Clay, Z., & Zuberbühler, K. (2012). Communication during sex among female bonobos: Effects of dominance, solicitation and audience. *Scientific Reports, 2,* Article 291. Retrieved from http://www.ncbi.nlm.nih.gov/pmc/articles/PMC3291041/

Clemente, M., Espinosa, P., & Vidal, M. Á. (2008). The media and violent behavior in young people: Effects of the media on antisocial aggressive behavior in a Spanish sample. *Journal of Applied Social Psychology, 38,* 2395–2409.

Coan, J. A. (2010). Emergent ghosts of the emotion machine. *Emotion Review, 2,* 274–285.

Cochrane, R. E., Tett, R. P., & Vandecreek, L. (2003). Psychological testing and the selection of police officers: A national survey. In C. R. Bartol & A. M. Bartol (Eds.), *Current perspectives in forensic psychology and criminal justice* (pp. 25–34). Thousand Oaks, CA: Sage.

Cohen, D. (2011). Applied knowledge: NASA aids the Chilean rescue effort. *ASK Magazine, 41,* 5–9.

Cohen, D. A., Wang, W., Wyatt, J. K., Kronauer, R. E., Dijk, D. J., Czeisler, C. A., & Klerman, E. B. (2010). Uncovering residual effects of chronic sleep loss on human performance. *Science Translational Medicine, 13,* 14ra3.

Cohen, H. W., Gibson, G., & Alderman, M. H. (2000). Excess risk of myocardial infarction in patients treated with antidepressant medications: Association with use of tricyclic agents. *American Journal of Medicine, 108,* 2–8.

Cohen, J. (2013, March 18). Gay marriage support hits new high in Post-ABC poll. *The Washington Post.* Retrieved from: http://www.washingtonpost.com/blogs/the-fix/wp/2013/03/18/gay-marriage-support-hits-new-high-in-post-abc-poll/

Cohen, S., Doyle, W., Frank, E., Gwaltney, J. M. Jr., Rabin, B. S., & Skoner, D. P. (1998). Types of stressors that increase susceptibility to the common cold in healthy adults. *Health Psychology, 17,* 214–223.

Cohen, S., Kamarck, T., & Mermelstein, R. (1983). A global measure of perceived stress. *Journal of Health and Social Behavior, 24,* 385–396.

Cohen, S., Miller, G. E., & Rabin, B. S. (2001). Psychological stress and antibody response to immunization: A critical review of the human literature. *Psychosomatic Medicine, 63,* 7–18.

Colapinto, J. (2000). *As nature made him: The boy who was raised as a girl.* New York: HarperCollins.

Cole, C. F., Labin, D. B., & del Rocio Galarza, M. (2008). Begin with the children: What research on *Sesame Street's* international coproductions reveals about using media to promote a new more peaceful world. *International Journal of Behavioral Development, 32*(4), 359–365.

Collins, D. W., & Kimura, D. (1997). A large sex difference on a two-dimensional mental rotation task. *Behavioral Neuroscience, 111,* 845–849.

Collins, P. A., & Gibbs, A. C. C. (2003). Stress in police officers: A study of the origins, prevalence and severity of stress-related symptoms within a county police force. *Occupational Medicine, 53,* 256–264.

Colrain, I. M. (2005). The k-complex: A 7-decade history. *SLEEP, 28,* 255–273.

Compton, W. M., Grant, B. F., Colliver, J. D., Glantz, M. D., & Stinson, F. S. (2004). Prevalence of marijuana use disorders in the United States: 1991–1992 and 2001–2002. *Journal of the American Medical Association, 291,* 2114–2121.

Cone, B. K., Wake, M., Tobin, S., Poulakis, Z., & Rickards, F. W. (2010). Slight–mild sensorineural hearing loss in children: Audiometric, clinical, and risk factor profiles. *Ear and Hearing, 31,* 202–212.

Congdon, E., Service, S., Wessman, J., Seppänen, J. K., Schönauer, S., Miettunen, J., . . . Nelson B. (2012). Early environment and neurobehavioral development predict adult temperament clusters. *PLoS ONE, 7,* e38065. doi: 10.1371/journal.pone.0038065

Conley, A. M. (2012). Patterns of motivation beliefs: Combining achievement goal and expectancy-value perspectives. *Journal of Educational Psychology, 104,* 32–47.

Conley, T. D., Ziegler, A., Moors, A. C., Matsick, J. L., & Valentine, B. (2013). A critical examination of popular assumptions about the benefits and outcomes of monogamous relationships. *Personality and Social Psychology Review, 17,* 124–141.

Conway, M. A., Cohen, G., & Stanhope, N. (1991). On the very long-term retention of knowledge acquired through formal education: Twelve years of cognitive psychology. *Journal of Experimental Psychology: General, 120*, 395–409.

Copeland, W., Shanahan, L., Costello, J., & Angold, A. (2011). Cumulative prevalence of psychiatric disorders by young adulthood: A prospective cohort analysis from the Great Smoky Mountain Study. *Journal of the American Academy of Child & Adolescent Psychiatry, 50*, 252–261.

Copen, C. E., Daniels, K., Vespa, J., & Mosher, W. D. (2012). *First marriages in the United States: Data from the 2006–2010 National Survey of Family Growth.* Washington, DC: U.S. Department of Health and Human Services, Centers for Disease Control and Prevention, National Center for Health Statistics.

Corballis, P. M. (2003). Visuospatial processing and the right-hemisphere interpreter. *Brain and Cognition, 53*, 171–176.

Corballis, P. M., Funnell, M. G., & Gazzaniga, M. S. (2002). Hemispheric asymmetries for simple visual judgments in the split brain. *Neuropsychologia, 40*, 401–410.

Coren, S. (2008, October 20). Can dogs see colors? *Psychology Today.* Retrieved from http://www.psychologytoday.com/blog/canine-corner/200810/can-dogs-see-colors

Corey, G. (2013). *Theory and practice of counseling and psychotherapy* (9th ed.). Belmont, CA: Brooks/Cole, Cengage Learning.

Corkin, S. (2002). What's new with the amnesic patient H.M.? *Nature Reviews Neuroscience, 3*, 153–160.

Cornelius, S. W., & Caspi, A. (1987). Everyday problem solving in adulthood and old age. *Psychology and Aging, 2*, 144–153.

Correll, C. U., Leucht, S., & Kane, J. M. (2004). Lower risk for tardive dyskinesia associated with second-generation antipsychotics: A systematic review of 1-year studies. *American Journal of Psychiatry, 161*, 414–425.

Corrigan, P. (2005). How stigma interferes with mental health care. *American Psychologist, 59*, 614–625.

Corti, R., Binggeli, C., Sudano, I., Spieker, L., Hänseler, E., Ruschitzka, F., . . . Noll, G. (2002). Coffee acutely increases sympathetic nerve activity and blood pressure independently of caffeine content: Role of habitual versus nonhabitual drinking. *Circulation, 106*, 2935–2940.

Corwin, E. J., & Pajer, K. (2008). The psychoneuroimmunology of postpartum depression. *Journal of Women's Health, 17*, 1529–1534.

Costa, G. (2003). Shift work and occupational medicine: An overview. *Occupational Medicine, 53*, 83–88.

Costa, P. T. Jr., Terracciano, A., & McCrae, R. R. (2001). Gender differences in personality traits across cultures: Robust and surprising findings. *Journal of Personality and Social Psychology, 81*, 322–331.

Costandi, M. (2009, February 10). Where are old memories stored in the brain? *Scientific American Online.* Retrieved from http://www.scientificamerican.com/article.cfm?id=the-memory-trace

Costanzo, E. S., Lutgendorf, S. K., & Roeder, S. L. (2011). Common-sense beliefs about cancer and health practices among women completing treatment for breast cancer. *Psychooncology, 20*, 53–61.

Cotman, C. W., & Berchtold, N. C. (2002). Exercise: A behavioral intervention to enhance brain health and plasticity. *Trends in Neurosciences, 25*, 295–301.

Coulson, S., & Van Petten, C. (2007). A special role for the right hemisphere in metaphor comprehension? ERP evidence from hemifield presentation. *Brain Research, 1146*, 128–145.

Couperus, J. W. (2011). Perceptual load influences selective attention across development. *Developmental Psychology, 47*, 1431–1439.

Cowan, N. (1988). Evolving conceptions of memory storage, selective attention, and their mutual constraints within the human information-processing system. *Psychological Bulletin, 104*, 163–191.

Cowan, N. (2008). What are the differences between long-term, short-term, and working memory? *Progress in Brain Research, 169*, 323–338.

Cowan, N., Chen, Z., & Rouder, J. N. R. (2004). Constant capacity in an immediate serial-recall task a logical sequel to Miller (1956). *Psychological Science, 15*, 634–640.

Cowan, N., Nugent, L. D., & Elliott, E. M. (2000). Memory-search and rehearsal processes and the word length effect in immediate recall: A synthesis in reply to service. *Quarterly Journal of Experimental Psychology, 53*, 666–670.

Craddock, N., O'Donovan, M. C., & Owen, M. J. (2005). The genetics of schizophrenia and bipolar disorder: Dissecting psychosis. *Journal of Medical Genetics, 42*, 193–204.

Craik, F. I. M., & Lockhart, R. S. (1972). Levels of processing: A framework for memory research. *Journal of Verbal Learning and Verbal Behavior, 11*, 671–684.

Craik, F. I. M., & Tulving, E. (1975). Depth of processing and the retention of words in episodic memory. *Journal of Experimental Psychology, 104*, 268–294.

Cramer, P. (2000). Defense mechanisms in psychology today: Further processes for adaptation. *American Psychologist, 55*, 637–646.

Cramer, P. (2008). Identification and the development of competence: A 44-year longitudinal study from late adolescence to late middle age. *Psychology and Aging, 23*, 410–421.

Craske, M. G., Kircanski, K., Epstein, A., Wittchen, H.-U., Pine, D. S., Lewis-Fernández, . . . DSM–V Anxiety, OC Spectrum, Posttraumatic and Dissociative Disorder Work Group. (2010). Panic disorder: A review of *DSM–IV* panic disorder and proposals for *DSM–V. Depression and Anxiety, 27*, 93–112.

Craze, M., & Crooks, N. (2010, October 13). Chile is rescuing trapped miners through escape tube. *Bloomberg.com.* Retrieved from http://www.bloomberg.com/news/2010-10-13/chile-frees-first-of-33-miners-in-world-s-longest-underground-mine-rescue.html

Crick, N. R., & Grotpeter, J. K. (1995). Relational aggression, gender, and social-psychological adjustment. *Child Development, 66*, 710–722.

Croce, P. J. (2010). Reaching beyond Uncle William: A century of William James in theory and in life. *History of Psychology, 13*, 351–377.

Crooks, R., & Baur, K. (2014). *Our sexuality* (12th ed.). Belmont, CA: Wadsworth, Cengage Learning.

Crowell, S. E., Beauchaine, T. P., & Linehan, M. M. (2009). A biosocial developmental model of borderline personality: Elaborating and extending Linehan's theory. *Psychological Bulletin, 135*, 495–510.

Culbertson, J. (2009, October 15). Numerology number 33—The master healer. *Suite 101.com.* Retrieved from http://suite101.com/article/numerology-number-33-the-master-healer-a146089

Cunha, J. P., & Stöppler, M. C. (Eds.) (2011). Jetlag. *Medicine.net.com.* Retrieved from http://www.medicinenet.com/jet_lag/article.htm

Cunningham, M., & Cox, E. O. (2003). Hearing assessment in infants and children: Recommendations beyond neonatal screening. *Pediatrics, 111*, 436–440.

Cunningham, M. R., Shamblen, S. R., Barbee, A. P, & Ault, L. K. (2005). Social allergies in romantic relationships: Behavioral repetition, emotional sensitization, and dissatisfaction in dating couples. *Personal Relationships, 12*, 273–295.

Curtiss, S., Fromkin, V., Krashen, S., Rigler, D., & Rigler, M. (1974). The linguistic development of Genie. *Language, 50*, 528–554.

Cyna, A. M., McAuliffe, G. L., & Andrew, M. I. (2004). Hypnosis for pain relief in labour and childbirth: A systematic review. *British Journal of Anesthesia, 93*, 505–511.

Cynkar, A. (2007). The changing gender composition of psychology. *Monitor on Psychology, 38*, 46. Retrieved from http://www.apa.org/monitor/jun07/changing.aspx

Cyrzyk, T. (2013). Electroconvulsive therapy: Why it is still controversial. *Mental Health Practice, 16*, 22–27.

Czarnowski, C., Bailey, J., & Bal, S. (2007). Curare and a Canadian connection. *Canadian Family Physician, 53*, 1531–1532.

Czeisler, C. A., Duffy, J. F., Shanahan, T. L., Brown, E. N., Mitchell, J. F., Rimmer, D. W., . . . Kronauer, R. E. (1999). Stability, precision, and near-24-hour period of the human circadian pacemaker. *Science, 284,* 2177–2181.

Daffner, K. R., Chong, H., Riis, J., Rentz, D. M., Wolk, D. A., Budson, A. E., & Holcomb, P. J. (2007). Cognitive status impacts age-related changes in attention to novel and target events. *Neuropsychology, 21,* 291–300.

Dalrymple, T. (2012). *Jeremy Lin: The reason for the Linsanity.* New York: Center Street.

Dalton, P. H., Opiekun, R. E., Gould, M., McDermott, R., Wilson, T., Maute, C., . . . Moline, J. (2010, May 18). Chemosensory loss: Functional consequences of the World Trade Center disaster. *Environmental Health Perspectives, 118,* 1251–1256. doi: 10.1289/ehp.1001924

Damasio, A. R., Grabowski, T. J., Bechara, A., Damasio, H., Ponto, L. L. B., Parvizi, J., & Hichwa, R. D. (2000). Subcortical and cortical brain activity during the feeling of self-generated emotions. *Nature Neuroscience, 3,* 1049–1056.

Damasio, H., Grabowski, T., Frank, R., Galaburda, A. M., & Damasio, A. R. (1994). The return of Phineas Gage: Clues about the brain from the skull of a famous patient. *Science, 264,* 1102–1105.

D'Angiulli, A., Lipina, S. J., & Olesinska, A. (2012, September 6). Explicit and implicit issues in the developmental cognitive neuroscience of social inequality. *Frontiers in Human Neuroscience,* Article 254. Retrieved from http://www.ncbi.nlm.nih.gov/pmc/articles/PMC3434357/pdf/fnhum-06-00254.pdf

Dang-Vu, T. T., Schabus, M., Desseilles, M., Albouy, G., Boly, M., Darsaud, A., . . . Maquet, P. (2008). Spontaneous neural activity during human slow wave sleep. *Proceeding of the National Academy of Sciences, 105,* 15160–15165.

Danker, J. F., & Anderson, J. R. (2010). The ghosts of brain states past: Remembering reactivates the brain regions engaged during encoding. *Psychological Bulletin, 136,* 87–102.

Dapretto, M., Lee, S. S., & Caplan, R. (2005). A functional magnetic resonance imaging study of discourse coherence in typically developing children. *NeuroReport, 16,* 1661–1665.

Darcy, A. M., Doyle, A. C., Lock, J., Peebles, R., Doyle, P., & Le Grange, D. (2012). The eating disorders examination in adolescent males with anorexia nervosa: How does it compare to adolescent females? *International Journal of Eating Disorders, 45,* 110–114.

Darley, J. M., & Latané, B. (1968). Bystander intervention in emergencies: Diffusion of responsibility. *Journal of Personality and Social Psychology, 8,* 377–383.

Dar-Nimrod, I., & Heine, S. J. (2011). Genetic essentialism: On the deceptive determinism of DNA. *Psychological Bulletin, 137,* 800–818.

Darwin, C. (2002). *The expression of the emotions in man and animals.* New York: Oxford University Press. (Original work published 1872)

Davidson, A. R., & Jaccard, J. J. (1979). Variables that moderate the attitude–behavior relation: Results of a longitudinal survey. *Journal of Personality and Social Psychology, 37,* 1364–1376.

Davidson, R. J., Kabat-Zinn, J., Schumacher, J., Rosenkranz, M., Muller, D., Santorelli, S. F., . . . Sheridan, J. F. (2003). Alterations in brain and immune function produced by mindfulness meditation. *Psychosomatic Medicine, 65,* 564–570.

Davidson, R. J., & Lutz, A. (2008). Buddha's brain: Neuroplasticity and meditation. *IEEE Signal Process Magazine, 25,* 176–174.

Davidson, R. J., Scherer, K. R., & Goldsmith, H. H. (Eds.). (2002). *Handbook of affective sciences.* New York: Oxford University Press.

d'Avila, J., Lam, T., Bingham, D., Shi, J., Won, S., Kauppinen, T., . . . Swanson, R. (2012). Microglial activation induced by brain trauma is suppressed by post-injury treatment with a PARP inhibitor. *Journal of Neuroinflammation, 9,* 31–42.

Davis, E. P., & Sandman, C. A. (2010). The timing of prenatal exposure to maternal cortisol and psychosocial stress is associated with human infant cognitive development. *Child Development, 81,* 131–148.

Davis, M., & Whalen, P. J. (2001). The amygdala: Vigilance and emotion. *Molecular Psychiatry, 6,* 13–34.

Deary, I. J., Penke, L., & Johnson, W. (2010). The neuroscience of human intelligence differences. *Nature Reviews Neuroscience, 11,* 201–211.

de Boysson-Bardies, B., Halle, P., Sagart, L., & Durand, C. (1989). A cross-linguistic investigation of vowel formats in babbling. *Journal of Child Language, 16,* 1–17.

DeCasper, A. J., & Fifer, W. P. (1980). Of human bonding: Newborns prefer their mothers' voices. *Science, 208,* 1174–1176.

Deci, E. L., Koestner, R., & Ryan, R. M. (1999). A meta-analytic review of experiments examining the effects of extrinsic rewards on intrinsic motivation. *Psychological Bulletin, 125,* 627–668.

Deci, E. L., Koestner, R., & Ryan, R. M. (2001). Extrinsic rewards and intrinsic motivation in education: Reconsidered once again. *Review of Educational Research, 71,* 1–27.

Deci, E. L., & Ryan, R. M. (2008). Self-determination theory: A macrotheory of human motivation, development, and health. *Canadian Psychology, 49,* 182–185.

Deckers, L. (2005). *Motivation: Biological, psychological, and environmental* (2nd ed.). New York: Pearson.

Deeb, S. S. (2005). The molecular basis of variation in human color vision. *Clinical Genetics, 67,* 369–377.

Deer, B. (2011). How the case against the MMR vaccine was fixed. *British Medical Journal, 342,* c5347.

Deese, J., & Kaufman, R. A. (1957). Serial effects in recall of unorganized and sequentially organized verbal material. *Journal of Experimental Psychology, 54,* 180–187.

Degnan, K. A., Hane, A. A., Henderson, H. A., Moas, O. L., Reeb-Sutherland, B. C., & Fox, N. A. (2011). Longitudinal stability of temperamental exuberance and social-emotional outcomes in early childhood. *Developmental Psychology, 47,* 765–780.

DeGregory, L. (2008). The girl in the window. *Tampa Bay Times.* Retrieved from http://www.tampabay.com/specials/2008/reports/danielle/

de Hoog, N., Stroebe, W., & de Wit, J. B. F. (2007). The impact of vulnerability to and severity of a health risk on processing and acceptance of fear-arousing communications: A meta-analysis. *Review of General Psychology, 11,* 258–285.

de Lauzon-Guillain, B., Wijndaele, K., Clark, M., Acerini, C. L., Hughes, I. A., Dunger, D. B., . . . Ong, K. K. (2012). Breastfeeding and infant temperament at age three months. *PLoS ONE, 7*(1), e29326. doi: 10.1371/journal.pone.0029326

Del Giudice, M., Booth, T., & Irwing, P. (2012). The distance between Mars and Venus: Measuring global sex differences in personality. *PLoS ONE, 7*(1), e29265. doi: 10.1371/journal.pone.0029265

DeLongis, A., Coyne, J. C., Dakof, G., Folkman, S., & Lazarus, R. S. (1982). Relationship of daily hassles, uplifts, and major life events to health status. *Health Psychology, 1,* 119–136.

DeLongis, A., Folkman, S., & Lazarus, R. S. (1988). The impact of daily stress on health and mood: Psychological and social resources as mediators. *Journal of Personality and Social Psychology, 54,* 486–495.

Dement, W., & Kleitman, N. (1957). The relation of eye movements during sleep to dream activity: An objective method for the study of dreaming. *Journal of Experimental Psychology, 53,* 339–346.

Dement, W. C., & Vaughan, C. (1999). *The promise of sleep.* New York: Delacorte Press.

Démonet, J.-F., Taylor, M. J., & Chaix, Y. (2004). Developmental dyslexia. *Lancet, 363,* 1451–1460.

Dennis, C. (2004). The most important sexual organ. *Nature, 427,* 390–392.

Denollet, J., & Conraads, V. M. (2011). Type D personality and vulnerability to adverse outcomes in heart disease. *Cleveland Clinic Journal of Medicine, 78,* S13–S19.

Department of Justice, Office of the Inspector General: Evaluation and Inspections Division. (2006). *Use of polygraph examinations in the Department of Justice* (I-2006-008). Retrieved from http://www.justice.gov/oig/reports/plus/e0608/final.pdf

De Robertis, M. M., & Delaney, P. A. (1993). A survey of the attitudes of university students to astrology and astronomy. *Journal of the Royal Astronomical Society of Canada, 87,* 34–50. Retrieved from http://adsabs.harvard.edu/full/1993JRASC..87. . .34D

Derringer, J., Krueger, R. F., Dick, D. M., Saccone, S., Grucza, R. A., Agrawal, A., . . . Bierut, L. J. (2010). Predicting sensation seeking from dopamine genes: A candidate system approach. *Psychological Science, 21,* 1282–1290.

Desai, M., Pratt, L.A., Lentzner, H., & Robinson, K. N. (2001). Trends in vision and hearing among older Americans. *Aging Trends, 2,* 1–8. Hyattsville, MD: National Center for Health Statistics. Retrieved from http://www.cdc.gov/nchs/data/ahcd/agingtrends/02vision.pdf

Deslandes, A., Moraes, H., Ferreira, C., Veiga, H., Silverira, H., Mouta, R., . . . Laks, J. (2009). Exercise and mental health: Many reasons to move. *Neuropsychobiology, 59,* 191–198.

Despins, L. A., Scott-Cawiezell, J., & Rouder, J. N. (2010). Detection of patient risk by nurses: A theoretical framework. *Journal of Advanced Nursing, 66,* 465–474.

Dessens, A. B., Slijper, F. M., & Drop, S. L. (2005). Gender dysphoria and gender change in chromosomal females with congenital adrenal hyperplasia. *Archives of Sexual Behavior, 34,* 389–397.

DeValois, R. L., & DeValois, K. K. (1975). Neural coding of color. *Handbook of Perception, 5,* 117–166.

Devaney, S. A., Palomaki, G. E., Scott, J. A., & Bianchi, D. W. (2011). Non-Invasive fetal sex determination using cell-free fetal DNA. *Journal of the American Medical Association, 306,* 627–636.

De Waal, F. B. M. (2009). Bonobo sex and society. *Scientific American Mind, 20,* 4–11.

DeWall, C. N., Baumeister, R. F., & Vohs, K. D. (2008). Satiated with belongingness? Effects of acceptance, rejection, and task framing on self-regulatory performance. *Journal of Personality Social Psychology, 95,* 1367–1382.

Dewar, M., Alber, J., Butler, C., Cowan, N., & Della Sala, S. (2012). Brief wakeful resting boosts new memories over the long term. *Psychological Science, 23,* 955–960.

Diamond, E. L. (1982). The role of anger and hostility in essential hypertension and coronary heart disease. *Psychological Bulletin, 92,* 410–433.

Diamond, L. M., & Dickenson, J. A. (2012). The neuroimaging of love and desire: Review and future directions. *Clinical Neuropsychiatry, 9,* 39–46.

Diamond, M. (2004). Sex, gender, and identity over the years: A changing perspective. *Child and Adolescent Psychiatric Clinics of North America, 13,* 591–607.

Diamond, M., & Sigmundson, H. K. (1997). Sex reassignment at birth: Long-term review and clinical implications. *Archives of Pediatric & Adolescent Medicine, 151,* 298–304.

Dickens, W. T., & Flynn, J. R. (2001). Heritability estimates vs. large environmental effects: The IQ paradox resolved. *Psychological Review, 108,* 346–369.

Dickens, W. T., & Flynn, J. R. (2006). Black Americans reduce the racial IQ gap: Evidence from standardization samples. *Psychological Science, 17,* 913–920.

Dickerson, F. B., Tenhula, W. N., & Green-Paden, L. D. (2005). The token economy for schizophrenia: Review of the literature and recommendations for future research. *Schizophrenia Research, 75,* 405–416.

Diekelmann, S., & Born, J. (2010). The memory function of sleep. *Nature Reviews Neuroscience, 11,* 114–126.

Diener, E. (1979). Deindividuation, self-awareness, and disinhibition. *Journal of Personality and Social Psychology, 3,* 1160–1171.

Diener, E., Fraser, S. C., Beaman, A. L., & Kelem, R. T. (1976). Effects of deindividuation variables on stealing among Halloween trick-or-treaters. *Journal of Personality and Social Psychology, 33,* 178–183.

Diener, E., Lucas, R. E., & Scollon, C. N. (2006). Beyond the hedonic treadmill. *American Psychologist, 6,* 305–314.

DiLalla, L. F. (2002). Behavior genetics of aggression in children: Review and future directions. *Developmental Review, 22,* 593–622.

Di Lorenzo, L., De Pergola, G., Zocchetti, C., L'Abbate, N., Basso, A., Pannacciulli, N., . . . Soleo, L. (2003). Effect of shift work on body mass index: Results of a study performed in 319 glucose-tolerant men working in a Southern Italian industry. *International Journal of Obesity, 27,* 1353–1358.

Dimberg, U., Thunberg, M., & Elmehed, K. (2000). Unconscious facial reactions to emotional facial expressions. *Psychological Science, 11,* 86–89.

Dimsdale, J. E. (2008). Psychological stress and cardiovascular disease. *Journal of the American College of Cardiology, 51,* 1237–1247.

DiSalvo, D. (2010, January/February). Are social networks messing with your head? *Scientific American Mind, 20,* 48–55.

Dixon, J. F., & Hokin, L. E. (1998). Lithium acutely inhibits and chronically up-regulates and stabilizes glutamate uptake by presynaptic nerve endings in mouse cerebral cortex. *Proceedings of the National Academy of Sciences, 95,* 8363–8368.

Dobkin, B. H. (2005). Rehabilitation after stroke. *New England Journal of Medicine, 352,* 1677–1684.

Doherty-Sneddon, G. (2008). The great baby signing debate. *Psychologist, 21,* 300–303. doi: 10.1371/journal.pone.0029265

Doidge, N. (2007). *The brain that changes itself.* New York: Penguin Books.

Dolbier, C. L., & Rush, T. E. (2012). Efficacy of abbreviated progressive muscle relaxation in a high-stress college sample. *International Journal of Stress Management, 19,* 48–68.

Dolder, C. R., & Nelson, M. H. (2008). Hypnosedative-induced complex behaviors: Incidence, mechanisms and management. *CNS Drugs, 22,* 1172–7047.

Dollard, J., Miller, N. E., Doob, L. W., Mowrer, O. H., & Sears, R. R. (1939). *Frustration and aggression.* New Haven, CT: Yale University Press.

Domhoff, G. W. (2001). A new neurocognitive theory of dreams. *Dreaming, 11,* 13–33.

Donlan, W., & Lee, J. (2010). Coraje, nervios, and susto: Culture-bound syndromes and mental health among Mexican migrants in the United States. *Advances in Mental Health, 9,* 288–302.

Dorgan, B. L. (2010). The tragedy of Native American youth suicide. *Psychological Services, 7,* 213–218.

Dougherty, D. M., & Lewis, P. (1991). Stimulus generalization, discrimination learning, and peak shift in horses. *Journal of the Experimental Analysis of Behavior, 56,* 97–104.

Dougherty, L. R., Klein, D. N., Olino, T. M., Dyson, M., & Rose, S. (2009). Increased waking salivary cortisol and depression risk in preschoolers: The role of maternal history of melancholic depression and early child temperament. *Journal of Child Psychology Psychiatry, 50,* 1495–1503.

Douglas, V. I., & Parry, P. A. (1983). Effects of reward on delayed reaction time task performance of hyperactive children. *Journal of Abnormal Child Psychology, 11,* 313–326.

Dovidio, J. F., Kawakami, K., & Gaertner, S. L. (2002). Implicit and explicit prejudice and interracial interaction. *Journal of Personality and Social Psychology, 82,* 62–68.

Drace, S., Ric, F., & Desrichard, O. (2010). Affective biases in likelihood perception: A possible role of experimental demand in mood-congruence effects. *International Review of Social Psychology, 23*(1), 93–109.

Driver, H. S., & Taylor, S. R. (2000). Exercise and sleep. *Sleep Medicine Reviews, 4,* 387–402.

drjilltaylor.com. (2010). *Dr. Jill Bolte Taylor.* Retrieved from http://drjilltaylor.com/about.html

Druckman, D., & Bjork, R. A. (Eds.). (1994). *Learning, remembering, believing: Enhancing human performance* [Study conducted by the National Research Council]. Washington, DC: National Academy Press.

Drug Abuse Warning Network. (2009). *Data, outcomes, and quality, 2004–2008* [Detailed tables on national estimates and drug-related emergency department visits]. Retrieved from http://www.samhsa.gov/data/DAWN.aspx

Drug Enforcement Administration. (2012). *Rohypnol* [Fact sheet]. Retrieved from http://www.justice.gov/dea/druginfo/drug_data_sheets/Rohypnol.pdf

Druss, B. G., Hwang, I., Petukhova, M., Sampson, N.A., Wang, P. S., & Keller, R. C. (2009). Impairment in role functioning in mental and chronic medical disorders in the United States: Results from the National Comorbidity Survey Replication. *Molecular Psychiatry, 14,* 728–737.

Duckworth, A. L., & Seligman, M. E. P. (2005). Self-discipline outdoes IQ in predicting academic performance of adolescents. *Psychological Science, 16,* 939–944.

Dugas, M. J., Brillon, P., Savard, P., Turcotte, J., Gaudet, A., Ladouceur, R., . . . Gervais, N. J. (2010). A randomized clinical trial of cognitive-behavioral therapy and applied relaxation for adults with generalized anxiety disorder. *Behavioral Therapies, 41,* 46–58.

Duijts, S. F. A., Zeegers, M. P.A., & Borne, B. V. (2003). The association between stressful life events and breast cancer risk: A meta-analysis. *International Journal of Cancer, 107,* 1023–1029. doi: 10.1002/ijc.11504

Dunlosky, J., Rawson, K. A., Marsh, E. J., Nathan, M. J., & Willingham, D. T. (2013). Improving students' learning with effective learning techniques promising directions from cognitive and educational psychology. *Psychological Science in the Public Interest, 14,* 4–58.

Durante, K. M., Griskevicius, V., Simpson, J. A., Cantú, S. M., & Li., N. P. (2012). Ovulation leads women to perceive sexy cads as good dads. *Journal of Personality and Social Psychology, 103,* 292–305.

Dusek, J. A., Out, H. H., Wohlhueter, A. L., Bhasin, M., Zerbini, L. F., Joseph, M. G., . . . Libermann, T. A. (2008). Genomic counter-stress changes induced by the relaxation response. *PLoS ONE, 3,* e2576. doi: 10.1371/journal.pone.0002576

Dyer, A. G., Neumeyer, C., & Chittka, L. (2005). Honeybee (*Apis mellifera*) vision can discriminate between and recognise images of human faces. *Journal of Experimental Biology, 208,* 4709–4714.

Eagly, A. H., & Crowley, M. (1986). Gender and helping behavior: A meta-analytic review of the social psychological literature. *Psychological Bulletin, 100,* 283–308.

Eastwick, P. W., Eagly, A. H., Finkel, E. J., & Johnson, S. E. (2011). Implicit and explicit preferences for physical attractiveness in a romantic partner: A double dissociation in predictive validity. *Journal of Personality and Social Psychology, 101,* 993–1011.

Eaton, N. R., Keyes, K. M., Krueger, R. F., Balsis, S., Skodol, A. E., Markon, K. E., . . . Hasin, D. S. (2012). An invariant dimensional liability model of gender differences in mental disorder prevalence: Evidence from a national sample. *Journal of Abnormal Psychology, 121,* 282–288.

Ebbinghaus, H. (1885/1913). *Memory: A contribution to experimental psychology.* H. A. Ruger & C. E. Bussenius (Trans.). New York: Teachers College, Columbia University.

eBizMBA. (2012). *Top 15 most popular social networking sites: October 2012.* Retrieved October 11, 2012, from http://www.ebizmba.com/articles/social-networking-websites

Eckert, M. A., Keren, N. I., Roberts, D. R., Calhoun, V. D., & Harris, K. C. (2010). Age-related changes in processing speed: Unique contributions of cerebellar and prefrontal cortex. *Frontiers in Human Neuroscience, 4,* 1–14.

Eckstein, D., Aycock, K. J., Sperber, M. A., McDonald, J., Van Wiesner V., III, Watts, R. E., & Ginsburg, P. (2010). A review of 200 birth-order studies: Lifestyle characteristics. *Journal of Individual Psychology, 6,* 408–434.

Eden, G. F., Jones, K. M., Cappell, K., Gareau, L., Wood, F. B., Zeffiro, T. A., . . . Flowers, D. L. (2004). Neural changes following remediation in adult developmental dyslexia. *Neuron, 44,* 411–422.

Editors of *The Lancet.* (2010). Retraction—Ileal-lymphoid-nodular hyperplasia, non-specific colitis, and pervasive developmental disorder in children. *Lancet, 375,* 445.

Egan, S. K., & Perry, D. G. (2001). Gender identity: A multidimensional analysis with implications for psychosocial adjustment. *Developmental Psychology, 37,* 451–463.

Eichenbaum, H. (2004). Hippocampus: Cognitive processes and neural representations that underlie declarative memory. *Neuron, 44,* 109–120.

Eisenberger, N. I., Lieberman, M. D., & Satpute, A. B. (2005). Personality from a controlled processing perspective: An fMRI study of neuroticism, extraversion, and self-consciousness. *Cognitive, Affective, & Behavioral Neuroscience, 5,* 169–181.

Ekman, P. (1992). Are there basic emotions? *Psychological Review, 99,* 550–553.

Ekman, P. (2003). *Emotions revealed.* New York: Times Books.

Ekman, P., & Friesen, W. V. (1971). Constants across cultures in the face and emotion. *Journal of Personality and Social Psychology, 17,* 124–129.

Ekman, P., Friesen, W. V., O'Sullivan, M., Chan, A., Diacoyanni-Tarlatzis, I., Heider, K., . . . Tzavaras, A. (1987). Universals and cultural differences in the judgments of facial expressions of emotion. *Journal of Personality and Social Psychology, 53,* 712–717.

Ekman, P., Levenson, R. W., & Friesen, W. V. (1983). Autonomic nervous system activity distinguishes among emotions. *Science, 221,* 1208–1210.

El Ansary, M., Steigerwald, I., & Esser, S. (2003). Egypt: Over 5000 years of pain management—Cultural and historic aspects. *Pain Practice, 3,* 84–87.

Elder, C. R., Gullion, C. M., Funk, K. L., DeBar, L. L., Lindberg, N. M., & Stevens, V. J. (2012). Impact of sleep, screen time, depression and stress on weight change in the intensive weight loss phase of the LIFE study. *International Journal of Obesity, 36,* 86–92.

Elkind, D. (1967). Egocentrism in adolescence. *Child Development, 38,* 1025–1034.

Elliott, D. B., Krivickas, K., Brault, M. W., & Kreider, R. M. (2012, May). *Historical marriage trends from 1890–2010: A focus on race differences.* Paper presented at Annual Meeting of the Population Association of America, San Francisco.

Ellis, A., & Dryden, W. (1997). *The practice of rational emotive behavior therapy* (2nd ed.). New York: Springer.

El Mansari, M., Guiard, B. P., Chernoloz, O., Ghanbari, R., Katz, N., & Blier, P. (2010). Relevance of norepinephrine–dopamine interactions in the treatment of major depressive disorder. *CNS Neuroscience & Therapeutics, 16,* e1–e17.

El Mercurio. (2010, October 15). *El Mercurio en fotos* [Photographs]. Retrieved from http://www.emol.com/mundografico/el-mercurio-en-fotos/951037/minero-rescatado-detallo-aspectos-organizacion-grupo-atrapado.html

Else-Quest, N. M., Higgins, A., Allison, C., & Morton, L. C. (2012). Gender differences in self-conscious emotional experience: A meta-analysis. *Psychological Bulletin, 138,* 947–981.

Emmons, R. A., & McCullough, M. E. (2003). Counting blessings versus burdens: An experimental investigation of gratitude and subjective well-being in daily life. *Journal of Personality and Social Psychology, 84,* 377–389. doi: 10.1037/0022-3514.84.2.377

Endicott, L., Bock, T., & Narvaez, D. (2003). Moral reasoning, intercultural development, and multicultural experiences: Relations and cognitive underpinnings. *International Journal of Intercultural Relations, 27,* 403–419.

Enea, V., & Dafinoiu, I. (2009). Motivational/solution-focused intervention for reducing school truancy among adolescents. *Journal of Cognitive and Behavioral Psychotherapies, 9*, 185–198.

Engel de Abreu, P. M., Cruz-Santos, A., Tourinho, C. J., Martin, R., & Bialystok, E. (2012). Bilingualism enriches the poor: Enhanced cognitive control in low-income minority children. *Psychological Science, 23*, 1364–1371.

Epstein, L., & Mardon, S. (2007). *The Harvard Medical School guide to a good night's sleep.* New York: McGraw Hill.

Erdberg, P. (1990). Rorschach assessment. In G. Goldstein & M. Hersen (Eds.), *Handbook of psychological assessment* (2nd ed.). New York: Pergamon.

Erickson, K. I., Voss, M. W., Prakash, R. S., Basak, C., Szabo, A., Chaddock, L., . . . Kramer, A. F. (2011). Exercise training increases size of hippocampus and improves memory. *Proceedings of the National Academy of Sciences, USA, 108*(7), 3017–3022.

Erickson-Schroth, L. (2010). The neurobiology of sex/gender-based attraction. *Journal of Gay & Lesbian Mental Health, 14*, 56–69.

Ericsson, K. A. (2003). The acquisition of expert performance as problem solving. In J. E. Davidson & R. J. Sternberg (Eds.), *The psychology of problem solving* (pp. 31–83). Cambridge, UK: Cambridge University Press.

Erikson, E. H. (1993). *Childhood and society.* New York: W. W. Norton.

Erikson, E. H., & Erikson, J. M. (1997). *The life cycle completed.* New York: W. W. Norton.

Eriksson, P. S., Perfilieva, E., Bjork-Eriksson, T., Alborn, A. M., Nordborg, C., Peterson, D. A., & Gage, F. H. (1998). Neurogenesis in the adult human hippocampus. *Nature Medicine, 4*, 1313–1317.

Ernst, C., & Angst, J. (1983). *Birth order: Its influence on personality.* Berlin: Springer Verlag.

ESPN.com. (2012, February 10). *Jeremy Lin pours in career-best 38 points, leads Knicks past Lakers.* Retrieved from http://scores.espn.go.com/nba/recap?gameId= 320210018

ESPN.com. (2013). *Jeremy Lin.* Retrieved from http://espn.go.com/nba/player/_/ id/4299/jeremy-lin

Etaugh, C. (2008). Women in the middle and later years. In F. L. Denmark & M. Paludi (Eds.), *Psychology of women: Handbook of issues and theories* (2nd ed., pp. 271–302). Westport, CT: Praeger.

Evans, V., & Green, M. (2006). *Cognitive linguistics: An introduction.* Mahwah, NJ: Erlbaum.

Exner, J. E. (1980). But it's only an inkblot. *Journal of Personality Assessment, 44*, 562–577.

Exner, J. E. (1986). *The Rorschach: A comprehensive system* (Vol. 1, 2nd ed.). New York: Wiley.

Eysenck, H. J. (1967). *The biological basis of personality.* Springfield, IL: Charles C Thomas.

Eysenck, H. J. (1990). *Biological dimensions of personality.* In L. A. Pervin (Ed.), *Handbook of personality: Theory of research* (pp. 244–276). New York: Guilford Press.

Eysenck, H. J., & Eysenck, B. G. (1968). *Manual for the Eysenck Personality Inventory.* San Diego, CA: Educational Industrial Testing Service.

Facebook. (2012). *Newsroom: Key facts.* Retrieved from http://newsroom.fb.com/ content/default.aspx?NewsAreaId=22

Falk, D., Lepore, F. E., & Noe, A. (2012, November 14). The cerebral cortex of Albert Einstein: A description and preliminary analysis of unpublished photographs. *Brain.* doi: 10.1093/brain/aws295

Fallows, Z. (n.d.). *MIT Medlinks.* Retrieved April 12, 2013, from http://ocw.mit. edu/ans7870/SP/SP.236/S09/lecturenotes/drugchart.htm

Fancher, R. E., & Rutherford, A. (2012). *Pioneers of psychology: A history* (4th ed.). New York: W. W. Norton.

Fantini, M. L., Corona, A., Clerici, S., & Ferini-Strambi, L. (2005). Aggressive dream content without daytime aggressiveness in REM sleep behavior disorder. *Neurology, 65*, 1010–1015.

Farha, B. (2007). *Paranormal claims: A critical analysis.* Lanham, MD: University Press of America.

Faria, M. A. (2013). Violence, mental illness, and the brain—A brief history of psychosurgery: Part 2. From the limbic system and cingulotomy to deep brain stimulation. *Surgical Neurology International, 4.* Retrieved from http://www.surgicalneurologyint.com/text.asp?2013/4/1/75/112825

Farmer, R. F., Kosty, D. B., Seeley, J. R., Olino, T. M., & Lewinsohn, P. M. (2013). Aggregation of lifetime axis I psychiatric disorders through age 30: Incidence, predictors, and associated psychosocial outcomes. *Journal of Abnormal Psychology, 122*, 573–586.

Farthing, G. W. (1992). *The psychology of consciousness.* Upper Saddle River, NJ: Prentice Hall.

Faymonville, M. E., Laureys, S., Degueldre, C., DelFiore, G., Luxen, A., Franck, G., . . . Maquet, P. (2000). Neural mechanisms of antinociceptive effects of hypnosis. *Anesthesiology, 92*, 1257–1267.

Fazel, S., Gulati, G., Linsell, L., Geddes, J. R., & Grann, M. (2009). Schizophrenia and violence: Systematic review and meta-analysis. *PLOS Med, 6*, e1000120. doi:10.1371/journal.pmed.1000120

Federal Bureau of Investigation. (2013). *Federal Bureau of Investigation careers.* Retrieved from https://www.fbijobs.gov/61.asp

Feigelman, S. (2011). The first year. In R. M. Kliegman, R. E. Behreman, H. B. Jenson, & B. F. Stanton (Eds.), *Nelson textbook of pediatrics* (19th ed.). Philadelphia: Saunders Elsevier.

Feinstein, J. S., Adolphs, R., Damasio, A., & Tranel, D. (2011). The human amygdala and the induction and experience of fear. *Current Biology, 21*(1), 34–38.

Feis, D. L., Brodersen, K. H., von Cramon, D. Y., Luders, E., & Tittgemeyer, M. (2013). Decoding gender dimorphism of the human brain using multimodal anatomical and diffusion MRI data. *NeuroImage, 70*, 250–257.

Feist, G. J. (2004). Creativity and the frontal lobes. *Bulletin of Psychology and the Arts, 5*, 21–28.

Feldman, R., Eidelman, A. I., Sirota, L., & Weller, A. (2002). Comparison of skin-to-skin (kangaroo) and traditional care: Parenting outcomes and preterm infant development. *Pediatrics, 110*, 16–26.

Feldman, R., Weller, A., Sirota, L., & Eidelman, A. I. (2002). Skin-to-skin contact (kangaroo care) promotes self-regulation in premature infants: Sleep–wake cyclicity, arousal modulation, and sustained exploration. *Developmental Psychology, 2*, 194–207.

Fennis, B. M., & Janssen, L. (2010). Mindlessness revisited: Sequential request techniques foster compliance by draining self-control resources. *Current Psychology, 29*, 235–246.

Ferguson, C. J. (2010). Genetic contributions to antisocial personality and behavior: A meta-analytic review from an evolutionary perspective. *Journal of Social Psychology, 150*, 160–180.

Ferrer, E., Shaywitz, B. A., Holahan, J. M., Marchione, K., & Shaywitz, S. E. (2010). Uncoupling of reading and IQ over time: Empirical evidence for a definition of dyslexia. *Psychological Science, 21*, 93–101

Ferri, C. P., Prince, M., Brayne, C., Brodaty, H., Fratiglioni, L., Ganguli, M., . . . Scazufca, M. (2005). Global prevalence of dementia: A Delphi consensus study. *Lancet, 366*, 2112–2117.

Ferris, P. A., Kline, T. J. B., & Bourdage, J. S. (2012). He said, she said: Work, biopsychosocial, and lifestyle contributions to coronary heart disease risk. *Health Psychology, 31*, 503–511.

Fessler, D. M. T., & Abrams, E. T. (2004). Infant mouthing behavior: The immunocalibration hypothesis. *Medical Hypotheses, 63*, 925–932.

Festinger, L. (1957). *A theory of cognitive dissonance.* New York: Harper & Row.

Festinger, L., & Carlsmith, J. M. (1959). Cognitive consequences of forced compliance. *Journal of Abnormal and Social Psychology, 58*, 203–210.

Festinger, L., Schachter, S., & Back, K. (1950). *Social pressures in informal groups: A study of human factors in housing.* Stanford, CA: Stanford University Press.

Feyerick, D., & Steffen, S. (2009, April 8). 'Sexting' lands teen on sex offender list. *CNN.* Retrieved from: http://www.cnn.com/2009/CRIME/04/07/sexting.busts/

Field, T. (1996). Attachment and separation in young children. *Annual Review of Psychology, 47*, 541–561.

Field, T. (2001). Massage therapy facilitates weight gain in preterm infants. *Current Directions in Psychological Science, 10*, 51–54.

Field, T., & Diego, M. (2008). Cortisol: The culprit prenatal stress variable. *International Journal of Neuroscience, 118*, 1181–1205.

Filkins, D. (2004, November 21). In Falluja, young marines saw the savagery of an urban war. *The New York Times.* Retrieved from http://www.nytimes.com/2004/11/21/international/middleeast/21battle.html?_r=0

Fine, E. J., Ionita, C. C., & Lohr, L. (2002). The history of the development of the cerebellar examination. *Seminars in Neurology, 22*, 375–384.

Finer, L. B. (2007). Trends in premarital sex in the United States, 1954–2003. *Public Health Reports, 122*, 73–78.

Finger, S. (2001). *Origins of neuroscience: A history of explorations into brain function.* New York: Oxford University Press.

Fink, G. (2011). Stress controversies: Post-traumatic stress disorder, hippocampal volume, gastroduodenal ulceration. *Journal of Neuroendocrinology, 23*, 107–117.

Fink, M., & Taylor, M. A. (2007). Electroconvulsive therapy: Evidence and challenges. *Journal of the American Medical Association, 298*, 330–332.

Finkel, E. J., Eastwick, P. W., Karney, B. R., Reis, H. T., & Sprecher, S. (2012). Online dating: A critical analysis from the perspective of psychological science. *Psychological Science in the Public Interest, 13*, 3–66.

Finucane, A. M. (2011). The effect of fear and anger on selective attention. *Emotion, 11*, 970–974.

Firestein, S. (2001). How the olfactory system makes sense of scents. *Nature, 413*, 211–218.

Firth, S. (2005). End-of-life: A Hindu view. *Lancet, 366*, 682–686.

Fischer, B., & Rehm, J. (2007). Illicit opioid use in the 21st century: Witnessing a paradigm shift? *Addiction, 102*, 499–501.

Fischer, P., Krueger, J. I., Greitemeyer, T., Vogrincic, C., Kastenmüller, A., Frey, D., . . . Kainbacher, M. (2011). The bystander effect: A meta-analytic review on bystander intervention in dangerous and non-dangerous emergencies. *Psychological Bulletin, 137*, 517–537.

Fisher, S. E., & DeFries, J. E. (2002). Developmental dyslexia: Genetic dissection of a complex cognitive trait. *Nature Reviews Neuroscience, 3*, 767–780.

Fitzpatrick, M. J., & McPherson, B. J. (2010). Coloring within the lines: Gender stereotypes in contemporary coloring books. *Sex Roles, 62*, 127–137.

Flaherty, C. (2011, October 29). Soldier's best friend: Dogs boost therapy program for wounded. *Lubbock Avalanche-Journal.* Retrieved from http://lubbockonline.com/life/2011-10-29/soldiers-best-friend-dogs-boost-therapy-program-wounded#.UXl89HApsVs

Flegal, K. M., Carroll, M. D., Kit, B. K., & Ogden, C. L. (2012). Prevalence of obesity and trends in the distribution of body mass index among US adults, 1999–2010. *Journal of the American Medical Association, 307*, 491–497.

Flegal, K. M., Carroll, M. D., Ogden, C. L., & Curtin, L. R. (2010). Prevalence and trends in obesity among US adults, 1999–2008. *Journal of the American Medical Association, 303*, 235–241.

Flor, H., & Birbaumer, N. (1993). Comparison of the efficacy of electromyographic biofeedback, cognitive-behavioral therapy, and conservative medical interventions in the treatment of chronic musculoskeletal pain. *Journal of Consulting and Clinical Psychology, 61*, 653–658.

Flor, H., Nikolajsen, L., & Jensen, T. S. (2006). Phantom limb pain: A case of maladaptive CNS plasticity? *Nature Reviews Neuroscience, 7*, 873–881.

Florida Museum of Natural History. (2011). *2010 Worldwide shark attack summary.* Retrieved March 23, 2012, from http://www.flmnh.ufl.edu/fish/sharks/isaf/isaf.htm

Fogel, S. M., & Smith, C. T. (2011). The function of the sleep spindle: A psychological index of intelligence and a mechanism for sleep-dependent memory consolidation. *Neuroscience & Biobehavioral Reviews, 35*, 1154–1165.

Folkman, S., & Lazarus, R. S. (1985). If it changes it must be a process: Study of emotion and coping during three stages of a college examination. *Journal of Personality and Social Psychology, 48*, 150–170.

Foos, P. W., & Goolkasian, P. (2008). Presentation format effects in a levels-of-processing task. *Experimental Psychology, 55*, 215–227.

Forgas, J. P. (2008). Affect and cognition. *Perspectives on Psychological Science, 3*, 94–101.

Forger, D. B., & Peskin, C. S. (2003). A detailed predictive model of the mammalian circadian clock. *Proceedings of the National Academy of Sciences, 100*, 14806–14811.

Fournier, J. C., DeRubeis, R. J., Hollon, S. D., Dimidjian, S., Amsterdam, J. D., Shelton, R. C., & Fawcett, J. (2010). Antidepressant drug effects and depression severity. *Journal of the American Medical Association, 303*, 47–53.

Fowlkes, C. C., Martin, D. R., & Malik, J. (2007). Local figure–ground cues are valid for natural images. *Journal of Vision, 7*, 1–9.

Fox, A. B., Rosen, J., & Crawford, M. (2009). Distractions, distractions: Does instant messaging affect college students' performance on a concurrent reading comprehension task? *CyberPsychology & Behavior, 12*, 51–53.

Fox, M. (2013, July 25). Virginia Johnson, Masters' collaborator in sex research, dies at 88. *The New York Times.* Retrieved from: http://www.nytimes.com/2013/07/26/us/virginia-johnson-masterss-collaborator-in-sex-research-dies-at-88.html?pagewanted=all&_r=0 .

Fox News. (2012, September 19). *Pacifier use can lead to emotional problems in boys, study finds.* Retrieved from http://www.foxnews.com/health/2012/09/19/pacifier-use-can-lead-to-emotional-problems-in-boys-study-finds/

Fox News. (2013, March 20). *Social media anxiety: Sites like Facebook, Twitter stressing teens out?* Retrieved from http://www.foxnews.com/health/2013/03/20/social-media-anxiety-sites-like-facebook-twitter-stressing-teens-out/

Fozard, J. L. (1990). Vision and hearing in aging. *Handbook of the Psychology of Aging, 3*, 143–156.

Fraga, M. F., Ballestar, E., Paz, M. F., Ropero, S., Setien, F., Ballestar, M. L., . . . Esteller, M. (2005). Epigenetic differences arise during the lifetime of monozygotic twins. *Proceedings of the National Academy of Sciences, 102*, 10604–10609.

Francis, W. S., & Gutiérrez, M. (2012). Bilingual recognition memory: Stronger performance but weaker levels-of-processing effects in the less fluent language. *Memory Cognition, 40*, 496–503.

Frankenburg, W. K., Dodds, J., Archer, P., Shapiro, H., & Bresnick, B. (1992). The Denver II: A major revision and restandardization of the Denver Developmental Screening Test. *Pediatrics, 89*(1), 91–97.

Franklin, J. (2010, September 9). We know best: Doctors tussle with miners. *The Sydney Morning Herald.* Retrieved from http://www.smh.com.au/world/we-know-best-doctors-tussle-with-miners-20100917-15g9b.html

Franklin, J. (2011). *33 Men: Inside the miraculous survival and dramatic rescue of the Chilean miners.* New York: G.P. Putnam's Sons.

Fratiglioni, L., Paillard-Borg, S., & Winblad, B. (2004). An active and socially integrated lifestyle in late life might protect against dementia. *Lancet Neurology, 3*, 343–353.

Frawley, T. J. (2008). Gender schema and prejudicial recall: How children misremember, fabricate, and distort gendered picture book information. *Journal of Research in Childhood Education, 22,* 291–303.

Freberg, K., Adams, R., McGaughey, K., & Freberg, L. (2010). The rich get richer: Online and offline social connectivity predicts subjective loneliness. *Media Psychology Review, 3*(1), 105–111.

Freedman, J. L., & Fraser, S. C. (1966). Compliance without pressures: The foot-in-the-door technique. *Journal of Personality and Social Psychology, 4,* 195–202.

FreedomFlores. (2010, October 18). The Chilean miners' rescue, or masonic ritual? [Web log post]. Retrieved from http://www.davidicke.com/forum/showthread.php?t=140011

Freud, S. (1949). *An outline of psychoanalysis.* (James Strachey, Trans.). New York: W. W. Norton. (Original work published 1940)

Freud, S. (1953). The interpretation of dreams. In J. Strachey (Ed. & Trans.), *The standard edition of the complete psychological works of Sigmund Freud* (Vol. 4, pp. 1–338; Vol. 5, pp. 339–621). London: Hogarth Press. (Original work published 1900)

Freud, S. (1953). Three essays on the theory of sexuality. In J. Strachey (Ed. & Trans.), *The standard edition of the complete psychological works of Sigmund Freud* (Vol. 7, pp. 123–245). London: Hogarth Press. (Original work published 1905)

Freud, S. (1960). *The ego and the id.* (Joan Riviere, Trans., & James Strachey, Ed.). New York: W. W. Norton. (Original work published 1923)

Freud, S. (1961). The ego and the id. In J. Strachey (Ed. & Trans.), *The standard edition of the complete psychological works of Sigmund Freud* (Vol. 19, pp. 1–66). London: Hogarth Press. (Original work published 1923)

Freud, S. (1964). New introductory lectures on psycho-analysis. In J. Strachey (Ed. & Trans.), *The standard edition of the complete psychological works of Sigmund Freud* (Vol. 22, pp. 1–182). London: Hogarth Press. (Original work published 1933)

Freud, S. (1966). *Introductory lectures on psycho-analysis. The standard edition.* New York: W. W. Norton. (Original work published 1917)

Freud Museum. (2013). *About the museum.* Retrieved from http://www.freud.org.uk/about/

Friedman, L. F. (2011). The taste of immune suppression. *Scientific American Mind, 22,* 11. doi: 10.1038/scientificamericanmind0112-11a

Friedman, M., & Rosenman, R. H. (1974). *Type A behavior and your heart.* New York: Knopf.

Friedman, M. J., Resick, P. A., Bryant, R. A., & Brewin, C. R. (2011). Considering PTSD for *DSM–5. Depression and Anxiety, 28,* 750–769.

Friend farming. (n.d.). In *Merriam-Webster.com: The Open Dictionary.* Retrieved December 3, 2012, from http://nws.merriam-webster.com/opendictionary/newword_search.php

Fries, C. J. (2011, September 23). Brian Sinclair was 'ignored to death.' *The Huffington Post.* Retrieved from http://www.huffingtonpost.ca/christopher-j-fries/brian-sinclair-ignored-to-death_b_969550.html

Frith, M. (2006, April 3). Beckham reveals his battle with obsessive disorder. *The Independent.* Retrieved from http://www.independent.co.uk/news/uk/this-britain/beckham-reveals-his-battle-with-obsessive-disorder-472573.html

Funnell, M. G., Corballis, P. M., & Gazzaniga, M. S. (1999). A deficit in perceptual matching in the left hemisphere of a callosotomy patient. *Neuropsychologia, 37,* 1143–1154.

Furness, W. H. (1916). Observations on the mentality of chimpanzees and orangutans. *Proceedings of the American Philosophical Society, 55,* 281–290.

Gabrieli, J. D. E., Corkin, S., Mickel, S. F., & Growdon, J. H. (1993). Intact acquisition and long-term retention of mirror-tracing skill in Alzheimer's disease and in global amnesia. *Behavioral Neuroscience, 107,* 899–910.

Gackenbach, J., & LaBerge, S. (Eds.). (1988). *Conscious mind, sleeping brain: Perspectives on lucid dreaming.* New York: Plenum Press.

Galanter, E. (1962). Contemporary psychophysics. In R. Brown, E. Galanter, E. H. Hess, & G. Mandler (Eds.), *New directions in psychology* (pp. 87–156). New York: Holt, Rinehart & Winston.

Galati, D., Scherer, K. R., & Ricci-Bitti, P. E. (1997). Voluntary facial expression of emotion: Comparing congenitally blind with normally sighted encoders. *Journal of Personality and Social Psychology, 73,* 1363–1379.

Gale, C., & Martyn, C. (1998). Larks and owls and health, wealth, and wisdom. *British Medical Journal, 317,* 1675–1677

Gale, C. R., Batty, G. D., & Deary, I. J. (2008). Locus of control at age 10 years and health outcomes and behaviors at age 30 years: The 1970 British Cohort Study. *Psychosomatic Medicine, 70,* 397–403.

Gamer, M. (2009, February). Building a portrait of a lie in the brain. *Scientific American Mind, 20,* 50–55.

Gangestad, S. W., & Scheyd, G. J. (2005). The evolution of human physical attractiveness. *Annual Review of Anthropology, 34,* 523–548.

Ganis, G., Thompson, W. L., & Kosslyn, S. M. (2004). Brain areas underlying visual mental imagery and visual perception: An fMRI study. *Cognitive Brain Research, 20,* 226–241.

Ganzel, B. L., Morris, P. A., & Wethington, E. (2010). Allostasis and the human brain: Integrating models of stress from the social and life sciences. *Psychological Review, 117,* 134–174.

Garcia, J., Ervin, F. R., & Koelling, R. A. (1966). Learning with prolonged delay of reinforcement. *Psychonomic Science, 5,* 121–122.

Garcia, J. R., Reiber, C., Massey, S. G., & Merriwether, A. M. (2012). Sexual hookup culture: A review. *Review of General Psychology, 16,* 161–176.

García-Lázaro, H., Ramirez-Carmona, R., Lara-Romero, R., & Roldan-Valadez, E. (2012). Neuroanatomy of episodic and semantic memory in humans: A brief review of neuroimaging studies. *Neurology India, 60,* 613–617.

Gardner, H. (1999). *Intelligence reframed: Multiple intelligences for the 21st century.* New York: Basic Books.

Gardner, H. (2006). *Multiple intelligences: New horizons in theory and practice.* New York: Basic Books.

Gardner, H. (2011). *Frames of mind: The theory of multiple intelligences.* New York: Basic Books.

Gardner, H., & Hatch, T. (1989). Educational implications of the theory of multiple intelligences. *Educational Researcher, 18,* 4–10.

Gardner, S., & Wade, T. (2010, October 18). Cracks appear in Chile miners' 'pact of silence.' *Reuters.* Retrieved from http://www.reuters.com/article/2010/10/18/us-chile-miners-pact-idUSTRE69G1TT20101018

Garry, M., & Gerrie, M. P. (2005). When photographs create false memories. *Current Directions in Psychological Science, 14,* 321–325.

Gassmann, P. (1991, December 21). Somalia: The agony of a dying nation. *The New York Times.* Retrieved from http://www.nytimes.com/1991/12/21/opinion/21iht-edga.html?scp=2&sq=somalia%201991&st=cse

Gastil, J. (1990). Generic pronouns and sexist language: The oxymoronic character of masculine generics. *Sex Roles, 23,* 629–643.

Gatchel, R. J., & Maddrey, A. M. (2004). The biopsychosocial perspective of pain. In J. M. Raczynski & L. C. Leviton (Eds.), *Handbook of clinical health psychology: Vol. 2. Disorders of behavior and health* (pp. 357–378). Washington, DC: American Psychological Association.

Gatchel, R. J., Peng, Y. B., Peters, M. L., Fuchs, P. N., & Turk, D. C. (2007). The biopsychosocial approach to chronic pain: Scientific advances and future directions. *Psychological Bulletin, 133,* 581–624.

Gates, G. J. (2011). *How many people are lesbian, gay, bisexual, and transgendered?* Los Angeles: Williams Institute, UCLA School of Law. Retrieved from http://

williamsinstitute.law.ucla.edu/research/census-lgbt-demographics-studies/how-many-people-are-lesbian-gay-bisexual-and-transgender/

Gaval-Cruz, M., & Weinshenker, D. (2009). Mechanisms of disulfiram-induced cocaine abstinence: Antabuse and cocaine relapse. *Molecular Interventions, 9*, 175–187.

Gavie, J., & Revonsuo, A. (2010). The future of lucid dreaming treatment [Commentary on "The neurobiology of consciousness: Lucid dreaming wakes up" by J. Allan Hobson]. *International Journal of Dream Research, 3*, 13–15.

Gay, P. (1988). *Freud: A life for our time.* New York: W. W. Norton.

Gayton, S. D., & Lovell, G. P. (2012). Resilience in ambulance service paramedics and its relationships with well-being and general health. *Traumatology, 18*, 58–64. doi: 10.1177/1534765610396727

Gazzaniga, M. S. (1967). The split brain in man. *Scientific American, 217*, 24–29.

Gazzaniga, M. S. (1998). The split brain revisited. *Scientific American, 279*, 50–55.

Gazzaniga, M. S., Bogen, J. E., & Sperry, R. W. (1965). Observations on visual perception after disconnection of the cerebral hemispheres in man. *Brain, 88*, 221–236.

Geake, J. (2008). Neuromythologies in education. *Educational Research, 50*, 123–133.

Geary, D. C., Vigil, J., & Byrd-Craven, J. (2004). Evolution of human mate choice. *Journal of Sex Research, 41*, 27–42.

Geddes, L. (2011, November 29). Banishing consciousness: The mystery of anaesthesia. *New Scientist.* Retrieved from http://www.newscientist.com/article/mg21228402.300-banishing-consciousness-the-mystery-of-anaesthesia.html?full=true

Gegenfurtner, K. R. (2003). Cortical mechanisms of color vision. *Nature Reviews Neuroscience, 4*, 563–572.

Geier, A., Wansink, B., & Rozin, P. (2012). Red potato chips: Segmentation cues can substantially decrease food intake. *Health Psychology, 31*, 398–401.

Genetics Home Reference. (2008). *5-alpha reductase deficiency.* Retrieved from http://ghr.nlm.nih.gov/condition/5-alpha-reductase-deficiency

George, M. S. (2003, September). Stimulating the brain. *Scientific American, 289*, 67–73.

Georgiadis, J. R., Reinders, A. A. T., Paans, A. M., Renken, R., & Korte-kaas, R. (2009). Men versus women on sexual brain function: Prominent differences during tactile genital stimulation, but not during orgasm. *Human Brain Mapping, 30*, 3089–3101.

Gerdes, A. B. M., Uhl, G., & Alpers, G. W. (2009) Spiders are special: Fear and disgust evoked by pictures of arthropods. *Evolution and Human Behavior, 30*, 66–73.

German, T. P., & Defeyter, M. A. (2000). Immunity to functional fixedness in young children. *Psychonomic Bulletin & Review, 7*, 707–712.

Gerressu, M., Mercer, C. H., Graham, C. A., Wellings, K., & Johnson, A. M. (2008). Prevalence of masturbation and associated factors in a British National Probability Survey. *Archives of Sexual Behavior, 37*, 266–278.

Gershoff, E. T. (2002). Corporal punishment by parents and associated child behaviors and experiences: A meta-analytic and theoretical review. *Psychological Bulletin, 128*, 539–579.

Gershoff, E. T. (2008). *Report on physical punishment in the United States: What research tells us about its effects on children.* Columbus, OH: Center for Effective Discipline. Retrieved from http://www.phoenixchildrens.com/sites/default/files/PDFs/principles_and_practices_of_effective_discipline.pdf

Gershoff, E. T., & Bitensky, S. H. (2008). The case against corporal punishment of children. *Psychology, Public Policy, and Law, 13*, 231–272.

Gerstorf, D., Ram, N., Hoppmann, C., Willis, S. L., & Schaie, K W. (2011). Cohort differences in cognitive aging and terminal decline in the Seattle Longitudinal Study. *Developmental Psychology, 47*, 1026–1041.

Gibson, E. J., & Walk, R. D. (1960). The "visual cliff." *Scientific American, 202*, 80–92.

Giedd, J. N., Lalonde, F. M., Celano, M. J., White, S. L., Wallace, G. L., Lee, N. R., & Lenroot, R. K. (2009). Anatomical brain magnetic resonance imaging of typically developing children and adolescents. *Journal of the American Academy of Child and Adolescent Psychiatry, 48*, 465–475.

Gigerenzer, G. (2004). Dread risk, September 11, and fatal traffic accidents. *Psychological Science, 15*, 286–287.

Gilligan, C. (1982). *In a different voice: Psychological theory and women's development.* Cambridge, MA: Harvard University Press.

Gillin, J. C. (2002, March 25). How long can humans stay awake ? *Scientific American.* Retrieved from http://www.scientificamerican.com/article.cfm?id=how-long-can-humans-stay

Girodo, M., & Henry, D. R. (1976). Cognitive, physiological and behavioural components of anxiety in flooding. *Canadian Journal of Behavioural Science/Revue Canadienne des Sciences du Comportement, 8*, 224–231.

Glahn, D. C., Laird, A. R., Ellison-Wright, I., Thelen, S. M., Robinson, J. L., Lancaster, J. L., . . . Fox, P. (2008). Meta-analysis of gray matter anomalies in schizophrenia: Application of anatomic likelihood estimation and network analysis. *Biological Psychiatry, 64*, 774–781.

Glaser, R., & Kiecolt-Glaser, J. K. (2005). Stress-induced immune dysfunction: Implications for health. *Nature Reviews Immunology, 5*, 243–251.

Glass, R. M. (2001). Electroconvulsive therapy: Time to bring it out of the shadows. *Journal of the American Medical Association, 285*, 1346–1348.

Glenn, A. L., Raine, A., Schug, R. A., Gao, Y., & Granger, D. A. (2011). Increased testosterone-to-cortisol ratio in psychopathy. *Journal of Abnormal Psychology, 120*, 389–399.

Global Sex Survey (2005). *Frequency of sex.* Retrieved September 1, 2012, from http://www.durex.com/en-jp/sexualwellbeingsurvey/documents/gss2005result.pdf

Go, A. S., Mozaffarian, D., Roger, V. L., Benjamin, E. J., Berry, J. D., Borden, W. B., . . . Turner, M. B. (2013). Heart disease and stroke statistics—2013 update: A report from the American Heart Association. *Circulation, 127*, e6–e245.

Go, V. F., Srikrishnan, A. K., Sivaram, S., Murugavel, G. K., Galai, N., Johnson, S. C., . . . Celentano, D. D. (2004). High HIV prevalence and risk behaviors in men who have sex with men in Chennai, India. *Journal of Acquired Immune Deficiency Syndrome, 35*, 314–319.

Gockley, R., Bruce, A., Forlizzi, J., Michalowski, M., Mundell, A., Rosenthal, S., . . . Wang, J. (2005). Designing robots for long-term social interaction. In *2005 IEEE/RSJ International Conference on Intelligent Robots and Systems (IROS 2005;* pp. 2199–2204). New York: IEEE.

Godden, D. R., & Baddeley, A. D. (1975). Context-dependent memory in two natural environments: On land and underwater. *British Journal of Psychology, 66*, 325–331.

Godlee, F., Smith, J., & Marcovitch, H. (2011). Wakefield's article linking MMR vaccine and autism was fraudulent. *British Medical Journal, 342*, c7452.

Goel, N., Rao, H., Durmer, J. S., & Dinges, D. F. (2009, September). Neurocognitive consequences of sleep deprivation. *Seminars in Neurology, 29*, 320–339.

Gogtay, N., Vyas, N. S., Testa, R., Wood, S. J., & Pantelis, C. (2011). Age of onset of schizophrenia: Perspectives from neural structural neuroimaging studies. *Schizophrenia Bulletin, 37*, 504–513.

Gold, R. B. (2005). The implications of defining when a woman is pregnant. *Guttmacher Report on Public Policy, 8*, 7–10.

Goldin-Meadow, S. (1978). Review: A study in human capacities. *Science, 200*, 649–651.

Goldsmith, H. H., Buss, A. H., Plomin, R., Rothbart, M. K., Chess, S., Hinde, R. A., & McCall, R. B. (1987). What is temperament? Four approaches. *Child Development, 58*, 505–529.

Goldstein, E. B. (2011). *Cognitive psychology: Connecting mind, research, and everyday experience* (3rd ed.). Belmont, CA: Wadsworth, Cengage Learning.

Goldstein, I. (2000). Male sexual circuitry. *Scientific American, 283*, 70–75.

Goldstein, J. M., Seidman, L. J., Horton, N. J., Makris, N., Kennedy, D. N., Caviness, V. S. Jr., . . . Tsuang, M. T. (2001). Normal sexual dimorphism of the adult human brain assessed by in vivo magnetic resonance imaging. *Cerebral Cortex, 11*, 490–497.

Goleman, D. (1995). *Emotional intelligence.* New York: Bantam Books.

Goodfriend, W. (2012, May 22). Mental hospitals in "One Flew Over the Cuckoo's Nest." *Psychology Today.* Retrieved from http://www.psychologytoday.com/blog/psychologist-the-movies/201205/mental-hospitals-in-one-flew-over-the-cuckoo-s-nest

Google. (2012, February 15). *Google+.* Retrieved from https://plus.google.com/app/basic/stream/z12ozd4rjor0fh3t322hcvzimtebslkul

Gordon, J. (2010). Testing the glutamate hypothesis of schizophrenia. *Nature Neuroscience, 13*, 2–4.

Gordon, S. M. (2001, July 5). What are the effects of the drug Ecstasy? *Scientific American Online.* Retrieved from http://www.scientificamerican.com/article.cfm?id=what-are-the-effects-of-t

Gordon-Messer, D., Bauermeister, J. A., Grodzinski, A., & Zimmerman, M. A. (2013). Sexting among young adults. *Journal of Adolescent Health, 52*, 301–306. doi: 10.1016/j.jadohealth.2012.05.013

Gordon-Salant, S., & Callahan, J. S. (2009). The benefits of hearing aids and closed captioning for television viewing by older adults with hearing loss. *Ear & Hearing, 30*, 458–465.

Gottesman, I. I. (2001). Psychopathology through a life span—Genetic prism. *American Psychologist, 56*, 867–878.

Gottesman, I. I., Laursen, T. M., Bertelsen, A., & Mortensen, P. B. (2010). Severe mental disorders in offspring with 2 psychiatrically ill parents. *Archives of General Psychiatry, 67*, 252–257.

Gottfried, J. A., Smith, A. P. R., Rugg, M. D., & Dolan, R. J. (2004). Remembrance of odors past: Human olfactory cortex in cross-modal recognition memory. *Neuron, 42*, 687–895.

Gould, E., Beylin, A., Tanapat, P., Reeves, A., & Shors, T. J. (1999). Learning enhances adult neurogenesis in the hippocampal formation. *Nature Neuroscience, 2*, 260–265.

Grabner, R. H., Ansari, D., Reishofer, G., Stern, E., Ebner, F., & Neuper, C. (2007). Individual differences in mathematical competence predict parietal brain activation during mental calculation. *NeuroImage, 38*, 346–356.

Gracheva, E. O., Ingolia, N. T., Kelly, Y. M., Cordero-Morales, J. F., Hollopeter, G., Chesler, A. T., . . . Julius, D. (2010). Molecular basis of infrared detection by snakes. *Nature, 464*, 1006–1011.

Gradin, M., & Eriksson, M. (2011). Neonatal pain assessment in Sweden—A fifteen-year follow up. *Acta Pædiatrica, 100*, 204–208.

Grady, J. S., Ale, C. M., & Morris, T. L. (2012). A naturalistic observation of social behaviours during preschool drop-off. *Early Child Development and Care, 182*, 1683–1694.

Grammer, K., & Thornhill, R. (1994). Human (Homo sapiens) facial attractiveness and sexual selection: The role of symmetry and averageness. *Journal of Comparative Psychology, 108*, 233–242.

Granich, R., Kahn, J. G., Bennett, R., Holmes, C. B., Garg, N., Serenata, C., . . . Williams, B. G. (2012). Expanding ART for treatment and prevention of HIV in South Africa: Estimated cost and cost-effectiveness 2011–2050. *PloS ONE, 7*, e30216. doi:10.1371/journal.pone.0030216

Granrud, C. E. (2009). Development of size constancy in children: A test of the metacognitive theory. *Perception & Psychophysics, 71*, 644–654.

Grant, B. F., Stinson, F. S., Dawson, D. A., Chou, S. P., Dufour, M. C., Compton, W., . . . Kaplan, K. (2004). Prevalence and co-occurrence of substance use disorders and independent mood and anxiety disorders: Results from the National Epidemiologic Survey on Alcohol and Related Conditions. *Archives of General Psychiatry, 61*, 807–816.

Grant, P. R. (1991). Natural selection and Darwin's finches. *Scientific American, 265*, 82–87.

Gravotta, L. (2013, February 12). Be mine forever: Oxytocin may help build long-lasting love. *Scientific American Mind & Brain.* Retrieved from http://www.scientificamerican.com/article.cfm?id=be-mine-forever-oxytocin

Green, J. P. (1999). Hypnosis and the treatment of smoking cessation and weight loss. In I. Kirsch, A. Capafons, E. Cardeña-Buelna, & S. Amigó (Eds.), *Clinical hypnosis and self-regulation: Cognitive-behavioral perspectives* (pp. 249–276; Dissociation, Trauma, Memory, and Hypnosis Book Series). Washington, DC: American Psychological Association.

Green, M., & Elliott, M. (2010). Religion, health, and psychological well-being. *Journal of Religious Health, 49*, 149–163.

Greenberg, L., Warwar, S., & Malcolm, W. (2010). Emotion-focused couples therapy and the facilitation of forgiveness. *Journal of Marital and Family Therapy, 36*, 28–42.

Greenblatt, S. H., Dagi, T. F., & Epstein, M. H. (1997). *A history of neurosurgery.* Park Ridge, IL: American Association of Neurological Surgeons.

Greenfieldboyce, N. (2005, December 26). Robot receptionist dishes directions and attitude. *NPR.org.* Retrieved from http://www.npr.org/templates/story/story.php?storyId=5067678

Gregson, S., & Blacker, J. (2011). Kangaroo care in pre-term or low birth weight babies in a postnatal ward. *British Journal of Midwifery, 19*, 568–577.

Greitemeyer, T. (2009). Effects of songs with prosocial lyrics on prosocial thoughts, affect, and behavior. *Journal of Experimental Social Psychology, 45*, 186–190.

Grimm, J., & W. Grimm. (1884). *Grimm's household tales* (Margaret Hunt, Trans. & Ed.; Vol. 1). London: George Bell and Sons.

Groeger, L. (2012). Physically out of tune. *Scientific American Mind, 22*, 12. doi:10.1038/scientificamericanmind0112-12b

Groopman, J. (2008). *How doctors think.* Boston: Houghton Mifflin.

Gross, C. G. (2007). The discovery of motor cortex and its background. *Journal of the History of the Neurosciences, 16*, 320–331.

Grossman, R. P., & Till, B. D. (1998). The persistence of classically conditioned brand attitudes. *Journal of Advertising, 27*, 23–31.

Grotenhermen, F., & Müller-Vahl, K. (2012). The therapeutic potential of cannabis and cannabinoids. *Deutsches Ärzteblatt International, 109*, 495–501.

Gruber, D. F. (2009). Three's company. *Nature Medicine, 15*, 232–235.

Grusec, J. E., & Goodnow, J. J. (1994). Impact of parental discipline methods on the child's internalization of values: A reconceptualization of current points of view. *Developmental Psychology, 30*, 4–19.

Grusec, J. E., Goodnow, J. J., & Kuczynski, L. (2000). New directions in analyses of parenting contributions to children's acquisition of values. *Child Development, 71*, 205–211.

Guilford, J. P. (1967). *The nature of human intelligence.* New York: McGraw-Hill.

Guilford, J. P., Christensen, P. R., Merrifield, P. R., & Wilson, R. C. (1960). *Alternate uses.* Beverly Hills, CA: Sheridan Psychological Services.

Guillot, C. (2007). Is recreational ecstasy (MDMA) use associated with higher levels of depressive symptoms? *Journal of Psychoactive Drugs, 39*, 31–39.

Guinness Book of World Records News. (2012, February 6). *Royal mail group workers set charity record.* Retrieved from http://www.guinnessworldrecords.com/news/2012/2/royal-mail-group-workers-set-charity-record/

Gulevich, G., Dement, W., & Johnson, L. (1966). Psychiatric and EEG observations on a case of prolonged (264 hours) wakefulness. *Archives of General Psychiatry, 15*, 29–35.

Gundel, J. (2003). The migration–development nexus: Somalia case study. *International Migration, 40,* 255–281.

Gunderson, E. A., Ramirez, G., Levine, S. C., & Beilock, S. L. (2012). The role of parents and teachers in the development of gender-related math attitudes. *Sex Roles, 66,* 153–166.

Gurpegui, M., Aguilar, M. C., Martínez-Ortega, J. M., Diaz, F. J., & de Leon, J. (2004). Caffeine intake in outpatients with schizophrenia. *Schizophrenia Bulletin, 30,* 935–945.

Gurven, M., von Rueden, C., Massenkoff, M., Kaplan, H., & Lero Vie, M. (2013). How universal is the Big Five? Testing the five-factor model of personality variation among forager-farmers in the Bolivian Amazon. *Journal of Personality and Social Psychology, 104,* 354–370.

Güss, D. (2011). Fire and ice: Testing a model on culture and complex problem solving. *Journal of Cross-Cultural Psychology, 42,* 1279–1298.

Haedt-Matt, A. A., & Keel, P. K. (2011). Revisiting the affect regulation model of binge eating: A meta-analysis of studies using ecological momentary assessment. *Psychological Bulletin, 137,* 660–681.

Hagar, S. (2013, September 19). Washington State Penitentiary psychologist earns national acclaim for programs. Union-Bulletin.com. Retrieved from: http://union-bulletin.com/news/2013/sep/19/washington-state-penitentiary-psychologist-earns-n/

Hakun, J. G., Ruparel, K., Seelig, D., Busch, E., Loughead, J. W., Gur, R. C., & Langleben, D. D. (2009). Towards clinical trials of lie detection with fMRI. *Social Neuroscience, 4,* 518–527.

Hall, J. A., & Matsumoto, D. (2004). Gender differences in judgments of multiple emotions from facial expressions. *Emotion, 4,* 201–206.

Hall, J. K., Hutton, S. B., & Morgan, M. J. (2010). Sex differences in scanning faces: Does attention to the eyes explain female superiority in facial expression recognition? *Cognition and Emotion, 24,* 629–637.

Hall, J. W., Smith, S. D., & Popelka, G. R. (2004). Newborn hearing screening with combined otoacoustic emissions and auditory brainstem responses. *Journal of the American Academy of Audiology, 15,* 414–425.

Halpern, D. F., Benbow, C. P., Geary, D. C., Gur, R. C., Hyde, J. S., & Gernsbacher, M. A. (2007). The science of sex differences in science and mathematics. *Psychological Science in the Public Interest, 8,* 1–51.

Halpern, L. (2013). What it's like to have schizophrenia. *Ladies Home Journal.* Retrieved from http://www.lhj.com/health/conditions/mental-health/symptoms-treatment-schizophrenia/?page=1

Hamer, D. H., Hu, S., Magnuson, V. L., Hu, N., & Pattatucci, A. M. (1993). A linkage between DNA markers on the X chromosome and male sexual orientation. *Science, 261,* 321–327.

Hamilton, W. D. (1964). The genetical evolution of social behavior. *Journal of Theoretical Biology, 12,* 12–45.

Hammond, S. I., Müller, U., Carpendale, J. I. M., Bibok, M. B., & Liebermann-Finestone, D. P. (2012). The effects of parental scaffolding on preschoolers' executive function. *Developmental Psychology, 48,* 271–281.

Hampton, A. N., & O'Doherty, J. P. (2007). Decoding the neural substrates of reward-related decision making with functional MRI. *Proceedings of the National Academy of Sciences, 104,* 1377–1382.

Hampton, J. A. (1998). Similarity-based categorization and fuzziness of natural categories. *Cognition, 65,* 137–165.

Haney, C., Banks, C., & Zimbardo, P. (1973). Interpersonal dynamics in a simulated prison. *International Journal of Criminology and Penology, 1,* 69–97.

Haney, C., & Zimbardo, P. (1998). The past and future of U. S. prison policy: Twenty-five years after the Stanford prison experiment. *American Psychologist, 53,* 709–727.

Hanish, L. D., Sallquist, J., DiDonato, M., Fabes, R. A., & Martin, C. L. (2012). Aggression by whom—Aggression toward whom: Behavioral predictors of same- and other-gender aggression in early childhood. *Developmental Psychology, 48,* 1450–1462. doi: 10.1037/a0027510

Hanley, J. R., & Chapman, E. (2008). Partial knowledge in a tip-of-the-tongue state about two- and three-word proper names. *Psychonomic Bulletin & Review, 15,* 156–160.

Hanna-Pladdy, B., & MacKay, A. (2011). The relation between instrumental musical activity and cognitive aging. *Neuropsychology, 25,* 378–386.

Hanscombe, K. B., Trzaskowski, M., Haworth, C. M. A., Davis, O. S. P., Dale, P. S., & Plomin, R. (2012). Socioeconomic status (SES) and children's intelligence (IQ): In a UK-representative sample SES moderates the environmental, not genetic, effect on IQ. *PLoS ONE, 7,* e30320. doi: 10.1371/journal.pone.0030320

Hansen, C. J., Stevens, L. C., & Coast, J. R. (2001). Exercise duration and mood state: How much is enough to feel better? *Health Psychology, 20,* 267–275.

Harcourt, B. E. (2011). An institutionalization effect: The impact of mental hospitalization and imprisonment on homicide in the United States, 1934–2001. *Journal of Legal Studies, 40,* 39–83.

Harden, K. P., & Mendle, J. (2012). Gene–environment interplay in the association between pubertal timing and delinquency in adolescent girls. *Journal of Abnormal Psychology, 121,* 73–87.

Hariri, A. R., Tessitore, A., Mattay, V. S., Fera, F., & Weinberger, D. R. (2002). The amygdala response to emotional stimuli: A comparison of faces and scenes. *NeuroImage, 17,* 317–323.

Harlow, H. F. (1958). The nature of love. *American Psychologist, 13,* 673–685.

Harlow, H. F., Harlow, M. K., & Meyer, D. R. (1950). Learning motivated by a manipulation drive. *Journal of Experimental Psychology, 40,* 228–234.

Harlow, H. F., Harlow, M. K., & Suomi, S. J. (1971). From thought to therapy: Lessons from a primate laboratory. *American Scientist, 59,* 538–549.

Harlow, H. F., & Zimmerman, R. R. (1959). Affectional responses in the infant monkey. *Science, 130,* 421–432.

Harmon, D. K., Masuda, M., & Holmes, T. H. (1970). The social readjustment rating scale: A cross-cultural study of Western Europeans and Americans. *Journal of Psychosomatic Research, 14,* 391–400.

Harrington, A. (2012). The fall of the schizophrenogenic mother. *Lancet, 379,* 1292–1293.

Harrington, J. M. (2001). Health effects of shift work and extended hours of work. *Occupational and Environmental Medicine, 58,* 68–72. doi: 10.1136/oem.58.1.68

Harrington, R. (2013). *Stress, health & well-being: Thriving in the 21st century.* Belmont, CA: Wadsworth, Cengage Learning.

Harris, B. (1979). Whatever happened to Little Albert? *American Psychologist, 34,* 151–160.

Harris, B. (2011). Letting go of Little Albert: Disciplinary memory, history, and the uses of myth. *Journal of the History of the Behavioral Sciences, 47,* 1–17.

Harris, E. C., & Barraclough, B. (1998). Excess mortality of mental disorder. *British Journal of Psychiatry, 173,* 11–53.

Harris, J. A., Petersen, R. S. & Diamond, M. E. (2001). The cortical distribution of sensory memories. *Neuron, 30,* 315–318.

Harris Interactive/Health Day Poll. (2011). *Vaccine–autism link: Sound science or fraud?* [Press release]. Retrieved from http://www.harrisinteractive.com/NewsRoom/PressReleases/tabid/446/mid/1506/articleId/674/ctl/ReadCustom%20Default/Default.aspx

Hart, B., & Risley, T. R. (1995). *Meaningful differences in the everyday experience of young American children.* Baltimore, MD: Paul H. Brookes.

Hart, B., & Risley, T. R. (1999). *The social world of children learning to talk.* Baltimore, MD: P. H. Brookes Publishers.

Hartlage, S., Alloy, L. B., Vázquez, C., & Dykman, B. (1993). Automatic and effortful processing in depression. *Psychological Bulletin, 113,* 247–278.

Hartshorne, J. K. (2010). How birth order affects your personality. *Scientific American Online.* Retrieved from http://www.scientificamerican.com/article.cfm?id=ruled-by-birth-order&print=true

Hartshorne, J. K., Salem-Hartshorne, N., & Hartshorne, T. S. (2009). Birth order effects in the formation of long-term relationships. *Journal of Individual Psychology, 65,* 156–176.

Harvard Medical School. (2007). *Healthy sleep: Jet lag and shift work.* Retrieved from http://healthysleep.med.harvard.edu/healthy/science/variations/jet-lag-and-shift-work

Harvey, M. A., Sellman, J. D., Porter, R. J., & Frampton, C. M. (2007). The relationship between non-acute adolescent cannabis use and cognition. *Drug and Alcohol Review, 26,* 309–319.

Hasher, L., & Zacks, R. T. (1979). Automatic and effortful processes in memory. *Journal of Experimental Psychology: General, 108,* 356–388.

Hassett, J. M., Siebert, E. R., & Wallen, K. (2008). Sex differences in rhesus monkey toy preferences parallel those of children. *Hormones and Behavior, 54,* 359–364.

Hassin, R. R., Bargh, J. A., & Zimerman, S. (2009). Automatic and flexible: The case of non-conscious goal pursuit. *Social Cognition, 27,* 20–36.

Hatch, S. L., & Dohrenwend, B. P. (2007). Distribution of traumatic and other stressful life events by race/ethnicity, gender, SES and age: A review of the research. *American Journal of Community Psychology, 40,* 313–332.

Hatfield, E., Bensman, L., & Rapson, R. L. (2012). A brief history of social scientists' attempts to measure passionate love. *Journal of Social and Personal Relationships, 29,* 143–164.

Hatfield, E., Luckhurst, C., & Rapson, R. L. (2010). Sexual motives: Cultural, evolutionary, and social psychological perspectives. *Sexuality & Culture, 14,* 173–190.

Hau, M., & Wikelski, M. (2001). Darwin's finches. In *Encyclopedia of Life Sciences* (pp. 1–8). Chichester, UK: Wiley.

Havelka, M., Lučanin, J. D., & Lučanin, D. (2009). Biopsychosocial model-the integrated approach to health and disease. *Collegium Antropologicum, 33,* 303–310.

Hawthorne, W. B., Folsom, D. P., Sommerfeld, D. H., Lanouette, N. M., Lewis, M., Aarons, G. A., . . . Jeste, D. V. (2012). Incarceration among adults who are in the public mental health system: Rates, risk factors, and short-term outcomes. *Psychiatric Services, 63,* 26–32.

Hayano, F., Nakamura, M., Asami, T., Uehara, K., Yoshida, T., Roppongi, T., . . . Hirayasu, Y. (2009). Smaller amygdala is associated with anxiety in patients with panic disorder. *Psychiatry and Clinical Neurosciences, 63,* 266–276.

He, Y., Jones, C. R., Fujiki, N., Xu, Y., Guo, B., Holder, J. L., . . . Fu, Y. (2009). The transcriptional repressor DEC2 regulates sleep length in mammals. *Science, 325,* 866–870.

Healey, M. D., & Ellis, B. J. (2007). Birth order, conscientiousness, and openness to experience: Tests of the family-niche model of personality using a within-family methodology. *Evolution and Human Behavior, 28,* 55–59.

Health Resources and Services Administration. (2010). *The registered nurse population findings from the 2008 National Sample Survey of Registered Nurses.* Retrieved from http://bhpr.hrsa.gov/healthworkforce/rnsurveys/rnsurveyfinal.pdf

Healy, J. (2010, August 23). Chileans will work to sustain miners. *The New York Times.* Retrieved from http://www.nytimes.com/2010/08/24/world/americas/24chile.html?_r=0

Hecht, S., & Mandelbaum, J. (1938). Rod–cone dark adaptation and vitamin A. *Science, 88,* 219–221.

Hegarty, P., & Buechel, C. (2006). Androcentric reporting of gender differences in APA journals: 1965–2004. *Review of General Psychology, 10,* 377–389.

Heiman, J. R. (2002). Sexual dysfunction: Overview of prevalence, etiological factors, and treatments. *Journal of Sex Research, 39,* 73–78.

Heller, N. (2012, June 18). Emma Stone makes her Vogue cover debut in the July issue. *Vogue.* Retrieved from http://www.vogue.com/magazine/article/emma-stone-comic-relief/#1

Hendricks, M. L., & Testa, R. J. (2012). A conceptual framework for clinical work with transgender and gender nonconforming clients: An adaptation of the minority stress model. *Professional Psychology: Research and Practice, 43,* 460–467. doi: 10.1037/a0029597

Henneman, W. J., Sluimer, J. D., Barnes, J., van der Flier, W. M., Sluimer, I. C., Fox, N. C., . . . Barkhof, F. (2009). Hippocampal atrophy rates in Alzheimer disease: Added value over whole brain volume measures. *Neurology, 72,* 999–1007.

Henry, D. B., Kobus, K., & Schoeny, M. E. (2011). Accuracy and bias in adolescents' perceptions of friends' substance use. *Psychology of Addictive Behaviors, 25,* 80–89.

Herbenick, D., Reece, M., Schick, V., Sanders, S. A., Dodge, B., & Fortenberry, J. D. (2010). Sexual behavior in the United States: Results from a national probability sample of men and women ages 14–94. *Journal of Sexual Medicine, 7* (Suppl. 5), 255–265.

Hergenhahn, B. R. (2005). *An introduction to the history of psychology* (5th ed.). Belmont, CA: Thomson Wadsworth.

Herman, C. P., Roth, D. A., & Polivy, J. (2003). Effects of the presence of others on food intake: A normative interpretation. *Psychological Bulletin, 129,* 873–886.

Hersh, S. M. (2004, May 10). Torture at Abu Ghraib. *The New Yorker.* Retrieved from http://www.newyorker.com/archive/2004/05/10/040510fa_fact?printable=true&currentPage=all

Hertenstein, M. J., & McCullough, M. A. (2005). Separation anxiety. In N. J. Salkind (Ed.), *Encyclopedia of human development* (Vol. 3, pp. 1146–1147). Thousand Oaks, CA: Sage.

Hertzog, C., Kramer, A. F., Wilson, R. S., & Lindenberger, U. (2009, July/August). Fit body, fit mind? *Scientific American Mind, 20,* 24–31.

Herz, R. (2007). *The scent of desire: Discovering our enigmatic sense of smell.* New York: William Morrow/HarperCollins.

Herz, R. S. (1998). Are odors the best cues to memory? A cross-modal comparison of associative memory stimuli. *Annals of the New York Academy of Sciences, 855,* 670–674.

Herz, R. S., Eliassen, J., Beland, S., & Souza, T. (2004). Neuroimaging evidence for the emotional potency of odor-evoked memory. *Neuropsychologia, 42,* 371–378.

Hess, E. H. (1975). The role of pupil size in communication. *Scientific American, 233,* 110–119.

Hess, U., & Thibault, P. (2009). Darwin and emotion expression. *American Psychologist, 64,* 120–128.

Hettema, J. M., Kettenmann, B., Ahluwalia, V., McCarthy, C., Kates, W. R., Schmitt, J. E., . . . Fatouros, P. (2012). Pilot multimodal twin imaging study of generalized anxiety disorder. *Depression and Anxiety, 29,* 202–209.

Hettema, J. M., Neale, M. C., & Kendler, K. S. (2001). A review and meta-analysis of the genetic epidemiology of anxiety disorders. *American Journal of Psychiatry, 158,* 1568–1578.

Hetzel, L., & Smith, A. (2001). The 65 years and over populations: 2000. *Census 2000 Brief.* Retrieved from http://www.census.gov/prod/2001pubs/c2kbr01-10.pdf

Heyes, C. (2012). What's social about social learning. *Journal of Comparative Psychology, 126,* 193–202.

Hickok, G., & Poeppel, D. (2000). Towards a functional neuroanatomy of speech perception. *Trends in Cognitive Sciences, 4,* 131–138.

Higgens, A., Nash, M., & Lynch, A. M. (2010). Antidepressant-associated sexual dysfunction: Impact, effects, and treatment. *Drug, Healthcare and Patient Safety, 2,* 141–150. doi: 10.2147/DHPS.S7634

Hilgard, E. R. (1977). *Divided consciousness.* New York: Wiley.

Hilgard, E. R. (1987). *Psychology in America: A historical survey.* Orlando, FL: Harcourt Brace Jovanovich.

Hilgard, E. R. (1994). Neodissociation theory. In S. J. Lynn & J. W. Rhue (Eds.), *Dissociation: Clinical, theoretical and research perspectives.* New York: Guilford Press.

Hilgard, E. R., Morgan, A. H., & Macdonald, H. (1975). Pain and dissociation in the cold pressor test: A study of hypnotic analgesia with "hidden reports" through automatic key pressing and automatic talking. *Journal of Abnormal Psychology, 84,* 280–289.

Hines, M. (2011a). Gender development and the human brain. *Annual Review of Neuroscience, 34,* 69–88.

Hines, M. (2011b). Prenatal endocrine influences on sexual orientation and on sexually differentiated childhood behavior. *Frontiers in Neuroendocrinology, 32,* 170–182.

Hingson, R. W., Zha, W., & Weitzman, E. R. (2009). Magnitude of and trends in alcohol-related mortality and morbidity among U.S. college students ages 18–24, 1998–2005. *Journal of Studies on Alcohol and Drugs, 16* (Suppl.), 12–20.

Hirsh-Pasek, K., Golinkoff, R. M., & Eyer, D. (2003). *Einstein never used flash cards.* Emmaus, PA: Rodale Press.

Hirst, W., Buckner, R. L., Cuc, A., Johnson, M. K., Lyle, K. B., Meksin, R., . . . Mitchell, K. (2009). Long-term memory for the terrorist attack of September 11: Flashbulb memories, event memories, and the factors that influence their retention. *Journal of Experimental Psychology: General, 138,* 161–176.

Hjerrild, B. E., Mortensen, K. H., & Gravholt, C. H. (2008). Turner syndrome and clinical treatment. *British Medical Bulletin, 86,* 77–93.

Hobson, J. A. (1989). *Sleep.* New York: Scientific American Library.

Hobson, J. A. (2006, April/May). Freud returns? Like a bad dream. *Scientific American Mind, 17,* 35.

Hobson, J. A., & McCarley, R. W. (1977). The brain as a dream state generator: An activation–synthesis hypothesis of the dream process. *American Journal of Psychiatry, 134,* 1335–1348.

Hock, R. R. (2012). *Human sexuality* (3rd ed.). Upper Saddle River, NJ: Pearson Education.

Hodis, F. A., Meyer, L. H., McClure, J., Weir, K. F., & Walkey, F. H. (2011). A longitudinal investigation of motivation and secondary school achievement using growth mixture modeling. *Journal of Educational Psychology, 103,* 312–323.

Hoff, E. (2003). The specificity of environmental influence: Socioeconomic status affects early vocabulary development via maternal speech. *Child Development, 74,* 1368–1378.

Hoffman, I. Z. (2009). Therapeutic passion in the countertransference. *Psychoanalytic Dialogues, 19,* 617–636.

Hofmann, S. G., Asnaani, M. A., & Hinton, D. E. (2010). Cultural aspects in social anxiety and social anxiety disorder. *Depression and Anxiety, 27,* 1117–1127.

Hofmann, W., Vohs, K. D., & Baumeister, R. F. (2012). What people desire, feel conflicted about, and try to resist in everyday life. *Psychological Science, 23,* 582–588.

Hofstede, G. (1993). Cultural constraints in management theories. *The Executive, 7,* 81–94.

Holahan, C. K., & Sears, R. R. (1995). *The gifted group in later maturity.* Stanford, CA: Stanford University Press.

Holland, R. W., Verplanken, B., & Van Knippenberg, A. (2002). On the nature of attitude–behavior relations: The strong guide, the weak follow. *European Journal of Social Psychology, 32,* 869–876.

Hollywood Reporter. (2012, February 15). *George Clooney's big surprises: Small paychecks, insomnia, bouts of loneliness.* Retrieved from http://www.hollywoodreporter.com/news/george-clooney-oscars-brad-pitt-stacy-keibler-descendants-290676

Holmes, T. H., & Rahe, R. H. (1967). The Social Readjustment Rating Scale. *Journal of Psychosomatic Research, 11,* 213–318.

Holowka, S., & Petitto, L. A. (2002). Left hemisphere cerebral specialization for babies while babbling. *Science, 297,* 1515

Holsen, L. M., Spaeth, S. B., Lee, J.-H., Ogden, L. A., Klibanski, A., Whitfield-Gabrieli, S., & Goldstein, J. M. (2011). Stress response circuitry hypoactivation related to hormonal dysfunction in women with major depression. *Journal of Affective Disorders, 131,* 379–387.

Hölzel, B. K., Carmody, J., Vangel, M., Congleton, C., Yerramsetti, S. M., Gard, T., & Lazar, S. W. (2011). Mindfulness practice leads to increases in regional brain gray matter density. *Psychiatry Research: Neuroimaging, 191,* 36–43.

Honberg, R., Diehl, S., Kimball, A., Gruttadaro, D., & Fitzpatrick, M. (2011). *State mental health cuts: A national crisis* [Report by the National Alliance on Mental Illness]. Retrieved from http://www.nami.org/Template.cfm?Section=state_budget_cuts_report

Honda, H., Shimizu, Y., & Rutter, M. (2005). No effect of MMR withdrawal on the incidence of autism: A total population study. *Journal of Child Psychology and Psychiatry, 46,* 572–579.

Honey, A., Emerson, E., & Llewellyn, G. (2011). The mental health of young people with disabilities: Impact of social conditions. *Social Psychiatry and Psychiatric Epidemiology, 46,* 1–10.

Hong, Y.-y., Wyer, R. S. Jr., & Fong, C. P. S. (2008). Chinese working in groups: Effort dispensability versus normative influence. *Asian Journal of Social Psychology, 11,* 187–195.

Hoppel, A. M. (2012). HIV: Still epidemic after 30 years. *Clinician Reviews, 22*(C1), 11–14, 33–35.

Hor, H., & Tafti, M. (2009). How much sleep do we need? *Science, 325,* 825–826.

Horne, J. (2006). *Sleepfaring.* Oxford, UK: Oxford University Press.

Horney, K. (1967). The flight from womanhood: The masculinity-complex in women as viewed by men and by women. In H. Kelmam (Ed.), *Feminine psychology* (pp. 54–70). New York: W. W. Norton. (Original work published 1926)

Horney, K. (1945). *Our inner conflicts: A constructive theory of neurosis.* New York: W. W. Norton.

Horoscope.com. (2012). *Monthly horoscope: Cancer.* Retrieved from http://my.horoscope.com/astrology/free-monthly-horoscope-cancer.html

Horwitz, B., Amuntsb, K., Bhattacharyya R., Patkin, D., Jeffries, K., Zilles, K., & Braun, A. R. (2003). Activation of Broca's area during the production of spoken and signed language: A combined cytoarchitectonic mapping and PET analysis. *Neuropsychologia, 41,* 1868–1876.

Horwitz, D., Lovenberg, W., Engelman, K., & Sjoerdsma, A. (1964). Monoamine oxidase inhibitors, tyramine, and cheese. *Journal of the American Medical Association, 188,* 1108–1110.

Horwood, L. J., & Fergusson, D. M. (1998). Breastfeeding and later cognitive and academic outcomes. *Pediatrics, 101,* 1–7.

Hothersall, D. (2004). *History of psychology* (4th ed.). New York: McGraw-Hill.

House, J. S., Landis, K. R., & Umberson, D. (1988). Social relationships and health. *Science, 241,* 540–545.

Hovland, C. I., Janis, I. L., & Kelley, H. H. (1953). *Communication and persuasion: Psychological studies of opinion change.* New Haven, CT: Yale University Press.

Hovland, C. I., & Weiss, W. (1951). The influence of source credibility on communication effectiveness. *Public Opinion Quarterly, 15,* 635–650.

Howes, O. D., & Kapur, S. (2009). The dopamine hypothesis of schizophrenia: Version III—The final common pathway. *Schizophrenia Bulletin, 35,* 549–562.

Howland, J., Rohsenow, D. J., Greece, J. A., Littlefield, C. A., Almeida, A., Heeren, T., . . . Hermos, J. (2010). The effects of binge drinking on college students' next-day academic test-taking performance and mood state. *Addiction, 105,* 655–665.

Howland, M., Hunger, J. M., & Mann, T. (2012). Friends don't let friends eat cookies: Effects of restrictive eating norms on consumption among friends. *Appetite, 59,* 505–509.

Hoyert, D., & Xu, J. (2012). Deaths: Preliminary data for 2011. *National Vital Statistics Reports, 61,* 1–64.

Hubbard, T. L. (2010). Auditory imagery: Empirical findings. *Psychological Bulletin, 136,* 302–329.

Hubel, D. H., & Wiesel, T. N. (1979, September). Brain mechanisms of vision. *Scientific American, 241,* 150–162.

Huber, V. L., Neale, M. A., & Northcraft, G. B. (1987). Decision bias and personnel selection strategies. *Organizational Behavior and Human Decision Processes, 40,* 136–137.

Hudson, C., & Paul, J. (Producers). (2007). *Through your eyes.* [DVD]. Los Angeles: Global Universal Film Group.

Huesmann, L. R., Moise-Titus, J., Podolski, C., & Eron, L. D. (2003). Longitudinal relations between children's exposure to TV violence and their aggressive and violent behavior in young adulthood: 1977–1992. *Developmental Psychology, 39,* 201–221.

Huffington Post. (2012, February 14). *Stephen Wiltshire's unbelievably detailed drawings made from memory.* Retrieved from http://www.huffingtonpost.com/2012/02/07/stephen-wiltshires-detailed-drawings_n_1260041.html

Huffington Post. (2012, July 16). *Ramadan 2012: History, dates, greeting and rules of the Muslim fast.* Retrieved from http://www.huffingtonpost.com/2012/07/16/ramadan-top-ten_n_1676639.html

Hull, C. L. (1952). *A behavior system: An introduction to behavior theory concerning the individual organism.* New Haven, CT: Yale University Press.

Humphries, T., Kushalnagar, P., Mathur, G., Napoli, D. J., Padden, C., Rathmann, C., & Smith, S. R. (2012). Language acquisition for deaf children: Reducing the harms of zero tolerance to the use of alternative approaches. *Harm Reduction Journal, 9,* 1–9.

Hunsley, J., Lee, C. M., & Wood, J. M. (2003). Controversial and questionable assessment techniques. In S. O. Lilienfeld, J. M. Lohr, & S. J. Lynn (Eds.), *Science and pseudoscience in clinical psychology* (pp. 39–76). New York: Guilford Press.

Hunt, W. A. (1939). A critical review of current approaches to affectivity. *Psychological Bulletin, 36,* 807–828.

Hupp, J. M., Smith, J. L, Coleman, J. M., & Brunell, A. B. (2010). That's a boys' toy: Gender-typed knowledge in toddlers as a function of mother's marital status. *Journal of Genetic Psychology, 171,* 389–401.

Hurst, L. C. (1982). What was wrong with Anna O? *Journal of the Royal Society of Medicine, 75,* 129–131.

Hyde, J. S. (2005). The gender similarities hypothesis. *American Psychologist, 60,* 581–592.

Hyde, J. S. (2007). New directions in the study of gender similarities and differences. *Current Directions in Psychological Science, 16,* 259–263.

Hyde, J. S., & Linn, M. C. (1988). Gender differences in verbal ability: A meta-analysis. *Psychological Bulletin, 104,* 53–69.

Hyman, I. E. Jr., Husband, T. H., & Billings, F. J. (1995). False memories of childhood experiences. *Applied Cognitive Psychology, 9,* 181–197.

IMDB. (2012a). *Orlando Bloom.* Retrieved from http://www.imdb.com/name/nm0089217/bio

IMDB. (2012b). *Quotes for Legolas Greenleaf.* Retrieved from http://www.imdb.com/character/ch0000137/quotes

iminmotion.net. (2012). *Ivonne Marcela Mosquera-Schmidt.* Retrieved from http://iminmotion.net/about.html

Ingold, J. (2013, September 30). Sides debate lengthy witness lists for James Holmes trial. *The Denver Post.* Retrieved from http://www.denverpost.com/breakingnews/ci_24205468/psychiatric-exam-up-debate-new-aurora-theater-shooting#

Interlandi, J. (2012, June 22). When my crazy father actually lost his mind. *The New York Times.* Retrieved from http://www.nytimes.com/2012/06/24/magazine/when-my-crazy-father-actually-lost-his-mind.html?_r=0

International Dyslexia Association. (2012). *Dyslexia basics* [Fact sheet]. Retrieved from http://www.interdys.org/ewebeditpro5/upload/DyslexiaBasicsREV-May2012.pdf

International Organization for Migration. (2013). *Facts and figures* [Fact sheet]. Retrieved from http://www.iom.int/cms/en/sites/iom/home/about-migration/facts--figures-1.html

Intersex Society of North America. (2008). *How common is intersex?* Retrieved May 28, 2013, from http://www.isna.org/faq/frequency

Inui, K., Urakawa, T., Yamahiro, K., Otsuru, N., Takeshima, Y., Nishihara, M., . . . Kakigi, R. (2010). Echoic memory of a single pure tone by change-related brain activity. *BMS Neuroscience, 11,* 135–145.

Ireland, M. (2012). Meditation and psychological health and functioning: A descriptive and critical review. *Scientific Review of Mental Health Practice, 9,* 4–19.

Isen, A. (2008). Some ways in which positive affect influences decision making and problem solving. In M. Lewis, J. M. Haviland-Jones, & L. F. Barrett (Eds.), *Handbook of emotions* (3rd ed., pp. 548–573). New York: Guilford Press.

Ivcevic, Z., & Ambady, N. (2012). Personality impressions from identity claims on Facebook. *Psychology of Popular Media Culture, 1,* 38–45.

Iversen, L. (2003). Cannabis and the brain. *Brain, 126,* 1252–1270.

Izard, C. E. (1992). Basic emotions, relations among emotions, and emotion–cognition relations. *Psychological Review, 99,* 561–565.

Izard, C. E. (2007). Basic emotions, natural kinds, emotion schemas, and a new paradigm. *Perspectives on Psychological Science, 2,* 260–280.

Jaaro-Peled, H., Ayhan, Y., Pletnikov, M. V., & Sawa, A. (2010). Review of pathological hallmarks of schizophrenia: Comparison of genetic models with patients and nongenetic models. *Schizophrenia Bulletin, 36,* 301–313.

Jacobs, H. (2012, May 1). Don't ask, don't tell, don't publish. *EMBO Reports, 13*(5), 393.

Jacobson, E. (1938). *Progressive relaxation.* Chicago: University of Chicago Press.

Jacobson, N. S., & Addis, M. E. (1993). Research on couples and couple therapy. What do we know and where are we going? *Journal of Consulting and Clinical Psychology, 61,* 85–93.

James, L. E., & Burke, D. M. (2000). Phonological priming effects on word retrieval and tip-of-the-tongue experiences in young and older adults. *Journal of Experimental Psychology: Learning, Memory, and Cognition, 26,* 1378–1391.

James, S. D. (2008, May 7). Wild child speechless after tortured life. *ABC News.* Retrieved from http://abcnews.go.com/Health/story?id=4804490&page=1#.UW4DxHApsVs

James, W. J. (1983). *The principles of psychology.* Cambridge, MA: Harvard University Press. (Original work published 1890)

Jameson, D., & Hurvich, L. M. (1989). Essay concerning color constancy. *Annual Review of Psychology, 40,* 1–24.

Janata, P., & Paroo, K. (2006). Acuity of auditory images in pitch and time. *Perception & Psychophysics, 68,* 829–844.

Jang, K. L., Livesley, W. J., & Vernon, P. A. (1996). Heritability of the Big Five personality dimensions and their facets: A twin study. *Journal of Personality, 64,* 577–592.

Janis, I. L. (1972). *Victims of groupthink: A psychological study of foreign-policy decisions and fiascoes.* Oxford, UK: Houghton Mifflin.

Janis, I. L., & Feshbach, S. (1953). Effects of fear-arousing communications. *Journal of Abnormal and Social Psychology, 48,* 78–92.

Janis, I. L., Kaye, D., & Kirschner, P. (1965). Facilitating effects of "eating-while-reading" on responsiveness to persuasive communication. *Journal of Personality and Social Psychology, 1,* 181–186.

Jasper, J. D., Goel, R., Einarson, A., Gallo, M., & Koren, G. (2001). Effects of framing on teratogenic risk perception in pregnant women. *Lancet, 358,* 1237–1238.

Jenaro, C., Flores, N., & Arias, B. (2007). Burnout and coping in human service practitioners. *Professional Psychology: Research and Practice, 38,* 80–87.

Jeste, D. V., Savla, G. N., Thompson, W. K., Vahia, I. V., Glorioso, D. K., Palmer, B. W., . . . Depp, C. A. (2013). Association between older age and more successful aging: Critical role of resilience and depression. *American Journal of Psychiatry, 170,* 188–196. doi: 10.1176/appi.ajp.2012.12030386

Jiang, Y., Chew, S. H., & Ebstein, R. P. (2013). The role of D4 receptor gene exon lll polymorphisms in shaping human altruism and prosocial behavior. *Frontiers in Human Neuroscience, 7,* 1–7.

Joelving, F. (2010). More than just a bad dream. *Scientific American Mind, 20,* 14. doi: 10.1038/scientificamericanmind0110-14

Johnson, D. M. (2005). *Introduction to and review of simulator sickness research* (Research Report 1832, Army Project No. 2O262785A790). Arlington, VA: U.S. Army Research Institute for the Behavioral and Social Sciences. Retrieved from http://www.dtic.mil/cgi-bin/GetTRDoc?AD=ADA434495

Johnson, H. D., McNair, R., Vojick, A., Congdon, D., Monacelli, J., & Lamont, J. (2006). Categorical and continuous measurement of sex-role orientation: Differences in associations with young adults' reports of well-being. *Social Behavior and Personality, 34,* 59–76.

Johnson, H. D., Sholcosky, D., Gabello, K., Ragni, R., & Ogonosky, N. (2003). Sex differences in public restroom handwashing behavior associated with visual behavior prompts. *Perceptual and Motor Skills, 97,* 805–810.

Johnson, L. R., LeDoux, J. E., & Doyère, V. (2009). Hebbian reverberations in emotional memory micro circuits. *Frontiers in Neuroscience, 3,* 198–205.

Johnson, P. L., Truitt, W., Fitz, S. D., Minick, P. E., Dietrich, A., Sanghani, S., . . . Shekhar, A. (2010). A key role for orexin in panic anxiety. *Nature Medicine, 16,* 111–115.

Johnson, R. D. (1987). Making judgments when information is missing: Inferences, biases, and framing effects. *Acta Psychologica, 66,* 69–72.

Johnson, W., & Bouchard, T. J. (2011). The MISTRA data: Forty-two mental ability tests in three batteries. *Intelligence, 39,* 82–88.

Johnston, L. D., O'Malley, P. M., Bachman, J. G., & Schulenberg, J. E. (2012). *Monitoring the future national results on adolescent drug use: Overview of key findings, 2011.* Ann Arbor: Institute for Social Research, University of Michigan.

Johnston, M. V. (2009). Plasticity in the developing brain: Implications for rehabilitation. *Developmental Disabilities Research Reviews, 15,* 94–101.

Jones, B. E. (2003). Arousal systems. *Frontiers in Bioscience, 8,* 438–451.

Jones, E. E., & Harris, V. A. (1967). The attribution of attitudes. *Journal of Experimental Social Psychology, 3,* 1–24.

Jones, K. (2013). Discouraging social loafing during team-based assessments. *Teaching Innovation Projects, 3*(1), Article 13. Retrieved from http://ir.lib.uwo.ca/tips/vol3/iss1/13

Jordan-Young, R. M. (2012). Hormones, context, and "brain gender": A review of evidence from congenital adrenal hyperplasia. *Social Science & Medicine, 74,* 1738–1744.

Joseph, N. T., Matthews, K. A., & Myers, H. F. (2013, March 25). Conceptualizing health consequences of Hurricane Katrina from the perspective of socioeconomic status decline. *Health Psychology.* doi: 10.1037/a0031661

Josephs, R. A., Newman, M. L., Brown, R. P., & Beer, J. M. (2003). Status, testosterone, and human intellectual performance: Stereotype threat as status concern. *Psychological Science, 14,* 158–163.

Joshua, A. M., Cotroneo, A., & Clarke, S. (2005). Humor and oncology. *Journal of Clinical Oncology, 23,* 645–648.

Jouvet, M. (1979). What does a cat dream about? *Trends in Neurosciences, 2,* 280–282.

Juberg, D. R., Alfano, K., Coughlin, R. J., & Thompson, K. M. (2001). An observational study of object mouthing behavior by young children. *Pediatrics, 107,* 135–142.

Julien, R. M., Advokat, C. D. & Comaty, J. E. (2011). *A primer of drug action* (12th ed.). New York: Worth Publishers.

Julien, R. M., & DiCecco, K. (2010). To intend or not to intend: That is the question. *Journal of Legal Nurse Consulting, 21,* 10–14.

Junco, R., & Cotten, S. R. (2012). No A 4 U: The relationship between multitasking and academic performance. *Computers and Education, 59,* 505–514.

Jung, C. G. (1969). *Collected works: Vol. 8. The structure and dynamics of the psyche* (R. F. C. Hull, Ed.; 2nd ed.). Princeton, NJ: Princeton University Press.

Jussim, L., & Harber, K. D. (2005). Teacher expectations and self-fulfilling prophecies: Knowns and unknowns, resolved and unresolved controversies. *Personality and Social Psychology Review, 9,* 131–155.

Juul, A., Main, K. M., & Skakkebaek, N. E. (2011). Disorders of sex development—The tip of the iceberg? *Nature, 7,* 504–505.

Kaduvettoor-Davidson, A., & Inman, A. G. (2013). South Asian Americans: Perceived discrimination, stress, and well-being. *Asian American Journal of Psychology, 4,* 155–165. doi: 10.1037/a0030634

Kafka, M. P. (2009). The *DSM* diagnostic criteria for paraphilia not otherwise specified. *Archives of Sexual Behavior, 39,* 373–376.

Kagan, J. (1985). The human infant. In A. M. Rogers & C. J. Scheirer (Eds.), *The G. Stanley Hall lecture series* (Vol. 5, pp. 55–86). Washington, DC: American Psychological Association.

Kagan, J. (2003). Biology, context, and developmental inquiry. *Annual Review of Psychology, 54,* 1–23.

Kagan, J., & Snidman, N. (1991). Temperamental factors in human development. *American Psychologist, 46,* 856–862.

Kahlenberg, S. G., & Hein, M. M. (2010). Progression on Nickelodeon? Gender-role stereotypes in toy commercials. *Sex Roles, 62,* 830–847.

Kahn, J. (2012, January). Born to run back. *Runner's World.* Retrieved from http://www.runnersworld.com/runners-stories/born-run-back?page=single

Kahneman, D., & Tversky, A. (1973). On the psychology of prediction. *Psychological Review, 80,* 238–251.

Kahneman, D., & Tversky, A. (1984). Choices, values, and frames. *American Psychologist, 39,* 341–350.

Kahneman, D., & Tversky, A. (1996). On the reality of cognitive illusions. *Psychological Review, 103,* 582–591.

Kalin, N. H., Shelton, S. E., & Davidson, R. J. (2004). The role of the central nucleus of the amygdala in mediating fear and anxiety in the primate. *Journal of Neuroscience, 24,* 5506–5515.

Kaminski, J., Call, J., & Fischer, J. (2004). Word learning in a domestic dog: Evidence for "fast mapping." *Science, 304,* 1682–1683.

Kanai, R., Bahrami, B., Roylance, R., & Rees, G. (2012). Online social network size is reflected in human brain structure. *Proceedings of the Royal Society B, 279,* 1327–1334.

Kandel, E. R. (2009). The biology of memory: A forty-year perspective. *Journal of Neuroscience, 29,* 12748–12756.

Kandel, E. R., & Pittenger, C. (1999). The past, the future and the biology of memory storage. *Philosophical Transactions: Biological Sciences, 354,* 2027–2052.

Kandler, C., Bleidorn, W., & Riemann, R. (2012). Left or right? Sources of political orientation: The roles of genetic factors, cultural transmission, assortative mating, and personality. *Journal of Personality and Social Psychology, 102,* 633–645.

Kandler, C., Bleidorn, W., Riemann, R., Spinath, F. M., Thiel, W., & Angleitner, A. (2010). Sources of cumulative continuity in personality: A longitudinal multiple-rater twin study. *Journal of Personality and Social Psychology, 98,* 995–1008.

Kane, D. B. (2004, June 10). Rico's remarkable "vocabulary" raises new questions about language learning in animals. *AAAS News.* Retrieved from http://www.aaas.org/news/releases/2004/0610rico.shtml

Kaneda, H., Maeshima, K., Goto, N., Kobayakawa, T. Ayabe-Kanamura, S., & Saito, S. (2000). Decline in taste and odor discrimination abilities with age, and relationship between gustation and olfaction. *Chemical Senses, 25,* 331–337.

Kanwisher, N., McDermott, J., & Chun, M. M. (1997). The fusiform face area: A module in human extrastriate cortex specialized for face perception. *Journal of Neuroscience, 17,* 4302–4311.

Kapur, S. (2003). Psychosis as a state of aberrant salience: A framework linking biology, phenomenology, and pharmacology in schizophrenia. *American Journal of Psychiatry, 160,* 13–23.

Karam, E. G., Mneimneh, Z. N., Dimassi, H., Fayyad, J. A., Karam, A. N., Nasser, S. C., . . . Kessler, R. C. (2008). Lifetime prevalence of mental disorders in Lebanon: First onset, treatment, and exposure to war. *PLOS Medicine, 5,* 0579–0586.

Karlen, S. J., Kahn, D. M., & Krubitzer, L. (2006). Early blindness results in abnormal cortico-cortical and thalamocortical connections. *Neuroscience, 142,* 843–858.

Karremans, J. C., Stroebe, W., & Claus, J. (2006). Beyond Vicary's fantasies: The impact of subliminal priming and brand choice. *Journal of Experimental Social Psychology, 42,* 792–798.

Kasisomayajula, V., Herbst, R. S., Land, S. R., Leischow, S. J., Shields, P. G., & Writing Committee for the American Association for Cancer Research Task Force on Tobacco and Cancer. (2010). Tobacco and cancer: An American Association for Cancer Research policy statement. *Cancer Research, 70,* 3419–3430.

Kassin, S., Fein, S., & Markus, H. R. (2011). *Social psychology* (8th ed.). Belmont, CA: Wadsworth, Cengage Learning.

Kastenbaum, R., & Costa, P. T. Jr. (1977). Psychological perspectives on death. *Annual Review of Psychology, 28,* 225–249.

Kaufman, M. T. (2007, July 25). Albert Ellis, 93, influential psychotherapist, dies. *The New York Times.* Retrieved from http://www.nytimes.com/2007/07/25/nyregion/25ellis.html?pagewanted=all&_r=0

Kawa, S., & Giordano, J. (2012). A brief historicity of the *Diagnostic and Statistical Manual of Mental Disorders:* Issues and implications for the future of psychiatric canon and practice. *Philosophy, Ethics, and Humanities in Medicine, 7,* 1–9.

Kay, L. M., & Sherman, S. M. (2007). An argument for an olfactory thalamus. *Trends in Neurosciences, 30,* 47–53.

Kazdin, A. E. (1982). The token economy: A decade later. *Journal of Applied Behavior Analysis, 15,* 431–45.

Keel, P. K., & Klump, K. L. (2003). Are eating disorders culture-bound syndromes? Implications for conceptualizing their etiology. *Psychological Bulletin, 129,* 747–769.

Keesey, R. E., & Hirvonen, M. D. (1997). Body weight set-points: Determination and adjustment. *Journal of Nutrition, 127,* 1875S–1883S.

Keirstead, H. S., Nistor, G., Bernal, G., Totoiu, M., Cloutier, F., Sharp, K., & Oswald S. (2005). Human embryonic stem cell-derived oligodendrocyte progenitor cell transplants remyelinate and restore locomotion after spinal cord injury. *Journal of Neuroscience, 25,* 4694–4705.

Keith, S. E., Michaud, D. S., & Chiu, V. (2008). Evaluating the maximum playback sound levels from portable digital audio players. *Journal of the Acoustical Society of America, 123,* 4227–4237.

Kellner, C. H., Knapp, R. G., Petrides, G., Rummans, T. A., Husain, M. M., Rasmussen, K., . . . Fink, M. (2006). Continuation electroconvulsive therapy vs. pharmacotherapy for relapse prevention in major depression: A multisite study from the Consortium for Research Electroconvulsive Therapy (CORE). *Archives of General Psychiatry, 63,* 1337–1344.

Kemeny, M. E., & Shestyuk, A. (2008). Emotions, the neuroendocrine and immune systems, and health. In M. Lewis, J. M. Haviland-Jones, & L. F. Barrett (Eds.), *Handbook of emotions* (3rd ed., pp. 661–675). New York: Guilford Press.

Kempton, M. J., Salvador, Z., Munafò, M. R., Geddes, J. R. Simmons, A., Frangou, S., & Williams, S. C. R. (2011). Structural neuroimaging studies in major depressive disorder. *Archives of General Psychiatry, 68,* 675–690.

Kendall, A. E. (2012). *U.S. response to the global threat of HIV/AIDS: Basic facts.* Washington, DC: Congressional Research Service.

Kennedy, N., Boydell, J., Kalidindi, S., Fearon, P., Jones, P. B., van Os, J., & Murray, R. M. (2005). Gender differences in incidence and age at onset of mania and bipolar disorder over a 35-year period in Camberwell, England. *American Journal of Psychiatry, 162,* 257–262.

Kennedy, P. G. E., & Chaudhuri, A. (2002). Herpes simplex encephalitis. *Journal of Neurology, Neurosurgy & Psychiatry, 73,* 237–238.

Kennedy, S. H., Giacobbe, P., Rizvi, S. J., Placenza, F. M., Nishikawa, Y., Mayberg, H. S., & Lozano, A. M. (2011). Deep brain stimulation for treatment-resistant depression: Follow-up after 3 to 6 years. *American Journal of Psychiatry, 168,* 502–510.

Kerr, N. L., & Tindale, R. S. (2004). Group performance and decision making. *Annual Review of Psychology, 55,* 623–655.

Kessler, R. C. (2010). The prevalence of mental illness. In T. L. Scheid & T. N. Brown (Eds.), *A handbook for the study of mental health: Social contexts, theories, and systems* (2nd ed., pp. 46–63). Cambridge, UK: Cambridge University Press.

Kessler, R. C., Berglund, P., Demler, O., Jin, R., Koretz, D., Merikangas, K. R., . . . Wang, P. S. (2003). The epidemiology of major depressive disorder: Results from the National Comorbidity Survey Replication (NCS-R). *Journal of the American Medical Association, 289,* 3095–3105.

Kessler, R. C., Berglund, P., Demler, O., Jin, R., Merikangas, K. R., & Walters, E. E. (2005). Lifetime prevalence and age-of-onset distributions of *DSM–IV* disorders in the National Comorbidity Survey Replication. *Archives of General Psychiatry, 62,* 593–602.

Kessler, R. C., Chiu, W. T., Demler, O., & Walters, E. E. (2005). Prevalence, severity, and comorbidity of 12-month *DSM–IV* disorders in the National Comorbidity Survey Replication. *Archives of General Psychiatry, 62,* 617–627.

Kessler, R. C., & Wang, P. S. (2008). The descriptive epidemiology of commonly occurring mental disorders in the United States. *Annual Review of Public Health, 29,* 115–129.

Key, M. S., Edlund, J. E., Sagarin, B. J., & Bizer, G. Y. (2009). Individual differences in susceptibility to mindlessness. *Personality and Individual Differences, 46,* 261–264.

Keys, T. E. (1945). *The history of surgical anesthesia.* New York: Schuman's.

Kidd, S. A., Eskenazi, B., & Wyrobek, A. J. (2001). Effects of male age on semen quality and fertility: A review of the literature. *Fertility and Sterility, 75,* 237–248.

Kihara, T., & Shimohama, S. (2004). Alzheimer's disease and acetylcholine receptors. *Acta Neurobiologiae Experimentalis, 64,* 99–106.

Kihlstrom, J. F. (1985). Hypnosis. *Annual Review of Psychology, 36,* 385–418.

Kim, D.-Y., Oh, B.-M., & Paik, N.-J. (2006). Central effect of botulinum toxin type A in humans. *International Journal of Neuroscience, 116,* 667–680.

King, B. M. (2006). The rise, fall, and resurrection of the ventromedial hypothalamus in the regulation of feeding behavior and body weight [Invited review]. *Physiology & Behavior, 87,* 221–244.

King Humphrey, E. (2011). Laughter leads to insight. *Scientific American Mind, 22,* 5. doi: 10.1038/scientificamericanmind0511-5a

Kingsbury, M. K., & Coplan, R. J. (2012). Mothers' gender-role attitudes and their responses to young children's hypothetical display of shy and aggressive behaviors. *Sex Roles, 66,* 506–517.

Kinoshita, Y., Chen, J., Rapee, R. M., Bögels, S., Schneier, F. R., Choy, Y., . . . Furukawa, T. A. (2008). Cross-cultural study of conviction subtype Taijin Kyofu: Proposal and reliability of Nagoya–Osaka diagnostic criteria for social anxiety disorder. *Journal of Nervous and Mental Diseases, 196,* 307–313.

Kinsey, A. C., Pomeroy, W. B., & Martin, C. E. (1948). *Sexual behavior in the human male.* Philadelphia: W. B. Saunders.

Kinsey, A. C., Pomeroy, W. B., Martin, C. E., & Gebhard, P. H. (1953). *Sexual behavior in the human female.* Philadelphia: W. B. Saunders.

Kisilevsky, B. S., Hains, M. J., Brown, C.A., Lee, C. T., Cowperthwaite, B., Stutzman, S. S., . . . Wang, Z. (2008). Fetal sensitivity to properties of maternal speech and language. *Infant Behavior and Development, 32,* 59–71.

Kisilevsky, B. S., Hains, S. M. J., Lee, K., Xie, X., Huang, H., Ye, H. H., . . . Wang, Z. (2003). Effects of experience on fetal voice recognition. *Psychological Science, 14,* 220–224.

Klass, P. (2011, October 10). Hearing bilingual: How babies sort out language. *The New York Times.* Retrieved from http://www.nytimes.com/2011/10/11/health/views/11klass.html?_r=1

Klaver, C. C., Wolfs, R. C., Vingerling, J. R., Hoffman, A., & de Jong, P. T. (1998). Age-specific prevalence and causes of blindness and visual impairment in an older population: The Rotterdam Study. *Archives of Opthamology, 116,* 653–658.

Kleber, H. D., & DuPont, R. (2012). Physicians and medical marijuana. *American Journal of Psychiatry, 169,* 564–568.

Kleiner, K. (2011). Lunchtime leniency. *Scientific American Mind, 22,* 7. doi: 10.1038/scientificamericanmind0911-7b

Kleinman, A. (2004). Culture and depression. *New England Journal of Medicine, 351,* 951–953.

Klerman, E. B., & Dijk, D. J. (2004). Interindividual variation in sleep duration and its association with sleep debt in young adults. *Sleep, 28,* 1253–1259.

Klimstra, T. A., Luyckx, K., Hale III, W. W., Frijns, T., van Lier, P. A. C., & Meeus, W. H. J. (2010). Short-term fluctuations in identity: Introducing a micro-level approach to identity formation. *Journal of Personality and Social Psychology, 99,* 191–202.

Klugman, A., & Gruzelier, J. (2003). Chronic cognitive impairment in users of "ecstasy" and cannabis. *World Psychiatry, 2,* 184–190.

Kluver, H., & Bucy, P. (1939). Preliminary analysis of function of the temporal lobe in monkeys. *Archives of Neurology, 42,* 979–1000.

Knafo, A., & Israel, S. (2010). Genetic and environmental influences on prosocial behavior. In M. Mikulincer & P. R. Shaver (Eds.), *Prosocial motives, emotions, and behavior: The better angels of our nature* (pp. 149–167). Washington, DC: American Psychological Association.

Knapp, S., & VandeCreek, L. (2000). Recovered memories of childhood abuse: Is there an underlying professional consensus? *Professional Psychology: Research and Practice, 31,* 365–371.

Knecht, S., Dräger, B., Deppe, M., Bobe, L., Lohmann, H., Flöel, A., . . . Henningsen, H. (2000). Handedness and hemispheric language dominance in healthy humans. *Brain, 123,* 74–81.

Kneer, J., Glock, S., & Rieger, D. (2012). Fast and not furious? Reduction of cognitive dissonance in smokers. *Social Psychology, 43,* 81–91.

Knickmeyer, R. C., Gouttard, S., Kang, C., Evans, D., Wilber, J., Smith, K., . . . Gilmore, J. H. (2008). A structural MRI study of human brain development from birth to 2 years. *Journal of Neuroscience, 47*(28), 12176–12182.

Knudsen, E. I. (2004). Sensitive periods in the development of the brain and behavior. *Journal of Cognitive Neuroscience, 16,* 1412–1425.

Knutsson, A. (2003). Health disorders of shift workers. *Occupational Medicine, 53,* 103–108. Retrieved from http://occmed.oxfordjournals.org/content/53/2/103.long

Ko, H. J., & Youn, C. H. (2011). Effects of laughter therapy on depression, cognition and sleep among the community-dwelling elderly. *Geriatrics & Gerontology International, 3,* 267–274.

Kobasa, S. C. (1979). Stressful life events, personality, and health: An inquiry into hardiness. *Journal of Personality and Social Psychology, 37,* 1–11.

Koch, I., Lawo, V., Fels, J., & Vorländer, M. (2011). Switching in the cocktail party: Exploring intentional control of auditory selective attention. *Journal of Experimental Psychology: Human Perception and Performance, 37,* 1140–1147.

Kochanek, K. D., Xu, J., Murphy, S. L., Miniño, A. M., & Kung, H.-C. (2011). *Deaths: Final data for 2009* (National Vital Statistics Reports, Vol. 60, No. 3). Hyattsville, MD: National Center for Health Statistics. Retrieved from http://www.cdc.gov/nchs/data/nvsr/nvsr59/nvsr59_04.pdf

Koelsch, S., Gunter, T. C., Cramon, D. Y., Zysset, S., Lohmann, G., & Friederici, A. D. (2002). Bach speaks: A cortical "language-network" serves the processing of music. *NeuroImage, 17,* 956–966.

Koenig, B. A., & Gates-Williams, J. (1995). Understanding cultural difference in caring for dying patients. *Western Journal of Medicine, 163,* 244–249.

Kofman, J., & Hopper, K. (2010, October 13). Chile's successful rescue sets example for other countries. *ABC News International.* Retrieved from http://abcnews.go.com/International/chilean-miners-rescued-united-states-success/story?id=11874238

Kohlberg, L. (1981). *The philosophy of moral development: Vol. 1. Essays on moral development.* San Francisco: Harper & Row.

Kohlberg, L., & Hersh, R. H. (1977). Moral development: A review of the theory. *Theory into Practice, 16,* 53–59.

Kohler, P. K., Manhart, L. E., & Lafferty, W. E. (2008). Abstinence-only and comprehensive sex education in the initiation of sexual activity and teen pregnancy. *Journal of Adolescent Health, 42,* 344–351.

Köhler, W. (1925). *The mentality of apes.* New York: Harcourt Brace Jovanovich.

Kolb, B., & Gibb, R. (2011). Brain plasticity and behaviour in the developing brain. *Journal of the Canadian Academy of Child and Adolescent Psychiatry, 20,* 265–276.

Kolb, B., & Whishaw, I. Q. (1998). Brain plasticity and behavior. *Annual Review of Psychology, 49,* 43–64.

Kolb, B., & Whishaw, I. Q. (2009). *Fundamentals of human neuropsychology* (6th ed.). New York: Worth Publishers.

Kolb B., & Whishaw, I. Q. (2011). *An introduction to brain and behavior* (3rd ed.). New York: Worth Publishers.

Kolmes, K. (2012, December). Social media in the future of professional psychology. *Professional Psychology: Research and Practice, 43*(6), 606–612. doi: 10.1037/a0028678

Komai, T. (1951). Notes on lingual gymnastics. *Journal of Heredity, 42,* 293–297.

Kornheiser, A. S. (1976). Adaptation to laterally displaced vision: A review. *Psychological Bulletin, 5,* 783–816.

Kosslyn, S. M. (1978). Measuring the visual angle of the mind's eye. *Cognitive Psychology, 10,* 356–389.

Kosslyn, S. M., Ball, T. M., & Reiser, B. J. (1978). Visual images preserve metric spatial information: Evidence from studies of image scanning. *Journal of Experimental Psychology: Human Perception and Performance, 4,* 47–60.

Kosslyn, S. M., Thompson, W. L., Costantini-Ferrando, M. F., Alpert, N. M., & Spiegel, D. (2000). Hypnotic visual illusion alters color processing in the brain. *American Journal of Psychiatry, 157,* 1279–1284.

Kossoff, E. H., Vining, E. P. G., Pillas, D. J., Pyzik, P. L., Avellino, A. M., Carson, B. S., & Freeman, J. M. (2003). Hemispherectomy for intractable unihemispheric epilepsy: Epilepsy vs. outcome. *Neurology, 61,* 887–890.

Kothadia, J. P., Chhabra, S., Marcus, A., May, M., Saraiya, B., & Jabbour, S. K. (2012). Anterior mediastinal mass in a young marijuana smoker: A rare case of small-cell lung cancer. *Case Reports in Medicine,* Article 754231, 1–4.

Kouider, S., & Dehaene, S. (2007). Levels of processing during non-conscious perception: A critical review of visual masking. *Philosophical Transactions of the Royal Society B: Biological Sciences, 362,* 857–875.

Kounios, J., & Beeman, M. (2009). The *Aha!* moment: The cognitive neuroscience of insight. *Current Directions in Psychological Science, 18,* 210–216.

Kovács, A. M., & Mehler, J. (2009). Cognitive gains in 7-month-old bilingual infants. *Proceedings of the National Academy of Sciences, 106,* 6556–6560.

Kozel, A. F., Johnson, K. A., Grenesko, E. L., Laken, S. J., Kose, S., Lu, X., . . . George, M. S. (2009). Functional MRI detection of deception after committing a mock sabotage crime. *Journal of Forensic Science, 54,* 220–231.

Kraft, D. (2012). Successful treatment of heavy smoker in one hour using split screen imagery, aversion, and suggestions to eliminate cravings. *Contemporary Hypnosis and Integrative Therapy, 29,* 175–188.

Kramer, A. F., Erickson, K. I., & Colcombe, S. J. (2006). Exercise, cognition, and the aging brain. *Journal of Applied Physiology, 101,* 1237–1242.

Krasnova, I. N., & Cadet, J. L. (2009). Methamphetamine toxicity and messengers of death. *Brain Research Reviews, 60,* 379–407.

Kraul, C. (2010, October 11). Health experts monitoring trapped miners in Chile brace for unexpected ailments. *Los Angeles Times.* Retrieved from http://articles.latimes.com/2010/oct/11/world/la-fg-chile-miners-medical-20101011

Krebs, D. L., & Denton, K. (2005). Toward a more pragmatic approach to morality: A critical evaluation of Kohlberg's model. *Psychological Review, 112,* 629–649.

Krech, D., & Crutchfield, R. S. (1958). *Elements of psychology.* New York: Alfred A. Knopf.

Kreiman, G., Koch, C., & Fried, I. (2000). Imagery neurons in the human brain. *Nature, 408,* 357–361.

Krijn, M., Emmelkamp, P. M. G., Olafsson, R. P., & Biemond, R. (2004). Virtual reality exposure therapy of anxiety disorders: A review. *Clinical Psychology Review, 24,* 259–281.

Kripke, D. F., Langer, R. D., & Kline, L. E. (2012). Hypnotics' association with mortality or cancer: A matched cohort study. *BMJ Open, 2,* e000850.

Krizan, Z., & Windschitl, P. D. (2007). The influence of outcome desirability on optimism. *Psychological Bulletin, 133,* 95–121.

Krosnick, J. A., Betz, A. L., Jussim, L. J., & Lynn, A. R. (1992). Subliminal conditioning of attitudes. *Personality and Social Psychology Bulletin, 18,* 152–162.

Kross, E., & Grossmann, I. (2012). Boosting wisdom: Distance from the self enhances wise reasoning, attitudes, and behavior. *Journal of Experimental Psychology: General, 141,* 43–48.

Kruger, J., Blanck, H. M., & Gillespie, C. (2006). Dietary and physical activity behaviors among adults successful at weight loss maintenance. *International Journal of Behavioral Nutrition and Physical Activity, 3,* 17–27.

Kruk, M. R., Halász, J., Meelis, W. & Haller, J. (2004). Fast positive feedback between the adrenocortical stress response and a brain mechanism involved in aggressive behavior. *Behavioral Neuroscience, 118,* 1062–1070.

Kubinec, V-L. (2013, September 5). Brian Sinclair ignored by Winnipeg ER: Report. *CBC News.* Retrieved from http://www.cbc.ca/news/canada/manitoba/brian-sinclair-ignored-by-winnipeg-er-report-1.1385107

Kübler-Ross, E. (2009). *On death and dying. What the dying have to teach doctors, nurses, clergy, and their own families* (40th Anniversary Ed.). London: Routledge.

Kucharski, A. (1984). History of frontal lobotomy in the United States, 1935–1955. *Neurosurgery, 14,* 765–772.

Kuhl, P. K., Conboy, B. T., Padden, D., Nelson, T., & Pruitt, J. (2005). Early speech perception and later language development: Implications for the "critical period." *Language Learning and Development, 1,* 237–264.

Kujawa, S. G., & Liberman, M. C. (2006). Acceleration of age-related hearing loss by early noise exposure: Evidence of a misspent youth. *Journal of Neuroscience, 26,* 2115–2123.

Kuo, Z. Y. (1921). Giving up instincts in psychology. *Journal of Philosophy, 18,* 654–664.

Laan, E., & Janssen, E. (2007). How do men and women feel? Determinants of subjective experience of sexual arousal. In E. Janssen (Ed.), *The psychophysiology of sex* (pp. 278–290). The Kinsey Institute Series. Bloomington: Indiana University Press.

Ladouceur, C. D. (2012). Neural systems supporting cognitive–affective interactions in adolescence: The role of puberty and implications for affective disorders. *Frontiers in Integrative Neuroscience, 6,* 1–11.

Laeng, B., & Falkenberg, L. (2007). Women's pupillary responses to sexually significant others during the hormonal cycle. *Hormones and Behavior, 52,* 520–530.

Laeng, B., Profeti, I., Sæther, L., Adolfsdottir, S., Lundervold, A. J., Vangberg, T., . . . Waterloo, K. (2010). Invisible expressions evoke core impressions. *Emotion, 10,* 573–386.

Lahav, O., & Mioduser, D. (2008). Construction of cognitive maps of unknown spaces using a multi-sensory virtual environment for people who are blind. *Computers in Human Behavior, 24,* 1139–1155.

Lakdawalla, D. N., & Schoeni, R. F. (2003). Is nursing home demand affected by the decline in age difference between spouses? *Demographic Research, 8,* 279–304.

Lakes, K., Lopez, S. R., & Garro, L. C. (2006). Cultural competence and psychotherapy: Applying anthropologically informed conceptions of culture. *Psychotherapy: Theory, Research, Practice, Training, 43,* 380–396.

Lal, S. (2002). Giving children security: Mamie Phipps Clark and the racialization of child psychology. *American Psychologist, 57,* 20–28.

Lambert, M. J., Hansen, N. B., & Finch, A. E. (2001). Patient-focused research: Using patient outcome data to enhance treatment effects. *Journal of Consulting and Clinical Psychology, 69,* 159–172.

Landau, J. D., & Bavaria, A. J. (2003). Does deliberate source monitoring reduce students' misconceptions about psychology? *Teaching of Psychology, 30,* 311–314.

Lando, H. A. (1976). On being sane in insane places: A supplemental report. *Professional Psychology, 7,* 47–52.

Landolt, H. P., Dijk, D. J., Gaus, S. E., & Borbély, A. A. (1995). Caffeine reduces low-frequency delta activity in the human sleep EEG. *Neuropsychopharmacology, 12,* 229–238.

Landrum, R. E. (2001). I'm getting my bachelor's degree in psychology—What can I do with it? *Eye on Psi Chi, 6,* 22–24.

Lange, C. G., & James, W. (1922). The emotions. In K. Dunlap (Ed.), *Psychology classics: A series of reprints and translations.* Baltimore, MD: Williams & Wilkins.

Langer, E., Blank, A., & Chanowitz, B. (1978). The mindlessness of ostensibly thoughtful action: The role of "placebic" information in interpersonal interaction. *Journal of Personality and Social Psychology, 36,* 635–642.

Langer, E. J., & Rodin, J. (1976). The effects of choice and enhanced personal responsibility for the aged: A field experiment in an institutional setting. *Journal of Personality and Social Psychology, 34,* 191–198.

Langlois, J. H., Kalakanis, L., Rubenstein, A. J., Larson, A., Hallam, M., & Smoot, M. (2000). Maxims or myths of beauty? A meta-analytic and theoretical review. *Psychological Bulletin, 126,* 390–423.

Långström, N., Rahman, Q., Carlström, E., & Lichtenstein, P. (2010). Genetic and environmental effects on same-sex sexual behavior: A population study of twins in Sweden. *Archives of Sexual Behavior, 39,* 75–80.

Langwith, J. (2010). *Perspectives on diseases and disorders.* Farmington Hills, MI: Greenhaven Press.

Lara, D. R. (2010). Caffeine, mental health, and psychiatric disorders. *Journal of Alzheimer's Disease, 20,* S239–S248.

Larsen, L., Hartmann, P., & Nyborg, H. (2008). The stability of general intelligence from early adulthood to middle-age. *Intelligence, 36*, 29–34.

Larsson, M., Finkel, D., & Pederson, N. L. (2000). Odor identification: Influences of age, gender, cognition, and personality. *Journal of Gerontology: Psychological Sciences, 55B*, P304–P310.

Larsson, M., & Willander, J. (2009). Autobiographical odor memory. *Annals of the New York Academy of Sciences, 1170*, 318–323.

Larzelere, R. E., & Baumrind. (2010). Are spanking injunctions scientifically supported? *Law and Contemporary Problems, 73*, 57–87.

Lashley, K. D. (1950). In search of the engram. *Symposia of the Society for Experimental Biology, 4*, 454–482.

Las Vegas Sun. (2011, January 12). *Chilean miner Edison Pena at Viva Elvis.* Retrieved from http://www.lasvegassun.com/photos/galleries/2011/jan/12/chilean-miner-edison-pena-viva-elvis-aria/#102054

Latané, B., & Darley, J. M. (1968). Group inhibition of bystander intervention in emergencies. *Journal of Personality and Social Psychology, 10*, 215–221.

Latané, B., Williams, K., & Harkins, S. (1979). Many hands make light the work: The causes and consequences of social loafing. *Journal of Personality and Social Psychology, 37*, 822–832.

Laumann, E. O., Gagnon, J. H., Michael, R.T., & Michaels, S. (1994). *The social organization of sexuality: Sexual practices in the United States.* Chicago: University of Chicago Press.

Laumann, E. O., Paik, A., & Rosen, R. C. (1999). Sexual dysfunction in the United States: Prevalence and predictors. *Journal of the American Medical Association, 281*, 537–544.

Laureys, S., Perrin, F., & Brédart, S. (2007). Self-consciousness in non-communicative patients. *Consciousness and Cognition, 16*, 722–741.

Lavee, Y., & Ben-Ari, A. (2008). The association of daily hassles and uplifts with family and life satisfaction: Does cultural orientation make a difference? *American Journal of Community Psychology, 41*, 89–98.

Lawler-Row, K. A., & Elliott, J. (2009). The role of religious activity and spirituality in the health and well-being of older adults. *Journal of Health Psychology, 14*, 43–52.

Lawn, J. E., Blencowe, H., Pattinson, R., Cousens, S., Kumar, S, Ibiebele, I., . . . Stanton, C. (2011). Stillbirths: Where? When? Why? How to make the data count? *Lancet, 377*, 1448–1463.

Lazarus, R. S. (1984). On the primacy of cognition. *American Psychologist, 39*, 124–129.

Lazarus, R. S. (1991a). Cognition and motivation in emotion. *American Psychologist, 46*, 352–367.

Lazarus, R. S. (1991b). Progress on a cognitive–motivational–relational theory of emotion. *American Psychologist, 46*, 819–834.

Lazarus, R. S. (1993). From psychological stress to the emotions: A history of changing outlooks. *Annual Review of Psychology, 44*, 1–21.

Lazarus, R. S., & Folkman, S. (1984). *Stress, appraisal, and coping.* New York: Springer.

LeBeau, R. T., Glenn, D., Liao, B., Wittchen, H.-U., Beesdo-Baum, K., Ollendick, T., & Craske, M. G. (2010). Specific phobia: A review of *DSM–IV* specific phobia and preliminary recommendations for *DSM–V*. *Depression and Anxiety, 27*, 148–167.

Lebrecht, N. (2010, February 1). Sony pays $3 million to win pianist Lang Lang: Norman Lebrecht. *Bloomberg.com.* Retrieved from http://www.bloomberg.com/apps/news?pid=newsarchive&sid=a7bLa9pIgrek

LeDoux, J. E. (1996). *The emotional brain: The mysterious underpinnings of emotional life.* New York: Simon & Schuster.

LeDoux, J. E. (2000). Emotion circuits in the brain. *Annual Review of Neuroscience, 23*, 155–184.

LeDoux, J. E. (2002). Emotion, memory and the brain. *Scientific American Special Edition, 12*, 62–71.

LeDoux, J. E. (2012). Rethinking the emotional brain. *Neuron, 73*, 653–676.

Lee, J. H., Chang, Y. S., Yoo, H. S., Ahn, S. Y., Seo, H. J., Choi, S. H., . . . Park, W. S. (2011). Swallowing dysfunction in very low birth weight infants with oral feeding desaturation. *World Journal of Pediatrics, 7*, 337–343.

Lee, J. H., O'Keefe, J. H., Bell, D., Hensrud, D. D., & Holick, M. F. (2008). Vitamin D deficiency an important, common, and easily treatable cardiovascular risk factor? *Journal of the American College of Cardiology, 52*, 1949–1956.

Lee, M. (2006, December 19). Anthony suspended 15 games for brawl. *The Washington Post.* Retrieved from http://www.washingtonpost.com/wp-dyn/content/article/2006/12/18/AR2006121800424.html

Lee, M. K., Kiesler, S. B., & Forlizzi, J. (2010). Receptionist or information kiosk: How do people talk with a robot? In K. Inkpen, C. Gutwin, & J. Tang (Eds.), *Proceedings of the 2010 ACM Conference on Computer-Supported Cooperative Work, Savannah, Georgia* (pp. 31–40). New York: Association for Computing Machinery.

Lee, P. A., Houk, C. P., Ahmed, S. F., & Hughes, I. A. (2006). Consensus statement on management of intersex disorders. *Pediatrics, 118*, e488–e500.

Lee, V. E., & Burkam, D. T. (2002). *Inequality at the starting gate.* Washington, DC: Economic Policy Institute.

Lee, W., Reeve, J., Xue, Y., & Xiong, J. (2012). Neural differences between intrinsic reasons for doing versus extrinsic reasons for doing: An fMRI study. *Neuroscience Research, 73*, 68–72.

Lehrner, J., Eckersberger, C., Walla, P., Pötsch, G., & Deecke, L. (2000). Ambient odor of orange in a dental office reduces anxiety and improves mood in female patients. *Physiology & Behavior, 71*, 83–86.

Leichsenring, F., & Rabung, S. (2008). Effectiveness of long-term psychodynamic psychotherapy. *Journal of the American Medical Association, 300*, 1551–1565.

Leighty, K. A., Grand, A. P., Pittman Courte, V. L., Maloney, M. A., & Bettinger, T. L. (2013). Relational responding by eastern box turtles (*Terrapene carolina*) in a series of color discrimination tasks. *Journal of Comparative Psychology, 127*, 256–264. doi: 10.1037/a0030942

Leinninger, G. (2011). Lateral thinking about leptin: A review of leptin action via the lateral hypothalamus. *Physiology & Behavior, 104*, 572–581.

Lenhart, A. (2012). *Teens, smartphones & texting.* Washington, DC: Pew Internet & American Life Project.

Lenhart, A., Madden, M., Smith, A., Purcell, K., Zickuhr, K., & Rainie, L. (2011). *Teens, kindness and cruelty on social network sites.* Washington, DC: Pew Internet & American Life Project.

Lenzenweger, M. F., Lane, M. C., Loranger, A. W., & Kessler, R. C. (2007). *DSM–IV* personality disorders in the National Comorbidity Survey Replication. *Biological Psychiatry, 62*, 553–564.

Leontopoulou, S., Jimerson, S. R., & Anderson, G. E. (2011). An international exploratory investigation of students' perceptions of stressful life events: Results from Greece, Cyprus, and the United States. *School Psychology International, 32*, 632–644.

Lerman, C., & Audrain-McGovern, J. (2010). Reinforcing effects of smoking: More than a feeling. *Biological Psychiatry, 67*, 699–701.

Lessmoellmann, A. (2006, October 4). Can we talk? *Scientific American Mind, 17*, 44–49. Retrieved from http://www.scientificamerican.com/article.cfm?id=can-we-talk

Levänen, S., Uutela, K., Salenius, S., & Hari, R. (2001). Cortical representations of sign language: Comparison of deaf signers and hearing non-signers. *Cerbral Cortex, 11*, 506–512.

LeVay, S. (1991). A difference in hypothalamic structure between heterosexual and homosexual men. *Science, 253*, 1034–1037.

Levenson, R. W. (1992). Autonomic nervous system differences among emotions. *Psychological Science, 3*, 23–27.

Levenson, R. W., Carstensen, L. L., Friesen, W. V., & Ekman, P. (1991). Emotion, physiology, and expression in old age. *Psychology and Aging, 6,* 28–35.

Leventhal, H., Watts, J. C., & Pagano, F. (1967). Effects of fear an instructions on how to cope with danger. *Journal of Personality and Social Psychology, 6,* 313–321.

Levett-Jones, T., Sundin, D., Bagnall, M., Hague, K., Schuman, W., Taylor, C., & Wink, J. (2010). Learning to think like a nurse. *HNE Handover: For Nurses and Midwives, 3,* 15–20.

Levin, R. J. (2008). Critically revisiting aspects of the human sexual response cycle of Masters and Johnson: Correcting errors and suggesting modifications. *Sexual and Relationship Therapy, 23,* 393–399.

Levine, M. P., & Troiden, R. R. (1988). The myth of sexual compulsivity. *Journal of Sex Research, 25,* 347–363.

Levinson, D. F. (2006). The genetics of depression: A review. *Biological Psychiatry, 60,* 84–92.

Levy, R. A., & Ablon, S. J. (2010, February 23). Talk therapy: Off the couch and into the lab. *Scientific American Online.* Retrieved from http://www.scientificamerican.com/article.cfm?id=talk-ther

Lewis, D. J., & Duncan, C. P. (1956). Effect of different percentages of money reward on extinction of a lever-pulling response. *Journal of Experimental Psychology, 52,* 23–27.

Ley, J., Bennett, P., & Coleman, G. (2008). Personality dimensions that emerge in companion canines. *Applied Animal Behaviour Science, 110,* 305–317.

Li, A., Montaño, Z., Chen, V. J., & Gold, J. I. (2011). Virtual reality and pain management: Current trends and future directions. *Pain Management, 1,* 147–157.

Li, J. (2005). Mind or virtue: Western and Chinese beliefs about learning. *Current Directions in Psychological Science, 14,* 190–194.

Lichtwarck-Aschoff, A., Kunnen, S. E., & van Geert, P. L. C. (2009). Here we go again: A dynamic systems perspective on emotional rigidity across parent–adolescent conflicts. *Developmental Psychology, 45,* 1364–1375.

Licis, A. K., Desruisseau, D. M., Yamada, K. A., Duntley, S. P., & Gurnett, C. A. (2011). Novel findings in an extended family pedigree with sleepwalking. *Neurology, 76,* 49–52.

Liddle, J. R., Shackelford, T. K., & Weekes-Shackelford, V. A. (2012). Why can't we all just get along? Evolutionary perspectives on violence, homicide, and war. *Review of General Psychology, 16,* 24–36.

Lieberson, A. D. (2004, November 8). How long can a person survive without food? *Scientific American.* Retrieved from http://www.scientificamerican.com/article.cfm?id=how-long-can-a-person-sur

Lilienfeld, S. O. (2012). Public skepticism of psychology: Why many people perceive the study of human behavior as unscientific. *American Psychologist, 67,* 111–129.

Lilienfeld, S. O., & Arkowitz, H. (2011, January/February). The insanity verdict on trial. *Scientific American Mind,* 64–65.

Lilienfeld, S. O., Lynn, S. J., Ruscio, J., & Beyerstein, B. L. (2010). Busting big myths in popular psychology. *Scientific American Mind, 21,* 42–49.

Lilienfeld, S. O., Lynn, S. J., Ruscio, J., & Beyerstein, B. L. (2011). *50 great myths of popular psychology: Shattering widespread misconceptions about human behavior.* Hoboken, NJ: Wiley-Blackwell.

Lilienfeld, S. O., Wood, J. M., & Garb, H. N. (2005). What's wrong with this picture? *Scientific American Mind, 16,* 50–57.

Lillard, A. S., & Peterson, J. (2011). The immediate impact of different types of television on young children's executive function. *Pediatrics, 128,* 644–649.

Lim, J., & Dinges, D. F. (2010). A meta-analysis of the impact of short-term sleep deprivation on cognitive variables. *Psychological Bulletin, 136,* 375–389.

Lindau, S. T., Schumm, L. P., Laumann, E. O., Levinson, W., O'Muircheartaigh, C. A., & Waite, L. J. (2007). A study of sexuality and health among older adults in the United States. *New England Journal of Medicine, 357,* 762–774.

Lindberg, S. M., Hyde, J. S., Petersen, J. L., & Linn, M. C. (2010). New trends in gender and mathematics performance: A meta-analysis. *Psychological Bulletin, 136,* 1123–1135.

Linden, J. (2012, July 5). Profile: Olympics-Lochte unfazed by challenge of tackling Phelps. *Reuters.com.* Retrieved from http://www.reuters.com/article/2012/07/05/oly-swim-lochte-profile-idUSL6E8I208620120705

Lineberry, T. W., & Bostwick, J. M. (2006). Methamphetamine abuse: A perfect storm of complications. *Mayo Clinic Proceedings, 81,* 77–84.

Linhares, J. M., Pinto, P. D., & Nascimento, S. M. (2008). The number of discernible colors in natural scenes. *Journal of the Optical Society of America, 25,* 2918–2924.

Linnenbrink, E. A., & Pintrich, P. R. (2002). Motivation as an enabler for academic success. *School Psychology Review, 31,* 313–327.

Linnerooth, P. J., Mrdjenovich, A. J., & Moore, B. A. (2011). Professional burnout in clinical military psychologists: Recommendations before, during, and after deployment. *Professional Psychology: Research and Practice, 42,* 87–93.

Lipina, S. J., & Posner, M. I. (2012, August 17). The impact of poverty on the development of brain networks. *Frontiers in Human Neuroscience,* Article 238. Retrieved from http://www.frontiersin.org/Human_Neuroscience/10.3389/fnhum.2012.00238/abstract

Littlewood, R. (2004). Commentary: Globalization, culture, body image, and eating disorders. *Culture, Medicine and Psychiatry, 28,* 597–602.

Liu, S., Chow, H. M., Xu, Y., Erkkinen, M. G., Swett, K. E., Eagle, M. W., . . . Braun, A. R. (2012). Neural correlates of lyrical umprovisation: An fMRI study of freestyle rap. *Scientific Reports, 2.* doi: 10.1038/srep00834

Liu, Y., Yu, C., Liang, M., Li, J., Tian, L., Zhou, Y., . . . Jiang, T. (2007). Whole brain functional connectivity in the early blind. *Brain, 130,* 2085–2096.

Livingston, I., Doyle, J., & Mangan, D. (2010, April 25). Stabbed hero dies as more than 20 people stroll past him. *New York Post.* Retrieved from http://www.nypost.com/p/news/local/queens/passers_by_let_good_sam_die_5SGkf5XDP5ooudVuEd8fbl

Lloyd, M. A. (1997, July 16). *Entry level positions obtained by psychology majors.* Retrieved from http://www.psywww.com/careers/entry.htm

Loftus, E. F. (1994). The repressed memory controversy. *American Psychologist, 49,* 443–445.

Loftus, E. F. (1997). Creating false memories. *Scientific American, 277,* 70–75.

Loftus, E. F. (2005). Planting misinformation in the human mind: A 30-year investigation of the malleability of memory. *Learning and Memory, 12,* 361–366.

Loftus, E. F., & Bernstein, D. M. (2005). Rich false memories. In A. F. Healy (Ed.), *Experimental cognitive psychology and its applications* (pp. 101–113). Washington, DC: American Psychological Association Press.

Loftus, E., & Ketcham, K. (1994). *The myth of repressed memory.* New York: St. Martin's Griffin.

Loftus, E. F., Miller, D. G., & Burns, H. J. (1978). Semantic integration of verbal information into a visual memory. *Journal of Experimental Psychology: Human Learning and Memory, 4,* 19–31.

Loftus, E. F., & Palmer, J. C. (1974). Reconstruction of automobile destruction. *Journal of Verbal Learning and Verbal Behavior, 13,* 585–589.

Loftus, E. F., & Pickrell, J. E. (1995). The formation of false memories. *Psychiatric Annals, 25,* 720–725.

Looker, K. J., Garnett, G. P., & Schmid, G. P. (2008). An estimate of the global prevalence and incidence of herpes simplex virus type 2 infection. *Bulletin of the World Health Organization, 86*(10), 805-812.

Lorenz, K. Z. (1937). The companion in the bird's world. *The Auk, 54,* 245–273.

Los Angeles Times. (2010, October 12). *Editorial: Inspiration below ground and above.* Retrieved from http://articles.latimes.com/2010/oct/12/opinion/la-ed-1012-chile-20101012

Lott, A. J., & Lott, B. E. (1965). Group cohesiveness as interpersonal attraction: A review of relationships with antecedent and consequent variables. *Psychological Bulletin, 64,* 259–309.

Lou, S., & Zhang, G. (2009). What leads to romantic attractions: Similarity, reciprocity, security, or beauty? Evidence from a speed-dating study. *Journal of Personality, 77,* 933–964.

Lowenstein, J. A., Blank, H., & Sauer, J. D. (2010). Uniforms affect the accuracy of children's eyewitness identification and decisions. *Journal of Investigative Psychology and Offender Profiling, 7,* 59–73.

Lu, Z.-L., Williamson, S. J., & Kaufman, L. (1992). Behavioral lifetime of human auditory sensory memory predicted by physiological measures. *Science, 258,* 1668–1670.

Ludel, J. (1978). *Introduction to sensory processes.* San Francisco: W. H. Freeman and Company.

Lund, C., De Silva, M., Plagerson, S., Cooper, S., Chisholm, D., Das, J., . . . Patel, V. (2011). Poverty and mental disorders: Breaking the cycle in low-income and middle-income countries. *Lancet, 78,* 1502–1514.

Lyckholm, L. J. (2004). Thirty years later: An oncologist reflects on Kübler-Ross's work. *American Journal of Bioethics, 4,* 29–31.

Lynch, G. (2002). Memory enhancement: The search for mechanism-based drugs. *Nature Neuroscience 5* (Suppl.), 1035–1038.

Lynch, K. (1960). *The image of the city.* Cambridge, MA: MIT Press.

Lynn, S. J., Lilienfeld, S. O., Merckelbach, H., Giesbrecht, T., & van der Kloet, D. (2012). Dissociation and dissociative disorders: Challenging conventional wisdom. *Current Directions in Psychological Science, 21,* 48–53.

Lyubomirsky, S., Dickerhoof, R., Boehm, J. K., & Sheldon, K. M. (2011). Becoming happier takes both a will and a proper way: An experimental longitudinal intervention to boost well-being. *Emotion, 11,* 391–402.

Lyubomirsky, S., Sheldon, S. M., & Schkade, D. (2005). Pursuing happiness: The architecture of sustainable change. *Review of General Psychology, 9,* 111–131.

MacCann, C., Fogarty, G. J., Zeidner, M., & Roberts, R. D. (2011). Coping mediates the relationship between emotional intelligence (EI) and academic achievement. *Contemporary Educational Psychology, 36,* 60–70.

Maccoby, E. E., & Martin, J. A. (1983). Socialization in the context of the family: Parent–child interaction. In P. Mussen & E. M. Hetherington (Eds.), *Handbook of child psychology: Vol. IV. Socialization, personality and social development* (pp. 1–101). New York: Wiley.

Mack, A. (2003). Inattentional blindness: Looking without seeing. *Current Directions in Psychological Science, 12,* 180–184.

Macmillan, M. (2000). Restoring Phineas Gage: A 150th retrospective. *Journal of the History of the Neurosciences, 9,* 46–66.

Madden, S., Morris, A., Zurynski, Y. A., Kohn, M., & Elliot, E. J. (2009). Burden of eating disorders in 5–13-year-old children in Australia. *Medical Journal of Australia, 190,* 410–414.

Madden, T. J., Hewett, K., & Roth, M. S. (2000). Managing images in different cultures: A cross-national study of color meanings and preferences. *Journal of International Marketing, 8,* 90–107.

Madsen, K. M., Hviid, A., Vestergaard, M., Schendel, D., Wohlfahrt, J., Thorsen, P., . . . Melbye, M. (2002). A population-based study of measles, mumps, and rubella vaccination and autism. *New England Journal of Medicine, 347,* 1477–1482.

Maguen, S., Metzler, T. J., McCaslin, S. E., Inslicht, S. S., Henn-Haase, C., Neylan, T. C., & Marmar, C. R. (2009). Routine work environment stress and PTSD symptoms in police officers. *Journal of Nervous and Mental Disease, 197,* 754–760.

Maguire, E. A., Valentine, E. R., Wilding, J. M., & Kapur, N. (2003). Routes to remembering: The brains behind superior memory. *Nature Neuroscience, 6,* 90–95.

Maguire, E. A., Woollett, K., & Spiers, H. J. (2006). London taxi drivers and bus drivers: A structural MRI and neuropsychological analysis. *Hippocampus, 16,* 1091–1101

Mah, K., & Binik, Y. M. (2001). Do all orgasms feel alike? Evaluating a two-dimensional model of orgasm experience across gender and sexual context. *Journal of Sex Research, 39,* 104–113.

Maher, W. B., & Maher, B. A. (2003). Abnormal psychology. In D. K. Freedheim (Ed.), *Handbook of psychology: History of psychology* (Vol. 1, pp. 303–336). New York: Wiley.

Maheu, M. M., Pulier, M. L., McMenamin, J. P., & Posen, L. (2012). Future of telepsychology, telehealth, and various technologies in psychological research and practice. *Professional Psychology: Research and Practice, 43,* 613–621.

Mahmood, N. (2010, March 31). Here's how easily a hacker can crack your weak passwords. *Tech Journal.* Retrieved from http://thetechjournal.com/electronics/computer/security-computer-electronics/heres-how-easily-a-hacker-can-crack-your-weak-passwords.xhtml#ixzz1F7chbAEr

Mahoney, J. (2010). Strategic communication and anti-smoking campaigns. *Public Communication Review, 1,* 33–48.

Mai, E., & Buysse, D. J. (2008). Insomnia: Prevalence, impact, pathogenesis, differential diagnosis, and evaluation. *Sleep Medicine Clinics, 3,* 167–174.

Maiden, B., & Perry, B. (2011). Dealing with free-riders in assessed group work: Results from a study at a UK university. *Assessment & Evaluation in Higher Education, 36,* 451–464.

Maine Suicide Prevention Program. (2006). *Maine teen suicide prevention: I'm worried about . . . a friend.* Retrieved from http://maine.gov/suicide/youth/friend/

Majid, A. (2012). Current emotion research in the language sciences. *Emotion Review, 4,* 432–443.

Ma-Kellams, C., & Blascovich, J. (2012). Enjoying life in the face of death: East–West differences in responses to mortality salience. *Journal of Personality and Social Psychology, 103,* 773–786.

Makin, J. W., & Porter, R. H. (1989). Attractiveness of lactating females' breast odors to neonates. *Child Development, 60,* 803–810.

Malenka, R. C., & Nicoll, R. A. (1999). Long-term potentiation—A decade of progress? *Science, 285,* 1870–1874.

Malkoff-Schwartz, S., Frank, E., Anderson, B., Sherrill, J. T., Siegel, L., Patterson, D., & Kupfer, D. J. (1998). Stressful life events and social rhythm disruption in the onset of manic and depressive bipolar episodes. *Archives of General Psychiatry, 55,* 702–707.

Manago, A. M., Taylor, T., & Greenfield, P. M. (2012). Me and my 400 friends: The anatomy of college students' Facebook networks, their communication patterns, and well-being. *Developmental Psychology, 48*(2), 369–380. doi: 10.1037/a0026338

Manber, R., Kraemer, H. C., Arnow, B. A., Trivedi, M. H., Rush, A. J., Thase, M. E., . . . Keller, M. E. (2008). Faster remission of chronic depression with combined psychotherapy and medication than with each therapy alone. *Journal of Consulting and Clinical Psychology, 76,* 459–467.

Mancini, A. D., Bonanno, G. A., & Clark, A. E. (2011). Stepping off the hedonic treadmill: Individual differences in response to major life events. *Journal of Individual Differences, 32,* 144–152.

Mandler, J. M. (2008). On the birth and growth of concepts. *Philosophical Psychology, 21,* 207–230.

Mandoki, M. W., Sumner, G. S., Hoffman, R. P., & Riconda, D. L. (1991). A review of Klinefelter's syndrome in children and adolescents. *Psychiatry, 30,* 167–172.

Manickam, L. S. S. (2010). Psychotherapy in India. *Indian Journal of Psychiatry, 52,* S366–S370.

Mann, J. J., Apter, A., Bertolote, J., Beautrais, A., Currier, D., Haas, A., . . . Hendin, H. (2005). Suicide prevention strategies. *Journal of the American Medical Association, 294,* 2064–2074. doi: 10.1001/jama.294.16.2064

Manninen, B. A. (2011). Parental, medical, and sociological responsibilities: "Octomom" as a case study in the ethics of fertility treatments. *Journal of Clinical Research & Bioethics, S1*, 1–11.

Manning, J. T., Kilduff, L. P., & Trivers, R. (2013). Digit ratio (2D:4D) in Klinefelter's syndrome. *Andrology, 1*, 1–6.

Manning, R., Levine, M., & Collins, A. (2007). The Kitty Genovese murder and the social psychology of helping: The parable of the 38 witnesses. *American Psychologist, 62*, 555–562.

Manns, J. R., Hopkins, R. O., & Squire, L. R. (2003). Semantic memory and the human hippocampus. *Neuron, 38*, 127–133.

Maquet, P. (2000). Functional neuroimaging of normal human sleep by positron emission tomography. *Journal of Sleep Research, 9*, 208–231.

Marceau, K., Ram, N., Houts, R. M., Grimm, K. J., & Susman, E. J. (2011). Individual differences in boys' and girls' timing and tempo of puberty: Modeling development with nonlinear growth models. *Developmental Psychology, 47*, 1389–1409.

March of Dimes. (2012). *Prematurity campaign: What we know about prematurity*. Retrieved from http://www.marchofdimes.com/mission/prematurity_indepth.html

Marmurek, H. C., & Grant, R. D. (1990). Savings in a recognition test. *Canadian Journal of Psychology, 44*, 414–419.

Maron, E., Hettema, J. M., & Shlik, J. (2010). Advances in molecular genetics of panic disorder. *Molecular Psychiatry, 15*, 681–701.

Marris, E. (2006, March 28). ACS: Are you a supertaster? [Web log comment]. Retrieved from http://blogs.nature.com/inthefield/2006/03/acs_are_you_a_supertaster.html

Marsh, H. W., Nagengast, B., & Morin, A. J. (2012). Measurement invariance of Big-Five factors over the life span: ESEM tests of gender, age, plasticity, maturity, and La Dolce Vita effects. *Developmental Psychology, 49*, 1194–1218.

Marshall, L., & Born, L. (2007). The contribution of sleep to hippocampus-dependent memory consolidation. *Trends in Cognitive Sciences, 10*, 442–450.

Martin, C. L., & Halverson, C. F. (1983). The effects of sex-typing schemas on young children's memory. *Child Development, 54*, 563–574.

Martin, C. L., & Ruble, D. N. (2010). Patterns of gender development. *Annual Review of Psychology, 61*, 353–381.

Martin, C. L., Ruble, D. N., & Szkrybalo, J. (2002). Cognitive theories of early gender development. *Psychological Bulletin, 128*, 903–933.

Martin, L. A., Doster, J. A., Critelli, J. W., Purdum, M., Powers, C., Lambert, P. L., & Miranda, V. (2011). The "distressed" personality, coping and cardiovascular risk. *Stress and Health, 27*, 64–72.

Martin, R. A., Puhlik-Doris, P., Larsen, G., Gray, J., & Weir, K. (2003). Individual differences in uses of humor and their relation to psychological well-being: Development of the Humor Styles Questionnaire. *Journal of Research in Personality, 37*, 48–75.

Mashour, G. A., Walker, E. E., & Martuza, R. L. (2005). Psychosurgery: Past, present, and future. *Brain Research Reviews, 48*, 409–419.

Maslow, A. H. (1943). A theory of human motivation. *Psychological Review, 50*, 370–396.

Maslow, A. H. (1971). *The farther reaches of human nature*. New York: Viking Press.

Masterpasqua, F. (2009). Psychology and epigenetics. *Review of General Psychology, 13*, 194–201.

Masters, W., & Johnson, V. (1966). *Human sexual response*. Boston: Little, Brown.

Masters, W., & Johnson, V. (1979). *Homosexuality in perspective*. Boston: Little, Brown.

Matlin, M. W. (2009). *Cognition* (7th ed.). Hoboken, NJ: Wiley.

Matsumoto, D., & Willingham, B. (2009). Spontaneous facial expressions of emotion of congenitally and noncongenitally blind individuals. *Journal of Personality and Social Psychology, 96*, 1–10.

Matsumura, S., Bito, S., Liu, H., Kahn, K., Fukuhara, S., Kagawa-Singer, M., & Wenger, N. (2002). Acculturation of attitudes toward end-of-life care: A cross-cultural survey of Japanese Americans and Japanese. *Journal of General Internal Medicine, 17*, 531–539.

Mattarella-Micke, A., Mateo, J., Kozak, M. N., Foster, K., & Beilock, S. L. (2011). Choke or thrive? The relation between salivary cortisol and math performance depends on individual differences in working memory and math-anxiety. *Emotion, 11*(4), 1000–1005.

Maulia, E. (2013, February 15). Social media addiction a new "pathological" disorder. *The Jakarta Globe*. Retrieved from http://www.thejakartaglobe.com/news/social-media-addiction-a-new-pathological-disorder/571887

Maxmen, A. (2012). Generic HIV drugs will widen US treatment net. *Nature, 488*, 267.

Mayo Clinic. (2011). *Presbyopia*. Retrieved July 9, 2011, from http://www.mayoclinic.com/health/presbyopia/DS00589/DSECTION=causes

Mayo Clinic. (2011, May 21). Fetal alcohol syndrome: Symptoms. Retrieved from: http://www.mayoclinic.com/health/fetal-alcohol-syndrome/DS00184/DSECTION=symptoms

Mayo Clinic. (2012, May 11). *Cochlear implants a good next step when hearing aids are no longer effective*. Retrieved from http://www.mayoclinic.org/medical-edge-newspaper-2012/may-11b.html

Mazur, T. (2005). Gender dysphoria and gender change in androgen insensitivity or micropenis. *Archives of Sexual Behavior, 34*, 411–421.

McAdams, D. P., & Olson, B. D. (2010). Personality development: Continuity and change over the life course. *Annual Review of Psychology, 61*, 5.1–5.26.

McAnulty, R. D., Dillon, J., & Adams, H. E. (2002). Sexual deviation: Paraphilias. In P. B. Sutker & H. E. Adams (Eds.), *Comprehensive handbook of psychopathology* (Third Edition, 749–773). New York: Springer.

McCarthy, C. (2013). Pediatricians and television: It's time to rethink our messaging and our efforts. *Pediatrics, 131*, 589–590.

McCarthy, J. R., & Skowronski, J. J. (2011). The interplay of controlled and automatic processing in the expression of spontaneously inferred traits: A PDP analysis. *Journal of Personality and Social Psychology, 100*, 229–240.

McCauley, E., & Sybert, V. (2006). Social and behavioral development of girls and women with Turner syndrome. *International Congress Series, 1298*, 93–99.

McClelland, D. C., Atkinson, J. W., Clark, R. W., & Lowell, E. L. (1976). *The achievement motive*. New York: Irvington.

McCormick, J. G. (2007). Behavioral observations of sleep and anesthesia in the dolphin: Implications for bispectral index monitoring of unihemispheric effects in dolphins. *Anesthesia & Analgesia, 104*, 239–241.

McCosker, B., & Moran, C. C. (2012). Differential effects of self-esteem and interpersonal competence on humor styles. *Psychology Research and Behavior Management, 5*, 143–150.

McCrae, R. R., & Costa, P. T. Jr. (1987). Validation of the five-factor model of personality across instruments and observers. *Journal of Personality and Social Psychology, 49*, 81–90.

McCrae, R. R., & Costa, P. T. Jr. (1990). *Personality in adulthood*. New York: Guilford Press.

McCrae, R. R., Costa, P. T. Jr., Ostendorf, F., Angleitner, A., Hřebíčková, M., Avia, M. D., . . . Smith, P. B. (2000). Nature over nurture: Temperament, personality, and life span development. *Journal of Personality and Social Psychology, 78*, 173–186.

McCrae, R. R., Scally, M., Terracciano, A., Abecasis, G. R., & Costa, P. T. Jr. (2010). An alternative to the search for single polymorphisms: Toward molecular personality scales for the five-factor model. *Journal of Personality and Social Psychology, 99*, 1014–1024.

McCrae, R. R., Terracciano, A., & 78 Members of the Personality Profiles of Cultures Project. (2005). Universal features of personality traits from the observer's perspective: Data from 50 cultures. *Journal of Personality and Social Psychology, 88*, 547–561.

McDougall, D., & Allen-Mills, T. (2010, October 18). "I fight to live": Trapped miner Edison Pena ran for survival. *The Australian.* Retrieved from http://www.theaustralian.com.au/news/world/i-fight-to-live-trapped-miner-edison-pena-ran-for-survival/story-e6frg6so-1225939876501

McDougall, W. (1912). *An introduction to social psychology* (4th ed., rev.). Boston: John W. Luce.

McEwen, B. S. (2000). The neurobiology of stress: From serendipity to clinical relevance. *Brain Research, 886,* 172–189.

McGregor, J. (2012, February 15). How Jeremy Lin's star power could go unnoticed for so long. *The Washington Post.* Retrieved from http://www.washingtonpost.com/blogs/post-leadership/post/how-jeremy-lin-could-go-unnoticed-by-the-new-york-knicks-for-so-long/2011/04/01/gIQAAscmFR_blog.html

McGue, M., Bouchard, T. J. Jr., Iacono, W. G., & Lykken, D. T. (1993). Behavioral genetics of cognitive ability: A life-span perspective. In R. Plomin & G. E. McClearn (Eds.), *Nature, nurture & psychology* (pp. 59–76). Washington, DC: American Psychological Association.

McHugh, P. R., & Slavney, P. R. (2012). Mental illness—Comprehensive evaluation or checklist? *New England Journal of Medicine, 366,* 1853–1855.

McKenzie, S. (2012, October 23). A weighty issue: Hidden world of jockey heaving bowls. CNN.com. Retrieved from http://edition.cnn.com/2012/10/23/sport/jockey-diets-weight-horse-racing

McKinney, A., & Coyle, K. (2006). Alcohol hangover effects on measures of affect the morning after a normal night's drinking. *Alcohol & Alcoholism, 41,* 54–60.

McMurray, B. (2007). Defusing the childhood vocabulary explosion. *Science, 317,* 631.

McMurray, B., & Mitchell, C. (2008). A stochastic model for the vocabulary explosion. *Cognitive Science Proceedings,* 1919–1926.

McNally, R. J., & Clancy, S.A. (2005). Sleep paralysis, sexual abuse, and space alien abduction. *Transcultural Psychiatry, 42,* 113–122.

McPherson, M., Smith-Lovin, L., & Cook, J. M. (2001). Birds of a feather: Homophily in social networks. *Annual Review of Sociology, 27,* 415–444.

Medline Plus. (2010). *Osteomalacia.* Bethesda, MD: U.S. National Library of Medicine. Retrieved from http://www.nlm.nih.gov/medlineplus/ency/article/000376.htm

Medline Plus. (2011). *Brain surgery.* Bethesda, MD: U.S. National Library of Medicine. Retrieved from http://www.nlm.nih.gov/medlineplus/ency/article/003018.htm

Mehta, C. M., & Strough, J. (2010). Gender segregation and gender-typing in adolescence. *Sex Roles, 63*(3–4), 251–263.

Melzack, R. (1993). Pain: Past present and future. *Canadian Journal of Experimental Psychology, 47,* 615–629.

Melzack, R. (2008). The future of pain. *Nature Reviews, 7,* 629.

Melzack, R., & Wall, P. D. (1965). Pain mechanisms: A new theory. *Science, 150,* 971–979.

Mendle, J., & Ferrero, J. (2012). Detrimental psychological outcomes associated with pubertal timing in adolescent boys. *Developmental Review, 32,* 49–66.

Mendle, J., Harden, K. P., Brooks-Gunn, J., & Graber, J. A. (2010). Development's tortoise and hare: Pubertal timing, pubertal tempo, and depressive symptoms in boys and girls. *Developmental Psychology, 46,* 1341–1353.

Menken, J., Trussell, J., & Larsen, U. (1986). Age and infertility. *Science, 233,* 1389–1394.

Mennella, J. A., Coren P., Jagnow, M. S., & Beauchamp, G. K. (2001). Prenatal and postnatal flavor learning by human infants. *Pediatrics, 107,* e88.

Merikangas, K. R., Akiskal, H. S., Angst, J., Greenberg, P. E., Hirschfeld, R. M. A., Petukhova, M., & Kessler, R. C. (2007). Lifetime and 12-month prevalence of bipolar spectrum disorder in the National Comorbidity Survey Replication. *Archives of General Psychiatry, 64,* 543–552.

Mervis, C. B., & Rosch, E. (1981). Categorization of natural objects. *Annual Review of Psychology, 32,* 89–115.

Michael, R. T., Laumann, E. O., Kolata, G. B., & Gagnon, J. H. (1994). *Sex in America: A definitive survey.* Boston: Little, Brown.

Michalski, D., Kohout, J., Wicherski, M., & Hart, B. (2011). *2009 Doctorate employment survey.* APA Center for Workforce Studies. Retrieved from http://www.apa.org/workforce/publications/09-doc-empl/index.aspx

Milgram, S. (1963). Behavioral study of obedience. *Journal of Abnormal and Social Psychology, 67,* 371–378.

Milgram, S. (1964). Issues in the study of obedience: A reply to Baumrind. *American Psychologist, 19,* 848–852.

Milgram, S. (1965). Some conditions of obedience and disobedience to authority. *Human Relations, 18,* 57–76.

Milgram, S. (1974). *Obedience to authority: An experimental view.* New York: Harper & Row.

Miller, G. (1956). The magical number seven, plus or minus two: Some limits on our capacity for processing information. *Psychological Review, 63,* 81–97.

Miller, G. E., Chen, E., & Parker, K. J. (2011). Psychological stress in childhood and susceptibility to the chronic diseases of aging: Moving toward a model of behavioral and biological mechanisms. *Psychological Bulletin, 137,* 959–997.

Milrod, B., Leon, A. C., Busch, F., Rudden, M., Schwalberg, M., Clarkin, J., . . . Shear, M. K. (2007). A randomized control trial of psychoanalytic psychotherapy for panic disorder. *American Journal of Psychiatry, 164,* 265–272.

Mineka, S., Davidson, M., Cook, M., & Keir, R. (1984). Observational conditioning of snake fear in rhesus monkeys. *Journal of Abnormal Psychology, 93,* 355–372.

Mirsky, A. F., Bieliauskas L. A., French, L. M., Van Kammen, D. P., Jönsson, E., & Sedvall G. A. (2000). A 39-year followup of the Genain quadruplets. *Schizophrenia Bulletin, 26,* 699–708.

Mirsky, A. F., & Quinn, O. W. (1988). The Genain triplets. *Schizophrenia Bulletin, 14,* 595–612.

Mischel, W., & Shoda, Y. (1995). A cognitive-affective system theory of personality: Reconceptualizing the invariances in personality and the role of situations. *Psychological Review, 102,* 229–258.

Mistry, R. S., & Wadsworth, M. E. (2011). Family functioning and child development in the context of poverty. *Prevention Researcher, 18,* 11–15.

Mita, T. H., Dermer, M., & Knight, J. (1977). Reversed facial images and the mere-exposure hypothesis. *Journal of Personality and Social Psychology, 35,* 597–601.

Mitler, M. M., & Miller, J. C. (1996). Methods of testing for sleeplessness. *Behavioral Medicine, 21,* 171–183.

Moisse, K. (2011, September 20). Drug deaths exceed traffic deaths. *ABC News.* Retrieved from http://abcnews.go.com/Health/Drugs/drug-deaths-exceed-traffic-deaths/story?id=14554903

Mokdad, A. H., Marks, J. S., Stroup, D. F., & Gerberding, J. L. (2004). Actual causes of deaths in the United States, 2000. *Journal of the American Medical Association, 291,* 1238–1245.

Mollon, J. D. (1982). Color vision. *Annual Review of Psychology, 33,* 41–85.

Monroe, S. M., & Harkness, K. L. (2011). Recurrence in major depression: A conceptual analysis. *Psychological Review, 118,* 655–674.

Monteleone, G. T., Phan, L., Nusbaum, H. C., Gitzgerald, D., Irick, J.-S., Fienberg, S. E., & Cacioppo, J. T. (2009). Detection of deception using fMRI: Better than chance, but well below perfection. *Social Neuroscience, 4,* 528–538.

Montemayor, R. (1983). Parents and adolescents in conflict: All families some of the time and some families most of the time. *Journal of Early Adolescence, 3,* 83–103.

Montoya, E. R., Terburg, D., Bos, P. A., & van Honk, J. (2012). Testosterone, cortisol, and serotonin as key regulators of social aggression: A review and theoretical perspective. *Motivation and Emotion, 36,* 65–73.

Moore, E. G. J. (1986). Family socialization and the IQ test performance of traditionally and transracially adopted Black children. *Developmental Psychology, 22,* 317–326.

Morales, A., Heaton, J. P. W., & Carson III, C. C. (2000). Andropause: A misnomer for a true clinical entity. *Journal of Urology, 163,* 705–712.

Moreira-Almeida, A., Neto, F. L., & Cardeña, E. (2008). Comparison of Brazilian spiritist mediumship and dissociative identity disorder. *Journal of Nervous and Mental Disease, 196,* 420–424.

Moreland, R. L., & Zajonc, R. B. (1982). Exposure effects in person perception: Familiarity, similarity, and attraction. *Journal of Experimental Social Psychology, 18,* 395–415.

Morin, C. M., Bootzin, R. R., Buysse, D. J., Edinger, J. D., Espie, C. A., & Lichstein, K. L. (2006). Psychological and behavioral treatment of insomnia: Update of the recent evidence (1998–2004). *Sleep, 29,* 1398–1414.

Morone, N. E., & Greco, C. M. (2007). Mind–body interventions for chronic pain in older adults: A structured review. *Pain Medicine, 8,* 359–375.

Morrot, G., Brochet, F., & Dubourdieu, D. (2001). The color of odors. *Brain and Language, 79,* 309–320.

Morry, M. M., Kito, M., & Ortiz, L. (2011). The attraction-similarity model and dating couples: Projection, perceived similarity, and psychological benefits. *Personal Relationships, 18,* 125–143.

Mos Def. (2011, February 28). Kanye West: "I'm Scared of the Grammys" [Video file embedded in article]. *Rolling Stone.* Retrieved from http://www.rollingstone.com/music/news/kanye-west-im-scared-of-the-grammys-20110228

Moseley, G. L., Gallace, A., & Spence, C. (2008). *Pain, 138,* 7–10.

Mosher, W. D., Chandra, A., & Jones, J. (2005). *Sexual behavior and selected health measures: Men and women 15–44 years of age, United States, 2002* (Advance Data from Vital and Health Statistics, No. 362). Washington, DC: Centers for Disease Control and Prevention, National Center for Health Statistics. Retrieved from http://www.cdc.gov/nchs/data/ad/ad362.pdf

Most, S. B., Simons, D. J., Scholl, B. J., Jimenez, R., Clifford, E., & Chabris, C. F. (2001). How not to be seen: The contribution of similarity and selective ignoring to sustained inattentional blindness. *Psychological Science, 12,* 9–17.

Moyer, M. W. (2012). Rudeness on the Internet. *Scientific American Mind, 23,* 9.

MSN.com. (2012). *Famous middle children.* Retrieved from http://specials.msn.com/a-list/lifestyle/famous-middle-children-ss

MSNBC.com. (2011, July 26). *Girl, 6, on shark that bit her: "I forgive him"* [Video file]. Retrieved from http://today.msnbc.msn.com/id/43892097/ns/today-today_people/t/girl-shark-bit-her-i-forgive-him/#.TqR3Sc33LjQ

Mukamal, K. J., Maclure, M., Muller, J. E., Sherwood, J. B., & Mittleman, M. A. (2001). Prior alcohol consumption and mortality following acute myocardial infarction. *Journal of the American Medical Association, 285,* 1965–1970.

Mulder, E. J. H., Robles de Medina, P. G., Huizink, A. C., Van den Bergh, B. R. H., Buitelaar, J. K., & Visser, G. H. A. (2002). Prenatal maternal stress: Effects on pregnancy and the (unborn) child. *Early Human Development, 70,* 3–14.

Mulvey, S. (2006, May 15). Cakes and jokes at Cafe d'Europe. *BBC News.* Retrieved from http://news.bbc.co.uk/2/hi/europe/4755659.stm

Murdock, B. (1962). The serial position effect of free recall. *Journal of Experimental Psychology, 64,* 482–488.

Murdock, N. L., Edwards, C., & Murdock, T. B. (2010). Therapists' attributions for client premature termination: Are they self-serving? *Psychotherapy Theory, Research, Practice, Training, 47,* 221–234.

Murray, R. M., Morrison, P. D., Henquet, C., & Di Forti, M. (2007). Cannabis, the mind and society: The hash realities. *Nature Reviews Neuroscience, 8,* 885–895.

Mustanski, B. S., Chivers, M. L., & Bailey, J. M. (2002). A critical review of recent biological research on human sexual orientation. *Annual Review of Sex Research, 13,* 89–140.

Musto, D. F. (1991). Opium, cocaine and marijuana in American history. *Scientific American, 265,* 41–47.

Myers, D. G., & Lamm, H. (1976). The group polarization phenomenon. *Psychological Bulletin, 83,* 602–627.

Mysterud, I. (2003). Long live nature via nurture! *Evolutionary Psychology, 1,* 188–191.

Nagel, I. E., Chicherio, C., Li, S., von Oertzen, T., Sander, T., Villringer, A., . . . Lindenberger, U. (2008). Human aging magnifies genetic effects on executive functioning and working memory. *Frontiers in Human Neuroscience, 2,* 1–8.

Nahemow, L., & Lawton, M. P. (1975). Similarity and propinquity in friendship formation. *Journal of Personality and Social Psychology, 32,* 205–213.

Naimi, T. S., Brewer, R. D., Mokdad, A., Denny, C., Serdula, M. K., & Marks, J. S. (2003). Binge drinking among US adults. *Journal of the American Medical Association, 289,* 70–75.

Nakajima, M., & al'Absi, M. (2012). Predictors of risk for smoking relapse in men and women: A prospective examination. *Psychology of Addictive Behaviors, 26,* 633–637. doi: 10.1037/z0027280

Nash, M. R. (2001). The truth and the hype of hypnosis. *Scientific American, 285,* 44–55.

Nathanson, V., Jayesinghe, N., & Roycroft, G. (2007). Is it all right for women to drink small amounts of alcohol in pregnancy? No. *British Medical Journal, 335,* 857.

National Alliance on Mental Illness. (2012). *Treatment and services: Continuum model housing options.* Retrieved from http://www.nami.org/Template.cfm?Section=About_Treatments_and_Supports&Template=/ContentManagement/ContentDisplay.cfm&ContentID=144020

National Cancer Institute. (2010). The downside of diagnostic imaging. *NCI Cancer Bulletin, 7*(2).

National Eye Institute. (2009). *Facts about retinopathy of prematurity (ROP).* Retrieved from: http://www.nei.nih.gov/health/rop/rop.asp

National Eye Institute. (2012). *Facts about the cornea and corneal disease.* Retrieved June 8, 2012, from http://www.nei.nih.gov/health/cornealdisease/

National Geographic. (2013). *Dia de los muertos.* Retrieved from http://education.nationalgeographic.com/education/media/dia-de-los-muertos/?ar_a=1

National Heart, Lung, and Blood Institute. (2011). *What is CPAP?* Retrieved from http://www.nhlbi.nih.gov/health/health-topics/topics/cpap/

National Institute of Mental Health. (2007). *Medications.* Bethesda, MD: Author. Retrieved from http://solsticenyc.com/pdfs/medications.pdf

National Institute of Mental Health. (2011). *Eating disorders.* Bethesda, MD: Author. Retrieved from http://www.nimh.nih.gov/health/publications/eating-disorders/eating-disorders.pdf

National Institute of Mental Health. (2012). *The numbers count: Mental disorders in America.* Bethesda, MD: Author. Retrieved from http://www.nimh.nih.gov/health/publications/the-numbers-count-mental-disorders-in-america/index.shtml#ConwellSuiAging

National Institute of Mental Health. (2013). *Antidepressant medications for children and adolescents: Information for parents and caregivers.* Bethesda, MD: Author. Retrieved from http://www.nimh.nih.gov/health/topics/child-and-adolescent-mental-health/antidepressant-medications-for-children-and-adolescents-information-for-parents-and-caregivers.shtml

National Institute of Neurological Disorders and Stroke. (2011a). *Narcolepsy* [Fact sheet]. Bethesda, MD: National Institutes of Health. Retrieved from http://www.ninds.nih.gov/disorders/narcolepsy/detail_narcolepsy.htm

National Institute of Neurological Disorders and Stroke. (2011b). *NINDS Rasmussen's encephalitis information page.* Bethesda, MD: National Insitutes of Health. Retrieved from http://www.ninds.nih.gov/disorders/rasmussen/rasmussen.htm

National Institute of Neurological Disorders and Stroke. (2012). *Arteriovenous malformations and other vascular lesions of the central nervous system fact sheet.* Bethesda, MD: National Institutes of Health. Retrieved from http://www.ninds.nih.gov/disorders/avms/detail_avms.htm

National Institute on Aging. (2013). *About Alzheimer's disease: Alzheimer's basics.* Retrieved from http://www.nia.nih.gov/alzheimers/topics/alzheimers-basics

National Institute on Deafness and Other Communication Disorders. (2011, March). *Cochlear implants.* Retrieved from http://www.nidcd.nih.gov/health/hearing/pages/coch.aspx

National Institute on Drug Abuse. (2006). *Research report series—Methamphetamine abuse and addiction* (NIH Publication No. 06-4210). Bethesda, MD: National Institutes of Health.

National Institute on Drug Abuse. (2009). *Research report series—Tobacco addiction, glossary.* Bethesda, MD: National Institutes of Health. Retrieved from http://www.drugabuse.gov/researchreports/nicotine/glossary.html

National Institute on Drug Abuse. (2010a). *Cocaine.* Bethesda, MD: National Institutes of Health. Retrieved from http://www.nida.nih.gov/infofacts/cocaine.html

National Institute on Drug Abuse. (2010b). *MDMA (Ecstasy).* Bethesda, MD: National Institutes of Health. Retrieved from http://www.drugabuse.gov/publications/drugfacts/mdma-ecstasy

National Institute on Drug Abuse. (2010c). *Marijuana abuse.* Bethesda, MD: National Institutes of Health. Retrieved from http://www.drugabuse.gov/publications/research-reports/marijuana-abuse

National Institute on Drug Abuse. (2011). *Topics in brief: Prescription drug abuse.* Bethesda, MD: National Institutes of Health. Retrieved from http://www.nida.nih.gov/tib/prescription.html

National Institute on Drug Abuse. (2012, July). *Nationwide trends.* Retrieved November 24, 2012, from http://www.drugabuse.gov/sites/default/files/drugfactsnationtrends_1.pdf

National Institute on Drug Abuse. (2013). *DrugFacts: Heroin.* Bethesda, MD: National Institutes of Health. Retrieved from: http://www.drugabuse.gov/publications/drugfacts/heroin

National Institutes of Health. (2012). Tips for getting a good night's sleep. *Medline Plus, 7,* 20.

National Institutes of Health, Eunice Kennedy Shriver National Institute of Child Health and Human Development. (n.d.). *Turner syndrome.* Retrieved May 28, 2013, from http://turners.nichd.nih.gov/

National Institutes of Health, National Institute on Alcohol Abuse and Alcoholism. (2013). *Alcohol use disorders.* Retrieved from http://www.niaaa.nih.gov/e/alcohol-health/overview-alcohol-consumption/alcohol-use-disorders

National Safety Council. (2012). *Injury facts 2012 edition.* Itasca, IL: Author.

National Science Foundation, Division of Science Resources Statistics. (2011). Women, minorities, and persons with disabilities in science and engineering: 2011. In *Special Report NSF 11-309.* Arlington, VA. Available at http://www.nsf.gov/statistics/wmpd/.

National Sleep Foundation. (2009). *Sleep in America poll.* Retrieved from http://www.sleepfoundation.org/sites/default/files/2009%20Sleep%20in%20America%20SOF%20EMBARGOED.pdf

National Sleep Foundation. (2012a). *Children and sleep.* Retrieved from http://www.sleepfoundation.org/article/sleep-topics/children-and-sleep

National Sleep Foundation. (2012b). *Myths and facts.* Retrieved from http://www.sleepfoundation.org/sleep-facts-information/myths-and-facts

National Sleep Foundation. (2012c). *Teens and sleep.* Retrieved from http://www.sleepfoundation.org/article/sleep-topics/teens-and-sleep

Nature. (2004, April 15). True lies. *Nature, 428,* 679.

NBA.com. (2007, November 20). *2007–08 Player survey: Weight.* Retrieved from http://www.nba.com/news/survey_weight_2007.html

NBA.com. (2007, November 27). *2007–08 Player survey: Height.* Retrieved from http://www.nba.com/news/survey_height_2007.html

NBC Universal. (2013, February 12). *UK clinics treating patients for social-media addiction.* Retrieved from http://www.9news.com/news/article/31659

Ndubaku, U., & de Bellard, M. (2008). Glial cells: Old cells with new twists. *Acta Histochemica, 110,* 182–195.

Neal, R. (2009, February 11). Personality traits linked to birth order. *CBS News.* Retrieved from http://www.cbsnews.com/2100-500172_162-511694.html

Neary, L. (2013, March 25). How Ellen DeGeneres helped change the conversation about gays. *NPR.* Retrieved from: http://www.npr.org/2013/03/25/175265720/how-ellen-degeneres-helped-change-the-conversation-about-gays.

Neisser, U. (1979). The control of information pickup in selective looking. In A. D. Pick (Ed.), *Perception and its development: A tribute to Eleanor J. Gibson* (pp. 201–219). Hillsdale, NJ: Erlbaum.

Neisser, U. (1991). A place of misplaced nostalgia. *American Psychologist, 46,* 34–36.

Neisser, U., & Becklen, R. (1975). Selective looking: Attending to visually specified events. *Cognitive Psychology, 7,* 480–494.

Nelson, S. M., Telfer, E. E., & Anderson, R. A. (2013). The ageing ovary and uterus: New biological insights. *Human Reproduction Update, 19,* 67–83.

Nes, R. B., Czajkowski, N., & Tambs, K. (2010). Family matters: Happiness in nuclear families and twins. *Behavioral Genetics, 40,* 577–590.

Newell, A., Shaw, J. C., & Simon, H. A. (1958). Elements of a theory of human problem solving. *Psychological Review, 65,* 151–166.

Newell, B. R., & Andrews, S. (2004). Levels of processing effects on implicit and explicit memory tasks: Using question position to investigate the lexical-processing hypothesis. *Experimental Psychology, 51,* 132–144.

Newton, K. M., Reed, S. D., LaCroix, A. Z., Grothaus, L. C., Ehrlich, K., & Guiltinan, J. (2006). Treatment of vasomotor symptoms of menopause with black cohosh, multibotanicals, soy, hormone therapy, or placebo. *Annals of Internal Medicine, 145,* 869–879.

New York Times. (2009, May 6). *Times topics: Sichuan earthquake.* Retrieved from http://topics.nytimes.com/topics/news/science/topics/earthquakes/sichuan_province_china/index.html

Neylan, T. C. (1999). Frontal lobe function: Mr. Phineas Gage's famous injury. *Journal of Neuropsychiatry and Clinical Neurosciences, 11,* 280–281.

Ng, D. M., & Jeffery, R. W. (2003). Relationships between perceived stress and health behaviors in a sample of working adults. *Health Psychology, 22,* 638–642.

Ngun, T. C., Ghahramani, N., Sánchez, F. J., Bocklandt, S., & Vilain, E. (2011). The genetics of sex differences in brain and behavior. *Frontiers in Neuroendocrinology, 32,* 227–248.

NHL.com. (2013). *Oilers team: Joey Moss dressing room attendant.* Retrieved from http://oilers.nhl.com/club/page.htm?id=33055

Nickerson, R. S., & Adams, J. J. (1979). Long-term memory for a common object. *Cognitive Psychology, 11,* 287–307.

Niedenthal, P. M., Augustinova, M., Rychlowska, M., Droit-Volet, S., Zinner, L., Knafo, A., & Brauer, M. (2012). Negative relations between pacifier use and emotional competence. *Basic and Applied Social Psychology, 34,* 387–394.

Nielsen, N. R., Kristensen, T. S., Strandberg-Larsen, K., Zhang, Z.-F., Schnohr, P., & Grønbæk, M. (2008). Perceived stress and risk of colorectal cancer in men and women: A prospective cohort study. *Journal of Internal Medicine, 263,* 192–202.

Niemi, M.-B. (2009). Placebo effect: A cure in the mind. *Scientific American Mind, 20,* 42–49. Retrieved from http://www.scientificamerican.com/article.cfm?id=placebo-effect-a-cure-in-the-mind

Nieves, E. (2007, June 9). Indian reservation reeling in wave of youth suicides and attempts. *The New York Times.* Retrieved from http://www.nytimes.com/2007/06/09/us/09suicide.html?_r=0

Nisbett, R. E., Aronson, J., Blair, C., Dickens, W., Flynn, J., Halpern, D. F., & Turkehimer, E. (2012). Intelligence: New findings and theoretical developments. *American Psychologist, 67,* 130–159.

Nishitani, S., Miyamura, T., Tagawa, M., Sumi, M., Takase, R., Doi, H., . . . Shinohara, K. (2009). The calming effect of a maternal breast milk odor on the human newborn infant. *Neuroscience Research, 63,* 66–71.

Niskar, A. S., Kieszak, S. M., Holmes, A. E., Esteban, E., Rubin, C., & Brody, D. J. (2001). Estimated prevalence of noise-induced hearing threshold shifts among children 6 to 19 years of age: The Third National Health and Nutrition Examination Survey, 1988–1994, United States. *Pediatrics, 108,* 40–43.

Nohynek, H., Jokinen, J., Partinen, M., Vaarala, O., Kirjavainen, T., Sundman, J., . . . Kilpi, T. (2012). AS03 Adjuvanted AH1N1 vaccine associated with an abrupt increase in the incidence of childhood narcolepsy in Finland. *PLoS ONE, 7,* e33536. doi: 10.1371/journal.pone.0033536

Nolen-Hoeksema, S. (1991). Responses to depression and their effects on the duration of depressive episodes. *Journal of Abnormal Psychology, 100,* 569–582.

Noller, G. (2009). *Literature review and assessment report on MDMA/Ecstasy.* Wellington, New Zealand: Ministry of Health. Retrieved from http://www.ndp.govt.nz/moh.nsf/pagescm/7708/$File/July2010Literature-Review-Assessment-Report-MDMA-Ecstasy.pdf

Nonnemaker, J., Hersey, J., Homsi, G., Busey, A., Hyland, A., Juster, H., & Farrelly, M. (2011). Self-reported exposure to policy and environmental influences on smoking cessation and relapse: A 2-year longitudinal population-based study. *International Journal of Environmental Research and Public Health, 8,* 3591–3608.

Norcross, J. C., & Beutler, L. E. (2014). Integrative psychotherapies. In R. J. Corsini & D. Wedding (Eds.), *Current psychotherapies* (10th ed., pp. 499–532). Belmont, CA: Brooks/Cole, Cengage Learning.

Norcross, J. C., & Castle, P. H. (2002). Appreciating the PsyD: The facts. *Eye on Psi Chi, 7,* 2–26.

Norcross, J. C., & Wampold, B. E. (2011). What works for whom: Tailoring psychotherapy to the person. *Journal of Clinical Psychology, 67,* 127–132

Northoff, G. (2012). Genes, brains, and environment—Genetic neuroimaging of depression. *Current Opinion in Neurobiology, 23,* 1–10.

Northoff, G., Schneider, F., Rotte, M., Matthiae, C., Tempelmann, C., Wiebking, C., . . . Panksepp, J. (2009). Differential parametric modulation of self-relatedness and emotions in different brain regions. *Human Brain Mapping, 30,* 369–382.

Nour, N. M. (2009). Child marriage: A silent health and human rights issue. *Reviews in Obstetrics & Gynecology, 2,* 51–56.

Nusbaum, E. C., & Silvia, P. J. (2011). Are intelligence and creativity really so different? Fluid intelligence, executive processes, and strategy use in divergent thinking. *Intelligence, 39,* 36–45.

nyc.gov. (2013). *The NYC experience: Queens.* Retrieved from http://www.nyc.gov/html/ocnyc/html/experience/queens.shtml

Oatley, K., Keltner, D., & Jenkins, J. (2006). *Understanding emotions.* Malden, MA: Blackwell.

Öberg, M., Jaakkola, M. S., Woodward, A., Peruga, A., & Prüss-Ustün, A. (2011). Worldwide burden of disease from exposure to second-hand smoke: A retrospective analysis of data from 192 countries. *Lancet, 377,* 139–146.

O'Brien, D. (2005). *How to develop a brilliant memory.* London: Duncan Baird.

O'Brien, P. (2007). Is it all right for women to drink small amounts of alcohol in pregnancy? Yes. *British Journal of Medicine, 335,* 857.

Oda, R., Matsumoto-Oda, A., & Kurashima, O. (2005). Effects of belief in genetic relatedness on resemblance judgments by Japanese raters. *Evolution of Human Behavior, 26,* 441–450.

O'Donnell, S., Webb, J. K., & Shine, R. (2010). Conditioned taste aversion enhances the survival of an endangered predator imperiled by a toxic invader. *Journal of Applied Ecology, 47,* 558–565.

Oerlemans, W. G. M., Bakker, A. B., & Veenhoven, R. (2011). Finding the key to happy aging: A day reconstruction study of happiness. *Journal of Gerontology: Psychological Sciences, 6,* 665–674. doi: 10.1093/geronb/gbr040

Office of the Surgeon General, National Center for Injury Prevention and Control, National Institute of Mental Health, & Center for Mental Health Services. (2001). *Youth violence: A report of the Surgeon General (Risk factors for youth violence,* chapter 4). Rockville, MD: Office of the Surgeon General. Retrieved from http://www.ncbi.nlm.nih.gov/books/NBK44293/

Ogden, M. (2013, February 27). Jeremy Lin continues to prove NBA legitimacy as Rockets starting point guard. *Bleacher Report.* Retrieved from http://bleacherreport.com/articles/1546896-jeremy-lin-continues-to-prove-nba-legitimacy-as-rockets-starting-point-guard

O'Hanlon, I. (2010, August 31). Chilean miners suffering like soldiers. *Discovery News.* Retrieved from http://news.discovery.com/human/trapped-miners-psychology.html

Ohayon, M. (2011). Epidemiological overview of sleep disorders in the general population. *Sleep Medicine Reviews, 2,* 1–9.

Ohayon, M., Carskadon, M. A., Guilleminault, C., & Vitiello, M. V. (2004). Meta-analysis of quantitative sleep parameters from childhood to old age in healthy individuals: Developing normative sleep values across the human life-span. *Sleep, 27,* 1255–1273.

Ohbuchi, K., Fukushima, O., & Tedeschi, J. T. (1999). Cultural values in conflict management: Goal orientation, goal attainment, and tactical decision. *Journal of Cross-Cultural Psychology, 30,* 51–70.

O'Keefe, D. J. (2008). Elaboration likelihood model. In W. Donsbach (Ed.), *International encyclopedia of communication* (Vol. IV, pp. 1475–1480). Malden, MA: Blackwell.

O'Keeffe, G. S., Clarke-Pearson, K., & Council on Communications and Media. (2011). The impact of social media on children, adolescents, and families. *Pediatrics, 127,* 800–804.

Ollendick, T. H., Öst, L. G., Reuterskiöld, L., Costa, N., Cederlund, R., Sirbu, C., . . . Jarrett, M. A. (2009). One-session treatment of specific phobias in youth: A randomized clinical trial in the United States and Sweden. *Journal of Consulting and Clinical Psychology, 77,* 504–516.

Olson, J. M., Vernon, P. A., Harris, J. A., & Jang, K. L. (2001). The heritability of attitudes: A study of twins. *Journal of Personality and Social Psychology, 80,* 845–860.

Olson, R. L., Hanowski, R. J., Hickman, J. S., & Bocanegra, J. (2009). *Driver distraction in commercial vehicle operations* (Document No. FMCSA-RRT-09-042). Washington, DC: U.S. Department of Transportation, Federal Motor Carrier Safety Administration. Retrieved from http://www.distraction.gov/research/PDF-Files/Driver-Distraction-Commercial-Vehicle-Operations.pdf

O'Neil, D. (2009, December 10). Immigrant dream plays out through son. *ESPN.com.* Retrieved from http://sports.espn.go.com/ncb/columns/story?columnist=oneil_dana&id=4730385

Organisation for Economic Co-operation and Development. (2008). *Mental health in OECD countries* (OECD Policy Brief). Retrieved from http://www.oecd.org/els/health-systems/41686440.pdf

O'Riordan, K. (2012). The life of the gay gene: From hypothetical genetic marker to social reality. *Journal of Sex Research, 49,* 362–368.

Orzeł-Gryglewska, J. (2010). Consequences of sleep deprivation. *International Journal of Occupational Medicine & Environmental Health, 23,* 94–114.

Öst, L. G. (1989). One-session treatment for specific phobias. *Behaviour Research and Therapy, 27,* 1–7.

Otta, E., da Silva Queiroz, R., de Sousa Campos, L., da Silva, M. W. D., & Silveira, M. T. (1999). Age differences between spouses in a Brazilian marriage sample. *Evolution and Human Behavior, 20,* 99–103.

Overmier, J. B., & Seligman, M. E. P. (1967). Effects of inescapable shock upon subsequent escape and avoidance responding. *Journal of Comparative and Physiological Psychology, 63*, 28–33.

Oyserman, D., Coon, H. M., & Kemmelmeier, M. (2002). Rethinking individualism and collectivism: Evaluation of theoretical assumptions and meta-analyses. *Psychological Bulletin, 128*, 3–72.

Ozsungur, S., Brenner, D., & El-Sohemy, A. (2009). Fourteen well-described caffeine withdrawal symptoms factor into three clusters. *Psychopharmacology, 201*, 541–548.

Pachana, N. A., Brilleman, S. L., & Dobson, A. J. (2011). Reporting of life events over time: Methodological issues in a longitudinal sample of women. *Psychological Assessment, 23*, 277–281.

Paikoff, R. L., & Brooks-Gunn, J. (1991). Do parent–child relationships change during puberty? *Psychological Bulletin, 110*, 47–66.

Palermo, T. M., Eccleston, C., Lewandowski, A. S., Williams, A. C. D. C., & Morley, S. (2010). Randomized controlled trials of psychological therapies for management of chronic pain in children and adolescents: An updated meta-analytic review. *Pain, 148*, 387–397.

Pan, J.-Y., & Wong, D. F. K. (2011). Acculturative stressors and acculturative strategies as predictors of negative affect among Chinese international students in Australia and Hong Kong: A cross-cultural comparative study. *Academic Psychiatry, 35*, 376–381.

Pape, H.-C., & Pare, D. (2010). Plastic synaptic networks of the amygdala for the acquisition, expression, and extinction of conditioned fear. *Physiological Review, 90*, 419–463.

Papsin, B. C., & Gordon, K. A. (2007). Cochlear implants for children with severe-to-profound hearing loss. *New England Journal of Medicine, 357*, 2380–2387.

Parker, E. S., Cahill, L., & McGaugh, J. L. (2006). A case of unusual autobiographical remembering. *Neurocase, 12*, 35–49.

Parmentier, F. B. R., & Andrés, P. (2010). The involuntary capture of attention by sound: Novelty and postnovelty distraction in young and older adults. *Experimental Psychology, 57*, 68–76.

Parrott, A. C. (2004). MDMA (3,4-Methylenedioxymethamphetamine) or Ecstasy: The neuropsychobiological implications of taking it at dances and raves. *Neuropsychobiology, 50*, 329–335.

Parry, M. S. (2006). Dorothea Dix (1802–1887). *American Journal of Public Health, 96*, 624–625.

Parsons, T. D., & Rizzo, A. A. (2008). Affective outcomes of virtual reality exposure therapy for anxiety and specific phobias: A meta-analysis. *Journal of Behavior Therapy and Experimental Psychiatry, 39*, 250–261.

Pashler, H., Rohrer, D., Cepeda, N. J., & Carpenter, S. K. (2007). *Psychonomic Bulletin & Review, 14*, 187–193.

Patorno, E., Bohn, R. L., Wahl, P. M., Avorn, J., Patrick, A. R., Liu, J., & Schneeweiss, S. (2010). Anticonvulsant medications and the risk of suicide, attempted suicide, or violent death. *Journal of the American Medical Association, 303*, 1401–1409.

Patterson, D. R., & Jensen, M. P. (2003). Hypnosis and clinical pain. *Psychological Bulletin, 129*, 495–521.

Pavlov, I. (1906). The scientific investigation of the psychical faculties or processes in the higher animals. *Science, 24*, 613–619.

Pavlov, I. (1927/1960). *Conditioned reflexes.* New York: Dover.

Pavlovich-Danis, S. J., & Patterson, K. (2006, January 9). For a good night's sleep. *Nurseweek News.*

PBS. (1997, March 4). Secret of the wild child. *NOVA: Transcripts.* Retrieved from http://www.pbs.org/wgbh/nova/transcripts/2112gchild.html

PBS. (2005, January 27). American experience: Kinsey. Retrieved from: http://www.pbs.org/wgbh/amex/kinsey/peopleevents/p_kinsey.html.

PBS. (2013). Other notorious insanity cases. *Frontline.* Retrieved from http://www.pbs.org/wgbh/pages/frontline/shows/crime/trial/other.html

Pearce, J. M. (2009). Marie-Jean-Pierre Flourens (1794–1867) and cortical localization. *European Journal of Neurology, 61*, 311–314.

Pearlstein, T., Howard, M., Salisbury, A., & Zlotnick, C. (2009). Postpartum depression. *American Journal of Obstetrics & Gynecology, 200*, 357–364.

Pearson, E., & Siemaszko, C. (2010, November 6). Chilean miner Edison Pena is on top of world and ready for New York Marathon. *New York Daily News.* Retrieved from http://articles.nydailynews.com/2010-11-06/local/27080418_1_miner-observation-deck-elvis-presley

Peck, M. (2012). Changing social roles can reverse aging. *Scientific American Mind, 23*, 6. doi: 10.1038/scientificamericanmind1112-6

Pedersen, A., Zachariae, R., & Bovbjerg, D. H. (2010). Influence of psychological stress on upper respiratory infection: A meta-analysis of prospective studies. *Psychosomatic Medicine, 72*, 823–832.

Penfield, W., & Boldrey E. (1937). Somatic motor and sensory representation in the cerebral cortex of man as studied by electrical stimulation. *Brain, 60*, 389–443.

Penhaul, K. (2010, September 18). Trapped miners celebrate independence. *CNN.com.* Retrieved from http://www.cnn.com/2010/WORLD/americas/09/18/chile.mine.independence/index.html

Pennisi, E. (2012, September 5). Human genome is much more than just genes. *Science NOW.* Retrieved from http://news.sciencemag.org/sciencenow/2012/09/human-genome-is-much-more-than-j.html

Peplau, L. A. (2003). Human sexuality: How do men and women differ? *Current Directions in Psychological Science, 12*, 37–40.

Perkins, K. A., Karelitz, J. L., Conklin, C. A., Sayette, M. A., & Giedgowd, G. E. (2010). Acute negative affect relief from smoking depends on the affect measure and situation, but not on nicotine. *Biological Psychiatry, 67*, 707–714.

Peters, W. (1971). *A class divided: Then and now.* New Haven, CT: Yale University Press.

Peterson, B. S., Warner, V., Bansal, R., Zhu, H., Hao, X., Liu, J., . . . Weissman, M. M. (2009). Cortical thinning in persons at increased familial risk for major depression. *Proceedings of the National Academy of Sciences, 106*, 6273–6278.

Peterson, G. B. (2004). A day of great illumination: B. F. Skinner's discovery of shaping. *Journal of the Experimental Analysis of Behavior, 82*, 317–328.

Peterson, L. R., & Peterson, M. J. (1959). Short-term retention of individual verbal items. *Journal of Experimental Psychology, 58*, 193–198.

Peterson, M. J., Meagher, R. B. Jr., & Ellsbury, S. W. (1970). Repetition effects in sensory memory. *Journal of Experimental Psychology, 84*, 15–23.

Petitto, L. A. (1994). Are signed languages "real" languages? *International Quarterly of the Sign Linguistics Association, 7*, 1–10.

Petitto, L. A., & Marentette, P. F. (1991). Babbling in the manual mode: Evidence for the ontogeny of language. *Science, 251*, 1493–1496.

Petronis, A. (2004). The origin of schizophrenia: Genetic thesis, epigenetic antithesis, and resolving synthesis. *Biological Psychiatry, 55*, 965–970.

Petronis, A. (2010). Epigenetics as a unifying principle in the aetiology of complex traits and diseases. *Nature, 465*, 721–727.

Petty, R. E., & Cacioppo, J. T. (1986). The elaboration likelihood model of persuasion. *Advances in Experimental Social Psychology, 19*, 123–205.

Pevere, G. (2013, January 11). Last Tango in Paris: 40 years later, sexual controversy isn't so controversial any more. *The Globe and Mail.* Retrieved from: http://www.theglobeandmail.com/arts/film/last-tango-in-paris-40-years-later-sexual-controversy-isnt-so-controversial-any-more/article7171925/.

Pfeifer, C. (2012). Physical attractiveness, employment and earnings. *Applied Economics Letters, 19*, 505–510.

Phillips, J. (2013). Prescription drug abuse: Problem, policies, and implications. *Nursing Outlook, 61*, 78–84.

Phillips, R. G., & LeDoux, J. E. (1992). Differential contribution of amygdala and hippocampus to cued and contextual fear conditioning. *Behavioral Neuroscience, 106,* 274–285.

Phonecrastinate. (n.d.). In *Merriam-Webster.com: The open dictionary.* Retrieved December 3, 2012, from http://nws.merriam-webster.com/opendictionary/new-word_search.php

Piaget, J. (1936/1952). *The origins of intelligence in children.* New York: W. W. Norton.

Pich, E. M., Pagliusi, S. R., Tessari, M., Talabot-Ayer, D., Van Huijsduijnen, R. H., & Chiamulera, C. (1997). Common neural substrates for the addictive properties of nicotine and cocaine. *Science, 275,* 83–86.

Pierre, J. M. (2012). Mental illness and mental health: Is the glass half empty of half full? *Canadian Journal of Psychiatry, 57,* 651–658.

Pilley, J. W., & Reid, A. K. (2011). Border collie comprehends object names as verbal referents. *Behavioural Processes, 86,* 184–195.

Pines, A. (2011). Male menopause: Is it a real clinical syndrome? *Climacteric, 14,* 15–17.

Pinker, S. (1994). *The language instinct.* New York: Harper Perennial.

Pinker, S. (2003). Language as an adaptation to the cognitive niche. In M. H. Christiansen & S. Kirby (Eds.), *Language evolution: The states of the art* (pp. 16–37). New York: Oxford University Press.

Piper, A., Lillevik, L., & Kritzer, R. (2008). What's wrong with believing in repression?: A review for legal professionals. *Psychology, Public Policy, and Law, 14,* 223–242.

Pittenger, D. J. (1993). Measuring the MBTI and coming up short. *Journal of Career Planning & Placement, 54,* 48–52.

Pittenger, D. J. (2005). Cautionary comments regarding the Myers–Briggs Type Indicator. *Consulting Psychology Journal: Practice and Research, 57,* 210–221.

Platt, J. R. (2011, December, 27). Lions vs. cattle: Taste aversions could solve African predator problem [Web log post]. *Scientific American.* Retrieved from http://blogs.scientificamerican.com/extinction-countdown/2011/12/27/lions-vs-cattle-taste-aversion/

Pletcher, M. J., Vittinghoff, E., Kalhan, R., Richman, J., Safford, M., Sidney, S., . . . Kertesz, S. (2012). Association between marijuana exposure and pulmonary function over 20 years. *Journal of the American Medical Association, 307,* 173–181.

Plomin, R., & DeFries, J. C. (1998). Genetics of cognitive abilities and disabilities. *Scientific American, 278*(5), 62–69.

Plomin, R., DeFries, J. C., Knopik, V. S., & Neiderhiser, J. M. (2013). *Behavioral genetics* (6th ed.). New York: Worth Publishers.

Plomin, R., Haworth, C. M. A., Meaburn, E. L., Price, T. S., Wellcome Trust Case Control Consortium 2, & Davis, O. S. P. (2013). Common DNA markers can account for more than half of the genetic influence on cognitive abilities. *Psychological Science, 24,* 562–568. doi: 10.1177/0956797612457952

Poisson, J. (2011, December 26). The 'genderless baby' who caused a storm of controversy in 2011. *Toronto Star.* Retrieved from: http://www.thestar.com/news/gta/2011/12/26/the_genderless_baby_who_caused_a_storm_of_controversy_in_2011.html.

Polidori, M. C., Nelles, G., & Pientka, L. (2010). Prevention of dementia: Focus on lifestyle. *International Journal of Alzheimer's Disease, 2010,* 1–9. doi: 10.4061/2010/393579

Pope, K. S., & Wedding, D. (2014). Contemporary challenges and controversies. In R. J. Corsini & D. Wedding (Eds.), *Current psychotherapies* (10th ed., pp. 569–604). Belmont, CA: Brooks/Cole, Cengage Learning.

Porter, J. S., Stern, M., & Zak-Place, J. (2009). Prematurity, stereoptyping, and perceived vulnerability at 5 months: Relations with mothers and their premature and full-term infants at 9 months. *Journal of Reproductive and Infant Psychology, 27,* 168–181.

Porter, R. H., & Winberg, J. (1999). Unique salience of maternal breast odors for newborn infants. *Neuroscience & Biobehavioral Reviews, 23,* 439–449.

Postuma, R. B., Gagnon, J. F., Vendette, M., Fantini, M. L., Massicotte-Marquez, J., & Montplaisir, J. (2009). Quantifying the risk of neurodegenerative disease in idiopathic REM sleep behavior disorder. *Neurology, 72,* 1296–1300.

Potter, R. H. (2006). "As firecrackers to atom bombs": Kinsey, science, and authority. *Sexuality & Culture, 10,* 29–38.

Powell, L. H., Shahabi, L., & Thoresen, C. E. (2003). Religion and spirituality: Linkages to physical health. *American Psychologist, 58,* 36–52.

Powell, R. A. (2010). Little Albert still missing. *American Psychologist, 65,* 299–300.

Premack, A. J., & Premack, D. (1972). Teaching language to an ape. *Scientific American, 227,* 92–99.

Prengaman, P. (2010, September 3). NASA's advice to trapped Chile miners: Sleep, exercise, vitamin D. *Associated Press.* Retrieved from http://www.msnbc.msn.com/id/39000893/ns/world_news-americas/

Prinstein, M. J., Meade, C. S., & Cohen, G. L. (2003). Adolescent oral sex, peer popularity, and perceptions of best friends' sexual behavior. *Journal of Pediatric Psychology, 28,* 243–249.

Prochaska, J. J., Velicer, W. F., Prochaska, J. O., Delucchi, K., & Hall, S. M. (2006). Comparing intervention outcomes in smokers treated for single versus multiple behavioral risks. *Health Psychology, 25,* 380–388.

Prochaska, J. O., & Norcross, J. C. (2014). *Systems of psychotherapy* (8th ed.). Pacific Grove, CA: Brooks/Cole, Cengage Learning.

Prüfer, K., Munch, K., Hellmann, I., Akagi, K., Miller, J. R., Walenz, B., . . . Pääbo, S. (2012). The bonobo genome compared with the chimpanzee and human genomes. *Nature, 486,* 527–531.

Pryor, K. (2002). *Don't shoot the dog!* Dorking, UK: Ringpress Books.

Pryzgoda, J., & Chrisler, J. C. (2000). Definitions of gender and sex: The subtleties of meaning. *Sex Roles, 43,* 553–569.

Przybelski, R. J., & Binkley, N. C. (2007). Is vitamin D important for preserving cognition? A positive correlation of serum 25-hydroxyvitamin D concentration with cognitive function. *Archives of Biochemistry and Biophysics, 460,* 202–205.

Puig, J., Englund, M. M., Simpson, J. A., & Collins, W. A. (2013). Predicting adult physical illness from infant attachment: A prospective longitudinal study. *Health Psychology, 32,* 409–417.

Pullum, G. K. (1991). *The great Eskimo vocabulary hoax and other irreverent essays on the study of language.* Chicago: University of Chicago Press.

Qin, S., Ge, S., Yin, H., Xia, J., & Heynderickx, I. (2010). Just noticeable difference in black level, white level and chroma for natural images measured in two different countries. *Displays, 31,* 25–34.

Quilodran, F. (2010, August 24). Dinner for Chile miners—2 spoonfuls of tuna. *Associated Press.* Retrieved from http://www.msnbc.msn.com/id/38830593/ns/world_news-americas/t/dinner-chile-miners-spoonfuls-tuna/

Quinn, O. W. (1963). The public image of the family. In David Rosenthal (Ed.), *The Genain quadruplets: A case study and theoretical analysis of heredity and environment in schizophrenia* (pp. 355–372). New York: Basic Books.

Rabkin, J. G., & Struening, E. L. (1976). Life events, stress, and illness. *Science, 194,* 1013–1020.

Radak, Z., Hart, N., Sarga, L., Koltai, E., Atalay, M., Ohno, H., & Boldough, I. (2010). Exercise plays a preventive role against Alzheimer's disease. *Journal of Alzheimer's Disease, 20,* 777–783.

Radua, J., & Mataix-Cols, D. (2009). Voxel-wise meta-analysis of grey matter changes in obsessive-compulsive disorder. *British Journal of Psychiatry, 195,* 393–402.

Raichle, K. A., Hanley, M., Jensen, M. P., & Cardenas, D. D. (2007). Cognitions, coping, and social environment predict adjustment to pain in spinal cord injury. *Journal of Pain, 8,* 718–729.

Raine, A., Lencz, T., Bihrle, S., LaCasse, L., & Colletti, P. (2000). Reduced prefrontal gray matter volume and reduced autonomic activity in antisocial personality disorder. *Archives of General Psychiatry, 57,* 119–127.

Rainville, P., Duncan, G. H., Price, D. D., Carrier, B., & Bushnell, M. C. (1997, August 15). Pain affect encoded in human anterior cingulate but not somatosensory cortex. *Science, 277* (5328), 968–971.

Rajah, A., Kumar, R. S., Somasundaram, C. P., & Kumar, A. A. (2009). Dissociative fugue in the elderly. *Indian Journal of Psychiatry, 51,* 305–307.

Ramachandran, V. S., & Brang, D. (2009). Sensations evoked in patients with amputation from watching an individual whose corresponding intact limb is being touched. *Archives of Neurology, 66,* 1281–1284.

Ramachandran, V. S., & Rogers-Ramachandran, D. (2009). I see, but I don't know. Patients with unusual visual deficits provide insights into how we normally see. *Scientific American Mind, 19,* 20–22.

Ramchandran, K., & Hauser, J. (2010). Phantom limb pain #212. *Journal of Palliative Medicine, 13,* 1285–1287.

Rameson, L. T., Morelli, S. A., & Lieberman, M. D. (2012). The neural correlates of empathy: Experience, automaticity, and prosocial behavior. *Journal of Cognitive Neuroscience, 24,* 235–245.

Randall, D. K. (2012, September 22). Rethinking sleep. *The New York Times.* Retrieved from http://www.nytimes.com/2012/09/23/opinion/sunday/rethinking-sleep.html?pagewanted=all&_r=0

Rapee, R. M., & Spence, S. H. (2004). The etiology of social phobia: Empirical evidence and an initial model. *Clinical Psychology Review, 24,* 737–767.

Rasmussen, S. C. (2007). The history of science as a tool to identify and confront pseudoscience. *Journal of Chemical Education, 84,* 949–951.

Ratnesar, R. (2011, July/August). The menace within. *Stanford Magazine.* Retrieved from http://alumni.stanford.edu/get/page/magazine/article/?article_id=40741

Read, J., & Bentall, R. (2010). The effectiveness of electroconvulsive therapy: A literature review. *Epidemiologia e Psichiatria Sociale, 19,* 333–347.

Reber, S., Allen, R., & Reber, E. S. (2009). Appendix A: Simple phobias. In S. Reber, R. Allen, & E. S. Reber (Eds.). *The Penguin dictionary of psychology* (4th ed.). London: Penguin.

Rechtschaffen, A., & Bergmann, B. M. (1995). Sleep deprivation in the rat by the disk-over-water method. *Behavioural Brain Research, 69,* 55–63.

Reece, A. S. (2009). Chronic toxicology of cannabis. *Clinical Toxicology, 47,* 517–524.

Rees, J. L. (2003). Genetics of hair and skin color. *Annual Review of Genetics, 37,* 67–90.

Reese, H. W. (2010). Regarding Little Albert. *American Psychologist, 65,* 300–301.

Regalado, M., Sareen, H., Inkelas, M., Wissow, L. S., & Halfon, N. (2004). Parents' discipline of young children: Results from the National Survey of Early Childhood Health. *Pediatrics, 113,* 1952–1958.

Reich, S. M., Subrahmanyam, K., & Espinoza, G. (2012). Friending, IMing, and hanging out face-to-face: Overlap in adolescents' online and offline social networks. *Developmental Psychology, 48,* 356–368.

Reiche, E. M. V., Nunes, S. O. V., & Morimoto, H. K. (2004). Stress, depression, the immune system, and cancer. *Lancet Oncology, 5,* 617–625.

Reisenzein, R. (1983). The Schachter theory of emotion: Two decades later. *Psychological Bulletin, 94,* 239–264.

Ren, J., Wu, Y. D., Chan, J. S., & Yan, J. H. (2013). Cognitive aging affects motor performance and learning. *Geriatrics & Gerontology International, 13,* 19–27. doi: 10.1111/j.1447-0594.2012.00914.x

Reneman, L., Booij, J., de Bruin, K., Reitsma, J. B., de Wolff, F. A., Gunning, W. B., . . . van den Brink, W. (2001). Effects of dose, sex, and long-term abstention from use on toxic effects of MDMA (ecstasy) on brain serotonin neurons. *Lancet, 358,* 1864–1869.

Renner, M. J., & Macklin, R. S. (1998). A life stress instrument for classroom use. *Teaching of Psychology, 25,* 46–48.

Renner, W., Laireiter, A.-R., & Maier, M. (2012). Social support as a moderator of acculturative stress among refugees and asylum seekers. *Social Behavior and Personality, 40,* 129–146.

Reuter-Lorenz, P. A. (2013). Aging and cognitive neuroimaging: A fertile union. *Perspectives on Psychological Science, 8,* 68–71.

Reuters. (2010, August 22). *Trapped Chilean miners send message.* Retrieved from http://www.nytimes.com/2010/08/23/world/americas/23chile.html

Reynolds, B. A., & Weiss, S. (1992). Generation of neurons and astrocytes from isolated cells of the adult mammalian central nervous system. *Science, 255,* 1707–1710.

Rhudy, J. L., & Meagher, M. W. (2000). Fear and anxiety: Divergent effects on human pain thresholds. *Pain, 84,* 65–75.

Ricaurte, G. A., & McCann, U. D. (2001). Experimental studies on 3,4-methylenedioxymethamphetamine (MDMA, "ecstasy") and its potential to damage brain serotonin neurons. *Neurotoxicity Research, 3,* 85–99.

Rice, E., Rhoades, H., Winetrobe, H., Sanchez, M., Montoya, J., Plant, A., & Kordic, T. (2012). Sexually explicit cell phone messaging associated with sexual risk among adolescents. *Pediatrics, 130,* 667–673.

Rich, A. N., & Mattingley, J. B. (2002). Anomalous perception in synaesthesia: A cognitive neuroscience perspective. *Nature Reviews Neuroscience, 3,* 43–52.

Richardson, E. G., & Hemenway, D. (2011). Homicide, suicide, and unintentional firearm fatality: Comparing the United States with other high-income countries, 2003. *Journal of Trauma Injury, Infection, and Critical Care, 70,* 238–243.

Riedel, G., Platt, B., & Micheau, J. (2003). Glutamate receptor function in learning and memory. *Behavioural Brain Research, 140,* 1–47.

Rieger, G., & Savin-Williams, R. C. (2012). The eyes have it: Sex and sexual orientation differences in pupil dilation patterns. *PLoS One, 7.* doi: 10.1371/journal.pone.0040256

Rieke, F., & Baylor, D. A. (1998). Single-photon detection by rod cells of the retina. *Reviews of Modern Physics, 70,* 1027–1036.

Rietschel, M., Maier, W., & Schulze, T. G. (2013). *Phenotype refinement in bipolar affective disorder as a prerequisite for the identification of disease genes.* Federal Ministry of Education and Research, Disease-Oriented Genome Networks. Retrieved from http://www.science.ngfn.de/6_148.htm

Riggio, H. R., & Garcia, A. L. (2009). The power of situations: Jonestown and the fundamental attribution error. *Teaching of Psychology, 36,* 108–112.

Ritchie, J. (2009, January 12). Fact or fiction: Elephants never forget. *Scientific American Online.* Retrieved from http://www.scientificamerican.com/article.cfm?id=elephants-never-forget

Ritchie, S. J., Wiseman, R., & French, C. C. (2012). Replication, replication, replication. *Psychologist, 25*(5), 346–348.

Rivkees, S. A. (2003). Editorial: Time to wake-up to the individual variation in sleep needs. *Journal of Clinical Endocrinology & Metabolism, 88,* 24–25.

Robbins, B. D. (2008). What is the good life? Positive psychology and the renaissance of humanistic psychology. *Humanistic Psychologist, 36,* 96–112. Retrieved from http://www.mythosandlogos.com/Goodlife.pdf

Robbins, R. N., & Bryan, A. (2004). Relationships between future orientation, impulsive sensation seeking, and risk behavior among adjudicated adolescents. *Journal of Adolescent Research, 19,* 428–445.

Roberti, J. W. (2004). A review of behavioral and biological correlates of sensation seeking. *Journal of Research in Personality, 38,* 256–279.

Roberts, B. W., & DelVecchio, W. F. (2000). The rank-order consistency of personality traits from childhood to old age: A quantitative review of longitudinal studies. *Psychological Bulletin, 126,* 3–25.

Roberts, F. (2011, July 28). He's definitely got his figure back: World's first pregnant man unveils muscular physique after three babies in three years. *MailOnline.com.* Retrieved from http://www.dailymail.co.uk/news/article-2019579/Worlds-pregnant-man-Thomas-Beatie-unveils-muscular-body-3-babies.html

Roberts, F. D., Newcomb, P. A., Trentham-Dietz, A., & Storer, B. E. (1995). Self-reported stress and risk of breast cancer. *Cancer, 77,* 1089–1093.

Robertson, L. A., McAnally, H. M., & Hancox, R. J. (2013). Childhood and adolescent television viewing and antisocial behavior in early adulthood. *Pediatrics, 131,* 439–446.

Robinson, D. K. (2010). Gustav Fechner: 150 years of Elemente der Psychophysik. *History of Psychology, 13,* 409–410.

Rockett, I. R. H., Regier, M. D., Kapusta, N., Coben, J., Miller, T. R., Hanzlick, R. L., . . . Smith, G. S. (2012). Leading causes of unintentional and intentional injury mortality: United States, 2000–2009. *American Journal of Public Health, 102,* e84–e92. Retrieved from http://www.ncbi.nlm.nih.gov/pmc/articles/PMC3477930/

Rodin, J., & Langer, E. J. (1977). Long-term effects of a control-relevant intervention with the institutionalized aged. *Journal of Personality and Social Psychology, 12,* 897–902.

Rodriguez, T. (2012). Open mind, longer life. *Scientific American Mind, 23,* 18. doi: 10.1038/scientificamericanmind0912-18b

Roediger, H. L., & Bergman, E. T. (1998). The controversy over recovered memories. *Psychology, Public Policy, and Law, 4,* 1091–1109.

Roediger, H. L., III, Putnam, A. L., & Smith, M. A. (2011). Ten benefits of testing and their applications to educational practice. *Psychology of Learning and Motivation: Advances in Research and Theory, 55,* 1–36.

Roehrs, T., Hyde, M., Blaisdell, B., Greenwald, M., & Roth, T. (2006). Sleep loss and REM sleep loss are hyperalgesic. *Sleep, 29,* 145–151.

Roemer, L., Orsillo, S. M., & Salters-Pedneault, K. (2008). Efficacy of an acceptance-based behavior therapy for generalized anxiety disorder: Evaluation in a randomized controlled trial. *Journal of Consulting and Clinical Psychology, 76,* 1083–1089.

Rogers, C. R. (1951). *Client-centered therapy: Its current practice, implications, and theory.* Boston: Houghton Mifflin.

Rogers, C. R. (1959). A theory of therapy, personality, and interpersonal relationships as developed in the client-centered framework. In S. Koch (Ed.), *Psychology: A study of a science: Vol. 3. Formulations of the person and the social context* (pp. 184–256). New York: McGraw-Hill.

Rogers, C. R. (1961). *On becoming a person.* New York: Houghton Mifflin.

Rogers, C. R. (1979). The foundations of the person-centered approach. *Education, 100,* 98–107.

Rohrer, D., & Taylor, K. (2006). The effects of overlearning and distributed practice on the retention of mathematics knowledge. *Applied Cognitive Psychology, 20,* 1209–1224.

Rohwedder, S., & Willis, R. J. (2010). Mental retirement. *Journal of Economic Perspective, 24,* 119–138.

Roid, G. H. (2003). *Stanford–Binet Intelligence Scales* (5th ed.). Itasca, IL: Riverside.

Romero, A. J., Cuéllar, I., & Roberts, R. E. (2000). Ethnocultural variables and attitudes toward cultural socialization of children. *Journal of Community Psychology, 28,* 79–89.

Romero, M., Simón, R., Garcia-Recuero, I., & Romance, A. (2008). Dental management of oral self-mutilation in neurological patients: A case of congenital insensitivity to pain with anhidrosis. *Medicina Oral Patologia Oral y Cirugia Bucal, 13,* E644–E647.

Rosales-Lagarde, A., Armony, J. L., del Río-Portilla, Y., Trejo-Martínez, D., Conde, R., & Corsi-Cabrera, M. (2012). Enhanced emotional reactivity after selective REM sleep deprivation in humans: An fMRI study. *Frontiers in Behavioral Neuroscience, 6,* 1–13.

Rosch, E. (1973). Natural categories. *Cognitive Psychology, 4,* 328–350.

Rosch, E., & Mervis, C. B. (1975). Family resemblances: Studies in the internal structure of categories. *Cognitive Psychology, 7,* 573–605.

Rosch, E., Mervis, C. B., Gray, W. D., Johnson, D. M., & Boyes-Braem, P. (1976). Basic objects in natural categories. *Cognitive Psychology, 8,* 382–439.

Rose, J. D. (2011). Diverse perspectives on the groupthink theory—A literary review. *Emerging Leadership Journeys, 4,* 37–57.

Rose, N., Myerson, J., Roediger, H. L., & Hale, S. (2010). Similarities and differences between working memory and long-term memory: Evidence from the levels-of-processing span task. *Journal of Experimental Psychology: Learning, Memory, and Cognition, 36,* 471–483.

Rosenberg, R. S., & Kosslyn, S. M. (2011). *Abnormal psychology.* New York: Worth Publishers.

Rosenblum, L. D. (2010). *See what I'm saying: The extraordinary powers of our five senses.* New York: W. W. Norton.

Rosenhan, D. L. (1973). On being sane in insane places. *Science, 179,* 250–258.

Rosenkranz, M. A. (2007). Substance P at the nexus of mind and body in chronic inflammation and affective disorders. *Psychological Bulletin, 133,* 1007–10037.

Rosenman, R. H., Brand, R. J., Jenkins, D., Friedman, M., Straus, R., & Wurm, M. (1975). Coronary heart disease in the Western Collaborative Group Study: Final follow-up experience of 8½ years. *Journal of the American Medical Association, 233,* 872–877.

Rosenthal, R. (2002a). Covert communication in classrooms, clinics, courtrooms, and cubicles. *American Psychologist, 57,* 839–849.

Rosenthal, R. (2002b). Experimenter and clinician effects in scientific inquiry and clinical practice. *Prevention & Treatment, 5,* 1–12.

Rosenthal, R. (2003). Covert communication in laboratories, classrooms, and the truly real world. *Current Directions in Psychological Science, 12,* 151–154.

Rosenthal, R., & Jacobson, L. (1966). Teachers' expectancies: Determinants of pupils' IQ gains. *Psychological Reports, 19,* 115–118.

Rosenthal, R., & Jacobson, L. (1968). *Pygmalion in the classroom: Teacher expectation and pupils' intellectual development.* New York: Holt, Rinehart, & Winston.

Rosenzweig, M. R. (1984). Experience, memory, and the brain. *American Psychologist, 39,* 365–376.

Roseth, C. J., Johnson, D. W., & Johnson, R. T. (2008). Promoting early adolescents' achievement and peer relationships: The effects of cooperative, competitive, and individualistic goal structures. *Psychological Bulletin, 134,* 223–246.

Ross, L. (1977). The intuitive psychologist and his shortcomings: Distortions in the attribution process. In L. Berkowitz (Ed.), *Advances in experimental social psychology* (Vol. 10, pp. 173–220). New York: Academic Press.

Ross, L., Amabile, T. M., & Steinmetz, J. L. (1977). Social roles, social control, and biases in social-perception processes. *Journal of Personality and Social Psychology, 33,* 485–494.

Ross, L., Greene, D., & House, P. (1977). The "false consensus effect": An egocentric bias in social perception and attribution processes. *Journal of Experimental Social Psychology, 13,* 279–301.

Rosso, A., Mossey, J., & Lippa, C. F. (2008). Review: Caffeine: Neuroprotective functions in cognition and Alzheimer's disease. *American Journal of Alzheimer's Disease and Other Dementias, 23,* 417–422.

Rotge, J.-Y., Guehl, D., Dilharreguy, B., Tignol, J., Bioulac, B., Allard, M., . . . Aouizerate, B. (2009). Meta-analysis of brain volume changes in obsessive-compulsive disorder. *Biological Psychiatry, 65,* 75–83.

Roth, T. (2007). Insomnia: Definition, prevalence, etiology, and consequences. *Journal of Clinical Sleep Medicine, 3,* 7–10.

Rothbaum, B. O., Hodges, L., Smith, S., Lee, J. H., & Price, L. (2000). A controlled study of virtual reality exposure therapy for the fear of flying. *Journal of Consulting and Clinical Psychology, 68*, 1020–1026.

Rothbaum, F., Weisz, J., Pott, M., Miyake, K., & Morelli, G. (2000). Attachment and culture: Security in the United States and Japan. *American Psychologist, 55*, 1093–1104.

Rotter, J. B. (1954). *Social learning and clinical psychology.* Englewood Cliffs, NJ: Prentice-Hall.

Rotter, J. B. (1966). Generalized expectancies for internal versus external control of reinforcement. *Psychological Monographs: General and Applied, 80*, 1–28.

Rotter, J. B. (1990). Internal versus external control of reinforcement: A case history of a variable. *American Psychologist, 45*, 489–493.

Routh, D. K., & Reisman, J. M. (2003). Clinical psychology. In D. K. Freedheim (Ed.), *Handbook of psychology: Vol. 1. History of psychology* (pp. 337–355). Hoboken, NJ: Wiley.

Rowe, D. C., Almeida, D. M., & Jacobson, K. C. (1999). School context and genetic influences on aggression in adolescence. *Psychological Science, 10*, 277–280.

Rowe, M. H. (2002). Trichromatic color vision in primates. *News in Physiological Sciences, 17*, 93–98.

Rowe, R., Maughan, B., Worthman, C. M., Costello, E. J., & Angold, A. (2004). Testosterone, antisocial behavior, and social dominance in boys: Pubertal development and biosocial interaction. *Biological Psychiatry, 55*, 546–552.

Roy, D., Hazarika, S., Bhattacharya, A., Das, S., Nath, K., & Saddichha, S. (2011). Koro: Culture bound or mass hysteria? *Royal Australian & New Zealand Journal of Psychiatry, 45*, 683.

Rubin, Z., & Peplau, L. A. (1975). Who believes in a just world? *Journal of Social Issues, 31*, 65–89.

Rugg, D. (1941). Experiments in wording questions: II. *Public Opinion Quarterly, 5*(1), 91–92.

Rupert, P. A., Stevanovic, P., & Hunley, H. A. (2009). Work–family conflict and burnout among practicing psychologists. *Professional Psychology: Research and Practice, 40*, 54–61.

Rusbult, C. E. (1983). A longitudinal test of the investment model: The development (and deterioration) of satisfaction and commitment in heterosexual involvements. *Journal of Personality and Social Psychology, 45*, 101.

Rusbult, C. E., & Martz, J. M. (1995). Remaining in an abusive relationship: An investment model analysis of nonvoluntary dependence. *Personality and Social Psychology Bulletin, 21*, 558–571.

Rushton, J. P., & Jensen, A. R. (2010). Race and IQ: A theory-based review of the research in Richard Nisbett's *Intelligence and how to get it. Open Psychology Journal, 3*, 9–35.

Russell, J. A. (1980). A circumplex model of affect. *Journal of Personality and Social Psychology, 39*(6), 1161–1178.

Rutter, M., & O'Connor, T. G. (2004). Are there biological programming effects for psychological development findings from a study of Romanian adoptees? *Developmental Psychology, 40*, 81–94.

Ruxton, C. H. S. (2008). The impact of caffeine on mood, cognitive function, performance and hydration: A review of benefits and risks. *Nutrition Bulletin, 33*, 15–25.

Ryan, R. M., & Deci, E. L. (2000). Intrinsic and extrinsic motivations: Classic definitions and new directions. *Contemporary Educational Psychology, 25*, 54–67.

Sabah, M., Mulcahy, J., & Zeman, A. (2012). Herpes simplex encephalitis. *British Medical Journal, 344*, e3166. doi: 10.1136/bmj.e3166

Sable, P., & Akcay, O. (2010). Color: Cross-cultural marketing perspectives as to what governs our response to it. *Proceedings of American Society of Business and Behavioral Sciences, 17*, 950–954.

Sable, P., & Akcay, O. (2011). Response to color: Literature review with cross-cultural marketing perspective. *International Bulletin of Business Administration, 11*, 34–41.

Sacher, J., Neumann, J., Fünfstück, T., Soliman, A., Villringer, A., & Schroeter, M. L. (2012). Mapping the depressed brain: A meta-analysis of structural and functional alterations in major depressive disorder. *Journal of Affective Disorders, 140*, 142–148.

Sacks, O. (2007, September 24). The abyss. *The New Yorker.* Retrieved from http://www.newyorker.com/reporting/2007/09/24/070924fa_fact_sacks

Sagiv, M., Vogelaere, P. P., Soudry, M., & Ehrsam, R. (2000). Role of physical activity training in attenuation of height loss through aging. *Gerontology, 46*, 266–270.

Saha, S., Chant, D., Welham, J., & McGrath, J. (2005). A systematic review of the prevalence of schizophrenia. *PLoS Medicine, 2*, e141.

Sai, F. Z. (2005). The role of the mother's voice in developing mother's face preference: Evidence for intermodal perception at birth. *Infant and Child Development, 14*, 29–50.

Saini, R., Saini, S., & Sharma, S. (2010). Oral sex, oral health and orogenital infections. *Journal of Global Infection Diseases, 2*, 57–62.

Salimpoor, V. N., Benovoy, M., Larcher, K., Dagher, A., & Zatorre, R. J. (2011). Anatomically distinct dopamine release during anticipation and experience of peak emotion to music. *Nature Neuroscience, 14*, 257–264.

Salmon, P. (2001). Effects of physical exercise on anxiety, depression, and sensitivity to stress: A unifying theory. *Clinical Psychology Review, 21*, 33–61.

Salovey, P., Mayer, J. D., & Caruso, D. (2002). The positive psychology of emotional intelligence. In C. R. Snyder & S. J. Lopez (Eds.), *Handbook of positive psychology* (pp. 159–171). New York: Oxford University Press.

Salthouse, T. A. (2006). Mental exercise and mental aging: Evaluating the validity of the "use it or lose it" hypothesis. *Perspectives on Psychological Science, 1*, 68–87.

Salva, O. R., Farroni, T., Regolin, L., Vallortigara, G., & Johnson, M. H. (2011). The evolution of social orienting: Evidence from chicks (*gallus gallus*) and human newborns. *PLoS ONE 6*, e18802. doi: 10.1371/journal.pone.0018802

Sanders, G., Sjodin, M., & de Chastelaine, M. (2002). On the elusive nature of sex differences in cognition: Hormonal influences contributing to within-sex variation. *Archives of Sexual Behavior, 31*, 145–152.

Sansom-Daly, U. M., Peate, M., Wakefield, C. E., Bryant, R. A., & Cohn, R. (2012). A systematic review of psychological interventions for adolescents and young adults living with chronic illness. *Health Psychology, 31*, 380–393.

Santa Maria, C. (2012, February 14). Bonobo love: Valentine's advice from Christopher Ryan. *Huffington Post.* Retrieved from: http://www.huffingtonpost.com/2012/02/14/bonobo-love_n_1275381.html?ref=science. 458

Saper, C. B., Schammell, T. E., & Lu, J. (2005). Hypothalamic regulation of sleep and circadian rhythms. *Nature, 437*, 1257–1263.

Sar, V. (2011). Epidemiology of dissociative disorders: An overview. *Epidemiology Research International, 2011*, 1–8.

Sastre, J. P., & Jouvet, M. (1979). Le comportement onirique du chat [Oneiric behavior in cats]. *Physiology & Behavior, 22*, 979–989.

Sattler, J. M. (1990). *Assessment of children* (3rd ed.). San Diego, CA: Author.

Savic, I., & Lindström, P. (2008). PET and MRI show differences in cerebral asymmetry and functional connectivity between homo-and heterosexual subjects. *Proceedings of the National Academy of Sciences, 105*, 9403–9408.

Savin-Williams, R. C. (2009). How many gays are there? It depends. In D. A. Hope (Ed.), *Contemporary perspectives on lesbian, gay, and bisexual identities* (pp. 5–41). New York: Springer Science + Business Media.

Saxe, L. (1994). Detection of deception: Polygraph and integrity tests. *Current Directions in Psychological Science, 3*, 69–73.

Scarr, S., & McCartney, K. (1983). How people make their own environments: A theory of genotype–environment effects. *Child Development, 54*, 424–435.

Schachner, A., & Hannon, E. E. (2011). Infant-directed speech drives social preferences in 5-month-old infants. *Developmental Psychology, 47,* 19–25.

Schachter, S., & Singer, J. E. (1962). Cognitive, social, and physiological determinants of emotional state. *Psychological Review, 69,* 379–399.

Schaie, K. W. (1993). The Seattle longitudinal studies of adult intelligence. *Current Directions in Psychological Science, 2,* 171–175.

Schaie, K. W. (2008). Historical processes ad patterns of cognitive aging. In S. M. Hofer & D. F. Alwin (Eds.), *Handbook of cognitive aging: Interdisciplinary perspectives.* Thousand Oaks, CA: Sage.

Schalock, R. L., Borthwick-Duffy, S., Bradley, V. J., Bunting, W. H. E., Coulter, D. L., & Craig, E. M. (2010). *Intellectual disability: Definition classification, and systems of supports* (11th ed.). Washington, DC: American Association on Intellectual and Developmental Disabilities.

Scheffer, P. G., van der Schoot, C. E., Page-Christiaens, G. C., Bossers, B., van Erp, F., & de Haas, M. (2010). Reliability of fetal sex determination using maternal plasma. *Obstetrics & Gynecology, 115,* 117–126.

Schell, T. L., & Marshall, G. N. (2008). Survey of individuals previously deployed for OEF/OIF. In T. Tanielian & L. H. Jacycox (Eds.), *Invisible wounds of war: Psychological and cognitive injuries, their consequences, and services to assist recovery* (pp. 86–115). Santa Monica, CA: Rand Corporation.

Schellenberg, E. G. (2011). Music lessons, emotional intelligence, and IQ. *Music Perception, 29,* 185–194.

Schellenberg, E. G., & Winner, E. (2011). Music training and nonmusical abilities. *Music Perception, 29,* 129–132.

Schenck, C. H., & Mahowald, M. W. (2002). REM sleep behavior disorder: Clinical, developmental, and neuroscience perspectives 16 years after its formal identification in *SLEEP. SLEEP, 25,* 120–138.

Scherer, A. M., Windschitl, P. D., O'Rourke, J., & Smith, A. R. (2012). Hoping for more: The influence of outcome desirability on information seeking and predictions about relative quantities. *Cognition, 125,* 113–117.

Schiffman, S. S. (1997). Taste and smell losses in normal aging and disease. *Journal of American Medical Association, 278,* 1357–1362.

Schlaepfer, T. E., Bewernick, B. H., Kayser, S., Mädler, B., & Coenen, V. A. (2013). Rapid effects of deep brain stimulation for treatment-resistant major depression. *Biological Psychiatry, 73,* 1204–1212.

Schleppenbach, M., Flevares, L. M., Sims, L. M., & Perry, M. (2007). Teachers' responses to student mistakes in Chinese and U.S. mathematics classrooms. The Elementary School Journal, 108, 131–147.

Schmidt, H. G., Peeck, V. H., Paas, F., & van Breukelen, G. J. P. (2000). Remembering the street names of one's childhood neighbourhood: A study of very long-term retention. *Memory, 8,* 37–49.

Schmidt, R., & Cain, W. S. (2010). Making scents: Dynamic olfactometry for threshold measurement. *Chemical Senses, 35,* 109–120.

Schmidt-Daffy, M. (2011). Modeling automatic threat detection: Development of a face-in-the-crowd task. *Emotion, 11,* 153–168.

Schmitt, D. P., Realo, A., Voracek, M., & Allik, J. (2008). Why can't a man be more like a woman? Sex differences in Big Five personality traits across 55 cultures. *Journal of Personality and Social Psychology, 94,* 168–182.

Schnall, S., Roper, J., & Fessler, D. M. (2010). Elevation leads to altruistic behavior. *Psychological Science, 21,* 315–320.

Schneidman, E. S. (1973). *Deaths of man.* New York: Quadrangle/New York Times Book Co.

Schnider, A., Guggisberg, A., Nahum, L., Gabriel, D., & Morand, S. (2010). Dopaminergic modulation of rapid reality adaptation in thinking. *Neuroscience, 167,* 583–587.

Schommer-Aikins, M., & Easter, M. (2008). Epistemological beliefs' contributions to study strategies of Asian Americans and European Americans. *Journal of Educational Psychology, 100,* 920–929.

Schreiner, A. M., & Dunn, M. E. (2012). Residual effects of cannabis use on neurocognitive performance after prolonged abstinence: A meta-analysis. *Experimental and Clinical Psychopharmacology, 20,* 420–429.

Schultz, D. P., & Schultz, S. E. (2012). *A history of modern psychology* (10th ed.). Belmont, CA: Wadsworth, Cengage Learning.

Schultz, D. P., & Schultz, S. E. (2013). *Theories of personality* (10th ed.). Belmont, CA: Wadsworth, Cengage Learning.

Schultz, W. W., van Andel, P., Sabelis, I., & Mooyaart, E. (1999). Magnetic resonance imaging of male and female sexual arousal. *British Medical Journal, 319,* 1596–1600.

Schwartz, B. L. (2012). *Tip-of-the-tongue states: Phenomenology, mechanism, and lexical retrieval.* Mahwah, NJ: Psychology Press.

Schwartz, C. E., Keyl, P. M., Marcum, J. P., & Bode, R. (2009). Helping others shows differential benefits on health and well-being for male and female teens. *Journal of Happiness Studies, 10,* 431–448.

Schwartz, C. E., Meisenhelder, J. B., Yunsheng, M., & Reed, G. (2003). Altruistic social interest behaviors are associated with better mental health. *Psychosomatic Medicine, 65,* 778–785.

Schwartz, S. J. (2001). The evolution of Eriksonian and Neo-Eriksonian identity theory and research: A review and integration. *Identity: An International Journal of Theory and Research, 1,* 7–58.

Schwarz, S., & Hassebrauck, M. (2012). Sex and age differences in mate-selection preferences. *Human Nature, 23,* 447–466.

Schwarz, S., Hassebrauck, M., & Dörfler, R. (2010). Let us talk about sex: Prototype and personal templates. *Personal Relationships, 17,* 533–555.

Schweinsburg, A. D., Brown, S. A., & Tapert, S. F. (2008). The influence of marijuana use on neurocognitive functioning in adolescents. *Current Drug Abuse Reviews, 1,* 99–111.

Scott, S. B., Rhoades, G. K., Stanley, S. M., Allen, E. S., & Markman, H. J. (2013). Reasons for divorce and recollections of premarital intervention: Implications for improving relationship education. *Couple and Family Psychology: Research and Practice, 2,* 131–145.

Scott, S. K., Blank, C. C., Rosen, S., & Wise, R. J. S. (2000). Identification of a pathway for intelligible speech in the left temporal lobe. *Brain, 123,* 2400–2406.

Scoville, W. B., & Milner, B. (1957). Loss of recent memory after bilateral hippocampal lesions. *Journal of Neurology, Neurosurgery, & Psychiatry, 20,* 11–21.

Scribner, C. M. (2001). Rosenhan revisited. *Professional Psychology: Research and Practice, 32,* 215–216.

Scully, J. A., Tosi, H., & Banning, K. (2000). Life event checklists: Revisiting the Social Readjustment Rating Scale after 30 years. *Educational and Psychological Measurement, 60,* 864–876.

Searight, H. R., & Gafford, J. (2005). Cultural diversity at the end of life: Issues and guidelines for family physicians. *American Family Physician, 71,* 515–522.

Searleman, A. (2007, March 12). Is there such a thing as a photographic memory? And if so, can it be learned? *Scientific American Online.* Retrieved from http://www.scientificamerican.com/article.cfm?id=is-there-such-a-thing-as

Sedlmeier, P., Eberth, J., Schwarz, M., Zimmermann, D., Haarig, F., Jaeger, S., & Kunze, S. (2012). The psychological effects of meditation: A meta-analysis. *Psychological Bulletin, 138,* 1139–1171. doi: 10.1037/a0028168

Seely, R. (2012, September 19). UW study says boys' pacifier use limits social development. *Wisconsin State Journal.* Retrieved from http://host.madison.com/news/local/education/university/uw-study-says-boys-pacifier-use-limits-social-development/article_c44e3998-01f9-11e2-9b69-0019bb2963f4.html

Seery, M. D. (2011). Resilience: A silver lining to experiencing adverse life events? *Current Directions in Psychological Science, 20,* 390–394.

Segal, D. L., Coolidge, F. L., & Mizuno, H. (2007). Defense mechanism differences between younger and older adults: A cross-sectional investigation. *Aging and Mental Health, 11,* 415–422.

Segall, M. H., Campbell, D. T., & Herskovits, M. J. (1968). The influence of culture on visual perception. In H. Toch and C. Smith (Eds.), *Social perception* (pp. 1–5). Oxford, UK: Bobbs-Merrill.

Segerstrom, S. C., & Miller, G. E. (2004). Psychological stress and the human immune system: A meta-analytic study of 30 years of inquiry. *Psychological Bulletin, 130*, 601–630.

Segraves, R. T. (2010). Considerations for a better definition of male orgasmic disorder in DSM–V. *Journal of Sexual Medicine, 7*, 690–699.

Seligman, M. E. P. (1975). *Helplessness: On depression, development, and death.* San Francisco: W. H. Freeman and Company.

Seligman, M. E. P. (1995). The effectiveness of psychotherapy: The *Consumer Reports* study. *American Psychologist, 50*, 965–974.

Seligman, M. E. P., & Csikszentmihalyi, M. (2000). Positive psychology: An introduction. *American Psychologist, 55*, 5–14.

Seligman, M. E. P., & Maier, S. F. (1967). Failure to escape traumatic shock. *Journal of Experimental Psychology, 74*, 1–9.

Seligman, M. E. P., & Steen, T. A. (2005). Positive psychology progress. *American Psychologist, 60*, 410–421.

Sella, M. (2005). The epic life of Orlando Bloom. *GQ.com*. Retrieved from http://www.gq.com/entertainment/celebrities/200510/orlando-bloom-errol-flynn?currentPage=1

Selye, H. (1936). A syndrome produced by diverse nocuous agents. *Nature, 138*, 32.

Selye, H. (1953). The general adaptation syndrome in its relationships to neurology, psychology, and psychopathology. In A. Weider (Ed.), *Contributions toward medical psychology: Vol. 1. Theory and psychodiagnostic methods* (pp. 234–274). New York: Ronald Press.

Seyle, H. (1956). *The stress of life.* New York: McGraw-Hill.

Selye, H. (1976). Forty years of stress research: Principal remaining problems and misconceptions. *Canadian Medical Association Journal, 115*, 53–56.

Selye, H., & Fortier, C. (1950). Adaptive reaction to stress. *Psychosomatic Medicine, 12*, 149–157.

Shackelford, T. K., Schmitt, D. P., & Buss, D. M. (2005). Mate preferences of married persons in the newlywed year and three years later. *Cognition and Emotion, 19*, 1262–1270.

Shadish, W. R., & Baldwin, S. A. (2003). Meta-analysis of MFT interventions. *Journal of Marital and Family Therapy, 29*, 547–570.

Shah, A. K., & Oppenheimer, D. M. (2008). Heuristics made easy: An effort-reduction framework. *Psychological Bulletin, 134*, 207–222.

Shapiro, D. H. Jr., Schwartz, C. E., & Astin, J. A. (1996). Controlling ourselves, controlling our world: Psychology's role in understanding positive and negative consequences of seeking and gaining control. *American Psychologist, 51*, 1213–1230.

Shargorodsky, J., Curhan, S. G., Curhan, G. C., & Eavey, R. (2010). Change in prevalence of hearing loss in US adolescents. *Journal of the American Medical Association, 304*, 772–778.

Sharp, A. (2011, December 12). Liverpool mum tells how swine flu jab could have destroyed her son's life. *Click Liverpool*. Retrieved from http://www.click-liverpool.com/news/local-news/1214938-liverpool-mum-tells-how-swine-flu-jab-could-have-destroyed-her-sons-life.html

Shaw, G. (2013, March 13). Amanda Todd's mother speaks out about her daughter, bullying (with video). *The Vancouver Sun*. Retrieved from: http://www.vancouversun.com/news/Amanda+Todd+mother+speaks+about+daughter+bullying+with+video/7384521/story.html.

Shaywitz, S. E. (1996). Dyslexia. *Scientific American, 275*, 98–104.

Shaywitz, S. E. (2003). *Overcoming dyslexia: A new and complete science-based program for reading problems at any level.* New York: Vintage Books.

Shaywitz, S. E., Mody, M., & Shaywitz, B. A. (2006). Neural mechanisms in dyslexia. *Current Directions in Psychological Science, 15*, 278–281.

Shaywitz, S. E., & Shaywitz, B. A. (2005). Dyslexia (specific reading disability). *Biological Psychiatry, 57*, 1301–1309.

Sheard, M. (2009). Hardiness commitment, gender, and age differentiate university academic performance. *British Journal of Educational Psychology, 79*, 189–204.

Shedler, J. (2010). The efficacy of psychodynamic psychotherapy. *American Psychologist, 63*, 98–109.

Shelton, K. H., & van den Bree, M. B. M. (2010). The moderating effects of pubertal timing on the longitudinal associations between parent-child relationships' quality and adolescent substance use. *Journal of Research on Adolescence, 20*, 1044–1064.

Shepard, R. N., & Metzler, J. (1971). Mental rotation of three-dimensional objects. *Science, 171*, 701–703.

Sherwood, C. C., Subiaul, F., & Zawidzki, T. W. (2008). A natural history of the human mind: Tracing evolutionary changes in brain and cognition. *Journal of Anatomy, 212*, 426–454.

Sherwood, L. (2010). *Human physiology: From cells to systems* (7th ed.). Belmont, CA: Brooks/Cole, Cengage Learning.

Shiv, B., & Fedorikhin, A. (1999). Heart and mind in conflict: The interplay of affect and cognition in consumer decision making. *Journal of Consumer Research, 26*, 278–291.

Shonkoff, J. P., Garner, A. S., The Committee on Psychosocial Aspects of Child and Family Health, Committee on Early Childhood, Adoption, and Dependent Care, and Section on Developmental and Behavioral Pediatrics, Siegel, B. S., Dobbins, M. I., Earls, M. F., . . . Wood, D. L. (2012). The lifelong effects of early childhood adversity and toxic stress. *Pediatrics, 129*, e232–e246.

Siegel, J. M. (2005). Clues to the functions of mammalian sleep. *Nature, 437*, 1264–1271.

Sigelman, C. K., & Rider, E. A. (2009). *Life-span human development* (6th ed.). Belmont, CA: Brooks/Cole, Cengage Learning.

Sigurdson, K., & Ayas, N. T. (2007). The public health and safety consequences of sleep disorders. *Canadian Journal of Physiology and Pharmacology, 85*, 179–183.

Silva, C. E., & Kirsch, I. (1992). Interpretive sets, expectancy, fantasy proneness, and dissociation predictors of hypnotic response. *Journal of Personality and Social Psychology, 63*, 847–856.

Silverstein, C. (2009). The implications of removing homosexuality from the *DSM* as a mental disorder. *Archives of Sexual Behavior, 38*, 131–163.

Simmer, J. J. (2012, October). Cocaine topical anesthetic. *eMedicine*. Retrieved from http://emedicine.medscape.com/article/874104-overview#aw2aab6b5

Simmons, R., Makatchev, M., Kirby, R., Lee, M. K., Fanaswala, I., Browning, B., . . . Sakr, M. (2011). Believable robot characters. *AI Magazine, 32*(4), 39–52.

Simons, D. J. (2010). Monkeying around with the gorillas in our midst: Familiarity with an inattentional-blindness task does not improve the detection of unexpected events. *i-Perception, 1*, 3–6.

Simons, D. J., & Chabris, C. F. (1999). Gorillas in our midst: Sustained inattentional blindness for dynamic events. *Perception, 28*, 1059–1074.

Simonton, D. K. (2000). Creativity: Cognitive, personal, developmental, and social aspects. *American Psychologist, 55*, 151–158.

Simonton, D. K. (2012, November/December). The science of genius. *Scientific American Mind, 23*, 35–41.

Simpson, J. A., & Rholes, W. S. (2010). Attachment and relationships: Milestones and future directions. *Journal of Social and Personal Relationships, 27*, 173–180.

Simpson, J. R. (2008). Functional MRI lie detection: Too good to be true? *Journal of the American Academy of Psychiatry and the Law, 36*, 491–498.

Simpson, K. J. (2002). Anorexia nervosa and culture. *Journal of Psychiatric and Mental Health Nursing, 9*, 65–71.

Singh, L., Nestor, S., Parikh, C., & Yull, A. (2009). Influences of infant-directed speech on early word recognition. *Infancy, 14*, 654–666.

Singh, M. K., Kesler, S. R., Hosseini, S. M. H., Kelley, R. G., Amatya, D., Hamilton, J. P., . . . Gotlib, I. H. (2013). Anomalous gray matter structural networks in major depressive disorder. *Biological Psychiatry, 74*, 777–785. doi: 0.1016/j.biopsych.2013.03.005

Singh-Manoux, A., Kivimaki, M., Glymour, M. M., Elbaz, A., Berr, C., Ebmeier, K. P., . . . Dugravot, A. (2012). Timing of onset of cognitive decline: Results from Whitehall II prospective cohort study. *British Medical Journal, 334*, 1–8.

Sinn, D. L., & Moltschaniwskyj, N. A. (2005). Personality traits in dumpling squid (*Euprymna tasmanica*): Context-specific traits and their correlation with biological characteristics. *Journal of Comparative Psychology, 119*, 99–110.

Sio, U. N., & Ormerod, T. C. (2009). Does incubation enhance problem solving? A meta-analytic review. *Psychological Bulletin, 135*, 94–120.

Sivacek, J., & Crano, W. D. (1982). Vested interest as a moderator of attitude-behavior consistency. *Journal of Personality and Social Psychology, 43*, 210–221.

Skinner, B. F. (1953). *Science and human behavior.* New York: Macmillan.

Skinner, B. F. (1956). A case history in scientific method. *American Psychologist, 11*, 221–233.

Skinner, B. F. (1957). *Verbal behavior.* New York: Macmillan.

Skinner, B. F. (1976). *Particulars of my life.* New York: Knopf.

Skinner, N. F. (2009). Academic folk wisdom: Fact, fiction and falderal. *Psychology Learning and Teaching, 8*, 46–50.

Skirbekk, V., Loichinger, E., & Weber, D. (2012). Variation in cognitive functioning as a refined approach to comparing aging across countries. *Proceedings of the National Academy of Sciences, 109*, 770–774.

Skoog, G., & Skoog, I. (1999). A 20-year follow-up of patients with obsessive-compulsive disorder. *Archives of General Psychiatry, 56*, 121–127.

Slaney, K. L., & Racine, T. P. (2011). On the ambiguity of concept use in psychology: Is the concept "concept" a useful concept? *Journal of Theoretical and Philosophical Psychology, 31*, 73–89.

Slatcher, R. B., & Robles, T. F. (2012). Preschoolers' everyday conflict at home and diurnal cortisol patterns. *Health Psychology, 31*, 834–838. doi: 10.1037/a0026774

Slife, B. D. (1990). Introduction and overview of the special issue on Aristotle. *Theoretical & Philosophical Psychology, 10*, 1990, 3–6.

Slotema, C. W., Blom, J. D., Hoek, H. W., & Sommer, I. E. C. (2010). Should we expand the toolbox of psychiatric treatment methods to include repetitive transcranial magnetic stimulation (rTMS)? A meta-analysis of the efficacy of rTMS in psychiatric disorders. *Journal of Clinical Psychiatry, 71*, 873–884.

Sloter, E., Schmid, T. E., Marchetti, F., Eskenazi, B., Nath, J., & Wyrobek, A. J. (2006). Quantitative effects of male age on sperm motion. *Human Reproduction, 21*, 2868–2875.

Slovic, P., & Weber, E. U. (2002, April). *Perception of risk posed by extreme events.* Paper presented at Conference on Risk Management Strategies in an Uncertain World, Palisades, NY.

Small, B. J., Dixon, R. A., & McArdle, J. J. (2011). Tracking cognition–health changes from 55 to 95 years of age. *Journals of Gerontology Series B: Psychological Sciences and Social Sciences, 66*, i153.

Small, B. J., Dixon, R. A., McArdle, J. J., & Grimm, K. J. (2012). Do changes in lifestyle engagement moderate cognitive decline in normal aging? Evidence from the Victoria Longitudinal Study. *Neuropsychology, 26*, 144–155. doi: 10.1037/a0026579

Smink, F. R. E., van Hoeken, D., & Hoek, H. W. (2012). Epidemiology of eating disorders: Incidence, prevalence, and mortality rates. *Current Psychiatry Reports, 14*, 406–414.

Smith, B. L. (2012). The case against spanking. *Monitor on Psychology, 43*, 60.

Smith, C. N., & Squire, L. R. (2009). Medial temporal lobe activity during retrieval of semantic memory is related to the age of the memory. *Journal of Neuroscience, 29*, 930–938.

Smith, D. (2001). Shock and disbelief. *Atlantic Monthly, 287*, 79–90.

Smith, J. (2009, March 23). Can robots be programmed to learn from their own experiences? *Scientific American Online.* Retrieved from http://www.scientificamerican.com/article.cfm?id=robot-learning

Smith, S. M., Glenberg, A. M., & Bjork, R. A. (1978). Environmental context and human memory. *Memory and Cognition, 6*, 342–353.

Smith, T. W., Birmingham, W., & Uchino, B. N. (2012). Evaluative threat and ambulatory blood pressure: Cardiovascular effects of social stress in daily experience. *Health Psychology, 31*, 763–766.

Smith, T. W., & MacKenzie, J. (2006). Personality and risk of physical illness. *Annual Review of Clinical Psychology, 2*, 435–467.

Smith, T. W., & Ruiz, J. M. (2002). Psychosocial influences on the development and course of coronary heart disease: Current status and implications for research and practice. *Journal of Consulting and Clinical Psychology, 70*, 548–568.

Smithsonian Institution. (2013). *5 Reasons to revere, not fear, the shark.* Washington, DC: Smithsonian National Museum of National History. Retrieved from http://ocean.si.edu/ocean-news/5-reasons-revere-not-fear-shark

Smrt, D. L., & Karau, S. J. (2011). Protestant work ethic moderates social loafing. *Group Dynamics: Theory, Research, and Practice, 15*, 267–274.

Snyder, C. R., Ilardi, S. S., Cheavens, J., Michael, S. T., Yamhure, L., & Sympson, S. (2000). The role of hope in cognitive-behavior therapies. *Cognitive Therapy and Research, 24*, 747–762.

Snyder, T. D., & Dillow, S. A. (2011). *Digest of education statistics 2010* (NCES 2011-015). Washington, DC: U.S. Department of Education, National Center for Education Statistics, Institute of Education Sciences. Retrieved from http://nces.ed.gov/pubs2011/2011015.pdf

Society for Neuroscience. (2012). Sensation and perception. In *Brain facts* (6th ed., pp. 15–21). Washington, DC: Author.

Socolar, R. R. S., Savage, R., & Evans, H. (2007). A longitudinal study of parental discipline of children. *Southern Medical Journal, 100*, 472–477.

Solms, M. (2006, May). Freud returns. *Scientific American*, 82–88.

Solomon, S. G., & Lennie, P. (2007). The machinery of color vision. *Nature Reviews Neuroscience, 8*, 276–286.

Somatosensory function. (2004). In *Corsini encyclopedia of psychology.* Hoboken, NJ: Wiley. doi: 10.1002/9780470479216

Sørensen, K., Aksglaede, L., Petersen, J. H., & Juul, A. (2010). Recent changes in pubertal timing in healthy Danish boys: Associations with body mass index. *Journal of Clinical Endocrinology & Metabolism, 95*, 263–270.

Sorhagen, N. S. (2013). Early teacher expectations disproportionately affect poor children's high school performance. *Journal of Educational Psychology, 105*, 465–477.

Southworth, M. R., Kortepeter, C., & Hughes, A. (2008). Nonbenzodiazepine hypnotic use and cases of sleep driving. *Annals of Internal Medicine, 148*, 486–487.

Spangenberg, E. R., Sprott, D. E., Grohmann, B., & Tracy, D. L. (2006). Gender-congruent ambient scent influences on approach and avoidance behaviors in a retail store. *Journal of Business Research, 59*, 1281–1287

Sparling, J., Wilder, D. A., Kondash, J., Boyle, M., & Compton, M. (2011). Effects of interviewer behavior on accuracy of children's responses. *Journal of Applied Behavior Analysis, 44*, 587–592.

Sparrow, B., Liu, J., & Wegner, D. W. (2011). Google effects on memory: Cognitive consequences of having information at our fingertips. *Science, 333*, 776–778. doi: 10.1126/science.1207745

Sparrow, R. (2005). Defending deaf culture: The case of cochlear implants. *Journal of Political Philosophy, 13*, 135–152.

Speakman, J. R., Levitsky, D. A., Allison, D. B., Bray, M. S., de Castro, J. M., Clegg, D. J., . . . Westerterp-Plantenga, M. S. (2011). Set points, settling points and some alternative models: Theoretical options to understand how genes and environments combine to regulate body adiposity. *Disease Models & Mechanisms, 4*, 733–745.

Spears, M. J. (2012, February 18). Jeremy Lin's high school inspired by Linsanity. *Yahoo Sports.* Retrieved from http://sports.yahoo.com/nba/news?slug=mc-spears-jeremy_lin_high_school_coach_021812

Specht, J., Egloff, B., & Schmukle, S. C. (2011). Stability and change of personality across the life course: The impact of age and major life events on mean-level and rank-order stability of the Big Five. *Journal of Personality and Social Psychology, 101*, 862–882.

Sperling, G. (1960). The information available in brief visual presentations. *Psychological Monographs: General and Applied, 74*, 1–29.

Spiegel, D., Loewenstein, R. J., Lewis-Fernández, R., Sar, V., Simeon, D., Vermetten, E., . . . Dell, P. F. (2011). Dissociative disorders in *DSM–5. Depression and Anxiety, 28*, 824–852.

Spitzer, R. L. (1975). On pseudoscience in science, logic in remission, and psychiatric diagnosis: A critique of Rosenhan's "On Being Sane in Insane Places." *Journal of Abnormal Psychology, 84*, 442–451.

Spotts, P. (2010, September 7). Trapped miners impress NASA team. *Christian Science Monitor.* Retrieved from http://www.csmonitor.com/Science/2010/0907/Trapped-miners-impress-NASA-team

Squire, L. R., & Bayley, P. J. (2007). The neuroscience of remote memory. *Current Opinion in Neurobiology, 17*, 185–196.

Squire, L. R., Stark, C. E. L., & Clark, R. E. (2004). The medial temporal lobe. *Annual Review of Neuroscience, 27*, 279–306.

Squire, L. R., & Wixted, J. T. (2011). The cognitive neuroscience of human memory since HM. *Annual Review of Neuroscience, 34*, 259–288.

Srinivasa, S. S., Ferguson, D., Helfrich, C. J., Berenson, D., Collet, A., Diankov, R., . . . Vande Weghe, J. (2009). HERB: A home exploring robotic butler. *Autonomous Robots, 28*, 5–20.

Stanford Center for Narcolepsy. (2012). About narcolepsy. *Stanford School of Medicine.* Retrieved from http://med.stanford.edu/school/Psychiatry/narcolepsy/symptoms.html

Stanger-Hall, K., & Hall, D. W. (2011). Abstinence-only education and teen pregnancy rates: Why we need comprehensive sex education in the U.S. *PLoS ONE, 6*, e24658. doi: 10.1371/journal.pone.0024658

Staniloiu, A., & Markowitsch, H. J. (2012). The remains of the day in dissociative amnesia. *Brain Sciences, 2*, 101–129.

Stanovich, K. E. (2010). *How to think straight about psychology* (9th ed.). Boston: Pearson.

Starr, B. (2005, June 10). Is it possible for two parents who cannot roll their tongues to have a tongue-roller child? *Tech Museum of Innovation.* Retrieved from http://genetics.thetech.org/ask/ask125

Steele, C. M. (1997). A threat in the air: How stereotypes shape intellectual identity and performance. *American Psychologist, 52*, 613–629.

Steele, C. M. (2010). *Whistling Vivaldi: How stereotypes affect us and what we can do.* New York: W. W. Norton.

Steele, J. D., Christmas, D., Elijamel, M. S., & Matthews, K. (2008). Anterior cingulotomy for major depression: Clinical outcome and relationship to lesion characteristics. *Biological Psychology, 63*, 670–677.

Stein, B. E., Stanford, T. R., & Rowland, B. A. (2009). The neural basis of multisensory integration in the midbrain: Its organization and maturation. *Hearing Research, 258*, 4–15.

Stein, D. J., Seedat, S., Herman, A., Moomal, H., Heeringa, S. G., Kessler, R. C., & Williams, D. R. (2008). Lifetime prevalence of psychiatric disorders in South Africa. *British Journal of Psychiatry, 192*, 112–117.

Steinberg, L. (2010). Commentary: A behavioral scientist looks at the science of adolescent brain development. *Brain and Cognition, 72*, 160–164.

Steinberg, L. (2012). Should the science of adolescent brain development inform public policy? *Issues in Science & Technology, 28*, 76–78.

Steiner, M. (2012, September 4). The importance of pragmatic communication. *Monocracy Neurodevelopmental Center.* Retrieved from http://monocacycenter.com/the-importance-of-pragmatic-communication/

Stern, K., & Karraker, K. H. (1989). Sex stereotyping of infants: A review of gender labeling studies. *Sex Roles, 20*, 501–522.

Sternberg, R. J. (1986). A triangular theory of love. *Psychological Review, 93*, 119–135.

Sternberg, R. J. (1988). *The triarchic mind: A new theory of human intelligence.* New York: Viking.

Sternberg, R. J. (2004). Culture and intelligence. *American Psychologist, 59*, 325–338.

Sternberg, R. J. (2006a). Creating a vision of creativity: The first 25 years. *Psychology of Aesthetics, Creativity, and the Arts, S*(1), 2–12.

Sternberg, R. J. (2006b). The nature of creativity. *Creativity Research Journal, 18*, 87–98.

Sternberg, R. J., & Grigorenko, E. L. (2005). Intelligence and wisdom. In M. L. Johnson (Ed.), *The Cambridge Handbook of Age and Ageing* (pp. 209–213). Cambridge, UK: Cambridge University Press.

Stice, E., Marti, C. N., Shaw, H., & Jaconis, M. (2009). An 8-year longitudinal study of the natural history of threshold, subthreshold, and partial eating disorders from a community sample of adolescents. *Journal of Abnormal Psychology, 118*, 587–597.

St. John, K. (2003, August 19). Yosemite landmark falls/Sentinel Dome's oft-photographed Jeffrey pine topples. *San Francisco Chronicle.* Retrieved from http://www.sfgate.com/news/article/Yosemite-landmark-falls-Sentinel-Domes-2574496.php#ixzz2HLMo2N31

Stone, A. A., Schwartz, J. E., Broderick, J. E., & Deaton, A. (2010). A snapshot of the age distribution of psychological well-being in the United States. *Proceedings of the National Academy of Sciences, 107*, 9985–9990.

Stone, D. (2009). Brainy Bonnie. *Smithsonian Zoogoer.* Retrieved from http://nationalzoo.si.edu/Publications/ZooGoer/2009/1/BrainyBonnie.cfm

Stone, D. N., Deci, E. L., & Ryan, R. M. (2009). Beyond talk: Creating autonomous motivation through self-determination theory. *Journal of General Management, 34*, 75–102.

Stoner, J. A. F. (1961). *A comparison of individual and group decisions involving risk.* Unpublished master's thesis, Alfred P. Sloan School of Management, Massachusetts Institute of Technology. Retrieved from http://dspace.mit.edu/bitstream/handle/1721.1/11330/33120544.pdf

Stoner, J. A. F. (1968). Risky and cautious shifts in group decisions: The influence of widely held values. *Journal of Experimental Psychology, 4*, 442–459.

Storaasli, R. D., & Markman, H. J. (1990). Relationship problems in the early stages of marriage: A longitudinal investigation. *Journal of Family Psychology, 4*, 80–98.

Storm, B. C., Bjork, E. L., & Bjork, R. A. (2008). Accelerated relearning after retrieval-induced forgetting: The benefit of being forgotten. *Journal of Experimental Psychology: Learning, Memory, and Cognition, 34*, 230–236.

Stout, H. (2010, April 30). Antisocial networking? *The New York Times.* Retrieved from http://www.nytimes.com/2010/05/02/fashion/02BEST.html?pagewanted=all&_r=0

Strack, F., Martin, L. L., & Stepper, S. (1988). Inhibiting and facilitating conditions of the human smile: A nonobtrusive test of the facial feedback hypothesis. *Journal of Personality and Social Psychology, 54*, 768–777.

Strain, G. M. (2003). *How well do dogs and other animals hear?* Department of Comparative Biomedical Sciences, School of Veterinary Medicine,

Louisiana State University. Retrieved from http://www.lsu.edu/deafness/HearingRange.html

Strassberg, D. S., McKinnon, R. K., Sustaíta, M. A., & Rullo J. (2013). Sexting by high school students: An exploratory and descriptive study. *Archives of Sexual Behavior, 42,* 15–21.

Stratton, G. (1896, August). *Some preliminary experiments on vision without inversion of the retinal image.* Paper presented at the Third International Congress for Psychology, Munich.

Straub, R. O. (2012). *Health psychology: A biopsychosocial approach* (3rd ed.). New York: Worth Publishers.

Straus, M. A. (2005). Children should never, ever, be spanked no matter what the circumstances. In D. R. Loseke, R. J. Gelles, & M. M. Cavanaugh (Eds.), *Current controversies about family violence* (2nd ed., pp. 137–157). Thousand Oaks, CA: Sage.

Straus, M. A., & Paschall, M. J. (2009). Corporal punishment by mothers and development of children's cognitive ability: A longitudinal study of two nationally representative age cohorts. *Journal of Aggression, Maltreatment & Trauma, 18,* 459–483.

Strayer, D. L., & Watson, J. M. (2012, March). Top multitaskers help explain how brain juggles thoughts. *Scientific American Mind, 23,* 22–29.

Streit, W. J. (2000). Microglial response to brain injury: A brief synopsis. *Toxicologic Pathology, 28,* 28–30.

Stright, A. D., Gallagher, K. C., & Kelley, K. (2008). Infant temperament moderates relations between maternal parenting in early childhood and children's adjustment in first grade. *Child Development, 79,* 186–200.

Stroebe, W., van Koningsbruggen, G. M., Papies, E. K., & Aarts, H. (2013). Why most dieters fail but some succeed: A goal conflict model of eating behavior. *Psychological Review, 120,* 110–138.

Strube, M. J. (2005). What did Triplett really find? A contemporary analysis of the first experiment in social psychology. *American Journal of Psychology, 118,* 271–286.

Struthers, R., & Lowe, J. (2003). Nursing in the Native American culture and historical trauma. *Issues in Mental Health Nursing, 24,* 257–272.

Stuart, H. (2003). Violence and mental illness: An overview. *World Psychiatry, 2,* 121–124.

Stuen, C., & Faye, E. E. (2003). Vision loss: Normal and not normal changes among older adults. *Generations, 27,* 8–14.

Stump, S. (2011, July 26). Girl, 6, on shark that bit her: 'I forgive him.' *Today.com.* Retrieved from http://today.msnbc.msn.com/id/43892097/ns/today-today_people/t/girl-shark-bit-her-i-forgive-him/#.Tpnf6s1lYjw

Stuss, D. T., & Alexander, M. P. (2000). Executive functions and the frontal lobes: A conceptual view. *Psychological Research, 63,* 289–298.

Su, K. G., Banker, G., Bourdette, D., & Forte, M. (2009). Axonal degeneration in multiple sclerosis: The mitochondrial hypothesis. *Current Neurological Neuroscience, 9,* 411–417.

Substance Abuse and Mental Health Services Administration. (2008). *National Survey on Drug Use and Health.* Retrieved from http://www.oas.samhsa.gov/NSDUH/2k4nsduh/2k4tabs/Sect1peTabs1to66.htm#tab1.20a

Substance Abuse and Mental Health Services Administration. (2010). *The DAWN report: Trends in emergency department visits involving nonmedical use of narcotic pain relievers.* Retrieved from http://oas.samhsa.gov/2k10/DAWN016/OpioidEdHTML.pdf

Substance Abuse and Mental Health Services Administration. (2011). *Results from the 2010 National Survey on Drug Use and Health: Summary of national findings* (NSDUH Series H-41, HHS Publication No. (SMA) 11-4658). Retrieved from http://www.samhsa.gov/data/nsduh/2k10nsduh/2k10results.htm

Substance Abuse and Mental Health Services Administration. (2012). *Results from the 2011 National Survey on Drug Use and Health: Summary of national findings* (NSDUH Series H-44, HHS Publication No. (SMA) 12-4713). Retrieved from http://www.samhsa.gov/data/nsduh/2k11results/nsduhresults2011.htm

Sucala, M., Schnur, J. B., Constantino, M. J., Miller, S. J., Brackman, E. H., & Montgomery, G. H. (2012). The therapeutic relationship in e-therapy for mental health: A systematic review. *Journal of Medical Internet Research, 14,* e110. doi: 10.2196/jmir.2084

Sue, S., Fujino, D. C., Hu, L., Takeuchi, D. T., & Zane, N. W. S. (1991). Community mental health services for ethnic minority groups: A test of the cultural responsiveness hypothesis. *Journal of Consulting and Clinical Psychology, 59,* 533–540.

Sun-Edelstein, C., & Mauskop, A. (2011). Alternative headache treatments: Nutraceuticals, behavioral, and physical treatments. *Headache, 25,* 469–483.

Susuki, K. (2010). Myelin: A specialized membrane for cell communication. *Nature Education, 3,* 59–63.

Sutherland, S. (2012). Brain freeze explained. *Scientific American Mind, 23,* 7. doi: 10.1038/scientificamericanmind0912-7c

Sutton, R. E. (2010, September 6). Boss Luis Urzua and the trapped miners in Chile. *Psychology Today.* Retrieved from http://www.psychologytoday.com/blog/work-matters/201009/boss-luis-urzua-and-the-trapped-miners-in-chile

Suwanrath, C., & Suntharasaj, T. (2010). Sleep–wake cycles in normal fetuses. *Archives of Gynecology and Obstetrics, 281,* 449–454.

Swan, S. H., Liu, F., Hines, M., Kruse, R. L., Wang, C., Redmon, J. B., . . . Weiss, B. (2010). Prenatal phthalate exposure and reduced masculine play in boys. *International Journal of Andrology, 3,* 259–269.

Swanson, L. (1997). Cochlear implants: The head-on collision between medical technology and the right to be deaf. *Canadian Medical Association Journal, 157,* 929–932.

Swendsen, J. D., Tennen, H., Carney, M. A., Affleck, G., Willard, A., & Hromi, A. (2000). Mood and alcohol consumption: An experience sampling test of the self-medication hypothesis. *Journal of Abnormal Psychology, 109,* 198–204.

Swift, J. K., & Greenberg, R. P. (2012). Premature discontinuation in adult psychotherapy: A meta-analysis. *Journal of Consulting and Clinical Psychology, 80,* 547–559.

Swinburn, B. A., Sacks, G., Hall, K. D., McPherson, K., Finegood, D. T., Moodie, M. L., & Gortmaker, S. L. (2011). The global obesity pandemic: Shaped by global drivers and local environments. *Lancet, 378,* 804–814

Szalavitz, M. (2011, May 13). Q&A: Positive psychologist Martin Seligman on the good life. *Time.* Retrieved from: http://healthland.time.com/2011/05/13/mind-reading-positive-psychologist-martin-seligman-on-the-good-life/print/

Szabo, R., & Hall, M. (2007). *Behind happy faces.* Los Angeles: Volt Press.

Szasz, T. (2011). The myth of mental illness: 50 years later. *Psychiatrist Online, 35,* 179–182.

Tackett, J. L., Waldman, I. D., & Lahey, B. B. (2009). Etiology and measurement of relational aggression: A multi-informant behavior genetic investigation. *Journal of Abnormal Psychology, 118,* 722–733.

Takeda, A. (2013, July 12). Catherine Zeta-Jones wows on first red carpet after treatment for bipolar II: Picture. *US Weekly.* Retrieved from http://www.usmagazine.com/celebrity-style/news/catherine-zeta-jones-wows-on-first-red-carpet-after-treatment-for-bipolar-ii-picture-2013127

Talarico, J. M., & Rubin, D. C. (2003). Confidence, not consistency, characterizes flashbulb memories. *Psychological Science, 14,* 455–461.

Tallandini, M. A., & Caudek, C. (2010). Defense mechanisms development in typical children. *Psychotherapy Research, 20,* 535–545.

Tandon, P. S., Zhou, C., Lozano, P., & Christakis, D. A. (2011). Preschoolers' total daily screen time at home and by type of child care. *Journal of Pediatrics, 158,* 297–300.

Tandon, R., Keshavan, M. S., & Nasrallah, H. A. (2008a). Schizophrenia, "just the facts": What we know in 2008. Part 1: Overview. *Schizophrenia Research, 100,* 4–19.

Tandon, R., Keshavan, M. S., & Nasrallah, H. A. (2008b). Schizophrenia," just the facts": What we know in 2008. Part 2. Epidemiology and etiology. *Schizophrenia Research, 102,* 1–18.

Tandon, R., Nasrallah, H. A., & Keshavan, M. S. (2009). Schizophrenia, "just the facts." Part 4. Clinical features and conceptualization. *Schizophrenia Research, 110,* 1–23.

Tang, Y., Nyengaard, J. R., De Groot, D. M., & Gundersen, H. J. G. (2001). Total regional and global number of synapses in the human brain neocortex. *Synapse, 41*(3), 258–273.

Taverniers, J., Smeets, T., Van Ruysseveldt, J., Syroit, J., & von Grumbkow, J. (2011). The risk of being shot at: Stress, cortisol secretion, and their impact memory and perceived learning during reality-based practice for armed officers. *International Journal of Stress Management, 18,* 113–132.

Taylor, B., Miller, E., Lingam, R., Andrews, N., Simmons, A., & Stowe, J. (2002). Measles, mumps, and rubella vaccination and bowel problems or developmental regression in children with autism: Population study. *British Medical Journal, 324,* 393–396.

Taylor, C. A., Manganello, J. A., Lee, S. J., & Rice, J. (2010). Mothers' spanking of 3-year-old children and subsequent risk of children's aggressive behavior. *Pediatrics, 125,* e1057–e1065.

Taylor, J. B. (2006). *My stroke of insight.* New York: Plume.

Taylor, S. E., Klein, L. C., Lewis, B. P., Gruenewald, T. L., Gurung, R. A., & Updegraff, J. A. (2000). Biobehavioral responses to stress in females: Tend-and-befriend, not fight-or-flight. *Psychological Review, 107,* 411–429.

Teachman, B. A., Marker, C. D., & Clerkin, E. M. (2010). Catastrophic misinterpretations as a predictor of symptom change during treatment for panic disorder. *Journal of Consulting and Clinical Psychology, 78,* 964–973.

TED.com. (2008). *Jill Bolte Taylor's stroke of insight* [Video file]. Retrieved from http://www.ted.com/talks/jill_bolte_taylor_s_powerful_stroke_of_insight.html

Tenenbaum, H. R., & Leaper, C. (2002). Are parents' gender schemas related to their children's gender-related cognitions? A meta-analysis. *Developmental Psychology, 38,* 615–630.

Tennis, M. (2012, February 19). Jeremy Lin and the 2006 All-State Team. *ESPN.com.* Retrieved from http://espn.go.com/blog/high-school/california/post/_/id/631/jeremy-lin-and-the-2006-all-state-team

Terman, L. M. (1916). *The measurement of intelligence.* Boston: Houghton Mifflin.

Terman, L. M. (1925). *Genetic studies of genius. Mental and physical traits of a thousand gifted children.* Palo Alto, CA: Stanford University Press.

Terman, L. M., & Oden, M. H. (1947). *The gifted child grows up: Twenty-five years' follow-up of a superior group.* Palo Alto, CA: Stanford University Press.

Terracciano, A., Abdel-Khalek, A. M., Ádám, N., Adamovová, L., Ahn, C.-k., Ahn, H.-n., . . . McCrae, R. R. (2005). National character does not reflect mean personality trait levels in 49 cultures. *Science, 310,* 96–100.

Terry, W. S. (2005). Serial position effects in recall of television commercials. *Journal of General Psychology, 132,* 151–163.

Thelen, E., & Fisher, D. M. (1982). Newborn stepping: An explanation for a "disappearing" reflex. *Developmental Psychology, 18,* 760–775.

Thibaut, J., & Kelly, H. (1959). *The social psychology of groups.* New York: Wiley.

Thomas, A., & Chess, S. (1986). The New York Longitudinal Study: From infancy to early adult life. In R. Plomin & J. Dunn (Eds.), *The study of temperament: Changes, continuities, and challenges* (pp. 39–52). Hillsdale, NJ: Erlbaum.

Thomas, M. (December 30, 2009). 'I'm just trying to be honest about who I am': Lambert. *Daily Xtra.* Retrieved from: http://dailyxtra.com/vancouver/arts-and-entertainment/im-just-trying-honest-lambert?market=210.

Thomas, T. L., Garland, F. C., Molé, D., Cohen, B. A., Gudewicz, T. M., Spiro, R. T., & Zahm, S. H. (2003). Health of U.S. Navy submarine crew during periods of isolation. *Aviation, Space, and Environmental Medicine, 74,* 260–265.

Thompson, P. M., Giedd, J. N., Woods, R. P., MacDonald, D., Evans, A. C., & Toga, A.W. (2000). Growth patterns in the developing brain detected by using continuum mechanical tensor maps. *Nature, 404,* 190–193.

Thompson, R. F., & Kim, J. J. (1996). Memory systems in the brain and localization of a memory. *Proceedings of the National Academy of Sciences, USA, 93,* 13438–13444.

Thompson, R. F., & Steinmetz, J. E. (2009). The role of the cerebellum in classical conditioning of discrete behavioral responses. *Neuroscience, 162,* 732–755.

Thorndike, E. L. (1898). Animal intelligence: An experimental study of the associative process in animals. *Psychological Review Monograph Supplement, 2*(8).

Thorndike, E. L. (1920). A constant error in psychological ratings. *Journal of Applied Psychology, 4,* 25–29.

Thorne, B. (1993). *Gender play: Girls and boys in school.* Cambridge, UK: Open University Press.

Thorne, M., & Henley, T. B. (2005). *Connections in the history and systems of psychology* (3rd ed.). Boston: Houghton Mifflin.

Thurlow, H. J., & Girvin, J. P. (1971). Use of anti-epileptic medication in treating "flashbacks" from hallucinogenic drugs. *Canadian Medical Association Journal, 105,* 947–948.

Tian, L., Wang, J., Yan, C., & He, Y. (2011). Hemisphere-and gender-related differences in small-world brain networks: A resting-state functional MRI study. *NeuroImage, 54,* 191–202.

Tobin, D. D., Menon, M., Menon, M., Spatta, B. C., Hodges, E. V. E., & Perry, D. G. (2010). The intrapsychics of gender: A model of self-socialization. *Psychological Review, 117,* 601–622.

Toga, A. W., Thompson, P. M., & Sowell, E. R. (2006). Mapping brain maturation. *Trends in Neuroscience, 29,* 148–159.

Tollenaar, M. S., Beijers, R., Jansen, J., Riksen-Walraven, J. M. A., & De Weerth, C. (2011). Maternal prenatal stress and cortisol reactivity to stressors in human infants. *Stress, 14,* 53–65.

Tolman, E. C. (1948). Cognitive maps in rats and men. *Psychological Review, 55*(4), 189–208.

Tolman, E. C., & Honzik, C. H. (1930). Introduction and removal of reward, and maze performance in rats. *University of California Publications in Psychology, 4,* 257–275.

Tombs, S., & Silverman, I. (2004). Pupillometry: A sexual selection approach. *Evolution and Human Behavior, 25,* 221–228.

Tomoda, A., Suzuki, H., Rabi, K., Sheu, Y., Polcari, A., & Teicher, M. H. (2009). Reduced prefrontal cortical gray matter volume in young adults exposed to harsh corporal punishment. *NeuroImage, 47,* T66–T71.

Tondo, L., Isacsson, G., & Baldessarini, R. J. (2003). Suicidal behaviour in bipolar disorder: Risk and prevention. *CNS Drugs, 17,* 491–511.

Topp, S. S. (2013). Against the quiet revolution: The rhetorical construction of intersex individuals as disordered. *Sexualites, 16,* 180–194.

Torrente, M. P., Gelenberg, A. J., & Vrana, K. E. (2012). Boosting serotonin in the brain: Is it time to revamp the treatment of depression? *Journal of Psychopharmacology, 26,* 629–635.

Torry, Z. D., & Billick, S. B. (2010). Overlapping universe: Understanding legal insanity and psychosis. *Psychiatric Quarterly, 81,* 253–262.

Toufexis, A. (2001, June 24). Why men can outdrink women. *TIME Magazine.* Retrieved from http://content.time.com/time/magazine/article/0,9171,153672,00.html

Tourangeau, R., & Yan, T. (2007). Sensitive questions in surveys. *Psychological Bulletin, 133,* 859–883.

Tränkner, D., Jägle, H., Kohl, S., Apfelstedt-Sylla, E., Sharpe, L. T., Kaupp, U. B., . . . Wissinger, B. (2004). Molecular basis of an inherited form of incomplete achromatopsia. *Journal of Neuroscience, 24,* 138–147.

Treffert, D. A. (2009). The savant syndrome: An extraordinary condition. A synopsis: Past, present, future. *Philosophical Transactions of the Royal Society, 364,* 1351–1357.

Trelawny, P. (2008, June 5). China's love affair with the piano. *BBC News.* Retrieved from http://news.bbc.co.uk/2/hi/programmes/from_our_own_correspondent/7436434.stm

Trivers, R. L. (1971). The evolution of reciprocal altruism. *Quarterly Review of Biology, 46,* 35–57.

Tsaw, D., Murphy, S., & Detgen, J. (2011). Social loafing and culture: Does gender matter? *International Review of Business Research, 7,* 1–8.

Tsuang, M. T., Stone, W. S., & Faraone, S. V. (2001). Genes, environment and schizophrenia. *British Journal of Psychiatry, 178,* s18–s24.

Tsukayama, H. (2012, February 3). Your Facebook friends have more friends than you. *The Washington Post.* Retrieved from http://www.washingtonpost.com/business/technology/your-facebook-friends-have-more-friends-than-you/2012/02/03/gIQAuNUlmQ_print.html

Tulving, E. (1972). Episodic and semantic memory. In E. Tulving & W. Donaldson (Eds.), *Organization of memory* (pp. 381–403). New York: Academic Press.

Tulving, E. (1985). Memory and consciousness. *Canadian Psychology/Psychologice Canadienne, 26,* 1–11.

Tulving, E., & Osler, S. (1968). Effectiveness of retrieval cues in memory for words. *Journal of Experimental Psychology, 77,* 593–601.

Tulving, E., & Thomson, D. M. (1973). Encoding specificity and retrieval processes in episodic memory. *Psychological Review, 80,* 352–373.

Tummala-Narra, P., Alegria, M., & Chen, C.-N. (2012). Perceived discrimination, acculturative stress, and depression among South Asians: Mixed findings. *Asian American Journal of Psychology, 3,* 3–16.

Turgeon, J. K. (2011, July 14). 11 celebrities with dyslexia who made it big. *The Huffington Post.* Retrieved from http://www.huffingtonpost.com/2011/07/14/famous-people-with-dyslexia_n_897475.html#s308246&title=Whoopi_Goldberg

Turk, J., Marks, I. M., & Horder, J. (1990). Obsessive-compulsive disorder: Case study and discussion of treatment. *British Journal of General Practice, 40,* 210–212.

Tversky, A., & Kahneman, D. (1981). The framing of decisions and the psychology of choice. *Science, 211,* 453–458.

Tversky, A., & Kahneman, D. (1982). Judgment under uncertainty: Heuristics and biases. In D. Kahneman, P. Slovic, & A. Tversky (Eds.), *Judgment under uncertainty: Heuristics and biases* (pp. 3–20). New York: Cambridge University Press.

Twenge, J. M., Baumeister, R. F., DeWall, C. N., Ciarocco, N. J., & Bartels, J. M. (2007). Social exclusion decreases prosocial behavior. *Journal of Personality and Social Psychology, 92,* 56–66.

Uchino, B. N., Berg, C. A., Smith, T. W., Pearce, G., & Skinner, M. (2006). Age-related differences in ambulatory blood pressures during daily stress: Evidence for greater blood pressure reactivity with age. *Psychology and Aging, 21,* 231–239.

Üçok, A., & Gaebel, W. (2008). Side effects of atypical antipsychotics: A brief overview. *World Psychiatry, 7,* 58–62.

UCSF Medical Center. (2012). *FAQ: Cochlear implants.* Retrieved from http://www.ucsfhealth.org/education/cochlear_implants/index.html

UNAIDS. (2011). *Malawi: HIV and AIDS estimates (2011).* Retrieved from: http://www.unaids.org/en/regionscountries/countries/malawi/#3

UNAIDS. (2012a). *Malawi: HIV and AIDS estimates (2012).* Retrieved from: http://www.unaids.org/en/regionscountries/countries/malawi/#3

UNAIDS. (2012b). *UNAIDS report on the global AIDS epidemic.* Accessed July 6, 2013 at http://www.unaids.org/en/media/unaids/contentassets/documents/

epidemiology/2012/gr2012/20121120_UNAIDS_Global_Report_2012_with_annexes_en.pdf

Underdown, A., Barlow, J., & Stewart-Brown, S. (2010). Tactile stimulation in physically healthy infants: Results of a systematic review. *Journal of Reproductive and Infant Psychology, 1,* 11–29.

United Nations. (2012). *World drug report 2012* (No. E.12.XI.1). Vienna: Office on Drugs and Crime.

United Nations Office for the Coordination of Humanitarian Affairs. (2011, September 5). *Key facts on Somalia.* Retrieved from http://reliefweb.int/report/somalia/key-figures-somalia-05-september-2011

United States Senate. (2010, January 28). *Unemployment on Indian reservations at 50 percent: The urgent need to create jobs in Indian country: Hearing before the Committee on Indian Affairs,* 111th Cong., 2nd Sess.

University of Chicago. (2013). *Human performance level.* Retrieved from http://hpl.uchicago.edu/

Urso, A. M. (2007). The reality of neonatal pain and the resulting effects. *Journal of Neonatal Nursing, 13,* 236–238.

U.S. Census Bureau. (2011 and earlier). *Current Population Survey (CPS) data on educational attainment* (Annual Social and Economic [ASEC] or March Supplements). Retrieved from http://www.census.gov/hhes/socdemo/education/data/cps/

U.S. Census Bureau. (2012). Table 41, Foreign-born population—selected characteristic by region of origin: 2010. *The 2012 statistical abstract of the United States.* Retrieved from http://www.census.gov/compendia/statab/2012/tables/12s0041.pdf

U.S. Fish & Wildlife Service. (2006). *Laysan Albatross* Phoebastria immutabilis *conservation status* (Alaska Seabird Information Series, 3–4). Retrieved from http://www.fws.gov/alaska/mbsp/mbm/seabirds/pdf/laal.pdf

U.S. Food and Drug Administration. (2008). *Mandate: Information for healthcare professionals: Suicidal behavior and ideation and antiepileptic drugs.* Retrieved from http://www.fda.gov/Drugs/DrugSafety/PostmarketDrugSafetyInformationforPatientsandProviders/ucm100192.htm

Vaillant, G. E. (1992). *Ego mechanisms of defense: A guide for clinicians and researchers.* Arlington, VA: American Psychiatric Association.

Vaillant, G. E. (2000). Adaptive mental mechanisms: Their role in a positive psychology. *American Psychologist, 55,* 89–98.

Valenza, E., Leo, I., Gava, L., & Simion, F. (2006). Perceptual completion in newborn human infants. *Child Development, 77,* 1810–1821.

VanderVeen, J. W., Reddy, L. F., Veileux, J. C., January, A. M., & DiLillo, D. (2012). Clinical PhD graduate student views of their scientist-practitioner training. *Journal of Clinical Psychology, 68,* 1048–1057.

Van Doorn, M. D., Branje, S. J. T., & Meeus, W. H. (2011). Developmental changes in conflict resolution styles in parent–adolescent relationships: A four-wave longitudinal study. *Journal of Youth and Adolescence, 40,* 97–107.

van Os, J., & Kapur, S. (2009). Schizophrenia. *Lancet, 374,* 635–645.

van Praag, H., Kempermann, G., & Gage, F. H. (2000). Neural consequences of environmental enrichment. *Nature Reviews Neuroscience, 1,* 191–198.

Vartanian, L. R., Herman, C. P., & Wansink, B. (2008). Are we aware of the external factors that influence our food intake? *Health Psychology, 27,* 533–538.

Vasalou, A., Joinson, A. N., & Courvoisier, D. (2010). Cultural differences, experience with social networks and the nature of "true commitment" in Facebook. *International Journal of Human–Computer Studies, 68,* 719–728.

Velagaleti, G. V. N., & Moore, C. M. (2011). Role of array comparative genomic hybridization of cytogenetic causes of pregnancy loss. *Pathology Case Reviews, 16,* 214–221.

Vennard, M. (2011, November 20). How can musicians keep playing despite amnesia? *BBC World Service.* Retrieved from http://www.bbc.co.uk/news/magazine-15791973

Vernon, P. (2010, September 18). Mad Men: Jon Hamm on life as Don Draper and the blessings of late fame. *The Observer*. Retrieved from http://www.theguardian.com/tv-and-radio/2010/sep/19/jon-hamm-mad-men-don-draper

Vernon, P. A., Martin, R. A., Schermer, J. A., Cherkas, L. F., & Spector, T. D. (2008). Genetic and environmental contributions to humor styles: A replication study. *Twin Research and Human Genetics, 11,* 44–47.

Vgontzas, A. N., Liao, D., Pejovic, S., Calhoun, S., Karataraki, M., & Bixler, E. O. (2009). Insomnia with objective short sleep duration is associated with type 2 diabetes: A population-based study. *Diabetes Care, 32,* 1980–1985.

Viera, M. (2011, November 3). After tough year, a Chilean miner returns to run. *The New York Times*. Retrieved from http://www.nytimes.com/2011/11/04/sports/edison-pena-returns-to-new-york-to-run-marathon-again.html?_r=0

Viera, M. (2012, February 12). For Lin, erasing a history of being overlooked. *The New York Times*. Retrieved from http://www.nytimes.com/2012/02/13/sports/basketball/for-knicks-lin-erasing-a-history-of-being-overlooked.html

Vigilant Citizen. (2010, October 14). *The odd masonic imagery of the 33 Chilean miners' rescue.* Retrieved from http://vigilantcitizen.com/latestnews/the-odd-masonic-imagery-surrounding-the-33-chilean-miners-rescue/

Vilain, E. J. N. (2008). Genetics of sexual development and differentiation. In D. L. Rowland & L. Incrocci (Eds.), *Handbook of sexual and gender identity disorders* (pp. 329–353). Hoboken, NJ: Wiley.

Vingtdeux, V., Davies, P., Dickson, D. W., & Marambaud, P. (2011). AMPK is abnormally activated in tangle-and pre-tangle-bearing neurons in Alzheimer's disease and other tauopathies. *Acta Neuropathologica,, 121,* 337–349.

Violanti, J. M. (1992). Coping strategies among police recruits in a high-stress training environment. *Journal of Social Psychology, 132*(6), 717–729.

Visser, B. A., Ashton, M. C., & Vernon, P. A. (2006). Beyond *g:* Putting multiple intelligences theory to the test. *Intelligence, 34,* 487–502.

Visweswaraiah, N. K., & Telles, S. (2006). Psychophysiological effects of colored light used in healing. *World Journal of Medical Science, 1,* 21–23.

Vlahos, J. (2007, September 9). Scent and sensibility. *The New York Times*. Retrieved from http://query.nytimes.com/gst/fullpage.html?res=9D07EFDC1E3AF93AA3575AC0A9619C8B63&pagewanted=all

Volkow, N. D., Chang, L., Wang, G. J., Fowler, J. S., Leonido-Yee, M., Franceschi, D., . . . Miller, E. N. (2001). Association of dopamine transporter reduction with psychomotor impairment in methamphetamine abusers. *American Journal of Psychiatry, 158,* 377–382.

von Dawans, B., Fischbacher, U., Kirschbaum, C., Fehr, E., & Heinrichs, M. (2012). The social dimension of stress reactivity: Acute stress increases prosocial behavior in humans. *Psychological Science, 23,* 829–839.

von Stumm, S., & Deary, I. J. (2012). Typical intellectual engagement and cognition in the ninth decade of life: The Lothian Birth Cohort 1921. *Psychology and Aging, 27,* 761–767.

Vredeveldt, A., Baddeley, A. D., & Hitch, G. J. (2013, February). The effectiveness of eye-closure in repeated interviews. *Legal and Criminological Psychology*. doi: 10.1111/lcrp.12013

Vygotsky, L. S. (1934/1962). *Thought and language* (Eugenia Hanfmann & Gertrude Vakar, Eds. & Trans.). Cambridge, MA: Massachusetts Institute of Technology.

Wagenmakers, E. J., Wetzels, R., Borsboom, D., & van der Maas, H. L. (2011). Why psychologists must change the way they analyze their data: The case of psi [Peer commentary on the paper "Feeling the future: Experimental evidence for anomalous retroactive influences on cognition and affect" by D. J. Bem]. *Journal of Personality and Social Psychology, 100,* 426–432.

Wagner, J. A. III, Humphrey, S. E., Meyer, C. J., & Hollenbeck, J. R. (2011). Individualism–collectivism and team member performance: Another look. *Journal of Organizational Behavior, 33,* 946–963.

Wai, J., Cacchio, M., Putallaz, M., & Makel, M. C. (2010). Sex differences in the right tail of cognitive abilities: A 30 year examination. *Intelligence, 38,* 412–423.

Wakefield, A. J., Murch, S. H., Anthony, A., Linnell, J., Casson, D. M., Malik, M., . . . Walker-Smith, J. A. (1998). Ileal-lymphoid-nodular hyperplasia, non-specific colitis, and pervasive developmental disorder in children. *Lancet, 28,* 637–641.

Wakefield, J. C. (1992). The concept of mental disorder: On the boundary between biological facts and social values. *American Psychologist, 47,* 373–388.

Wallentin, M. (2009). Putative sex differences in verbal abilities and language cortex: A critical review. *Brain and Language, 108,* 175–183.

Wallin, P. (1949). An appraisal of some methodological aspects of the Kinsey report. *American Sociological Review, 14,* 197–210.

Walma van der Molen, J. H., & van der Voort, T. H. A. (2000). The impact of television, print, and audio on children's recall of the news: A study of three alternative explanations for the dual-coding hypothesis. *Human Communication Research, 26,* 3–26.

Walsh, R. (2011). Lifestyle and mental health. *American Psychologist, 66,* 579–592.

Wang, H.-X., Karp, A., Winblad, B., & Fratiglioni, L. (2002). Late-life engagement in social and leisure activities is associated with a decreased risk of dementia: A longitudinal study from the Kungsholmen Project. *American Journal of Epidemiology, 155,* 1081–1087.

Wang, L., Swank, J. S., Glick, I. E., Gado, M. H., Miller, M. I., Morris, J. C. W., & Csernansky, J. G. (2003). Changes in hippocampal volume and shape across time distinguish dementia of the Alzheimer type from healthy aging. *NeuroImage, 20,* 667–682.

Wang, Q., & Conway, M. A. (2004). The stories we keep: Autobiographical memory in American and Chinese middle-aged adults. *Journal of Personality, 72,* 911–938.

Wansink, B., & Kim, J. (2005). Bad popcorn in big buckets: Portion size can influence intake as much as taste. *Journal of Nutrition Education and Behavior, 37,* 242–245.

Warburton, D. E. R., Charlesworth, S., Ivey, A., Nettlefold, L., & Bredin, S. S. D. (2010). A systematic review of the evidence for Canada's physical activity guidelines for adults. *International Journal of Behavioral Nutrition and Physical Activity, 7,* 1–220.

Ward, O. (2006, June 10). The man who heard his paintbox hiss. *The Telegraph*. Retrieved from http://www.telegraph.co.uk/culture/art/3653012/The-man-who-heard-his-paintbox-hiss.html

Warneken, F., & Tomasello, M. (2006). Altruistic helping in human infants and young chimpanzees. *Science, 311,* 1301–1303.

Washburn, D. A. (2010). Book reviews: The animal mind at 100. *Psychological Record, 60,* 369–376.

Wasserstein, R. L. (2013, May 16). A statistician's view: What are your chances of winning the Powerball lottery? *The Huffington Post, Science*. Retrieved from: http://www.huffingtonpost.com/ronald-l-wasserstein/chances-of-winning-powerball-lottery_b_3288129.html.

Waterhouse, L. (2006). Multiple intelligences, the Mozart effect, and emotional intelligence: A critical review. *Educational Psychologist, 41,* 207–225.

Watson, J. B. (1930). *Behaviorism.* New York: W. W. Norton.

Watson, J. B., & Rayner, R. (1920). Conditioned emotional reactions. *Journal of Experimental Psychology, 3,* 1–14. (Reprinted in *American Psychologist, 55,* 313–317.)

Watson, J. M., & Strayer, D. L. (2010). Supertaskers: Profiles in extraordinary multi-tasking ability. *Psychonomic Bulletin and Review, 17,* 479–485.

Watson, R. I. (1968). *The great psychologists* (2nd ed.). Philadelphia: J. B. Lippincott.

Waugh, N. C., & Norman, D. A. (1965). Primary memory. *Psychological Review, 72,* 89–104.

Wearing, D. (2005). *Forever today: A memoir of love and amnesia.* London: Corgi Books.

Weathington, B. L., Cunningham, C. J. L., & Pittenger, D. J. (2010). *Research methods for the behavioral and social sciences.* Hoboken, NJ: Wiley.

Weaver, J. (2011). Crying women turn men off. *Scientific American Mind, 22,* 6. doi: 10.1038/scientificamericanmind0511-6a

Weaver, J. (2012). Happy in the morning. *Scientific American Mind, 23,* 9. doi: 10.1038/scientificamericanmind0312-9a

Webb, S. J., Monk, C. S., & Nelson, C. A. (2001). Mechanisms of postnatal neurobiological development: Implications for human development. *Developmental Neuropsychology, 19,* 147–171.

Webber, J. (2010, October 11). Chile miners knew of dangers but needed money. *The Financial Times.* Retrieved from http://www.ft.com/intl/cms/s/0/f3ea0c16-d557-11df-8e86-00144feabdc0.html#axzz2HigyKjnk

Weber, H., Scholz, C. J., Domschke, K., Baumann, C., Klauke, B., Jacob, C. P., . . . Reif, A. (2012). Gender differences in associations of glutamate decarboxylase 1 gene (GAD1) variants with panic disorder. *PLoS ONE, 7,* e37651.

Webster's New International Dictionary of the English Language. (1925). W. T. Harris & F. Sturges Allen (Eds.). Springfield, MA: G. & C. Merriam.

Weiner, J. (2011). Chilean mine rescue makes Golborne, SEP '96, a star. *Stanford Graduate School of Business News.* Retrieved from http://www.gsb.stanford.edu/news/headlines/golborne010311.html

Weiss, A., King, J. E., & Perkins, L. (2006). Personality and subjective well-being in orangutans (*Pongo pygmaeus* and *Pongo abelii*). *Journal of Personality and Social Psychology, 90,* 501–511.

Weisskirch, R. S., & Delevi, R. (2011). "Sexting" and adult romantic attachment. *Computers in Human Behavior, 27,* 1697–1701.

Wellings, K., Collumbien, M., Slaymaker, E., Singh, S., Hodges, Z., Patel, D., & Bajos, N. (2006). Sexual behaviour in context: A global perspective. *Lancet, 368,* 1706–1728.

Wen, C. P., Wai, J. P., Tsai, M. K., Yang, Y. C., Cheng, T. Y., Lee, M. C., . . . Wu, X. (2011). Minimum amount of physical activity for reduced mortality and extended life expectancy: A prospective cohort study. *Lancet, 378,* 1244–1253.

Wen, X. J., Kanny, D., Thompson, W. W., Okoro, C. A., Town, M., & Balluz, L.S. (2012). Binge drinking intensity and health-related quality of life among US adult binge drinkers. *Preventing Chronic Disease, 9,* 1–11.

Wenner Moyer, M. (2010). Electric surprise. *Scientific American Mind, 20,* 10. doi: 10.1038/scientificamericanmind0110-10b

Wenner Moyer, M. (2012). Rudeness on the Internet. *Scientific American Mind, 23,* 10. doi: 10.1038/scientificamericanmind0912-10a

Wentzel, K. R., McNamara Barry, C., & Caldwell, K. A. (2004). Friendships in middle school: Influences on motivation and school adjustment. *Journal of Educational Psychology, 96,* 195–203.

Werker, J. F., & Tees, R. C. (1984). Cross-language speech perception: Evidence for perceptual reorganization during the first year of life. *Infant Behavior and Development, 7,* 49–63.

Wernig, M., Zhao, J. P., Pruszak, J., Hedlund, E., Fu, D., Soldner, F., . . . & Jaenisch, R. (2008). Neurons derived from reprogrammed fibroblasts functionally integrate into the fetal brain and improve symptoms of rats with Parkinson's disease. *Proceedings of the National Academy of Sciences, 105,* 5856–5861.

Wertheimer, M. (2012). *A brief history of psychology* (5th ed.). New York: Taylor & Francis.

Westen, D. (1990). Psychoanalytic approaches to personality. In L. A. Pervin (Ed.), *Handbook of personality* (pp. 21–65). New York: Guilford Press.

Westen, D., Gabbard, G. O., & Ortigo, K. M. (2008). Psychoanalytic approaches to personality. In O. P. John, R. W. Robins, & L. A. Pervin (Eds.), *Handbook of personality: Theory of research* (pp. 61–113). New York: Guilford Press.

Westly, E. (2011, July/August). The bilingual advantage. *Scientific American Mind.*

Whisman, M. A., & Synder, D. K. (2007). Sexual infidelity in a national survey of American women: Differences in prevalence and correlates as a function of method of assessment. *Journal of Family Psychology, 21,* 147–154.

White, T. (2013, April 22). Finding hope on the Rosebud Indian Reservation [Web log post]. Retrieved from http://scopeblog.stanford.edu/2013/04/22/finding-hope-on-the-rosebud-indian-reservation/

Whitley, R. J., & Gnann, J. W. (2002). Viral encephalitis: Familiar infections and emerging pathogens. *Lancet, 359,* 507–513.

Whitlock, J. R., Heynen, A. J., Shuler, M. G., & Bear, M. F. (2006). Learning induces long-term potentiation in the hippocampus. *Science, 313,* 1093–1097.

Whitman, R. D. (2011). *Cognition.* Hoboken, NJ: Wiley.

WHO Multicentre Growth Reference Study Group, & de Onis, M. (2006). WHO Motor Development Study: Windows of achievement for six gross motor development milestones. *Acta Paediatrica, 95,* 86–95.

Whorf, B. L. (1956). *Language, thought, and reality.* Cambridge, MA: MIT Press.

Wich, S.A., Swartz, K. B., Hardus, M. E., Lameira, A. R., Stromberg, E., & Shumaker, R.W. (2009). Case of spontaneous acquisition of a human sound by an orangutan. *Primates, 50,* 56–64.

Wicker, A. W. (1969). Attitudes versus actions: The relationship of verbal and overt behavioral responses to attitude objects. *Journal of Social Issues, 24,* 41–78.

Widmer, E. D., Treas, J., & Newcomb, R. (1998). Attitudes toward nonmarital sex in 24 countries. *Journal of Sex Research, 35,* 349–358.

Wilkins, C. H., Sheline, Y. I., Roe, C. M., Birge, S. J., & Morris, J. C. (2006). Vitamin D deficiency is associated with low mood and worse cognitive performance in older adults. *American Journal of Geriatric Psychiatry, 14,* 1032–1340.

Williams, P. G., Suchy, Y., & Kraybill, M. L. (2010). Five-factor model personality traits and executive functioning among older adults. *Journal of Research in Personality, 44,* 485–491.

Williams, R. (2012). What marijuana reveals about memory. *Scientific American Mind, 23,* 10. doi: 10.1038/scientificamericanmind0712-10b

Williamson, A. M., & Feyer, A. M. (2000). Moderate sleep deprivation produces impairments in cognitive and motor performance equivalent to legally prescribed levels of alcohol intoxication. *Occupational and Environmental Medicine, 57,* 649–655.

Willoughby, K. A., Desrocher, M., Levine, B., & Rovet, J. F. (2012). Episodic and semantic autobiographical memory and everyday memory during late childhood and early adolescence. *Frontiers in Psychology, 3,* 1–15.

Willyard, C. (2008). Hungry for sleep. *Nature Medicine, 14,* 477–480.

Wilson, B. A., Baddeley, A. D., & Kapur, N. (1995). Dense amnesia in a professional musician following herpes simplex virus encephalitis. *Journal of Clinical and Experimental Neuropsychology, 17,* 668–681.

Wilson, B. A., Kopelman, M., & Kapur, N. (2008). Prominent and persistent loss of past awareness in amnesia: Delusion, impaired consciousness or coping strategy. *Neuropsychological Rehabilitation, 18,* 527–540.

Wilson, B. A., & Wearing, D. (1995). Prisoner of consciousness: A state of just awakening following herpes simplex encephalitis. In R. Campbell & M. Conway (Eds.), *Broken memories: Case studies in memory impairment* (pp. 14–30). Oxford, UK: Blackwell.

Wilson, R. S., & Bennett, D. A. (2003). Cognitive activity and risk of Alzheimer's disease. *Current Directions in Psychological Science, 12,* 87–91.

Winickoff, J. P., Friebely, J., Tanski, S. E., Sherrod, C., Matt, G. E., Hovell, M. F., & McMillen, R. C. (2009). Beliefs about the health effects of "thirdhand" smoke and home smoking bans. *Pediatrics, 123,* e74–e79.

Wiseman, R., & Watt, C. (2006) Belief in psychic ability and the misattribution hypothesis: A qualitative review. *British Journal of Psychology, 97,* 323–338.

Witelson S., Kigar, D., & Harvey, T. (1999). The exceptional brain of Albert Einstein. *Lancet, 353,* 2149–2153.

Witelson, S. F., Kigar, D. L., Scamvougeras, A., Kideckel, D. M., Buck, B., Stanchev, P. L., . . . Black, S. (2008). Corpus callosum anatomy in right-handed homosexual and heterosexual men. *Archives of Sexual Behavior, 37,* 857–863.

Wittchen, H.-U., & Jacobi, F. (2005). Size and burden of mental disorders in Europe. *European Neuropsychopharmacology, 15,* 357–376.

Wobst, A. H. K. (2007). Hypnosis and surgery: Past, present, and future. *Anesthesia & Analgesia, 104,* 1199–1208.

Wodrich, D. L., & Tarbox, J. (2008). Psychoeducational implications of sex chromosome anomalies. *School Psychology Quarterly, 23,* 301–311.

Wojcicki, J. M., van der Straten, A., & Padian, N. (2010). Bridewealth and sexual and reproductive practices among women in Harare, Zimbabwe. *AIDS Care, 22,* 705–710.

Wolf, M. (2007). *Proust and the squid: The story and science of the reading brain.* New York: HarperCollins.

Wolman, D. (2012, March 15). The split brain: A tale of two halves. *Nature, 483,* 260–263.

Wolpert, D. M., Goodbody, S. J., & Husain, M. (1998). Maintaining internal representations: The role of the human superior parietal lobe. *Nature Neuroscience, 1,* 529–533.

Wong, B. (2011). Point of view: Color blindness. *Nature Methods, 8,* 441.

Wood, G., & Pennington, J. (1973). Encoding and retrieval from long-term storage. *Journal of Experimental Psychology, 99,* 243–254.

Wood, W., & Eagly, A. H. (2002). A cross-cultural analysis of the behavior of women and men: Implications for the origins of sex differences. *Psychological Bulletin, 128,* 699–727.

Woon, T.-H., Masuda, M., Wagner, N. N., & Holmes, T. H. (1971). The Social Readjustment Rating Scale: A cross-cultural study of Malaysians and Americans. *Journal of Cross-Cultural Psychology, 2,* 373–386.

World Health Organization. (2008a). *Global incidence and prevalence of selected curable sexually transmitted infections.* Accessed July 6, 2013 at http://apps.who.int/iris/bitstream/10665/75181/1/9789241503839_eng.pdf

World Health Organization. (2008b). Table A2, Burden of disease in DALYs by cause, sex and income group in WHO regions, estimates for 2004. *The global burden of disease: 2004 update.* Retrieved from http://www.who.int/healthinfo/global_burden_disease/GBD_report_2004update_AnnexA.pdf

World Health Organization. (2008c). *WHO report on the global tobacco epidemic, 2008: The MPOWER package.* Retrieved from http://www.who.int/tobacco/mpower/mpower_report_full_2008.pdf

World Health Organization. (2009). *UNAIDS: Global facts & figures* [Fact sheet]. Retrieved from http://data.unaids.org/pub/factsheet/2009/20091124_fs_global_en.pdf

World Memory Statistics. (2013). *60 Minute/hour numbers.* Retrieved from http://www.world-memory-statistics.com/discipline.php?id=num60

Worringham, C. J., & Messick, D. M. (1983). Social facilitation of running: An unobtrusive study. *Journal of Social Psychology, 121,* 23–29.

Worthy, D. A., Gorlick, M. A., Pacheco, J. L., Schnyer, D. M., & Maddox, W. T. (2011). With age comes wisdom: Decision making in younger and older adults. *Psychological Science, 22,* 1375–1380.

WRAL.com. (2011, July 26). *NC shark attack victim asked, 'Am I going to die?'* Retrieved from http://www.wral.com/news/local/story/9907709/

Wright, K. (2002). The times of our lives. *Scientific American, 287,* 59–65.

Wuethrich, B. (1999, November 29). Telling an ovenbird by its nest. *Science NOW.* Retrieved from http://news.sciencemag.org/sciencenow/1999/11/29-02.html

Xu, J., Gannon, P. J., Emmorey, K., Smith, J. F., & Braun, A. R. (2009). Symbolic gestures and spoken language are processed by a common neural system. *Proceedings of the National Academy of Sciences, USA, 106,* 20664–20669.

Yalom, I. D. and Leszcz, M. (2005). *The theory and practice of group psychotherapy* (5th ed.). New York: Basic Books.

Yamagata, S., Suzuki, A., Ando, J., Ono, Y., Kijima, N., Yoshimura, K., . . . Jang, K. (2006). Is the genetic structure of human personality universal? A cross-cultural twin study from North America, Europe, and Asia. *Journal of Personality and Social Psychology, 90,* 987–998.

Yanchar, S. C., Slife, B. D., & Warne, R. (2008). Critical thinking as disciplinary practice. *Review of General Psychology, 12,* 265–281.

Yardi, S., & Bruckman, A. (2011). Social and technical challenges in parenting teens' social media use. In *Proceedings of the SIGCHI Conference on Human Factors in Computing Systems, May 7–12, 2011, Vancouver, BC* (pp. 3237–3246). New York: Association for Computing Machinery.

Yasmin, M., Sharif, M., Masood, S., Raza, M., & Mohsin, S. (2012). Brain image enhancement—A survey. *World Applied Sciences Journal, 17,* 1192–1204.

Yee, M., & Brown, R. (1994). The development of gender differentiation in young children. *British Journal of Social Psychology, 33,* 183–196.

Yen, H. (2012, May 18). Minority birth rate: Racial and ethnic minorities surpass Whites in U.S. births for first time, Census reports. *The Huffington Post.* Retrieved from http://www.huffingtonpost.com/2012/05/17/census-minority-birth-rate_n_1523150.html

Yolken, R. H., & Torrey, E. F. (1995). Viruses, schizophrenia, and bipolar disorder. *Clinical Microbiology Reviews, 8,* 131–145.

Yoon, C., Feinberg, F., Hu, P., Gutchess, A. H., Hedden, T., Chen, H.-Y. M., . . . Park, D. C. (2004). Category norms as a function of culture and age: Comparisons of item responses to 105 categories by American and Chinese adults. *Psychology and Aging, 19,* 379–393.

Yost, W. A. (2007). *Fundamentals of hearing* (5th ed.). San Diego: Academic Press.

Young, M. E., Mizzau, M., Mai, N. T., Sirisegaram, A., & Wilson, M. (2009). Food for thought: What you eat depends on your sex and eating companions. *Appetite, 53,* 268–271.

Young-Bruehl, E. (2009). Women and children first! *Modern Psychoanalysis, 34,* 52–74.

Youngstedt, S. D., & Kline, C. E. (2006). Epidemiology of exercise and sleep. *Sleep and Biological Rhythms, 4,* 215–221.

Youth Suicide Prevention Program. (2011). *Helping a friend. Youth: Make a difference.* Retrieved from http://www.yspp.org/for_youth/helping_friend.htm

Yu, C. K. C., & Fu, W. (2011). Sex dreams, wet dreams, and nocturnal emissions. *Dreaming, 21,* 197–212.

Yu, D., Ponomarev, A., & Davis R. L. (2004). Altered representation of the spatial code for odors after olfactory classical conditioning: Memory trace formation by synaptic recruitment. *Neuron, 42,* 437–449.

Yue, S., Duncan, I. J. H., & Moccia, R. D. (2008). Investigating fear in rainbow trout (*Oncorhynchus mykiss*) using the conditioned-suppression paradigm. *Journal of Applied Animal Welfare Science, 11*(1), 14–27.

Yuhas, D., & Jabr, F. (2012). Know your neurons: What is the ration of glia to neurons in the brain? Retrieved from http://blogs.scientificamerican.com/brainwaves/2012/06/13/know-your-neurons-what-is-the-ratio-of-glia-to-neurons-in-the-brain/

Yule, G. (1996). *Pragmatics.* Oxford, UK: Oxford University Press.

Zajonc, R. B. (1980). Feeling and thinking: Preferences need no inferences. *American Psychologist, 35,* 151–175.

Zajonc, R. B. (1984). On the primacy of affect. *American Psychologist, 39,* 117–123.

Zammit, G. (2009). Comparative tolerability of newer agents for insomnia. *Drug Safety, 32,* 735–748.

Zaretskii, V. K. (2009). The zone of proximal development: What Vygotsky did not have time to write. *Journal of Russian and East European Psychology, 47,* 70–93.

Zhang, L., Dong, Y., Doyon, W. M, & Dani, J. A. (2012). Withdrawal from chronic nicotine exposure alters dopamine signaling dynamics in the nucleus accumbens. *Biological Psychiatry, 71,* 184–191.

Zhang, T.-Y., & Meaney, M. J. (2010). Epigenetics and the environmental regulation of the genome and its function. *Annual Review of Psychology, 61,* 439–466.

Zhang, Y., Picetti, R., Butelman, E. R., Schlussman, S. D., Ho, A., & Kreek, J. (2009). Behavioral and neurochemical changes induced by oxycodone differ between adolescent and adult mice. *Neuropsychopharmacology, 34,* 912–922.

Zimbardo, P. (2007). *The Lucifer effect: Understanding how good people turn evil.* New York: Random House.

Zosuls, K. M., Miller, C. F., Ruble, D. N., Martin, C. L., & Fabes, R. A. (2011). Gender development research in *Sex Roles:* Historical trends and future directions. *Sex Roles, 64,* 826–842.

Zuckerman, M. (1979). *Sensation seeking: Beyond the optimal level of arousal.* Hillsdale, NJ: Erlbaum.

Zuckerman, M. (1994). *Behavioral expressions and biosocial bases of sensation seeking.* Cambridge, UK: Cambridge University Press.

Zupec, R. (2008, October 22). Can birth order determine your career? *CNN.com.* Retrieved from http://www.cnn.com/2008/LIVING/worklife/10/22/cb.birth.order.career/index.html

Name Index

Note: Page numbers followed by f indicate figures; i indicates infographics; c indicates connections; t indicates tables.

AA. *See* Alcoholics Anonymous
AAIDD. *See* American Association on Intellectual and Developmental Disabilities
Aarts, H., 399
Aase, H., 211
Abdul-Jabbar, K., 219, 219f
Abecasis, G. R., 490–491
Abel, K. M., 569
Ablon, S. J., 593
Abou-Khalil, B. W., 69
Abrams, E. T., 352f
Acebo, C., 148
Achon, J., 624, 634–636, 635f, 637, 640, 643, 643f, 647, 650, 652, 653f, 654, 658, 658f
Achon Uganda Children's Fund (AUCF), 658
Ackerman, P. L., 373
Active Minds, 577–578
Adams, J. J., 260
Adams, R., 394
Addis, M. E., 605
Addy, S., 511
Adie-Ikor, I., 207
Adler, A., 479, 479f, 481, 501
Adolphs, R., 415, 416i
Advokat, C. D., 60
Aeschbach, D., 154
Agam, G., 563
Agrawal, Y., 116
Aguilar, M. C., 167
Ahima, R. S., 85
Ahmed, S. F., 431
Aiello, J. R., 647
Ainsworth, M. D. S., 358–359, 430
Ainsworth, S. E., 443
Ajzen, I., 630, 633
Akcay, O., 109, 109f
Akii-Bua, J., 635f
Akinola, M., 523
Aksglaede, L., 362f
Al Firdaus, M. M., 239t
al'Absi, M., 521
Al-Anon, 604
Alber, J., 253
Albert, D., 364
Alcoholics Anonymous (AA), 604
Alderman, M. H., 608
Aldrete, J. A., 140
Ale, T. M., 28

Alegria, M., 513
Alexander, D. A., 528
Alexander, G. M., 436f, 437
Alexander, M. P., 80
Alexander, R. D., 651t
Alfano, K., 476f
Allegood, J., 405
Allen, D. L., 531
Allen, E. S., 605
Allen, L., 93, 94, 96, 100–101, 110, 110f, 111, 113, 117, 118, 134, 134f
Allen, N., 480f
Allen, R., 555t
Allen, S., 312, 312f
Allen-Mills, T., 25
Allik, J., 491–492
Allison, C., 419, 435
Alloy, L. B., 250
Allport, Gordon W., 489, 490, 502
Almeida, D., 6t
Almeida, D. M., 511, 652
Alpers, G. W., 556
Alpert, N. M., 179
Alpert, P., 450f
Alpert, P. T., 167
Althoff, S. E., 427f
Altshuler, L. L., 567
Alzheimer, A., 274
Alzheimer's Association, 274f, 275t
Amabile, T. M., 628
Amaral, D. G., 415
Ambady, N., 498
Amdam, G., 375f
American Academy of Pediatrics, 221
American Academy of Sleep Medicine, 157f
American Art Therapy Association, 594f
American Association on Intellectual and Developmental Disabilities (AAIDD), 321
American Foundation for Suicide Prevention, 562i
American Group Psychotherapy Association, 606t
American Heart Association, 399, 520
American Humane Association, 187f
American Psychiatric Association, 151, 155, 156, 157, 158, 176, 178, 400, 401, 426, 431, 438–439, 452,

453, 453t, 454, 458, 459, 463, 511, 542, 543, 544, 547, 548i, 549, 551, 551f, 553, 553t, 554, 556, 556f, 557, 558, 559, 560, 561, 561f, 563, 561t, 566–569, 566t, 568t, 569t, 573, 574, 575, 576, 573t, 587, 607, 612, 613, 613f
American Psychological Association (APA), 5, 10f, 11, 41, 155, 171f, 266, 363f, 394f, 401f, 404f, 410, 426 438–439, 442, 443, 461, 511, 514f, 534i, 546–547, 571f, 616, 657, B-2, B-4, B-5, B-6, B-7, B-8
Amesbury, E. C., 106
Amin, Z., 500
Anastasi, A., 316, 498
Anastasio, A., 608
Anderson, A., 238
Anderson, B., 661
Anderson, C. A., 28
Anderson, G. E., 510
Anderson, G. S., 522
Anderson, J. R., 257
Anderson, R. A., 370
Anderson, R. C., 236
Anderson, V., 14
Anderson-Hanley, C., 647, 647f
Andre, T., 257
Andrés, P., 145
Andrew, M. I., 178
Andrews, S., 237
Andrus, B. M., 563
Angold, A., 431, 550
Angst, F., 608
Angst, J., 480, 608
Anis, A. H., 399
Anna O., 478f
Annan, J., 643
Annese, J., 271f
Ansbacher, H. L., 479
Ansbacher, R. R., 479
Anthony, C., 215
Antwi, D. A., 85
APA. *See* American Psychological Association
Araque, A., 54
Archer, J., 430, 431f, 652
Arciero, P. J., 647, 647f
Ardelt, M., 375
Ardila, A., 430
Arias, B., 525
Aristotle, 8–9, 13i
Arkowitz, H., 6t, 545, 546, 546f, 589i
Arlin, P. K., 372
Armitage, C. J., 633
Arnett, J. J., 368, 374
Arnold, C., 653f
Aronson, E., 633, 638, 642, 644, 654, 662, 663
Asch, S. E., 641–642, 641f, 646
Ashton, M. C., 313
ASL. *See* American Sign Language
Asnaani, M. A., 556
Associated Press, 2, 3, 24, 401f

Association for Psychological Science, 5, 41, B-8
Astin, J. A., 529
Atienza, M., 151
Atkinson, R. C., 236, 243
Attarian, H. P., 156
Attia, E., 401
AUCF. *See* Achon Uganda Children's Fund
Audrain-McGovern, J., 520
Ault, L. K., 661
Aurora, R. N., 157
Austin Community College, 331
Ávalos, F., 15f, 16–17, 43, 44
Ávalos, S., 16–17
Awikunprasert, C., 152
Ayas, N. T., 160
Ayhan, Y., 571

Bach, J. S., 267
Bachman, J. G., 175
Back, K., 660
Back, M. D., 498, 661
Baddeley, A. D., 231, 237, 244, 245–246, 245f, 256–257, 257f, 266, 278, 279
Badie, D., 650
Baer, J. M., 324, 325
Bahrami, B., 77
Bahrick, H. P., 260
Bahrick, L. E., 145, 219
Baibazarova, E., 522
Bailey, J., 167
Bailey, J. M., 444
Bailey, S. J., 521
Baillargeon, R., 354
Baker, L. A., 335, 652
Baker, M., 612
Baker, T. B., 598
Bakker, A. B., 376
Bal, S., 167
Baldessarini, R. J., 608
Baldwin, S. A., 606
Ball, A. L., 77
Ball, M., 142
Ball, T. M., 290, 289f
Ballantyne, C., 162
Bandell, M., 122
Bandura, A., 186, 219, 220, 220f, 221, 227, 229, 309, 435, 486–488, 487i, 488f, 501, A-2
Banker, G., 57
Banks, C., 656–657, 656f
Banks, M. S., 345
Banks, S., 147, 162
Banning, K., 510
Banuazizi, A., 657
Banyard, V. L., 651
Barak, A., 617
Barash, P. G., 170
Barbee, A. P., 661
Barber, C., 610
Barberá, E., 436
Bard, P., 406, 407, 407f, 409i, 413, 421, 423
Bargh, J. A., 144, 661

Barker, E. T., 511
Barlow, D. H., 554
Barlow, J., 344
Barnes, A. J., 175
Barnes, S. K., 349f
Barnum, P. T., 499
Barraclough, B., 401
Barre, S., 383
Barredo, J. L., 347
Barrett, B., 532f
Barrett, L. F., 418, 419
Barrionuevo, A., 43
Barrios, C., 43f
Barrios, Y., 16, 19
Barrowman, S., 519f
Bartels, J. M., 392
Bartels, M., 417
Bateman, A., 593
Batson, C. D., 651t
Batty, G. D., 530
Bauer, P. J., 272
Bauermeister, J. A., 451
Baughman, H. M., 469, 469f
Bauman, M. D., 415
Baumeister, R. F., 176, 392, 443, 484
Baumrind, D., 216, 374
Baur, K., 442, 458t
Bavaria, A. J., 5
Bayley, N., 346i
Bayley, P. J., 272
Baylor, D. A., 106
BBC. See British Broadcasting
    Company
Beaman, A. L., 648–649, 648f
Bear, M. F., 273
Beauchaine, T. P., 575
Beauchamp, G. K., 121
Beauchamp, M. H., 14
Bech, P., 608
Beck, A. T., 564, 601–604, 601f,
    602t, 619, 621
Beck, H., 200, 201
Becker, K. A., 316
Beckham, D., 200, 558f
Becklen, R., 145
Beebe-Center, J. G., 407
Beeman, M., 295
Beer, J. M., 65
Beethoven, L., 267, 590f
Beijers, R., 522
Beilock, S. L., 20f, 438
Beissinger, S. R., 311
Bekk, M., 637
Beland, S., 119
Belizaire, L. S., 512
Bell, D., 35
Bell, S. M., 358
Belmaker, R. H., 563, 567
Beltz, A. M., 444
Bem, D., 133
Bem, S. L., 436
Ben-Ari, A., 514
Benchley, P., 414
Benedek, M., 324
Benedict, R. H. B., 268
Benham, G., 520
Benjamin, L. T., 9, 10, 11

Bennett, A. T. D., 102
Bennett, D. A., 274
Bennett, P., 491
Benovoy, M., 406
Bensman, L., 663
Benson, H., 531
Bentall, R., 613
Ben-Zvi, A., 517
Berchtold, N. C., 275t
Berenbaum, S. A., 444
Berg, C. A., 514
Berg, K. S., 311
Berger, W., 511
Bergh, C., 396
Berglund, P., 550, 561
Bergman, E. T., 266
Bergmann, B. M., 160
Berkeley Lab, 101t
Bernard, L. L., 388
Bernier, A., 355
Bernstein, D. M., 265
Berry, J. W., 512
Berscheid, E., 663
Bertelsen, A., 571
Berthoz, S., 406
Besedovsky, L., 160
Betsch, C., 637
Betz, A. L., 99
Betz, N., 418f
Beutler, L. E., 589i, 590
Bewernick, B. H., 612
Beyerstein, B. L., 6t, 71
Beylin, A., 74
Beyonce, 112
Bezdjian, S., 335, 652
Bhatnagar, S., 109, 109f
Bialystok, E., 306, 306f
Bianchi, D. W., 429
Bibok, M. B., 355
Biemond, R., 597
Bihm, E. M., 205f
Bihrle, S., 574
Bikle, D. D., 121
Billick, S. B., 545
Billings, F. J., 265
Bindemann, M., 629
Binet, A., 315, 315f
Bing, 262
Binik, Y. M., 441
Binkley, N. C., 35
Binns, C., 564f, 590f
Birbaumer, N., 533
Bird, L., 219, 219f
Birge, S. J., 35
Birmingham, W., 520
Bitensky, S. H., 216
Bizer, G. Y., 638–639
Bjork, E. L., 258
Bjork, R. A., 179, 257, 258
Black, H., 532f
Blacker, J., 344
Blackmore, S. J., 143
Blackwell, B., 608
Blackwell Publishing, 625f
Blair, C., 512
Blair, R. J. R., 406
Blaisdell, B., 160

Blake, R., 145
Blakemore, J. E. O., 444
Blanchard, R., 444, 444f
Blanck, H. M., 400t
Blank, A., 639
Blank, C. C., 83
Blank, H., 266
Blascovich, J., 377
Blasi, A., 367
Blass, T., 644f, 646
Blatchley, B., 626
Blattman, C., 643
Blecher, S. R., 429
Blehar, M. C., 358–359
Bleidorn, W., 633, 633f
Blickenstaff, J. C., 65
Bliss-Moreau, E., 415, 418, 419
Bloch, M. H., 559
Block, C. J., 654
Blom, J. D., 612
Bloom, O., 304–305, 304f, 312, 315,
    326
Bloomberg, M., 27f
Blumenthal, H., 362
Bocanegra, J., 244
Boccella, K., 185
Bock, T., 365f
Bocklandt, S., 428
Bode, R., 533, 659
Boehm, J. K., 417
Boeve, B. F., 157
Bogaert, A. F., 444
Bogen, J. E., 71
Bold, K. W., 177
Boldrey, E., 82, 83
Bolen, R. M., 266
Bolton, P., 615
Bonanno, G. A., 20, 417, 511
Bond, R., 642
Boniel-Nissim, M., 617
Bonnie, R. J., 363
Booth, T., 492
Borbély, A. A., 162
Borges, G., 561
Boring, E. G., 10
Born, J., 160, 161, 253
Born, L., 253
Borne, B. V., 519
Bornstein, R. F., 478
Borra, J. E., 363
Borsboom, D., 133
Bos, P. A., 430, 652
Bostwick, J. M., 172
Bottos, S. H., 514
Bouchard, T. J., 323, 323f
Bourdage, J. S., 520
Bourdette, D., 57
Bouton, M. E., 554
Bovbjerg, D. H., 514
Bowden, C. L., 609
Bower, G. H., 249, 258
Bower, J. M., 86
Bowers, J. S., 259
Bowman, L. L., 243–244
Boyes-Braem, P., 286
Boylan, J., 264f
Boyle, M., 266

Bradbury, J. W., 311
Bradley, L. A., 438
Brady, R. E., 558
The Brain Observatory, 271f
Branan, N., 19
Brand, B. L., 575
Brandone, A. C., 307
Brandt, J., 268
Brang, D., 125
Branje, S. J. T., 364
Brantley, D., III, B–3f
Brascamp, J. W., 145
Brault, M. W., 368
Braun, A. R., 72
Brave at Heart, 604f
Breazeal, C., 485
Bredin, S. S. D., 531
Breland, K., 205, 205f
Breland, M., 205, 205f
Brendgen, M., 431
Brenner, D., 60
Brent, R. L., 343t
Breuer, J., 478f
Breus, M. J., 160
Brewin, C. R., 20, 511
Brewster, K. L., 450
Bridge, H., 83
Briggs, K. C., 499
Brilleman, S. L., 510
Broadbelt, K. G., 86
Broca, P. P., 72
Brochet, F., 127
Broderick, A. C., 388
Broderick, G., 517
Broderick, J. E., 375
Brodersen, K. H., 429–430
Brody, S., 448, 448t
Brogaard, P., 29f
Brooks-Gunn, J., 362, 364, 429
Brotto, L. A., 453
Brown, A. S., 260, 572
Brown, P. K., 102
Brown, R., 247, 436
Brown, R. P., 65
Brown, S. A., 176
Brown, S. L., 533
Brown, T. T., 175
Brownell, P., 588
Bruck, D., 142
Bruckman, A., 365
Brunell, A. B., 435
Brunstein, J. C., 417
Bryan, A., 363, 531
Bryan, S. M., 197
Bryant, K., 200
Bryant, R. A., 511
Buchanan, T. W., 415
Buck, L. B., 118
Buck, R., 413
Bucy, P., 84
Buechel, C., 310
Buehler, S., 425, 426, 427f, 439–440,
    439f, 442, 452, 458, 460
Buffardi, L. E., 394, 498
Bui, N. H., 630
Bulpitt, C. J., 370
Bunk, K., 235f

Bureau of Labor Statistics, B–1
Burgaleta, M., 430
Burger, J. M., 484, 646
Burkam, D. T., 349
Burke, D. M., 260
Burkley, M., 574f
Burlingame, G. M., 606
Burnette, J. L., 650
Burns, B., 49, 50f, 51, 51f, 52, 52f, 53, 58, 60, 61, 63, 65, 66, 68, 69, 71, 71f, 74, 75, 79, 84, 86, 87, 87f, 90
Burns, H. J., 264
Burns, L., 50, 87
Burstein, A. G., 496i
Burton, H., 74
Bushman, B. J., 28
Bushnell, M. C., 179
Buss, D. M., 445, 460
Buss, L., 342
Bussey, K., 435
Butcher, J. N., 498, 525
Butler, C., 253
Butler, R. A., 390
Butte, K. S., 610f
Butte, W. S., 610f
Buysse, D. J., 158
Byers, E. S., 427, 451
Bynum, H., 140
Byrd-Craven, J., 460

Cabanatuan, M., 405
Cacchio, M., 430
Cáceres, C., 445
Cacioppo, J. T., 638, 638f
Cadet, J. L., 172
Cahalan, M., 170
Cahill, L., 65, 261
Cain, W. S., 118
Calderwood, C., 373
Caldicott, D. G., 405
Caldwell, K. A., 364
Calhoun, V. D., 371
Calkins, M. W., 10–11, 13i
Call, J., 311
Callahan, J. S., 116
Callan, M. J., 629
Campbell, A., 652
Campbell, D. T., 128
Campbell, G. A., 175
Campbell, J. D., 484
Campbell, W. K., 394, 498
Canli, T., 500
Cannon, D. S., 598
Cannon, W. B., 396, 396f, 406, 407, 407f, 409i, 413, 421, 423
Cantero, J. L., 151
Cantú, S. M., 662
Caplan, R., 72
Card, N. A., 430
Cardeña, E., 576, 576f
Cardenas, D. D., 125
Carey, B., 271
Carlsmith, J. M., 633–634
Carlson, S. M., 355
Carlsson, K., 406
Carlström, E., 443

Carlton, L., 155f
Carnevale, A. P., B–2
Carpendale, J. I. M., 355
Carpenter, C. J., 394
Carpenter, S. K., 252
Carr, P. B., 654
Carrey, J., 22f, 480
Carrier, B., 179
Carroll, M. D., 399, 399f
Carskadon, M. A., 148, 154
Carson, C. C., III, 371
Carstensen, L. L., 375, 415
Carter, C. J., 567
The Carter Center, 511f
Caruso, D., 321
Caruso, R., 107
Case, B. G., 612
Caspani, M., 395
Caspi, A., 356, 372, 467
Cassidy, J., 359
Castel, A. D., 336
Castellanos, M., 58
Castle, P. H., B–4
Catalino, L. I., 44
Catholic Church, 482f
Cattell, R. B., 489, 489f, 490, 499, 499f, 502, 503
Caudek, C., 475
Cavallini, A., 345
CDC. See Centers for Disease Control and Prevention
Ceci, S., 318
Centers for Disease Control and Prevention (CDC), 153i, 170f, 171, 174, 362, 454–455, 455r, 457i, 562i
Centola, D., 209
Cepeda, N. J., 252
Cerny, J. A., 443
Cervilla, J. A., 171
Chaiken, S., 637
Chaimay, B., 345
Chaix, Y., 305
Chamorro-Premuzic, T., 661
Champagne, F. A., 340
Chan, J. S., 372
Chan, M.-p. S., 529
Chandra, A., 443
Chandrashekar, J., 120
Chanowitz, B., 639
Chant, D., 569
Chapman, E., 260
Chapman, G. B., 177
Charles, Prince of Wales, 231
Charlesworth, S., 531
Charlton, B., 376
Chaser (the Border Collie), 311f
Chatterjee, A., 445
Chaudhuri, A., 235
Chawan, I., 209f
Chawla, D., 104
Cheah, B., B–2
Chechik, G., 347
Chein, J., 364
Chen, C.-N., 513
Chen, E., 512
Chen, V. J., 125f

Chen, Z., 244
Cheng, C., 529
Cheng, D. T., 414
Chepa, 583–585, 587, 588, 591, 601, 607
Cherkas, L. F., 469
Cherney, I. D., 430
Chess, S., 356
Cheung, S.-f., 529
Chew, S. H., 659
Cheyne, J. A., 155, 156
Chiao, J. Y., 414
Child Mind Institute, 304, 312, 315
Chin, H. B., 451
Chio, J. H.-m., 529
Chirawatkul, S., 561
Chittka, L., 187
Chiu, V., 111f
Chiu, W. T., 550, 561f, 563
Chivers, M. L., 427, 444
Cho, H. J., 608
Choi, C. Q., 69, 74
Chomnirat, W., 561
Chomsky, N., 309, 348, 349, 360, 379
Chrisler, J. C., 426
Christakis, D. A., 222
Christensen, P. R., 324
Christian, J., 633
Christmas, D., 611i
Chua, A., 483f
Chun, M. M., 72
Chung, F., 157
Cialdini, R. B., 639
Ciarocco, N. J., 392
Cisler, J. M., 558
Clancy, S. A., 155, 156
Clapp, W. C., 244
Clare College (Cambridge), 268
Clark, A. E., 417
Clark, D. M., 555, 603
Clark, K. B., 11
Clark, M. C., 249
Clark, M. P., 11, 11f, 12, 13i
Clark, R. E., 83
Clarke, S., 406f
Clarke-Pearson, K., 365
Classen, C. C., 575
Claus, J., 99
Clay, Z., 446
Clemente, M., 221
Clerici, S., 156
Clerkin, E. M., 555
Cleveland Clinic, 312
Clinton, B., 287
Clooney, G., 158f
Coan, J. A., 404, 414
Coast, J. R., 531
Cochrane, R. E., 525
Coenen, V. A., 612
Cohen, D., 2
Cohen, D. A., 162
Cohen, G., 260
Cohen, G. L., 450
Cohen, H. W., 608
Cohen, J., 445f
Cohen, S., 516i, 518, 520, 523, 534i
Cohn, R., 511

Colapinto, J., 437
Colcombe, S. J., 275t
Cole, C. F., 222, 222f
Coleman, G., 491
Coleman, J. M., 435
Colletti, P., 574
Collins, A., 650
Collins, D. W., 430
Collins, P. A., 511
Collins, W. A., 359
Colliver, J. D., 175
Colrain, I. M., 152
Comaty, J. E., 60
Compton, M., 266
Compton, W. M., 175
Conboy, B. T, 335
Cone, B. K., 116
Conklin, C. A., 520
Conley, A. M., 385
Conley, T. D., 447
Conraads, V. M., 528
Constable, R. T., 500
Conway, M. A., 252, 253f, 260
Cook, J. M., 364
Cook, M., 555
Cool, N., 265
Coolidge, F. L., 474i
Coon, H. M., 615
Cooper, A., 312f
Copeland, W., 550
Copen, C. E., 447
Coplan, R. J., 435
Corballis, P. M., 72
Coren, P., 121
Coren, S., 102
Corey, G., 595, 605
Corkin, S., 271
Cornelius, S. W., 372
Corona, A., 156
Correll, C. U., 609
Corrigan, P., 546
Corti, R., 60, 64
Cortopassi, K. A., 311
Corwin, E. J., 563
Cosgrove, D., 312, 315
Costa, G., 150f
Costa, P. T., Jr., 376, 490–491, 490f, 492
Costa, R. M., 448, 448t
Costandi, M., 269
Costantini-Ferrando, M. F., 179
Costanzo, E. S., 529
Costello, E. J., 431
Costello, J., 550
Cotman, C. W., 275t
Cotroneo, A., 406f
Cotten, S. R., 96, 244
Coughlin, R. J., 476f
Coulson, S., 72
Couperus, J. W., 145
Courvoisier, D., 32, 34f
Covell, K., 521
Cowan, N., 237, 244, 245, 248, 253
Cowan, P. A., 216
Cox, E. O., 116
Coyle, K., 171
Coyne, J. C., 514

Coyne, M. S., 388
Coyne, S. M., 430, 431f, 652
Craddock, N., 340, 567
Craig, D., 258f
Craik, F. I. M., 237
Cramer, P., 475
Crano, W. D., 633
Craske, M. E., 554
Crawford, M., 244
Craze, M., 43
Crick, N. R., 430
Croce, P. J., 10
Crockett, D., 350
Crook, A., 594f
Crooks, N., 43
Crooks, R., 442, 458t
Crowell, S. E., 575
Crowley, M., 650
Cruise, T., 312f
Crutchfield, R. S., 407
Cruz-Santos, A., 306
Csikszentmihalyi, M., 44, 417, 535
Cuéllar, I., 615
Culbertson, J., 17
Cullen, B. F., 170
Cunha, J. P., 150, 150f
Cunningham, C. J. L., A–4
Cunningham, M., 116
Cunningham, M. R., 661
Curhan, G. C., 116
Curhan, S. G., 116
Curie, P., 312
Curry, A., 411
Curtin, L. R., 399
Curtiss, S., 350
Cuthill, I. C., 102
Cyna, A. M., 178
Cynkar, A., 11
Cyrus, M., 480
Cyrzyk, T., 612
Czajkowski, N., 417
Czarnowski, C., 167
Czeisler, C. A., 148

Da Costa, L. A., 260
da Silva, M. W. D., 460
da Silva Queiroz, R., 460
Daffner, K. R., 145
Dafinoiu, I., 205
Dagher, A., 406
Dagi, T. F., 72
Dahmer, J., 545
Dakof, G., 514
Dalgin, M. H., 109, 109f
Dalrymple, T., 185, 200, 201
Dalton, P. H., 118
Damasio, A. R., 80, 406, 416i
Damasio, H., 80
D'Angiulli, A., 512
Dang-Vu, T. T., 77
Dani, J. A., 174
Daniels, K., 447
Danker, J. F., 257
Dapretto, M., 72
Darcy, A. M., 401
Darley, J. M., 650
Dar-Nimrod, I., 444

Darwin, C., 10, 12, 13i, 47, 388, 411,
    421, 480, 481
Davidson, A. R., 633
Davidson, M., 555
Davidson, R. J., 84, 404, 531, 532
Davies, P., 274
d'Avila, J., 53
Davis, E. P., 522
Davis, M., 414
Davis, R. L., 274
de Bellard, M., 53
de Boysson-Bardies, B., 306
de Chastelaine, M., 430
De Groot, D. M., 50
de Hoog, N., 638
de Jong, P. T., 107
de Lauzon-Guillain, B., 345
de Leon, J., 167
De Robertis, M. M., 18
de Rossi, Portia, 445f
de Sousa Campos, L., 460
De Waal, F. B. M., 446
De Weerth, C., 522
de Wit, J. B. F., 638
Deary, I. J., 334, 372, 430, 530
Deaton, A., 375
DeCasper, A. J., 345
Deci, E. L., 386–387, 393, 394f
Deckers, L., 388
Deckie, S. S., 108
Deecke, L., 119
Deeg, K. E., 347
Deer, B., 22
Deese, J., 256
Defeyter, M. A., 297
DeFries, J. C., 323, 388, 467, 555f
DeFries, J. E., 322
DeGeneres, E., 445f
Degnan, K. A., 356
DeGregory, L., 350
Dehaene, S., 99
Del Giudice, M., 492
del Rocio Galarza, M., 222
Delaney, P. A., 18
Delevi, R., 451
Delgado, S., 311
Della Sala, S., 253
DeLongis, A., 514, 514f
Delucchi, K., 521
Dement, W., 153i, 160, 166
Demler, O., 550
Démonet, J. -F., 305
Dennis, C., 429
Denollet, J., 528
Denton, K., 367
Department of Justice, U. S., 410
Dermer, M., 661
Derringer, J., 386f
Desai, M., 116
Descartes, R., 9, 9f, 13i
Deslandes, A., 371
Despins, L. A., 100
Desrichard, O., 258
Desrocher, M., 272
Desruisseau, D. M., 158
Dessens, A. B., 431
Detgen, J., 648

DeValois, K. K., 109
DeValois, R. L., 109
Devaney, S. A., 429
DeWall, C. N., 392
Dewar, M., 253
Dewey, D., 514
Di Forti, M., 176
Di Lorenzo, L., 150, 151
Diagnostic and Statistical Manual of
    Mental Disorders (DSM-5), 547,
    548i, 551, 551f, 553, 553t, 556,
    560, 561t, 566t, 568t, 569, 569t,
    573, 573t, 574, 587, 587f
Diamond, E. L., 528
Diamond, L. M., 443
Diamond, M., 437
Diamond, M. E., 270i
Diaz, C., 480
Diaz, F. J., 167
Diaz, J., 25
DiCecco, K., 142
Dickens, W. T., 318, 323
Dickenson, J. A., 443
Dickerhoof, R., 417
Dickerson, F. B., 600
Dickson, D. W., 274
DiDonato, M., 430
Diego, M., 522
Diehl, S., 588
Diekelmann, S., 161, 253
Diener, E., 417, 648–649, 648f
Diepenbrock, P., 185, 201, 201f, 207,
    219
Dijk, D. J., 154, 162
DiLalla, L. F., 431
DiLillo, D., B–4
Dillow, S. A., B–2
Dimberg, U., 408
Dimsdale, J. E., 519, 520
Dinges, D. F., 147, 159, 160, 162
Dioscorides, 170
Dirie, M., 383–385, 384f, 385f, 386,
    387, 388–390, 392, 393, 395,
    412–413, 419, 419f, 512
DiSalvo, D., 394
Dix, D., 587, 587f
Dixon, J. F., 608
Dixon, R. A., 334, 336
Dobkin, B. H., 291
Dobs, A. S., 175
Dobson, A. J., 510
Doherty-Sneddon, G., 349f
Dohrenwend, B. P., 509
Doidge, N., 86
Dolan, R. J., 257, 257f
Dolbier, C. L., 531
Dolder, C. R., 142
Dollard, J., 652
Domhoff, G. W., 165
Dong, Y., 174
Donlan, W., 544
Donlon, C., 617f
Doob, L. W., 652
Dörfler, R., 450
Dorgan, B. L., 610
Dougherty, D. M., 206
Dougherty, L. R., 563

Douglas, V. I., 211
Douthitt, E. A., 647
Dovidio, J. F., 654
Doyère, V., 415
Doyle, J., 651
Doyon, W. M., 174
Drace, S., 258
Drake, R., 569
Driver, H. S., 162
Drop, S. L., 431
Druckman, D., 179
Druss, B. G., 550
Dryden, W., 603
DSM-5. See Diagnostic and Statistical
    Manual of Mental Disorders
Dubourdieu, D., 127
Duckworth, A. L., 320
Dugas, M. J., 603
Duijts, S. F. A., 519
Duncan, C. P., 211
Duncan, G. H., 179
Duncan, I. J. H., 187
Dunlosky, J., 238
Dunn, E., 93, 94, 94f, 96, 100–101,
    101f, 104, 105i, 110, 110f, 111,
    113, 114i, 116, 118, 121, 126,
    127, 134, 134f, 625
Dunn, M. E., 176
Dunn, S. (Sarah), 100, 110f, 134, 134f
Dunn, S. (Sophie), 93, 94, 94f, 96,
    100–101, 101f, 104, 105i, 110,
    110f, 111, 113, 114i, 116, 118,
    126, 127, 134, 134f, 625
Dunn, Zoe, 93, 94, 94f, 96, 100–101,
    101f, 104, 105i, 110, 110f, 111,
    113, 114i, 116, 117, 117f, 118,
    121, 121i, 126, 127, 134, 134f,
    625
Duntley, S. P., 158
DuPont, R., 175
Durand, C., 306
Durante, K. M., 662
Durmer, J. S., 159
Dusek, J. A., 531
Dweck, C. S., 654
Dyer, A. G., 187
Dykman, B., 250
Dyson, M., 563

Eagly, A. H., 431, 637, 650, 662
Easter, M., 252
Eastwick, P. W., 625, 625f, 662
Eaton, N. R., 565
Eavey, R., 116
Ebbinghaus, H., 252, 258–259, 259f,
    262
Eber, H. W., 489f
Ebstein, R. P., 659
eBizMBA, 32
Eccleston, C., 533
Eckersberger, C., 119
Eckert, M. A., 371
Eckstein, D., 480
Eden, G. F., 323
Edlund, J. E., 638–639
Edwards, C., 630
Egan, S. K., 435

Egloff, B., 335, 491, 660
Ehrsam, R., 370
Eichenbaum, H., 84
Eidelman, A. I., 344, 344f
Einarson, A., 303
Einstein, A., 82, 82f
Eisenberger, N. I., 500
Ekman, P., 406, 411, 412f, 413, 414, 415, 423
El Ansary, M., 139, 141f
El Mansari, M., 563
Elder, C. R., 400
Eliassen, J., 119
Elijamel, M. S., 611i
Elkind, D., 363, 368
Elliot, E. J., 401
Elliott, D. B., 368
Elliott, E. M., 244
Elliott, J., 535
Elliott, J., 655i
Elliott, M., 535
Ellis, A., 602–603, 619
Ellis, B. J., 480
Ellsbury, S. W., 242
Elmehed, K., 408
Elsaid, H., 157
Else-Quest, N. M., 419, 435
El-Sohemy, A., 60
Emerson, E., 551
Emmelkamp, P. M. G., 597
Emmons, R. A., 23i, 417
Emmorey, K., 72
Emory, G., 602
Endicott, L., 365f, 367
Enea, V., 205
Engel de Abreu, P. M., 306
Engelhardt, W., 511
Engelmann, K., 608
Englund, M. M., 359
Epstein, L. J., 151, 154, 162
Epstein, M. H., 72
Erdberg, P., 496i
Erickson, K. I., 275t
Erickson, R. P., 429
Erickson-Schroth, L., 446
Ericsson, K. A., 293
Erikson, E, H., 359, 360t, 364, 368, 374, 378, 379, 380, 381, 373, 393, 479f, 481
Erikson, J. M., 359, 360t, 364
Eriksson, M., 345
Eriksson, P. S., 6t, 74, 84
Ernst, C., 480
Eron, L. D., 221
Ervin, F. R., 195
Eskenazi, B., 370
Espinosa, P., 221
Espinoza, G., 661, 661f
ESPN.com, 200, 201
Esser, S., 139
Etaugh, C., 371
Evans, H., 215
Evans, V., 307
Exner, J. E., 497
Eyer, D., 6t, 75
Eysenck, B. G., 490f
Eysenck, H. J., 490, 490f, 502, 503

Fabes, R. A., 430, 435
Fagan, P., 661
Falk, D., 82f
Falkenberg, L., 104
Fancher, R. E., 189, 315, 321
Fantini, M. L., 156, 157
Faraone, S. V., 571
Farha, B., 133
Faria, M. A., 611i
Farmer, A., 610f
Farmer, R. F., 550
FarmersOnly.com, 625
Farroni, T., 345
Farthing, G. W., 141, 142, 143, 161
Favre, B., 451
Faye, E. E., 334
Faymonville, M. E., 179
Fazel, S., 546, 546f
Fechner, G. T., 9, 13i
Fedorikhin, A., 303
Fehr, E., 65
Feigelman, S., 346i
Fein, S., 637
Feinstein, J. S., 416i
Feis, D. L., 429–430
Feist, G. J., 325
Feldman, R., 344, 344f
Fels, J., 145
Feng, W., 255f
Fennis, B. M., 639
Fera, F., 414
Ferguson, C. J., 574
Ferguson, H. J., 629
Fergusson, D. M., 345
Ferini-Strambi, L., 156
Ferrer, E., 312
Ferrero, J., 362f
Ferri, C. P., 275t
Ferris, P. A., 520
Feshbach, S., 637
Fessler, D. M., 352f, 651t
Festinger, L., 633–634, 660
Fey, T., 263f
Feyer, A. M., 160
Feyerick, D., 450f
Field, T., 344, 359, 522
Fields, R. D., 272
Fifer, W. P., 345
Filkins, D., 51f
Finch, A. E., 616
Fine, E. J., 86
Finer, L. B., 447, 448f
Finger, S., 80
Fink, G., 519
Fink, M., 613
Finkel, D., 118
Finkel, E. J., 625, 625f, 660, 661–662
Finucane, A. M., 145
Firestein, S., 118
Firth, S., 377
Fischbacher, U., 65
Fischer, B., 168
Fischer, J., 311
Fischer, P., 651
Fisher, D. M., 344
Fisher, S. E., 322
Fitzpatrick, M., 588

Fitzpatrick, M. J., 438
Flaherty, C., 187f
Flansburg, E., 505–509, 509f, 513, 526, 533, 535
Flegal, K. M., 399, 399f
Flevares, L. M., 487i
Flor, H., 125, 533
Flores, N., 525
Flourens, P., 75–76
Flynn, J. R., 318, 323
Fogarty, G. J., 321
Fogel, S. M., 152
Folkman, S., 408, 514, 514f, 526
Fonagy, P., 593
Fong, C. P. S., 648
Foos, P. W., 237
Ford, J. I., 639f
Forgas, J. P., 410, 414
Forger, D. B., 148
Forlizzi, J., 465
Forsyth, D. R., 650
Forte, M., 57
Fortier, C., 517
Foster, B., 618
Foster, D., 542, 583–586, 585f, 587, 591, 600, 601–602, 607, 609, 610, 614–615, 618, 618f
Fournier, J. C., 608
Fowlkes, C. C., 128
Fox, A. B., 244
Fox, M., 440f
Fozard, J. L., 371
Fraga, M. F., 340
Frampton, C. M., 175
Francis, Pope, 482f
Francis, W. S., 237
Frank, R., 80
Frankenburg, W. K., 346i
Franklin, J., 1–3, 15, 16, 24, 25, 27, 43
Franz, F., 324
Fraser, S. C., 639, 648f
Fratiglioni, L., 275t
Frawley, T. J., 436
Freberg, K., 394
Freberg, L., 394
Fredrickson, B. L., 44
Freedman, J. L., 639
Freeman, J., 68, 69
French, C. C., 133
Freud, A., 473
Freud, J., 470f
Freud, S., 11, 11f, 13i, 29t, 164, 165, 166, 172, 182, 183, 469, 470–478, 470f, 471f, 472f, 474i, 475f, 475t, 476f, 477f, 478f, 479, 479f, 480, 481, 483, 485, 501, 503, 551, 591–593, 592f, 601, 619, 621
Freud Museum (London), 592f
Fried, I., 291
Friedman, L. F., 197
Friedman, M., 526, 528
Friedman, M. J., 511
Fries, C. J., 629f
Friesen, W. V., 411, 412f, 415
Frith, M., 558f
Fritsch, G., 80, 82
Fromkin, V., 350

Fu, W., 165
Fuchs, P. N., 124
Fuertes, J. N., 512
Fujino, D. C., 614–615
Fukushima, O., 297
Fuller, W. J., 388
Funnell, M. G., 72
Furness, W. H., 223

Gabbard, G. O., 470–471
Gabriel, D., 609
Gabrieli, J. D. E., 271
Gackenbach, J., 166
Gaebel, W., 609
Gaertner, S. L., 654
Gafford, J., 377
Gage, F. H., 347f
Gage, P., 29t, 80, 81i, 83
Gage, S. H., 259
Gagnon, J. H., 447–448
Gais, S., 253
Galaburda, A. M., 80
Galanter, E., 97, 98i
Galati, D., 412
Gale, C., 150, 530
Gall, J., 75–76, 91
Gallace, A., 125f
Gallagher, K. C., 357
Gallo, M., 303
Gamer, M., 410
Gamma, A., 608
Gangestad, S. W., 662
Ganis, G., 291
Gannon, P. J., 72
Ganzel, B. L., 528
Gao, Y., 652
Garb, H. N., 495, 496i
Garcia, A. L., 629
Garcia, J., 195, 196
Garcia, J. R., 449, 449t
Garcia-Lázaro, H., 271–272
Garcia-Recuero, I., 123
Gardner, H., 313, 313f, 313t, 314t, 327
Gardner, R., 160f
Gardner, S., 15
Garnett, G. P., 457i
Garro, L. C., 615
Garry, M., 265f
Gassmann, P., 384f, 388
Gastil, J., 310
Gatchel, R. J., 124, 125
Gates, G. J., 438, 443, 445
Gates-Williams, J., 377
Gaus, S. E., 162
Gava, L., 128
Gaval-Cruz, M., 598
Gavie, J., 166
Gay, P., 11, 470
Gayton, S. D., 522, 525
Gazzaley, A., 244
Gazzaniga, M., 70, 71, 72, 91
Ge, S., 99
Geake, J., 314
Geary, D. C., 460
Geddes, J. R., 546, 546f
Geddes, L., 140f

Gegenfurtner, K. R., 109
Geier, A., 398
Gelenberg, A. J., 563
Genain, H., 29t, 570
Genain, I., 29t, 570
Genain, M., 29t, 570
Genain, N., 29t, 570
Gendron, M., 243–244
Genetics Home Reference, 433t
Genovese, C. (Kitty), 650, 651f
George, M. S., 611i
Georgiadis, J. R., 441
Gerberding, J. L., 171
Gerber-Werder, R., 608
Gerdes, A. B. M., 556
German, T. P., 297
German StudiVZ, 498
Gerressu, M., 448
Gerrie, M. P., 265f
Gershoff, E. T., 215, 216
Gerstorf, D., 372
Ghahramani, N., 428
Gibb, R., 346i, 347
Gibbs, A. C. C., 511
Gibson, E. J., 130, 130f
Gibson, G., 608
Giedd, J. N., 363
Giedgowd, G. E., 520
Giesbrecht, T., 576
Gigerenzer, G., 301
Gilbert, R., 445
Gillaspy, J. A., 205f
Gillespie, C., 400t
Gilligan, C., 365f, 367
Gilligan, S. G., 258
Gillin, J. C., 160
Gino, A., 598
Giordano, J., 551
Girodo, M., 596
Girvin, J. P., 175
Glahn, D. C., 571
Glantz, M. D., 175
Glaser, R., 514
Glass, R. M., 612
Glen, F., 388
Glenberg, A. M., 257
Glenn, A. L., 652
Global Sex Survey, 449, 449f
Glock, S., 634
Gnann, J. W., 232
Go, A. S., 520
Go, V. F., 445
Gockley, R., 467
Godden, D. R., 256, 257f, 279
Godlee, F., 22, 24
Godley, B. J., 388
Goel, N., 159, 160
Goel, R., 303
Gogate, L. J., 219
Gogtay, N., 569
Gold, J. I., 125f
Gold, R. B., 342
Goldin-Meadow, S., 350
Goldsmith, H. H., 404, 467
Goldstein, E. B., 293
Goldstein, I., 65
Goldstein, J. M., 65, 569

Goldstein, N. J., 639
Goleman, D., 321
Golinkoff, R. M., 6t, 75, 307
Gomez, C. M., 151
Gomez, M., 24f
Gondolf, L. P., 265
Goodbody, S. J., 82
Goodfriend, W., 549f
Goodnow, J. J., 374
Google, 200, 230, 261–262, 302
Google Hangout, 617f
Goolkasian, P., 237
Gordon, J., 58
Gordon, K. A., 115
Gordon, S. M., 175
Gordon-Messer, D., 451
Gordon-Salant, S., 116
Gorlick, M. A., 375
Gottesman, I. I., 571, 571f
Gottfried, J. A., 257, 257f
Gould, E., 74
Graber, J. A., 362, 429
Grabner, R. H., 82
Grabowski, T., 80
Gracheva, E. O., 102, 102f
Gradin, M., 345
Grady, J. S., 28
Graham, C. A., 448
Grammer, K., 662
Granger, D. A., 652
Granich, R., 456
Grann, M., 546, 546f
Granrud, C. E., 132
Grant, B. F., 170, 175
Grant, E., 629f
Grant, P. R., 12f
Grant, R. D., 258
Gravholt, C. H., 433
Gray, J., 469
Gray, W. D., 286
Greco, C. M., 533
Green, J. P., 179
Green, M., 307, 535
Greenberg, J. S., 511
Greenberg, L., 605
Greenberg, R. P., 615
Greenblatt, S. H., 72
Greene, D., 630
Greenfield, P. M., 21i
Greenfieldboyce, N., 465
Green-Paden, L. D., 600
Greenwald, M., 160
Gregson, S., 344
Greider, C., 312, 312f
Greitemeyer, T., 222
Grigorenko, E. L., 372
Grimbos, T., 427
Grimm, J., 629
Grimm, K. J., 336, 362
Grimm, W., 629
Griskevicius, V., 662
Grodzinski, A., 451
Groeger, L., 112
Grohmann, B., 119
Groopman, J., 629
Gross, C. G., 80
Grossman, R. P., 199, 199f

Grossmann, I., 375
Grotenhermen, F., 176
Grotpeter, J. K., 430
Growdon, J. H., 271
Gruber, D. F., 54
Grusec, J. E., 374
Gruttadaro, D., 588
Guggenheim Museum, 372f
Guggisberg, A., 609
Guilford, J. P., 324
Guilleminault, C., 154
Guillot, C., 175
Gulati, G., 546, 546f
Gulevich, G., 160, 160f
Gundel, J., 388, 388f, 389f
Gundersen, H. J. G., 50
Gunderson, E. A., 438
Gurnett, C. A., 158
Gurpegui, M., 167
Gurven, M., 491, 491f
Güss, D., 297–298
Gutiérrez, M., 237
Gruzelier, J., 175

Haas, B., 500
Haedt-Matt, A. A., 401
Hakun, J. G., 410
Halász, J., 28
Hale, S., 245
Halfon, N., 215
Hall, D. W., 451
Hall, J. A., 419
Hall, J. K., 419
Hall, J. W., 345
Hall, L. K., 260
Hall, M., 541, 577
Hall, S. M., 521
Halle, P., 306
Haller, J., 28
Halpern, D. F., 430
Halpern, L., 568
Halverson, C. F., 436
Hamer, D. H., 443
Hamilton, W. D., 651t
Hamm, J., 561f
Hammond, S. I., 355
Hampton, A. N., 77
Hancox, R. J., 221
Haney, C., 656–657, 656f
Hanish, L. D., 430
Hanley, J. R., 260
Hanley, M., 125
Hanna-Pladdy, B., 373
Hannon, E. E., 348
Hanowski, R. J., 244
Hanscombe, K. B., 318
Hansen, C. J., 531
Hansen, N. B., 616
Harber, K. D., 637
Harcourt, B. E., 587f
Harden, K. P., 362, 429
Hari, R., 309
Hariri, A. R., 414
Harkins, S., 647
Harkness, K. L., 561
Harlow, H. F., 357–358, 358f, 390
Harlow, J. M., 80

Harlow, M. K., 357–358, 358f, 390
Harmon, D. K., 510
Harrington, A., 570, 587
Harrington, J. M., 149i
Harrington, R., 506
Harris, B., 198
Harris, E. C., 401
Harris, J. A., 270i, 632
Harris, K. C., 371
Harris, V. A., 628
Harrold, S., 83
Hart, B., 349
Hartlage, S., 250
Hartmann, P., 371
Hartshorne, J. K., 480
Hartshorne, T. S., 480
Harvey, M. A., 175
Harvey, T., 82, 82f
Hasher, L., 250
Hassebrauck, M., 450, 460
Hassett, J. M. 436f
Hassin, R. R., 144
Hatch, S. L., 509
Hatch, T., 313t
Hatfield, E., 459, 663
Hauser, J., 125
Havelka, M., 523
Hawthorne, W. B., 587
Hayano, F., 554
Haydn, J., 267
Hayes, C., 223
He, Y., 154, 429
Healey, M. D., 480
Healy, J., 15
Heaton, J. P. W., 371
Hecht, S., 107
Hecker, L., 307
Heene, M., 324
Hegarty, P., 310
Heiman, J. R., 453
Hein, M. M., 438
Heine, S. J., 444
Heinrichs, M., 65
Heller, N., 554f
Hellers, G., 396
Helmstetter, F. J., 414
Hemenway, D., 638
Hen, L., 617
Hendricks, M. L., 439
Henley, T. B., 9, 9f
Henneman, W. J., 84
Henquet, C., 176
Henríquez, J., 15, 16
Henry, D. B., 630
Henry, D. R., 596
Hensrud, D. D., 35
HERB (the Home Exploring Robot
    Butler), 485
Herbenick, D., 447, 449
Hergenhahn, B. R., 586
Hering, E., 108
Herman, C. P., 398
Hersch, R. H., 366
Hersh, S. M., 657
Herskovits, M. J., 128
Hertenstein, M. J., 356
Hertzog, C., 274, 275t

Herz, R. S., 119
Hess, E. H., 104
Hess, U., 414
Hettema, J. M., 554, 557
Hetzel, L., 375
Hewett, K., 109
Heyes, C., 555
Heynderickx, I., 99
Heynen, A. J., 273
Hickman, J. S., 244
Hickok, G., 83
Higgins, A., 419, 435, 608
Hilgard, E. R., 180, 406, 481
Hinckley, J., Jr., 545
Hines, M., 429, 436, 436f, 437
Hingson, R. W., 170
Hinton, D. E., 556
Hirsh-Pasek, K., 6t, 75, 307
Hirvonen, M. D., 399
Hitch, G. J., 244, 245, 266
Hitzig, E., 80, 82
Hjerrild, B. E., 433
H. M. (Henry Molaison), 269, 270i,
   271, 271f
Hobson, J. A., 11f, 161, 165
Hock, R. R., 453
Hockney, D., 95f
Hodges, L., 597
Hodis, F. A., 385
Hoek, H. W., 401, 612
Hoff, E., 349
Hoffman, A., 107
Hoffman, R. P., 433
Hofman, W., 176
Hoffmann, I. Z., 592
Hofmann, S. G., 556
Hofstede, G., 298
Hokin, L. E., 608
Holahan, C. K., 321
Holahan, J. M., 312
Holick, M. F., 35
Holland, A., 35
Holland, R. W., 633
Hollenbeck, J. R., 648
Holmes, E. A., 83
Holmes, J., 545f
Holmes, T. H., 509, 510, 536
Holowka, S., 309
Holsen, L. M., 563
Hölzel, B. K., 532
the Home Exploring Robot Butler. See
   HERB
Honberg, R., 588
Honda, H., 22
Honey, A., 551
Hong, Y.-y, 648
Honzik, C. H., 224
Hoon, M. A., 120
Hopely, M., 541, 552, 552f, 557, 558–
   560, 560f, 576, 578, 578f
Hopkins, A., 546f
Hopkins, R. O., 268
Hoppel, A. M., 456
Hopper, K., 34
Hoppmann, C., 372
Hor, H., 154
Horder, J., 558

Horemheb, 141f
Horne, J., 147, 148, 150, 160
Horney, K., 481, 501
Horoscope.com, 18
Horton, R., 643
Horwitz, B., 309
Horwitz, D., 608
Horwood, L. J., 345
Hothersall, D., 10, 192, 201
Houk, C. P., 431
House, J. S., 533
House, P., 630
Houts, R. M., 362
Hovland, C. I., 637, 667
Howard, M., 563
Howes, O. D., 571, 572
Howland, J., 171
Howland, M., 398
Hoyert, D., 376
Hu, L., 614–615
Hu, N., 443
Hu, S., 443
Hua T'o, 176
Hubbard, T. L., 290
Hubble Space Telescope, 470, 478
Hubel, D. H., 107
Huber, V. L., 303
Hudson, C., 113
Huesmann, L. R., 221
Huffman, S. P., 205f
Hughes, A., 142
Hughes, I. A., 431
Hull, C. L., 389f
Humphrey, E. K., 295
Humphrey, S. E., 648
Humphries, T., 309
Hunger, J. M., 398
Hunley, H. A., 525
Hunsly, J., 499
Hunt, W. A., 407
Hupp, J. M., 435
Hurst, L. C., 478f
Hurvich, L. M., 109
Husain, M., 82
Husband, T. H., 265
Hutchison, K. E., 531
Hutton, S. B., 419
Hyde, J. S., 430, 431
Hyde, M., 160
Hyman, I. E., Jr., 265

Iacono, W. G., 323, 323f
Ibañez, C., 27
Illanes, J., 15, 43
iminmotion.net, 185
Indian Health Services, 607f
Ingold, J., 545f
Ingram, A., 187f
Inkelas, M., 215
Inman, A. G., 513
Inozemtseva, O., 430
Institute for Sex Research, 447f
Interlandi, J., 588
Inui, K., 242
Ionita, C. C., 86
Ireland, M., 532
Irving, J., 312, 315

Irwing, P., 492
Isacsson, G., 608
Isen, A., 297
Israel, S., 659
Iturra, A., 24–25, 27
Ivcevic, Z., 498
Iversen, L., 175, 176
Ivey, A., 531
Izard, C. E., 404, 414

Jaakkola, M. S., 174
Jaaro-Peled, H., 571
Jabr, F., 53
Jaccard, J. J., 633
Jacobi, F., 550
Jacobs, H., 444
Jacobsen, E., 531
Jacobson, K. C., 652
Jacobson, L., 636
Jacobson, N. S., 605
Jaconis, M., 401
Jagnow, M. S., 121
James, L. E., 260
James, S. D., 350
James, W., 10, 13i, 45, 47, 143, 183,
   388, 406, 406f, 407
Jameson, D., 109
Janata, P., 290
Jang, K. L., 491t, 632, 633f
Janis, I. L., 637, 638, 649
Jansen, J., 522
Janssen, E., 85, 443
Janssen, L., 639
January, A. M., B–4
Jasper, J. D., 303
Jayesinghe, N., 342
Jeffrey, R. W., 520
Jenaro, C., 525
Jenkins, J., 404
Jensen, A. R., 318
Jensen, M. P., 125, 179
Jensen, T. S., 125
Jeste, D. V., 375
JFK Hospital (Liberia), 511f
Jiang, Y., 659
Jimerson, S. R., 510
Jin, R., 550
Joan of Arc, 481f
Joels, S., 171
Joelving, F., 159
Johnson, A. M., 448
Johnson, D. M., 126, 286
Johnson, D. W., 364
Johnson, H. D., 28f, 438
Johnson, L., 160
Johnson, L. R., 415
Johnson, M. H., 345
Johnson, M., 219
Johnson, P. L., 554
Johnson, R. D., 303
Johnson, R. T., 364
Johnson, S. E., 662
Johnson, V., 440, 440f, 441–442,
   443, 451, 461, 463
Johnson, W., 323, 430
Johnson, W. O., 133
Johnston, L. D., 175

Johnston, M. V., 73
Joinson, A. N., 32, 34f
Jolie, A., 103, 103f
Jones, B. E., 58
Jones, E. E., 628
Jones, J., 443
Jones, K., 647
Jordan-Young, R. M., 444
Joseph, N. T., 520
Josephs, R. A., 65
Joshua, A. M., 406f
Jouvet, Michel, 152, 156
Juberg, D. R., 476f
Julien, R. M., 60, 139, 140f, 142, 166,
   167, 168, 168f, 171, 172, 173,
   174, 179, 180, 181
Junco, R., 96, 244
Jung, C. G., 480–481, 481f, 501
Junior World Memory Champion,
   276, 276f
Jussim, L., 637
Jussim, L. J., 99
Juul, A., 362f, 431, 433

Kaduverttoor-Davidson, A., 513
Kafka, M. P., 458
Kagan, J., 356, 359, 467
Kahlenberg, S. G., 438
Kahn, D. M., 74
Kahn, J., 635
Kahneman, D., 300–301, 302
Kalin, N. H., 84
Kaminski, J., 311
Kamprad, I., 312f
Kanai, R., 77
Kanas, N., 25
Kandel, E. R., 269, 272, 273–274
Kandler, C., 491, 633, 633f
Kane, D. B., 311, 311f
Kane, J. M., 609
Kaneda, H., 121
Kanfer, R., 373
Kaniasty, K., 20
Kanwisher, N., 72
Kaplan, H., 491, 491f
Kapur, N., 231, 236
Kapur, S., 571, 572
Karam, E. G., 550, 550f
Karau, S. J., 648
Kardashian, K., 199f
Karelitz, J. L., 520
Karlen, S. J., 74
Karney, B. R., 625, 625f
Karp, A., 275t
Karraker, K. H., 132
Karremans, J. C., 99
Kasisomayajula, V., 174
Kassin, S., 637
Kastenbaum, R., 376
Kaufman, L., 242
Kaufman, M. T., 603
Kaufman, R. A., 256
Kaurashima, O., 132
Kawa, S., 551
Kawakami, K., 654
Kay, L. M., 85
Kaye, D., 638

Kayser, S., 612
Kazdin, A. E., 600
Keel, P. K., 401, 402, 402f
Keesey, R. E., 399
Keir, R., 555
Keirstead, H. S., 74
Keith, S. E., 111f
Kelem, R. T., 648–649, 648f
Kelley, H. H., 637
Kelley, K., 357
Kelley, K., 564f
Kellner, C. H., 611i
Kelly, H., 651t
Keltner, D., 404
Kemeny, M. E., 404
Kemmelmeier, M., 615
Kempermann, G., 347f
Kempton, M. J., 563
Kendall, A. E., 456
Kendler, K. S., 557
Kennard, C., 83
Kennedy, J. F., 267
Kennedy, N., 567
Kennedy, P. G. E., 235f
Kennedy, S. H., 612, 612f
Keren, N. I., 371
Kerr, L. N., 648
Keshavan, M. S., 340, 569
Kessler, R. C., 550, 550t, 561, 561f,
    563, 573, 597
Ketcham, K., 263, 264, 265, 266
Key, M. S., 638–639
Keyl, P. M., 533, 659
Keys, T. E., 139, 170, 172, 176
Kidd, S. A., 370
Kiecolt-Glaser, J. K., 514
Kiesler, S. B., 465
Kigar, D., 82, 82f
Kihara, T., 58
Kihlstrom, J. F., 179
Kilduff, L. P., 433
Kim, D.-Y., 60
Kim, J., 398
Kim, J. J., 271
Kimball, A., 588
Kimura, D., 430
King, B. M., 396, 397i
King, J. E., 491
King, M. L., Jr., 258, 655i
Kingsbury, M. K., 435
Kinney, H. C., 86
Kinoshita, Y., 557
Kinsey, A. C., 442, 443f, 447, 447f
The Kinsey Institute, 443f, 447f
Kirby, K., 506, 513, 513f, 521–522,
    525, 530, 530f, 533, 535
Kirkpatrick, L. A., 460
Kirsch, I., 179
Kirschbaum, C., 65
Kirschner, P., 638
Kisilevsky, S. B. S., 187, 345
Kit, B. K., 399f
Kito, M., 661
Klass, P., 306
Klaver, C. C., 107
Kleber, H. D., 175
Klein, D. N., 563

Klein, S., 528
Kleiner, K., 398f
Kleinman, A., 561
Kleitman, N., 166
Klerman, E. B., 154
Klimstra, T. A., 364
Kline, C. E., 162
Kline, L. E., 162
Kline, T. J. B., 520
Klugman, E. B., 175
Klump, K. L., 402, 402f
Kluver, H., 84
Knafo, A., 659
Knapp, S., 266
Knecht, S., 72
Kneer, J., 634
Knickmeyer, R. C., 346i
Knight, D. C., 414
Knight, J., 661
Knopik, V. S., 323, 388, 467, 555f
Knudsen, E. I., 335
Knutsson, A., 151
Ko, H. J., 406f
Kobasa, S. C., 509, 528
Kobus, K., 630
Koch, C., 291
Koch, I., 145
Koch, S. M., 654
Kochanek, K. D., 169i, 173f
Koelling, R. A., 195
Koelsch, S., 72
Koenig, B. A., 377
Koestner, R., 386–387
Kofman, J., 34
Kohlberg, L., 365–366, 365f, 367,
    367f, 379
Kohler, P. K., 451
Köhler, W., 224, 229, 295, 295f
Kohn, M., 401
Kolb, B., 340, 346i, 347, 407
Kolmes, K., 617
Komai, T., 341f
Konda, K., 445
Kondash, J., 266
Kopelman, M., 231
Koren, G., 303
Kornheiser, A. S., 106
Kortekaas, R., 441
Kortepeter, C., 142
Kosslyn, S. M., 179, 289–290, 289f,
    291, 608
Kossoff, E. H., 69
Kosty, D. B., 550
Kothadia, J. P., 175
Kouider, S., 99
Kounios, J., 295
Kovács, A. M., 306
Kozel, A. F., 77
Kraft, D., 179
Kramer, A. F., 274, 275t
Krashen, S., 350
Krasnova, I. N., 172
Kraul, C., 34, 43
Kraybill, M. L., 80
Krebs, D. L., 367
Krech, D., 407
Kreider, R. M., 368

Kreiman, G., 291
Krijn, M., 597
Kripke, D. F., 162
Krishna, 109
Kristina Acuma Achon Clinic, 658
Kristjánsson, Á, 145
Kritzer, R., 266
Krivickas, K., 368
Krizan, Z., 302
Krosnick, J. A., 99
Kross, E., 375
Krueger, J. I., 484
Kruger, J., 400
Kruk, M. R., 28
Kübler-Ross, E., 376
Kucharski, A., 613
Kuczynski, L., 374
Kuhl, P. K., 335
Kuhn, M., 405
Kujawa, S. G., 370
Kulik, J., 247
Kumar, A. A., 576
Kumar, R. S., 576
Kunis, M., 240
Kunnen, S. E., 364
Kuo, Z. Y., 388
Kurashima, O., 132
Kurashima, O., 132

La Greca, A. M., 20
Laan, E., 85, 427
Labayak, S. E., 148
LaBerge, S., 166
Labin, D. B., 222
LaCasse, L., 574
Ladouceur, C. D., 429
Laeng, B., 104, 414
Lafferty, W. E., 451
Lahav, O., 224
Lahey, B. B., 431
Laireiter, A.-R., 513
Lakdawalla, D. N., 460
Lakes, K., 615
Lal, S., 11, 12
Lalumiere, M. L., 427
Lambert, A., 438f
Lambert, M. J., 616
Lamm, H., 649
Lammers, W. J., 205f
Landau, J. D., 5
Landeros-Weisenberger, A., 559
Landis, K. R., 533
Lando, H. A., 549
Landolt, H. P., 162
Landrum, R. E., B–1
Lane, M. C., 573
Lange, C. G., 406, 406f, 407, 409i,
    413, 421, 423
Lange, T., 160
Langer, E. J., 529, 529f, 639
Langer, R. D., 162
Langlois, J. H., 662
Långström, N., 443
Langwith, J., 343t
Lapidot-Lefler, N., 657f
Lara, D. R., 173

Lara-Romero, R., 271
Larcher, K., 406
Larsen, G., 469
Larsen, L., 371
Larsen, R. J., 460
Larsen, U., 370
Larsson, M., 118, 119
Larzelere, R. E., 216
Lashley, K. D., 269, 270i
Latané, B., 647, 650
Laumann, E. O., 447–448, 452
Laursen, T. M., 571
Lavee, Y., 514
Lawler-Row, K. A., 535
Lawn, J. E., 344
Lawo, V., 145
Lawrence, J., 481f
Lawrence Erlbaum Publications, 510f
Lawton, M. P., 660
Lazarus, R. S., 408, 506, 509, 514,
    514f, 526
Le Clec'h, G., 406
Leaper, C., 435, 436
LeBeau, E. J., 555
Lebrecht, N., 74
Leckman, J. F., 559
LeDoux, J. E., 84, 414, 415
Lee, C. M., 499
Lee, J., 544
Lee, J. H., 35, 345, 597
Lee, M., 215
Lee, M. K., 465
Lee, P. A., 431
Lee, S. J., 215
Lee, S. S., 72
Lee, V. E., 349
Lee, W., 387t
LeFleur, M. (Tank), 465, 466–467,
    470, 478, 484–485, 489, 494
Lehrner, J., 119
Leichsenring, F., 593
Leighty, K. A., 206
Leininger, G., 396
Leinninger, T., 574
Lenhart, A., 365, 450
Lennie, P., 109
Leno, J., 160, 312f
Lentzner, H., 116
Lenzenweger, M. F., 573, 574
Leo, I., 128
Leontopoulou, S., 510
Lepore, F. E., 82f
Lerman, C., 520
Lero Vie, M., 491, 491f
Lesgold, A. M., 249
Lessmoellmann, A., 246, 305, 311
Leszcz, M., 604, 606, 606t
Leucht, S., 609
Levänen, S., 309
Levav, J., 398f
LeVay, S., 444
Levenson, R. W., 415
Leventhal, H., 638
Levett-Jones, T., 629
Levin, R. J., 441, 442
Levine, B., 272
Levine, L. E., 243–244

Levine, M., 650
Levine, M. P., 459
Levine, S. C., 438
Levinson, D. F., 563
Levy, R. A., 593
Lewandowski, A. S., 533
Lewinsohn, P. M., 550
Lewis, D. J., 211
Lewis, P., 206
Ley, J., 491
Li, A., 125f
Li, J., 487i
Li, N. P., 662
Liberato, O., 125f
Liberman, B. E., 654
Liberman, M. C., 370
Lichtenstein, P., 443
Lichti, L., 591, 591f, 593, 594, 618,
    618f
Lichtwarck-Aschoff, A., 364
Licis, A. K., 158
Liddle, J. R., 653
Lieberman, M. D., 500, 659
Liebermann-Firestone, D. P., 355
Lieberson, A. D., 3
Lilienfeld, S. O., 5, 6, 6t, 71, 495,
    496i, 497, 545, 546, 546f, 576,
    589i
Lillard, A. S., 40, 41
Lillevik, L., 266
Lim, J., 160
Lin, G.-M., 219, 219f
Lin, J., 184, 185, 186f, 188, 200, 200f,
    201, 201f, 205, 207, 215, 218,
    219, 219f, 225, 225f, 226, 630
Lindau, S. T., 375, 449
Lindberg, S. M., 430
Linden, J., 528f
Lindenberger, U., 274
Lindström, P., 444
Lineberry, T. W., 172
Linehan, M. M., 575
Linhares, J. M., 103
LinkedIn, 617
Linn, M. C., 430
Linnenbrink, E. A., 385
Linnerooth, P. J., 525
Linsell, L., 546, 546f
Lipina, S. J., 512
Lippa, C. F., 173
Little, T. D., 430
Little Albert, 29t, 186, 197, 198, 198f,
    200, 226, 228, 596, 596f
Littlewood, R., 402
Litzenberger, R., 522
Liu, J., 262
Liu, S., 325, 325f
Liu, Y., 74
Livesley, W. J., 491t
Livingston, I., 651
Llewellyn, G., 551
Lloyd, M. A., B–1
Lochte, R., 528f
Lockhart, R. S., 237
Loftus, E. F., 263–265, 266, 279
Lohr, J. M., 558
Lohr, L., 86

Loichinger, E., 334
London Lassus Ensemble, 269
Looker, K. J., 457i
Lopez, S. R., 615
Loranger, A. W., 573
Lorenz, K. Z., 29t, 335, 335f
Lott, A. J., 6t, 661
Lott, B. E., 6t, 661
Lou, S., 662
Loucks, S., 496i
Lovell, G. P., 522, 525
Lovenberg, W., 608
Lovestone, S., 171
Lowe, J., 586
Lowenstein, J. A., 266
Lozano, P., 222
Lu, J., 85
Lu, Z.-L., 242
Lučanin, D., 523
Lučanin, J. D., 523
Lucas, R. E., 417
Luckhurst, C., 459
Ludel, J., 107, 111, 113
Luders, E., 429–430
Lund, C., 551
Luria, Gil, 19
Lutgendorf, S. K., 529
Lutz, A., 532
Luwanda, F., 456f
Lyckholm, L. J., 376
Lyerla, R., 445
Lykken, D. T., 323, 323f
Lynch, A. M., 608
Lynch, G., 224, 273
Lynn, A. R., 99
Lynn, S. J., 6t, 71, 576
Lyubomirsky, S., 394f, 417

MacCann, C., 321
Maccoby, E. E., 374
Macdonald, H., 180
Mack, A., 145
MacKay, A., 373
MacKenzie, J., 528
Mackin, R. S., 510, 510f
Maclure, M., 171
Macmillan, M., 80
Macpherson, L. J., 122
Madden, S., 401
Madden, T. J., 109
Maddox, W. T., 375
Maddrey, A. M., 124
Mädler, B., 612
Madonna, 160, 480
Madsen, K. M., 22
Maggio, J., 623–625, 624f, 627–628,
    629–630, 658, 660, 660f, 661,
    663, 664f
Maggio, S., 623–625, 624f, 627–628,
    629–630, 658, 660, 660f, 661,
    663, 664f
Magnuson, V. L., 443
Maguen, S., 511
Maguire, E. A., 236, 273
Mah, K., 441
Mahajani, R., 405
Maher, B. A., 586

Maher, W. B., 586
Maheu, M. M., 617
Mahmood, N., 294
Mahoney, J., 521
Mahowald, M. H., 156, 157
Mai, E., 158
Mai, N. T., 398
Maiden, B., 647
Maier, E. J., 102
Maier, M., 513
Maier, S. F., 564
Maier, W., 567f
Main, K. M., 431
Maine Suicide Prevention Program,
    562i
Majid, A., 404
Makel, M. C., 430
Ma-Kellams, C., 377
Makin, J. W., 119
Malcolm, W., 605
Malenka, R. C., 273
Malik, J., 128
Malkoff-Schwartz, S., 567
Mamani, C., 43
Manago, A. M., 21i
Manber, R., 610
Mancini, A. D., 417, 511
Mandela, N., 372, 372f
Mandelbaum, J., 107
Mandler, J. M., 286
Mandoki, M. W., 433
Maner, J. K., 430
Mangan, D., 651
Manganello, J. A., 215
Mangum, C., 403, 411
Mangum, J., 403, 404
Mangum, L., 403, 405, 406, 411
Manhart, L. E., 451
Manickam, L. S. S., 615
Mann, A., 171
Mann, J. J., 562i
Mann, T., 398
Manninen, B. A., 341
Manning, J. T., 433
Manning, R., 650
Manns, J. R., 268
Maquet, P., 161
Marambaud, P., 274
Marceau, K., 362
Marchione, K., 312
Marcovitch, H., 22
Marcum, J. P., 533, 659
Mardon, S., 151, 154, 162
Marentette, P. F., 309, 309f, 349
Marker, C. D., 555
Markman, H. J., 605
Markowe, H. L. J., 370
Markowitsch, H. J., 575
Marks, I. M., 558
Marks, J. S., 171
Markus, H. R., 637
Marley, C., 608
Marlow, K., 29f
Marmurek, H. C., 258
Maron, E., 554
Marris, E., 121f
Marron, G. M., 140

Marsh, E. J., 238
Marsh, H. W., 491
Marshall, G. N., 510
Marshall, L., 253
Marsicano, G., 272
Marti, C. N., 401
Martin, A., 312
Martin, C. E., 442
Martin, C. L., 430, 435, 436, 437, 438
Martin, D. R., 128
Martin, J. A., 374
Martin, L. A., 528
Martin, L. L., 413
Martin, R., 306
Martin, R. A., 469
Martínez-Ortega, J. M., 167
Martinot, J. -L., 406
Martuza, R. L., 613
Martyn, C., 150
Martz, J. M., 664
Marx, K., 481
Mashoodh, R., 340
Mashour, G. A., 613
Maslow, A. H., 12, 13i, 383, 385,
    392, 395, 420, 423, 390, 391i,
    392f, 393, 393f, 442, 482, 482f,
    501, 640
Masood, S., 76
Massenkoff, M., 491, 491f
Massey, S. G., 449, 449t
Masterpasqua, F., 340
Masters, W., 440, 440f, 441–442,
    443, 451, 461, 463
Masuda, M., 510
Mataix Cols, D., 559
Match.com, 624, 624f, 627, 660
Matlin, M. W., 284, 292, 404
Matsick, J. L., 447
Matsumoto, D., 412, 419
Matsumoto-Oda, A., 132
Matsumura, S., 377
Mattarella-Micke, A., 522f
Mattay, V. S., 414
Matthews, K., 611i
Mattingley, A. B., 95f
Mattys, S. L., 259
Matute, E., 430
Maughan, B., 431
Maulia, E., 176
Mauskop, A., 533
Maxmen, A., 456
Mayer, J. D., 321
Mayo Clinic, 104, 113, 342f
Mazur, T., 431
McAdams, D. P., 335
McAnally, H. M., 221
McArdle, J. J., 334, 336
McAuliffe, G. L., 178
McCann, U. D., 175
McCarley, R. W., 165
McCarthy, C., 222
McCarthy, D. E., 177
McCarthy, J., 22, 22f
McCarthy, J. R., 144
McCartney, K., 340
McCauley, E., 433
McClelland, D. C., 394

McClure, J., 385
McCosker, B., 469
McCrae, R. R., 490–491, 490f, 492
McCullough, M. A., 356
McCullough, M. E., 23i, 417
McDermott, J., 72
McDougall, D., 25
McDougall, W., 388
McEwen, B. S., 318
McGaugh, J. L., 261
McGaughey, K., 394
McGrath, J., 569
McGregor, J., 201
McGue, M., 323, 323f
McGuire, J., 559
McHugh, P. R., 549, 550
McKenna, K. Y. A., 661
McKenzie, S., 401f
McKinney, A., 171
McKinnon, R. K., 450
McMenamin, J. P., 617
McMurray, B., 350, 350f
McNally, R. J., 155, 156
McNamara Barry, C., 364
McNary, S. W., 575
McPherson, B. J., 438
McPherson, M., 364
Meade, C. S., 450
Meagher, M. W., 415
Meagher, R. B., Jr., 242
Meaney, M. J., 340
Medline Plus, 35, 292
Meelis, W., 28
Meeus, W. H., 364
Mehler, J., 306
Mehta, C. M., 435
Meilijson, I., 347
Meisenhelder, J. B., 533, 659
Melzack, R., 124
Mendes, W. B., 523
Mendle, J., 362, 362f, 429
Menken, J., 370
Mennella, J. A., 121
Menteiro, K. P., 258
Mercer, C. H., 448
Merckelbach, H., 576
Merikangas, K. R., 567
Merrifield, P. R., 324
Merrill, M., 315f
Merritte, D., 198
Merriweather, A. M., 449, 449t
Merriweather, T. J., 654
Mervis, C. B., 286, 287, 288i
Mesmer, F., 179f
Messick, D. M., 647
Metzler, J., 289, 289f
Meyer, C. J., 648
Meyer, D. R., 390
Meyer, L. H., 385
Michael, R. T., 447–448
Michaels, S., 447–448
Michaud, D. S., 111f
Micheau, J., 58
Michelle (Sergeant), 515, 522
Mickel, S. F., 271
Milgram, S., 626f, 643–646, 644f,
    645i, 646, 665, 667

Miller, C. F., 435
Miller, D. G., 264
Miller, G., 12, 13i, 244, 244f, 278
Miller, G. E., 512, 518, 519, 523
Miller, J. C., 148
Miller, N. E., 652
Milner, B., 271
Milrod, G. E., 593
Minding Your Mind, 578f
Mineka, S., 554, 555
Mioduser, D., 224
Mirsky, A. F., 570
Mischel, W., 492
Mistry, R. S., 512
Mita, T. H., 661
Mitchell, C., 350f
Mitchell, E., 331, 333, 334, 341, 344,
    344f, 349, 352, 355–357, 376
Mitchell, J. (Jasmine), 331–334, 332f,
    338–339, 341, 344, 344f, 345,
    348, 349, 352, 354, 356–357,
    361, 369, 375, 376
Mitchell, J. (Jocelyn), 331, 333, 334,
    338–339, 341, 344, 348, 349,
    352, 354, 355–356, 361, 376
Mitler, M. M., 148
Mittleman, M. A., 171
Miyake, K., 359
Mizuno, H., 474i
Mizzau, M., 398
Moccia, R. D., 187
Mody, M., 307
Mohammadian, P., 590f
Mohsin, S., 76
Moise-Titus, J., 221
Moisse, K., 168
Mokdad, A. H., 171
Molaison, H. (H. M.), 269, 270i, 271,
    271f
Mollon, J. D., 108
Moltschaniwskyj, N. A., 491
Money, J., 437
Monino, J., 26f
Monk, C. S., 347
Monroe, M., 662
Monroe, S. M., 561
Montaño, Z., 125f
Monteleone, G. T., 410
Montemayor, R., 364
Montoya, E. R., 430, 652
Moore, B. A., 525
Moore, C. M., 342
Moore, E. C. J., 318
Moors, A. C., 447
Mooyaart, E., 427
Morales, A., 371
Moran, C. C., 469
Morand, S., 609
Moreira-Almeida, A., 576, 576f
Moreland, R. L., 661
Morelli, G., 359
Morelli, S. A., 659
Morgan, A. H., 180
Morgan, M. J., 419
Morimoto, H. K., 519
Morin, A. J., 491
Morin, C. M., 151

Morley, S., 533
Morone, N. E., 533
Morris, A., 401
Morris, J. C., 35
Morris, P. A., 528
Morris, T. L., 28
Morrison, A., 152, 156
Morrison, P. D., 176
Morrot, G., 127
Morry, M. M., 661
Mortensen, K. H., 433
Mortensen, P. B., 571
Morton, L. C., 419, 435
Mos Def, 325
Moseley, G. L., 125f
Mosher, W. D., 443, 447
Mosquera-Schmidt, I., 185, 186f, 188,
    188f, 194, 195, 195f, 209, 210,
    210f, 220, 220f, 223, 223f, 225,
    225f
Mossey, J., 173
Most, S. B., 145, 146f
Mother Teresa, 372
Movahedi, S., 657
Mowrer, O. H., 652
Moynihan, M. M., 651
Mozart, L. A., 74–75, 267
Mrdjenovich, A. J., 525
Mugisha, S. (Sam), 650, 658
Mukamal, K. J., 171
Mulba, K., 511f
Mulcahy, J., 232
Mulder, E. J. H., 522
Muller, J. E., 171
Müller, U., 355
Müller-Vahl, K., 176
Mulvey, S., 492
Murdock, B., 256
Murdock, N. L., 630
Murdock, T. B., 630
Murphy, S., 648
Murray, H., 394, 497
Murray, R. M., 176
Mustanski, B. S., 444
Musto, D. F., 171f, 172
Myers, D. G., 649
Myers, I. B., 499
Myerson, J., 245
Mysterud, I., 335

Nagel, I. E., 372
Nagengast, B., 491
Nahemow, L., 660
Nahum, L., 609
Naimi, T. S., 170
Nakajima, M., 521
Narvaez, D., 365f
Nascimento, S. M., 103
Nash, M., 608
Nash, M. R., 179
Nasrallah, H. A., 340, 569
Nathan, M. J., 238
Nathan, P. E., 598
Nathanson, V., 342
National Aeronautics and Space
    Administration (NASA), 35, 465,
    470, 494

National Alliance on Mental Illness
    (NAMI), 588, 601
National Association of Clinical
    Nurse Specialists, 426f
National Cancer Institute, 76t
National Center for Injury Prevention
    and Control, 562i
National Eye Institute, 104, 105i
National Health and Social Life
    Survey (NHSLS), 447, 452
National Heart, Lung, and Blood
    Institute, 157f
National Institute of Mental Health
    (NIMH), 401, 402t, 561, 563,
    570, 607, 608f, 609
National Institute of Neurological
    Disorders and Stroke, 68, 155,
    283, 283f
National Institute on Aging, 274
National Institute on Alcohol Abuse
    and Alcoholism, 171f
National Institute on Drug Abuse, 168,
    168f, 172, 173, 175, 176, 177f
National Institutes of Health (NIH),
    162, 163t
National Institutes of Health, Eunice
    Kennedy Shriver National
    Institute of Child Health and
    Human Development, 433t
National Safety Council, 301, 301f
National Science Foundation, 66f
National Sleep Foundation, 154, 160,
    162
National Suicide Prevention Lifeline,
    561f, 562i
The National Mental Health
    Consumers' Self-Help
    Clearinghouse, 604
Navarrete, M., 54
Ndubaku, U., 53
Neal, R., 480
Neale, M. A., 303
Neale, M. C., 557
Neary, L., 445f
Neeson, L., 304
Neiderhiser, J. M., 323, 388, 467, 555f
Neisser, U., 145, 247
Nelles, G., 275t
Nelson, C. A., 347
Nelson, M. H., 142
Nelson, S. M., 370
Nelson, T., 335
Nes, R. B., 417
Nesse, R. M., 533
Nestor, S., 348
Neto, F. L., 576, 576f
Nettlefold, L., 531
Neubauer, A. C., 324
Neumeyer, C., 187
Newby-Clark, I. R., 155
Newcomb, P. A., 519
Newcomb, R., 459, 459f
Newell, A., 292
Newell, B. R., 237
Newell, L. C., 145
Newman, M. L., 65
Newsom, G., 445

Newton, K. M., 371
Neylan, T. C., 80
Ng, D. M., 520
Ngun, T. C., 428
Nicholson, J., 549f
Nickerson, R. S., 260
Nicoll, R. A., 273
Niedenthal, P. M., 42
Nielsen, N. R., 519
Nielsen, T., 159
Niemann, A., 172
Niemi, M-B., 38
Nieves, E., 610f
NIH. See National Institutes of Health
Nikolajsen, L., 125
NIMH. See National Institute of Mental Health
Nimon, J. P., 647, 647f
Niparko, J. K., 116
Nisbett, R. E., 318, 373
Nishitani, S., 345
Niskar, A. S., 370
Nix, L. A., 260
Noe, A., 82f
Nolen-Hoeksema, S., 565
Noller, G., 175
Nonnemaker, J., 174
Norcross, J. C., 589i, 590, 597, 602–604, 615, B–4
Norman, D. A., 261
Northcraft, G. B., 303
Northoff, G., 407, 563
Nour, N. M., 361
Nugent, L. D., 244
Nunes, S. O. V., 519
Nusbaum, E. C., 324
Nyborg, H., 371
Nyengaard, J. R., 50

Oatley, K., 404
Öberg, M., 174
O'Brien, D., 236, 237, 249, 252i
O'Brien, K. R., 626
O'Brien, P., 342
Occupy Wall Street, 542f, 543
O'Connor, T. G., 348
Oda, R., 132
Odbert, H. S., 489
O'Doherty, J. P., 77
O'Donnell, S., 196
O'Donovan, M. C., 340, 567
Oerlemans, W. G. M., 376
Office of the Surgeon General, 221
Ogden, C. L., 399, 399f
Ogden, M., 225
Ogin, M., 220f
Oh, B.-M, 60
O'Hanlon, L., 25
Ohayon, M., 154, 156
Ohbuchi, K., 297
Ojeah, C., 331–332, 332f, 334, 338, 369, 369f, 375, 376
O'Keefe, D. J., 638
O'Keeffe, G. S., 365
O'Keefe, J. H., 35
Olafsson, R. P., 597

Olatunji, B. O., 558
Olesinska, A., 512
Olino, T. M., 550, 563
Ollendick, T. H., 600
Olson, B. D., 335
Olson, J. M., 632, 633f
Olson, R. L., 244
Olympics (2000), 635, 635f
O'Malley, P. M., 175
Omura, K., 500
O'Neal, S., 157f
O'Neil, D., 219, 219f
Oppenheimer, D. M., 301
Organisation for Economic Co-operation and Development, 550
O'Riordan, K., 443
Ormerod, T. C., 295
O'Rourke, J., 302
Orsillo, S. M., 531
Ortigo, K. M., 470–471
Ortiz, L., 661
Orzel-Gryglewska, J., 160
Osler, S., 255
Öst, L. G., 600
Otta, E., 460
Otto, S. 511f
Overmier, J. B., 564
Owen, M. J., 340, 567
Oyserman, D., 615
Ozsunger, S., 60

Paans, A. M., 441
Paas, F., 246
Pachana, N. A., 510
Pacheco, J. L., 375
Padden, D., 335
Padian, N., 663
Pagano, F., 638
Paik, A., 452
Paik, N.-J., 60
Paikoff, R. L., 364
Paillard-Borg, S., 275t
Pajer, K., 563
Palermo, T. M., 533
Palin, S., 263f
Palinkas, L., 25
Palmer, J. C., 263–264, 266, 279
Palomaki, G. E., 429
Pan, J.-Y., 512
Pantelis, C., 569
Pape, H.-C., 414
Papies, E. K., 399
Pappenheim, B., 478f
Papsin, B. C., 115
Pare, D., 414
Parents without Partners, 604
Parikh, C., 348
Parker, E. S., 261
Parker, K. J., 512
Parmentier, F. B. R., 145
Paroo, K., 290
Parrott, A. C., 175
Parry, M. S., 587, 587f
Parry, P. A., 211
Parsons, L. M., 86
Parsons, T. D., 597

Partridge, J. C., 102
Paschall, M. J., 216
Pashler, H., 252
Pasley, L., 265
Patapoutian, A., 122
Paterno, E., 609
Paterson, D. S., 86
Pattatucci, A. M., 443
Patten, S., 425–426, 426f, 434, 460
Patterson, D. R., 179
Patterson, K., 162
Patterson, P. H., 572
Pauker, K., 654
Paul, J., 113
Paupore, N., 125f
Pavlov, I., 11, 13i, 186, 188, 189, 189f, 190, 191i, 192, 193, 194, 197, 203, 218, 225, 226
Pavlovich-Danis, S. J., 162
Peace Corps, 577f, 578
Pearce, G., 514
Pearce, J. M., 75
Pearlstein, T., 563
Pearson, E., 43
Pearson Education, Inc., 320f
Peate, M., 511
Pecheny, M., 445
Peck, M., 375f
Pedersen, A., 514
Pedersen, N. L., 118
Peeck, V. H., 246
Peek, K., 29f
Peña, E., 16, 43
Penfield, W., 82, 83
Peng, Y. B., 124
Penguin Group (USA) Inc., 282
Penhaul, K., 26f
Penke, L., 430
Pennington, J., 236
Pennisi, E., 340f
Peplau, L. A., 448, 629
Perkins, K. A., 520
Perkins, L., 491
Perry, B., 647
Perry, D. G., 435
Perry, M., 487i
Peruga, A., 174
Peskin, C. S., 148
Peters, M. L., 124
Peters, W., 655i
Petersen, J. H., 362f
Petersen, J. L., 430
Petersen, R. S., 270i
Peterson, B. S., 563
Peterson, G. B., 203
Peterson, J., 40, 41
Peterson, L. R., 243, 243f
Peterson, M. J., 242, 243, 243f
Petitto, L. A., 309, 309f, 349
Petronis, A., 340, 571
Petty, R. E., 638, 638f
Pfeifer, J., 662
Phillips, J., 610
Phillips, R. G., 415
Piaget, J., 351, 351f, 352, 353i, 354–355, 360, 362, 365, 368, 372, 379, 381, 512

Pich, E. M., 174
Pickrell, J. E., 265
Pientka, L., 275t
Pierre, J. M., 587
Pilley, J. W., 311f
Pinel, P., 586
Piñera, S., 34, 43
Pines, A., 371
Pinker, S., 246, 305, 311, 348
Pinto, P. D., 103
Pintrich, P. R., 385
Piper, A., 266
Pittenger, C., 269, 272, 559
Pittenger, D. J., 499, A–4
Plato, 8–9, 13i, 47
Platt, B., 58
Platt, J. R., 197
Platz, E. A., 116
Plecas, D., 522
Pletcher, M. J., 175
Pletnikov, M. V., 571
Plomin, R., 323, 388, 399, 467, 555f
Podolski, C., 221
Poeppel, D., 83
Poisson, J., 435f
Polidori, M. C., 275t
Polivy, J., 398
Pollack, J. M., 650
Pomeroy, W. B., 442
Ponomarev, A., 274
Pope, K. S., 616
Popelka, G. R., 345
Porter, J. S., 133
Porter, R. H., 119
Porter, R. J., 175
Posen, L., 617
Posner, M. I., 512
Postuma, R. B., 157
Pötsch, G., 119
Pott, M., 359
Potter, R. H., 447
Poulakis, Z., 116
Powell, A. A., 651t
Powell, L. H., 535
Powell, R. A., 198
Prakhaw, P., 561
Pratt, L. A., 116
Premack, A. J., 311
Premack, D., 311
Prengaman, P., 35
Presley, E., 43
Price, D. D., 179
Price, J., 608
Price, L., 597
Prince, M., 171
Prinstein, M. J., 450
Prochaska, J. J., 521
Prochaska, J. O., 521, 597, 602–604, 615
Prüfer, K., 446
Pruitt, J., 335
Prüss-Ustün, A., 174
Pryor, K., 217
Pryzgoda, J., 426
Przybelski, R. J., 35
Puhlik-Doris, P., 469

Puig, J., 359
Pulier, M. L., 617
Pullum, G. K., 310
Putallaz, M., 430
Putnam, A. L., 238, 239t
Pyc, M., 238

Qin, S., 99
Quilodran, F., 25f
Quinn, O. W., 570

Rabin, B. S., 518
Rabkin, J. G., 509
Rabung, S., 593
Racine, T. P., 285
Radak, Z., 371
Radua, J., 559
Rahe, R. H., 509, 536
Rahman, Q., 443
Raichle, K. A., 125
Raine, A., 574, 652
Rainville, P., 179
Rajah, A., 576
Ram, N., 362, 372
Ramachandran, K., 125
Ramachandran, V. S., 107, 125
Rameson, L. T., 659
Ramirez, G., 438
Ramirez-Carmona, R., 271
Randall, D. K., 160f
Rao, H., 159
Rapace, N., 574f
Rapee, R. M., 557
Rapson, R. L., 459, 663
Rasch, B., 253
Rasmussen, S. C., 18
The "Rat Man,", 29t
Ratnesar, R., 657
Raver, C. C., 512
Rawson, K. A., 238
Rayner, R., 198, 198f, 200, 228, 596,
    596f
Raza, M., 76
Read, J., 613
Reagan, R., 545
Realo, A., 491–492
Reber, E. S., 555t
Reber, S., 555t
Rechtschaffen, A., 160
Reddy, L. F., B–4
Reece, A. S., 175
Reed, G., 533, 659
Rees, G., 77
Rees, J. L., 340
Reese, H. W., 198
Reeves, A., 74
Regalado, M., 215
Regolin, L., 345
Rehm, J., 168
Reiber, C., 449, 449t
Reich, S. M., 661, 661f
Reiche, E. M. V., 519
Reid, A. K., 311f
Reimer, B., 437
Reimer, D., 437
Reinders, A. A. T., 441
Reis, H. T., 625, 625f

Reisenzein, R., 408
Reiser, B. J., 290, 289f
Reisman, J. M., 586
Ren, J., 372
Reneman, L., 175
Renken, R., 441
Renner, M. J., 510, 510f
Renner, W., 513
Resick, P. A., 511
Reuter-Lorenz, P. A., 372
Reuters, 17, 528f
Revonsuo, A., 166
Reynolds, B. A., 74
Rhoades, G. K., 605
Rholes, W. S., 359
Rhudy, J. L., 415
Ric, F., 258
Ricaurte, G. A., 175
Ricci-Bitti, P. E., 412
Rice, E., 450
Rice, J., 215
Rich, J. N., 95f
Richard, J. M., 332, 369–370, 369f,
    371
Richard, Mrs., 369, 369f
Richards, S. I. V., B–8f
Richardson, E. J., 638
Rickards, F. W., 116
Rico (the Border Collie), 311, 311f
Riconda, D. L., 433
Rider, E. A., 467
Riedel, G., 58
Rieger, D., 634
Rieger, G., 427
Rieke, F., 106
Riemann, R., 633, 633f
Rietschel, M., 567f
Riggio, H. R., 629
Rigler, D., 350
Rigler, M., 350
Riksen-Walraven, J. M. A., 522
Risley, T. R., 349
Ritchie, J., 254, 254f
Ritchie, S. J., 133
Rivera, K. D., 86
Rivkees, S. A., 154
Rizzo, A. A., 597
Robbins, B. D., 44
Robbins, R. N., 363
Roberson, L., 654
Roberti, J. W., 390
Roberto, C. A., 401
Roberts, B. W., 356, 467
Roberts, D., 275t
Roberts, D. R., 371
Roberts, F. D., 519
Roberts, R. D., 321
Roberts, R. E., 615
Robertson, L. A., 221
Robinson, D. K., 9
Robinson, K. N., 116
Robles, T. F., 522
Rockett, I. R. H., 562i
Rodin, J., 529, 529f
Rodriguez, T., 493f
Roe, C. M., 35
Roeder, S. L., 529

Roediger, H. L., III, 238, 239t, 245,
    266
Roehrs, T., 160
Roemer, L., 531
Rogers, C. R., 12, 13i, 482–483, 483f,
    501, 503, 594–595, 595f, 595t
Rogers-Ramachandran, V., 107
Rohrer, D., 239t, 252
Rohwedder, S., 373
Roid, G. H., 316
Roldan-Valadez, E., 271
Romance, A., 123
Romero, A. J., 615
Romero, M., 123
Roper, J., 651t
Rorschach, H., 497
Rosales-Lagarde, A., 160
Rosch, E., 286, 287, 288i, 310
Rose, J. D., 649
Rose, N., 245
Rose, S., 563
Rose, S. J., B–2
Rosen, J., 244
Rosen, R. C., 452
Rosen, S., 83
Rosenberg, R. S., 608
Rosenblum, L. D., 119, 120, 125
Rosenhan, D. L., 549
Rosenkranz, M. A., 125
Rosenman, R. H., 526, 528
Rosenthal, D., 570
Rosenthal, R., 38, 636–637, 637f, 665
Rosenzweig, M. R., 347
Roseth, C. J., 364
Rosner, M. H., 175
Ross, D., 220
Ross, L., 628, 630
Ross, S. A., 220
Rosselli, M., 430
Rosso, A., 173
Rotge, J. -Y., 559
Roth, D. A., 398
Roth, M. S., 109
Roth, T., 158, 158f, 160
Rothbaum, B. O., 597
Rothbaum, F., 359
Rotter, J. B., 486, 488, 501, 529
Rouder, J. N., 100
Rouder, J. N. R., 244
Rouse, S. V., 498, 525
Routh, D. K., 586
Rovet, J. F., 272
Rowe, D. C., 652
Rowe, M. H., 102
Rowe, R., 431
Rowland, B. A., 85
Roy, D., 544
Roycroft, G., 342
Roylance, R., 77
Rozin, P., 398
Rubens, M. T., 244
Rubin, D. C., 247
Rubin, Z., 629
Ruble, D. N., 435, 437, 438
Rueffer, S. D., 155
Rugg, D., 30f
Rugg, M. D., 257, 257f

Ruiz, I., 219
Ruiz, J. M., 528
Rullo, J., 450
Rupert, P. A., 525
Ruppin, E., 347
Rusbult, Caryl E., 664
Ruscio, J., 6t, 71
Rush, A. J., 602
Rush, T. E., 531
Rushton, J. P., 318
Russell, J. A., 404f
Russell, T., B–4f
Rutherford, A., 189, 315, 321
Rutter, M., 22, 348
Ruxton, C. H. S., 173
Ryan, R. M., 386–387, 393, 394f
Ryba, N. J., 120
Ryder, W., 574f

Sabah, M., 232, 235f
Sabelis, I., 427
Sabharwal, J., 244
Sable, P., 109
Sacher, J., 563
Sachse, K., 637
Sacks, O., 231
Sagarin, B. J., 638–639
Sagart, L., 306
Sagiv, M., 370
Sagvolden, T., 211
Saha, S., 569
Sai, F. Z., 345
Saini, R., 450
Saini, S., 450
St. John, K., 8f
Salapatek, P., 345
Salas, R. M., 151
Salem-Hartshorne, N., 480
Salenius, S., 309
Salimpoor, V. N., 406
Salisbury, A., 563
Salkind, S. J., 307
Sallquist, J., 430
Salmon, P., 531
Salovey, P., 321
Salters-Pedneault, K., 531
Salthouse, T. A., 373
Salva, O. R., 345
SAMHSA. See Substance Abuse
    and Mental Health Services
    Administration
Sánchez, F. J., 428
Sanders, G., 430
Sandman, C. A., 522
Sandy Hook Elementary School, 247
Sansom-Daly, U. M., 511
Santa Maria, C., 446f
Santhouse, C., 50, 68, 68f, 69, 69f,
    72, 72f, 73, 73f, 74, 75, 79, 80,
    86, 87, 87f
Saper, C. B., 85
Sar, V., 576
Sareen, H., 215
Sastre, J. P., 152
Satpute, A. B., 500
Sattler, J. M., 315f, 318
Sauer, J. D., 266

Savage, R., 215
Savic, I., 444
Savin-Williams, R. C., 427, 443
Sawa, A., 571
Sawalani, G. M., 430
Saxe, L., 410, 410f
Sayette, M. A., 520
Scally, M., 490–491
Scammell, T. E., 85
Scannapieco, M., 266
Scarr, S., 340
Scassellati, B., 485
Schachner, A., 348
Schachter, S., 407, 408, 409i, 413, 421, 422, 423, 660
Schaie, K. W., 372
Schallhorn, S. C., 106
Schalock, R. L., 320
Schedlowski, M., 197
Scheffer, P. G., 429
Schell, T. L., 510
Schellenberg, E. G., 75
Schenck, C. H., 156, 157
Scherer, A. M., 302
Scherer, K. R., 404, 412
Schermer, J. A., 469
Scheyd, G. J., 662
Schiffman, S. S., 118, 120
Schkade, D., 394f,
Schlaepfer, T. E., 612
Schleppenbach, M., 487i
Schmid, G. P., 457i
Schmidt, H. G., 246, 260
Schmidt, J., 210f, 223f
Schmidt, R., 118
Schmidt-Daffy, M., 144
Schmitt, D. P., 460, 491–492
Schmukle, S. C., 335, 491, 660
Schnall, S., 651t
Schneidman, E. S., 376
Schnider, A., 609, A–2
Schnyer, D. M., 375
Schoeni, R. F., 460
Schoeny, M. E., 630
Schommer-Aikins, M., 252
Schreiner, A. M., 176
Schug, R. A., 652
Schulenberg, J. E., 175
Schultz, D. P., 10, 471, 479f, 483t, 484, 488, 497
Schultz, S. E., 10, 471, 479f, 483t, 484, 488, 497
Schultz, W. W., 427
Schulze, T. G., 567f
Schwab, C., 312, 312f
Schwartz, B. L., 260
Schwartz, C. E., 529, 533, 659
Schwartz, J. E., 375
Schwartz, S. J., 374
Schwarz, S., 450, 460
Schweinsburg, A. D., 176
Scollon, C. N., 417
Scott, E. S., 363
Scott, J. A., 429
Scott, S. B., 605
Scott, S. K., 83
Scott-Cawiezell, J., 100

Scoville, W. B., 271
Scribner, C. M., 549
Scully, J. A., 510
Seals, D. R., 531
Searight, H. R., 377
Searleman, A., 242
Sears, R. R., 321, 652
Sebastian, S., 405
Sedlmeier, P., 531–532
Seeley, J. R., 550
Seely, R., 42
Seery, M. D., 510
Segal, D. L., 474i
Segall, M. H., 128
Segerstrom, S. C., 519, 523
Segovia, D., 1–2, 32f, 44f
Segraves, R. T., 453
Seifer, R., 148
Seitz, D., 232, 235, 248–249, 250, 276, 276f
Seligman, M. E. P., 44, 320, 417, 417f, 535, 564, 565f, 615
Sella, M., 304
Sellman, J. D., 175
Selye, H., 506, 515–517, 516i, 517f, 526
Selzer, M. M., 511
Sepúlveda, M., 15, 16, 43
Serrador, Jorge, 122
Seto, M. C., 427
Shackelford, T. K., 460, 653
Shadish, W. R., 606
Shah, A. K., 301
Shahabi, L., 535
Shakira, 112
Shamblen, S. R., 661
Shanahan, L., 550
Shapira, N. A., 617
Shapiro, D. H., Jr., 529
Shargorodsky, J., 116
Sharif, M., 76
Sharma, S., 450
Shaw, B. F., 602
Shaw, G., 431f
Shaw, H., 401
Shaw, J. C., 292
Shaywitz, B. A., 304, 307, 312
Shaywitz, S. E., 304–305, 306, 307, 312, 315, 322, 323
Sheard, M., 528
Shedler, J., 478, 593
Sheldon, K. M., 417
Sheldon, S. M., 394f
Sheline, Y. I., 35
Shelton, K. H., 362
Shelton, S. E., 84
Shepard, R. N., 289, 289f
Sherman, S. M., 85
Sherwood, C. C., 343
Sherwood, J. B., 171
Sherwood, L., 339
Shestyuk, A., 404
Shiffrin, R. M., 236, 243
Shimizu, Y., 22
Shimohama, S., 58
Shine, R., 196
Shiner, R. L., 356, 467

Shipley, M. J., 370
Shiv, B., 303
Shlik, J., 554
Shoda, Y., 492
Shonkoff, J. P., 515
Shors, T. J., 74
Shuler, M. G., 273
Siebert, E. R., 436f
Siegel, J. M., 147, 147f, 154, 160
Siemaszko, C., 43
Sigelman, C. K., 467
Sigmundson, H. K., 437
Sigurdson, K., 160
Silva, C. E., 179
Silveira, M. T., 460
Silverman, I., 104
Silverstein, C., 544
Silvia, P. J., 324
Simion, F., 128
Simmer, J. J., 171
Simmons, R., 465, 466–467, 466f, 485, 489
Simon, H. A., 292
Simón, R., 123
Simon, T., 315, 315f
Simons, D. J., 145
Simonton, D. K., 321, 325
Simpson, J. A., 359, 662
Simpson, J. R., 402, 410
Sims, L. M., 487i
Sinclair, Brian, 629f
Singer, J. E., 407, 408, 409i, 413, 421, 423
Singh, L., 348
Singh, M K., 563
Singh-Manoux, A., 338
Sinn, D. L., 491
Sio, U. N., 295
Sirisegaram, A., 398
Sirota, L., 344, 344f
Sittiprapaporn, W., 152
Sivacek, J., 633
Sjodin, M., 430
Sjoerdsma, A., 608
Sjöstedt, S., 396
Skakkebaek, N. E., 431, 433
Skinner, B. F., 11–12, 13i, 143, 143f, 203, 203f, 204i, 205, 205f, 207, 208, 211, 212, 218, 224, 225, 226, 227, 309, 485
Skinner, C., 511
Skinner, M., 514
Skinner, N. F., 18
Skirbekk, V., 334
Skoog, G., 559
Skoog, I., 559
Skowronski, J. J., 144
Skype, 617f
Slaney, K. L., 285
Slatcher, R. B., 522
Slavney, P. R., 549, 550
Slife, B. D., 9, 18
Slijper, F. M., 431
Slotema, C. W., 612
Sloter, E., 370
Slovic, P., 301
Small, B. J., 334, 336

Smart, K., 201
Smeets, T., 523
Smink, F. R. F., 401
Smith, A., 375
Smith, A. P. R., 257, 257f
Smith, A. R., 302
Smith, B. L., 216
Smith, C. N., 272, 414
Smith, C. T., 152
Smith, D., 612
Smith, D. M., 533
Smith, J., 22, 485
Smith, J. F., 72
Smith, J. L., 435
Smith, M. A., 238, 239t
Smith, P. B., 642
Smith, S., 597
Smith, S. D., 345
Smith, S. M., 257
Smith, T. W., 514, 520, 528
Smith-Lovin, L., 364
Smithsonian Institute, 403f
Smrt, D. L., 648
Snape, J., B–8f
Snidman, N., 356, 467
Snyder, A. L., 647, 647f
Snyder, C. R., 588
Snyder, D. K., 30
Snyder, T. D., B–2
Sobel, Noam, 441f
Society for Neuroscience, 120, 590f
Society of Clinical Psychology, Division 12, B–4
Socolar, R. R. S., 215
Söderøten, P., 396
Sola, J., 257
Solms, M., 591
Solomon, S. G., 109
Somali Student Association, 393
Somasundaram, C. P., 576
Sommer, I. E. C., 612
Sony Pictures, 322f
Sørenson, K., 362f
Sorhagen, N. S., 637, 637f
Soudry, M., 370
Southworth, M. R., 142
Souza, T., 119
Sowell, E. R., 347
Spangenberg, E. R., 119
Sparling, J., 266
Sparrow, B., 262
Sparrow, R., 115
Speakman, J. R., 399
Spearman, C., 313, 314t, 327
Spears, M. J., 201
Specht, J., 335, 491
Spector, T. D., 469
Spelke, E. S., 354
Spence, C., 125f
Spence, S. H., 557
Spencer, Lady Diana, 231
Sperling, G., 240, 241i, 278
Sperry, Roger, 70, 71, 91
Spiderworld, 597f
Spiegel, D., 179, 575
Spiers, H. J., 273
Spitzer, R. L., 549

Spörrle, M., 637
Spotts, P., 25, 35
Sprecher, S., 625, 625f
Sprott, D. E., 119
Squire, L. R., 83, 268, 272
Srinivasa, S. S., 485
Stanford, T. R., 85
Stanford Center for Narcolepsy, 164
Stanger-Hall, K., 451
Stanhope, N., 260
Stanilou, A., 575
Stanley, S. M., 605
Stanovich, K. E., 5, 11f, 18, 20, 30
Starbucks, 400
Stark, C. E. L., 83
Starr, B., 341f
Steele, C. M., 654
Steele, J. D., 611i
Steen, T. A., 417, 535
Steffen, S., 450f
Steigerwald, I., 139
Stein, B. E., 85
Stein, D. J., 550
Steinberg, L., 363, 364
Steiner, M., 309
Steinmetz, J. E., 271
Steinmetz, J. L., 628
Stepper, S., 413
Stern, K., 132
Stern, M., 133
Stern, W., 316
Sternberg, R. J., 312, 314, 314f, 314t,
    315, 318, 320, 324, 327, 372,
    663, 663f, 667
Stevanovic, P., 525
Stevens, L. C., 531
Stewart-Brown, S., 344
Stice, E., 401
Stinson, F. S., 175
Stocker, D., 435f
Stocker, J., 435f
Stocker, S., 435f
Stoelting, R. K., 170
Stokes, M., 83
Stone, A. A., 375
Stone, D., 223
Stone, D. N., 393
Stone, E., 554f
Stone, W. S., 571
Stoner, J., A. F., 649
Stöppler, M. C., 150, 150f
Storaasli, R. D., 605
Storer, B. E., 519
Storm, B. C., 258
Stout, H., 365
Strack, F., 413
Strain, 112t
Strassberg, D. S., 450
Stratton, G., 106
Straub, R. O., 518, 520, 528
Straus, M. A., 216
Strayer, D. L., 96, 244
Streisand, B., 478
Streit, W. J., 53
Stright, A. D., 357
Stroebe, W., 99, 399, 400, 638
Stromberg, E., 223

Strough, J., 435
Stroup, D. F., 171
Struening, E. L., 509
Struthers, R., 586
Stuart, H., 546
Stucky, B. D., 430
Stuen, C., 334
Stump, S., 403, 405
Stuss, D. T., 80
Su, K. G., 57
Subiaul, F., 343
Subrahmanyam, K., 661, 661f
Subramaniam, K., 295
Substance Abuse and Mental Health
    Services Administration
    (SAMHSA), 167, 168, 169i, 175,
    562i
Sucala, M., 617
Suchy, Y., 80
Sue, S., 614–615
Sumner, G. S., 433
Sun-Edelstein, C., 533
Suntharasaj, T., 343
Suomi, S. J., 357–358
Supreme Court, U. S., 363, 363f
Susman, E. J., 362
Sustaíta, M. A., 450
Susuki, K., 57, 57f
Sutherland, S., 122
Suwanrath, C., 343
Swan, S. H., 436
Swanson, L., 115
Swendsen, J. D., 521
Swift, J. K., 615
Swinburn, B. A., 399f
Sybert, V., 433
Syroit, J., 523
Szabo, R., 541–546, 542f, 547, 566,
    576, 577–578, 577f, 608
Szalavitz, M., 417f
Szasz, T., 551
Szkrybalo, J., 437

Tackett, J. L., 431
Tafti, M., 154
Takeda, A., 567f
Takeuchi, D. T., 614–615
Talarico, J. M., 247
Tale-Yax, H., 651, 651f
Tallandini, M. A., 475
Tambs, K., 417
Tanapat, P., 74
Tandon, P. S., 222
Tandon, R., 340, 569, 570–571, 572
Tang, Y., 50
Tank. See LeFleur, M.
Tapert, S. F., 176
Tarbox, J., 433
Tatsuoka, M. M., 489f
Taverniers, J., 523
Taylor, B., 22
Taylor, C. A., 215
Taylor, D., 608
Taylor, G. G., 284–287, 299, 299f
Taylor, J. B., 281–287, 282f, 283f,
    285f, 290–294, 299, 299f, 304,
    314, 321, 322, 322f, 326

Taylor, K., 239t, 252
Taylor, M. A., 613
Taylor, M. J., 305
Taylor, S. E., 65
Taylor, S. R., 162
Taylor, T., 21i
Teachman, B. A., 555
TED.com, 284
Tedeschi, J. T., 297
Tees, R. C., 306
Telfer, E. E., 370
Telles, S., 109
Tenenbaum, H. R., 435, 436
Tenhula, W. N., 600
Tennis, M., 201
Terburg, D., 430, 652
Terman, L. M., 315f, 316, 321
Terracciano, A., 490–491, 492
Terry, W. S., 256
Tessitore, A., 414
Testa, R., 569
Testa, R. J., 439
Tett, R. P., 525
Thelen, E., 344
Thibault, P., 414
Thibaut, J., 651t
Thomas, A., 356
Thomas, M., 438f
Thomas, T. L., 7f
Thompson, K. M., 476f
Thompson, P. M., 347
Thompson, R. F., 271
Thompson, W. L., 179, 291
Thomson, D. M., 257
Thoresen, C. E., 535
Thorndike, E. L., 186, 201, 202,
    202f, 203, 205, 206, 207, 218,
    227, 662
Thorne, B., 438
Thorne, M., 9, 9f
Thornhill, R., 662
Thunberg, M., 408
Thurlow, H. J., 175
Tian, L., 429
Till, B. D., 199, 199f
Tillman, K. H., 450
Tindale, R. S., 648
Titchener, E., 10–11, 13i, 45, 143
Tittgemeyer, M., 429–430
Tobin, D. D., 435, 438
Tobin, S., 116
Todd, A., 431f
Toga, A. W., 347
Tollenaar, M. S., 522
Tolman, E., 224, 228
Tomasello, M., 659
Tombs, S., 104
Tomoda, A., 216
Tondo, L., 608
Topp, S. S., 431
Torrente, M. P., 563
Torrey, E. F., 567
Torry, Z. D., 545
Tosi, H., 510
Toufexis, A., 171
Tourangeau, R., 30
Tourinho, C. J., 306

Trachtenberg, F. L., 86
Tracy, D. L., 119
Tranel, D., 415, 416i
Tränkner, D., 108
Treas, J., 459, 459f
Treffert, D. A., 314
Trelawny, P., 74
Trentham-Dietz, A., 519
Trivers, R., 433
Trivers, R. L., 651t
Troiden, R. R., 459
Trussell, J., 370
Tsao, J., 125f
Tsaw, D., 648
Tsuang, M. T., 571
Tsukayama, H., 77
Tulving, E., 237, 247, 255, 257
Tummala-Narra, P., 513
Turgeon, J. K., 312f
Turiano, N., 493f
Turk, D. C., 124
Turk, J., 558
Tuvblad, C., 335, 652
Tversky, A., 300–301, 302
Twenge, J. M., 392
Twitter, 365, 418f, 617

Uchino, B. N., 514, 520
Üçok, A., 609
UCSF Medical Center, 93
Uhl, G., 556
Umberson, D., 533
UNAIDS, 456f
Underdown, A., 344
Urbina, S., 316, 498
Urso, A. M., 345
Urzúa, Luis, 15, 16, 43
U.S. Census, 512
U.S. Food and Drug Administration
    (USFDA), 608f, 609
U.S. Marine Corps, 519f
Utesch, M., 140, 147, 147f, 152, 155,
    155f, 156, 156f, 159, 163, 164,
    164f
Utts, J., 133
Uutela, K., 309

Valentine, B., 447
Valentine, E. R., 236
Valenza, E., 128
Valliant, G. E., 474i, 475
Vallortigara, G., 345
van Andel, P., 427
van Breukelen, G. J. P., 246
van den Bree, M. B. M., 362
van der Kloet, D., 576
van der Maas, H. L. J., 133
van der Straten, A., 663
van der Voort, T. H. A., 250
Van Doorn, M. D., 364
van Geert, P. L. C., 364
van Hoeken, D., 401
van Honk, J., 430, 652
Van Knippenberg, A., 633
van Koningsbruggen, G. M., 399
van Os, J., 572
Van Petten, C., 72

van Praag, H., 347f
Van Ruysseveldt, J., 523
VandeCreek, L., 266
Vandecreek, L., 525
VanderVeen, J. W., B–4
Vartanian, L. R., 398
Vasalou, A., 32, 34, 34f
Vásquez, C., 250
Veenhoven, R., 376
VeggieDate.org, 625
Veileux, J. C., B–4
Velagaleti, G. V. N., 342
Velicer, W. F., 521
Vennard, M., 248, 248f, 276f
Verghese, A., 376
Vernon, P., 561f
Vernon, P. A., 313, 469, 491t, 632, 633f
Vernon, S. D., 517
Verplanken, B., 633
Vespa, J., 447
Vgontzas, A. N., 151
Vidal, M. A., 221
Viera, M., 201
ViewFinder Exis, LLC, 108f
Vigil, J., 460
Viking Penguin, 282
Vilain, E., 428
Vilain, E. J. N., 431
Villaroel, R., 15
Vincent, S., 284–285
Vingerling, J. R., 107
Vingtdeux, V., 274
Vinokur, A. D., 533
Violanti, J. M., 515
Visser, B. A., 313
Visweswaraiah, N. K., 109
Vitiello, M. V., 154
Vlahos, J., 119
Vogalaere, P. P., 370
Vohs, K. D., 176, 392, 484
Volkow, N. D., 172
von Cramon, D. Y., 429–430
von Dawans, B., 65
von Grumbkow, J., 523
von Helmholtz, H., 107
von Rueden, C., 491, 491f
von Stumm, S., 334, 372
Voracek, M., 491–492
Vorländer, M., 145
Vrana, K. E., 563
Vredeveldt, A., 266
Vyas, N. S., 569
Vygotsky, Lev S., 12, 13i, 355, 360, 379, 381

Wade, T., 15
Wadsworth, M. E., 512
Wagenmakers, E. J., 133
Wagner, J. A., III, 648
Wagner, N. N., 510
Wai, J., 430
Waite, B. M., 243–244
Wake, M., 116
Wakefield, A. J., 22, 24
Wakefield, C. E., 511
Wakefield, J. C., 543

Wald, G., 102
Waldman, I. D., 431
Walk, R. D., 130, 130f
Walker, E. E., 613
Walkey, F. H., 385
Wall, P. D., 124
Wall, S., 358–359
Walla, P., 119
Wallen, K., 436f
Wallenda, N., 126
Wallentin, M., 430
Wallin, P., 447
Walma van der Molen, J. H., 250
Walsh, R., 417, 531, 533
Walters, E. E., 550
Wampold, B. E., 615
Wang, H-X., 275t
Wang, J., 429
Wang, L., 84
Wang, M. C., 28
Wang, P. S., 550
Wang, Q., 252, 253f
Wansink, B., 398
Warburton, D. E. R., 531
Ward, O., 95f
Warne, R., 18
Warne, S., B–8f
Warneken, F., 659
Warwar, S., 605
Washburn, A. L., 396, 396f, 403
Washburn, D. A., 10f, 11f
Washburn, M. F., 10–11, 10f, 13i
Washington State Penitentiary, B–4f
Wasserman, S., 354
Wasserstein, R. L., 385
Waterhouse, L., 314
Waters, E., 358–359
Watson, J. M., 96, 244
Watson, J. B., 11–12, 13i, 143, 198, 198f, 200, 203, 227, 228, 596, 596f
Watson, R. I., 189, 193, 315
Watt, C., 133
Watts, J. C., 638
Waubonsee Community College, 331, 376
Waugh, N. C., 261
Wearing, C., 230–235, 238, 248, 253, 255, 267, 267f, 268–269, 271, 276, 276f, 625
Wearing, D., 231–233, 253, 255, 267, 267f, 269, 271, 276, 276f
Weathington, B. I., A–4
Weaver, J., 418f, 441f
The Weavers, 444
Webb, J. K., 196
Webb, S. J., 347
Webber, J., 32f
Weber, D., 334
Weber, E. U., 301
Weber, E., H., 99, 135
Weber, M., 554
Wechsler, David, 316, 317, 320
Wedding, D., 616
Weekes-Shackelford, V. A., 653
Wegner, D. W., 262
Weight Watchers, 604

Weinberger, D. R., 414
Weiner, A., 451
Weiner, J., 34
Weinshenker, D., 598
Weir, K., 469
Weir, K. F., 385
Weisel, T. N., 107
Weishaar, M. E., 601–602, 602t
Weiss, A., 491
Weiss, S., 74
Weiss, W., 637
Weisskirch, R. S., 451
Weisz, J., 359
Weitzman, E. R., 170
Weizmann Institute of Science, 441f
Welham, J., 569
Weller, A., 344, 344f
Wellings, K., 445, 448
Wen, C. P., 370f
Wen, X. J., 170, 171f
Wenner, M., 77
Wenner Moyer, M., 657f
Wentzel, K. R., 364
Werker, J. F., 306
Wernicke, K., 72, 72f, 73, 79, 81i, 89, 91
Wernig, M., 74
Wertheimer, M., 12
West, K., 325
Westen, D., 470–471, 480, 488
Westly, E., 306
Westphal, M., 511
Wethington, E., 528
Wetzels, R., 133
Whalen, P. J., 414
Whipple, N., 355
Whishaw, I. Q., 340, 347, 407
Whisman, M. A., 30
White, T., 610f
Whitley, R. J., 232
Whitlock, J. R., 273
Whitman, R. D., 295
WHO. See World Health Organization
WHO Multicentre Growth Reference Study Group, 334, 334f
Whorf, B. L., 310
Wich, S. A., 187, 223
Wicker, A. W., 630
Widmer, E. D., 459, 459f
Wikipedia, 390
Wilcox, T., 437
Wilde, O., 304
Wilder, D. A., 266
Wilding, J. M., 236
Wilkins, C. H., 35
Willander, J., 119
Williams, A. C. D. C., 533
Williams, K., 647
Williams, P. G., 80
Williams, R., 272
Williams, W. M., 318
Williamson, A. M., 160
Williamson, S. J., 242
Willingham, B., 412
Willingham, D. T., 238
Willis, R. J., 373

Willis, S. L., 372
Willoughby, K. A., 272
Willyard, C., 160
Wilson, B. A., 231, 232–233, 267–268, 269, 271
Wilson, M., 398
Wilson, R. C., 324
Wilson, R. S., 274
Winberg, J., 119
Winblad, B., 275t
Windschitl, P. D., 302
Winfrey, O., 106, 480f
Winickoff, J. P., 174
Winner, E., 75
Winzenz, D., 249
Wise, R. J. S., 83
Wiseman, R., 133
Wissow, L. S., 215
Witelson, S. F., 82, 82f, 444
Wittchen, H.-U., 550
Witterick, K., 435f
Wixted, J. T., 268
Wobst, A. H. K., 179, 179f
Wodrich, D. L., 433
Wojcicki, J. M., 663
Wolf, M., 305
Wolfs, R. C., 107
Wolman, D., 69
Wolpert, D. M., 82
Wong, B., 108
Wong, D. F. K., 512
Wong, J. S., 108f
Wood, G., 236
Wood, J. M., 495, 496i, 499
Wood, S. J., 569
Wood, W., 431
Woodnutt, T., 661
Woods, R., 437
Woods, T., 200, 451
Woodward, A., 174
Woollett, K., 273
Woon, T. H., 510
World Health Organization (WHO), 173, 456, 457i, 561
Worringham, C. J., 647
Worthman, C. M., 431
Worthy, D. A., 375
Wright, A., 140
Wright, F. L., 372, 372f
Wright, K., 148
Wu, Y. D., 372
Wuethrich, B., 388f
Wundt, W., 9–10, 9f, 13i, 16, 45, 143
Wyer, R. S., Jr., 648
Wyrobek, A. J., 370

Xia, J., 99
Xu, J., 72, 376

Yalom, I. D., 604, 606, 606t
Yamada, K. A., 158
Yamagata, S., 491
Yan, C., 429
Yan, J. H., 372
Yan, T., 30
Yanchar, S. C., 18
Yardi, S., 365

Yasmin, M., 76t
Yee, M., 436
Yen, H., 614
Yin, H., 99
Yizhou, W., 321f
Yolken, R. H., 567
Yoon, C., 287
Yoon, H., 177
Yost, W. A., 111
Youn, C. H., 406f
Young, A., 285
Young, M. E., 398
Young, T., 107
Young-Bruehl, E., 478
Youngstedt, S. D., 162
Youth Outreach for the National
    Health Awareness Campaign, 577

Youth Suicide Prevention Program,
    562i
Yu, C. K. C., 165
Yu, D., 274
Yue, S., 187
Yuhas, D., 53
Yule, G., 309
Yull, A., 348
Yunsheng, M., 533, 659

Zachariae, R., 514
Zacks, R. T., 250
Zajonc, R. B., 408, 661
Zaki, J., 653f
Zak-Place, J., 133
Zammit, G., 142

Zamora, V., 2
Zandian, M., 396
Zane, N. W. S., 614–615
Zaretskii, V. K., 355
Zatorre, R. J., 406
Zaveri, P., 575
Zawidzki, T. W., 343
Zeegers, M. P. A., 519
Zeidner, M., 321
Zeman, A., 232
Zeri, R., 405
Zeta-Jones, C., 567f
Zha, W., 170
Zhang, G., 662
Zhang, L., 174
Zhang, T.-Y., 340

Zhang, Y., 168
Zhou, C., 222
Ziegler, A., 447
Zimbardo, P., 656–657, 656f
Zimerman, S., 144
Zimmerman, M. A., 451
Zimmerman, R. R., 358
Zlotnick, C., 563
Zosuls, K. M., 435
Zuberbühler, K., 446
Zuckerman, M., 390
Zuker, C. S., 120
Zupek, R., 480
Zurynski, Y. A., 401

Subject Index

Note: Page numbers followed by f indicate figures; i indicates infographics; c indicates connections; t indicates tables; and boldface indicates key terms.

AAIDD. *See* American Association on Intellectual and Developmental Disabilities
abnormal behavior
  as continuum, 544
  culture and, 544–545
  defined, 542–544, **543**t, 579
  identifying, 552
  introduction, 541
abnormal psychology, 542
absolute thresholds, 96–97, 98i, 121, 135
Abu Ghraib prison, 656f, 657
ACC. *See* anterior cingulate cortex
accommodation, 104, 351
acculturative stress, 512–513
acetylcholine, 58, 59i, 60, 67, 167c
achievement, 315. *See also* need for achievement
  adulthood, 372f
  tests, 317f
acquired immune deficiency syndrome (AIDS), 456, 456f, 462
acquisition, 190
  classical conditioning, 206t
  operant conditioning, 205–209, 206t
acronyms, 248, 249f, 251i
acrophobia, 555t
action potential, 53, 54, 55i, **56,** 57f, 59i, 66, 114i, 116, 117, 117c, 120
activation-synthesis model, 164, 165, 165f, 182
active listening, 595, 595t
adaptive value, 195, 195c
ADHD. *See* attention-deficit hyperactivity disorder
addiction. *See* overuse and addiction
additive model, 300
adenosine, 60
adolescence, 361
  brain in, 363
  bickering, 364f
  cognitive development, 362–363
  digital communication and, 365
  egocentrism and, 363
  emerging adulthood, 367–368, 368f
  Erikson's theory of development, 364, 379, 393
  friends and, 364
  hearing loss in, 370
  Kohlberg's moral development, 365–367, 365f, 367f, 379
  marriage and, 368f
  parents and, 364, 364f
  physical development, 361–362
  sexting and, 450
  social networking and, 365
  socioemotional development, 363–365
adoption studies, 318, 323, 491, 567
adrenal cortex, 516i

adrenal glands, 66, 67, 67f
adrenal medulla, 516i
adulthood. *See also* adolescence; children
  achievement in, 372f
  aging with grace, 375–376
  cognitive development, 371–373
  death and dying, 376
  early, 370
  emerging, 367, **368**
  exercise, 370f, 371f
  late, 371
  middle, 370–371
  overview of, 369–370
  parenting, 374–375, 380
  reversing aging, 375
  romance and relationships, 374
  socioemotional development, 373–376, 380
advertising, 199, 199f, 199t. *See also* media; social media
  classical conditioning and, 199, 199t
afferent neurons, 63
afterimage, 108–109
age of viability, 344
aggression, 6t, 475t, **652,** 665
  biology and, 58, 66, 84, 554, 563c
  drugs and, 167f, 168, 175c, 178t
  frustration-aggression hypothesis, 652
  gender differences, 652, 652c
  heritability and, 430, 430c
  identical twins and, 652, 652c
  observational learning and, 220f, 221, 222, A-2c
  online, 657
  psychoanalysis on, 591, 593c
  relational, 430–431, 431f
  sex differences, 430–431
  spanking and, 215–216
  stereotypes and discrimination, 652–657, 653f, 655i
  stigma, 546
aging, 6t, 493
  with grace, 375–376
  reversing, 375
  sexual activity and, 449
  wisdom and, 375
agonists, 59i, 60, 609, 609c
agoraphobia, 556
agreeableness, 490–491, 490f, 490t
aha moments, 294. *See also* insight
AIDS. *See* acquired immune deficiency syndrome
alcohol
  altered states of consciousness and, 167, 170–171, 178t
  anesthesia as, 170
  BAC, 170f

  barbiturates and, 169i
  binge drinking, 170, 171f
  body and, 171
  consequences of drinking, 169i, 171
  GABA and, 169i, 171
  pregnancy, 171, 321, 342, 342f
  sleep and, 162
  stress and, 521, 521f
  warning signs of problem, 171f
algorithms, 293–294, 296i, 327
all-or-none, 56–57
alpha waves, 151, 153i
altered states of consciousness, 140, 146
  alcohol and, 167, 170–171, 178t
  barbiturates and, 168, 178t
  depressants and, 142, 166, 167–168, 182
  hypnosis, 178–180, 182, 265c
  introduction to, 166–167
  opioids and, 168, 168f, 178t
  prescription drug abuse and, 168
  psychoactive drugs and, 166–167
  stimulants and hallucinogens, 171–177, 178t, 182
alternate uses task, 324f
altruism, 445, 533, 533f, 651t, 658, **659,** 659c, 666
Alzheimer's disease, 58, 84, 274, 274f, 369–370, 369f. *See also* dementia
amenorrhea, 401
American Association on Intellectual and Developmental Disabilities (AAIDD), 321
American Psychiatric Association, 151, 155, 156, 157, 158, 176, 178, 400, 401, 426, 431, 438–439, 452, 453, 453t, 454, 458, 459, 463, 511, 542, 543, 544, 547, 548i, 549, 551, 551f, 553, 553t, 554, 556, 556f, 557, 558, 559, 560, 561, 561f, 561t, 563, 566–569, 566t, 568t, 569t, 573, 574, 575, 576, 573t, 581i, 587, 607, 612, 613, 613f
American Psychological Association (APA), 5, 5f, 10f, 11, 41, 155, 171f, 266, 363f, 394f, 401f, 404f, 410, 426, 438–439, 442, 443, 461, 511, 514f, 534i, 546–547, 571f, 616, 657, B-2, B-4, B-5, B-6, B-7, B-8
  on repressed memories, 266
  resources, B-2, B-3
American Sign Language (ASL), 309, 309f
amnesia, 271f. *See also* electroconvulsive therapy
  anterograde, 268–269, 268f, 271, 278, 613, 613c
  biology of memory and, 267–269
  infantile, 272
  retrograde, 268–269, 268f, 271, 278, 613, 613c
amphetamines, 172–173
amplitude, 102, 102f, 103
amygdala, 84, 84f, 123f, 124, 270i
  fear and, 416i
amyloid plaques, 274
anal stage, 475t, 476
analytic intelligence, 314
analytic psychology, 480
androgen insensitivity syndrome, 431, 432i, 433t
androgens, 429, 431, 432i, 444
androgyny, 438, 438f
anesthesia, 140, 142f
  alcohol and, 170
  cocaine as, 172
  marijuana as, 176
  psychedelic anesthetics, 174
anesthesiologist, 139, 140f
anger, 6t. *See also* aggression

The Animal Mind (Washburn, M. F.), 10f
animals, 10f, 411, 436f
  Animal Welfare Committee, 26, 73c, 188c
  behavior, 10, 205, 388f, 446f
  classical conditioning, 196, 196f, 198
  Harlows' attachment study, 357–358, 358f
  hearing, 112t
  insight, 224, 295, 295f
  language and, 311, 311f
  observational learning by, 222–223, 223f
  operant conditioning, 205f
  problem solving, 295f
  REM sleep, 152f
  rescuing with classical conditioning, 196
  research, 188
  sleep, 147, 147f, 152f
  therapy, 187f
animus, 481
anorexia nervosa, 400, **401**, 402f
anosmia, 117
antagonists, 59i, 60, 572c, 609, 609c
anterior cingulate cortex (ACC), 295
anterograde amnesia, 268–269, 268f, 271, 278,
    613, 613c
antianxiety drugs, 609–**610**
antibodies, 444
antidepressant drugs, 607–608
antimanic drugs, 608
antipsychotic drugs, 608, **609**
  atypical, 608
  traditional, 608
antisocial personality disorder, **574**, 574f, 580
anvil, 113, 114i. *See also* ear, hearing, auditory system.
anxiety disorders, **553**, 579
  basic anxiety, 481
  etiology, 550–551, 551f
  generalized anxiety disorder, 553t, 556, 557
  math anxiety, 522f
  panic disorder, 553–554, 553t
  separation anxiety, 356, 553t
  social anxiety disorder, 553t, 556–557
  specific phobias, 553t, 554–556, 555f, 555t
APA. *See* American Psychological Association
applied behavior analysis, 598
applied research, 5, 197c, B-2
approach-approach conflict, **524**
approach-avoidance conflict, **524**, 524f
APS. *See* Association for Psychological Science
aptitude, **315**
arbitrary inference, 602t
archetypes, 480, **481**, 481f
arousal
  sex and problems with, 453
  arousal level of emotion, 404f, 405
arousal theory, **390**, 391i, 420, 509, 509c
art therapy, 594f
arteriovenous malformation (AVM), 283, 283f, 292
artificial concepts, 287
ASL. *See* American Sign Language
assimilation, **351**, 512, 512c, 512f. *See also*
    acculturative stress
association areas, 79–80, 89, 290c. *See also*
    cognition
Association for Psychological Science (APS), 5, 41
association neurons, 63
assumptions, 629f

astraphobia, 555t
astrocytes, 54
astrology, 17–18
asylums, 586–587
ataque de nervios, 557f
atheoretical approach and the *DSM*, 549–550
atherosclerosis, 520
atoms of the mind, 143
attachment, **358**–359
  ambivalent, 358
  avoidant, 358
  secure, 358
attention, 187, 243, 243c
  inattentional blindness, 145, 146f
  selective attention, 144, 145, 181
attention-deficit hyperactivity disorder (ADHD),
    211, 548i
attitudes, **630**, 633f, 655i
  cognitive dissonance and, 633–634, 634f
  nature and nurture, 632–633
  origin, 632
  predicting behavior, 633
  prejudice, 654, 655i
  same-sex marriage, 445f
  stress, 534i
attraction and love
  companionate love, 663, 633f
  consummate love, 663, 633f
  interpersonal attraction, 660–663
  passionate love, 663, 633f
  physical attractiveness, 653, 662
  romantic love, 663
  Sternberg triangular model of love, 663–664,
    663f
attributions, **627**, 631i, 664
  dimensions, 628
  dispositional, 628, 631i
  errors in, 631i
  false consensus effect, 630, 631i
  fundamental attribution error, 628–629, 631i
  just-world hypothesis, 628–629, 631i
  self-serving bias, 628–630, 630f, 631i
  situational, 628
  types of, 627
atypical antipsychotics, 608, **609**
audition, **110**–111, 114i
auditory canal, 113, 114i
auditory cortex, 83, 270i
auditory imagery, 290
auditory nerve, 113, 114i, 116
auditory system, 116f
  pitch, 111
  structure of, 114i
authoritarian parenting, **374**
authoritative parenting, **374**
autism, 22, 22f, 548i
autoeroticism, 475t
automatic cognitive activity, 639
automatic processing, **144**–145, 144c, 145f, 250c,
    639c
  long-term memory and, 250
automatic thoughts, 601
autonomic nervous system, 61, 61f, **63**–64, 64f
    88, **95**, 189c, 405c
  fear and, 415
  salivating dogs and, 189–190

availability heuristic, **300**–301, 301f, 545c, 630c.
    See also false consensus effect
aversion therapy, **598**, 599i
AVM. *See* arteriovenous malformation
avoidance-avoidance conflict, **524**
avoidant attachment, 358
awareness, 141, 181, 577
axon, **53**, 53f, 60
  firing, 56
  growth, 346i, 347
  myelinated, 57, 57f, 78i
  unmyelinated, 57, 123, 123c
axon buds, 53
axon hillock, 55i, 56

B lymphocytes, **518**–519, 518f
babbling, 309f, 348, **349**
baby blues, 563f
baby proofing, 390f
BAC. *See* blood alcohol concentration
bachelor's degrees, 66f, B-1t, B-2, B-3
balance and the cerebellum, 86
bar graph, A-8, A-8f, A-9
barbiturates, **168**
  alcohol and, 169i
  altered states of consciousness and, 168, 178t
Barnum effect, 499
base rate, 302
basic anxiety, Horneye's theory of, 481
basic research, 5, 197c, B-2
basilar membrane, 113, 114i, 116
bats, 112f
Battle Hymn of the Tiger Mother (Chua), 483f
behavior, 24t, 143, 143f, 197, 487i, 657. *See also*
    abnormal behavior; biology and behavior;
    prosocial behaviors
  animal, 10, 205, 388f
  attitudes predicting, 633
  behavior modification, 598
  behavioral addictions, 176
  behavioral change, 96
  cognitive behavioral therapy, 603
  complexity, 14
  consequences, 11
  contagious behaviors, 209
  helping behavior, 651f
  hookup behavior, 449t
  maladaptive behaviors, 543
  observation, 12
  positive, 209f, 222f
  REBT, 602–603, 603f
  reflexive, 189
  sex, 450
  voluntary, 189
behavior modification, **598**, 600
behavior therapies, **588**, 589i, 619
  appraisal, 600
  aversion therapy, 598, 599i
  behavior modification, 598, 600
  classical conditioning in, 599i
  exposure and response prevention, 596–597,
    597f, 599i
  Little Albert study and, 596, 596f
  systematic desensitization, 598, 599i
behavioral medicine, 519
behavioral neuroscience, 51

behavioral perspective, introduction of, 11–12, 13i, 14t, 45

behaviorism, 10–**11,** 12, 143f, 202–**203,** 203f, 205, 227

language and, 348

rise of, 284

Behind Happy Faces (Szabo), 577

bell curve, 316, **317, A-6**

benzodiazepine, 167

beta waves, 151, 153i

bias

confirmation, 302

correspondence, 628

experimenter, 38, 39i, 40

hindsight, 5, 494

memory and, 263, 263c

observer bias, 28–29, 494c

self-serving bias, 628, 629, 630, 630f, 631i

sexual orientation and, 445

Bigger Trees Near Water (Hockney), 95f

bilingualism, 306, 306f

bimodal distribution, A-10, A-10f, A-11

Binet-Simon test, 315, 315f

binge drinking, 170, 171f

binge-eating disorder, 400, **401**

binocular cues, 130, **131**

biofeedback, 533, 533f

biological model of psychological disorders, 551

biological perspective, introduction of, 12, 13i, 14t, 45

biological preparedness, 196

biological psychology, 50, **51**

biological theories,
personality and, 468, 468t

biology, 188, 226

of cognition, 290–291, 327

of depression, 563

of fear, 414–415, 416i

gender and, 436–437

of happiness, 417

of memory, 267–272, 269c, 278

of OCD, 559

of panic disorder, 554

of sexual determination, 428–431, 461

specific phobias and, 555–556

biology and behavior. *See also* brain

endocrine system, 66–67, 67f, 86, 88, 563c

neurons and neural communication, 52–57, 55i, 59i, 95, 95c, 117, 117c, 234c, 273c, 291c, 607c

neuroscience and, 50, 51, 52

neurotransmitters and, 58–60, 175c

supporting systems, 61–65

biology of memory, 278, 318c

amnesia and, 267–269, 268f, 271

hippocampus role, 269c, 271–272

introduction, 267

limbic system, 84, 84f

macro perspective of memories in brain, 269, 270i, 271–273

micro perspective of memories in brain, 273–275

biomedical therapy, 588, 589i, 607f, 611i, 619

deep brain stimulation, 611i, 612, 612f

ECT, 589i, 607–610

evaluation of, 613

neurosurgery, 589i, 611i, 612, 613

psychopharmacology, 589i, 607–610, 689i

rTMS, 611i, 612

bionic ears, 93

biopsychology, 51

biopsychosocial perspective, 13i, **14,** 14t, 15, 45, 334

color and, 109, 109c

pain and, 124, 135

psychological disorders, 551, 551f, 586

bipolar cells, 105i, 106

bipolar disorder, 542, 543, 566t, 567f, 579

brain and, 567f

cycling, 567

DSM-5 and, 566–567

genetics and, 567

stigma, 545–546

birth order, 444, 479–480, 480f, 480c

bisexual, 442

Black Swan (film), 574, 574f

blind spot, 105i, **106**–107, 108f

blindness, 93–94, 94f, 185, 186f

blood alcohol concentration (BAC), 170f

BMI. *See* body mass index

Bobo doll experiment

Bandura and, 220–221, 220f, 227

body

alcohol and, 171

BMI, 399, 399f

mind-body connection, 3f, 8–9, 9f

regulating body movements, 187

stress and, 515, 516i, 517

whole-body response, 84

body mass index (BMI), 399, 399f

bonobos, 446, 446f

borderline personality disorder, 574, 575, 574f

boredom, 391i

Botox, 60

bottom-up processing, 96

brain, 12, 50–52, 61f, 95. *See also* amygdala; cerebellum; cortex; hippocampus; neurons

in adolescence, 363

bipolar disorder and, 567f

brainstem, 85–87, 86f, 89, 124, 270i

cerebrum, 68–69, 69f

deep brain stimulation, 611i, 612, 612f

depressive disorders and, 563

during dreams, 165–166, 165f

Ecstasy and, 175

electricity and, 77

Facebook study, 76–77

freeze, 122

Google brain, 262

growth of in infants, 345, 346i, 347

healing and regeneration ability, 73

imaging, 20f

injuries of, 52f, 234f, 276

introduction to, 49

language and left hemisphere, 70f, 71–72

learning and, 187

left and right hemispheres, 68–73, 69f, 70f, 72f,73, 88–90

limbic system, 84–85, 84f, 89, 123f

lobes of, 79–83, 81i, 270i

macro perspective of memories in brain, 269, 271i, 271–273

male and female, 65

measuring cognition, 291

micro perspective of memories in brain, 273–275

musical training of children, 74–75, 74f, 79

neuroplasticity, 73–75, 117, 117c

olfaction and, 118, 118f

processing, 104

right hemisphere role, 72

scans, 75

schizophrenia and, 571

sex differences, 429–430, 430c

sexual orientation and, 444

split-brain, 69–71, 70f, 89, 613c

stem cells, 74, 74f

study technologies, 75–79, 76t, 78i, 89

superbrain of Einstein, 82, 82f

supporting systems, 61–65

surgery, 612

trauma, 73

Brain, Behavior, and Immunity, 197

breast milk, 119

brightness of light, 102

British Psychological Society (BPS), 41

Broca's area, 72, 72f, 79, 81i, 89, 285f, 290, 290c

brontophobia, 555t

bulimia nervosa, 400, **401**

bullying, 365, 431f, 578f

bungee jumping, 386f

buried alive, 2

burnout, 524, **525,** 525f

bystander effect, 650–651, 651f, 665

caffeine, 60, 167, 173, 178i

callosotomy, 69

cancer, 396, 406f, 448, 455, 455t, 511, 518, 519, 523, 529, 531, 564

cane toad, 196, 196f

cannabis, 176, 176f

Cannon-Bard theory of emotion, 407, 407f, 409i

cardiovascular disease, 158

stressors and, 519–520

careers in psychology, B-1–B-8

with bachelor's degree, B-1t, B-2, B-3

clinical psychology, 4, 616, B-4, B-5

cognitive psychology, B-5

counseling psychology, 4, B-5

developmental psychology, B-5

educational and school psychology, B-5, B-6

engineering psychology, B-6, B-6f

environmental psychology, B-6

experimental psychology, B-6

forensic psychology, B-6

gender and, 66f

health psychology, B-7

industrial-organizational psychology, B-7

with master's degree, B-3, B-3t

media psychology, B-7

neuropsychology and psychobiology, B-7, B-7f

with PhD and PsyD degrees, B-3f, B-4, B-4f

psychologists, 4, B-2

rehabilitation psychology, B-7

social psychology, B-8

sport psychology, B-8, B-8f

caregiving, 331–332, 333f
cartoons, and children's attention span, 40–41
case study, 29, 29f, 82, 82c, 258, 258c
    classic, 29t, 478, 478c
    providing clues, 30
    psychoanalytic theories, 478f
CAT scan. *See* computerized axial tomography
cataplexy, 155–156, 155f
catecholamines, 516i
categorical variables, A-4
categories, 285
cause-and-effect
    auditory imagery and, 290
    experimental method and, 35, 38, 42f, 46, 75,
        75c, 190c, 593c, 662c
    relationships, 28
    spanking and, 216, 216f
CCK. *See* cholecystokinin
CDC. *See* Centers for Disease Control and
    Prevention
cell body, 53, 53f, 55i
Centers for Disease Control and Prevention (CDC),
    174, 362, 454
central executive, 245f, 246, 574
central nervous system (CNS), 61–62, 61f, 67, 88,
    95, 95c
    interneurons, 107, 107c
    processing by, 95
    spinal cord, **61,** 61f, 62, 62f
cerebellum, 85, **86,** 86f, 87, 89, 124, 270i
cerebral cortex, 77, **79,** 85, 270i, 272
cerebrum, 68–69, 69f
chemical senses, 117, 120–121
child abuse, 350
child development and children, 5, 11
    altruism and toddlers, 659
    attachment, 358–359
    cortisol and, 522
    Erikson's psychosocial stages, 359–360, 360t,
        379, 393c, 479c
    feral children, 350
    growth hormone, 148, 152, 161, 161t
    infant brain and sensorimotor development,
        346i
    infant research, 41f
    kangaroo care, 344, 344f
    language explosion, 348–350, 350f, 379
    milestones, 334f, 345, 346i
    musical training and, 74–75, 74f, 79
    newborn growth and development, 344–348
    Piaget's cognitive development, 351–352, 353i,
        354–355, 379
    premature birth, 344, 344f
    sleep terrors, 157t, **158**
    temperament, 356–358, 356f, 417c, 467c
    vaccines and, 22, 22f
    Vygotsky's cognitive development, 355–356,
        379
chlamydia, 455, 455t, 457i
cholecystokinin (CCK), 397i
chromosomes, 338, **339,** 339f, 340–341
    intersexuality and, 431, 432i, 433
    sex, 428, 428f, 432i
chronic pain, 124
chunking, 244, 248, 251i, 277
circadian rhythm, 147–**148,** 181, 343c
    sleep-wake disorders, 151

classical conditioning, 11, 188, **190,** 191i, 199f,
    248c, 274c, 598c, 632, 632c. *See also*
        attitudes
    acquisition, 206t
    in behavior therapies, 599i
    conditioned emotional response and, 197–198,
        198f, 596f
    conditioned taste aversion, 195–196, 196c, 226
    extending understanding, 194–195
    extinction, 193, 195, 206t
    higher order conditioning, 193–194, 194f
    implicit memory and, 248
    introduction to, 192–194
    operant conditioning, comparison with, 218,
        218f
    real-life examples, 198–200, 200t
    rescuing animals with, 196
    salivating dogs experiment, 189–190, 191i,
        192–193
    spontaneous recovery, 193, 206t
    stimulus discrimination, 192–193, 193c, 195
    stimulus generalization, 192, 193–194
    terms, 190, 192, 198
classical music and depression, 590
claustrophobia, 555t
client-centered therapy, 595
clinical psychologists, 4, 4f
clinical psychology, 543, B-4, B-5
closure, 129i, **130**
club drugs, 175
CNS. *See* central nervous system
cocaine, 171f, 172, 176t
cochlea, 113, 114i
    pitch and, 115–116
cochlear implants, 93, 94f, 113, 114i, 115
cocktail-party effect, 145
codeine, 139
cognition, 228, **284,** 487i, 627c. *See also*
        introspection; social cognition
    biology of, 290–291, 327
    children, 351f
    concepts and, 285–287, 286f, 326
    culture and, 355f
    emotion and, 407–408, 410
    gender and, 436
    introduction, 281–284
    learning and, 223–225
    measuring in brain, 291
    neurons and, 290–291
    observational learning and, 219–225
    panic disorder and, 555
    sex differences, 429–430, 430c
    thinking and, 284–287, 326, 627
cognitive behavioral therapy, 603
cognitive decline, 373
cognitive development, 334
    adolescence, 362–363
    adulthood, 371–373
    Piaget's theory of, 351–352, 353i, 354–355,
        379
    Vygotsky's theory of, 355–356, 379
cognitive dissonance, 633–634, 634f
cognitive distortions, 601f, 602, 602t
cognitive equilibrium, 351
cognitive function in children, 40f
cognitive map, 222, **223**–224, 223f
cognitive neuroscience, 12, 284, 284c

cognitive perspective, introduction to, 12, 13i, 14t
cognitive psychology, 12, 143
    careers in psychology, B-5
cognitive revolution, 284
cognitive therapy, 601, 619
    appraisal, 603–604
    concepts, 601–602, 602t
    REBT, 602–603, 603f
    schema and, 602, 602c
cognitive appraisal approach, 408, 409i, 410,
    526, 526c. *See also* coping
cohort effect, 336
collective unconscious, 480, **481**
collectivist cultures, 252, 253f, 297, 298, 529, 557,
    615, 642, 648
College Undergraduate Stress Scale (CUSS), 510,
    510f
color
    biopsychosocial perspective and, 109, 109c
    blindness, 108, 108f
    brightness, 102
    culture and, 97f, 109, 109f
    deficiencies, 106, 108f
    hue, 102, 103
    light and, 102–103
    mixing, 108f
    perception of, 103, 103f, 107–110
    saturation, 102, 103, 103f
    vision and, 102–104, 107–110
color constancy, 132
color deficiency, 108, 108f
commitment, 528
common sense, 5–6
    myths, 6t
comorbidity, 550, 551
companionate love, 663
compliance, 638–639, 642t, 665
compulsion, 558
computerized axial tomography (CAT scan), 76t,
    78i, 89, 235f, 284, 284c, 285f
conception, 338–339, 341
concepts, 285, 286f
    artificial, 287
    defined, 285–286
    formal, 286–287, 288i, 326
    hierarchies, 286, 288i
    natural, 286–287, 288i, 326
    prototypes, 287, 288i
    subordinate, 286, 288i
    superordinate, 286, 288i
concrete operational stage, 352, 353i, 354
conditioned emotional response, 197–198, 198f,
    596f
conditioned reinforcers, 208
conditioned response (CR), 190, 191i, 192, 194,
    198–200, 199t, 226
conditioned stimulus (CS), 190, 191i, 192–195,
    198–200, 199t, 226
conditioned taste aversion, 195–197, 196c, 226
conditioning, 189, 191f, 226. *See also* classical
        conditioning; higher order conditioning;
        operant conditioning
    Pavlovian, 190
cones, 104, 105i, **106**–107, 106f, 135, 148c,
    345c
    light-sensitive in newborns, 345
    in opponent-process theory, 109

SNC and, 148
types in trichromatic theory, 108
confederates, 408, 626, 626f, 641, 643, 644, 645i, 648, 649
confirmation bias, 302
conflict
approach-approach, 524
approach-avoidance, 524, 524f
avoidance-avoidance, 524
sensory conflict theory, 126
stress and, 525–526, 537
conformity, 641, 642t, 665
Asch's study of, 641–642, 641f
conditions, 642
following crowd, 640–641
confounding variables, 36, **37,** 39i, 336c, 480, 480c. *See also* cross-sectional method
connectedness, 129i, **130**
connectionism, 269
conscience, 472
conscientiousness, 490–491, 490f, 490t
conscious, 470–471
consciousness, 10, **141.** *See also* altered states of consciousness; dreams; sleep
automatic processing, 144–145, 145f
changing nature of, 143
defined, 141–142
divided, 180
inattentional blindness, 145, 146f
introduction to, 139–140
levels of, 146, 181
memory and, 142
selective attention, 144, 145, 181
stream of, 143–144
studying, 143
as subjective, 143, 143c
understanding, 143–147
waking, 146
conservation, 352, 659
conservation of volume test, 353i
Piaget's study of, 353i
tasks, 354f
consolidation theory of sleep, 161, 161t
constitutional vulnerability, 571
consummate love, 663
contagious behaviors, 209
context
context-dependent memory, 257
retrieval and, 256–257, 257f
continuity, 129i, **130**
continuous reinforcement, 210–211, 212f, 227
control, 528, 529f
controlling a variable, 37, 190c
in psychology, 7, 51
control group, 36, 37f, **39i,** 641, 641c
controlled stimulus, 190, 190c
conventional moral reasoning, 366
convergence, 130, **131**
convergent thinking, 324
cooing, 348, **349**
coping, 525, **526**
appraisal and, 526, 537
hardiness and, 528–529
process of, 527i
Type A and B personalities, 526, 528, 528f, 537

cornea, 103–104, 105i
corpus callosum, 68, **69,** 70f, 71, 73
correlation, 31, 33i, 244, 489, 489c. *See also* multitasking
causation and, 74f, 82c, 173c, 244c, 290c, 373c, 660c, 662c
correlation coefficient, 31–32, 33i, A-12t
correlational method, 31
advantages and disadvantages, 40f
correlation coefficient, 31–32, 33i
third variable, 32, 33i, 75, 75c,173c
correspondence bias, 628
coronary heart disease, 520, 528, 564
cortex
association areas, 79–80, 89, 290c
auditory cortex, 83, 270i
cerebral cortex, 79, 270i
lobes of, 79–83, 81i, 89
motor cortex, 80, 81i, 82f
prefrontal cortex, 270i
somatosensory cortex, 81i, 82–83, 82f, 123f
visual cortex, 107, 270i, 291, 291c, 416i
corticosteroids, 516i
cortisol, 20f, 66, 148, 516i, 517, 522f, 537, 563
children and, 522
on the job, 523
psychoneuroimmunology and, 522, 523
counseling, 591, 591f
counseling psychologists, 4
counseling psychology, B-5
countertransference, 592
couples therapy, 605
CR. *See* conditioned response
creative intelligence, 314, 314f
creativity, 324–325, 325f, 328, 492f
critical period, 334, **335,** 335f
critical thinking, 17, **18,** 311, 362, 638, A-8
scientific method and, 19, 45
subliminal stimuli and, 99, 99c
cross-cultural, 28, 32–34, 75–76, 115, 297–298, 318, 399f, 402, 402f, 411–413, 412f, 449, 449f, 457i, 491f, 553t, 556f, 576f, 614f
cross-sectional method, 336, 337i
cross-sequential method, 336, 337i, 338
crystallized intelligence, 372
CS. *See* conditioned stimulus
culture, 13i, 14, 14f, 44t
abnormal behavior and, 544–545
cognition and, 355f
collectivist, 253f, 648
color and, 97f, 109, 109f
death and dying, 377, 377f
eating disorders and, 402, 402f
emotion and, 412–413
homosexuality and, 445
hunger and eating, 396–398
individualistic, 252, 297, 648
major depressive disorder and, 561
memory and, 252–253, 253f
of personality, 492
problem solving and, 297–298
psychotherapy and, 614, 614f, 619–620
sex and, 459
sleep and, 160f
specific phobias and, 555–556
culture-fair intelligence tests, 318, 320, 320f
curve of forgetting, 259, 259f

CUSS. *See* College Undergraduate Stress Scale
cynophobia, 555t

daily hassles, 513–514, 514f
dark adaptation, 107
data. *See also* statistics
collection in scientific method, 20, 23i, 46
raw data, 22f
data analysis, 6
in scientific method, 20, 22, 23i, 46
data-based processing, 96, **127**
dB. *See* decibels
deafness, 93–94, 94f, 111f, 116f, 309f
as gift, 115
conduction, 370c
sensorineural, 116, 370c
death and dying
adulthood and, 376
in different cultures, 377, 377f
stages, 376, 380
debate, 20, 334–336
debriefing, 26–**27,** 42, 626, 626c
deception, 38, 42, 410, 625, 626, 626c, 643, 645i, 646
decibels (dB), 111, 111f
decision making, 299, 327
additive model, 300
availability heuristic, 300–301, 301f, 545c, 630c
confirmation bias, 302
defined, 299
external demands, 303
framing effect, 302
predicting future, 299
representativeness heuristic, 301–302
single feature and, 299
wording of question, 303
declarative memory, 246
deep brain stimulation, 611i, 612, 612f
deep processing, 237–239
deep-breathing, 178
defense mechanisms, 473, 475, 474i, 591c
deindividuation, 648–**649,** 648f
deinstitutionalization, 586, **587**–588, 587f
delayed ejaculation, 453, 453c
delirium tremens (DTs), 177
delta waves, 152, 153i
delusions, 568, **569,** 569t
dementia, 142, 157, 275t
dendrites, 53, 53f, 55i, 56–57, 57f
denial, 474i
deoxyribonucleic acid (DNA), 53, 338, **339,** 339f, 340f
dependent variable (DV), 36, **37,** 39i, 41, 480c
depressants, 142, 166, **167**–168, 182. *See also* alcohol
depressive disorders
biology of depression, 563
brain and, 563
genetic factors and, 563
hormones and, 563
HPA and, 563
immune system and, 564
major depressive disorder, 560–563, 561f, 561t, 579
major depressive episode,
psychological roots of depression, 564–565

deprivation, 391i. *See also* drive-reduction theory.
depth perception, 130f, 131f, 132–133, 136
describe
  goal of psychology, 7, 51
  San José, Chile, copper mine disaster, 7
descriptive research, 28, 46
  advantages and disadvantages, 40f, 82c, 478c
  case study, 29–30, 29t, 478c
  correlation method, 31–32, 33i, 34
  naturalistic observation, 28–29, 28f, 398c, 648c
  survey method, 30–31
descriptive statistics, 22, A-1, A-2
desire
  sex and problems with, 453, 453t
development. *See also* adolescence; adulthood; child
    development
  biopsychosocial perspective, 334
  brain and experiences, 347, 347f, 348
  chromosomes and genes, 338–341, 339f
  cognitive development, 334
  cohort effect, 336, 336c, 337i
  debates over, 334–336
  developmental psychology, 333
  genetics, conception, prenatal development,
    338–339
  hereditary and environmental influences, 335
  introduction to, 333–334
  milestones, 334f, 345, 346i
  personality, 356–357, 468, 468t
  physical development, 333–334
  progression of prenatal development, 341–343,
    378
  research methods, 336, 337i, 338
  socioemotional development, 334
  stability and change, 335–336
  stages or continuity, 334–335
  study of, 331–332
developmental psychology, 333, 378
  careers in psychology, B-5
developmental reading disorder, 304
deviance, 543f, 543t, 544
*Diagnostic and Statistical Manual of Mental
    Disorders (DSM-5),* 548i, 587, 587c
  anxiety disorders and, 553
  atheoretical approach, 549–550
  bipolar disorder and, 566–567
  criticisms of, 547, 549
  major depressive disorder and, 560–563
  OCD and, 558
  reliability and validity, 549
  revisions to, 547, 548i
  schizophrenia and, 569
  social anxiety disorder and, 553t, 556–557
diamondback rattlesnake vision, 102f
diathesis-stress model, 571, 586c
dichotomous thinking, 602t
difference thresholds, 96, 97, 97f, 98i, 99, 135,
    193c
diffusion and the neuron, 54
diffusion of responsibility, 647, 650
diffusion spectrum imaging (DSI), 78i
Digit Span test, 244, 244f
disability, 94
  intellectual, 320–321
  mental, 543
discrimination, 12, 206–207, 654
  stereotypes and, 652–657, 655i

disease. *See also specific diseases*
  Alzheimer's disease, 58, 84, 274, 274f, 369–370,
    369f
  cardiovascular disease, 158, 519–520
  immunity, 7f
  neurodegenerative disease, 157
  Parkinson's disease, 58, 60, 74, 157
disequilibrium and cognitive balance, 351
disidentification, 654
displacement, 308i, 310, 474i
display rules, 412, 421
dispositional attributions, 628, 631i
dissociation, 575
dissociative amnesia, 575–576
dissociative disorders, 575, 576f, 580
  causes, 576
  dissociative amnesia, 575–576
  dissociative identity disorder, 576, 577
dissociative fugue, 575
dissociative identity disorder, 576, 577
dissociative symptoms, 511
distress
  abonormal behavior and, 543t, 544
  stressors, **509**
distributed practice, 251i, 252, 253
distribution shapes, A-6, A-7
divergent thinking, 324
divided consciousness, 180
dizygotic twins, 341
DNA. *See* deoxyribonucleic acid
dominant gene, 340–341, 341f
door-in-the-face technique, 639
dopamine, 58, 60, 187c, 386f
dopamine hypothesis, 572, 573
dot problem, 296i, 298f
double-blind study, 38, 39i, 45,626c, A-2
Down syndrome, 321f
dreams
  activation-synthesis model, 164, 166, 182
  brain during, 165–166, 165f
  during REM, 165–166, 165f
  interpretation, 471
  introduction, 163–164
  lucid, 166
  neurocognitive theory of dreams, 165
  psychoanalysis and, 164, 592
  unconsciousness and, 166, 592
drive, 389
drive-reduction theory, 389, 391i, 420, 472, 472c
drug dependence, 177f
drugs in combination, 169i
DSI. *See* diffusion spectrum imaging
*DSM-5. See Diagnostic and Statistical Manual of
    Mental Disorders*
DTs. *See* delirium tremens
dualism, 9f
DV. *See* dependent variable
dysfunction, 543t
dyslexia, 304, 312, 312f
  nature and nurture and, 322–324

ear, 114i
  cochlea, 113, 114i, 115–116
  hearing and, 112–115, 114i
  sound waves and, 112–113, 135
earbuds, 116, 116f
eardrum, 113, 114i

early adulthood, 370
Early Childhood Educator Award, 207f
eating disorders, 421, 551c
  anorexia nervosa, 400–401, 402f
  binge-eating disorder, 400–401
  bulimia nervosa, 400–401
  culture and, 402, 402f
  jockeys and, 401f
  overview, 400–401
  treatment, 402t
echoic memory, 241i, 242, 242c, 243
eclectic approach to therapy, 589i, 590
Ecstasy, 167, 175
ECT. *See* electroconvulsive therapy
educational and school psychology, B-5, B-6
EEG. *See* electroencephalogram
efferent neurons, 63
effortful processing, 250
ego, 471–**472,** 474i
ego defense mechanisms, 472, 473, 474i
ego identity *versus* role confusion, 364
egocentrism, 352, 353i, 363
eidetic imagery, 242
ejaculation
  delayed, 453, 453t
  premature, 453t, 454
elaboration likelihood model, 638
elaborative rehearsal, 250, 251i
Electra complex, 477
electrical and chemical signals, 95, 95c
electricity, 77
electroconvulsive therapy (ECT), 612–613
electroencephalogram (EEG), 76t, 78i, 89
electromagnetic (EM) waves, 101, 101t, 102f,
    107–110, 135
electrostatic pressure, 54
elephants, 254, 254f
embryo, 341
embryonic period, 341, 342f
emergency medical service (EMS), 513
Emergency Vehicle Operations Course (EVOC),
    505, 526
emerging adulthood, 367–**368,** 368f
emotion, 11, 404, 409i, 421, 506, 506c. *See also*
    stress; *specific emotions*
  arousal level, 404f, 405
  cognition and, 407–408, 410
  culture and, 412–413, 412f
  defined, 403–404
  dimensions of, 404f
  facial expressions and, 411–413, 412f
  fMRI and, 410, 410c
  gender and, 418–419, 418f
  language and, 404–405
  moods and, 404
  physiology and, 405–407
  polygraphs and, 410–411, 410f
  study of, 12
  theories of, 405–414, 409i
  types of, 414–419
  valence, 404–405, 404f
emotional intelligence, 42f, 321, 385c
emotion-focused coping, 526, 527i
empathy, 42, 595, 595t, 651t, 659
empirical evidence, 19, 23i
empiricism, 9
empowerment, 529f

EMS. *See* emergency medical service
EMS providers, 513, 521–522, 530
    burnout, 525
encephalitis, 232, 232f, 233f, 235f, 248f
encoding, 142, **234**–235, 237, 255, 276
    failure, 259–260
encoding specificity principle, 256–**257**
endocrine system, 66–67, 67f, 86, 88, 563c
endorphins, 60, 125, 125c
engineering psychology, B-6, B-6f
English as a Second Language (ESL), 384
engram, 269
enriched environments, 347–348, 347i
entorhinal cortex, 77
environment, 487i
    changes in, 96–97
    in learning and social cognitive theories, 485–486, 487i
    schizophrenia triggers, 572
    sex differences, 430, 430c
environmental psychology, B-6
epigenetics, 340, 341
epilepsy, 271
episodic buffer, 245f, 246, 471c
episodic memory, 246, **247,** 247f, 263
epistemophobia, 555t
erectile disorder, 453, 453t
Erikson's psychosocial stages, 359–360, 360t, 379, 393c, 479c
Erikson's theory of development, 364, 379, 393, 393c
erogenous zone, 475t
ESL. *See* English as a Second Language
ESP. *See* extrasensory perception
esteem needs, 392
estrogen, 429
e-therapy, 616, **617,** 617f
Ethical Review Board, 26, 73c, 188c, 646c
ethnocentrism, 652, 653
etiology of psychological disorders, 550, 551, 586c
eustress, 509
EVOC. *See* Emergency Vehicle Operations Course
evolution
    fear and, 415, 555f
    mate selection, 662
    physical attractiveness and, 662
    taste and, 121
evolutionary perspective, 12, 13i, 14t, 45, 97c, 142, 142c, 388, 388c. *See also* instincts
    conditioned taste aversion and, 195, 196c
    sensory adaptation and, 97, 242c, 663c
evolutionary theory of sleep, 161, 161t
excitatory signal, 56, 117c, 118f
executive functioning, 40, 306, 306f, 574c
exercise, 275t
    adulthood, 370f, 371f
    neurogenesis and, 371, 371c
    sleep and, 162
    stress and, 531
exhibitionism, 458t
expectancy, 486, 487i, 501
expectations, 38f, 263c, 626c, 636–637, 637f
experiment, 19
experimental group, 36, 37, 39i
experimental method, 35, 190c, 593c
    advantages and disadvantages, 40f
    cause-and-effect and, 35, 38, 46, 75, 75c, 662c

confounding variables, 36–37, 39i, 336c
control group, 36, 37f, 39i
dependent variable (DV), 36–37, 39i
double-blind study, 38, 39i, 45, 626c
experimental bias, 38, 39i, 40
experimental group, 36, 39i
extraneous variables, 36–38, 192c
generalize, 26, 31, 82c, A-3
independent variable (IV), 37–38, 39i
random assignment, 36, 39i
SpongeBob SquarePants experiment, 40–41, 40f
stimulus and, 190
weaknesses, 38
experimental psychology, B-6
experimental psychopathology, 543
experimental research
    method, 35–41, 39i, 40f
    overview, 34–35
experimenter bias, 38, 39i, 40
experimenter effect, 38
explain, in psychology, 7, 51
explanatory variable, 37
explicit memory, 246, **247,** 247f, 255
exposure therapy, 596–597, 597f, 599i
The Expression of the Emotions in Man and Animals
    (Darwin), 411
external locus of control, 529, 529c
extinction, 193, 596
    classical conditioning, 193, 195, 206t
    operant conditioning, 205–206, 206t
extraneous variables, 36–38, **37,** 192c, 480c. *See also* salivating dogs experiment
extrasensory perception (ESP), 133, 136
extraversion, 490, 490t
extreme sleepers, 160
extrinsic motivation, 386–387, 387t
extroversion, 490–491, 490f
eye, 105i. *See also* cones; rods
    cornea, 103–104, 105i
    iris and pupil, 104, 105i
    lens and accommodation, 104, 105i
    as machine, 9f
    retina, 106–107
    San José, Chile miners, 15f, 148
    vision and, 103–107
eyewitness testimony, 264, 266, B-6

Facebook, 21i, 32, 34, 34f, 96, 302, 305, 336, 617, 661
    brain study, 76–77
    clustered network, 209
    GPA and, 244
    grades and, 96
    as habit forming, 176
    narcissism and, 394
    peer pressure and, 364
    personality assessment and, 498
facial expressions, 411–413, 412f
facial feedback hypothesis, 413, 413f
factor analysis, 489, 489c
false consensus effect, 630, 631i
false memories, 264–265, 265f
familiarity, 300
family counseling, 605
family therapy, 589i, 605–606
famine, 388f, 395f
FAS. *See* fetal alcohol syndrome

fast nerve fibers, 123, 123c, 123f
fasting, 393
father-son relationship, 470f
favorable attitudes, 199
fear
    amygdala and, 416i
    anatomy of, 416i
    autonomic nervous system and, 415
    biology of, 414–415, 416i
    classical conditioning, 199t
    evolution and, 415, 555f
    fear of flying, 301, 301f
    pathways to, 414–415
    theories of, 409i
feature detectors, 107
female orgasmic disorder, 453, 453t
female sexual interest/arousal disorder, 453, 453t
feral children, 350
fetal alcohol syndrome (FAS), 342, 342f
fetal period, 342f, 343
fetishes, 458, 458t
fetus, 342, **343**
fight-or-flight, 64–65, 64f, 65f, 88, 405, 405c, 515, 515c, 516i, 536
figure-ground, 128, 130
firefighters, 530, 530f, 535
firing down axon, 56
firstborns, 480f
first-generation antipsychotic medications, 608
first-letter technique, 248, 249f, 251i
5-alpha reductase deficiency, 432i, 433t
five-factor model of personality, 490–492, 490f, 491f, 491t, 502
    agreeableness, 490, 490f, 491, 491t, 493
    conscientiousness, 490, 490f, 491, 491t, 493
    extraversion, 490, 490f, 491, 491t, 493, 498
    neuroticism, 490, 490f, 491, 491t, 493
    openness, 490, 490f, 491, 491t, 493, 498
fixation, 475t, 476
fixed-interval schedule, 212f, 213
fixed-ratio schedule, 212, 212f
flashbulb memory, 246, **247**
flow of information, 236
fluid intelligence, 372
fMRI. *See* functional Magnetic Resonance Imaging
foot-in-the-door technique, 638, 639, 639f
forebrain, 85, 165
forensic psychology, B-6
forgetting, 277
    curve of forgetting, 259, 259f
    encoding failure, 259–260
    hyperthymestic syndrome, 261
    memory and, 259–662
    proactive interference, 260, 261, 262f
    retroactive interference, 260, 261, 262f
    storage failure and memory decay, 260
    tip-of-the-tongue phenomenon, 260, 261f
formal concepts, **286**–287, 288i, 326
formal operational stage, 353i, 354
fovea, 105i, 106, 106f
framing effect, 302
free association, 471, 592, 593
frequency
    availability heuristic and, 300, 300c
    pitch and, **111,** 112t, 115
frequency distribution, A-4, **A-5,** A-5t, A-7t
frequency polygon, A-4, **A-5,** A-6f

frequency theory, 115–116
Freudian slip, 475f
frontal lobes, 79, 80, 81i, 216c, 574, 574c. *See also*
    antisocial personality disorder; punishment
frotteurism, 458t
frustration-aggression hypothesis, 652
functional fixedness, 296i, 297, 297f, 324
functional Magnetic Resonance Imaging (fMRI),
    20f, 76t, 78i, 89, 257f, 291. *See also* context
    emotion and, 410, 410c
functionalism, 10, 13i
fundamental attribution error, 628–629, 631i

gamma-aminobutyric acid (GABA), 58
    alcohol and, 169i, 171
    receptors, 169i
gamophobia, 555t
ganglion cells, 105i, 106
gastric ulcers, 518–519
gate control theory, 124–125
gender, 26, 37, 44t, 65c, 66f, 426
    aggression and, 652c
    androgyny, 438
    biology and, 436–437
    cognition and, 436
    defined, 434–435, 461
    emotion and, 418–419, 418f
    imbalance, 65
    introduction, 425–426
    panic disorder and, 554
    sexual activity and gender differences, 448–449,
        449t
    social cognition, 429–430, 430c, 627c
    transgender and transsexual, 438–439, 461
gender dysphoria, 438
gender identity, 434, 435, 435f
gender roles, 434
    encouragement and discouragement and, 435,
        435c
    learning and, 435
    observational learning and, 435
    operant conditioning and, 435
gender schema, 436–437, 436c
gender similarities hypothesis, 431, 492c
gender typing, 435
gender-role stereotypes, 418f, 437–438, 452
gender-specific toy preference, 436–437, 436f
gene, 338, 339, 339f, 340–341, 378
    dominant, 340–341
    recessive, 340–341
    sex, 428–429
general adaptation syndrome (GAS), 515, 516i,
    517, 517f, 536
general intelligence (*g* factor), 313, 314t
generalized anxiety disorder, 553t, 556, 557
generativity *versus* stagnation, 373
genes, 12, 340f, 341f
genetic hypothesis, 318
genetic sex, 428
genetics, 338–339
    bipolar disorder and, 567
    depressive disorders and, 563
    panic disorder and, 554
    schizophrenia and, 570–571, 571f
    sexual orientation and, 443
genital stage, 475t, 477
genito-genital rubbing (G-G rubbing), 446

genito-pelvic pain/penetration disorder, 453t,
    454
genome, 340f
genotype, 338, 339, 340, 378
genuineness, 595, 595t
germinal period, 341, 342f
Gestalt, 128, 129i
G-G rubbing. *See* genito-genital rubbing
ghrelin, 397i
gifted
    intelligence and, 321, 321f, 385, 385c
The Girl with the Dragon Tattoo, 574, 574f
glial cells, 53–54, 54f, 272
Global Sex Survey, 6t, 449, 449f
glomeruli, 118, 118f
glutamate, 58, 124
goal state, 292
gonads, 429, 432i, 444
gonorrhea, 455, 455t, 457i
Google, 21i, 200, 261, 262, 302, 336, 617f, 660,
    A-4
GPA, Facebook and, 244
Graduate Study in Psychology, B-2–B-3
grammar, 307, 308i
group polarization, 649
group therapy, 589i, 604–605
    benefits and drawbacks, 606t, 619
groups and relationships
    bystander effect, 650–651, 651f
    deindividuation, 648–649, 648f
    diffusion of responsibility, 647
    group polarization, 649
    groupthink, 649–650, 649f
    helping behavior, 651f
    overview, 647
    risky shift, 649
    social facilitation, 647, 647f
    social loafing, 647
    worldwide, 648
groupthink, 649–650, 649f
growth hormone, 148, 152, 161, 161t
gustation, 120, 121
    sensory neurons and, 120c, 120f

H. pylori, 519
habituation, 187, 273, 663c. *See also* passionate
    love; sensory adaptation
    happiness and, 417, 417c
hair follicle receptors, 122f
hallucination, 151, 173, 568, 569, 569t, 584,
    588c
    auditory, 549, 568
    hypnagogic, 152, 155–156, 164
hallucinogens, 174, 182
    altered states of consciousness and, 171–177,
        178t, 182
    ketamine, 174
    LSD, 174–175, 175f, 178t
    MDMA, 174, 175, 178t
    PCP, 174
halo effect, 662
hammer, 113, 114i
handedness, 72–73, 444, 444f
handwriting, 19f
happiness, 406f, 417f
    biology of, 417
    habituation and, 417, 417c

increasing, 417–418, 514c, 659
    in morning, 418
    laughter, 406f
    temperament and, 417, 417c
hardiness, 528–529
Harvard Brain Tissue Resource Center, 322f
health, 447, 493
    mental, 4t, 24–25, 577, 616
    stress and, 3, 518–523
    weight loss, 400t
health psychology, 518–519, B-7
hearing, 94f, 96, 98i. *See also* ear
    ear, 112–116, 114i
    sound and, 110–112
    of triplets, 110
hearing aids, 113. *See also* cochlear implants
hearing loss, 111f, 116, 116f, 370, 370c. *See also*
    deafness
helping behavior, 651f
hemispherectomy, 68–69, 68f, 69f, 70f
hemispheres. *See* left and right hemispheres
heredity, 335, 399. *See also* genetics
heritability, 322, 323, 340, 340c, 469f, 632c. *See*
    also attitudes
    aggression and, 430, 430c
    obesity and, 399, 399c
    personality and, 491, 491c, 491t
heroin, 168f, 178f
herpes, 455, 455t, 457i
heterosexual, 442
heuristics, 294, 296i, 327, 629c. *See also*
    fundamental attribution error
    availability heuristic, 300–301, 545c, 630c
    representativeness heuristic, 301–302
hierarchical structures, 249, 251i
hierarchy of needs, 390, 390i, 393f, 420, 640c. *See*
    also conformity
    esteem needs, 391i, 392
    exceptions, 393
    love and belongingness, 391i, 392, 392f, 442,
        442c, 640c
    personality and, 482, 482c, 501
    psychological needs, 391i, 392
    safety needs, 391i, 392
    self-actualization, 391i, 392, 393
    self-transcendence, 391i, 393
higher order conditioning, 193–194, 194f
high-quality learning, 387
hindbrain, 85, 86f
hindsight bias, 5, 494c
hippocampus, 84, 84f, 269, 270i
    in biology of memory, 84f, 269c, 271–272
    nerve cells, 371
    history of psychology, 9
    case studies in, 28t
    early psychologists, 8–11, 13i, 143
    perspectives, 11–14, 13i, 14t
    treatment in, 586–587
    women and minorities in, 10–11, 11f, 13i
histogram, A-4, A-5, A-5f
HIV. *See* human immunodeficiency virus
homeostasis, 389, 391i, 472, 472c
homosexual, 442
    culture and, 445
    older brothers and, 444, 444f
homunculus, 82–83, 82f
hookup behavior, 449t

hormones, 12, **66,** 67f, 393c
  depressive disorders and, 563, 563c
  hunger and, 396
  sex, 428–429
  sexual orientation and, 444
horoscope, 17–18
HPA. *See* hypothalamic-pituitary-adrenal
HPA axis. *See* hypothalamic-pituitary-adrenal axis
HPV. *See* human papillomavirus
hue, 102, 103
human factors engineers, 98i, 141, 141c
human immunodeficiency virus (HIV), 456,
    456f, 457i, 462
human papillomavirus (HPV), 455, 455t, 457i
human sexual response, 440–442, 440f, 461
humanistic movement, 390, 484c, 594
humanistic perspective, 12, 13i, 14t, 45, 390c,
    468t, 594, 594c
humanistic psychology, 12, 390, 390c, 484c,
    595f
humanistic theories, 390c, 468, 468t
  appraisal, 484
  self-actualizers, 482, 482f, 483t
  self-concept, 482–483, 501
humanistic therapy, 589i, **593, 595f**
  appraisal, 595
  overview, 593–594
  person-centered therapy, 594–595, 619
  positive psychology and, 484c, 594c
hunger, 388f, 397i, 421. *See also* eating disorders;
    obesity
  appetite, 397i
  blood chemistry and, 396
  culture and eating, 396–398
  hormones and, 396, 396c
  hypothalamus and, 396
  introduction, 395
  judges' rulings and, 398
  mechanisms in regulation, 397i
  naturalistic observation and, 398, 398c
  portion distortion, 398
  satiety, 396, 397i
  stomach and, 396, 396f
  study, 395–396, 396f
Hunger Games, 481f
hypertension, 158
hyperthymestic syndrome, 261
hypnagogic hallucinations, 152, 155–156, 164
hypnosis, 179, 182, 471
  altered states of consciousness, 178–180
  characteristics, 179
  controversies, 179–180
  divided consciousness, 180
  introduction, 178–179
  memory and, 265, 265c
  Mesmer and, 179f
  for pain, 180, 180f
  as role-playing exercise, 180
  theories of, 180
hypothalamic-pituitary-adrenal (HPA), 516i,
    517, 537
  axis of, 516i, 517
  depression and, 563, 563c
hypothalamus, 67, 67f, 84f, **85,** 123f, 124, 148c,
    149i
  hunger and, 396
  lateral, 396, 397i

  SCN within, 148, 149i
  ventromedial, 396, 397i
hypothesis, 20
  case study and, 30
  genetic, 318
  in scientific method, 20, 23i, 46
  supporting, 22
hypothesis testing, A-1

"I Have a Dream" speech, 258
iconic memory, 240, 241i
id, 471–472, 474i
ideal self, 483
identical twins, 323f, 469f
  aggression and, 652, 652c
  intelligence, 491c
identification, 474i, 477, 477f
identity, 362, **363,** 364
IDS. *See* infant-directed speech
illusion, 127–128, 128f, 132
illusory correlation, 133
imaging techniques, 76t, 78i, 567f
immune suppression, 197
immune system, 197, 518, 518f
  depressive disorders and, 564
implicit memory, 247f, **248,** 255
imprinting, 335, 335f
inattentional blindness, 145, 146f
incentive, 386, 386c, 387t
Independent Ethics Committee, 26, 73c, 188c,
    358c
independent variable (IV), 37, 38, 39i, 40–41,
    480c
individualistic cultures, 252, 297, 648
individual psychology, 479, 479f
induction, 168
industrial-organizational psychology, B-7
infant-directed speech (IDS), 348
infantile amnesia, 272
infants
  depth perception in, 130, 130f, 344
  motor development, 344, 345, 346i,
inferential statistics, 22, A-1, A-2
inferiority complex, 479
information-processing model, 236–239, 236f, 277
informed consent, 26–27, 41f
in-group, 652, **653**
inhibitory signal, 56
initial state, 292
inner ear, 114i
insanity, 545, 545f
insight, 224, **225, 294**
  laughter and, 295
  problem solving and, 294–295, 295f
insight therapies, 588, 589i
  psychoanalysis, 589i, 591–593, 592f
  psychodynamic therapy, 593
insomnia, 150–151, 157t, **158**–159, 158f, 164
  debilitation, 162
instinct theory, 388, 420
instinctive drift, 205, 205f
instincts, 388–389, 388f
Institutional Review Boards (IRB), 26, 27, 73c,
    188c, 646, 646c. *See also* Milgram's obedience
    study
insulin, 396, 397i
integrative approach to therapy, 591

integrity *versus* despair, 373
intellectual disability, 320–321
intelligence, 312
  analytic, 314, 314f
  creative, 314, 314f
  crystallized, 372
  defined, 312–313
  emotional, 321, 385
  evaluation of testing, 316–318, 320i
  fairness of testing, 318, 319i
  fluid, 372
  life smarts, 321
  measuring brainpower, 315–316
  motivation and, 385
  multiple, 313–314, 313f, 313t, 314t
  nature and nurture impact, 323f, 491c
  origins, 323–324
  practical, 314, 314f
  survival smarts, 312f
  tests, 315
  theories, 313–315, 327
intelligence quotient (IQ), 316, 385
interference and memory, 243, 261, 262f
intermediate processing, 237–239
intermittent reinforcement, 210
internal locus of control, 529, 529c, 629, 629c. *See
    also* self-serving bias
internal malaise, 196
Internet, 21i, 101t, 144, 199, 200, 221, 262, 317,
    365, 452, 525, 616, 617, 624, 625, 657
interneurons, 62–63, 62f, 107, 107c
interpersonal attraction, 660–663
interposition, 131
interpretation, 496i, **592,** 593
The Interpretation of Dreams (Freud), 164
interrater reliability, 494, 494c
intersexual, 431–433, 432i, 433t, 461
interviews, personality assessment, 495, 495f
intimacy *versus* isolation, 373
intrinsic motivation, 386–387, 386f, 387t
intrinsic processing areas, 79
introspection, 8, **9,** 10, 143c, 284, 284c
introversion, 490, 490f
investment model of commitment, 664
ions, 54, 55i, 56–57
IQ. *See* intelligence quotient
Iraq War, 49, 51f
IRB. *See* Institutional Review Boards
iris, 104, 105i
Ishihara color plate, 108f
IV. *See* independent variable

James-Lange theory of emotion, 406, 406f,
    409i
Jaws, 414, 414f
Jeffrey pines, 8f
jet lag, 150f
jigsaw classroom, 654
jockeys, 401f
just noticeable differences, 96, 97, 97f, 99
just-world hypothesis, 628–629, **631i**

kangaroo care, 344, 344f
K-complexes, 152, 153i
keraunophobia, 555t
ketamine, 174
kin altruism, 445

kin selection, 651t
kinesthesia, 126, 126f, 127, 136
Kinsey Institute, 447f
Kinsey Sexuality Rating Scale, 442, 443f
Klinefelter's syndrome, 432i, 433, 433t
knowledge, 8, 273
knowledge-based processing, 96, 127, 127f
koro, 544

LAD. *See* language acquisition device
language, 52, 299f, **305,** 348c
    animals and, 311, 311f
    behaviorism and, 348
    bilingualism, 306, 306f
    building blocks, 308i
    child development explosion, 348–350, 350f, 379
    defined, 305
    displacement, 308i, 310
    elements of, 305–310, 327
    in environment, 348–349
    grammar and semantics, 307, 308i
    infant-directed speech, 348
    language acquisition device, 309, 348
    left hemisphere and, 71–72, 72f
    linguistic relativity hypothesis, 310
    morphemes, 307, 308i
    overview, 304–305
    phonemes, 306, 308i
    pragmatics, 308i, 309
    production and comprehension, 89
    reading, 307
    sequence of acquisition, 349–350
    without sound, 309, 309f, 349f
    syntax, 307, 308i
language acquisition device (LAD), 309, 348
languishing physical bonds, 605
larks, 150
late adulthood, 371
latency period, 475t, 477
latent content, 164, 592, 592c
latent learning, 224–225, 224f
lateral hypothalamus, 396, 397i
lateralization, 70f, **71,** 89
laudanum, 170
laughter, insight and, 295. *See also* happiness
law of effect, 201, **202,** 202f, 227
learned helplessness, 564, 565f
learning, 187, 226, 551c. *See also* classical
        conditioning; neurons; observational learning;
        operant conditioning
    brain and, 187
    cognition and, 223–225
    defining, 187–188
    gender roles and, 435, 535c
    high-quality, 387
    introduction, 185
    latent, 224–225, 224f
    panic disorder and, 554–555
    reinforcement, 205i, 485
    relearning, 258
    social, 188
    specific phobias and, 555
    testing and, 238
    therapy animals and, 187f
learning and social cognitive theories, 468, 468t,
        484–485, 501
    appraisal, 488

    role of learning, thought, environment, 485–
        486, 487i, 488
left and right hemispheres. *See* hemispheres, brain
lens, 104, 105i, 106
leptin, 396, 397i
levels of processing framework, 237–239, 237f
    elaborative rehearsal and, 250
    retrieval and, 257
life events, 509–510
light
    color and, 102–103
    features, 102–103
    seeing and, 105i
    vision and, 101–102, 102f
light adaptation, 107
light mixing, 108f
limbic system, 84, 84f, 89, 123f
    amygdala, 84, 84f, 123f, 124
    hippocampus, 84, 84f, 269, 270i, 271–272
    hypothalamus, 85, 123f, 124
    thalamus, 84f, 85, 123f, 416i
linear perspective, 131
linguistic relativity hypothesis, 310, 327
LinkedIn, 32
Little Albert study, 198, 198f, 200, 226–227, 554c
    behavior therapy and, 596, 596f
lobes, of brain, 79–83, 81i, 89
    frontal lobes, 79, 80, 81i, 216c, 270i, 574c
    motor cortex, 80
    occipital lobes, 79, 81i, 83, 83f
    parietal lobes, 79, 80, 81i, 82–83, 82f
    temporal lobes, 79, 81i, 83
localization of function, 76, 81i
locus of control, 486, 529–530, 529c
longitudinal method, 336, 337i
long-term memory, 236–237, 241i, 247f, 277
    automatic processing and, 250, 250c
    distributed practice for, 251i, 252, 253
    effortless processing for, 250
    elaborative rehearsal for, 250, 250i
    episodic memory, 246, 247, 247f, 263
    explicit memory, 246, 247, 247f, 255
    flashbulb memory, 246–247
    implicit memory, 247f, 248, 255
    improving, 239t, 249–250, 252–253
    maintenance rehearsal for, 250
    procedural memory, 247f, 248, 248f
    semantic memory, 246, 247, 247f
    sleep for, 251i, 253
long-term potentiation, 273, 278, 291, 291c
    Alzheimer's disease and, 274, 274f
    sea slugs and, 273–274, 273f
Lord of the Rings, 304
loudness, 111, 111f, 116f
love. *See also* attraction and love
    as emotion, 415, 44c
    in Maslow's hierarchy of needs, 381i, 392, 392f,
        393, 394, 442, 442c
LSD. *See* lysergic acid diethylamide
lucid dream, 166
lying, 19, 410, 410c
lymphocytes, 518–519
lysergic acid diethylamide (LSD), 167, **174**–175,
    175f, 178t

MA. *See* mental age
macrophages, 518, 518f

Magnetic Resonance Imaging (MRI), 76t, 77, 78i,
        89, 567f
magnification-minimization, 602t
maintenance rehearsal, 250
major depressive disorder, 560, 579
    culture and, 561
    DSM-5 and, 560–563
    suicide and, 561, 562i, 563
major depressive episode, 560
maladaptive behaviors, 543
male hypoactive sexual desire disorder, 453t
malleability of memory, 263–264, 277, 495, 495c,
    519c
manic episodes, 566
manifest content, 164, 592, 592c
MAOIs. *See* monoamine oxidase inhibitors
marijuana, 175–176, 176f, 178t
    memory and, 272
marital therapy, 605
massed practice, 252, 253
Match.com, 624f
mate selection, 662
math anxiety, 522f
maturation, 333, 429f
MBTI. *See* Myers-Briggs Type Indicator
mean, A-9
means-ends analysis, 294
measures of central tendency, A-3, **A-9,** A-10
measures of position, A-11, A-12
measures of variation, A-3, **A-10,** A-10f, A-11
media, 42, 221–222. *See also* social media
media psychology, B-7
median, A-9
medical model, 551, 586c
medicine, 532
meditation, 178, 531–532
medulla, 85–86, 86f
Meissner's corpuscles, 122, 122f
melatonin, 67, 148, 154
memory, 7f, 52, **234.** *See also* biology of memory;
        long-term memory; retrieval; sensory memory;
        short-term memory; working memory
    bias and, 263
    consciousness and, 142
    context-dependent, 257
    culture and, 252–253, 253f
    declarative, 246, 248
    defined, 276
    echoic memory, 241i, 242, 242c, 243
    eidetic imagery, 242
    of elephants, 254, 254f
    encoding, 142, 234–235, 237, 255, 276
    false memories, 264–265, 265f
    forgetting and, 259–262
    hypnosis and, 265, 265c
    information-processing model, 236–239, 236f
    introduction to, 231–234
    levels of processing framework, 237–239, 237f
    loss, 142, 275t
    malleability, 263–264, 277, 495, 519c
    marijuana and, 272
    memory decay, 260
    neurogenesis and, 269c, 371c
    neurons and, 273
    olfaction and, 119
    overview, 234–235
    reconstructionist model, 263

reliability, 263–266
REM and, 253
repressed memories, 265–266, 473c
savings, 258–259
shallow, intermediate, deep processing, 237–239
state-dependence, 258
states, 240–254
storage, 234–235, 237, 255, 276
memory aids
  acronyms, 248, 249f, 251i
  chunking, 244, 248, 251i, 277
  first-letter technique, 248, 249f, 251i
  hierarchical structures, 249, 251i
  method of loci, 249, 251i
  mnemonics, 248–249, 249f, 251i
memory consolidation, 253c, 270i, 272
memory sketches, 264f
memory trace, 269
menarche, 362, 429, 429f
meninges, 79, 81i
menopause, 371
mental age (MA), 315
mental disorder, 543
Mental Health Parity and Addiction Equity Act
  (MHPAEA), 616
mental health professionals, 4t, 4f, 511f, 542c, B-2t
mental illness, 543
mental images, 83, 287, 289–290, 289f
  mental rotation and, 289f, 430, 430c
mental manipulation, 289
mental processes, 12
mental rehearsal, 244
mental set, 296i, 297
mere-exposure effect, 660, 661
mesmerizing, 179f
meta-analysis, A-4
meth mouth, 173
methamphetamine, 172, 172f, 178t
method of loci, 248–249, 251i
methylenedioxymethamphetamine (MDMA),
  174, **175,** 178t. *See also* Ecstasy
metronomes, 189f
MHPAEA. *See* Mental Health Parity and Addiction
  Equity Act
microglia, 53
microsleeps, 160
midbrain, 85, 86f
middle adulthood, 370–371
middle ear, 113, 114i
Middle Eastern market, 14f
midlife crisis, 6t
milestones, in child development
  motor, 334, 334c, 346i
  sensory, 346i
Milgram's obedience study, 626f, 643–644, 644f,
  645i, 646, 665
mind, 578f. *See also* perception
  atoms of mind, 143
  measuring, 9
  mind-body connection, 3f, 8–9, 9f
  mind's eye, 289
  structure of, 10
mindfulness, 532
Minding Your Mind, 578f
Minnesota Multiphasic Personality Inventory
  (MMPI-2), 498–499
Minnesota twin studies, 323, 491

mirror therapy, 125f
misguided marchers, 22f
misinformation effect, 263–264, 495. *See also*
  personality assessment
MMPI-2. *See* Minnesota Multiphasic Personality
  Inventory
mnemonic, 248–249, 249f, 251i
mode, A-10, A-11
models, 14, 219, 236c, 348
  information-processing model, 236–239
  of psychologists, 236
monoamine oxidase inhibitors (MAOIs),
  607–608
monocular cues, 130, 131, 131f
monozygotic twins, 323f, **341**
mood, 7f, 651t
  congruence, 258
  emotion and, 404
mood-stabilizing drugs, 608
morphemes, 307, 308i, 348
morphine, 139
mother surrogate study, 357–358, 358f
motherese, 348
motion sickness, 126
motivation, 386, 420, 649. *See also*
  deindividuation
  defined, 385–388
  extrinsic, 386–387, 387t
  incentive and, 386
  intelligence and, 385
  intrinsic, 386–387, 386f, 387t
  introduction, 383–385
  theories, 388–394, 391i
motor areas, 79
motor cortex, 80, 81i, 82f
motor neurons, 62–63, 62f
mouthing, 352f
MRI. *See* Magnetic Resonance Imaging
Müller-Lyer illusion, 127, 128f, 132
multiple intelligences, 313–314, 313f, 313t, 314t
multitasking, 96, 243–244
muscarine, 60
My Stroke of Insight (Taylor), 281, 322f
myelin, 57f
myelin sheath, 53, 53f, 55i, 57, 347c
  pain and, 123, 123c
myelinated axons, 57, 57f, 78i, 123c
Myers-Briggs Type Indicator (MBTI), 499

n-Ach. *See* need for achievement
narcissism, 394
narcolepsy, 155–156, 155f, 157t, 159, 181
  power naps and, 163–164, 164f
National Aeronautics and Space Administration
  (NASA), 35
National Health and Social Life Survey (NHSLS),
  447
National Institute on Drug Abuse, 176
natural concepts, 286–287, 288i, 326
natural killer cells (NK cells), 518, 518f, 519f
natural selection, 12, 12, 12f, 142c, 195c,
  388c
naturalistic observation, 28, 29, 648.
  hunger and, 398, 398c
nature and nurture, 8f, 13i, 44t, 45, 65c, 216c
  attitudes, 632–633, 633c
  biology and, 188, 188c

dyslexia and, 322–324
  humor, 469, 469f
  impact on intelligence, 323f, 491c, 512c, 637c
  schizophrenia, 570
  sex reassignment, 437
  sleep patterns, 154
near-death experiences, 84
need for achievement (n-Ach), 394, 395
need for power (n-Pow), 394, 395, 649c
needs, 389, 391i. *See also* hierarchy of needs
  social media and, 394
negative correlation, 31, 33i, 244c
negative punishment, 214i, 215, 216f, 217t
negative reinforcement, 208, 214i, 227, 386,
  555c, 558c, 596c. *See also* behavior therapies
  OCD and, 558
  punishment and, 216, 217t, 227
negative symptoms, 569, 569, 569t
negative thinking, 564–565
negatively skewed, A-7
neo-Freudian theories, 479–481, 501, 593c
nerves, 63
nervous system, 50, 52, 61f, 86. *See also* autonomic
  nervous system; central nervous system;
  parasympathetic nervous system; peripheral
  nervous system; somatic nervous system;
  sympathetic nervous system
neural chatter, 165
neurocognitive disorder, 275t
neurocognitive theory of dreams, 165
neurodegenerative disease, 157
neurofibrillary tangles, 274, 274f
neurogenesis, 74, 187c, 269c. *See also* learning;
  memory
  exercise and, 371, 371c
neuroimaging, 99
neuron generation, 6t
neurons, 52, 53f, 54f, 55i, 88, 95
  afferent, 63
  association, 63
  cognition and, 290–291
  communication within and between, 54, 55i,
    56–57, 59i, 234
  creation of new, 347
  efferent, 63
  glial cells and, 53–54, 54f, 272
  hippocampus and, 84
  in infants, 346i
  interneurons, 62–63, 62f, 107, 107c
  memory and, 273
  motor, 62–63, 62f
  neural communication and, 52–57, 95, 95c, 104,
    104c, 117c, 234c, 273c, 291c
  olfactory receptor, 118–119
  photoreceptors and, 104, 106, 148c, 345c
  receiving, 117
  recovering, 116
  relay, 63
  of sea slugs, 273–274, 273f
  sensory neurons, 62–63, 62f, 120c
  structure and parts, 53, 53f, 347c
neurophysiologist, 142f
neuroplasticity, 72, 73–75, 87, 89
  healing ability, 117c
neuropsychology, 51, B-7, B-7f
neuroscience, 50, 51, 52, 88. *See also* cognitive
  neuroscience

neurosurgery, 611i, 612, **613**
neuroticism, 490–491, 490f, 490t
neurotoxin, 174
neurotransmitters, 57, 57f, 59i, 88, 124–125, 175c, 273c, 607, 607c, 611i. *See also* antidepressant drugs
   acetylcholine, 58, 59i, 167, 167c
   adenosine, 60
   agonists and, 59i, 60, 609c
   antagonists and, 59i, 60, 609c
   biology and behavior and, 58–60
   caffeine and, 60
   dopamine, 58, 60, 386f
   endorphins and, 60, 125, 125c
   GABA, 58
   glutamate, 58
   norepinephrine, 58
   schizophrenia and, 572, 572c
   serotonin, 175, 175c
   sleep and, 161
neutral stimulus, 190, 191i, 194, 198
NHSLS. *See* National Health and Social Life Survey
nicotine, 59i, 60, 167, 174
night owls, 150
night terrors, 158
nightmares, 158–159
NK cells. *See* natural killer cells
nociceptive pain, 122
nodes of Ranvier, 53, 53f, 55i, 57, 57f
nondeclarative memory, 248
nondirective, 594
non-rapid eye movement (non-REM), 151–152, 153i, 156
nonstandard treatment, 616–617
nonvisual pathway, 149i
noradrenaline, 58
norepinephrine, 58
normal curve, 316, **317,** 319i, **A-6**
normal distribution, 317
norms, 643
Northside Center for Child Development, 11f
n-Pow. *See* need for power
numerology, San José, Chile, copper mine disaster and, 17, 18
nursing, 426f, 434, 525

obedience, 642t, **643,** 645i
   boy soldiers, 643
   Milgram's study, 643–644, 644f, 645i, 646, 665
obesity, 158
   epidemic, 399f
   overeating, and, 399–400
   screen time as contribution to, 399–400
   set point settling point, heredity, 399
object permanence, 351–352, 353i
objective personality tests, 502
   evaluation of, 499
   MBTI, 499
   MMPI-2, 498–499
   16PF, 499, 499f
objective reporting, 143, 143c, 192c
objective scientific study, 192, 192c
observational learning, 188, 219, 348, 348c, 435c, A-2
   by animals, 222–223, 223f

Bobo doll experiment, 220f, 227, A-2
   cognition and, 219–225
   gender roles and, 435
   power of, 219–223
   prosocial behaviors, 222
   violence in media, 221–222
observations, 5–6, 19, 23i
   behavior, 12
   measurement and, 10
observer bias, 28–29, 494c
obsession, 558
obsessive-compulsive disorder (OCD), 558–560, 558f, 578, 579
obstructive sleep apnea hypopnea, 157–158, 157f, 157t
occipital lobes, 79, 81i, 83, 83f
Occupy Wall Street, 543f, 544
OCD. *See also* obsessive-compulsive disorder
odontophobia, 555t
odor molecules, 118, 118f
Oedipus complex, 476–477, 477f
oenology, 127
olfaction, 85, 98i, 100, 116, **117,** 135
   brain and, 118, 118f
   chemical sense, 117
   memory and, 119
   olfactory receptor neurons, 118–119
   scent marketing, 119
   September 11, 2001 terrorist attacks and, 118
   taste and, 119–120
   transduction and, 117
olfactory bulb, 118, 118f
olfactory epithelium, 117, 118f
olfactory receptors, 118–119
On Becoming a Person (Rogers), 594
"On Being a Sane in Insane Places" study, 549
One Flew Over the Cuckoo's Nest, 549f
"One Hour Numbers," 255, 255f, 259
on-line dating, 623–624, 624f, 625f, 627
   social media and, 660–661, 661f
openness, 490–491, 490f, 490t, 492f, 493
operant chambers, 202
operant conditioning, 11, 188, **201,** 204i, 206t, 348, 348c
   acquisition phase, 205–209, 206t
   applying, 217
   behaviorism and, 202, 203, 203f, 205
   classical conditioning differences, 218, 218f
   continuous reinforcement, 210–211, 212f, 227
   extinction, 205–206, 206t
   gender roles and, 435, 435c
   law of effect and, 201–202, 202f, 227
   negative reinforcement, 208, 214i, 216, 217t, 227, 386c, 555c, 558c, 596c
   overview, 200
   partial reinforcement and, 209–211, 227
   positive reinforcement, 206, 207, 207f, 214i, 217, 217f, 227, 386c, 598c
   primary reinforcer, 208–209, 227
   punishment and, 213, 215–216
   reinforcement schedules, 211–213, 212f
   robots and, 485, 485c
   secondary reinforcers, 208–209, 227, 600c
   spontaneous recovery, 206t
   stimulus generalization and discrimination, 206–207

operational definitions, 20, 190c, 286c, 590c. *See also* concepts
   treatment and, 590
ophidiophobia, 555t
opiates, 141f, **168**
opioids, 168, 168f, 178t
opium, 139, 141f, 168f
opossums study, 73–74
opponent-process theory, 108–109, 135
optic chiasm, 107
optic disc, 105i, 106
optic nerve, 105i, **106**–107
optimum arousal, 390, 391i
oral fixation, 476f
oral stage, 475t, 476, 476f
orexins, 397i
orgasm, 440f, **441,** 453
outcome research, 590
outer ear, 113, 114i
out-group, 652, **653**
oval window, 113, 114i
ovaries, 67, 67f
overeating, 399–400
overgeneralization, 602, 602t
overuse and addiction, 182. *See also* alcohol; altered states of consciousness
   drug dependence, 177f
   introduction, 176
   MHPAEA, 616
   physiological dependence, 177–178, 521c, 610c
   psychological dependence, 177–178, 610c
   social media and, 176
OxyContin, 168, 177f

pacifier study, 42, 42f, 45
Pacinian corpuscles, 122, 122f
pain
   biopsychosocial perspective and, 124, 135
   chronic, 124
   gate control theory, 124–125
   genito-pelvic pain/penetration disorder, 453t
   hypnosis for, 180, 180f
   myelin sheath and, 123, 123c
   nociceptive, 122
   not feeling, 123
   pathways, 123–124, 123f
   phantom limb pain, 125, 125f
   psychology of, 125
   relief, 139
   touch and, 122–125
   virtual reality for, 125f
pancreas, 67, 67f
panic attack, 554, 554f
panic disorder, 553, 553t, **554.** *See also* classical conditioning
   biology of, 554
   cognition and, 555
   genetics, gender and, 554
   learning and, 554–555
papillae, 120, 120f
paradoxical sleep, 152
parallel distributed processing, 269
paramedics, 513, 513f, 520f
parameters, A-2, A-3
paraphilia, 458–459, 458t
parapsychology, 133

parasympathetic nervous system, 61f, **64**–65, 64f, 88, 405c, 515c. *See also* fight-or-flight
parenting
    adolescence and, 364, 364f
    adulthood, 374–375, 380
    authoritarian, 374
    authoritative, 374
    permissive, 374
    uninvolved, 374
parietal lobes, 79, 80, 81i, 82–83, 82f
Parkinson's disease, 58, 60, 74, 157
partial reinforcement, 210
    operant conditioning and, 209–211, 227
    partial reinforcement effect, 210–211, 211f
partial reinforcement effect, 210, **211,** 211f
partial reinforcement schedules, 211–212, 212f
partial report, 240
passionate love, 663, 633f
passive smoke, 174
Pavlovian conditioning, 190. *See also* classical conditioning.
PCP. *See* phencyclidine
pedophilia, 458t, 459
peer-review process, 22, 23i
penis envy, 477
The People You Meet in Real Life (Hopely), 578, 578f
perception, 13i, **94,** 102f, 129i, 140, 237c. *See also* hearing; information-processing model; olfaction; taste; vision
    of color, 103, 103f, 107–110
    defined, 94–96, 134
    depth perception, 103f, 131f, 132–133, 136
    of environment, 3
    extrasensory, 133, 136
    introduction, 93
    mind's imperfect eye, 127–128
    organization, 128, 129i, 130, 136
    perceptual constancy, 132–133
    problem solving and, 295
    reality through, 8–9
    risk, 301
    sensation and, 94–95, 100
perceptual constancy, 132–133
perceptual set, 132–133, 132f
peripartum onset, 560, 563f
peripheral nervous system (PNS), 61–63, 61f, 88, 95, 95c
    autonomic nervous system, 63–64, 405c
    communication, 62
    fight-or-flight, 64–65, 64f, 65f, 88, 405, 405c, 515, 515c, 516i, 536
    somatic nervous system, 63
    rest-and-digest, 64, 64f, 88, 405c, 515c
    tend and befriend, 65, 67
permissive parenting, 374
personal unconscious, 480
personality, 11, 216c, **467.** *See also* humanistic theories; learning and social cognitive theories; neo-Freudian theories; psychoanalytic theories; trait theories
    birth-order and, 480
    Cattell's factors, 489, 489f
    culture of, 491f, 492
    defined, 467, 500
    Eysenck's dimensions of, 490, 490f

five-factor model of personality, 490–492, 490f, 491f, 491t, 502
    hierarchy of needs and, 482, 501
    introduction, 465–467
    perspectives, 468–469, 486i, 500–501
    roboceptionist and, 500
    temperament and, 467c
    theories, 468t
personality assessment
    Facebook and, 498
    interviews, 495, 495f
    objective personality tests, 498–499, 502
    projective personality tests, 495, 496i, 497, 502, 592c
    reliability and validity, 494–495, 494c, 502, 549c
    technology and, 500
personality disorders, 573, 573t
    antisocial personality disorder, 573t, 574, 574f, 580
    borderline personality disorder, 573t, 574–575, 574f
personalizing, 602t
person-centered therapy, 594–595, 619
persuasion, 636, **637,** 642t
    audience, 638
    elaboration likelihood model, 638
    message of, 637–638
    routes of, 638f
    source of, 637
PET. *See* position emission tomography
phallic stage, 475t, 476–477
phantom limb pain, 125, 125f
phencyclidine (PCP), 174
phenotype, 340, 341, 378
philosophy, 8–9, 13i
phonemes, 306, 308i, 348
phonological loop, 245–246, 245f
photons, 106
photoreceptors, 104, 105i, 148, 345c
    neurons and, 104, 104c, 106
phrenology, 74, **75,** 75f
physical attractiveness, 653, 662
physical development, 333–334, 361–362
physiological dependence, 177–178, 521, 521c, 610c. *See also* smoking
physiological psychology, 51
physiology, 8–9, 13i. *See also* nervous system
pie charts, A-8, A-8f, A-9
pineal gland, 67, 67f, 149i
Pirates of the Caribbean, 304
pitch, 111–112, 135
    cochlea and, 115–116
pituitary gland, 66–67, 67f, 516i
place theory, 115–116
placebo, 36, 37, 38f, 45, 626
    SSRIs and, 608, 608c
placebo effect, 36, 532, 608c
pleasure principle, 472
PNS. *See* peripheral nervous system
polarity, 54
police cadets, 507f
polygraph, 410–411, 410f
pons, 85, 86f
popular wisdom, 5
population, 26
position emission tomography (PET), 76t, 78i, 89, 274f, 291

positive behavior, 209f, 222f
positive correlation, 31, 33i, 509, 509c
positive psychology, 27, **43**–45, 44t, 417f, 484, 484c, 535, 594c. *See also* humanistic theories
    humanistic therapy and, 594
positive punishment, 214i, **215,** 216f, 217t, 569c
positive reinforcement, 206–**207,** 207f, 214i, 217f, 227, 386, 386c, 598c
    behavior modification and, 598
positive symptoms, 569, **569,** 569t
positively skewed, A-7
postconventional moral reasoning, 366–367
posthypnotic suggestion, 180
posttraumatic stress disorder (PTSD), 43, **510**–511, 511f, 551c
    poverty, 511–512, 512c, 536, 584f, 637, 637c, 637f. *See also* expectations
power naps, 163–164, 164f
practical intelligence, 314, 314f
pragmatics, 308i, **309**
preconscious, 470–471
preconventional moral reasoning, 366
prediction, 18
    meeting, 22
    in psychology, 7, 51
    San José, Chile, copper mine disaster, 7
    testable, 23i
predictive validity, 317
premature newborns, 101f, 105i
prejudice, 12, **654,** 655i
premature ejaculation, 453t, 454
prenatal development, 338–339
    critical growth periods, 342f
    progression of, 341–343, 378
preoperational stage, 352, 353i, 354f
presbyopia, 104
prescription drug abuse, 168
primacy effect, 256
primary appraisal, 526, 527i
primary reinforcer, 208–209, 227
primary sex characteristics, 361, 429, 429c, 429f, 432i
primary visual cortex, 83
priming, 99, **255**
proactive interference, 260, **261,** 262f
problem solving, 292
    algorithms, 293–294, 296i, 327
    approaches to, 293–295
    barriers to, 296i, 297–298
    components, 292–293
    culture and, 297–298
    heuristics, 294, 296i, 327
    insight and, 294–295, 295f
    overview, 292
    perception and, 295
    steps to, 293, 296i
    trial and error, 293, 293f, 296i, 327
problem-focused coping, 526, 527i
procedural memory, 247f, **248,** 248f
progressive muscle relaxation, 531, 598, 598c
projection, 473, 474i
projective personality tests, 495, 496i, 502, 592c
    appraisal, 497
    test interpretation, 496i
    Rorschach inkblots, 496i, 497
    TAT, 497
Propofol, 167

proprioceptors, **126,** 127
prosocial behaviors, 222, 222f, **658**–659, 666
prototypes, 287, 288i
proximity, 129i, 130, **660**
pseudopsychology, 17–18, 45, 75f
pseudosciences, 17–18, 18f, 75f
pseudotheories, 45
psychedelic anesthetics, 174
psychedelic drugs, 174
psychiatric disorders, 543
psychic energy, 472
psychoactive drugs, 166, **167,** 178t, 182, 610. *See also* antianxiety drugs
psychoanalysis, 11f, **470,** 589i, **591,** 619, 627c
    dreams and, 164, 592c
    as insight therapy, 591–593, 592f
    rigidity, 12
psychoanalytic, 11, 13i, 14t, 45
psychoanalytic theories, 468, 468t, 501, 551
    appraisal of, 478
    case studies, 478f
    conscious, preconscious, unconscious, 470–471, 471f
    defense mechanisms, 473, 474i, 475, 591c
    id, ego, superego, 471–473, 471f, 474i
    overview, 470
    psychosexual stages, 475–478, 475t
psychobiology, 51
    careers in psychology, B-7, B-7f
psychodynamic, 11
psychodynamic therapy, 589i, **593,** 619
psychological dependence, 177–178, 610c
psychological disorders, 542, 543. *See also* abnormal behavior; treatment
    anxiety disorders, 553–557, 553t, 555f, 555t, 579
    biopsychosocial perspective, 551, 551f, 586c
    bipolar disorder, 566–567, 566t, 567f, 579
    causes, 550–552
    childhood, 548i
    classifying, 547–550, 579
    comorbidity, 550–551
    defined, 542, 579
    depressive disorders, 560–565, 561f, 561t, 563f
    dissociative disorders, 575–576, 576f, 580
    eating disorders, 402t, 551c
    etiology, 550, 579, 586
    introduction, 541
    medical model, 551, 596c
    OCD, 558–560, 558f, 578, 579
    personality disorders, 573–575, 573t
    psychological factors, 551
    rates, 550, 550t
    schizophrenia, 568–572, 568t, 569t, 580
    sociocultural factors, 551
    violence and, 550f
psychological needs, 391i, 392, 394, 394f
psychological perspectives. *See also* biopsychosocial perspective; evolutionary perspective
    behavioral, 11–12, 13i, 14t, 45
    biological, 12, 13i, 14t, 45
    cognitive, 12, 13i, 14t
    humanistic, 12, 13, 14t, 45, 390c
    psychoanalytic, 11, 13i, 14t, 45
    sociocultural, 12, 13i, 14, 14t, 45, 99, 99c
    summary of, 14

psychologists, 4, 4t
    basic and applied research, 5, 197c
    careers in psychology, 4, B-2
    with China earthquake survivors, 4f
    clinical, 4, 4f
    counseling, 4
    defined, 4–5
    focus, 44
    models, 236
    workplace and specialization, 4f
psychology, 4, 96. *See also* careers in psychology; cognitive psychology; research ethics
    abnormal psychology, 542
    biological, 50, 51
    as boys' club, 10
    clinical psychology, 543, B-5–B-6
    control in, 7, 51
    counseling psychology, B-5
    defined, 4–6, 45
    describe in, 7, 51
    developmental, 333, 378, B-5
    educational and school psychology, B-5–B-6
    engineering psychology, B-6, B-6f
    environmental psychology, B-6
    experimental psychology, B-6
    fields of, 4f
    forensic psychology, B-6
    goals of, 7–8, 45, 51c
    health psychology, 518–519, B-7
    humanistic, 12, 390, 390c
    industrial-organizational psychology, B-7
    key issues in, 41–45
    media psychology, B-7
    misconceptions, 5–6
    of pain, 125
    physiological, 51
    positive psychology, 27, 43–45, 44t, 417f, 484c, 594c
    prediction in, 7, 51
    presenting, 1–4
    pseudopsychology, 17–18, 45
    rehabilitation psychology, B-7
    roots in philosophy and physiology, 8–9, 13i, 45
    schools of, 9–11, 13i
    as science, 6, 16–17
    social, 17
    social media and, 176, 209
    sport psychology, B-8, B-8f
    subfields, 5, 45
    as womens' club, 11
psychomythology, 6, 99, 99c
psychoneuroimmunology, 522, **523**
psychopath, 575
psychopharmacology, 589i, 607–610, 680i
psychosexual stages, 475, 475t, 501
    anal stage, 475t, 476
    genital stage, 475t, 477
    latency period, 475t, 477
    oral stage, 475t, 476, 476f
    phallic stage, 475t, 476–477
psychosis, 568, 569, 588c
psychosurgery, 612
psychotherapy, 588, 589i
    culture and, 614, 614f, 619–620
    effectiveness, 615–616, 620
    online, 617, 617f, 620
    worldwide, 614–615

psychoticism, 490, 490c
psychotropic medication, 610, 611i, 612
PsycINFO, 21i
pterygium syndrome, 594f
PTSD. *See* posttraumatic stress disorder
puberty, 361, 362f, 429, 429f
publishing findings in scientific method, 22, 23i, 24, 46
punishment, 213
    negative, 214i, 215, 217t
    negative reinforcement and, 216, 217t, 227
    operant conditioning and, 213, 215–216, 435c
    positive, 214i, 215, 217t
    reinforcement and, 214i, 217t, 348
    spanking, 215–216, 216f
    time-out, 216f
pupil, 104, 105i, 106
puzzle box cat experiment, 201–202, 202f

qualitative data displays, A-7–A-9
qualitative variables, A-4
quantitative data displays, A-5–A-6
questions
    asking new, 24
    in scientific method, 20, 23i
quoll, 196, 196f

Rain Man, 29f
Ramadan, 393, 393f
random assignment, 36, 39i
random sample, 26, 36, 39i, 46
random sampling, A-3
randomized controlled trials, 593
range, A-11
rap music, 325, 325f
rapid eye movement (REM), 152, 153i, 156, 181
    dreams during, 165–166, 165f
    memory and, 253
Rasmussen's encephalitis, 68, 69
rational-emotive behavior therapy (REBT), 602–603, 603f
rationalization, 474i
ratios, 99
Raven's Progressive Matrices test, 320f
reaction time
    Wundt's experiment, 9, 9f
    sleep and, 160
reading, 307
reality principle, 472
recall, 255–256, 336, 336c
recency effect, 256, 300c
receptor sites, 56, **57,** 59i
recessive gene, 340–341
reciprocal altruism, 651t
reciprocal concessions, 639
reciprocal determinism, 487i, **488,** 489
recognition, 255, **256**
reconstructionist model of memory, 263
recycling, 659
red, 109, 109f
references, 5f, **21i**
reflex arc, 62–**63,** 62f, 67
reflexes, 344–345
reflexive behavior, 62f, 189, 248c
refractory period, 440f, **441**–442
regulating body movements, 187
rehabilitation psychology, B-7

reinforcement, 187, **202,** 204i, 214i
  OCD and, 559
  positive, 206, 207, 207f, 214i, 217
  punishment and, 204i, 217t, 348
  reinforcement value, 486
reinforcement learning, 485
reinforcement schedules, 227
  fixed-interval schedule, 212f, 213
  fixed-ratio schedule, 212f
  operant conditioning, 211–213, 212f
  variable-interval schedule, 212f, 213
  variable-ratio schedule, 212–213, 212f
reinforcers, 202, 203, 204i, 205, 386, 485. *See also*
    motivation
relational aggression, 430–431, 431f
relationships, 374. *See also* groups and relationships
  father-son relationship, 470f
  sexual activity, 447–448, 448f, 448t
relative size, 131
relaxation response, 531
relay neurons, 63
relearning, 258
reliability, 316, **317,** 319i, 494c, 549, 549c
REM. *See* rapid eye movement
REM deprivation, 160
REM rebound, 160–161
REM sleep behavior disorder, 156–157, 157t
repetitive transcranial magnetic stimulation
    (rTMS), 611i, 612
replicate, 24, 25, 133, 133c
representative sample, 26, 39i, 82c, 367, 367c,
    478, 478c, A-3
  availability heuristic and, 300, 300c
  in sex research, 428, 428c, 447, 447c
  in survey method, 31
representativeness heuristic, 301–302
repressed memories, 265–266, 473, 473c
repression, 472, **473,** 473c, 474i, 475, 591, 591c
reproduction roles, 459–460
research, 159. *See also* correlational method;
    descriptive research; experimental method,
    scientific method
  animal, 73c, 188
  applied, 5, 197
  basic research, 5, 197c
  basics, 26–27
  debriefing, 26–27, 42, 626c
  designs, 24–25
  expectations, 263c, 626
  Human Subjects Research, 26
  infant, 41f
  informed consent, 26–27
  methods for human development, 336, 337i,
      338
  operational definitions, 190c
  outcome, 590
  population, 26
  question in scientific method, 20, 23i
  sample, 26, 27f
  in scientific articles, 21i
  sex research, 427–428, 440f, 447, 447f
  social psychology, 625–626, 626f
  variables, 26, 426c
research ethics, 41f, 46, 73f, 358c
  confidentiality, 41–42
  deception and, 42
  positive psychology, 43–45

researcher expectancy effect, 38, 263
resentment, 387
resistance, 592, 593
response. *See also* conditioned emotional response;
    conditioned response; unconditioned
    response
  in classical and operant conditioning, 206t
  human sexual, 440–442, 440f, 461
  rates, 31
  relaxation, 531
  response prevention, 596–597, 597f
  short-term, 516i, 554
  stimulus and, 189
  variable, 37
  whole-body, 84
rest-and-digest process, 64, 64f, 88, 405c, 515c
resting potential, 54, 55i, 56
restorative theory of sleep, 161, 161t
reticular activating system, 85, 148c
reticular formation, 85, 86f, 123f, 148c
retina, 104, 106–107
retinal disparity, 130, **131**
retinal ganglion cells, 148
retinopathy of prematurity (ROP), 104, 105i
retrieval, 234, **235,** 237, 282, 282c
  context and, 257f
  cues and priming, 255, 258f, 277, 336
  forgetting and, 254
  levels of processing framework and, 257
  mood congruence, 258
  recall and recognition, 255–256
  serial position effect, 256, 256f
  World Memory Championships and, 254–
      256
retrieval cues, 255, 336c
retroactive interference, 260, **261,** 262f
retrograde amnesia, 268–269, 268f, 271, 278,
    613, 613c
reuptake, 56, 57
reviewing committee, 26, 27
rich false memories, 264, 265
risk perception, 301
risky shift, 649
roboceptionist, 465–467, 466f, 478, 484
  mishaps, 494
  personality and, 500
robots, 485, 485f
rods, 104, 105i, **106**–107, 106f, 135, 148c
  SNC and, 148
Rohypnol, 168
romantic attraction, 6t
romantic love, 374, **663**
roofies, 168
rooting reflex, 345
ROP (retinopathy of prematurity), 104
Roper v. Simmons, 363
Rorschach inkblots, 496i, 497
Rosebud Indian Reservation, 583–586, 584f, 586f,
    610f, 618
rTMS. *See* repetitive transcranial magnetic
    stimulation
running, 209–210, 210f

safety, 3
safety needs, 391i, 392
St. Thomas Boy's Choir, 362f
salivating dogs experiment, 189–190, 191i, 192–193

sample, 26, 27f, 82. *See also* representative
    sample
  random sample, 26, 36, 39i, 46
  representative, 26, 31, 39i, 82c, 300c, 367c,
      428c, 447, 447c, 478c
sampling techniques, A-2–A-4
San José, Chile, copper mine disaster, 1–3, 2f, 3f,
    300
  empanadas for miners, 26, 26f
  eyes of miner, 15f, 148
  first 17 days, 15
  letters to miners, 24f, 25, 25f
  lifelines, 25f
  mental health of miners, 24–25
  miners' celebrity status, 43
  miners' families, 44, 44f
  miners' psychological problems, 43–44
  miners' roles and responsibilities, 16–17
  miners' social structure, 27
  navigating through dark mine, 3f
  note from miner, 15, 15f
  numerology and, 17, 18
  prediction in, 7
  PTSD and, 43
  el refugio, 2f
  rescue, 34–35, 35f, 43, 43f
  trapped miners, 2f
Sandy Hook Elementary School shootings,
    247
saturation, 102, 103
Saturday Night Live, 263, 263f
savant syndrome, 313
savings score, 258
scaffolding, 354, 355
scalp, 81i
scapegoat, 654
scatterplots, 32, 33i
scent marketing, 119
Schachter-Singer theory of emotion, 407–408,
    409i
schema, 351
  cognitive therapy and, 602, 602c
  gender, 436, 436c
schizophrenia, 6t, 58, 340, **568,** 585, 585c
  brain and, 571
  DSM-5 and, 569
  environmental triggers, 572
  features and symptoms, 568–569
  genetics and, 570–571, 571f
  nature and nurture, 570
  neurotransmitters and, 572
  as psychological disorder, 568–572, 568t, 569t,
      580
  roots of, 569–570, 571f
schools of psychology, 9–11, 13i. *See also*
    functionalism; structuralism
Schwann cells, 54
science, 5, 41. *See also* cognitive neuroscience;
    neuroscience
  pseudosciences, 17–18, 18f, 75c
  psychology as, 6, 16–17
science, math, and engineering (STEM), 65c,
    66f
scientific articles
  locating, reading, elements, 21i
  research in, 21i
  retractions, 22

scientific method, 19, 192, 192c. *See also* salivating
    dogs experiment
    critical thinking and, 19, 45
    cyclical nature, 23i
    data analysis, 20, 22, 23i, 46
    data collection, 20, 23i, 46
    hypothesis in, 20, 23i, 46
    publishing findings, 22, 23i, 24, 46
    research question, 20, 23i
    steps of, 20–24, 23i
    study design and data collection, 20, 23i
SDT. *See* self-determination theory
sea slugs (Aplysia), 273–274, 273f
Seattle Longitudinal Study, 372
secondary appraisal, 526, 527i
secondary reinforcers, 208–209, 227
    tokens, 600, 600c
secondary sex characteristics, 361, 429, 429c,
    429f, 432i
second-generation antipsychotic medications,
    608
secondhand smoke, 174
secure attachment, 358
secure base, 358–359, 359f
seeing. *See also* eye, vision.
seeing stars, 83, 83f
segregation, 12
seizures, 68–69, 73
selective abstraction, 602t
selective attention, 144, 145, 181
selective serotonin reuptake inhibitors (SSRIs), 608,
    608f, 611i
self-actualization, 391i, 392, 393, 595f
self-actualizers, 482, 482f. *See also* hierarchy of
    needs
    attributes, 483t
self-concept, 482–483, 501
self-determination theory (SDT), 393–394, 394f,
    420–421
self-efficacy, 486, 487i, 508c
self-help groups, 604–605
    Alcoholics Anonymous (AA),
    self-medication hypothesis, 521, 521f
self-serving bias, 628, 629, 630, 630f, 631i
self-transcendence, 391i, 393
semantic memory, 246, 247, 247f
semantics, 307, 308i, 348
semicircular canals, 126
sensation, 9, 94, 140, 237c, 584, 584c. *See also*
    hearing; information-processing model;
    olfaction; taste; vision
    absolute thresholds, 96–97, 98i, 121, 135
    defined, 94–96, 134
    difference thresholds, 96–97, 97f, 98i, 99, 135,
    193c
    human, 96
    introduction, 93
    perception and, 94–95, 100, 129i
    sensory adaptation, 96, 97, 97c, 97f, 144c, 187c,
    242c
    signal detection theory, 98i, 99–100
    studying, 96–100, 115f
    subliminal stimuli, 98i, 99
    transduction and, 95, 102f, 234c
    Weber's law, 99
sensation seeking, 386f, 390, 390f, 391i,
    509c

senses. *See also* vestibular sense; *specific senses*
    chemical, 117, 120–121
    common sense, 5–6, 6t
    in newborns and infants, 345, 346i
sensorimotor stage, 351–352, 353i
sensorineural deafness, 116, 370c
sensory adaptation, 96–97, 97f, 144, 144c, 187,
    187c, 242c, 277, 663c. *See also* echoic memory;
    passionate love
sensory areas, 79
sensory blending, 95f
sensory conflict theory, 126
sensory experience, 584
sensory memory, 236–237, 241i
    iconic, 240, 241i
    more seen than remembered, 240–241
sensory neurons, 62–63, 62f
    gustation and, 120–121, 120c
sensory register, 236
sensory systems, 144
sensory toolkit, 99
separation anxiety, 356, 553t
September 11, 2001 terrorist attacks
    flashbulb memory of, 247
    olfaction and, 118
serial position effect, 256, 256f
serotonin, 175, 175c
SES. *See* socioeconomic status
Sesame Street, 222, 222f
set point, 399
settling point, 399
sex, 426
    activity and age, 449
    activity and gender differences, 448–449,
    449t
    activity in relationships, 447–448, 448f, 448t
    biology of sexual determination, 428–431,
    461
    among bonobos, 446, 446f
    chromosomes, 428, 428f, 432i
    contemporary trends in behavior, 450
    culture and, 459
    defined, 425–428, 461
    education, 451
    evolutionary psychology and, 445–446
    fetishes, 458, 458t
    genes and hormones, 428–429
    genetic, 428
    history of research, 447, 447f
    human sexual response, 440–442, 440f, 461
    introduction, 425–426
    paraphilia, 458–459, 458t
    reproduction roles, 459–460
    research and, 427–428, 440f
    self-report surveys, 450, 450c
    sex differences, 429–433
    sexting, 450–451, 450f
    sexual scripts, 456, 462
    therapy, 427f
    variables and, 426, 426c
    worldwide, 449–450, 449f
sex differences
    aggression and, 430–431
    brains, 429–430, 430c
    cognition, 430
    environmental factors, 430
    experience and, 430

    mental rotation and, 430, 430c
    in sex development, 431, 433, 433t
    social cognition, 429–430, 430c, 527c
sex reassignment, 437, 439
sex therapy, 439–440, 439f, 605c
sexting, 450–451, 450f
sexual determination
    biology of, 428–431
    layers of, 432i
sexual dysfunctions, 452, 551c
    symptoms, 452–453, 462
    types, 453–454, 453t
sexual masochism, 458t
sexual orientation, 442
    bias and, 445
    brain and, 444
    development, 443–446, 461–462
    genetics and, 443
    handedness, 444, 444c
    hormones, antibodies and, 444
    introduction, 442
    numbers, 442–443
sexual sadism, 458t
sexual scripts, 456, 462
sexuality, 426–427, 475t
sexually transmitted infections (STIs), 362, 454,
    455t, 457i, 462
    bacterial infections, 455
    viral infections, 455
shallow processing, 237–239
shape constancy, 132, 132f
shaping, 202, 203, 204i, 227, 482c
shark attacks, 403f
shift work, 149i, 150–151, 150f
short-term memory, 236–237, 241i, 256, 277. *See
    also* attention
    chunking and, 244
    duration, 243, 243f
    multitasking and, 243–244
    working memory and, 244–246, 523c
SIDS. *See* sudden infant death syndrome
siestas, 160f
sign language, 93, 349f
signal detection theory, 98i, 99–100
The Silence of the Lambs, 546f
similarity, 129i, 130, 661
single feature, 299
single-blind study, 38
sitting, 334f
situational attributions, 628, 631i
Sixteen Personality Factor Questionnaire (16PF),
    489f, 499, 499f
size constancy, 132
skewed distribution, A-7, A-7f
skimming surface, 30–31
skin, 122, 122f
Skinner boxes, 202, 203
skull, 81i
sleep
    aids, 162
    age, 153i
    animal, 147, 147f, 152f
    attacks, 155, 155f
    brain waves, 151f
    circadian rhythm, 147–148, 151, 181, 343c
    culture and, 160f
    debt, 154

deprivation, 160, 160f
disturbances, 156–158, 157t
eight hours of, 152i, 162
exercise and, 162
extreme sleepers, 160
good night's sleep, 159, 163t
habits, 154f
hormone, 154
introduction to, 147–151
jet lag, 150–151, 150f
larks and night owls, 150
light sleep, 151
for long-term memory, 251i, 253
myths, 162
neurotransmitters and, 161
non-REM, 151–152, 153i, 156
obesity and, 399–400
paradoxical, 152
paralysis, 155–156
patterns, 154
purpose and function of, 161–162
reaction time and, 160
REM, 152, 153i, 156, 181
screen time and, 162, 399–400
shift work, 149i, 150–151, 150f
sleep deprivation, 7, 58, 160f, 231
sleep drive, 142
sleep-wake cycles, 3, 85, 148c, 343, 343c
SNC, 148, 149i
spindles, 152, 153i, 253c
stages of, 151–156, 153i, 181
talking, 158
theories of, 161–162, 161t
who needs, 159–162
sleep terrors, 157t, **158**–159
sleepwalking, 157t, 158
slow nerve fibers, 123, 123c, 123f
smell. *See* olfaction
smiley face texting, 127, 127f
smoking, 167f, 173–174, 173f, 634c. *See also*
cognitive dissonance
stress and, 520–521
SNC. *See* suprachiasmatic nucleus
social anxiety disorder, 553t, 556–557
social browsing, 34, 34f
social cognition, 627, 664
attitudes, 630–634, 632f, 633f, 634f
attributions, 627–630, 631i, 664
gender, 429–430, 430c, 627c
social exchange theory, 651t
social facilitation, 647, 647f
social identity, 652, **653**
social influence, 636
compliance, 638–639, 642t, 665
conformity, 640–642, 641f, 642t, 665
obedience, 642t, 643–646, 643f
overview, 635
persuasion, 636–638, 638f, 642t
power of others, 636–637
social learning, 188
social loafing, 647
social media, 76–77, 176, 209, 209f
adolescence and, 365
needs and, 394
on-line dating and, 660–661, 661f
overuse and addiction and, 176
therapy and, 617

social psychology, 17, **625.** *See also* aggression;
attraction and love; groups and relationships;
prosocial behavior; social cognition; social
influence
careers in psychology, B-8
defined, 624–626, 664
introduction, 623–624
research methods, 625–626, 626f
sociology and, 625–626, 664
Social Readjustment Rating Scale (SRRS), 509–
510, 536
social roles, 656
social searching, 34, 34f
social support, 513, 533, 533f
social-cognitive perspective, 486, 487i, 488f, 501
social-evaluative threats, 520
sociocultural perspective, 12, 13i, 14, 14t, 45, 252c.
See also distributed practice
difference thresholds and, 99, 99c
socioeconomic status (SES), 317–318, 512, 512c
socioemotional development, 334, 363–365,
373–376, 380
sociology, social psychology and, 625–626, 664
sociopath, 574f, 575
sole participant, 258
soma, 53
Somalia, 384f, 388f, 389f
famine, 395
food aid, 395f
somatic nervous system, 61, 61f, **63,** 88, **95**
somatosensory cortex, 81i, **82–83,** 82f, 123f
somnambulism, 158
sound. *See also* audition, auditory system, ear,
hearing
hearing and, 110–112, 114i
loudness, 111, 111f
pitch, 111–112, 115–116, 135
sound waves, 110–111
timbre, 112
sound waves, human ear and, 112–113, 135
source traits, 489, 489f
spacing effect, 253
spanking, 215–216, 216f
spatial knowledge, 273
specialization of hemispheres, 69–71, 69f, 81i
specific phobias, 553t, 554, 555f
biology, culture and, 555–556
learning and, 555
speech therapy, 71f
spermarche, 362, 429, 429f
spinal cord, 61, 61f, 95, 123f, 124–125
communication, 62
reflex arc, 62–63, 62f
split-brain operation, 68, **69,** 70f, 613, 613c
lateralization and, 71, 89
specializations and, 69–71
SpongeBob SquarePants experiment, 40–41, 40f, A-1
spontaneous recovery, 193, 206t
sports psychology, B-8, B-8f
SSRIs. *See* selective serotonin reuptake inhibitors
SSRS. *See* Social Readjustment Rating Scale
standard deviation, A-11, A-11t
standardization, 317, 319i
Stanford prison study, 656–657, 656f
Stanford-Binet test, 316
state of readiness, 407
state-dependence memory, 258

statistical analysis, 22
statistical significance, A-2
statistics, A-1
description of data, A-9–A-12
descriptive, 22, A-1–A-2
distribution shapes, A-6–A-7, A-6f
inferential, 22, A-1–A-2
language, A-12
presentation of data, A-4–A-5
qualitative data displays, A-7–A-9
quantitative data displays, A-5–A-6
sampling techniques, A-2–A-4
symbols, A-12f
variables, A-4
STEM. *See* science, math, and engineering
stem cells, 74, 74f
stem-and-leaf plot, A-6, A-6f, A-7
stereotype threat, 654, 656
stereotypes, 418f, 546f, **652,** 653f, 665
discrimination and, 652–657, 655i
Sternberg triangular model of love, 663–664,
663f
stigma, 546, 546f, 547
bipolar disorder and, 545–546
defined, 546
stimulants, 170, 171
altered states of consciousness and, 171–177,
178t, 182
amphetamines, 172–173
caffeine, 173, 178f
cocaine, 171f, 172, 176t
marijuana, 175–176, 176f, 178t
tobacco, 173–174, 173f, 178t
stimulation, 390f, 391i
stimulus, 95, 96, **187**
controlled, 190
experimental method and, 190
ignoring unchanging, 97
neutral, 190, 191i, 194
potential, 56
response and, 189
subliminal, 98i, 99
threshold, 56
stimulus discrimination, 192–193, 193c, 195. *See
also* difference thresholds
stimulus generalization, 192, 193–194, 206–207
stirrup, 113, 114i
STIs. *See* sexually transmitted infections
storage, 234, **235,** 237, 255, 276
failure, 260
Strange Situation, 358–359
stratified sampling, A-3
stream of consciousness, 143–144
stress, 159, **506,** 508f
acculturative, 512–513
alcohol and, 521, 521f
altruism and,533f, 659
biofeedback and, 533, 533f
body and, 64f, 515, 516i, 517
chronic stressors, 511–513, 520f, 584f
conflict and, 525–526, 537
controlling, 529–530
coping and, 525–526, 527i, 528–529
daily hassles, 513–514, 514f
defined, 506–509, 536
exercise and, 531
faith, religion, prayer and, 535

stress *(cont.)*
  health and, 3, 518–523
  introduction, 505
  life events and, 509–510
  meditation and, 531–532
  prolonged, 516i
  PTSD, 43, 510–511, 511f
  reducing, 659
  relaxation and, 531
  short-term responses, 516i, 554
  smoking and, 520–521
  social support and, 533, 533f
  sources, 534i
  tools for reducing, 530–535, 537
  worldwide, 512–513
stressors, 506, 507f, 508, 516i, 534i, 536, 586, 586c
  aging and, 534i
  cancer and, 519
  cardiovascular disease and, 519–520
  chronic, 511–513
  long-term, 519f
stress-vulnerability model, 571
stroboscopic motion, 128, 128f
structural model, 471–472, 471f
structuralism, 10, 13i
study design, in scientific method, 20, 23i
study tips, 239t
subjective awareness, 141
sublimation, 474i
subliminal stimuli, 98i, 99
submarines, 7, 7f
subordinate concepts, 286, 288i
substance P, 124–125
successive approximations, 202, 203
sucking reflex, 345
sudden infant death syndrome (SIDS), 174
suicide, 431f, 560f, 561, 562i, 563, 608f, 610f
superego, 471–**472,** 474i
superior temporal sulcus, 77
supermom, 332–333, 332f
superordinate concepts, 286, 288i
supersized sugary drinks, 27, 27f
supertasters, 121f
support groups, 604f, 605
suprachiasmatic nucleus (SNC), 148, 149i
Supreme Court, U.S., 363
surah, 385f
surface traits, 489
survey method, 30
  representative sample, 31
  skimming surface, 30–31
  self-report, 450c
  wording and honesty, 30, 30f
survival, 97, 388, 388c, 389f
sustainability, 659
Swedish twin study, 443
sympathetic nervous system, 61f, **64**–**65,** 64f, 67,
    88, 405, 405c, 416i, 515i, 516i, 554c
synapse, 53, 53f, 273, 273c, 572c, 611i. *See also*
    memory
  growth, 346i
synaptic cleft, 53, 60
synaptic gap, 53, 57, 59i, 607c
synaptic knobs, 53
synaptic pruning, 347
synesthesia, 95f
syntax, 307, 308i

syphilis, 455, 455t, 457i
systematic desensitization, 598, 599i

T lymphocytes, 518–519, 518f
taijin kyofu, 553t, **556**
taijin kyofusho, 556
taste, 98i, 120f, 135
  chemical sense, 117, 120–121
  evolution and, 121
  as gustation, 120
  losing, 121
  olfaction and, 119–120
  sweet, salty, sour, bitter, umami, 120–121
  transduction and, 120
taste buds, 120, 120f
TAT. *See* thematic apperception test
technology
  brain study, 75–79, 76t, 78i, 89
  personality assessment and, 500
telegraphic speech, 348, **349**
television, 40–41, 221–222
temperament, 356–358, 356f
  happiness and, 417, 417c
  personality and, 467
temporal lobes, 79, 81i, 83, 270i
tend and befriend, 65, 67
teratogens, 342, 343t
Terman Study of the Gifted, 321
terminal buds, 53, 53f
terminal buttons, 53
testes, 67, 67f
testing effect, 238
testosterone, 429
test-retest reliability, 494, 494c
tetrahydrocannabinol (THC), 176
text messaging, 96
texture gradient, 131
thalamus, 84f, **85,** 123f, 416i
THC. *See* tetrahydrocannabinol
thematic apperception test (TAT), 496i, 497
theories, 20, 23i, 24. *See also* specific theories
therapeutic alliance, 595, 595t
therapists, 5
therapy animals, 187f
thermoreceptors, 122, 122f
theta waves, 151, 153i
thinking, 284. *See also* critical thinking
  cognition and, 284–287, 326, 627c
  convergent, 324
  defined, 285
  dichotomous, 602t
  divergent, 324
  groupthink, 649–650, 649f
  negative, 564–565
third eye task, 353i, 354
third factor, 32, 173, 244, 244c, 290c
third variable, 32, 32f, 33i, 42f, 74f, 75, 75c, 173c,
    244c, 290c, 371c
thirdhand smoke, 174
three mountains task test, 352, 353i
threshold potential, 56
thyroid gland, 66, **67,** 67f
thyroxin, 67
timbre, 112
time-out, 216f
tip-of-the-tongue phenomenon, 260, 261f
tobacco, 173–174, 173f, 178t. *See also* smoking

toilet training, 475t
token economy, 600, 600f, 601
tokens, 600
tolerance, 177, 521, 521c, 610c. *See also* smoking
tone-deaf, 112
tongue, 120–121, 120f
tongue-rolling, 341f
top-down processing, 96
topographical model, 470, 471f
touch, 98i, 122f
  epidermis and, 121–122
  pain and, 122–125
Tower of Hanoi task, 40
trait theories, 468t, 469, **489,** 502
  appraisal, 492
  biological basis, 489–492, 386f
traits, 489, 386f, 489f
tranquilizers, 167–168
transduction, 95, 102f, 104, 134, 234c, 584c. *See*
    also memory
  olfaction and, 117
  taste and, 120
transference, 592, 593, 643c. *See also* obedience
transgender, 438–439, 461
transsexual, 438–**439,** 461
treatment. *See also specific therapies; specific*
    treatments
  costs, 616
  history, 586–588, 618
  introduction, 583–585
  nonstandard, 616–617
  operational definition, 590, 590c
  overview of major approaches, 588, 589i, 590,
    618–619
  seeking help, 616
  treatment group, 37
  who gets, 585–586
trephination, 586
trial and error, 293, 293f, 296i, 327
triarchic theory of intelligence, 314–315, 314f,
    314t
trichromatic theory, 107–109, 135
triplets, 93–94, 96, 100–101, 101f
  cochlear implants, 113, 114i, 115
  ear poisoning, 110
  eating, 121
  frequency and, 111
  hearing of, 110
  medication damage, 116
  at play, 117, 117f
  ROP and, 104, 105i
  toddlers, 110f
Turner's syndrome, 432i, 433, 433t
twins
  dizygotic twins, 341
  identical, 323f, 491c, 469f, 652
  Minnesota twin studies, 323, 491c
  monozygotic, 341
  personality, 491
  studies, 659
  Swedish twin study, 443
Twitter, 32, 176
  clustered network, 209
  on emotional rhythms, 418
two-string problem, 296i, 298f
Type A personality, 526, **528,** 537
Type B personality, 526, **528,** 528f, 537

typical antipsychotic medications, 608
typicality, 543t

Uganda, 635f, 658f
uncertainty avoidance, 298
unconditional positive regard, 483, 483f, 595t
unconditioned stimulus (US), 190, 191i, 192–195, 198–200, 199t, 226
unconditioned response (UR), 190, 191i, 192, 195, 198–200, 199t, 226
unconscious, 141, 470–**471**
   dreams and, 166
   processes, 144
uninvolved parenting, 374
unmyelinated axons, 57, 123c
unusual uses test, 324, 324f
uplifts, 514, 514f, 515
UR. See unconditioned response
urban myths, 99, 99c
US. See also unconditioned stimulus.
USS *Annapolis,* 7f

vaccinations, 22, 22f
valence, 404–405, 404f
validity, 316–317, 319i, 549, 549c
Valium, 168
variable-interval schedule, 212f, **213**
variable-ratio schedule, 212–213, 212f
variables, 26, 28, 39i. See also confounding
   variables; dependent variable; extraneous
   variables; independent variable
   controlling, 37, 190c
   dependent variable (DV), 36–37, 39i, 41
   explanatory, 37
   extraneous, 36–38, 480c
   independent variable (IV) 37–38, 39i, 40–41
   qualitative, A-4
   research, 26
   response, 37
   sex and, 426, 426c

statistics, A-4
   third variable, 32, 32f, 33i, 75, 75c, 173c
ventromedial hypothalamus, 396, 397i
Versed, 142
vertigo, 110
vesicles, 57
vestibular sacs, 126
vestibular sense, 126, 127, 165c,166
Vicodin, 168, 177f
violence. See also aggression
   in media, 221–222
   psychological disorders and, 550f
vision, 98i
   color and, 102–104, 103f, 107–**110**
   human eye and, 103–107
   introduction, 100–101
   light and, 101–102, 102f
visual cliff, 130, 130f
visual cortex, 107, 270i, 291, 291c, 416i
visual illusion, 128f
visual impressions, 240
visual pathway, 105i, 106
visual processing center, 83f
visualization, 250
visuospatial sketchpad, 245f, 246
vitamin D, 35–36, 38
vividness, 300, 545c
volley principle, 116
volume and sound, 111, 111f, 116f
voluntary behavior, 189
voyeurism, 458t

WAIS. See Wechsler Adult Intelligence Scale
waking consciousness, 146
wavelength, 101t, **102,** 102f, 103
weaning, 475t
Weber's law, 99, 135
Wechsler Adult Intelligence Scale (WAIS), 316
Wechsler Intelligence Scale for Children
   (WISC-IV), 316, 320f

weeping, sexual response and, 441
weight
   obesity, 160, 371, 396, 399, 399f, 400
   tips for losing, 400t
Wernicke-Korsakoff Syndrome, 171
Wernicke's area, 72, 72f, 79, 81i, 89, 285f, 290,
   290c
WHO Multicentre Growth Reference Study
   Group, 334
whole-body response, 84
Wikipedia, 390
wish fulfillment, 164
withdrawal, 177, 610c
women
   bachelor's degrees, 66f
   female brain, 65
   in STEM fields, 66f
wording and honesty, 30, 30f
wording of question, 303
working memory, 244, 245f, 271, 277, 522f, 523,
   523c. See also cortisol
   central executive, 245f, 246, 574
   episodic buffer, 245f, 471c
   phonological loop, 245–246, 245f
   short-term memory and, 244–246
   visuospatial sketchpad, 245f, 246
World Memory Championships, 233, 235–236,
   235f, 236f, 248, 250
   retrieval and, 254–256

Xanax, 168
xenophobia, 555t

Yosemite National Park, 8f
Youth Outreach for the National Mental Health
   Awareness Campaign, 577
YouTube, 390, 431f

zygote, 341, 428, 428c